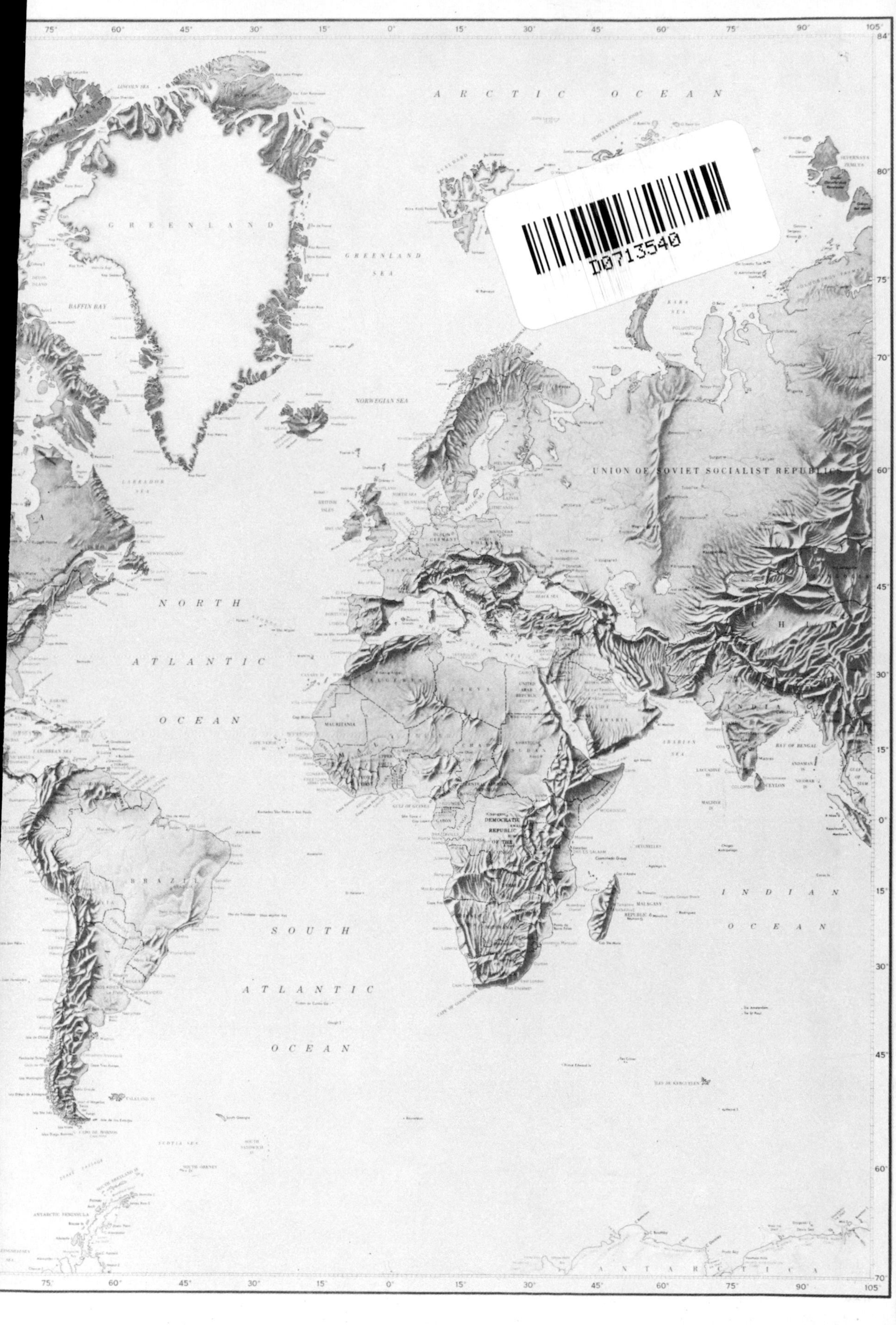

ARCTIC OCEAN
GREENLAND
GREENLAND SEA
LINCOLN SEA
BAFFIN BAY
LABRADOR SEA
NORWEGIAN SEA
NORTH SEA
BRITISH ISLES
KARA SEA
UNION OF SOVIET SOCIALIST REPUBLICS
BLACK SEA
NORTH ATLANTIC OCEAN
CARIBBEAN SEA
MAURITANIA
UNITED ARAB REPUBLIC
ARABIA
ARABIAN SEA
INDIA
BAY OF BENGAL
CHINA
CEYLON
ANDAMAN IS.
NICOBAR IS.
LACCADIVE IS.
MALDIVE IS.
SEYCHELLES
GULF OF GUINEA
DEMOCRATIC REPUBLIC OF THE CONGO
MALAGASY REPUBLIC
BRAZIL
SOUTH ATLANTIC OCEAN
INDIAN OCEAN
FALKLAND IS.
SCOTIA SEA
SOUTH GEORGIA
SOUTH ORKNEY
ANTARCTIC PENINSULA
ANTARCTICA
75° 60° 45° 30° 15° 0° 15° 30° 45° 60° 75° 90° 105°
84° 80° 75° 70° 60° 45° 30° 15° 0° 15° 30° 45° 60° 70°

The World In Figures

Figure 1. The earth photographed from the Apollo 16 spacecraft while orbiting the moon. (Credit: US National Aeronautics and Space Administration.)

THE WORLD IN FIGURES

VICTOR SHOWERS

A WILEY-INTERSCIENCE PUBLICATION

JOHN WILEY & SONS, New York · London · Sydney · Toronto

Library of Congress Cataloging in Publication Data:

Showers, Victor, 1910–
The world in figures.

"A Wiley-Interscience publication."
Bibliography: p.
1. Geography—Tables, etc. I. Title.

G109.S52 910'.21'2 73-9
ISBN 0-471-78859-7

Printed in the United States of America

10 9 8 7 6 5 4 3 2 1

To THELMA,
who gave me valuable advice
on the preparation of the manuscript
and loving care throughout the period of research

Acknowledgments

First I want to thank the many librarians at the Library of Congress who made available to me a great majority of the books, maps, and periodicals of which I had need and who generously assisted my research in many other ways.

In addition to the magnificent resources of that institution, I made frequent profitable use of specialized collections in a number of other libraries in the metropolitan Washington area, most notably the Bureau of the Census Library and the Atmospheric Sciences Library of the Department of Commerce; the main libraries of the Departments of Interior, Transportation, and Health, Education, and Welfare; the National Geographic Society Library; the Columbus Memorial Library of the Organization of American States; the Public Library of the District of Columbia; the Alexandria (Virginia) Library; and the United Nations Information Office. In all of these, I found the librarians to be unstintingly helpful.

For the latest information about foreign countries, I paid repeated visits to the various embassies in Washington, which invariably were most cooperative. I especially want to thank for their assistance the Embassies of Argentina, Australia, Bangladesh, Brazil, Canada, Ceylon, Chile, Denmark, Egypt, Finland, Iceland, India, Indonesia, Iran, Japan, Malaysia, Mexico, New Zealand, Nigeria, Norway, Pakistan, Portugal, Romania, South Africa, South Korea, Sweden, Switzerland, Taiwan, Thailand, Turkey, the United Kingdom, the USSR, Venezuela, and West Germany.

Finally, I should like to extend my thanks to the many correspondents in this country and abroad who took the pains to ascertain and forward to me the answers to specific questions that could not be found in published materials or who located and lent or gave photographs for the book.

V.S.

Alexandria, Virginia
April 1973

Contents

TABULAR GAZETTEERS

Illustrations

The World In Figures

Introduction

The World in Figures is a digest of useful and up-to-date statistical information about every country in the world, 1600 of the most important cities, and 2000 other geographic and cultural features. Comprising forty comparative tables and two tabular gazetteers, it is the first known work in any language that provides such information on a worldwide and strictly comparable basis.

The work is divided into three main parts, the first of which contains tables relating to physical geography, demography, climate, engineering, and education. The second part consists of the two tabular gazetteers, giving significant data about countries and cities, respectively. The countries are listed alphabetically by continent, and the cities are entered alphabetically by country. Alphabetized by more than 6800 names, the third main part is a complete cross-referenced index to the individual entries in parts one and two.

Each statistical table has been constructed to give as much practical information as is consonant with clarity. To cite one example, the principal table of rivers, listing 418 of the longest rivers on earth, gives, in addition to the length of each river, the area of its drainage basin, its average discharge rate, its outflow (sea, lake, river, etc.) and the subdivision and country in which it is located, the latitude and longitude at its mouth, and its alternate and former names.

In compiling the tables in this book, the latest official data have been used whenever they were available. When of necessity unofficial figures are given, they have been verified for authenticity to the greatest possible extent, but they are still identified as unofficial. Wherever appropriate, the date of the information supplied is given, and all information is revised to November 1972. Although each table is reasonably self-explanatory, its exact contents, arrangement, and coverage are described at the beginning of the table.

Because Arabic numerals are now universally employed, *The World in Figures* can be understood without difficulty by people in all countries. To increase its usefulness in countries that have adopted the metric system and to obviate the necessity of conversion, all measurement data are given in both English and metric units, and temperature data in both Fahrenheit and Celsius (centigrade).

Another important feature of the book is the provision of latitude and longitude (to the nearest minute) for every city and almost every physiographic feature listed. This has been done to facilitate their location on maps and to make possible a rapid comparison of geographic positions. Many of the features cited, and even a few of the cities, cannot be found in current world atlases, either because the maps in these atlases have too small a scale or because they are not sufficiently up-to-date, but supplied with latitude and longitude, the reader can still locate them with respect to better-known cities and features that are shown in these atlases.

No effort has been spared to make this digest as accurate and complete as possible. The Selected Bibliography, beginning on page 535, cities some of the more important soucres from which information has been derived. Arranged as it is by subject and including only the most useful publications in each field, this bibliography should prove most valuable to readers who seek more detailed information on any subject covered by *The World in Figures.* Yet, many of the figures supplied in this book are not found in any of the works cited in the Selected Bibliography. A considerable number of the dates of foundation for libraries here provided, for example, are not given in any of the standard library directories listed in the bibliography.

It is for this reason – to uncover more information – as well as for purposes of verification, that innumerable books and periodicals of a more specialized nature – population census reports, guidebooks and histories of particular localities, meteorological and water supply bulletins, and civil engineering and architectural journals – have also been consulted in the preparation of this work. In addition, correspondence with governmental agencies here and abroad has yielded some basic data published neither in the official statistical yearbooks nor elsewhere. The areas of some of the largest Alaskan islands, for instance, have never been published, yet they are readily obtainable from the US Coast and Geodetic Survey (see bibliography, number 165).

The World in Figures gives striking evidence of a shrinking earth. Only a few years ago the compilation of an authoritative digest of comparative statistics of this scope would have been impossible. Now, with jet aircraft flying travelers to every corner of the globe and television flashing instant pictures of important events by satellite, there is no longer a *terra incognita* anywhere. Census-taking has become almost universal, meteorological data are collected in nearly every important community, and some of the most underdeveloped nations vie with the most "advanced" in the production of official statistical yearbooks.

Nor is it only that we know more about the remote regions of the world. We have simultaneously acquired far greater knowledge of our own and neighboring countries. Thirty-five years ago the longest watercourse of the Mississippi River (from the source of the Red Rock to the Gulf of Mexico) was universally regarded as the longest river in the world; its length was officially stated to be 4221 mi, or 6793 km. By 1939, however, the US Geological Survey had reduced that figure to 3988 mi (6418 km), and 10 years later it was again reduced to 3872 mi (6231 km). Further revisions have decreased the length to 3741 mi (6021 km), and the Mississippi is now known to rank well behind the Nile and the Amazon as the third longest of the world's great rivers.

It will be noted that this work contains no statistics on production, trade, or monetary matters. Since such statistics are subject to rapid change and would be misleading after a short lapse of time, their presentation here would be of questionable value. Moreover, official and adequate data in these fields are already published annually in the *Statistical Yearbook* of the United Nations (bibliography, number 90).

Abbreviations Used in This Work

AD	anno Domini (i.e., since the birth of Christ)
alt	alternate name (or names)
Apr	April
Aug	August
avg	average
B	bay
BC	before Christ (other dates listed are AD)
bef	before
bldg	building
c	century
C	Celsius (or centigrade)
cfs	cubic feet per second
ctry	country
Dec	December
e	estimated (other population data are from census returns)
E	east
ed	edition
Ed	editor
elev	elevation (i.e., altitude above sea level)
exc	excluding
F	Fahrenheit
Feb	February
for	former name (or names)
ft	feet
ft^2	square feet
G	gulf
I	island
in.	inches
inc	including
Jan	January
Jul	July
Jun	June
km	kilometers
km^2	square kilometers
L	lake
lag	lagoon
lib	library
m	meters
m^3	cubic meters
m^3/sec	cubic meters per second
Mar	March
mi	miles
mi^2	square miles
mm	millimeters
mt	mountain (peak or massif)
mts	mountains (range or system)
N	north
ND	no date
Nov	November
NP	no place
nr	near (i.e., within approximately 10 mi, or 16 km)
O	ocean
Oct	October
off	official name (or names)
p	page
pp	pages
R	river
s	with adjacent suburban areas
S	south

sec	second
Sep	September
UC	under construction
UK	United Kingdom of Great Britain and Northern Ireland
univ	university
unp	unpaged
USA	United States of America
USSR	Union of Soviet Socialist Republics
v	volume (or volumes)
volc	active volcano
W	west
wf	waterfall
yd^3	cubic yards
yrs	years
°	degrees (of temperature)
●	unofficial data
*	capital (of a country or subdivision)
* * *	(used to divide tables into two parts, the portion above the division representing all-inclusive coverage and that below the division, selective coverage)

GENERAL EXPLANATORY NOTES

An explanation of the contents, arrangement, and coverage of each statistical table and tabular gazetteer in this work precedes the table or gazetteer in question. The notes in this section are of a more general nature or pertain to more than one table or gazetteer.

Spelling

The spelling of geographic names accords generally with that in the various gazetteers prepared by the US Office of Geography (see bibliography, number 126). Accent and other diacritical marks are omitted for simplicity.[1] Exception to this spelling rule is, of course, made when the name has been changed since publication of the relevant gazetteer and when, as evidenced by a consensus of later authorities, the spelling is manifestly outdated. The spelling of nongeographic names is that adopted officially or that approved by recognized authorities in the appropriate field. The names of dams, for example, are either given their official spelling or spelled in conformity with the *World Register of Dams* (bibliography, number 212).

Conventional and Other Names

Many cities, countries, and physiographic features have conventional names in English that differ from their official (sometimes called vernacular) names. The difference may be marked (as Albania for Shqiperi) or minimal (as Lyons for Lyon). In either case, the conventional English name is always given in this work, and the initial citation of the city, country, or physiographic feature is by this name if it is in general use. The official name or names, marked "off," are also given, however, in appropriate places in the tables and gazetteers, and if no "off" name appears in these places, it may be assumed that the conventional name is also an official one.

Two other sorts of names appear in the tables: alternate ("alt") names and former ("for") names. If no "off" name is listed, the "alt" name or names are other official names or (rarely) English names infrequently used. Often these other official names will be names used in another country. The Danube River, flowing through eight countries in Europe, has no fewer than six official names, none of which is Danube, the conventional English name. Sometimes, however, there will be two or three official names within a single country. Helsinki and Helsingfors are both official names for the capital of Finland, since both Finnish and Swedish are official languages in that country.

[1] Readers versed in foreign languages will inevitably notice the omission of these diacritical marks. Since their primary function, however, is to indicate proper pronunciation, with which this work is not concerned, their inclusion would be of limited value at best. On the other hand, the marks are so numerous and so frequent in occurrence that their inclusion would serve to clutter the book, confuse the English-speaking reader, and raise serious problems in alphabetizing.

Former ("for") names are, as the term implies, names that were once in general use but have become obsolete. Ancient (i.e., classical) names are not given in this book, but names dating from more recent historical periods are entered unless the name in question was used for a very brief time.

The conventional and other names given for countries are their so-called short names, for example, Mexico (official spelling identical), not United Mexican States (off Estados Unidos Mexicanos). To save space and because the abbreviations are in common use, three large countries are identified by abbreviations, as follows:

UK, for United Kingdom of Great Britain and Northern Ireland
USA, for United States of America
USSR, for Union of Soviet Socialist Republics

In the citation of foreign physiographic features, that portion of the name signifying river, mountain (or mount), lake, or the like is usually deleted, and an abbreviation for the English-language equivalent is substituted for it, unless, of course, this equivalent is a tabular heading. Thus, the river known in Brazil as Rio Negro is listed simply as Negro in Tables 5, 7, and 8 and as Negro R (for River) in Tabular Gazetteer 2. Similarly, the Chinese lake Poyang Hu is cited as Poyang or Poyang L.[2] When, however, the foreign designation for the physiographic feature is but little known and especially when the particular feature is almost never cited in English-language works without its full name, even though this makes the citation redundant, that portion of the name signifying river, and so forth, is retained but is parenthesized, for example, (Tonle) Sap L, Kizil (Irmak) R. Portions of conventional geographic names that are redundant or misleading but are invariably used are also retained and parenthesized, for example, Dead (Sea). The Dead Sea is in actuality a salt-water lake.

It goes without saying that a cross-referenced entry appears in the index for each unconventional name, whether it is an alternate, former, or official one.

Alphabetizing

Some of the individual tables, as well as the index, are arranged alphabetically. Alphabetizing in this work is letter-by-letter, in accordance with the English alphabet, without regard for spaces, punctuation marks, or foreign combination letters. Thus, Newark precedes New Britain, and Chile precedes Cienfuegos, even though the latter words are Spanish and in Spanish "ch" is a separate letter that follows the letter "c." Abbreviations are alphabetized as they are spelled: for example, UAR falls among the "ua's," not among the "un's." When, however, names begin with words like "Saint" that are often abbreviated in other books, these words are spelled out. And names beginning with Arabic numerals (e.g., 345 Park Avenue) are alphabetized as if the numerals were spelled out.

Translation and Transliteration

Since the spelling of geographic names is in accord with the pattern set by the gazetteers prepared by the US Office of Geography, it follows that the systems of transliteration adopted by that office have been employed in this work. This accounts, for instance, for the spelling "Gorkiy" in preference to "Gorki," "Gorkii," or "Gorky" in the names of dams, universities, and libraries. Personal names aside, however, the official designations of universities and libraries in countries that do not use the Roman alphabet are not transliterated. In line with the rule followed by many authorities in the field of education, these designations are translated into English, whereas the names of like institutions in countries where the Roman alphabet prevails are left unchanged.[3] Thus, the national library of Thailand is listed under

[2] But note that foreign-language designations for river, and so on, used in countries where the language in question does not prevail, are not deleted. For example, Rio Grande R, not Grande R, designates the river in the southwestern USA.

[3] This is not the case with capitalization, which for consistency and to avoid confusion follows English-language rules. In some foreign languages, proper adjectives are not capitalized, and there are many other differences.

Bangkok (in Tabular Gazetteer 2) as "National Library," but the national library of France is entered under Paris as "Bibliotheque Nationale." When universities and libraries are commonly known by two names, as sometimes happens in countries with two official languages, both names are given. For example, under Bloemfontein, South Africa, there is listed: "University of the Orange Free State (alt Universiteit van die Oranje-Vrystaat)."

"University" defined

For purposes of inclusion in and exclusion from this work, a university is defined as an educational institution that, either of itself or in conjunction with constituent or affiliated institutions, offers undergraduate work leading to a bachelor's degree and graduate work leading to at least a master's degree. This broad definition of "university" includes some institutions that call themselves colleges, but it is felt that a more restrictive definition would be too exclusive. In 1970 there were in the United States only 298 universities that offered graduate work leading to a doctor's degree (universities in the narrow sense), whereas there were 826 that offered graduate work leading to at least a master's or a second professional degree (universities in the broad sense employed in this book). Because of the different standards that prevail in various countries, it is not always possible to apply this definition to the letter, but every effort has been made to adhere to it as closely as possible.

So-called colleges that meet the definition, as well as other institutions of university level that do not have the word "university" or its foreign-language equivalent in their names, are therefore listed in Tabular Gazetteer 2, and also in Table 39 if they qualify by size. These institutions, however, are identified by the designation "univ" placed in parentheses after their names. On the other hand, a number of so-called universities offer no graduate work. These are also included in the listings if they are independent institutions, but they are identified by the designation "college" placed in parentheses after their names. Branch campuses of a university centered elsewhere are not listed, unless they are of university level in the sense already defined.

Rounding

Many of the statistical figures in this book are rounded. This means, for example, that a population of 151,743 is given as 152,000 (151,499 would, of course, become 151,000). Population data are invariably rounded to the nearest 1000. However, when the original figure is less than 1000, the rounding is done to the nearest 100. Other figures in the book may be rounded to the nearest 10 ft (m) (mountain elevations) or to the nearest three significant digits[4] (island areas). The extent of the rounding is described in the explanatory notes preceding each table and tabular gazetteer.

Although the rounding of all population figures to the nearest 1000 obviously saves print and space, since the word "thousands" can be inserted into the tabular heading and the figure printed as 152 instead of 152,000, the main purpose of rounding is to promote understanding – to make the statistical tables easier to read and the data they contain easier to comprehend. To one untrained in statistics, it might appear that rounding sacrifices accuracy, but this is not necessarily so. If done with discrimination, it may actually enhance statistical significance. To say that Mount Lucania is 17,147 feet high is really misleading, for mountain elevations cannot be determined with such accuracy. As for populations, they tend to grow so fast and the census techniques by which they are ascertained are so inexact that expressions of their size to the last digit are meaningless.

Subdivisions of countries

No statistical data are given for political or regional subdivisions of countries, nor are they listed in the index. Nevertheless, such subdivisions are cited throughout the book for the larger

[4]This means, for example, that the area of Madagascar, which is greater than 100,000 mi^2 and 100,000 km^2, is given as 227,000 mi^2, or 587,000 km^2; and that of Reunion, which is less than 1000 mi^2 and less than 10,000 km^2, is given as 969 mi^2, or 2510 km^2.

countries, to facilitate the location of cities and physiographic features and for general interest. Only "great" subdivisions are listed (e.g., regions rather than departments for France), and these are cited by conventional or official[5] names without alternative designations. The following kinds of subdivisions are listed:

Argentina — provinces
Australia — states and territories
Brazil — states and territories
Canada — provinces and territories
China — provinces and regions
Czechoslovakia — regions
France — regions
India — states
Indonesia — islands
Italy — regions
Japan — islands
Libya — provinces
Malaysia — divisions
Mexico — states and territories
New Zealand — islands
Philippines — islands
Saudi Arabia — regions
South Africa — provinces
Spain — regions
Tanzania — divisions
UK — divisions
USA — states
USSR — republics
West Germany — states
Yugoslavia — republics

Latitude and Longitude

Further to facilitate geographic location, latitude and longitude to the nearest minute are given for all cities and almost all physiographic features. Almost exclusively, the latitudes and longitudes are derived from the gazetteers prepared by the US Office of Geography; these are based on official large-scale maps of the relevant countries and regions. They can therefore be depended upon for accuracy. For reasons of simplicity, they are given in this form: 50.46N, 6.06E (this defines the geographic position of Aachen, West Germany, and means 50 degrees 46 minutes north of the equator and 6 degrees 6 minutes east of Greenwich, a section of London).

Special Symbols

Every effort has been made to obtain official data for the various statistical tables. When such data are unavailable, the most reliable unofficial figures are given. In Tables 3 through 13, unofficial data are identified by the symbol ● placed before the name of the physiographic feature in question.

All population figures are from census returns except those for which an "e" is placed after the year of record; the "e," of course, indicates that the figure has been estimated, usually by official sources. For many cities, two sets of population figures are given. Figures without a symbol are for the city proper; those followed by an "s" are for the city and adjacent

[5] Official names are used for the subdivisions of France, Italy, Spain, and West Germany because only a few of these have different conventional English names.

suburban areas. Preferably, the latter figures are for the urbanized area or conurbation only, but some officially reported suburban areas include rural districts.

The asterisk (*) is another special symbol used in this work. This symbol indicates that the city cited is the capital of a country or subdivision. If the asterisk is placed before the name of the city, it is the capital of the country under which it is listed. If the asterisk is placed before the name of a subdivision, the city cited is the capital of that subdivision. It should be noted that some countries have more than one capital.

Finally, most of the tables that are arranged by some measurement, rather than alphabetically, are divided into two parts separated by three centered asterisks (***). When this division is made, the portion of the table that is above the asterisks represents all-inclusive coverage, and the portion that is below, selective coverage.

Figure 2. The earth photographed from the Apollo 11 spacecraft about halfway to the moon (98,000 nautical miles from earth). (Credit: US National Aeronautics and Space Administration.)

1
Continents, Including Adjacent Islands

Contents

Conventional name of continent.

Area, including inland waters and adjacent islands, in thousands of square miles and square kilometers, and percentage of world total.

Latest population, in thousands, and percentage of world total.

Density of population, per square mile and per square kilometer.

World totals.

Arrangement

By continent, alphabetically.

Coverage

All continents.

Rounding

Areas are rounded to the nearest 1000 mi^2 and km^2; populations, to the nearest 1000; densities of population, to the nearest two significant digits.

Special Feature

World totals are equivalent to world land area, population, and density of population.

Entries

7.

TABLE 1. CONTINENTS, INCLUDING ADJACENT ISLANDS

Continent	Area (1000 mi²)	Area (1000 km²)	Area (%)	Population (thousands)	Population (%)	Density of Population (per mi²)	Density of Population (per km²)
Africa	11,709	30,319	20.2	352,764	9.8	30	12
Antarctica	5,396	13,975	9.3	0	0	0	0
Asia	17,069	44,211	29.5	2,075,726	57.8	122	47
Europe	3,954	10,239	6.8	636,529	17.7	161	62
North America	9,416	24,386	16.3	314,748	8.8	33	13
Oceania	3,452	8,942	6.0	21,166	0.6	6.1	2.4
South America	6,884	17,834	11.9	189,252	5.3	27	11
World	57,880	149,906	100	3,590,185	100	62	24

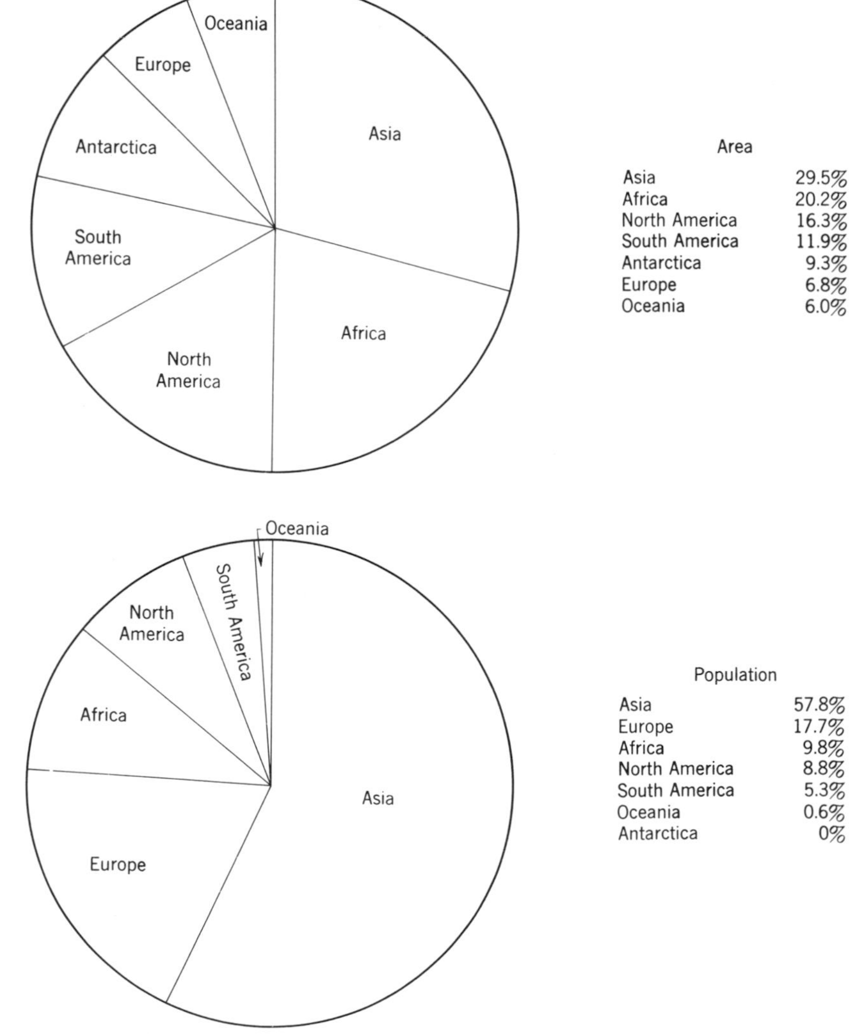

Figure 3. Area and population of continents.

2
Largest Seas

Contents

Conventional and alternate names of sea.

Area in thousands of square miles and square kilometers.

Arrangement

By area.

Coverage

All large seas, including those commonly designated as oceans, gulfs, bays, straits, and the like, generally recognized by oceanographic authorities.

Rounding

Areas are rounded to the nearest 1000 mi^2 and km^2.

Entries

65.

TABLE 2. LARGEST SEAS

Sea	Area (1000 mi²)	Area (1000 km²)	Sea	Area (1000 mi²)	Area (1000 km²)
Pacific O			Timor Sea	237	615
with adjacent seas	70,017	181,344	Andaman (alt Burma) Sea	232	602
without adjacent seas	64,186	166,241	North Sea	232	600
Atlantic O			Chukchi (alt Chuckchee) Sea	225	582
with adjacent seas	36,415	94,314	Great Australian Bight	187	484
without adjacent seas	33,420	86,557	Beaufort Sea	184	476
Indian O			Celebes (alt Sulawesi) Sea	182	472
with adjacent seas	28,617	74,118	Black Sea	178	461
without adjacent seas	28,350	73,427	Red Sea	174	450
Arctic O			Java (alt Djawa) Sea	167	433
with adjacent seas	4,732	12,257	Sulu Sea	162	420
without adjacent seas	3,662	9,485	Yellow (alt Huang, Hwang) Sea	161	417
Coral Sea	1,850	4,791	Baltic Sea	149	386
Arabian Sea	1,492	3,863	G of Carpentaria	120	311
South China (alt Nan) Sea	1,423	3,685	Molucca (alt Maluku) Sea	119	307
Caribbean Sea	1,063	2,754	Persian G (alt G of Iran)	93	241
Mediterranean Sea	971	2,516	G of Siam (alt G of Thailand)	92	239
Bering Sea	890	2,304	G of Saint Lawrence	92	238
B of Bengal	839	2,172	G of Aden	85	220
Sea of Okhotsk	614	1,590	Makassar (alt Macassar, Makasar) Strait	75	194
G of Mexico	596	1,543	Ceram (alt Seram) Sea	72	187
G of Guinea	592	1,533	B of Biscay	71	184
Barents Sea	542	1,405	G of Oman	70	181
Norwegian Sea	534	1,383	Aegean Sea	69	179
G of Alaska	512	1,327	G of California	68	177
Hudson B	476	1,232	Adriatic Sea	51	132
Greenland Sea	465	1,205	Flores Sea	47	121
Arafura Sea	400	1,037	Bali Sea	46	119
Philippine Sea	400	1,036	G of Bothnia	45	117
Sea of Japan	378	978	G of Tonkin	45	117
East Siberian Sea	348	901	Savu Sea	41	105
Kara Sea	341	883	Irish Sea	40	103
East China (alt Tung) Sea	290	752	White Sea	35	90
Solomon Sea	278	720	Bass Strait	29	75
Banda Sea	268	695	English Channel	29	75
Baffin B	266	689	Sea of Azov	15	38
Laptev Sea	251	650			

3
Largest Islands, by Continent

Contents

Latitude and longitude, in degrees and minutes, at center of island.
Conventional and other (alternate, former, and official) names of island.
Principal body of water, and subdivision and country in which located.
Area in thousands of square miles and square kilometers.

Arrangement

By area, under continent.

Coverage

Above * * *, all islands with at least the following areas:
- Africa – 2000 mi^2 (5180 km^2)
- Antarctica – 2000 mi^2 (5180 km^2)
- Asia – 2000 mi^2 (5180 km^2)
- Europe – 2000 mi^2 (5180 km^2)
- North America – 1500 mi^2 (3880 km^2)
- Oceania – 2000 mi^2 (5180 km^2)
- South America – 2000 mi^2 (5180 km^2)

Below * * *, other well-known islands, including the largest in certain countries.

Rounding

Areas are rounded to the nearest three significant digits.

Entries

212.

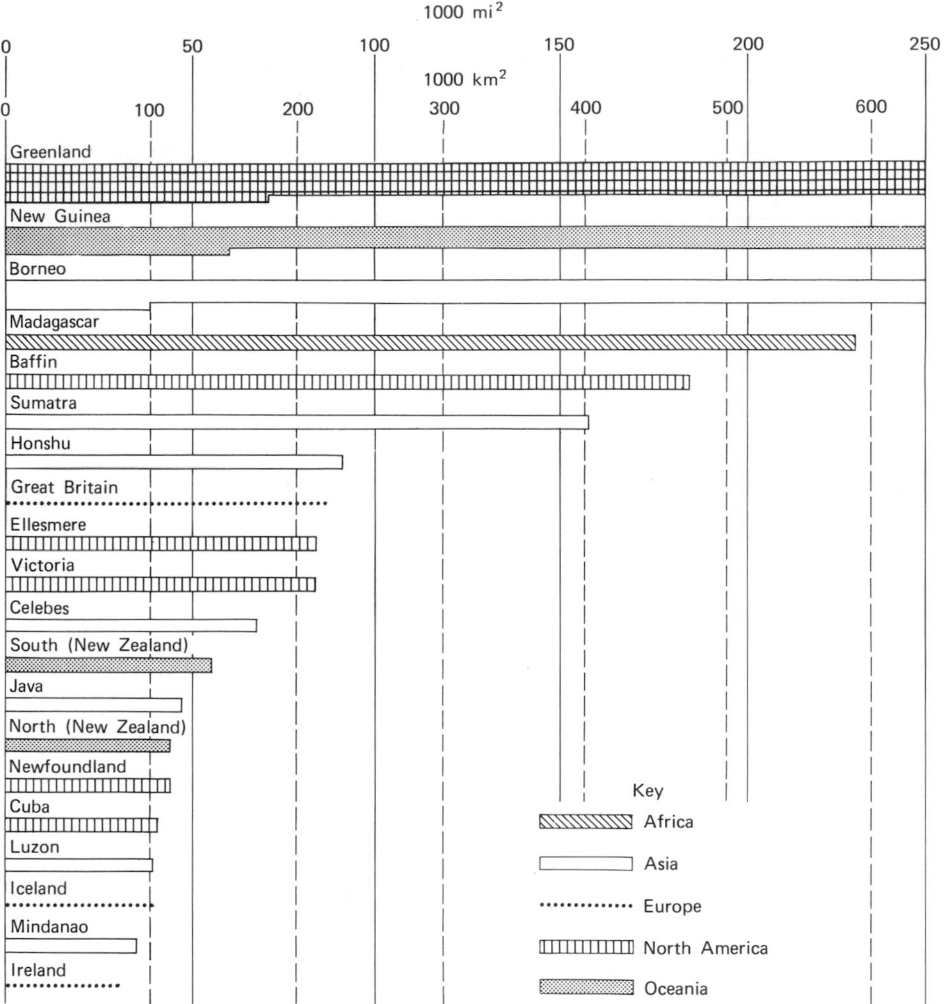

Figure 4. Twenty largest islands.

TABLE 3. LARGEST ISLANDS, BY CONTINENT

AFRICA

Latitude and Longitude	Island	Principal Body of Water	Location	Area (1000 mi²)	Area (1000 km²)
20.00S/47.00E	Madagascar (alt Madagaskara)	Indian O	Malagasy Republic	227	587
49.30S, 69.30E	• Kerguelen	Indian O	French Southern and Antarctic Lands	2.32	6.00
		* * *			
21.06S, 55.36E	Reunion (for Bourbon)	Indian O	Reunion	0.969	2.51
3.30N, 8.42E	Fernando Po (off Fernando Poo)	Bight of Biafra of G of Guinea	Equatorial Guinea	0.779	2.02
28.19N, 16.34W	Tenerife (for Teneriffe)	Atlantic O	(Canary Islands), Spain	0.745	1.93
20.18S, 57.35E	Mauritius [for (Ile de) France]	Indian O	Mauritius	0.720	1.86
28.20N, 14.00W	Fuerteventura	Atlantic O	(Canary Islands), Spain	0.642	1.66
6.10S, 39.20E	Zanzibar (alt Unguja)	Indian O	Zanzibar, Tanzania	0.640	1.66
28.00N, 15.36W	Gran Canaria (alt Grand Canary)	Atlantic O	(Canary Islands), Spain	0.592	1.53
11.35S, 43.20E	• Grande Comore	Mozambique Channel	Comoro Islands	0.442	1.14
15.05N, 23.40W	Santiago (alt Sao Tiago)	Atlantic O	Cape Verde Islands	0.384	0.994
5.10S, 39.48E	• Pemba	Indian O	Zanzibar, Tanzania	0.380	0.984
15.42N, 40.08E	• Dahlac (alt Grand Dahlac)	Red Sea	Ethiopia	0.347	0.900
0.12N, 6.39E	Sao Tome (for Sao Thome)	G of Guinea	Sao Tome and Principe	0.323	0.836
17.05N, 25.10W	Santo Antao	Atlantic O	Cape Verde Islands	0.302	0.782
32.44N, 17.00W	Madeira	Atlantic O	(Madeira Islands), Portugal	0.286	0.741

ANTARCTICA

Latitude and Longitude	Island	Principal Body of Water	Location	Area (1000 mi²)	Area (1000 km²)
71.00S, 70.00W,	• Alexander (for Alexander I)	Bellingshausen Sea	Antarctica	16.7	43.2

ASIA

Latitude and Longitude	Island	Principal Body of Water	Location	Area (1000 mi²)	Area (1000 mi²)
1.00N, 114.00E	• Borneo (alt Kalimantan)	South China Sea	Brunei-Indonesia-Malaysia	287	742
0.00, 102.00E	• Sumatra (off Sumatera)	Andaman Sea	Indonesia	156	405
36.00N, 138.00E	• Honshu (alt Hondo)	Pacific O	Japan	88.0	228
2.00S, 121.00E	• Celebes (off Sulawesi)	Celebes Sea	Indonesia	67.4	174
7.30S, 110.00E	• Java (off Djawa)	Indian O	Indonesia	48.8	126
15.00N, 121.00E	Luzon	Pacific O	Philippines	40.4	105

ASIA

Latitude and Longitude	Island	Principal Body of Water	Location	Area (1000 mi^2)	Area (1000 km^2)
8.00N, 125.00E	Mindanao	Pacific O	Philippines	36.5	94.6
44.00N, 143.00E	• Hokkaido (for Ezo, Yezo)	Pacific O	Japan	30.1	78.0
51.00N, 143.00E	Sakhalin (for Karafuto, Saghalien)	Sea of Okhotsk	Russia, USSR	29.5	76.4
7.30N, 80.30E	Ceylon (for Serendib; off Lanka)	Indian O	Ceylon	25.2	65.3
23.30N, 121.00E	Taiwan (alt Formosa)	Pacific O	Taiwan	13.8	35.8
33.00N, 131.00E	• Kyushu (alt Kiushu)	Pacific O	Japan	13.8	35.7
19.00N, 109.30E	Hainan	South China Sea	Kwangtung, China	13.1	34.0
8.50S, 126.00E	• Timor	Timor Sea	Indonesia-Portuguese Timor	10.2	26.3
1.00N, 128.00E	• Halmahera (off Djailolo)	Molucca Sea	Indonesia	6.95	18.0
33.45N, 133.30E	• Shikoku	Pacific O	Japan	6.86	17.8
3.00S, 129.00E	• Ceram (off Seram)	Banda Sea	Indonesia	6.62	17.2
8.30S, 121.00E	• Flores	Flores Sea	Indonesia	6.60	17.1
8.40S, 118.00E	• Sumbawa (for Soembawa)	Indian O	Indonesia	5.75	14.9
79.30N, 97.00E	Oktyabrskoy Revolyutsii (alt October Revolution)	Arctic O	Russia, USSR	5.48	14.2
12.00N, 125.00E	Samar	Pacific O	Philippines	5.05	13.1
10.00N, 123.00E	Negros	Sulu Sea	Philippines	4.90	12.7
10.30N, 118.30E	Palawan	South China Sea	Philippines	4.55	11.8
75.45N, 138.44E	Kotelnyy	Arctic O	Russia, USSR	4.48	11.6
2.15S, 106.00E	• Banka (off Bangka)	Java Sea	Indonesia	4.45	11.5
10.42N, 122.33E	Panay	Sulu Sea	Philippines	4.45	11.5
78.40N, 102.30E	Bolshevik	Arctic O	Russia, USSR	4.44	11.5
10.00S, 120.00E	• Sumba (for Sandalwood, Soemba)	Indian O	Indonesia	4.31	11.2
12.50N, 121.10E	Mindoro	South China Sea	Philippines	3.76	9.73
3.24S, 126.40E	• Buru (for Boeroe)	Banda Sea	Indonesia	3.71	9.60
35.05N, 33.15E	Cyprus (off Kibris, Kypros)	Mediterranean Sea	Cyprus	3.57	9.25
80.30N, 95.00E	Komsomolets	Arctic O	Russia, USSR	3.57	9.25
71.00N, 179.30W	Wrangel (off Vrangelya)	Chukchi Sea	Russia, USSR	2.82	7.30
10.50N, 124.52E	Leyte	Visayan Sea	Philippines	2.78	7.21
45.00N, 148.00E	Iturup (for Etorofu)	Pacific O	Russia, USSR	2.60	6.72
75.00N, 149.00E	Novaya Sibir (alt New Siberia)	East Siberian Sea	Russia, USSR	2.39	6.20
8.30S, 115.00E	• Bali	Indian O	Indonesia	2.15	5.56
73.35N, 142.00E	Bolshoy Lyakhovskiy	Arctic O	Russia, USSR	2.08	5.40
75.30N, 144.00E	Faddeyevskiy	Arctic O	Russia, USSR	2.05	5.30
		* * *			
7.00S, 113.30E	• Madura (for Madoera)	Java Sea	Indonesia	1.85	4.80
8.45S, 116.30E	• Lombok	Indian O	Indonesia	1.83	4.73
2.50S, 108.00E	• Billiton (off Belitung)	Java Sea	Indonesia	1.81	4.70
10.23N, 123.50E	Cebu (for Zebu)	Visayan Sea	Philippines	1.71	4.42
9.50N, 124.10E	Bohol	Mindanao Sea	Philippines	1.49	3.86
12.30N, 54.00E	• Socotra (alt Sokotra; off Suqutra)	Indian O	Southern Yemen	1.40	3.63

ASIA

Latitude and Longitude	Island	Principal Body of Water	Location	Area (1000 mi^2)	Area (1000 km^2)
19.06N, 93.48E	• Ramree (off Yanbye)	B of Bengal	Burma	0.888	2.30
33.20N, 126.30E	• Cheju (for Quelpart, Saishu)	East China Sea	South Korea	0.710	1.84
12.30N, 92.50E	Middle Andaman	B of Bengal	Andaman and Nicobar, India	0.593	1.54
13.15N, 92.55E	North Andaman	B of Bengal	Andaman and Nicobar, India	0.531	1.38
11.45N, 92.10E	South Andaman	B of Bengal	Andaman and Nicobar, India	0.520	1.35
26.45N, 55.45E	• Qeshm (for Kishm, Tawilah)	Strait of Hormuz	Iran	0.515	1.33
26.42N, 128.11E	Okinawa	Pacific O	Ryukyu Islands	0.454	1.18
7.00N, 93.50E	Great Nicobar	Indian O	Andaman and Nicobar, India	0.403	1.04
26.00N, 50.30E	• Bahrain (alt Bahrein; off Bahrayn)	Persian G	Bahrain	0.210	0.544
1.22N, 103.48E	• Singapore (off Singapura)	South China Sea	Singapore	0.210	0.543

EUROPE

Latitude and Longitude	Island	Principal Body of Water	Location	Area (1000 mi^2)	Area (1000 km^2)
53.30N, 2.30W	• Great Britain (alt Britain)	Atlantic O	UK	84.4	219
65.00N, 18.00W	Iceland (off Island)	Atlantic O	Iceland	39.8	103
53.25N, 8.00W	• Ireland (alt Eire)	Atlantic O	Ireland-UK	32.5	84.1
75.00N, 61.30E	Novaya Zemlya (north island)	Kara Sea	Russia, USSR	18.6	48.1
78.45N, 16.00E	West Spitsbergen (off Vestspitsbergen)	Arctic O	Svalbard	15.3	39.5
72.00N, 54.00E	Novaya Zemlya (south island)	Barents Sea	Russia, USSR	12.8	33.2
37.30N, 14.00E	Sicily (off Sicilia)	Mediterranean Sea	Sicilia, Italy	9.81	25.4
40.00N, 9.00E	Sardinia (off Sardegna)	Mediterranean Sea	Sardegna, Italy	9.19	23.8
79.48N, 22.24E	North East Land (off Nordaustlandet)	Barents Sea	Svalbard	5.79	15.0
42.00N, 9.00E	Corsica (off Corse)	Mediterranean Sea	Provence-Cote d'Azur-Corse, France	3.37	8.72
35.29N, 24.42E	Crete (for Candia; off Kriti)	Mediterranean Sea	Greece	3.22	8.33
55.30N, 11.45E	Zealand (off Sjaelland)	Baltic Sea	Denmark	2.71	7.02
		* * *			
77.45N, 22.30E	Edge	Barents Sea	Svalbard	1.94	5.03
39.30N, 3.00E	Majorca (off Mallorca)	Mediterranean Sea	Baleares, Spain	1.40	3.63
38.34N, 24.24E	Euboea (off Evvoia)	Aegean Sea	Greece	1.40	3.62
57.30N, 18.33E	Gotland (for Gottland)	Baltic Sea	Sweden	1.16	3.00
55.20N, 10.30E	Fyn (for Funen)	Baltic Sea	Denmark	1.15	2.98
58.25N, 22.30E	Sarema (alt Saaremaa)	Baltic Sea	Estonia, USSR	1.05	2.71

Figure 5. Icebergs floating along the west coast of Greenland, the largest island in the world. (Credit: Danish National Tourist Office.)

EUROPE

Latitude and Longitude	Island	Principal Body of Water	Location	Area (1000 mi²)	Area (1000 km²)
68.30N, 16.00E	Hinn(oya)	Norwegian Sea	Norway	0.849	2.20
58.05N, 6.40W	• Lewis with Harris	Atlantic O	Scotland, UK	0.825	2.14
57.20N, 6.15W	• Skye	Sea of the Hebrides	Scotland, UK	0.643	1.67
39.10N, 25.50E	Lesbos (off Lesvos)	Aegean Sea	Greece	0.623	1.61
36.10N, 28.00E	Rhodes (off Rodhos)	Aegean Sea	Greece	0.541	1.40
56.45N, 16.38E	Oland	Baltic Sea	Sweden	0.519	1.34
54.46N, 11.30E	Lolland (for Laaland)	Baltic Sea	Denmark	0.479	1.24
54.25N, 13.24E	Rugen	Baltic Sea	East Germany	0.358	0.926
38.22N, 26.00E	Chios (off Khios)	Aegean Sea	Greece	0.325	0.842
37.47N, 25.30W	Sao Miguel	Atlantic O	(Azores), Portugal	0.288	0.747
60.15N, 20.00E	• Ahvenanmaa (alt Aaland, Aland)	G of Bothnia of Baltic Sea	Finland	0.285	0.738
40.00N, 4.00E	Minorca (off Menorca)	Mediterranean Sea	Baleares, Spain	0.266	0.689
39.40N, 19.42E	Corfu (off Kerkira)	Ionian Sea	Greece	0.229	0.592
54.14N, 4.33W	(Isle of) Man	Irish Sea	Isle of Man	0.227	0.588
55.10N, 15.00E	Bornholm	Baltic Sea	Denmark	0.227	0.587
38.28N, 28.20W	Pico	Atlantic O	(Azores), Portugal	0.167	0.433
38.43N, 27.13W	Terceira	Atlantic O	(Azores), Portugal	0.153	0.397
50.40N, 1.17W	• (Isle of) Wight	English Channel	England, UK	0.147	0.381

NORTH AMERICA

Latitude and Longitude	Island	Principal Body of Water	Location	Area (1000 mi²)	Area (1000 km²)
73.00N, 42.00W	• Greenland (off Gronland)	Atlantic O	Greenland	823	2131
68.00N, 70.00W	Baffin (for Baffin Land)	Baffin B	Northwest Territories, Canada	184	476
81.00N, 80.00W	Ellesmere	Arctic O	Northwest Territories, Canada	82.1	213
71.00N, 114.00W	Victoria	Melville Sound	Northwest Territories, Canada	81.9	212
49.00N, 56.00W	Newfoundland	Atlantic O	Newfoundland, Canada	43.4	112
21.30N, 80.00W	Cuba	Caribbean Sea	Cuba	41.7	108
19.00N, 71.00W	Hispaniola (for Hayti; off Haiti, Santo Domingo)	Atlantic O	Dominican Republic-Haiti	29.2	75.6
73.15N, 121.30W	Banks	Arctic O	Northwest Territories, Canada	23.2	60.2
87.00N, 75.00W	Devon	Baffin B	Northwest Territories, Canada	20.9	54.0
75.15N, 110.00W	Melville	Melville Sound	Northwest Territories, Canada	16.4	42.4
80.30N, 92.00W	Axel Heiberg	Arctic O	Northwest Territories, Canada	15.8	40.9
64.20N, 84.40W	Southampton	Hudson B	Northwest Territories, Canada	15.7	40.7
72.40N, 99.00W	Prince of Wales	Melville Sound	Northwest Territories, Canada	12.8	33.2

NORTH AMERICA

Latitude and Longitude	Island	Principal Body of Water	Location	Area (1000 mi^2)	Area (1000 km^2)
49.00N, 125.00W	Vancouver	Pacific O	British Columbia, Canada	12.4	32.1
73.15N, 93.30W	Somerset	Lancaster Sound	Northwest Territories, Canada	9.37	24.3
76.00N, 100.30W	Bathurst	Melville Sound	Northwest Territories, Canada	7.61	19.7
76.45N, 119.30W	Prince Patrick	Arctic O	Northwest Territories, Canada	6.08	15.7
78.30N, 104.00W	Ellef Ringnes	Arctic O	Northwest Territories, Canada	5.14	13.3
69.00N, 97.30W	King William	Queen Maud G	Northwest Territories, Canada	4.95	12.8
18.15N, 77.30W	Jamaica	Caribbean Sea	Jamaica	4.41	11.4
73.13N, 78.34W	Bylot	Baffin B	Northwest Territories, Canada	4.20	10.9
46.00N, 60.30W	Cape Breton	Atlantic O	Nova Scotia, Canada	3.97	10.3
57.30N, 153.30W	Kodiak	Pacific O	Alaska, USA	3.67	9.51
67.50N, 76.00W	Prince Charles	Foxe Basin	Northwest Territories, Canada	3.64	9.43
18.15N, 66.45W	Puerto Rico (for Porto Rico)	Atlantic O	Puerto Rico	3.35	8.67
69.45N, 53.20W	Disco (alt Disko)	Davis Strait	Greenland	3.31	8.58
49.30N, 63.00W	Anticosti	G of Saint Lawrence	Quebec, Canada	3.04	7.88
73.17N, 106.45W	Stefansson	Melville Sound	Northwest Territories, Canada	2.89	7.49
75.15N, 94.30W	Cornwallis	Barrow Strait	Northwest Territories, Canada	2.67	6.92
55.30N, 132.45W	Prince of Wales	Pacific O	Alaska, USA	2.59	6.70
78.00N, 97.00W	Amund Ringnes	Peary Channel	Northwest Territories, Canada	2.51	6.51
53.00N, 132.00W	Graham	Pacific O	British Columbia, Canada	2.49	6.45
62.30N, 83.00W	Coats	Hudson B	Northwest Territories, Canada	2.21	5.71
46.30N, 63.00W	Prince Edward	G of Saint Lawrence	Prince Edward Island, Canada	2.18	5.66
57.50N, 135.40W	Chichagof	G of Alaska	Alaska, USA	2.08	5.40
77.45N, 111.00W	Mackenzie King	Hazen Strait	Northwest Territories, Canada	1.92	4.98
10.30N, 61.15W	Trinidad	Caribbean Sea	Trinidad and Tobago	1.86	4.83
63.30N, 170.30W	Saint Lawrence	Bering Sea	Alaska, USA	1.71	4.43
57.45N, 134.25W	Admiralty	Chatham Strait	Alaska, USA	1.65	4.27
60.06N, 166.20W	Nunivak	Bering Sea	Alaska, USA	1.62	4.21
70.45N, 26.00W	Milne Land	Greenland Sea	Greenland	1.62	4.20
54.45N, 164.00W	Unimak	Pacific O	Alaska, USA	1.61	4.16
24.26N, 77.57W	Andros[1]	Great Bahama Bank	Bahama Islands	1.60	4.14
57.00N, 135.00W	Baranof	G of Alaska	Alaska, USA	1.60	4.14

* * *

[1] Actually several (unnamed) islands.

NORTH AMERICA

Latitude and Longitude	Island	Principal Body of Water	Location	Area (1000 mi^2)	Area (1000 km^2)
40.50N, 73.00W	Long	Atlantic O	New York, USA	1.40	3.63
21.40N, 82.50W	(Isle of) Pines (off Pinos)	Caribbean Sea	Cuba	1.18	3.06
55.35N, 131.20W	Revillagigedo	Behm Canal	Alaska, USA	1.14	2.97
56.46N, 133.25W	Kupreanof	Frederick Sound	Alaska, USA	1.09	2.82
45.50N, 82.20W	Manitoulin	Huron L	Ontario, Canada	1.07	2.77
53.45N, 167.00W	Unalaska	Pacific O	Alaska, USA	1.06	2.76
26.28N, 77.05W	Abaco (alt Great Abaco)	Atlantic O	Bahama Islands	0.776	2.01
21.05N, 73.18W	Inagua (alt Great Inagua)	Windward Passage	Bahama Islands	0.560	1.45
26.38N, 78.25W	Grand Bahama	Northwest Providence Channel	Bahama Islands	0.430	1.11
14.40N, 61.00W	Martinique	Caribbean Sea	Martinique	0.425	1.10
16.10N, 61.40W	Basse-Terre	Caribbean Sea	Guadeloupe	0.364	0.943
29.20N, 113.25W	Angel de la Guarda	G of California	Baja California, Mexico	0.330	0.855
15.25N, 61.20W	Dominica	Caribbean Sea	Dominica	0.305	0.790
29.00N, 112.25W	Tiburon	G of California	Baja California, Mexico	0.290	0.751
13.55N, 60.59W	Saint Lucia	Caribbean Sea	Saint Lucia	0.238	0.616
16.20N, 61.25W	Grande-Terre	Caribbean Sea	Guadeloupe	0.219	0.566
48.00N, 88.50W	(Isle) Royale	Superior L	Michigan, USA	0.210	0.544
12.10N, 69.00W	Curacao	Caribbean Sea	Netherlands Antilles	0.182	0.472
13.10N, 59.33W	Barbados	Caribbean Sea	Barbados	0.166	0.430
44.20N, 68.18W	Mount Desert	Atlantic O	Maine, USA	0.108	0.280

OCEANIA

Latitude and Longitude	Island	Principal Body of Water	Location	Area (1000 mi^2)	Area (1000 km^2)
5.00S, 140.00E	• New Guinea (alt Irian, Papua)	Pacific O	Indonesia-New Guinea (Australia)-Papua	311	806
44.00S, 170.00E	South (New Zealand)	Pacific O	New Zealand	58.1	150
38.00S, 175.40E	North (New Zealand)	Pacific O	New Zealand	44.3	115
42.00S, 147.00E	Tasmania (for Van Diemen's Land)	Indian O	Tasmania, Australia	24.6	63.8
5.40S, 151.00E	New Britain (for Neu Pommern)	Bismarck Sea	New Guinea (Australia)	14.6	37.8
21.30S, 165.30E	New Caledonia (off Nouvelle-Caledonie)	Coral Sea	New Caledonia	6.53	16.9
7.53S, 138.23E	• Dolak (alt Kolepon; for Frederik Hendrik)	Arafura Sea	West Irian, Indonesia	4.16	10.8
19.30N, 155.30W	Hawaii	Pacific O	Hawaii, USA	4.02	10.4
18.00S, 178.00E	Viti Levu	Pacific O	Fiji	4.01	10.4
6.00S, 155.00E	Bougainville	Pacific O	New Guinea (Australia)	3.88	10.0
3.20S, 152.00E	New Ireland (for Neu Mecklenburg)	Pacific O	New Guinea (Australia)	3.34	8.65
9.32S, 160.12E	Guadalcanal	Solomon Sea	British Solomon Islands	2.50	6.47
11.40S, 131.00E	Melville	Timor Sea	Northern Territory, Australia	2.40	6.22
16.33S, 179.15E	Vanua Levu	Pacific O	Fiji	2.14	5.53

* * *

OCEANIA

Latitude and Longitude	Island	Principal Body of Water	Location	Area (1000 mi^2)	Area (1000 km^2)
15.15S, 166.50E	Espiritu Santo (alt Santo; for Marina)	Coral Sea	New Hebrides	1.93	5.00
8.00S, 159.00E	Santa Isabel (alt Ysabel)	Pacific O	British Solomon Islands	1.80	4.67
35.50S, 137.06E	Kangaroo	Indian O	South Australia, Australia	1.68	4.35
9.00S, 161.00E	Malaita	Pacific O	British Solomon Islands	1.57	4.07
16.15S 167.30E	Malekula (alt Mallicolo)	Coral Sea	New Hebrides	0.965	2.50
20.48N, 156.20W	Maui	Pacific O	Hawaii, USA	0.728	1.89
13.36S, 172.22W	Savaii	Pacific O	Western Samoa	0.703	1.82
47.00S, 167.40E	Stewart	Pacific O	New Zealand	0.670	1.74
21.30N, 158.00W	Oahu	Pacific O	Hawaii, USA	0.604	1.56
22.03N, 159.30W	Kauai	Pacific O	Hawaii, USA	0.555	1.44
13.55S, 171.45W	Upolu	Pacific O	Western Samoa	0.430	1.11
17.37S, 149.27W	Tahiti	Pacific O	French Polynesia	0.402	1.04
13.26N, 144.43E	Guam	Pacific O	Guam	0.203	0.526

SOUTH AMERICA

Latitude and Longitude	Island	Principal Body of Water	Location	Area (1000 mi^2)	Area (1000 km^2)
54.00S, 69.00W	• Grande de Tierra del Fuego	Atlantic O	Argentina-Chile	18.7	48.4
1.00S, 49.30W	• Marajo	Amazon R	Para, Brazil	18.5	48.0
11.30S, 50.15W	• Bananal	Araguaia R	Goias, Brazil	7.72	20.0
42.30S, 73.55W	• Chiloe	Pacific O	Chile	3.24	8.39
49.20S, 74.40W	• Wellington	Pacific O	Chile	2.61	6.75
51.55S, 58.45W	• East Falkland (alt Malvina del Este)	Atlantic O	Falkland Islands	2.44	6.31
0.30S, 91.06W	• Isabela (alt Albemarle)	Pacific O	Ecuador[1]	2.25	5.82
53.45S, 72.45W	• Santa Ines	Pacific O	Chile	2.12	5.50
		* * *			
0.10N, 50.10W	• Caviana	Amazon R	Para, Brazil	1.90	4.92
1.00S, 51.30W	• Grande de Gurupa	Amazon R	Para, Brazil	1.88	4.86
51.50S, 60.00W	• West Falkland (alt Malvina del Oeste)	Atlantic O	Falkland Islands	1.68	4.35
54.15S, 36.45W	• South Georgia	Atlantic O	Falkland Islands	1.45	3.76
11.00N, 64.00W	Margarita	Caribbean Sea	Venezuela	0.355	0.920

[1] Galapagos (off Colon) Islands.

4
Largest Island in Each Country

Contents

Conventional name of country.
Conventional and other (alternate, former, and official) names of island.
Principal body of water in which located.
Country (if any) with which island is shared.
Area in thousands of square miles and square kilometers.

Arrangement

By country, alphabetically.

Coverage

All countries with an area of at least 5000 mi^2 (12,950 km^2) having or sharing an island of significant size.

Rounding

Areas are rounded to the nearest three significant digits.

Entries

87.

TABLE 4. LARGEST ISLAND IN EACH COUNTRY

Country	Island	Principal Body of Water	Country with which Shared	Area (1000 mi²)	Area (1000 km²)
Argentina	•Grande de Tierra del Fuego	Atlantic O	Chile	18.7	48.4
Australia	Tasmania	Indian O		24.6	63.8
Bangladesh	•Dakhin Shahbazpur	B of Bengal		0.612	1.59
Brazil	•Marajo	Amazon R		18.5	48.0
British Honduras	•Turneffe	Caribbean Sea		0.115	0.298
British Solomon Islands	Guadalcanal	Solomon Sea		2.50	6.47
Brunei	•Borneo (alt Kalimantan)	South China Sea	Indonesia, Malaysia	287	742
Burma	•Ramree (off Yanbye)	B of Bengal		0.888	2.30
Canada	Baffin (for Baffin Land)	Baffin B		184	476
Ceylon	Ceylon (for Serendib; off Lanka)	Indian O		25.2	65.3
Chile	•Grande de Tierra del Fuego	Atlantic O	Argentina	18.7	48.4
China	Hainan	South China Sea		13.1	34.0
Costa Rica	Chira	G of Nicoya of Pacific O		0.020	0.052
Cuba	Cuba	Caribbean Sea		41.7	108
Cyprus	Cyprus (off Kibris, Kypros)	Mediterranean Sea		3.57	9.25
Denmark	Zealand (off Sjaelland)	Baltic Sea		2.71	7.02
Dominican Republic	Hispaniola (for Hayti; off in Dominican Republic Santo Domingo)	Atlantic O	Haiti	29.2	75.6
Ecuador	•Isabela (alt Albemarle)	Pacific O		2.25	5.82
Egypt	•Tiran	Red Sea		0.030	0.070
Equatorial Guinea	Fernando Po (off Fernando Poo)	Bight of Biafra of G of Guinea		0.779	2.02
Ethiopia	•Dahlac (alt Grand Dahlac)	Red Sea		0.347	0.900
Falkland Islands	•East Falkland (alt Malvina del Este)	Atlantic O		2.44	6.31
Fiji	Viti Levu	Pacific O		4.01	10.4
Finland	•Ahvenanmaa (alt Aaland, Aland)	G of Bothnia of Baltic Sea		0.285	0.738
France	Corsica (off Corse)	Mediterranean Sea		3.37	8.72
French Guiana	•Cayenne	Atlantic O		0.060	0.155
Germany					
East	Rugen	Baltic Sea		0.358	0.926
West	Fehmarn	Baltic Sea		0.071	0.185
Greece	Crete (off Kriti)	Mediterranean Sea		3.22	8.33

Country	Island	Principal Body of Water	Country with which Shared	Area (1000 mi²)	Area (1000 km²)
Greenland	•Greenland (off Gronland)	Atlantic O		823	2131
Haiti	Hispaniola (for Hayti; off in Haiti Haiti)	Atlantic O	Dominican Republic	29.2	75.6
Honduras	•Roatan	Caribbean Sea		0.077	0.200
Iceland	Iceland (off Island)	Atlantic O		39.8	103
India	Middle Andaman	B of Bengal		0.593	1.54
Indonesia					
in Asia	•Borneo (alt Kalimantan)	South China Sea	Brunei, Malaysia	287	742
in Oceania (West Irian)	•New Guinea (alt Irian, Papua)	Pacific O	New Guinea (Australia), Papua	311	806
Iran	•Qeshm (for Kishm, Tawilah)	Strait of Hormuz		0.515	1.33
Ireland	•Ireland (alt Eire)	Atlantic O	UK	32.5	84.1
Italy	Sicily (off Sicilia)	Mediterranean Sea		9.81	25.4
Jamaica	Jamaica	Caribbean Sea		4.41	11.4
Japan	•Honshu (alt Hondo)	Pacific O		88.0	228
Korea					
North	•Sinmi (for Shimmi; off Shinmi)	Korea B of Yellow Sea		0.020	0.053
South	•Cheju (for Quelpart, Saishu)	East China Sea		0.710	1.84
Kuwait	•Bubiyan	Persian G		0.250	0.650
Malagasy Republic	Madagascar (alt Madagaskara)	Indian O		227	587
Malaysia					
East	•Borneo (alt Kalimantan)	South China Sea	Brunei, Indonesia	287	742
West	•Langkawi	Strait of Malacca		0.203	0.526
Mexico	Angel de la Guarda	G of California		0.330	0.855
Netherlands	•Schouwen-Duiveland	North Sea		0.086	0.222
New Caledonia	New Caledonia (off Nouvelle-Caledonie)	Coral Sea		6.53	16.9
New Guinea (Australia)	•New Guinea (alt Irian, Papua)	Pacific O	Indonesia, Papua	311	806
New Hebrides	Espiritu Santo (alt Santo; for Marina)	Coral Sea		1.93	5.00
New Zealand	South (New Zealand)	Pacific O		58.1	150
Nicaragua	•Ometepe	Nicaragua L		0.106	0.275
Norway	Hinn(oya)	Norwegian Sea		0.849	2.20
Oman	• Masirah	Arabian Sea		0.250	0.650
Panama	•Coiba	Pacific O		0.200	0.518
Papua	•New Guinea (alt Irian, Papua)	Pacific O	Indonesia, New Guinea (Australia)	311	806
Philippines	Luzon	Pacific O		40.4	105

Country	Island	Principal Body of Water	Country with which Shared	Area (1000 mi²)	Area (1000 km²)
Portugal					
in Africa (Madeira Islands)	Madeira	Atlantic O		0.286	0.741
in Europe	Sao Miguel	Atlantic O		0.288	0.747
Portuguese Guinea	•Orango	Atlantic O		0.120	0.300
Portuguese Timor	•Timor	Timor Sea	Indonesia	10.2	26.3
Puerto Rico	Puerto Rico (for Porto Rico)	Atlantic O		3.35	8.67
Saudi Arabia	•Farasan al Kabir	Red Sea		0.120	0.300
Sierra Leone	•Sherbro	Atlantic O		0.260	0.670
South Africa	•Marion	Indian O		0.140	0.350
Southern Yemen	•Socotra (alt Sokotra; off Suqutra)	Indian O		1.40	3.63
Spain					
in Africa (Canary Islands)	Tenerife (for Teneriffe)	Atlantic O		0.745	1.93
in Europe	Majorca (off Mallorca)	Mediterranean Sea		1.40	3.63
Svalbard	West Spitsbergen (off Vestspitsbergen)	Arctic O		15.3	39.5
Sweden	Gotland (for Gottland)	Baltic Sea		1.16	3.00
Taiwan	Taiwan (alt Formosa)	Pacific O		13.8	35.8
Tanzania	Zanzibar (alt Unguja)	Indian O		0.640	1.66
Thailand	•Phuket (for Salang)	Andaman Sea		0.206	0.534
Trinidad and Tobago	Trinidad	Caribbean Sea		1.86	4.83
Tunisia	•Djerba (off Jarbah)	Mediterranean Sea		0.197	0.510
Turkey (in Asia)	•Imbros (off Imroz)	Aegean Sea		0.108	0.280
UK	•Great Britain (alt Britain)	Atlantic O		84.4	219
USA					
in North America	Kodiak	Pacific O		3.67	9.51
in Oceania (Hawaii)	Hawaii	Pacific O		4.02	10.4
USSR					
in Asia	Sakhalin (for Karafuto, Saghalien)	Sea of Okhotsk		29.5	76.4
in Europe	Novaya Zemlya (north island)	Kara Sea		18.6	48.1
Venezuela	Margarita	Caribbean Sea		0.355	0.920
Vietnam (South)	•Phu Quoc	G of Siam		0.230	0.596
Yemen	•Zuqar	Red Sea		0.070	0.180
Yugoslavia	Krk	Adriatic Sea		0.158	0.408

5
Longest Rivers, by Continent

Contents

Latitude and longitude, in degrees and minutes, at mouth of river.

Conventional and other (alternate, former, and official) names of river and of its tributaries (if any) constituting the longest watercourse.

Outflow (sea, lake, river, etc.), and subdivision and country in which located.

Total length of watercourse, in miles and kilometers.

Area of drainage basin of river and all its tributaries, in thousands of square miles and square kilometers.

Average discharge rate, in thousands of cubic feet per second and in cubic meters per second. The discharge rate given is that of the main stream, preferably averaged over several recent years and measured at the gauging station registering the greatest discharge (or nearest the mouth of the river).

Arrangement

By length of watercourse, under continent.

Coverage

Above * * *, all rivers with continuous watercourses of at least the following lengths:

Africa – 600 mi (970 km)
Asia – 600 mi (970 km)
Europe – 500 mi (800 km)
North America – 500 mi (800 km)
Oceania – 600 mi (970 km)
South America – 500 mi (800 km)

Below * * *, other well-known rivers, including the longest in certain countries and certain border rivers of strategic importance. Also included are all nontributary rivers in the USA at least 250 mi long.

Rounding

Lengths are rounded to the nearest 10 mi (km); drainage basin areas, to the nearest 1000 mi² (km²); average discharge rates, to the nearest 1000 cfs (100 when less than 10,000) and to the nearest 10 m³/sec (one when less than 1000).

Entries

418.

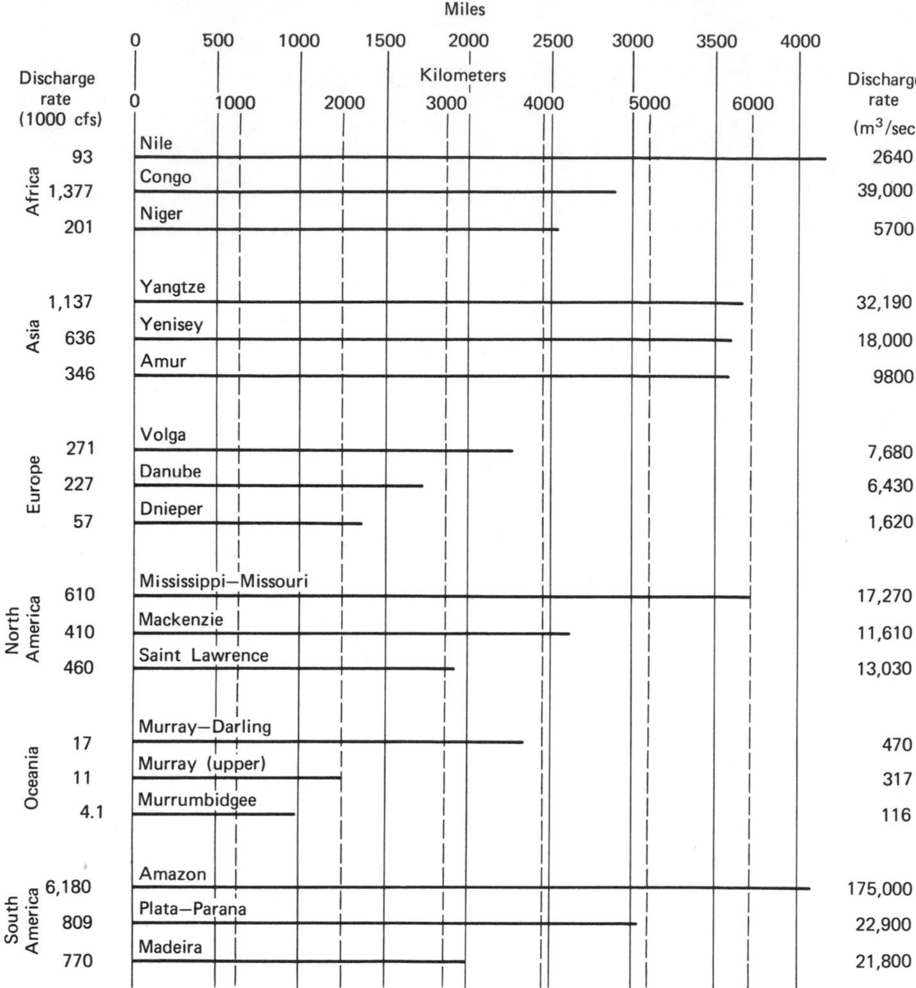

Figure 6. Three longest rivers of each continent, showing average discharge rate of each river.

TABLE 5. LONGEST RIVERS, BY CONTINENT

AFRICA

Latitude and Longitude		River	Outflow and Location	Length (mi)	Length (km)	Drainage Basin (1000 mi²)	Drainage Basin (1000 km²)	Discharge Rate (1000 cfs)	Discharge Rate (m³/sec)
31.32N,	31.51E[1]	•Nile (off Nil)-Kagera-Ruvuvu-Luvironza	Mediterranean Sea, Egypt	4160	6690	1082	2802	93	2,640
6.04S,	12.24E	Congo (alt Zaire; for Kongo)-Lualaba	Atlantic O, Angola-Zaire	2880	4630	1476	3822	1377	39,000
4.20N,	6.00E	•Niger	G of Guinea, Nigeria	2550	4100	808	2092	201	5,700
18.50S,	36.17E	•Zambezi (alt Zambesi, Zambeze)	Mozambique Channel, Mozambique	1650	2650	514	1331	565	16,000
0.26N,	42.48E	•Shebeli (alt Shabale, Shibeli; for Scebeli)	Balli Swamp, Somalia	1550	2490	77	200	11	320
0.30S,	17.42E	•Ubangi (alt Oubangui)-Uele-Kibali	Congo R, Congo-Zaire	1530	2460	298	773	265	7,500
28.38S,	16.27E	•Orange (alt Oranje)	Atlantic O, South Africa – South-West Africa	1300	2090	261	677	12	345
3.02S,	16.57E	•Kasai (alt Cassai)	Congo R, Zaire	1200	1930	349	904	351	9,950
15.48N,	16.32W	Senegal-Bafing	Atlantic O, Mauritania-Senegal	1050	1700	170	440		
15.38N,	32.31E	•Blue Nile (off Abay, Azraq)	Nile R, Sudan	1000	1610	128	331	57	1,620
18.53S,	22.24E	•Okovanggo (alt Cubango, Okavango)	Okovanggo Basin, Botswana	1000	1610	303	785	9.0	255
5.47N,	0.43E	•Volta-Black Volta (alt Volta Noire)	G of Guinea, Ghana	990	1600	150	388	41	1,170
25.12S,	33.32E	•Limpopo (alt Crocodile)	Indian O, Mozambique	990	1590	170	440		
0.16S,	42.35E	•Juba (alt Ganana; for Giuba)–Ganale-Dorya	Indian O, Somalia	970	1560	76	196	7.1	200
6.46S,	26.58E	•Luvua-Luapula-Chambezi	Lualaba R, Zaire	930	1500	97	250		
0.46N,	24.16E	•Lomami	Congo R, Zaire	900	1450	42	110		
12.58N,	14.31E	•Shari (alt Chari)-Sara (alt Ouham)	Chad L, Cameroon-Chad	900	1450	270	700	43	1,230
8.00S,	39.20E	•Rufiji-Luwegu	Indian O, Tanganyika, Tanzania	870	1400	69	178		
7.50N,	6.50E	•Benue (alt Benoue)	Niger R, Nigeria	810	1300	130	337	112	3,170
1.13N,	23.36E	•Aruwimi-Ituri	Congo R, Zaire	800	1290	45	116		
0.05N,	18.17E	•Ruki-Busira-Tshuapa	Congo R, Zaire	800	1290	67	174		
0.49S,	9.00E	•Ogooue (alt Ogowe)	G of Guinea, Gabon	750	1210	83	216	353	10,000
4.17S,	20.25E	•Sankuru-Lubilash	Kasai R, Zaire	750	1210	60	156	88	2,500

[1]For Damietta (off Dumyat) R distributary; for Nile R proper: 30.10N, 31.06E.

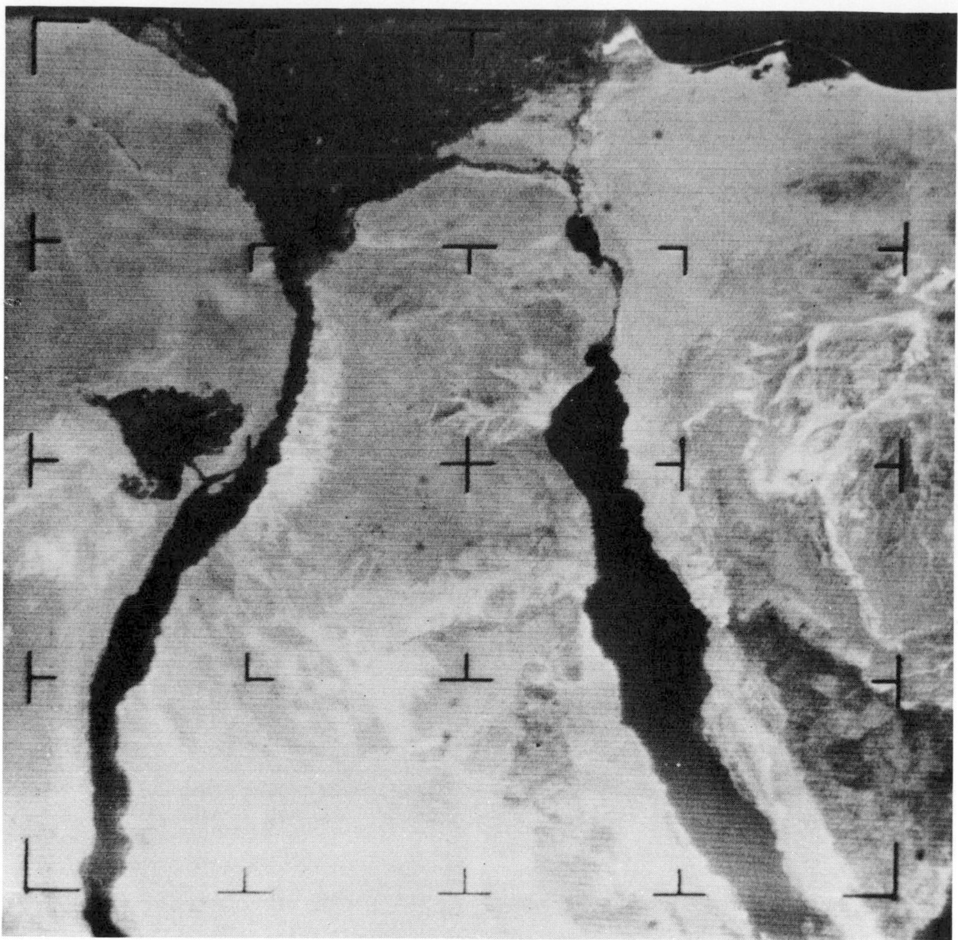

Figure 7. Lower course of the Nile, the earth's longest river, photographed from a Nimbus weather satellite during flooding conditions. The Nile delta (top left) is entirely inundated except for a few small islands. The Gulf of Suez and the Sinai Peninsula are to the right. (Credit: US National Aeronautics and Space Administration.)

AFRICA

Latitude and Longitude		River	Outflow and Location	Length (mi)	Length (km)	Drainage Basin (1000 mi^2)	Drainage Basin (1000 km^2)	Discharge Rate (1000 cfs)	Discharge Rate (m^3/sec)
29.04S,	23.38E	•Vaal	Orange R, Cape of Good Hope, South Africa	750	1210				
11.12N,	41.40E	Awash (alt Hawash)	Abbe (alt Abe) L, Ethiopia	750	1200	21	55	5.7	160
13.27N,	16.37W	Gambia (alt Gambie)	Atlantic O, Gambia	700	1130	70	182		
3.14S,	17.22E	•Kwango (alt Cuango)	Kasai R, Zaire	700	1130	102	263	95	2,700
3.01S,	16.58E	•Fimi-Lukenie	Kasai R, Zaire	660	1070	51	132		
3.22S,	17.22E	•Kwilu (alt Cuilo)	Kwango R, Zaire	650	1050	35	90	2.5	71
17.47S,	25.10E	•Chobe (alt Linyanti)-Kwando (alt Cuando)	Zambezi R, Botswana-South-West Africa	620	1000				
15.56S,	28.55E	•Kafue	Zambezi R, Zambia	600	970				
28.31S,	20.13E	•Molopo	Orange R, Cape of Good Hope, South Africa	600	970				
9.19S,	13.08E	Cuanza	Atlantic O, Angola	600	960	60	156		
			* * *						
17.20S,	11.50E	Cunene (alt Kunene)	Atlantic O, Angola-South-West Africa	590	940				
5.02S,	21.07E	•Lulua	Kasai R, Zaire	550	890	25	65		
25.46S,	32.43E	•Komati (alt Incomati)	Delagoa B of Indian O, Mozambique	500	800				
17.40N,	33.56E	•Atbara (alt Atbarah)	Nile R, Sudan	480	780			1.1	32
10.29S,	40.28E	Ruvuma (alt Rovuma)	Indian O, Mozambique-Tanzania	450	730	58	150		
2.32S,	40.31E	•Tana	Indian O, Kenya	440	710				
36.02N,	0.08E	•Sheliff (alt Cheliff; off Shalaf)	Mediterranean Sea, Algeria	430	700	14	35		
33.19N,	8.20W	•Oum er Rbia	Atlantic O, Morocco	370	600			1.4	40
17.42S,	35.19E	•Shire (alt Chire)	Zambezi R, Mozambique	370	600				
4.22N,	7.32W	•Cavally (alt Cavalla)	Atlantic O, Ivory Coast-Liberia	320	510				
16.03S,	46.36E	•Betsiboka	Mozambique Channel, Malagasy Republic	270	440				

AFRICA

Latitude and Longitude		River	Outflow and Location	Length (mi)	Length (km)	Drainage Basin (1000 mi²)	Drainage Basin (1000 km²)	Discharge Rate (1000 cfs)	Discharge Rate (m³/sec)
37.07N,	10.13E	•Medjerda (off Majardah)	G of Tunis of Mediterranean Sea, Tunisia	230	360				

ASIA

Latitude and Longitude		River	Outflow and Location	Length (mi)	Length (km)	Drainage Basin (1000 mi²)	Drainage Basin (1000 km²)	Discharge Rate (1000 cfs)	Discharge Rate (m³/sec)
31.48N,	121.10E	Yangtze (off Chang)	East China Sea, Kiangsu, China	3720	5980	705	1827	1137	32,190
71.50N,	82.40E	Yenisey (alt Yenisei)-Angara[1]-Selenga (alt Selenge)-Ider (off Ideriin)	Yenisey G of Kara Sea, Russia, USSR	3650	5870	1011	2619	636	18,000
52.56N,	141.10E	Amur (alt Heilung)-Argun (alt Oerhkuna)-Kerulen (off Hereleng, Kolulun)	Tatar Strait, Russia, USSR	3590	5780	792	2050	346	9,800
66.45N,	69.30E	Ob-Irtysh[2] (alt Irtish)	G of Ob of Kara Sea, Russia, USSR	3360	5410	954	2470	360	10,200
37.32N,	118.19E	Yellow (alt Hwang; off Huang)	Yellow Sea, Shantung, China	3010	4840	297	771	54	1,530
72.25N,	126.40E	Lena	Laptev Sea, Russia, USSR	2730	4400	957	2478	569	16,100
10.33N,	105.24E	•Mekong (alt Khong, Lantsang, Tien Giang)	South China Sea, South Vietnam	2600	4180	313	811	424	12,000
46.03N,	61.00E	Syr (Darya)-Naryn	Aral (Sea) L, Kazakhstan, USSR	1910	3080	178	462	17	473
65.48N,	88.04E	Lower Tunguska (off Nizhnyaya Tunguska)	Yenisey R, Russia, USSR	1860	2990	182	471	118	3,330
22.50N,	90.50E[3]	•Brahmaputra (alt Tsangpo, Yalutsangpu)	B of Bengal, Bangladesh	1800	2900	361	935	678	19,200
24.20N,	67.47E	•Indus (alt Yintu)	Arabian Sea, Pakistan	1790	2880	455	1178	127	3,590
16.31N,	97.37E	•Salween (alt Khong, Lu, Nu)	G of Martaban of Andaman Sea, Burma	1750	2820	125	324	86[4]	2,450[4]

[1] Data for Angara-Selenga-Ider: 2120 mi, 3410 km; 408,000 mi², 1,056,000 km²; 147,000 cfs, 4150 m³/sec.

[2] Data for Irtysh: 2640 mi, 4250 km; 615,000 mi², 1,592,000 km²; 76,000 cfs, 2150 m³/sec.

[3] For Meghna R distributary; for Brahmaputra R proper: 24.02N, 90.59E.

[4] In China.

ASIA

Latitude and Longitude		River	Outflow and Location	Length		Drainage Basin		Discharge Rate	
				(mi)	(km)	(1000 mi^2)	(1000 km^2)	(1000 cfs)	(m^3/sec)
41.05N,	86.40E	Tarim (off Talimu)-Yarkand (alt Yeherhchiang)	Tarim Basin, Sinkiang, China	1710	2750	173	447	5.2	146
21.55N,	88.05E[1]	•Ganges (alt Ganga)-Bhagirathi	B of Bengal, Bangladesh-India	1650	2650	409	1059	410	11,610
64.24N,	126.26E	Vilyuy (alt Vilyui)	Lena R, Russia, USSR	1650	2650	190	491	54	1,530
43.40N,	59.01E	Amu (Darya) (alt Oxus)-Panja (alt Pyandzh)-Vakhsh	Aral (Sea) L, Uzbekistan, USSR	1630	2620	180	465	54	1,520
69.30N,	161.00E	Kolyma (alt Kolima)	East Siberian Sea, Russia, USSR	1610	2600	249	644	87	2,450
47.00N,	51.48E	Ural	Caspian (Sea) L, Kazakhstan, USSR	1570	2530	85	220	8.7	246
61.04N,	68.52E	Ob (upper)-Katun	Ob R, Russia, USSR	1560	2520	295	765	174	4,920
57.42N,	71.12E	Ishim	Irtysh R, Russia, USSR	1520	2450	56	144	1.9	53
29.57N,	48.34E	(Shatt al) Arab-Euphrates (off Firat, Furat)-Kara (Su)	Persian G, Iran-Iraq	1510	2430	427	1105	101	2,860
63.28N,	129.35E	Aldan	Lena R, Russia, USSR	1410	2270	271	702	177	5,000
73.00N,	119.55E	Olenek	Laptev Sea, Russia, USSR	1410	2270	89	231	30	840
15.50N,	95.06E	•Irrawaddy (off Iyawadi)-Nmai	Andaman Sea, Burma	1300	2090	158	409	447	12,660
70.48N,	148.54E	Indigirka-Khastakh	East Siberian Sea, Russia, USSR	1230	1980	140	362	54	1,520
59.26N,	112.34E	Vitim	Lena R, Russia, USSR	1230	1980	88	227	53	1,510
22.45N,	113.37E	Pearl (alt Canton, Yueh; off Chu)-Si (off Hsi)-Hung (Shui)	South China Sea, Kwangtung, China	1220	1960	173	448	409	11,590
47.42N,	132.30E	Sungari (off Sunghua)	Amur R, Heilungkiang, China	1160	1860	202	524	71	2,000
31.00N,	47.25E	Tigris (off Dicle, Dijlah)	(Shatt al) Arab R, Iraq	1150	1850	145	373	44	1,250
61.36N,	90.18E	Stony Tunguska (off Podkamennaya Tunguska)	Yenisey R, Russia, USSR	1140	1830	96	249	59	1,680

[1] For Hooghly R distributary; for Ganges R proper: 23.20N, 90.30E.

ASIA

Latitude and Longitude		River	Outflow and Location	Length		Drainage Basin		Discharge Rate	
				(mi)	(km)	(1000 mi^2)	(1000 km^2)	(1000 (cfs)	(m^3/sec)
57.43N,	83.51E	Chulym (alt Chulim)	Ob R, Russia, USSR	1120	1800	52	134	27	775
72.55N,	106.00E	Khatanga-Kotuy	Khatanga G of Laptev Sea, Russia, USSR	1020	1640	163	422	135	3,820
58.06N,	93.00E	Yenisey (upper)	Yenisey R, Russia, USSR	1010	1630	115	299	103	2,910
58.55N,	81.32E	Ket	Ob R, Russia, USSR	1010	1620	31	81	15	415
70.51N,	153.34E	Alazeya-Nelkan	East Siberian Sea, Russia, USSR	990	1590	25	64	11	320
58.10N,	68.12E	Tobol	Irtysh R, Russia, USSR	990	1590	153	395	29	830
53.20N,	121.26E	Shilka-Onon	Amur R. Russia, USSR	970	1570	78	201	18	504
25.30N,	81.53E	•Yamuna (alt Jumna)-Chambal	Ganges R, Uttar Pradesh, India	950	1530	144	372		
28.57N,	70.30E	•Panjnad-Sutlej	Indus R, Pakistan	940	1520	206	533	51	1,450
30.34N,	114.17E	Han (Shui)	Yangtze R, Hupeh, China	930	1500	67	174	42	1,200
71.31N,	136.32E	Yana-Sartang	Laptev Sea, Russia, USSR	930	1490	95	245	32	915
62.38N,	134.32E	Amga	Aldan R, Russia, USSR	910	1460	29	74	6.0	170
17.00N,	81.45E	Godavari	B of Bengal, Andhra Pradesh, India	900	1450	121	313	30	850
60.22N,	120.42E	Olekma	Lena R, Russia, USSR	890	1440	78	202	34	955
45.24N,	74.08E	Ili-Tekes	Balkhash L, Kazakhstan, USSR	870	1400	52	134	17	470
67.32N,	78.40E	Taz	Kara Sea, Russia, USSR	870	1400	55	142	43	1,210
40.40N,	122.15E	Liao	G of Liaotung of Yellow Sea, Liaoning, China	840	1340	83	215	22	624
58.06N,	94.01E	Taseyeva-Chuna	Angara R, Russia, USSR	820	1320	49	128	26	735
26.37N,	101.48E	Yalung	Yangtze R, Szechwan, China	820	1320				
15.57N,	80.59E	Krishna (alt Kistna)	B of Bengal, Andhra Pradesh, India	800	1290	100	259		
21.38N,	72.36E	Narmada (alt Narbada)	G of Cambay of Arabian Sea, Gujarat, India	800	1290	38	98	43	1,230

ASIA

Latitude and Longitude	River	Outflow and Location	Length (mi)	Length (km)	Drainage Basin (1000 mi²)	Drainage Basin (1000 km²)	Discharge Rate (1000 cfs)	Discharge Rate (m³/sec)
50.15N, 127.35E	Zeya	Amur R, Russia, USSR	770	1240	90	233	63	1,770
58.48N, 130.35E	Uchur	Aldan R, Russia, USSR	750	1210	44	113	50	1,410
41.45N, 35.59E	Kizil (Irmak)	Black Sea, Turkey	730	1180	30	77	4.7	133
63.28N, 118.50E	Markha	Vilyuy R, Russia, USSR	730	1180	38	99	11	299
45.26N, 124.39E	Nonni (alt Nun; off Nen)	Sungari R, Heilungkiang, China	730	1170				
68.42N, 158.36E	Omolon	Kolyma R, Russia, USSR	710	1150	46	119		
20.17N, 106.34E	Red (alt Coi, Koi; off Hong, Yuan)	G of Tonkin of South China Sea, North Vietnam	710	1150	46	120		
29.26N, 113.08E	Siang (off Hsiang)	Tungting L, Hunan, China	710	1150	39	100		
64.54N, 176.13E	Anadyr (alt Anadir)	G of Anadyr of Bering Sea, Russia, USSR	710	1140	77	200	35	978
37.24N, 60.38E	Hari (Rud) (alt Tedzhen)	Kara (Kum) Desert, Turkmenia, USSR	700	1120	30	78	0.9	24
50.21N, 106.05E	Orhon (alt Orkhon)	Selenga R, Mongolia	700	1120	51	133	4.2	120
60.45N, 76.45E	Vakh	Ob R, Russia, USSR	700	1120	26	67	16	448
31.12N, 61.34E	•Helmand (alt Helmund, Hirmand)	Seistan Basin, Afghanistan-Iran	690	1110	193	500		
40.30N, 80.48E	•Khotan (off Hotien) - Kara-Kash (off Kalakashih)	Tarim R, Sinkiang, China	680	1100				
60.40N, 69.46E	Konda	Irtysh R, Russia, USSR	680	1100	28	73	9.5	270
33.12N, 118.33E	Hwai (off Huai)	Hungtze L, Anhwei, China	680	1090	81	210	38	1,090
54.30N, 134.38E	Maya	Aldan R, Russia, USSR	680	1090	66	171	41	1,170
54.59N, 73.22E	Om	Irtysh R, Russia, USSR	680	1090	20	53	2.2	61
59.07N, 80.46E	Vasyugan	Ob R, Russia, USSR	670	1080	25	66	12	343
45.00N, 67.44E	Chu	Sauma(kol) L, Kazakhstan, USSR	640	1030	10	27	2.1	61
25.47N, 84.37E	•Ghaghara (alt Gogra)	Ganges R, Bihar-Uttar Pradesh, India	640	1030				

ASIA

Latitude and Longitude		River	Outflow and Location	Length		Drainage Basin		Discharge Rate	
				(mi)	(km)	(1000 mi^2)	(1000 km^2)	(1000 cfs)	(m^3/sec)
57.12N,	66.56E	Tura	Tobol R, Russia, USSR	640	1030	31	80	6.1	174
0.25S,	109.40E	Kapuas (alt Kapuas-Besar; for Kapoeas)	South China Sea, Borneo I, Indonesia	630	1010	39	102		
29.34N,	106.35E	Kialing (off Chialing)	Yangtze R, Szechwan, China	620	1000	62	160		
13.32N,	100.36E	Chao Phraya (alt Menam)-Nan	G of Siam, Thailand	620	990	58	150		
29.23N,	71.02E	•Chenab	Panjnad R, Pakistan	610	970	53	138	32	919
38.57N,	117.43E	Hai-Pai (alt Pei)	G of Chihli of Yellow Sea, Hopeh, China	600	970	80	208	8.3	234
63.46N,	121.35E	Tyung	Vilyuy R, Russia, USSR	600	970	17	44		

* * *

Latitude and Longitude		River	Outflow and Location	Length (mi)	Length (km)	Drainage Basin (1000 mi^2)	Drainage Basin (1000 km^2)	Discharge Rate (1000 cfs)	Discharge Rate (m^3/sec)
21.06N,	72.41E	Tapti	G of Cambay of Arabian Sea, Gujarat, India	560	910	25	64	23	654
48.28N,	135.02E	Ussuri (alt Wusuli)-Ulakhe	Amur R, China-USSR	560	910	72	187	34	953
30.25N,	48.12E	•Karun	(Shatt al) Arab R, Iran	530	850	22	57	27	766
20.19N,	86.45E	Mahanadi	B of Bengal, Orissa, India	520	840	51	132	69	1,950
73.50N,	87.10E	Pyasina	Kara Sea, Russia, USSR	510	820	69	178	94	2,650
41.07N,	30.39E	Sakarya	Black Sea, Turkey	510	820	21	55	9.1	257
39.55N,	124.20E	Yalu (alt Amnok)	Korea B of Yellow Sea, China-North Korea	500	810	24	63	19	526
25.32N,	83.10E	•Gomati (alt Gumti)	Ganges R, Uttar Pradesh, India	500	800				
1.16S,	104.05E	•Hari (for Djambi)	Berhala Strait, Sumatra I, Indonesia	500	800	15	40		
11.09N,	78.52E	•Kaveri (alt Cauvery)	B of Bengal, Madras, India	470	760	31	80	33	934
30.35N,	71.49E	•Ravi	Chenab R, Pakistan	470	760			8.8	250
25.42N,	84.52E	•Son	Ganges R, Bihar, India	470	760	21	55		
31.12N,	72.08E	•Jhelum	Chenab R, Pakistan	450	720			31	883

ASIA

Latitude and Longitude		River	Outflow and Location	Length (mi)	Length (km)	Drainage Basin (1000 mi^2)	Drainage Basin (1000 km^2)	Discharge Rate (1000 cfs)	Discharge Rate (m^3/sec)
0.35S,	117.17E	•Mahakam (alt Kutai)	Makassar Strait, Borneo I, Indonesia	450	720				
6.47S,	112.33E	•Solo	Java Sea, Java I, Indonesia	340	540	6	15		
35.07N,	128.57E	•Naktong (for Rakuti)	Korea Strait, South Korea	330	520	9	24		
36.02N,	35.58E	Orontes (off Asi)	Mediterranean Sea, Turkey	300[1]	470[1]	9	23	2.2	62
37.57N,	139.04E	Shinano	Sea of Japan, Honshu I, Japan	230	370	5	12		
43.15N,	141.23E	Ishikari	Sea of Japan, Hokkaido I, Japan	230	360	5	14		
35.44N,	140.51E	Tone	Pacific O, Honshu I, Japan	220	360	6	16		
18.22N,	121.37E	•Cagayan (alt Grande de Cagayan)	Babuyan Channel, Luzon I, Philippines	220	350	14	37		
7.07N,	124.24E	•Mindanao	Moro G of Celebes Sea, Mindanao I, Philippines	200	320	2	5		
31.46N,	35.33E	•Jordan (off Urdunn, Yarden)	Dead (Sea) L, Jordan	160	250	6	16	1.3	37

EUROPE

Latitude and Longitude		River	Outflow and Location	Length (mi)	Length (km)	Drainage Basin (1000 mi^2)	Drainage Basin (1000 km^2)	Discharge Rate (1000 cfs)	Discharge Rate (m^3/sec)
45.45N,	47.52E	Volga	Caspian (Sea) L, Russia, USSR	2300	3700	533	1380	271	7,680
45.20N,	29.40E	Danube (off Donau, Duna, Dunaj, Dunarea, Dunav, Dunay)	Black Sea, Romania-USSR	1770	2850	298	773	227	6,430
46.30N,	32.18E	Dnieper (off Dnepr)	Black Sea, Ukraine, USSR	1370	2200	194	503	57	1,620
47.04N,	39.18E	Don	Sea of Azov of Black Sea, Russia, USSR	1160	1870	163	422	30	851

[1] Average of lengths officially given by Syria (350 mi, 570 km) and Turkey (240 mi, 380 km).

EUROPE

Latitude and Longitude		River	Outflow and Location	Length (mi)	Length (km)	Drainage Basin (1000 mi²)	Drainage Basin (1000 km²)	Discharge Rate (1000 cfs)	Discharge Rate (m³/sec)
68.13N,	54.15E	Pechora (for Petchora)	Barents Sea, Russia, USSR	1120	1810	126	327	141	4,000
55.25N,	50.40E	Kama	Volga R, Russia, USSR	1120	1800	202	522	128	3,620
64.32N,	40.30E	Northern Dvina (off Severnaya Dvina) - Vychegda (alt Vichegda)	White Sea, Russia, USSR	1120	1800	139	360	120	3,400
56.20N,	43.59E	Oka	Volga R, Russia, USSR	920	1480	95	245	39	1,110
55.54N,	53.33E	Belaya	Kama R, Russia, USSR	890	1430	55	142	30	850
39.24N,	49.19E	Kura	Caspian (Sea) L, Azerbaijan, USSR	850	1360	73	188	18	514
46.18N,	30.17E	Dniester (off Dnestr)	Black Sea, Moldavia, USSR	840	1350	28	72	11	310
51.47N,	4.10E[1]	Rhine (off Rhein, Rhin, Rijn)	North Sea, Netherlands	820	1320	97	252	88	2,490
55.36N,	51.30E	Vyatka (alt Viatka)	Kama R, Russia, USSR	820	1310	50	129	29	830
54.21N,	18.56E	Vistula (for Visla, Weichsel; off Wisla)-Bug (alt Zapadnyy Bug)	G of Danzig of Baltic Sea, Poland	760	1220	75	194	33	930
53.50N,	9.00E	Elbe (alt Labe)	North Sea, Niedersachsen-Schleswig-Holstein, West Germany	710	1140	56	144	25	703
50.33N,	30.32E	Desna	Dnieper R, Ukraine, USSR	700	1130	34	88	12	330
39.56N,	48.20E	Araks (alt Aras)	Kura R, Azerbaijan, USSR	670	1070	39	100	7.5	212
47.35N,	40.54E	Donets (alt Northern Donets; off Severnyy Donets)	Don R, Russia, USSR	650	1050	38	99	5.4	153
47.16N,	2.11W	Loire	B of Biscay, Pays de la Loire, France	630	1020	46	120	31	871
57.00N,	24.00E	Western Dvina (alt Daugava; for Duna; off Zapadnaya Dvina)	G of Riga of Baltic Sea, Latvia, USSR	630	1020	33	85	25	697
49.36N,	42.19E	Khoper	Don R, Russia, USSR	630	1010	24	61	5.3	151

[1] For Haringvliet Estuary distributary; for Rhine R proper: 51.52N, 6.02E.

EUROPE

Latitude and Longitude		River	Outflow and Location	Length (mi)	Length (km)	Drainage Basin (1000 mi²)	Drainage Basin (1000 km²)	Discharge Rate (1000 cfs)	Discharge Rate (m³/sec)
38.40N,	9.24W	Tagus (off Tajo, Tejo)	Atlantic O, Portugal	630	1010	31	81	4.5	128
45.15N,	20.17E	Tisza (alt Tisa, Tissa; for Theiss)	Danube R, Serbia, Yugoslavia	600	970	61	157	27	771
51.47N	4.10E[1]	Meuse (alt Maas)	North Sea, Netherlands	590	950	19	49	9.5	269
55.18N,	21.23E	Neman (alt Nemunas; for Memel, Niemen)	Baltic Sea, Lithuania-Russia, USSR	580	940	38	98	22	629
44.50N,	20.28E	Sava (alt Save; for Sau, Szava)	Danube R, Serbia, Yugoslavia	580	940	37	96	43	1,210
54.40N,	56.00E	Ufa	Belaya R, Russia, USSR	580	930	20	53	12	351
45.30N,	28.12E	Prut (alt Prutul; for Pruth)	Danube R, Romania-USSR	570	920	11	27	2.5	70
40.43N,	0.54E	Ebro	Mediterranean Sea, Cataluna, Spain	570	910	32	83	6.1	173
66.11N,	43.59E	Mezen	White Sea, Russia, USSR	570	910	30	76	23	648
45.20N,	37.22E	Kuban	Sea of Azov of Black Sea, Russia, USSR	560	910	24	61	8.4	238
41.08N,	8.40W	Douro (alt Duero)	Atlantic O, Portugal	560	890	38	98	11	312
53.32N,	14.38E	Oder (alt Odra)	Baltic Sea, East Germany-Poland	540	870	46	119	17	480
51.10N,	30.30E	Pripet (off Pripyat)	Dnieper R, Ukraine, USSR	540	860	44	114	13	372
56.06N,	46.00E	Sura	Volga R, Russia, USSR	540	860	26	68	7.6	215
46.59N,	31.58E	Southern Bug (off Yuzhnyy Bug)	Dnieper R, Ukraine, USSR	530	860	27	69	2.9	83
59.57N,	30.20E	Neva-Svir-Suna	G of Finland of Baltic Sea, Russia, USSR	520	830	108	281	89	2,530
49.01N,	33.32E	Psel	Dnieper R, Ukraine, USSR	500	810	9	23	1.9	54
43.20N,	4.50E	Rhone	Mediterranean Sea, Provence-Cote d' Azur-Corse, France	500	810	38	99	53	1,500
52.35N,	14.39E	Warta (for Warthe)	Oder R, Poland	500	810	21	55	6.6	188
58.13N,	56.22E	Chusovaya	Kama R, Russia, USSR	500	800	18	48	8.0	226
56.18N,	46.24E	Vetluga	Volga R, Russia, USSR	500	800	15	40	8.2	231

* * *

[1] For Haringvliet Estuary distributary; for Meuse R proper: 51.49N, 5.01E.

EUROPE

Latitude and Longitude		River	Outflow and Location	Length		Drainage Basin		Discharge Rate	
				(mi)	(km)	(1000 mi²)	(1000 km²)	(1000 cfs)	(m³/sec)
64.08N,	41.54E	Pinega	Northern Dvina R, Russia, USSR	480	780	17	43	12	353
49.26N,	0.26E	Seine	English Channel, Haute-Normandie, France	480	780	31	79	9.6	273
46.15N,	20.12E	Maros (alt Mures, Muresul)	Tisza R, Hungary	470	750	12	30	5.7	161
53.32N,	8.34E	Weser-Werra	North Sea, Niedersachsen, West Germany	460	730	17	45	10	292
45.24N,	28.01E	Siret (for Sereth; off Seret, Siretul)	Danube R, Romania	450	730	18	48	14	400
57.42N,	11.52E	Gota-Klar	Kattegat Strait, Sweden	450	720	19	50	18	500
45.33N,	18.55E	Drava (alt Drau, Drave)	Danube R, Croatia, Yugoslavia	440	710	15	40	12	335
43.43N,	24.51E	Olt (for Aluta)	Danube R, Romania	420	670	9	24		
36.47N,	6.22W	Guadalquivir	G of Cadiz of Atlantic O, Andalucia, Spain	410	660	22	57	6.4	182
45.35N,	1.03W	Gironde-Garonne (alt Garona)	B of Biscay, Aquitaine - Poitou–Charentes, France	400	650	33	85	21	590
44.57N,	12.04E	Po	Adriatic Sea, Veneto, Italy	380	620	29	75	54	1,540
59.12N,	10.57E	Glomma (off Glama)	Skagerrak Strait, Norway	380	610	16	41	16	450
37.14N,	7.22W	Guadiana	G of Cadiz of Atlantic O, Portugal-Spain	360	580	26	68	3.2	91
65.48N,	24.08E	Torne (alt Tornio)-Muonio-Konkama (alt Kongama)	G of Bothnia of Baltic Sea, Finland-Sweden	350	570	16	40	2.7	76
65.47N,	24.30E	•Kemi	G of Bothnia of Baltic Sea, Finland	340	550	20	51	19	534
50.22N,	7.36E	Moselle (alt Mosel)	Rhine R, Rheinland-Pfalz, West Germany	340	550	11	28	10	292
50.00N,	8.18E	Main	Rhine R, Hessen, West Germany	330	520	10	27	3.5	100

EUROPE

Latitude and Longitude		River	Outflow and Location	Length (mi)	Length (km)	Drainage Basin (1000 mi²)	Drainage Basin (1000 km²)	Discharge Rate (1000 cfs)	Discharge Rate (m³/sec)
48.49N,	2.24E	Marne	Seine R, Region Parisienne, France	330	520	5	14	3.7	104
39.09N,	0.14W	Jucar	Mediterranean Sea, Valencia, Spain	310	500	12	31	2.1	60
40.52N,	26.12E	Maritsa (alt Evros, Meric)	Aegean Sea, Greece-Turkey	300	490	14	35		
51.22N,	4.15E	Scheldt (alt Escaut, Schelde)	North Sea, Netherlands	270	430	8	20	5.5	155
50.22N,	14.28E	Vltava (alt Moldau)	Elbe R, Bohemia, Czechoslovakia	270	430	11	28	5.4	153
45.10N,	12.20E	Adige	Adriatic Sea, Veneto, Italy	250	410	6	15	9.3	262
41.44N,	12.14E	Tiber (off Tevere)	Tyrrhenian Sea, Lazio, Italy	250	410	7	17	8.4	239
52.30N,	9.55W	Shannon	Atlantic O, Ireland	230	370	5	13	7.6	198
51.25N,	3.00W	Severn	Bristol Channel, England, UK	210	340	8	21	2.3	64
51.30N,	0.45E	Thames	North Sea, England, UK	200	320	6	16	2.7	76
41.45N,	19.34E	Drin	Adriatic Sea, Albania	170	280	2	6		
63.47N,	20.48W	•Thjorsa	Atlantic O, Iceland	140	230			14	385
56.29N,	10.13E	Gudena	Kattegat Strait, Denmark	100	160	1	3		

NORTH AMERICA

Latitude and Longitude		River	Outflow and Location	Length (mi)	Length (km)	Drainage Basin (1000 mi²)	Drainage Basin (1000 km²)	Discharge Rate (1000 cfs)	Discharge Rate (m³/sec)
29.00N,	89.10W	Mississippi-Missouri[1]-Jefferson-Beaverhead-Red Rock	G of Mexico, Louisiana, USA	3740	6020	1244	3222	610	17,270
69.15N,	134.08W	Mackenzie-Slave-Peace-Finlay	Beaufort Sea, Northwest Territories, Canada	2630	4240	681	1764	410	11,610
49.09N,	67.10W	Saint Lawrence (alt Saint-Laurent)-(Great Lakes) - Saint Louis	G of Saint Lawrence, Quebec, Canada	1900[2]	3060[2]	508	1316	460	13,030

[1] Data for Missouri-Jefferson-Beaverhead-Red Rock: 2560 mi, 4130 km; 530,000 mi², 1,373,000 km²; 79,000 cfs, 2250 m³/sec.

[2] For Saint Lawrence R proper: 590 mi, 960 km.

NORTH AMERICA

Latitude and Longitude		River	Outflow and Location	Length (mi)	Length (km)	Drainage Basin (1000 mi²)	Drainage Basin (1000 km²)	Discharge Rate (1000 cfs)	Discharge Rate (m³/sec)
25.55N,	97.09W	Rio Grande (alt Bravo)	G of Mexico, Mexico-USA	1880	3030	182	471	2.7	77
62.32N,	163.54W	Yukon-Lewes-Teslin-Nisutlin	Bering Sea, Alaska, USA	1870	3020	330	855	188	5,320
57.04N,	92.30W	Nelson-Saskatchewan - South Saskatchewan - Bow	Hudson B, Manitoba, Canada	1600	2570	414	1072	72	2,030
33.48N,	91.09W	Arkansas	Mississippi R, Arkansas, USA	1450	2330	160	414	40	1,150
31.54N,	114.57W	Colorado	G of California, Baja California - Sonora, Mexico	1450	2330	246	637	3.7	104
46.14N,	124.00W	Columbia-Snake[1]	Pacific O, Oregon-Washington, USA	1320	2130	259	671	195	5,520
36.59N,	89.08W	Ohio—Allegheny	Mississippi R, Illinois-Kentucky, USA	1310	2100	203	526	258	7,310
30.59N,	91.39W	Red	Mississippi R, Louisiana, USA	1220	1970	90	233	31	880
28.57N,	95.18W	Brazos	G of Mexico, Texas, USA	1210	1950	35	91	5.3	149
38.49N,	90.07W	Mississippi (upper)	Mississippi R, Missouri, USA	1170	1880	172	446	93	2,640
58.47N,	94.12W	Churchill	Hudson B, Manitoba, Canada	1000	1610	109	282	28	790
41.02N,	95.51W	Platte-North Platte	Missouri R, Nebraska, USA	990	1590	86	223	5.0	142
29.41N,	101.22W	Pecos	Rio Grande R, Texas, USA	930	1490	30	78	0.1	3
37.03N,	88.33W	Tennessee-Holston	Ohio R, Kentucky, USA	910	1470	40	104	64	1,810
35.28N,	95.03W	Canadian	Arkansas R, Oklahoma, USA	910	1460	48	124	6.3	179
28.41N,	96.00W	Colorado	Matagorda B of G of Mexico, Texas, USA	890	1440	42	109	2.4	67

[1] Data for Snake: 1000 mi 1610 km; 109,000 mi², 282,000 km²; 54,000 cfs, 1530 m³/sec.

NORTH AMERICA

Latitude and Longitude	River	Outflow and Location	Length (mi)	Length (km)	Drainage Basin (1000 mi^2)	Drainage Basin (1000 km^2)	Discharge Rate (1000 cfs)	Discharge Rate (m^3/sec)
46.12N, 119.03W	Columbia (upper)	Columbia R, Washington, USA	890	1430	96	249	120	3,410
49.04N, 123.07W	Fraser	Strait of Georgia, British Columbia, Canada	850	1370	90	231	95	2,700
60.05N, 162.25W	Kuskokwim	Kuskokwim B of Bering Sea, Alaska, USA	800	1290	31	80	42	1,180
30.41N, 88.00W	Mobile-Alabama-Coosa-Etowah	Mobile B of G of Mexico, Alabama, USA	780	1260	43	111	38	1,080
35.16N, 95.28W	North Canadian	Canadian R, Oklahoma, USA	780	1260	14	36	0.8	22
58.40N, 110.50W	Athabasca	Athabasca L, Alberta, Canada	760	1230	63	163	23	651
53.15N, 105.05W	North Saskatchewan	Saskatchewan R, Saskatchewan, Canada	760	1220	46	119	8.5	241
61.51N, 121.18W	Liard	Mackenzie R, Northwest Territories, Canada	750	1210	86	223	40	1,120
37.09N, 88.24W	Cumberland	Ohio R, Kentucky, USA	740	1190	18	47	27	774
38.11N, 109.53W	Green	Colorado R, Utah, USA	730	1170	41	106	6.5	185
39.06N, 94.36W	Kansas (alt Kaw) - Smoky Hill	Missouri R, Kansas, USA	730	1170	60	155	6.6	186
48.02N, 106.18W	Milk	Missouri R, Montana, USA	730	1170	23	58	0.7	20
29.45N, 94.43W	Trinity	Galveston B of G of Mexico, Texas, USA	710	1150	18	47	7.4	209
42.52N, 97.14W	James (alt Dakota)	Missouri R, South Dakota, USA	710	1140	22	57	0.3	9
36.11N, 96.16W	Cimarron	Arkansas R, Oklahoma, USA	700	1120	19	49	1.8	50
45.25N, 74.00W	Ottawa (alt Outaouais)	Saint Lawrence R, Quebec, Canada	700	1120	55	142	69	1,950
50.24N, 96.48W	Red - Otter Tail	Winnipeg L, Manitoba, Canada	690	1120	111	287	8.2	231

NORTH AMERICA

Latitude and Longitude		River	Outflow and Location	Length		Drainage Basin		Discharge Rate	
				(mi)	(km)	(1000 mi^2)	(1000 km^2)	(1000 cfs)	(m^3/sec)
18.24N,	92.38W	Usumacinta-Chixoy	B of Campeche of G of Mexico, Tabasco, Mexico	690	1110	40	103	59	1,680
33.56N,	91.02W	White	Mississippi R, Arkansas, USA	680	1100	28	73	28	795
47.58N,	104.01W	Yellowstone	Missouri R, North Dakota, USA	670	1080	70	181	13	365
58.30N,	68.10W	Koksoak-Caniapiskau	Ungava B of Hudson Strait, Quebec, Canada	660	1060	56	145	85	2,410
32.43N,	114.35W	Gila	Colorado R, Arizona, USA	630	1010	58	150	0.02	0.6
21.36N,	105.26W	Santiago (alt Grande de Santiago)-Lerma	Pacific O, Nayarit, Mexico	630	1010	35	90	2.7	76
33.53N,	96.35W	Washita	Red R, Oklahoma, USA	630	1010	8	21	1.5	44
47.37N,	102.18W	Little Missouri	Missouri R, North Dakota, USA	620	1010	9	23	0.6	16
52.17N,	81.31W	Albany-Cat	James B of Hudson B, Ontario, Canada	610	980	26	69	0.8	22
56.02N,	87.36W	Severn-Black Birch	Hudson B, Ontario, Canada	610	980	39	102		
67.15N,	95.15W	Back	Arctic O, Northwest Territories, Canada	600	970	35	91	18	521
53.20N,	60.20W	Churchill (for Hamilton)-Ashuanipi	Atlantic O, Newfoundland, Canada	600	970	31	80	56	1,600
31.16N,	91.50W	Ouachita	Red R, Louisiana, USA	600	970	18	47	18	515
49.53N,	97.07W	Assiniboine	Red R, Manitoba, Canada	590	950	63	163	1.6	46
64.33N,	100.06W	Dubawnt	Baker L, Northwest Territories, Canada	580	930	27	69	13	365
64.55N,	157.32W	Koyukuk	Yukon R, Alaska, USA	550	890				
66.34N,	145.19W	Porcupine	Yukon R, Alaska, USA	550	890				
39.02N,	96.51W	Republican-Arikaree	Kansas R, Kansas, USA	550	890	25	65	1.1	31
29.43N,	85.00W	Apalachicola-Chattahoochee	G of Mexico, Florida, USA	550	880	19	49	21	603
31.08N,	87.56W	Tombigbee	Mobile R, Alabama, USA	550	880	19	49	26	743

NORTH AMERICA

Latitude and Longitude		River	Outflow and Location	Length		Drainage Basin		Discharge Rate	
				(mi)	(km)	(1000 mi^2)	(1000 km^2)	(1000 cfs)	(m^3/sec)
44.47N,	100.45W	Cheyenne - Belle Fourche	Missouri R, South Dakota, USA	530	850	25	65	0.9	26
60.51N,	115.44W	Hay	Great Slave L, Northwest Territories, Canada	530	850	19	49	2.9	83
65.09N,	151.57W	Tanana	Yukon R, Alaska, USA	530	850				
67.49N,	115.04W	Coppermine	Arctic O, Northwest Territories, Canada	520	840	16	40	4.1	116
52.15N,	78.32W	Eastmain	James B of Hudson B, Quebec, Canada	510	820	18	47	29	810
43.45N,	99.25W	White	Missouri R, South Dakota, USA	510	820	10	26	0.5	15
49.00N,	117.36W	Pend Oreille-Clark Fork	Columbia R, British Columbia, Canada	500	810	25	65	27	760
38.35N,	91.58W	Osage-Marais des Cygnes	Missouri R, Missouri, USA	500	800	15	39	10	283
			* * *						
30.11N,	89.36W	Pearl	G of Mexico, Louisiana-Mississippi, USA	490	790	8	21	8.8	249
46.44N,	105.24W	Powder	Yellowstone R, Montana, USA	490	780	13	34	0.6	17
17.55N,	102.10W	Balsas	Pacific O, Guerrero-Michoacan, Mexico	480	770	42	108	8.2	231
48.10N,	69.45W	Saguenay-Peribonca	Saint Lawrence R, Quebec, Canada	470	760	39	101	53	1,490
37.46N,	88.02W	Wabash	Ohio R, Illinois-Indiana, USA	470	760	14	36	11	326
15.00N,	83.10W	•Coco (alt Segovia)	Caribbean Sea, Honduras-Nicaragua	470	750			18	500
62.12N,	159.43W	Innoko	Yukon R, Alaska, USA	460	750				
28.27N,	96.46W	Guadalupe	San Antonio B of G of Mexico, Texas, USA	460	740	9	23	2.1	59
39.33N,	76.05W	Susquehanna	Chesapeake B of Atlantic O, Maryland, USA	460	740	28	73	37	1,040

NORTH AMERICA

Latitude and Longitude		River	Outflow and Location	Length		Drainage Basin		Discharge Rate	
				(mi)	(km)	(1000 mi²)	(1000 km²)	(1000 cfs)	(m³/sec)
31.20N,	81.17W	Altamaha-Ocmulgee-South	Atlantic O, Georgia, USA	450	720	14	36	13	362
35.48N,	95.18W	Neosho (alt Grand)	Arkansas R, Oklahoma, USA	450	720	13	33	6.5	184
41.07N,	100.42W	South Platte	Platte R, Nebraska, USA	440	710	24	63	0.2	6
33.09N,	79.14W	Santee-Wateree-Catawba	Atlantic O, South Carolina, USA	440	700	15	39	2.3	64
33.22N,	79.15W	Pee Dee-Yadkin	Winyah B of Atlantic O, South Carolina, USA	430	700	9	23	9.0	256
70.27N,	150.07W	Colville	Beaufort Sea, Alaska, USA	430	690				
42.45N,	98.00W	Niobrara	Missouri R, Nebraska, USA	430	690	12	31	1.4	40
34.38N,	90.35W	Saint Francis	Mississippi R, Arkansas, USA	430	690	8	22	5.9	167
43.00N,	91.15W	Wisconsin	Mississippi R, Wisconsin, USA	430	690	12	31	8.5	241
42.30N,	96.25W	Big Sioux	Missouri R, South Dakota, USA	420	680	9	23	0.8	23
45.15N,	66.04W	Saint John	B of Fundy of Atlantic O, New Brunswick, Canada	420	670	22	56	26	736
36.56N,	76.26W	James-Jackson	Chesapeake B of Atlantic O, Virginia, USA	410	670	7	18	7.5	213
41.17N,	72.21W	Connecticut	Long Island Sound of Atlantic O, Connecticut, USA	410	650	11	28	17	471
49.15N,	117.39W	Kootenay (alt Kootenai)	Columbia R, British Columbia, Canada	410	650	15	39	16	450
45.51N,	116.46W	Salmon	Snake R, Idaho, USA	400	650	14	36	11	309
35.55N,	76.42W	Roanoke	Albemarle Sound of Atlantic O, North Carolina, USA	380	610	10	26	8.2	232
29.59N,	93.46W	Sabine	G of Mexico, Louisiana-Texas, USA	380	610	10	26	8.8	249

NORTH AMERICA

Latitude and Longitude	River	Outflow and Location	Length (mi)	Length (km)	Drainage Basin (1000 mi^2)	Drainage Basin (1000 km^2)	Discharge Rate (1000 cfs)	Discharge Rate (m^3/sec)
38.03N, 121.55W	Sacramento	Suisun B of Pacific O, California, USA	380	610	27	70	24	669
39.20N, 75.25W	Delaware	Delaware B of Atlantic O, Delaware-New Jersey, USA	370	600	12	31	12	338
38.00N, 76.20W	Potomac	Chesapeake B of Atlantic O, Maryland-Virginia, USA	360	580	14	36	11	314
32.03N, 80.55W	Savannah-Seneca	Atlantic O, Georgia-South Carolina, USA	360	580	10	26	11	320
39.07N, 113.03W	Sevier	Sevier L, Utah, USA	350	570	6	16	0.2	6
41.27N, 112.15W	Bear	Great Salt L, Utah, USA	350	560	7	18	1.7	48
67.00N, 162.30W	Noatak	Kotzebue Sound of Chukchi Sea, Alaska, USA	350	560	8	21		
38.02N, 121.50W	San Joaquin	Suisun B of Pacific O, California, USA	350	560	14	36	4.7	133
27.48N, 97.34W	Nueces	Nueces B of G of Mexico, Texas, USA	340	550	19	49	0.9	24
40.42N, 74.02W	Hudson	New York B of Atlantic O, New Jersey-New York, USA	310	490	13	34	14	394
60.18N, 145.03W	Copper	G of Alaska, Alaska, USA	300	480	21	54	38	1,080
61.15N, 150.36W	Susitna	G of Alaska, Alaska, USA	300	480	6	16	9.8	279
40.03N, 118.30W	Humboldt	Humboldt L, Nevada, USA	290	470	17	44	0.07	2
35.05N, 76.30W	Neuse-Flat	Pamlico Sound of Atlantic O, North Carolina, USA	280	460	3	8	2.9	82
29.58N, 93.50W	Neches	Sabine L, Texas, USA	280	450	8	21	6.4	182
59.03N, 158.23W	Nushagak	Bristol B of Bering Sea, Alaska, USA	280	450				
30.23N, 81.25W	Saint Johns	Atlantic O, Florida, USA	280	440	3	8	3.3	94

NORTH AMERICA

Latitude and Longitude		River	Outflow and Location	Length (mi)	Length (km)	Drainage Basin (1000 mi^2)	Drainage Basin (1000 km^2)	Discharge Rate (1000 cfs)	Discharge Rate (m^3/sec)
43.04N,	86.15W	Grand	Michigan L, Michigan, USA	260	420	5	13	3.5	100
41.34N,	124.05W	Klamath	Pacific O, California, USA	250	400	12	31	17	490
31.53N,	81.04W	Ogeechee	Atlantic O, Georgia, USA	250	400	3	8	2.2	62
13.14N,	88.49W	Lempa	Pacific O, El Salvador	190	300				
17.32N,	88.14W	•Belize	Caribbean Sea, British Honduras	180	290				
19.15N,	72.47W	Artibonite	G of Gonaives of Caribbean Sea, Haiti	170	280	4	10		
19.51N,	71.41W	Yaque del Norte	Atlantic O, Dominican Republic	170	280				
20.17N,	75.56W	Cauto	G of Guacanayabo of Caribbean Sea, Cuba	160	250	4	11		

OCEANIA

Latitude and Longitude		River	Outflow and Location	Length (mi)	Length (km)	Drainage Basin (1000 mi^2)	Drainage Basin (1000 km^2)	Discharge Rate (1000 cfs)	Discharge Rate (m^3/sec)
35.22S,	139.22E	Murray-Darling[1]-Culgoa-Balonne-Condamine	Indian O, South Australia, Australia	2330	3750	414	1072	17	470
34.07S,	141.55E	Murray (upper)	Murray R, New South Wales, Australia	1210	1950			11	317
34.43S,	143.12E	Murrumbidgee	Murray R, New South Wales, Australia	980	1580	52	135	4.1	116
34.21S,	143.57E	Lachlan	Murrumbidgee R, New South Wales, Australia	920	1480			1.1	31
8.25S,	143.10E	•Fly-Strickland	G of Papua of Coral Sea, Papua	800	1290			318	9,000
3.51S,	144.34E	•Sepik	Pacific O, New Guinea (Australia)	700	1130				

* * *

[1] Data for Darling-Culgoa-Balonne-Condamine: 1930 ml, 3110 km; 250,000 mi^2, 647,000 km^2; 4,000 cfs, 113 m^3/sec.

OCEANIA

Latitude and Longitude		River	Outflow and Location	Length (mi)	Length (km)	Drainage Basin (1000 mi²)	Drainage Basin (1000 km²)	Discharge Rate (1000 cfs)	Discharge Rate (m³/sec)
30.07S,	147.24E	Macquarie	Darling R, New South Wales, Australia	590	950			1.3	37
1.26S,	137.53E	•Mamberamo-Taritatu (for Idenburg)	Pacific O, West Irian, Indonesia	420	670				
37.23S,	174.42E	Waikato	Tasman Sea, North I, New Zealand	270	440	6	14	13	368

SOUTH AMERICA

Latitude and Longitude		River	Outflow and Location	Length (mi)	Length (km)	Drainage Basin (1000 mi²)	Drainage Basin (1000 km²)	Discharge Rate (1000 cfs)	Discharge Rate (m³/sec)
0.10S,	49.00W	•Amazon (off Amazonas)-Ucayali-Tambo-Ene-Apurimac	Atlantic O, Amapa-Para, Brazil	4080	6570	2375	6150	6180	175,000
35.00S,	57.00W	Plata-Parana-Grande	Atlantic O, Argentina-Uruguay	3030	4880	1197	3100	809	22,900
3.22S,	58.45W	•Madeira-Mamore-Grande (alt Guapay)	Amazon R, Amazonas, Brazil	1990	3200	463	1200	770	21,800
2.37S,	65.44W	•Jurua (alt Yurua)	Amazon R, Amazonas, Brazil	1860	3000	03	240	141	4,000
3.42S,	61.28W	•Purus	Amazon R, Amazonas, Brazil	1860	3000	154	400		
10.30S,	36.24W	Sao Francisco	Atlantic O, Alagoas-Sergipe, Brazil	1730	2780	236	611	95	2,690
1.00S,	48.30W	Para-Tocantins	Atlantic O, Para, Brazil	1710	2750	323	836	305	8,630
27.18S,	58.38W	Paraguay	Parana R, Argentina-Paraguay	1610	2600	425	1100	155	4,400
3.08S,	64.46W	•Caqueta (alt Japura, Yapura)	Amazon R, Amazonas, Brazil	1420	2280	120	310	247	7,000
2.24S,	54.41W	•Tapajos-Juruena	Amazon R, Para, Brazil	1380	2220	179	463	212	6,000
5.21S,	48.41W	•Araguaia	Tocantins R, Para, Brazil	1370	2200				
34.12S,	58.18W	Uruguay-Canoas	Plata R, Argentina-Uruguay	1370	2200	119	307	194	5,500
1.30S,	51.53W	•Xingu	Amazon R, Para, Brazil	1300	2100	174	450	73	2,060

SOUTH AMERICA

Latitude and Longitude		River	Outflow and Location	Length		Drainage Basin		Discharge Rate	
				(mi)	(km)	(1000 mi^2)	(1000 km^2)	(1000 cfs)	(m^3/sec)
8.37N,	62.15W	Orinoco	Atlantic O, Venezuela	1280	2060	340	880	636	18,000
3.08S,	59.55W	•Negro (alt Guainia)	Amazon R, Amazonas, Brazil	1240	2000	386	1000	1236	35,000
3.07S,	67.58W	•Putumayo (alt Ica)	Amazon R, Amazonas, Brazil	1240	2000	43	112	177	5,000
11.54S,	65.01W	•Guapore (alt Itenez)	Mamore R, Bolivia-Brazil	1120	1800	232	600	71	2,000
3.00S,	41.50W	•Parnaiba	Atlantic O, Maranhao-Piaui, Brazil	1060	1700	135	350		
4.30S,	73.27W	•Maranon	Amazon R, Peru	1000	1610				
4.21S,	70.02W	•Javari (alt Yacarana, Yavari)	Amazon R, Brazil-Peru	990	1600	35	91	4.2	120
11.06N,	74.51W	•Magdalena	Caribbean Sea, Colombia	960	1540	100	260	283	8,000
31.42S,	60.44W	Salado (alt Salado del Norte)	Parana R, Santa Fe, Argentina	930	1500	309	800	1.3	38
1.24S,	61.51W	•Branco-Uraricoera	Negro R, Roraima, Brazil	920	1470				
39.50S,	62.08W	Colorado-Salado-Desaguadero-Bermejo	Atlantic O, Buenos Aires, Argentina	890	1430	42	110	4.7	133
7.21S,	58.03W	•Teles Pires (alt Sao Manuel, Tres Barras)	Tapajos R, Mato Grosso-Para, Brazil	870	1400			62	1,750
8.54N,	74.28W	•Cauca	Magdalena R, Colombia	840	1350	24	63	78	2,200
4.03N,	67.44W	•Guaviare	Orinoco R, Colombia	840	1350	56	145		
25.36S,	54.36W	Iguazu (alt Iguacu; for Iguassu)	Parana R, Argentina-Brazil	820	1320	24	62	62	1,750
7.24N,	66.35W	Arauca	Orinoco R, Venezuela	810	1300	7	18		
5.07S,	60.24W	•Aripuana-Roosevelt	Madeira R, Amazonas, Brazil	800	1290				
10.23S,	65.24W	•Beni-Madre de Dios	Madeira R, Bolivia	800	1290				
20.07S,	51.05W	Paranaiba	Parana R, Mato Grosso-Minas Gerais, Brazil	790	1270				
41.02S,	62.47W	Negro-Neuquen	Atlantic O, Buenos Aires-Rio Negro, Argentina	750	1210	48	125	36	1,010

SOUTH AMERICA

Latitude and Longitude		River	Outflow and Location	Length (mi)	Length (km)	Drainage Basin (1000 mi²)	Drainage Basin (1000 km²)	Discharge Rate (1000 cfs)	Discharge Rate (m³/sec)
2.52S,	44.12W	•Itapecuru	Sao Jose B of Atlantic O, Maranhao, Brazil	750	1200	17	45		
2.43S,	66.57W	•Jutai	Amazon R, Amazonas, Brazil	750	1200	12	·31	18	500
21.37S,	41.03W	Paraiba (alt Paraiba do Sul)	Atlantic O, Rio de Janeiro, Brazil	710	1140	22	57	12	331
5.10S,	75.32W	•Huallaga	Maranon R, Peru	700	1130	37	95		
20.40S,	51.35W	•Tiete	Parana R, Sao Paulo, Brazil	700	1130	28	72	13	378
3.04S,	44.35W	•Mearim	Sao Marcos B of Atlantic O, Maranhao, Brazil	680	1100	39	100		
25.21S,	57.42W	Pilcomayo	Paraguay R, Paraguay	680	1100	74	192	3.3	93
15.51S,	38.53W	•Jequitinhonha	Atlantic O, Bahia, Brazil	680	1090	24	62	20	557
26.52S,	58.23W	·Bermejo	Paraguay R, Chaco-Formosa, Argentina	660	1060	36	94	11	325
7.37N,	66.25W	Apure-Uribante	Orinoco R, Venezuela	620	1000	50	130	7.4	210
19.37S,	39.49W	•Doce	Atlantic O, Espirito Santo, Brazil	620	1000	32	83	34	969
3.52S,	52.37W	•Iriri	Xingu R, Para, Brazil	620	1000				
6.12N,	67.28W	Meta	Orinoco R, Colombia-Venezuela	620	1000	40	104		
0.02N,	67.16W	•Vaupes (alt Uaupes)	Negro R, Amazonas, Brazil	620	1000				
6.58N,	58.23W	•Essequibo	Atlantic O, Guyana	600	970	4	11		
8.21N,	62.43W	Caroni	Orinoco R, Venezuela	570	920	37	95	177	5,000
38.49S,	64.57W	Colorado (upper)-Grande	Colorado R, La Pampa, Argentina	570	920	10	25		
1.29S,	48.30W	•Guama-Capim	Para R, Para, Brazil	560	900				
22.40S,	53.09W	•Paranapanema	Parana R, Parana-Sao Paulo, Brazil	560	900	22	56	12	348

SOUTH AMERICA

Latitude and	Longitude	River	Outflow and Location	Length (mi)	Length (km)	Drainage Basin (1000 mi²)	Drainage Basin (1000 km²)	Discharge Rate (1000 cfs)	Discharge Rate (m³/sec)
3.35S,	64.47W	•Tefe	Amazon R, Amazonas, Brazil	560	900				
1.23S,	69.25W	•Apaporis	Caqueta R, Colombia	550	880				
6.25N,	58.37W	•Mazaruni-Cuyuni	Essequibo R, Guyana	550	880				
3.20S,	72.40W	•Napo	Amazon R, Peru	550	880				
6.15S,	42.52W	•Caninde	Parnaiba R, Piaui, Brazil	530	860				
23.18S,	53.42W	•Ivai	Parana R, Parana, Brazil	530	860	14	36	12	340
43.20S,	65.03W	Chubut	Atlantic O, Chubut, Argentina	500	810	12	31	1.7	49
10.25S,	58.20W	•Arinos	Juruena R, Mato Grosso, Brazil	500	800			45	1,280
10.58S,	66.09W	•Beni (upper)	Beni R, Bolivia	500	800				
3.41S,	44.48W	•Grajau	Mearim R, Maranhao, Brazil	500	800				
1.13S,	46.06W	•Gurupi	Atlantic O, Maranhao-Para, Brazil	500	800	24	61		
11.47S,	37.32W	•Itapicuru	Atlantic O, Bahia, Brazil	500	800	15	39	0.6	17
11.45S,	50.44W	•Mortes	Araguaia R, Mato Grosso, Brazil	500	800				
33.24S,	58.22W	•Negro	Uruguay R, Uruguay	500	800				
15.39S,	38.57W	•Pardo	Atlantic O, Bahia, Brazil	500	800	17	45	2.2	62
1.33S,	52.38W	•Paru	Amazon R, Para, Brazil	500	800				
			* * *						
12.28S,	64.24W	•Itonamas-San Miguel	Guapore R, Bolivia	470	760				
17.13S,	44.49W	•Velhas	Sao Francisco R, Minas Gerais, Brazil	470	760				
5.43N,	53.58W	•Maroni (alt Marowyne)	Atlantic O, French Guiana-Surinam	420	680	23	60		
1.55S,	55.35W	•Trombetas	Amazon R, Para, Brazil	340	550	48	124	53	1,500
47.49S,	73.37W	Baker	G of Penas of Pacific O, Chile	270	440	10	25	21	600
6.00N,	57.04W	•Courantyne (alt Corantijn)	Atlantic O, Guyana-Surinam	270	440				
21.26S,	70.04W	Loa	Pacific O, Chile	270	440	13	34	0.06	1.6

6
Longest Rivers, Irrespective of Continent

Contents

Rank.

Conventional and other (alternate, former, and official) names of river and of its tributaries (if any) constituting the longest watercourse.

Outflow (sea, lake, river, etc.), and subdivision and country in which located.

Total length of watercourse, in miles and kilometers.

Arrangement

By length of watercourse.

Coverage

50 longest rivers.

Rounding

Lengths are rounded to the nearest 10 mi (km).

Entries

50.

TABLE 6. LONGEST RIVERS, IRRESPECTIVE OF CONTINENT

Rank	River	Outflow and Location	Length (mi)	Length (km)
1.	•Nile (off Nil)-Kagera-Ruvuvu-Luvironza	Mediterranean Sea, Egypt	4160	6690
2.	•Amazon (off Amazonas)-Ucayali-Tambo-Ene-Apurimac	Atlantic O, Amapa-Para, Brazil	4080	6570
3.	Mississippi-Missouri-Jefferson-Beaverhead-Red Rock	G of Mexico, Louisiana, USA	3740	6020
4.	Yangtze (off Chang)	East China Sea, Kiangsu, China	3720	5980
5.	Yenisey (alt Yenisei)-Angara-Selenga (alt Selenge)-Ider (off Ideriin)	Yenisey G of Kara Sea, Russia, USSR	3650	5870
6.	Amur (alt Heilung)-Argun (alt Oerhkuna)-Kerulen (off Hereleng, Kolulun)	Tatar Strait, Russia, USSR	3590	5780
7.	Ob-Irtysh (alt Irtish)	G of Ob of Kara Sea, Russia, USSR	3360	5410
8.	Plata-Parana-Grande	Atlantic O, Argentina-Uruguay	3030	4880
9.	Yellow (alt Hwang; off Huang)	Yellow Sea, Shantung, China	3010	4840
10.	Congo (alt Zaire; for Kongo)-Lualaba	Atlantic O, Angola-Zaire	2880	4630
11.	Lena	Laptev Sea, Russia, USSR	2730	4400
12.	Mackenzie-Slave-Peace-Finlay	Beaufort Sea, Northwest Territories, Canada	2630	4240
13.	•Mekong (alt Khong, Lantsang, Tien Giang)	South China Sea, South Vietnam	2600	4180
14.	•Niger	G of Guinea, Nigeria	2550	4100
15.	Murray-Darling-Culgoa-Balonne-Condamine	Indian O, South Australia, Australia	2330	3750
16.	Volga	Caspian (Sea) L, Russia, USSR	2300	3700
17.	•Madeira-Mamore-Grande (alt Guapay)	Amazon R, Amazonas, Brazil	1990	3200
18.	Syr (Darya)-Naryn	Aral (Sea) L, Kazakhstan, USSR	1910	3080
19.	Saint Lawrence (alt Saint-Laurent)-(Great Lakes)-Saint Louis	G of Saint Lawrence, Quebec, Canada	1900	3060
20.	Rio Grande (alt Bravo)	G of Mexico, Mexico-USA	1880	3030
21.	Yukon-Lewes-Teslin-Nisutlin	Bering Sea, Alaska, USA	1870	3020
22.	•Jurua (alt Yurua)	Amazon R, Amazonas, Brazil	1860	3000
22.	•Purus	Amazon R, Amazonas, Brazil	1860	3000
24.	Lower Tunguska (off Nizhnyaya Tunguska)	Yenisey R, Russia, USSR	1860	2990
25.	•Brahmaputra (alt Tsangpo, Yalutsangpu)	B of Bengal, Bangladesh	1800	2900
26.	•Indus (alt Yintu)	Arabian Sea, Pakistan	1790	2880
27.	Danube (off Donau, Duna, Dunaj, Dunarea, Dunav, Dunay)	Black Sea, Romania-USSR	1770	2850
28.	•Salween (alt Khong, Lu, Nu)	G of Martaban of Andaman Sea, Burma	1750	2820
29.	Sao Francisco	Atlantic O, Alagoas-Sergipe, Brazil	1730	2780
30.	Para-Tocantins	Atlantic O, Para, Brazil	1710	2750
30.	Tarim (off Talimu)-Yarkand (alt Yeherchiang)	Tarim Basin, Sinkiang, China	1710	2750
32.	•Ganges (alt Ganga)-Bhagirathi	B of Bengal, Bangladesh-India	1650	2650
32.	Vilyuy (alt Vilyui)	Lena R, Russia, USSR	1650	2650
32.	•Zambezi (alt Zambesi, Zambeze)	Mozambique Channel, Mozambique	1650	2650
35.	Amu (Darya) (alt Oxus)-Panja (alt Pyandzh)-Vakhsh	Aral (Sea) L, Uzbekistan, USSR	1630	2620
36.	Kolyma (alt Kolima)	East Siberian Sea, Russia, USSR	1610	2600
36.	Paraguay	Parana R, Argentina-Paraguay	1610	2600
38.	Nelson-Saskatchewan-South Saskatchewan-Bow	Hudson B, Manitoba, Canada	1600	2570
39.	Ural	Caspian (Sea) L, Kazakhstan, USSR	1570	2530
40.	Ob (upper)-Katun	Ob R, Russia, USSR	1560	2520
41.	•Shebeli (alt Shabale, Shibeli; for Scebeli)	Balli Swamp, Somalia	1550	2490

Rank	River	Outflow and Location	Length (mi)	(km)
42.	•Ubangi (alt Oubangui)-Uele-Kibali	Congo R, Congo-Zaire	1530	2460
43.	Ishim	Irtysh R, Russia, USSR	1520	2450
44.	(Shatt al) Arab-Euphrates (off Firat, Furat)-Kara (Su)	Persian G, Iran-Iraq	1510	2430
45.	Arkansas	Mississippi R, Arkansas, USA	1450	2330
45.	Colorado	G of California, Baja California-Sonora, Mexico	1450	2330
47.	•Caqueta (alt Japura, Yapura)	Amazon R, Amazonas, Brazil	1420	2280
48.	Aldan	Lena R, Russia, USSR	1410	2270
48.	Olenek	Laptev Sea, Russia, USSR	1410	2270
50.	•Tapajos-Juruena	Amazon R, Para, Brazil	1380	2220

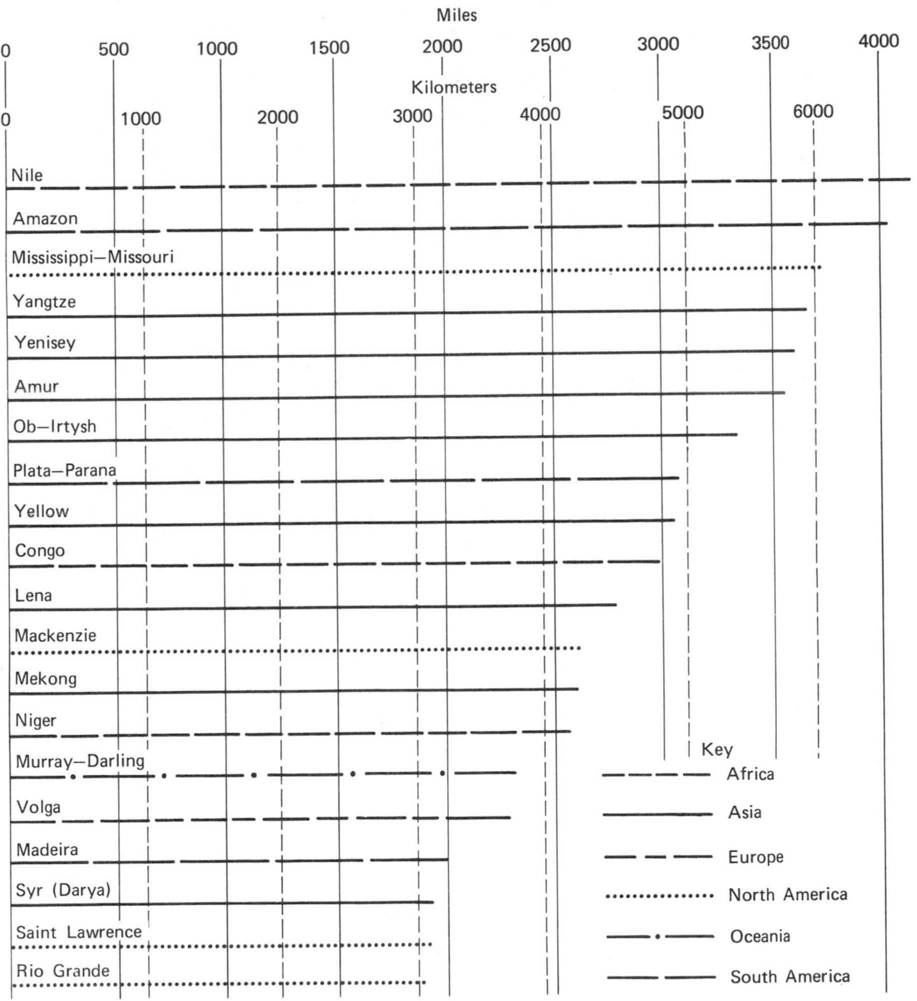

Figure 8. Twenty longest rivers.

Figure 9. At the mouth of the Amazon, the river with the largest drainage basin and the highest discharge rate. (Credit: Organization of American States.)

7
Rivers with Largest Drainage Basins

Contents

Rank.

Conventional and other (alternate, former, and official) names of river and of its tributaries (if any) constituting the longest watercourse.

Outflow (sea, lake, river, etc.), and subdivision and country in which located.

Area of drainage basin of river and all its tributaries, in thousands of square miles and square kilometers.

Arrangement

By area of drainage basin.

Coverage

50 rivers with the largest drainage basins.

Rounding

Areas are rounded to the nearest 1000 mi^2 (km^2).

Entries

50.

TABLE 7. RIVERS WITH LARGEST DRAINAGE BASINS

Rank	River	Outflow and Location	Drainage Basin (1000 mi²)	(1000 km²)
1.	•Amazon (off Amazonas)-Ucayali-Tambo-Ene-Apurimac	Atlantic O, Amapa-Para, Brazil	2375	6150
2.	Congo (alt Zaire; for Kongo)-Lualaba	Atlantic O, Angola-Zaire	1476	3822
3.	Mississippi-Missouri-Jefferson-Beaverhead-Red Rock	G of Mexico, Louisiana, USA	1244	3222
4.	Plata-Parana-Grande	Atlantic O, Argentina-Uruguay	1197	3100
5.	•Nile (off Nil)-Kagera-Ruvuvu-Luvironza	Mediterranean Sea, Egypt	1082	2802
6.	Yenisey (alt Yenisei)-Angara-Selenga (alt Selenge)-Ider (off Ideriin)	Yenisey G of Kara Sea, Russia, USSR	1011	2619
7.	Lena	Laptev Sea, Russia, USSR	957	2478
8.	Ob-Irtysh (alt Irtish)	G of Ob of Kara Sea, Russia, USSR	954	2470
9.	•Niger	G of Guinea, Nigeria	808	2092
10.	Amur (alt Heilung)-Argun (alt Oerhkuna)-Kerulen (off Hereleng, Kolulun)	Tatar Strait, Russia, USSR	792	2050
11.	Yangtze (off Chang)	East China Sea, Kiangsu, China	705	1827
12.	Mackenzie-Slave-Peace-Finlay	Beaufort Sea, Northwest Territories, Canada	681	1764
13.	Volga	Caspian (Sea) L, Russia, USSR	533	1380
14.	•Zambezi (alt Zambesi, Zambeze)	Mozambique Channel, Mozambique	514	1331
15.	Saint Lawrence (alt Saint-Laurent)-(Great Lakes)-Saint Louis	G of Saint Lawrence, Quebec, Canada	508	1316
16.	•Madeira-Mamore-Grande (alt Guapay)	Amazon R, Amazonas, Brazil	463	1200
17.	•Indus (alt Yintu)	Arabian Sea, Pakistan	455	1178
18.	(Shatt al) Arab-Euphrates (off Firat, Furat)-Kara (Su)	Persian G, Iran-Iraq	427	1105
19.	Paraguay	Parana R, Argentina-Paraguay	425	1100
20.	Murray-Darling-Culgoa-Balonne-Condamine	Indian O, South Australia, Australia	414	1072
20.	Nelson-Saskatchewan-South Saskatchewan-Bow	Hudson B, Manitoba, Canada	414	1072
22.	•Ganges (alt Ganga)-Bhagirathi	B of Bengal, Bangladesh-India	409	1059
23.	•Negro (alt Guainia)	Amazon R, Amazonas, Brazil	386	1000
24.	•Brahmaputra (alt Tsangpo, Yalutsangpu)	B of Bengal, Bangladesh	361	935
25.	•Kasai (alt Cassai)	Congo R, Zaire	349	904
26.	Orinoco	Atlantic O, Venezuela	340	880
27.	Yukon-Lewes-Teslin-Nisutlin	Bering Sea, Alaska, USA	330	855
28.	Para-Tocantins	Atlantic O, Para, Brazil	323	836
29.	•Mekong (alt Khong, Lantsang, Tien Giang)	South China Sea, South Vietnam	313	811
30.	Salado (alt Salado del Norte)	Parana R, Santa Fe, Argentina	309	800
31.	•Okovanggo (alt Cubango, Okavango)	Okovanggo Basin, Botswana	303	785
32.	Danube (off Donau, Duna, Dunaj, Dunarea, Dunav, Dunay)	Black Sea, Romania-USSR	298	773
32.	•Ubangi (alt Oubangui)-Uele-Kibali	Congo R, Congo-Zaire	298	773
34.	Yellow (alt Hwang; off Huang)	Yellow Sea, Shantung, China	297	771
35.	Ob (upper)-Katun	Ob R, Russia, USSR	295	765
36.	Aldan	Lena R, Russia, USSR	271	702
37.	•Shari (alt Chari)-Sara (alt Ouham)	Chad L, Cameroon-Chad	270	700
38.	•Orange (alt Oranje)	Atlantic O, South Africa–South-West Africa	261	677
39.	Columbia-Snake	Pacific O, Oregon-Washington, USA	259	671

Rank	River	Outflow and Location	Drainage Basin (1000 mi²)	
			(1000 mi^2)	(1000 km^2)
40.	Kolyma (alt Kolima)	East Siberian Sea, Russia, USSR	249	644
41.	Colorado	G of California, Baja California-Sonora, Mexico	246	637
42.	Sao Francisco	Atlantic O, Alagoas-Sergipe, Brazil	236	611
43.	•Guapore (alt Itenez)	Mamore R, Bolivia-Brazil	232	600
44.	•Panjnad-Sutlej	Indus R, Pakistan	206	533
45.	Ohio-Allegheny	Mississippi R, Illinois-Kentucky, USA	203	526
46.	Sungari (off Sunghua)	Amur R, Heilungkiang, China	202	524
47.	Kama	Volga R, Russia, USSR	202	522
48.	Dnieper (off Dnepr)	Black Sea, Ukraine, USSR	194	503
49.	•Helmand (alt Helmund, Hirmand)	Seistan Basin, Afghanistan-Iran	193	500
50.	Vilyuy (alt Vilyui)	Lena R, Russia, USSR	190	491

8
Rivers with Highest Discharge Rates

Contents

Rank.

Conventional and other (alternate, former, and official) names of river and of its tributaries (if any) constituting the longest watercourse.

Outflow (sea, lake, river, etc.), and subdivision and country in which located.

Average discharge rate, in thousands of cubic feet per second and in cubic meters per second. The discharge rate given is that of the main stream, preferably averaged over several recent years and measured at the gauging station registering the greatest discharge (or nearest the mouth of the river).

Arrangement

By discharge rate.

Coverage

50 rivers with the highest average discharge rates.

Rounding

Discharge rates are rounded to the nearest 1000 cfs and to the nearest 10 m^3/sec.

Entries

50.

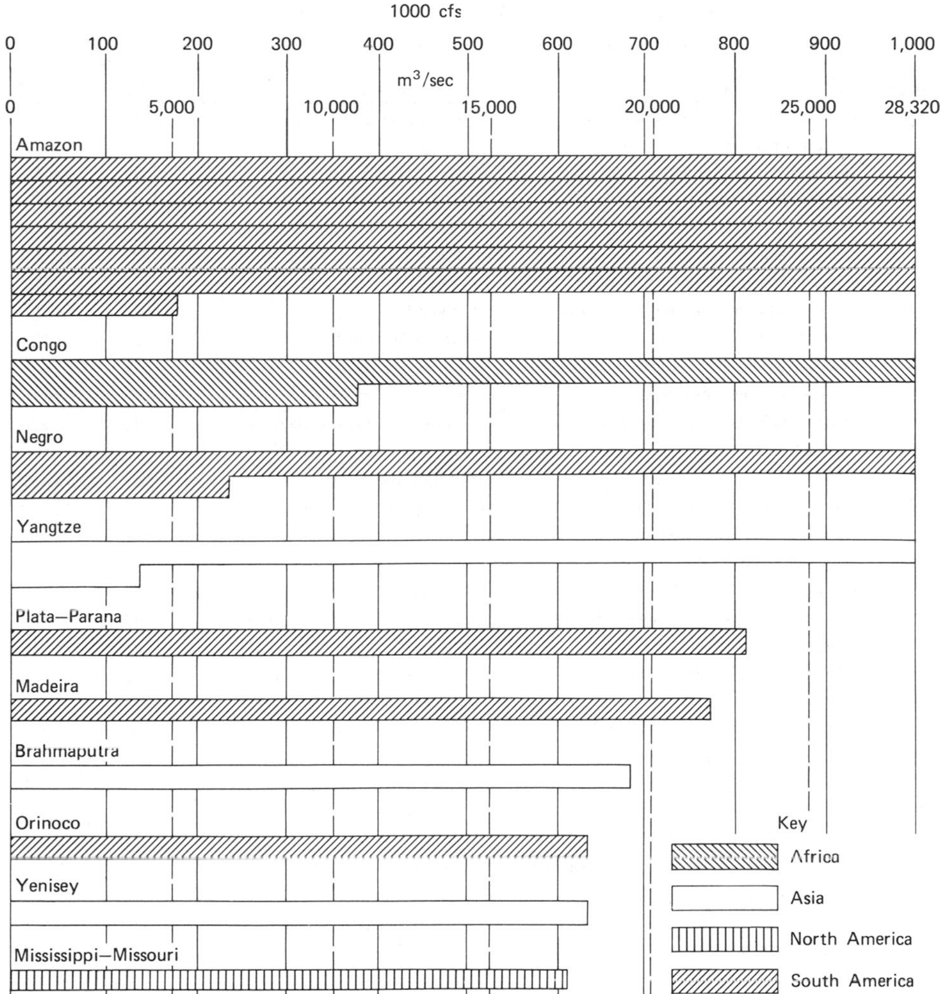

Figure 10. Ten rivers with highest discharge rates.

TABLE 8. RIVERS WITH HIGHEST DISCHARGE RATES

Rank	River	Outflow and Location	Discharge Rate (1000 cfs)	Discharge Rate (m^3/sec)
1.	•Amazon (off Amazonas)-Ucayali-Tambo-Ene-Apurimac	Atlantic O, Amapa-Para, Brazil	6180	175,000
2.	Congo (alt Zaire; for Kongo)-Lualaba	Atlantic O, Angola-Zaire	1377	39,000
3.	•Negro (alt Guainia)	Amazon R, Amazonas, Brazil	1236	35,000
4.	Yangtze (off Chang)	East China Sea, Kiangsu, China	1137	32,190
5.	Plata-Parana-Grande	Atlantic O, Argentina-Uruguay	809	22,900
6.	•Madeira-Mamore-Grande (alt Guapay)	Amazon R, Amazonas, Brazil	770	21,800
7.	•Brahmaputra (alt Tsangpo, Yalutsangpu)	B of Bengal, Bangladesh	678	19,200
8.	Orinoco	Atlantic O, Venezuela	636	18,000
8.	Yenisey (alt Yenisei)-Angara-Selenga (alt Selenge)-Ider (off Ideriin)	Yenisey G of Kara Sea, Russia, USSR	636	18,000
10.	Mississippi-Missouri-Jefferson-Beaverhead-Red Rock	G of Mexico, Louisiana, USA	610	17,270
11.	Lena	Laptev Sea, Russia, USSR	569	16,100
12.	•Zambezi (alt Zambesi, Zambeze)	Mozambique Channel, Mozambique	565	16,000
13.	Saint Lawrence (alt Saint-Laurent)-(Great Lakes)-Saint Louis	G of Saint Lawrence, Quebec, Canada	460	13,030
14.	•Irrawaddy (off Iyawadi)-Nmai	Andaman Sea, Burma	447	12,660
15.	•Mekong (alt Khong, Lantsang, Tien Giang)	South China Sea, South Vietnam	424	12,000
16.	•Ganges (alt Ganga)-Bhagirathi	B of Bengal, Bangladesh-India	410	11,610
16.	Mackenzie-Slave-Peace-Finlay	Beaufort Sea, Northwest Territories, Canada	410	11,610
18.	Pearl (alt Canton, Yueh; off Chu)-Si (off Hsi)-Hung (Shui)	South China Sea, Kwangtung, China	409	11,590
19.	Ob-Irtysh (alt Irtish)	G of Ob of Kara Sea, Russia, USSR	360	10,200
20.	•Ogooue (alt Ogowe)	G of Guinea, Gabon	353	10,000
21.	•Kasai (alt Cassai)	Congo R, Zaire	351	9,950
22.	Amur (alt Heilung)-Argun (alt Oerhkuna)-Kerulen (off Hereleng, Kolulun)	Tatar Strait, Russia, USSR	346	9,800
23.	•Fly-Strickland	G of Papua of Coral Sea, Papua	318	9,000
24.	Para-Tocantins	Atlantic O, Para, Brazil	305	8,630
25.	•Magdalena	Caribbean Sea, Colombia	283	8,000
26.	Volga	Caspian (Sea) L, Russia, USSR	271	7,680
27.	•Ubangi (alt Oubangui)-Uele-Kibali	Congo R, Congo-Zaire	265	7,500
28.	Ohio-Allegheny	Mississippi R, Illinois-Kentucky, USA	258	7,310
29.	•Caqueta (alt Japura, Yapura)	Amazon R, Amazonas, Brazil	247	7,000
30.	Danube (off Donau, Duna, Dunaj, Dunarea, Dunav, Dunay)	Black Sea, Romania-USSR	227	6,430
31.	•Tapajos-Juruena	Amazon R, Para, Brazil	212	6,000
32.	•Niger	G of Guinea, Nigeria	201	5,700
33.	Columbia-Snake	Pacific O, Oregon-Washington, USA	195	5,520
34.	Uruguay-Canoas	Plata R, Argentina-Uruguay	194	5,500
35.	Yukon-Lewes-Teslin-Nisutlin	Bering Sea, Alaska, USA	188	5,320
36.	Aldan	Lena R, Russia, USSR	177	5,000
36.	Caroni	Orinoco R, Venezuela	177	5,000
36.	•Putumayo (alt Ica)	Amazon R, Amazonas, Brazil	177	5,000
39.	Ob (upper)-Katun	Ob R, Russia, USSR	174	4,920
40.	Paraguay	Parana R, Argentina-Paraguay	155	4,400
41.	•Jurua (alt Yurua)	Amazon R, Amazonas, Brazil	141	4,000
41.	Pechora (for Petchora)	Barents Sea, Russia, USSR	141	4,000
43.	Khatanga-Kotuy	Khatanga G of Laptev Sea, Russia, USSR	135	3,820

Rank	River	Outflow and Location	Discharge Rate (1000 cfs)	Discharge Rate (m^3/sec)
44.	Kama	Volga R, Russia, USSR	128	3,620
45.	•Indus (alt Yintu)	Arabian Sea, Pakistan	127	3,590
46.	Columbia (upper)	Columbia R, Washington, USA	120	3,410
47.	Northern Dvina (off Severnaya Dvina)-Vychegda (alt Vichegda)	White Sea, Russia, USSR	120	3,400
48.	Lower Tunguska (off Nizhnyaya Tunguska)	Yenisey R, Russia, USSR	118	3,330
49.	•Benue (alt Benoue)	Niger R, Nigeria	112	3,170
50.	Yenisey (upper)	Yenisey R, Russia, USSR	103	2,910

9
Longest River in Each Country

Contents

Conventional name of country.

Conventional and other (alternate, former, and official) names of river and of its tributaries (if any) constituting the longest watercourse.

Outflow (sea, lake, river, etc.), and subdivision and country in which located.

Total length of watercourse, in miles and kilometers.

Arrangement

By country, alphabetically.

Coverage

All countries with an area of at least 1000 mi^2 (2590 km^2) having a river of significant length.

Rounding

Lengths are rounded to the nearest 10 mi (km).

Entries

146.

TABLE 9. LONGEST RIVER IN EACH COUNTRY

Country	River	Outflow and Location	Length (mi)	Length (km)
Afghanistan	Amu (Darya) (alt Oxus)-Panja (alt Pyandzh)-Vakhsh	Aral (Sea) L, Uzbekistan, USSR	1630	2620
Albania	Drin	Adriatic Sea, Albania	170	280
Algeria	•Sheliff (alt Cheliff; off Shalaf)	Mediterranean Sea, Algeria	430	700
Angola	Congo (alt Zaire; for Kongo)-Lualaba	Atlantic O, Angola-Zaire	2880	4630
Argentina	Plata-Parana-Grande	Atlantic O, Argentina-Uruguay	3030	4880
Australia	Murray-Darling-Culgoa-Balonne-Condamine	Indian O, South Australia, Australia	2330	3750
Austria	Danube (off in Austria Donau)	Black Sea, Romania-USSR	1770	2850
Bangladesh	•Brahmaputra (alt Tsangpo, Yalutsangpu)	B of Bengal, Bangladesh	1800	2900
Belgium	Meuse (alt Maas)	North Sea, Netherlands	590	950
Bhutan	•Manas	Brahmaputra R, Assam, India	220	350
Bolivia	•Guapore (alt Itenez)	Mamore R, Bolivia-Brazil	1120	1800
Botswana	•Zambezi (alt Zambesi, Zambeze)	Mozambique Channel, Mozambique	1650	2650
Brazil	•Amazon (off Amazonas)-Ucayali-Tambo-Ene-Apurimac	Atlantic O, Amapa-Para, Brazil	4080	6570
British Honduras	•Belize	Caribbean Sea, British Honduras	180	290
Brunei	•Limbang	South China Sea, Brunei-Malaysia	120	200
Bulgaria	Danube (off in Bulgaria Dunav)	Black Sea, Romania-USSR	1770	2850
Burma	•Mekong (alt Khong, Lantsang, Tien Giang)	South China Sea, South Vietnam	2600	4180
Burundi	•Nile (off Nil)-Kagera-Ruvuvu-Luvironza	Mediterranean Sea, Egypt	4160	6690
Cambodia	•Mekong (alt Khong, Lantsang, Tien Giang)	South China Sea, South Vietnam	2600	4180
Cameroon	•Shari (alt Chari)-Sara (alt Ouham)	Chad L, Cameroon-Chad	900	1450
Canada	Mackenzie-Slave-Peace-Finlay	Beaufort Sea, Northwest Territories, Canada	2630	4240
Central African Republic	•Ubangi (alt Oubangui)-Uele-Kibali	Congo R, Congo-Zaire	1530	2460
Ceylon	Mahaweli Ganga	Indian O, Ceylon	210	330
Chad	•Shari (alt Chari)-Sara (alt Ouham)	Chad L, Cameroon-Chad	900	1450
Chile	Baker	G of Penas of Pacific O, Chile	270	440
	Loa	Pacific O, Chile	270	440
China	Yangtze (off Chang)	East China Sea, Kiangsu, China	3720	5980
Colombia	•Amazon (off Amazonas)-Ucayali-Tambo-Ene-Apurimac	Atlantic O, Amapa-Para, Brazil	4080	6570
Congo	Congo (alt Zaire; for Kongo)-Lualaba	Atlantic O, Angola-Zaire	2880	4630
Costa Rica	•San Juan	Caribbean Sea, Costa Rica-Nicaragua	140	220
Cuba	Cauto	G of Guacanayabo of Caribbean Sea, Cuba	160	250
Cyprus	•Pedias	Mediterranean Sea, Cyprus	62	100
Czechoslovakia	Danube (off in Czechoslovakia Dunaj)	Black Sea, Romania-USSR	1770	2850
Dahomey	•Niger	G of Guinea, Nigeria	2550	4100
Denmark	Gudena	Kattegat Strait, Denmark	100	160
Dominican Republic	Yaque del Norte	Atlantic O, Dominican Republic	170	280
Ecuador	•Putumayo (alt Ica)	Amazon R, Amazonas, Brazil	1240	2000
Egypt	•Nile (off Nil)-Kagera-Ruvuvu-Luvironza	Mediterranean Sea, Egypt	4160	6690
El Salvador	Lempa	Pacific O, El Salvador	190	300
Equatorial Guinea	•Benito	G of Guinea, Equatorial Guinea	200	320

Country	River	Outflow and Location	Length (mi)	Length (km)
Ethiopia	•Shebeli (alt Shabale, Shibeli; for Scebeli)	Balli Swamp, Somalia	1550	2490
Fiji	Rewa	Pacific O, Viti Levu I, Fiji	95	150
Finland	Torne (alt Tornio)-Muonio-Konkama (alt Kongama)	G of Bothnia of Baltic Sea, Finland-Sweden	350	570
France	Rhine (off in France Rhin)	North Sea, Netherlands	820	1320
French Guiana	•Maroni (alt Marowyne)	Atlantic O, French-Guiana-Surinam	420	680
Gabon	•Ogooue (alt Ogowe)	G of Guinea, Gabon	750	1210
Gambia	Gambia (alt Gambie)	Atlantic O, Gambia	700	1130
Germany				
East	Elbe (alt Labe)	North Sea, Niedersachsen–Schleswig-Holstein, West Germany	710	1140
West	Danube (off in Germany Donau)	Black Sea, Romania-USSR	1770	2850
Ghana	•Volta-Black Volta (alt Volta Noire)	G of Guinea, Ghana	990	1600
Greece	Maritsa (off in Greece Evros)	Aegean Sea, Greece-Turkey	300	490
Guatemala	Usumacinta-Chixoy	B of Campeche of G of Mexico, Tabasco, Mexico	690	1110
Guinea	•Niger	G of Guinea, Nigeria	2550	4100
Guyana	•Essequibo	Atlantic O, Guyana	600	970
Haiti	Artibonite	G of Gonaives of Caribbean Sea, Haiti	170	280
Honduras	•Coco (alt Segovia)	Caribbean Sea, Honduras-Nicaragua	470	750
Hungary	Danube (off in Hungary Duna)	Black Sea, Romania-USSR	1770	2850
Iceland	•Thjorsa	Atlantic O, Iceland	140	230
India	•Brahmaputra (alt Tsangpo, Yalutsangpu)	B of Bengal, Bangladesh	1800	2900
Indonesia				
in Asia	Kapuas (alt Kapuas Besar; for Kapoeas)	South China Sea, Borneo I, Indonesia	630	1010
in Oceania (West Irian)	•Mamberamo-Taritatu (for Idenburg)	Pacific O, New Guinea I, Indonesia	420	670
Iran	(Shatt al) Arab-Euphrates (off in Iran Furat)-Kara (Su)	Persian G, Iran-Iraq	1510	2430
Iraq	(Shatt al) Arab-Euphrates (off in Iraq Furat)-Kara (Su)	Persian G, Iran-Iraq	1510	2430
Ireland	Shannon	Atlantic O, Ireland	230	370
Israel	•Jordan (off in Israel Yarden)	Dead (Sea) L, Jordan	160	250
Italy	Po	Adriatic Sea, Veneto, Italy	380	620
Ivory Coast	•Volta-Black Volta (alt Volta Noire)	G of Guinea, Ghana	990	1600
Jamaica	Black	Caribbean Sea, Jamaica	44	71
Japan	Shinano	Sea of Japan, Honshu I, Japan	230	370
Jordan	•Jordan (off in Jordan Urdunn)	Dead (Sea) L, Jordan	160	250
Kashmir-Jammu	•Indus (alt Yintu)	Arabian Sea, Pakistan	1790	2880
Kenya	•Tana	Indian O, Kenya	440	710
Korea				
North	Yalu (alt Amnok)	Korea B of Yellow Sea, China-North Korea	500	810
South	•Naktong (for Rakuti)	Korea Strait, South Korea	330	520
Laos	•Mekong (alt Khong, Lantsang, Tien Giang)	South China Sea, South Vietnam	2600	4180
Lebanon	Orontes (off Asi)	Mediterranean Sea, Turkey	300	470
Lesotho	•Orange (alt Oranje)	Atlantic O, South Africa–South-West Africa	1300	2090
Liberia	•Cavally (alt Cavalla)	Atlantic O, Ivory Coast-Liberia	320	510

Country	River	Outflow and Location	Length (mi)	Length (km)
Luxembourg	Moselle (alt Mosel)	Rhine R, Rheinland-Pfalz, West Germany	340	550
Malagasy Republic	•Betsiboka	Mozambique Channel, Malagasy Republic	270	440
Malawi	•Shire (alt Chire)	Zambezi R, Mozambique	370	600
Malaysia				
East	Kinabatangan	Sulu Sea, Sabah, Malaysia	350	560
	Rajang	South China Sea, Sarawak, Malaysia	350	560
West	•Pahang	South China Sea, West Malaysia, Malaysia	200	320
Mali	•Niger	G of Guinea, Nigeria	2550	4100
Mauritania	Senegal-Bafing	Atlantic O, Mauritania-Senegal	1050	1700
Mexico	Rio Grande (alt Bravo)	G of Mexico, Mexico-USA	1880	3030
Mongolia	Yenisey (alt Yenisei)-Angara-Selenga (alt Selenge)-Ider (off Ideriin)	Yenisey G of Kara Sea, Russia, USSR	3650	5870
Morocco	•Oum er Rbia	Atlantic O, Morocco	370	600
Mozambique	•Zambezi (off in Mozambique Zambeze)	Mozambique Channel, Mozambique	1650	2650
Nepal	•Ghaghara (alt Gogra)	Ganges R, Bihar-Uttar Pradesh, India	640	1030
Netherlands	Rhine (off in Netherlands Rijn)	North Sea, Netherlands	820	1320
New Caledonia	Diahot	Coral Sea, New Caledonia	56	90
New Guinea (Australia)	•Sepik	Pacific O, New Guinea (Australia)	700	1130
New Zealand	Waikato	Tasman Sea, North I, New Zealand	270	440
Nicaragua	•Coco (alt Segovia)	Caribbean Sea, Honduras-Nicaragua	470	750
Niger	•Niger	G of Guinea, Nigeria	2550	4100
Nigeria	•Niger	G of Guinea, Nigeria	2550	4100
Norway	Glomma (off Glama)	Skagerrak Strait, Norway	380	610
Pakistan	•Indus (alt Yintu)	Arabian Sea, Pakistan	1790	2880
Panama	•Chepo (alt Bayano)	G of Panama of Pacific O, Panama	100	160
Papua	•Fly-Strickland	G of Papua of Coral Sea, Papua	800	1290
Paraguay	Plata-Parana-Grande	Atlantic O, Argentina-Uruguay	3030	4880
Peru	•Amazon (off Amazonas)-Ucayali-Tambo-Ene-Apurimac	Atlantic O, Amapa-Para, Brazil	4080	6570
Philippines	•Cagayan (alt Grande de Cagayan)	Babuyan Channel, Luzon I, Philippines	220	350
Poland	Vistula (for Visla, Weichsel; off Wisla)-Bug (alt Zapadnyy Bug)	G of Danzig of Baltic Sea, Poland	760	1220
Portugal (in Europe)	Tagus (off in Portugal Tejo)	Atlantic O, Portugal	630	1010
Portuguese Guinea	•Geba-Corubal	Atlantic O, Portuguese Guinea	350	560
Portuguese Timor	•Laclo do Norte	Banda Sea, Portuguese Timor	50	80
Puerto Rico	•Plata	Atlantic O, Puerto Rico	45	72
Rhodesia	•Zambezi (alt Zambesi, Zambeze)	Mozambique Channel, Mozambique	1650	2650
Romania	Danube (off in Romania Dunarea)	Black Sea, Romania-USSR	1770	2850
Rwanda	•Nile (off Nil)-Kagera-Ruvuvu-Luvironza	Mediterranean Sea, Egypt	4160	6690
Senegal	Senegal-Bafing	Atlantic O, Mauritania-Senegal	1050	1700
Sierra Leone	•Sierra Leone-Rokel	Atlantic O, Sierra Leone	270	440
Sikkim	•Tista	Brahmaputra R, Bangladesh	250	400
Somalia	•Shebeli (alt Shabale, Shibeli; for Scebeli)	Balli Swamp, Somalia	1550	2490
South Africa	•Orange (alt Oranje)	Atlantic O, South Africa-South-West Africa	1300	2090

Country	River	Outflow and Location	Length (mi)	Length (km)
South-West Africa	•Zambezi (alt Zambesi, Zambeze)	Mozambique Channel, Mozambique	1650	2650
Spain (in Europe)	Tagus (off in Spain Tajo)	Atlantic O, Portugal	630	1010
Sudan	•Nile (off Nil)-Kagera-Ruvuvu-Luvironza	Mediterranean Sea, Egypt	4160	6690
Surinam	•Maroni (off in Surinam Marowyne)	Atlantic O, French Guiana-Surinam	420	680
Swaziland	•Komati (alt Incomati)	Delagoa B of Indian O, Mozambique	500	800
Sweden	Gota-Klar	Kattegat Strait, Sweden	450	720
Switzerland	Rhine (off in Switzerland Rhein, Rhin)	North Sea, Netherlands	820	1320
Syria	(Shatt al) Arab-Euphrates (off in Syria Furat)-Kara (Su)	Persian G, Iran-Iraq	1510	2430
Taiwan	Choshui	Formosa Strait, Taiwan	120	190
Tanzania	•Nile (off Nil)-Kagera-Ruvuvu-Luvironza	Mediterranean Sea, Egypt	4160	6690
Thailand	•Mekong (off in Thailand Khong)	South China Sea, South Vietnam	2600	4180
Togo	•Oti	Volta R, Ghana	320	510
Trinidad and Tobago	•Ortoire	Atlantic O, Trinidad I, Trinidad and Tobago	31	50
Tunisia	•Medjerda (off Majardah)	G of Tunis of Mediterranean Sea, Tunisia	230	360
Turkey				
in Asia	(Shatt al) Arab-Euphrates (off in Turkey Firat)-Kara (Su)	Persian G, Iran-Iraq	1510	2430
in Europe	Maritsa (off in Turkey Meric)	Aegean Sea, Greece-Turkey	300	490
Uganda	•Nile (off Nil)-Kagera-Ruvuvu-Luvironza	Mediterranean Sea, Egypt	4160	6690
UK	Severn	Bristol Channel, England, UK	210	340
Upper Volta	•Volta-Black Volta (alt Volta Noire)	G of Guinea, Ghana	990	1600
Uruguay	Plata-Parana-Grande	Atlantic O, Argentina-Uruguay	3030	4880
USA				
in North America	Mississippi-Missouri-Jefferson-Beaverhead-Red Rock	G of Mexico, Louisiana, USA	3740	6020
in Oceania (Hawaii)	•Kaukonahua (Stream)	Pacific O, Oahu I, Hawaii, USA	33	53
USSR				
in Asia	Yenisey (alt Yenisei)-Angara-Selenga (alt Selenge)-Ider (off Ideriin)	Yenisey G of Kara Sea, Russia, USSR	3650	5870
in Europe	Volga	Caspian (Sea) L, Russia, USSR	2300	3700
Venezuela	Orinoco	Atlantic O, Venezuela	1280	2060
Vietnam				
North	Red (alt Coi, Koi; off Hong, Yuan)	G of Tonkin of South China Sea, North Vietnam	710	1150
South	•Mekong (off in Vietnam Tien Giang)	South China Sea, South Vietnam	2600	4180
Yugoslavia	Danube (off in Yugoslavia Dunav)	Black Sea, Romania-USSR	1770	2850
Zaire	Congo (for Kongo; off in Zaire Zaire)-Lualaba	Atlantic O, Angola-Zaire	2880	4630
Zambia	•Zambezi (alt Zambesi, Zambeze)	Mozambique Channel, Mozambique	1650	2650

10
Highest Mountains (Peaks), by Continent

Contents

Latitude and longitude of mountain peak, in degrees and minutes.

Conventional and other (alternate, former, and official) names of peak and of massif, if any (in brackets).

Mountain range or system (unconventional names are given only for initial entry), and subdivision and country in which located.

Elevation (i.e., altitude of summit above sea level), in feet and meters.

Date of first successful ascent.

Arrangement

By elevation, under continent.

Coverage

Above * * *, all named peaks rising to at least the following elevations:

- Africa – 15,000 ft (4570 m)
- Antarctica – 14,000 ft (4270 m)
- Asia – 25,500 ft (7770 m)
- Europe – 14,800 ft (4510 m)
- North America – 14,250 ft (4340 m)
- Oceania – 14,000 ft (4270 m)
- South America – 20,700 ft (6310 m)

Below * * *, other well-known peaks, including the highest in certain countries and in important ranges.

Rounding

Elevations are rounded to the nearest 10 ft (m).

Special Features

When peak is the highest in a particular range, the name of the range is italicized.

Active volcanoes are indicated by the abbreviation "volc."

Entries

441.

TABLE 10. HIGHEST MOUNTAINS (PEAKS), BY CONTINENT

AFRICA

Latitude and Longitude		Peak and [Massif]	Mountain Range or System	Location	Elevation (ft)	Elevation (m)	First Ascent
3.04S,	37.21E	Kibo (volc[1]) [Kilimanjaro]	–	Tanganyika, Tanzania	19,340	5890	1889
3.06S,	37.27E	Mawensi (volc[1]) [Kilimanjaro]	–	Tanganyika, Tanzania	17,100	5210	1912
0.09S,	37.18E	Batian [Kenya]	–	Kenya	17,050	5200	1899
0.09S,	37.18E	•Nelion [Kenya]	–	Kenya	17,020	5190	1929
0.23N,	29.52E	Margherita [Stanley]	*Ruwenzori*	Uganda-Zaire	16,760	5110	1906
0.23N,	29.52E	Alexandra [Stanley]	Ruwenzori	Uganda-Zaire	16,700	5090	1906
0.23N,	29.52E	Albert [Stanley]	Ruwenzori	Zaire	16,690	5090	1932
0.23N,	29.52E	Savoia [Stanley]	Ruwenzori	Uganda	16,330	4980	1906
0.23N,	29.52E	Elena [Stanley]	Ruwenzori	Uganda	16,300	4970	1906
0.23N,	29.52E	Elizabeth [Stanley]	Ruwenzori	Uganda	16,170	4930	1953
0.23N,	29.52E	Philip [Stanley]	Ruwenzori	Uganda	16,140	4920	1954
0.23N,	29.52E	Moebius [Stanley]	Ruwenzori	Uganda	16,130	4920	1906
0.24N,	29.53E	Vittorio Emanuele [Speke]	Ruwenzori	Uganda	16,040	4890	1906
0.24N,	29.53E	Ensonga [Speke]	Ruwenzori	Uganda	15,960	4860	1926
0.22N,	29.53E	Edward [Baker]	Ruwenzori	Uganda	15,890	4840	1906
0.24N,	29.53E	Johnston [Speke]	Ruwenzori	Uganda	15,860	4830	1926
0.26N,	29.54E	Umberto [Emin]	Ruwenzori	Zaire	15,740	4800	1906
0.22N,	29.53E	Semper [Baker]	Ruwenzori	Uganda	15,730	4790	1906
0.26N,	29.54E	Kraepelin [Emin]	Ruwenzori	Zaire	15,720	4790	1932
0.26N,	29.55E	Iolanda [Gessi]	Ruwenzori	Uganda	15,470	4720	1906
0.26N,	29.55E	Bottego [Gessi]	Ruwenzori	Uganda	15,420	4700	1906
0.20N,	29.53E	Sella [Luigi di Savoia]	Ruwenzori	Uganda	15,180	4630	1906
0.22N,	29.53E	Wollaston [Baker]	Ruwenzori	Uganda	15,180	4630	1906
0.22N,	29.53E	Moore [Baker]	Ruwenzori	Uganda	15,170	4620	1906
0.20N,	29.53E	Weismann [Luigi di Savoia]	Ruwenzori	Uganda	15,160	4620	1935
0.23N,	29.52E	Great Tooth [Stanley]	Ruwenzori	Uganda	15,100	4600	
0.22N,	29.51E	Wasuwameso [Mugule]	Ruwenzori	Zaire	15,030	4580	
0.19N,	29.52E	Okusoma [Luigi di Savoia]	Ruwenzori	Uganda	15,020	4580	
0.24N,	29.53E	Trident [Speke]	Ruwenzori	Uganda	15,000	4570	
			* * *				
3.14S,	36.45E	•Meru (volc)	–	Tanganyika, Tanzania	14,980	4570	
13.15N,	38.24E	Ancua [Ras Dashan (off Rasdajan)]	*Semien*	Ethiopia	14,930	4550	
1.30S,	29.27E	Karisimbi (volc)	*Virunga*	Rwanda-Zaire	14,790	4510	
1.27S,	29.26E	Mikeno (volc)	Virunga	Zaire	14,560	4440	
10.36N,	37.54E	•Talo	*Choke*	Ethiopia	14,480	4410	
1.08N,	34.33E	Elgon	–	Kenya-Uganda	14,180	4320	1911
6.55N,	39.49E	Batu	*Mendebo*	Ethiopia	14,130	4310	
31.03N,	7.57W	Toubkal: W peak [Toubkal]	*Atlas*	Morocco	13,650	4160	
1.23S,	29.40E	Muhavura (volc)	Virunga	Rwanda-Uganda	13,540	4130	
4.12N,	9.11E	Fako (volc) [Cameroon (alt Cameroun)]	*Cameroon* (alt Cameroun)	Cameroon	13,350	4070	1861
0.19S,	36.37E	Lesatima	*Aberdare*	Kenya	13,100	3990	
28.16N,	16.38W	Teide (volc)	–	(Canary Islands), Spain[2]	12,170	3710	

[1] No known eruption.

[2] Tenerife I.

AFRICA

Latitude and Longitude	Peak and [Massif]	Mountain Range or System	Location	Elevation (ft)	Elevation (m)	First Ascent
19.50N, 18.30E	(Emi) Koussi (volc)	*Tibesti*	Chad	11,470	3490	
29.28S, 29.16E	Thabana Ntlenyana (alt Thabantshonyana)	*Drakens(berg)*	Lesotho	11,420	3480	
29.12S, 29.22E	•Injasuti	Drakens(berg)	Lesotho-South Africa	11,310	3450	
3.57N, 32.54E	• Kinyeti	*Imatong*	Sudan	10,460	3190	
21.25N, 18.42E	•Kegueur Terbi (alt Chegor Tedi, Hessi)	Tibesti	Chad-Libya	10,330	3150	
21.05S, 55.29E	Neiges (volc)	–	Reunion	10,070	3070	
15.59S, 35.36E	Mlanje	*Mlanje*	Malawi	10,000	3050	
3.35N, 8.46E	Santa Isabel (volc)	–	Equatorial Guinea[1]	9,840	3000	
23.18N, 5.32E	•Tahat	*Ahaggar* (alt Hoggar)	Algeria	9,570	2920	1912?
14.01S, 48.58E	Maromokotro	*Tsaratanana*	Malagasy Republic	9,470	2890	
14.56N, 24.21W	Cano (volc)	–	Cape Verde Islands[2]	9,280	2830	
28.31N, 33.57E	Katrinah (alt Catherine) [Musa]	*Sinai*	Egypt	8,650	2640	
12.30S, 15.19E	Moco	*Upanda*	Angola	8,600	2620	
21.10S, 14.33E	Konigstein [Brand(berg)]	*Kaokoveld*	South-West Africa	8,550	2610	
18.18S, 32.54E	•Inyangani	*Inyanga*	Rhodesia	8,520	2600	
19.47S, 33.09E	Binga	*Chimanimani*	Mozambique-Rhodesia	7,990	2440	
10.42N, 47.09E	•Surad Ad (off Surud Ad)	*Ogo*	Somalia	7,900	2410	
35.20N, 6.40E	Chelia	*Aures* (off Awras)	Algeria	7,640	2330	
20.00N, 8.35E	•Greboun	*Air* (alt Azbine)	Niger	7,550	2300	
8.20N, 11.45E	Vogel	*Banglang*	Nigeria	6,700	2040	
9.13N, 11.07W	• Bintimani	*Loma*	Sierra Leone	6,390	1940	
32.45N, 16.56W	Ruivo de Santana	–	(Madeira Islands), Portugal[3]	6,110	1860	
25.57S, 31.11E	•Emlembe	Drakens(berg)	Swaziland	6,100	1860	
7.37N, 8.25W	Nimba	*Nimba*	Guinea-Ivory Coast-Liberia	5,780	1760	
35.13N, 8.41E	Shanabi (alt Chambi)	*Dorsale*	Tunisia	5,070	1540	

ANTARCTICA

Latitude and Longitude	Peak and [Massif]	Mountain Range or System	Location	Elevation (ft)	Elevation (m)	First Ascent
78.35S, 85.25W	•–[Vinson]	*Sentinel*	Antarctica	16,860	5140	1966
78.24S, 85.55W	•Tyree	Sentinel	Antarctica	16,290	4970	1967
78.27S, 85.46W	•Shinn	Sentinel	Antarctica	15,750	4800	1966
78.23S, 86.02W	•Gardner	Sentinel	Antarctica	15,380	4690	1966
78.26S, 85.53W	•Epperly	Sentinel	Antarctica	15,100	4600	
84.20S, 166.19E	•Kirkpatrick	*Queen Alexandra*	Antarctica	14,850	4530	
83.54S, 168.23E	•Elizabeth	Queen Alexandra	Antarctica	14,700	4480	
82.51S, 161.21E	•Markham	*Queen Elizabeth*	Antarctica	14,270	4350	
84.04S, 167.30E	•Bell	Queen Alexandra	Antarctica	14,120	4300	
83.59S, 166.39E	•Mackellar	Queen Alexandra	Antarctica	14,100	4300	

* * *

84.33S, 175.18E	• Kaplan	*Hughes*	Antarctica	13,880	4230	

[1] Fernando Po I.

[2] Fogo I.

[3] Madeira I.

Figure 11. Peaks of the incomparable Everest massif photographed by a Swiss expedition in 1952: at the left, Mount Everest, or Chumulangma, the world's highest peak; in the middle, Lhotse, or Lotzu; at the right, Nuptse. (Credit: Swiss Foundation for Alpine Research.)

ANTARCTICA

Latitude and Longitude	Peak and [Massif]	Mountain Range or System	Location	Elevation (ft)	Elevation (m)	First Ascent
71.23S, 63.22W	•Jackson	*Gutenko*	Antarctica	13,740	4190	
77.02S, 126.00W	•Sidley	*Executive Committee*	Antarctica	13,720	4180	
71.47S, 168.45E	•Minto	*Admiralty*	Antarctica	13,660	4160	
77.32S, 167.09E	•Erebus (volc)	–	Antarctica	12,450	3790	1908

ASIA

Latitude and Longitude	Peak and [Massif]	Mountain Range or System	Location	Elevation (ft)	Elevation (m)	First Ascent
27.59N, 86.56E	Everest (alt Chumulangma) [Everest]	*Nepal Himalaya*	China-Nepal	29,030	8850	1953
35.53N, 76.31E	K^2 (alt Chogori, Dapsang, Godwin Austen)	*Karakoram*	Kashmir-Jammu	28,250	8610	1954
27.42N, 88.09E	Kangchenjunga (alt Kanchenjunga): highest peak [Kangchenjunga]	Nepal Himalaya	Nepal-Sikkim	28,170	8590	1955
27.58N, 86.56E	Lhotse (alt E^1, Lotzu) [Everest]	Nepal Himalaya	China-Nepal	27,890	8500	1956
27.41N, 88.09E	Kangchenjunga: S peak [Kangchenjunga]	Nepal Himalaya	Nepal-Sikkim	27,800	8470	
27.53N, 87.05E	Makalu I [Makalu]	Nepal Himalaya	China-Nepal	27,790	8470	1955
27.42N, 88.09E	•Kangchenjunga: W peak [Kangchenjunga]	Nepal Himalaya	Nepal-Sikkim	27,620	8420	
27.57N, 86.57E	•Lhotse Shar (alt Lhotse: E peak) [Everest]	Nepal Himalaya	China-Nepal	27,500	8380	1970
28.42N, 83.30E	Dhaulagiri I (alt Daulagiri I)	Nepal Himalaya	Nepal	26,810	8170	1960
28.06N, 86.39E	Cho Oyu (alt Choaoyu): highest peak	Nepal Himalaya	China-Nepal	26,750	8150	1954
28.33N, 84.34E	Manaslu (alt Kutang I): highest peak [Manaslu]	Nepal Himalaya	Nepal	26,660	8130	1956
35.14N, 74.35E	Nanga Parbat: highest peak	*Punjab Himalaya*	Kashmir-Jammu	26,660	8130	1953
28.36N, 83.49E	Annapurna I	Nepal Himalaya	Nepal	26,500	8080	1950
35.43N, 76.42E	Gasherbrum I (alt Hidden) [Gasherbrum]	Karakoram	Kashmir-Jammu	26,470	8070	1958
35.49N, 76.34E	Broad: highest peak [Gasherbrum]	Karakoram	Kashmir-Jammu	26,400	8050	1957
35.46N, 76.39E	Gasherbrum II: highest peak [Gasherbrum]	Karakoram	Kashmir-Jammu	26,360	8030	1956
28.21N, 85.47E	Gosainthan (alt Shishma Pangma; off Kaosengtsan)	Nepal Himalaya	Tibet, China	26,290	8010	1964
35.49N, 76.34E	•Broad: mittel(gipfel) peak [Gasherbrum]	Karakoram	Kashmir-Jammu	26,250	8000	
35.46N, 76.39E	Gasherbrum III [Gasherbrum]	Karakoram	Kashmir-Jammu	26,090	7950	
28.32N, 84,07E	Annapurna II	Nepal Himalaya	Nepal	26,040	7940	1960
35.46N, 76.37E	Gasherbrum IV [Gasherbrum]	Karakoram	Kashmir-Jammu	26,000	7920	1958
28.06N, 86.45E	Gyachung Kang	Nepal Himalaya	China-Nepal	25,990	7920	1964

ASIA

Latitude and Longitude	Peak and [Massif]	Mountain Range or System	Location	Elevation (ft)	Elevation (m)	First Ascent
35.14N, 74.35E	•Nanga Parbat: vor(gipfel) peak	Punjab Himalaya	Kashmir-Jammu	25,950	7910	
27.43N, 88.07E	Kangbachen [Kangchenjunga]	Nepal Himalaya	India-Nepal	25,930	7900	
28.33N, 84.34E	•Manaslu: E pinnacle [Manaslu]	Nepal Himalaya	Nepal	25,900	7900	
36.20N, 75.11E	Distaghil Sar	Karakoram	Kashmir-Jammu	25,870	7890	1960
27.58N, 86.53E	Nuptse (alt E^2) [Everest]	Nepal Himalaya	Nepal	25,850	7880	1961
28.26N, 84.39E	Himalchuli: highest peak	Nepal Himalaya	Nepal	25,800	7860	1956
36.11N, 75.13E	•Khiangyang Kish (alt Khinyang Chhish)	Karakoram	Kashmir-Jammu	25,760	7850	
28.06N, 86.41E	Ngojumba Ri (alt Cho Oyu: E peak)	Nepal Himalaya	China-Nepal	25,720	7840	1965
28.30N, 84.34E	Dakura (alt Kutang II) [Manaslu]	Nepal Himalaya	Nepal	25,710	7840	
35.39N, 76.19E	Masherbrum: E peak	Karakoram	Kashmir-Jammu	25,660	7820	1960
30.23N, 79.58E	Nanda Devi: W peak	*Kumaun Himalaya*	Uttar Pradesh, India	25,650	7820	1936
35.15N, 74.35E	Nanga Parbat: N peak	Punjab Himalaya	Kashmir-Jammu	25,650	7820	
27.55N, 87.08E	Chomo Lonzo (alt Makalu) [Makalu]	Nepal Himalaya	China-Nepal	25,640	7820	1954
35.38N, 76.18E	Masherbrum: W peak	Karakoram	Kashmir-Jammu	25,610	7810	
36.09N, 74.29E	Rakaposhi	*Haramosh (Ridge)*	Kashmir-Jammu	25,550	7790	1958
36.31N, 74.31E	Batura Mustagh I (alt Hunza-Kunji I)	Karakoram	Kashmir-Jammu	25,540	7790	1959?
35.46N, 76.39E	•Gasherbrum II: E peak [Gasherbrum]	Karakoram	Kashmir-Jammu	25,500	7770	

* * *

Latitude and Longitude	Peak and [Massif]	Mountain Range or System	Location	Elevation (ft)	Elevation (m)	First Ascent
30.56N, 79.35E	Kamet (alt Kameite)	*Zaskar*	China-India	25,440	7760	1931
29.40N, 95.10E	Namcha Barwa (off Namuchopaerhwa)	*Assam Himalaya*	Tibet, China	25,440	7760	
30.26N, 81.18E	Gurla Mandhata (off Kualamantata)	*Nepal-Tibet (Watershed)*	Tibet, China	25,350	7730	
36.25N, 87.25E	•Ulugh Mustagh (off Wulukomushih)	*Kunlun*	Sinkiang-Tibet, China	25,340	7720	
38.40N, 75.21E	Kungur II (off Kungkoerh II)	*Mustagh Ata* (off Mussutakoate)	Sinkiang, China	25,330	7720	1955
36.15N, 71.50E	•Tirich Mir: W peak	*Hindu Kush*	Pakistan	25,260	7700	1950
36.15N, 71.50E	•Tirich Mir: E peak	Hindu Kush	Pakistan	25,230	7690	1964
34.52N, 77.45E	•Saser Kangri I	*Saser (Ridge)*	Kashmir-Jammu	25,170	7670	
29.34N, 101.53E	•Minya Konka (alt Minyag Gangkar; off Kungka)	*Tahsueh*	Szechwan, China	24,890	7590	1932
28.14N, 90.36E	Khula Kangri I (alt Kula Gangri I)	Assam Himalaya	Bhutan-China	24,780	7550	
38.16N, 75.09E	•Mustagh Ata (off Mussutakoate)	Mustagh Ata	Sinkiang, China	24,760	7550	1956
28.01N, 86.54E	Changtse (alt Changtzu, E^3) [Everest]	Nepal Himalaya	China-Nepal	24,730	7540	
38.56N, 72.02E	Kommunizma (for Garmo, Stalina)	*Pamir-Alai* (off Pamir-Alay)	Tadzhikistan, USSR	24,590	7490	1933
36.26N, 71.50E	•Noshaq: highest peak	Hindu Kush	Afghanistan-Pakistan	24,580	7490	1960

ASIA

Latitude and Longitude	Peak and [Massif]	Mountain Range or System	Location	Elevation (ft)	Elevation (m)	First Ascent
42.03N, 80.11E	Pobedy (alt Shengli)	*Tien* (alt Tyan)	China-USSR	24,410	7440	1956
32.46N, 81.02E	•Alung Gangri (off Aling)	*Alung* (off Aling)	Tibet, China	24,000	7320	
27.50N, 89.16E	Chomo Lhari (alt Chonolali)	Assam Himalaya	Bhutan-China	24,000	7310	1937
39.20N, 72.55E	Lenina (for Kaufmann)	Pamir-Alai	Kirgizia-Tadzhikistan, USSR	23,380	7130	1928
34.24N, 100.10E	Amne Machin (alt Animaching; off Chishih)	*Amne Machin* (off Chishih)	Tsinghai, China	23,300	7100	1960
30.27N, 90.33E	•Nyenchhen Thanglha (off Nienchingtangkula)	*Nyenchhen Thanglha* (off Nienchingtang-kula)	Tibet, China	23,250	7090	
29.56N, 84.33E	•Lombo Kangra (off Lungpu)	*Kailas* (off Kangtissu)	Tibet, China	23,160	7060	
42.15N, 80.10E	Khan-Tengri	Tien	Kirgizia, USSR	22,950	6990	1931
31.04N, 81.19E	Kailas (off Kangtissu)	Kailas	Tibet, China	22,030	6710	
37.09N, 72.26E	Karla Marksa	*Vakhan*	Tadzhikistan, USSR	21,980	6700	1946
38.35N, 97.45E	•Sulo	*Nan*	Tsinghai, China	20,820	6350	
28.17N, 97.46E	•Hkakabo Razi	*Kumon*	Burma	19,300	5880	
35.56N, 52.08E	•Damavand (alt Demavend)	*Alborz* (alt Elburz)	Iran	18,610	5670	1837
39.42N, 44.18E	Great Ararat (off Buyukagri) (volc[1])	–	Turkey	16,920	5160	1829
30.50N, 51.35E	•Dinar	*Zagros*	Iran	16,400	5000	
56.04N, 160.38E	Klyuchevskaya (volc)	*Kamchatka*	Russia, USSR	15,670	4770	1931
49.10N, 87.55E	Khuitun (off Kuyten) [Taban Bogdo]	*Altai* (alt Altay)	Mongolia	15,270	4650	
49.48N, 86.35E	Belukha: W peak	Altai	Kazakhstan-Russia, USSR	15,160	4620	1903
37.30N, 44.00E	Geliasin [Resko (alt Cilo)]	*Hakkari*	Turkey	13,680	4170	
6.05N, 116.33E	Kinabalu: highest peak	*Crocker*	Sabah, Malaysia	12,450	4100	1924
23.28N, 120.57E	Yu (alt Hsinkao, Morrison)	*Central* (off Chungyang)	Taiwan	13,110	4000	1896?
38.32N, 35.28E	Erciyas (volc)	–	Turkey	12,850	3920	
1.42S, 101.16E	Kerintji (for Indrapura) (volc)	*Barisan*	Sumatra I, Indonesia	12,480	3800	
35.22N, 138.44E	Fuji (alt Huzi) (volc)	–	Honshu I, Japan	12,400	3780	7th c?
15.20N, 43.55E	•Hadur Shuayb	*Yemen (Highlands)*	Yemen	12,340	3760	
36.43N, 44.50E	• Algurd (alt Halgurd)	Zagros	Iraq	12,250	3730	
8.24S, 116.28E	Sangkarijan (volc[1]) [Rindjani]	–	Lombok I, Indonesia	12,220	3730	
8.06S, 112.55E	Mahameru (volc)	*Semeru*	Java I, Indonesia	12,060	3680	
16.52N, 43.22E	•Razikh	Yemen (Highlands)	Saudi Arabia-Yemen	11,990	3650	
51.45N, 100.20E	Munku-Sardyk	*Sayan*	Mongolia-USSR	11,450	3490	1868
3.21S, 120.01E	Rante Kombola	*Quarles*	Celebes I, Indonesia	11,340	3450	
36.48N, 139.08E	Oku-Hotaka [Hotaka]	*Mikuni*	Honshu I, Japan	10,530	3210	
15.04N, 107.59E	•(Ngoc) Linh	*Annamese* (off Trungphan)	South Vietnam	10,500	3200	
8.21S, 115.30E	Agung (volc)	–	Bali I, Indonesia	10,310	3140	

[1] No known eruption.

ASIA

Latitude and Longitude	Peak and [Massif]	Mountain Range or System	Location	Elevation (ft)	Elevation (m)	First Ascent
22.18N, 103.46E	Fan Si Pan	*Fan Si Pan*	North Vietnam	10,310	3140	
23.13N, 57.16E	•Sham	*Akhdar*	Oman	10,190	3110	
34.18N, 36.07E	Qurnat al Sawda	*Lebanon* (off Lubnan)	Lebanon	10,130	3090	
8.55S, 125.30E	Tata Mailau (alt Rameau)	–	Portuguese Timor	9,720	2960	
6.59N, 125.16E	Apo (volc[1])	–	Mindanao I, Philippines	9,690	2950	
16.36N, 120.54E	Pulog	*Central*	Luzon I, Philippines	9,610	2930	
18.59N, 103.10E	•Bia	*Tranninh*	Laos	9,240	2820	
33.24N, 35.50E	Hermon (off Shaykh)	*Anti-Lebanon* (off Sharqi)	Lebanon-Syria	9,230	2810	
41.59N, 128.04E	•Paitou (alt Paektu)	*Changpai* (alt Changbaek)	China-North Korea	8,900	2710	1886
18.35N, 98.29E	Inthanon (alt Angka)	*Phi Pan Nam*	Thailand	8,450	2580	
7.00N, 80.46E	Pidurutalagala	*Piduru (Ridges)*	Ceylon	8,280	2520	
13.53N, 45.12E	•Thamar (off Thamir)	Yemen (Highlands)	Southern Yemen	8,240	2510	
4.38N, 102.14E	Tahan	*Cameron (Highlands)*	West Malaysia, Malaysia	7,190	2190	
34.55N, 32.52E	Khionistra (alt Olympus)	*Troodos*	Cyprus	6,410	1950	
33.22N, 126.32E	•Halla	–	South Korea[2]	6,400	1950	
12.02N, 104.10E	•Aural	*Cardamomes*	Cambodia	5,950	1810	
29.36N, 35.24E	•Ramm	*Sharah*	Jordan	5,750	1750	
33.00N, 35.25E	•Meron (for Jarmaq, Sharqi)	*Galilee*	Israel	3,960	1210	

EUROPE

Latitude and Longitude	Peak and [Massif]	Mountain Range or System	Location	Elevation (ft)	Elevation (m)	First Ascent
43.21N, 42.26E	Elbrus (for Elborus): W peak (volc[1]) [Elbrus (for Elborus)]	*Caucasus* (off Kavkaz)	Russia, USSR	18,480	5630	1874
43.21N, 42.26E	Elbrus: E peak (volc[1]) [Elbrus]	Caucasus	Russia, USSR	18,360	5590	1829
43.00N, 43.06E	Shkhara: E peak	Caucasus	Georgia-Russia, USSR	17,060	5200	1888
43.03N, 43.08E	Dykh(-Tau): W peak	Caucasus	Russia, USSR	17,050	5200	1888
43.03N, 43.08E	Dykh(-Tau): E peak	Caucasus	Russia, USSR	16,900	5150	1938
43.03N, 43.13E	Koshtan(-Tau)	Caucasus	Russia, USSR	16,880	5140	1888
43.00N, 43.06E	Shkhara: W peak	Caucasus	Georgia-Russia, USSR	16,880	5140	
43.03N, 43.10E	Pushkina	Caucasus	Russia, USSR	16,730	5100	1938
43.02N, 43.03E	Dzhangi(-Tau): NW peak	Caucasus	Georgia, USSR	16,570	5050	1903
42.42N, 44.31E	Kazbek: E peak	Caucasus	Georgia, USSR	16,560	5050	1868
43.02N, 43.03E	Dzhangi(-Tau): SE peak	Caucasus	Georgia, USSR	16,520	5030	1888
43.02N, 43.02E	Katyn(-Tau)	Caucasus	Georgia-Russia, USSR	16,310	4970	1888
43.02N, 43.05E	Shota Rustaveli	Caucasus	Georgia-Russia, USSR	16,270	4960	1937
43.02N, 43.09E	Mizhirgi: W peak	Caucasus	Russia, USSR	16,170	4930	1934
43.02N, 43.09E	Mizhirgi: E peak	Caucasus	Russia, USSR	16,140	4920	1889
43.04N, 43.13E	Kundyum-Mizhirgi	Caucasus	Russia, USSR	16,010	4880	1946
43.03N, 43.01E	Gestola	Caucasus	Georgia-Russia, USSR	15,930	4860	1886

[1] No known eruption.

[2] Cheju I.

EUROPE

Latitude and Longitude		Peak and [Massif]	Mountain Range or System	Location	Elevation (ft)	Elevation (m)	First Ascent
43.02N,	42.58E	Tetnuld	Caucasus	Georgia, USSR	15,920	4850	1887
45.50N,	6.52E	(Mont-)Blanc (alt Bianco) [Blanc (alt Bianco)]	*Alps* (off Alpe, Alpen, Alpes, Alpi)	France-Italy	15,770	4810	1786
42.43N,	44.25E	Dzhimariy(-Khokh)	Caucasus	Georgia, USSR	15,680	4780	1890
43.02N,	43.04E	Adish	Caucasus	Georgia-Russia, USSR	15,570	4750	1931
43.08N,	42.40E	Ushba: SW peak	Caucasus	Georgia, USSR	15,450	4710	1903
43.08N,	42.40E	Ushba: NE peak	Caucasus	Georgia, USSR	15,400	4690	1888
43.05N,	43.13E	Ullu-Auz(-Bashi)	Caucasus	Russia, USSR	15,360	4680	1888
43.05N,	43.12E	Panoramnyy	Caucasus	Russia, USSR	15,350	4680	1946
43.02N,	43.10E	Krumkol	Caucasus	Russia, USSR	15,320	4670	1937
42.42N,	44.31E	Kazbek: W peak	Caucasus	Georgia, USSR	15,250	4650	1890
42.46N,	43.48E	Uilpata [for Aday(-Khokh)]	Caucasus	Russia, USSR	15,240	4650	1890
42.45N,	44.25E	Shau(-Khokh)	Caucasus	Georgia, USSR	15,240	4640	1936
45.56N,	7.52E	Dufour(spitze) [Rosa]	Alps	Italy-Switzerland	15,200	4630	1855
45.56N,	7.52E	Grenz(gipfel) [Rosa]	Alps	Italy-Switzerland	15,190	4630	1851
43.20N,	42.25E	Kyukyurtlyukol(-Bashi) [Elbrus]	Caucasus	Russia, USSR	15,170	4620	1936
45.56N,	7.51E	Nordend [Rosa]	Alps	Italy-Switzerland	15,130	4610	1861
43.08N,	42.59E	Tikhtengen: S peak	Caucasus	Georgia-Russia, USSR	15,130	4610	1935
43.08N,	42.59E	Tikhtengen: N peak	Caucasus	Georgia-Russia, USSR	15,130	4610	1936
42.42N,	44.28E	Mayli(-Khokh)	Caucasus	Georgia, USSR	15,100	4600	1903
42.45N,	43.47E	Dubl: N peak	Caucasus	Russia, USSR	15,030	4580	1933
45.56N,	7.52E	Zumstein(spitze) [Rosa]	Alps	Italy-Switzerland	15,000	4570	1820
45.55N,	7.52E	Signal(kuppe) [Rosa]	Alps	Italy-Switzerland	14,960	4560	1842
43.06N,	43.13E	Dumala(-Tau)	Caucasus	Russia, USSR	14,950	4560	1930
43.03N,	43.15E	Tyutyun(-Bashi)	Caucasus	Russia, USSR	14,930	4550	1933
46.06N,	7.51E	Dom [Mischabel]	Alps	Switzerland	14,910	4540	1858
42.57N,	43.11E	Aylama	Caucasus	Georgia-Russia, USSR	14,890	4540	1889
43.12N,	42.57E	Dzhaylyk(-Bashi)	Caucasus	Russia, USSR	14,890	4540	1936
45.55N,	7.50E	Lyskamm [Rosa]	Alps	Italy-Switzerland	14,890	4540	1861
43.01N,	43.15E	Tyutyun(-Tau)	Caucasus	Russia, USSR	14,890	4540	1933
42.45N,	43.47E	Dubl: S peak	Caucasus	Russia, USSR	14,880	4530	1933
43.01N,	43.03E	Lakutsa	Caucasus	Georgia, USSR	14,830	4520	1931
42.47N,	43.46E	Karaugom: E peak	Caucasus	Russia, USSR	14,810	4510	1890
42.20N,	46.15E	Addala Shukhgelmeer	Caucasus	Russia, USSR	14,800	4510	1935
42.47N,	43.46E	Karaugom: W peak	Caucasus	Russia, USSR	14,800	4510	1937
42.42N,	44.29E	Spartak	Caucasus	Georgia, USSR	14,800	4510	1940

* * *

Latitude and Longitude		Peak and [Massif]	Mountain Range or System	Location	Elevation (ft)	Elevation (m)	First Ascent
46.07N,	7.43E	Weiss(horn)	Alps	Switzerland	14,780	4500	1861
46.05N,	7.51E	Tasch(horn) [Mischabel]	Alps	Switzerland	14,730	4490	1862
45.58N,	7.39E	Matter(horn) [Cervino]	Alps	Italy-Switzerland	14,690	4480	1865
45.51N,	6.53E	Maudit [Blanc]	Alps	France-Italy	14,650	4470	1878
41.13N,	47.51E	Bazar-Dyuzi	Caucasus	Azerbaijan-Russia, USSR	14,550	4430	1873
46.02N,	7.37E	(Dent) Blanche	Alps	Switzerland	14,300	4360	1862
46.32N,	8.08E	Finsteraar(horn)	Alps	Switzerland	14,020	4270	1812
46.28N,	8.00E	Aletsch(horn)	Alps	Swtizerland	13,760	4190	1859
46.33N,	7.58E	Jungfrau	Alps	Switzerland	13,640	4160	1811
46.33N,	8.01E	Monch	Alps	Switzerland	13,450	4100	1857
46.34N,	8.01E	Eiger	Alps	Switzerland	13,020	3970	1858
47.04N,	12.42E	Grossglockner	Alps	Austria	12,460	3800	1800
37.03N,	3.19W	Mulhacen	*Nevada*	Andalucia, Spain	11,410	3480	

EUROPE

Latitude and Longitude	Peak and [Massif]	Mountain Range or System	Location	Elevation (ft)	Elevation (m)	First Ascent
42.38N, 0.40E	Aneto	*Pyrenees* (alt Pirineos)	Aragon, Spain	11,170	3400	1842
37.50N, 14.55E	Etna (volc)	–	Sicilia, Italy[1]	10,760	3280	
47.25N, 10.59E	Zug(spitze)	Alps	Austria-West Germany	9,720	2960	1820
42.11N, 23.34E	Musala	*Rhodope* (off Rodhopis, Rodopi)	Bulgaria	9,600	2920	
42.28N, 13.34E	Corno Grande	*Apennines* (off Appennino)	Abruzzi e Molise, Italy	9,560	2910	
40.05N, 22.21E	Mytikas [Olympus (off Olimbos)]	*Olympus* (off Olimbos)	Greece	9,550	2910	1915?
46.23N, 13.50E	Triglav	Alps	Slovenia, Yugoslavia	9,390	2860	1778
41.44N, 20.32E	Korab	*Korab*	Albania-Yugoslavia	9,050[2]	2760[2]	
42.23N, 8.56E	Cinto	–	Provence-Cote d'Azur-Corse, France[3]	8,890	2710	
49.09N, 20.05E	Gerlachovsky (alt Gerlachovka; for Stalin)	*Tatra* (off Tatry)	Slovakia, Czechoslovakia	8,710	2650	
43.12N, 4.48W	Cerredo [Europa]	*Cantabrian* (off Cantabrica)	Asturias-Castilla la Vieja-Leon, Spain	8,690	2650	1892
45.36N, 24.44E	Moldoveanu	*Transylvanian Alps* (off Carpatii Meridionali)	Romania	8,340	2540	
45.35N, 24.34E	Negoiu	Transylvanian Alps	Romania	8,320	2530	
49.12N, 20.04E	Rysy	Tatra	Czechoslovakia-Poland	8,200	2500	
61.39N, 8.33E	Glittertinden	*Jotunheimen*	Norway	8,110	2470	
61.37N, 8.17E	Galdhopiggen	Jotunheimen	Norway	8,100	2470	
42.43N, 24.55E	Botev	*Balkan* (off Stara)	Bulgaria	7,800	2380	
38.28N, 28.25W	Ponta do Pico (alt Pico) (volc)	–	(Azores), Portugal[4]	7,710	2350	
64.01N, 16.41W	Hvannadalshnukur	–	Iceland	6,950	2120	
67.53N, 18.31E	Kebnekaise	*Kolen*	Sweden	6,930	2110	1883
40.19N, 7.37W	Estrela	*Estrela*	Portugal	6,530	1990	
65.04N, 60.09E	Narodnaya	*Ural*	Russia, USSR	6,210	1890	
45.32N, 2.50E	Sancy	*Auvergne*	Auvergne, France	6,190	1890	
79.02N, 17.30E	Newton	–	Svalbard[5]	5,630	1720	
56.48N, 5.00W	(Ben) Nevis	*Grampian*	Scotland, UK	4,410	1340	
69.18N, 21.16E	Haltiatunturi (alt Reisduoddarhaldde)	Haltia (alt Halddia)	Finland-Norway	4,340	1320	
40.49N, 14.26E	Vesuvius (off Vesuvio) (volc)	–	Campania, Italy	4,190	1280	
50.26N, 12.57E	Fichtel(-berg)	*Erz(gebirge)*	East Germany	3,980	1220	
52.00N, 9.45W	Carrantuohill (alt Carrantual)	*Macgillicuddy's Reeks*	Ireland	3,410	1040	
47.52N, 20.01E	Kekes	*Matra*	Hungary	3,330	1010	

[1] Sicily I.

[2] Average of elevations officially given by Albania (9030 ft, 2750 m) and Yugoslavia (9070 ft, 2760 m).

[3] Corsica I.

[4] Pico I.

[5] West Spitsbergen I.

NORTH AMERICA

Latitude and Longitude	Peak and [Massif]	Mountain Range or System	Location	Elevation (ft)	Elevation (m)	First Ascent
63.04N, 151.00W	McKinley: S peak [McKinley]	*Alaska*	Alaska, USA	20,320	6190	1913
60.34N, 140.24W	Logan: central peak [Logan]	*Saint Elias*	Yukon Territory, Canada	19,850	6050	1925
60.34N, 140.25W	•Logan: W peak [Logan]	Saint Elias	Yukon Territory, Canada	19,800	6040	1925
60.34N, 140.22W	•Logan: E peak [Logan]	Saint Elias	Yukon Territory, Canada	19,750	6020	1957
63.04N, 151.00W	McKinley: N peak [McKinley]	Alaska	Alaska, USA	19,470	5930	1910
19.02N, 97.16W	Citlatepetl (alt Orizaba) (volc[1])	*Neovolcanica*	Puebla-Veracruz, Mexico	18,700	5700	1848
60.35N, 140.24W	•Logan: N peak [Logan]	Saint Elias	Yukon Territory, Canada	18,600	5670	1959
60.17N, 140.55W	Saint Elias	Saint Elias	Canada-USA	18,010	5490	1897
19.01N, 98.32W	Popocatepetl (volc)	Neovolcanica	Puebla, Mexico	17,890	5450	1520
62.58N, 151.24W	Foraker	Alaska	Alaska, USA	17,400	5300	1934
19.11N, 98.38W	Ixtacihuatl (alt Iztaccihuatl)	Neovolcanica	Puebla, Mexico	17,340	5290	16th c?
	•Queen [Logan]	Saint Elias	Yukon Territory, Canada	17,300	5270	1966
61.01N, 140.28W	Lucania	Saint Elias	Yukon Territory, Canada	17,150	5230	1937
60.35N, 140.39W	King [Logan]	Saint Elias	Yukon Territory, Canada	17,130	5220	1952
61.06N, 140.23W	Steele	Saint Elias	Yukon Territory, Canada	16,640	5070	1935
61.23N, 141.45W	Bona	Saint Elias	Alaska, USA	16,500	5030	1930
61.44N, 143.26W	Blackburn: highest peak	*Wrangell*	Alaska, USA	16,390	5000	1958
61.44N, 143.26W	Blackburn: SE peak	Wrangell	Alaska, USA	16,290	4960	1912
62.13N, 144.08W	Sanford	Wrangell	Alaska, USA	16,240	4950	1938
61.14N, 140.30W	Wood	Saint Elias	Yukon Territory, Canada	15,880	4840	1941
60.20N, 139.42W	Vancouver	Saint Elias	Canada-USA	15,700	4790	1949
61.25N, 141.43W	Churchill	Saint Elias	Alaska, USA	15,640	4770	1951
61.11N, 140.33W	•Slaggard	Saint Elias	Yukon Territory, Canada	15,570	4750	1959
61.12N, 140.30W	•McCauley (alt Macauly)	Saint Elias	Yukon Territory, Canada	15,470	4720	1959
58.54N, 137.31W	Fairweather	Saint Elias	Canada-USA	15,300	4660	1931
61.20N, 141.48W	University	Saint Elias	Alaska, USA	15,030	4580	1955
60.19N, 139.04W	Hubbard	Saint Elias	Canada-USA	15,010	4580	1951
61.17N, 141.09W	Bear	Saint Elias	Alaska, USA	14,850	4530	1951
61.00N, 140.01W	Walsh	Saint Elias	Yukon Territory, Canada	14,780	4500	1941
19.14N, 98.02W	Malinche (alt Matlalcueyetl)	Neovolcanica	Puebla-Tlaxcala, Mexico	14,640	4460	
62.57N, 151.05W	Hunter	Alaska	Alaska, USA	14,570	4440	1954
60.21N, 139.04W	Alverstone	Saint Elias	Canada-USA	14,530[2]	4430[2]	1951

[1] Dormant since 1687.

[2] Average of elevations officially given by Canada (14,500 ft, 4420 m) and USA (14,560 ft, 4440 m).

NORTH AMERICA

Latitude and Longitude	Peak and [Massif]	Mountain Range or System	Location	Elevation (ft)	(m)	First Ascent
63.06N, 150.56W	Browne Tower [McKinley]	Alaska	Alaska, USA	14,530	4430	1913
36.35N, 118.17W	Whitney	*Sierra Nevada*	California, USA	14,490	4420	1873
61.22N, 141.54W	•Aello	Saint Elias	Alaska, USA	14,440	4400	1967
39.07N, 106.28W	Elbert	*Rocky*	Colorado, USA	14,430	4400	1874
38.56N, 106.19W	Harvard	Rocky	Colorado, USA	14,420	4390	1869
39.11N, 106.28W	Massive	Rocky	Colorado, USA	14,420	4390	1874
46.52N, 121.45W	Rainier (volc)	*Cascade*	Washington, USA	14,410	4390	1870
19.06N, 99.46W	Toluca (alt Zinantecatl)	Neovolcanica	Mexico, Mexico	14,410	4390	
36.39N, 118.21W	Williamson	Sierra Nevada	California, USA	14,370	4380	1884?
39.02N, 106.28W	La Plata	Rocky	Colorado, USA	14,370	4380	
37.34N, 105.29W	Blanca	Rocky	Colorado, USA	14,320	4360	1874
38.04N, 107.28W	Uncompahgre	Rocky	Colorado, USA	14,310	4360	1874
37.59N, 105.35W	Crestone	Rocky	Colorado, USA	14,290	4360	1916
39.21N, 106.06W	Lincoln	Rocky	Colorado, USA	14,290	4350	1861
38.41N, 106.15W	Antero	Rocky	Colorado, USA	14,270	4350	
39.38N, 105.49W	Grays	Rocky	Colorado, USA	14,270	4350	1869
39.39N, 105.49W	Torreys	Rocky	Colorado, USA	14,270	4350	
39.00N, 106.56W	Castle	Rocky	Colorado, USA	14,260	4350	bef 1875
39.35N, 105.38W	Evans	Rocky	Colorado, USA	14,260	4350	
40.15N, 105.37W	Longs	Rocky	Colorado, USA	14,260	4350	1868
39.24N, 106.12W	Quandary	Rocky	Colorado, USA	14,260	4350	
60.37N, 140.11W	McArthur [Logan]	Saint Elias	Yukon Territory, Canada	14,250	4340	1961
		* * *				
41.25N, 122.12W	Shasta (volc)	Cascade	California, USA	14,160	4320	1854
62.00N, 144.00W	Wrangell (volc)	Wrangell	Alaska, USA	14,160	4320	1908
38.50N, 105.02W	Pikes (Peak)	Rocky	Colorado, USA	14,110	4300	1820
60.19N, 139.00W	Kennedy	Saint Elias	Yukon Territory, Canada	13,900	4240	1965
15.02N, 91.55W	Tajumulco (volc)	Madre	Guatemala	13,850	4220	
43.45N, 110.50W	Grand Teton	*Teton*	Wyoming, USA	13,770	4200	1872
51.22N, 125.14W	Waddington	*Coast*	British Columbia, Canada	13,260	4040	1936
53.07N, 119.08W	Robson	*Canadian Rocky*	British Columbia, Canada	12,970	3950	1913
9.29N, 83.30W	Chirripo Grande	*Talamanca*	Costa Rica	12,530	3820	
68.50N, 29.45W	Gunnbjorn	–	Greenland	12,140	3700	1935
8.48N, 82.38W	•Chiriqui (alt Baru) (volc)	*Central*	Panama	11,410	3480	
45.24N, 121.41W	Hood	Cascade	Oregon, USA	11,240	3430	1854
40.30N, 121.30W	Lassen (volc)	Cascade	California, USA	10,460	3190	
19.02N, 70.59W	Duarte (for Trujillo)	*Central*	Dominican Republic	10,420	3170	
18.22N, 71.59W	Selle	*Selle*	Haiti	8,790	2680	
13.50N, 89.38W	Santa Ana (volc)	*Apaneca Lamatepeque*	El Salvador	7,730	2360	
18.03N, 76.35W	Blue (Mountain)	*Eastern*	Jamaica	7,400	2260	
13.45N, 86.23W	•Mogoton	*Dipilto*	Honduras-Nicaragua	6,910	2110	
35.47N, 82.16W	Mitchell	*Blue (Ridge) (Appalachian)*	North Carolina, USA	6,680	2040	
19.59N, 76.50W	Turquino	*Maestra*	Cuba	6,470	1970	
44.17N, 71.19W	Washington	*White* (Appalachian)	New Hampshire, USA	6,290	1920	1642

NORTH AMERICA

Latitude and Longitude	Peak and [Massif]	Mountain Range or System	Location	Elevation (ft)	Elevation (m)	First Ascent
16.03N, 61.40W	Soufriere (volc)	–	Guadeloupe[1]	4,870	1480	
14.48N, 61.10W	Pelee (volc)	–	Martinique	4,580	1400	
18.10N, 66.36W	Punta	*Central*	Puerto Rico	4,390	1340	

OCEANIA

Latitude and Longitude	Peak and [Massif]	Mountain Range or System	Location	Elevation (ft)	Elevation (m)	First Ascent
4.05S, 137.11E	Ngga Pulu [Sukarno (for Carstensz)]	*Sudirman* (for Nassau)	West Irian, Indonesia	16,500	5030	1936
4.21S, 138.26E	Daam	*Djajawidjaja* (for Orange)	West Irian, Indonesia	16,150	4920	
4.03S, 137.02E	Pilimsit (for Idenburg)	Sudirman	West Irian, Indonesia	15,750	4800	
4.15S, 138.45E	Trikora (for Wilhelmina)	Djajawidjaja	West Irian, Indonesia	15,580	4750	1913
4.44S, 140.20E	Mandala (for Juliana)	Djajawidjaja	West Irian, Indonesia	15,420	4700	1959
5.43S, 145.03E	•Wilhelm	*Bismarck*	New Guinea (Australia)	15,400	4690	
4.25S, 139.56E	Wisnumurti (for Jan Pieterszoon Coen)	Djajawidjaja	West Irian, Indonesia	15,080	4590	
4.42S, 140.06E	Yamin (for Prins Hendrik)	Djajawidjaja	West Irian, Indonesia	14,860	4530	
6.07S, 144.42E	•Kubor	*Kubor*	New Guinea (Australia)	14,300	4360	
5.38S, 145.01E	•Herbert	Bismarck	New Guinea (Australia)	14,000	4270	

* * *

Latitude and Longitude	Peak and [Massif]	Mountain Range or System	Location	Elevation (ft)	Elevation (m)	First Ascent
19.50N, 155.28W	(Mauna) Kea: highest peak	–	Hawaii, USA[2]	13,800	4210	
19.28N, 155.36W	(Mauna) Loa (volc)	–	Hawaii, USA[2]	13,680	4170	
6.04S, 143.53E	•Giluwe	*Hagen*	Papua	13,660	4160	
6.16S, 147.04E	•Bangeta	*Saruwaged*	New Guinea (Australia)	13,470	4110	
8.53S, 147.33E	•Victoria	*Owen Stanley*	Papua	13,360	4070	
43.37S, 170.08E	Cook (alt Aorangi): highest peak	*Southern Alps*	South I, New Zealand	12,350	3760	1894
5.55S, 154.59E	•Balbi (volc[3])	*Emperor*	New Guinea (Australia)[4]	10,210	3110	
9.42S, 160.03E	Popomanasiu	*Kavo*	British Solomon Islands[5]	7,660	2330	
17.37S, 149.28W	Orohena	–	French Polynesia[6]	7,340	2240	
36.27S, 148.16E	Kosciusko	*Great Dividing*	New South Wales, Australia	7,330	2230	1840?
13.35S, 172.27W	•Silisili (alt Hertha)	–	Western Samoa[7]	6,090	1860	
20.36S, 164.46E	Panie	–	New Caledonia	5,380	1640	
17.37S, 178.01E	Tomaniivi (alt Victoria)	–	Fiji[8]	4,340	1320	

[1] Basse-Terre I.
[2] Hawaii I.
[3] No known eruption.
[4] Bougainville I.
[5] Guadalcanal I.
[6] Tahiti I.
[7] Savaii I.
[8] Viti Levu I.

SOUTH AMERICA

Latitude and Longitude		Peak and [Massif]	Mountain Range or System	Location	Elevation (ft)	Elevation (m)	First Ascent
32.39S,	70.01W	Aconcagua	*Andes*	Mendoza, Argentina	22,840	6960	1897
27.06S,	68.32W	Ojos del Salado: SE peak (volc[1])	Andes	Argentina-Chile	22,560[2]	6870[2]	1937
27.51S,	68.47W	Bonete	Andes	La Rioja, Argentina	22,550	6870	1913
27.47S,	68.51W	Pissis	Andes	Catamarca-La Rioja, Argentina	22,240	6780	1937
9.07S,	77.37W	Huascaran: S peak	*Blanca* (Andes)	Peru	22,210	6770	1932
31.59S,	70.07W	Mercedario	Andes	San Juan, Argentina	22,210	6770	1934
24.43S,	68.33W	Llullaillaco (volc)	Andes	Argentina-Chile	22,100[3]	6730[3]	bef 1550
24.58S,	66.22W	Libertador (for Cachi: N peak) [Cachi]	Andes	Salta, Argentina	22,050	6720	1950
27.06S,	68.32W	•Ojos del Salado: NW peak (volc[1])	Andes	Argentina-Chile	22,050	6720	1937
33.22S,	69.47W	Tupungato	Andes	Argentina-Chile	21,900[4]	6670[4]	1897
27.03S,	68.27W	•Gonzalez: highest peak	Andes	Argentina-Chile	21,850	6660	
9.07S,	77.37W	Huascaran: N peak	Blanca (Andes)	Peru	21,840	6650	1908 or 1939
27.04S,	68.29W	Muerto	Andes	Argentina-Chile	21,820[5]	6650[5]	1950?
10.16S,	76.54W	Yerupaja: N peak	*Huayhuash* (Andes)	Peru	21,760	6630	1950
27.02S,	68.18W	Incahuasi (alt Incaguasi)	Andes	Argentina-Chile	21,700[6]	6610[6]	1859 or 1913
25.55S,	66.52W	Galan	Andes	Catamarca, Argentina	21,650	6600	
27.06S,	68.47W	Tres Cruces: central peak	Andes	Argentina-Chile	21,540[7]	6560[7]	1937
27.03S,	68.27W	•Gonzalez: N peak	Andes	Argentina-Chile	21,490	6550	1955
18.06S,	68.54W	•Sajama	*Occidental* (Andes)	Bolivia	21,390	6520	1939
10.16S,	76.54W	•Yerupaja: S peak	Huayhuash (Andes)	Peru	21,380	6510	1958
27.16S,	68.32W	Nacimiento	Andes	Catamarca, Argentina	21,300	6490	1937
16.39S,	67.48W	•Illimani: S peak	*Real* (Andes)	Bolivia	21,200	6460	1898
16.39S,	67.48W	•Illimani: N peak	Real (Andes)	Bolivia	21,130	6440	1915
15.51S,	68.36W	•Ancohuma [Sorata]	Real (Andes)	Bolivia	21,100	6430	1919
15.31S,	72.42W	Coropuna: highest peak	*Occidental* (Andes)	Peru	21,080	6420	1911
27.08S,	68.49W	Puntiagudo	Andes	Argentina-Chile	21,060[8]	6420[8]	
32.05S,	69.59W	Ramada	Andes	San Juan, Argentina	21,030	6410	1934
9.07S,	77.36W	Chopilcalqui (alt Huascaran: E peak)	Blanca (Andes)	Peru	21,000	6400	1932
26.30S,	68.32W	Laudo	Andes	Catamarca, Argentina	21,000	6400	
9.32S,	77.18W	•Huantsan: S peak	Blanca (Andes)	Peru	20,980	6390	1952
13.48S,	71.14W	Ausangate: highest peak	*Vilcanota* (Andes)	Peru	20,950	6380	1953
29.08S,	69.48W	Toro	Andes	Argentina-Chile	20,930	6380	
15.50S,	68.34W	•Illampu [Sorata]	Real (Andes)	Bolivia	20,870	6360	1928
9.02S,	77.41W	Huandoy: central peak	Blanca (Andes)	Peru	20,850	6360	1932
9.02S,	77.41W	•Huandoy: W peak	Blanca (Andes)	Peru	20,850	6360	1954
10.17S,	76.54W	Siula: N peak	Huayhuash (Andes)	Peru	20,850	6360	1936
27.06S,	68.47W	•Tres Cruces: S peak	Andes	Argentina-Chile	20,850	6360	1937
15.31S,	72.42W	•Coropuna: NW peak	Occidental (Andes)	Peru	20,790	6340	1952
13.48S,	71.14W	•Ausangate: E peak	Vilcanota (Andes)	Peru	20,770	6330	1952

[1] No known eruption.

[2] Average of elevations officially given by Argentina (22,540 ft, 6870 m) and Chile (22,570 ft, 6880 m).

[3] Average of elevations officially given by Argentina (22,060 ft, 6720 m) and Chile (22,150 ft, 6750 m).

[4] Average of elevations officially given by Argentina (22,310 ft, 6800 m) and Chile (21,490 ft, 6550 m).

[5] Average of elevations officially given by Argentina (21,460 ft, 6540 m) and Chile (22,200 ft, 6760 m).

[6] Average of elevations officially given by Argentina (21,720 ft, 6620 m) and Chile (21,690 ft, 6610 m).

[7] Average of elevations officially given by Argentina (20,850 ft, 6360 m) and Chile (22,210 ft, 6770 m).

[8] Average of elevations officially given by Argentina (19,360 ft, 5900 m) and Chile (22,770 ft, 6940 m).

SOUTH AMERICA

Latitude and Longitude		Peak and [Massif]	Mountain Range or System	Location	Elevation (ft)	(m)	First Ascent
18.10S,	69.09W	Parinacota [Payachata]	Andes	Bolivia-Chile	20,770	6330	1928
29.56S,	69.54W	Tortolas	Andes	Argentina-Chile	20,760[1]	6330[1]	1924 or 1952
15.20S,	72.40W	•Solimana	Occidental (Andes)	Peru	20,750	6320	1952?
15.50S,	71.52W	Ampato: highest peak	Occidental (Andes)	Peru	20,700	6310	1950
			* * *				
1.28S,	78.48W	•Chimborazo	*Occidental* (Andes)	Ecuador	20,580	6270	1880
18.25S,	69.08W	Guallatiri (volc)	Andes	Chile	19,880	6060	1926?
0.40S,	78.26W	•Cotopaxi (volc)	*Oriental* (Andes)	Ecuador	19,340	5900	1872
22.26S,	67.55W	Tocorpuri: highest peak	Andes	Bolivia-Chile	19,140	5830	1939
16.18S,	71.24W	Misti (volc)	Occidental (Andes)	Peru	19,100	5820	1677?
3.00N,	76.00W	Huila (volc[2])	*Central* (Andes)	Colombia	18,870	5750	1944
23.23S,	67.45W	Lascar (volc)	Andes	Chile	18,420	5610	
6.26N,	72.18W	Guican [Cocuy]	*Oriental* (Andes)	Colombia	18,020	5490	
10.48N,	73.41W	Bolivar [Horqueta]	*Santa Marta*	Colombia	17,390	5300	1939
10.49N,	73.41W	Colon (alt Cristobal Colon) [Horqueta]	*Santa Marta*	Colombia	17,390	5300	1939
8.33N,	71.03W	Bolivar (alt Columna)	*Merida*	Venezuela	16,430	5010	1935 or 1936
0.50N,	65.25W	•Neblina	*Imeri*	Amazonas, Brazil	9,890	3010	
20.26S,	41.47W	Bandeira	*Caparao*	Espirito Santo-Minas Gerais, Brazil	9,480	2890	
31.59S,	64.59W	Champaqui	*Cordoba*	Cordoba, Argentina	9,460	2880	
5.12N,	60.44W	Roraima	*Pacaraima*	Brazil-Guyana-Venezuela	9,430	2870	1884
22.23S,	44.38W	Agulhas Negras [Itatiaia]	*Mantiqueira*	Minas Gerais-Rio de Janeiro, Brazil	9,140	2790	

[1] Average of elevations officially given by Argentina (20,740 ft, 6320 m) and Chile (20,770 ft, 6330 m).

[2] No known eruption.

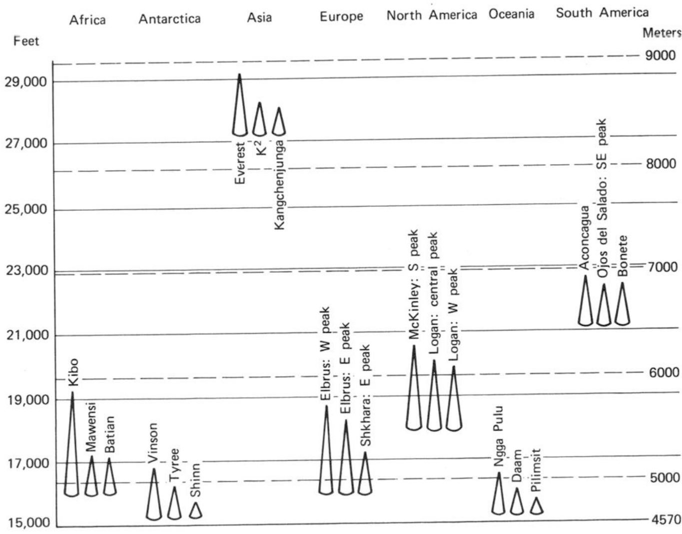

Figure 12. Three highest mountains of each continent.

11
Highest Mountain, or Elevation, in Each Country

Contents

Conventional name of country.
Conventional and other (alternate, former, and official) names of mountain peak and of massif, if any (in brackets).
Conventional and other names of mountain range or system.
Country (if any) with which mountain is shared.
Elevation (i.e., altitude of summit above sea level), in feet and meters.

Arrangement

By country, alphabetically.

Coverage

All countries with an area of at least 1000 mi^2 (2590 km^2), except a few countries consisting of a number of small islands.

Rounding

Elevations are rounded to the nearest 10 ft (m).

Entries

161.

TABLE 11. HIGHEST MOUNTAIN, OR ELEVATION, IN EACH COUNTRY

Country	Peak and [Massif]	Mountain Range or System	Country with which Shared	Elevation (ft)	Elevation (m)
Afghanistan	•Noshaq: highest peak	Hindu Kush	Pakistan	24,580	7490
Albania	Korab	Korab	Yugoslavia	9,050	2760
Algeria	•Tahat	Ahaggar (alt Hoggar)		9,570	2920
Angola	Moco	Upanda		8,600	2620
Argentina	Aconcagua	Andes		22,840	6960
Australia	Kosciusko	Great Dividing		7,330	2230
Austria	Grossglockner	Alps (off in Austria Alpen)		12,460	3800
Bangladesh	•Keokradong	Chittagong (Hills)		4,030	1230
Belgium	•Botrange	Ardennes		2,270	690
Bhutan	Khula Kangri I (alt Kula Gangri I)	Assam Himalaya	China	24,780	7550
Bolivia	•Sajama	Occidental (Andes)		21,390	6520
Botswana	?	?		5,000	1520
Brazil	•Neblina	Imeri		9,890	3010
British Honduras	Victoria	Maya		3,680	1120
British Solomon Islands	Popomanasiu	Kavo		7,660	2330
Brunei	•Pagon	Crocker	Sarawak (Malaysia)	6,070	1850
Bulgaria	Musala	Rhodope (off in Bulgaria Rodopi)		9,600	2920
Burma	•Hkakabo Razi	Kumon		19,300	5880
Burundi	•Heha	?		8,750	2670
Cambodia	•Aural	Cardamomes		5,950	1810
Cameroon	Fako [Cameroon (alt Cameroun)]	Cameroon (alt Cameroun)		13,350	4070
Canada	Logan: central peak [Logan]	Saint Elias		19,850	6050
Central African Republic	Gaou	Yade		4,660	1420
Ceylon	Pidurutalagala	Piduru (Ridges)		8,280	2520
Chad	(Emi) Koussi	Tibesti		11,470	3490
Chile	Ojos del Salado: SE peak	Andes	Argentina	22,560	6870
China	Everest (alt Chumulangma) [Everest]	Nepal Himalaya	Nepal	29,030	8850
Colombia	Huila	Central (Andes)		18,870	5750
Congo	?	Mayombe		2,620	800
Costa Rica	Chirripo Grande	Talamanca		12,530	3820
Cuba	Turquino	Maestra		6,470	1970
Cyprus	Khionistra (alt Olympus)	Troodos		6,410	1950
Czechoslovakia	Gerlachovsky (alt Gerlachovka; for Stalin)	Tatra (off Tatry)		8,710	2650
Dahomey	• ?	Atakora		2,620	800
Denmark	•Ejer Bavnehoj	–		560	170
Dominican Republic	Duarte (for Trujillo)	Central		10,420	3170
Ecuador	•Chimborazo	Occidental (Andes)		20,580	6270
Egypt	Katrinah (alt Catherine)	Sinai		8,650	2640
El Salvador	Santa Ana	Apaneca Lamatepeque		7,730	2360
Equatorial Guinea	Santa Isabel	–		9,840	3000
Ethiopia	Ancua [Ras Dashan (off Rasdajan)]	Semien		14,930	4550
Fiji	Tomaniivi (alt Victoria)	–		4,340	1320

Country	Peak and [Massif]	Mountain Range or System	Country with which Shared	Elevation (ft)	Elevation (m)
Finland	Haltiatunturi (alt Reisduoddarhaldde)	Haltia (alt Halddia)	Norway	4,340	1320
France	(Mont-)Blanc (alt Bianco) [Blanc (alt Bianco)]	Alps (off in France Alpes)	Italy	15,770	4810
French Guiana	– [Timotakem]	Tumuc-Humac		2,620	800
French Territory of the Afars and the Issas	Gouda (alt Goudah)	?		5,500	1670
Gabon	Iboundji	Chaillu		5,160	1570
Gambia	• ?	–		230	70
Germany					
East	Fichtel(-berg)	Erz(gebirge)		3,980	1220
West	Zug(spitze)	Alps (off in Germany Alpen)	Austria	9,720	2960
Ghana	•Afadjoto	Akwapim-Togo		2,900	890
Greece	Mytikas [Olympus (off Olimbos)]	Olympus (off Olimbos)		9,550	2910
Greenland	Gunnbjorn	–		12,140	3700
Guatemala	Tajumulco	Madre		13,850	4220
Guinea	Nimba	Nimba	Ivory Coast, Liberia	5,780	1760
Guyana	Roraima	Pacaraima	Brazil, Venezuela	9,430	2870
Haiti	Selle	Selle		8,790	2680
Honduras	• ?	Celaque		9,400	2870
Hungary	Kekes	Matra		3,330	1010
Iceland	Hvannadalshnukur	–		6,950	2120
India	Kangbachen [Kangchenjunga (alt Kanchenjunga)]	Nepal Himalaya	Nepal	25,930	7900
Indonesia					
in Asia	Kerintji (for Indrapura)	Barisan		12,480	3800
in Oceania (West Irian)	Ngga Pulu [Sukarno (for Carstensz)]	Sudirman (for Nassau)		16,500	5030
Iran	•Damavand (alt Demavend)	Alborz (alt Elburz)		18,610	5670
Iraq	•Algurd (alt Halgurd)	Zagros		12,250	3730
Ireland	Carrantuohill (alt Carrantual)	Macgillicuddy's Reeks		3,410	1040
Israel	•Meron (for Jarmaq, Sharqi)	Galilee		3,960	1210
Italy	(Mont-)Blanc (alt Bianco) [Blanc (alt Bianco)]	Alps (off in Italy Alpi)	France	15,770	4810
Ivory Coast	Nimba	Nimba	Guinea, Liberia	5,780	1760
Jamaica	Blue (Mountain)	Eastern		7,400	2260
Japan	Fuji (alt Huzi)	–		12,400	3780
Jordan	•Ramm	Sharah		5,750	1750
Kashmir-Jammu	K^2 (alt Chogori, Dapsang, Godwin Austen)	Karakoram		28,250	8610
Kenya	Batian [Kenya]	–		17,050	5200
Korea					
North	•Paitou (alt Paektu)	Changpai (alt Changbaek)	China	8,900	2710
South	•Halla	–		6,400	1950
Kuwait	• ?	–		950	290
Laos	•Bia	Tranninh		9,240	2820

Country	Peak and [Massif]	Mountain Range or System	Country with which Shared	Elevation (ft)	Elevation (m)
Lebanon	Qurnat al Sawda	Lebanon (off Lubnan)		10,130	3090
Lesotho	Thabana Ntlenyana (alt Thabantshonyana)	Drakens(berg)		11,420	3480
Liberia	Nimba	Nimba	Guinea, Ivory Coast	5,780	1760
Libya	•Kegueur Terbi (alt Chegor Tedi, Hessi)	Tibesti	Chad	10,330	3150
Luxembourg	•Burgplatz	Ardennes		1,840	560
Malagasy Republic	Maromokotro	Tsaratanana		9,470	2890
Malawi	Mlanje	Mlanje		10,000	3050
Malaysia					
East	Kinabalu: highest peak	Crocker		13,450	4100
West	Tahan	Cameron (Highlands)		7,190	2190
Mali	• ?	Iforas		3,150	960
Mauritania	•Ijill (alt Idjil)	?		2,900	880
Mexico	Citlaltepetl (alt Orizaba)	Neovolcanica		18,700	5700
Mongolia	Khuitun (off Kuyten) [Taban Bogdo]	Altai (alt Altay)		15,270	4650
Morocco	Toubkal: W peak [Toubkal]	Atlas		13,650	4160
Mozambique	Binga	Chimanimani	Rhodesia	7,990	2440
Nepal	Everest (alt Chumulangma) [Everest]	Nepal Himalaya	China	29,030	8850
Netherlands	•Vaalser(berg)	–		1,060	320
New Caledonia	Panie	–		5,380	1640
New Guinea (Australia)	•Wilhelm	Bismarck		15,400	4690
New Zealand	Cook (alt Aorangi): highest peak	Southern Alps		12,350	3760
Nicaragua	•Mogoton	Dipilto	Honduras	6,910	2110
Niger	•Greboun	Air (alt Azbine)		7,550	2300
Nigeria	Vogel	Banglang		6,700	2040
Norway	Glittertinden	Jotunheimen		8,110	2470
Oman	•Sham	Akhdar		10,190	3110
Pakistan	•Tirich Mir: W peak	Hindu Kush		25,260	7700
Panama	•Chiriqui (alt Baru)	Central		11,410	3480
Papua	•Giluwe	Hagen		13,660	4160
Paraguay	–[Villa Rica]	?		2,790	850
Peru	Huascaran: S peak	Blanca (Andes)		22,210	6770
Philippines	Apo	–		9,690	2950
Poland	Rysy	Tatra (off Tatry)	Czechoslovakia	8,200	2500
Portugal					
in Africa (Madeira Islands)	Ruivo de Santana	–		6,110	1860
In Europe	Ponta do Pico (alt Pico)	–		7,710	2350
Portuguese Guinea	• ?	Fouta Djallon		980	300
Portuguese Timor	Tata Mailau (alt Rameau)	–		9,720	2960
Puerto Rico	Punta	Central		4,390	1340
Qatar	• ?	–		250	80
Rhodesia	•Inyangani	Inyanga		8,520	2600
Romania	Moldoveanu	Transylvanian Alps (off Carpatii Meridionali)		8,340	2540
Rwanda	Karisimbi	Virunga	Zaire	14,790	4510
Saudi Arabia	•Razikh	Yemen (Highlands)	Yemen	11,990	3650
Senegal	?	Fouta Djallon		1,640	500

Country	Peak and [Massif]	Mountain Range or System	Country with which Shared	Elevation (ft)	Elevation (m)
Sierra Leone	•Bintimani	Loma		6,390	1940
Sikkim	Kangchenjunga (alt Kanchenjunga): highest peak [Kangchenjunga]	Nepal Himalaya	Nepal	28,170	8590
Somalia	•Surad Ad (off Surud Ad)	Ogo		7,900	2410
South Africa	•Injasuti	Drakens(berg)	Lesotho	11,310	3450
Southern Yemen	•Thamar (off Thamir)	Yemen (Highlands)		8,240	2510
South-West Africa	Konigstein [Brand(berg)]	Kaokoveld		8,550	2610
Spain					
in Africa (Canary Islands)	Teide	–		12,170	3710
in Europe	Mulhacen	Nevada		11,410	3480
Spanish Sahara	?	–		1,640	500
Sudan	•Kinyeti	Imatong		10,460	3190
Surinam	•–[Wilhelmina]	Wilhelmina		4,200	1280
Svalbard	Newton	–		5,630	1720
Swaziland	•Emlembe	Drakens(berg)		6,100	1860
Sweden	Kebnekaise	Kolen		6,930	2110
Switzerland	Dufour(spitze) [Rosa]	Alps (off in Switzerland Alpen, Alpes, Alpi)	Italy	15,200	4630
Syria	Hermon (off Shaykh)	Anti-Lebanon (off Sharqi)	Lebanon	9,230	2810
Taiwan	Yu (alt Hsinkao, Morrison)	Central (off Chungyang)		13,110	4000
Tanzania	Kibo [Kilimanjaro]	–		19,340	5890
Thailand	Inthanon (alt Angka)	Phi Pan Nam		8,450	2580
Togo	Baumann (alt Agou)	Togo		3,350	1020
Trinidad and Tobago	Aripo	–		3,080	940
Tunisia	Shanabi (alt Chambi)	Dorsale		5,070	1540
Turkey					
in Asia	Great Ararat (off Buyukagri)	–		16,920	5160
in Europe	Mahya	Istranca		3,380	1030
Uganda	Margherita [Stanley]	Ruwenzori	Zaire	16,760	5110
UK	(Ben) Nevis	Grampian		4,410	1340
United Arab Emirates	•Adhan	?		3,700	1130
Upper Volta	?	–		1,000	300
Uruguay	•Animas	Animas		1,640	500
USA					
in North America	McKinley: S peak [McKinley]	Alaska		20,320	6190
in Oceania (Hawaii)	(Mauna) Kea: highest peak	–		13,800	4210
USSR					
in Asia	Kommunizma (for Garmo, Stalina)	Pamir-Alai (off Pamir-Alay)		24,590	7490
in Europe	Elbrus (for Elborus): W peak [Elbrus (for Elborus)]	Caucasus (off Kavkaz)		18,480	5630
Venezuela	Bolivar (alt Columna)	Merida		16,430	5010
Vietnam					
North	Fan Si Pan	Fan Si Pan		10,310	3140
South	•(Ngoc) Linh	Annamese (off Trungphan)		10,500	3200

Country	Peak and [Massif]	Mountain Range or System	Country with Which Shared	Elevation (ft)	Elevation (m)
Yemen	•Hadur Shuayb	Yemen (Highlands)		12,340	3760
Yugoslavia	Triglav	Alps (off in Yugoslavia Alpe)		9,390	2860
Zaire	Margherita [Stanley]	Ruwenzori	Uganda	16,760	5110
Zambia	?	Mapinga		7,800	2380

12
Largest Natural Lakes, by Continent

Contents

Latitude and longitude, in degrees and minutes, at center of lake.
Conventional and other (alternate, former, and official) names of lake.
Subdivision and country (or countries) in which located.
Area in square miles and square kilometers.
Elevation (i.e., altitude of surface above sea level), in feet and meters.
Greatest recorded depth of water, in feet and meters.

Arrangement

By area, under continent.

Coverage

Above * * *, all natural lakes with at least the following areas:
Africa – 500 mi² (1290 km²)
Asia – 500 mi² (1290 km²)
Europe – 400 mi² (1040 km²)
North America – 300 mi² (780 km²)
Oceania – 500 mi² (1290 km²)
South America – 300 mi² (780 km²)
Below * * *, other well-known natural lakes, including the largest in certain countries.

Rounding

Areas are rounded to the nearest 10 mi² (km²).

Special Features

Saltwater lakes are indicated by the word "salt," and lagoons, by the abbreviation "lag."
When area and/or depth vary from season to season, the normal minima and maxima are shown as follows: 4,000/10,000.

Entries

190.

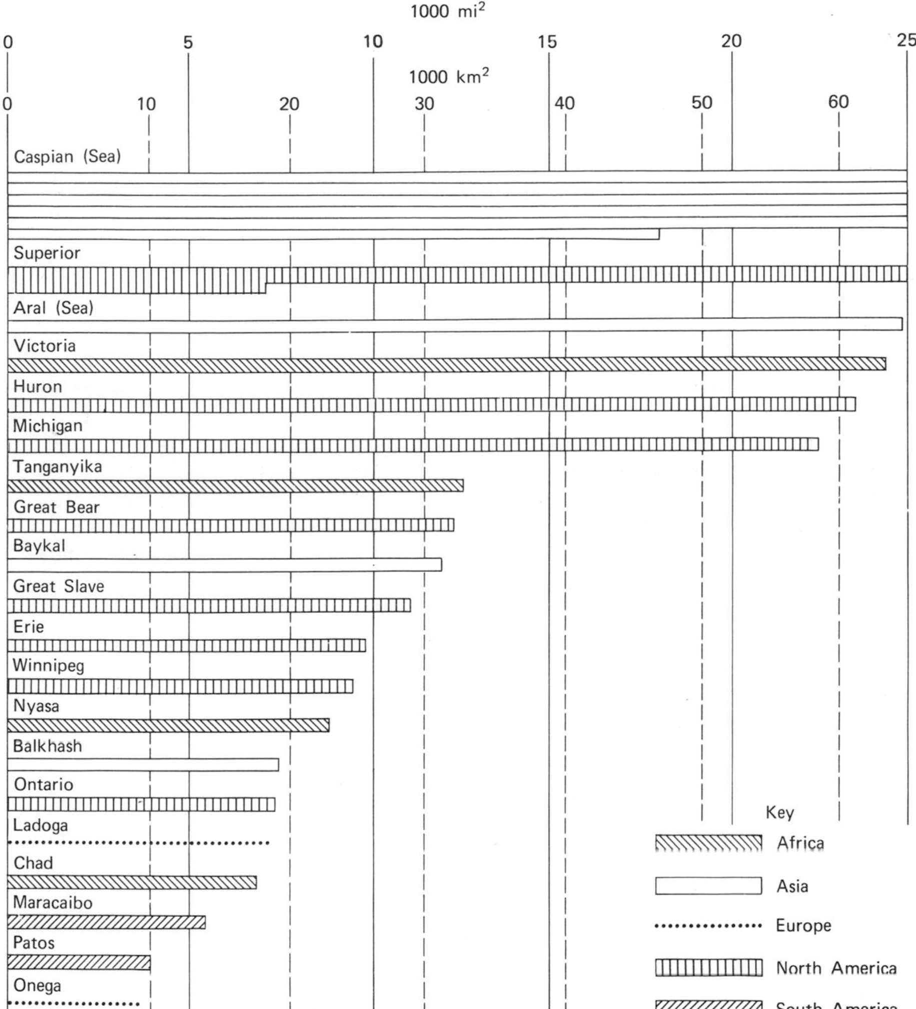

Figure 13. Twenty largest natural lakes.

TABLE 12. LARGEST NATURAL LAKES, BY CONTINENT

AFRICA

Latitude and Longitude	Lake	Location	Area (mi²)	Area (km²)	Elevation (ft)	Elevation (m)	Greatest Depth (ft)	Greatest Depth (m)
1.00S, 33.00E	Victoria	Kenya-Tanzania-Uganda	24,300	62,940	3,721	1134	266	81
6.00S, 29.30E	Tanganyika	Burundi-Tanzania-Zaire-Zambia	12,350	32,000	2,539	774	4825	1471
12.00S, 34.30E	Nyasa (alt Malawi, Niassa)	Malawi-Mozambique-Tanzania	8,680	22,490	1,558	475	2316	706
13.20N, 14.00E	Chad (alt Tchad)	Cameroon-Chad-Niger-Nigeria	4,000/ 10,000	10,360/ 25,900	787	240	36/13	11/4
3.30N, 36.00E	Rudolf (salt)	Ethiopia-Kenya	2,470	6,410	1,401	427	240	73
1.40N, 31.00E	Albert	Uganda-Zaire	2,160	5,590	2,024	617	197/164	60/50
2.00S, 18.20E	Leopold II	Zaire	900/ 3,170	2,070/ 8,210	1,116	340	39/33	12/10
11.05S, 29.45E	Bangweulu	Zambia	1,930	5,000	3,740	1140	16	5
1.30N, 33.00E	•Kyoga (alt Kioga)	Uganda	1,710	4,430	3,400	1036	26	8
9.00S, 28.45E	Mweru	Zaire-Zambia	1,680	4,350	3,025	922	10/6	3/2
12.10N, 37.20E	Tana (alt Tsana)	Ethiopia	1,390	3,600	6,037	1840	30	9
2.00S, 29.10E	Kivu	Rwanda-Zaire	860	2,200	4,790	1460	1575	480
0.21S, 29.35E	Edward	Uganda-Zaire	830	2,150	2,992	912	384	117
8.00S, 32.25E	•Rukwa (salt)	Tanganyika, Tanzania	290/ 1,160	750/ 3,000	2,602	793	shallow	
31.15N, 32.00E	•Manzala (off Manzilah) (salt, lag)	Egypt	530	1,360	0	0	shallow	
		* * *						
6.20N, 37.55E	Abaya (for Margherita)	Ethiopia	450	1,160	4,160	1268	43	13
15.12S, 35.50E	Chilwa (alt Chirua, Shirwa) (salt)	Malawi-Mozambique	400	1,040	1,805	550	shallow	

ASIA

Latitude and Longitude	Lake	Location	Area (mi²)	Area (km²)	Elevation (ft)	Elevation (m)	Greatest Depth (ft)	Greatest Depth (m)
42.00N, 50.00E	Caspian (Sea) (off Kaspiyskoye, Khazar) (salt)	Iran-USSR	143,240	371,000	–91	–28	3215	980
45.00N, 60.00E	Aral (Sea) (off Aralskoye) (salt)	Kazakhstan-Uzbekistan, USSR	24,900	64,500	174	53	223	68
54.00N, 109.00E	Baykal (alt Baikal)	Russia, USSR	12,160	31,500	1,496	456	5315	1620
46.00N, 74.00E	Balkhash (alt Balkash) (salt)	Kazakhstan, USSR	6,560/ 8,490	17,000/ 22,000	1,116	340	87	26
13.00N, 104.00E	•(Tonle) Sap	Cambodia	1,040/ 3,860	2,700/ 10,000			39	12
42.25N, 77.15E	Issyk(-Kul) (salt)	Kirgizia, USSR	2,390	6,190	5,279	1609	2303	702
37.40N, 45.30E	•Urmia (off Rezaiyeh) (salt)	Iran	1,500/ 2,300	3,880/ 5,960	4,183	1275	52	16
74.30N, 102.30E	Taymyr (alt Taimyr)	Russia, USSR	1,540/ 1,930	4,000/ 5,000	20	6	85	26
37.00N, 100.20E	Koko (alt Tsing; off Ching) (salt)	Tsinghai, China	1,720	4,460	10,489	3197	125	38

ASIA

Latitude and Longitude	Lake	Location	Area (mi²)	Area (km²)	Elevation (ft)	Elevation (m)	Greatest Depth (ft)	Greatest Depth (m)
45.00N, 132.24E	Khanka (alt Hsingkai)	China-USSR	1,540/ 1,700	4,000/ 4,400	226	69	33	10
29.18N, 112.45E	Tungting	Hunan, China	1,200/ 2,010	3,100/ 5,200	36	11		
54.50N, 77.30E	Chany (salt)	Russia, USSR	970/ 1,930	2,500/ 5,000	345	105	39/23	12/7
38.33N, 42.46E	Van (salt)	Turkey	1,440	3,740	5,401	1646	82	25
29.00N, 116.25E	Poyang	Kiangsi, China	1,290	3,350	5,906	1800	66	20
50.20N, 92.45E	Ubsa (alt Ubsu) (salt)	Mongolia	1,290	3,350	2,490	759	shallow	
40.30N, 90.30E	Lop (alt Lob; off Lopu) (salt)	Sinkiang, China	1,160	3,010	2,520	768	7	2
33.18N, 118.41E	Hungtze (off Hungtse)	Anhwei-Kiangsu, China	1,040	2,700				
51.00N, 100.30E	Hobsogol (alt Khubsugul, Kosogol)	Mongolia	1,010	2,620	5,328	1624	807	246
30.45N, 90.30E	Nam (alt Tengri; off Namu) (salt)	Tibet, China	970	2,500	15,181	4627		
31.15N, 120.10E	Tai	Chekiang-Kiangsu, China	850	2,210			16	5
46.10N, 81.50E	Ala(kol) (salt)	Kazakhstan, USSR	810	2,100	1,116	340	174	53
30.50N, 47.10E	•Hammar	Iraq	750	1,940			7	2
31.50N, 89.00E	•Zilling (alt Goring, Seling; off Chilin) (salt)	Tibet, China	720	1,860	14,748	4495	26	8
48.00N, 84.00E	Zaysan	Kazakhstan, USSR	690	1,800	1,266	386	26	8
48.00N, 92.10E	Hara Usa (alt Khara-Us)	Mongolia	680	1,760	3,783	1153		
38.45N, 33.25E	Tuz (salt)	Turkey	630	1,640	3,035	925	shallow	
49.00N, 117.27E	•Hulun (alt Dalai) (salt)	Inner Mongolia, China	620	1,590	4,183	1275	5	2
50.24N, 68.57E	Tengiz (salt)	Kazakhstan, USSR	610	1,590	997	304	22	7
31.00N, 86.22E	•Tangra (alt Dangrayum; off Tangkulayumu) (salt)	Tibet, China	540	1,400	15,499	4724		
42.00N, 87.00E	Possuteng (alt Baghrash) (salt)	Sinkiang, China	530	1,380	3,406	1038		
49.12N, 93.24E	Hirgis (alt Khirgis) (salt)	Mongolia	530	1,360	3,373	1028		
7.30N, 100.15E	•(Thale) Luang (alt Sap) (salt, lag)	Thailand	500	1,290	0	0	shallow	

* * *

Latitude and Longitude	Lake	Location	Area (mi²)	Area (km²)	Elevation (ft)	Elevation (m)	Greatest Depth (ft)	Greatest Depth (m)
2.35N, 98.50E	Toba	Sumatra I, Indonesia	440	1,150	2,973	906	1736	529
19.45N, 85.25E	•Chilka (salt, lag)	Orissa, India	350/450	910/1,170	0	0	shallow	
31.30N, 35.30E	Dead (Sea) (off Lut, Mayyit, Melah) (salt)	Israel-Jordan	390	1,020	−1,289	−393	1168	356
14.23N, 121.15E	Bay (salt)	Luzon I, Philippines	360	920	7	2	21	6
35.15N, 136.05E	Biwa	Honshu I, Japan	260	680	285	87	314	96

EUROPE

Latitude and Longitude		Lake	Location	Area (mi²)	Area (km²)	Elevation (ft)	Elevation (m)	Greatest Depth (ft)	Greatest Depth (m)
61.00N,	31.30E	Ladoga (off Ladozhskoye)	Russia, USSR	7,100	18,400	13	4	738	225
61.30N,	35.45E	Onega (off Onezhskoye)	Russia, USSR	3,710	9,600	108	33	377	115
58.55N,	13.30E	Vanern (alt Vaner, Vener)	Sweden	2,160	5,580	144	44	328	100
57.19N,	30.52E	Peipus (off Chudskoye)	Estonia-Russia, USSR	1,660	4,300	98	30	49	15
58.24N,	14.36E	Vattern (alt Vatter, Vetter)	Sweden	740	1,910	289	88	389	119
61.15N,	28.15E	Saimaa (alt Saima)	Finland	680	1,760	249	76	269	82
55.00N,	21.00E	•Kurisches (Haff) (off Kurskiy) (salt, lag)	Lithuania-Russia, USSR	630	1,620	0	0	33	10
40.20N,	45.20E	Sevan (for Gokcha)	Armenia, USSR	540	1,400	6,254	1906	282	86
58.17N,	31.20E	Ilmen	Russia, USSR	230/810	600/2,100	59	18	36/11	11/3
63.40N,	34.40E	Vyg(ozero)	Russia, USSR	500	1,280	292	89	40	12
52.35N,	5.30E	•IJssel(meer)[for Zuider (Zee)]	Netherlands	470	1,210			shallow	
59.30N,	17.12E	Malaren (alt Malar)	Sweden	440	1,140	1	0.3	210	64
60.15N,	37.40E	White (off Beloye)	Russia, USSR	430	1,120	371	113	13	4
61.35N,	25.30E	Paijanne	Finland	410	1,060	256	78	305	93
65.40N,	32.00E	Top(ozero)	Russia, USSR	410	1,050	358	109	184	56
		* * *							
69.00N,	28.00E	Inari (alt Enare)	Finland	390	1,000	374	114	197	60
53.46N,	14.14E	Oder(-Haff) [alt Szczecinski; for Stettiner (Haff)] (salt, lag)	East Germany-Poland	350	900	0	0	30	9
64.20N,	27.15E	Oulu(jarvi) (alt Ule)	Finland	350	900	400	122	125	38
46.50N,	17.45E	Balaton (alt Platten)	Hungary	230	590	341	104	36	11
46.25N,	6.30E	Geneva (off Geneve, Leman)	France-Switzerland	220	580	1,221	372	1017	310
47.35N,	9.25E	Constance [alt Boden(see)]	Austria-Switzerland-West Germany	210	540	1,299	396	827	252
54.40N,	6.25W	• Neagh	Northern Ireland, UK	150	400	49	15	102	31
44.54N,	28.57E	Razelm (alt Razim) (salt)	Romania	150	390	10	3	10	3
42.10N,	19.20E	Scutari (off Shkodres, Skadarsko) (salt)	Albania-Yugoslavia	150[1]	380[1]	20	6	144	44

[1] Average of areas officially given by Albania (140 mi², 370 km²) and Yugoslavia (150 mi², 390 km²).

EUROPE

Latitude and Longitude	Lake	Location	Area (mi²)	Area (km²)	Elevation (ft)	Elevation (m)	Greatest Depth (ft)	Greatest Depth (m)
45.40N, 10.41E	•Garda	Lombardia-Trentino-Alto Adige-Veneto, Italy	140	370	213	65	1135	346
60.40N, 11.00E	Mjosa	Norway	140	370	400	122	1473	449
41.00N, 20.45E	Ohrid (off Ohridsko, Ohrit)	Albania-Yugoslavia	140[1]	360[1]	2,280	695	938	286
47.50N, 16.45E	Neusiedler (alt Ferto)	Austria-Hungary	120	320	377	115	5	1
40.55N, 21.00E	Prespa (off Megal Prespa, Prespansko, Prespes)	Albania-Greece-Yugoslavia	110[2]	280[2]	2,799	853	177	54
46.54N, 6.52E	Neuchatel [alt Neuenburger (see)]	Switzerland	84	220	1,408	429	502	153
45.57N, 8.39E	Maggiore	Italy-Switzerland	82	210	633	193	1221	372
53.25N, 12.42E	Muritz	East Germany	45	120	203	62	108	33
47.00N, 8.28E	Lucerne (alt Vierwaldstatter)	Switzerland	44	110	1,424	434	702	214
47.13N, 8.45E	Zurich(see) (alt Zurigo)	Switzerland	35	90	1,332	406	469	143
56.08N, 4.38W	•Lomond	Scotland, UK	27	70	23	7	623	190

NORTH AMERICA

Latitude and Longitude	Lake	Location	Area (mi²)	Area (km²)	Elevation (ft)	Elevation (m)	Greatest Depth (ft)	Greatest Depth (m)
48.00N, 88.00W	Superior	Canada-USA	32,150[3]	83,270[3]	602	183	1302	397
44.30N, 82.15W	Huron	Canada-USA	23,430[4]	60,700[4]	581	177	750	229
44.00N, 87.00W	Michigan	Illinois-Indiana-Michigan-Wisconsin, USA	22,400	58,020	581	177	923	281
66.00N, 121.00W	Great Bear	Northwest Territories, Canada	12,270	31,790	511	156	1356	413
61.30N, 114.00W	Great Slave	Northwest Territories, Canada	10,980	28,440	513	156	2015	614
42.15N, 81.00W	Erie	Canada-USA	9,910[5]	25,680[5]	572	174	210	64
52.00N, 97.30W	Winnipeg	Manitoba, Canada	9,460	24,510	713	217	92	28
43.45N, 78.00W	Ontario	Canada-USA	7,430[6]	19,230[6]	246	75	778	237
11.30N, 85.30W	Nicaragua (alt Cocibolca)	Nicaragua	3,190	8,260	105	32	230	70
59.05N, 109.30W	Athabasca	Alberta-Saskatchewan, Canada	3,120	8,080	699	213	407	124
57.15N, 102.40W	Reindeer	Manitoba-Saskatchewan, Canada	2,470	6,390	1,150	351		
52.30N, 100.00W	Winnipegosis	Manitoba, Canada	2,100	5,450	833	254	39	12
66.30N, 70.40W	Nettilling	Northwest Territories, Canada[7]	1,960	5,080	100	30		

[1] Average of areas officially given by Albania (140 mi², 370 km²) and Yugoslavia (130 mi², 350 km²).

[2] Average of areas officially given by Albania (110 mi², 280 km²) and Yugoslavia (110 mi², 270 km²).

[3] Average of areas officially given by Canada (32,480 mi², 84,120 km²) and USA (31,820 mi², 82,410 km²).

[4] Average of areas officially given by Canada (23,860 mi², 61,800 km²) and USA (23,010 mi², 59,600 km²).

[5] Average of areas officially given by Canada (9890 mi², 25,620 km²) and USA (9940 mi², 25,740 km²).

[6] Average of areas officially given by Canada (7310 mi², 18,930 km²) and USA (7540 mi², 19,530 km²).

[7] Baffin I.

NORTH AMERICA

Latitude and Longitude	Lake	Location	Area (mi²)	Area (km²)	Elevation (ft)	Elevation (m)	Greatest Depth (ft)	Greatest Depth (m)
49.50N, 88.30W	Nipigon	Ontario, Canada	1,870	4,840	855	261	541	165
51.00N, 98.45W	Manitoba	Manitoba, Canada	1,820	4,710	814	248	92	28
63.08N, 101.30W	Dubawnt	Northwest Territories Canada	1,600	4,140	764	233		
49.15N, 94.45W	Woods	Canada-USA	1,590[2]	4,120[2]	1,060	323	69	21
65.00N, 71.00W	Amadjuak	Northwest Territories, Canada[1]	1,400	3,630				
53.45N, 59.30W	Melville (salt)	Newfoundland, Canada	1,130	2,930	0	0	840	256
57.10N, 98.40W	Southern Indian	Manitoba, Canada	1,060	2,750	835	255	59	18
41.10N, 112.30W	Great Salt (salt)	Utah, USA	950/ 1,050	2,460/ 2,720	4,200	1280	48	15
59.30N, 155.00W	Iliamna	Alaska, USA	1,000	2,590	50	15		
66.00N, 100.00W	Garry	Northwest Territories, Canada	980	2,540				
64.10N, 95.20W	Baker	Northwest Territories, Canada	970	2,530	30	9	756	230
62.41N, 98.00W	Yathkyed	Northwest Territories, Canada	860	2,230	461	141		
60.30N, 99.30W	Nueltin	Manitoba-Northwest Territories, Canada	850	2,200	875	267		
51.00N, 73.30W	Mistassini	Quebec, Canada	840	2,180	1,220	372	410	125
58.15N, 103.20W	Wollaston	Saskatchewan, Canada	800	2,060	1,300	396	233	71
26.57N, 80.52W	Okeechobee	Florida, USA	700	1,810	19	6	20	6
63.15N, 116.55W	La Martre	Northwest Territories, Canada	680	1,770	870	265		
30.13N, 90.07W	Pontchartrain (salt, lag)	Louisiana, USA	620	1,620	0	0	15	5
18.37N, 91.33W	•Terminos (salt, lag)	Campeche, Mexico	600	1,550	0	0	shallow	
54.00N, 64.00W	Michikamau	Newfoundland, Canada	570	1,470	1,521	464	262	80
55.10N, 105.00W	La Ronge	Saskatchewan, Canada	550	1,430	1,198	365	135	41
53.47N, 94.25W	Island	Manitoba, Canada	550	1,420	744	227		
58.35N, 112.05W	Claire	Alberta, Canada	540	1,410	699	213		
61.40N, 95.10W	Maguse	Northwest Territories, Canada	540	1,400				
50.20N, 92.30W	Seul	Ontario, Canada	540	1,400	1,170	357	112	34
56.00N, 74.30W	Eau Clair	Quebec, Canada	530	1,390	790	241		
54.00N, 100.10W	Moose	Manitoba, Canada	520	1,360	838	255		
53.20N, 100.00W	Cedar	Manitoba, Canada	520	1,340	830	253		
57.30N, 75.00W	Minto	Quebec, Canada	480	1,260	450	137		
64.27N, 99.00W	Aberdeen	Northwest Territories, Canada	470	1,230	261	80		
57.56N, 156.23W	Becharof	Alaska, USA	460	1,190	14	4		
55.25N, 115.25W	Lesser Slave	Alberta, Canada	460	1,190	1,892	577	10	3
48.02N, 94.55W	Red	Minnesota, USA	450	1,170	1,175	358	31	9

[1] Baffin I.

[2] Average of areas officially given by Canada (1690 mi², 4390 km²) and USA (1480 mi², 3850 km²).

NORTH AMERICA

Latitude and Longitude	Lake	Location	Area (mi²)	Area (km²)	Elevation (ft)	Elevation (m)	Greatest Depth (ft)	Greatest Depth (m)
57.30N, 106.30W	Cree	Saskatchewan, Canada	450	1,160	1,570	479	148	45
42.28N, 82.40W	Saint Clair	Canada-USA	450[1]	1,160[1]	575	175	21	6
20.15N, 103.00W	Chapala	Jalisco-Michoacan, Mexico	440	1,140	5,004	1525	108	33
44.35N, 73.20W	Champlain	Canada-USA	420[2]	1,100[2]	100	30	399	122
48.35N, 72.05W	Saint-Jean	Quebec, Canada	410	1,070	321	98	207	63
15.23N, 83.55W	•Caratasca (salt, lag)	Honduras	400	1,040	0	0	16	5
12.21N, 86.21W	Managua (alt Xolotlan)	Nicaragua	400	1,040	120	37	262	80
55.10N, 73.15W	Bienville	Quebec, Canada	390	1,020	1,400	427		
65.04N, 118.29W	Hottah	Northwest Territories, Canada	380	980	640	195		
48.42N, 79.45W	Abitibi	Ontario-Quebec, Canada	370	960	868	265		
45.50N, 60.50W	Bras d'Or (salt, lag)	Nova Scotia, Canada[3]	360	930	0	0	230	70
63.00N, 95.40W	Kaminuriak	Northwest Territories, Canada	360	930	320	98		
46.17N, 79.45W	Nipissing	Ontario, Canada	350	910	640	195	72	22
63.02N, 98.15W	Nutarawit	Northwest Territories, Canada	350	910				
48.42N, 93.10W	Rainy	Canada-USA	350[4]	910[4]	1,105	337	112	34
33.13N, 115.51W	Salton (Sea) (salt)	California, USA	350	910	-231	-70	46	14
9.05N, 82.05W	•Chiriqui (salt, lag[5])	Panama	350	900	0	0	deep	
64.30N, 110.30W	Gras	Northwest Territories, Canada	340	890	1,365	416		
64.05N, 108.30W	Aylmer	Northwest Territories, Canada	340	880	1,230	375		
65.59N, 101.12W	Pelly	Northwest Territories, Canada	330	860	501	153		
54.45N, 94.00W	Gods	Manitoba, Canada	320	830	585	178		
70.35N, 153.26W	Teshekpuk	Alaska, USA	310	820	5	2		
55.55N, 108.44W	Peter (Pond)	Saskatchewan, Canada	300	780	1,382	421		
		* * *						
15.30N, 89.10W	•Izabal	Guatemala	280	730	26	8	69	21
44.25N, 79.20W	Simcoe	Ontario, Canada	280	730	718	219	136	41
58.38N, 155.52W	Naknek	Alaska, USA	240	630	34	10		
44.00N, 88.27W	Winnebago	Wisconsin, USA	210	560	747	228	21	6
46.13N, 93.40W	Mille Lacs	Minnesota, USA	210	540	1,249	381	36	11
47.54N, 114.07W	Flathead	Montana, USA	200	510	2,892	881	220	67
18.27N, 71.39W	Enriquillo (salt)	Dominican Republic	190	500	-144	-44		
39.05N, 120.03W	Tahoe	California-Nevada, USA	190	500	6,229	1899	1645	501

[1] Average of areas officially given by Canada (430 mi², 1110 km²) and USA (460 mi², 1190 km²).

[2] Average of areas officially given by Canada (360 mi², 930 km²) and USA (490 mi², 1270 km²).

[3] Cape Breton I.

[4] Average of areas officially given by Canada (360 mi², 930 km²) and USA (340 mi², 890 km²).

[5] Actually a bay.

NORTH AMERICA

Latitude and Longitude	Lake	Location	Area (mi²)	Area (km²)	Elevation (ft)	Elevation (m)	Greatest Depth (ft)	Greatest Depth (m)
40.03N, 119.33W	Pyramid (salt)	Nevada, USA	180	470	3,802	1159	330	101
47.10N, 94.25W	Leech	Minnesota, USA	180	460	1,290	393		
48.09N, 116.25W	Pend Oreille	Idaho, USA	150	380	2,063	629	1150	351
42.22N, 121.56W	Upper Klamath	Oregon, USA	140	370	4,139	1262	40	12
40.12N, 111.50W	Utah	Utah, USA	140	360	4,487	1368	16	5
44.26N, 110.24W	Yellowstone	Wyoming, USA	140	350	7,733	2357	300	91
42.56N, 122.06W	Crater	Oregon, USA	21	54	6,176	1882	1932	589

OCEANIA

Latitude and Longitude	Lake	Location	Area (mi²)	Area (km²)	Elevation (ft)	Elevation (m)	Greatest Depth (ft)	Greatest Depth (m)
31.00S, 137.50E	Torrens (salt)	South Australia, Australia	2,230	5,780	98	30	shallow	
31.35S, 136.00E	Gairdner (salt)	South Australia, Australia	1,840	4,770	112	34	shallow	
28.40S, 137.10E	Eyre (salt)	South Australia, Australia	0/3,430	0/8,880	-39	-12	4/0	1/0
30.44S, 139.48E	Frome (salt)	South Australia, Australia	930	2,410	160	49	4/1	1/0.3
		* * *						
38.50S, 175.56E	Taupo	North I, New Zealand	230	610	1,172	357	522	159

SOUTH AMERICA

Latitude and Longitude	Lake	Location	Area (mi²)	Area (km²)	Elevation (ft)	Elevation (m)	Greatest Depth (ft)	Greatest Depth (m)
9.40N, 71.30W	•Maracaibo (salt, lag)	Venezuela	5,520	14,300	0	0	197	60
31.06S, 51.15W	•Patos (salt, lag)	Rio Grande do Sul, Brazil	3,860	10,000	0	0	15	5
15.48S, 69.24W	Titicaca	Bolivia-Peru	3,220	8,340	12,497	3809	997	304
32.45S, 52.50W	•Mirim (alt Merin) (salt, lag)	Brazil-Uruguay	1,140	2,970	0	0	shallow	
18.45S, 67.07W	Poopo	Bolivia	1,080	2,800	12,107	3690	10	3
46.30S, 72.00W	Buenos Aires (alt General Carrera)	Argentina-Chile	860	2,240	712	217		
30.42S, 62.36W	(Mar) Chiquita (salt)	Cordoba, Argentina	720	1,850	230	70	13/10	4/3
50.13S, 72.25W	Argentino	Santa Cruz, Argentina	550	1,410	656	200	984	300
49.35S, 72.35W	Viedma	Santa Cruz, Argentina	420	1,090	820	250		
48.52S, 72.40W	San Martin (alt O'Higgins)	Argentina-Chile	390	1,010	656	200	558	170
41.08S, 72.48W	Llanquihue	Chile	310	800	171	52	1148	350
		* * *						
40.58S, 71.30W	Nahuel Huapi	Neuquen-Rio Negro, Argentina	210	550	2,517	767	1437	438

13
Largest Natural Lake in Each Country

Contents

Conventional name of country.
Conventional and other (alternate, former, and official) names of lake.
Country (if any) with which lake is shared.
Area in square miles and square kilometers.

Arrangement

By country, alphabetically.

Coverage

All countries with an area of at least 5000 mi^2 (12,950 km^2) having or sharing a natural lake of significant size.

Rounding

Areas are rounded to the nearest 10 mi^2 (km^2) [to the nearest square mile and square kilometer if less than 100 mi^2 (km^2)].

Special Features

Saltwater lakes are indicated by the word "salt," and lagoons, by the abbreviation "lag."
When area varies from season to season, the normal minimum and maximum are shown as follows: 4,000/10,000.

Entries

98.

TABLE 13. LARGEST NATURAL LAKE IN EACH COUNTRY

Country	Lake	Country with Which Shared	Area (mi²)	Area (km²)
Afghanistan	•(Ab-i-)Istada (salt)		200?	520?
Albania	Scutari (off in Albania Shkodres)	Yugoslavia	150	380
Algeria	•Oran (off Ouahran) (salt, lag)		120	320
Angola	•Dilolo		20?	60?
Argentina	Buenos Aires (alt General Carrera)	Chile	860	2,240
Australia	Torrens (salt)		2,230	5,780
Austria	Constance [off in Austria Boden(see)]	Switzerland, West Germany	210	540
Bangladesh	•Chalan (Bil)		20/150	52/390
Bolivia	Titicaca	Peru	3,220	8,340
Botswana	Dow		70?	180?
Brazil	•Patos (salt, lag)		3,860	10,000
Burma	•Indawgyi		80	210
Burundi	Tanganyika	Tanzania, Zaire, Zambia	12,350	32,000
Cambodia	•(Tonle) Sap		1,040/3,860	2,700/10,000
Cameroon	Chad (alt Tchad)	Chad, Niger, Nigeria	4,000/10,000	10,360/25,900
Canada	Superior	USA	32,150	83,270
Ceylon	•Batticaloa (salt, lag)		46	120
Chad	Chad (alt Tchad)	Cameroon, Niger, Nigeria	4,000/10,000	10,360/25,900
Chile	Buenos Aires (off in Chile General Carrera)	Argentina	860	2,240
China	Koko (alt Tsing; off Ching) (salt)		1,720	4,460
Colombia	•Tota		23	59
Cuba	•Leche (salt, lag)		30	78
Denmark	•Arre		16	41
Dominican Republic	Enriquillo (salt)		190	500
Egypt	•Manzala (off Manzilah) (salt, lag)		530	1,360
El Salvador	•Guija		120	310
Ethiopia	Rudolf (salt)	Kenya	2,470	6,410
Finland	Saimaa (alt Saima)		680	1,760
France	Geneva (off in France Geneve)	Switzerland	220	580
French Territory of the Afars and the Issas	•Abbe (alt Abe) (salt)	Ethiopia	300?	780?
Gabon	•Onangue		90?	250?
Germany				
East	(Oder(-Haff) [alt Szczecinski; for Stettiner (Haff)] (salt, lag)	Poland	350	900
West	Constance [off in Germany Boden(see)]	Austria, Switzerland	210	540
Ghana	•Bosumtwi		18	48
Greece	Prespa (off in Greece Megal Prespa)	Albania, Yugoslavia	110	280
Guatemala	•Izabal		280	730
Haiti	Saumatre (alt Azuel)		65	170
Honduras	•Caratasca (salt, lag)		400	1,040
Hungary	Balaton (alt Platten)		230	590
Iceland	•Thingvallavatn		32	83
India	•Chilka (salt, lag)		350/450	910/1,170
Indonesia (in Asia)	Toba		440	1,150

Country	Lake	Country with Which Shared	Area (mi²)	Area (km²)
Iran	Caspian (Sea) (off in Iran Khazar) (salt)	USSR	143,240	371,000
Iraq	•Hammar		750	1,940
Ireland	Corrib		65	170
Israel	Dead (Sea) (off in Israel Melah) (salt)	Jordan	390	1,020
Italy	•Garda		140	370
Ivory Coast	•Aby (salt, lag)		300?	780?
Japan	Biwa		260	680
Jordan	Dead (Sea) (off in Jordan Lut, Mayyit) (salt)	Israel	390	1,020
Kashmir-Jammu	•Pangong (alt Pangkong, Pankung) (salt)	China	230	600
Kenya	Victoria	Tanzania, Uganda	24,300	62,940
Liberia	•Fisherman's		30	78
Malagasy Republic	•Alaotra		70	180
Malawi	Nyasa (off in Malawi Malawi)	Mozambique, Tanzania	8,680	22,490
Malaysia	•(Tasek) Dampar		40?	100?
Mali	•Faguibine		140?	350?
Mauritania	•Rkiz (alt Cayar)		60?	160?
Mexico	•Terminos (salt, lag)		600	1,550
Mongolia	Ubsa (alt Ubsu) (salt)		1,290	3,350
Mozambique	Nyasa (off in Mozambique Niassa)	Malawi, Tanzania	8,680	22,490
Netherlands	•IJssel(meer) [for Zuider (Zee)]		470	1,210
New Guinea (Australia)	•Chambri		20?	50?
New Zealand	Taupo		230	610
Nicaragua	Nicaragua (alt Cocibolca)		3,190	8,260
Niger	Chad (alt Tchad)	Cameroon, Chad, Nigeria	4,000/10,000	10,360/25,900
Nigeria	Chad (alt Tchad)	Cameroon, Chad, Niger	4,000/10,000	10,360/25,900
Norway	Mjosa		140	370
Pakistan	•Manchhar		30/100	78/260
Panama	•Chiriqui (salt, lag[1])		350	900
Papua	•Murray		120?	300?
Paraguay	•Ipoa		100	260
Peru	Titicaca	Bolivia	3,220	8,340
Philippines	Bay (salt)		360	920
Poland	Oder(-Haff) [off in Poland Szczecinski; for Stettiner (Haff)] (salt, lag)	East Germany	350	900
Romania	Razelm (alt Razim) (salt)		150	390
Rwanda	Kivu	Zaire	860	2,220
Senegal	•Guiers		60?	150?
South Africa	•Saint Lucia (salt, lag)		150?	390?
Sweden	Vanern (alt Vaner, Vener)		2,160	5,580
Switzerland	Geneva (off in Switzerland Geneve, Leman)	France	220	580
Syria	Jabbul		58	150
Tanzania	Victoria	Kenya, Uganda	24,300	62,940
Thailand	•(Thale) Luang (alt Sap) (salt, lag)		500	1,290

[1] Actually a bay.

Country	Lake	Country with Which Shared	Area (mi²)	(km²)
Tunisia	•Bizerta (alt Bizerte; off Banzart) (salt, lag)		42	110
Turkey				
in Asia	Van (salt)		1,440	3,740
in Europe	Terkos		9	24
Uganda	Victoria	Kenya, Tanzania	24,300	62,940
UK	•Neagh		150	400
Uruguay	•Mirim (off in Uruguay Merin) (salt, lag)	Brazil	1,140	2,970
USA (in North America)	Superior	Canada	32,150	83,270
USSR				
in Asia	Caspian (Sea) (off in USSR Kaspiyskoye)	Iran	143,240	371,000
in Europe	Ladoga (off Ladozhskoye)		7,100	18,400
Venezuela	•Maracaibo (salt, lag)		5,520	14,300
Vietnam (South)	•Cau Hai (salt, lag)		40	100
Yugoslavia	Scutari (off in Yugoslavia	Albania	150	380
	Skadarsko)		150	380
Zaire	Tanganyika	Burundi, Tanzania, Zambia	12,350	32,000
Zambia	Tanganyika	Burundi, Tanzania, Zaire	12,350	32,000

Figure 14. Beach at Bandar Pahlavi, Iran, on the south shore of the Caspian Sea, the largest lake in the world. (Credit: Iran National Tourist Organization.)

14
Highest Waterfalls (Individual Leaps), by Continent

Contents

Latitude and longitude, in degrees and minutes.
Conventional and alternate names of waterfall.
River, and subdivision and country in which located.
Height of greatest individual leap, in feet and meters.

Arrangement

By height, under continent.

Coverage

Above * * *, all known and named waterfalls with a height of at least 300 ft (91 m).
Below * * *, other well-known waterfalls.

Entries

151.

TABLE 14. HIGHEST WATERFALLS (INDIVIDUAL LEAPS), BY CONTINENT

AFRICA

Latitude and Longitude		Waterfall	River and Location	Height (ft)	Height (m)
28.45S,	28.56E	Tugela: highest fall	Tugela R, Natal, South Africa	1350	411
		Shire (alt Chire)	Shire (alt Chire) R, Malawi	1200?	366?
10.12S,	27.27E	Kaloba (alt Lofoi)	Lofoi R, Zaire	1115	340
18.36S,	32.42E	Mtarazi	Mtarazi R, Mozambique-Rhodesia	1000	305
8.36S,	31.14E	Kalambo	Kalambo R, Tanzania-Zambia	704	215
29.52S,	28.04E	Maletsunyane	Maletsunyane R, Lesotho	630	192
		Fincha	Fincha R, Ethiopia	508	155
28.35S,	20.23E	Aughrabies (alt King George's)	Orange (alt Oranje) R, Cape of Good Hope, South Africa	480	146
5.22N,	40.03E	Baratieri	Ganale-Dorya R, Ethiopia	459	140
31.26S,	29.38E	Magwa	Magwa R, Cape of Good Hope, South Africa	450	137
8.50S,	31.22E	Chirombo	Ieisa (alt Iza) R, Zambia	440	134
31.15S,	28.57E	Tsitsa	Tsitsa R, Cape of Good Hope, South Africa	375	114
17.23S,	14.15E	Ruacana	Cunene (alt Kunene) R, Angola–South-West Africa	352?	107?
29.29S,	30.14E	Howick	Umgeni R, Natal, South Africa	311	95
17.55S,	25.51E	Victoria	Zambezi (alt Zambesi, Zambeze) R, Rhodesia-Zambia	304	92
			* * *		
9.06S,	15.57E	Dianzundu (alt Duque de Braganca)	Lucala R, Angola	200?	61?
2.17N,	31.41E	Murchison	Nile (off Nil) R, Uganda	130	40

ASIA

Latitude and Longitude		Waterfall	River and Location	Height (ft)	Height (m)
25.10N,	91.45E	Mawsmai	? R, Assam, India	1148?	350?
6.04N,	116.29E	Kalupis	? R, Sabah, Malaysia	1100?	335?
25.30N,	91.40E	Thylliejlongwa	? R, Assam, India	997?	304?
14.14N,	74.50E	Gersoppa (alt Jog): highest fall	Sharavati R, Maharashtra-Mysore, India	829	253
7.05N,	80.50E	Kurundu Oya	Kurundu (Oya) R, Ceylon	620	189
6.44N,	81.02E	Diyaluma	? R, Ceylon	560	171
6.46N,	80.50E	Bambarakanda: highest fall	? R, Ceylon	461	141
33.40N,	135.53E	Nachi	Nachi R, Honshu I, Japan	430	131
6.54N,	80.30E	Laksapana	? R, Ceylon	377	115
24.32N,	81.18E	Bihar	Bihar R, Madhya Pradesh, India	370	113
7.22N,	80.55E	Ratna Ella	Ratna (Ella) R, Ceylon	365	111
36.44N,	139.27E	Kegon	Daiya R, Honshu I, Japan	348	106
6.38N,	80.34E	Kirindi Ela	Kirindi (Ela) R, Ceylon	347	106
36.48N,	139.26E	Yudaki	? R, Honshu I, Japan	335	102
7.04N,	80.42E	Ramboda	? R, Ceylon	329	100
12.15N,	77.10E	Kaveri (alt Cauvery)	Kaveri (alt Cauvery) R, Madras-Mysore, India	320	98

ASIA

Latitude and Longitude		Waterfall	River and Location	Height (ft)	Height (m)
11.27N,	76.35E	Pykara	? R, Madras, India	300	91
			* * *		
13.56N,	105.56E	Khone	Mekong (alt Khong, Lantsang, Tien Giang) R, Cambodia-Laos	70	21

EUROPE

Latitude and Longitude		Waterfall	River and Location	Height (ft)	Height (m)
		Ormeli	? R, Norway	1847	563
		Tysse	Tyssa R, Norway	1749	533
62.34N,	8.11E	Vestre Mardola (alt Western Mardola)	? R, Norway	1535	468
42.42N,	0.00	Gavarnie: highest fall	Pau R, Midi-Pyrenees, France	1385	422
62.21N,	8.04E	Verma	? R, Norway	1250	381
		Austerbo	? R, Norway	1247	380
		Serio	Serio R, Italy	1034	315
60.31N,	7.15E	Rembesdals: highest fall	? R, Norway	984	300
60.07N,	6.44E	Tyssestrengene	Tysso R, Norway	984	300
46.36N,	7.54E	Staubbach	Staub(bach) Creek, Switzerland	980	299
62.34N,	8.11E	Ostre Mardola (alt Eastern Mardola): upper fall	? R, Norway	974	297
61.22N,	7.55E	Vettis: highest fall	Morkedola R, Norway	902	275
60.22N,	7.08E	Valur	? R, Norway	892	272
		Mollius	? R, Norway	883	269
		Austerkrok	? R, Norway	843	257
		Seculejo	? R, Spain	820	250
60.29N,	7.15E	Skykkje	Skykkjua R, Norway	820	250
		Kjos	? R, Norway	738	225
62.34N,	8.11E	Ostre Mardola: lower fall	? R, Norway	722	220
61.23N,	7.26E	Feigum	? R, Norway	715	218
		Rogaland: highest fall	? R, Norway	689	210
		Teverone	? R, Italy	680?	207?
61.27N,	7.59E	Maradals	? R, Norway	656	200
		Aurstaupet	? R, Norway	633	193
60.26N,	7.15E	Voring	Bjoreia R, Norway	597	182
		Stauber	Stauber R, Switzerland	590?	180?
		Sote: highest fall	? R, Norway	577	176
61.07N,	10.30E	Mesna	? R, Norway	525	160
60.07N,	6.44E	Skjeggedals	Tysso R, Norway	525	160
58.13N,	4.52W	Eas Coul Aulin	? R, Scotland, UK	511	156
59.02N,	7.51E	Kjel (alt Kile): highest fall	Kjel (alt Kile) R, Norway	502	153
46.24N,	8.24E	Frua (alt Toce)	Toce R, Piemonte, Italy	470?	143?
		Hundkastet: highest fall	? R, Norway	459	140

EUROPE

Latitude and Longitude		Waterfall	River and Location	Height (ft)	Height (m)
60.44N,	6.53E	Rjoande: highest fall	? R, Norway	459	140
47.12N,	12.10E	Krimmler: lower fall	Krimmler R, Austria	459	140
47.12N,	12.10E	Krimmler: upper fall	Krimmler R, Austria	459	140
60.50N,	6.40E	Stalheims	? R, Norway	413	126
46.24N,	7.26E	Iffigen	Iffigen(bach) Creek, Switzerland	394	120
57.16N,	5.18W	Glomach	Glomach R, Scotland, UK	370	113
59.52N,	8.34E	Rjukan	Mane R, Norway	345	105
		Fagerbakk	Fager(bakk) Creek, Norway	328	100
		Heis	? R, Norway	328	100
47.12N,	12.10E	Krimmler: middle fall	Krimmler R, Austria	328	100
			* * *		
47.07N,	13.08E	Gastein: lower fall	Gasteiner Ache R, Austria	280	85

NORTH AMERICA

Latitude and Longitude		Waterfall	River and Location	Height (ft)	Height (m)
37.44N,	119.39W	Ribbon	Ribbon Creek, California, USA	1612	491
37.45N,	119.36W	Yosemite: upper fall	Yosemite Creek, California, USA	1430	436
51.30N,	116.29W	Takakkaw: highest fall	Yoho R tributary, British Columbia, Canada	1200	366
37.42N,	119.40W	Silver Strand (alt Widow's Tears)	Meadow Brook, California, USA	1170	357
28.13N,	108.14W	Basaseachic	(Arroyo) Basaseachic Creek, Chihuahua, Mexico	1020	311
51.33N,	116.33W	Twin	Twin Falls Creek, British Columbia, Canada	900	274
		Mystery	? R, British Columbia, Canada	830	253
46.47N,	121.42W	Fairy	Stevens Creek, Washington, USA	700	213
39.34N,	121.17W	Feather	Fall R, California, USA	640	195
37.43N,	119.39W	Bridalveil	Bridalveil Creek, California, USA	620	189
52.11N,	117.03W	Panther	Nigel Creek, Alberta, Canada	600	183
37.43N,	119.32W	Nevada	Merced R, California, USA	594	181
45.34N,	122.06W	Multnomah: highest fall	Multnomah R, Oregon, USA	542	165
37.43N,	119.36W	Sentinel: lower fall	Sentinel Creek, California, USA	500?	152?
51.57N,	120.11W	Helmcken	Murtle R, British Columbia, Canada	450	137
37.43N,	119.34W	Illilouette	Illilouette Creek, California, USA	370	113
46.47N,	121.47W	Comet	Van Trump Creek, Washington, USA	320	98
37.45N,	119.36W	Yosemite: lower fall	Yosemite Creek, California, USA	320	98
37.44N,	119.33W	Vernal	Merced R, California, USA	317	97
61.38N,	125.42W	Virginia	South Nahanni R, Northwest Territories, Canada	315	96
44.43N,	110.28W	Yellowstone: lower fall	Yellowstone R, Wyoming, USA	308	94
10.44N,	61.24W	Maracas	? R, Trinidad I, Trinidad and Tobago	300	91
46.47N,	121.43W	Sluiskin	Paradise R, Washington, USA	300	91

* * *

Figure 15. Angel Falls on the Churun River, Venezuela, the highest waterfall on earth. (Credit: Embassy of Venezuela Information Service, Washington.)

NORTH AMERICA

Latitude and Longitude		Waterfall	River and Location	Height (ft)	Height (m)
46.55N,	71.10W	Montmorency	Montmorency R, Quebec, Canada	273	83
47.33N,	121.49W	Snoqualmie	Snoqualmie R. Washington, USA	270	82
35.39N,	85.22W	Fall Creek	Fall Creek, Tennessee, USA	256	78
53.30N,	64.10W	Churchill (for Grand)	Churchill (for Hamilton) R, Newfoundland, Canada	245	75
42.33N,	76.34W	Taughannock	Taughannock Creek, New York, USA	215	66
42.36N,	114.26W	Shoshone	Snake R, Idaho, USA	195	59
43.04N,	79.04W	Niagara	Niagara R, Canada-USA	186	57

OCEANIA

Latitude and Longitude		Waterfall	River and Location	Height (ft)	Height (m)
		Cleve-Garth	? R, New Zealand	1476?	450?
30.32S,	152.03E	Wollomombi: highest fall	Wollomombi R, New South Wales, Australia	1100	334
18.17S,	146.03E	Wallaman (alt Stony Creek)	Stony Creek, Queensland, Australia	970	296
17.43S,	145.35E	Elizabeth Grant	Tully R, Queensland, Australia	900	274
45.28S,	167.10E	Helena	Helena R, South I, New Zealand	830	253
44.48S,	167.44E	Sutherland: upper fall	Arthur R, South I, New Zealand	815	248
16.50S,	145.39E	Barron	Barron R, Queensland, Australia	770	235
44.48S,	167.44E	Sutherland: middle fall	Arthur R, South I, New Zealand	751	229
17.47S,	145.35E	Tully: highest fall	Tully R, Queensland, Australia	550?	168?
44.40S,	167.55E	Bowen	Bowen R, South I, New Zealand	520	158
44.36S,	167.52E	Stirling	Stirling R, South I, New Zealand	480	146
19.51N,	155.09W	Akaka	Kolekole Stream, Hawaii I, Hawaii, USA	418	127
34.39S,	150.29E	Fitzroy: highest fall	? R, New South Wales, Australia	400	122
33.43S,	150.23E	Wentworth: upper fall	Wentworth R, New South Wales, Australia	360	110
44.48S,	167.44E	Sutherland: lower fall	Arthur R, South I, New Zealand	338	103

SOUTH AMERICA

Latitude and Longitude		Waterfall	River and Location	Height (ft)	Height (m)
5.57N,	62.30W	Angel: upper fall	Churun R, Venezuela	2648	807
23.07S,	48.36W	Itatinga	Itatinga R, Sao Paulo, Brazil	2060	628
5.13N,	60.51W	Cuquenan (alt Kukenaam)	Cuquenan (alt Kukenaam) R, Guyana-Venezuela	2000	610
		Pilao	Itajai R, Santa Catarina, Brazil	1719	524
		Roraima	Potaro R, Guyana	1500?	457?
5.46N,	61.08W	King George VI	Utshi R, Guyana	1200?	366?
5.22N,	72.45W	Candelas	Cusiana R, Colombia	984	300
		King Edward VIII	Semang R, Guyana	840	256
5.09N,	59.29W	Kaieteur	Potaro R, Guyana	741	226
		Casca d'Anta	Sao Francisco R, Minas Gerais, Brazil	666	203
		Sakaika	? R, Guyana	629	192
5.57N,	62.30W	Angel: lower fall	Churun R, Venezuela	564	172

SOUTH AMERICA

Latitude and Longitude		Waterfall	River and Location	Height (ft)	Height (m)
4.35N,	74.18W	Tequendama	Bogota (alt Funza) R, Colombia	515	157
		Wakowaieng	? R, Guyana	440	134
		Fagundes	Piabanha R, Rio de Janeiro, Brazil	413	126
		Kumarow	Kamarang R, Guyana	400	122
		Itiquira	Itiquira R, Brazil	394	120
5.25N,	59.30W	Marina	Ipobe R, Guyana	360	110
		Papagaio	Papagaio R, Mato Grosso, Brazil	350?	107?
2.22N,	52.40W	Manoa (alt Manaua)	Oyapock (alt Oiapoque) R, Brazil–French Guiana	345	105
5.42N,	61.07W	Great	? R, Guyana	300	91
			* * *		
9.24S,	38.13W	Paulo Afonso	Sao Francisco R, Alagoas-Bahia, Brazil	262	80
25.41S,	54.26W	Iguazu (alt Iguacu; for Iguassu)	Iguazu (alt Iguacu; for Iguassu) R, Argentina-Brazil	230	70
24.02S,	54.16W	Sete Quedas (alt Guaira)	Parana R, Brazil-Paraguay	213	65
20.18S,	49.10W	Marimbondo	Grande R, Minas Gerais-Sao Paulo, Brazil	115	35
31.14S,	57.55W	Grande	Uruguay R, Argentina-Uruguay	75	23
20.36S,	51.33W	Urubupunga	Parana R, Mato Grosso-Sao Paulo, Brazil	27	9

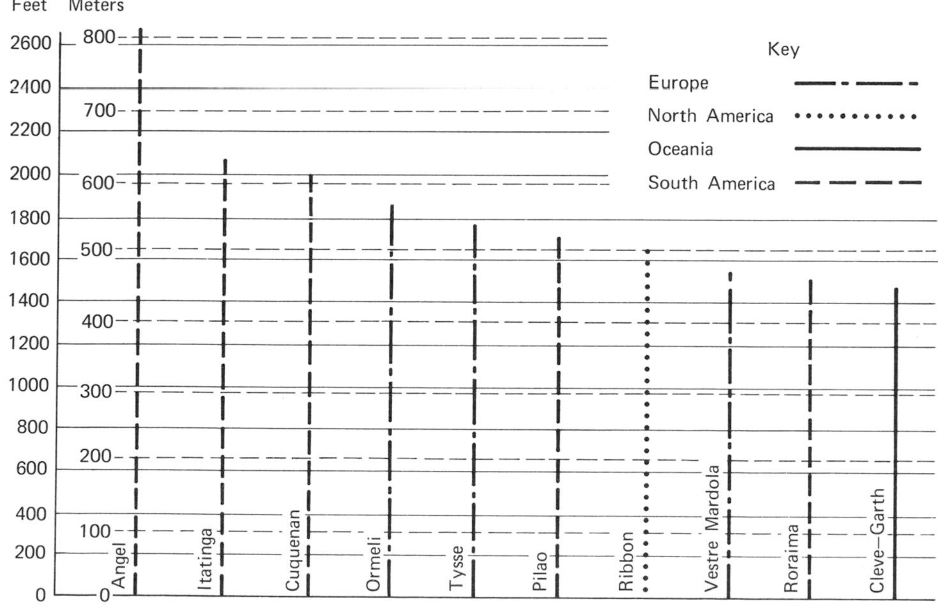

Figure 16. Ten highest waterfalls.

15
Greatest Waterfalls (Volume of Water)

Contents

Rank.
Conventional and alternate names of waterfall.
River, and subdivision and country in which located.
Average rate of flow, in thousands of cubic feet per second and in cubic meters per second.
Height of greatest individual leap, in feet and meters.

Arrangement

By average rate of flow.

Coverage

All waterfalls with an average rate of flow of at least 20,000 cfs (566 m^3/sec).

Rounding

Rates of flow are rounded to the nearest 1000 cfs.

Entries

12.

TABLE 15. GREATEST WATERFALLS (VOLUME OF WATER)

Rank	Waterfall	River and Location	Average Flow (1000 cfs)	Average Flow (m^3/sec)	Height (ft)	Height (m)
1.	Sete Quedas (alt Guaira)	Parana R, Brazil-Paraguay	470	13,310	213	65
2.	Khone	Mekong (alt Khong, Lantsang, Tien Giang) R, Cambodia-Laos	410	11,610	70	21
3.	Niagara	Niagara R, Canada-USA	212	6,000	186	57
4.	Grande	Uruguay R, Argentina-Uruguay	106	3,000	75	23
5.	Urubupunga	Parana R, Mato Grosso-Sao Paulo, Brazil	97	2,750	27	9
6.	Iguazu (alt Iguacu; for Iguassu)	Iguazu (alt Iguacu; for Iguassu) R, Argentina-Brazil	60	1,700	230	70
7.	Marimbondo	Grande R, Minas Gerais-Sao Paulo, Brazil	53	1,500	115	35
8.	Victoria	Zambezi (alt Zambesi, Zambeze) R, .Rhodesia-Zambia	38	1,090	304	92
9.	Churchill (for Grand)	Churchill (for Hamilton) R, Newfoundland, Canada	35	991	245	75
10.	Kaveri (alt Cauvery)	Kaveri (alt Cauvery) R, Madras-Mysore, India	33	934	320	98
11.	Paulo Afonso	Sao Francisco R, Alagoas-Bahia, Brazil	25	700	262	80
12.	Kaieteur	Potaro R, Guyana	23	650	741	226

Figure 17. Sete Quedas, or Guaira, on the Parana River, the waterfall with the greatest volume of water. (Credit: Organization of American States.)

16
Largest Countries in Area

Contents

Rank.
Conventional name of country.
Area, including inland waters, in thousands of square miles and square kilometers.
Percentage of world land area represented by the given area.

Arrangement

By area.

Coverage

50 largest countries in area.

Rounding

Areas are rounded to the nearest 1000 mi^2 (km^2); percentages, to the nearest two significant digits.

Entries

50.

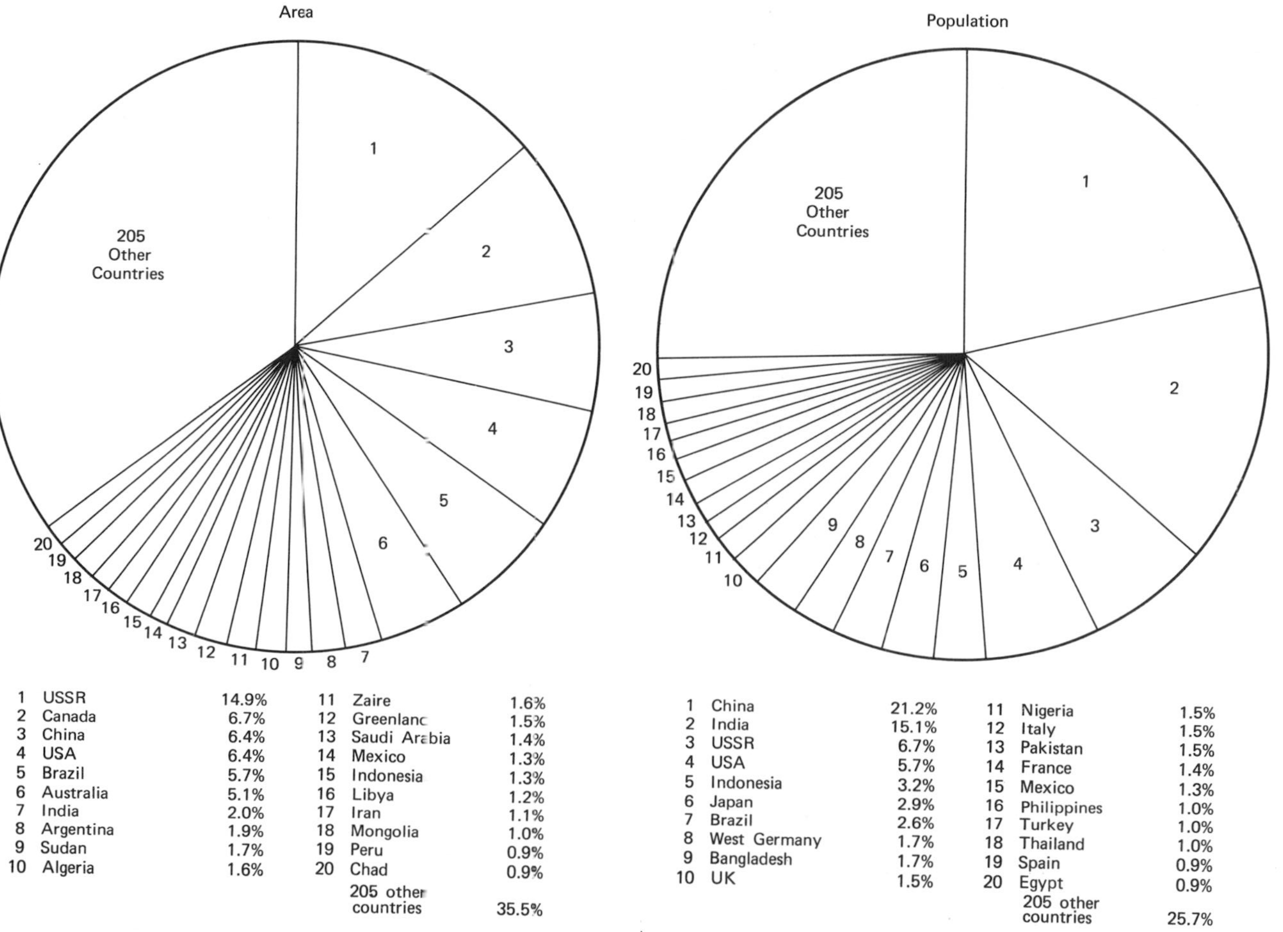

	Area	%		Area	%
1	USSR	14.9%	11	Zaire	1.6%
2	Canada	6.7%	12	Greenland	1.5%
3	China	6.4%	13	Saudi Arabia	1.4%
4	USA	6.4%	14	Mexico	1.3%
5	Brazil	5.7%	15	Indonesia	1.3%
6	Australia	5.1%	16	Libya	1.2%
7	India	2.0%	17	Iran	1.1%
8	Argentina	1.9%	18	Mongolia	1.0%
9	Sudan	1.7%	19	Peru	0.9%
10	Algeria	1.6%	20	Chad	0.9%
				205 other countries	35.5%

	Population	%		Population	%
1	China	21.2%	11	Nigeria	1.5%
2	India	15.1%	12	Italy	1.5%
3	USSR	6.7%	13	Pakistan	1.5%
4	USA	5.7%	14	France	1.4%
5	Indonesia	3.2%	15	Mexico	1.3%
6	Japan	2.9%	16	Philippines	1.0%
7	Brazil	2.6%	17	Turkey	1.0%
8	West Germany	1.7%	18	Thailand	1.0%
9	Bangladesh	1.7%	19	Spain	0.9%
10	UK	1.5%	20	Egypt	0.9%
				205 other countries	25.7%

Figure 18. Area and population of countries as percentage of world land area and population.

TABLE 16. LARGEST COUNTRIES IN AREA

Rank	Country	Area (1000 mi²)	Area (1000 km²)	% of World Land Area	Rank	Country	Area (1000 mi²)	Area (1000 km²)	% of World Land Area
1.	USSR	8,649	22,402	14.9	27.	Bolivia	424	1,099	0.73
2.	Canada	3,852	9,976	6.7	28.	Mauritania	398	1,031	0.69
3.	China	3,692	9,561	6.4	29.	Egypt	387	1,001	0.67
4.	USA	3,676	9,520	6.4	30.	Tanzania	363	940	0.63
5.	Brazil	3,286	8,512	5.7	31.	Nigeria	357	924	0.62
6.	Australia	2,968	7,687	5.1	32.	Venezuela	352	912	0.61
7.	India	1,176	3,045	2.0	33.	South-West Africa	318	824	0.55
8.	Argentina	1,072	2,777	1.9	34.	Pakistan	310	804	0.54
9.	Sudan	967	2,506	1.7	35.	Mozambique	302	783	0.52
10.	Algeria	920	2,382	1.6	36.	Turkey	301	781	0.52
11.	Zaire	906	2,345	1.6	37.	Chile	292	757	0.50
12.	Greenland	840	2,176	1.5	38.	Zambia	291	753	0.50
13.	Saudi Arabia	830	2,150	1.4	39.	Burma	262	678	0.45
14.	Mexico	762	1,972	1.3	40.	Afghanistan	250	647	0.43
15.	Indonesia	735	1,904	1.3	41.	Somalia	246	638	0.43
16.	Libya	679	1,759	1.2	42.	Central African Republic	241	623	0.42
17.	Iran	636	1,648	1.1					
18.	Mongolia	604	1,565	1.0	43.	Botswana	232	600	0.40
19.	Peru	496	1,285	0.86	44.	Malagasy Republic	227	587	0.39
20.	Chad	496	1,284	0.86	45.	Kenya	225	583	0.39
21.	Niger	489	1,267	0.85	46.	France	211	547	0.36
22.	Angola	481	1,247	0.83	47.	Thailand	198	514	0.34
23.	Mali	479	1,240	0.83	48.	Spain	195	505	0.34
24.	Ethiopia	472	1,222	0.82	49.	Cameroon	184	475	0.32
25.	South Africa	471	1,221	0.81	50.	Sweden	174	450	0.30
26.	Colombia	440	1,139	0.76	Total		46,814	121,248	80.9

17
Largest Countries in Population

Contents

Rank.
Conventional name of country.
Latest population in thousands, and year of estimate (e) or census.
Percentage of world population represented by the given population.

Arrangement

By population.

Coverage

50 largest countries in population.

Rounding

Populations are rounded to the nearest 1000; percentages, to the nearest two significant digits.

Entries

50.

TABLE 17. LARGEST COUNTRIES IN POPULATION

Rank	Country	Population (thousands)	Year	% of World Population	Rank	Country	Population (thousands)	Year	% of World Population
1.	China	759,619	1970e	21.2	27.	Zaire	21,638	1970	0.60
2.	India	542,753	1971	15.1	28.	Canada	21,568	1971	0.60
3.	USSR	241,748	1970	6.7	29.	South Africa	21,448	1970	0.60
4.	USA	204,816	1970	5.7	30.	North Vietnam	21,154	1970e	0.59
5.	Indonesia	114,950	1970	3.2	31.	Colombia	21,117	1970e	0.59
6.	Japan	103,720	1970	2.9	32.	Yugoslavia	20,505	1971	0.57
7.	Brazil	94,509	1970	2.6	33.	Romania	20,253	1970e	0.56
8.	West Germany	60,651	1970	1.7	34.	South Vietnam	18,332	1970e	0.51
9.	Bangladesh	59,547	1969e	1.7	35.	Afghanistan	17,125	1970e	0.48
10.	UK	55,364	1971	1.5	36.	East Germany	17,041	1971	0.47
11.	Nigeria	55,074	1970e	1.5	37.	Sudan	15,695	1970e	0.44
12.	Italy	53,770	1971	1.5	38.	Morocco	15,379	1971	0.43
13.	Pakistan	52,282	1969e	1.5	39.	Czechoslovakia	14,362	1970	0.40
14.	France	50,775	1970e	1.4	40.	Taiwan	14,035	1970e	0.39
15.	Mexico	48,377	1970	1.3	41.	Algeria	14,012	1970e	0.39
16.	Philippines	36,684	1970	1.0	42.	North Korea	13,892	1970e	0.39
17.	Turkey	35,667	1970	0.99	43.	Peru	13,586	1970e	0.38
18.	Thailand	34,152	1970	0.95	44.	Tanzania	13,273	1970e	0.37
19.	Spain	33,832	1970	0.94	45.	Netherlands	13,019	1970e	0.36
20.	Egypt	33,329	1970e	0.93	46.	Ceylon	12,748	1971	0.36
21.	Poland	32,589	1970	0.91	47.	Australia	12,728	1971	0.35
22.	South Korea	31,469	1970	0.88	48.	Nepal	11,290	1971	0.31
23.	Iran	28,662	1970e	0.80	49.	Kenya	11,247	1970e	0.31
24.	Burma	27,584	1970e	0.77	50.	Malaysia	10,434	1970	0.29
25.	Ethiopia	25,046	1970e	0.70	Total		3,226,173		89.9
26.	Argentina	23,323	1970	0.65					

18
Most Densely Populated Countries

Contents

Rank.
Conventional name of country.
Continent in which located.
Year of data, and density of population per square mile and per square kilometer.

Arrangement

By density of population.

Coverage

50 most densely populated countries.

Entries

50.

TABLE 18. MOST DENSELY POPULATED COUNTRIES

Rank Country	Continent	Year	Density of Population (per mi²)	(per km²)
1. Monaco	Europe	1970	41,440	16,000
2. Macao	Asia	1970	40,145	15,500
3. Melilla	Africa	1970	13,166	5,083
4. Gibraltar	Europe	1970	11,655	4,500
5. Hong Kong	Asia	1971	10,105	3,902
6. Singapore	Asia	1970	9,250	3,571
7. Ceuta	Africa	1970	8,588	3,316
8. Vatican City	Europe	1970	6,475	2,500
9. Malta	Europe	1970	2,672	1,032
10. Bermuda	North America	1970	2,590	1,000
11. Johnston and Sand Islands	Oceania	1970	2,500	965
12. Gaza Strip	Asia	1967	2,440	942
13. Channel Islands	Europe	1971	1,660	641
14. Barbados	North America	1970	1,434	553
15. Ryukyu Islands	Asia	1970	1,107	428
16. Bangladesh	Asia	1969	1,080	417
17. Mauritius	Africa	1970	1,061	410
18. Taiwan	Asia	1970	1,010	390
19. Midway Islands	Oceania	1970	1,000	386
20. Maldives	Asia	1970	991	383
21. Bahrain	Asia	1971	940	363
22. Nauru	Oceania	1970	863	333
23. South Korea	Asia	1970	828	319
24. Netherlands	Europe	1970	826	319
25. Belgium	Europe	1970	822	317
26. San Marino	Europe	1970	807	311
27. Martinique	North America	1970	794	307
28. Puerto Rico	North America	1970	790	305
29. Lebanon	Asia	1970	737	285
30. Japan	Asia	1970	726	280
31. Grenada	North America	1970	708	273
32. Wake Island	Oceania	1970	667	257
33. West Germany	Europe	1970	632	244
34. Netherlands Antilles	North America	1970	598	231
35. Saint Vincent	North America	1970	594	229
36. UK	Europe	1971	588	227
37. Tokelau Islands	Oceania	1970	518	200
38. Ceylon	Asia	1971	503	194
39. Trinidad and Tobago	North America	1970	477	184
40. Guadeloupe	North America	1970	476	184
41. Virgin Islands (USA)	North America	1970	466	180
42. Italy	Europe	1971	462	179
43. India	Asia	1971	462	178
44. Reunion	Africa	1970	460	178
45. Jamaica	North America	1970	438	169
46. Saint Kitts-Nevis	North America	1970	437	169
47. El Salvador	North America	1971	429	165
48. Saint Lucia	North America	1970	425	164
49. East Germany	Europe	1971	408	157
50. Guam	Oceania	1970	401	155

19
Least Densely Populated Countries

Contents

Rank.
Conventional name of country.
Continent in which located.
Year of data, and density of population per square mile and per square kilometer.

Arrangement

By density of population, inversely.

Coverage

50 least densely populated countries.

Rounding

Densities of population are rounded to the nearest two significant digits if between 1 and 100 per square mile or per square kilometer, and to the nearest significant digit if less than 1 per square mile or per square kilometer.

Entries

50.

TABLE 19. LEAST DENSELY POPULATED COUNTRIES

Rank	Country	Continent	Year	Density of Population (per mi²)	(per km²)
1.	Greenland	North America	1970	0.06	0.02
2.	French Southern and Antarctic Lands	Africa	1970	0.07	0.03
3.	Svalbard	Europe	1970	0.1	0.05
4.	Falkland Islands	South America	1970	0.5	0.2
5.	Spanish Sahara	Africa	1970	0.7	0.3
6.	French Guiana	South America	1970	1.5	0.6
7.	South-West Africa	Africa	1970	2.0	0.8
8.	Mongolia	Asia	1970	2.1	0.8
9.	Botswana	Africa	1971	2.7	1.0
10.	Libya	Africa	1970	2.8	1.1
11.	Mauritania	Africa	1970	2.9	1.1
12.	Australia	Oceania	1971	4.3	1.7
13.	Gabon	Africa	1970	4.8	1.9
14.	Iceland	Europe	1970	5.2	2.0
15.	United Arab Emirates	Asia	1968	5.5	2.1
16.	Canada	North America	1971	5.6	2.2
17.	Surinam	South America	1972	6.1	2.4
18.	Central African Republic	Africa	1970	6.3	2.4
19.	Chad	Africa	1970	7.5	2.9
20.	Papua	Oceania	1970	7.8	3.0
21.	Oman	Asia	1970	8.0	3.1
22.	Congo	Africa	1970	8.2	3.2
22.	Niger	Africa	1970	8.2	3.2
24.	Guyana	South America	1970	8.6	3.3
25.	Qatar	Asia	1970	9.3	3.6
25.	Saudi Arabia	Asia	1970	9.3	3.6
27.	Mali	Africa	1970	10	4.0
28.	Canton and Enderbury Islands	Oceania	1960	11	4.3
28.	French Territory of the Afars and the Issas	Africa	1970	11	4.3
30.	Somalia	Africa	1970	11	4.4
31.	Bolivia	South America	1970	12	4.5
31.	Southern Yemen	Asia	1970	12	4.5
33.	Angola	Africa	1970	12	4.6
34.	British Honduras	North America	1970	14	5.2
35.	British Solomon Islands	Oceania	1970	14	5.4
36.	New Caledonia	Oceania	1970	15	5.7
36.	New Hebrides	Oceania	1970	15	5.7
36.	Zambia	Africa	1970	15	5.7
39.	Algeria	Africa	1970	15	5.9
39.	Paraguay	South America	1970	15	5.9
41.	Sudan	Africa	1970	16	6.3
42.	New Guinea (Australia)	Oceania	1970	19	7.3
43.	Argentina	South America	1970	22	8.4
44.	Zaire	Africa	1970	24	9.2
45.	Equatorial Guinea	Africa	1970	27	10
46.	Mozambique	Africa	1970	27	11
46.	Peru	South America	1970	27	11
48.	New Zealand	Oceania	1971	28	11
48.	USSR	Europe and Asia	1970	28	11
50.	Brazil	South America	1970	29	11

20
Countries with Highest Birth Rates

Contents

Rank.
Conventional name of country.
Continent in which located.
Period of data, and number of live births per thousand of population.

Arrangement

By birth rate.

Coverage

50 countries with the highest birth rates.

Entries

51.

TABLE 20. COUNTRIES WITH HIGHEST BIRTH RATES

Rank	Country	Continent	Period	Birth Rate	Rank	Country	Continent	Period	Birth Rate
1.	Swaziland	Africa	1965-70	52.3e	28.	Kenya	Africa	1965-70	47.8e
2.	Niger	Africa	1965-70	52.2e	29.	Chad	Africa	1965-70	47.7e
3.	Rwanda	Africa	1965-70	51.8e	30.	Pakistan	Asia	1964-65	47.6e
4.	Dahomey	Africa	1965-70	50.9e	31.	Syria	Asia	1965-70	47.5e
4.	Togo	Africa	1965-70	50.9e	32.	Guinea	Africa	1965-70	47.2e
6.	Bangladesh	Asia	1964-65	50.6e	33.	Tanzania	Africa	1967	47e
7.	Afghanistan	Asia	1965-70	50.5e	34.	Ghana	Africa	1965-70	46.6e
8.	Angola	Africa	1965-70	50.1e	35.	Senegal	Africa	1965-70	46.3e
8.	Sao Tome and Principe	Africa	1966-68	50.1	36.	Central African Republic	Africa	1965-70	46.1e
10.	Liberia	Africa	1969-70	50e	37.	Ivory Coast	Africa	1965-70	46.0e
10.	Saudi Arabia	Asia	1965-70	50.0e	37.	Malagasy Republic	Africa	1966	46e
10.	Southern Yemen	Asia	1965-70	50.0e					
10.	Yemen	Asia	1965-70	50.0e	37.	Nicaragua	North America	1965-70	46.0e
14.	Mali	Africa	1965-70	49.8e					
14.	Zambia	Africa	1965-70	49.8e	40.	Libya	Africa	1965-70	45.9e
16.	Nigeria	Africa	1965-70	49.6e	40.	Somalia	Africa	1965-70	45.9e
17.	Morocco	Africa	1965-70	49.5e	42.	Ethiopia	Africa	1965-70	45.6e
18.	Upper Volta	Africa	1965-70	49.4e	43.	Iran	Asia	1965-70	45.4e
19.	Iraq	Asia	1965-70	49.3e	44.	New Hebrides	Oceania	1966	45.0e
20.	Jordan	Asia	1965-70	49.1e	45.	Ecuador	South America	1965-70	44.9e
21.	Honduras	North America	1965-70	49.0e					
					46.	Sierra Leone	Africa	1965-70	44.8e
21.	Malawi	Africa	1965-70	49.0e	47.	Philippines	Asia	1965-70	44.7e
23.	Sudan	Africa	1965-70	48.9e	48.	Cambodia	Asia	1965-70	44.6e
24.	Dominican Republic	North America	1965-70	48.5e	48.	Colombia	South America	1965-70	44.6e
25.	Rhodesia	Africa	1965-70	48.4e	48.	Nepal	Asia	1965-70	44.6e
26.	Indonesia	Asia	1965-70	48.3e	48.	Paraguay	South America	1965-70	44.6e
27.	Burundi	Africa	1965-70	48.1e					

21
Countries with Lowest Birth Rates

Contents

Rank.
Conventional name of country.
Continent in which located.
Period of data, and number of live births per thousand of population.

Arrangement

By birth rate, inversely.

Coverage

50 countries with the lowest birth rates.

Entries

50.

TABLE 21. COUNTRIES WITH LOWEST BIRTH RATES

Rank	Country	Continent	Period	Birth Rate	Rank	Country	Continent	Period	Birth Rate
1.	Christmas Island (Australia)	Oceania	1966-69	11.6	28.	USA	North America	1966-70	17.9
2.	Canal Zone	North America	1966-70	12.0	29.	Greece	Europe	1966-69	18.0
					30.	Canada	North America	1966-69	18.1
3.	Norfolk Island	Oceania	1966-70	13.7					
4.	Isle of Man	Europe	1966-69	13.9	31.	Netherlands	Europe	1966-70	18.9
5.	Luxembourg	Europe	1966-70	14.2	32.	Yugoslavia	Europe	1966-70	19.0
6.	East Germany	Europe	1966-70	14.5	33.	Bermuda	North America	1966-69	19.5
6.	Sweden	Europe	1966-70	14.5					
8.	Hungary	Europe	1966-70	14.6	34.	Australia	Oceania	1966-70	19.9
9.	Belgium	Europe	1966-70	15.1	35.	Portugal	Europe	1966-70	20.4
10.	Melilla	Africa	1966-70	15.3	36.	Spain	Europe	1966-70	20.5
11.	Czechoslovakia	Europe	1966-70	15.4	37.	Argentina	South America	1966-67	20.8
11.	Finland	Europe	1966-70	15.4					
13.	West Germany	Europe	1966-70	15.7	38.	Ryukyu Islands	Asia	1966-69	21.2
14.	Denmark	Europe	1966-70	15.9	39.	Uruguay	South America	1965-70	21.3e
15.	Bulgaria	Europe	1966-70	16.0					
16.	Channel Islands	Europe	1966-69	16.2	40.	Ireland	Europe	1966-70	21.4
17.	Malta	Europe	1966-70	16.3	41.	Gibraltar	Europe	1966-69	21.7
18.	Ceuta	Africa	1966-70	16.4	42.	Iceland	Europe	1966-69	22.0
18.	Poland	Europe	1966-70	16.4	43.	Montserrat	North America	1966-69	22.1
20.	Austria	Europe	1966-70	16.8					
21.	France	Europe	1966-70	16.9	44.	Hong Kong	Asia	1966-70	22.3
22.	Switzerland	Europe	1966-70	17.1	45.	Barbados	North America	1966-69	22.4
22.	UK	Europe	1966-70	17.1					
24.	Norway	Europe	1966-70	17.4	45.	New Zealand	Oceania	1966-70	22.4
24.	USSR	Europe and Asia	1966-70	17.4	47.	Romania	Europe	1966-70	22.5
					48.	Cyprus	Asia	1965-70	23.3e
26.	Italy	Europe	1966-70	17.8	49.	Singapore	Asia	1966-70	25.6
26.	Japan	Asia	1966-70	17.8	50.	Israel	Asia	1966-70	25.7

22
Countries with Highest Death Rates

Contents

Rank.
Conventional name of country.
Continent in which located.
Period of data, and number of deaths per thousand of population.

Arrangement

By death rate.

Coverage

50 countries with the highest death rates.

Entries

50.

TABLE 22. COUNTRIES WITH HIGHEST DEATH RATES

Rank	Country	Continent	Period	Death Rate	Rank	Country	Continent	Period	Death Rate
1	Angola	Africa	1965-70	30.2e	26.	Congo	Africa	1965-70	22.8e
2.	Portuguese Guinea	Africa	1965-70	29.9e	26.	Senegal	Africa	1965-70	22.8e
3.	Upper Volta	Africa	1965-70	29.1e	29.	Ivory Coast	Africa	1965-70	22.7e
4.	Mali	Africa	1965-70	26.6e	29.	Mauritania	Africa	1965-70	22.7e
5.	Afghanistan	Asia	1965-70	26.5e	29.	Saudi Arabia	Asia	1965-70	22.7e
6.	Dahomey	Africa	1965-70	25.5e	29.	Sierra Leone	Africa	1965-70	22.7e
6.	Togo	Africa	1965-70	25.5e	29.	Southern Yemen	Asia	1965-70	22.7e
8.	Portuguese Timor	Asia	1965-70	25.4e	29.	Yemen	Asia	1965-70	22.7e
9.	Burundi	Africa	1965-70	25.2e	29.	Zaire	Africa	1965-70	22.7e
10.	Central African Republic	Africa	1965-70	25.1e	36.	Botswana	Africa	1965-70	22.6e
10.	Guinea	Africa	1965-70	25.1e	37.	Equatorial Guinea	Africa	1965-70	22.1e
12.	Chad	Africa	1965-70	25.0e	38.	Tanzania	Africa	1967	22e
12.	Ethiopia	Africa	1965-70	25.0e	39.	Bangladesh	Asia	1964-65	21.0e
12.	Gabon	Africa	1965-70	25.0e	39.	Lesotho	Africa	1965-70	21.0e
12.	Malagasy Republic	Africa	1966	25e	41.	Zambia	Africa	1965-70	20.7e
12.	Malawi	Africa	1965-70	25.0e	42.	New Hebrides	Oceania	1966	20.0e
12.	South-West Africa	Africa	1965-70	25.0e	43.	Haiti	North America	1965-70	19.7e
18.	Nigeria	Africa	1965-70	24.9e	44.	Indonesia	Asia	1965-70	19.4e
19.	Somalia	Africa	1965-70	24.0e	45.	Bolivia	South America	1965-70	19.1e
20.	Swaziland	Africa	1965-70	23.5e	46.	Sudan	Africa	1965-70	18.4e
21.	Niger	Africa	1965-70	23.3e	47.	Liberia	Africa	1969-70	18e
21.	Rwanda	Africa	1965-70	23.3e	48.	Ghana	Africa	1965-70	17.8e
23.	Gambia	Africa	1965-70	23.1e	49.	Uganda	Africa	1965-70	17.6e
24.	Mozambique	Africa	1965-70	22.9e	50.	Kenya	Africa	1965-70	17.5e
24.	Nepal	Asia	1965-70	22.9e					
26.	Cameroon	Africa	1965-70	22.8e					

23
Countries with Lowest Death Rates

Contents

Rank.
Conventional name of country.
Continent in which located.
Period of data, and number of deaths per thousand of population.

Arrangement

By death rate, inversely.

Coverage

50 countries with the lowest death rates.

Entries

53.

TABLE 23. COUNTRIES WITH LOWEST DEATH RATES

Rank	Country	Continent	Period	Death Rate
1.	Canal Zone	North America	1966-70	2.3
2.	Christmas Island (Australia)	Oceania	1966-69	2.6
3.	Guam	Oceania	1966-70	3.8
4.	American Samoa	Oceania	1966-70	4.6
5.	Hong Kong	Asia	1966-70	5.1
5.	Ryukyu Islands	Asia	1966-69	5.1
7.	Fiji	Oceania	1965-70	5.3e
7.	Taiwan	Asia	1966-70	5.3
9.	Singapore	Asia	1966-70	5.4
10.	Puerto Rico	North America	1966-69	6.0
11.	Brunei	Asia	1966-69	6.2
11.	Ceuta	Africa	1966-70	6.2
11.	Melilla	Africa	1966-70	6.2
14.	Israel	Asia	1966-70	6.7
15.	Japan	Asia	1966-70	6.8
16.	Trinidad and Tobago	North America	1966-69	6.9
17.	Costa Rica	North America	1966-69	7.0
17.	Iceland	Europe	1966-69	7.0
19.	Bahama Islands	North America	1966-69	7.3
19.	Bermuda	North America	1966-69	7.3
21.	Canada	North America	1966-69	7.4
21.	Jamaica	North America	1966-70	7.4
21.	Kuwait	Asia	1965-70	7.4e
24.	Cuba	North America	1965-70	7.5e
24.	Martinique	North America	1966-70	7.5
24.	Nauru	Oceania	1966-68	7.5
24.	Surinam	South America	1965-66	7.5
28.	Virgin Islands (USA)	North America	1966-70	7.7
29.	Cyprus	Asia	1965-70	7.8e
29.	Guadeloupe	North America	1966-70	7.8
29.	Poland	Europe	1966-70	7.8
29.	USSR	Europe and Asia	1966-70	7.8
29.	Venezuela	South America	1965-70	7.8e
34.	Ceylon	Asia	1966-68	7.9
34.	Dominica	North America	1966-68	7.9
34.	Grenada	North America	1966-69	7.9
34.	Saint Lucia	North America	1965-66	7.9
38.	Barbados	North America	1966-69	8.1
38.	Greece	Europe	1966-69	8.1
40.	Cook Islands	Oceania	1966-68	8.2
40.	Netherlands	Europe	1966-70	8.2
42.	Albania	Europe	1966-68	8.3
42.	Guyana	South America	1966-68	8.3
42.	Malaysia	Asia	1966-68	8.3e
42.	Saint Kitts-Nevis	North America	1966-69	8.3
46.	Argentina	South America	1966-67	8.4
46.	Mauritius	Africa	1966-70	8.4
48.	Norfolk Island	Oceania	1966-70	8.5
49.	Antigua	North America	1963-65	8.7
49.	New Zealand	Oceania	1966-70	8.7
49.	Saint-Pierre and Miquelon	North America	1966-69	8.7
49.	Virgin Islands (UK)	North America	1963-64	8.7
49.	Yugoslavia	Europe	1966-70	8.7

24
Countries with Highest Life Expectancies

Contents

Rank.
Conventional name of country.
Continent in which located.
Period of data, and expectation of life at birth, in years, for men, for women, and for both (average).

Arrangement

By life expectancy.

Coverage

50 countries with the highest life expectancies.

Entries

50.

TABLE 24. COUNTRIES WITH HIGHEST LIFE EXPECTANCIES

Rank	Country	Continent	Period	Life Expectancy (yrs)		
				Men	Women	Avg
1.	Sweden	Europe	1967	71.8	76.5	74.2
2.	Netherlands	Europe	1968	71.0	76.4	73.7
3.	Iceland	Europe	1961-65	70.8	76.2	73.5
3.	Norway	Europe	1961-65	71.0	76.0	73.5
5.	Denmark	Europe	1967-68	70.6	75.4	73.0
6.	Ryukyu Islands	Asia	1965	68.9	75.6	72.3
7.	Canada	North America	1965-67	68.7	75.2	72.0
8.	France	Europe	1968	68.0	75.5	71.7
8.	Japan	Asia	1968	69.0	74.3	71.7
10.	UK	Europe	1967-69	68.5	74.7	71.6
11.	Switzerland	Europe	1958-63	68.7	74.1	71.4
12.	East Germany	Europe	1965-66	68.7	73.7	71.2
13.	New Zealand	Oceania	1960-62	68.4	73.7	71.1
14.	Australia	Oceania	1960-62	67.9	74.2	71.0
14.	Israel	Asia	1969	69.2	72.8	71.0
16.	Bulgaria	Europe	1965-67	68.8	72.7	70.7
17.	Belgium	Europe	1959-63	67.7	73.5	70.6
17.	West Germany	Europe	1966-68	67.5[1]	73.6[1]	70.6[1]
19.	Czechoslovakia	Europe	1966	67.3	73.6	70.4
20.	Malta	Europe	1967-69	68.4	72.2	70.3
20.	USA	North America	1968	66.6	74.0	70.3
22.	Hong Kong	Asia	1968	66.7	73.3	70.0
22.	Ireland	Europe	1960-62	68.1	71.9	70.0
22.	USSR	Europe and Asia	1967-68	65	74	70
25.	Austria	Europe	1969	66.5	73.3	69.9
26.	Italy	Europe	1960-62	67.2	72.3	69.8
26.	Poland	Europe	1965-66	66.8	72.8	69.8
28.	Spain	Europe	1960	67.3	71.9	69.6
29.	Puerto Rico	North America	1959-61	67.1	71.9	69.5
30.	Hungary	Europe	1964	67.0	71.8	69.4
31.	Greece	Europe	1960-62	67.5	70.7	69.1
32.	Bermuda	North America	1965-66	65.6	72.3	69.0
32.	Finland	Europe	1961-65	65.4	72.6	69.0
34.	Romania	Europe	1964-67	66.4	70.5	68.5
34.	Uruguay	South America	1963-64	65.5	71.6	68.5
36.	Yugoslavia	Europe	1966-67	67.7	69.0	68.4
37.	Singapore	Asia	1965-70			68.2e
38.	Fiji	Oceania	1965-70			68.1e
38.	Taiwan	Asia	1965	65.8	70.4	68.1
40.	Argentina	South America	1965-70	64.1	70.2	67.1
41.	Cuba	North America	1965-70			66.8e
42.	Cyprus	Asia	1948-50	63.6	68.8	66.2
43.	Albania	Europe	1965-66	64.9	67.0	65.9
44.	Barbados	North America	1959-61	62.7	67.4	65.1
45.	Jamaica	North America	1959-61	62.6	66.6	64.6
45.	Surinam	South America	1963	62.5	66.7	64.6
47.	Guadeloupe	North America	1959-63	62.5	66.5	64.5
47.	Martinique	North America	1959-63	62.5	66.5	64.5
49.	Kuwait	Asia	1965-70			64.4e
50.	Trinidad and Tobago	North America	1959-61	62.1	66.3	64.2

[1] Exc West Berlin.

25
Countries with Lowest Life Expectancies

Contents

Rank.
Conventional name of country.
Continent in which located.
Period of data, and expectation of life at birth, in years, for men, for women, and for both (average).

Arrangement

By life expectancy, inversely.

Coverage

50 countries with the lowest life expectancies.

Entries

52.

TABLE 25. COUNTRIES WITH LOWEST LIFE EXPECTANCIES

Rank	Country	Continent	Period	Life Expectancy (yrs)		
				Men	Women	Avg
1.	Guinea	Africa	1955	26e	28e	27e
2.	Upper Volta	Africa	1961	32.1	31.1	31.6
3.	Chad	Africa	1963-64	29e	35e	32e
4.	Angola	Africa	1965-70			33.5e
4.	Portuguese Guinea	Africa	1965-70			33.5e
6.	Central African Republic	Africa	1959-60	33e	36e	34.5e
7.	Gabon	Africa	1960-61	25e	45e	35e
7.	Togo	Africa	1961	31.6	38.5	35.0
9.	Burundi	Africa	1965	35.0e	38.5e	36.7e
10.	Nigeria	Africa	1965-66	37.2	36.7	36.9
11.	Mali	Africa	1965-70			37.2e
12.	Liberia	Africa	1962	36.1e	38.6e	37.3e
13.	Afghanistan	Asia	1965-70			37.5e
13.	Portuguese Timor	Asia	1965-70			37.5e
15.	Malagasy Republic	Africa	1966	37.5e	38.3e	37.9e
16.	Dahomey	Africa	1965-70			38.5e
16.	Ethiopia	Africa	1965-70			38.5e
16.	Malawi	Africa	1965-70			38.5e
16.	Somalia	Africa	1965-70			38.5e
16.	South-West Africa	Africa	1965-70			38.5e
21.	Zaire	Africa	1950-52	37.6	40.0	38.8
22.	Tanzania	Africa	1967			40.5e
23.	Nepal	Asia	1965-70			40.6e
24.	Botswana	Africa	1965-70			41.0e
24.	Cameroon	Africa	1965-70			41.0e
24.	Congo	Africa	1965-70			41.0e
24.	Equatorial Guinea	Africa	1965-70			41.0e
24.	Gambia	Africa	1965-70			41.0e
24.	Ivory Coast	Africa	1965-70			41.0e
24.	Mauritania	Africa	1965-70			41.0e
24.	Mozambique	Africa	1965-70			41.0e
24.	Niger	Africa	1965-70			41.0e
24.	Rwanda	Africa	1965-70			41.0e
24.	Senegal	Africa	1965-70			41.0e
24.	Sierra Leone	Africa	1965-70			41.0e
24.	Swaziland	Africa	1965-70			41.0e
37.	India	Asia	1951-60	41.9	40.5	41.2
38.	Saudi Arabia	Asia	1965-70			42.3e
38.	Southern Yemen	Asia	1965-70			42.3e
38.	Yemen	Asia	1965-70			42.3e
41.	Cambodia	Asia	1958-59	42.2	43.3	42.7
42.	Lesotho	Africa	1965-70			43.5e
42.	Zambia	Africa	1965-70			43.5e
44.	Haiti	North America	1965-70			44.5e
45.	Colombia	South America	1950-52	44.2	45.9	45.1
46.	Ghana	Africa	1965-70			46.0e
47.	British Honduras	North America	1944-48	45.0	49.0	47.0
48.	Burma	Asia	1965-70			47.5e
48.	Indonesia	Asia	1960	47.5	47.5	47.5
48.	Kenya	Africa	1965-70			47.5e
48.	Laos	Asia	1965-70			47.5e
48.	Uganda	Africa	1965-70			47.5e

26
Largest Cities

Contents

Rank.

Conventional name of city, and subdivision and country in which located.

Year of data. If the year is followed by the letter "e," the population has been estimated; otherwise, the figure given is from census returns.

Latest population, in thousands, of city proper.[1]

Arrangement

By population.

Coverage

All cities with populations exceeding 1,000,000.

Rounding

Populations are rounded to the nearest 1000.

Entries

104.

[1] Occasionally, population data are conventionally given only for a city with suburbs included (indicated by the letter "s").

TABLE 26. LARGEST CITIES

Rank	City and Location	Year	Population (thousands)
1.	Shanghai, China	1968e	10,700
2.	Peking, China	1968e	10,000
3.	Tokyo, Honshu I, Japan	1970	8,841
4.	New York, New York, USA	1970	7,895
5.	London, England, UK	1971	7,393s
6.	Moscow, Russia in Europe, USSR	1970	6,942
7.	Bombay, Maharashtra, India	1971	5,969
8.	Seoul, South Korea	1970	5,536
9.	Sao Paulo, Sao Paulo, Brazil	1970	5,241
10.	Cairo, Egypt	1970e	4,961
11.	Djakarta, Java I, Indonesia	1970	4,386
12.	Rio de Janeiro, Guanabara, Brazil	1970	4,316
13.	Tientsin, Hopeh, China	1968e	4,000
14.	Hong Kong, Hong Kong	1971	3,951
15.	Lushun-Talien, Liaoning, China	1965e	3,600
16.	Leningrad, Russia in Europe, USSR	1970	3,513
17.	Chicago, Illinois, USA	1970	3,367
18.	Delhi, Delhi, India	1971	3,280
19.	Berlin, East and West Germany	1970-71	3,207
	East Berlin, East Germany	1971	1,085
	West Berlin, West-Berlin, West Germany	1970	2,122
20.	Calcutta, West Bengal, India	1971	3,141
21.	Madrid, Castilla la Nueva, Spain	1970	3,121
22.	Karachi, Pakistan	1969e	3,060
23.	Canton, Kwangtung, China	1965e	3,000
24.	Osaka, Honshu I, Japan	1970	2,980
25.	Buenos Aires, Distrito Federal, Argentina	1970	2,972
26.	Mexico, Distrito Federal, Mexico	1970	2,903
27.	Los Angeles, California, USA	1970	2,816
28.	Mukden, Liaoning, China	1968?e	2,800
28.	Rome, Lazio, Italy	1971	2,800
30.	Sydney, New South Wales, Australia	1971	2,717s
31.	Teheran, Iran	1966	2,695
32.	Paris, Region Parisienne, France	1968	2,591
33.	Santiago, Chile	1970	2,582s
34.	Madras, Tamil Nadu, India	1971	2,470
35.	Lima, Peru	1969e	2,416s
36.	Melbourne, Victoria, Australia	1971	2.389s
37.	Istanbul, Turkey	1970	2,248
38.	Yokohama, Honshu I, Japan	1970	2,238
39.	Bangkok, Thailand	1970	2,228
40.	Wuhan, Hupeh, China	1958e	2,226
41.	Chungking, Szechwan, China	1958e	2,165
42.	Singapore, Singapore	1970	2,075
43.	Bogota, Colombia	1969e	2,038
44.	Nagoya, Honshu I, Japan	1970	2,036
45.	Alexandria, Egypt	1970e	2,032
46.	Philadelphia, Pennsylvania, USA	1970	1,949
47.	Budapest, Hungary	1970	1,940
48.	Pusan, South Korea	1970	1,881
49.	Lahore, Pakistan	1969e	1,823
50.	Hamburg, Hamburg, West Germany	1970	1,794
51.	Saigon, South Vietnam	1970e	1,761
52.	Rangoon, Burma	1970e	1,759
53.	Barcelona, Cataluna, Spain	1970	1,742
54.	Milan, Lombardia, Italy	1971	1,724
55.	Taipei, Taiwan	1969e	1,712
56.	Kiev, Ukraine, USSR	1970	1,632
57.	Hyderabad, Andhra Pradesh, India	1971	1,612
58.	Vienna, Austria	1971	1,603
59.	Sian, Shensi, China	1968?e	1,600
60.	Harbin, Heilungkiang, China	1958e	1,595
61.	Ahmedabad, Gujarat, India	1971	1,588
62.	Detroit, Michigan, USA	1970	1,511
63.	Baghdad, Iraq	1965	1,491
64.	Bucharest, Romania	1970e	1,475
65.	Nanking, Kiangsu, China	1958e	1,455

Rank	City and Location	Year	Population (thousands)
66.	Surabaja, Java I, Indonesia	1970	1,442
67.	Kyoto, Honshu I, Japan	1970	1,419
68.	Changchun, Kirin, China	1968?e	1,400
69.	Casablanca, Morocco	1970e	1,395
70.	Tashkent, Uzbekistan, USSR	1970	1,385
71.	Manila, Luzon I, Philippines	1970	1,331
72.	Kinshasa, Zaire	1970	1,323
73.	Warsaw, Poland	1970	1,308
74.	Munich, Bayern, West Germany	1970	1,294
75.	Kobe, Honshu, I Japan	1970	1,289
76.	Montevideo, Uruguay	1967e	1,280
77.	Houston, Texas, USA	1970	1,233
77.	Naples, Campania, Italy	1971	1,233
79.	Kharkov, Ukraine, USSR	1970	1,223
80.	Pyongyang, North Korea	1965e	1,221
81.	Montreal, Quebec, Canada	1971	1,214
82.	Ankara, Turkey	1970	1,209
83.	Tsinan, Shantung, China	1968?e	1,200
84.	Guadalajara, Jalisco, Mexico	1970	1,195
85.	Turin, Piemonte, Italy	1971	1,178
86.	Gorkiy, Russia in Europe, USSR	1970	1,170
87.	Novosibirsk, Russia in Asia, USSR	1970	1,161
88.	Kanpur, Uttar Pradesh, India	1971	1,152
89.	Tsingtao, Shantung, China	1958e	1,144
90.	Chengtu, Szechwan, China	1958e	1,135
91.	Bandung, Java I, Indonesia	1970	1,126
91.	Belo Horizonte, Minas Gerais, Brazil	1970	1,126
93.	Taegu, South Korea	1970	1,083
94.	Prague, Bohemia, Czechoslovakia	1970	1,078
95.	Recife, Pernambuco, Brazil	1970	1,070
96.	Taiyuan, Shansi, China	1958e	1,053
97.	Kuybyshev, Russia in Europe, USSR	1970	1,047
98.	Kitakyushu, Kyushu I, Japan	1970	1,042
99.	Bangalore, Mysore, India	1969e	1,027
100.	Sverdlovsk, Russia in Asia, USSR	1970	1,026
101.	Fushun, Liaoning, China	1958e	1,019
102.	Salvador, Bahia, Brazil	1970	1,018
103.	Birmingham, England UK	1971	1,013
104.	Sapporo, Hokkaido I, Japan	1970	1,010

27
Largest Cities, Including Adjacent Suburban Areas

Contents

Rank.

Conventional name of city, and subdivision and country in which located.

Year of data. If the year is followed by the letter "e," the population has been estimated; otherwise, the figure given is from census returns.

Latest population, in thousands, of city and adjacent suburban areas.[1] Preferably, this is the population of the urbanized area or conurbation only; some officially reported suburban areas, however, include rural districts.

Arrangement

By population.

Coverage

150 largest cities, including adjacent suburban areas, in population.

Rounding

Populations are rounded to the nearest 1000.

Entries

151.

[1] When population data are not officially supplied for adjacent suburban areas, the letter "s" is omitted, and the population of the city proper is given.

TABLE 27. LARGEST CITIES, INCLUDING ADJACENT SUBURBAN AREAS

Rank	City and Location	Year	Population (thousands)
1.	New York, New York, USA	1970	16,207s
2.	Tokyo, Honshu I, Japan	1970	11,161s
3.	Shanghai, China	1968e	10,700
4.	Peking, China	1968e	10,000
5.	Buenos Aires, Distrito Federal, Argentina	1970	8,353s
6.	Los Angeles, California, USA	1970	8,351s
7.	Paris, Region Parisienne, France	1968	8,197s
8.	London, England, UK	1971	7,393s
9.	Moscow, Russia in Europe, USSR	1970	7,061s
10.	Calcutta, West Bengal, India	1971	7,040s
11.	Mexico, Distrito Federal, Mexico	1970	7,006s
12.	Chicago, Illinois, USA	1970	6,715s
13.	Sao Paulo, Sao Paulo, Brazil	1970	5,979s
14.	Bombay, Maharashtra, India	1971	5,969
15.	Seoul, South Korea	1970	5,536
16.	Cairo, Egypt	1970e	4,961
17.	Djakarta, Java I, Indonesia	1970	4,386
18.	Rio de Janeiro, Guanabara, Brazil	1970	4,316s
19.	Philadelphia, Pennsylvania, USA	1970	4,021s
20.	Tientsin, Hopeh, China	1968e	4,000
21.	Detroit, Michigan, USA	1970	3,971s
22.	Hong Kong, Hong Kong	1971	3,951
23.	Leningrad, Russia in Europe, USSR	1970	3,950s
24.	Delhi, Delhi, India	1971	3,630s
25.	Lushun-Talien, Liaoning, China	1965e	3,600
26.	Berlin, East and West Germany	1970-71	3,207
	East Berlin, East Germany	1971	1,085
	West Berin, West-Berlin, West Germany	1970	2,122
27.	Madrid, Castilla la Nueva, Spain	1970	3,121
28.	Karachi, Pakistan	1969e	3,060
29.	Canton, Kwangtung, China	1965e	3,000
30.	Manila, Luzon I, Philippines	1969e	2,989s
31.	San Francisco, California, USA	1970	2,988s
32.	Osaka, Honshu I, Japan	1970	2,980
33.	Mukden, Liaoning, China	1968?e	2,800
33.	Rome, Lazio, Italy	1971	2,800
35.	Montreal, Quebec, Canada	1971	2,743s
36.	Sydney, New South Wales, Australia	1971	2,717s
37.	Teheran, Iran	1966	2,695
38.	Boston, Massachusetts USA	1970	2,653s
39.	Toronto, Ontario, Canada	1971	2,628s
40.	Santiago, Chile	1970	2,582s
41.	Athens, Greece	1971	2,530s
42.	Washington, District of Columbia, USA	1970	2,481s
43.	Madras, Tamil Nadu, India	1971	2,470
44.	Lima, Peru	1969e	2,416s
45.	Melbourne, Victoria, Australia	1971	2,389s
46.	Bogota, Colombia	1969e	2,294s
47.	Istanbul, Turkey	1970	2,248
48.	Yokohama, Honshu I, Japan	1970	2,238
49.	Bangkok, Thailand	1970	2,228
50.	Wuhan, Hupeh, China	1958e	2,226
51.	Chungking, Szechwan, China	1958e	2,165
52.	Singapore, Singapore	1970	2,075
53.	Caracas, Venezuela	1969e	2,064s
54.	Nagoya, Honshu I, Japan	1970	2,036
55.	Alexandria, Egypt	1970e	2,032
56.	Cleveland, Ohio, USA	1970	1,960s
57.	Budapest, Hungary	1970	1,940
58.	Saint Louis, Missouri, USA	1970	1,883s
59.	Pusan, South Korea	1970	1,881
60.	Pittsburgh, Pennsylvania, USA	1970	1,846s
61.	Lahore, Pakistan	1969e	1,823
62.	Hyderabad, Andhra Pradesh, India	1971	1,799s
63.	Hamburg, Hamburg, West Germany	1970	1,794
64.	Monterrey, Nuevo Leon, Mexico	1970	1,777s

Rank	City and Location	Year	Population (thousands)
65.	Saigon, South Vietnam	1970e	1,761
66.	Rangoon, Burma	1970e	1,759
67.	Havana, Cuba	1970	1,755s
68.	Ahmedabad, Gujarat, India	1971	1,746s
69.	Barcelona, Cataluna, Spain	1970	1,742
70.	Milan, Lombardia, Italy	1971	1,724
71.	Taipei, Taiwan	1969e	1,712
72.	Minneapolis, Minnesota, USA	1970	1,704s
73.	Houston, Texas, USA	1970	1,678s
74.	Baghdad, Iraq	1965	1,657s
75.	Bangalore, Mysore, India	1971	1,648s
76.	Kiev, Ukraine, USSR	1970	1,632
77.	Vienna, Austria	1971	1,603
78.	Sian, Shensi, China	1968?e	1,600
79.	Harbin, Heilungkiang, China	1958e	1,595
80.	Baltimore, Maryland, USA	1970	1,580s
81.	Bucharest, Romania	1970e	1,575s
82.	Guadalajara, Jalisco, Mexico	1970	1,487s
83.	Nanking, Kiangsu, China	1958e	1,455
84.	Surabaja, Java I, Indonesia	1970	1,442
85.	Johannesburg, Transvaal, South Africa	1970	1,433s
86.	Kyotó, Honshu I, Japan	1970	1,419
87.	Changchun, Kirin, China	1968?e	1,400
88.	Casablanca, Morocco	1970e	1,395
89.	Tashkent, Uzbekistan, USSR	1970	1,385
90.	Copenhagen, Denmark	1971e	1,379s
91.	Stockholm, Sweden	1970	1,345s
92.	Dallas, Texas, USA	1970	1,339s
93.	Lisbon, Portugal	1960	1,335s
94.	Kinshasa, Żaire	1970	1,323
95.	Warsaw, Poland	1970	1,308
96.	Munich, Bayern, West Germany	1970	1,294
97.	Kobe, Honshu I, Japan	1970	1,289
98.	Montevideo, Uruguay	1967e	1,280
99.	Kanpur, Uttar Pradesh, India	1971	1,273s
100.	Baku, Azerbaijan, USSR	1970	1,261s
101.	Belo Horizonte, Minas Gerais, Brazil	1970	1,255s
102.	Milwaukee, Wisconsin, USA	1970	1,252s
103.	Seattle, Washington, USA	1970	1,238s
104.	Naples, Campania, Italy	1971	1,233
105.	Kharkov, Ukraine, USSR	1970	1,223
106.	Pyongyang, North Korea	1965e	1,221
107.	Miami, Florida, USA	1970	1,220s
108.	Ankara, Turkey	1970	1,209
109.	Tsinan, Shantung, China	1968?e	1,200
110.	San Diego, California USA	1970	1,198s
111.	Turin, Piemonte, Italy	1971	1,178
112.	Atlanta, Georgia, USA	1970	1,173s
113.	Gorkiy, Russia in Europe, USSR	1970	1,170
114.	Novosibirsk, Russia in Asia, USSR	1970	1,161
115.	Tsingtao, Shantung, China	1958e	1,144
116.	Chengtu, Szechwan, China	1958e	1,135
117.	Bandung, Java I, Indonesia	1970	1,126
118.	Poona, Maharashtra, India	1971	1,123s
119.	Cincinnati, Ohio, USA	1970	1,111s
120.	Kansas City, Missouri, USA	1970	1,102s
121.	Cape Town, Cape of Good Hope, South Africa	1970	1,097s
122.	Buffalo, New York, USA	1970	1,087s
123.	Recife, Pernambuco, Brazil	1970	1,084s
124.	Taegu, South Korea	1970	1,083
125.	Vancouver, British Columbia, Canada	1971	1,082s

Rank	City and Location	Year	Population (thousands)
126.	Prague, Bohemia, Czechoslovakia	1970	1,078
127.	Lyons, Rhone-Alpes, France	1968	1,075s
128.	Brussels, Belgium	1969e	1,073s
129.	Rotterdam, Netherlands	1970e	1,061s
130.	Taiyuan, Shansi, China	1958e	1,053
131.	Denver, Colorado, USA	1970	1,047s
131.	Kuybyshev, Russia in Europe, USSR	1970	1,047
133.	Kitakyushu, Kyushu I, Japan	1970	1,042
134.	Amsterdam, Netherlands	1970e	1,040s
135.	Salvador, Bahia, Brazil	1970	1,027s
136.	Sverdlovsk, Russia in Asia, USSR	1970	1,026
137.	San Jose, California, USA	1970	1,025s
138.	Fushun, Liaoning, China	1958e	1,019
139.	Birmingham, England, UK	1971	1,013
140.	Sapporo, Hokkaido I, Japan	1970	1,010
141.	Kawasaki, Honshu I, Japan	1970	973
141.	Sofia, Bulgaria	1970e	973s
143.	Medellin, Colombia	1969e	968
144.	New Orleans, Louisiana, USA	1970	962s
145.	Marseilles, Provence-Cote d'Azur-Corse, France	1968	954s
146.	Algiers, Algeria	1966	943s
147.	Nagpur, Maharashtra, India	1969e	933s
148.	Minsk, White Russia, USSR	1970	916s
149.	Porto Alegre, Rio Grande do Sul, Brazil	1970	903s
150.	Anshan, Liaoning, China	1962e	900
150.	Kunming, Yunnan, China	1958e	900

28
Highest Cities

Contents

Rank.

Conventional name of city, and subdivision and country in which located.

Elevation (i.e., altitude above sea level), in feet and meters. When available, the given elevation is that of the city center or principal business district, or is an average of elevations at several points in the city; otherwise, it is that of the meteorological station.

Arrangement

By elevation.

Coverage

All cities listed in Tabular Gazetteer 2 of this work with an elevation of at least 3000 ft (914 m).

Entries

109.

TABLE 28. HIGHEST CITIES

Rank	City and Location	Elevation (ft)	Elevation (m)	Rank	City and Location	Elevation (ft)	Elevation (m)
1.	Lhasa, Tibet, China	12,002	3658	51.	Albuquerque, New Mexico,	4,945	1507
2.	La Paz, Bolivia	11,910	3630		USA		
3.	Cuzco, Peru	11,152	3399	52.	Guatemala, Guatemala	4,928	1502
4.	Sucre, Bolivia	9,331	2844	53.	Salisbury, Rhodesia	4,831	1472
5.	Quito, Ecuador	9,249	2819	54.	Vereeniging, Transvaal,	4,725	1440
6.	Toluca, Mexico, Mexico	8,793	2680		South Africa		
7.	Bogota, Colombia	8,675	2644	55.	Chihuahua, Chihuahua,	4,692	1430
8.	Cochabamba, Bolivia	8,390	2557		Mexico		
9.	Addis Ababa, Ethiopia	7,900	2408	56.	Pueblo, Colorado, USA	4,690	1430
10.	Asmara, Ethiopia	7,789	2374	57.	Jalapa, Veracruz, Mexico	4,682	1427
11.	Arequipa, Peru	7,559	2304	58.	Bloemfontein, Orange Free	4,678	1426
12.	Mexico, Distrito Federal, Mexico	7.546	2300		State, South Africa		
13.	Netzahualcoyotl, Mexico, Mexico	7,474	2278	59.	Pereira, Colombia	4,672	1424
14.	Sining, Tsinghai, China	7.363	2244	60.	Kashgar, Sinkiang, China	4,629	1411
15.	Gustavo A. Madero, Distrito Federal,	7,356	2242	61.	Provo, Utah, USA	4,549	1387
	Mexico			62.	Tananarive, Malagasy Republic	4,531	1381
16.	Sana, Yemen	7,260	2242	63.	Reno, Nevada, USA	4,490	1369
17.	Puebla, Puebla, Mexico	7,094	2162	64.	Tabriz, Iran	4,469	1362
18.	Manizales, Colombia	7,021	2140	65.	Pocatello, Idaho, USA	4,464	1361
19.	Santa Fe, New Mexico, USA	6,950	2118	66.	Bulawayo, Rhodesia	4,405	1343
20.	Morelia, Michoacan, Mexico	6,368	1941	67.	Salt Lake City, Utah, USA	4,390	1338
21.	Kunming, Yunnan, China	6,211	1893	68.	Katmandu, Nepal	4,388	1337
22.	Durango, Durango, Mexico	6,198	1889	69.	Pretoria, Transvaal, South	4,375	1333
23.	Aguascalientes, Aguascalientes, Mexico	6,195	1888		Africa		
24.	Leon, Guanajuato, Mexico	6,185	1885	70.	Kermanshah, Iran	4,337	1322
25.	San Luis Potosi, San Luis Potosi,	6,158	1877	71.	Ogden, Utah, USA	4,295	1309
	Mexico			71	Ulan-Bator, Mongolia	4,295	1309
26.	Cheyenne, Wyoming, USA	6,100	1859	73.	Orizaba, Veracruz, Mexico	4,213	1284
27.	Colorado Springs, Colorado, USA	5,980	1823	74.	Lusaka, Zambia	4,196	1279
28.	Kabul, Afghanistan	5,903	1799	75.	Ibague, Colombia	4,098	1249
29.	Hamadan, Iran	5,824	1775	76.	Lubumbashi, Zaire	4,035	1230
30.	Johannesburg, Transvaal, South Africa	5,750	1753	77.	Kampala, Uganda	3,910	1192
31.	Kokiu, Yunnan, China	5,709	1740	78.	Teheran, Iran	3,908	1191
32.	Irapuato, Guanajuato, Mexico	5,656	1724	79.	Salta, Salta, Argentina	3,878	1182
33.	Queretaro, Queretaro, Mexico	5,528	1685	80.	San Jose, Costa Rica	3,845	1172
34.	Nairobi, Kenya	5,453	1662	81.	Brasilia, Distrito Federal,	3,809	1161
35.	Germiston, Transvaal, South Africa	5,450	1661		Brazil		
36.	Boulder, Colorado, USA	5,430	1655	82.	Ciudad Juarez, Chihuahua,	3,734	1138
37.	Lakewood, Colorado, USA	5,355	1632		Mexico		
38.	Denver, Colorado, USA	5,280	1609	83.	Torreon, Coahuila, Mexico	3,708	1130
39.	Saltillo, Coahuila, Mexico	5,246	1599	84.	El Paso, Texas, USA	3,695	1126
40.	Isfahan, Iran	5,217	1590	85.	Amarillo, Texas, USA	3,685	1123
41.	Srinagar, Kashmir-Jammu	5,205	1586	86.	Yinchwan, Ningsia, China	3,645	1111
42.	Guadalajara, Jalisco, Mexico	5,141	1567	87.	Kayseri, Turkey	3,514	1071
43.	Casper, Wyoming, USA	5,123	1561	87.	Kweiyang, Kweichow, China	3,514	1071
44.	Siakwan, Yunnan, China	5,118	1560	89.	Blantyre, Malawi	3,501	1067
45.	Leninakan, Armenia, USSR	5,105	1556	90.	Huhehot, Inner Mongolia,	3,484	1062
46.	Oaxaca, Oaxaca, Mexico	5,086	1550		China		
47.	Cuernavaca, Morelos, Mexico	5,059	1542	91.	Kandahar, Afghanistan	3,462	1055
48.	Medellin, Colombia	5,056	1541	92.	Tatung, Shansi, China	3,442	1049
49.	Shiraz, Iran	5,049	1539	93.	Cali, Colombia	3,432	1046
50.	Lanchow, Kansu, China	4,948	1508	94.	Calgary, Alberta, Canada	3,428	1045

Rank	City and Location	Elevation (ft)	Elevation (m)	Rank	City and Location	Elevation (ft)	Elevation (m)
95.	Paotow, Inner Mongolia, China	3,425	1044	103.	Billings, Montana, USA	3,120	951
96.	Yenan, Shensi, China	3,400	1036	104.	Curitiba, Parana, Brazil	3,117	950
97.	Konya, Turkey	3,366	1026	105.	Bucaramanga, Colombia	3,035	925
98.	Great Falls, Montana, USA	3,330	1015	106.	Caracas, Venezuela	3,025	922
99.	Tegucigalpa, Honduras	3,304	1007	106.	Herat, Afghanistan	3,025	922
100.	Meshed, Iran	3,232	985	108.	Bangalore, Mysore, India	3,021	921
101.	Rapid City, South Dakota, USA	3,231	985	109.	Tepic, Nayarit, Mexico	3,002	915
102.	Lubbock, Texas, USA	3,195	974				

Figure 19. Panorama of Lhasa, Tibet, China, the world's highest city, showing the famous Potala Palace. (Credit: Foreign Languages Press, Peking.)

29
Oldest Cities, by Continent

Contents

Rank.

Conventional name of city, and subdivision and country in which located.

Year or century in which the first permanent settlement within present city limits was made. A question mark following a given date usually indicates that, although its exact origin is unknown, the city in question was first mentioned in historical records at that date. When the time of settlement cannot be ascertained but the city is known to have existed before a certain date, that date is given, preceded by the abbreviation "bef." It should be observed that the settlement date of a city bears no relation either to the date when the city was formally established (or chartered) or to the date when the present name was adopted.

Arrangement

By date, under continent.

Coverage

All cities listed in Tabular Gazetteer 2 of this work that were settled as early as the following dates:

Africa – 1600 AD
Asia – 300 BC
Europe – 300 BC
North America – 1640 AD
Oceania – 1850 AD
South America – 1640 AD

Entries

289.

TABLE 29. OLDEST CITIES, BY CONTINENT

AFRICA

Rank	City and Location	Date Settled
1.	Giza, Egypt	bef 2568 BC
2.	Asyut, Egypt	bef 2160 BC
2.	Luxor, Egypt	bef 2160 BC
4.	Tangier, Morocco	15th c BC?
5.	Tripoli, Tripolitania, Libya	7th c BC?
6.	Aswan, Egypt	6th c BC?
6.	Bengasi, Cyrenaica, Libya	6th c BC
8.	Tunis, Tunisia	4th c BC?
9.	Alexandria, Egypt	332 BC
10.	Constantine, Algeria	3rd c BC?
11.	Sfax, Tunisia	2nd c AD?
12.	Cairo, Egypt	641?
13.	Annaba, Algeria	7th c
14.	Mombasa, Kenya	8th c?
15.	Fez, Morocco	808
16.	Mogadishu, Somalia	908?
17.	Algiers, Algeria	10th c
17.	Oran, Algeria	10th c
19.	Mahalla al Kubra, Egypt	985?
20.	Meknes, Morocco	11th c
20.	Rabat-Sale, Morocco	11th c
22.	Marrakesh, Morocco	1062
23.	Tanta, Egypt	12th c?
24.	Timbuktu, Mali	1215?
25.	Mansurah, Egypt	1221
26.	Ouagadougou, Upper Volta	14th c?
27.	Funchal, (Madeira Islands), Portugal	1425
28.	Suez, Egypt	15th c
29.	Las Palmas, (Canary Islands), Spain	1478
30.	Santa Cruz de Tenerife, (Canary Islands), Spain	1494
31.	Casablanca, Morocco	1515
32.	Lourenco Marques, Mozambique	1544
33.	Kano, Nigeria	16th c?
33.	Niamey, Niger	16th c?
33.	Porto-Novo, Dahomey	16th c
33.	Zanzibar, Zanzibar, Tanzania	16th c
33.	Zaria, Nigeria	16th c
38.	Luanda, Angola	1575

ASIA

Rank	City and Location	Date Settled
1.	Gaziantep, Turkey	3650 BC?
2.	Jerusalem, Israel	3000 BC?
2.	Kirkuk, Iraq	3000 BC?
4.	Konya, Turkey	2600 BC?
5.	Sian, Shensi, China	2205 BC?
6.	Shaohing, Chekiang, China	2000 BC?
7.	Loyang, Honan, China	1900 BC?
8.	Amman, Jordan	17th c BC?
8.	Ankara, Turkey	17th c BC?
10.	Changchih, Shansi, China	16th c BC?
11.	Tel Aviv–Jaffa, Israel	bef 1472 BC
12.	Gaza, Gaza Strip	1468 BC?
13.	Beirut, Lebanon	15th c BC?
13.	Liaoyang, Liaoning, China	15th c BC?
15.	Damascus, Syria	bef 14th c BC
16.	Varanasi, Uttar Pradesh, India	12th c BC?
17.	Pyongyang, North Korea	1122 BC?
18.	Hamadan, Iran	1100 BC?
19.	Izmir, Turkey	11th c BC?
19.	Peking, China	11th c BC?
21.	Aleppo, Syria	bef 1000 BC
22.	Changchow, Fukien, China	10th c BC?
22.	Chengchow, Honan, China	10th c BC?
22.	Foochow, Fukien, China	10th c BC?
22.	Hofei, Anhwei, China	10th c BC?
22.	Nanchung, Szechwan, China	10th c BC?
22.	Nanning, Kwangsi, China	10th c BC?
22.	Tatung, Shansi, China	10th c BC?
29.	Canton, Kwangtung, China	9th c BC?
30.	Adana, Turkey	8th c BC?
31.	Hengyang, Hunan, China	7th c BC?
31.	Kaifeng, Honan, China	7th c BC?
31.	Osaka, Honshu I, Japan	7th c BC?
31.	Shaoyang, Hunan, China	7th c BC?
31.	Suchow, Kiangsu, China	7th c BC?
31.	Tripoli, Lebanon	7th c BC
31.	Yangchow, Kiangsu, China	7th c BC?
38.	Sialkot, Pakistan	600 BC?
39.	Patna, Bihar, India	6th c BC?
39.	Gaya, Bihar, India	545 BC?
41.	Colombo, Ceylon	543 BC?
42.	Soochow, Kiangsu, China	525 BC?
43.	Isfahan, Iran	5th c BC?
43.	Madurai, Tamil Nadu, India	5th c BC?
43.	Omiya, Honshu I, Japan	5th c BC?
46.	Hantan, Hopeh, China	4th c BC
46.	Herat, Afghanistan	4th c BC?
46.	Kabul, Afghanistan	4th c BC?
46.	Kweilin, Kwangsi, China	4th c BC?
46.	Samarkand, Uzbekistan, USSR	4th c BC?
51.	Antioch, Turkey	300 BC?

EUROPE

Rank	City and Location	Date Settled
1.	Zurich, Switzerland	3000 BC?
2.	Lisbon, Portugal	2000 BC?
2.	Porto, Portugal	2000 BC?
4.	Athens, Greece	bef 13th c BC
5.	La Coruna, Galicia, Spain	bef 12th c BC
6.	Malaga, Andalucia, Spain	12th c BC
7.	Cadiz, Andalucia, Spain	1100 BC?
8.	Pisa, Toscana, Italy	11th c BC?
9.	Metz, Lorraine, France	1000 BC?
9.	Rome, Lazio, Italy	1000 BC?
11.	Toulon, Provence-Cote d'Azur-Corse, France	9th c BC
12.	Cordova, Andalucia, Spain	bef 8th c BC
13.	Cannes, Provence-Cote d'Azur-Corse, France	8th c BC?
13.	Catania, Sicilia, Italy	8th c BC
13.	Messina, Sicilia, Italy	8th c BC
13.	Palermo, Sicilia, Italy	8th c BC
13.	Ravenna, Emilia-Romagna, Italy	8th c BC
13.	Reggio di Calabria, Calabria, Italy	8th c BC
19.	Syracuse, Sicilia, Italy	734 BC
20.	Taranto, Puglia, Italy	708 BC?
21.	Terni, Umbria, Italy	672 BC?
22.	Istanbul, Turkey	658 BC
23.	Constanta, Romania	7th c BC?
23.	Huelva, Andalucia, Spain	7th c BC?
23.	Jerez de la Frontera, Andalucia, Spain	7th c BC?
23.	Seville, Andalucia, Spain	7th c BC?
23.	Vigo, Galicia, Spain	7th c BC?
28.	Marseilles, Provence-Cote d'Azur-Corse, France	600 BC?
28.	Naples, Campania, Italy	600 BC?
30.	Besancon, Franche-Comte, France	6th c BC?
30.	Brescia, Lombardia, Italy	6th c BC
30.	Bristol, England, UK	6th c BC
30.	Kerch, Ukraine, USSR	6th c BC
30.	Kutaisi, Georgia, USSR	6th c BC
30.	Monaco, Monaco	6th c BC?
30.	Perugia, Umbria, Italy	6th c BC?
30.	Stara Zagora, Bulgaria	6th c BC?
30.	Varna, Bulgaria	6th c BC
39.	Cagliari, Sardegna, Italy	540 BC
40.	Bologna, Emilia-Romagna, Italy	510 BC?
41.	Bergamo, Lombardia, Italy	5th c BC?
41.	Genoa, Liguria, Italy	5th c BC?
41.	Granada, Andalucia, Spain	5th c BC?
41.	Le Mans, Pays de la Loire, France	5th c BC?
41.	Mainz, Rheinland-Pfalz, West Germany	5th c BC?
41.	Modena, Emilia-Romagna, Italy	5th c BC?
41.	Monza, Lombardia, Italy	5th c BC?
41.	Neuss, Nordrhein-Westfalen, West Germany	5th c BC?
41.	Nice, Provence-Cote d' Azur-Corse, France	5th c BC?
41.	Patras, Greece	5th c BC?
41.	Piraeus, Greece	5th c BC
41.	Regensburg, Bayern, West Germany	5th c BC?
41.	Salamanca, Leon, Spain	5th c BC?
54.	Rimini, Emilia-Romagna, Italy	400 BC?
55.	Ancona, Marche, Italy	390 BC?
56.	Milan, Lombardia, Italy	4th c BC
56.	Novara, Piemonte, Italy	4th c BC?
56.	Turin, Piemonte, Italy	4th c BC?
56.	Vienna, Austria	4th c BC?
60.	Plovdiv, Bulgaria	341 BC?
61.	Cosenza, Calabria, Italy	bef 331 BC
62.	Salonika, Greece	315 BC
63.	Padua, Veneto, Italy	302 BC?
64.	Rheims, Champagne, France	300 BC?
64.	Toulouse, Midi-Pyrenees, France	300 BC?

NORTH AMERICA

Rank	City and Location	Date Settled
1.	Toluca, Mexico, Mexico	1120 AD?
2.	Jalapa, Veracruz, Mexico	1313?
3.	Mexico, Distrito Federal, Mexico	1325
4.	Queretaro, Queretaro, Mexico	1440
5.	Orizaba, Veracruz, Mexico	1457
6.	Oaxaca, Oaxaca, Mexico	1486
7.	Santo Domingo, Dominican Republic	1496
8.	Santiago de los Caballeros, Dominican Republic	1504
9.	Santiago de Cuba, Cuba	1514
10.	Havana, Cuba	1519
11.	Cuernavaca, Morelos, Mexico	bef 1521
11.	Managua, Nicaragua	bef 1521
13.	San Juan, Puerto Rico	1521

NORTH AMERICA

Rank	City and Location	Date Settled	Rank	City and Location	Date Settled
14.	San Salvador, El Salvador	1525	42.	Veracruz, Veracruz, Mexico	1599
15.	Willemstad, Netherlands Antilles	1527	43.	Quebec, Quebec, Canada	1608
16.	Camaguey, Cuba	1528	44.	Santa Fe, New Mexico, USA	1609
17.	San Miguel, El Salvador	1530	45.	Hampton, Virginia, USA	1610
18.	Tepic, Nayarit, Mexico	1531	46.	Newport News, Virginia, USA	1621
19.	Puebla, Puebla, Mexico	1532	47.	Albany, New York, USA	1624
20.	Culiacan, Sinaloa, Mexico	1533	47.	New York, New York, USA	1624
21.	San Pedro Sula, Honduras	1536	49.	Quincy, Massachusetts, USA	1625
22.	Tallahassee, Florida, USA	bef 1539	50.	Salem, Massachusetts, USA	1626
23.	Mazatlan, Sinaloa, Mexico	bef 1541	51.	Bridgetown, Barbados	1628
24.	Morelia, Michoacan, Mexico	1541	52.	Jersey City, New Jersey, USA	1629?
25.	Guadalajara, Jalisco, Mexico	1542	52.	Lynn, Massachusetts, USA	1629
25.	Merida, Yucatan, Mexico	1542	54.	Boston, Massachusetts, USA	1630
27.	Irapuato, Guanajuato, Mexico	1547	54.	Cambridge, Massachusetts, USA	1630
28.	Acapulco, Guerrero, Mexico	1550	54.	Somerville, Massachusetts, USA	1630
28.	Netzahualcoyotl, Mexico, Mexico	16th c?	57.	Williamsburg, Virginia, USA	1633
30.	Durango, Durango, Mexico	1563	58.	Trois-Rivieres, Quebec, Canada	1634
31.	Saint Augustine, Florida, USA	1565	59.	Hartford, Connecticut, USA	1635
32.	Aguascalientes, Aguascalientes, Mexico	1575	60.	Providence, Rhode Island, USA	1636
32.	Saltillo, Coahuila, Mexico	1575	60.	Springfield, Massachusetts, USA	1636
34.	Leon, Guanajuato, Mexico	1576	62.	New Haven, Connecticut, USA	1638
34.	San Luis Potosi, San Luis Potosi, Mexico	1576	62.	Wilmington, Delaware, USA	1638
			64.	Yonkers, New York, USA	bef 1639
34.	Santa Ana, El Salvador	1576?	65.	Bridgeport, Connecticut, USA	1639
37.	Tegucigalpa, Honduras	1578	65.	Chihuahua, Chihuahua, Mexico	1639
38.	Monterrey, Nuevo Leon, Mexico	1579?	65.	Newport, Rhode Island, USA	1639
39.	Saint John's, Newfoundland, Canada	1583?	65.	Newton, Massachusetts, USA	1639
40.	Port of Spain, Trinidad and Tobago	bef 1595	69.	New Bedford, Massachusetts, USA	1640
41.	Villahermosa, Tabasco, Mexico	1596			

OCEANIA

Rank	City and Location	Date Settled	Rank	City and Location	Date Settled
1.	Hilo, Hawaii, USA	bef 1778 AD	9.	Melbourne, Victoria, Australia	1835
2.	Sydney, New South Wales, Australia	1788	10.	Adelaide, South Australia, Australia	1836
3.	Honolulu, Hawaii, USA	bef 1794	11.	Geelong, Victoria, Australia	1837
4.	Hobart, Tasmania, Australia	1804	12.	Papeete, French Polynesia	1840?
4.	Newcastle, New South Wales, Australia	1804	12.	Wellington, North I, New Zealand	1840
6.	Brisbane, Queensland, Australia	1824	14.	Auckland, North I, New Zealand	1841
6.	Canberra, Australian Capital Territory, Australia	1824?	15.	Apia, Western Samoa	bef 1850
8.	Perth, Western Australia, Australia	1829	16.	Christchurch, South I, New Zealand	1850

SOUTH AMERICA

Rank	City and Location	Date Settled	Rank	City and Location	Date Settled
1.	Quito, Ecuador	1000 AD?	3.	Cartagena, Colombia	1533
2.	Cuzco, Peru	11th c	4.	Lima, Peru	1535

SOUTH AMERICA

Rank	City and Location	Date Settled	Rank	City and Location	Date Settled
4.	Olinda, Pernambuco, Brazil	1535	30.	Niteroi, Rio de Janeiro, Brazil	1565
4.	Recife, Pernambuco, Brazil	1535?	30.	Rio de Janeiro, Guanabara, Brazil	1565
4.	Vitoria, Espirito Santo, Brazil	1535	32.	Caracas, Venezuela	1567
8.	Cali, Colombia	1536	32.	Nova Iguacu, Rio de Janeiro, Brazil	1567?
8.	Santos, Sao Paulo, Brazil	1536	34.	Maracaibo, Venezuela	1571
10.	Asuncion, Paraguay	1537	35.	Cordoba, Cordoba, Argentina	1573
10.	Callao, Peru	1537	35.	Santa Fe, Santa Fe, Argentina	1573
10.	Guayaquil, Ecuador	1537	37.	Cochabamba, Bolivia	1574
13.	Sucre, Bolivia	bef 1538	38.	Buenos Aires, Distrito Federal, Argentina	1580
14.	Bogota, Colombia	1538	39.	Salta, Salta, Argentina	1582
15.	Arequipa, Peru	1540	40.	Joao Pessoa, Paraiba, Brazil	1585
15.	Paramaribo, Surinam	1540?	41.	Vina del Mar, Chile	1586?
17.	Santiago, Chile	1541	42.	Seis de Septiembre, Buenos Aires, Argentina	1600
18.	Valparaiso, Chile	1544?	43.	Fortaleza, Ceara, Brazil	1609
19.	La Paz, Bolivia	1548	44.	Sao Luis, Maranhao, Brazil	1612
20.	Salvador, Bahia, Brazil	1549	45.	Belem, Para, Brazil	1616
21.	Concepcion, Chile	1550	45.	Medellin, Colombia	1616
22.	Ibague, Colombia	1551	47.	Bucaramanga, Colombia	1622
22.	Santo Andre, Sao Paulo, Brazil	1551	48.	Georgetown, Guyana	1625
24.	Barquisimeto, Venezuela	1552	49.	Barranquilla, Colombia	1629
24.	Sao Bernardo do Campo, Sao Paulo, Brazil	1552	50.	Campos, Rio de Janeiro, Brazil	1634
26.	Sao Paulo, Sao Paulo, Brazil	1554			
27.	Valencia, Venezuela	1555			
28.	Guarulhos, Sao Paulo, Brazil	1560			
29.	Mendoza, Mendoza, Argentina	1561			

30
Warmest Cities

Contents

Rank.
Conventional name of city, and subdivision and country in which located.
Average temperature throughout the year, in degrees Fahrenheit and in degrees Celsius (centigrade).

Arrangement

By temperature, from high to low.

Coverage

All cities listed in Tabular Gazetteer 2 of this work with an average temperature of at least 80° F (26.7° C).

Entries

90.

TABLE 30. WARMEST CITIES

Rank	City and Location	Average Temperature (°F)	Average Temperature (°C)
1.	Timbuktu, Mali	84.7	29.3
1.	Tirunelveli, Tamil Nadu, India	84.7[1]	29.3[1]
3.	Khartoum, Sudan	84.6	29.2
3.	Omdurman, Sudan	84.6[2]	29.2[2]
5.	Madurai, Tamil Nadu, India	84.0	28.9
5.	Niamey, Niger	84.0	28.9
7.	Aden, Southern Yemen	83.9	28.8
8.	Tiruchirapalli, Tamil Nadu, India	83.8	28.8
9.	Madras, Tamil Nadu, India	83.5	28.6
9.	Ouagadougou, Upper Volta	83.5	28.6
11.	Bamako, Mali	82.6	28.1
11.	Bangkok, Thailand	82.6	28.1
11.	Teresina, Piaui, Brazil	82.6	28.1
11.	Thon Buri, Thailand	82.6[3]	28.1[3]
15.	Fort-Lamy, Chad	82.4	28.0
15.	Maracaibo, Venezuela	82.4	28.0
15.	Salem, Tamil Nadu, India	82.4	28.0
18.	Jidda, Hejaz, Saudi Arabia	82.2	27.9
19.	Barranquilla, Colombia	82.0	27.8
19.	George Town, West Malaysia, Malaysia	82	27.8
19.	Guntur, Andhra Pradesh, India	82.0[4]	27.8[4]
19.	Vijayawada, Andhra Pradesh, India	82.0[4]	27.8[4]
23.	Cuttack, Orissa, India	81.9	27.7
23.	Rajahmundry, Andhra Pradesh, India	81.9[5]	27.7[5]
23.	Surat, Gujarat, India	81.9	27.7
23.	Warangal, Andhra Pradesh, India	81.9	27.7
23.	Willemstad, Netherlands Antilles	81.9	27.7
28.	Ipoh, West Malaysia, Malaysia	81.7	27.6
28.	Mandalay, Burma	81.7	27.6
30.	Iloilo, Panay I, Philippines	81.5	27.5
30.	Kuala Lumpur, West Malaysia, Malaysia	81.5	27.5
30.	Phnom-Penh, Cambodia	81.5	27.5
30.	San Miguel, El Salvador	81.5	27.5
34.	Acapulco, Guerrero, Mexico	81.3	27.4
34.	Pontianak, Borneo I, Indonesia	81.3	27.4
34.	Rangoon, Burma	81.3	27.4
37.	Ahmedabad, Gujarat, India	81.1	27.3
37.	Bombay, Maharashtra, India	81.1	27.3
37.	Calicut, Kerala, India	81.1	27.3
37.	Cucuta, Colombia	81.1	27.3
37.	Kalyan, Maharashtra, India	81.1[6]	27.3[6]
37.	Medina, Hejaz, Saudi Arabia	81.1	27.3
37.	Paramaribo, Surinam	81.1	27.3
37.	Tjirebon, Java I, Indonesia	81.1	27.3
45.	Amravati, Maharashtra, India	81.0	27.2
45.	Bhavnagar, Gujarat, India	81.0	27.2
45.	Hyderabad, Pakistan	81.0	27.2
45.	Mogadishu, Somalia	81.0	27.2
45.	Porto-Novo, Dahomey	81.0	27.2
45.	Visakhapatnam, Andhra Pradesh, India	81.0	27.2
51.	Cartagena, Colombia	80.8	27.1
51.	Cebu, Cebu I, Philippines	80.8	27.1
51.	Ernakulam, Kerala, India	80.8[7]	27.1[7]
51.	Fortaleza, Ceara, Brazil	80.8	27.1
51.	Mangalore, Mysore, India	80.8	27.1
51.	Sholapur, Maharashtra, India	80.8	27.1
51.	Trivandrum, Kerala, India	80.8	27.1
58.	Baroda, Gujarat, India	80.6	27.0
58.	Georgetown, Guyana	80.6	27.0
58.	Jamshedpur, Bihar, India	80.6	27.0
58.	Kota, Rajasthan, India	80.6	27.0
58.	Singapore, Singapore	80.6	27.0
63.	Aswan, Egypt	80.4	26.9
63.	Calcutta, West Bengal, India	80.4	26.9
63.	Colombo, Ceylon	80.4	26.9
63.	Cotonou, Dahomey	80.4	26.9
63.	Davao, Mindanao I, Philippines	80.4	26.9
63.	Durg, Madhya Pradesh, India	80.4[8]	26.9[8]
63.	Howrah, West Bengal, India	80.4[9]	26.9[9]
63.	Managua, Nicaragua	80.4	26.9
63.	Nagpur, Maharashtra, India	80.4	26.9
63.	Panama, Panama	80.4[10]	26.9[10]
63.	Port Moresby, Papua	80.4	26.9
63.	Raipur, Madhya Pradesh, India	80.4	26.9
63.	Saigon, South Vietnam	80.4	26.9
63.	Semarang, Java I, Indonesia	80.4	26.9
63.	South Suburban, W Bengal, India	80.4[9]	26.9[9]
78.	Bacolod, Negros I, Philippines	80.2	26.8
78.	Bandjermasin, Borneo I, Indonesia	80.2	26.8

1 Data for Palayamcottai, nr Tirunelveli.
2 Data for Khartoum, nr Omdurman.
3 Data for Bangkok, nr Thon Buri.
4 Data for Masulipatnam, nr Guntur and Vijayawada.
5 Data for Kakinada, nr Rajahmundry.
6 Data for Bombay, nr Kalyan.
7 Data for Cochin, nr Ernakulam.
8 Data for Raipur, nr Durg.
9 Data for Calcutta, nr Howrah and South Suburban.
10 Data for Balboa Heights, Canal Zone, nr Panama.

Rank	City and Location	Average Temperature (°F)	(°C)
78.	Charlotte Amalie, Virgin Islands, USA	80.2	26.8
78.	Djakarta, Java I, Indonesia	80.2	26.8
78.	Lagos, Nigeria	80.2	26.8
78.	Surabaja, Java I, Indonesia	80.2	26.8
84.	Conakry, Guinea	80.1	26.7
84.	Enugu, Nigeria	80.1	26.7
84.	Holguin, Cuba	80.1[1]	26.7[1]
84.	Ibadan, Nigeria	80.1	26.7
84.	Jodhpur, Rajasthan, India	80.1	26.7
84.	Rajkot, Gujarat, India	80.1	26.7
90.	Quezon City, Luzon I, Philippines	80.0	26.7

[1] Data for Gibara, nr Holguin.

31
Coolest Cities

Contents

Rank.
Conventional name of city, and subdivision and country in which located.
Average temperature throughout the year in degrees Fahrenheit and in degrees Celsius (centigrade).

Arrangement

By temperature, from low to high.

Coverage

All cities listed in Tabular Gazetteer 2 of this work with an average temperature of 40° F (4.4° C) or lower.

Entries

91.

TABLE 31. COOLEST CITIES

Rank	City and Location	Average Temperature (°F)	Average Temperature (°C)
1.	Ulan-Bator, Mongolia	24.8	-4.0
2.	Chita, Russia in Asia, USSR	27.1	-2.7
3.	Bratsk, Russia in Asia, USSR	28.0	-2.2
4.	Ulan-Ude, Russia in Asia, USSR	28.9	-1.7
5.	Angarsk, Russia in Asia, USSR	29.7	-1.3
6.	Irkutsk, Russia in Asia, USSR	30.0	-1.1
7.	Komsomolsk-na-Amure, Russia in Asia, USSR	30.7	-0.7
8.	Tomsk, Russia in Asia, USSR	30.9	-0.6
9.	Kemerovo, Russia in Asia, USSR	31.3	-0.4
10.	Novosibirsk, Russia in Asia, USSR	31.8	-0.1
11.	Omsk, Russia in Asia, USSR	32.0	0.0
12.	Kurgan, Russia in Asia, USSR	32.4[1]	0.2[1]
12.	Murmansk, Russia in Europe, USSR	32.4	0.2
14.	Prokopyevsk, Russia in Asia, USSR	32.7[2]	0.4[2]
15.	Biysk, Russia in Asia, USSR	32.9	0.5
15.	Petropavlovsk, Kazakhstan, USSR	32.9	0.5
17.	Zlatoust, Russia in Asia, USSR	33.1	0.6
18.	Novokuznetsk, Russia in Asia, USSR	33.3	0.7
19.	Archangel, Russia in Europe, USSR	33.4	0.8
19.	Krasnoyarsk, Russia in Asia, USSR	33.4	0.8
21.	Barnaul, Russia in Asia, USSR	34.0	1.1
22.	Tyumen, Russia in Asia, USSR	34.3	1.3
23.	Khabarovsk, Russia in Asia, USSR	34.5	1.4
23.	Tselinograd, Kazakhstan, USSR	34.5	1.4
25.	Kamensk-Uralskiy, Russia in Asia, USSR	34.7[3]	1.5[3]
25.	Kirov, Russia in Europe, USSR	34.7	1.5
25.	Sverdlovsk, Russia in Asia, USSR	34.7	1.5
28.	Anchorage, Alaska, USA	35.2	1.8
28.	Chelyabinsk, Russia in Asia, USSR	35.2	1.8
28.	Kopeysk, Russia in Asia, USSR	35.2[4]	1.8[4]
28.	Perm, Russia in Europe, USSR	35.2	1.8
32.	Pavlodar, Kazakhstan, USSR	35.4	1.9
32.	Petropavlovsk-Kamchatskiy, Russia in Asia, USSR	35.4	1.9
32.	Saskatoon, Saskatchewan, Canada	35.4	1.9
35.	Izhevsk, Russia in Europe, USSR	35.8	2.1
36.	Petrozavodsk, Russia in Europe, USSR	36.0	2.2
37.	Karaganda, Kazakhstan, USSR	36.1	2.3
37.	Regina, Saskatchewan, Canada	36.1	2.3
37.	Temir-Tau, Kazakhstan, USSR	36.1[5]	2.3[5]
37.	Yoshkar-Ola, Russia in Europe, USSR	36.1	2.3
41.	Vologda, Russia in Europe, USSR	36.3	2.4
42.	Winnipeg, Manitoba, Canada	36.6	2.6
43.	Cherepovets, Russia in Europe, USSR	36.7	2.6
43.	Sterlitamak, Russia in Europe, USSR	36.7	2.6
43.	Ufa, Russia in Europe, USSR	36.7	2.6
46.	Edmonton, Alberta, Canada	36.8	2.7
46.	Thunder Bay, Ontario, Canada	36.8	2.7
48.	Kostroma, Russia in Europe, USSR	36.9	2.7
48.	Tsitsihar, Heilungkiang, China	36.9	2.7
48.	Yaroslavl, Russia in Europe, USSR	36.9[6]	2.7[6]
51.	Mutankiang, Heilungkiang, China	37.0	2.8
52.	Cheboksary, Russia in Europe, USSR	37.2	2.9
53.	Orsk, Russia in Europe, USSR	37.4	3.0
53.	Ust-Kamenogorsk, Kazakhstan, USSR	37.4	3.0
55.	Dzerzhinsk, Russia in Europe, USSR	37.6[7]	3.1[7]
55.	Gorkiy, Russia in Europe, USSR	37.6	3.1
57.	Chicoutimi, Quebec, Canada	37.8	3.2
57.	Semipalatinsk, Kazakhstan, USSR	37.8	3.2
57.	Ulyanovsk, Russia in Europe, USSR	37.8	3.2
60.	Duluth, Minnesota, USA	37.9	3.3
60.	Harbin, Heilungkiang, China	37.9	3.3
60.	Ivanovo, Russia in Europe, USSR	37.9	3.3
60.	Vladimir, Russia in Europe, USSR	37.9	3.3
64.	Kiamusze, Heilungkiang, China	38.1	3.4
65.	Aktyubinsk, Kazakhstan, USSR	38.5	3.6
65.	Kaluga, Russia in Europe, USSR	38.5	3.6
65.	Kazan, Russia in Europe, USSR	38.5	3.6
68.	Saransk, Russia in Europe, USSR	38.7	3.7

[1] Data for Staro-Sidorovo, nr Kurgan.

[2] Data for Kiselevsk, nr Prokopyevsk.

[3] Data for Sverdlovsk, nr Kamensk-Uralskiy.

[4] Data for Chelyabinsk, nr Kopeysk.

[5] Data for Karaganda, nr Temir-Tau.

[6] Data for Kostroma, nr Yaroslavl.

[7] Data for Gorkiy, nr Dzerzhinsk.

Rank	City and Location	Average Temperature	
		(°F)	(°C)
69.	Kisi, Heilungkiang, China	38.8	3.8
69.	Kuybyshev, Russia in Europe, USSR	38.8	3.8
69.	Tampere, Finland	38.8	3.8
72.	Calgary, Alberta, Canada	39.0	3.9
72.	Kalinin, Russia in Europe, USSR	39.0	3.9
72.	Novgorod, Russia in Europe, USSR	39.0	3.9
72.	Orenburg, Russia in Europe, USSR	39.0	3.9
72.	Penza, Russia in Europe, USSR	39.0	3.9
72.	Sudbury, Ontario, Canada	39.0	3.9
72.	Yinchwan, Ningsia, China	39.0	3.9
79.	Smolensk, Russia in Europe, USSR	39.2	4.0
79.	Vladivostok, Russia in Asia, USSR	39.2	4.0
81.	Grand Forks, North Dakota, USA	39.4	4.1
82.	Moscow, Russia in Europe, USSR	39.6	4.2
82.	Podolsk, Russia in Europe, USSR	39.6[1]	4.2[1]
84.	Leningrad, Russia in Europe, USSR	39.7	4.3
84.	Tula, Russia in Europe, USSR	39.7	4.3
86.	Vitebsk, White Russia, USSR	39.8[2]	4.3[2]
87.	Kirin, Kirin, China	39.9	4.4
87.	Syzran, Russia in Europe, USSR	39.9	4.4
87.	Tolyatti, Russia in Europe, USSR	39.9	4.4
90.	Trois-Rivieres, Quebec, Canada	40	4.4
90.	Turku, Finland	40	4.4

1 Data for Moscow, nr Podolsk.

2 Data for Novoye Korolevo, nr Vitebsk.

32
Cities with Most Precipitation

Contents

Rank.
Conventional name of city, and subdivision and country in which located.
Average annual precipitation (i.e., rainfall plus the rain equivalent of snowfall), in inches and in millimeters.

Arrangement

By precipitation.

Coverage

All cities listed in Tabular Gazetteer 2 of this work with annual precipitation averaging at least 70 in (1778 mm).

Entries

92.

TABLE 32. CITIES WITH MOST PRECIPITATION

Rank	City and Location	Annual Precipitation	
		(in)	(mm)
1.	Monrovia, Liberia	202.01	5131
2.	Padang, Sumatra I, Indonesia	187.56	4764
3.	Conakry, Guinea	170.91	4341
4.	Bogor, Java I, Indonesia	166.34	4225
5.	Douala, Cameroon	161.77	4109
6.	Freetown, Sierra Leone	141.14	3585
7.	Hilo, Hawaii, USA	136.62	3470
8.	Mangalore, Mysore, India	133.78	3398
9.	Manado, Celebes I, Indonesia	131.97	3352
10.	Makasar, Celebes I, Indonesia	125.51	3188
11.	Calicut, Kerala, India	125.12	3178
12.	Suva, Fiji	124.41	3160
13.	Ernakulam, Kerala, India	120.55	3062
14.	Pontianak, Borneo I, Indonesia	120.31	3056
15.	Keelung, Taiwan	119.80	3043
16.	Hue, South Vietnam	118.78	3017
17.	Apia, Western Samoa	115.28	2928
18.	Bandjermasin, Borneo I, Indonesia	108.46	2755
19.	George Town, West Malaysia, Malaysia	107.7	2736
20.	Chittagong, Bangladesh	107.63	2734
21.	Rangoon, Burma	104.45	2653
22.	Libreville, Gabon	104.25	2648
23.	Kochi, Shikoku I, Japan	104.17	2646
24.	Ipoh, West Malaysia, Malaysia	101.60	2581
25.	Miyazaki, Kyushu I, Japan	101.22	2571
26.	Kanazawa, Honshu I, Japan	100.75	2559
27.	Kuala Lumpur, West Malaysia, Malaysia	96.1	2441
28.	Shizuoka, Honshu I, Japan	95.51	2426
29.	Singapore, Singapore	95.08	2415
30.	Colombo, Ceylon	94.3	2395
30.	Port Harcourt, Nigeria	94.3	2395
32.	Palembang, Sumatra I, Indonesia	93.74	2381
33.	Toyama, Honshu I, Japan	93.31	2370
34.	Kalyan, Maharashtra, India	92.72	2355
35.	Fukui, Honshu I, Japan	92.64	2353
36.	Kagoshima, Kyushu I, Japan	92.01	2337
37.	Quezon City, Luzon I, Philippines	91.62	2327
38.	Paramaribo, Surinam	88.90	2258
39.	Georgetown, Guyana	87.44	2221
40.	Belem, Para, Brazil	86.10	2187
41.	Bacolod, Negros I, Philippines	85.55	2173
42.	Surakarta, Java I, Indonesia	85.24	2165
43.	Bandung, Java I, Indonesia	85.00	2159
44.	Hong Kong, Hong Kong	84.92	2157
44.	Manila, Luzon I, Philippines	84.92	2157
46.	Dehra Dun, Uttar Pradesh, India	84.58	2149
47.	Abidjan, Ivory Coast	84.41	2144
48.	Iloilo, Panay I, Philippines	83.54	2122
48.	Petropolis, Rio de Janeiro, Brazil	83.54	2122
50.	Orizaba, Veracruz, Mexico	83.27	2115
51.	Naha, Ryukyu Islands	82.80	2103
52.	Taipei, Taiwan	82.68	2100
53.	Numazu, Honshu I, Japan	82.44	2094
54.	Santos, Sao Paulo, Brazil	82.05	2084
55.	Da Nang, South Vietnam	81.61	2073
56.	Manizales, Colombia	80.91	2055
57.	Pereira, Colombia	80.87	2054
58.	Ibague, Colombia	80.83	2053
59.	Semarang, Java I, Indonesia	80.04	2033
60.	Kandy, Ceylon	79.7	2024
61.	Hamamatsu, Honshu I, Japan	79.45	2018
62.	Jogjakarta, Java I, Indonesia	78.82	2002
63.	Kweilin, Kwangsi, China	77.40	1966
63.	Sasebo, Kyushu I, Japan	77.40	1966
65.	Bergen, Norway	77.09	1958
65.	Medan, Sumatra I, Indonesia	77.09	1958
67.	Nagasaki, Kyushu I, Japan	76.50	1943
68.	Davao, Mindanao I, Philippines	76.47	1942
69.	Yokosuka, Honshu I, Japan	76.34	1939
70.	Saigon, South Vietnam	76.26	1937
70.	San Jose, Costa Rica	76.26	1937
72.	Salvador, Bahia, Brazil	76.06	1932
73.	Kaohsiung, Taiwan	75.71	1923
74.	Villahermosa, Tabasco, Mexico	75.51	1918
75.	Tjirebon, Java I, Indonesia	74.96	1904
76.	Sao Luis, Maranhao, Brazil	74.05	1881
77.	Narayanganj, Bangladesh	73.79	1874
78.	Kumamoto, Kyushu I, Japan	73.58	1869
79.	Dacca, Bangladesh	73.35	1863
80.	Fort-de-France, Martinique	73.19	1859
81.	Gifu, Honshu I, Japan	73.11	1857
82.	Vientiane, Laos	72.83	1850
83.	Papeete, French Polynesia	72.60	1844
84.	Niigata, Honshu I, Japan	72.48	1841
85.	Tainan, Taiwan	72.40	1839
86.	Trivandrum, Kerala, India	71.34	1812
87.	Manaus, Amazonas, Brazil	71.3	1811
88.	Hanoi, North Vietnam	71.22	1809
89.	Bombay, Maharashtra, India	71.06	1805
90.	San Salvador, El Salvador	70.98	1803
91.	Akita, Honshu I, Japan	70.43	1789
92.	Taichung, Taiwan	70.24	1784

33
Cities with Least Precipitation

Contents

Rank.
Conventional name of city, and subdivision and country in which located.
Average annual precipitation (i.e., rainfall plus the rain equivalent of snowfall), in inches and in millimeters.

Arrangement

By precipitation, inversely.

Coverage

All cities listed in Tabular Gazetteer 2 of this work with annual precipitation averaging 12 in (305 mm) or less.

Entries

77.

TABLE 33. CITIES WITH LEAST PRECIPITATION

Rank	City and Location	Annual Precipitation (in)	(mm)	Rank	City and Location	Annual Precipitation (in)	(mm)
1.	Luxor, Egypt	0.02	0.5	41.	Herat, Afghanistan	7.91	201
2.	Aswan, Egypt	0.04	1	42.	Ulan-Ude, Russia in Asia, USSR	7.95	202
3.	Asyut, Egypt	0.20	5	43.	Yinchwan, Ningsia, China	7.99	203
4.	Suez, Egypt	0.87	22	44.	Albuquerque, New Mexico, USA	8.13	206
5.	Giza, Egypt	1.10	28	44.	Karachi, Pakistan	8.13	206
6.	Cairo, Egypt	1.14	29	46.	Meshed, Iran	8.23	209
7.	Zagazig, Egypt	1.18	30	47.	Ciudad Obregon, Sonora, Mexico	8.31	211
8.	Lima, Peru	1.22	31	48.	Ashkhabad, Turkmenia, USSR	8.70	221
9.	Aden, Southern Yemen	1.51	38	49.	Timbuktu, Mali	8.86	225
10.	Tanta, Egypt	1.65	42	50.	Damascus, Syria	8.98	228
11.	Mansurah, Egypt	2.13	54	51.	Ulan-Bator, Mongolia	9.02	229
12.	Medina, Hejaz, Saudi Arabia	2.44	62	52.	Almeria, Andalucia, Spain	9.09	231
13.	Manama, Bahrain	2.9	74	53.	Urumtsi, Sinkiang, China	9.17	233
14.	Mexicali, Baja California, Mexico	2.99	76	54.	Baku, Azerbaijan, USSR	9.37	238
15.	Kashgar, Sinkiang, China	3.07	78	55.	Kirovabad, Azerbaijan, USSR	9.76	248
16.	Riyadh, Nejd, Saudi Arabia	3.14	80	55.	Marrakesh, Morocco	9.76	248
17.	Jidda, Hejaz, Saudi Arabia	3.15	80	57.	Long Beach, California, USA	9.84	250
18.	Port Said, Egypt	3.27	83	57.	Teheran, Iran	9.84	250
19.	Las Vegas, Nevada, USA	3.90	99	59.	Santa Cruz de Tenerife, (Canary Islands), Spain	9.88	251
20.	Arequipa, Peru	4.31	109	60.	Pavlodar, Kazakhstan, USSR	10.00	254
21.	Isfahan, Iran	4.61	117	61.	San Diego, California, USA	10.39	264
22.	Kuwait, Kuwait	4.69	119	62.	Bengasi, Cyrenaica, Libya	10.47	266
23.	Baghdad, Iraq	6.14	156	63.	Semipalatinsk, Kazakhstan, USSR	10.51	267
24.	Basra, Iraq	6.34	161	64.	Amman, Jordan	10.75	273
25.	Bakersfield, California, USA	6.36	162	65.	Pocatello, Idaho, USA	10.85	276
26.	Torreon, Coahuila, Mexico	6.50	165	66.	Tucson, Arizona, USA	11.00	279
27.	Multan, Pakistan	6.6	168	67.	Riverside, California, USA	11.04	280
28.	Abadan, Iran	6.65	169	68.	Fresno, California, USA	11.14	283
29.	Astrakhan, Russia in Europe, USSR	6.89	175	68.	Tabriz, Iran	11.14	283
30	Kandahar, Afghanistan	7.0	178	70.	Dzhambul, Kazakhstan, USSR	11.30	287
31.	Khartoum, Sudan	7.05	179	71.	Boise City, Idaho, USA	11.43	290
32.	Reno, Nevada, USA	7.15	182	72.	Hama, Syria	11.77	299
33.	Hyderabad, Pakistan	7.20	183	73.	Casper, Wyoming, USA	11.80	300
33.	Phoenix, Arizona, USA	7.20	183	74.	Pueblo, Colorado, USA	11.84	301
35.	Ciudad Juarez, Chihuahua, Mexico	7.36	187	75.	Bratsk, Russia in Asia, USSR	11.85	301
36.	Alexandria, Egypt	7.40	188	75.	Murcia, Murcia, Spain	11.85	301
37.	Ahvaz, Iran	7.48	190	77.	Paotow, Inner Mongolia, China	11.97	304
38.	Mendoza, Mendoza, Argentina	7.76	197				
38.	Sfax, Tunisia	7.76	197				
40.	El Paso, Texas, USA	7.89	200				

34 Highest Buildings

Contents

Conventional and alternate names of building.
City, and subdivision and country in which located.
Year of completion.
Height above street level, in feet and meters.

Arrangement

By height.

Coverage

Above * * *, all buildings standing or under construction, excluding observation and television towers, with a height of at least 600 ft (183 m).

Below * * *, other well-known high buildings.

Entries

113.

Figure 20. Twin towers of the World Trade Center, New York, the highest completed building on earth. (Credit: New York Convention and Visitors Bureau, Inc.)

Figure 21. Architect's rendering of the Sears Tower, Chicago. Scheduled for completion in 1974, it will surpass New York's World Trade Center in height. (Credit: Skidmore, Owings & Merrill, Chicago.)

TABLE 34. HIGHEST BUILDINGS

Building	Location	Year Completed[1]	Height (ft)	Height (m)
Sears Tower	Chicago, Illinois, USA	UC (1974?)	1450	442
World Trade Center	New York, New York, USA	1972	1350[2]	411[2]
Empire State	New York, New York, USA	1931	1250	381
Standard Oil (Indiana)	Chicago, Illinois, USA	1971	1136	346
John Hancock Center	Chicago, Illinois, USA	1967	1107	337
Chrysler	New York, New York, USA	1930	1046	319
Eiffel Tower (off Tour Eiffel)[3]	Paris, Region Parisienne, France	1889	984	300
60 Wall Tower	New York, New York, USA	1934	950	290
Dallas Tower	Dallas, Texas, USA	UC	913	278
Bank of Manhattan (alt 40 Wall Tower)	New York, New York, USA	1930	900	274
Transamerica	San Francisco, California, USA	UC	853	260
First National Bank	Chicago, Illinois, USA	1969	850	259
RCA	New York, New York, USA	1933	850	259
United States Steel	Pittsburgh, Pennsylvania, USA	1969	841	256
Chase Manhattan	New York, New York, USA	1960	813	248
Pan Am	New York, New York, USA	1961	808	246
Woolworth	New York, New York, USA	1913	792	241
John Hancock Tower	Boston, Massachusetts, USA	1970	790	241
Canadian Imperial Bank of Commerce	Toronto, Ontario, Canada	1971	784	239
Bank of America	San Francisco, California, USA	1969	778	237
IDS Center	Minneapolis, Minnesota, USA	1971	772	235
Palace of Culture and Science (off Palac Kultury i Nauki)	Warsaw, Poland	1955	768	234
One Penn Plaza	New York, New York, USA	1972	766	233
Prudential Tower	Boston, Massachusetts, USA	1964	750	229
United States Steel (alt One Liberty Plaza)	New York, New York, USA	1971	743	226
Farmers Loan and Trust (alt 20 Exchange Place)	New York, New York, USA	1931	741	226
Toronto-Dominion Bank Tower	Toronto, Ontario, Canada	1967	740	226
Esso (alt 1251 Avenue of the Americas)	New York, New York, USA	1971	735	224
One Astor Place	New York, New York, USA	1971	731	223
Nine West 57th Street	New York, New York, USA	1972	725	221
Moscow M. V. Lomonosov State University	Moscow, Russia, USSR	1953	720	219
One Shell Plaza	Houston, Texas, USA	1971	714	218
Embarcadero Center Number 2	San Francisco, California, USA	1970	710	216
Terminal Tower	Cleveland, Ohio, USA	1930	708	216
Union Carbide	New York, New York, USA	1960	707	215
General Motors	New York, New York, USA	1967	705	215
Metropolitan Life	New York, New York, USA	1909	700	213
500 Fifth Avenue	New York, New York, USA	1930	697	212
IBM	Chicago, Illinois, USA	1971	695	212
Chemical Bank New York Trust	New York, New York, USA	1964	687	209
Chanin	New York, New York, USA	1928	680	207
55 Water Street	New York, New York, USA	1972	680	207
Tour Maine-Montparnasse	Paris, Region Parisienne, France	1972	680	207
Gulf and Western	New York, New York, USA	1969	679	207
Marine Midland	New York, New York, USA	1966	677	206

[1] UC, under construction.

[2] Two buildings of equal height.

[3] Primarily an observation tower.

Building	Location	Year Completed	Height (ft)	Height (m)
McGraw-Hill (alt 1221 Avenue of the Americas)	New York, New York, USA	1972	674	205
Lincoln	New York, New York, USA	1929	673	205
1633 Broadway	New York, New York, USA	1971	670	204
Atlantic Richfield Plaza	Los Angeles, California, USA	1971	667[1]	203[1]
Civic Center (alt City Hall)	Chicago, Illinois, USA	1965	662	202
Carlton Centre Tower	Johannesburg, Transvaal, South Africa	1971	656	200
Ukraina Hotel	Moscow, Russia, USSR	bef 1961	650	198
American Tobacco	New York, New York, USA	1967	648	198
Lake Point Tower	Chicago, Illinois, USA	1967	645	197
Irving Trust	New York, New York, USA	1930	640	195
345 Park Avenue	New York, New York, USA	1968	634	193
Gateway Arch	Saint Louis, Missouri, USA	1965	630	192
Home Insurance Company	New York, New York, USA	1966	630	192
One New York Plaza	New York, New York, USA	1969	630	192
1114 Avenue of the Americas (alt Monsanto)	New York, New York, USA	1972	630	192
Burlington House	New York, New York, USA	1969	625	190
First National Bank	Dallas, Texas, USA	1965	625	190
Waldorf-Astoria Hotel	New York, New York, USA	1931	625	190
Stock Exchange (alt Bourse)	Montreal, Quebec, Canada	1965	624	190
Canadian Imperial Bank of Commerce (alt Banque Canadienne Imperiale de Commerce)	Montreal, Quebec, Canada	1962	620	189
Crocker-Citizens Plaza	Los Angeles, California, USA	1967	620	189
Ten East 40th Street	New York, New York, USA	1928	620	189
General Electric	New York, New York, USA	1939	616	188
Royal Bank of Canada (alt Banque Royale du Canada)	Montreal, Quebec, Canada	1962	616	188
New York Life	New York, New York, USA	1928	615	187
Celanese (alt 1205 Avenue of the Americas)	New York, New York, USA	1972	611	186
Development Bank of Singapore (alt DBS)	Singapore, Singapore	UC (1973?)	610	186
Penney	New York, New York, USA	1964	609	186
Seattle-First National Bank	Seattle, Washington, USA	1969	609	186
Qantas	Sydney, New South Wales, Australia	1971	607	185
Humble Oil	Houston, Texas, USA	1961	606	185
Board of Trade	Chicago, Illinois, USA	1930	605	184
Australia Square Tower	Sydney, New South Wales, Australia	1968	602	183
Boston Company	Boston, Massachusetts, USA	1970	601	183
First Wisconsin Center and Office Tower	Milwaukee, Wisconsin, USA	UC	601	183
Prudential	Chicago, Illinois, USA	1954	601	183
Columbia Plaza	Denver, Colorado, USA	1970	600	183
Royal Trust Tower	Toronto, Ontario, Canada	1969	600	183
One Hammarskjold Plaza	New York, New York, USA	1972	(50 stories)	
(Edificio) Italia	Sao Paulo, Sao Paulo, Brazil	1966	(45 stories)	
	* * *			
Torre Latino Americana	Mexico, Distrito Federal, Mexico	1950	597	182
Marina City Apartments	Chicago, Illinois, USA	1962	587[1]	179[1]
Connaught Centre	Hong Kong, Hong Kong	UC (1973?)	585	178
Post Office Tower	London, England, UK	1966	580	177

[1] Two buildings of equal height.

Building	Location	Year Completed	Height (ft)	(m)
Keio Plaza Hotel	Tokyo, Honshu I, Japan	1971	558	170
Washington Monument	Washington, District of Columbia, USA	1884	555	169
Vehicle Assembly	Cape Kennedy, Florida, USA	1966	552	168
United Nations Secretariat	New York, New York, USA	1950	550	168
Mole Antonelliana	Turin, Piemonte, Italy	1863	550	167
City Hall	Philadelphia, Pennsylvania, USA	1901	548	167
Torre de Madrid	Madrid, Castilla la Nueva. Spain	1959	541	165
Cathedral of Learning (alt University of Pittsburgh)	Pittsburgh, Pennsylvania, USA	1956	535	163
Cathedral (off Munster)	Ulm, Baden-Wurttemberg, West Germany	1890	529	161
Banco do Estado de Sao Paulo	Sao Paulo, Sao Paulo, Brazil	1946	528	161
Seagram	New York, New York, USA	1958	525	160
Cathedral (off Dom Sankt Peter)	Cologne, Nordrhein-Westfalen, West Germany	1880	515	157
Cathedrale Notre-Dame	Rouen, Haute-Normandie, France	1530	512	156
World Trade Center	Tokyo, Honshu I, Japan	1969	499	152
CBS	New York, New York, USA	1965	491	150
Kasumigaseki	Tokyo, Honshu I, Japan	1968	482	147
Tribune Tower	Chicago, Illinois, USA	1925	462	141
Pyramid of Khufu (alt Pyramid of Cheops)	Giza, Egypt	2568 BC?	450	137
Saint Peter's Basilica (off Basilica di San Pietro)	Vatican City	1615	435	132
Bayer A. G.	Leverkusen, Nordrhein-Westfalen, West Germany	1962	434	132
Pirelli	Milan, Lombardia, Italy	1960	414	126
Shwedagon Pagoda	Rangoon, Burma	1774	326	99
Statue of Liberty	New York, New York, USA	1886	305	93
Leaning Tower (alt Torre Pendente; off Campanile)	Pisa, Toscana, Italy	1350	179	54

35
Longest Bridges (Span)

Contents

Conventional and alternate names of bridge.
Body of water spanned, and subdivision and country in which located.
Type of bridge.
Use to which bridge is put.
Year of completion.
Longest span, in feet and meters.

Arrangement

By length of span.

Coverage

All bridges standing or under construction with spans of at least the following lengths:

- Suspension bridges – 1200 ft (366 m)
- Cantilever bridges – 1100 ft (335 m)
- Cable-stayed girder bridges – 900 ft (274 m)
- Continuous truss bridges – 900 ft (274 m)
- Steel arch bridges – 900 ft (274 m)
- Concrete arch bridges – 750 ft (229 m)
- Continuous plate and box girder bridges – 750 ft (229 m)

Additionally, the longest span bridge is listed for each of the following types: bascule, simple truss, swing span, and vertical lift.

Entries

106.

Figure 22. Verrazano-Narrows Bridge, New York. The span, suspended across New York Bay between Brooklyn and Staten Island, is the longest ever erected. (Credit: New York Convention and Visitors Bureau, Inc.)

TABLE 35. LONGEST BRIDGES (SPAN)

Bridge	Body of Water and Location	Type[1]	Use[2]	Year Completed[3]	Span (ft)	Span (m)
Verrazano-Narrows	New York B of Atlantic O, New York, USA	S	H	1964	4260	1298
Golden Gate	San Francisco B of Pacific O, California, USA	S	H	1937	4200	1280
Mackinac	Straits of Mackinac, Michigan, USA	S	H	1957	3800	1158
Bosporus	Bosporus Strait, Turkey	S	H	UC (1973?)	3524	1074
George Washington	Hudson R, New Jersey-New York, USA	S	H	1931	3500	1067
Salazar	Tagus R, Portugal	S	H;RR	1966	3323	1013
Forth Road	Forth R, Scotland, UK	S	H	1964	3300	1006
Severn	Severn R, England-Wales, UK	S	H	1966	3240	988
Tacoma Narrows II	Puget Sound of Pacific O, Washington, USA	S	H	1952	2800	853
Kammon	Kammon Strait, Honshu I-Kyushu I, Japan	S	H	UC (1973?)	2350	716
Angostura	Orinoco R, Venezuela	S	H	1967	2336	712
San Francisco-Oakland Bay (alt Transbay)	San Francisco B of Pacific O, California, USA	S	H;RT	1936	2310[4]	704[4]
Bronx-Whitestone	East R, New York, USA	S	H	1939	2300	701
Frontenac (alt Quebec Road)	Saint Lawrence R, Quebec, Canada	S	H	1970	2190	668
Delaware Memorial I	Delaware R, Delaware-New Jersey, USA	S	H	1951	2150	655
Delaware Memorial II	Delaware R, Delaware-New Jersey, USA	S	H	1968	2150	655
Seaway Skyway	Saint Lawrence R, Canada-USA	S	H	1960	2150	655
Walt Whitman	Delaware R, New Jersey-Pennsylvania, USA	S	H	1957	2000	610
Tancarville	Seine R, Haute-Normandie, France	S	H	1959	1995	608
Little Belt (off Lillebaelt)	Little Belt Strait, Denmark	S	H	1969	1969	600
Ambassador	Detroit R, Canada-USA	S	H	1929	1850	564
Quebec	Saint Lawrence R, Quebec, Canada	C	H; RR[5]	1918	1800	549
Throgs Neck	Long Island Sound of Atlantic O, New York, USA	S	H	1961	1800	549
Benjamin Franklin	Delaware R, New Jersey-Pennsylvania, USA	S	H;RT	1926	1750	533
Skjomen	Skjomen Fjord of Norwegian Sea, Norway	S	H	1971	1723	525
Forth	Forth R, Scotland, UK	C	RR	1890	1710[6]	521[6]
Bayonne (alt Kill van Kull)	Kill van Kull, New Jersey-New York, USA	SA	H	1931	1652	504

[1] B, bascule; C, cantilever; CA, concrete arch; CPBG, continuous plate and box girder; CSG, cable-stayed girder; CT, continuous truss; S, suspension; SA, steel arch; SS, swing span; ST, simple truss; VL, vertical lift.

[2] H, highway; RR, railroad; RT, rapid transit.

[3] UC, under construction.

[4] Two spans of this length, and two additional spans each of 1160 ft, 354 m.

[5] Railroad traffic only since opening of Frontenac Bridge in 1970.

[6] Two spans of this length.

Bridge	Body of Water and Location	Type[1]	Use[2]	Year Completed[3]	Span (ft)	Span (m)
Sydney Harbour	Sydney Harbor of Pacific O, New South Wales, Australia	SA	H; RR	1932	1650	503
Chester	Delaware R, New Jersey–Pennsylvania, USA	C	H	UC (1973?)	1644	501
Kleve-Emmerich	Rhine R, Nordrhein-Westfalen, West Germany	S	H	1965	1640	500
Bear Mountain	Hudson R, New York, USA	S	H	1924	1632	497
Chesapeake Bay I (alt William Preston Lane Memorial)	Chesapeake B of Atlantic O, Maryland, USA	S	H	1952	1600	488
Chesapeake Bay II	Chesapeake B of Atlantic O, Maryland, USA	S	H	UC (1973?)	1600	488
Newport	Narragansett B of Atlantic O, Rhode Island, USA	S	H	1969	1600	488
Williamsburg	East R, New York, USA	S	H; RT	1903	1600	488
Brooklyn	East R, New York, USA	S	H; RT	1883	1595	486
Greater New Orleans	Mississippi R, Louisiana, USA	C	H	1958	1575	480
Lions Gate	Burrard Inlet of Strait of Georgia, British Columbia, Canada	S	H	1939	1550	472
Howrah	Hooghly R, West Bengal, India	C	H; RT	1943	1500	457
Mid-Hudson (alt Poughkeepsie)	Hudson R, New York, USA	S	H	1930	1500	457
Vincent Thomas (alt San Pedro–Terminal Island)	San Pedro B of Pacific O, California, USA	S	H	1964	1500	457
Manhattan	East R, New York, USA	S	H; RT	1909	1470	448
Angus L. MacDonald (alt Halifax Harbour)	Halifax Harbor of Atlantic O, Nova Scotia, Canada	S	H	1955	1447	441
A. Murray MacKay	Halifax Harbor of Atlantic O, Nova Scotia, Canada	S	H	1970	1400	427
San Francisco–Oakland Bay (alt Transbay)	San Francisco B of Pacific O, California, USA	C	H; RT	1936	1400	427
Triborough	East R, New York, USA	S	H	1936	1380	421
Alvsborg	Gota R, Sweden	S	H	1966	1368	417
Aquitaine	Garonne R, Aquitaine, France	S	H	1967	1293	394
Zdakov (alt Orlik)	Vltava R, Bohemia, Czechoslovakia	SA	H	1967	1247	380
Cologne–Rodenkirchen (off Koln–Rodenkirchen)	Rhine R, Nordrhein-Westfalen, West Germany	S	H	1954	1240	378
Baton Rouge	Mississippi R, Louisiana, USA	C	H	1969	1235	376
Astoria	Columbia R, Oregon–Washington, USA	CT	H	1966	1232	376
Tappan Zee (alt Nyack-Tarrytown)	Hudson R, New York, USA	C	H	1955	1212	369
Saint Johns	Willamette R, Oregon, USA	S	H	1931	1207	368
Wakato	Dokai B of Korea Strait, Kyushu I, Japan	S	H	1962	1204	367
Longview	Columbia R, Oregon–Washington, USA	C	H	1930	1200	366
Mount Hope	Mount Hope B of Atlantic O, Rhode Island, USA	S	H	1929	1200	366

[1] B, bascule; C, cantilever; CA, concrete arch; CPBG, continuous plate and box girder; CSG, cable-stayed girder; CT continuous truss; S, suspension; SA, steel arch; SS, swing span; ST,simple truss; VL, vertical lift.

[2] H, highway; RR, railroad; RT, rapid transit.

[3] UC, under construction.

Bridge	Body of Water and Location	Type[1]	Use[2]	Year Completed[3]	Span (ft)	Span (m)
Port Mann	Fraser R, British Columbia, Canada	SA	H	1964	1200	366
Queensboro	East R, New York, USA	C	H; RT	1909	1182[4]	360[4]
Duisburg-Neuenkamp	Rhine R, Nordrhein-Westfalen, West Germany	CSG	H	1970	1148	350
Thatcher Ferry	Panama Canal, Canal Zone	SA	H	1962	1128	344
Mesopotamia	Parana R, Chaco-Corrientes, Argentina	CSG	H	UC	1116	340
Hercilio Luz (alt Florianopolis)	Strait between Norte B and Sul B, Santa Catarina, Brazil	S	H; RT	1926	1114	340
West Gate	Yarra R, Victoria, Australia	CSG	H	UC[5]	1102	336
Carquinez I	Carquinez Strait, California, USA	C	H	1927	1100[6]	335[6]
Carquinez II	Carquinez Strait, California, USA	C	H	1958	1100[6]	335[6]
Lagiolette (alt Trois-Rivieres)	Saint Lawrence R, Quebec, Canada	SA	H	1967	1100	335
Second Narrows	Burrard Inlet of Strait of Georgia, British Columbia, Canada	C	H	1960	1100	335
Jacques Cartier (alt Montreal Harbour)	Saint Lawrence R, Quebec, Canada	C	H; RR	1930	1097	334
Runcorn-Widnes	Mersey R, England, UK	SA	H	1961	1082	330
Birchenough	Sabi R, Rhodesia	SA	H	1935	1080	329
Richmond-San Rafael	San Francisco B of Pacific O, California, USA	C	H	1957	1070[6]	326[6]
Cincinnati-Covington	Ohio R, Kentucky-Ohio, USA	S	H	1867[7]	1057	322
Knie	Rhine R, Nordrhein-Westfalen, West Germany	CSG	H	1969	1050	320
Glen Canyon	Colorado R, Arizona, USA	SA	H	1959	1028	313
Wheeling	Ohio R, Ohio-West Virginia, USA	S	H	1849[8]	1010	308
Erskine	Clyde R, Scotland, UK	CSG	H	1970	1000	305
Gladesville	Parramatta R, New South Wales, Australia	CA	H	1964	1000	305
Lewiston-Queenston	Niagara R, Canada-USA	SA	H	1962	1000	305
Bratislava	Danube R, Slovakia, Czechoslovakia	CSG	H	1971	994	303
Severin	Rhine R, Nordrhein-Westfalen, West Germany	CSG	H	1959	991	302
Rio de Janeiro-Niteroi	Guanabara B of Atlantic O, Guanabara-Rio de Janeiro, Brazil	CPBG	H	1971	984	300
Temmon-Kyo	Misumi Strait, Kyushu I, Japan	CT	H	1966	984	300
Hell Gate	East R, New York, USA	SA	RR	1917	977	298
Foz do Iguacu	Parana R, Brazil-Paraguay	CA	H	1965	951	290
Mannheim-Nord	Rhine R, Baden-Wurttemberg-Rheinland-Pfalz, West Germany	CSG	H	1969	951	290
Rainbow	Niagara R, Canada-USA	SA	H	1941	950	290

[1] B, bascule; C, cantilever; CA, concrete arch; CPBG, continuous plate and box girder; CSG, cable-stayed girder; CT, continuous truss; S, suspension; SA, steel arch; SS, swing span; ST, simple truss; VL, vertical lift.

[2] H, highway; RR, railroad; RT, rapid transit.

[3] UC, under construction.

[4] A second span of 984 ft, 300 m.

[5] Completion originally scheduled for 1972 but delayed by collapse of side span in October 1970.

[6] Two spans of this length.

[7] Reconstructed in 1898.

[8] Reconstructed in 1856.

Bridge	Body of Water and Location	Type[1]	Use[2]	Year Completed[3]	Span (ft)	Span (m)
Bonn-Nord	Rhine R, Nordrhein-Westfalen, West Germany	CSG	H	1967	919	280
Leverkusen	Rhine R, Nordrhein-Westfalen, West Germany	CSG	H	1965	919	280
Tjorn	Askero Fjord of Skagerrak Strait, Sweden	SA	H	1960	912	278
Arrabida	Douro R, Portugal	CA	H	1963	885	270
Royal Gorge[4]	Arkansas R, Colorado, USA	S	H	1929	880	268
Sando	Angerman R, Sweden	CA	H	1943	866	264
Sava I	Sava R, Serbia, Yugoslavia	CPBG	H	1956	856	261
Zoo	Rhine R, Nordrhein-Westfalen, West Germany	CPBG	H	1966	850	259
Dubuque	Mississippi R, Illinois-Iowa, USA	CT	H	1943	845	258
Sava II	Sava R, Serbia, Yugoslavia	CPBG	H	1970	820	250
Sibenik	Krka R, Croatia, Yugoslavia	CA	H	1967	808	246
Saikai	Inoura Strait, Kyushu I, Japan	SA	H	1955	800	244
Fiumarella	Fiumarella R, Calabria, Italy	CA	H	1961	758	231
Bonn-Sud	Rhine R, Nordrhein-Westfalen, West Germany	CPBG	H	1971	755	230
San Mateo–Hayward II	San Francisco B of Pacific O, California, USA	CPBG	H	1967	750	229
Metropolis	Ohio R, Illinois-Kentucky, USA	ST	RR	1917	720	219
Arthur Kill	Arthur Kill, New Jersey–New York, USA	VL	RR	1959	558	170
Ferdan	Suez Canal, Egypt	SS	H; RR	1965	550	168
Sault Sainte Marie	Sault Sainte Marie Canal, Canada-USA	B	RR	1914	336	102

[1] B, bascule; C, cantilever; CA, concrete arch; CPBG, continuous plate and box girder; CSG, cable-stayed girder, CT, continuous tress; S, suspension; SA, steel arch; SS, swing span; ST, simple truss; VL, vertical lift.

[2] H, highway, RR, railroad; RT, rapid transit.

[3] UC, under construction.

[4] Height of deck above water; 1053 ft, 321 m—a record.

36
Longest Railroad, Highway, and Canal Tunnels

Contents

Conventional and alternate names of tunnel.
Subdivision and country in which located.
Use to which tunnel is put.
Year of completion.
Length from portal to portal, in miles and kilometers.

Arrangement

By length.

Coverage

Above * * *, all railroad, highway, and canal tunnels, built or under construction, with a length of at least 4.5 mi (7.24 km).

Below * * *, other such tunnels that are long and well known.

Entries

68.

Figure 23. Seikan Tunnel, which will eventually connect the two largest Japanese islands by a bore under Tsugaru Strait and thereby become the world's longest railroad tunnel: (a) site of the Honshu Island approach. (Credit: Japanese National Railways.)

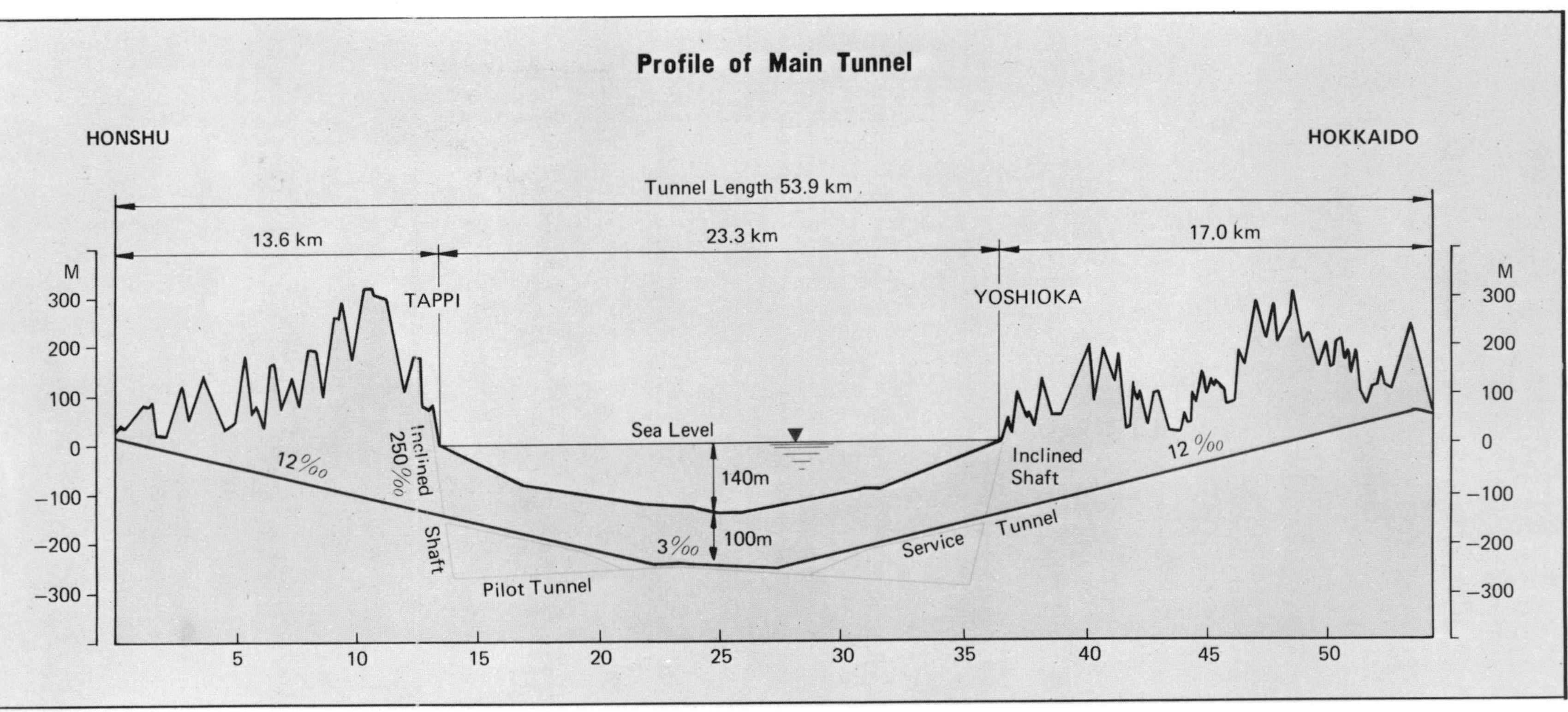

Figure 23. Seikan Tunnel (Continued) (b) profile of the main tunnel. (Credit: Japanese National Railways.)

TABLE 36. LONGEST RAILROAD, HIGHWAY, AND CANAL TUNNELS

Tunnel	Location	Use[1]	Year Completed[2]	Length (mi)	Length (km)
Seikan (underwater)	Hokkaido I–Honshu I, Japan	RR	UC (1979?)	33.49	53.9
Simplon II (alt Sempione II)	Italy-Switzerland	RR	1922	12.31	19.82
Simplon I (alt Sempione I)	Italy-Switzerland	RR	1906	12.30	19.80
New Kammon (off Shin Kammon) (underwater)	Honshu I–Kyushu I, Japan	RR	UC (1975?)	11.56	18.6
Apennine (off Appennino)	Emilia-Romagna–Toscana, Italy	RR	1934	11.49	18.51
Rokko	Honshu I, Japan	RR	1970	10.06	16.2
Gotthard (alt Saint-Gotthard)	Switzerland	RR	1882	9.32	15.00
Lotschberg	Switzerland	RR	1913	9.08	14.61
Hokuriku	Honshu I, Japan	RR	1962	8.61	13.87
Mont-Cenis (alt Frejus, Monte Cenisio)	France-Italy	RR	1871	8.48	13.66
Shimizu II	Honshu I, Japan	RR	1967	8.38	13.49
Cascade	Washington, USA	RR	1929	7.79	12.54
Mont-Blanc (alt Monte Bianco)	France-Italy	H	1965	7.25	11.67
Kubiki	Honshu I, Japan	RR	1969	7.05	11.35
Flathead	Montana, USA	RR	1970	7.0	11.26
Arlberg	Austria	RR	1884	6.37	10.25
Gran Sasso	Abruzzi e Molise, Italy	H	UC	6.21	10.0
Shimizu I	Honshu I, Japan	RR	1931	6.03	9.70
Moffat	Colorado, USA	RR	1928	5.97	9.62
Kvineshei	Norway	RR	1943	5.63	9.06
Kaimai	North I, New Zealand	RR	1970	5.49	8.84
Rimutaka	North I, New Zealand	RR	1955	5.46	8.79
Otira	South I, New Zealand	RR	1923	5.37	8.65
Ricken	Switzerland	RR	1910	5.35	8.60
Grenchenberg	Switzerland	RR	1915	5.33	8.58
Tauern	Austria	RR	1909	5.31	8.55
Ena	Honshu I, Japan	H	UC	5.30	8.53
Haegebostad	Norway	RR	1943	5.23	8.42
Ronco (alt Giovi)	Liguria, Italy	RR	1889	5.14	8.27
Hauenstein	Switzerland	RR	1916	5.05	8.13
Colle di Tenda (alt Col de Tende)	France-Italy	RR	1900[3]	5.03	8.10
Connaught	British Columbia, Canada	RR	1916	5.00	8.05
Kobe	Honshu I, Japan	RR	1970	4.97	8.0
Karawanken (alt Karavanke)	Austria-Yugoslavia	RR	1906	4.95	7.98
Tanna II	Honshu I, Japan	RR	1963	4.91	7.90
Somport	France-Spain	RR	1928	4.89	7.87
Tanna I	Honshu I, Japan	RR	1934	4.85	7.81
Ulriken	Norway	RR	1964	4.76	7.66
Hozaka	Honshu I, Japan	RR	1970	4.72	7.6
Hoosac	Massachusetts, USA	RR	1875	4.70	7.56
Monte Orso	Lazio, Italy	RR	1927	4.68	7.53
Lupacino	Italy	RR	1958	4.67	7.52
Vivola	Lazio, Italy	RR	1927	4.63	7.45
* * *					
Jungfrau	Switzerland	RR	1912	4.43	7.12

[1] C, canal; H, highway; RR, railroad.

[2] UC, under construction.

[3] Closed since World War II.

Tunnel	Location	Use[1]	Year Completed[2]	Length (mi)	Length (km)
Rove	Provence-Cote d'Azur-Corse, France	C	1927	4.42	7.11
Severn (underwater)	England-Wales, UK	RR	1886	4.36	7.01
Tauern	Austria	H	UC	4.35	7.0
San Bernardino (alt Bernhardin)	Switzerland	H	1967	4.10	6.6
Grand Saint-Bernard (alt Gran San Bernardo)	Italy-Switzerland	H	1964	3.64	5.85
Felber-Tauern	Austria	H	1967	3.48	5.6
Viella	Cataluna, Spain	H	1941	3.13	5.04
Katschberg	Austria	H	UC	3.11	5.0
Kammon (underwater)	Honshu I-Kyushu I, Japan	RR	1942	2.24	3.6
Kammon (underwater)	Honshu I-Kyushu I, Japan	H	1958	2.15	3.46
Mersey (alt Queensway) (underwater)	England, UK	H	1934	2.13	3.43
Elbe (underwater)	Hamburg-Niedersachsen, West Germany	H	UC (1973?)	1.99	3.21
Transandine Summit (off Cumbre)	Argentina-Chile	RR	1910	1.97	3.17
Pyrenees (alt Pirineos)	France-Spain	H	1970	1.87	3.01
Sasago II	Honshu I, Japan	H	1958	1.84	2.95
Rokko	Honshu I, Japan	H	1967	1.77	2.84
Brooklyn-Battery (underwater)	New York, USA	H	1950	1.73	2.78
Straight Creek	Colorado, USA	H	1971	1.70	2.74
Kuriko II	Honshu I, Japan	H	1966	1.66	2.67
Holland (underwater)	New Jersey-New York, USA	H	1927	1.62	2.61
Lincoln I (underwater)	New Jersey-New York, USA	H	1937	1.56	2.50
Lincoln III	New Jersey-New York, USA	H	1957	1.52	2.44
Baltimore Harbor (underwater)	Maryland, USA	H	1958	1.45	2.33
Lincoln II (underwater)	New Jersey-New York, USA	H	1945	1.42	2.28

[1] C, canal; H, highway; RR, railroad.

[2] UC, under construction.

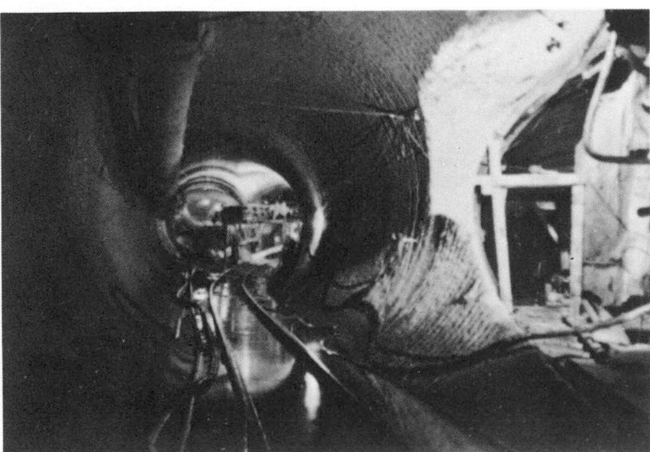

Figure 23. Seikan Tunnel (Continued) (c) site of the Hokkaido Island approach. (Credit: Japanese National Railways.)

37
Highest Dams

Contents

Rank.
Conventional and alternate names of dam.
River dammed, and subdivision and country in which located.
Type of dam.
Year of completion.
Height of dam, excluding projections, in feet and meters.
Volume of structure, in millions of cubic yards and cubic meters.

Arrangement

By height.

Coverage

Above * * *, all dams in place or under construction with a height of at least 500 ft (152 m).
Below * * *, other well-known high dams.

Rounding

Volumes are rounded to the nearest 100,000 yd^3 (m^3).

Entries

65.

Figure 24. Grande Dixence Dam, Switzerland, the highest completed dam on earth. (Credit: Swiss National Tourist Office.)

TABLE 37. HIGHEST DAMS

Rank	Dam	River and Location	Type[1]	Year Completed[2]	Height (ft)	Height (m)	Volume[3] (yd³)	Volume[3] (m³)
1.	Nurek	Vakhsh R, Tadzhikistan, USSR	R	UC	1017	310	70.8	54.1
2.	Grande Dixence	Dixence R, Switzerland	CG	1962	932	284	7.8	6.0
3.	Inguri	Inguri R, Georgia, USSR	CA	UC	892	272	5.0	3.8
4.	Vaiont	Vaiont R, Veneto, Italy	CA	1961	858	262	0.5	0.4
5.	Mica	Columbia R, British Columbia, Canada	R	UC	800	244	42.0	32.1
6.	Mauvoisin	Drance de Bagnes R, Switzerland	CA	1958	777	237	2.7	2.0
7.	Sayansk	Yenisey R, Russia, USSR	CA	UC	774	236	11.9	9.1
8.	Oroville	Feather R, California, USA	E	1968	770	235	80.3	61.4
9.	Chirkey	Sulak R, Russia, USSR	CA	UC	764	233	1.6	1.2
10.	Contra	Verzasca R, Switzerland	CA	1965	754	230	0.9	0.7
11.	Bhakra	Sutlej R, Himachal Pradesh, India	CG	1962	740	226	5.4	4.1
12.	Hoover (for Boulder)	Colorado R, Arizona-Nevada, USA	CA	1936	726	221	4.4	3.4
13.	Mratinje	Piva R, Yugoslavia	CA	UC	721	220	1.0	0.8
14.	Dworshak	North Fork Clearwater R, Idaho, USA	CG	UC	717	219	6.5	5.0
15.	Glen Canyon	Colorado R, Arizona, USA	CA	1964	710	216	4.9	3.7
16.	Toktogul	Naryn R, Kirgizia, USSR	CA	UC	705	215	3.5	2.7
17.	Daniel Johnson	Manicouagan R, Quebec, Canada	CA	1967	703	214	2.9	2.2
18.	Luzzone	Brenno di Luzzone R, Switzerland	CA	1963	682	208	1.8	1.4
19.	Auburn	North Fork American R, California, USA	CA	UC	680	207	6.0	4.6
20.	Keban	Euphrates R, Turkey	R	UC	679	207	19.6	15.0
21.	Mohammed Reza Shah Pahlavi	Dez R, Iran	CA	1963	668	204	0.6	0.5
22.	Reza Shah Kabir	Karun R, Iran	CA	UC	656	200		
22.	Tachien	Tachia R, Taiwan	CA	UC	656	200	0.9	0.7
24.	Almendra (alt Vallarino)	Tormes R, Leon, Spain	CA	UC	650	198	3.3	2.5
25.	Bullard's Bar	North Yuba R, California, USA	CA	1968	635	194	2.7	2.1
26.	Melones	Stanislaus R, California, USA	R	1968	625	190	16.0	12.2
27.	Kurobe Number 4	Kurobe R, Honshu I, Japan	CA	1964	610	186	1.8	1.4
28.	Kolnbrein	Malta (Bach) Creek, Austria	CA	UC	607	185	1.8	1.4
29.	Mossyrock	Cowlitz R, Washington, USA	CA	1969	605	184	1.2	0.9
30.	Shasta	Sacramento R, California, USA	CG	1945	602	183	8.7	6.7
31.	W. A. C. Bennett	Peace R, British Columbia, Canada	E	1967	600	183	56.7	43.3
32.	Amir Kabir	Karaj R, Iran	CA	1962	591	180	0.9	0.7
32.	Emosson	Barberine R, Switzerland	CA	UC	591	180	1.4	1.1
32.	Grande Maison	Eau d'Olle (Ruisseau) Creek, Rhone-Alpes, France	E	UC	591	180	24.9	19.0
32.	Tignes	Isere R, Rhone-Alpes, France	CA	1952	591	180	0.8	0.6
36.	Don Pedro	Tuolumne R, California, USA	R	UC	585	178	16.8	12.8
37.	Alpe Gera	Cormor R, Friuli-Venezia Giulia, Italy	CG	1965	584	178	2.3	1.7
38.	Hungry Horse	South Fork Flathead R, Montana, USA	CA	1953	564	172	3.1	2.4
39.	Idikki	Periyar R, Kerala, India	CA	UC	560	171	0.6	0.5

[1] A, arch; C, concrete; E, earth; G, gravity; R, rock.

[2] UC, under construction.

[3] In millions of cubic yards and cubic meters.

Rank	Dam	River and Location	Type[1]	Year Completed[2]	Height (ft)	Height (m)	Volume[3] (yd³)	Volume[3] (m³)
40.	Charvak	Chirchik R, Uzbekistan, USSR	E	UC	551	168	25.0	19.1
41.	Grand Coulee	Columbia R, Washington, USA	CG	1942	550	168	10.6	8.1
42.	Vidraru	Arges R, Romania	CA	1963	545	166	0.7	0.5
43.	Ross	Skagit R, Washington, USA	CA	1949	540	165	0.9	0.7
44.	Trinity	Trinity R, California, USA	E	1962	537	164	30.0	22.9
45.	Talbingo (alt Yalwal)	Tumut R, New South Wales, Australia	R	UC	530	162	18.5	14.1
46.	Cabora Bassa	Zambezi R, Mozambique	CA	UC	525	160	0.6	0.5
46.	King Paul (alt Kremasta)	Akheloos R, Greece	E	1965	525	160	10.2	7.8
46.	Yellowtail	Bighorn R, Montana, USA	CA	1966	525	160	1.5	1.1
49.	Gokcekaya	Sakarya R, Turkey	CA	UC	518	158	0.8	0.6
50.	Oku-Tadami	Tadami R, Honshu I, Japan	CG	1961	515	157	2.1	1.6
50.	Speccheri	Leno di Vallarsa R, Trentino-Alto Adige, Italy	CA	1957	515	157	0.2	0.1
52.	Guri	Caroni R, Venezuela	E	1968	512	156	4.9	3.8
52.	Swift	Lewis R, Washington, USA	E	1958	512	156	15.4	11.8
52.	Tseuzier (alt Zeuzier)	Liene R, Switzerland	CA	1957	512	156	0.4	0.3
55.	Goscheneralp	Goschenerreuss R, Switzerland	E	1960	509	155	12.2	9.4
55.	Monteynard	Drac R, Rhone-Alpes, France	CA	1962	509	155	0.6	0.5
55.	Nagawado	Azusa R, Honshu I, Japan	CA	UC	509	155	0.9	0.7
55.	Sakuma	Tenryu R, Honshu I, Japan	CG	1956	509	155	1.5	1.1
59.	Bhumiphol (alt Yanhee)	Ping R, Thailand	CG	1964	505	154	1.3	1.0
60.	Flaming Gorge	Green R, Utah, USA	CA	1964	502	153	1.0	0.8
60.	Place Moulin	Buthier R, Valle d'Aosta, Italy	CG	1965	502	153	2.0	1.5
62.	Gepatsch	Faggen(bach) Creek, Austria	E	1964	500	152	9.2	7.1
62.	Santa Giustina	Noce R, Trentino-Alto Adige, Italy	CA	1950	500	152	0.1	0.1
		* * *						
Akosombo		Volta R, Ghana	R	1965	463	141	10.4	8.0
Kariba		Zambezi R, Rhodesia-Zambia	CG	1959	420	128	1.3	1.0

1 A, arch; C, concrete; E, earth; G, gravity; R, rock.

2 UC, under construction.

3 In millions of cubic yards and cubic meters.

38
Largest Dams (Volume of Structure)

Contents

Rank.
Conventional and alternate names of dam.
River dammed, and subdivision and country in which located.
Type of dam.
Year of completion.
Volume of structure, in millions of cubic yards and cubic meters.
Height of dam, excluding projections, in feet and meters.

Arrangement

By volume of structure.

Coverage

All dams in place or under construction with a volume of at least 20,000,000 yd^3 (15,291,100 m^3).

Rounding

Volumes are rounded to the nearest 100,000 yd^3 (m^3).

Entries

44.

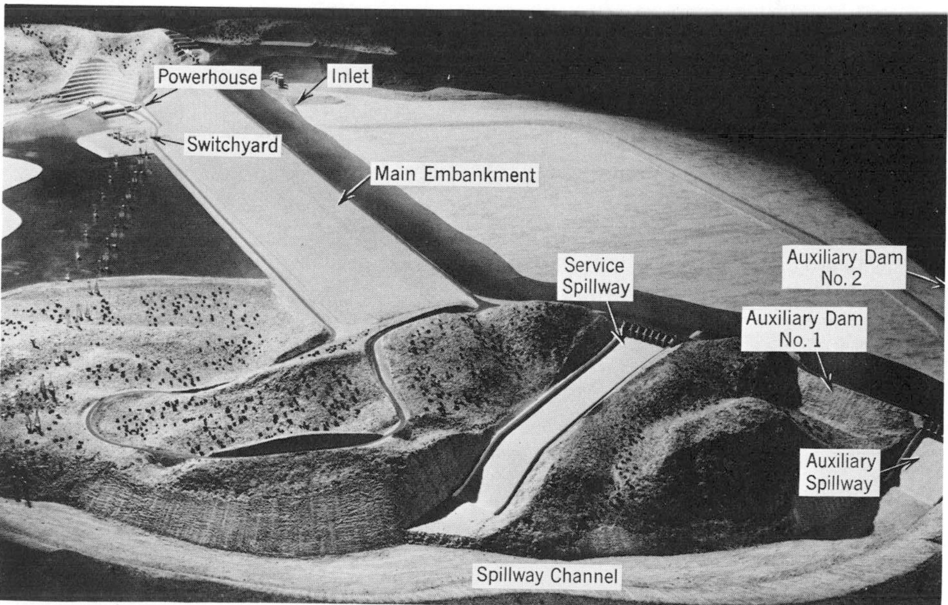

Figure 25. Scale model of the Tarbela Dam, now under construction on the Indus River, Pakistan, and destined to be the world's largest in volume of structure. (Credit: Tippetts-Abbett-McCarthy-Stratton, New York.)

TABLE 38. LARGEST DAMS (VOLUME OF STRUCTURE)

Rank	Dam	River and Location	Type[1]	Year Completed[2]	Volume[3] (yd³)	Volume[3] (m³)	Height (ft)	Height (m)
1.	Tarbela	Indus R, Pakistan	E	UC	186.0	142.2	485	148
2.	Fort Peck	Missouri R, Montana, USA	E	1940	125.6	96.1	251	77
3.	Mangla	Jhelum R, Pakistan	E	1968	108.3	82.8	380	116
4.	Oahe	Missouri R, South Dakota, USA	E	1963	92.0	70.3	245	75
5.	Gardiner	South Saskatchewan R, Saskatchewan, Canada	E	1966	85.7	65.5	223	68
6.	Oroville	Feather R, California, USA	E	1968	80.3	61.4	770	235
7.	San Luis	San Luis Creek, California, USA	E	1967	77.7	59.4	382	116
8.	Nagajunasagar	Krishna R, Andhra Pradesh, India	E	1966	73.6	56.3	409	125
9.	Nurek	Vakhsh R, Tadzhikistan, USSR	R	UC	70.8	54.1	1017	310
10.	Gorkiy	Volga R, Russia, USSR	E	1955	58.0	44.3	112	34
10.	Kiev	Dnieper R, Ukraine, USSR	E	1964	58.0	44.3	62	19
12.	Garrison	Missouri R, North Dakota, USA	E	1956	66.5	50.8	210	64
13.	W. A. C. Bennett	Peace R, British Columbia, Canada	E	1967	56.7	43.3	600	183
14.	Aswan High [off (Sadd al) Aali]	Nile R, Egypt	R	UC	55.8	42.7	364	111
15.	Fort Randall	Missouri R, South Dakota, USA	E	1956	50.2	38.4	165	50
16.	Kanev	Dnieper R, Ukraine, USSR	E	UC	49.5	37.9	82	25
17.	Kakhovka	Dnieper R, Ukraine, USSR	E	1955	46.6	35.6	121	37
18.	Tsimlyansk	Don R, Russia, USSR	E	1952	44.3	33.9	135	41
18.	Volga - V. I. Lenin	Volga R, Russia, USSR	E	1955	44.3	33.9	148	45
20.	Beas	Beas R, Punjab, India	E	UC	44.2	33.8	380	116
21.	Castaic	Castaic Creek, California, USA	E	UC	42.6	32.6	340	104
22.	Jari	Jari R, Pakistan	E	1967	42.4	32.4	234	71
23.	Mica	Columbia R, British Columbia, Canada	R	UC	42.0	32.1	800	244
24.	Cochiti	Rio Grande R, New Mexico, USA	E	1969	41.1	31.4	251	77
25.	Kremenchug	Dnieper R, Ukraine, USSR	E	1961	36.3	27.7	98	30
26.	Dneprodzerzhinsk	Dnieper R, Ukraine, USSR	E	1964	35.9	27.4	115	35
27.	Ukai	Tapti R, Gujarat, India	E	UC	33.4	25.5	225	69
28.	Volga - 22nd Congress	Volga R, Russia, USSR	E	1958	33.0	25.2	154	47
29.	Ilha Solteira	Parana R, Sao Paulo, Brazil	E	UC	32.8	25.1	262	80
30.	Kingsley	North Platte R, Nebraska, USA	E	1942	32.0	24.5	170	52
31.	Diablo	Rio Grande R, Texas, USA	E	UC	30.0	22.9	280	85
31.	Trinity	Trinity R, California, USA	E	1962	30.0	22.9	537	164
33.	Balimela	Sileru R, Orissa, India	E	UC	29.7	22.7	230	70
34.	Navajo	San Juan R, New Mexico, USA	E	1963	26.8	20.5	402	123
35.	Hirakud	Mahanadi R, Orissa, India	E	1956	25.1	19.2	202	62
36.	Charvak	Chirchik R, Uzbekistan, USSR	E	UC	25.0	19.1	551	168
37.	Grande Maison	Eau d'Olle (Ruisseau) Creek, Rhone-Alpes, France	E	UC	24.9	19.0	591	180
38.	Marimbondo	Grande R, Minas Gerais, Brazil	E	UC	24.3	18.6	295	90
39.	Gatun	Chagres R, Canal Zone	E	1912	23.0	17.6	115	35
40.	Bratsk	Angara R, Russia, USSR	E	1964	22.2	17.0	410	125
40.	Twin Buttes	Concho R, Texas, USA	E	1963	22.2	17.0	134	41
42.	Tuttle Creek	Big Blue R, Kansas, USA	E	1962	21.0	16.1	157	48
43.	Mingechaur	Kura R, Azerbaijan, USSR	E	1953	20.4	15.6	262	80
44.	Ivankovo	Volga R, Russia, USSR	E	1937	20.2	15.4	98	30

[1] E, earth; R, rock. [2] UC, under construction. [3] In millions of cubic yards and cubic meters.

39
Largest Universities

Contents

Rank.

Name of university.

City, and subdivision and country in which located.

Student enrollment (i.e., thousands of full-time and part-time students, excluding correspondence students, enrolled in the university and its affiliated institutions[1]).

Academic staff (i.e., number of full-time and part-time teachers).

Date of foundation. The date given is the year in which the institution itself or (preferably) its oldest constituent college or the educational institution from which it directly evolved was established (or chartered). This date may precede by several years the date when the first instruction was given. Also, it bears no necessary relation to the length of time during which the university has been operative, since many universities have been closed for periods of years or even decades.

Arrangement

By student enrollment.

Coverage

100 largest universities (as defined in the General Explanatory Notes, p. 5) in student enrollment.

Rounding

Enrollments are rounded to the nearest 1000 students.

Entries

104.

[1] In India and Pakistan most universities include as affiliates numerous educational institutions of lower level, such as preparatory schools and other secondary schools; thus the size of these universities may be exaggerated with respect to that of universities in other countries, where only college-level students are included in the enrollment statistics.

Figure 26. Albany campus of the State University of New York, the university with the largest student enrollment in the world. The Academic Podium (center) is 1600 ft (488 m) long and 600 ft (183 m) wide and comprises 13 interconnected buildings. All but one of the four 23-story towers and all of the low-rise units surrounding them are residence space. (Credit: State University of New York at Albany.)

TABLE 39. LARGEST UNIVERSITIES

Rank	University	Location	Students (thousands)	Teachers	Date Founded
1.	State University of New York	Albany, New York, USA	314	12,435	1844
	Albany campus	Albany, New York, USA	13	758	1844
	Buffalo campus	Buffalo, New York, USA	41	2,818?	1846
2.	University of Calcutta	Calcutta, West Bengal, India	196		1817
3.	Panjab University	Chandigarh, Chandigarh, India	166		1947
3.	Universite de Paris	Paris, Region Parisienne, France	166	5,848	1200
5.	University of California	Berkeley, California, USA	147	13,582	1855
	Berkeley campus	Berkeley, California, USA	29	3,648	1873
	Los Angeles campus	Los Angeles, California, USA	29	3,587	1881
6.	University of Wisconsin	Madison, Wisconsin, USA	137	7,369	1849
	Madison campus	Madison, Wisconsin, USA	34	2,119	1849
7.	City University of New York	New York, New York, USA	123	12,350	1847
8.	University of Madras	Madras, Tamil Nadu, India	118		1794
9.	University of Kerala	Trivandrum, Kerala, India	114		1937
10.	Universidad Nacional Autonoma de Mexico	Mexico, Distrito Federal, Mexico	105	10,500	1551
11.	University of Bombay	Bombay, Maharashtra, India	88		1832
12.	Universidad de Buenos Aires	Buenos Aires, Distrito Federal, Argentina	80	8,408	1821
12.	Instituto Politecnico Nacional (univ)	Mexico, Distrito Federal, Mexico	80	5,996	1931
14.	University of Texas	Austin, Texas, USA	74	4,525	1881
	Austin campus	Austin, Texas, USA	45	2,724	1881
15.	Agra University	Agra, Uttar Pradesh, India	72		1927
15.	Nihon University	Tokyo, Honshu I, Japan	72	3,077	1889
17.	University of Mysore	Mysore, Mysore, India	70		1833
18.	University of Minnesota	Minneapolis, Minnesota, USA	69	7,593	1851
	Minneapolis campus	Minneapolis, Minnesota, USA	61	7,228	1851
19.	Nagpur University	Nagpur, Maharashtra, India	67	2,480	1923
20.	Universita degli Studi di Roma	Rome, Lazio, Italy	66	4,955	1303
21.	Andhra University	Waltair, Andhra Pradesh, India	64		1926
22.	University of Rajasthan	Jaipur, Rajasthan, India	63	2,433	1873
23.	Osmania University	Hyderabad, Andhra Pradesh, India	62	2,543	1887
24.	Gujarat University	Ahmedabad, Gujarat, India	61		1949
25.	Indiana University	Bloomington, Indiana, USA	59	5,375	1820
	Bloomington campus	Bloomington, Indiana, USA	30		1820
26.	University of Illinois	Urbana and Champaign, Illinois, USA	58	8,169	1867
	Urbana-Champaign campus	Urbana and Champaign, Illinois, USA	36	4,887	1867
26.	Kanpur University	Kanpur, Uttar Pradesh, India	58		1966
26.	Karnatak University	Dharwar, Mysore, India	58		1917
26.	University of Poona	Poona, Maharashtra, India	58		1885
30.	University of Delhi	Delhi, Delhi, India	56		1881
31.	University of the East	Manila, Luzon I, Philippines	55	1,422	1946
31.	Pennsylvania State University	State College, Pennsylvania, USA	55	5,523	1855
	State College campus	State College, Pennsylvania, USA	36		1855
33.	Madurai University	Madurai, Tamil Nadu, India	54		1958
34.	University of Maryland	College Park, Maryland, USA	52	3,363	1807
	College Park campus	College Park, Maryland, USA	45	2,718	1856
35.	Universidad de Chile	Santiago, Chile	51	9,220	1738
35.	Ohio State University	Columbus, Ohio, USA	51	5,754	1870
	Columbus campus	Columbus, Ohio, USA	46		1870
37.	University of Calicut	Calicut, Kerala, India	50		1968

Rank	University	Location	Students (thousands)	Teachers	Date Founded
38.	University of Missouri	Columbia, Missouri, USA	49	4,557	1839
	Columbia campus	Columbia, Missouri, USA	23	3,029	1839
39.	University of Gauhati	Jhalukbari, Assam, India	47	2,457	1914
39.	Universidad Nacional de la Plata	La Plata, Buenos Aires, Argentina	47	1,209	1884
41.	University of North Carolina	Chapel Hill, North Carolina, USA	46	6,556	1789
	Chapel Hill campus	Chapel Hill, North Carolina, USA	18	4,385	1789
41.	Waseda University	Tokyo, Honshu I, Japan	46	2,037	1882
43.	University of Cairo	Giza, Egypt	45	2,892	1908
43.	University of Dacca	Dacca, Bangladesh	45		1910
45.	Meerut University	Meerut, Uttar Pradesh, India	44	1,942	1966
45.	Michigan State University	East Lansing, Michigan, USA	44	3,450	1855
47.	Universidad de Puerto Rico (alt University of Puerto Rico)	San Juan, Puerto Rico	43	2,785	1903
	San Juan campus	San Juan, Puerto Rico	29		1903
48.	University of Bihar	Muzaffarpur, Bihar, India	42	1,009	1889
48.	Universidad Complutense de Madrid	Madrid, Castilla la Nueva, Spain	42	2,200	1498
48.	Universita degli Studi di Napoli	Naples, Campania, Italy	42	3,000?	1224
48.	University of the Punjab	Lahore, Pakistan	42		1858
48.	Shivaji University	Kolhapur, Maharashtra, India	42	1,712	1962
53.	Univerzitet u Beogradu	Belgrade, Serbia, Yugoslavia	41	2,876	1808
53.	Universidad Veracruzana	Jalapa, Veracruz, Mexico	41	4,103	1846
55.	University of Michigan	Ann Arbor, Michigan, USA	40	4,469	1817
	Ann Arbor campus	Ann Arbor, Michigan, USA	37	4,154	1837
56.	Bangalore University	Bangalore, Mysore, India	39	1,614	1864
56.	University of London	London, England, UK	39	3,000?	13th c
56.	Southern Illinois University	Carbondale, Illinois, USA	39	2,932	1869
	Carbondale campus	Carbondale, Illinois, USA	25		1869
59.	Far Eastern University	Manila, Luzon I, Philippines	38	1,300	1928
59.	Universite de Lyon	Lyons, Rhone-Alpes, France	38	2,433	1809
59.	Northeastern University	Boston, Massachusetts, USA	38	2,345	1898
59.	Purdue University	Lafayette, Indiana, USA	38	4,303	1869
	Lafayette campus	Lafayette, Indiana, USA	26		1869
59.	University of Tennessee	Knoxville, Tennessee, USA	38	2,597	1794
	Knoxville campus	Knoxville, Tennessee, USA	28	1,456	1794
64.	Ain Shams University	Cairo, Egypt	37	1,079	1950
64.	Universite d'Aix-Marseille	Aix-en-Provence and Marseilles, Provence-Cote d'Azur-Corse, France	37	2,225	1409
64.	Bhagalpur University	Bhagalpur, Bihar, India	37		1960
64.	Ranchi University	Ranchi, Bihar, India	37	1,571	1899
68.	Universite de Montreal	Montreal, Quebec, Canada	36	3,585	1876
68.	University of Toronto	Toronto, Ontario, Canada	36	4,700	1827
68.	Wayne State University	Detroit, Michigan, USA	36	2,700	1868
71.	Universita degli Studi di Bari	Bari, Puglia, Italy	35	2,506	1924
71.	Universita degli Studi di Bologna	Bologna, Emilia-Romagna, Italy	35	2,095	11th c
71.	University of Burdwan	Burdwan, West Bengal, India	35	850?	1960
71.	Istanbul Universitesi	Istanbul, Turkey	35	1,327	1453
71.	Louisiana State University	Baton Rouge, Louisiana, USA	35	4,508	1853
	Baton Rouge campus	Baton Rouge, Louisiana, USA	20	2,500	1869
71.	Magadh University	Bodh Gaya, Bihar, India	35		1942
71.	University of Nebraska	Lincoln, Nebraska, USA	35	1,518	1869
	Lincoln campus	Lincoln, Nebraska, USA	21	1,000	1869
71.	San Diego State College (univ)	San Diego, California, USA	35	978	1897

Rank	University	Location	Students (thousands)	Teachers	Date Founded
71.	Sri Venkateswara University	Tirupati, Uttar Pradesh, India	35		1954
71.	Universite de Toulouse	Toulouse, Midi-Pyrenees, France	35	1,127	1229
81.	University of Alexandria	Alexandria, Egypt	34	2,604	1942
81.	Universite de Bordeaux	Bordeaux, Aquitaine, France	34	736	1441
81.	University of Cincinnati	Cincinnati, Ohio, USA	34	2,763	1819
	Cincinnati campus	Cincinnati, Ohio, USA	32		1819
81.	San Jose State College (univ)	San Jose, California, USA	34	874	1857
85.	Chuo University	Tokyo, Honshu I, Japan	33	1,235	1885
85.	University of Hawaii	Honolulu, Hawaii, USA	33	2,109	1907
	Honolulu campus	Honolulu, Hawaii, USA	23		1907
85.	Rutgers, the State University	New Brunswick, New Jersey, USA	33	4,442	1766
	New Brunswick campus	New Brunswick, New Jersey, USA	24		1766
85.	Vikram University	Ujjain, Madhya Pradesh, India	33		1896
85.	University of Washington	Seattle, Washington, USA	33	3,146	1861
90.	University of Colorado	Boulder, Colorado, USA	32	2,689	1861
	Boulder campus	Boulder, Colorado, USA	21		1861
90.	Meiji University	Tokyo, Honshu I, Japan	32	1,083	1881
90.	New York University	New York, New York, USA	32	6,100	1831
90.	Universita degli Studi di Padova	Padua, Veneto, Italy	32	3,293	1222
90.	University of Pittsburgh	Pittsburgh, Pennsylvania, USA	32	2,532	1787
	Pittsburgh campus	Pittsburgh, Pennsylvania, USA	28		1787
90.	University of Santo Tomas	Manila, Luzon I, Philippines	32	1,260	1611
90.	Temple University	Philadelphia, Pennsylvania, USA	32	3,318	1884
97.	Damascus University	Damascus, Syria	31	677	1902
97.	University of Gorakhpur	Gorakhpur, Uttar Pradesh, India	31		1933
99.	Arizona State University	Tempe, Arizona, USA	30	1,377	1885
99.	Universidad Central de Venezuela	Caracas, Venezuela	30	3,060	1696
99.	Hosei University	Tokyo, Honshu I, Japan	30	911	1880
99.	McGill University	Montreal, Quebec, Canada	30	2,227	1821
99.	Kungliga Universitetet i Stockholm	Stockholm, Sweden	30	995	1877
99.	Sveuciliste u Zagrebu	Zagreb, Croatia, Yugoslavia	30	4,409	1669

40
Largest Libraries

Contents

Rank.

Name of library.

City, and subdivision and country in which located.

Size of collection (i.e., thousands of volumes of books and pamphlets, usually excluding bound and unbound periodicals[1]).

Date of foundation. The date given is preferably the year in which the library was opened on a permanent basis, that is, the one since which it has been continuously operative. By "library," however, is meant the nucleus of the present book collection, not necessarily the institution under its name today.

Arrangement

By size of collection.

Coverage

100 largest libraries in size of collection.

Rounding

Collections are rounded to the nearest 1000 volumes.

Entries

100.

[1] In the USSR the size of a library's collection is often expressed in the number of separate items rather than in the number of volumes; thus the size of the library may be exaggerated with respect to that of libraries in other countries. In 1957, for example, the V. I. Lenin State Library of the USSR had 19,816,000 items, but only 8,900,000 of these were books.

(a)

(b)

Figure 27. Two of the world's largest libraries: (a) V. I. Lenin State Library of the USSR, Moscow (the building at the far left was originally an 18th-century palace); (b) Library of Congress, Washington. (Credit: (a) Embassy of the USSR, Washington: (b) US, Library of Congress.)

TABLE 40. LARGEST LIBRARIES

Rank	Library	Location	Volumes (thousands)	Date Founded
1.	V. I. Lenin State Library of the USSR	Moscow, Russia in Europe, USSR	25,226	1828
2.	M. E. Saltykov-Shchedrin State Public Library	Leningrad, Russia in Europe, USSR	15,144	1795
3.	Library of Congress	Washington, District of Columbia, USA	14,846	1800
4.	USSR Academy of Sciences Library	Leningrad, Russia in Europe, USSR	10,343	1714
5.	University of California Library	Berkeley, California, USA	10,072	1868
	Berkeley campus	Berkeley, California, USA	3,635	1873?
	Los Angeles campus	Los Angeles, California, USA	2,793	1919
6.	National K. Marx State Library of the Georgian SSR	Tbilisi, Georgia, USSR	9,720	1846
7.	Harvard University Library	Cambridge, Massachusetts, USA	8,088	1638
8.	British Museum Library	London, England, UK	8,000	1753
9.	New York Public Library	New York, New York, USA	7,179	1848
10.	Bibliotheque Nationale	Paris, Region Parisienne, France	7,000	1480
11.	Institute of Scientific Information and Central Library of Social Sciences of the USSR Academy of Sciences	Moscow, Russia in Europe, USSR	6,723	1918
12.	Biblioteca Academiei Republicii Socialiste Romania	Bucharest, Romania	6,624	1867
13.	Bibliotheque de l'Universite de Paris	Paris, Region Parisienne, France	6,076	1570?
	Bibliotheque Sainte-Genevieve	Paris, Region Parisienne, France	3,000	1624
14.	Central Scientific Library of the Ukrainian SSR Academy of Sciences	Kiev, Ukraine, USSR	6,051	1919
15.	A. M. Gorkiy Scientific Library of the Moscow M. V. Lomonosov State University	Moscow, Russia in Europe, USSR	5,995	1755
16.	National Diet Library	Tokyo, Honshu I, Japan	5,840	1948
17.	National A. F. Myashnikyan State Library of the Armenian SSR	Yerevan, Armenia, USSR	5,698	1921
18.	Biblioteca Centrala de Stat	Bucharest, Romania	5,642	1955
19.	State University of New York Library	Albany, New York, USA	5,579	1844
	Albany campus	Albany, New York, USA	543	1844
	Buffalo campus	Buffalo, New York, USA	1,111	1922
20.	State Public Scientific-Technical Library	Moscow, Russia in Europe, USSR	5,500	1958
21.	Yale University Library	New Haven, Connecticut, USA	5,453	1701
22.	State Public Scientific-Technical Library of the Siberian Department of the USSR Academy of Sciences	Novosibirsk, Russia in Asia, USSR	5,021	1918
23.	National Library of Peking	Peking, China	4,600	1909
24.	V. I. Lenin State Library of the White Russian SSR	Minsk, White Russia, USSR	4,513	1922
25.	University of Illinois Library	Urbana and Champaign, Illinois, USA	4,429	1868
	Urbana-Champaign campus	Urbana and Champaign, Illinois, USA	4,089	1868
26.	Lvov State Scientific Library	Lvov, Ukraine, USSR	4,371	1940
27.	Statni Knihovna	Prague, Bohemia, Czechoslovakia	4,213	1366?
28.	Public Library	Chicago, Illinois, USA	4,184	1873
29.	Cape Provincial Library Service (alt Kaapse Provinsiale Biblioteekdiens)	Cape Town, Cape of Good Hope, South Africa	4,073	1945
30.	Columbia University Library	New York, New York, USA	4,014	1761
31.	New York State Library	Albany, New York, USA	4,000	1818

Rank	Library	Location	Volumes (thousands)	Date Founded
32.	M. Gorkiy Scientific Library of the Leningrad A. A. Zhdanov State University	Leningrad, Russia in Europe, USSR	3,867	1819
33.	N. I. Lobachevskiy Scientific Library of the Kazan V. I. Ulyanov-Lenin State University	Kazan, Russia in Europe, USSR	3,858	1798
34.	Biblioteca Nazionale Centrale	Florence, Toscana, Italy	3,831	1747
35.	Public Library	Boston, Massachusetts, USA	3,784	1854
36.	V. G. Korolenko State Scientific Library	Kharkov, Ukraine, USSR	3,760	1886
37.	Lancashire County Library	Preston, England, UK	3,731	1925
38.	All-Union State Library of Foreign Literature	Moscow, Russia in Europe, USSR	3,547	1921
39.	Shanghai Library	Shanghai, China	3,500	1952
40.	National Library of New Zealand	Wellington, North I, New Zealand	3,484	1856
41.	Cornell University Library	Ithaca, New York, USA	3,445	1865
42.	Alisher Navoi State Library of the Uzbek SSR	Tashkent, Uzbekistan, USSR	3,410	1870
43.	Public Library	Los Angeles, California, USA	3,371	1872
44.	University of Michigan Library	Ann Arbor, Michigan, USA	3,365	1838
45.	Vilis Lacis State Library of the Latvian SSR	Riga, Latvia, USSR	3,352	1919
46.	University of Tokyo Library	Tokyo, Honshu I, Japan	3,300	1893
47.	Stanford University Library	Palo Alto, California, USA	3,275	1891
48.	Public Library	Cleveland, Ohio, USA	3,217	1869
49.	Mirabeau B. Lamar Library of the University of Texas	Austin, Texas, USA	3,209	1883
	Austin campus	Austin, Texas, USA	2,166	1883
50.	Bayerische Staatsbibliothek	Munich, Bayern, West Germany	3,200	1558
51.	Deutsche Bucherei	Leipzig, East Germany	3,151	1912
52.	Odessa A. M. Gorkiy State Scientific Library	Odessa, Ukraine, USSR	3,140	1830
53.	Kentucky Department of Libraries	Frankfort, Kentucky, USA	3,134	1856?
54.	University of Toronto Library	Toronto, Ontario, Canada	3,088	1842
55.	Los Angeles County Public Library	Los Angeles, California, USA	3,080	1912
56.	Yorkshire (West Riding) County Library	Wakefield, England, UK	3,068	1922
57.	University of North Carolina Library	Chapel Hill, North Carolina, USA	3,049	1795
	Chapel Hill campus	Chapel Hill, North Carolina, USA	1.923	1795
58.	Deutsche Staatsbibliothek	Berlin, East Germany	3,024	1661
59.	Bodleian Library (alt University of Oxford Library)	Oxford, England, UK	3,000	1602
59.	University of Cambridge Library	Cambridge, England, UK	3,000	1400
59.	Central House of the Soviet Army Library	Moscow, Russia in Europe, USSR	3,000	
59.	Central State Medical Library	Moscow, Russia in Europe, USSR	3,000	1919
59.	National Library of Scotland	Edinburgh, Scotland, UK	3,000	1682
59.	Bibliotheque Nationale et Universitaire	Strasbourg, Alsace, France	3,000	1872
65.	University of Wisconsin Library	Madison, Wisconsin, USA	2,990	1850
	Madison campus	Madison, Wisconsin, USA	2,160	1850
66.	Statni Vedecka Knihovna	Brno, Moravia, Czechoslovakia	2,973	1899
67.	Biblioteca Nacional	Madrid, Castilla la Nueva, Spain	2,923	1712
68.	Kyoto University Library	Kyoto, Honshu I, Japan	2,917	1899

Rank	Library	Location	Volumes (thousands)	Date Founded
69.	Central Scientific Library of the Kazakh SSR Academy of Sciences	Alma-Ata, Kazakhstan, USSR	2,866	1933
70.	University of Chicago Library	Chicago, Illinois, USA	2,854	1891
71.	Universitetsbiblioteket	Oslo, Norway	2,836	1811
72.	Hertfordshire County Library	Hertford, England, UK	2,833	1925
73.	University of Minnesota Library	Minneapolis, Minnesota, USA	2,813	1851
	Minneapolis campus	Minneapolis, Minnesota, USA	2,489	1851
74.	Scientific Library of the Tartu State University	Tartu, Estonia, USSR	2,779	1802
75.	Center for Research Library	Chicago, Illinois, USA	2,750	1949
76.	Brooklyn Public Library	New York, New York, USA	2,745	1897
77.	City University of New York Library	New York, New York, USA	2,694	1849
78.	Scientific Library of the Tomsk V. V. Kuybyshev State University	Tomsk, Russia in Asia, USSR	2,677	1888
79.	Transvaal Provincial Library Service (alt Transvaalse Provinsiale Biblioteekdiens)	Pretoria, Transvaal, South Africa	2,655	1943
80.	Public Library of Cincinnati and Hamilton County	Cincinnati, Ohio, USA	2,615	1856
81.	Bibliotheque Royale de Belgique	Brussels, Belgium	2,600	1837
82.	Gorkiy Province V. I. Lenin Library	Gorkiy, Russia in Europe, USSR	2,572	1930
83.	Karl Marx State Library of the Turkmen SSR	Ashkhabad, Turkmenia, USSR	2,555	1895
84.	Central Scientific Library of the Kharkov A. M. Gorkiy State University	Kharkov, Ukraine, USSR	2,552	1805
85.	Free Library	Philadelphia, Pennsylvania, USA	2,535	1891
85.	Fovarosi Szabo Ervin Konyvtar	Budapest, Hungary	2,535	1904
87.	Central Scientific Agricultural Library of the All-Union Lenin Academy of Agricultural Sciences	Moscow, Russia in Europe, USSR	2,500	1930
87.	Central Polytechnic Library of the All-Union Society for the Dissemination of Political and Scientific Knowledge	Moscow, Russia in Europe, USSR	2,500	1864
87.	Central Library of the Chinese Academy of Sciences	Peking, China	2,500	1951
87.	Scientific Library of the Odessa I. I. Mechnikov State University	Odessa, Ukraine, USSR	2,500	1817
91.	Buffalo and Erie County Public Library	Buffalo, New York, USA	2,478	1836
92.	Queens Borough Public Library	New York, New York, USA	2,464	1896
93.	Princeton University Library	Princeton, New Jersey, USA	2,436	1746
94.	F. R. Kreutzwald State Library of the Estonian SSR	Tallin, Estonia, USSR	2,434	1940
95.	Biblioteka Narodowa	Warsaw, Poland	2,416	1928
96.	Scientific Library of the Vilnyus V. Kapsukas State University	Vilnyus, Lithuania, USSR	2,407	1570
97.	Biblioteca Centrala Universitara Cluj	Cluj, Romania	2,401	1872
98.	Nanking Library	Nanking, Kiangsu, China	2,400	1908
99.	National A. S. Pushkin State Library of the Kazakh SSR	Alma-Ata, Kazakhstan, USSR	2,317	1931
100.	National N. G. Chernyshevskiy State Library of the Kirgiz SSR	Frunze, Kirgizia, USSR	2,261	1934

1
Countries, by Continent

Contents

This gazetteer consists of four parts.

I. Latest Area, Population, and Density of Population

Conventional name of country.

Area, including inland waters, in thousands of square miles and square kilometers.

Latest population, in thousands, by census and by estimate, with year of data for each. If the census date is 1970 or 1971, no estimate is given.

Density of population, based on latest available data, per square mile and per square kilometer.

II. Evolution of Population

Conventional name of country.

Population, in thousands, for the years 1960, 1950, 1930, 1900, 1850, and 1800, or for the times nearest to those years for which reliable data are available, with the exact year stated. All populations are for the country as it existed at the time when the population was determined, not for its present-day area. For populations "circa 1960," a 1956 census figure is normally given in preference to a 1960 estimate. Question marks are used when the exact year is unknown; for example, the notation "(00?e)" below the tabular heading "Circa 1900" indicates that the population preceding it was estimated about but not necessarily during the year 1900.

III. Miscellaneous Statistics

Conventional name of country.

Period of record for birth and death rates.

Number of live births per thousand of population.

Number of deaths per thousand of population.

Period of record for life expectancies.

Expectation of life at birth, in years, for men, for women, and for both (average).

Year of data for length of roads.

Length of all roads, in miles and kilometers.

Year of data for railroad route length.

Length of all railroad routes (not tracks), in miles and kilometers.

IV. Supplemental Information

Conventional name of country.

[a]Alternate, former, and official names of country. See General Explanatory Notes, p. 3, for explanation. In addition, formerly separate countries now included in the country cited and component parts of the country that are sometimes regarded as separate countries (e.g., Guernsey, a part of the Channel Islands) are listed after the abbreviation "inc."

[b]Conventional and other (alternate, former, and official) names of capital (or capitals), and its latest population in thousands, with year of census or estimate (e).

[c]Conventional and other (alternate, former, and official) names of the largest city other than the capital (or capitals), and its latest population, in thousands, with year of census or estimate (e).[1]

Arrangement

By country, alphabetically under continent.

[1] In some countries the "largest city" is actually a small town or even a village. No attempt has been made to differentiate in the index, where each is identified simply as a city.

Coverage

All countries, regardless of sovereignty, but excluding provinces, states, and regions generally recognized as subdivisions of another country, for example, Tibet, a subdivision of China, and Ukraine, a subdivision of the USSR. For historical reasons, however, some states and so forth that once were separate countries are entered under the names of the countries of which they are now subdivisions. All countries located in more than one continent are listed under each applicable continent.

Rounding

Areas are rounded to the nearest 1000 mi^2 and km^2 if more than 100,000 mi^2 or km^2, to the nearest 100 if between 10,000 and 100,000, to the nearest 10 if between 1000 and 10,000, and to the nearest square mile and square kilometer if less than 1000 mi^2 or km^2.

Populations are rounded to the nearest 1000, except that when the original figure is less than 1000 the rounding is done to the nearest 100.

Densities of population are rounded to the nearest two significant digits if between 1 and 100 per square mile or per square kilometer, and to the nearest significant digit if less than 1 per square mile or per square kilometer.

Entries

254.

TABULAR GAZETTEER 1. COUNTRIES, BY CONTINENT

Part I. Latest Area, Population, and Density of Population

AFRICA

Country	Area		Latest Population (thousands)				Density of Population	
	(1000 mi²)	(1000 km²)	Census		Estimate		(per mi²)	(per km²)
Algeria	920	2382	11,822	(1966)	14,012	(1970)	15	5.9
Angola	481	1247	5,673	(1970)			12	4.6
Botswana	232	600	626	(1971)			2.7	1.0
British Indian Ocean Territory	0.030	0.078	1	(1960-62)	2	(1970)	66	26
Burundi	10.7	27.8	3,400	(1970)			317	122
Cameroon	184	475	5,017	(1960-65)	5,836	(1970)	32	12
Cape Verde Islands	1.56	4.03	272	(1970)			175	67
Central African Republic	241	623	1,203	(1959-60)	1,522	(1970)	6.3	2.4
Ceuta	0.007	0.019	63	(1970)			8,588	3,316
Chad	496	1284	3,254	(1963-64)	3,706	(1970)	7.5	2.9
Comoro Islands	0.838	2.17	244	(1966)	271	(1970)	323	125
Congo	132	342	1,089	(1970)			8.2	3.2
Dahomey	43.5	113	2,106	(1961)	2,686	(1970)	62	24
Egypt	387	1001	30,076	(1966)	33,329	(1970)	86	33
Equatorial Guinea	10.8	28.1	246	(1960)	290	(1970)	27	10
Ethiopia	472	1222			25,046	(1970)	53	20
Eritrea	45.4	118	598	(1931)	1,589	(1967)	35	14
French Southern and Antarctic Lands	2.90	7.56	0.2	(1970)			0.07	0.03
French Territory of the Afars and the Issas	8.49	22.0	81	(1960-61)	95	(1970)	11	4.3
Gabon	103	268	449	(1960-61)	500	(1970)	4.8	1.9
Gambia	4.36	11.3	315	(1963)	364	(1970)	83	32
Ghana	92.1	238	8,546	(1970)			93	36
Guinea	94.9	246	2,570	(1955)	3,921	(1970)	41	16
Ivory Coast	125	322	3,100	(1957-58)	4,310	(1970)	35	13
Kenya	225	583	10,943	(1969)	11,247	(1970)	50	19
Lesotho	11.7	30.3	852	(1966)	1,043	(1970)	89	34
Liberia	43.0	111	1,523	(1970)			35	14
Libya	679	1759	1,564	(1964)	1,900	(1970)	2.8	1.1
Malagasy Republic	227	587	6,200	(1966)	6,750	(1970)	30	11
Malawi	45.8	118	4,040	(1966)	4,530	(1970)	99	38
Mali	479	1240	4,100	(1960-61)	5,022	(1970)	10	4.0
Mauritania	398	1031	1,050	(1964-65)	1,171	(1970)	2.9	1.1
Mauritius	0.788	2.04	701	(1962)	836	(1970)	1,061	410
Melilla	0.005	0.012	61	(1970)			13,166	5,083
Morocco	172	446	15,379	(1971)			89	34
Mozambique	302	783	8,234	(1970)			27	11
Niger	489	1267	2,766	(1959-60)	4,016	(1970)	8.2	3.2
Nigeria	357	924	55,670	(1963)	55,074	(1970)	154	60
Portugal (in Africa: Madeira Islands)	0.308	0.797	253	(1970)			822	317
Portuguese Guinea	13.9	36.1	487	(1970)			35	13
Reunion	0.969	2.51	417	(1967)	446	(1970)	460	178
Rhodesia	150	389	5,099	(1969)	5,270	(1970)	35	14
Rwanda	10.2	26.3	3,724	(1970)			367	142

AFRICA

Country	Area		Latest Population (thousands)				Density of Population	
	(1000 mi²)	(1000 km²)	Census		Estimate		(per mi²)	(per km²)
Saint Helena	0.162	0.419	5	(1966)	6	(1970)	37	14
Sao Tome and Principe	0.372	0.964	74	(1970)			199	77
Senegal	75.8	196	3,110	(1960-61)	3,925	(1970)	52	20
Seychelles	0.145	0.376	52	(1971)			359	138
Sierra Leone	27.7	71.7	2,180	(1963)	2,550	(1970)	92	36
Somalia	246	638	1,022	(1931)	2,789	(1970)	11	4.4
South Africa	471	1221	21,448	(1970)			45	18
South-West Africa	318	824	526	(1960)	632	(1970)	2.0	0.8
Spain (in Africa: Canary Islands)	2.81	7.27	1,125	(1970)			401	155
Spanish Sahara	103	266	76	(1970)			0.7	0.3
Sudan	967	2506	10,263	(1956)	15,695	(1970)	16	6.3
Swaziland	6.72	17.4	395	(1966)	420	(1970)	63	24
Tanzania	363	940	12,313	(1967)	13,273	(1970)	37	14
Tanganyika	362	937	11,959	(1967)	12,896	(1970)	36	14
Zanzibar	1.02	2.64	355	(1967)	377	(1970)	370	143
Togo	21.6	56.0	1,956	(1970)			90	35
Tunisia	63.4	164	4,533	(1966)	5,137	(1970)	81	31
Uganda	91.1	236	9,549	(1969)	9,764	(1970)	107	41
Upper Volta	106	274	4,400	(1960-61)	5,384	(1970)	51	20
Zaire	906	2345	21,638	(1970)			24	9.2
Zambia	291	753	4,057	(1969)	4,295	(1970)	15	5.7

ASIA

Country	Area		Latest Population (thousands)				Density of Population	
	(100 mi²)	(1000 km²)	Census		Estimate		(per mi²)	(per km²)
Afghanistan	250	647			17,125	(1970)	69	26
Bahrain	0.231	0.598	217	(1971)			940	363
Bangladesh[1]	55.1	143	50,854	(1961)	59,547	(1969)	1,080	417
Bhutan	18.1	47.0			836	(1970)	46	18
Brunei	2.23	5.76	136	(1971)			61	24
Burma	262	678	16,824	(1941)	27,584	(1970)	105	41
Cambodia	69.9	181	5,729	(1962)	6,818	(1970)	98	38
Ceylon	25.3	65.6	12,748	(1971)			503	194
China	3692	9561	582,603	(1953)	759,619	(1970)	206	79
Cyprus	3.57	9.25	578	(1960)	637	(1970)	178	69
Gaza Strip	0.146	0.378	356	(1967)			2,440	942
Hong Kong	0.391	1.01	3,951	(1971)			10,105	3,902
India	1176	3045	542,753	(1971)			462	178
Indonesia								
Total	735	1904	114,950	(1970)			156	60
in Asia	576	1492	114,126	(1970)			198	77
Iran	636	1648	25,785	(1966)	28,662	(1970)	45	17
Iraq	168	435	8,047	(1965)	9,440	(1970)	56	22
Israel	7.99	20.7	2,183	(1961)	2,889	(1970)	362	140
Japan	143	370	103,720	(1970)			726	280
Jordan	37.7	97.7	1,706	(1961)	2,317	(1970)	61	24
Kashmir-Jammu	86.0	223	4,022	(1941)	5,255	(1970)	61	24
Korea								
North Korea	46.5	120			13,892	(1970)	299	115
South Korea	38.0	98.5	31,469	(1970)			828	319

[1] East Pakistan until December 1971.

ASIA

Country	Area (1000 mi²)	Area (1000 km²)	Latest Population (thousands) Census		Estimate		Density of Population (per mi²)	Density of Population (per km²)
Kuwait	6.18	16.0	739	(1970)			120	46
Laos	91.4	237	944	(1931)	2,962	(1970)	32	13
Lebanon	4.02	10.4	629	(1921-22)	2,963	(1970)	737	285
Macao	0.006	0.016	248	(1970)			40,145	15,500
Malaysia	128	333	10,434	(1970)			81	31
Sabah	29.4	76.1	656	(1970)			22	8.6
Sarawak	48.3	125	977	(1970)			20	7.8
West Malaysia	50.7	131	8,801	(1970)			174	67
Maldives	0.115	0.298	114	(1970)			991	383
Mongolia	604	1565	1,198	(1969)	1,248	(1970)	2.1	0.8
Nepal	54.4	141	11,290	(1971)			208	80
Oman	82.0	212			657	(1970)	8.0	3.1
Pakistan[1]	310	804	42,978	(1961)	52,282	(1969)	168	65
Philippines	116	300	36,684	(1970)			317	122
Portuguese Timor	5.75	14.9	517	(1960)	611	(1970)	106	41
Qatar	8.49	22.0			79	(1970)	9.3	3.6
Ryukyu Islands	0.848	2.20	945	(1970)			1,107	428
Saudi Arabia	830	2150			7,740	(1970)	9.3	3.6
Sikkim	2.75	7.11	205	(1971)			75	29
Singapore	0.224	0.581	2,075	(1970)			9,250	3,571
Southern Yemen	111	288			1,281	(1970)	12	4.5
Syria	71.5	185	6,294	(1970)			88	34
Taiwan	13.9	36.0	13,161	(1966)	14,035	(1970)	1,010	390
Thailand	198	514	34,152	(1970)			172	66
Turkey								
Total	301	781	35,667	(1970)			118	46
in Asia	292	757	32,292	(1970)			110	43
United Arab Emirates	32.3	83.6	178	(1968)			5.5	2.1
USSR (in Asia)	6608	17,114	66,902	(1970)			10	3.9
Vietnam								
North Vietnam	61.3	159	15,917	(1960)	21,154	(1970)	345	133
South Vietnam	67.1	174	9,606	(1931)	18,332	(1970)	273	105
Yemen	75.3	195			5,733	(1970)	76	29

EUROPE

Country	Area (1000 mi²)	Area (1000 km²)	Latest Population (thousands) Census		Estimate		Density of Population (per mi²)	Density of Population (per km²)
Albania	11.1	28.7	1,626	(1960)	2,168	(1970)	195	75
Andorra	0.175	0.453	6	(1954)	15	(1970)	86	33
Austria	32.4	83.8	7,444	(1971)			230	89
Belgium	11.8	30.5	9,190	(1961)	9,676	(1970)	822	317
Bulgaria	42.8	111	8,228	(1965)	8,490	(1970)	198	77
Channel Islands	0.075	0.195	125	(1971)			1,660	641
Czechoslovakia	49.4	128	14,362	(1970)			291	112
Denmark	16.6	43.1	4,768	(1965)	4,921	(1970)	296	114
Faeroe Islands	0.540	1.40	37	(1966)	38	(1970)	70	27
Finland	130	337	4,706	(1970)			36	14
France	211	547	49,779	(1968)	50,775	(1970)	240	93

[1] Data are for West Pakistan only; East Pakistan became Bangladesh in December 1971.

EUROPE

Country	Area (1000 mi²)	Area (1000 km²)	Latest Population (thousands) Census		Estimate		Density of Population (per mi²)	Density of Population (per km²)
Germany								
East Germany	41.8	108	17,041	(1971)			408	157
West Germany	95.9	248	60,651	(1970)			632	244
Gibraltar	0.002	0.006	27	(1970)			11,655	4,500
Greece	50.9	132	8,745	(1971)			172	66
Hungary	35.9	93.0	10,316	(1970)			287	111
Iceland	39.8	103	205	(1970)			5.2	2.0
Ireland	27.1	70.3	2,971	(1971)			109	42
Isle of Man	0.227	0.588	50	(1971)			220	85
Italy	116	301	53,770	(1971)			462	179
Liechtenstein	0.062	0.157	21	(1970)			346	134
Luxembourg	1.00	2.59	340	(1970)			340	131
Malta	0.122	0.316	316	(1967)	326	(1970)	2,672	1,032
Monaco	0.0006	0.0015	23	(1968)	24	(1970)	41,440	16,000
Netherlands	15.8	40.8	11,462	(1960)	13,019	(1970)	826	319
Norway	125	324	3,591	(1960)	3,879	(1970)	31	12
Poland	121	313	32,589	(1970)			270	104
Portugal								
Total	35.6	92.1	8,668	(1970)			244	94
in Europe	35.3	91.3	8,415	(1970)			239	92
Azores	0.905	2.34	291	(1970)			322	124
Romania	91.7	237	19,103	(1966)	20,253	(1970)	221	85
San Marino	0.024	0.061	12	(1947)	19	(1970)	807	311
Spain								
Total	195	505	33,832	(1970)			174	67
in Europe	192	497	32,707	(1970)			170	66
Balearic Islands	1.94	5.01	533	(1970)			275	106
Svalbard	24.1	62.4	3	(1960)	3	(1970)	0.1	0.05
Sweden	174	450	8,077	(1970)			47	18
Switzerland	15.9	41.3	6,270	(1970)			393	152
Turkey (in Europe)	9.11	23.6	3,375	(1970)			370	143
UK	94.2	244	55,364	(1971)			588	227
England and Wales	58.3	151	48,604	(1971)			833	322
Northern Ireland	5.44	14.1	1,536	(1971)			282	109
Scotland	30.4	78.8	5,224	(1971)			172	66
USSR								
Total	8,649	22,402	241,748	(1970)			28	11
in Europe	2,042	5,288	174,846	(1970)			86	33
Vatican City	0.0002	0.0004	0.9	(1948)	1	(1970)	6,475	2,500
Yugoslavia	98.8	256	20,505	(1971)			208	80

NORTH AMERICA

Country	Area (1000 mi²)	Area (1000 km²)	Latest Population (thousands) Census		Estimate		Density of Population (per mi²)	Density of Population (per km²)
Anguilla	0.035	0.091	6	(1960)	5	(1966)	143	55
Antigua	0.171	0.442	54	(1960)	60	(1970)	352	136
Bahama Islands	4.40	11.4	175	(1970)			40	15
Barbados	0.166	0.430	238	(1970)			1,434	553
Bermuda	0.020	0.053	53	(1970)			2,590	1,000
British Honduras	8.88	23.0	120	(1970)			14	5.2

NORTH AMERICA

Country	Area (1000 mi²)	Area (1000 km²)	Latest Population (thousands) Census		Estimate		Density of Population (per mi²)	(per km²)
Canada	3852	9976	21,568	(1971)			5.6	2.2
Newfoundland	156	405	522	(1971)			3.3	1.3
Canal Zone	0.553	1.43	44	(1970)			80	31
Cayman Islands	0.100	0.259	11	(1970)			110	42
Costa Rica	19.6	50.7	1,336	(1963)	1,710	(1970)	87	34
Cuba	44.2	114	8,553	(1970)			193	75
Dominica	0.290	0.751	70	(1970)			241	93
Dominican Republic	18.8	48.7	4,006	(1970)			213	82
El Salvador	8.26	21.4	3,541	(1971)			429	165
Greenland	840	2176	40	(1965)	47	(1970)	0.06	0.02
Grenada	0.133	0.344	94	(1970)			708	273
Guadeloupe	0.687	1.78	313	(1967)	327	(1970)	476	184
Guatemala	42.0	109	4,284	(1964)	5,111	(1970)	122	47
Haiti	10.7	27.7	4,206	(1971)			393	152
Honduras	43.3	112	1,885	(1961)	2,582	(1970)	60	23
Jamaica	4.25	11.0	1,861	(1970)			438	169
Martinique	0.425	1.10	320	(1967)	338	(1970)	794	307
Mexico	762	1972	48,377	(1970)			64	25
Montserrat	0.038	0.098	12	(1970)			317	122
Netherlands Antilles	0.371	0.961	189	(1960)	222	(1970)	598	231
Nicaragua	50.2	130	1,536	(1963)	1,986	(1970)	40	15
Panama	29.2	75.6	1,425	(1970)			49	19
Puerto Rico	3.43	8.90	2,712	(1970)			790	305
Saint Kitts-Nevis	0.103	0.267	45	(1970)			437	169
Saint Lucia	0.238	0.616	101	(1970)			425	164
Saint-Pierre and Miquelon	0.093	0.242	5	(1967)	5	(1970)	54	21
Saint Vincent	0.150	0.388	89	(1970)			594	229
Trinidad and Tobago	1.98	5.13	945	(1970)			477	184
Turks and Caicos Islands	0.166	0.430	6	(1970)			36	14
USA								
Total	3676	9520	204,816	(1970)			56	22
in North America	3669	9503	204,031	(1970)			56	21
Alaska	586	1519	304	(1970)			0.5	0.2
Virgin Islands (UK)	0.059	0.153	10	(1970)			169	65
Virgin Islands (USA)	0.133	0.344	62	(1970)			466	180

OCEANIA

Country	Area (1000 mi²)	Area (1000 km²)	Latest Population (thousands) Census		Estimate		Density of Population (per mi²)	(per km²)
American Samoa	0.076	0.197	27	(1970)			355	137
Australia	2968	7687	12,728	(1971)			4.3	1.7
Tasmania	26.4	68.4	390	(1971)			15	5.7
British Solomon Islands	11.5	29.8	161	(1970)			14	5.4
Canton and Enderbury Islands	0.027	0.070	0.3	(1960)	0.3	(1970)	11	4.3
Christmas Island (Australia)	0.052	0.135	3	(1971)			58	22
Cocos Islands	0.005	0.014	0.7	(1966)	1	(1970)	185	71

OCEANIA

Country	Area		Latest Population (thousands)				Density of Population	
	(1000 mi²)	(1000 km²)	Census		Estimate		(per mi²)	(per km²)
Cook Islands	0.090	0.234	19	(1966)	24	(1970)	266	103
Fiji	7.07	18.3	477	(1966)	520	(1970)	74	28
French Polynesia	1.54	4.00	119	(1971)			77	30
Gilbert and Ellice Islands	0.342	0.886	54	(1968)	56	(1970)	164	63
Guam	0.212	0.549	85	(1970)			401	155
Indonesia (in Oceania: West Irian)	159	413	824	(1970)			5.2	2.0
Johnston and Sand Islands	0.0004	0.001	1	(1970)			2,500	965
Midway Islands	0.002	0.005	2	(1970)			1,000	386
Nauru	0.008	0.021	6	(1966)	7	(1970)	863	333
New Caledonia	7.34	19.0	101	(1969)	109	(1970)	15	5.7
New Guinea (Australia)	92.2	239	1,579	(1966)	1,752	(1970)	19	7.3
New Hebrides	5.70	14.8	78	(1967)	84	(1970)	15	5.7
New Zealand	104	269	2,863	(1971)			28	11
Niue	0.100	0.259	5	(1966)	6	(1970)	60	23
Norfolk Island	0.014	0.036	1	(1966)	1	(1970)	72	28
Pacific Islands (USA)	0.717	1.86	95	(1970)			132	51
Papua	86.1	223	606	(1966)	669	(1970)	7.8	3.0
Pitcairn Island	0.002	0.005	0.1	(1947)	0.1	(1970)	52	20
Tokelau Islands	0.004	0.010	2	(1966)	2	(1970)	518	200
Tonga	0.270	0.699	77	(1966)	87	(1970)	322	124
USA (in Oceania: Hawaii)	6.45	16.7	785	(1970)			122	47
Wake Island	0.003	0.008	2	(1970)			667	257
Wallis and Futuna Islands	0.077	0.200	9	(1969)	9	(1970)	117	45
Western Samoa	1.10	2.84	144	(1971)			131	51

SOUTH AMERICA

Country	Area		Latest Population (thousands)				Density of Population	
	(1000 mi²)	(1000 km²)	Census		Estimate		(per mi²)	(per km²)
Argentina	1072	2777	23,323	(1970)			22	8.4
Bolivia	424	1099	3,019	(1950)	4,931	(1970)	12	4.5
Brazil	3286	8512	94,509	(1970)			29	11
Chile	292	757	8,827	(1970)			30	12
Colombia	440	1139	17,485	(1964)	21,117	(1970)	48	19
Ecuador	109	284	4,650	(1962)	6,093	(1970)	56	21
Galapagos Islands	3.03	7.84	2	(1962)			0.7	0.3
Falkland Islands	6.22	16.1	3	(1962)	3	(1970)	0.5	0.2
French Guiana	35.1	91	44	(1967)	51	(1970)	1.5	0.6
Guyana	83.0	215	714	(1970)			8.6	3.3
Paraguay	157	407	1,854	(1962)	2,396	(1970)	15	5.9
Peru	496	1285	10,008	(1961)	13,586	(1970)	27	11
Surinam	63.1	163	385	(1972)			6.1	2.4
Uruguay	68.5	177	2,596	(1963)	2,886	(1970)	42	16
Venezuela	352	912	7,556	(1961)	10,431	(1970)	30	11

TABULAR GAZETTEER 1. COUNTRIES, BY CONTINENT
Part II. Evolution of Population
AFRICA

Country	Population (thousands)											
	Circa 1960		Circa 1950		Circa 1930		Circa 1900		Circa 1850		Circa 1800	
Algeria	10,784	(60)	8,682	(48)	6,553	(31)	4,429	(96)	2,496	(56)	1,500	(00?e)
Angola	4,841	(60)	4,145	(50)	2,615	(29)	4,119	(00?e)	2,500	(50?e)		
Botswana	543	(64)	296	(46)	153	(21)	121	(04)				
British Indian Ocean Territory	1	(60-62)										
Burundi[1]	2,224	(60e)	1,908	(52)								
Cameroon	5,017	(60-65)	4,085	(50e)	2,996	(31)	3,500	(00?e)				
Cape Verde Islands	200	(60)	148	(50)	146	(30)	147	(00)	83	(73)	42	(00?e)
Central African Republic	1,203	(59-60)	1,072	(50e)	1,066	(26)	2,130	(06e)				
Ceuta	73	(60)	60	(50)	51	(30)	13	(00)	7	(57)		
Chad	3,254	(63-64)	2,241	(50e)	974	(26)	885	(06e)				
Comoro Islands	183	(58)	166	(51)	130	(31)	96	(06)	28	(50)	21	(00?e)
Congo	797	(60-61)	684	(50e)	699	(26)	259	(06e)				
Dahomey	2,106	(61)	1,535	(51e)	980	(26)	749	(06)				
Egypt	26,085	(60)	19,022	(47)	14,218	(27)	9,794	(97)	4,476	(46)	2,460	(00e)
Equatorial Guinea	246	(60)	199	(50)	167	(32)	161	(00e)				
Ethiopia	20,600	(60e)	15,000	(50e)	5,500	(30?e)	4,500	(00?e)	3,000	(31e)	1,800	(00?e)
Eritrea	[1,422	(62e)]	1,104	(50e)	598	(31)	330	(99)				
French Southern and Antarctic Lands	0.1	(63e)										
French Territory of the Afars and the Issas	81	(60-61)	56	(51e)	70	(31)	208	(06)				
Gabon	449	(60-61)	409	(50e)	389	(26)	376	(06e)				
Gambia	315	(63)	280	(51)	200	(31)	103	(01)				
Ghana	6,727	(60)	3,736	(48)	2,870	(31)	1,503	(11)	408	(71e)		
Guinea	3,072	(60e)	2,570	(55)	2,096	(26)	1,498	(06)				

[1] Burundi with Rwanda: 3,406 (1935e).

AFRICA

Country	Population (thousands)											
	Circa 1960		Circa 1950		Circa 1930		Circa 1900		Circa 1850		Circa 1800	
Ivory Coast	3,100	(57-58)	2,169	(51e)	1,725	(26)	889	(06)				
Kenya	8,636	(62)	5,406	(48)	3,025	(31)	3,000	(00?e)				
Lesotho	642	(56)	564	(46)	562	(36)	349	(04)	128	(75)		
Liberia	1,016	(62)	1,648	(49e)	2,500	(30?e)	2,060	(00?e)	250	(50e)		
Libya	1,564	(64)	1,089	(54)	704	(31)	1,000	(00?e)	750	(50?e)	1,000	(00?e)
Malagasy Republic	5,393	(60e)	4,256	(50e)	3,759	(31)	2,505	(01)	3,000	(50?e)	4,000	(00?e)
Malawi	3,460	(60e)	2,330	(50e)	1,604	(31)	970	(11)				
Mali[1]	4,100	(60-61)	3,347	(51e)	2,635	(26)						
Mauritania	1,050	(64-65)	657	(51e)	289	(26)	223	(06)				
Mauritius	701	(62)	517	(52)	403	(31)	371	(01)	181	(51)	20	(90e)
Melilla	79	(60)	81	(50)	63	(30)	9	(00)	2	(57)		
Morocco	11,626	(60)	9,125	(52)	6,235	(31)	7,000	(00?e)	8,500	(50?e)	5,000	(00?e)
Mozambique	6,604	(60)	5,732	(50)	4,006	(30)	3,120	(00?e)	300	(50?e)		
Niger[2]	2,766	(59-60)	2,127	(51e)	1,219	(26)						
Nigeria	55,670	(63)	29,731	(52-53)	19,158	(31)	17,133	(11e)				
Portugal (in Africa: Madeira Islands)	268	(60)	267	(50)	212	(30)	151	(00)	107	(54)	90	(00?e)
Portuguese Guinea	521	(60)	511	(50)	377	(31)	820	(00?e)				
Reunion	349	(61)	242	(46)	198	(31)	173	(02)	106	(52)	65	(04)
Rhodesia	3,857	(62)	1,765	(48)	1,109	(31)	613	(04e)				
Rwanda[3]	2,665	(60e)	2,148	(52)								
Saint Helena	5	(56)	5	(46)	4	(31)	4	(04)	7	(61)	2	(05)
Sao Tome and Principe	64	(60)	60	(50)	59	(21)	42	(00)	17	(50?e)	5	(00?e)
Senegal	3,110	(60-61)	2,093	(51e)	1,358	(26)	1,247	(11)				
Seychelles	41	(60)	35	(47)	27	(31)	19	(01)	7	(50)	7	(25)
Sierra Leone	2,180	(63)	1,858	(48)	1,769	(31)	1,403	(11)				

[1] Mali with Niger: 5,059 (1906).
[2] Niger with Mali: 5,059 (1906).
[3] Rwanda with Burundi: 3,406 (1935e).

AFRICA

Country	Circa 1960		Circa 1950		Circa 1930		Circa 1900		Circa 1850		Circa 1800	
	Population (thousands)											
Somalia	2,010	(60e)	1,747	(51e)	1,022	(31)	400	(00?e)				
South Africa	16,003	(60)	12,668	(51)	9,588	(36)	5,176	(04)	267[1]	(56)	62[1]	(98)
South-West Africa	526	(60)	418	(51)	259	(26)	207	(04e)				
Spain (in Africa: Canary Islands)	944	(60)	793	(50)	555	(30)	359	(00)	234	(57)	174	(97)
Spanish Sahara	24	(60)	37	(50e)	32	(30?e)	115	(00?e)				
Sudan	10,263	(56)	8,350	(50e)	5,508	(31e)	3,000	(10e)				
Swaziland	237	(56)	185	(46)	157	(36)	85	(11)				
Tanzania												
Tanganyika	8,788	(57)	7,408	(52)	5,023	(31)	4,145	(13)				
Zanzibar	299	(58)	264	(48)	235	(31)	197	(10)	130	(46e)	200	(11e)
Togo	1,440	(58-60)	1,395	(50e)	1,044	(31e)	2,250	(00?e)				
Tunisia	4,113	(56)	3,231	(46)	2,411	(31)	1,939	(11)	1,520	(81)	1,000	(00?e)
Uganda	6,537	(59)	4,959	(48)	3,553	(31)	2,843	(11)				
Upper Volta	4,400	(60-61)	3,109	(51e)	3,240	(26)						
Zaire	12,769	(55-58)	11,258	(50e)	8,764	(30e)	9,000	(10e)				
Zambia	3,490	(63)	1,878	(50)	1,345	(31)	497	(00?e)				

ASIA

Country	Circa 1960		Circa 1950		Circa 1930		Circa 1900		Circa 1850		Circa 1800	
Afghanistan	14,483	(61e)	12,000	(50e)	7,000	(30?e)	4,550	(00?e)	4,000	(50?e)	3,000	(00?e)
Bahrain	143	(59)	110	(50)	120	(30?e)	70	(00?e)				
Bangladesh[2]												
Bhutan	670	(60e)	300	(50e)	250	(30?e)	200	(00?e)	20	(64e)		
Brunei	84	(60)	41	(47)	30	(31)	22	(11)				
Burma	22,325	(60e)	16,824	(41)	14,667	(31)	10,491	(01)	7,722	(91)	4,231	(26e)

[1] For Cape of Good Hope Province only.

[2] East Pakistan until December 1971 (see under Pakistan).

ASIA

Country	Population (thousands)											
	Circa 1960		Circa 1950		Circa 1930		Circa 1900		Circa 1850		Circa 1800	
Cambodia	5,729	(62)	3,640	(51e)	2,806	(31)	1,194	(06)	1,000	(50?e)	1,000	(00?e)
Ceylon	10,582	(63)	8,099	(53)	5,307	(31)	3,566	(01)	2,400	(71)	852	(24)
China	646,530	(57e)	582,603	(53)	438,933	(31e)	372,563	(10e)	429,931	(50e)	295,273	(00e)
Cyprus	578	(60)	450	(46)	348	(31)	237	(01)	186	(81)	[84	(00?e)]
Gaza Strip	377	(60e)	198	(50e)								
Hong Kong	3,133	(61)	2,015	(51e)	840	(31)	399	(01)	33	(50)		
India	435,512[1]	(61)	357,303[1]	(51)	338,061[2]	(31)	283,870[2]	(01)	203,415[2]	(67-72)	131,000[2]	(20e)
Indonesia												
Total	97,069	(61)	77,271	(50e)	60,727	(30)	37,694	(00e)	19,319	(63e)	13,476	(00?e)
in Asia	96.319	(61)	76,571	(50e)	60,413	(30)	37,494	(00e)	19,119	(63e)		
Iran	18,955	(56)	16,550	(40)	15,055	(33)	9,000	(97e)	5,000	(50?e)		
Iraq	6,340	(57)	4,816	(47)	3,300	(30?e)	[1,398	(10e)]				
Israel	2,183	(61)	1,258	(50e)	1,036	(31)						
Japan	93,419	(60)	83,419	(50)	64,450	(30)	43,756	(98)	33,111	(72)	15,000	(00?e)
Jordan	1,706	(61)	1,329	(52)	300	(29e)						
Kashmir-Jammu	4,835	(61e)	4,022	(41)	[3,646	(31)]	[2,906	(01)]				
Korea					20,438	(30)	12,934	(09)	10,519	(83)		
North Korea	10,600	(60e)	9,102	(49e)								
South Korea	24,989	(60)	20,167	(49)								
Kuwait	322	(61)	170	(50e)	51	(30?e)						
Laos	1,805	(60e)	1,360	(51e)	944	(31)	664	(06)	1,000	(50?e)	3,000	(00?e)
Lebanon	2,152	(61e)	1,257	(50e)	629	(21–22)	[200	(00?e)]				
Macao	169	(60)	188	(50)	158	(27)	64	(99)	52	(62e)	34	(22e)
Malaysia												
Sabah	454	(60)	334	(51)	270	(31)	105	(01)				
Sarawak	745	(60)	546	(47)	440	(37e)	500	(01e)				
West Malaysia	6,279	(57)	4,908	(47)	3,788	(31)	2,351	(11)				

[1] Exc Burma and Kashmir-Jammu.

[2] Exc Burma.

ASIA

Country	Population (thousands)											
	Circa 1960		Circa 1950		Circa 1930		Circa 1900		Circa 1850		Circa 1800	
Maldives	82	(56)	82	(46)	79	(31)	72	(11)	175	(50?e)		
Mongolia	1,017	(63)	732	(50)	648	(18)						
Nepal	9,413	(61)	8,432	(52–54)	5,574	(20)	5,639	(11)	2,000	(50?e)	2,000	(20e)
Oman	565	(60e)	550	(50e)	500	(30?e)	1,000	(00?e)				
Pakistan	93,832[3]	(61)	75,842[3]	(51)	[56,887[1]	(31)]	[45,504[1]	(01)]				
East Pakistan	50,854	(61)	42,063	(51)	[35,604[1]	(31)]	[28,928[1]	(01)]				
West Pakistan	42,978[3]	(61)	33,779[3]	(51)	[21,283[1]	(31)]	[16,577[1]	(01)]				
Philippines	27,088	(60)	19,234	(48)	16,000	(39)	7,635	(03)	6,171	(77)	1,522	(99e)
Portuguese Timor	517	(60)	442	(50)	442	(26)	300	(00?e)				
Qatar	55	(63e)	17	(51e)	26	(30?e)						
Ryukyu Islands	883	(60)	918	(50)	[785[2]	(30)]	[454[2]	(98)]				
Saudi Arabia	6,400	(62e)	6,000	(51e)	4,200	(30?e)	[3,000	(00?e)]	[4,000	(50?e)]		
Sikkim	162	(61)	138	(51)	110	(31)	59	(01)				
Singapore	1,446	(57)	938	(47)	560	(31)	229	(01)	54	(50)	0.2	(00?e)
Southern Yemen	1,000	(60e)	750	(50e)	650	(37e)	194	(00?e)				
Syria	4,565	(60)	3,503	(50e)	1,506	(21–22)	[2,690	(00?e)]				
Taiwan	9,368	(56)	7,618	(50)	4,593	(30)	2,925	(01)				
Thailand	26,258	(60)	17,443	(47)	11,506	(29)	8,266	(11)	5,000	(54e)	1,900	(00?e)
Turkey												
Total	27,755	(60)	20,947	(50)	13,648	(27)	23,813	(10e)	26,636	(44–50?e)	20,912	(00?e)
in Asia	25,470	(60)	19,363	(50)	12,608	(27)	17,683[4]	(10e)	16,050[4]	(50?e)	11,090[4]	(00?e)
United Arab Emirates	111	(62e)	80	(49e)								
USSR (in Asia)	54,648	(59)	38,614	(39)	26,752	(26)	13,506	(97)	4,103	(56)	2,500	(95?e)
Vietnam					17,702	(31)	14,281	(06)	10,000	(50?e)	17,000	(00?e)
North Vietnam	15,917	(60)	16,114	(53e)								
South Vietnam	14,100	(60e)	9,766	(53e)								

[1] Included with India.
[2] Included with Japan.
[3] Exc Kashmir-Jammu.
[4] Inc Iraq, Lebanon, Saudi Arabia, Syria, and Yemen.

ASIA

Country	Population (thousands)											
	Circa 1960		Circa 1950		Circa 1930		Circa 1900		Circa 1850		Circa 1800	
Yemen	5,000	(60e)	4,500	(50e)	2,000	(30?e)	[750	(10e)]				

EUROPE

Country	Population (thousands)											
	Circa 1960		Circa 1950		Circa 1930		Circa 1900		Circa 1850		Circa 1800	
Albania	1,626	(60)	1,122	(45)	1,003	(30)						
Andorra	8	(60e)	6	(54)	5	(21)	8	(01)	7	(50?e)		
Austria	7,074	(61)	6,934	(51)	6,760	(34)	26,151	(00)	17,535	(50)	8,511	(00)
Belgium	9,190	(61)	8,512	(47)	8,092	(30)	6,694	(00)	4,337	(46)	3,763	(30)
Bulgaria	7,614	(56)	7,029	(46)	5,479	(26)	3,744	(00)	[2,008	(80)]	[1,800	(00?e)]
Channel Islands	111	(61)	103	(51)	93	(31)	96	(01)	91	(51)	49	(21)
Czechoslovakia	13,746	(61)	12,338	(50)	14,730	(30)						
Denmark	4,585	(60)	4,281	(50)	3,544	(30)	2,450	(01)	1,408	(50)	926	(01)
Faeroe Islands	35	(60)	32	(50)	24	(30)	15	(01)	8	(50)	5	(01)
Finland	4,446	(60)	4,030	(50)	3,463	(30)	2,713	(00)	1,637	(50)	833	(00)
France	46,528	(62)	42,844	(54)	41,835	(31)	38,962	(01)	35,783	(51)	27,349	(01)
Germany					65,218	(33)	56,367	(00)	29,800	(49)	24,833	(16)
East Germany	17,004	(64)	18,388	(50)								
West Germany	56,175	(61)	49,843	(50)								
Gibraltar	25	(61)	23	(51)	17	(31)	20	(01)	16	(44)	3	(87)
Greece	8,389	(61)	7,633	(51)	6,205	(28)	2,434	(96)	987	(48)	[753	(28)]
Hungary	9,961	(60)	9,205	(49)	8,685	(30)	19,255	(00)	13,192	(50)	8,003	(85)
Iceland	176	(60)	144	(50)	109	(30)	78	(01)	59	(50)	47	(01)
Ireland	2,818[1]	(61)	2,961[1]	(51)	2,972[1]	(26)	4,459	(01)	6,552	(51)	6,802	(21)
Isle of Man	48	(61)	55	(51)	49	(31)	55	(01)	52	(51)	28	(92)
Italy	49,904	(61)	47,159	(51)	40,310	(31)	33,172	(01)	25,017	(61)	14,134	(00?e)
Liechtenstein	17	(60)	14	(50)	10	(30)	10	(01)	8	(52)	6	(12)

[1] Exc Northern Ireland.

EUROPE

Country	Population (thousands)											
	Circa 1960		Circa 1950		Circa 1930		Circa 1900		Circa 1850		Circa 1800	
Luxembourg	315	(60)	291	(47)	300	(30)	235	(00)	195	(51)	134	(21)
Malta	320	(57)	306	(48)	242	(31)	185	(01)	123	(51)	114	(98)
Monaco	22	(62)	20	(51)	25	(28)	15	(97)	8	(57)	6	(00?e)
Netherlands	11,462	(60)	9,625	(47)	7,936	(30)	5,104	(99)	3,057	(49)	1,880	(95)
Norway	3,591	(60)	3,279	(50)	2,814	(30)	2,240	(00)	1,490	(55)	883	(01)
Poland	29,776	(60)	25,008	(50)	32,107	(31)	9,402	(97)	4,852	(51e)	2,600	(15e)
Portugal												
Total	8,851	(60)	8,441	(50)	6,826	(30)	5,423	(00)	3,844	(54)	3,115	(01e)
in Europe	8,583[1]	(60)	8,174[1]	(50)	6,614[1]	(30)	5,272[1]	(00)	3,737[1]	(54)	3,025[1]	(01e)
Azores	[328	(60)]	[319	(50)]	[255	(30)]	[256	(00)]	[238	(54)]	[142	(00?e)]
Romania	17,489	(56)	15,873	(48)	14,282	(30)	5,957	(99)	[3,865	(59)]	[2,200	(00?e)]
San Marino	15	(60e)	12	(47)	13	(30e)	10	(06)	7	(64)	7	(00?e)
Spain												
Total	30,431	(60)	27,977	(50)	23,564	(30)	18,594	(00)	15,455	(57)	10,541	(97)
in Europe	29,486	(60)	27,183	(50)	23,009	(30)	18,235	(00)	15,220	(57)	10,367	(97)
Balearic Islands	443	(60)	422	(50)	366	(30)	312	(00)	263	(57)	187	(97)
Svalbard	3	(60)	2	(46)	0.6	(30)						
Sweden	7,495	(60)	7,042	(50)	6,142	(30)	5,136	(00)	3,483	(50)	2,347	(00)
Switzerland	5,429	(60)	4,715	(50)	4,066	(30)	3,315	(00)	2,393	(50)	1,843	(95)
Turkey (in Europe)	2,285	(60)	1,584	(50)	1,041	(27)	6,130	(10e)	10,586[2]	(44e)	9,822[3]	(00?e)
UK	52,709	(61)	50,225	(51)	46,052	(31)	37,000[4]	(01)	20,817[4]	(51)	10,501[4]	(01)
England and Wales	46,105	(61)	43,758	(51)	39,952	(31)	32,528	(01)	17,928	(51)	8,893	(01)
Northern Ireland	1,425	(61)	1,371	(51)	1,257	(26)						
Scotland	5,179	(61)	5,096	(51)	4,843	(31)	4,472	(01)	2,889	(51)	1,608	(01)

1 Inc Azores.

2 Inc Bulgaria and Romania.

3 Inc Bulgaria, Greece, and Romania.

4 Exc Ireland.

EUROPE

Country	Population (thousands)											
	Circa 1960		Circa 1950		Circa 1930		Circa 1900		Circa 1850		Circa 1800	
USSR												
Total	208,827	(59)	170,557	(39)	147,028	(26)	116,238	(97)	64,903	(56)	33,000	(95?e)
in Europe	154,179	(59)	131,943	(39)	120,276	(26)	102,732	(97)	60,800	(56)	30,500	(95?e)
Vatican City	0.9	(60e)	0.9	(48)	0.6	(30)						
Yugoslavia	18,549	(61)	15,772	(48)	13,934	(31)						

NORTH AMERICA

Country	Population (thousands)											
	Circa 1960		Circa 1950		Circa 1930		Circa 1900		Circa 1850		Circa 1800	
Anguilla	6	(60)	5	(46)	4	(21)	4	(01)	3	(71)	3	(25)
Antigua	54	(60)	42	(46)	30	(21)	35	(01)	36	(44)	36	(17)
Bahama Islands	136	(63)	85	(53)	60	(31)	54	(01)	28	(51)	14	(03)
Barbados	232	(60)	193	(46)	156	(21)	183	(91)	136	(51)	82	(11)
Bermuda	43	(60)	37	(50)	28	(31)	18	(01)	11	(51)	10	(90)
British Honduras	90	(60)	59	(46)	51	(31)	37	(01)	11	(45)		
Canada	18,238	(61)	14,009	(51)	10,377[1]	(31)	5,371[1]	(01)	2,561[1]	(52)	430[1]	(14e)
Newfoundland	[458	(61)]	[361	(51)]	290	(35)	221	(01)	96	(45)	70	(16e)
Canal Zone	42	(60)	53	(50)	39	(30)	63	(12)				
Cayman Islands	8	(60)	7	(43)	5	(21)	4	(91)	2	(34e)	0.9	(02)
Costa Rica	1,336	(63)	801	(50)	472	(27)	243	(92)	80	(44)		
Cuba	6,826	(60e)	5,829	(53)	3,962	(31)	1,573	(99)	1,008	(41)	272	(92)
Dominica	60	(60)	48	(46)	37	(21)	29	(01)	22	(44)	26	(05)
Dominican Republic	3,047	(60)	2,136	(50)	1,479	(35)	610	(00?e)	136	(50?e)	153	(85)
El Salvador	2,511	(61)	1,856	(50)	1,434	(30)	1,007	(01)	300	(50?e)		

[1] Exc Newfoundland.

NORTH AMERICA

Country	Population (thousands)											
	Circa 1960		Circa 1950		Circa 1930		Circa 1900		Circa 1850		Circa 1800	
Greenland	33	(60)	24	(51)	17	(30)	12	(01)	10	(55)	6	(05)
Grenada	89	(60)	72	(46)	66	(21)	63	(01)	33	(51)	31	(11)
Guadeloupe	283	(61)	278	(46)	267	(31)	182	(01)	125	(52)	115	(12)
Guatemala	4,284	(64)	2,791	(50)	2,005	(21)	1,365	(93)	850	(55e)	396	(1778)
Haiti	4,156	(60e)	3,097	(50)	1,631	(18)	1,294	(01)	572	(50?e)	511	(89e)
Honduras	1,885	(61)	1,369	(50)	854	(30)	544	(01)	202	(50?e)		
Jamaica	1,610	(60)	1,237	(43)	858	(21)	639	(91)	380	(44)	360	(12e)
Martinique	292	(61)	262	(46)	234	(31)	204	(01)	130	(53)	84	(89)
Mexico	34,923	(60)	25,791	(50)	16,553	(30)	13,607	(00)	6,382	(31)	5,800	(03e)
Montserrat	12	(60)	14	(46)	12	(21)	12	(01)	7	(46)	11	(00?e)
Netherlands Antilles	189	(60)	162	(50e)	72	(30)	55	(11)	32	(63)	37	(00?e)
Nicaragua	1,536	(63)	1,057	(50)	638	(20)	505	(06)	257	(67)	107	(1778)
Panama	1,076	(60)	805	(50)	467	(30)	337	(11)				
Puerto Rico	2,350	(60)	2,211	(50)	1,544	(30)	953	(99)	448	(46)	155	(00)
Saint Kitts-Nevis	51	(60)	41	(46)	34	(21)	43	(01)	33	(50)	44	(00?e)
Saint Lucia	86	(60)	70	(46)	52	(21)	50	(01)	24	(51)	17	(03)
Saint-Pierre and Miquelon	5	(62)	5	(51)	4	(31)	6	(06)	3	(61)	2	(00?e)
Saint Vincent	80	(60)	62	(46)	48	(31)	41	(91)	30	(51)	24	(12?)
Trinidad and Tobago	834	(60)	563	(46)	413	(31)	274	(01)	83	(51)	34	(02)
Turks and Caicos Islands	6	(60)	6	(43)	6	(21)	5	(01)	4	(61)	2	(03e)
USA												
Total	180,698	(60)	151,132[1]	(50)	122,775[1]	(30)	75,995[1]	(00)	23,192[1]	(50)	5,308[1]	(00)
in North America	180,065	(60)	151,132[2]	(50)	122,775[2]	(30)	75,995[2]	(00)	23,192[2]	(50)	5,308[2]	(00)
Alaska	[226	(60)]	129	(50)	59	(29)	64	(00)	11	(56)	0.8	(00?e)
Virgin Islands (UK)	7	(60)	7	(46)	5	(21)	5	(01)	7	(41)		
Virgin Islands (USA)	32	(60)	27	(50)	22	(30)	31	(01)	40	(50)	43	(35)

[1] Exc Alaska and Hawaii.

[2] Exc Alaska.

OCEANIA

Country	Population (thousands)											
	Circa 1960		Circa 1950		Circa 1930		Circa 1900		Circa 1850		Circa 1800	
American Samoa	20	(60)	19	(50)	10	(30)	6	(00)				
Australia	10,596	(61)	7,626	(47)	6,690	(33)	3,954	(01)	1,063[1]	(61)	37[1]	(28)
Tasmania	[350	(61)]	[257	(47)]	[228	(33)]	[172	(01)]	70	(51)	6	(21)
British Solomon Islands	124	(59)	100	(50e)	95	(31)	150	(11e)				
Canton and Enderbury Islands	0.3	(60)	0.3	(50)	0.04	(40)						
Christmas Island (Australia)	3	(61)	0.9	(47)	1	(26)	0.04	(98e)				
Cocos Islands	0.6	(61)	2	(47)	0.9	(24)	0.6	(98)				
Cook Islands	18	(61)	15	(51)	10	(26)	8	(02)	16	(50?e)		
Fiji	346	(56)	260	(46)	198	(36)	120	(01)	127	(81)		
French Polynesia	85	(62)	63	(51)	40	(31)	31	(06)	16	(76)	120	(00?e)
Gilbert and Ellice Islands	49	(63)	36	(47)	34	(31)	31	(11)				
Guam	67	(60)	59	(50)	19	(30)	10	(01)				
Indonesia (in Oceania: West Irian)	750	(60e)	700	(50e)	314	(30)	200	(00?e)	200	(65e)		
Johnston and Sand Islands	0.2	(60)	0.05	(50)	0.07	(40)						
Midway Islands	2	(60)	0.4	(50)	0.04	(30)						
Nauru	5	(61)	3	(49)	3	(33)						
New Caledonia	87	(63)	68	(56)	57	(31)	51	(01)	42	(50?e)		
New Guinea (Australia)	1,402	(60e)	1,080	(50e)	520	(33e)						
New Hebrides	63	(60e)	49	(50e)	60	(30e)	50	(00?e)			110	(00?e)
New Zealand	2,415	(61)	1,939	(51)	1,408	(26)	816	(01)	102	(61)	100	(00?e)
Niue	5	(61)	5	(51)	4	(28)	4	(00)	1	(54e)		
Norfolk Island	0.8	(61)	0.9	(47)	1	(33)	0.9	(01)	0.5	(71)	0.9	(05)
Pacific Islands (USA)	71	(58)	55	(50)	70	(30)						
Papua	503	(60e)	373	(50e)	280	(30?e)	350	(91e)				
Pitcairn Island	0.1	(63e)	0.1	(47)	0.2	(21)	0.2	(05)	0.2	(51)	0.03	(00)
Tokelau Islands	2	(61)	2	(51)	1	(26)	1	(00?e)				
Tonga	57	(56)	34	(39)	29	(31)	21	(00)	18	(50?e)	200	(00?e)

[1] Exc Tasmania and exc aborigines in Australia.

OCEANIA

Country	Population (thousands)											
	Circa 1960		Circa 1950		Circa 1930		Circa 1900		Circa 1850		Circa 1800	
USA (in Oceania: Hawaii)	633	(60)	500	(50)	368	(30)	154	(00)	84	(50)	130	(32)
Wake Island	1	(60)	0.3	(50)								
Wallis and Futuna Islands	11	(62e)	8	(55)	6	(31)						
Western Samoa	114	(61)	85	(51)	40	(26)	33	(00)	34	(50?e)		

SOUTH AMERICA

Country	Population (thousands)											
	Circa 1960		Circa 1950		Circa 1930		Circa 1900		Circa 1850		Circa 1800	
Argentina	20,011	(60)	15,894	(47)	7,924	(14)	4,045	(95)	1,830	(69)	311	(97e)
Bolivia	3,453	(60e)	3,019	(50)	2,397	(30e)	1,696	(00)	1,544	(54)	1,019	(31)
Brazil	70,992	(60)	51,989	(50)	30,636	(20)	17,438	(00)	9,930	(72)	3,200	(06e)
Chile	7,375	(60)	5,933	(52)	4,287	(30)	2,712	(95)	1.439	(54)	1,010	(35)
Colombia	17,485	(64)	11,356	(51)	7,851	(28)	4,355	(05)	2,244	(51)	1,224	(25)
Ecuador	4,650	(62)	3,203	(50)	2,500	(30e)	1,272	(92e)	870	(46e)	558	(25)
Galapagos Islands	2	(62)	1	(50)	2	(34e)	0.2	(00?e)	0.2	(35e)	0	(00)
Falkland Islands	3	(62)	2	(53)	3	(31)	2	(01)	0.3	(47)		
French Guiana	34	(61)	29	(46)	28	(31)	33	(01)	21	(41)	16	(15e)
Guyana	560	(60)	376	(46)	311	(31)	278	(91)	136	(51)	98	(31)
Paraguay	1,854	(62)	1,358	(50)	932	(36)	656	(99)	1,337	(57)	560	(00?e)
Peru	10,008	(61)	7,969	(50e)	6,558	(40)	4,610	(96e)	2,001	(50)	1,076	(91–95)
Surinam	324	(64)	210	(50)	119	(21)	87	(01)	58	(63)		
Uruguay	2,596	(63)	2,193	(50e)	1,877	(30e)	916	(00)	132	(52)	31	(96e)
Venezuela	7,556	(61)	5,092	(50)	3,027	(26)	2,324	(91)	1,888	(57)	660	(25)

TABULAR GAZETTEER 1. COUNTRIES, BY CONTINENT
Part III. Miscellaneous Statistics
AFRICA

Country	Birth and death rates			Life Expectancy (yrs)				Length of roads			Railroad route length		
	Period	Births	Deaths	Period	Men	Women	Avg	Year	(mi)	(km)	Year	(mi)	(km)
Algeria	1966-68	43.3		1965-70			50.7e	1969	47,116	75,825	1969	2,455	3,951
	1965-70		16.9e										
Angola	1965-70	50.1e	30.2e	1965-70			33.5e	1965?	22,991	37,000	1969	1,712	2,755
Botswana	1965-70	44.2e	22.6e	1965-70			41.0e	1969	4,840	7,779	1969	399	642
British Indian Ocean Territory												0	0
Burundi	1965-70	48.1e	25.2e	1965	35.0e	38.5e	36.7e	1965?	4,350	7,000		0	0
Cameroon	1965-70	43.1e	22.8e	1965-70			41.0e	1969	27,414[1]	44,119[1]	1969	444	715
Cape Verde Islands	1966-68	42.0	10.0					1965?	311	500		0	0
Central African Republic	1965-70	46.1e	25.1e	1959-60	33e	36e	34.5e	1969	13,235	21,300		0	0
Ceuta	1966-70	16.4	6.2									0	0
Chad	1965-70	47.7e	25.0e	1963-64	29e	35e	32e	1969	19,091	30,725		0	0
Comoro Islands								1965?	621	1,000		0	0
Congo	1965-70	44.4e	22.8e	1965-70			41.0e	1965?	6,835	11,000	1968?	497	800
Dahomey	1965-70	50.9e	25.5e	1965-70			38.5e	1969	4,301	6,922	1969	360	579
Egypt	1965-70	44.1e	16.5e	1961	51.6	53.8	52.7	1965?	18,641	30,000	1968?	3,185	5,126
Equatorial Guinea	1965-70	35.0e	22.1e	1965-70			41.0e	1965?	621	1,000		0	0
Ethiopia	1965-70	45.6e	25.0e	1965-70			38.5e	1965?	49,710	80,000	1969	675	1,087
Eritrea											1968	190	306
French Southern and Antarctic Lands												0	0
French Territory of the Afars and the Issas								1965?	1,864	3,000	1969	62	100
Gabon	1965-70	32.5e	25.0e	1960–61	25e	45e	35e	1969	3,566	5,739		0	0
Gambia	1965-70	42.5e	23.1e	1965-70			41.0e	1965?	1,243	2,000		0	0

[1] For East Cameroon only; data for West Cameroon unavailable.

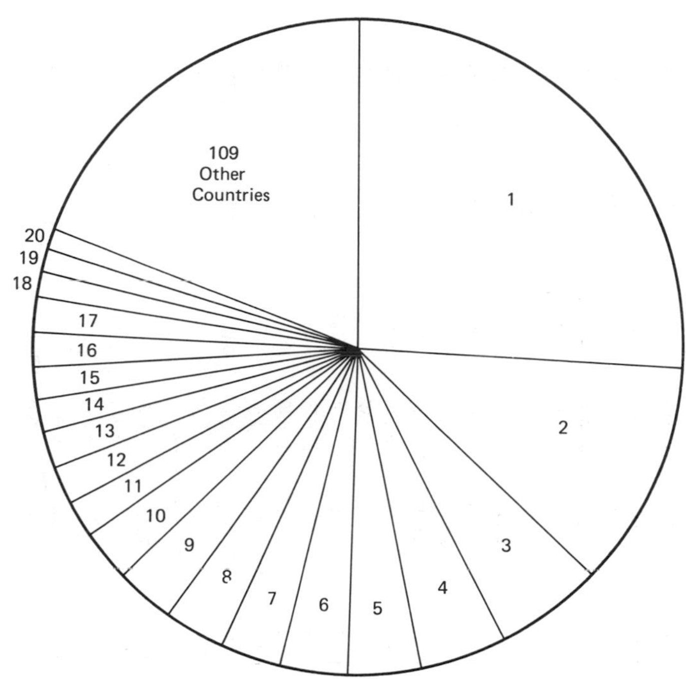

1	USA	26.6%	8	France	2.9%	15	UK	1.6%
2	USSR	10.4%	9	West Germany	2.7%	16	South Africa	1.6%
3	Canada	5.7%	10	Brazil	2.6%	17	Spain	1.4%
4	India	4.7%	11	Poland	2.1%	18	East Germany	1.2%
5	Argentina	3.3%	12	Japan	2.1%	19	Cuba	1.2%
6	Australia	3.3%	13	Mexico	1.9%	20	Czechoslovakia	1.1%
7	China	3.1%	14	Italy	1.6%		109 other countries	18.9%

Figure 28. Railroad route length of countries as percentage of world railroad route length.

AFRICA

Country	Birth and death rates			Life Expectancy (yrs)				Length of roads			Railroad route length		
	Period	Births	Deaths	Period	Men	Women	Avg	Year	(mi)	(km)	Year	(mi)	(km)
Ghana	1965-70	46.6e	17.8e	1965-70			46.0e	1965?	14,233	22,907	1969	592	953
Guinea	1965-70	47.2e	25.1e	1955	26e	28e	27e	1965?	6,214	10,000	1968	411	661
Ivory Coast	1965-70	46.0e	22.7e	1965-70			41.0e	1969	21,719	34,954	1968	743	1,196
Kenya	1965-70	47.8e	17.5e	1965-70			47.5e	1969	26,008	41,856	1967	1,286	2,069
Lesotho	1965-70	38.8e	21.0e	1965–70			43.5e	1965?	932	1,500	1967	1	2
Liberia	1969-70	50e	18e	1962	36.1e	38.6e	37.3e	1965?	3,728	6,000	1968?	216	348
Libya	1965-70	45.9e	15.8e	1965-70			52.1e	1965?	9,321	15,000	1968?	108	174
Malagasy Republic	1966	46e	25e	1966	37.5e	38.3e	37.9e	1969	23,680	38,110	1969	549	884
Malawi	1965-70	49.0e	25.0e	1965-70			38.5e	1969	6,517	10,488	1969	289	465
Mali	1965-70	49.8e	26.6e	1965-70			37.2e	1965?	8,078	13,000	1969	398	641
Mauritania	1965-70	44.4e	22.7e	1965-70			41.0e	1965?	3,728	6,000	1969	404	650
Mauritius	1966-70	30.1	8.4	1961-63	58.7	61.9	60.3	1966	1,076	1,732		0	0
Melilla	1966-70	15.3	6.2					1960?	9	14	1960?	7	12
Morocco	1965-70	49.5e	16.5e	1965-70			50.5e	1969	15,334	24,678	1969	1,104	1,777
Mozambique	1965-70	43.3e	22.9e	1965-70			41.0e	1965?	26,719	43,000	1969	2,096	3,373
Niger	1965-70	52.2e	23.3e	1965-70			41.0e	1969	4,192	6,746		0	0
Nigeria	1965-70	49.6e	24.9e	1965-66	37.2	36.7	36.9	1965	55,538	89,380	1969	2,178	3,505
Portugal (in Africa: Madeira Islands)								1968	312[1]	502[1]		0	0
Portuguese Guinea	1965-70	40.7e	29.9e	1965-70			33.5e	1965?	1,864	3,000		0	0
Reunion	1966-70	36.4	9.0	1959-63	54.1	60.6	57.3	1965?	1,243	2,000	1968?	37	59
Rhodesia	1965-70	48.4e	14.4e	1965-70			51.4e	1969	48,759	78,470	1969	1,611	2,592
Rwanda	1965-70	51.8e	23.3e	1965-70			41.0e	1965?	3,107	5,000		0	0
Saint Helena								1965?	62	100		0	0
Sao Tome and Principe	1966-68	50.1	15.5					1965?	249	400		0	0
Senegal	1965-70	46.3e	22.8e	1965-70			41.0e	1969	9,583	15,422	1968?	641	1,032
Seychelles				1960	60.8	65.9	63.3	1965?	75	120		0	0

[1] Exc local and urban roads.

AFRICA

Country	Birth and death rates			Life Expectancy (yrs)				Length of roads			Railroad route length		
	Period	Births	Deaths	Period	Men	Women	Avg	Year	(mi)	(km)	Year	(mi)	(km)
Sierra Leone	1965-70	44.8e	22.7e	1965-70			41.0e	1965?	3,107	5,000	1969	311	500
Somalia	1965-70	45.9e	24.0e	1965-70			38.5e	1969	8,324	13,396		0	0
South Africa	1965-70	40.3e	16.6e	1965-70			49.0e	1967	115,321[1]	185,590[1]	1968	12,274	19,753
South-West Africa	1965-70	44.4e	25.0e	1965-70			38.5e	1966	37,357	60,121	1965?	1,453	2,338
Spain (in Africa: Canary Islands)								1968	1,430	2,302		0	0
Spanish Sahara								1965?	932	1,500		0	0
Sudan	1965-70	48.9e	18.4e	1965-70			47.6e	1965	46,603	75,000	1969	2,972	4,783
Swaziland	1965-70	52.3e	23.5e	1965-70			41.0e	1965?	1,243	2,000	1969	139	224
Tanzania	1967	47e	22e	1967			40.5e	1969	10,404	16,743	1967	1,599	2,573
Tanganyika	1957	46e	24.5e	1957			37.5e				1967	1,599	2,573
Zanzibar	1970	47e	21e	1958			42.8					0	0
Togo	1965-70	50.9e	25.5e	1961	31.6	38.5	35.0	1968	4,529	7,289	1969	309	497
Tunisia	1966-69	39.7		1965-70			51.7e	1969	11,052	17,786	1969	1,429	2,300
	1965-70		16.0e										
Uganda	1965-70	43.2e	17.6e	1965-70			47.5e	1967	15,020	24,173	1967	786	1,265
Upper Volta	1965-70	49.4e	29.1e	1961	32.1	31.1	31.6	1965?	8,078	13,000	1967	323	520
Zaire	1965-70	44.4e	22.7e	1950-52	37.6	40.0	38.8	1969	87,799	141,298	1969	3,144	5,060
Zambia	1965-70	49.8e	20.7e	1965-70			43.5e	1969	21,532	34,653	1969	649	1,044

ASIA

Country	Birth and death rates			Life expectancy (yrs)				Length of roads			Railroad route length		
	Period	Births	Deaths	Period	Men	Woman	Avg	Year	(mi)	(km)	Year	(mi)	(km)
Afghanistan	1965-70	50.5e	26.5e	1965-70			37.5e	1967?	7,000	11,265		0	0
Bahrain	1968	30e						1965?	124	200		0	0

[1] Exc local and urban roads.

ASIA

Country	Birth and death rates			Life Expectancy (yrs)				Length of roads			Railroad route length		
	Period	Births	Deaths	Period	Men	Women	Avg	Year	(mi)	(km)	Year	(mi)	(km)
Bangladesh	1964-65	50.6e	21.0e	1962-65	49.2e	49.2e	49.2e	1967	2,588[1]	4,165[1]	1969	1,751	2,818
Bhutan												0	0
Brunei	1966-69	40.9	6.2					1965?	311	500		0	0
Burma	1965-70	40.3e	17.4e	1965-70			47.5e	1965?	24,855	40,000	1969	1,925	3,098
Cambodia	1965-70	44.6e	15.6e	1958-59	42.2	43.3	42.7	1965?	4,350	7,000	1969	405	652
Ceylon	1966-68	32.0	7.9	1962	61.9	61.4	61.6	1969	13,114	21,105	1969	940	1,513
China	1965-70	33.1e	15.3e	1965-70			50.0e	1966	342,000	550,393	1967	23,900	38,463
Cyprus	1965-70	23.3e	7.8e	1948-50	63.6	68.8	66.2	1969	5,306	8,539		0	0
Gaza Strip												0	0
Hong Kong	1966-70	22.3	5.1	1968	66.7	73.3	70.0	1969	593	955	1969	22	35
India	1965-70	42.8e	16.7e	1951-60	41.9	40.5	41.2	1967	413,062	664,763	1968	36,872	59,339
Indonesia													
Total	1965-70	48.3e	19.4e	1960	47.5	47.5	47.5	1969	52,362	84,268	1969	4,926	7,927
in Asia	1965-70	48.3e	19.4e	1960	47.5	47.5	47.5				1969	4,926	7,927
Iran	1965-70	45.4e	16.6e	1965-70			50.0e	1969	24,309	39,122	1969	2,181	3,510
Iraq	1965-70	49.3e	15.5e	1965-70			51.6e	1968	11,118	17,893	1969	1,462	2,353
Israel	1966-70	25.7	6.7	1969	69.2	72.8	71.0	1968	5,661	9,110	1969	490	789
Japan	1966-70	17.8	6.8	1968	69.0	74.3	71.7	1968	624,748	1,005,436	1969	16,206	26,082
Jordan	1965-70	49.1e	16.0e	1959-63	52.6	52.0	52.3	1969	3,322	5,346	1969	227	365
Kashmir-Jammu													
Korea													
North Korea	1965-70	38.8e	11.2e	1965-70			57.7e	1961	12,427	20,000	1962	2,429	3,910
South Korea	1965-70	35.6e	11.0e	1955-60	51.1	53.7	52.4	1965?	24,855	40,000	1969	1,983	3,192
Kuwait	1965-70	43.3e	7.4e	1965-70			64.4e	1968	946	1,523		0	0
Laos	1965-70	42.1e	17.2e	1965-70			47.5e	1965?	1,864	3,000		0	0
Lebanon								1969	4,520	7,275	1969	259	417
Macao								1965?	62	100		0	0
Malaysia	1966-68	37.7e	8.3e	1966			63.2e	1965-67	13,018	20,950	1969	1,132	1,822

[1] Exc earth roads.

ASIA

Country	Birth and death rates			Life expectancy (yrs)				Length of roads			Railroad route length		
	Period	Births	Deaths	Period	Men	Women	Avg	Year	(mi)	(km)	Year	(mi)	(km)
Sabah	1965-70	48.0e	12.5e	1965-70			55.1e	1965	1,497	2,409	1969	96	154
Sarawak	1965-70	48.0e	12.5e	1965-70			55.1e	1965	1,355	2,180		0	0
West Malaysia	1966-68	35.9	7.6	1966	63.1	66.0	64.6	1967	10,166	16,361	1969	1,036	1,667
Maldives								1965?	62	100		0	0
Mongolia	1965-70	41.5e	11.2e	1965-70			57.7e	1960	46,733	75,209	1963	887	1,427
Nepal	1965-70	44.6e	22.9e	1965-70			40.6e	1965?	373	600	1969	63	101
Oman												0	0
Pakistan[1]	1964-65	47.6e	16.3e	1962-65	53.4e	52.3e	52.8e	1967	22,508[2]	36,223[2]	1969	5,383	8,663
Philippines	1965-70	44.7e	12.0e	1946-49	48.8	53.4	51.1	1965?	34,176	55,000	1969	710	1,143
Portuguese Timor	1965-70	43.0e	25.4e	1965-70			37.5e	1965?	1,367	2,200		0	0
Qatar								1965?	932	1,500		0	0
Ryukyu Islands	1966-69	21.2	5.1	1965	68.9	75.6	72.3	1960	1,967	3,165	1967?	13	21
Saudi Arabia	1965-70	50.0e	22.7e	1965-70			42.3e	1969	6,847	11,020	1969	376	605
Sikkim	1954	28.8e	15.9e									0	0
Singapore	1966-70	25.6	5.4	1965-70			68.2e	1967?	525	845	1967	16	26
Southern Yemen	1965-70	50.0e	22.7e	1965-70			42.3e					0	0
Syria	1965-70	47.5e	15.3e	1965-70			52.8e	1969	9,278	14,932	1969	336	541
Taiwan	1966-70	29.3	5.3	1965	65.8	70.4	68.1	1968	10,492	16,885	1968	621	1,000
Thailand	1965-70	42.8e	10.4e	1960	53.6	58.7	56.1	1967	8,332	13,409	1967	2,339	3,765
Turkey													
Total	1967	39.6e	14.6e	1965-70			54.5e	1967	36,532[3]	58,792[3]	1969	4,976	8,008
in Asia								1967	34,029[3]	54,763[3]			
United Arab Emirates												0	0
USSR (in Asia)													

[1] Data are for West Pakistan only; East Pakistan became Bangladesh in December 1971.

[2] Exc earth roads.

[3] Exc local and urban roads.

ASIA

Country	Birth and death rates			Life Expectancy (yrs)				Length of roads			Railroad route length		
	Period	Births	Deaths	Period	Men	Women	Avg	Year	(mi)	(km)	Year	(mi)	(km)
Vietnam													
North Vietnam	1965-70	37.5e	16.1e	1965-70			50.0e	1963	4,076	6,560	1960	485	780
South Vietnam	1965-70	37.5e	16.1e	1965-70			50.0e	1968	12,984	20,896	1969	777	1,250
Yemen	1965-70	50.0e	22.7e	1965-70			42.3e	1965?	3,728	6,000		0	0

EUROPE

Country	Birth and death rates			Life expectancy (yrs)				Length of roads			Railroad route length		
	Period	Births	Deaths	Period	Men	Women	Avg	Year	(mi)	(km)	Year	(mi)	(km)
Albania	1966-68	35.0	8.3	1965-66	64.9	67.0	65.9	1963	2,237[1]	3,600[1]	1968	135	218
Andorra												0	0
Austria	1966-70	16.8	13.0	1969	66.5	73.3	69.9	1969	119,128	191,718	1969	4,070	6,550
Belgium	1966-70	15.1	12.4	1959-63	67.7	73.5	70.6	1969	57,068	91,843	1969	2.649	4,263
Bulgaria	1966-70	16.0	8.9	1965-67	68.8	72.7	70.7	1968	18,529	29,821	1969	3,736	6,013
Channel Islands	1966-69	16.2	12.3									0	0
Czechoslovakia	1966-70	15.4	10.7	1966	67.3	73.6	70.4	1968	90,688	145,948	1969	8,275	13,317
Denmark	1966-70	15.9	9.9	1967-68	70.6	75.4	73.0	1969	38,332	61,690	1969	1,796	2,890
Faeroe Islands												0	0
Finland	1966-70	15.4	9.5	1961-65	65.4	72.6	69.0	1969	47,342[2]	76,190[2]	1969	3,575	5,754
France	1966-70	16.9	11.0	1968	68.0	75.5	71.7	1967-69	919,064	1,479,090	1969	22,829	36,740
Germany													
East Germany	1966-70	14.5	13.7	1965-66	68.7	73.7	71.2	1969	88,176	141,905	1969	9,264	14,909
West Germany	1966-70	15.7	11.9	1966-68	67.5[3]	73.6[3]	70.6[3]	1969	257,667	414,673	1969	20,955	33,724
Gibraltar	1966-69	21.7	8.8					1966	19	31		0	0
Greece	1966-69	18.0	8.1	1960-62	67.5	70.7	69.1	1969	21,556[4]	34,692[4]	1969	1,598	2,571
Hungary	1966-70	14.6	11.0	1964	67.0	71.8	69.4	1969	68,430	110,128	1969	5,754	9,261

[1] Motor roads only.
[2] Exc private roads and local and urban roads.
[3] Exc West Berlin.
[4] Exc local and urban roads.

EUROPE

Country	Birth and death rates			Life expectancy (yrs)				Length of roads			Railroad route length		
	Period	Births	Deaths	Period	Men	Women	Avg	Year	(mi)	(km)	Year	(mi)	(km)
Iceland	1966-69	22.0	7.0	1961-65	70.8	76.2	73.5	1969	6,826[1]	10,986[1]		0	0
Ireland	1966-70	21.4	11.5	1960-62	68.1	71.9	70.0	1968	53,704	86,427	1969	1,333	2,145
Isle of Man	1966-69	13.9	17.4					1969?	500	805	1968	39	63
Italy	1966-70	17.8	9.8	1960-62	67.2	72.3	69.8	1969	177,173	285,138	1969	12,614	20,301
Liechtenstein											1967	11	18
Luxembourg	1966-70	14.2	12.4	1946-48	61.7	65.7	63.7	1969	2,759	4,440	1969	203	327
Malta	1966-70	16.3	9.2	1967-69	68.4	72.2	70.3	1967	721	1,160		0	0
Monaco											1967	1	2
Netherlands	1966-70	18.9	8.2	1968	71.0	76.4	73.7	1967	59,824	96,278	1969	1,956	3,148
Norway	1966-70	17.4	9.8	1961-65	71.0	76.0	73.5	1969	44,180	71,101	1969	2,636	4,242
Poland	1966-70	16.4	7.8	1965-66	66.8	72.8	69.8	1969	192,028	309,042	1969	16,512	26,574
Portugal													
Total	1966-70	20.4	10.3	1959-62	60.7	66.3	63.5	1968	23,220[1]	37,369[1]	1969	2,238	3,602
in Europe								1968	22,908[1]	36,867[1]	1969	2,238	3,602
Azores								1968	1,030[1]	1,658[1]		0	0
Romania	1966-70	22.5	9.4	1964-67	66.4	70.5	68.5	1969	47,576	76,566	1969	6,839	11,006
San Marino												0	0
Spain													
Total	1966-70	20.5	8.8	1960	67.3	71.9	69.6	1968	86,165	138,670	1968	10,827	17,425
in Europe								1968	84,735	136,368	1968	10,827	17,425
Balearic Islands								1968	1,191	1,917	1969?	20	32
Svalbard												0	0
Sweden	1966-70	14.5	10.2	1967	71.8	76.5	74.2	1969	107,859	173,582	1969	7,794	12,543
Switzerland	1966-70	17.1	9.2	1958-63	68.7	74.1	71.4	1969	36,382	58,550	1969	3,144	5,060
Turkey (in Europe)								1967	2,504[1]	4,029[1]			
UK	1966-70	17.1	11.7	1967-69	68.5	74.7	71.6	1969	219,509	353,266	1969	12,301	19,796
England and Wales	1966-70	16.8	11.7	1967-69	68.7	74.9	71.8	1969	176,232	283,613	1969	10,099	16,252
Northern Ireland	1966-70	21.9	10.6	1967-69	68.3	73.7	71.0	1969	14,273	22,970	1969	203	327

[1] Exc local and urban roads.

EUROPE

Country	Birth and death rates			Life expectancy (yrs)				Length of roads			Railroad route length		
	Period	Births	Deaths	Period	Men	Women	Avg	Year	(mi)	(km)	Year	(mi)	(km)
Scotland	1966-70	17.9	12.1	1967-69	67.1	73.2	70.1	1969	29,004	46,678	1969	1,999	3,217
USSR													
Total in Europe	1966-70	17.4	7.8	1967-68	65	74	70	1968	843,323[1]	1,357,200[1]	1969	80,927[2]	130,240[2]
Vatican City											1968	1	1
Yugoslavia	1966-70	19.0	8.7	1966-67	67.7	69.0	68.4	1968	60,640	97,591	1969	6,497	10,456

NORTH AMERICA

Country	Birth and death rates			Life expectancy (yrs)				Length of roads			Railroad route length		
	Period	Births	Deaths	Period	Men	Women	Avg	Year	(mi)	(km)	Year	(mi)	(km)
Anguilla								1969?	20	32		0	0
Antigua	1963-65	30.5	8.7	1959-61	60.5	64.3	62.4	1969?	150	241	1969?	50	80
Bahama Islands	1966-69	29.7	7.3					1969?	620	998		0	0
Barbados	1966-69	22.4	8.1	1959-61	62.7	67.4	65.1	1969?	840	1,352		0	0
Bermuda	1966-69	19.5	7.3	1965-66	65.6	72.3	69.0	1969?	132	212		0	0
British Honduras				1944-48	45.0	49.0	47.0	1968?	1,250	2,012		0	0
Canada	1966-69	18.1	7.4	1965-67	68.7	75.2	72.0	1969	513,157	825,842	1969	44,131	71,022
Newfoundland	1966-68	26.5	6.2	1966	68.9	74.4	71.7	1968	6.234	10,033			
Canal Zone	1966-70	12.0	2.3					1965?	124	200		0	0
Cayman Islands								1969?	117	188		0	0
Costa Rica	1966-69	37.1	7.0	1962-64	61.9	64.8	63.3	1969?	3,795	6,107	1969	437	703
Cuba	1965-70	26.6e	7.5e	1965-70			66.8e	1968	9,681	15,580	1969?	9,006	14,493
Dominica	1966,68	38.2		1958-62	57.0	59.2	58.1	1969?	449	723		0	0
	1966-68		7.9										
Dominican Republic	1965-70	48.5e	14.7e	1959-61	57.1	58.6	57.9	1957	4,094	6,588	1969	137	220

[1] Motor roads only.

[2] Exc industrial railroad routes, totaling 73,011 mi, 117,500 km.

NORTH AMERICA

Country	Birth and death rates			Life expectancy (yrs)				Length of roads			Railroad route length		
	Period	Births	Deaths	Period	Men	Women	Avg	Year	(mi)	(km)	Year	(mi)	(km)
El Salvador	1966-70	43.0	9.6	1960-61	56.6	60.4	58.5	1969?	5,132	8,259	1969	387	623
Greenland				1952-59	51.4	53.6	52.5					0	0
Grenada	1966-69	27.9	7.9	1959-61	60.1	65.6	62.9	1969?	566	911		0	0
Guadeloupe	1966-70	31.3	7.8	1959-63	62.5	66.5	64.5	1969?	1,171	1,885		0	0
Guatemala	1966-68	43.9	16.0	1963-65	48.3	49.7	49.0	1964	7,575	12,191	1969	510	821
Haiti	1965-70	43.9e	19.7e	1965-70			44.5e	1965?	2,175	3,500	1969	187	301
Honduras	1965-70	49.0e	17.1e	1965-70			49.0e	1965	2,261	3,639	1969	639	1,028
Jamaica	1966-70	35.0	7.4	1959-61	62.6	66.6	64.6	1969?	9,729	15,657	1969	205	330
Martinique	1966-70	29.4	7.5	1959-63	62.5	66.5	64.5	1968	808	1,300		0	0
Mexico	1966-70	42.8	9.4	1965-70	61.0	63.7	62.4	1969	43,321	69,719	1969	14,950	24,059
Montserrat	1966-69	22.1	9.3	1946	49.5	54.8	52.1	1969?	150	241		0	0
Netherlands Antilles								1965?	497	800		0	0
Nicaragua	1965-70	46.0e	16.5e	1965-70			49.9e	1968	6,270	10,091		0	0
Panama	1966-70	37.9		1960-61	57.6	60.9	59.2	1968	4,176	6,720	1969	152	245
	1965-70		8.8e										
Puerto Rico	1966-69	26.3	6.0	1959-61	67.1	71.9	69.5	1968	4,404	7,088	1968?	31	50
Saint Kitts-Nevis	1966-69	26.1	8.3	1959-61	58.0	61.9	59.9	1969?	125	201	1968?	36	58
Saint Lucia	1965-66	43.9	7.9	1959-61	55.1	58.5	56.8	1964	418	673		0	0
Saint-Pierre and Miquelon	1966-69	27.6	8.7									0	0
Saint Vincent	1966-68	39.2	8.9	1959-61	58.5	59.7	59.1	1969?	366	589		0	0
Trinidad and Tobago	1966-69	26.5	6.9	1959-61	62.1	66.3	64.2	1969?	4,000	6,437		0	0
Turks and Caicos Islands												0	0
USA													
Total	1966-70	17.9	9.5	1968	66.6	74.0	70.3	1969	3,710,299	5,971,114	1969	207,005	333,143
in North America								1969	3,706,787	5,965,463	1969	207,005	333,143
Alaska	1966-69	23.7	4.8					1969	7,123	11,463	1968	20	32
Virgin Islands (UK)	1963-64	29.3	8.7	1946	49.5	54.8	52.1	1969?	55[1]	89[1]		0	0
Virgin Islands (USA)	1966-70	42.5	7.7					1968	316	509		0	0

[1] Motor roads only.

OCEANIA

Country	Birth and death rates			Life expectancy (yrs)				Length of roads			Railroad route length		
	Period	Births	Deaths	Period	Men	Women	Avg	Year	(mi)	(km)	Year	(mi)	(km)
American Samoa	1966-70	33.7	4.6					1965?	62	100		0	0
Australia	1966-70	19.9	8.9	1960-62	67.9	74.2	71.0	1968	561,180	903,139	1969	25,523	41,075
Tasmania	1966-69	20.9	8.5					1968	13,411	21,582	1969	500	805
British Solomon Islands								1967	335	539		0	0
Canton and Enderbury Islands												0	0
Christmas Island (Australia)	1966-69	11.6	2.6									0	0
Cocos Islands												0	0
Cook Islands	1966-67	41.8										0	0
	1966-68		8.2										
Fiji	1966-70	31.7		1965-70			68.1e	1967?	1,168	1,880	1968?	420	676
	1965-70		5.3e										
French Polynesia								1967?	81	130		0	0
Gilbert and Ellice Islands				1958-62	56.9	59.0	57.9					0	0
Guam	1966-70	28.2	3.8					1965?	249	400		0	0
Indonesia (in Oceania: West Irian)												0	0
Johnston and Sand Islands												0	0
Midway Islands												0	0
Nauru	1966-68	40.3	7.5									0	0
New Caledonia								1966	2,796	4,500		0	0
New Guinea (Australia)								1967	5,800	9,334		0	0
New Hebrides	1966	45.0e	20.0e					1967?	150	241		0	0
New Zealand	1966-70	22.4	8.7	1960-62	68.4	73.7	71.1	1969	58,261	93,763	1969	3,067	4,936
Niue												0	0
Norfolk Island	1966-70	13.7	8.5									0	0
Pacific Islands (USA)	1967	40e						1966	473	761		0	0
Papua								1966	1,250	2,012		0	0
Pitcairn Island												0	0
Tokelau Islands												0	0
Tonga								1967	255	410		0	0

OCEANIA

Country	Birth and death rates			Life expectancy (yrs)				Length of roads			Railroad route length		
	Period	Births	Deaths	Period	Men	Women	Avg	Year	(mi)	(km)	Year	(mi)	(km)
USA (in Oceania: Hawaii)	1966-69	19.8	5.3					1969	3,512	5,652		0	0
Wake Island												0	0
Wallis and Futuna Islands												0	0
Western Samoa				1961-66	60.8	65.2	63.0	1967?	463	745		0	0

SOUTH AMERICA

Country	Birth and death rates			Life expectancy (yrs)				Length of roads			Railroad route length		
	Period	Births	Deaths	Period	Men	Women	Avg	Year	(mi)	(km)	Year	(mi)	(km)
Argentina	1966-67	20.8	8.4	1965-70	64.1	70.2	67.1	1969	124,908	201,020	1969	25,578	41,164
Bolivia	1965-70	44.0e	19.1e	1949-51	49.7	49.7	49.7	1964	15,094	24,291	1969	2,236	3,599
Brazil	1965-70	37.8e	9.5e	1965-70			60.7e	1969	676,953	1,089,452	1969	19,893	32,015
Chile	1966-68	29.7	9.6	1960-61	54.4	59.9	57.1	1969	43,946	70,725	1969	6,040	9,720
Colombia	1965-70	44.6e	10.6e	1950-52	44.2	45.9	45.1	1965	23,988	38,605	1969	2,164	3,483
Ecuador	1965-70	44.9e	11.4e	1961-63	51.0	53.7	52.4	1965	10,393	16,726	1969	661	1,064
Galapagos Islands												0	0
Falkland Islands												0	0
French Guiana								1965?	311	500		0	0
Guyana	1966-68	38.1	8.3	1959-61	59.0	63.0	61.0	1969?	1,685	2,712	1969	79	127
Paraguay	1965-70	44.6e	10.8e	1965-70			59.4e	1965	7,786	12,530	1969	309	497
Peru	1965-70	41.8e	11.1e	1960-65	52.6	55.5	54.0	1964	25,761	41,458	1969	1,327	2,136
Surinam	1965-66	42.1	7.5	1963	62.5	66.7	64.6	1968?	1,777	2,860	1969	53	85
Uruguay	1965-70	21.3e	9.1e	1963-64	65.5	71.6	68.5	1964	30,407	48,935	1969	1,848	2,974
Venezuela	1965-70	40.9e	7.8e	1965-70			63.8e	1964	29,949	48,198	1969	109	175

TABULAR GAZETTEER 1. COUNTRIES, BY CONTINENT

Part IV. Supplemental Information

AFRICA

Algeria: [a]off Jazair. [b] Algiers (alt Alger; off Jazair): 904, 943s (1966). [c]Oran (off Ouahran): 327, 328s (1966).

Angola: [a] alt Portuguese West Africa; inc Cabinda. [b] Luanda (for Loanda, Sao Paulo de Loanda): 475 (1970); proposed capital: Nova Lisboa (for Huambo): 48 (1967e). [c] Lobito: 43 (1967e).

Botswana: [a] for Bechuanaland. [b] Gaborone (for Gaberones): 18 (1971). [c] Kanye: 34 (1964); Serowe: 34 (1964).

British Indian Ocean Territory: [a] none. [b] Victoria (in Seychelles). [c] none.

Burundi: [a] for Urundi. [b] Bujumbura (for Usumbura): 80, 100s (1970e). [c] Bururi: 5 (1958e).

Cameroon: [a] alt Cameroun; for Kamerun. [b] Yaounde (alt Yaunde): 101 (1965e), 166s (1969e). [c] Douala (alt Duala): 250s (1970e).

Cape Verde Islands: [a] off Cabo Verde. [b] Praia (on Santiago I): 13 (1960). [c]Mindelo (on Sao Vicente I): 18 (1960).

Central African Republic: [a] for Ubangi-Shari; off Republique Centrafricaine. [b] Bangui: 111 (1964), 299s (1968). [c]Berberati: 38s (1968).

Ceuta: [a] alt Spanish North Africa (in part). [b]Ceuta: 63 (1970). [c] none.

Chad: [a] off Tchad. [b] Fort-Lamy: 133s (1968). [c] Fort-Archambault: 37 (1968).

Comoro Islands: [a] for Mayotte; off Comores. [b] Moroni (on Grande Comore I): 12 (1966). [c] Mutsamudu (on Anjouan I): 8 (1966).

Congo: [a] for Congo (Brazzaville), Middle Congo. [b] Brazzaville: 175 (1970). [c] Pointe-Noire: 79 (1962).

Dahomey: [a] none. [b]Porto-Novo: 87 (1970e); Cotonou (for Kotonu): 139 (1970e). [c]Abomey: 34 (1970e).

Egypt: [a] alt Arab Republic of Egypt; for UAR, United Arab Republic; off Jumhuriyat Misr al Arabiyah, Misr. [b] Cairo (off Qahirah): 4961 (1970e). [c] Alexandria (off Iskandariyah): 2032 (1970e).

Equatorial Guinea: [a] for Spanish Guinea; inc Fernando Po (off Fernando Poo), Rio Muni; off Guinea Ecuatorial. [b] Santa Isabel (on Fernando Po I): 23 (1960). [c] Bata: 8 (1960).

Ethiopia: [a] for Abyssinia; inc Eritrea; off Ityopya. [b] Addis Ababa: 644 (1967). [c] Asmara: 190 (1968).

French Southern and Antarctic Lands: [a] inc Kerguelen; off Terres Australes et Antarctiques Francaises. [b] Port-aux-Francais (on Kerguelen I): 0.07 (1967?). [c] none.

French Territory of the Afars and the Issas: [a] for French Somaliland; off Territoire Francais des Afars et des Issas. [b] Djibouti (alt Jibuti): 62s (1970e). [c] Tadjoura: 1 (1948e).

Gabon: [a] for Gabun. [b] Libreville: 57s (1967e). [c] Port-Gentil: 25 (1965).

Gambia: [a] none. [b] Bathurst: 32, 48s (1967e). [c] Brikama: 4 (1963).

Ghana: [a] for Gold Coast. [b] Accra (for Akkra): 634, 849s (1970). [c] Kumasi (for Coomassie): 343 (1970), 340s (1968e).

Guinea: [a] for French Guinea; off Guinee. [b] Conakry (for Konakry): 43 (1960), 197s (1967e). [c] Kankan: 29 (1960e).

Ivory Coast: [a] off Cote d'Ivoire. [b] Abidjan: 330s (1965e). [c] Bouake: 80s (1965e).

Kenya: [a] for British East Africa. [b] Nairobi: 350 (1967e), 478s (1969). [c] Mombasa (alt Mvita): 180 (1962), 246s (1969).

Lesotho: [a] for Basutoland. [b] Maseru: 14, 18s (1966). [c] Leribe: 2 (1956).

Liberia: [a] none. [b] Monrovia: 100 (1967e). [c] Harbel: 32 (1962).

Libya: [a] inc Cyrenaica, Tripolitania; off Libiyah. [b] Bengasi (alt Benghazi; off Banghazi): 150 (1968e); Tripoli (off Tarabulus): 247 (1968e); proposed capital: Beida (off Bayda): 13 (1964). [c] Derna (off Darnah): 21 (1964).

Malagasy Republic: [a] alt Madagascar, Madagaskara; off Repoblika Malagasy, Republique Malgache. [b]Tananarive (alt Antananarivo): 333 (1968e). [c] Tamatave: 50 (1966e).

Malawi: [a] for Nyasaland. [b] Zomba: 20 (1966); proposed capital: Lilongwe: 19 (1966). [c]Blantyre (inc Limbe since 1949): 109 (1966).

Mali: [a] for French Sudan. [b] Bamako: 182s (1968e). [c] Mopti: 32 (1967e).

Mauritania: [a] alt Islamic Republic of Mauritania, Mauretania; off Jumhuriyat Muritaniyah al Islamiyah, Mauritanie, Muritaniyah, Republique Islamique de Mauritanie. [b] Nouakchott: 35 (1970e). [c] F'Derik (for Fort-Gouraud): 16 (1970e).

Mauritius: [a] for Ile de France; inc Rodrigues (alt Rodriguez). [b] Port Louis: 89 (1962), 138s (1969e). [c] Beau Bassin-Rose Hill: 66 (1965e).

Melilla: [a] alt Spanish North Africa (in part). [b] Melilla: 61 (1970). [c] none.

Morocco: [a] for Marrocco; off Maghrib. [b] Rabat-Sale (Sale: for Sallee; off Sla): 460 (1970e). [c] Casablanca (off Dar al Baida): 1395 (1970e).

Mozambique: [a]alt Portuguese East Africa; off Mocambique. [b]Lourenco Marques: 92 (1967e), 184s (1960). Beira: 65, 80s (1967e).

Niger: [a] none. [b] Niamey: 79 (1968e). [c] Zinder: 24 (1964e).

Nigeria: [a] none. [b] Lagos: 875 (1970e). [c] Ibadan: 746 (1970e).

Portuguese Guinea: [a] off Guine Portuguesa. [b] Bissau: 62 (1970). [c] Bafata: 14 (1960).

Reunion: [a] for Bourbon. [b] Saint-Denis: 66, 85s (1967). [c] Saint-Pierre: 19, 40s (1967).

Rhodesia: [a] for Southern Rhodesia. [b] Salisbury: 180 (1968e), 385s (1969). [c] Bulawayo: 210 (1968e), 246s (1969).

Rwanda: [a] alt Ruanda. [b] Kigali: 59 (1970). [c] Astrida: 3 (1958e).

Saint Helena: [a] inc Ascension, Tristan da Cunha. [b] Jamestown (on Saint Helena I): 1 (1966). [c] Georgetown (on Ascension I): ? (Ascension I: 0.5 (1966).

Sao Tome and Principe: [a] off Sao Tome e Principe; Sao Tome: for Sao Thome. [b] Sao Tome (for Sao Thome) (on Sao Tome I): 6 (1960). [c] Santo Antonio (on Principe I): 0.9 (1960).

Senegal: [a] none. [b] Dakar: 581s (1969e). [c] Kaolack: 70 (1960-61); Thies: 69 (1960-61).

Seychelles: [a] none. [b] Victoria (alt Port Victoria) (on Mahe I): 14 (1971). [c] Cascade (on Mahe I): 4s (1931).

Sierra Leone: [a] none. [b] Freetown: 179 (1970e). [c] Bo Town (alt Bo): 27 (1963).

Somalia: [a] alt Somali Republic; inc British Somaliland, Italian Somaliland. [b] Mogadishu (alt Mogadiscio; off Hamar): 173 (1967e). [c] Merca: 56 (1964e).

South Africa: [a] alt Suid-Afrika; for Union of South Africa. [b] Cape Town (alt Kaapstad): 691, 1097s (1970); Pretoria: 544, 562s (1970). [c] Johannesburg: 655, 1433s (1970).

South-West Africa: [a] alt Namibia, Suidwes-Afrika. [b] Windhoek: 48s (1965e). [c] Walvis Bay (alt Walvisbaai): 20 (1967e).

Spanish Sahara: [a] inc Rio de Oro, Sekia el Hamrah (off Saguia el Hamra); off Sahara Espanol. [b] Aaiun (alt Aiun): 25 (1970). [c] Villa Cisneros (alt Cisneros): 2 (1960).

Sudan: [a] for Anglo-Egyptian Sudan. [b] Khartoum (off Khurtum): 194 (1968e), 246s (1956). [c] Omdurman (off Umm Durman): 206 (1968e).

Swaziland: [a] none. [b] Mbabane: 14s (1966). [c] Manzini (for Bremersdorp): 6s (1966).

Tanzania: [a] inc Tanganyika (for German East Africa), Zanzibar (alt Unguja). [b] Dar es Salaam: 273 (1967). [c] Zanzibar (alt Unguja) (on Zanzibar I): 68 (1967). *Tanganyika:* [b] Dar es Salaam: 273 (1967). [c] Tanga: 61 (1967). *Zanzibar:* [b] Zanzibar (alt Unguja) (on Zanzibar I): 68 (1967). [c] Wete (on Pemba I): 8 (1967).

Togo: [a] alt Togoland; for French Togo. [b] Lome: 148 (1970). [c] Sokode: 30 (1970).

Tunisia: [a] off Tunisiyah. [b] Tunis: 469, 648s (1966). [c] Sfax (off Safaqis): 80, 216s (1966).

Uganda: [a] inc Buganda. [b] Kampala: 80 (1967e), 331s (1969). [c] Jinja: 53 (1969).

Upper Volta: [a] alt Voltaic Republic; off Haute-Volta. [b] Ouagadougou (for Wagadugu): 79 (1967e). [c] Bobo Dioulasso: 68 (1967e).

Zaire: [a] for Belgian Congo, Congo (Kinshasa), Kongo. [b] Kinshasa (for Leopoldville): 1323 (1970). [c] Kananga (for Luluabourg): 429 (1970).

Zambia: [a] for Northern Rhodesia. [b] Lusaka: 238s (1969). [c] Kitwe: 179s (1969).

ASIA

Afghanistan: [a] none. [b] Kabul (for Cabul): 307, 489s (1970e). [c] Kandahar (alt Qandahar): 130 (1970e).

Bahrain: [a] alt Bahrein; off Bahrayn. [b] Manama (off Manamah) (on Bahrain I): 90 (1971). [c] Muharraq (on Muharraq I): 49 (1971).

Bangladesh: [a] for East Pakistan. [b] Dacca: 829 (1969e). [c] Chittagong: 437 (1969e).

Bhutan: [a] off Druk-yul. [b] Thimbu [alt Thimphu; off Tashi Chho (Dzong)]: 10 (1967?e); Paro (Dzong): ?. [c] Punakha: ?

Brunei: [a] none. [b] Bandar Seri Begawan (alt Brunei, Brunei Town): 37 (1971). [c] Seria: 18 (1960).

Burma: [a] alt Union of Burma; for Birmah; off Myanma. [b] Rangoon (off Yangon): 1759 (1970e). [c] Mandalay (off Mandale): 360 (1969e).

Cambodia: [a] alt Khmer Republic; for French Indo-China (in part); off Kampuchea. [b] Phnom-Penh: 650 (1969e). [c] Battambang: 45 (1969e).

Ceylon: [a] for Serendib; off Lanka, Sri Lanka. [b] Colombo: 564 (1971). [c] Dehiwala-Mount Lavinia: 122 (1968e).

China: [a] alt Mainland China; off Chunghua. [b] Peking (for Peiping; off Peiching): 10,000 (1968e). [c] Shanghai: 10,700 (1968e).

Cyprus: [a] off Kibris, Kypros. [b] Nicosia (off Levkosia): 46 (1960), 114s (1969e). [c] Limassol (off Lemesos): 51 (1969e).

Gaza Strip: [a] off Qita Ghazzah. [b] Gaza (alt Azzah; off Ghazzah): 118 (1967). [c] Khan Yunus: 53 (1967).

Hong Kong: [a] alt Hsiangchiang, Hsiangkang. [b] Hong Kong (alt Hsiangchiang, Hsiangkang; inc Kowloon, New Kowloon, Victoria): 3951 (1971). [c] none.

India: [a] off Bharat. [b] New Delhi: 293 (1971). [c] Bombay: 5969 (1971); Calcutta: 3141, 7005s (1971).

Indonesia: [a] for Dutch East Indies, Netherlands Indies; inc West Irian (for Netherlands New Guinea, West New Guinea; off Irian Barat). [b] Djakarta (alt Jakarta; for Batavia): 4386 (1970). [c] Surabaja (alt Surabaya; for Soerabaja): 1442 (1970).

Iran: [a] for Persia. [b] Teheran (off Tehran): 2695 (1966). [c] Isfahan (alt Ispahan; off Esfahan): 424 (1966).

Iraq: [a] alt Irak; for Mesopotamia. [b] Baghdad (alt Bagdad): 1491, 1657s (1965). [c] Basra (off Basrah): 311, 311s (1965).

Israel: [a] for Palestine. [b] Jerusalem (alt Quds ash Sharif; inc Jordanian Jerusalem; off Yerushalayim): 283 (1971e). [c] Tel Aviv-Jaffa (Jaffa: off Yafo): 383 (1971e), 838s (1968e).

Japan: [a] off Nihon, Nippon. [b] Tokyo (alt Tokio; for Edo, Yedo) (on Honshu I): 8841, 11,161s (1970). [c] Osaka (on Honshu I): 2980 (1970).

Jordan: [a] for Trans-Jordan; off Urdunn. [b] Amman: 330 (1967). [c] Zarqa (alt Zerka): 121 (1967).

Kashmir-Jammu: [a] alt Jammu and Kashmir; Kashmir: for Cashmere. [b] Srinagar (for Cashmere): 404 (1971); Jammu: 155 (1971). [c] Anantnag: 28 (1971).

Korea: [a] for Chosen, Choson, Corea; off Tae Han Min Guk. *North Korea*: [b] Pyongyang (for Heijo): 1221 (1965e). [c] Chongjin (for Seishin): 265 (1967e); Kimchaek (for Joshin, Songjin): 265 (1967e). *South Korea:* [b] Seoul (alt Kyongsong; for Keijo; off Soul): 5536 (1970). [c] Pusan (alt Busan; for Fusan): 1881 (1970).

Kuwait: [a] alt Kuweit; off Kuwayt. [b] Kuwait (alt Kuweit; off Kuwayt): 80 (1970), 295s (1965). [c] Hawalli: 107 (1970).

Laos: [a] for French Indo-China (in part); off Lao. [b] Vientiane: 132 (1966e), 162s (1962e); Luang-Prabang: 25 (1962e). [c] Pakse: 8 (1960?e); Savannakhet: 8 (1960?e).

Lebanon: [a] off Lubnan. [b] Beirut (for Beyrouth; off Bayrut): 700 (1964e). [c] Tripoli (off Tarabulus): 128 (1964e).

Macao: [a] alt Aomen; off Macau. [b] Macao (alt Aomen; off Macau): 227 (1970). [c] none.

Malaysia: [a] inc East Malaysia (inc Sabah, Sarawak; off Malaysia Timor), West Malaysia (off Malaysia Barat). [b] Kuala Lumpur: 452, 876s (1970). George Town (alt Penang; off Pinang): 270 (1970). *Sabah:* [a] for British North Borneo, North Borneo. [b] Kota Kinabalu (for Jesselton): 42 (1970). [c] Sandakan: 29 (1960). *Sarawak:* [a] none. [b] Kuching: 63 (1970). [c] Sibu: 30 (1960). *West Malaysia:* [a] for British Malaya, Malaya; off Malaysia Barat. [b] Kuala Lumpur: 452, 876s (1970). [c] George Town (alt Penang; off Pinang): 270 (1970).

Maldives: [a] for Maldive Islands; off Divehi Raaje. [b] Male [on Male (alt King's) I]: 14 (1970). [c] Gan (on Addu I): ? [Addu I: 10 (1966)].

Mongolia: [a] for Outer Mongolia; off Mongol. [b] Ulan-Bator (alt Ulaan Baatar; for Kulun, Urga): 269 (1968e). [c] Darhan (alt Darkhan): 35 (1967e).

Nepal: [a] for Nepaul. [b] Katmandu (alt Kathmandu): 153 (1971). [c] Patan (alt Lalitpur): 49 (1961).

Oman: [a] for Masqat wah Oman, Muscat and Oman. [b] Muscat (off Masqat): 6 (1962e). [c] Matrah: 14 (1962e).

Pakistan: [a] none. [b] Islamabad: 50 (1967e). [c] Karachi: 3060 (1969e).

Philippines: [a] off Pilipinas. [b] Quezon City (on Luzon I): 754 (1970). [c] Manila (on Luzon I): 1331 (1970), 2989s (1969e).

Portuguese Timor: [a] off Timor Portugues. [b] Dili: 29 (1970), 55s (1967e). [c] Vila Salazar (alt Salazar): 2 (1967e).

Qatar: [a] alt Katar. [b] Doha (off Dawhah): 55 (1967e). [c] Wakrah (alt Waqra): 5 (1950?e).

Ryukyu Islands: [a] alt Ryukyu Shoto; for Liuchiu Islands, Nansei Islands; inc Okinawa. [b] Naha (alt Nawa) (on Okinawa I): 276 (1970). [c] Koza (on Okinawa I): 56 (1965).

Saudi Arabia: [a] inc Asir, Hejaz, Nejd (alt Najd); off Arabiyah as Suudiyah. [b] Jidda (alt Jedda; off Juddah): 194 (1965e); Riyadh (off Riyad): 225 (1965e). [c] Mecca (alt Mekka; off Makkah): 185 (1965e).

Sikkim: [a] none. [b] Gangtok: 7 (1961). [c] Thango: ?

Singapore: [a] off Singapura. [b] Singapore (off Singapura): 2075 (1970). [c] none.

Southern Yemen: [a] for Hadhramaut, South Arabia; inc Aden; off Yaman al Janubi. [b] Aden: 150, 225s (1964e); Madinat ash Shab (for Ittihad): 10 (1966e). [c] Sheikh Othman (off Shaykh Uthman): 30 (1966?e).

Syria: [a] off Sham, Suriyah. [b] Damascus (off Dimashq): 835 (1970). [c] Aleppo (off Halab): 639 (1970).

Taiwan: [a] alt Formosa, Republic of China. [b] Taipei [for Taihoku; inc Daitotei, Moko (alt Banka, Manka)] : 1712 (1969e). [c] Kaohsiung (for Takao; inc Kigo): 785 (1969e).

Thailand: [a] for Siam; off Prathet Thai. [b] Bangkok (off Krung Thep): 2228 (1970). [c] Thon Buri: 866 (1968e).

Turkey: [a] for Ottoman Empire; off Turkiye. [b] Ankara (for Angora): 1209 (1970). [c] Istanbul (for Constantinople) (in Europe): 2248 (1970).

United Arab Emirates: [a] for Pirate Coast, Trucial Oman, Trucial States; inc Abu Dhabi (off Abu Zaby), Ajman, Dubai (off Dubayy), Fujairah (off Fujayrah), Ras al Khaimah (off Ras al Khaymah), Sharjah (alt Sharjah and Kalba; inc Kalba; off Shariqah), Umm al Qaiwain (off Umm al Qaywayn); off Amiiraat al Arabiyah al Muttahidah. [b] Abu Zaby (alt Abu Dhabi): 22 (1968?). [c] Dubayy (alt Dubai): 56 (1968?).

USSR: (see under Europe).

Vietnam: [a] for French Indo-China (in part); off Viet Nam. *North Vietnam:* [b] Hanoi (for Kecho): 415, 644s (1960). [c] Haiphong: 182, 369s (1960). *South Vietnam:* [b] Saigon (inc Cholon): 1761 (1970e). [c] Da Nang (for Tourane): 428 (1970e).

Yemen: [a] alt Northern Yemen; off Yaman. [b] Sana (alt Sanaa): 100 (1963e). [c] Hudaydah (alt Hodeida): 40 (1960e).

EUROPE

Albania: [a] off Shqiperi. [b] Tirane (alt Tirana): 169 (1967e). [c] Durres (alt Durazzo): 53 (1967e).

Andorra: [a] none. [b] Andorra (alt Andorra la Vella): 0.6 (1960e). [c] San Julian de Loria: 0.7 (1950?e); Las Escaldas: 0.6 (1961?e).

Austria: [a] off Osterreich. [b] Vienna (off Wien): 1603 (1971). [c] Graz: 249 (1971).

Belgium: [a] off Belgie, Belgique. [b] Brussels (off Brussel, Bruxelles): 164, 1073s (1969e). [c] Antwerp (off Antwerpen, Anvers): 230, 673s (1969e).

Bulgaria: [a] off Bulgariya. [b] Sofia (off Sofiya): 868, 973s (1970e). [c] Plovdiv (for Philippopolis): 247 (1970e).

Channel Islands: [a] inc Guernsey, Jersey. [b] Saint Helier (on Jersey I): 28 (1971); Saint Peter Port (on Guernsey I): 16 (1971). [c] Saint Saviour (on Jersey I): 11 (1971).

Czechoslovakia: [a] off Ceskoslovensko. [b] Prague (for Prag; off Praha): 1078 (1970). [c] Brno (for Brunn): 336 (1970).

Denmark: [a] off Danmark. [b] Copenhagen (off Kobenhavn): 621, 1379s (1971e). [c] Arhus (alt Aarhus): 238 (1971e).

Faeroe Islands: [a] alt Faroe Islands; off Faeroerne. [b] Torshavn (alt Thorshavn) (on Streymoy I): 10 (1966). [c] Klaksvik (alt Klakksvik) (on Bordhoy I): 4 (1960).

Finland: [a] alt Suomi. [b] Helsinki (alt Helsingfors): 524, 710s (1970). [c] Tampere (alt Tammerfors): 158, 220s (1970).

France: [a] none. [b] Paris: 2591, 8197s (1968). [c] Marseilles (off Marseille): 889, 954s (1968); Lyons (off Lyon): 528, 1075s (1968).

Germany: [a] off Deutschland. *East Germany*: [b] East Berlin (off Ost-Berlin): 1085 (1971). [c] Leipzig: 583 (1971). *West Germany:* [b] Bonn [inc Bad Godesberg (alt Godesberg) since 1968]: 274 (1970). [c] West Berlin (off West-Berlin): 2122 (1970).

Gibraltar: [a] none. [b] Gibraltar: 27 (1970). [c] none.

Greece: [a] off Ellas, Hellas. [b] Athens (off Athinai): 862, 2530s (1971). [c] Salonika (alt Salonica; off Thessaloniki): 339, 551s (1971).

Hungary: [a] off Magyarorszag. [b] Budapest [inc Buda (for Ofen), Pest]: 1940 (1970). [c] Miskolc: 173 (1970).

Iceland: [a] off Island. [b] Reykjavik: 82, 95s (1970). [c] Akureyri: 11 (1970).

Ireland: [a] off Eire. [b] Dublin (off Baile Atha Cliath): 566 (1971), 650s (1966). [c] Cork (off Corcaigh): 128 (1971), 125s (1966).

Isle of Man: [a] none. [b] Douglas: 20 (1971). [c] Ramsey: 5 (1971).

Italy: [a] Off Italia. [b] Rome (off Roma): 2800 (1971). [c] Milan (for Mailand; off Milano): 1724 (1971).

Liechtenstein: [a] none. [b] Vaduz: 4 (1970). [c] Schaan: 3 (1960).

Luxembourg: [a] alt Lutzelburg, Luxemburg. [b] Luxembourg (alt Lutzelburg, Luxemburg): 76 (1970). [c] Esch-sur-Alzette: 28 (1970).

Malta: [a] inc Gozo. [b] Valletta (alt Valetta) (on Malta I): 15 (1967). [c] Sliema (on Malta I): 21 (1967).

Monaco: [a] none. [b] Monaco (inc Monte-Carlo): 24 (1970e). [c] none.

Netherlands: [a] alt Holland; off Nederland. [b] Amsterdam: 831, 1040s (1970e); Hague (alt The Hague; off 's Gravenhage): 551, 719s (1970e). [c] Rotterdam: 687, 1061s (1970e).

Norway: [a] off Norge. [b] Oslo (for Christiania, Kristiania): 481 (1971e), 599s (1969e). [c] Trondheim (for Nidaros, Trondhjem): 128 (1971e); Bergen: 113 (1971e), 149s (1960).

Poland: [a] off Polska. [b] Warsaw (off Warszawa): 1308 (1970). [c] Lodz: 762 (1970).

Portugal: [a] inc Azores (off Acores), Madeira Islands (off Madeira). [b] Lisbon (off Lisboa): 782 (1970), 1335s (1960). [c] Porto (alt Oporto): 310 (1970), 746s (1960).

Romania: [a] alt Roumania, Rumania. [b] Bucharest (off Bucuresti): 1475, 1575s (1970e). [c] Cluj (for Klausenburg, Kolozsvar): 203, 203S (1970e); Constanta (alt Constantsa; for Kustendje): 172, 238s (1970e).

San Marino: [a] none. [b] San Marino: 3, 4s (1964e). [c] none.

Spain: [a] inc Balearic Islands (off Islas Baleares), Canary Islands (off Islas Canarias); off Espana. [b] Madrid: 3121 (1970). [c] Barcelona: 1742 (1970).

Svalbard: [a] inc Spitsbergen. [b] Longyearbyen [on West Spitsbergen (off Vestspitsbergen) I]: 1 (1958e). [c] Ny-Alesund (on West Spitsbergen I): 0.2 (1946e).

Sweden: [a] off Sverige. [b] Stockholm: 740, 1345s (1970). [c] Goteborg (alt Gothenburg): 452, 678s (1970).

Switzerland: [a] off Schweiz, Suisse, Svizzera. [b] Bern (alt Berna, Berne): 162, 259s (1970). [c] Zurich (alt Zurigo): 423, 675s (1970).

Turkey: (see under Asia).

UK: [a] alt Great Britain and Northern Ireland, United Kingdom; inc England and Wales (Wales: alt Cymru), Northern Ireland, Scotland; off United Kingdom of Great Britain and Northern Ireland. [b] London: 7393s (1971). [c] Birmingham: 1013 (1971). *England and Wales*: [b] London: 7393s (1971). [c] Birmingham: 1013 (1971). *Northern Ireland:* [b] Belfast: 362, 556s (1971). [c] Londonderry (alt Derry): 52 (1971). *Scotland:* [b] Edinburgh: 453 (1971). [c] Glasgow: 897 (1971).

USSR: [a] alt Soviet Union, Union of Soviet Socialist Republics; for Russia; off Soyuz Sovetskikh Sotsialisticheskikh Respublik. [b] Moscow (off Moskva): 6942, 7061s (1970). [c] Leningrad (for Petrograd, Saint Petersburg): 3513, 3950s (1970).

Vatican City: [a] alt Holy See; off Citta del Vaticano. [b] Vatican City (off Citta del Vaticano): 1 (1969e). [c] none.

Yugoslavia: [a] alt Jugoslavia; inc Bosnia and Herzegovina, Montenegro, Serbia; off Jugoslavija. [b] Belgrade (off Beograd): 742 (1971). [c] Zagreb (for Agram, Zagrab): 566 (1971).

NORTH AMERICA

Anguilla: [a] for Snake Island. [b] London (in UK). [c] Road Bay: ?

Antigua: [a] inc Barbuda. [b] Saint John's (on Antigua I): 21 (1960). [c] All Saints' Village (on Antigua I): 2 (1960).

Bahama Islands: [a] alt Bahamas. [b] Nassau (on New Providence I): 101s (1970). [c] Freeport (on Grand Bahama I): 2 (1963).

Barbados: [a] none. [b] Bridgetown: 9, 115s (1970). [c] Speightstown: 2 (1960).

Bermuda: [a] for Somers Islands. [b] Hamilton (on Bermuda I): 2 (1970), 17s (1965e). [c] Saint George's (on Saint George's I): 1 (1960).

British Honduras. [a] for Belize. [b] Belmopan: 5 (1971e). [c] Belize: 39 (1970), 48s (1966e).

Canada: [a] inc Newfoundland. [b] Ottawa (for Bytown): 302, 603s (1971). [c] Montreal: 1214, 2743s (1971).

Canal Zone: [a] alt Panama Canal Zone. [b] Balboa Heights: 0.2 (1970). [c] Balboa: 3 (1970).

Cayman Islands: [a] none. [b] George Town (on Grand Cayman I): 4 (1970). [c] West Bay (on Grand Cayman I): 2 (1960).

Costa Rica: [a] none. [b] San Jose: 203 (1969e), 355s (1967e). [c] Alajuela: 26 (1967e).

Cuba: [a] none. [b] Havana (alt Habana; off La Habana): 990 (1966e), 1755s (1970). [c] Marianao:[1] 369 (1970); Santiago de Cuba (alt Santiago): 276 (1970).

Dominica: [a] none. [b] Roseau: 10 (1970). [c] Portsmouth: 2 (1960).

Dominican Republic: [a] off Republica Dominicana. [b] Santo Domingo (for Ciudad Trujillo): 671 (1970). [c] Santiago de los Caballeros (alt Santiago): 155 (1970).

El Salvador: [a] alt Salvador. [b] San Salvador: 350, 350s (1969e). [c] Santa Ana: 102, 168s (1969e).

Greenland: [a] off Gronland. [b] Godthab: 5 (1965). [c] Egedesminde: 2 (1965); Holsteinsborg: 2 (1965).

Grenada: [a] none. [b] Saint George's (on Grenada I): 7, 20s (1960). [c] Gouyave (alt Charlotte Town) (on Grenada I): 2 (1960).

Guadeloupe: [a] none. [b] Basse-Terre (on Basse-Terre I): 15 (1967). [c] Pointe-a-Pitre (on Grande-Terre I): 29 (1967).

Guatemala: [a] none. [b] Guatemala (alt Guatemala City): 731 (1970e). [c] Quezaltenango: 57 (1964).

Haiti: [a] for Hayti. [b] Port-au-Prince: 340 (1969e). [c] Cap-Haitien: 30 (1961e).

Honduras: [a] none. [b] Tegucigalpa: 232 (1970e). [c] San Pedro Sula: 103 (1970e).

Jamaica: [a] none. [b] Kingston: 117, 550s (1970). [c] Montego Bay: 43 (1970).

Martinique: [a] none. [b] Fort-de-France (for Fort-Royal): 94, 97s (1967). [c] Schoelcher: 11, 13s (1967).

Mexico: [a] none. [b] Mexico (alt Mexico City): 2903, 7006s (1970). [c] Guadalajara: 1195, 1487s (1970); Monterrey: 858, 1777s (1970).

Montserrat: [a] none. [b] Plymouth: 3 (1970). [c] none.

Netherlands Antilles: [a] alt Dutch West Indies; for Curacao; off Nederlandse Antillen. [b] Willemstad (on Curacao I): 44, 94s (1960). [c] Oranjestad (on Aruba I): 16 (1966e).

Nicaragua: [a] none. [b] Managua: 323 (1969e). [c] Leon: 59 (1967e).

Panama: [a] none. [b] Panama (alt Panama City): 418 (1970). [c] Colon: 68 (1970).

Puerto Rico: [a] for Porto Rico. [b] San Juan (inc Rio Piedras): 453, 820s (1970). [c] Bayamon: 148 (1970).

Saint Kitts-Nevis: [a] Saint Kitts: alt Saint Christopher. [b] Basseterre (on Saint Kitts I): 16 (1966e). [c] Sandy Point (on Saint Kitts I): 4 (1960).

Saint Lucia: [a] none. [b] Castries: 4, 15s (1960). [c] Vieux Fort: 3 (1960).

Saint-Pierre and Miquelon: [a] off Saint-Pierre et Miquelon. [b] Saint-Pierre (on Saint-Pierre I): 5 (1967). [c] Miquelon (on Miquelon I): 0.6 (1967).

Saint Vincent: [a] none. [b] Kingstown (on Saint Vincent I): 4 (1960), 21s (1963e). [c] Georgetown (on Saint Vincent I): 1 (1960).

Trinidad and Tobago: [a] none. [b] Port of Spain (on Trinidad I): 68 (1970). [c] San Fernando (on Trinidad I): 40 (1960).

Turks and Caicos Islands: [a] none. [b] Grand Turk (on Grand Turk I): 2 (1970). [c] Cockburn Harbour (on South Caicos I): 0.9 (1960).

USA: [a] alt United States, US; inc Alaska (for Russian America). Hawaii (for Hawaiian Islands, Sandwich Islands); off United States of America. [b] Washington: 757, 2481s (1970). [c] New York (alt New York City; for New Amsterdam; inc Brooklyn since 1898): 7895, 16,207s (1970).

[1] Included in Havana urbanized area.

Virgin Islands (UK): [a] alt British Virgin Islands. [b] Road Town (on Tortola I): 2 (1970). [c] East End-Long Look (on Tortola I): 2 (1958e).

Virgin Islands (USA): [a] alt Virgin Islands of the United States; for Danish West Indies. [b] Charlotte Amalie (for Saint Thomas) (on Saint Thomas I): 12 (1970). [c] Christiansted (on Saint Croix I): 3 (1970).

OCEANIA

American Samoa: [a] alt Eastern Samoa. [b] Pago Pago (on Tutuila I): 2 (1970). [c] Nu'uuli (on Tutuila I): 2 (1970).

Australia: [a] inc Tasmania (for Van Diemen's Land). [b] Canberra: 141s (1971). [c] Sydney: 2717s (1971).

British Solomon Islands: [a] none. [b] Honiara (on Guadalcanal I): 11 (1970). [c] Auki (on Malaita I): ?

Canton and Enderbury Islands: [a] none. [b] Canton (on Canton I): 0.3 (1960). [c] none.

Christmas Island (Australia): [a] none. [b] Flying Fish Cove: ? [c] none.

Cocos Islands: [a] alt Keeling Islands. [b] Bantam Village (on Home I): ? [c] none.

Cook Islands: [a] for Harvey Islands. [b] Avarua (on Rarotonga I): 4 (1961e). [c] Avatiu (on Rarotonga I): ?

Fiji: [a] alt Fiji Islands; for Fidji, Viti. [b] Suva (on Viti Levu I): 54, 80s (1966). [c] Lautoka (on Viti Levu I): 11, 21s (1966).

French Polynesia: [a] for French Oceania; inc Marquesas Islands, Society Islands (inc Tahiti); off Polynesie Francaise. [b] Papeete (on Tahiti I): 23, 44s (1971). [c] Uturoa (on Raiatea I): 2 (1962).

Gilbert and Ellice Islands: [a] none. [b] Bairiki (on Tarawa I): 1 (1968). [c] Betio (on Tarawa I): 5 (1968).

Guam: [a] inc Marianas (alt Mariana) Islands (for Ladrone Islands) (in part). [b] Agana: 2 (1970). [c] Tamuning: 8 (1970).

Johnston and Sand Islands: [a] none. [b] Washington (in USA). [c] none.

Midway Islands: [a] none. [b] Washington (in USA). [c] none.

Nauru: [a] for Pleasant Island. [b] Nauru: 7 (1970e). [c] none.

New Caledonia: [a] off Nouvelle-Caledonie. [b] Noumea (for Port-de-France) [on New Caledonia (off Nouvelle-Caledonie) I]: 42, 48s (1969). [c] Lifou (on New Caledonia I): 7 (1969).

New Guinea (Australia): [a] inc Bismarck Archipelago (inc New Britain). [b] Port Moresby (in Papua). [c] Lae (on New Guinea I): 24 (1970).

New Hebrides: [a] alt Nouvelles-Hebrides. [b] Vila (alt Port-Vila) [on Efate (alt Vate) I]: 3, 8s (1967). [c] Santo (alt Luganville) [on Espiritu Santo (alt Santo) I]: 3, 5s (1967).

New Zealand: [a] none. [b] Wellington (on North I): 136, 137s (1971). [c] Christchurch (on South I): 166, 276s (1971); Auckland (on North I): 152, 650s (1971).

Niue: [a] for Savage Island. [b] Alofi: 1 (1958e), 5s (1966). [c] none.

Norfolk Island: [a] none. [b] Kingston: ? [c] none.

Pacific Islands (USA): [a] inc Caroline Islands (for New Philippines), Marianas (alt Mariana) Islands (for Ladrone Islands) (in part), Marshall Islands; off Trust Territory of the Pacific Islands. [b] Chalon Kanoa (on Saipan I): 3 (1970). [c] Ebeye (on Kwajalein I): 6 (1970).

Papua: [a] none. [b] Port Moresby (on New Guinea I): 56 (1970). [c] Daru (on Daru I): 4 (1966).

Pitcairn Island: [a] none. [b] Adamstown: ? [c] none.

Tokelau Islands: [a] alt Union Islands. [b] Wellington (in New Zealand). [c] Fakaofo (on Fakaofo I): ? [Fakaofo I: 0.8 (1961)].

Tonga: [a] alt Tonga Islands; for Friendly Islands. [b] Nukualofa (on Tongatapu I): 16 (1966). [c] Neiafu (on Vavau I): 3 (1956).

Wake Island: [a] none. [b] Washington (in USA). [c] none.

Wallis and Futuna Islands: [a] off Wallis et Futuna; Futuna Islands: for Hoorn Islands. [b] Mata-Utu (on Uvea I): 0.6 (1969). [c] Vaitupu (on Uvea I): 0.6 (1969).

Western Samoa: [a] for Navigators' Islands; off Samoa i Sisifo. [b] Apia (on Upolu I): 25s (1966). [c] Saleimoa (on Upolu I): 3 (1966).

SOUTH AMERICA

Argentina: [a] none. [b] Buenos Aires (for Buenos Ayres): 2972, 8353s (1970). [c] Cordoba: 799 (1970).

Bolivia: [a] none. [b] La Paz (alt Paz; off La Paz de Ayacucho): 562 (1970e); Sucre (for Chuquisaca): 85 (1970e). [c] Cochabamba: 150 (1970e).

Brazil: [a] off Brasil. [b] Brasilia: 277, 546s (1970). [c] Sao Paulo: 5241, 5979s (1970).

Chile: [a] for Chili. [b] Santiago (alt Santiago de Chile): 2582s (1970). [c] Valparaiso: 239 (1970).

Colombia: [a] for New Granada. [b] Bogota (for Santa Fe de Bogota): 2038, 2294s (1969e). [c] Medellin: 968 (1969e).

Ecuador: [a] inc Galapagos (off Colon) Islands. [b] Quito 496 (1969e). [c] Guayaquil (for Santiago de Guayaquil): 739 (1969e).

Falkland Islands: [a] alt Islas Malvinas; inc South Georgia. [b] Stanley (alt Port Stanley) (on East Falkland I): 1 (1966). [c] none.

French Guiana: [a] inc Inini; off Guyane Francaise. [b] Cayenne: 20, 25s (1967). [c] Saint-Laurent-du-Maroni: 3, 5s (1967).

Guyana: [a] for British Guiana. [b] Georgetown: 66, 167s (1970). [c] New Amsterdam: 14 (1960).

Paraguay: [a] none. [b] Asuncion (for Nuestra Senora de la Asuncion): 305 (1962), 437s (1970e). [c] Encarnacion: 19 (1962).

Peru: [a] none. [b] Lima: 2416s (1969e). [c] Callao: 322 (1969e).

Surinam: [a] alt Dutch Guiana, Netherlands Guiana; off Suriname. [b] Paramaribo: 102 (1972), 182s (1964). [c] Nieuw Nickerie: 5 (1964?e).

Uruguay: [a] alt Republica Oriental del Uruguay; for Banda Oriental. [b] Montevideo: 1280 (1967e). [c] Salto: 58 (1963).

Venezuela: [a] none. [b] Caracas (for Santiago de Leon de Caracas): 787 (1961), 2064s (1969e). [c] Maracaibo: 625 (1969e).

2
Cities, by Continent and Country

Contents

This gazetteer consists of four parts.

I. Date of Settlement and Evolution of Population

Conventional name of city.

Year or century in which the first permanent settlement within present city limits was made. A question mark following a given date usually indicates that, although its exact origin is unknown, the city in question was first mentioned in historical records at that date. When the time of settlement cannot be ascertained but the city is known to have existed before a certain date, that date is given, preceded by the abbreviation "bef." It should be observed that the settlement date of a city bears no relation either to the date when the city was formally established (or chartered) or to the date when the present name was adopted.

Latest population, in thousands, and year of data. If the year is followed by the letter "e," the population has been estimated; otherwise, the figure given is from census returns. For many cities, two population figures are listed for a given year; the first is for the city proper, and the second, followed by the letter "s," for the city and adjacent suburban areas. Preferably, this is the population of the urbanized area or conurbation only; some officially reported suburban areas, however, include rural districts.

Similar population data for the years 1960, 1950, 1930, 1900, 1850, and 1800, or the times nearest to those years for which reliable figures are available, with the exact year stated. All populations are for the city as it existed at the time the population was determined, not for its present-day area. For populations "circa 1960," a 1956 census figure is normally given in preference to a 1960 estimate. Question marks are used when the exact year is unknown; for example, the notation "(00?e)" below the tabular heading "circa 1900" indicates that the population preceding it was estimated about, but not necessarily during, the year 1900.

II. Location and Climatic Data (English Measure)

Conventional name of city.

Latitude and longitude, in degrees and minutes. The notation "50.46N, 6.06E" means 50 degrees 46 minutes north of the equator and 6 degrees 6 minutes east of Greenwich, a section of London.

Elevation (i.e., altitude above sea level), in feet. When available, the given elevation is that of the city center or principal business district, or it is an average of elevations at several points in the city; otherwise, it is that of the meteorological station.

Period of record for climatic data. The period cited refers to the average temperature statistics; extreme temperature and precipitation data frequently cover a longer period.

Average temperature throughout the year. This and all other temperatures in Part II are expressed in degrees Fahrenheit.

Average temperatures during the warmest and coolest months, and the specific months.

Highest and lowest temperatures of record (absolute high and low).

Highest and lowest average annual temperatures. These are, in effect, the extreme temperatures likely to occur during a given year.

Average annual precipitation (i.e., rainfall plus the rain equivalent of snowfall), in inches.

III. Location and Climatic Data (Metric Measure)

This part contains the same data as Part II, except that elevation is given in meters, temperatures are expressed in degrees Celsius (centigrade), and precipitation is shown in millimeters.

IV. Supplemental Information

Conventional name of city.

[a] Subdivision of country in which city is located. This information is given for cities in the larger countries; see General Explanatory Notes, p. 5, for further information.

b Alternate, former, and official names of city. See General Explanatory Notes, p. 3, for explanation. In addition, important formerly separate cities that have been incorporated into the city cited and certain well-known sections of the city sometimes regarded as separate cities (e.g., Cholon, a section of Saigon) are listed after the abbreviation "inc." If a date is given after the "inc," this is related to the populations entered in Part I. Thus, the notation (under New York, USA) that reads "inc Brooklyn since 1898" means that the populations given for New York before 1898 exclude Brooklyn.

[c] Hydrographic features within present city limits. These are listed in the following order: seas (including oceans, gulfs, bays, straits, etc.), by size; rivers, by length, except that main rivers are always listed before their tributaries; natural lakes (including lagoons), by size. Creeks and other small streams are cited only if there is no river. If there is no hydrographic feature within the city limits, the nearest sea, river, or lake within approximately 10 mi (16 km) is given, preceded by the abbreviation "nr." Unconventional (i.e., alternate, former, and official) names of rivers and lakes are not entered here if the river or lake in question is listed in Table 5 or 12, and thus in the index.

[d] Universities, with date of foundation (in parentheses), student enrollment (i.e, thousands of full-time and part-time students, excluding correspondence students, enrolled in the university and its affiliated institutions), and academic staff (i.e., number of full-time and part-time teachers). Universities are listed in order of student enrollment.

Except as noted in the gazetteer itself,[1] all universities, as defined in the General Explanatory Notes, p. 5, within approximately 10 mi (16 km) of the city are listed.[2] Those outside the city limits, however, are described like this example under Visakhapatnam, India: "Andhra University (at Waltair, nr Visakhapatnam)." If a university was founded other than at its present location, the notation reads as in this example under Greenville, USA: "Furman University (1825 at Edgefield, relocated 1851)."

The date given for the foundation of a university is the year in which the institution itself, or (preferably) its oldest constituent college or the educational institution from which it directly evolved, was established (or chartered). This date may precede by several years the date when instruction was first given. Also, it bears no necessary relation to the length of time during which the university has been operative, since many universities have been closed for periods of years or even decades.

If no university exists at or near a given city, the notation "none" appears after *d*.

[e] Largest libraries, with date of foundation (in parentheses) and size of collection (i.e., thousands of volumes of books and pamphlets, usually excluding bound and unbound periodicals) for each library. Libraries are listed by size of collection.

Although only the largest libraries are cited, if the city has a public library of any importance, it is listed along with all other libraries that are larger. The name of the city is omitted from the name of each city (or municipal) public library; otherwise, the names of libraries are given in full. To save space, however, the names of universities already entered under *d* are not repeated when a university library is listed unless it is impossible without the name to determine to which university the library belongs; instead, the library is entered simply as "... University Library" or "University ... Library," depending on whether the university in question is called, for example, New York University or University of New York.

As with universities, large libraries located within approximately 10 mi (16 km) of the city are also listed, but are identified as being "nr" the city. Again, as with universities, those founded elsewhere and subsequently moved to the city under which they are cited are entered as in this example under Camden, USA: "Camden County Free Library (1922 at Haddonfield, relocated 1931)."

The date of foundation given for libraries is preferably the year in which the library was opened on a permanent basis, that is, the one since which it has been continuously operative. By "library," however, is meant the nucleus of the present book collection, not necessarily the institution under its name today.

[f] Supplemental population data. These may include a recent population of the city with suburbs, where no suburban population has previously been computed; a population, as returned by a particular census, that will promote comparability with the data given for other cities in the same country; or a reliable population for a date earlier than "circa 1800." They may also include populations at various dates for the cities listed after "inc" in Section *b* of Part IV. All data are in thousands, followed by the year of record in parentheses.

Arrangement

By city, alphabetically under country, the countries being arranged alphabetically under continent.

Coverage

All cities with at least the following populations (including suburbs if the suburban population is officially determined):
Africa – 200,000
Asia, except USSR – 200,000
Europe, except USSR – 100,000
North America – 100,000
Oceania – 100,000
South America – 200,000
USSR – 150,000

[1] For a few large cities with many universities, only universities above a certain size are listed.

[2] Provided, of course, that the university in question is not located in another city entered in the gazetteer.

In addition, many other well-known cities almost as large, as well as a few smaller cities of historical importance, are included.

Rounding

Populations are rounded to the nearest 1000, except that when the original figure is less than 1000 the rounding is done to the nearest 100.

Highest and lowest temperatures of record and highest and lowest average annual temperatures are rounded to the nearest degree.

University student enrollments are rounded to the nearest 1000 students, except that enrollments of less than 1000 are rounded to the nearest 100 students.

Library collections are rounded to the nearest 1000 volumes.

Entries

1635.

TABULAR GAZETTEER 2. CITIES, BY CONTINENT AND COUNTRY

Part I. Date of Settlement and Evolution of Population

AFRICA

City	Date settled	Population (thousands)						
		Latest	Circa 1960	Circa 1950	Circa 1930	Circa 1900	Circa 1850	Circa 1800
ALGERIA								
*Algiers	10th c	904 (66)	722 (60)	266 (48)	221 (31)	97 (01)	97 (49)	117 (00?e)
		943s (66)	884s (60)	489s (48)	257s (31)	137s (01)		
Annaba	7th c	152 (66)	135 (60)	78 (48)	66 (31)	32 (01)	10 (47)	
		169s (66)	165s (60)	103s (48)	69s (31)			
Constantine	3rd c BC?	244 (66)	169 (60)	80 (48)	79 (31)	41 (01)	23 (49)	
		254s (66)	223s (60)	119s (48)	105s (31)	48s (01)		
Oran	10th c	327 (66)	357 (60)	245 (48)	154 (31)	88 (01)	25 (49)	16 (00?e)
		328s (66)	426s (60)	273s (48)	164s (31)			
ANGOLA								
*Luanda	1575	475 (70)	225 (60)	142 (50)	51 (30?)	20 (98)	16 (70)	
BURUNDI								
*Bujumbura	1897	80 (70e)	47s (60e)	17 (49e)				
CAMEROON								
Douala	bef 1884	250s (70e)	128s (62)	125s (56)	28 (31)	23 (02e)		
*Yaounde	1888	101 (65e)	93 (62)	30 (50e)	6 (36)			
(CANARY ISLANDS), SPAIN								
*Las Palmas	1478	263 (70)	194 (60)	153 (50)	78 (30)	45 (00)	13 (57)	9 (00?e)
Santa Cruz de Tenerife	1494	142 (70)	133 (60)	103 (50)	62 (30)	38 (00)	11 (57)	7 (1768)
CENTRAL AFRICAN REPUBLIC								
*Bangui	1890	299s (68)	111 (64)	41 (50e)	13 (26)			
CHAD								
*Fort-Lamy	1900	133s (68)	88s (62)	23 (50e)	6 (26)			

AFRICA

City	Date settled	Population (thousands)						
		Latest	Circa 1960	Circa 1950	Circa 1930	Circa 1900	Circa 1850	Circa 1800
CONGO								
*Brazzaville	1880	175 (70)	136s (61-2)	83 (50e)	4 (26)	5 (00?e)		
DAHOMEY								
*Cotonou	bef 1868	139 (70e)	78 (61)	23 (46-49e)	8 (32)	4 (11)		
*Porto-Novo	16th c	87 (70e)	64 (61)	31 (46-49e)	27 (32)	30 (00?e)		
EGYPT								
Alexandria	332 BC	2032 (70e)	1516 (60)	919 (47)	573 (27)	320 (97)	164 (62)	15 (00e)
Aswan	6th c BC?	201 (70e)	48 (60)	26 (47)	16 (27)	13 (97)	6 (82)	
Asyut	bef 2160 BC	176 (70e)	127 (60)	90 (47)	57 (27)	42 (97)	26 (62)	12 (00e)
*Cairo	641?	4961 (70e)	3349 (60)	2091 (47)	1065 (27)	570 (97)	257 (62)	260 (00e)
Giza	bef 2568 BC	712 (70e)	262 (60)	66 (47)	27 (27)	17 (97)	11 (72)	3 (00e)
Luxor	bef 2160 BC	77 (66)	35 (60)	24 (47)	13 (27)	11 (97)	4 (82)	
Mahalla al Kubra	985?	256 (70e)	178 (60)	116 (47)	46 (27)	32 (97)	28 (82)	17 (00e)
Mansurah	1221	212 (70e)	147 (60)	102 (47)	64 (27)	36 (97)	16 (72)	7 (00e)
Port Said	1859	313 (70e)	245 (60)	178 (47)	101 (27)	42 (97)	9 (72)	
Shubra al Khaymah		252 (70e)	101 (60)	15 (47)	7 (27?)	2 (97?)	2 (82)	
Suez	15th c	315 (70e)	204 (60)	107 (47)	41 (27)	17 (97)	13 (72)	
Tanta	12th c?	254 (70e)	184 (60)	140 (47)	90 (27)	57 (97)	19 (62)	10 (00e)
Zagazig		173 (70e)	124 (60)	82 (47)	53 (27)	36 (97)	20 (82)	
ETHIOPIA								
*Addis Ababa	1887	644 (67)	449 (61)	400 (51e)	70 (28e)	30 (00e)		
Asmara	bef 1889	190 (68)	130 (60e)	117 (48e)	22 (31)	9 (05)		
GABON								
*Libreville	1849	57s (67e)	31s (61)	10 (50e)	4 (26)	3 (03e)		

Figure 29. Buildings clustered around Liberation Square in Cairo, the largest city and the largest urbanized area in Africa. The Nile River and part of Zamalik Island can be seen in the background. (Credit: Government of Egypt Ministry of Culture.)

AFRICA

City	Date settled	Population (thousands)						
		Latest	Circa 1960	Circa 1950	Circa 1930	Circa 1900	Circa 1850	Circa 1800
GAMBIA								
*Bathurst	1816	32 (67e)	28 (63)	20 (51)	14 (31)	7 (01)	4 (50?e)	
		48s (67e)	40s (63)	27s (51)				
GHANA								
*Accra	17th c	634 (70)	338 (60)	134 (48)	51 (31)	15 (01)	3 (50?e)	
		849s (70)	388s (60)					
Kumasi	17th c	343 (70)	181 (60)	71 (48)	36 (31)	6 (06)	18 (50?e)	13 (17e)
		340s (68e)	218s (60)					
GUINEA								
*Conakry	1890	197s (67e)	43 (60)	38 (46–49e)	9 (31)	7 (11)		
IVORY COAST								
*Abidjan	1904	330s (65e)	180s (60e)	56 (46–49e)	10 (31)	1 (11)		
KENYA								
Mombasa	8th c?	246s (69)	180 (62)	85 (48)	56 (31)	27 (00?e)	6 (50?e)	
*Nairobi	1899	350 (67e)	267 (62)	75 (48)	48 (31)	5 (07)		
		478s (69)	315s (62)	119s (48)				
LIBERIA								
*Monrovia	1822	100 (67e)	81 (62)	20 (50?e)	10 (30?e)	5 (97e)	2 (52e)	
LIBYA								
*Bengasi	6th c BC	150 (68e)	137 (64)	70 (54)	31 (28)	15 (00?e)	3 (50?e)	5 (00?e)
*Tripoli	7th c BC?	247 (68e)	214 (64)	130 (54)	72 (31)	42 (00e)	15 (42e)	15 (05e)
(MADEIRA ISLANDS), PORTUGAL								
*Funchal	1425	44 (70)	43 (60)	37 (50)	31 (30)	21 (00)	17 (45)	15 (00e)

AFRICA

City	Date settled	Population (thousands)						
		Latest	Circa 1960	Circa 1950	Circa 1930	Circa 1900	Circa 1850	Circa 1800
MALAGASY REPUBLIC								
*Tananarive	17th c	333 (68e)	248 (60?)	174 (49e)	92 (31)	63 (11)	25 (50?e)	
MALAWI								
Blantyre	1876	109 (66)	62 (61e)	6 (49e)	8 (30e)	6 (00?e)		
MALI								
*Bamako	bef 1883	182s (68e)	130s (60e)	60 (46–49e)	20 (31)	7 (11)	0.8 (83)	
Timbuktu	1215?	7 (60e)	7 (60e)	7 (46–49e)	6 (31)	7 (11)	13 (54e)	60 (00?e)
MAURITIUS								
*Port Louis	1735	138s (69e)	89 (62)	70 (52)	54 (31)	53 (01)	35 (50?e)	20 (00?e)
MOROCCO								
Casablanca	1515	1395 (70e)	965 (60)	682 (52)	160 (31)	20 (00?e)	0.7 (50?e)	0.1 (00?e)
Fez	808	290 (70e)	216 (60)	179 (52)	107 (31)	145 (00?e)	88 (50?e)	100 (00?e)
Marrakesh	1062	305 (70e)	243 (60)	215 (52)	192 (31)	50 (00e)	80 (50e)	30 (00?e)
Meknes	11th c	245 (70e)	176 (60)	140 (52)	54 (31)	35 (00?e)	50 (50?e)	15 (00?e)
*Rabat-Sale	11th c	460 (70e)	303 (60)	203 (52)	79 (31)	51 (00e)	38 (50e)	
Tangier	15th c BC?	170 (70e)	142 (60)	85 (47e)	80 (26e)	35 (00e)	8 (50e)	12 (00?e)
MOZAMBIQUE								
*Lourenco Marques	1544	92 (67e)	79 (60)	94 (50)	43 (30)	6 (00)	1 (67e)	
		184s (60)	184s (60)	100s (50)				
NIGER								
*Niamey	16th c?	79 (68e)	30 (59)	9 (46–49e)	3 (31)			

AFRICA

City	Date settled	Population (thousands) Latest	Circa 1960	Circa 1950	Circa 1930	Circa 1900	Circa 1850	Circa 1800
NIGERIA								
Abeokuta	1825?	223 (70e)	187 (63)	84 (52)	46 (31)	60 (00?e)	60 (50e)	
Enugu	1909	165 (70e)	138 (63)	63 (53)	13 (31)			
Ibadan	bef 1821	746 (70e)	627 (63)	459 (52)	387 (31)	345 (11)	70 (51e)	
Ilesha	18th c?	197 (70e)	166 (63)	72 (52)	22 (31)	40 (00?e)		
Ilorin	18th c	248 (70e)	209 (63)	41 (52)	47 (31)	36 (11)	70 (51e)	
Kano	16th c?	351 (70e)	295 (63)	130 (52)	89 (31)	39 (11)	30 (51e)	35 (24e)
*Lagos	1700?	875 (70e)	665 (63)	267 (52)	126 (31)	42 (01)	29 (71)	5 (89e)
Ogbomosho	17th c	380 (70e)	320 (63)	140 (52)	87 (31)	60 (00?e)	25 (51e)	
Oshogbo		248 (70e)	209 (63)	123 (52)	50 (31)	35 (00?e)		
Port Harcourt	1912	213 (70e)	180 (63)	72 (53)	15 (31)			
Zaria	16th c	198 (70e)	166 (63)	54 (52)	22 (31)	45 (00?e)	50 (50?e)	
REUNION								
*Saint-Denis	1665	66 (67)	37 (61)	26 (54)	27 (31)	27 (02)	18 (51)	7 (04)
		85s (67)	65s (61)	42s (54)				
RHODESIA								
Bulawayo	1893	210 (68e)	125 (56e)	43 (46–48)	31 (31e)	5 (00?e)		
		246s (69)	190s (59e)	53s (46–48)				
*Salisbury	1890	180 (68e)	160 (56e)	90 (51)	29 (31e)	5 (00?e)		
		385s (69)	271s (59e)	119s (51)				
SENEGAL								
*Dakar	1857	581s (69e)	375s (61)	171 (46e)	54 (31)	18 (04)	3 (65)	
SIERRA LEONE								
*Freetown	1788	179 (70e)	128 (63)	65 (47e)	55 (31)	34 (01)	18 (60)	5s (20)

AFRICA

City	Date settled	Population (thousands)						
		Latest	Circa 1960	Circa 1950	Circa 1930	Circa 1900	Circa 1850	Circa 1800
SOMALIA								
*Mogadishu	908?	173 (67e)	91 (59e)	74 (48e)	36 (31)	7 (00?e)	4 (50?e)	4 (25e)
SOUTH AFRICA								
Bloemfontein	1846	148 (70)	113 (60)	81 (51)	53 (36)	34 (04)	1 (65?e)	
		180s (70)	145s (60)	109s (51)	64s (36)			
*Cape Town	1652	691 (70)	508 (60)	441 (51)	296 (36)	78 (04)	26 (56)	17 (00?)
		1097s (70)	807s (60)	578s (51)	344s (36)	170s (04)		
Durban	1824	495 (70)	560 (60)	435 (51)	240 (36)	68 (04)	5 (66)	
		721s (70)	681s (60)	480s (51)	260s (36)			
Germiston	1887	210 (70)	148 (60)	116 (51)	68 (36)	29 (04)		
		282s (70)	214s (60)	168s (51)	79s (36)			
Johannesburg	1886	655 (70)	595 (60)	632 (51)	475 (36)	99 (04)		
		1433s (70)	1153s (60)	884s (51)	519s (36)	156s (04)		
Pietermaritzburg	1839	113 (70)	92 (60)	73 (51)	47 (36)	31 (04)	5 (71?)	
		160s (70)	129s (60)	92s (51)	56s (36)			
Port Elizabeth	1820	387 (70)	249 (60)	169 (51)	99 (36)	33 (04)	12 (65)	
		469s (70)	291s (60)	189s (51)	110s (36)			
*Pretoria	1855	544 (70)	304 (60)	232 (51)	108 (36)	37 (04)	0.3 (67e)	
		562s (70)	423s (60)	285s (51)	129s (36)			
Vereeniging	1892	170 (70)	79 (60)	60 (51)	20 (36)	0.9 (04?)		
		196s (70)	135s (60)	123s (51)				
SUDAN								
*Khartoum	1823	194 (68e)	93 (56)	68 (47e)	50 (29e)	8 (00e)	25 (50e)	
			246s (56)	223s (47e)				
Omdurman	18th c?	206 (68e)	114 (55)	123 (47e)	104 (29e)	43 (09)		
TANZANIA								
*Dar es Salaam	1862	273 (67)	129 (57)	69 (48)	23 (31)	17 (00e)		

AFRICA

City	Date settled	Population (thousands) Latest		Circa 1960		Circa 1950		Circa 1930		Circa 1900		Circa 1850		Circa 1800	
Zanzibar	16th c	68	(67)	58	(58)	45	(48)	45	(31)	58	(00e)	25	(50?e)		
TOGO															
*Lome	bef 1884	148	(70)	77	(58-60)	33	(50)	18	(31)	4	(03)	6	(50?e)		
TUNISIA															
Sfax	2nd c?	80	(66)	66	(56)	55	(46)	40	(31)	15	(00?e)				
*Tunis	4th c BC?	469	(66)	410	(56)	365	(46)	202	(31)	228	(06)	130	(50?e)	125	(00e)
UGANDA															
*Kampala	1890	80	(67e)	47	(59)	22	(48)	5	(30e)	3	(11)				
		331s	(69)	123s	(59)										
UPPER VOLTA															
*Ouagadougou	14th c?	79	(67e)	59	(61)	21	(46-49e)	11	(31)						
ZAIRE															
Kananga	1884	429	(70)	115	(59e)	11	(48e)								
*Kinshasa	1887	1323	(70)	402	(59e)	209	(50e)	40	(32e)	5	(01e)				
Kisangani	1882	230	(70)	127	(60e)	25	(48e)	12	(30e)	0.4	(00?)				
Lubumbashi	1910	318	(70)	184	(59e)	103	(50e)	17	(32e)						
Mbuji-Mayi		256	(70)	41	(58e)										
ZAMBIA															
Kitwe	1931?	179s	(69)	116s	(63)	17s	(46)								
*Lusaka	1910?	238s	(69)	114s	(63)	32	(50)	2	(31)						

ASIA

City	Date settled	Population (thousands)						
		Latest	Circa 1960	Circa 1950	Circa 1930	Circa 1900	Circa 1850	Circa 1800
AFGHANISTAN								
Herat	4th c BC?	102 (70e)	35 (60e)	76 (48e)	30 (30?e)	45 (00?e)	45 (50?e)	100 (10e)
*Kabul	4th c BC?	307 (70e)	200 (60e)	206 (48e)	80 (30?e)	100 (00e)	40 (53e)	200 (00?e)
Kandahar	1747?	130 (70e)	50 (60e)	77 (48e)	45 (30?e)	40 (00e)	58 (50e)	100 (09e)
BAHRAIN								
*Manama	1507?	90 (71)	62 (59)	40 (50)	25 (30?e)	8 (00?e)	5 (50?e)	
BANGLADESH								
Chittagong	8th c?	437 (69e)	364 (61)	290 (51)	53 (31)	22 (01)	21 (72)	
*Dacca	1608?	829 (69e)	557 (61)	336 (51)	139 (31)	90 (01)	69 (72)	68 (38)
Khulna	18th c?	320 (69e)	128 (61)	41 (51)	19 (31)	10 (01)		
Narayanganj	17th c?	327 (69e)	162 (61)	68 (51)	34 (31)	24 (01)	11 (72)	6 (38)
BURMA								
Mandalay	1857	360 (69e)	195 (58e)	182 (53)	148 (31)	184 (01)	189 (91)	
*Rangoon	8th c	1759 (70e)	822 (57e)	712 (53)	400 (31)	235 (01)	99 (72)	30 (00?e)
CAMBODIA								
*Phnom-Penh	1371	650 (69e)	394 (62)	111 (48e)	96 (31)	50 (00e)	17 (66e)	
CEYLON								
*Colombo	543 BC?	564 (71)	511 (63)	426 (53)	284 (31)	155 (01)	100 (71)	50 (04e)
Kandy	13th c?	68 (63)	68 (63)	57 (53)	37 (31)	26 (01)		
CHINA								
Amoy	16th c?	308 (58e)	308 (58e)	224 (53)	196 (35e)	96 (97)	275 (47e)	
Anking	13th c	129 (58e)	129 (58e)	105 (53)	121 (32e)	40 (00?e)		
Anshan	1908	900 (62e)	833 (58e)	549 (53)	214 (40)			

ASIA

City	Date settled	Population (thousands)						
		Latest	Circa 1960	Circa 1950	Circa 1930	Circa 1900	Circa 1850	Circa 1800
Antung	1896?	420 (62e)	370 (58e)	360 (53)	315 (40)	20 (08e)		
Canton	9th c BC?	3000 (65e)	2200 (58e)	1599 (53)	1157 (35e)	900 (05e)	1236 (47e)	1500 (00?e)
Changchih	16th c BC?	180 (58e)	180 (58e)	98 (53)				
Changchow (Fukien)	10th c BC?	90 (56e)	90 (56e)	81 (53)	56 (22e)	500 (05e)	1000 (50e)	
Changchow (Kiangsu)	1st c?	300 (58e)	300 (58e)	296 (53)	79 (35e)	200 (00?e)		
Changchun	11th c?	1400 (68?e)	988 (58e)	855 (53)	555 (40)	80 (08e)		
Changsha	3rd c BC?	709 (58e)	709 (58e)	651 (53)	480 (35e)	230 (05e)		
Chefoo	bef 1862	140 (58e)	140 (58e)	116 (53)	140 (34e)	82 (05e)	10 (69e)	
Chengchow	10th c BC?	785 (58e)	785 (58e)	595 (53)	80 (31e)			
Chengtu	3rd c BC?	1135 (58e)	1135 (58e)	857 (53)	481 (36e)	475 (00?e)	800 (72e)	
Chinchow	12th c	400 (58e)	400 (58e)	352 (53)	142 (40)	14 (00?e)		
Chinkiang	12th c?	190 (58e)	190 (58e)	201 (53)	205 (36e)	168 (05e)	137 (50e)	
Chinwangtao	bef 1879	210 (58e)	210 (58e)	187 (53)	20 (31e)	5 (05e)		
Chuchow	bef 1912	190 (58e)	190 (58e)	127 (53)				
Chungking	250?	2165 (58e)	2165 (58e)	1772 (53)	281 (34e)	620 (05e)	200 (61e)	
Foochow	10th c BC?	623 (58e)	623 (58e)	553 (53)	359 (35e)	624 (05e)	600 (47e)	
Foshan		300 (68?e)	120 (58e)	122 (53)	96 (48e)	400 (00?e)	400 (69e)	
Fushun	1669	1019 (58e)	1019 (58e)	679 (53)	270 (40)			
Fusin	1900?	290 (58e)	290 (58e)	189 (53)	143 (40)			
Hangchow	606	794 (58e)	794 (58e)	697 (53)	576 (35e)	350 (05e)	700 (50?e)	1000 (00?e)
Hantan	4th c BC	380 (58e)	380 (58e)	90 (53)				
Harbin	1896?	1595 (58e)	1595 (58e)	1163 (53)	661 (40)	20 (02e)		
Hengyang	7th c BC?	240 (58e)	240 (58e)	235 (53)	102 (35e)	20 (00?e)		
Hofei	10th c BC?	500 (63?e)	360 (58e)	184 (53)	70 (34e)			
Hoihow	bef 1876	402 (58e)	402 (58e)	135 (53)	15 (30?e)	12 (00?e)		
Hokang		200 (58e)	200 (58e)	90 (53)	20 (40)			
Huhehot	9th c	320 (58e)	320 (58e)	148 (53)	84 (35e)	200 (05e)		
Hwainan	bef 1940	500 (63?e)	280 (58e)	287 (53)				
Hwangshih		200 (63?e)	135 (58e)	110 (53)	6 (20?e)			

ASIA

City	Date settled	Population (thousands)						
		Latest	Circa 1960	Circa 1950	Circa 1930	Circa 1900	Circa 1850	Circa 1800
Ichang	1st c?	90 (56e)	90 (56e)	73 (53)	108 (31e)	45 (05e)		
Ichun	1948?	200 (58e)	200 (58e)	35 (53)				
Ipin	1st c?	190 (58e)	190 (58e)	178 (53)	78 (35e)	50 (07e)		
Kaifeng	7th c BC?	318 (58e)	318 (58e)	299 (53)	303 (36e)	200 (08e)		
Kalgan	1429	480 (58e)	480 (58e)	229 (53)	145 (35e)	47 (00e)		
Kashgar	2nd c BC?	100 (58e)	100 (58e)	91 (53)	80 (30?e)	65 (00?e)	30 (50?e)	
Kiamusze		232 (58e)	232 (58e)	146 (53)	129 (40)			
Kingtehchen	6th c	266 (58e)	266 (58e)	92 (53)	140 (34e)	200 (05e)	1000 (50?e)	1000 (00?e)
Kirin	1673	583 (58e)	583 (58e)	435 (53)	173 (40)	120 (09e)	135 (64e)	300 (12e)
Kisi	1935?	253 (58e)	253 (58e)	35 (53)				
Kokiu		180 (58e)	180 (58e)	170 (53)	50 (22e)	10 (00?e)		
Kunming	1st c?	900 (58e)	900 (58e)	699 (53)	144 (34e)	45 (07)		
Kweilin	4th c BC?	170 (58e)	170 (58e)	145 (53)	75 (36e)	150 (07e)		
Kweiyang	14th c	530 (58e)	530 (58e)	271 (53)	117 (35e)	100 (00?e)		
Lanchow	1st c?	732 (58e)	732 (58e)	397 (53)	106 (36e)	337 (00e)		
Lhasa	400?	80 (63?e)	70 (58?e)	50 (53)	20 (30?e)	30 (00?e)	50 (50?e)	
Liaoyang	15th c BC?	169 (58e)	169 (58e)	147 (53)	100 (40)	60 (00?e)	80 (73e)	
Liaoyuan		177 (58e)	177 (58e)	120 (53)	32 (38e)			
Liuchow	3rd c BC?	300 (63?e)	190 (58e)	158 (53)	60 (22e)	35 (00?e)		
Loyang	1900 BC?	500 (58e)	500 (58e)	171 (53)	77 (35e)	20 (00?e)		
Luchow	2nd c?	130 (58e)	130 (58e)	289 (53)	74 (35e)	40 (00?e)		
Lushun-Talien	600?	3600 (65e)	1590 (58e)	892 (53)	327 (30)	54 (00?e)		
Malipo		196 (53)		196 (53)				
Mukden	4th c?	2800 (68?e)	2423 (58e)	2300 (53)	1134 (40)	158 (08e)	170 (64e)	
Mutankiang	bef 1903	251 (58e)	251 (58e)	151 (53)	178 (40)			
Nanchang	12th c?	520 (58e)	520 (58e)	398 (53)	277 (35e)	233 (00e)	300 (50?e)	
Nanchung	10th c BC?	206 (58e)	206 (58e)	165 (53)	53 (35e)			
Nanking	2nd c BC?	1455 (58e)	1455 (58e)	1092 (53)	1013 (35e)	270 (05e)	400 (50?e)	1000 (00?e)
Nanning	10th c BC?	300 (63?e)	260 (58e)	195 (53)	89 (36e)	25 (05e)		

ASIA

City	Date settled	Population (thousands)												
		Latest		Circa 1960		Circa 1950		Circa 1930		Circa 1900		Circa 1850		Circa 1800
Nantung	1st c?	240	(58e)	240	(58e)	260	(53)	133	(35e)					
Neikiang	1st c?	180	(58e)	180	(58e)	190	(53)	32	(48e)					
Ningpo	8th c	280	(58e)	280	(58e)	238	(53)	244	(33e)	260	(05e)	280	(50e)	
Paoki	3rd c BC?	180	(58e)	180	(58e)	130	(53)	56	(48e)					
Paoting	13th c	380	(58e)	380	(58e)	125	(53)	312	(28e)	60	(07e)	135	(66e)	
Paotow	11th c?	800	(63?e)	490	(58e)	149	(53)	67	(35e)	20	(00?e)			
*Peking	11th c BC?	10,000	(68e)	4148	(58e)	2768	(53)	1565	(35e)	700	(05e)	1649	(45)	700 (00?e)
Pengpu	bef 1912	330	(58e)	330	(58e)	253	(53)	105	(34e)					
Penki	bef 1726	449	(58e)	449	(58e)	449	(53)	100	(40)	3	(00?e)			
Shanghai	bef 11th c	10,700	(68e)	5977	(58e)	6204	(53)	3259	(31e)	423	(95)	149	(65)	
Shangkiu	3rd c BC?	165	(58e)	165	(58e)	134	(53)	74	(35e)					
Shaohing	2000 BC?	160	(58e)	160	(58e)	131	(53)	178	(33e)	500	(00?e)	500	(71e)	
Shaoyang	7th c BC?	170	(58e)	170	(58e)	118	(53)	76	(35e)					
Shihkiachwang	bef 1904	623	(58e)	623	(58e)	373	(53)	217	(35e)					
Shiukwan	3rd c BC?	200	(63?e)	200	(63?e)	82	(53)	208	(35e)	100	(00?e)			
Siakwan		400	(68?e)			26	(53)	10	(20e)					
Sian	2205 BC?	1600	(68?e)	1368	(58e)	787	(53)	155	(36e)	1000	(00?e)	1000	(72e)	
Siangtan	3rd c BC?	300	(68?e)	247	(58e)	184	(53)	123	(33e)	300	(00?e)	1000	(70e)	
Sinhailien	3rd c BC?	210	(58e)	210	(58e)	208	(53)							
Sining	2nd c BC?	300	(63?e)	150	(58e)	94	(53)	56	(46e)	60	(00?e)			
Sinsiang	1st c?	203	(58e)	203	(58e)	170	(53)							
Soochow	525 BC?	651	(58e)	651	(58e)	474	(53)	390	(36e)	500	(05e)	2000	(52e)	
Suchow	7th c BC?	710	(58e)	710	(58e)	373	(53)	160	(35e)	40	(00?e)			
Swatow	bef 1860	300	(68?e)	250	(58e)	280	(53)	190	(35e)	60	(05e)	45	(72e)	
Szeping	bef 1900	200	(63?e)	130	(58e)	126	(53)	68	(40)					
Taichow	1st c?	200	(58e)	200	(58e)	160	(53)	66	(35e)					
Taiyuan	3rd c BC	1053	(58e)	1053	(58e)	721	(53)	139	(34e)	230	(00?e)	250	(66e)	
Tangshan	1878?	812	(58e)	812	(58e)	693	(53)	149	(35e)					
Tatung	10th c BC?	243	(58e)	243	(58e)	228	(53)	50	(22e)					

Figure 30. The famous bund and waterfront along the Whangpoo River at Shanghai, the largest city in Asia. (Credit: Foreign Languages Press, Peking.)

ASIA

City	Date settled	Population (thousands) Latest	Circa 1960	Circa 1950	Circa 1930	Circa 1900	Circa 1850	Circa 1800
Tientsin	bef 13th c	4000 (68e)	3278 (58e)	2694 (53)	1068 (35e)	750 (05e)	300 (50e)	
Tsamkong	3rd c BC?	170 (58e)	170 (58e)	166 (53)	230s (26)	177s (06)		
Tsiaotso	bef 1953	250 (58e)	250 (58e)	35 (53)				
Tsinan	6th c	1200 (68?e)	882 (58e)	680 (53)	437 (35e)	100 (00?e)		
Tsingtao	bef 1891	1144 (58e)	1144 (58e)	917 (53)	318 (28e)	35 (07)		
Tsitsihar	1691	704 (58e)	704 (58e)	345 (53)	133 (40)	25 (00?e)	60 (68e)	
Tzekung	3rd c BC	400 (63?e)	280 (58e)	291 (53)				
Tzepo	1st c?	875 (58e)	875 (58e)	184 (53)				
Urumtsi		700 (66?e)	320 (58e)	141 (53)	60 (22e)	40 (00e)	150 (65e)	
Weifang	1st c?	190 (58e)	190 (58e)	149 (53)	83 (34e)	100 (00?e)	100 (69e)	
Wenchow	4th c?	210 (58e)	210 (58e)	202 (53)	203 (27e)	80 (05e)	500 (70e)	
Wuhan	3rd c	2226 (58e)	2226 (58e)	1427 (53)	1353 (35e)	1500 (00?e)	996 (50e)	
Wuhu	3rd c?	230 (56e)	230 (56e)	242 (53)	150 (33e)	137 (05e)		
Wusih	1st c?	616 (58e)	616 (58e)	582 (53)	272 (36e)	200 (00?e)		
Wutungkiao	bef 1912	140 (58e)	140 (58e)	199 (53)				
Yangchow	7th c BC?	160 (58e)	160 (58e)	180 (53)	138 (36e)	100 (00?e)	360 (68e)	
Yangchuan	bef 283 BC	200 (58e)	200 (58e)	177 (53)				
Yenan	1st c?	15 (62e)	15 (62e)	30 (50e)	30 (30e)			
Yinchwan	bef 2nd c BC	160 (63?e)	60 (56e)	84 (53)	85 (22e)	12 (00?e)		
Yingkow	1836	161 (58e)	161 (58e)	131 (53)	181 (40)	60 (00?e)	80 (64e)	
CYPRUS								
*Nicosia	12th c?	114s (69e)	46 (60)	34 (46)	24 (31)	15 (01)	16 (50?e)	12 (00?e)
GAZA STRIP								
*Gaza	1468 BC?	118 (67)		38 (46e)	17 (31)	21 (00e)	3 (50?e)	5 (00e)
HONG KONG								
*Hong Kong	5th c?	3951 (71)	3133 (61)	2015 (51e)	840 (31)	284 (01)	33 (50)	

ASIA

City	Date settled	Population (thousands) Latest	Circa 1960	Circa 1950	Circa 1930	Circa 1900	Circa 1850	Circa 1800
INDIA								
Agra	12th c?	595 (71)	462 (61)	334 (51)	230 (31)	188 (01)	149 (72)	
		638s (71)	509s (61)	376s (51)				
Ahmedabad	bef 1298	1588 (71)	1150 (61)	788 (51)	314 (31)	186 (01)	120 (72)	100 (20e)
		1746s (71)	1206s (61)	794s (51)				
Ajmer	145?	262 (71)	231 (61)	197 (51)	120 (31)	74 (01)	35 (72)	23 (37e)
Aligarh	12th c?	254 (71)	185 (61)	142 (51)	84 (31)	72 (01)	59 (72)	
Allahabad	240 BC?	492 (71)	413 (61)	312 (51)	184 (31)	172 (01)	144 (72)	20 (03e)
		514s (71)	431s (61)	332s (51)				
Ambala	14th c?	186 (71)	182 (61)	152 (51)	85 (31)	79 (01)	51 (68)	
Amravati	bef 1756	194 (71)	138 (61)	103 (51)	47 (31)	34 (01)	23 (67)	
Amritsar	1574	433 (71)	376 (61)	326 (51)	265 (31)	162 (01)	134 (68)	
		459s (69e)	398s (61)					
Asansol	bef 1881	157 (71)	103 (61)	76 (51)	31 (31)	15 (01)		
		278s (69e)	169s (61)	95s (51)				
Bangalore	1537	1027 (69e)	905 (61)	779 (51)	306 (31)	69 (01)	61 (71)	60 (05e)
		1648s (71)	1207s (61)			159s (01)	143s (71)	
Bareilly	1537?	296 (71)	260 (61)	195 (51)	144 (31)	131 (01)	103 (72)	66 (22)
		326s (71)	273s (61)	208s (51)				
Baroda	812?	467 (71)	298 (61)	211 (51)	113 (31)	104 (01)	112 (72)	100 (18e)
Belgaum	bef 1160	156 (69e)	128 (61)	104 (51)	41 (31)	26 (01)	32 (72)	8 (20)
		214s (71)	147s (61)	120s (51)				
Bhatpara	bef 1815	205 (71)	148 (61)	135 (51)	85 (31)	22 (01)	10 (81)	
Bhavnagar	1723	226 (71)	176 (61)	138 (51)	76 (31)	56 (01)	36 (72)	
Bhopal	11th c?	303 (71)	185 (61)	102 (51)	61 (31)	77 (01)	55 (81)	
		392s (71)	223s (61)					
Bikaner	1488	189 (71)	151 (61)	117 (51)	86 (31)	53 (01)	33 (81)	
Bombay	150?	5969 (71)	4152 (61)	2839 (51)	1161 (31)	776 (01)	644 (72)	162 (16)

ASIA

City	Date settled	Population (thousands) Latest	Circa 1960	Circa 1950	Circa 1930	Circa 1900	Circa 1850	Circa 1800
Calcutta	1495?	3141 (71)	2927 (61)	2549 (51)	1197 (31)	848 (01)	448 (72)	230 (37)
		7005s (71)	4405s (61)	4578s (51)	1486s (31)	949s (01)	795s (72)	
Calicut	7th c	334 (71)	193 (61)	159 (51)	99 (31)	77 (01)	48 (71)	
		381s (69e)	249s (61)					
Chandigarh	1950	219 (71)	89 (61)	5 (51)				
		233s (71)	120s (61)					
Coimbatore	bef 1768	353 (71)	286 (61)	198 (51)	95 (31)	53 (01)	35 (71)	
Cuttack	10th c?	194 (71)	146 (61)	103 (51)	65 (31)	51 (01)	43 (72)	
Dehra Dun	1699	166 (71)	127 (61)	116 (51)	40 (31)	28 (01)	7 (72)	
		199s (71)	156s (61)	144s (51)				
Delhi	993	3280 (71)	2062 (61)	915 (51)	348 (31)	209 (01)	154 (68)	
		3630s (71)	2359s (61)	1384s (51)	447s (31)			
Dhanbad	bef 1860	80 (71)	47 (61)	34 (51)	16 (31)	12 (21)		
		433s (71)	201s (61)	74s (51)				
Durg	10th c?	71 (71)	47 (61)	20 (51)	13 (31)	4 (01)	4 (81)	
		245s (71)	133s (61)					
Durgapur	1960?	207 (71)	42 (61)					
Ernakulam	14th c?	203 (69e)	117 (61)	62 (51)	37 (31)	22 (01)	14 (75)	
		438s (71)	313s (61)	193s (51)				
Gaya	545 BC?	180 (71)	151 (61)	134 (51)	88 (31)	71 (01)	67 (72)	
Gorakhpur	1400?	231 (71)	180 (61)	124 (51)	59 (31)	64 (01)	51 (72)	
Guntur	18th c	270 (71)	187 (61)	125 (51)	65 (31)	31 (01)	18 (71)	
Gwalior	525?	379 (71)	301 (61)	34 (51)	22 (31)	17 (01)		
		407s (71)		242s (51)	127s (31)	139s (01)	88s (81)	
Howrah	17th c?	741 (71)	513 (61)	434 (51)	225 (31)	158 (01)	84 (72)	
Hubli	11th c?	217 (69e)	171 (61)	130 (51)	90 (31)	60 (01)	38 (72)	15 (20e)
		380s (71)	248s (61)					
Hyderabad	1589	1612 (71)	1119 (61)	860 (51)	346 (31)	352 (01)	124 (81)	100 (00?e)
		1799s (71)	1251s (61)	1129s (51)	467s (31)	448s (01)	367s (81)	
Indore	1715	544 (71)	395 (61)	311 (51)	127 (31)	87 (01)	75 (81)	10 (18e)

ASIA

City	Date settled	Population (thousands) Latest	Circa 1960	Circa 1950	Circa 1930	Circa 1900	Circa 1850	Circa 1800
Jabalpur	1100?	425 (71)	295 (61)	204 (51)	124 (31)	90 (01)	55 (72)	
		534s (71)	367s (61)	357s (51)				
Jaipur	1728	613 (71)	403 (61)	291 (51)	144 (31)	160 (01)	138 (70)	
Jamnagar	1540	215 (71)	140 (61)	103 (51)	55 (31)	54 (01)	35 (72)	
		227s (71)	149s (61)	104s (51)				
Jamshedpur	1908?	341 (71)	304 (61)	194 (51)	84 (31)	6 (11)		
		465s (71)	328s (61)	218s (51)				
Jhansi	1553?	173 (71)	140 (61)	127 (51)	77 (31)	56 (01)	30 (72e)	
		198s (71)	170s (61)					
Jodhpur	1459	319 (71)	225 (61)	181 (51)	95 (31)	79 (01)	63 (81)	
Jullundur	100?	296 (71)	223 (61)	169 (51)	89 (31)	68 (01)	50 (68)	
		334s (69e)	265s (61)					
Kalyan	2nd c?	99 (71)	73 (61)	59 (51)	26 (31)	11 (01)	13 (72)	
		267s (71)	194s (61)	140s (51)				
Kanpur	1778	1152 (71)	895 (61)	636 (51)	244 (31)	197 (01)	123 (72)	
		1273s (71)	971s (61)	705s (51)				
Kolhapur	2nd c?	259 (71)	187 (61)	137 (51)	70 (31)	54 (01)	40 (72)	
		259s (69e)	193s (61)					
Kota	14th c?	213 (71)	120 (61)	65 (51)	38 (31)	34 (01)	40 (81)	
Lucknow	bef 1478	751 (71)	595 (61)	445 (51)	275 (31)	264 (01)	285 (69)	300 (00e)
		826s (71)	656s (61)	497s (51)				
Ludhiana	1480	401 (71)	244 (61)	154 (51)	69 (31)	49 (01)	40 (68)	
Madras	1504	2470 (71)	1729 (61)	1416 (51)	647 (31)	509 (01)	368 (71)	300 (94e)
Madurai	5th c BC?	548 (71)	425 (61)	362 (51)	182 (31)	106 (01)	52 (71)	20 (12)
Malegaon	1740	192 (71)	121 (61)	55 (51)	29 (31)	19 (01)	10 (72)	
Mangalore	6th c?	169 (69e)	143 (61)	117 (51)	67 (31)	44 (01)	30 (71)	20 (00?e)
		214s (71)	170s (61)					
Meerut	3rd c BC?	271 (71)	209 (61)	158 (51)	137 (31)	118 (01)	81 (72)	
		368s (71)	284s (61)	233s (51)				

ASIA

City	Date settled	Population (thousands) Latest	Circa 1960	Circa 1950	Circa 1930	Circa 1900	Circa 1850	Circa 1800
Moradabad	1625	258 (71)	180 (61)	154 (51)	111 (31)	75 (01)	62 (72)	
		272s (71)	192s (61)	162s (51)				
Mysore	10th c?	356 (71)	254 (61)	244 (51)	107 (31)	68 (01)	58 (71)	
Nagpur	1700?	866 (71)	644 (61)	449 (51)	215 (31)	128 (01)	84 (72)	80 (00?e)
		933s (69e)	690s (61)					
Nasik	100 BC?	176 (71)	131 (61)	97 (51)	49 (31)	21 (01)	22 (72)	30 (20e)
		283s (69e)	216s (61)					
*New Delhi	993	293 (71)	262 (61)	276 (51)	65 (31)	31 (21)		
Patna	6th c BC?	472 (71)	365 (61)	250 (51)	160 (31)	135 (01)	159 (72)	312 (11e)
Poona	1604?	853 (71)	598 (61)	481 (51)	234 (31)	153 (01)	119 (72)	100 (00?e)
		1123s (71)	737s (61)	589s (51)				
Raipur	750?	174 (71)	140 (61)	90 (51)	45 (31)	32 (01)	19 (72)	5 (18e)
Rajahmundry	11th c?	166 (71)	130 (61)	105 (51)	64 (31)	36 (01)	20 (71)	
Rajkot	17th c?	300 (71)	194 (61)	132 (51)	47 (31)	36 (01)	12 (72)	
Ranchi	bef 1834	176 (71)	122 (61)	94 (51)	51 (31)	26 (01)	12 (72)	
		256s (71)	140s (61)	107s (51)				
Saharanpur	1340?	226 (71)	185 (61)	143 (51)	79 (31)	66 (01)	44 (72)	
Salem	16th c?	308 (71)	249 (61)	202 (51)	102 (31)	71 (01)	50 (71)	19 (43)
Sholapur	1345?	398 (71)	338 (61)	266 (51)	145 (31)	75 (01)	53 (72)	
South Suburban	1495?	274 (71)	186 (61)	104 (51)	39 (31)	26 (01)		
		513s (69e)	342s (61)	213s (51)				
Surat	bef 150	472 (71)	288 (61)	223 (51)	99 (31)	119 (01)	108 (72)	250 (11e)
Tiruchirapalli	bef 200	306 (71)	250 (61)	219 (51)	143 (31)	105 (01)	77 (71)	80s (20e)
Tirunelveli	7th c?	109 (71)	88 (61)	73 (51)	57 (31)	40 (01)	21 (71)	
			190s (61)	161s (51)				
Trivandrum	bef 1196	410 (71)	240 (61)	187 (51)	96 (31)	58 (01)	38 (81)	
		436s (69e)	302s (61)					
Ujjain	bef 263 BC	208 (71)	144 (61)	130 (51)	54 (31)	40 (01)	33 (81)	

ASIA

City	Date settled	Population (thousands)						
		Latest	Circa 1960	Circa 1950	Circa 1930	Circa 1900	Circa 1850	Circa 1800
Varanasi	12th c BC?	560 (71)	485 (61)	342 (51)	205 (31)	209 (01)	175 (72)	183 (26e)
		583s (71)	490s (61)	356s (51)				
Vijayawada	17th c?	316 (71)	230 (61)	161 (51)	60 (31)	24 (01)	8 (71)	
Visakhapatnam	14th c?	351 (71)	182 (61)	108 (51)	57 (31)	41 (01)	32 (71)	20 (00?e)
Warangal	12th c	207 (71)	156 (61)	133 (51)	62 (31)	5 (01)	3 (91)	
INDONESIA								
Bandjermasin	14th c	254 (68e)	214 (61)	150 (51e)	66 (30)	45 (95)	30 (50?e)	
Bandung	1810	1126 (70)	973 (61)	686 (52e)	167 (30)	27 (95)		
Bogor	1745	172 (68e)	154 (61)	103 (51e)	65 (30)	25 (95)	5 (50?e)	
*Djakarta	5th c?	4386 (70)	2907 (61)	1861 (52e)	435 (30)	115 (95)	54 (42)	47s (15)
Jogjakarta	1749	324 (70)	313 (61)	228 (51e)	137 (30)	58 (95)	43 (50?e)	100 (15e)
Makasar	15th c?	402 (70)	384 (61)	214 (51e)	85 (30)	17 (95)	20 (45e)	100 (00?e)
Malang	13th c?	404 (68e)	341 (61)	265 (53e)	87 (30)	13 (95)		
Manado	17th c?	156 (70)	130 (61)	64 (54e)	28 (30)	9 (96)	2 (50?e)	
Medan	bef 1869	541 (70)	479 (61)	250 (51e)	77 (30)	13 (95)		
Padang	1637	190 (70)	144 (61)	109 (51e)	52 (30)	32 (95)	12 (50?e)	
Palembang	2nd c?	522 (70)	475 (61)	208 (51e)	108 (30)	54 (95)	42 (55)	27 (00e)
Pontianak	1772?	178 (68e)	150 (61)	121 (55e)	45 (30)	17 (95)	12 (50?e)	
Semarang	17th c?	611 (70)	503 (61)	309 (51e)	218 (30)	83 (95)	28 (50?e)	25 (00e)
Surabaja	14th c?	1442 (70)	1008 (61)	926 (53e)	342 (30)	125 (95)	85 (57)	25 (15)
Surakarta	1744	443 (70)	368 (61)	319 (51e)	165 (30)	105 (95)	100 (50?e)	105 (15e)
Tjirebon	15th c?	170 (70)	158 (61)	106 (55e)	54 (30)	21 (96)	12 (50e)	
IRAN								
Abadan	1047?	271 (66)	226 (56)	40 (40)	40 (33)			
Ahvaz	12th c?	207 (66)	120 (56)	46 (40)	32 (33)	2 (00?e)	2 (50?e)	
Hamadan	1100 BC?	124 (66)	100 (56)	104 (40)	100 (33)	30 (00e)	30 (50e)	40 (00?e)
Isfahan	5th c BC?	424 (66)	255 (56)	205 (40)	100 (33)	86 (00e)	150 (50?e)	300 (00e)
Kermanshah	4th c	188 (66)	125 (56)	89 (40)	70 (33)	35 (00e)	30 (50e)	9 (00?e)

ASIA

City	Date settled	Population (thousands)						
		Latest	Circa 1960	Circa 1950	Circa 1930	Circa 1900	Circa 1850	Circa 1800
Meshed	817?	409 (66)	242 (56)	167 (40)	139 (33)	62 (00e)	45 (50?e)	50 (00?e)
Shiraz	693?	269 (66)	171 (56)	129 (40)	120 (33)	31 (00e)	30 (50?e)	40 (00?e)
Tabriz	3rd c?	405 (66)	290 (56)	214 (40)	220 (33)	162 (00e)	37 (50e)	55 (11e)
*Teheran	12th c	2695 (66)	1512 (56)	540 (40)	360 (33)	204 (00e)	70 (60e)	15 (97e)
IRAQ								
*Baghdad	762?	1491 (65)	361 (57)	364 (47)	145 (20e)	156 (00e)	50 (53e)	96 (00?e)
		1657s (65)	1057s (57)					
Basra	636	311 (65)	165 (57)	94 (47)	50 (20e)	19 (00e)	60 (50?e)	40 (00?e)
Karbala	680?	84 (65)	61 (57)	44 (47)	65 (20e)	65 (00?e)	20 (50?e)	
Kirkuk	3000 BC?	175 (65)	121 (57)	69 (47)	20 (20?e)	30s (00?e)	13 (50?e)	18 (00?e)
Mosul	636?	264 (65)	178 (57)	203 (47)	65 (20e)	60 (00e)	40 (50?e)	35 (00?e)
ISRAEL								
Haifa	4th c?	214 (71e)	183 (61)	147 (51e)	51 (31)	11 (00e)	3 (50?e)	
*Jerusalem	3000 BC?	283 (71e)	228 (61)	207 (51e)	91 (31)	55 (00e)	14 (50e)	19 (97e)
Tel Aviv-Jaffa	bef 1472 BC	383 (71e)	386 (61)	345 (51e)	97 (31)	21 (00e)	5 (50e)	
JAPAN								
Akashi	16th c?	207 (70)	130 (60)	66 (50)	39 (30)	21 (98)	14 (74)	
Akita	733	236 (70)	204 (60)	126 (50)	51 (30)	29 (98)	38 (74)	
Amagasaki	16th c	554 (70)	406 (60)	279 (50)	50 (30)	43 (98)	12 (74)	
Aomori	16th c	240 (70)	202 (60)	106 (50)	77 (30)	28 (98)	11 (74)	
Asahigawa	1893	288 (70)	188 (60)	123 (50)	83 (30)	24 (03)		
Chiba	1126	482 (70)	242 (60)	134 (50)	49 (30)	26 (98)	3 (74)	
Fujisawa	14th c?	229 (70)	125 (60)	85 (50)	25 (30)	6 (98)	6 (74)	
Fukui	1575?	201 (70)	150 (60)	101 (50)	64 (30)	44 (98)	40 (74)	
Fukuoka	bef 1281	853 (70)	647 (60)	393 (50)	228 (30)	66 (98)	21 (74)	
Fukushima	1180?	227 (70)	139 (60)	93 (50)	46 (30)	21 (98)	6 (74)	
Fukuyama	1619	255 (70)	141 (60)	67 (50)	38 (30)	17 (98)	18 (74)	
Funabashi		325 (70)	135 (60)	83 (50)	23 (30)	10 (98)	9 (74)	
Gifu	1565?	336 (70)	304 (60)	212 (50)	90 (30)	32 (98)	11 (74)	

ASIA

City	Date settled	Population (thousands) Latest		Circa 1960		Circa 1950		Circa 1930		Circa 1900		Circa 1850		Circa 1800	
Hachinohe	bef 1664	209	(70)	174	(60)	104	(50)	53	(30)	11	(98)	10	(74)		
Hachioji	bef 1590	254	(70)	158	(60)	83	(50)	52	(30)	23	(98)	8	(74)		
Hakodate	15th c?	242	(70)	243	(60)	229	(50)	197	(30)	78	(98)	113	(74)		
Hamamatsu	1505?	432	(70)	333	(60)	152	(50)	109	(30)	12	(98)	11	(74)		
Higashiosaka		500	(70)	213	(60)	150	(50)	24	(30)						
Himeji	10th c?	408	(70)	329	(60)	212	(50)	62	(30)	35	(98)	25	(74)		
Hirakata		217	(70)	80	(60)	44	(50)	6	(30)	2	(98)				
Hiroshima	1559	542	(70)	431	(60)	286	(50)	270	(30)	122	(98)	74	(74)		
Hitachi		193	(70)	161	(60)	56	(50)	28	(30)						
Ichikawa		261	(70)	157	(60)	103	(50)	21	(30)	2	(98)				
Ichinomiya	7th c	219	(70)	183	(60)	71	(50)	42	(30)	10	(98)	7	(74)		
Ise	4 BC	104	(70)	99	(60)	69	(50)	51	(30)	28	(98)	22	(74)		
Iwaki	14th c?	327	(70)	58	(60)	27	(50)	10	(30)	6	(98)	3	(74)		
Kagoshima	764?	403	(70)	296	(60)	229	(50)	137	(30)	53	(98)	27	(74)		
Kamakura	7th c?	139	(70)	99	(60)	85	(50)	27	(30)	6	(98)	6	(74)		
Kanazawa	bef 1471	361	(70)	299	(60)	252	(50)	157	(30)	84	(98)	110	(74)		
Kawaguchi		306	(70)	170	(60)	125	(50)	22	(30)	3	(98)				
Kawasaki	1150?	973	(70)	633	(60)	319	(50)	104	(30)	4	(98)	3	(74)		
Kitakyushu	1318	1042	(70)	986	(60)	711	(50)	473	(30)	88	(98)				
Kobe	1160?	1289	(70)	1114	(60)	765	(50)	788	(30)	216	(98)	11	(77)		
Kochi	1600?	240	(70)	196	(60)	162	(50)	97	(30)	37	(98)	40	(74)		
Kofu	13th c?	183	(70)	161	(60)	122	(50)	79	(30)	38	(98)	16	(74)		
Koriyama		242	(70)	103	(60)	71	(50)	51	(30)	6	(98)	5	(74)		
Kumamoto	15th c	440	(70)	374	(60)	268	(50)	164	(30)	61	(98)	45	(74)		
Kurashiki	17th c?	340	(70)	125	(60)	53	(50)	30	(30)	7	(98)	6	(74)		
Kure	bef 1887	235	(70)	210	(60)	188	(50)	190	(30)	11	(98)				
Kurume	bef 1600	194	(70)	155	(60)	101	(50)	83	(30)	29	(98)	20	(74)		
Kushiro		192	(70)	151	(60)	93	(50)	52	(30)	3	(98)				
Kyoto	8th c	1419	(70)	1285	(60)	1102	(50)	765	(30)	353	(98)	239	(74)	530	(00?)
Machida		203	(70)	71	(60)	21	(50)	7	(30)						
Maebashi	bef 1582	234	(70)	182	(60)	97	(50)	85	(30)	34	(98)	15	(74)		
Matsudo	17th c?	254	(70)	86	(60)	53	(50)	11	(30)	3	(98)				

ASIA

City	Date settled	Population (thousands)						
		Latest	Circa 1960	Circa 1950	Circa 1930	Circa 1900	Circa 1850	Circa 1800
Matsuyama	1603	323 (70)	239 (60)	164 (50)	82 (30)	37 (98)	12 (74)	
Miyazaki		203 (70)	158 (60)	103 (50)	55 (30)	5 (98)	12 (74)	
Morioka	1596	196 (70)	157 (60)	118 (50)	62 (30)	33 (98)	21 (74)	
Nagano	7th c	285 (70)	161 (60)	101 (50)	74 (30)	31 (98)	7 (74)	
Nagasaki	12th c?	421 (70)	344 (60)	242 (50)	204 (30)	107 (98)	30 (74)	
Nagoya	1612?	2036 (70)	1592 (60)	1031 (50)	907 (30)	244 (98)	125 (74)	
Nara	7th c?	208 (70)	135 (60)	78 (50)	53 (30)	31 (98)	21 (74)	
Neyagawa		207 (70)	46 (60)	30 (50)	3 (30)			
Niigata	bef 1869	384 (70)	315 (60)	221 (50)	125 (30)	53 (98)	33 (74)	
Nikko	766	29 (70)	33 (60)	29 (50)	20 (30)	3 (98)	3 (74)	
Nishinomiya		377 (70)	263 (60)	127 (50)	39 (30)	12 (98)	9 (74)	
Numazu	1579	189 (70)	143 (60)	102 (50)	44 (30)	12 (98)	16 (74)	
Oita	13th c?	261 (70)	125 (60)	94 (50)	57 (30)	9 (98)	7 (74)	
Okayama	16th c?	375 (70)	261 (60)	163 (50)	139 (30)	58 (98)	32 (74)	
Okazaki	1455	211 (70)	166 (60)	96 (50)	66 (30)	15 (98)	13 (74)	
Omiya	5th c BC?	269 (70)	170 (60)	100 (50)	29 (30)	2 (98)	3 (74)	
Omuta		175 (70)	206 (60)	192 (50)	97 (30)	2 (98)		
Osaka	7th c BC?	2980 (70)	3012 (60)	1956 (50)	2454 (30)	821 (98)	272 (74)	
Otaru	bef 1874	192 (70)	199 (60)	178 (50)	145 (30)	57 (98)	4 (74)	
Sagamihara		278 (70)	102 (60)	69 (50)				
Sakai	bef 1336	594 (70)	340 (60)	214 (50)	120 (30)	50 (98)	39 (74)	
Sapporo	1871	1010 (70)	524 (60)	314 (50)	169 (30)	37 (98)	2 (74)	
Sasebo	bef 1890	248 (70)	262 (60)	194 (50)	133 (30)	37 (98)	10 (90)	
Sendai	1600	545 (70)	425 (60)	342 (50)	190 (30)	83 (98)	52 (74)	
Shimizu		235 (70)	143 (60)	88 (50)	56 (30)	5 (98)	4 (74)	
Shimonoseki	bef 1185	258 (70)	247 (60)	194 (50)	99 (30)	43 (98)	18 (74)	
Shizuoka	bef 1569	416 (70)	329 (60)	239 (50)	136 (30)	42 (98)	32 (74)	
Suita		260 (70)	117 (60)	78 (50)	24 (30)	4 (98)	3 (74)	
Takamatsu	1335	274 (70)	228 (60)	125 (50)	80 (30)	34 (98)	33 (74)	
Takasaki	15th c	193 (70)	142 (60)	93 (50)	60 (30)	31 (98)	11 (74)	
Takatsuki	16th c?	231 (70)	79 (60)	43 (50)	6 (30)	3 (98)		
Tokushima	bef 1585	223 (70)	183 (60)	121 (50)	91 (30)	62 (98)	49 (74)	

Figure 31. Marunouchi business center of Tokyo, the largest urbanized area in Asia. (Credit: Government of Japan Ministry of Foreign Affairs.)

ASIA

City	Date settled	Population (thousands) Latest	Circa 1960	Circa 1950	Circa 1930	Circa 1900	Circa 1850	Circa 1800
*Tokyo	12th c	8841 (70)	8310 (60)	5385 (50)	2071 (30)	1440 (98)	596 (74)	1000 (00?e)
		11,161s (70)	9124s (60)	6277s (50)	4971s (30)			
Toyama	1572?	269 (70)	207 (60)	154 (50)	75 (30)	60 (98)	45 (74)	
Toyohashi	15th c	259 (70)	216 (60)	146 (50)	99 (30)	22 (98)	8 (74)	
Toyonaka		368 (70)	199 (60)	86 (50)	16 (30)			
Toyota	bef 1681	197 (70)	47 (60)	32 (50)	14 (30)	4 (98)		
Urawa		269 (70)	169 (60)	115 (50)	25 (30)	6 (98)	2 (74)	
Utsunomiya	12th c?	301 (70)	239 (60)	107 (50)	81 (30)	32 (98)	15 (74)	
Wakayama	16th c	365 (70)	285 (60)	191 (50)	117 (30)	64 (98)	61 (74)	
Yamagata	764?	204 (70)	189 (60)	105 (50)	63 (30)	35 (98)	18 (74)	
Yao	bef 1337	228 (70)	123 (60)	67 (50)	11 (30)	4 (98)	3 (74)	
Yokkaichi	bef 17th c	229 (70)	196 (60)	124 (50)	52 (30)	25 (98)	10 (74)	
Yokohama	bef 1854	2238 (70)	1376 (60)	951 (50)	620 (30)	194 (98)	65 (74)	
Yokosuka	bef 1600	348 (70)	287 (60)	251 (50)	110 (30)	25 (98)	3 (74)	
JORDAN								
*Amman	17th c BC?	330 (67)	246 (61)	103 (52)	12 (30e)			
KASHMIR-JAMMU								
*Jammu	12th c?	155 (71)	103 (61)	50 (41)	39 (31)	36 (01)	8 (44e)	150 (80?e)
*Srinagar	6th c	404 (71)	285 (61)	210 (41)	174 (31)	123 (01)	133 (73)	175 (09e)
KOREA: NORTH								
Chongjin		265 (67e)	200 (61e)	184 (44)	33 (30)			
Hamhung		200 (55e)	200 (55e)	112 (44)	40 (30)	14 (08)		
Hungnam		174 (55e)	174 (55e)	144 (44)	23 (30)			
Kaesong	bef 919	238 (65e)	140 (60e)	89 (49)	49 (30)	56 (99)		
Kimchaek		265 (67e)		68 (44)	11 (30)			
*Pyongyang	1122 BC?	1221 (65e)	653 (60e)	343 (44)	137 (30)	74 (99)		
Sinuiju	1910?	165 (67e)		118 (44)	44 (30)			
Wonsan		215 (67e)		113 (44)	43 (30)	16 (08)		

ASIA

City	Date settled	Population (thousands) Latest	Circa 1960	Circa 1950	Circa 1930	Circa 1900	Circa 1850	Circa 1800
KOREA: SOUTH								
Chonju		263 (70)	188 (60)	101 (49)	38 (30)	37 (99)		
Inchon	bef 1883	646 (70)	401 (60)	266 (49)	64 (30)	27 (99)		
Kwangju		503 (70)	314 (60)	139 (49)	33 (30)	23 (99)		
Masan	bef 1899	191 (70)	158 (60)	91 (49)	26 (30)	17 (99)		
Mokpo	bef 1897	178 (70)	130 (60)	111 (49)	32 (30)	9 (99)		
Pusan	bef 1443	1881 (70)	1164 (60)	474 (49)	130 (30)	17 (99)		
*Seoul	1104	5536 (70)	2445 (60)	1446 (49)	355 (30)	201 (99)	90 (50e)	190 (93)
Taegu	bef 8th c	1083 (70)	677 (60)	314 (49)	101 (30)	45 (99)		
Taejon		415 (70)	229 (60)	127 (49)	21 (30)			
KUWAIT								
*Kuwait	17th c	80 (70)	97 (61)	80 (48e)	40 (30?e)	20 (92e)	30 (70e)	
		295s (65)	152s (61)					
LAOS								
*Vientiane	bef 1350	132 (66e)	162s (62e)	10 (48e)	10 (31)			
LEBANON								
*Beirut	15th c BC?	700 (64e)	400 (58e)	201 (49e)	162 (31)	126 (00e)	12 (50?e)	7 (00?e)
Tripoli	7th c BC	128 (64e)	115 (58e)	65 (49e)	37 (31)	29 (00e)	14 (50e)	16 (19e)
MACAO								
*Macao	1st c?	227 (70)	161 (60)	167 (50)	157 (27)	64 (99)	30 (50)	34s (00?e)
MALAYSIA								
George Town	1786	270 (70)	235 (57)	189 (47)	149 (31)	94 (01)	10 (50?e)	
Ipoh	19th c	248 (70)	126 (57)	81 (47)	54 (31)	13 (01)		
*Kuala Lumpur	1857	452 (70)	316 (57)	176 (47)	111 (31)	47 (11)		

ASIA

City	Date settled	Latest	Circa 1960	Circa 1950	Circa 1930	Circa 1900	Circa 1850	Circa 1800
		Population (thousands)						
MONGOLIA								
*Ulan-Bator	1649	269 (68e)	218 (63)	70 (51e)	30 (30?e)	34 (00e)	30 (50?e)	
NEPAL								
*Katmandu	723	153 (71)	123 (61)	107 (52)	109s (20)	60 (00e)	35 (50?e)	100 (00e)
PAKISTAN								
Gujranwala	630?	289 (69e)	196 (61)	121 (51)	59 (31)	29 (01)	19 (68)	
Hyderabad	bef 8th c	698 (69e)	435 (61)	242 (51)	102 (31)	69 (01)	43 (72)	15 (00?e)
*Islamabad	1961	50 (67e)						
Karachi	1729	3060 (69e)	1913 (61)	1065 (51)	248 (31)	109 (01)	57 (72)	15 (30e)
Lahore	1st c?	1823 (69e)	1296 (61)	849 (51)	430 (31)	203 (01)	99 (68)	
Lyallpur	1892	854 (69e)	425 (61)	179 (51)	43 (31)	9 (01)		
Multan	7th c?	597 (69e)	358 (61)	190 (51)	119 (31)	87 (01)	46 (68)	
Peshawar	400?	296 (69e)	219 (61)	151 (51)	122 (31)	95 (01)	81 (68)	100 (09e)
Rawalpindi	bef 1765	455 (69e)	340 (61)	237 (51)	119 (31)	88 (01)	19 (68)	
Sargodha	1903	194 (69e)	129 (61)	78 (51)	27 (31)	9 (11)		
Sialkot	600 BC?	167 (69e)	164 (61)	168 (51)	101 (31)	58 (01)	46 (81)	
PHILIPPINES								
Bacolod	bef 1849	187 (70)	119 (60)	101 (48)	57 (39)	12 (03)	7 (87)	
Basilan	1521?	144 (70)	156 (60)	110 (48)	58 (39)	1 (03)	1 (87)	
Caloocan	bef 1815	274 (70)	146 (60)	58 (48)	39 (39)	6 (03)	9 (87)	
Cebu	bef 1521	347 (70)	251 (60)	168 (48)	147 (39)	31 (03)	12 (87)	
Davao	1849?	323 (70)	226 (60)	111 (48)	96 (39)	9 (03)	2 (77)	
Iloilo	bef 1569	210 (70)	151 (60)	110 (48)	90 (39)	19 (03)	4 (49)	2 (18)
Manila	14th c?	1331 (70)	1139 (60)	984 (48)	623 (39)	204 (03)	154 (87)	14 (18)
Pasay	17th c?	206 (70)	133 (60)	89 (48)	55 (39)	7 (03)	8 (87)	
*Quezon City	bef 1903	754 (70)	398 (60)	108 (48)	39 (39)	3 (03)		

ASIA

City	Date settled	Population (thousands) Latest	Circa 1960	Circa 1950	Circa 1930	Circa 1900	Circa 1850	Circa 1800
Zamboanga	1719	200 (70)	131 (60)	103 (48)	74 (39)	21 (03)	5 (87)	1 (00?e)
RYUKYU ISLANDS								
*Naha	7th c?	276 (70)	223 (60)	76 (50)	61 (30)	35 (98)	15 (74)	
SAUDI ARABIA								
*Jidda	17th c	194 (65e)	148 (62-63)	60 (50?e)	40 (30?e)	25 (00e)	22 (50?e)	5 (00?e)
Mecca	2nd c?	185 (65e)	159 (62-63)	135 (50?e)	130 (30?e)	60 (00e)	35 (50e)	18 (00?e)
Medina	135?	60 (61e)	60 (61e)	40 (50?e)	30 (30?e)	44 (00e)	18 (50e)	6 (00?e)
*Riyadh	1824?	225 (65e)	169 (62)	80 (50?e)	30 (30?e)	30 (00?e)	28 (62e)	
SINGAPORE								
*Singapore	11th c?	2075 (70)	1446 (57)	680 (47)	446 (31)	193 (01)	26 (50)	0.2 (00?e)
				938s (47)	560s (31)	229s (01)	54s (50)	
SOUTHERN YEMEN								
*Aden	3rd c BC?	150 (64e)	99 (55)	57 (46)	32 (31)	44s (01)	16 (42)	
SYRIA								
Aleppo	bef 1000 BC	639 (70)	425 (60)	363 (50e)	249 (31)	117 (00e)	100 (50?e)	200 (00?e)
*Damascus	bef 14th c BC	835 (70)	530 (60)	335 (50e)	229 (31)	165 (00e)	150 (50?e)	130 (00?e)
Hama	3rd c BC?	137 (70)	102 (60)	96 (53e)	40 (31)	45 (00e)	40 (50?e)	85 (00?e)
Homs	1st c?	216 (70)	148 (60)	127 (53e)	53 (31)	48 (00e)	27 (50e)	25 (00?e)
TAIWAN								
Chiai	17th c	234 (69e)	152 (56)	86 (50)	58 (30)	20 (01)		
Hsinchu	bef 1731	202 (69e)	126 (56)	125 (50)	44 (30)	19 (01)		
Kaohsiung	bef 1864	785 (69e)	365 (56)	268 (50)	63 (30)	14 (11)		
Keelung	1626?	318 (69e)	194 (56)	145 (50)	75 (30)	13 (01)		

ASIA

City	Date settled	Population (thousands) Latest		Circa 1960		Circa 1950		Circa 1930		Circa 1900		Circa 1850		Circa 1800	
Sanchung		221	(69e)	166	(65e)										
Taichung	18th c	428	(69e)	247	(56)	200	(50)	54	(30)	8	(05)				
Tainan	1590	462	(69e)	284	(56)	221	(50)	95	(30)	48	(01)	90	(69e)		
*Taipei	1708	1712	(69e)	737	(56)	503	(50)	230	(30)	79	(01)				
THAILAND															
*Bangkok	1782	2228	(70)	1300	(60)	605	(47)	685	(29)	587	(11)	401	(28)	35	(00?e)
Thon Buri		866	(68e)	404	(60)	177	(47)								
TURKEY															
Adana	8th c BC?	352	(70)	232	(60)	118	(50)	73	(27)	47	(00e)	20	(50?e)	30	(00?e)
*Ankara	17th c BC?	1209	(70)	650	(60)	289	(50)	75	(27)	32	(00e)	20	(50?e)	20	(00?e)
Antioch	300 BC?	66	(70)	46	(60)	30	(50)	19	(31)	28	(00e)	20	(50e)	18	(00?e)
Bursa	3rd c BC	276	(70)	154	(60)	104	(50)	62	(27)	76	(00e)	65	(50?e)	60	(02e)
Eskisehir	3rd c?	216	(70)	153	(60)	90	(50)	32	(27)	19	(00?e)	village			
Gaziantep	3650 BC?	226	(70)	124	(60)	72	(50)	40	(27)	43	(00?e)	20	(50?e)	20	(00?e)
Izmir	11th c BC?	521	(70)	361	(60)	228	(50)	154	(27)	196	(00e)	140	(51e)	120	(00?e)
Kayseri	1082	168	(70)	103	(60)	65	(50)	39	(27)	72	(00e)	25	(50?e)	25	(00?e)
Konya	2600 BC?	201	(70)	120	(60)	64	(50)	48	(27)	44	(00e)	25	(50?e)	30	(00?e)
USSR															
Aktyubinsk	1869	150	(70)	97	(59)	49	(39)	21	(26)	3	(97)				
Alma-Ata	1854	730	(70)	456	(59)	231	(39)	45	(26)	23	(97)	10	(67)		
Andizhan	9th c	188	(70)	130	(59)	85	(39)	73	(26)	47	(97)				
Angarsk	1948	204	(70)	134	(59)	10	(51e)								
Ashkhabad	1881	253	(70)	170	(59)	127	(39)	52	(26)	19	(97)				
Barnaul	1738	439	(70)	305	(59)	148	(39)	74	(26)	29	(97)	11	(56)	7	(82)
Biysk	1709	186	(70)	146	(59)	80	(39)	46	(26)	17	(97)	3	(56)		
Bratsk	1631	155	(70)	51	(59)	2	(56e)								

ASIA

City	Date settled	Population (thousands)						
		Latest	Circa 1960	Circa 1950	Circa 1930	Circa 1900	Circa 1850	Circa 1800
Bukhara	630?	112 (70)	69 (59)	50 (39)	47 (26)	65 (00e)	70 (66e)	150 (32e)
Chelyabinsk	1736	874 (70)	689 (59)	273 (39)	59 (26)	20 (97)	4 (56)	3 (82)
Chimkent	8th c?	247 (70)	153 (59)	74 (39)	21 (26)	11 (97)	3 (67)	
Chita	1653	242 (70)	172 (59)	103 (39)	62 (26)	12 (97)	0.9 (56)	
Dushanbe	bef 1922	374 (70)	224 (59)	83 (39)	6 (26)			
Dzhambul	18th c	188 (70)	113 (59)	64 (39)	25 (26)	3 (97)	2s (67?)	
Frunze	1825	431 (70)	220 (59)	93 (39)	37 (26)	7 (97)		
Irkutsk	1669	451 (70)	366 (59)	243 (39)	99 (26)	51 (97)	24 (56)	10 (82)
Kamensk-Uralskiy	1682	169 (70)	141 (59)	51 (39)	5 (26)			
Karaganda	1857	522 (70)	397 (59)	166 (39)	0.1 (26)			
Kemerovo	1720	385 (70)	278 (59)	133 (39)	22 (26)		0.3 (60?)	
Khabarovsk	1858	437 (70)	323 (59)	199 (39)	52 (26)	15 (97)		
Kokand	10th c?	133 (70)	105 (59)	85 (39)	69 (26)	81 (97)	45 (50e)	
Komsomolsk-na-Amure	1858	218 (70)	177 (59)	71 (39)				
Kopeysk	bef 1917	156 (70)	161 (59)	60 (39)	9 (26)			
Krasnoyarsk	1628	648 (70)	412 (59)	190 (39)	72 (26)	27 (97)	6 (56)	4 (82)
Kurgan	1553	244 (70)	146 (59)	53 (39)	28 (26)	11 (97)	3 (56)	0.5 (82)
Magnitogorsk	1929	364 (70)	311 (59)	146 (39)				
Namangan	1610	175 (70)	123 (59)	80 (39)	74 (26)	62 (97)		
Nizhniy Tagil	1725	378 (70)	339 (59)	160 (39)	39 (26)	27 (97?)	2 (63)	
Novokuznetsk	1617	499 (70)	377 (59)	170 (39)	4 (26)	3 (97)	2 (56)	
Novosibirsk	1893	1161 (70)	886 (59)	406 (39)	121 (26)	8 (97)		
Omsk	1716	821 (70)	581 (59)	281 (39)	162 (26)	37 (97)	16 (56)	1 (82)
Pavlodar	1720	187 (70)	90 (59)	29 (39)	18 (26)	8 (97)	0.2 (63)	
Petropavlovsk	1752	173 (70)	131 (59)	92 (39)	47 (26)	20 (97)	7 (56)	
Petropavlovsk-Kamchatskiy	1740	154 (70)	86 (59)	35 (39)	2 (26)	0.4 (97)	2 (56)	
Prokopyevsk	18th c	275 (70)	282 (59)	107 (39)	11 (26)			
Samarkand	4th c BC?	267 (70)	196 (59)	134 (39)	105 (26)	55 (97)	18 (50e)	
Semipalatinsk	1718	236 (70)	156 (59)	110 (39)	57 (26)	26 (97)	7 (56)	0.3 (00?)

ASIA

City	Date settled	Latest		Circa 1960		Circa 1950		Circa 1930		Circa 1900		Circa 1850		Circa 1800	
		Population (thousands)													
Sverdlovsk	1721	1026	(70)	779	(59)	426	(39)	136	(26)	42	(97)	17	(56)	8	(82)
Tashkent	7th c	1385	(70)	912	(59)	585	(39)	324	(26)	156	(97)	64	(67)	30	(00?e)
Temir-Tau	1930	167	(70)	77	(59)	5	(39)								
Tomsk	1604	339	(70)	249	(59)	141	(39)	92	(26)	52	(97)	20	(56)	9	(82)
Tselinograd	1830	180	(70)	102	(59)	32	(39)	13	(26)	10	(97)	5	(62)		
Tyumen	1586	269	(70)	150	(59)	76	(39)	50	(26)	30	(97)	11	(56)	2	(82)
Ulan-Ude	1666	254	(70)	175	(59)	129	(39)	29	(26)	8	(97)	3	(56)	1	(82)
Ust-Kamenogorsk	1720	230	(70)	150	(59)	20	(39)	14	(26)	9	(97)	3	(56)	2	(82)
Vladivostok	1860	442	(70)	291	(59)	206	(39)	108	(26)	29	(97)	0.5	(73)		
Zlatoust	1754	181	(70)	161	(59)	99	(39)	48	(26)	21	(97)	10	(61)		
VIETNAM: NORTH															
Haiphong	bef 1882	182	(60)	182	(60)	143s	(48e)	70	(36)	16	(00)				
*Hanoi	599	415	(60)	415	(60)	237s	(48e)	149	(36)	103	(00)	70	(50?e)	40	(00?e)
VIETNAM: SOUTH															
Da Nang	17th c?	428	(70e)	105	(60e)	51	(43)	6	(26)	7	(11)				
Hue	200 BC?	209	(69e)	104	(60e)	96	(53e)	61	(21)	50	(00)	60	(50?e)	30	(22e)
*Saigon	bef 17th c	1761	(70e)	1400	(60e)	1179	(58e)	256	(36)	160	(00)	110	(50e)	35	(00?e)
YEMEN															
*Sana	740?	100	(63e)	89	(60e)	28	(48e)	22	(30?e)	59	(00e)	40	(50?e)		

EUROPE

City	Date settled	Population (thousands)						
		Latest	Circa 1960	Circa 1950	Circa 1930	Circa 1900	Circa 1850	Circa 1800
ALBANIA								
*Tirane	1604	169 (67e)	136 (60)	60 (45)	31 (30)	12 (05e)	10 (50?e)	2 (00?e)
AUSTRIA								
Graz	881?	249 (71)	237 (61)	226 (51)	153 (34)	138 (00)	55 (51)	40 (00?e)
Innsbruck	1170	115 (71)	101 (61)	95 (51)	61 (34)	27 (00)	13 (46)	9 (08e)
Linz	1st c	205 (71)	196 (61)	185 (51)	109 (34)	59 (00)	27 (46)	19 (00?e)
Salzburg	7th c?	127 (71)	108 (61)	103 (51)	40 (34)	33 (00)	17 (51)	13 (11)
*Vienna	4th c BC?	1603 (71)	1628 (61)	1766 (51)	1875 (34)	1675 (00)	431 (51)	231 (00)
BELGIUM								
Anderlecht	11th c?	104 (69e)	95 (61)	86 (47)	80 (30)	48 (00)	6 (46)	2 (06?)
Antwerp	660?	230 (69e)	253 (61)	263 (47)	284 (30)	273 (00)	88 (46)	56 (06)
		673s (69e)	652s (61)	590s (47)	484s (30)	400s (00)		
Bruges	865	51 (69e)	52 (61)	53 (47)	51 (30)	52 (00)	50 (46)	34 (06)
		114s (69e)	103s (61)	91s (47)				
*Brussels	6th c?	164 (69e)	170 (61)	185 (47)	200 (30)	184 (00)	126 (46)	66 (00)
		1073s (69e)	1023s (61)	956s (47)	869s (30)	626s (00)	212s (46)	70s (00)
Charleroi	bef 1665	24 (69e)	26 (61)	26 (47)	29 (30)	24 (00)	7 (46)	4 (00?)
		217s (69e)	217s (61)	209s (47)				
Ghent	7th c	152 (69e)	158 (61)	166 (47)	170 (30)	160 (00)	103 (46)	55 (06)
		228s (69e)	229s (61)	228s (47)	219s (30)			
La Louviere	1189	24 (69e)	23 (61)	22 (47)	24 (30)	18 (00)	12 (80)	
		115s (69e)	111s (61)	108s (47)				
Liege	558?	149 (69e)	153 (61)	156 (47)	166 (30)	158 (00)	76 (46)	50 (06)
		445s (69e)	445s (61)	425s (47)	252s (30)			
Schaerbeek	282?	120 (69e)	117 (61)	124 (47)	119 (30)	64 (00)	6 (46)	1 (15)

EUROPE

City	Date settled	Population (thousands)						
		Latest	Circa 1960	Circa 1950	Circa 1930	Circa 1900	Circa 1850	Circa 1800
BULGARIA								
Burgas	18th c	132 (70e)	73 (56)	44 (46)	31 (26)	12 (00)	6 (50?e)	
Plovdiv	341 BC?	247 (70e)	162 (56)	125 (46)	85 (26)	43 (00)	30 (50?e)	30 (17e)
Ruse	17th c	150 (70e)	83 (56)	54 (46)	46 (26)	33 (00)	30 (50?e)	24 (00?e)
*Sofia	100?	868 (70e)	608 (56)	435 (46)	213 (26)	68 (00)	43 (62e)	46 (00?e)
		973s (70e)	645s (56)					
Stara Zagora	6th c BC?	109 (70e)	55 (56)	37 (46)	29 (26)	20 (00)	20 (50?e)	20 (00?e)
Varna	6th c BC	219 (70e)	120 (56)	78 (46)	61 (26)	33 (00)	18 (50?e)	16 (00?e)
CZECHOSLOVAKIA								
Bratislava	892?	284 (70)	242 (61)	193 (50)	124 (30)	62 (00)	42 (51)	22 (00?)
Brno	9th c	336 (70)	314 (61)	285 (50)	264 (30)	109 (00)	45 (46)	24 (00?)
Karlovy Vary	1349	45 (69e)	43 (61)	36 (50)	24 (30)	15 (00)	4 (57)	2 (02)
Kosice	1235	145 (70)	79 (61)	63 (50)	70 (30)	36 (00)	13 (50)	12 (00?e)
Ostrava	1267	279 (70)	234 (61)	189 (50)	125 (30)	30 (00)	4 (57)	0.8 (00?e)
Plzen	976?	148 (70)	138 (61)	124 (50)	114 (30)	68 (00)	10 (45)	5 (01)
*Prague	9th c?	1078 (70)	1005 (61)	932 (50)	848 (30)	202 (00)	118 (51)	80 (93)
DENMARK								
Alborg	11th c?	155 (71e)	86 (60)	80 (50)	44 (30)	31 (01)	10 (60)	6 (01)
			96s (60)	88s (50)				
Arhus	10th c?	238 (71e)	120 (60)	116 (50)	81 (30)	52 (01)	8 (50)	15 (01?)
			177s (60)	151s (50)				
*Copenhagen	1043?	621 (71e)	721 (60)	768 (50)	617 (30)	378 (01)	130 (50)	101 (01)
		1379s (71e)	1262s (60)	1168s (50)	771s (30)	477s (01)		
Frederiksberg	bef 1621	100 (71e)	114 (60)	119 (50)	106 (30)	14 (01)	8 (60)	5 (01)
Odense	10th c	166 (71e)	111 (60)	101 (50)	57 (30)	40 (01)	11 (51)	6 (01)
			130s (60)	113s (50)				

EUROPE

City	Date settled	Population (thousands) Latest	Circa 1960	Circa 1950	Circa 1930	Circa 1900	Circa 1850	Circa 1800
FINLAND								
Espoo	1458?	96 (70)	57s (60)	25s (50)	8s (30)	6s (00)		
*Helsinki	1550	524 (70)	453 (60)	369 (50)	244 (30)	91 (00)	21 (50)	9 (05)
		710s (70)	566s (60)	414s (50)				
Tampere	1779	158 (70)	127 (60)	101 (50)	56 (30)	36 (00)	3 (50)	0.6 (05)
Turku	12th c?	155 (70)	124 (60)	102 (50)	67 (30)	38 (00)	17 (50)	11 (05)
FRANCE								
Ajaccio	7th c	42 (68)	41 (62)	33 (54)	24 (31)	22 (01)	12 (51)	6 (01)
Amiens	54 BC?	118 (68)	105 (62)	93 (54)	90 (31)	91 (01)	52 (51)	40 (01)
		137s (68)	113s (62)					
Angers	3rd c?	129 (68)	115 (62)	102 (54)	86 (31)	82 (01)	47 (51)	33 (01)
		163s (68)	134s (62)					
Avignon	2nd c BC?	86 (68)	73 (62)	63 (54)	57 (31)	47 (01)	36 (51)	21 (01)
Bayonne	3rd c?	43 (68)	37 (62)	33 (54)	32 (31)	28 (01)	18 (51)	13 (01)
Besancon	6th c BC?	113 (68)	96 (62)	73 (54)	60 (31)	55 (01)	41 (51)	30 (01)
Bethune	11th c	27 (68)	23 (62)	22 (54)	20 (31)	12 (01)	8 (51)	5 (01)
Bordeaux	3rd c BC	267 (68)	250 (62)	258 (54)	263 (31)	257 (01)	131 (51)	91 (01)
		555s (68)	462s (62)	416s (54)				
Boulogne-Billancourt	11th c	109 (68)	107 (62)	94 (54)	86 (31)	44 (01)	8 (51)	
Brest	3rd c?	154 (68)	136 (62)	111 (54)	70 (31)	84 (01)	61 (51)	27 (01)
Bruay-en-Artois	bef 1851	29 (68)	31 (62)	32 (54)	32 (31)	15 (01)	0.7 (51)	
		127s (68)	110s (62)					
Caen	9th c?	110 (68)	91 (62)	68 (54)	58 (31)	45 (01)	45 (51)	31 (01)
		152s (68)	117s (62)					
Cannes	8th c BC?	67 (68)	58 (62)	50 (54)	47 (31)	30 (01)	6 (51)	3 (01)
		213s (68)	74s (62)	62s (54)				
Clermont-Ferrand	20 BC?	149 (68)	128 (62)	113 (54)	103 (31)	53 (01)	34 (51)	24 (01)
		205s (68)	160s (62)	138s (54)				

EUROPE

City	Date settled	Population (thousands) Latest	Circa 1960	Circa 1950	Circa 1930	Circa 1900	Circa 1850	Circa 1800
Denain	8th c	28 (68)	29 (62)	27 (54)	28 (31)	23 (01)	9 (51)	0.9 (01?)
Dijon	bef 273	145 (68)	136 (62)	113 (54)	91 (31)	71 (01)	32 (51)	21 (01)
		184s (68)	154s (62)	117s (54)				
Douai	7th c?	49 (68)	48 (62)	43 (54)	42 (31)	34 (01)	21 (51)	18 (01)
		205s (68)	134s (62)	47s (54)				
Dunkerque	7th c?	28 (68)	28 (62)	21 (54)	32 (31)	39 (01)	29 (51)	21 (01)
		143s (68)	122s (62)					
Grenoble	1st c BC?	162 (68)	157 (62)	116 (54)	91 (31)	69 (01)	31 (51)	23 (01)
		332s (68)	233s (62)	147s (54)				
Le Havre	1517	200 (68)	184 (62)	140 (54)	165 (31)	130 (01)	29 (51)	16 (01)
		247s (68)	223s (62)	173s (54)				
Le Mans	5th c BC?	143 (68)	132 (62)	112 (54)	77 (31)	63 (01)	27 (51)	17 (01)
		166s (68)	142s (62)	113s (54)				
Lens	1096?	42 (68)	43 (62)	41 (54)	34 (31)	24 (01)	10 (51)	2 (01)
		326s (68)	261s (62)					
Lille	1030?	191 (68)	193 (62)	195 (54)	202 (31)	211 (01)	76 (51)	55 (01)
		881s (68)	431s (62)	359s (54)				
Limoges	bef 52 BC	133 (68)	118 (62)	106 (54)	93 (31)	84 (01)	42 (51)	21 (01)
		148s (68)	120s (62)					
Lyons	43 BC	528 (68)	529 (62)	471 (54)	580 (31)	459 (01)	177 (51)	109 (01)
		1075s (68)	886s (62)	650s (54)				
Marseilles	600 BC?	889 (68)	778 (62)	661 (54)	801 (31)	491 (01)	195 (51)	111 (01)
		954s (68)	807s (62)					
Metz	1000 BC?	108 (68)	103 (62)	86 (54)	79 (31)	58 (00)	43 (51)	32 (01)
		166s (68)	147s (62)	112s (54)				
Montbeliard	843?	24 (68)	22 (62)	17 (54)	13 (31)	10 (01)	6 (51)	4 (01)
Montpellier	8th c?	162 (68)	119 (62)	98 (54)	87 (31)	76 (01)	46 (51)	34 (01)
		171s (68)	124s (62)					
Montreuil	12th c?	96 (68)	92 (62)	76 (54)	70 (31)	32 (01)	4 (51)	

EUROPE

City	Date settled	Population (thousands) Latest	Circa 1960	Circa 1950	Circa 1930	Circa 1900	Circa 1850	Circa 1800
Mulhouse	717?	115 (68)	109 (62)	99 (54)	100 (31)	89 (00)	30 (51)	9 (06)
		199s (68)	165s (62)	111s (54)				
Nancy	947?	123 (68)	129 (62)	125 (54)	121 (31)	103 (01)	45 (51)	30 (01)
		258s (68)	209s (62)	176s (54)				
Nantes	1st c BC?	259 (68)	240 (62)	223 (54)	187 (31)	133 (01)	96 (51)	74 (01)
		394s (68)	328s (62)	242s (54)				
Nice	5th c BC?	322 (68)	293 (62)	244 (54)	220 (31)	105 (01)	34 (48)	18 (01)
		393s (68)	310s (62)					
Nimes	2nd c BC?	123 (68)	100 (62)	89 (54)	89 (31)	81 (01)	54 (51)	39 (01)
Orleans	273	96 (68)	84 (62)	76 (54)	72 (31)	67 (01)	47 (51)	36 (01)
		168s (68)	126s (62)	96s (54)				
*Paris	3rd c BC?	2591 (68)	2790 (62)	2850 (54)	2891 (31)	2714 (01)	1053 (51)	548 (01)
		8197s (68)	7369s (62)	6436s (54)			1227s (51)	
Pau	12th c?	74 (68)	60 (62)	48 (54)	39 (31)	34 (01)	16 (51)	9 (01)
Perpignan	10th c	102 (68)	83 (62)	70 (54)	74 (31)	36 (01)	22 (51)	11 (01)
Rennes	1st c BC?	181 (68)	152 (62)	124 (54)	89 (31)	75 (01)	40 (51)	26 (01)
		193s (68)	157s (62)					
Rheims	300 BC?	153 (68)	134 (62)	121 (54)	113 (31)	108 (01)	46 (51)	20 (01)
		168s (68)	144s (62)	126s (54)				
Roubaix	9th c?	115[1] (68)	113 (62)	110 (54)	117 (31)	124 (01)	35 (51)	8 (01)
			340s (62)	267s (54)				
Rouen	bef 4th c	120 (68)	121 (62)	117 (54)	123 (31)	116 (01)	100 (51)	87 (01)
		370s (68)	325s (62)	246s (54)				
Saint-Denis	3rd c?	99 (68)	95 (62)	81 (54)	82 (31)	61 (01)	16 (51)	4 (01)
Saint-Etienne	1195?	213 (68)	201 (62)	182 (54)	191 (31)	147 (01)	56 (51)	16 (01)
		331s (68)	290s (62)	185s (54)				
Saint-Nazaire	1st c BC?	63 (68)	58 (62)	39 (54)	40 (31)	36 (01)	5 (51)	3 (01)
Strasbourg	12 BC	249 (68)	229 (62)	201 (54)	181 (31)	151 (00)	76 (51)	49 (01)
		335s (68)	302s (62)	239s (54)				

[1] Urbanized area population for 1968 included in Lille urbanized area.

Figure 32. Aerial view of Paris, the largest urbanized area in Europe, showing the Eiffel Tower and the Palais de Chaillot. (Credit: French Government Tourist Office.)

EUROPE

City	Date settled	Population (thousands) Latest		Circa 1960		Circa 1950		Circa 1930		Circa 1900		Circa 1850		Circa 1800	
Thionville	870?	37	(68)	32	(62)	23	(54)	17	(31)	10	(00)	5	(51)	5	(01)
		136s	(68)	125s	(62)										
Toulon	9th c BC	175	(68)	162	(62)	141	(54)	133	(31)	102	(01)	69	(51)	20	(01)
		340s	(68)	221s	(62)										
Toulouse	300 BC?	371	(68)	324	(62)	269	(54)	195	(31)	150	(01)	93	(51)	50	(01)
		440s	(68)	329s	(62)										
Tourcoing	1080?	99	(68)	89	(62)	83	(54)	82	(31)	79	(01)	28	(51)	11	(89)
Tours	2nd c?	128	(68)	93	(62)	84	(54)	79	(31)	65	(01)	11	(51)	22	(01)
		202s	(68)	151s	(62)	117s	(54)								
Troyes	1st c BC?	75	(68)	67	(62)	59	(54)	59	(31)	53	(01)	27	(51)	24	(01)
Valenciennes	693?	47	(68)	45	(62)	43	(54)	42	(31)	31	(01)	23	(51)	17	(01)
		224s	(68)	172s	(62)	65s	(54)								
Versailles	1682	91	(68)	87	(62)	84	(54)	67	(31)	55	(01)	37	(51)	25	(01)
Villeurbanne	18th c?	120	(68)	105	(62)	82	(54)	82	(31)	29	(01)	5	(51)	2	(92)
GERMANY: EAST															
*Berlin (see under Germany: West)															
Brandenburg	928	94	(71)	90	(64)	82	(50)	64	(33)	49	(00)	18	(49)	10	(02)
Dessau	1213	98	(71)	95	(64)	92	(50)	79	(33)	51	(00)	13	(48)	9	(02)
Dresden	1206?	500	(71)	504	(64)	494	(50)	642	(33)	396	(00)	94	(49)	62	(00)
Erfurt	741?	196	(71)	190	(64)	189	(50)	145	(33)	85	(00)	32	(49)	17	(00?)
Gera	995?	112	(71)	107	(64)	99	(50)	84	(33)	46	(00)	11	(46)	7	(00)
Halle	806	257	(71)	274	(64)	289	(50)	209	(33)	157	(00)	34	(49)	18	(00?)
Karl-Marx-Stadt	1136	298	(71)	293	(64)	293	(50)	351	(33)	207	(00)	31	(49)	11	(00?)
Leipzig	10th c?	583	(71)	595	(64)	618	(50)	713	(33)	456	(00)	62	(49)	31	(00)
Magdeburg	805?	271	(71)	265	(64)	260	(50)	307	(33)	230	(00)	51	(49)	28	(12)
Potsdam	10th c?	111	(71)	110	(64)	118	(50)	74	(33)	60	(00)	40	(49)	18	(02)
Rostock	1160?	201	(71)	179	(64)	133	(50)	94	(33)	44	(00)	20	(45)	14	(03)
Schwerin	1018?	97	(71)	91	(64)	94	(50)	54	(33)	39	(00)	17	(45)	10	(03)

EUROPE

City	Date settled	Population (thousands) Latest	Circa 1960	Circa 1950	Circa 1930	Circa 1900	Circa 1850	Circa 1800
Zwickau	11th c	127 (71)	128 (64)	139 (50)	85 (33)	56 (00)	13 (49)	4 (01)
GERMANY: WEST								
Aachen	1st c?	173 (70)	170 (61)	130 (50)	163 (33)	135 (00)	51 (49)	24 (06)
Augsburg	11 BC	212 (70)	209 (61)	185 (50)	177 (33)	89 (00)	38 (49)	29 (00?)
Baden-Baden	214?	37 (70)	40 (61)	37 (50)	30 (33)	16 (00)	8 (61)	2 (04)
Berlin	1230?	3207 (70)[1]	3268 (61)[2]	3336 (50)	4243 (33)	1889 (00)	424 (49)	172 (00)
Bielefeld	1015?	169 (70)	175 (61)	154 (50)	121 (33)	63 (00)	10 (49)	5 (00?)
Bochum	1041?	344 (70)	361 (61)	290 (50)	315 (33)	66 (00)	5 (49)	2 (16e)
*Bonn	10 BC?	274 (70)	144 (61)	115 (50)	99 (33)	51 (00)	18 (49)	9 (01)
Bottrop	1092?	107 (70)	111 (61)	93 (50)	86 (33)	25 (00)	5 (71)	0.4 (19?)
Bremen	787?	582 (70)	565 (61)	445 (50)	323 (33)	163 (00)	53 (49)	36 (12)
Bremerhaven	1827	140 (70)	142 (61)	114 (50)	26 (33)	20 (00)	2 (49?)	1 (34?)
Brunswick	861	224 (70)	246 (61)	224 (50)	157 (33)	128 (00)	39 (49)	28 (11)
Cologne	38 BC?	848 (70)	809 (61)	595 (50)	757 (33)	373 (00)	95 (49)	44 (00)
Darmstadt	11th c?	141 (70)	136 (61)	95 (50)	93 (33)	72 (00)	27 (46)	11 (05)
Dortmund	885?	640 (70)	641 (61)	507 (50)	541 (33)	143 (00)	11 (49)	4 (95)
Duisburg	8th c	455 (70)	503 (61)	411 (50)	440 (33)	93 (00)	9 (49)	4 (00)
Dusseldorf	1159	664 (70)	703 (61)	501 (50)	499 (33)	214 (00)	41 (49)	19 (00)
Essen	852	698 (70)	727 (61)	605 (50)	654 (33)	119 (00)	9 (49)	4 (00)
Flensburg	12th c	95 (70)	99 (61)	103 (50)	67 (33)	49 (00)	16 (47)	15 (00?e)
Frankfurt am Main	1st c?	670 (70)	683 (61)	532 (50)	556 (33)	289 (00)	58 (49)	40 (11)
Freiburg im Breisgau	1120	162 (70)	145 (61)	110 (50)	99 (33)	62 (00)	15 (46)	8 (00?e)
Furth	793	95 (70)	98 (61)	100 (50)	77 (33)	54 (00)	15 (46)	13 (06)
Gelsenkirchen	1150?	348 (70)	383 (61)	315 (50)	333 (33)	37 (00)	0.8 (52)	0.5 (19?)
Gottingen	953?	110 (70)	81 (61)	79 (50)	47 (33)	30 (00)	11 (46)	9 (07)

[1] East Berlin, 1971; West Berlin, 1970.
[2] East Berlin, 1964; West Berlin, 1961.

EUROPE

City	Date settled	Population (thousands) Latest		Circa 1960		Circa 1950		Circa 1930		Circa 1900		Circa 1850		Circa 1800	
Hagen	14th c	201	(70)	196	(61)	146	(50)	148	(33)	51	(00)	5	(49)	2	(16)
Hamburg	811?	1794	(70)	1832	(61)	1606	(50)	1129	(33)	706	(00)	133	(50)	95	(11)
Hannover	1163?	524	(70)	573	(61)	444	(50)	444	(33)	236	(00)	45	(52)	23	(10)
Heidelberg	1196?	121	(70)	127	(61)	116	(50)	85	(33)	40	(00)	12	(45)	9	(00?)
Heilbronn	741?	102	(70)	89	(61)	65	(50)	60	(33)	38	(00)	12	(61)	5	(03)
Herne	8th c?	104	(70)	113	(61)	112	(50)	99	(33)	28	(00)	4	(71)	0.8	(19?)
Hildesheim	8th c?	94	(70)	96	(61)	72	(50)	63	(33)	43	(00)	15	(45)	11	(02)
Kaiserslautern	882?	100	(70)	86	(61)	63	(50)	63	(33)	48	(00)	11	(52)	2	(02)
Karlsruhe	1715	259	(70)	242	(61)	199	(50)	155	(33)	97	(00)	23	(49)	8	(00)
Kassel	913?	214	(70)	208	(61)	162	(50)	175	(33)	106	(00)	33	(46)	20	(10)
Kiel	10th c?	272	(70)	273	(61)	254	(50)	218	(33)	108	(00)	12	(50)	7	(03)
Koblenz	9 BC	119	(70)	99	(61)	66	(50)	65	(33)	45	(00)	23	(46)	11	(01?)
Krefeld	1105?	222	(70)	213	(61)	172	(50)	165	(33)	107	(00)	36	(49)	8	(00?)
Leverkusen	1107?	107	(70)	95	(61)	66	(50)	44	(33)	3	(00)	1	(71)		
Lubeck	1143	239	(70)	235	(61)	238	(50)	129	(33)	82	(00)	26	(51)	23	(07)
Ludwigshafen	17th c	176	(70)	169	(61)	124	(50)	107	(33)	62	(00)	2	(52?)		
Mainz	5th c BC?	172	(70)	134	(61)	88	(50)	143	(33)	84	(00)	31	(45)	22	(03)
Mannheim	766?	332	(70)	314	(61)	246	(50)	275	(33)	141	(00)	24	(52)	18	(00?)
Monchengladbach	972	151	(70)	152	(61)	125	(50)	127	(33)	58	(00)	3	(49?)	2	(19?)
Mulheim an der Ruhr	11th c?	191	(70)	186	(61)	150	(50)	133	(33)	38	(00)	10	(46)	3	(00?)
Munich	1158	1294	(70)	1085	(61)	832	(50)	735	(33)	500	(00)	96	(49)	40	(01)
Munster	800?	198	(70)	183	(61)	118	(50)	122	(33)	64	(00)	24	(46)	13	(00?)
Neuss	5th c BC?	115	(70)	93	(61)	63	(50)	56	(33)	28	(00)	10	(49?)	4	(01?)
Nuremberg	1040?	474	(70)	455	(61)	362	(50)	410	(33)	261	(00)	51	(49)	25	(06)
Oberhausen	1862	247	(70)	257	(61)	203	(50)	192	(33)	42	(00)	6	(52?)	0.2	(19?)
Offenbach am Main	977?	117	(70)	116	(61)	89	(50)	81	(33)	51	(00)	10	(46)	9	(07)
Oldenburg in Oldenburg	12th c?	131	(70)	125	(61)	123	(50)	67	(33)	27	(00)	8	(46)	4	(00)
Osnabruck	772	144	(70)	139	(61)	110	(50)	94	(33)	52	(00)	12	(45)	8	(05e)
Pforzheim	1067?	90	(70)	82	(61)	54	(50)	80	(33)	43	(00)	8	(43)	5	(00)

EUROPE

City	Date settled	Population (thousands) Latest		Circa 1960		Circa 1950		Circa 1930		Circa 1900		Circa 1850		Circa 1800	
Recklinghausen	1179	125	(70)	131	(61)	105	(50)	87	(33)	34	(00)	4	(49?)	1	(00?e)
Regensburg	5th c BC?	130	(70)	125	(61)	117	(50)	81	(33)	45	(00)	23	(45)	21	(00?)
Remscheid	13th c?	136	(70)	127	(61)	103	(50)	101	(33)	58	(00)	12	(43)	5	(04)
Rheydt	1180?	100	(70)	94	(61)	78	(50)	77	(33)	34	(00)	4	(49?)		
Saarbrucken	999?	128	(70)	131	(61)	90	(46)	127	(28)	23	(00)	9	(46)	3	(02)
Salzgitter	1504	118	(70)	110	(61)	101	(50)	3	(33)	2	(05)	2	(49?)		
Solingen	965?	176	(70)	170	(61)	148	(50)	140	(33)	45	(00)	9	(58)	4	(00?e)
Stuttgart	1150?	633	(70)	638	(61)	498	(50)	415	(33)	177	(00)	48	(49)	21	(01)
Trier	15 BC	104	(70)	87	(61)	76	(50)	77	(33)	43	(00)	20	(46)	9	(01?)
Ulm	854?	93	(70)	93	(61)	71	(50)	62	(33)	43	(00)	16	(40)	11	(03)
Wanne-Eickel	774	99	(70)	107	(61)	87	(50)	92	(33)	41	(00)	0.6	(49?)		
Wiesbaden	3rd c BC	250	(70)	253	(61)	221	(50)	160	(33)	86	(00)	12	(45)	5	(00?)
Wilhelmshaven	bef 1852	103	(70)	100	(61)	101	(50)	28	(33)	23	(00)	0.2	(55)		
Witten	bef 1825	97	(70)	96	(61)	76	(50)	73	(33)	34	(00)	5	(52)		
Wolfsburg	700?	89	(70)	65	(61)	25	(50)	7	(39)	0.3	(00?)	0.3	(71?)		
Wuppertal	1176?	418	(70)	421	(61)	363	(50)	409	(33)	299	(00)	76	(49,51)	35	(16)
Wurzburg	7th c	117	(70)	117	(61)	78	(50)	101	(33)	75	(00)	27	(46)	21	(00?)
GIBRALTAR															
*Gibraltar	711	27	(70)	25	(61)	23	(51)	17	(31)	20	(01)	16	(44)	3	(87)
GREECE															
*Athens	bef 13th c BC	862	(71)	628	(61)	555	(51)	396	(28)	111	(96)	31	(53)	12	(00e)
		2530s	(71)	1853s	(61)	1379s	(51)	802s	(28)						
Iraklion	832?	77	(71)	63	(61)	51	(51)	33	(28)	22	(00)	15	(50?e)	13	(00?e)
		84s	(71)	70s	(61)	58s	(51)								
Patras	5th c BC?	111	(71)	95	(61)	79	(51)	61	(28)	38	(96)	18	(61)	6	(00?e)
		120s	(71)	102s	(61)	88s	(51)								
Peristeri	1923	119	(71)	79	(61)	36	(51)	7	(28)						

EUROPE

City	Date settled	Population (thousands) Latest	Circa 1960	Circa 1950	Circa 1930	Circa 1900	Circa 1850	Circa 1800
Piraeus	5th c BC	186 (71)	184 (61)	186 (51)	193 (28)	42 (96)	6 (52)	
Salonika	315 BC	339 (71)	251 (61)	217 (51)	237 (28)	115 (00e)	70 (50?e)	70 (00?e)
		551s (71)	378s (61)	297s (51)	251s (28)			
HUNGARY								
*Budapest	bef 19 AD	1940 (70)	1805 (60)	1058 (49)	1006 (30)	716 (00)	178 (50)	54 (99)
Debrecen	1211	155 (70)	130 (60)	120 (49)	117 (30)	72 (00)	61 (51)	29 (87)
Miskolc	13th c	173 (70)	144 (60)	104 (49)	62 (30)	41 (00)	16 (50)	19 (87)
Pecs	1st c BC?	145 (70)	115 (60)	78 (49)	62 (30)	42 (00)	15 (50)	9 (87)
Szeged	1138?	119 (70)	99 (60)	133 (49)	135 (30)	100 (00)	51 (51)	22 (87)
ICELAND								
*Reykjavik	874	82 (70)	72 (60)	56 (50)	28 (30)	7 (01)	0.5 (50?e)	0.5 (00?e)
		95s (70)	79s (60)					
IRELAND								
Cork	7th c	128 (71)	78 (61)	75 (51)	78 (26)	76 (01)	88 (51)	101 (21)
		125s (66)	116s (61)	107s (51)				
*Dublin	836?	566 (71)	537 (61)	522 (51)	317 (26)	291 (01)	262 (51)	182 (98)
		650s (66)	593s (61)	570s (51)	419s (26)			
ITALY								
Alessandria	1168	102 (71)	93 (61)	82 (51)	80 (31)	72 (01)	42 (48)	19 (1774)
Ancona	390 BC?	110 (71)	100 (61)	86 (51)	83 (31)	55 (01)	23 (46)	17 (00?)
Bari	180 BC?	357 (71)	312 (61)	268 (51)	170 (31)	78 (01)	34 (61)	18 (00?)
Bergamo	5th c BC?	127 (71)	115 (61)	103 (51)	79 (31)	47 (01)	41 (61)	24 (05)
Bologna	510 BC?	490 (71)	445 (61)	341 (51)	239 (31)	148 (01)	97 (53)	63 (06)
Bolzano	14 BC?	103 (71)	89 (61)	71 (51)	37 (31)	14 (00)	8 (57)	8 (00?e)
Brescia	6th c BC	210 (71)	173 (61)	142 (51)	115 (31)	69 (01)	35 (57)	42 (00?)
Cagliari	540 BC	224 (71)	184 (61)	139 (51)	101 (31)	53 (01)	27 (48)	29 (10e)

EUROPE

City	Date settled	Population (thousands)						
		Latest	Circa 1960	Circa 1950	Circa 1930	Circa 1900	Circa 1850	Circa 1800
Catania	8th c BC	398 (71)	364 (61)	300 (51)	225 (31)	147 (01)	57 (50)	46 (98)
Como	bef 196 BC	97 (71)	82 (61)	70 (51)	51 (31)	38 (01)	18 (46)	15 (05)
Cosenza	bef 331 BC	102 (71)	79 (61)	57 (51)	35 (31)	21 (01)	17 (61)	8 (89)
Ferrara	753?	153 (71)	153 (61)	134 (51)	116 (31)	87 (01)	68 (53)	24 (05)
Florence	59 BC?	462 (71)	437 (61)	375 (51)	305 (31)	198 (01)	106 (49)	78 (00)
Foggia	1069?	142 (71)	119 (61)	98 (51)	56 (31)	53 (01)	32 (61)	17 (88)
Forli	188 BC?	105 (71)	92 (61)	78 (51)	60 (31)	43 (01)	37 (61)	16 (06)
Genoa	5th c BC?	812 (71)	784 (61)	688 (51)	591 (31)	220 (01)	100 (48)	91 (99)
La Spezia	12th c?	125 (71)	122 (61)	112 (51)	115 (31)	66 (01)	12 (61)	4 (06)
Leghorn	807?	174 (71)	161 (61)	142 (51)	120 (31)	96 (01)	80 (55)	51 (91)
Messina	8th c BC	258 (71)	255 (61)	221 (51)	180 (31)	147 (01)	97 (50)	45 (98)
Milan	4th c BC	1724 (71)	1583 (61)	1274 (51)	962 (31)	490 (01)	169 (54)	135 (00)
Modena	5th c BC?	171 (71)	139 (61)	111 (51)	90 (31)	63 (01)	53 (61)	27 (05)
Monza	5th c BC?	114 (71)	84 (61)	73 (51)	60 (31)	42 (01)	26 (61)	11 (05)
Naples	600 BC?	1233 (71)	1183 (61)	1011 (51)	832 (31)	548 (01)	416 (50)	331 (18)
Novara	4th c BC?	101 (71)	88 (61)	69 (51)	61 (31)	44 (01)	25 (61)	14 (14e)
Padua	302 BC?	231 (71)	198 (61)	168 (51)	127 (31)	81 (01)	54 (57)	31 (00?)
Palermo	8th c BC	651 (71)	588 (61)	491 (51)	380 (31)	306 (01)	179 (50)	148 (98)
Parma	183 BC	175 (71)	141 (61)	123 (51)	69 (31)	49 (01)	41 (54)	28 (00?)
Perugia	6th c BC?	129 (71)	113 (61)	95 (51)	77 (31)	61 (01)	43 (61)	16 (00?e)
Pescara	48 AD?	122 (71)	87 (61)	65 (51)	44 (31)	7 (01)	4 (61)	
Piacenza	218 BC	106 (71)	89 (61)	73 (51)	64 (31)	36 (01)	32 (61)	15 (00?e)
Pisa	11th c BC?	104 (71)	91 (61)	78 (51)	71 (31)	60 (01)	49 (61)	17 (00?e)
Prato	10th c	144 (71)	111 (61)	78 (51)	67 (31)	51 (01)	35 (61)	10 (00?e)
Ravenna	8th c BC	132 (71)	116 (61)	92 (51)	77 (31)	63 (01)	54 (53)	26 (05)
Reggio di Calabria	8th c BC	163 (71)	153 (61)	141 (51)	124 (31)	45 (01)	27 (61)	16 (89)
Reggio nell'Emilia	2nd c BC	129 (71)	116 (61)	107 (51)	90 (31)	59 (01)	47 (61)	15 (05)
Rimini	400 BC?	120 (71)	93 (61)	77 (51)	63 (31)	44 (01)	33 (61)	17 (05)
*Rome	1000 BC?	2800 (71)	2188 (61)	1652 (51)	937 (31)	425 (01)	176 (53)	147 (99)

EUROPE

City	Date settled	Population (thousands) Latest	Circa 1960	Circa 1950	Circa 1930	Circa 1900	Circa 1850	Circa 1800
Salerno	197 BC	154 (71)	117 (61)	91 (51)	61 (31)	42 (01)	19 (50)	9 (89)
Sassari	bef 12th c	107 (71)	90 (61)	70 (51)	52 (31)	38 (01)	26 (61)	30 (00?e)
Syracuse	734 BC	109 (71)	89 (61)	71 (51)	49 (31)	32 (01)	20 (61)	17 (00?e)
Taranto	708 BC?	229 (71)	195 (61)	169 (51)	112 (31)	60 (01)	28 (61)	18 (00?e)
Terni	672 BC?	107 (71)	95 (61)	84 (51)	62 (31)	30 (01)	14 (61)	7 (00?e)
Trieste	181 BC?	270 (71)	273 (61)	273 (51)	250 (31)	133 (00)	64 (50)	24 (01)
Turin	4th c BC?	1178 (71)	1026 (61)	719 (51)	591 (31)	330 (01)	143 (48)	78 (00)
Udine	983?	101 (71)	86 (61)	73 (51)	64 (31)	37 (01)	19 (59)	15 (15)
Venice	6th c	364 (71)	347 (61)	317 (51)	250 (31)	148 (01)	107 (51)	137 (97)
Verona	bef 89 BC	264 (71)	221 (61)	179 (51)	152 (31)	74 (01)	51 (51)	42 (10)
Vicenza	1st c BC?	116 (71)	98 (61)	80 (51)	64 (31)	44 (01)	33 (57)	4 (02)
LUXEMBOURG								
*Luxembourg	963	76 (70)	72 (60)	62 (47)	54 (30)	21 (00)	12 (40)	9 (00e)
MALTA								
*Valletta	1566	15 (67)	18 (57)	19 (48)	23 (31)	23 (01)	25 (51)	24 (98)
MONACO								
*Monaco	6th c BC?	24 (70e)	22 (62)	20 (51)	25 (28)	15 (97)	8 (57)	6 (00?e)
NETHERLANDS								
*Amsterdam	1275?	831 (70e)	865 (60)	804 (47)	757 (30)	511 (99)	224 (49)	217 (95)
		1040s (70e)	911s (60)	838s (47)				
Apeldoorn	793?	124 (70e)	104 (60)	63 (47)	60 (30)	26 (99)	10 (49)	2 (95)
Arnhem	893?	133 (70e)	125 (60)	97 (47)	78 (30)	57 (99)	19 (49)	10 (95)
		270s (70e)	152s (60)	114s (47)				
Breda	1198?	121 (70e)	108 (60)	82 (47)	45 (30)	26 (99)	15 (49)	8 (95)
		147s (70e)		85s (47)				

EUROPE

City	Date settled	Population (thousands)						
		Latest	Circa 1960	Circa 1950	Circa 1930	Circa 1900	Circa 1850	Circa 1800
Dordrecht	1018	89 (70e)	84 (60)	68 (47)	56 (30)	38 (99)	21 (49)	18 (95)
Eindhoven	1232?	189 (70e)	168 (60)	135 (47)	95 (30)	5 (99)	3 (49)	3 (30)
		335s (70e)		137s (47)				
Enschede	1118?	139 (70e)	124 (60)	80 (47)	52 (30)	24 (99)	4 (49)	3 (30)
Groningen	1006?	169 (70e)	145 (60)	132 (47)	105 (30)	67 (99)	34 (49)	24 (95)
		201s (70e)		143s (47)				
Haarlem	960?	172 (70e)	169 (60)	157 (47)	120 (30)	64 (99)	26 (49)	21 (95)
		239s (70e)	224s (60)	201s (47)				
*Hague	1242?	551 (70e)	605 (60)	533 (47)	438 (30)	206 (99)	72 (49)	38 (95)
		719s (70e)	692s (60)	592s (47)				
Heerlen	2nd c?	75 (70e)	72 (60)	57 (47)	47 (30)	6 (99)	2 (49?)	3 (01)
Hilversum	13th c	100 (70e)	101 (60)	85 (47)	57 (30)	19 (99)	5 (49)	3 (95)
Leiden	9th c?	101 (70e)	96 (60)	87 (47)	71 (30)	54 (99)	36 (49)	31 (95)
		163s (70e)	117s (60)	102s (47)				
Maastricht	50 AD?	94 (70e)	91 (60)	74 (47)	61 (30)	34 (99)	25 (49)	18 (01)
Nijmegen	70 AD?	149 (70e)	130 (60)	107 (47)	82 (30)	43 (99)	21 (49)	13 (95)
		203s (70e)	133s (60)					
Rotterdam	9th c?	687 (70e)	729 (60)	646 (47)	587 (30)	319 (99)	90 (49)	34 (95)
		1061s (70e)	827s (60)	716s (47)				
's Hertogenbosch	1134?	82 (70e)	73 (60)	53 (47)	42 (30)	31 (99)	22 (49)	13 (95)
Tilburg	709?	153 (70e)	138 (60)	114 (47)	79 (30)	34 (99)	15 (49)	9 (95)
Utrecht	630?	279 (70e)	255 (60)	185 (47)	155 (30)	102 (99)	48 (49)	32 (95)
		445s (70e)		223s (47)				
Zaandam	1398?	64 (70e)	50 (60)	42 (47)	33 (30)	21 (99)	11 (49)	10 (95)
NORWAY								
Bergen	1070	113 (71e)	116 (60)	113 (50)	98 (30)	72 (00)	22 (45)	17 (01)
		149s (60)	149s (60)	144s (50)				
*Oslo	1048	481 (71e)	476 (60)	434 (50)	253 (30)	228 (00)	33 (45)	10 (01)
		599s (69e)	579s (60)	506s (50)				

EUROPE

City	Date settled	Population (thousands)						
		Latest	Circa 1960	Circa 1950	Circa 1930	Circa 1900	Circa 1850	Circa 1800
Stavanger	9th c?	82 (69e)	53 (60)	51 (50)	47 (30)	31 (00)	9 (45)	2 (01)
Trondheim	997	128 (71e)	59 (60)	57 (50)	54 (30)	38 (00)	15 (45)	9 (01)
POLAND								
Bialystok	1310	167 (70)	121 (60)	69 (50)	91 (31)	64 (97)	14 (58)	3 (98e)
Bielsko-Biala	13th c	106 (70)	75 (60)	57 (50)	45 (31)	25 (00)	13 (57)	6 (00?)
Bydgoszcz	13th c?	281 (70)	232 (60)	163 (50)	117 (31)	47 (00)	13 (49)	4 (00?)
Bytom	1136?	187 (70)	183 (60)	174 (50)	101 (33)	51 (00)	6 (49)	3 (00?)
Chorzow	1798	151 (70)	147 (60)	129 (50)	81 (31)	58 (00)	4 (52)	
Czestochowa	1220?	188 (70)	165 (60)	112 (50)	118 (31)	45 (97)	3 (50?e)	2 (00)
Gdansk	997?	364 (70)	287 (60)	195 (50)	256 (29)	141 (00)	64 (49)	47 (02)
Gdynia	13th c?	190 (70)	148 (60)	103 (50)	30 (31)	0.9 (10)		
Gliwice	13th c	171 (70)	150 (60)	133 (50)	111 (33)	52 (00)	8 (46)	3 (03)
Katowice	1598?	303 (70)	270 (60)	176 (50)	126 (31)	32 (00)	8 (71)	3 (06)
Kielce	1084?	126 (70)	90 (60)	61 (50)	58 (31)	23 (97)	5 (50?e)	2 (00?e)
Krakow	700?	583 (70)	481 (60)	344 (50)	219 (31)	91 (00)	41 (57)	26 (10)
Lodz	1332?	762 (70)	710 (60)	620 (50)	605 (31)	314 (97)	16 (50)	0.8 (06)
Lublin	10th c?	236 (70)	181 (60)	117 (50)	112 (31)	50 (97)	18 (58)	7 (00?)
Olsztyn	1348	94 (70)	68 (60)	44 (50)	43 (33)	24 (00)	4 (49)	2 (02)
Poznan	968?	469 (70)	408 (60)	321 (50)	245 (31)	117 (00)	45 (49)	16 (00?)
Radom	1154?	159 (70)	130 (60)	80 (50)	78 (31)	29 (97)	6 (50?e)	2 (00?)
Ruda Slaska	1303?	142 (70)	132 (60)	110 (50)	24 (29)	12 (00)	0.4 (50?)	
Sosnowiec	18th c	145 (70)	132 (60)	96 (50)	109 (31)	57 (00)	12 (90)	
Szczecin	9th c	337 (70)	269 (60)	179 (50)	271 (33)	211 (00)	47 (49)	18 (09)
Torun	1231	129 (70)	105 (60)	81 (50)	54 (31)	30 (00)	13 (46)	8 (02)
Walbrzych	1290	125 (70)	117 (60)	94 (50)	47 (33)	15 (00)	4 (52)	2 (19?)
*Warsaw	1224?	1308 (70)	1139 (60)	804 (50)	1172 (31)	684 (97)	164 (51)	63 (01)
Wroclaw	980?	523 (70)	431 (60)	309 (50)	625 (33)	423 (00)	111 (49)	65 (00)
Zabrze	13th c	197 (70)	190 (60)	172 (50)	130 (33)	20 (00)	6 (71)	0.9 (19?)

EUROPE

City	Date settled	Population (thousands) Latest	Circa 1960	Circa 1950	Circa 1930	Circa 1900	Circa 1850	Circa 1800
PORTUGAL								
*Lisbon	2000 BC?	782 (70)	817 (60)	790 (50)	594 (30)	356 (00)	251 (58)	230 (02e)
Porto	2000 BC?	310 (70)	305 (60)	285 (50)	232 (30)	168 (00)	81 (58)	74 (02e)
ROMANIA								
Arad	11th c	137 (70e)	106 (56)	87 (48)	77 (30)	54 (00)	20 (50?)	4 (00?e)
Bacau	1408?	91 (70e)	54 (56)	34 (48)	31 (30)	16 (99)	15 (73)	
Baia Mare	12th c	77 (70e)	36 (56)	21 (48)	14 (30)	11 (00)	6 (50)	4 (87)
Braila	1368?	152 (70e)	102 (56)	96 (48)	68 (30)	58 (99)	9 (50?e)	30 (00?e)
Brasov	1225	182 (70e)	124 (56)	83 (48)	59 (30)	35 (00)	24 (51)	18 (89)
*Bucharest	630?	1475 (70e)	1178 (56)	886 (48)	639 (30)	276 (99)	122 (59)	42 (00?e)
		1575s (70e)	1291s (56)	1042s (48)				
Cluj	12th c	203 (70e)	155 (56)	118 (48)	101 (30)	47 (00)	19 (51)	15 (97)
Constanta	7th c BC?	172 (70e)	100 (56)	79 (48)	59 (30)	13 (99)	5 (50?e)	
		238s (70e)	126s (56)					
Craiova	15th c	175 (70e)	97 (56)	85 (48)	63 (30)	45 (99)	8 (50?e)	2 (00?e)
Galati	1418?	179 (70e)	96 (56)	80 (48)	101 (30)	63 (99)	36 (39?e)	5 (00?e)
Hunedoara	1267?	77 (70e)	36 (56)	7 (48)	5 (30)	4 (00)	2 (57)	
Iasi	1408?	184 (70e)	113 (56)	94 (48)	103 (30)	78 (99)	66 (59)	25 (00?)
Oradea	1080	138 (70e)	99 (56)	82 (48)	83 (30)	47 (00)	23 (50)	5 (87)
Petroseni	17th c	40 (70e)	23 (56)	14 (48)	15 (30)	8 (00)	0.6 (69?)	
Pitesti	16th c?	74 (70e)	38 (56)	29 (48)	20 (30)	16 (99)	7 (59)	
Ploesti	16th c	163 (70e)	115 (56)	96 (48)	79 (30)	45 (99)	27 (59)	
Resita	1768	68 (70e)	41 (56)	25 (48)	20 (30)	12 (00)	1 (50?)	
Sibiu	12th c	120 (70e)	90 (56)	61 (48)	49 (30)	26 (00)	16 (50)	13 (00?)
Timisoara	1212	193 (70e)	142 (56)	112 (48)	92 (30)	50 (00)	18 (50)	11 (15?)
Tirgu Mures	1332?	98 (70e)	65 (56)	47 (48)	39 (30)	18 (00)	9 (50)	8 (00?e)
SPAIN								
Alicante	713?	182 (70)	122 (60)	104 (50)	73 (30)	50 (00)	17 (57)	13 (04)

EUROPE

City	Date settled	Population (thousands) Latest		Circa 1960		Circa 1950		Circa 1930		Circa 1900		Circa 1850		Circa 1800	
Almeria	238 BC?	114	(70)	87	(60)	76	(50)	54	(30)	47	(00)	23	(57)	7	(00?e)
Badajoz	3rd c BC?	101	(70)	96	(60)	79	(50)	44	(30)	31	(00)	22	(57)	10	(00?e)
Badalona	3rd c BC?	163	(70)	92	(60)	62	(50)	44	(30)	19	(00)	10	(57)	2	(16)
Baracaldo	12th c?	109	(70)	78	(60)	42	(50)	34	(30)	15	(00)	0.3	(57)		
Barcelona	200 BC?	1742	(70)	1558	(60)	1280	(50)	1006	(30)	533	(00)	160	(57)	147	(00?)
Bilbao	1300?	406	(70)	298	(60)	229	(50)	162	(30)	83	(00)	18	(57)	11	(02)
Burgos	884	117	(70)	82	(60)	74	(50)	40	(30)	30	(00)	26	(57)	12	(22)
Cadiz	1100 BC?	134	(70)	118	(60)	100	(50)	76	(30)	69	(00)	62	(57)	58	(00?)
Cartagena	225 BC?	143	(70)	124	(60)	113	(50)	103	(30)	100	(00)	22	(57)	25	(00?e)
Cordova	bef 8th c BC	232	(70)	198	(60)	165	(50)	103	(30)	58	(00)	36	(57)	25	(00e)
Elche	3rd c BC?	124	(70)	73	(60)	56	(50)	38	(30)	27	(00)	20	(57)	17	(00?e)
Gijon	1st c BC	185	(70)	125	(60)	111	(50)	78	(30)	48	(00)	10	(57)	3	(00?e)
Granada	5th c BC?	186	(70)	157	(60)	154	(50)	118	(30)	76	(00)	62	(57)	67	(97)
Hospitalet	987?	241	(70)	123	(60)	72	(50)	38	(30)	5	(00)	3	(57)		
Huelva	7th c BC?	96	(70)	74	(60)	64	(50)	45	(30)	21	(00)	8	(57)	5	(00?e)
Jerez de la Frontera	7th c BC?	149	(70)	131	(60)	108	(50)	72	(30)	63	(00)	39	(57)	8	(00?e)
La Coruna	bef 12th c BC	189	(70)	178	(60)	134	(50)	74	(30)	44	(00)	27	(57)	4	(00?e)
Leon	70 AD	105	(70)	73	(60)	60	(50)	29	(30)	16	(00)	10	(57)	6	(86?)
*Madrid	931?	3121	(70)	2260	(60)	1618	(50)	953	(30)	540	(00)	271	(57)	168	(97)
Malaga	12th c BC	361	(70)	301	(60)	276	(50)	188	(30)	130	(00)	93	(57)	52	(05)
Murcia	825	244	(70)	250	(60)	218	(50)	159	(30)	112	(00)	27	(57)	40	(07)
Oviedo	761	152	(70)	127	(60)	106	(50)	75	(30)	48	(00)	14	(57)	7	(00?)
Palma	123 BC	218	(70)	159	(60)	137	(50)	88	(30)	64	(00)	40	(57)	32	(84)
Pamplona	1st c BC?	145	(70)	98	(60)	72	(50)	42	(30)	29	(00)	23	(57)	14	(00?)
Sabadell	13th c	158	(70)	105	(60)	59	(50)	46	(30)	23	(00)	14	(57)		
Salamanca	5th c BC?	122	(70)	90	(60)	80	(50)	47	(30)	26	(00)	15	(57)	15	(00?e)
San Sebastian	1014?	161	(70)	135	(60)	114	(50)	78	(30)	38	(00)	9	(57)	5	(00?)
Santa Coloma de Gramanet	11th c	106	(70)	33	(60)	15	(50)	13	(30)	2	(00)	1	(57)		
Santander	1068?	149	(70)	118	(60)	102	(50)	85	(30)	55	(00)	25	(57)	4	(00?e)
Saragossa	bef 25 BC	469	(70)	326	(60)	264	(50)	174	(30)	99	(00)	56	(57)	42	(00?e)

EUROPE

City	Date settled	Population (thousands) Latest	Circa 1960	Circa 1950	Circa 1930	Circa 1900	Circa 1850	Circa 1800
Seville	7th c BC?	546 (70)	442 (60)	377 (50)	229 (30)	148 (00)	82 (57)	80 (87)
Tarrasa	3rd c BC?	137 (70)	92 (60)	59 (50)	40 (30)	16 (00)	9 (57)	3 (00e)
Toledo	193 BC?	44 (70)	41 (60)	40 (50)	27 (30)	23 (00)	15 (57)	22 (00?e)
Valencia	137 BC	648 (70)	505 (60)	509 (50)	320 (30)	214 (00)	87 (57)	61 (00)
Valladolid	1074?	234 (70)	152 (60)	124 (50)	91 (30)	69 (00)	40 (57)	20 (00?e)
Vigo	7th c BC?	199 (70)	145 (60)	138 (50)	65 (30)	23 (00)	8 (57)	5 (00?e)
Vitoria	581	133 (70)	74 (60)	52 (50)	41 (30)	31 (00)	19 (57)	6 (00?e)
SWEDEN								
Goteborg	1619	452 (70)	405 (60)	354 (50)	244 (30)	131 (00)	26 (50)	13 (00)
		613s (70)	487s (60)	380s (50)				
Halsingborg	1085?	101 (70)	77 (60)	72 (50)	56 (30)	25 (00)	4 (50)	2 (00)
Jonkoping	13th c	108 (70)	51 (60)	44 (50)	31 (30)	23 (00)	6 (50)	3 (00)
Linkoping	12th c	105 (70)	65 (60)	55 (50)	30 (30)	15 (00)	5 (50)	3 (00)
Malmo	1150?	266 (70)	229 (60)	192 (50)	128 (30)	61 (00)	13 (50)	4 (00)
		445s (70)	246s (60)	196s (50)				
Norrkoping	bef 1384	116 (70)	91 (60)	85 (50)	61 (30)	41 (00)	17 (50)	9 (00)
Orebro	13th c	116 (70)	75 (60)	67 (50)	38 (30)	22 (00)	5 (50)	3 (00)
*Stockholm	1255	740 (70)	808 (60)	744 (50)	502 (30)	301 (00)	93 (50)	76 (00)
		1345s (70)	1149s (60)	928s (50)				
Uppsala	9th c?	127 (70)	78 (60)	63 (50)	30 (30)	23 (00)	7 (50)	5 (00)
Vasteras	1120?	117 (70)	78 (60)	60 (50)	30 (30)	12 (00)	4 (50)	3 (00)
SWITZERLAND								
Basel	374?	213 (70)	207 (60)	184 (50)	148 (30)	109 (00)	27 (50)	15 (00?)
		373s (70)	300s (60)	258s (50)				
*Bern	1191	162 (70)	163 (60)	146 (50)	112 (30)	64 (00)	28 (50)	13 (00?)
		259s (70)	221s (60)	195s (50)				

EUROPE

City	Date settled	Population (thousands)						
		Latest	Circa 1960	Circa 1950	Circa 1930	Circa 1900	Circa 1850	Circa 1800
Geneva	58 BC?	174 (70)	176 (60)	145 (50)	124 (30)	105 (00)	29 (50)	23 (06?)
		321s (70)	238s (60)	195s (50)				
Lausanne	3rd c?	137 (70)	126 (60)	107 (50)	76 (30)	47 (00)	17 (50)	10 (00?)
		219s (70)	163s (60)	137s (50)				
Luzern	8th c	70 (70)	67 (60)	61 (50)	47 (30)	29 (00)	10 (50)	4 (99)
		149s (70)	120s (60)	98s (50)				
Winterthur	1180	93 (70)	80 (60)	67 (50)	54 (30)	22 (00)	5 (50)	3 (00?e)
		106s (70)	91s (60)	75s (50)				
Zurich	3000 BC?	423 (70)	440 (60)	390 (50)	250 (30)	151 (00)	17 (50)	21 (99)
		675s (70)	537s (60)	495s (50)				
TURKEY								
Edirne	125?	55 (70)	39 (60)	30 (50)	35 (27)	80 (05e)	130 (50e)	100 (00?e)
Istanbul	658 BC	2248 (70)	1467 (60)	983 (50)	691 (27)	874 (00?e)	900 (50?e)	400 (00?e)
						1125s (00?e)	891s (44)	598s (00?e)
UK								
Aberdeen	700?	182 (71)	185 (61)	183 (51)	170 (31)	144 (01)	72 (51)	18 (01)
Basildon	bef 1510	129 (71)	89 (61)	43 (51)	40 (31)	18 (01)	2 (51)	1 (41)
Bath	bef 1st c	85 (71)	81 (61)	79 (51)	69 (31)	50 (01)	54 (51)	32 (01)
Belfast	1177	362 (71)	416 (61)	444 (51)	415 (26)	349 (01)	100 (51)	18 (98)
		556s (71)	529s (61)					
Birkenhead	1150?	138 (71)	142 (61)	143 (51)	148 (31)	111 (01)	24 (51)	0.1 (01)
Birmingham	11th c?	1013 (71)	1107 (61)	1113 (51)	1003 (31)	522 (01)	233 (51)	61 (01)
Blackburn	6th c?	102 (71)	106 (61)	111 (51)	123 (31)	128 (01)	47 (51)	12 (01)
Blackpool	16th c?	152 (71)	153 (61)	147 (51)	102 (31)	47 (01)	2 (51)	0.5 (01)
Bolton	11th c?	154 (71)	161 (61)	167 (51)	177 (31)	168 (01)	61 (51)	13 (01)
Bournemouth	1810?	153 (71)	154 (61)	145 (51)	117 (31)	47 (01)	6 (71)	

EUROPE

City	Date settled	Population (thousands)						
		Latest	Circa 1960	Circa 1950	Circa 1930	Circa 1900	Circa 1850	Circa 1800
Bradford	1066?	294 (71)	296 (61)	292 (51)	299 (31)	280 (01)	104 (51)	6 (01)
Brighton	1086?	160 (71)	163 (61)	156 (51)	147 (31)	123 (01)	70 (51)	7s (01)
Bristol	6th c BC	425 (71)	436 (61)	443 (51)	404 (31)	329 (01)	137 (51)	41 (01)
Cambridge	730?	99 (71)	95 (61)	81 (51)	70 (31)	38 (01)	28 (51)	10 (01)
Cardiff	1st c	278 (71)	257 (61)	244 (51)	227 (31)	164 (01)	18 (51)	2 (01)
Coventry	1043?	335 (71)	306 (61)	258 (51)	178 (31)	70 (01)	37 (51)	16 (01)
Derby	51 AD?	219 (71)	132 (61)	141 (51)	142 (31)	106 (01)	41 (51)	11 (01)
Dudley	8th c?	186 (71)	63 (61)	64 (51)	60 (31)	49 (01)	38 (51)	10 (01)
Dundee	12th c?	182 (71)	183 (61)	177 (51)	177 (31)	161 (01)	79 (51)	26 (01)
Edinburgh	617?	453 (71)	468 (61)	467 (51)	439 (31)	316 (01)	160 (51)	83 (01)
Exeter	200 BC?	96 (71)	80 (61)	76 (51)	66 (31)	53 (01)	41 (51)	17 (01)
Gateshead	1080?	94 (71)	103 (61)	115 (51)	122 (31)	110 (01)	26 (51)	9s (01)
Glasgow	1202?	897 (71)	1055 (61)	1090 (51)	1093 (31)	736 (01)	329 (51)	77 (01)
Gloucester	49 AD?	90 (71)	70 (61)	67 (51)	53 (31)	48 (01)	18 (51)	8 (01)
Grimsby	8th c?	95 (71)	97 (61)	95 (51)	92 (31)	63 (01)	12 (51)	2s (01)
Halifax	bef 1066	91 (71)	96 (61)	98 (51)	98 (31)	105 (01)	34 (51)	9 (01)
Hartlepool	649?	97 (71)	95 (61)	90 (51)	89 (31)	86 (01)	10 (51)	1 (01)
Havant and Waterloo	bef 1066	109 (71)	75 (61)	35 (51)	21 (31)	4 (01)	2 (51)	2 (01)
Huddersfield	1086?	131 (71)	131 (61)	129 (51)	123 (31)	95 (01)	31 (51)	7 (01)
Hull	13th c	286 (71)	303 (61)	299 (51)	314 (31)	240 (01)	85 (51)	22 (01)
Ipswich	991?	123 (71)	117 (61)	107 (51)	88 (31)	67 (01)	33 (51)	11 (01)
Leeds	bef 1080	495 (71)	511 (61)	505 (51)	483 (31)	429 (01)	172 (51)	53 (01)
Leicester	bef 43 AD	284 (71)	273 (61)	285 (51)	258 (31)	212 (01)	61 (51)	17 (01)
Liverpool	1190?	609 (71)	747 (61)	789 (51)	856 (31)	685 (01)	376 (51)	78 (01)
*London	43 AD?		3200 (61)	3348 (51)	4397 (31)	4537 (01)	2362 (51)	865 (01)
		7393s (71)	3172s (61)	8348s (51)	8216s (31)	6581s (01)		
Luton	1st c?	161 (71)	132 (61)	110 (51)	69 (31)	36 (01)	11 (51)	3s (01)
Manchester	80 AD	542 (71)	662 (61)	703 (51)	766 (31)	544 (01)	303 (51)	70 (01)
Newcastle upon Tyne	1080	222 (71)	270 (61)	292 (51)	286 (31)	215 (01)	88 (51)	28 (01)

Figure 33. The modern skyline of London, the largest city in Europe, with Saint Paul's Cathedral at right center. (Credit: British Information Services.)

EUROPE

City	Date settled	Population (thousands)						
		Latest	Circa 1960	Circa 1950	Circa 1930	Circa 1900	Circa 1850	Circa 1800
Newport	12th c	112 (71)	108 (61)	106 (51)	89 (31)	67 (01)	19 (51)	1 (01)
Northampton	6th c?	126 (71)	105 (61)	104 (51)	92 (31)	87 (01)	27 (51)	7 (01)
Norwich	570?	122 (71)	120 (61)	121 (51)	126 (31)	112 (01)	68 (51)	37 (01)
Nottingham	9th c	300 (71)	312 (61)	306 (51)	276 (31)	240 (01)	57 (51)	29 (01)
Oldham	11th c?	106 (71)	115 (61)	123 (51)	140 (31)	137 (01)	53 (51)	12 (01)
Oxford	912?	109 (71)	106 (61)	99 (51)	81 (31)	49 (01)	28 (51)	12 (01)
Paisley	1163	95 (71)	96 (61)	94 (51)	86 (31)	79 (01)	48 (51)	31 (01)
Plymouth	11th c?	239 (71)	204 (61)	208 (51)	213 (31)	108 (01)	52 (51)	16 (01)
Poole	1224?	107 (71)	92 (61)	83 (51)	57 (31)	19 (01)	9 (51)	5 (01)
Portsmouth	12th c	197 (71)	215 (61)	234 (51)	252 (31)	188 (01)	72 (51)	32 (01)
Preston	1094?	98 (71)	113 (61)	121 (51)	119 (31)	113 (01)	70 (51)	12 (01)
Reading	871	133 (71)	120 (61)	114 (51)	97 (31)	72 (01)	21 (51)	10 (01)
Rochdale	1st c?	91 (71)	86 (61)	88 (51)	90 (31)	83 (01)	29 (51)	6 (01)
Saint Helens	17th c?	104 (71)	109 (61)	113 (51)	107 (31)	84 (01)	15 (51)	
Salford	1086?	131 (71)	155 (61)	178 (51)	223 (31)	221 (01)	64 (51)	14 (01)
Sheffield	1086?	520 (71)	494 (61)	513 (51)	518 (31)	381 (01)	135 (51)	31 (01)
Solihull	13th c?	107 (71)	96 (61)	68 (51)	25 (31)	8 (01)	3 (51)	2s (01)
Southampton	755?	215 (71)	205 (61)	178 (51)	176 (31)	105 (01)	35 (51)	8 (01)
Southend-on-Sea	1121	162 (71)	165 (61)	152 (51)	120 (31)	29 (01)	1 (51)	
South Shields	1245	101 (71)	110 (61)	107 (51)	113 (31)	97 (01)	29 (51)	8 (01)
Stockport	12th c?	140 (71)	143 (61)	142 (51)	125 (31)	79 (01)	54 (51)	15 (01)
Stoke-on-Trent	1086?	265 (71)	265 (61)	275 (51)	277 (31)	268 (01)	132 (51)	23 (01)
Sunderland	674	217 (71)	190 (61)	182 (51)	186 (31)	146 (01)	67 (51)	12 (01)
Swansea	1099?	173 (71)	167 (61)	161 (51)	165 (31)	95 (01)	31 (51)	6 (01)
Swindon	1086?	91 (71)	92 (61)	69 (51)	62 (31)	45 (01)	5 (51)	1 (01)
Teesside	686?	396 (71)	361 (61)	329 (51)	298 (31)	178 (01)	21 (51)	5 (01)
Thurrock	1149?	125 (71)	114 (61)	82 (51)	35 (31)	19 (01)	2 (51)	0.7 (01)
Torbay	12th c?	109 (71)	54 (61)	53 (51)	46 (31)	34 (01)	8 (51)	0.8 (01)
Wallasey	10th c?	97 (71)	103 (61)	101 (51)	98 (31)	54 (01)	1 (51)	0.3 (01)
Walsall	996?	135 (71)	118 (61)	115 (51)	103 (31)	86 (01)	26 (51)	5 (01)

EUROPE

City	Date settled	Population (thousands) Latest		Circa 1960		Circa 1950		Circa 1930		Circa 1900		Circa 1850		Circa 1800	
Warley	1086?	163	(71)	170	(61)	179	(51)	161	(31)	115	(01)	8	(51)	1	(01)
West Bromwich	1086?	167	(71)	96	(61)	88	(51)	81	(31)	65	(01)	35s	(51)	6s	(01)
Wolverhampton	985?	269	(71)	151	(61)	163	(51)	133	(31)	94	(01)	50	(51)	13	(01)
York	71?	105	(71)	104	(61)	105	(51)	94	(31)	78	(01)	36	(51)	16	(01)
USSR															
Archangel	1553	343	(70)	256	(59)	281	(39)	73	(26)	21	(97)	15	(56)	7	(82)
Astrakhan	13th c	411	(70)	296	(59)	254	(39)	177	(26)	113	(97)	35	(56)	70	(82)
Baku	5th c?	847	(70)	643	(59)	809	(39)	453	(26)	112	(97)	8	(56)		
		1261s	(70)	971s	(59)										
Belgorod	1237?	151	(70)	72	(59)	34	(39)	31	(26)	22	(97)	13	(56)	7	(82)
Bryansk	1146	318	(70)	207	(59)	87	(39)	46	(26)	24	(97)	11	(56)	4	(82)
Cheboksary	1371?	216	(70)	104	(59)	31	(39)	9	(26)	5	(97)	5	(56)		
Cherepovets	14th c	189	(70)	92	(59)	32	(39)	22	(26)	7	(97)	3	(56)	0.5	(82)
Cherkassy	14th c	159	(70)	85	(59)	52	(39)	40	(26)	30	(97)	12	(56)	8	(82)
Chernigov	7th c?	159	(70)	90	(59)	69	(39)	35	(26)	27	(97)	4	(56)	5	(82)
Chernovtsy	1407?	187	(70)	146	(59)	106	(39)	112	(30)	70	(00)	26	(57)	5	(00?e)
Dneprodzerzhinsk	1750?	227	(70)	194	(59)	148	(39)	34	(26)	40	(13)	3	(61)		
Dnepropetrovsk	1783	863	(70)	660	(59)	501	(39)	233	(26)	113	(97)	13	(56)	2	(82)
Donetsk	1869	879	(70)	699	(59)	462	(39)	106	(26)	32	(97?)				
Dzerzhinsk	bef 1917	221	(70)	164	(59)	103	(39)	9	(26)						
Gomel	1142?	272	(70)	168	(59)	144	(39)	86	(26)	37	(97)	10	(56)		
Gorkiy	1221	1170	(70)	942	(59)	644	(39)	185	(26)	90	(97)	36	(56)	10	(82)
Gorlovka	1867	335	(70)	293	(59)	109	(39)	23	(26)	2	(97)				
Groznyy	1818	341	(70)	242	(59)	172	(39)	97	(26)	16	(97)	3	(67)		
Ivanovo	16th c	419	(70)	335	(59)	285	(39)	111	(26)	54	(97)	6	(61)		
Izhevsk	1760	422	(70)	285	(59)	176	(39)	63	(26)	21	(97)	21	(59)		
Kalinin	1135	345	(70)	261	(59)	216	(39)	106	(26)	54	(97)	13	(56)	5	(82)
Kaliningrad	1255	297	(70)	204	(59)	372	(39)	316	(33)	189	(00)	76	(50)	62	(02)
Kaluga	1389?	211	(70)	134	(59)	89	(39)	52	(26)	50	(97)	31	(56)	17	(82)

EUROPE

City	Date settled	Population (thousands) Latest		Circa 1960		Circa 1950		Circa 1930		Circa 1900		Circa 1850		Circa 1800	
Kaunas	1030	306	(70)	214	(59)	152	(39)	92	(23)	71	(97)	20	(56)	4	(00e)
Kazan	1437	869	(70)	647	(59)	402	(39)	179	(26)	130	(97)	56	(56)	14	(82)
Kerch	6th c BC	128	(70)	98	(59)	104	(39)	35	(26)	33	(97)	13	(56)		
Kharkov	1656	1223	(70)	934	(59)	833	(39)	417	(26)	174	(97)	31	(56)	11	(82)
Kherson	1778	261	(70)	158	(59)	97	(39)	59	(26)	59	(97)	34	(56)	15	(82)
Kiev	430?	1632	(70)	1104	(59)	846	(39)	514	(26)	248	(97)	62	(56)	22	(82)
Kirov	1174	332	(70)	252	(59)	143	(39)	62	(26)	25	(97)	15	(56)	5	(82)
Kirovabad	12th c?	190	(70)	116	(59)	99	(39)	57	(26)	33	(97)	11	(56)		
Kirovograd	1754	189	(70)	128	(59)	100	(39)	67	(26)	61	(97)	13	(56)		
Kishinev	1420?	357	(70)	216	(59)	112	(39)	115	(30)	108	(97)	63	(56)	7	(12e)
Klaypeda	1252	140	(70)	90	(59)	47	(39)	37	(31)	21	(05)	10	(46)	5	(02)
Kostroma	1152	223	(70)	172	(59)	121	(39)	74	(26)	41	(97)	15	(56)	9	(82)
Kramatorsk	1897	151	(70)	115	(59)	94	(39)	12	(26)						
Krasnodar	1794	465	(70)	313	(59)	204	(39)	163	(26)	66	(97)	9	(56)		
Kremenchug	1571	148	(70)	87	(59)	90	(39)	59	(26)	63	(97)	20	(56)	3	(82)
Krivoy Rog	17th c	573	(70)	388	(59)	198	(39)	31	(26)	10	(00e)				
Kursk	9th c	284	(70)	205	(59)	120	(39)	99	(26)	75	(97)	41	(56)	15	(82)
Kutaisi	6th c BC	161	(70)	128	(59)	78	(39)	48	(26)	32	(97)	8	(67)		
Kuybyshev	1586	1047	(70)	806	(59)	390	(39)	176	(26)	90	(97)	24	(56)	3	(82)
Leninakan	773	164	(70)	108	(59)	68	(39)	42	(26)	32	(97)	12	(56)		
Leningrad	1703	3513	(70)	2900	(59)	3191	(39)	1614	(26)	1265	(97)	491	(56)	271	(05)
		3950s	(70)	3321s	(59)										
Lipetsk	13th c	290	(70)	157	(59)	67	(39)	21	(26)	16	(97)	11	(56)	6	(82)
Lugansk	18th c	382	(70)	275	(59)	213	(39)	72	(26)	20	(97)	7	(61)	0.8	(82)
Lvov	1250?	553	(70)	411	(59)	318	(39)	316	(31)	160	(00)	71	(46)	41	(00?)
Makeyevka	1899	393	(70)	358	(59)	240	(39)	52	(26)						
Makhachkala	1844	186	(70)	119	(59)	87	(39)	34	(26)	10	(97)	4	(67)		
Minsk	1067?	907	(70)	509	(59)	239	(39)	132	(26)	91	(97)	26	(56)	2	(82)
Mogilev	1267	202	(70)	122	(59)	99	(39)	50	(26)	43	(97)	23	(56)	12	(82)
*Moscow	1147?	6942	(70)	5046	(59)	4137	(39)	2026	(26)	1039	(97)	369	(56)	270	(11)

EUROPE

City	Date settled	Population (thousands)						
		Latest	Circa 1960	Circa 1950	Circa 1930	Circa 1900	Circa 1850	Circa 1800
Murmansk	1915	309 (70)	222 (59)	117 (39)	9 (26)			
Nikolayev	1788	331 (70)	226 (59)	167 (39)	105 (26)	92 (97)	44 (56)	4 (20)
Novgorod	859?	128 (70)	61 (59)	45 (39)	33 (26)	26 (97)	13 (56)	11 (82)
Novocherkassk	1805	162 (70)	95 (59)	76 (39)	62 (26)	52 (97)	18 (56)	
Odessa	14th c	892 (70)	667 (59)	604 (39)	421 (26)	404 (97)	101 (56)	8 (03)
Ordzhonikidze	1784	236 (70)	164 (59)	127 (39)	78 (26)	44 (97)	6 (63)	
Orel	1566	232 (70)	150 (59)	111 (39)	78 (26)	70 (97)	35 (56)	16 (82)
Orenburg	1743	345 (70)	267 (59)	173 (39)	123 (26)	72 (97)	14 (56)	17 (82)
Orsk	1735	225 (70)	176 (59)	66 (39)	14 (26)	14 (97)	2 (63)	2 (00?e)
Penza	1666	374 (70)	255 (59)	157 (39)	92 (26)	60 (97)	24 (56)	8 (82)
Perm	1568	850 (70)	629 (59)	255 (39)	85 (26)	45 (97)	9 (56)	3 (82)
Petrozavodsk	1703	185 (70)	136 (59)	70 (39)	27 (26)	13 (97)	10 (56)	3 (82)
Podolsk	bef 1781	169 (70)	124 (59)	72 (39)	20 (26)	4 (97)	4 (56)	0.9 (82)
Poltava	1174?	220 (70)	143 (59)	128 (39)	92 (26)	53 (97)	21 (56)	8 (82)
Riga	1201?	733 (70)	605 (59)	393 (39)	378 (30)	282 (97)	70 (56)	30 (04)
Rostov-na-Donu	1761	789 (70)	600 (59)	510 (39)	308 (26)	119 (97)	13 (56)	
Ryazan	1095?	351 (70)	214 (59)	95 (39)	51 (26)	46 (97)	21 (56)	4 (82)
Rybinsk	1137?	218 (70)	182 (59)	139 (39)	55 (26)	25 (97)	9 (56)	2 (82)
Saransk	1641	190 (70)	91 (59)	41 (39)	15 (26)	14 (97)	5 (56)	6 (82)
Saratov	1590	758 (70)	581 (59)	376 (39)	215 (26)	137 (97)	62 (56)	5 (82)
Sevastopol	16th c	229 (70)	148 (59)	112 (39)	75 (26)	54 (97)	6 (56)	2 (82)
Shakhty	1839	205 (70)	196 (59)	155 (39)	41 (26)	16 (97)	4 (63)	
Simferopol	16th c?	250 (70)	186 (59)	143 (39)	88 (26)	49 (97)	26 (56)	2 (82)
Smolensk	865	211 (70)	147 (59)	157 (39)	79 (26)	47 (97)	9 (56)	12 (82)
Sochi	1910	224 (70)	127 (59)	50 (39e)	10 (26)			
Stavropol	1777	198 (70)	141 (59)	85 (39)	59 (26)	42 (97)	17 (56)	
Sterlitamak	1766	185 (70)	112 (59)	39 (39)	25 (26)	16 (97)	6 (56)	0.5 (82)
Sumy	1658	159 (70)	98 (59)	64 (39)	44 (26)	28 (97)	12 (56)	10 (82)
Syzran	1683	174 (70)	149 (59)	78 (39)	50 (26)	32 (97)	18 (56)	
Taganrog	1698	254 (70)	202 (59)	189 (39)	86 (26)	51 (97)	19 (56)	4 (82)

EUROPE

City	Date settled	Population (thousands) Latest		Circa 1960		Circa 1950		Circa 1930		Circa 1900		Circa 1850		Circa 1800	
Tallin	1154	363	(70)	282	(59)	176	(41)	125	(27)	65	(97)	20	(56)	12	(16)
Tambov	1636	229	(70)	172	(59)	121	(39)	76	(26)	48	(97)	22	(56)	11	(82)
Tartu	1030	91	(70)	74	(59)	60	(41)	60	(27)	41	(97)	13	(56)	5	(00?e)
Tbilisi	4th c?	889	(70)	695	(59)	519	(39)	293	(26)	160	(97)	38	(56)	22	(97e)
Tolyatti	1738	251	(70)	61	(59)	10	(39e)	6	(26)	6	(97)	4	(56)	2	(82)
Tula	1146?	462	(70)	316	(59)	272	(39)	153	(26)	115	(97)	51	(56)	18	(82)
Ufa	1586	773	(70)	547	(59)	246	(39)	99	(26)	49	(97)	13	(56)	4	(82)
Ulyanovsk	1648	351	(70)	206	(59)	102	(39)	72	(26)	42	(97)	27	(56)	11	(82)
Vilnyus	10th c	372	(70)	236	(59)	215	(39)	196	(31)	155	(97)	46	(56)	21	(88)
Vinnitsa	14th c	211	(70)	122	(59)	93	(39)	58	(26)	29	(97)	9	(56)	1	(82)
Vitebsk	1021?	231	(70)	148	(59)	167	(39)	99	(26)	66	(97)	21	(56)	12	(82)
Vladimir	1108?	234	(70)	164	(59)	67	(39)	35	(26)	28	(97)	13	(56)	1	(82)
Volgograd	1589	818	(70)	592	(59)	445	(39)	148	(26)	55	(97)	7	(56)		
Vologda	1147?	178	(70)	139	(59)	95	(39)	58	(26)	28	(97)	14	(56)	11	(82)
Voronezh	1586	660	(70)	448	(59)	327	(39)	120	(26)	81	(97)	38	(56)	12	(82)
Yaroslavl	1024	517	(70)	407	(59)	298	(39)	114	(26)	72	(97)	27	(56)	19	(82)
Yerevan	607?	767	(70)	509	(59)	200	(39)	66	(26)	29	(97)	13	(56)	15	(00?e)
Yoshkar-Ola	1578	166	(70)	89	(59)	27	(39)	15	(34e)						
Zaporozhye	1770	658	(70)	435	(59)	289	(39)	56	(26)	16	(97)	3	(56)		
Zhdanov	1779	417	(70)	284	(59)	222	(39)	64	(26)	31	(97)	7	(56)	0.9	(82)
Zhitomir	1240?	161	(70)	106	(59)	95	(39)	77	(26)	65	(97)	31	(56)	2	(82)
YUGOSLAVIA															
*Belgrade	3rd c BC	742	(71)	598	(61)	368	(48)	266	(31)	70	(00)	15	(50)	25	(89e)
Dubrovnik	7th c	26	(65e)	23	(61)	16	(48)	19	(31)	13	(00)	17	(57)	17	(98)
Ljubljana	34 BC	174	(71)	157	(61)	115	(48)	60	(31)	37	(00)	21	(57)	11	(00?e)
Maribor	1147?	95	(71)	85	(61)	65	(48)	33	(31)	25	(00)	6	(57)	5	(00?e)
Nis	140?	112	(71)	85	(61)	49	(48)	35	(31)	25	(00)	4	(50?e)	4	(00?e)
Novi Sad	1687	140	(71)	111	(61)	78	(48)	64	(31)	29	(00)	10	(50)	13	(08)
Osijek	8 AD?	92	(71)	73	(61)	49	(48)	40	(31)	25	(00)	13	(50)	8	(1757)

EUROPE

City	Date settled	Population (thousands) Latest	Circa 1960	Circa 1950	Circa 1930	Circa 1900	Circa 1850	Circa 1800
Rijeka	28 AD	130 (71)	101 (61)	73 (48)	53 (31)	38 (00)	11 (46)	9 (10)
Sarajevo	1262	210 (71)	199 (61)	114 (48)	78 (31)	42 (95)	50 (50e)	40 (00?e)
Skopje	2nd c?	312 (71)	172 (61)	92 (48)	65 (31)	20 (00?e)	10 (50?e)	8 (00?e)
Split	305	142 (71)	93 (61)	50 (48)	35 (31)	27 (00)	10 (45)	7 (00?)
Zagreb	7th c?	566 (71)	457 (61)	280 (48)	186 (31)	58 (00)	17 (57)	13 (00e)

NORTH AMERICA

City	Date settled	Population (thousands) Latest	Circa 1960	Circa 1950	Circa 1930	Circa 1900	Circa 1850	Circa 1800
BAHAMA ISLANDS								
*Nassau	1729	101s (70)	81s (63)	46s (53)	20s (31)	13s (01)	8s (51)	6s (00?)
BARBADOS								
*Bridgetown	1628	9 (70)	11 (60)	13 (46)	13 (21)	21 (91)	20 (51)	17 (00?e)
		115s (70)	94s (60)	69s (46)				
BERMUDA								
*Hamilton	1790	2 (70)	3 (60)	3 (50)	3 (31)	2 (01)		
		17s (65e)	14s (60)					
CANADA								
Calgary	1875	403 (71)	250 (61)	129 (51)	84 (31)	4 (01)		
		403s (71)	279s (61)	139s (51)				
Chicoutimi	1676	34 (71)	32 (61)	23 (51)	12 (31)	4 (01)	1 (71)	
		134s (71)	105s (61)					
Edmonton	1819?	438 (71)	281 (61)	160 (51)	79 (31)	3 (01)		
		496s (71)	338s (61)	173s (51)				
Halifax	1749	122 (71)	93 (61)	86 (51)	59 (31)	41 (01)	26 (52)	12 (00e)
		223s (71)	184s (61)	134s (51)				

NORTH AMERICA

City	Date settled	Population (thousands)						
		Latest	Circa 1960	Circa 1950	Circa 1930	Circa 1900	Circa 1850	Circa 1800
Hamilton	1813	309 (71)	274 (61)	208 (51)	156 (31)	53 (01)	14 (52)	
		499s (71)	395s (61)	260s (51)				
Kitchener	1806	112 (71)	74 (61)	45 (51)	31 (31)	10 (01)	1 (50?e)	
		227s (71)	155s (61)	63s (51)				
Laval	1699	228 (71)	125s (61)	38s (51)	16s (31)	10s (01)	10s (52)	
London	1826	223 (71)	170 (61)	95 (51)	71 (31)	38 (01)	7 (52)	
		286s (71)	181s (61)	122s (51)				
Longueuil	1657	98 (71)	24 (61)	11 (51)	5 (31)	3 (01)	1 (52)	
Mississauga	bef 1852	156 (71)	63s (61)	29s (51)	10s (31)	5s (01)	8s (52)	
Montreal	1642	1214 (71)	1191 (61)	1022 (51)	819 (31)	268 (01)	58 (52)	19 (21)
		2743s (71)	2110s (61)	1395s (51)	1010s (31)			
Oshawa	1791	92 (71)	62 (61)	42 (51)	23 (31)	4 (01)	1 (52)	
		120s (71)	81s (61)	52s (51)				
*Ottawa	1826	302 (71)	268 (61)	202 (51)	127 (31)	60 (01)	8 (52)	1 (30)
		603s (71)	430s (61)	282s (51)	166s (31)			
Quebec	1608	186 (71)	172 (61)	164 (51)	131 (31)	69 (01)	42 (52)	12 (00e)
		481s (71)	358s (61)	275s (51)	165s (31)			
Regina	1882	139 (71)	112 (61)	71 (51)	53 (31)	2 (01)		
Saint Catharines	1792	110 (71)	84 (61)	38 (51)	25 (31)	10 (01)	4 (52)	
		303s (71)	96s (61)	67s (51)				
Saint John	1783?	89 (71)	55 (61)	51 (51)	48 (31)	41 (01)	23 (52)	9 (21e)
		107s (71)	96s (61)	78s (51)				
Saint John's	1583?	88 (71)	64 (61)	53 (51)	40 (35)	30 (01)	21 (52)	12 (15e)
		132s (71)	91s (61)	68s (51)				
Saskatoon	1883	126 (71)	96 (61)	53 (51)	43 (31)	0.1 (01)		
Sudbury	1887	91 (71)	80 (61)	42 (51)	19 (31)	2 (01)		
		155s (71)	111s (61)	71s (51)				
Sydney	1784	33 (71)	34 (61)	31 (51)	23 (31)	10 (01)	2 (71)	
		91s (71)	106s (61)	104s (51)				

NORTH AMERICA

City	Date settled	Population (thousands) Latest	Circa 1960	Circa 1950	Circa 1930	Circa 1900	Circa 1850	Circa 1800
Thunder Bay	1678	108 (71)	90 (61)	66 (51)	46 (31)	7 (01)	2 (81)	
		112s (71)	93s (61)	71s (51)				
Toronto	1793	713 (71)	672 (61)	676 (51)	631 (31)	208 (01)	31 (52)	1 (17)
		2628s (71)	1824s (61)	1117s (51)	665s (31)			
Trois-Rivieres	1634	56 (71)	53 (61)	46 (51)	35 (31)	10 (01)	5 (52)	2 (00?e)
		98s (71)	87s (61)	68s (51)				
Vancouver	1870?	426 (71)	385 (61)	345 (51)	247 (31)	26 (01)		
		1082s (71)	790s (61)	531s (51)	273s (31)			
Victoria	1851?	62 (71)	55 (61)	51 (51)	39 (31)	21 (01)	3 (71)	
		196s (71)	154s (61)	104s (51)				
Windsor	1745?	203 (71)	114 (61)	120 (51)	63 (31)	12 (01)	0.1 (52)	
		259s (71)	193s (61)	158s (51)	106s (31)			
Winnipeg	1812	246 (71)	265 (61)	236 (51)	219 (31)	42 (01)	0.2 (71)	
		540s (71)	476s (61)	354s (51)	239s (31)			
COSTA RICA								
*San Jose	1736	203 (69e)	101 (63)	87 (50)	51 (27)	25 (03)	6 (44)	8 (23)
		355s (67e)	322s (63)	140s (50)	63s (27)			
CUBA								
Camaguey	1528	197 (70)	162 (62e)	110 (53)	62 (31)	25 (99)	19 (46)	49 (27)
Cienfuegos	1738?	85 (70)	70 (62e)	58 (53)	50 (31)	30 (99)	5 (53)	
Guantanamo	1819	130 (70)	82 (62e)	65 (53)	28 (31)	7 (99)		
*Havana	1519	990 (66e)	978 (62e)	785 (53)	521 (31)	236 (99)	151 (50)	94 (27)
		1755s (70)	1463s (62e)	1218s (53)				
Holguin	1754	131 (70)	80 (62e)	58 (53)	24 (31)	6 (99)	3 (46)	6 (00?e)
Marianao	17th c?	369 (70)	325 (62e)	219 (53)	71 (31)	5 (99)	0.3 (61?)	
Matanzas	1693	85 (70)	80 (62e)	64 (53)	50 (31)	36 (99)	17 (51)	11 (27)
San Miguel del Padron	bef 1870	120 (70)		61 (53)	3 (31)	2 (99)		
Santa Clara	1689	131 (70)	106 (62e)	77 (53)	38 (31)	14 (99)	6 (51)	9 (27)

NORTH AMERICA

City	Date settled	Population (thousands) Latest	Circa 1960	Circa 1950	Circa 1930	Circa 1900	Circa 1850	Circa 1800
Santiago de Cuba	1514	276 (70)	220 (62e)	163 (53)	102 (31)	43 (99)	24 (46)	27 (27)
DOMINICAN REPUBLIC								
Santiago de los Caballeros	1504	155 (70)	84 (60)	57 (50)	34 (35)	12 (00?e)	12 (50?e)	
*Santo Domingo	1496	671 (70)	367 (60)	182 (50)	71 (35)	22 (00e)	12 (50?e)	12 (00?e)
					94s (35)			22s (00?e)
EL SALVADOR								
San Miguel	1530	51 (69e)	40 (61)	27 (50)	18 (30)	25 (01)	6 (50?e)	
		108s (69e)	82s (61)	57s (50)	40s (30)			
*San Salvador	1525	350 (69e)	256 (61)	162 (50)	89 (30)	60 (01)	25 (50e)	5 (00?e)
		350s (69e)	256s (61)	171s (50)	96s (30)			
Santa Ana	1576?	102 (69e)	73 (61)	52 (50)	41 (30)	48 (01)	10 (50?e)	
		168s (69e)	121s (61)	97s (50)	76s (30)			
GUATEMALA								
*Guatemala	1776	731 (70e)	577 (64)	284 (50)	116 (21)	68 (93)	37 (50e)	31 (25)
HAITI								
*Port-au-Prince	1749	340 (69e)	240 (60e)	134 (50)	80 (29)	60 (00?e)	25 (50?e)	15 (90e)
HONDURAS								
San Pedro Sula	1536	103 (70e)	59 (61)	21 (50)	13 (30)	7 (01)		
			95s (61)	54s (50)	24s (30)			
*Tegucigalpa	1578	232 (70e)	134 (61)	72 (50)	17 (30)	24 (01)	8 (50?e)	
			165s (61)	100s (50)	34s (30)			
JAMAICA								
*Kingston	1692	117 (70)	123 (60)	109 (43)	63 (21)	47 (91)	33 (44)	26 (1778)
		550s (70)	377s (60)	202s (43)				

NORTH AMERICA

City	Date settled	Population (thousands) Latest		Circa 1960		Circa 1950		Circa 1930		Circa 1900		Circa 1850		Circa 1800	
MARTINIQUE															
*Fort-de-France	1672	94	(67)	78	(61)	40	(54)	48	(31)	22	(01)	13	(67?)	10	(00?e)
		97s	(67)	85s	(61)	61s	(54)								
MEXICO															
Acapulco	1550	174	(70)	49	(60)	28	(50)	7	(30)	5	(00)	4	(50e)	4	(00?e)
Aguascalientes	1575	181	(70)	127	(60)	93	(50)	62	(30)	35	(00)	7	(50?e)		
Chihuahua	1639	257	(70)	150	(60)	87	(50)	46	(30)	30	(00)	14	(50e)	12	(03e)
Ciudad Juarez	1662	407	(70)	262	(60)	123	(50)	40	(30)	8	(00)	2	(50?e)		
Ciudad Madero	bef 1910	91	(70)	54	(60)	41	(50)	22	(30)	15	(21)				
Ciudad Obregon	1907	114	(70)	68	(60)	31	(50)	8	(30)	0.2	(21)				
Cuernavaca	bef 1521	134	(70)	37	(60)	31	(50)	9	(30)	10	(00)	10	(50?e)		
Culiacan	1533	168	(70)	85	(60)	49	(50)	18	(30)	10	(00)	11	(58)	11	(00?e)
Durango	1563	151	(70)	97	(60)	59	(50)	36	(30)	31	(00)	22	(50?e)	12	(00?e)
Guadalajara	1542	1195	(70)	737	(60)	377	(50)	180	(30)	101	(00)	56	(50e)	19	(00?e)
Gustavo A. Madero	1706?	125	(70)	103	(60)	60	(50)	11	(21)	6	(00)				
Hermosillo	1750	177	(70)	96	(60)	44	(50)	20	(30)	11	(00)				
Irapuato	1547	117	(70)	84	(60)	49	(50)	29	(30)	20	(00)				
Jalapa	1313?	122	(70)	66	(60)	51	(50)	37	(30)	20	(00)	17	(50?e)	13	(00?e)
Leon	1576	365	(70)	210	(60)	123	(50)	69	(30)	63	(00)	6	(60?e)		
Matamoros	1748	138	(70)	92	(60)	46	(50)	10	(30)	8	(00)	20	(50?e)		
Mazatlan	bef 1541	120	(70)	76	(60)	41	(50)	29	(30)	18	(00)	11	(50?e)		
Merida	1542	213	(70)	171	(60)	143	(50)	95	(30)	44	(00)	23	(50e)	10	(00?e)
Mexicali	1901	267	(70)	175	(60)	65	(50)	15	(30)	7	(21)				
*Mexico	1325	2903	(70)	2832	(60)	2235	(50)	1029	(30)	345	(00)	210	(62)	113	(93)
		7006s	(70)	4871s	(60)	3050s	(50)								
Monterrey	1579?	858	(70)	597	(60)	333	(50)	133	(30)	62	(00)	14	(50e)	11	(00?e)
Morelia	1541	162	(70)	101	(60)	63	(50)	40	(30)	37	(00)	18	(50?e)	18	(00?e)
Netzahualcoyotl	16th c?	580	(70)	7	(60)	0.6	(50)								

NORTH AMERICA

City	Date settled	Population (thousands) Latest	Circa 1960	Circa 1950	Circa 1930	Circa 1900	Circa 1850	Circa 1800
Nuevo Laredo	1755	149 (70)	93 (60)	58 (50)	22 (30)	7 (00)		
Oaxaca	1486	100 (70)	72 (60)	47 (50)	33 (30)	35 (00)	25 (50)	24 (92)
Orizaba	1457	93 (70)	70 (60)	56 (50)	43 (30)	32 (00)	16 (68e)	
Poza Rica	1939?	120 (70)	20 (60)	15 (50)	4 (40)			
Puebla	1532	402 (70)	289 (60)	211 (50)	115 (30)	94 (00)	72 (50e)	53 (93)
Queretaro	1440	113 (70)	68 (60)	49 (50)	33 (30)	33 (00)	30 (50?e)	
Reinosa	bef 1870	137 (70)	74 (60)	34 (50)	5 (30)	2 (00)		
Saltillo	1575	161 (70)	99 (60)	70 (50)	45 (30)	24 (00)	20 (50?e)	6 (00?e)
San Luis Potosi	1576	230 (70)	160 (60)	126 (50)	74 (30)	61 (00)	40 (50e)	9 (93)
Tampico	1823	180 (70)	123 (60)	94 (50)	68 (30)	16 (00)	7 (50?e)	
Tepic	1531	88 (70)	54 (60)	25 (50)	15 (30)	15 (00)	10 (50?e)	
Tijuana	1830?	277 (70)	152 (60)	60 (50)	8 (30)	0.2 (00)		
Toluca	1120?	114 (70)	77 (60)	53 (50)	41 (30)	26 (00)	12 (50?e)	
Torreon	1893	223 (70)	180 (60)	129 (50)	66 (30)	14 (00)		
Veracruz	1599	214 (70)	145 (60)	101 (50)	68 (30)	29 (00)	8 (50e)	16 (00?e)
Villahermosa	1596	100 (70)	52 (60)	34 (50)	15 (30)	11 (00)	4 (50?e)	
NETHERLANDS ANTILLES								
*Willemstad	1527	44 (60)	44 (60)	41 (48e)	19 (31)	14 (05)	8 (50?e)	
NICARAGUA								
*Managua	bef 1521	323 (69e)	235 (63)	109 (50)	28 (20)	30 (05e)	12 (50?e)	
PANAMA								
*Panama	1673	418 (70)	273 (60)	128 (50)	74 (30)	38 (11)	18 (60)	17s (22)
PUERTO RICO								
Bayamon	1750	148 (70)	15 (60)	20 (50)	13 (30)	2 (99)		
Ponce	1680	128 (70)	114 (60)	99 (50)	53 (30)	28 (99)	30 (60)	
		128s (70)	114s (60)					

NORTH AMERICA

City	Date settled	Population (thousands) Latest	Circa 1960	Circa 1950	Circa 1930	Circa 1900	Circa 1850	Circa 1800
*San Juan	1521	453 (70)	432 (60)	225 (50)	115 (30)	32 (99)	19 (60)	39 (00?e)
		820s (70)	542s (60)					
TRINIDAD AND TOBAGO								
*Port of Spain	bef 1595	68 (70)	94 (60)	93 (46)	70 (31)	54 (01)	18 (52)	10 (00?e)
USA								
Abilene	1881	90 (70)	90 (60)	46 (50)	23 (30)	3 (00)	3 (90)	
		91s (70)	92s (60)					
Akron	1807	275 (70)	290 (60)	275 (50)	255 (30)	43 (00)	3 (50)	2 (40)
		543s (70)	458s (60)	367s (50)				
Albany (Georgia)	1836	73 (70)	56 (60)	31 (50)	15 (30)	5 (00)	2 (60)	
		77s (70)	58s (60)					
Albany (New York)	1624	116 (70)	130 (60)	135 (50)	127 (30)	94 (00)	51 (50)	5 (00)
		487s (70)	455s (60)	292s (50)				
Albuquerque	1706	244 (70)	201 (60)	97 (50)	27 (30)	6 (00)	6 (50e)	5 (99e)
		297s (70)	241s (60)					
Alexandria	1713?	111 (70)	91 (60)	62 (50)	24 (30)	15 (00)	9 (50)	5 (00)
Allentown	1762	110 (70)	108 (60)	107 (50)	93 (30)	35 (00)	4 (50)	1 (00)
		364s (70)	256s (60)	226s (50)				
Altoona	1849	63 (70)	69 (60)	77 (50)	82 (30)	39 (00)	4 (60)	
		82s (70)	83s (60)	87s (50)				
Amarillo	1887	127 (70)	138 (60)	74 (50)	43 (30)	1 (00)		
		127s (70)	138s (60)	74s (50)				
Anaheim	1857	167 (70)	104 (60)	15 (50)	11 (30)	1 (00)	0.9 (70)	
Anchorage	1914	48 (70)	44 (60)	11 (50)	2 (30)	2 (20)		
Anderson	1823	71 (70)	49 (60)	47 (50)	40 (30)	20 (00)	0.4 (50)	
Ann Arbor	1824	100 (70)	67 (60)	48 (50)	27 (30)	15 (00)	5 (50)	
		179s (70)	115s (60)					
Appleton	1835	57 (70)	48 (60)	34 (50)	25 (30)	15 (00)	2 (60)	
Arlington (Texas)	1876	91 (70)	45 (60)	8 (50)	4 (30)	1 (00)	0.7 (90)	

NORTH AMERICA

City	Date settled	Population (thousands)						
		Latest	Circa 1960	Circa 1950	Circa 1930	Circa 1900	Circa 1850	Circa 1800
Arlington (Virginia)	1700?	174 (70)	163 (60)	135 (50)	27 (30)	3s (00)		
Asheville	1794	58 (70)	60 (60)	53 (50)	50 (30)	15 (00)	1 (70)	
		72s (70)	69s (60)	58s (50)				
Atlanta	1837	497 (70)	487 (60)	331 (50)	270 (30)	90 (00)	3 (50)	
		1173s (70)	768s (60)	508s (50)				
Atlantic City	1790?	48 (70)	60 (60)	62 (50)	66 (30)	28 (00)	0.7 (60)	
		134s (70)	125s (60)	105s (50)				
Augusta	1735	60 (70)	71 (60)	72 (50)	60 (30)	39 (00)	12 (60)	2 (00)
		149s (70)	124s (60)	88s (50)				
Aurora	bef 1834	74 (70)	64 (60)	51 (50)	47 (30)	24 (00)	6 (60)	
		233s (70)	86s (60)					
Austin	1839	252 (70)	187 (60)	132 (50)	53 (30)	22 (00)	0.6 (50)	
		264s (70)	187s (60)	136s (50)				
Bakersfield	1868	70 (70)	57 (60)	35 (50)	26 (30)	5 (00)	0.8 (80)	
		176s (70)	142s (60)					
Baltimore	1730	906 (70)	939 (60)	950 (50)	805 (30)	509 (00)	169 (50)	27 (00)
		1580s (70)	1419s (60)	1162s (50)				
Baton Rouge	1719	166 (70)	152 (60)	126 (50)	31 (30)	11 (00)	4 (50)	4 (10)
		249s (70)	193s (60)	139s (50)				
Bay City	1831	49 (70)	54 (60)	53 (50)	47 (30)	28 (00)	2 (60)	
		78s (70)	73s (60)					
Beaumont	1835	116 (70)	119 (60)	94 (50)	58 (30)	9 (00)	0.1 (50?)	
		116s (70)	119s (60)	94s (50)				
Berkeley	1853	117 (70)	111 (60)	114 (50)	82 (30)	13 (00)	5 (90)	
Billings	1882	62 (70)	53 (60)	32 (50)	16 (30)	3 (00)	0.8 (90)	
		71s (70)	61s (60)					
Biloxi	1719	48 (70)	44 (60)	37 (50)	15 (30)	5 (00)	1 (70)	
Binghampton	1787	64 (70)	76 (60)	81 (50)	77 (30)	40 (00)	5 (50)	
		167s (70)	158s (60)	144s (50)				

NORTH AMERICA

City	Date settled	Population (thousands)						
		Latest	Circa 1960	Circa 1950	Circa 1930	Circa 1900	Circa 1850	Circa 1800
Birmingham	1871	301 (70)	341 (60)	326 (50)	260 (30)	38 (00)	3 (80)	
		558s (70)	521s (60)	445s (50)				
Bismarck	1872	35 (70)	28 (60)	19 (50)	11 (30)	3 (00)	2 (80)	
Bloomington	1815	43 (70)	31 (60)	28 (50)	18 (30)	6 (00)	1 (50)	
Boise City	1863	75 (70)	34 (60)	34 (50)	22 (30)	6 (00)	1 (70)	
Boston	1630	641 (70)	697 (60)	801 (50)	781 (30)	561 (00)	137 (50)	25 (00)
		2653s (70)	2413s (60)	2233s (50)				
Boulder	1859	67 (70)	38 (60)	20 (50)	11 (30)	6 (00)	0.3 (70)	
Bridgeport	1639	157 (70)	157 (60)	159 (50)	147 (30)	71 (00)	6 (50)	0.6 (10)
		413s (70)	367s (60)	237s (50)				
Bristol	1727	55 (70)	45 (60)	36 (50)	28 (30)	6 (00)	3 (50)	3 (00)
Brockton	1700	89 (70)	73 (60)	63 (50)	64 (30)	40 (00)	4 (50)	2 (30)
		149s (70)	111s (60)	92s (50)				
Brownsville	1846	53 (70)	48 (60)	36 (50)	22 (30)	6 (00)	3 (60)	
Buffalo	1803	463 (70)	533 (60)	580 (50)	573 (30)	352 (00)	42 (50)	2 (10)
		1087s (70)	1054s (60)	798s (50)				
Burbank	1887	89 (70)	90 (60)	79 (50)	17 (30)	0.3 (00e)		
Burlington	1773	39 (70)	36 (60)	33 (50)	25 (30)	19 (00)	6 (50)	0.8 (00)
Cambridge	1630	100 (70)	108 (60)	121 (50)	114 (30)	92 (00)	15 (50)	2 (00)
Camden	1681	103 (70)	117 (60)	125 (50)	119 (30)	76 (00)	9 (50)	1 (28)
Canton	1805	110 (70)	114 (60)	117 (50)	105 (30)	31 (00)	3 (50)	0.8 (10)
		244s (70)	214s (60)	174s (50)				
Casper	1888	39 (70)	39 (60)	24 (50)	17 (30)	0.9 (00)	0.5 (90)	
Cedar Rapids	1838	111 (70)	92 (60)	72 (50)	56 (30)	26 (00)	2 (60)	
		132s (70)	105s (60)	78s (50)				
Champaign	1854	57 (70)	50 (60)	40 (50)	20 (30)	9 (00)	2 (60)	
		100s (70)	78s (60)					
Charleston (South Carolina)	1670	67 (70)	66 (60)	70 (50)	62 (30)	56 (00)	43 (50)	19 (00)
		228s (70)	160s (60)	120s (50)				

NORTH AMERICA

City	Date settled	Population (thousands) Latest	Circa 1960	Circa 1950	Circa 1930	Circa 1900	Circa 1850	Circa 1800
Charleston (West Virginia)	1788	72 (70)	86 (60)	74 (50)	60 (30)	11 (00)	1 (50)	0.6 (00)
		158s (70)	169s (60)	131s (50)				
Charlotte	1748	241 (70)	202 (60)	134 (50)	83 (30)	18 (00)	1 (50)	0.1 (00)
		280s (70)	210s (60)	141s (50)				
Chattanooga	1815	119 (70)	130 (60)	131 (50)	120 (30)	30 (00)	3 (53)	
		224s (70)	205s (60)	168s (50)				
Cheyenne	1867	41 (70)	44 (60)	32 (50)	17 (30)	14 (00)	1 (70)	
Chicago	1803	3367 (70)	3550 (60)	3621 (50)	3376 (30)	1699 (00)	30 (50)	4 (40)
		6715s (70)	5962s (60)	4921s (50)				
Cincinnati	1789	453 (70)	503 (60)	504 (50)	451 (30)	326 (00)	115 (50)	0.7 (00)
		1111s (70)	994s (60)	813s (50)				
Cleveland	1796	751 (70)	876 (60)	915 (50)	900 (30)	382 (00)	17 (50)	0.5 (10)
		1960s (70)	1785s (60)	1384s (50)				
Colorado Springs	1859	135 (70)	70 (60)	45 (50)	33 (30)	21 (00)	4 (80)	
		205s (70)	100s (60)					
Columbia (Missouri)	1819	59 (70)	37 (60)	32 (50)	15 (30)	6 (00)	0.7 (50)	
Columbia (South Carolina)	1786	114 (70)	97 (60)	87 (50)	52 (30)	21 (00)	6 (50)	2 (16)
		242s (70)	163s (60)	121s (50)				
Columbus (Georgia)	1828	154 (70)	117 (60)	80 (50)	43 (30)	18 (00)	6 (50)	3 (40)
		209s (70)	158s (60)	118s (50)				
Columbus (Ohio)	1797	540 (70)	471 (60)	376 (50)	291 (30)	126 (00)	18 (50)	2 (30)
		790s (70)	617s (60)	438s (50)				
Corpus Christi	1839	205 (70)	168 (60)	108 (50)	28 (30)	5 (00)	0.5 (50)	
		213s (70)	177s (60)	123s (50)				
Dallas	1842	844 (70)	680 (60)	434 (50)	260 (30)	43 (00)	0.2 (50)	
		1339s (70)	932s (60)	539s (50)				
Davenport	1836	98 (70)	89 (60)	75 (50)	61 (30)	35 (00)	2 (50)	
		266s (70)	227s (60)	195s (50)				
Dayton	1796	244 (70)	262 (60)	244 (50)	201 (30)	85 (00)	11 (50)	0.4 (10)
		686s (70)	502s (60)	347s (50)				

NORTH AMERICA

City	Date settled	Population (thousands)						
		Latest	Circa 1960	Circa 1950	Circa 1930	Circa 1900	Circa 1850	Circa 1800
Dearborn	1795?	104 (70)	112 (60)	95 (50)	50 (30)	0.8 (00)	1 (50)	
Decatur	1829	90 (70)	78 (60)	66 (50)	58 (30)	21 (00)	4 (60)	
		100s (70)	90s (60)	74s (50)				
Denver	1858	515 (70)	494 (60)	416 (50)	288 (30)	134 (00)	5 (60)	
		1047s (70)	804s (60)	499s (50)				
Des Moines	1843	201 (70)	209 (60)	178 (50)	143 (30)	62 (00)	1 (50)	
		256s (70)	241s (60)	200s (50)				
Detroit	1701	1511 (70)	1670 (60)	1850 (50)	1569 (30)	286 (00)	21 (50)	0.8 (10)
		3971s (70)	3538s (60)	2659s (50)				
Downey	1873	88 (70)	83 (60)	9 (40)		1 (00e)		
Dubuque	1837	62 (70)	57 (60)	50 (50)	42 (30)	36 (00)	3 (50)	
		66s (70)	59s (60)					
Duluth	1852	101 (70)	107 (60)	105 (50)	101 (30)	53 (00)	0.1 (60)	
		138s (70)	145s (60)	143s (50)				
Durham	1852?	95 (70)	78 (60)	71 (50)	52 (30)	7 (00)	0.3 (70)	
		101s (70)	85s (60)	73s (50)				
East Los Angeles	1874?	105 (70)	104 (60)	42 (40)				
Elgin	1835	56 (70)	49 (60)	44 (50)	36 (30)	22 (00)	3 (60)	
Elizabeth	1664	113 (70)	108 (60)	113 (50)	115 (30)	52 (00)	6 (50)	3 (10)
El Paso	1827	322 (70)	277 (60)	130 (50)	102 (30)	16 (00)	0.7 (80)	
		337s (70)	277s (60)	137s (50)				
Erie	1795	129 (70)	138 (60)	131 (50)	116 (30)	53 (00)	6 (50)	0.1 (00)
		175s (70)	177s (60)	152s (50)				
Eugene	1851	76 (70)	51 (60)	36 (50)	19 (30)	3 (00)	0.9 (70)	
		139s (70)	96s (60)					
Evansville	1812	139 (70)	142 (60)	129 (50)	102 (30)	59 (00)	3 (50)	
		142s (70)	144s (60)	138s (50)				
Fall River	1656	97 (70)	100 (60)	112 (50)	115 (30)	105 (00)	12 (50)	1 (10)
		139s (70)	124s (60)	118s (50)				

NORTH AMERICA

City	Date settled	Population (thousands) Latest	Circa 1960	Circa 1950	Circa 1930	Circa 1900	Circa 1850	Circa 1800
Fargo	1871	53 (70)	47 (60)	38 (50)	29 (30)	10 (00)	3 (80)	
		85s (70)	73s (60)					
Fayetteville	1729?	54 (70)	47 (60)	35 (50)	13 (30)	5 (00)	5 (50)	4 (20)
Fitchburg	1730?	43 (70)	43 (60)	43 (50)	41 (30)	32 (00)	5 (50)	1 (00)
		78s (70)	72s (60)					
Flint	1819	193 (70)	197 (60)	163 (50)	156 (30)	13 (00)	2 (50)	
		330s (70)	278s (60)	198s (50)				
Fort Lauderdale	1838	140 (70)	84 (60)	36 (50)	9 (30)	0.1 (00)		
		614s (70)	320s (60)					
Fort Smith	1817	63 (70)	53 (60)	48 (50)	31 (30)	12 (00)	1 (50)	
		76s (70)	62s (60)	56s (50)				
Fort Wayne	bef 1685	178 (70)	162 (60)	134 (50)	115 (30)	45 (00)	4 (50)	2 (40)
		225s (70)	180s (60)	140s (50)				
Fort Worth	1843	393 (70)	356 (60)	279 (50)	163 (30)	27 (00)	7 (80)	
		677s (70)	503s (60)	316s (50)				
Fremont	1797	101 (70)	44 (60)	5 (50)	6 (40e)	2 (00e)		
Fresno	1872	166 (70)	134 (60)	92 (50)	53 (30)	12 (00)	1 (80)	
		263s (70)	213s (60)	131s (50)				
Gainesville	1830	65 (70)	30 (60)	27 (50)	10 (30)	4 (00)	0.3 (60)	
Galveston	1816	62 (70)	67 (60)	67 (50)	53 (30)	38 (00)	4 (50)	
		62s (70)	118s (60)	72s (50)				
Garden Grove	1876	123 (70)	84 (60)	4 (50)	2 (40?e)	0.1 (00e)		
Gary	1906	175 (70)	178 (60)	134 (50)	100 (30)	17 (10)		
Glendale	1886	133 (70)	119 (60)	96 (50)	63 (30)	3 (10)		
Grand Forks	1871	39 (70)	34 (60)	27 (50)	17 (30)	8 (00)	2 (80)	
Grand Rapids	1824?	198 (70)	177 (60)	177 (50)	169 (30)	88 (00)	3 (50)	
		353s (70)	294s (60)	227s (50)				
Great Falls	1883	60 (70)	55 (60)	39 (50)	29 (30)	15 (00)	4 (90)	
		71s (70)	58s (60)					

NORTH AMERICA

City	Date settled	Population (thousands)						
		Latest	Circa 1960	Circa 1950	Circa 1930	Circa 1900	Circa 1850	Circa 1800
Green Bay	bef 1669	88 (70)	63 (60)	53 (50)	37 (30)	19 (00)	2 (50)	
		129s (70)	97s (60)					
Greensboro	1749	144 (70)	120 (60)	74 (50)	54 (30)	10 (00)	0.5 (70)	0.4 (29)
		152s (70)	123s (60)	83s (50)				
Greenville	1797	61 (70)	66 (60)	58 (50)	29 (30)	12 (00)	1 (50)	0.2 (10)
		157s (70)	127s (60)					
Hamilton	1791	68 (70)	72 (60)	58 (50)	52 (30)	24 (00)	3 (50)	0.3 (10)
		91s (70)	90s (60)	63s (50)				
Hammond	1851	108 (70)	112 (60)	88 (50)	65 (30)	12 (00)	0.7 (80)	
Hampton	1610	121 (70)	89 (60)	6 (50)	6 (30)	3 (00)	1 (53?e)	
Harrisburg	1785	68 (70)	80 (60)	90 (50)	80 (30)	50 (00)	8 (50)	1 (00)
		241s (70)	210s (60)	170s (50)				
Hartford	1635	158 (70)	162 (60)	177 (50)	164 (30)	80 (00)	14 (50)	4 (10)
		465s (70)	382s (60)	301s (50)				
Hayward	1854	93 (70)	73 (60)	14 (50)	6 (30)	2 (00)	0.5 (70)	
Hialeah	1921	102 (70)	67 (60)	20 (50)	3 (30)			
High Point	1853	63 (70)	62 (60)	40 (50)	37 (30)	4 (00)	1 (80)	
		94s (70)	67s (60)					
Hollywood	1921	107 (70)	35 (60)	14 (50)	3 (30)			
Hot Springs	1807	36 (70)	28 (60)	29 (50)	20 (30)	10 (00)	0.2 (60)	
Houston	1836	1233 (70)	938 (60)	596 (50)	292 (30)	45 (00)	2 (50)	
		1678s (70)	1140s (60)	701s (50)				
Huntington	1871	74 (70)	84 (60)	86 (50)	76 (30)	12 (00)	3 (80)	
		168s (70)	166s (60)	156s (50)				
Huntington Beach	bef 1904	116 (70)	11 (60)	5 (50)	4 (30)	0.8 (10)		
Huntsville	1807	138 (70)	72 (60)	16 (50)	12 (30)	8 (00)	3 (50)	
		147s (70)	75s (60)					
Independence	1825	112 (70)	62 (60)	37 (50)	15 (30)	7 (00)	3 (60)	
Indianapolis	1820	745 (70)	476 (60)	427 (50)	364 (30)	169 (00)	8 (50)	3 (40)
		820s (70)	639s (60)	502s (50)				

NORTH AMERICA

City	Date settled	Population (thousands)						
		Latest	Circa 1960	Circa 1950	Circa 1930	Circa 1900	Circa 1850	Circa 1800
Inglewood	1887	90 (70)	63 (60)	46 (50)	19 (30)	2 (10)		
Irving	1902	97 (70)	46 (60)	3 (50)	0.7 (30)	0.4 (20)		
Jackson (Michigan)	1829	45 (70)	51 (60)	51 (50)	55 (30)	25 (00)	2 (50)	
		79s (70)	71s (60)					
Jackson (Mississippi)	bef 1800	154 (70)	144 (60)	98 (50)	48 (30)	8 (00)	3 (60)	
		190s (70)	147s (60)	100s (50)				
Jacksonville	1816	529 (70)	201 (60)	205 (50)	130 (30)	28 (00)	1 (50)	
		530s (70)	373s (60)	243s (50)				
Jersey City	1629?	261 (70)	276 (60)	299 (50)	317 (30)	206 (00)	7 (50)	1 (20)
Johnstown	1800	42 (70)	54 (60)	63 (50)	67 (30)	36 (00)	1 (50)	0.9 (40)
		96s (70)	96s (60)	93s (50)				
Joliet	1831	80 (70)	67 (60)	52 (50)	43 (30)	29 (00)	3 (50)	
		155s (70)	117s (60)					
Kalamazoo	1829	86 (70)	82 (60)	58 (50)	55 (30)	24 (00)	3 (50)	
		152s (70)	116s (60)	83s (50)				
Kansas City (Kansas)	1843	168 (70)	122 (60)	130 (50)	122 (30)	51 (00)	3 (80)	
Kansas City (Missouri)	1821	507 (70)	476 (60)	457 (50)	400 (30)	164 (00)	4 (60)	
		1102s (70)	921s (60)	698s (50)				
Kenosha	1835	79 (70)	68 (60)	54 (50)	50 (30)	12 (00)	3 (50)	0.3 (40)
		84s (70)	73s (60)					
Knoxville	1786	175 (70)	112 (60)	125 (50)	106 (30)	33 (00)	2 (50)	0.4 (00)
		191s (70)	173s (60)	148s (50)				
La Crosse	1841	51 (70)	48 (60)	48 (50)	40 (30)	29 (00)	4 (60)	
Lafayette (Indiana)	1825	45 (70)	42 (60)	36 (50)	26 (30)	18 (00)	6 (50)	
Lafayette (Louisiana)	bef 1804	69 (70)	40 (60)	34 (50)	15 (30)	3 (00)	2 (90)	
Lake Charles	1803?	78 (70)	63 (60)	41 (50)	16 (30)	7 (00)	0.8 (80)	
		88s (70)	89s (60)					
Lakewood	1872	93 (70)	19 (60)	4 (50)	1 (30)	0.5 (00)		
Lancaster	1709?	58 (70)	61 (60)	64 (50)	60 (30)	41 (00)	12 (50)	4 (00)
		117s (70)	94s (60)	76s (50)				

NORTH AMERICA

City	Date settled	Population (thousands)						
		Latest	Circa 1960	Circa 1950	Circa 1930	Circa 1900	Circa 1850	Circa 1800
Lansing	1843	132 (70)	108 (60)	92 (50)	78 (30)	16 (00)	1 (50)	
		230s (70)	169s (60)	134s (50)				
Laredo	1755	69 (70)	61 (60)	52 (50)	33 (30)	13 (00)	1 (60)	
		70s (70)	61s (60)					
Las Vegas	1905	126 (70)	64 (60)	25 (50)	5 (30)	2 (20)		
		237s (70)	89s (60)					
Lawrence	1655	67 (70)	71 (60)	81 (50)	85 (30)	63 (00)	8 (50)	
		200s (70)	167s (60)	112s (50)				
Lawton	1901	74 (70)	62 (60)	35 (50)	12 (30)	6 (07)		
		96s (70)	62s (60)					
Lewiston	1770	42 (70)	41 (60)	41 (50)	35 (30)	24 (00)	4 (50)	0.9 (00)
		65s (70)	65s (60)					
Lexington	1779	108 (70)	63 (60)	56 (50)	46 (30)	26 (00)	9 (60)	2 (00)
		160s (70)	112s (60)					
Lima	1831	54 (70)	51 (60)	50 (50)	42 (30)	22 (00)	0.8 (50)	
		70s (70)	63s (60)					
Lincoln	1864	150 (70)	129 (60)	99 (50)	76 (30)	40 (00)	13 (80)	
		153s (70)	138s (60)	100s (50)				
Little Rock	1820	132 (70)	108 (60)	102 (50)	82 (30)	38 (00)	2 (50)	
		223s (70)	185s (60)	154s (50)				
Livonia	1832	110 (70)	67 (60)	18 (50)	3s (30)	1s (00)		
Long Beach	1881	359 (70)	344 (60)	251 (50)	142 (30)	2 (00)		
Lorain	1807	78 (70)	69 (60)	51 (50)	45 (30)	16 (00)	2 (80)	
		192s (70)	143s (60)					
Los Angeles	1781	2816 (70)	2479 (60)	1970 (50)	1238 (30)	102 (00)	2 (50)	0.3 (00)
		8351s (70)	6489s (60)	3997s (50)				
Louisville	1778	361 (70)	391 (60)	369 (50)	308 (30)	205 (00)	43 (50)	0.4 (00)
		739s (70)	607s (60)	473s (50)				
Lowell	1653	94 (70)	92 (60)	97 (50)	100 (30)	95 (00)	33 (50)	6 (30)
		183s (70)	119s (60)	107s (50)				

NORTH AMERICA

City	Date settled	Population (thousands)						
		Latest	Circa 1960	Circa 1950	Circa 1930	Circa 1900	Circa 1850	Circa 1800
Lubbock	1891	149 (70)	129 (60)	72 (50)	21 (30)	2 (10)		
		150s (70)	129s (60)					
Lynchburg	1787?	54 (70)	55 (60)	48 (50)	41 (30)	19 (00)	8 (50)	5 (30)
		71s (70)	59s (60)					
Lynn	1629	90 (70)	94 (60)	100 (50)	102 (30)	69 (00)	14 (50)	3 (00)
Macon	1806	122 (70)	70 (60)	70 (50)	54 (30)	23 (00)	6 (50)	4 (40)
		128s (70)	114s (60)	93s (50)				
Madison	1837	173 (70)	127 (60)	96 (50)	58 (30)	19 (00)	2 (50)	
		205s (70)	158s (60)	110s (50)				
Manchester	1722	88 (70)	88 (60)	83 (50)	77 (30)	57 (00)	14 (50)	0.6 (00)
		95s (70)	92s (60)	85s (50)				
Mansfield	1808?	55 (70)	47 (60)	44 (50)	34 (30)	18 (00)	4 (50)	
Memphis	1819	624 (70)	498 (60)	396 (50)	253 (30)	102 (00)	9 (50)	0.7 (30)
		664s (70)	545s (60)	406s (50)				
Meriden	1661	56 (70)	52 (60)	44 (50)	38 (30)	24 (00)	4 (50)	
		98s (70)	52s (60)					
Metairie	bef 1892	136 (70)	73 (60)	3 (40)				
Miami	1870	335 (70)	292 (60)	249 (50)	111 (30)	2 (00)		
		1220s (70)	853s (60)	459s (50)				
Miami Beach	1913	87 (70)	63 (60)	46 (50)	6 (30)	0.6 (20)		
Milwaukee	1818	717 (70)	741 (60)	637 (50)	578 (30)	285 (00)	20 (50)	2 (40)
		1252s (70)	1150s (60)	829s (50)				
Minneapolis	1847	434 (70)	483 (60)	522 (50)	464 (30)	203 (00)	3 (60)	
		1704s (70)	1377s (60)	985s (50)				
Mobile	1710	190 (70)	195 (60)	129 (50)	68 (30)	38 (00)	21 (50)	1 (18)
		258s (70)	260s (60)	183s (50)				
Modesto	1870	62 (70)	37 (60)	17 (50)	14 (30)	2 (00)	2 (80)	
Monroe	1785	56 (70)	52 (60)	39 (50)	26 (30)	5 (00)	0.4 (50)	
		91s (70)	81s (60)					

NORTH AMERICA

City	Date settled	Population (thousands)						
		Latest	Circa 1960	Circa 1950	Circa 1930	Circa 1900	Circa 1850	Circa 1800
Montgomery	1817	133 (70)	134 (60)	107 (50)	66 (30)	30 (00)	5 (50)	2 (40)
		139s (70)	143s (60)	109s (50)				
Muncie	1827	69 (70)	69 (60)	58 (50)	47 (30)	21 (00)	0.7 (50)	
		90s (70)	78s (60)					
Muskegon	1812	45 (70)	46 (60)	48 (50)	41 (30)	21 (00)	0.5 (50)	
		106s (70)	95s (60)	85s (50)				
Nashua	1656	56 (70)	39 (60)	35 (50)	31 (30)	24 (00)	6 (50)	0.9 (00)
Nashville	1780	448 (70)	171 (60)	174 (50)	154 (30)	81 (00)	10 (50)	0.3 (00)
		448s (70)	347s (60)	259s (50)				
Newark	1666	382 (70)	405 (60)	439 (50)	442 (30)	246 (00)	39 (50)	7 (10)
New Bedford	1640	102 (70)	102 (60)	109 (50)	113 (30)	62 (00)	16 (50)	4 (00)
		134s (70)	127s (60)	125s (50)				
New Britain	1686	83 (70)	82 (60)	74 (50)	68 (30)	26 (00)	3 (50)	0.9 (00)
		131s (70)	100s (60)	123s (50)				
New Haven	1638	138 (70)	152 (60)	164 (50)	163 (30)	108 (00)	20 (50)	4 (00)
		348s (70)	279s (60)	245s (50)				
New Orleans	1718	593 (70)	628 (60)	570 (50)	459 (30)	287 (00)	116 (50)	8 (97)
		962s (70)	845s (60)	660s (50)				
Newport	1639	35 (70)	47 (60)	38 (50)	28 (30)	22 (00)	10 (50)	7 (00)
Newport News	1621	138 (70)	114 (60)	42 (50)	34 (30)	20 (00)	4 (90)	
		268s (70)	209s (60)					
Newton	1639	91 (70)	92 (60)	82 (50)	65 (30)	34 (00)	5 (50)	1 (00)
New York	1624	7895 (70)	7782 (60)	7892 (50)	6930 (30)	3437 (00)	516 (50)	60 (00)
		16,207s (70)	14,115s (60)	12,296s (50)				
Niagara Falls	1807	86 (70)	102 (60)	91 (50)	75 (30)	19 (00)	3 (70)	0.5 (20)
Norfolk	1682	308 (70)	305 (60)	214 (50)	130 (30)	47 (00)	14 (50)	7 (00)
		668s (70)	508s (60)	385s (50)				
Norwalk (California)	1874	92 (70)	89 (60)	4 (40)				
Norwalk (Connecticut)	1649	79 (70)	68 (60)	49 (50)	36 (30)	6 (00)	5 (50)	
		107s (70)	82s (60)	55s (50)				

Figure 34. Skyscrapers of midtown New York, the largest city and the largest urbanized area in North America, as seen from the East River. The United Nations Secretariat Building is in the foreground. In the background, from left to right, are the Empire State, Chrysler, and Pan Am Buildings. (Credit: New York Convention and Visitors Bureau, Inc.)

NORTH AMERICA

City	Date settled	Population (thousands)						
		Latest	Circa 1960	Circa 1950	Circa 1930	Circa 1900	Circa 1850	Circa 1800
Norwich	1659	41 (70)	39 (60)	23 (50)	23 (30)	17 (00)	6 (50)	3 (00)
Oakland	1848	362 (70)	368 (60)	385 (50)	284 (30)	67 (00)	2 (60)	
Odessa	1881	78 (70)	80 (60)	29 (50)	2 (30)			
		82s (70)	84s (60)					
Ogden	1845?	69 (70)	70 (60)	57 (50)	40 (30)	16 (00)	1 (60)	
		150s (70)	122s (60)					
Oklahoma City	1889	366 (70)	324 (60)	244 (50)	185 (30)	10 (00)	4 (90)	
		580s (70)	429s (60)	275s (50)				
Omaha	1854	347 (70)	302 (60)	251 (50)	214 (30)	103 (00)	2 (60)	
		492s (70)	392s (60)	310s (50)				
Orlando	1837	99 (70)	88 (60)	52 (50)	27 (30)	2 (00)		
		305s (70)	201s (60)	73s (50)				
Oshkosh	1836	53 (70)	45 (60)	41 (50)	40 (30)	28 (00)	6 (60)	
Oxnard	1898	71 (70)	40 (60)	22 (50)	6 (30)	3 (10)		
Parma	1826?	100 (70)	83 (60)	29 (50)	14 (30)	1 (00)	1 (50)	
Pasadena	1874	113 (70)	116 (60)	105 (50)	76 (30)	9 (00)	0.4 (80)	
Paterson	1679	145 (70)	144 (60)	139 (50)	139 (30)	105 (00)	11 (50)	0.3 (10)
Pensacola	1698	60 (70)	57 (60)	43 (50)	32 (30)	18 (00)	2 (50)	4 (22e)
		167s (70)	128s (60)					
Peoria	1691?	127 (70)	103 (60)	112 (50)	105 (30)	56 (00)	5 (50)	1 (40)
		247s (70)	181s (60)	155s (50)				
Petersburg	1646	36 (70)	37 (60)	35 (50)	29 (30)	22 (00)	14 (50)	4 (00)
Philadelphia	1677?	1949 (70)	2003 (60)	2072 (50)	1951 (30)	1294 (00)	121 (50)	41 (00)
		4021s (70)	3635s (60)	2922s (50)			340s (50)	69s (00)
Phoenix	1867	582 (70)	439 (60)	107 (50)	48 (30)	6 (00)	2 (80)	
		863s (70)	552s (60)	216s (50)				
Pittsburgh	1758?	520 (70)	604 (60)	677 (50)	670 (30)	322 (00)	47 (50)	2 (00)
		1846s (70)	1804s (60)	1533s (50)				
Pittsfield	1752	57 (70)	58 (60)	53 (50)	50 (30)	22 (00)	6 (50)	2 (00)
		63s (70)	62s (60)					

NORTH AMERICA

City	Date settled	Population (thousands)						
		Latest	Circa 1960	Circa 1950	Circa 1930	Circa 1900	Circa 1850	Circa 1800
Pocatello	1882	40 (70)	29 (60)	26 (50)	16 (30)	4 (00)		
Pomona	1875	17 (70)	67 (60)	35 (50)	21 (30)	6 (00)	4 (90)	
		[1] (70)	187s (60)					
Port Arthur	1895	57 (70)	67 (60)	58 (50)	51 (30)	0.9 (00)		
		116s (70)	116s (60)	82s (50)				
Portland (Maine)	1716	65 (70)	73 (60)	78 (50)	71 (30)	50 (00)	21 (50)	4 (00)
		107s (70)	112s (60)	113s (50)				
Portland (Oregon)	1845	383 (70)	373 (60)	374 (50)	302 (30)	90 (00)	0.8 (50)	
		825s (70)	652s (60)	513s (50)				
Portsmouth	1752	111 (70)	115 (60)	80 (50)	46 (30)	17 (00)	9 (50)	2 (20)
Providence	1636	179 (70)	207 (60)	249 (50)	253 (30)	176 (00)	42 (50)	8 (00)
		795s (70)	660s (60)	583s (50)				
Provo	1849	53 (70)	36 (60)	29 (50)	15 (30)	6 (00)	2 (60)	
		104s (70)	61s (60)					
Pueblo	1842	97 (70)	91 (60)	64 (50)	50 (30)	28 (00)	3 (80)	
		103s (70)	103s (60)	73s (50)				
Quincy	1625	88 (70)	87 (60)	84 (50)	72 (30)	24 (00)	5 (50)	1 (00)
Racine	1834	95 (70)	89 (60)	71 (50)	68 (30)	29 (00)	5 (50)	
		117s (70)	96s (60)	77s (50)				
Raleigh	bef 1771	122 (70)	94 (60)	66 (50)	37 (30)	14 (00)	5 (50)	0.7 (00)
		152s (70)	94s (60)	69s (50)				
Rapid City	1876	44 (70)	42 (60)	25 (50)	10 (30)	1 (00)	0.3 (80)	
Reading	1733	88 (70)	98 (60)	109 (50)	111 (30)	79 (00)	16 (50)	2 (00)
		168s (70)	160s (60)	155s (50)				
Reno	1868	73 (70)	51 (60)	32 (50)	19 (30)	4 (00)	1 (70)	
		100s (70)	70s (60)					

[1] Urbanized area population for 1970 included in Los Angeles urbanized area.

NORTH AMERICA

City	Date settled	Population (thousands) Latest	Circa 1960	Circa 1950	Circa 1930	Circa 1900	Circa 1850	Circa 1800
Richmond	1737	250 (70)	220 (60)	230 (50)	183 (30)	85 (00)	28 (50)	6 (00)
		417s (70)	333s (60)	258s (50)				
Riverside	1870	140 (70)	84 (60)	47 (50)	30 (30)	8 (00)	5 (90)	
		584s (70)	[1] (60)	[1] (50)				
Roanoke	1834	92 (70)	97 (60)	92 (50)	69 (30)	21 (00)	0.7 (80)	
		157s (70)	125s (60)	107s (50)				
Rochester	1812	296 (70)	319 (60)	332 (50)	328 (30)	163 (00)	36 (50)	9 (30)
		601s (70)	493s (60)	409s (50)				
Rockford	1834	147 (70)	127 (60)	93 (50)	86 (30)	31 (00)	2 (50)	
		206s (70)	172s (60)	122s (50)				
Sacramento	1839	254 (70)	192 (60)	138 (50)	94 (30)	29 (00)	7 (50)	
		634s (70)	452s (60)	212s (50)				
Saginaw	1816	92 (70)	98 (60)	93 (50)	81 (30)	42 (00)	1 (50)	
		148s (70)	129s (60)	106s (50)				
Saint Augustine	1565	12 (70)	15 (60)	14 (50)	12 (30)	4 (00)	2 (50)	5 (00e)
Saint Joseph	1826	73 (70)	80 (60)	79 (50)	81 (30)	103 (00)	9 (60)	
		77s (70)	81s (60)	82s (50)				
Saint Louis	1764	622 (70)	750 (60)	857 (50)	822 (30)	575 (00)	78 (50)	2 (10)
		1883s (70)	1668s (60)	1400s (50)				
Saint Paul	1838	310 (70)	313 (60)	311 (50)	272 (30)	163 (00)	1 (50)	
Saint Petersburg	1856	216 (70)	181 (60)	97 (50)	40 (30)	2 (00)	0.3 (90)	
		495s (70)	325s (60)	115s (50)				
Salem (Massachusetts)	1626	41 (70)	39 (60)	42 (50)	43 (30)	36 (00)	20 (50)	9 (00)
Salem (Oregon)	1841	68 (70)	49 (60)	43 (50)	26 (30)	4 (00)	1 (70)	
Salinas	1856	59 (70)	29 (60)	14 (50)	10 (30)	3 (00)	0.6 (70)	
Salt Lake City	1847	176 (70)	189 (60)	182 (50)	140 (30)	54 (00)	10 (53)	
		479s (70)	349s (60)	227s (50)				

[1] Urbanized area population for 1960 and 1950 included in San Bernardino urbanized area.

NORTH AMERICA

City	Date settled	Population (thousands) Latest	Circa 1960	Circa 1950	Circa 1930	Circa 1900	Circa 1850	Circa 1800
San Antonio	1718	654 (70)	588 (60)	408 (50)	232 (30)	53 (00)	3 (50)	2 (10?e)
		773s (70)	642s (60)	450s (50)				
San Bernardino	1851	104 (70)	92 (60)	63 (50)	37 (30)	6 (00)	2 (80)	
		[1] (70)	378s (60)	136s (50)				
San Diego	1769	697 (70)	573 (60)	334 (50)	148 (30)	18 (00)	3 (52)	2 (02)
		1198s (70)	836s (60)	433s (50)				
San Francisco	1776	716 (70)	740 (60)	775 (50)	634 (30)	343 (00)	35 (52)	1 (00?e)
		2988s (70)	2395s (60)	2022s (50)				
San Jose	1777	446 (70)	204 (60)	95 (50)	58 (30)	21 (00)	3 (52)	0.2 (00e)
		1025s (70)	603s (60)	176s (50)				
Santa Ana	1869	157 (70)	100 (60)	46 (50)	30 (30)	5 (00)	0.7 (80)	
Santa Barbara	1782	70 (70)	59 (60)	45 (50)	34 (30)	7 (00)	3 (80)	
		130s (70)	73s (60)					
Santa Fe	1609	41 (70)	33 (60)	28 (50)	11 (30)	6 (00)	5 (50e)	5 (99e)
Santa Monica	1875	88 (70)	83 (60)	72 (50)	37 (30)	3 (00)	0.4 (80)	
Santa Rosa	1833	50 (70)	31 (60)	18 (50)	11 (30)	7 (00)	0.4 (60)	
Savannah	1733	118 (70)	149 (60)	120 (50)	85 (30)	54 (00)	15 (50)	5 (00)
		164s (70)	170s (60)	128s (50)				
Scranton	1771?	104 (70)	111 (60)	126 (50)	143 (30)	102 (00)	2 (50)	
		204s (70)	211s (60)	236s (50)				
Seaside	1900	36 (70)	19 (60)	10 (50)	2 (40)			
Seattle	1851	531 (70)	557 (60)	468 (50)	366 (30)	81 (00)	1 (70)	
		1238s (70)	864s (60)	622s (50)				
Shreveport	1837	182 (70)	164 (60)	127 (50)	77 (30)	16 (00)	2 (50)	
		235s (70)	209s (60)	150s (50)				
Sioux City	1848	86 (70)	89 (60)	84 (50)	79 (30)	33 (00)	3 (70)	
		96s (70)	98s (60)	90s (50)				

[1] Urbanized area population for 1970 included in Riverside urbanized area.

NORTH AMERICA

City	Date settled	Population (thousands) Latest	Circa 1960	Circa 1950	Circa 1930	Circa 1900	Circa 1850	Circa 1800
Sioux Falls	1865	72 (70)	65 (60)	53 (50)	33 (30)	10 (00)	2 (80)	
		75s (70)	67s (60)					
Somerville	1630	89 (70)	95 (60)	102 (50)	104 (30)	62 (00)	4 (50)	
South Bend	1820	126 (70)	132 (60)	116 (50)	104 (30)	36 (00)	2 (50)	
		289s (70)	219s (60)	168s (50)				
Spokane	1872	171 (70)	182 (60)	162 (50)	116 (30)	37 (00)	0.3 (80)	
		230s (70)	227s (60)	176s (50)				
Springfield (Illinois)	1818	92 (70)	83 (60)	82 (50)	72 (30)	34 (00)	5 (50)	3 (40)
		121s (70)	111s (60)	97s (50)				
Springfield (Massachusetts)	1636	164 (70)	174 (60)	162 (50)	150 (30)	62 (00)	12 (50)	2 (00)
		514s (70)	459s (60)	357s (50)				
Springfield (Missouri)	1830	120 (70)	96 (60)	67 (50)	58 (30)	23 (00)	0.4 (50)	
		121s (70)	97s (60)	76s (50)				
Springfield (Ohio)	1799	82 (70)	83 (60)	79 (50)	69 (30)	38 (00)	5 (50)	2 (20)
		94s (70)	90s (60)	82s (50)				
Stamford	1641	109 (70)	93 (60)	74 (50)	46 (30)	16 (00)	5 (50)	4 (00)
		185s (70)	167s (60)	118s (50)				
Steubenville	1786	31 (70)	32 (60)	36 (50)	35 (30)	14 (00)	6 (50)	3 (30)
		85s (70)	82s (60)					
Stockton	1844	108 (70)	86 (60)	71 (50)	48 (30)	18 (00)	3 (52)	
		160s (70)	142s (60)	113s (50)				
Sunnyvale	bef 1901	95 (70)	53 (60)	10 (50)	3 (30)	2 (20)		
Syracuse	1797	197 (70)	216 (60)	221 (50)	209 (30)	108 (00)	22 (50)	3 (30)
		376s (70)	333s (60)	265s (50)				
Tacoma	1864?	155 (70)	148 (60)	144 (50)	107 (30)	38 (00)	1 (80)	
		333s (70)	215s (60)	168s (50)				
Tallahassee	bef 1539	72 (70)	48 (60)	27 (50)	11 (30)	3 (00)	2 (60)	2 (40)
Tampa	1823	278 (70)	275 (60)	125 (50)	101 (30)	16 (00)	1 (50)	
		369s (70)	302s (60)	179s (50)				

NORTH AMERICA

City	Date settled	Population (thousands)						
		Latest	Circa 1960	Circa 1950	Circa 1930	Circa 1900	Circa 1850	Circa 1800
Terre Haute	1811	70 (70)	72 (60)	64 (50)	63 (30)	37 (00)	4 (50)	
		81s (70)	81s (60)	78s (50)				
Toledo	1817	384 (70)	318 (60)	304 (50)	291 (30)	132 (00)	4 (50)	1 (40)
		488s (70)	438s (60)	364s (60)				
Topeka	1854	125 (70)	119 (60)	79 (50)	64 (30)	34 (00)	0.8 (60)	
		132s (70)	119s (60)	89s (50)				
Torrance	1911	135 (70)	101 (60)	22 (50)	7 (30)			
Trenton	1679	105 (70)	114 (60)	128 (50)	123 (30)	73 (00)	6 (50)	3 (10)
		274s (70)	242s (60)	189s (50)				
Tucson	1776	263 (70)	213 (60)	45 (50)	33 (30)	8 (00)	3 (70)	
		294s (70)	227s (60)					
Tulsa	1832?	332 (70)	262 (60)	183 (50)	141 (30)	1 (00)	0.3 (57)	
		371s (70)	299s (60)	206s (50)				
Tuscaloosa	1816	66 (70)	63 (60)	46 (50)	21 (30)	5 (00)	4 (60)	2 (40)
		86s (70)	77s (60)					
Utica	1786?	92 (70)	100 (60)	102 (50)	102 (30)	56 (00)	18 (50)	3 (10)
		180s (70)	188s (60)	117s (50)				
Virginia Beach	1887	172 (70)	8 (60)	5 (50)	2 (30)	0.2 (00e)		
Waco	1849	95 (70)	98 (60)	85 (50)	53 (30)	21 (00)	3 (70)	
		119s (70)	116s (60)	93s (50)				
Warren	1837?	179 (70)	89 (60)	0.7 (50)	0.5 (30)	0.3 (00)	0.7 (50)	
*Washington	1665?	757 (70)	764 (60)	802 (50)	487 (30)	279 (00)	40 (50)	3 (00)
		2481s (70)	1808s (60)	1287s (50)				
Waterbury	1674	108 (70)	107 (60)	104 (50)	100 (30)	46 (00)	5 (50)	3 (00)
		157s (70)	142s (60)	132s (50)				
Waterloo	1845	76 (70)	72 (60)	65 (50)	46 (30)	13 (00)	4 (70)	
		113s (70)	103s (60)	84s (50)				
West Palm Beach	1880	57 (70)	56 (60)	43 (50)	27 (30)	0.6 (00)		
		288s (70)	173s (60)					

NORTH AMERICA

City	Date settled	Population (thousands) Latest	Circa 1960	Circa 1950	Circa 1930	Circa 1900	Circa 1850	Circa 1800
Wheeling	1769	48 (70)	53 (60)	59 (50)	62 (30)	39 (00)	11 (50)	0.5 (00e)
		93s (70)	101s (60)	107s (50)				
Wichita	1864	277 (70)	255 (60)	168 (50)	111 (30)	25 (00)	5 (80)	
		302s (70)	292s (60)	194s (50)				
Wichita Falls	1876	98 (70)	102 (60)	68 (50)	44 (30)	2 (00)	2 (90)	
		98s (70)	102s (60)					
Wilkes-Barre	1769	59 (70)	64 (60)	77 (50)	87 (30)	52 (00)	3 (50)	0.8 (00)
		223s (70)	234s (60)	272s (50)				
Williamsburg	1633	9 (70)	7 (60)	7 (50)	4 (30)	2 (00)	0.9 (50)	1 (82)
Wilmington (Delaware)	1638	80 (70)	96 (60)	110 (50)	107 (30)	77 (00)	14 (50)	4 (10)
		371s (70)	284s (60)	187s (50)				
Wilmington (North Carolina)	1732	46 (70)	44 (60)	45 (50)	32 (30)	21 (00)	7 (50)	2 (00)
Winston-Salem	1766	133 (70)	111 (60)	88 (50)	75 (30)	14 (00)	0.4 (70)	0.2 (00)
		143s (70)	128s (60)	92s (50)				
Woodbridge	1665	99 (70)	79 (60)	36 (50)	25 (30)	8 (00)	5 (50)	4 (10)
Worcester	1713	177 (70)	187 (60)	203 (50)	195 (30)	118 (00)	17 (50)	2 (00)
		247s (70)	225s (60)	219s (50)				
Yonkers	bef 1639	204 (70)	191 (60)	153 (50)	135 (30)	48 (00)	4 (50)	1 (00)
York	1741	50 (70)	55 (60)	60 (50)	55 (30)	34 (00)	7 (50)	3 (00)
		123s (70)	101s (60)	79s (50)				
Youngstown	1797	140 (70)	167 (60)	168 (50)	170 (30)	45 (00)	3 (50)	1 (10)
		396s (70)	373s (60)	298s (50)				
VIRGIN ISLANDS (USA)								
*Charlotte Amalie	1666	12 (70)	13 (60)	11 (50)	7 (30)	9 (01)	11 (50)	11 (35)

OCEANIA

City	Date settled	Population (thousands) Latest	Circa 1960	Circa 1950	Circa 1930	Circa 1900	Circa 1850	Circa 1800
AUSTRALIA								
Adelaide	1836	809s (71)	588s (61)	382s (47)	313s (33)	163s (01)	18 (61)	7 (46)
Brisbane	1824	817s (71)	622s (61)	402s (47)	300s (33)	119s (01)	6 (61)	
*Canberra	1824?	141s (71)	56s (61)	15s (47)	7 (33)			
Geelong	1837	115s (71)	88s (61)	45s (47)	39s (33)	23s (01)	17 (61)	
Hobart	1804	130s (71)	116s (61)	77s (47)	60s (33)	34s (01)	19 (61)	
Melbourne	1835	2389s (71)	1912s (61)	1226s (47)	992s (33)	502s (01)	140s (61)	
Newcastle	1804	250s (71)	209s (61)	127s (47)	104s (33)	55s (01)	4s (61)	
Perth	1829	640s (71)	420s (61)	273s (47)	207s (33)	36 (01)	3 (61)	
Sydney	1788	2717s (71)	2183s (61)	1484s (47)	1235s (33)	488s (01)	93s (61)	3 (00)
Wollongong	1815	186s (71)[1]	132s (61)[1]	18 (47)	11 (33)	4 (01)	1 (61)	
FIJI								
*Suva	bef 1877	54 (66)	37 (56)	11 (46)	13 (31e)			
		80s (66)		24s (46)				
FRENCH POLYNESIA								
*Papeete	1840?	23 (71)	20 (62)	12 (46)	7 (31)	4 (97)	3 (65)	
		44s (71)	28s (62)					
(HAWAII), USA								
Hilo	bef 1778	26 (70)	26 (60)	27 (50)	19 (30)	7 (10)	4 (72)	
*Honolulu	bef 1794	325 (70)	294 (60)	248 (50)	138 (30)	39 (00)	14 (66)	
		442s (70)	351s (60)					
NEW CALEDONIA								
*Noumea	1854	42 (69)	22 (56)	10 (46)	10 (26)	7 (98)		

[1] For Greater Wollongong, established 1947; comparable populations: 63s (1947), 43s (1933), 29s (1911).

Figure 35. Aerial view of Sydney, the largest city and the largest urbanized area in Oceania, showing Sydney Harbour Bridge and (at left) the unconventional Opera House. (Credit: Australian Information Service.)

Figure 36. Buildings of the Ministries of War and State, with Plaza Colon in the foreground, at Buenos Aires, the largest urbanized area in South America. (Credit: Government of Argentina Ministry of Interior.)

OCEANIA

City	Date settled	Population (thousands) Latest	Circa 1960	Circa 1950	Circa 1930	Circa 1900	Circa 1850	Circa 1800
NEW ZEALAND								
Auckland	1841	152 (71)	144 (61)	127 (51)	88 (26)	34 (01)	5 (47)	
		650s (71)	448s (61)	329s (51)	193s (26)	67s (01)		
Christchurch	1850	166 (71)	152 (61)	124 (51)	83 (26)	18 (01)	1 (58)	
		276s (71)	221s (61)	174s (51)	119s (26)	57s (01)		
Dunedin	1845	82 (71)	73 (61)	69 (51)	68 (26)	25 (01)	0.4 (49)	
		111s (71)	105s (61)	95s (51)	85s (26)	52s (01)		
*Wellington	1840	136 (71)	124 (61)	120 (51)	99 (26)	44 (01)	3 (48)	
		137s (71)	151s (61)	133s (51)	122s (26)	49s (01)		
PAPUA								
*Port Moresby	1883	56 (70)	14 (56)	1 (49-50e)	2 (30?e)			
WESTERN SAMOA								
*Apia	bef 1850	25s (66)	22s (61)	12s (51)	5 (36)	1 (00?e)		

SOUTH AMERICA

City	Date settled	Population (thousands) Latest	Circa 1960	Circa 1950	Circa 1930	Circa 1900	Circa 1850	Circa 1800
ARGENTINA								
Almirante Brown	1874	245 (70)	137 (60)	36 (47)	11 (14)	4 (95)		
Avellaneda	1818	333 (70)	327 (60)	274 (47)	46 (14)	10 (95)	6 (69)	
Bahia Blanca	1828	151 (68e)	121 (60)	113 (47)	44 (14)	9 (95)	1 (69)	
*Buenos Aires	1580	2972 (70)	2967 (60)	2981 (47)	1561 (14)	663 (95)	178 (69)	40 (97e)
		8353s (70)	6739s (60)	4722s (47)	2034s (14)	781s (95)		
Cordoba	1573	799 (70)	586 (60)	370 (47)	105 (14)	48 (95)	29 (69)	
Lanus		450 (70)	375 (60)	244 (47)	33 (14)			
La Plata	1800	408 (70)	337 (60)	207 (47)	90 (14)	45 (95)	0.6 (69)	

SOUTH AMERICA

City	Date settled	Population (thousands) Latest	Circa 1960	Circa 1950	Circa 1930	Circa 1900	Circa 1850	Circa 1800
Lomas de Zamora	1864	411 (70)	272 (60)	126 (47)	22 (14)	9 (95)		
Mar del Plata	1862	317 (70)	211 (60)	115 (47)	28 (14)	5 (95)		
Mendoza	1561	119 (70)	109 (60)	97 (47)	59 (14)	29 (95)	8 (69)	
Merlo	1730	189 (70)	100 (60)	8 (47)	4 (14)	2 (95)		
Parana	1730	186 (68e)	125 (60)	84 (47)	36 (14)	24 (95)	10 (69)	
Quilmes	1670	355 (70)	318 (60)	115 (47)	19 (14)	4 (95)	2 (69)	
Rosario	1725	761 (68e)	591 (60)	468 (47)	223 (14)	94 (95)	23 (69)	
Salta	1582	180 (70e)	117 (60)	67 (47)	28 (14)	17 (95)	12 (69)	
San Isidro	1719	250 (70)	188 (60)	90 (47)	9 (14)	5 (95)	0.9 (69)	
San Justo	1784	659 (70)	402 (60)	89 (47)	2 (14)	2 (95)	1 (69)	
San Martin		361 (70)	279 (60)	270 (47)	12 (14)	3 (95)	1 (69)	
San Miguel	1862	315 (70)	167 (60)	11 (47)	6 (14)	2 (95)		
Santa Fe	1573	279 (68e)	209 (60)	169 (47)	60 (14)	22 (95)	11 (69)	
Seis de Septiembre	1600	486 (70)	342 (60)	110 (47)	11 (14)	4 (95)	1 (69)	
Tres de Febrero	bef 1851	313 (70)	263 (60)	15 (47e)	6 (14)			
Tucuman	1685	306 (70)	272 (60)	194 (47)	91 (14)	34 (95)	17 (69)	5 (00?e)
Vicente Lopez	1878	285 (70)	248 (60)	150 (47)	12 (14)			
BOLIVIA								
Cochabamba	1574	150 (70e)	87 (57e)	81 (50)	36 (29e)	22 (00)	41 (58)	25 (35e)
*La Paz	1548	562 (70e)	339 (57e)	321 (50)	147 (29e)	55 (00)	57 (45?)	30 (00?e)
*Sucre	bef 1538	85 (70e)	54 (57e)	40 (50)	35 (29e)	21 (00)	24 (58)	18 (26e)
BRAZIL								
Aracaju	1855	182 (70)	113 (60)	68 (50)	37 (20)	16 (90)	6 (72)	
		187s (70)	116s (60)	78s (50)	37s (20)	21s (00)	10s (72)	
Belem	1616	573 (70)	360 (60)	225 (50)	145 (20)		10 (40e)	12 (00?e)
		643s (70)	402s (60)	255s (50)	236s (20)	97s (00)	62s (72)	
Belo Horizonte	1701	1126 (70)	643 (60)	339 (50)	56 (20)		8 (64e)	
		1255s (70)	693s (60)	353s (50)	56s (20)	13s (00)		

SOUTH AMERICA

City	Date settled	Population (thousands) Latest	Circa 1960	Circa 1950	Circa 1930	Circa 1900	Circa 1850	Circa 1800
*Brasilia	1957	277 (70)	90 (60)					
		546s (70)	142s (60)					
Campina Grande	1697	165 (70)	116 (60)	72 (50)	42 (20)	21 (90)	15 (72)	
		193s (70)	207s (60)	173s (50)	71s (20)	38s (00)	15s (72)	
Campinas	1773	334 (70)	180 (60)	99 (50)		20 (90)	6 (50?e)	
		382s (70)	219s (60)	137s (50)	116s (20)	68s (00)	31s (72)	
Campos	1634	155 (70)	91 (60)	62 (50)	48 (20)	23 (90)	20 (72)	
		321s (70)	292s (60)	238s (50)	176s (20)	91s (00)	89s (72)	
Curitiba	1654	498 (70)	345 (60)	138 (50)	57 (20)	23 (90)	13 (72)	
		624s (70)	361s (60)	181s (50)	79s (20)	50s (00)	13s (72)	
Duque de Caxias	1886?	259 (70)	173 (60)	74 (50)				
		435s (70)	244s (60)	92s (50)				
Feira de Santana	bef 1696	129 (70)	62 (60)	27 (50)	14 (20)	11 (90)	8 (72)	
		190s (70)	142s (60)	107s (50)	78s (20)	63s (00)	52s (72)	
Florianopolis	1700	120 (70)	74 (60)	48 (50)	20 (20)	11 (90)	9 (72)	
		143s (70)	99s (60)	68s (50)	41s (20)	32s (00)	26s (72)	
Fortaleza	1609	530 (70)	355 (60)	205 (50)	68 (20)		21 (72)	
		873s (70)	515s (60)	270s (50)	79s (20)	48s (00)	42s (72)	
Goiania	1935	371 (70)	133 (60)	40 (50)				
		390s (70)	154s (60)	52s (50)				
Guarulhos	1560	222 (70)	78 (60)	16 (50)	6 (20)		3 (72)	
		238s (70)	101s (60)	35s (50)	6s (20)	3s (00)		
Jaboatao	1648	53 (70)	34 (60)	34 (50)	14 (20)	9 (90)	12 (72)	
		203s (70)	105s (60)	57s (50)	48s (20)	23s (00)		
Joao Pessoa	1585	204 (70)	136 (60)	96 (50)	39 (20)			
		228s (70)	167s (60)	119s (50)	53s (20)	29s (00)	25s (72)	
Juiz de Fora	1850?	224 (70)	125 (60)	85 (50)	51 (20)	23 (90)	19 (72)	
		244s (70)	182s (60)	127s (50)	118s (20)	91s (00)	38s (72)	
Londrina	1931	160 (70)	74 (60)	33 (50)	11 (40)			
		232s (70)	135s (60)	71s (50)				

SOUTH AMERICA

City	Date settled	Population (thousands) Latest	Circa 1960	Circa 1950	Circa 1930	Circa 1900	Circa 1850	Circa 1800
Maceio	1815	249 (70)	153 (60)	99 (50)	39 (20)			
		269s (70)	170s (60)	121s (50)	74s (20)	36s (00)	28s (72)	
Manaus	1669	286 (70)	154 (60)	90 (50)	44 (20)		18 (72)	
		314s (70)	175s (60)	108s (50)	76s (20)	65s (00)	29s (72)	
Natal	1669	256 (70)	154 (60)	95 (50)	31 (20)		9 (72)	1 (00?e)
		270s (70)	163s (60)	98s (50)	31s (20)	16s (00)	20s (72)	
Niteroi	1565	298 (70)	229 (60)	171 (50)	25 (20)		21 (72)	
		330s (70)	245s (60)	186s (50)	86s (20)	31s (00)	48s (72)	
Nova Iguacu	1567?	334 (70)	135 (60)	59 (50)	3 (20?)			
		732s (70)	359s (60)	146s (50)				
Olinda	1535	190 (70)	101 (60)	38 (50)	16 (20)		8 (45e)	
		199s (70)	110s (60)	62s (50)	52s (20)	19s (00)	13s (72)	
Osasco	bef 1908	285 (70)	116 (60)[1]	43 (50)[1]	15 (40)[1]			
		285s (70)	116s (60)[1]					
Pelotas	1780	155 (70)	121 (60)	78 (50)	48 (20)	23 (90)	15 (72)	
		213s (70)	178s (60)	128s (50)	82s (20)	45s (00)	21s (72)	
Petropolis	1814	119 (70)	94 (60)	61 (50)	38 (20)		7 (72)	
		193s (70)	150s (60)	108s (50)	68s (20)	40s (00)	7s (72)	
Porto Alegre	1740	887 (70)	618 (60)	375 (50)	154 (20)		25 (72)	
		903s (70)	641s (60)	394s (50)	179s (20)	74s (00)	44s (72)	
Recife	1535?	1070 (70)	789 (60)	512 (50)			74 (45)	28 (00?e)
		1084s (70)	797s (60)	525s (50)	239s (20)	113s (00)	117s (72)	
Ribeirao Preto	1856	197 (70)	116 (60)	63 (50)	62 (20)	12 (90)	6 (72)	
		219s (70)	147s (60)	92s (50)	69s (20)	59s (00)	6s (72)	
Rio de Janeiro	1565	4316 (70)	3223 (60)	2303 (50)				43 (99)
		4316s (70)	3307s (60)	2377s (50)	1158s (20)	811s (06)	275s (72)	
Salvador	1549	1018 (70)	631 (60)	389 (50)				
		1027s (70)	656s (60)	417s (50)	283s (20)	206s (00)	129s (72)	100s (03e)

[1] Included in Sao Paulo.

SOUTH AMERICA

City	Date settled	Population (thousands) Latest	Circa 1960	Circa 1950	Circa 1930	Circa 1900	Circa 1850	Circa 1800
Santo Andre	1551	417 (70)	230 (60)	97 (50)	7 (20)			
		421s (70)	245s (60)	107s (50)				
Santos	1536	345 (70)	262 (60)	198 (50)	103 (20)	13 (90)	9 (72)	6 (00?e)
		350s (70)	266s (60)	204s (50)	103s (20)	50s (00)	9s (72)	
Sao Bernardo do Campo	1552	188 (70)	62 (60)	20 (50)	6 (20)	7 (90)	3 (72)	
		203s (70)	82s (60)	29s (50)	25s (20)	10s (00)		
Sao Goncalo	1647	163 (70)	64 (60)	21 (50)	31 (20)	9 (90)		
		434s (70)	248s (60)	127s (50)	47s (20)	19s (00)		
Sao Joao de Meriti	1645	165 (70)	103 (60)	44 (50)		3 (90)	3 (72)	
		305s (70)	192s (60)	76s (50)				
Sao Luis	1612	171 (70)	125 (60)	80 (50)				
		271s (70)	160s (60)	104s (50)	53s (20)	29s (00)	32s (72)	
Sao Paulo	1554	5241 (70)	3165 (60)	2017 (50				9 (36)
		5979s (70)	3825s (60)	2198s (50)	579s (20)	240s (00)	31s (72)	22s (36)
Teresina	1851	190 (70)	100 (60)	51 (50)	57 (20)			
		230s (70)	145s (60)	91s (50)	57s (20)	45s (00)	22s (72)	
Vitoria	1535	125 (70)	83 (60)	50 (50)	19 (20)	7 (90)	4 (72)	
		136s (70)	85s (60)	51s (50)	22s (20)	12s (00)	16s (72)	
CHILE								
Concepcion	1550	185 (70)	148 (60)	120 (52)	78 (30)	40 (95)	14 (65)	10 (00?e)
*Santiago	1541	2582s (70)	1907s (60)	1350s (52)	696s (30)	256 (95)	115 (65)	46 (00?e)
Valparaiso	1544?	239 (70)	253 (60)	219 (52)	193 (30)	122 (95)	52 (54)	6 (00?e)
Vina del Mar	1586?	175 (70)	115 (60)	85 (52)	49 (30)	11 (95)	0.5 (54)	
COLOMBIA								
Barranquilla	1629	817 (69e)	498 (64)	280 (51)	150 (38)	49 (12)	6 (51)	
*Bogota	1538	2038 (69e)	1697 (64)	648 (51)	326 (38)	121 (12)	30 (51)	21 (01)
Bucaramanga	1622	280 (69e)	230 (64)	112 (51)	42 (38)	20 (12)	10 (51)	
Cali	1536	821 (69e)	638 (64)	284 (51)	88 (38)	28 (12)	12 (51)	
Cartagena	1533	229 (69e)	242 (64)	129 (51)	73 (38)	37 (12)	10 (51)	24 (00?e)
Cucuta	1733	207 (69e)	175 (64)	70 (51)	37 (38)	20 (12)	6 (51)	4 (93)

Figure 37. Central business area of Sao Paulo, the largest city in South America. (Credit: Real Airlines.)

SOUTH AMERICA

City	Date settled	Population (thousands) Latest	Circa 1960	Circa 1950	Circa 1930	Circa 1900	Circa 1850	Circa 1800
Ibague	1551	179 (69e)	164 (64)	99 (51)	27 (38)	24 (12)	7 (51)	2 (00?e)
Manizales	1849	268 (69e)	222 (64)	126 (51)	51 (38)	35 (12)	3 (51)	
Medellin	1616	968 (69e)	773 (64)	358 (51)	144 (38)	71 (12)	14 (51)	6 (26e)
Pereira	1863	224 (69e)	147 (64)	115 (51)	31 (38)	18 (12)	0.6 (70)	
ECUADOR								
Guayaquil	1537	739 (69e)	511 (62)	259 (50)	92 (19)	45 (90)	28 (50?e)	15 (00?e)
*Quito	1000?	496 (69e)	355 (62)	210 (50)	81 (22)	52 (06)	36 (57)	28 (80)
GUYANA								
*Georgetown	1625	66 (70)	73 (60)	74 (46)	63 (31)	49 (91)	26 (51)	8 (00?e)
		167s (70)	148s (60)	94s (46)		55s (91)		
PARAGUAY								
*Asuncion	1537	305 (62)	305 (62)	207 (50)	90 (30e)	52 (99)	10 (50?e)	7 (00e)
		437s (70e)		219s (50)				
PERU								
Arequipa	1540	187 (69e)	135 (61)	97 (50e)	61 (40)	35 (96e)	29 (76)	32 (00?e)
Callao	1537	322 (69e)	156 (61)	88 (50e)	69 (40)	29 (98)	34 (76)	5 (00?e)
Cuzco	11th c	105 (69e)	80 (61)	56 (50e)	41 (40)	30 (96e)	45 (58)	46 (26)
*Lima	1535	2416s (69e)	1436s (61)	835s (50e)	521s (40)	130 (03)	94 (57)	53 (95)
SURINAM								
*Paramaribo	1540?	102 (72)	111 (64)	74 (50)	48 (31)	32 (01)	18 (60)	20 (00?e)
URUGUAY								
*Montevideo	1726	1280 (67e)	1154 (63)	784 (49e)	482 (31)	268 (00)	34 (52)	5 (03)

SOUTH AMERICA

City	Date settled	Population (thousands) Latest	Circa 1960	Circa 1950	Circa 1930	Circa 1900	Circa 1850	Circa 1800
VENEZUELA								
Barquisimeto	1552	280 (69e)	199 (61)	105 (50)	36 (26)	27 (91)	26 (73)	15 (07)
*Caracas	1567	787 (61)	787 (61)	495 (50)	135 (26)	72 (91)	49 (73)	42 (02e)
		2064s (69e)	1336s (61)	694s (50)	168s (26)	98s (91)	68s (73)	
Maracaibo	1571	625 (69e)	422 (61)	236 (50)	84 (26)	35 (91)	26 (73)	22 (01e)
Maracay	17th c	186 (69e)	135 (61)	65 (50)	13 (26)	6 (91)	5 (73)	8 (00?e)
Valencia	1555	225 (69e)	164 (61)	89 (50)	45 (26)	54 (91)	29 (73)	8 (00?e)

TABULAR GAZETTEER 2. CITIES, BY CONTINENT AND COUNTRY
Part II. Location and Climatic Data (English Measure)
AFRICA

City	Latitude and longitude	Elev (ft)	Period of record	Temperature (°F) Avg	Avg warmest month	Avg coolest month	Absolute High	Absolute Low	Avg annual High	Avg annual Low	Annual precipitation (in)
ALGERIA											
*Algiers	36.47N, 3.03E	194	1935–49	66.2	78.6 Aug	55.2 Jan	107	32	102	38	27.87
Annaba	36.54N, 7.46E	10	1935–49	64.4	77.9 Aug	52.9 Jan	115	32			29.53
Constantine	36.22N, 6.37E	1906	1935–49	59.2	77.2 Aug	44.2 Jan	114	23	104	29	17.56
Oran	35.42N, 0.38W	295	1924-50	63.0	77.2 Aug	50.5 Jan	110	31	100	40	15.98
ANGOLA											
*Luanda	8.48S, 13.14E	140	1921-50	75.4	8 0.1 Mar	68.5 Aug	98	58	91	60	13.74
BURUNDI											
*Bujumbura	3.23S, 29.22E	2569	1951-60	73.8	75.2 Sep	72.5 Jul	94	53			32.72
CAMEROON											
Douala	4.03N, 9.42E	43	1951-60	79.5	81.7 Feb	76.3 Aug	96	65	91	68	161.77
*Yaounde	3.52N, 11.31E	2494	1951-60	74.1	76.1 Feb	71.8 Jul	96	56	92	59	60.91
(CANARY ISLANDS), SPAIN											
*Las Palmas	28.06N, 15.24W	43	1882-1920,1943-55	68.4	74.5 Aug	64.0 Jan	99	46	89	51	22.95
Santa Cruz de Tenerife	28.27N, 16.14W	13	1931-60	69.4	76.5 Jul	63.3 Jan	109	47			9.88
CENTRAL AFRICAN REPUBLIC											
*Bangui	4.23N, 18.35E	1250	1941-60	78.8	81.3 Mar	77.2 Jul	108	45	100	58	61.42
CHAD											
*Fort-Lamy	12.07N, 15.03E	984	1951-60	82.4	90.9 Apr	74.3 Jan	114	47	113	50	25.43

AFRICA

City	Latitude and longitude	Elev (ft)	Period of record	Temperature (°F) Avg	Avg warmest month	Avg coolest month	Absolute High	Absolute Low	Avg annual High	Avg annual Low	Annual precipitation (in)
CONGO											
*Brazzaville	4.16S, 15.17E	1683	1941-60	76.8	79.5 Apr	70.5 Jul	98	51	96	56	53.98
DAHOMEY											
*Cotonou	6.21N, 2.26E	43	1951-60	80.4	83.5 Mar	77.0 Aug	98	65	93	67	52.72
*Porto-Novo	6.29N, 2.37E	66	1897-1909	81.0	84.0 Mar	77.5 Jul					52.32
EGYPT											
Alexandria	31.12N, 29.54E	13	1901-34	68.0	78.6 Aug	56.5 Jan	111	37	103	43	7.40
Aswan	24.05N, 32.53E	433	1913-60	80.4	93.0 Jul	60.3 Jan	124	35	119	41	0.04
Asyut	27.11N, 31.11E	217	1900-34	71.1	84.9 Jul	52.9 Jan	121	32	112	36	0.20
*Cairo	30.03N, 31.15E	79	1909-34	69.1	81.5 Aug	53.8 Jan	117	31	108	39	1.14
Giza	30.01N, 31.13E	82	1909-34	67.5	79.9 Jul	52.0 Jan	117	25			1.10
Luxor	25.41N, 32.39E	256	1941-47	76.3	90.7 Jul	56.3 Jan	119	33	117	34	0.02
Mahalla al Kubra	30.58N, 31.10E		1907-29[1]	66.4	79.7 Jul	50.9 Jan	117	32			2.40
Mansurah	31.03N, 31.23E	23	1927-34	70.5	82.4 Aug	56.5 Feb	116	32			2.13
Port Said	31.16N, 32.18E	7	1901-34	69.1	80.2 Aug	56.5 Jan	113	32	100	43	3.27
Shubra al Khaymah	30.06N, 31.15E		(see Cairo)								
Suez	29.58N, 32.33E	13	1910-34	71.6	83.8 Aug	57.2 Jan	113	35	108	41	0.87
Tanta	30.47N, 31.00E	46	1927-34	67.8	79.9 Jul	53.2 Jan	116	33			1.65
Zagazig	30.35N, 31.31E	36	1913-18, 1925-34	67.6	79.9 Jul	52.7 Jan	114	31			1.18
ETHIOPIA											
*Addis Ababa	9.02N, 38.47E	7900	27 yrs bef 1960	60.4	64.2 Mar	59.0 Jul	94	32	85	35	49.06
Asmara	15.19N, 38.55E	7789	1922-39, 1945-52	62.5	65.5 May	59.0 Jan	88	31	84	36	19.37

[1] Climatic data for Qurashiyah, nr Mahalla al Kubra.

AFRICA

City	Latitude and longitude	Elev (ft)	Period of record	Temperature (°F) Avg	Avg warmest month	Avg coolest month	Absolute High	Absolute Low	Avg annual High	Avg annual Low	Annual precipitation (in)
GABON											
*Libreville	0.23N, 9.27E	10	1956-60	79.5	81.0 Apr	75.7 Jul	99	62	94	65	104.25
GAMBIA											
*Bathurst	13.27N, 16.34W	7	34 yrs bef 1961	77.9	80.8 Oct	73.6 Jan	106	45	104	49	48.19
GHANA											
*Accra	5.31N, 0.12W	213	1941-60	79.7	82.0 Mar	75.7 Aug	100	59	93	65	30.98
Kumasi	6.43N, 1.37W	961	1941-60	77.9	80.4 Mar	74.5 Aug	100	51	97	54	57.68
GUINEA											
*Conakry	9.31N, 13.43W	151	29 yrs bef 1961	80.1	82.0 Apr	77.0 Aug	96	63	94	65	170.91
IVORY COAST											
*Abidjan	5.19N, 4.02W	23	1941-60	79.7	82.0 Mar	75.7 Aug	97	56	93	64	84.41
KENYA											
Mombasa	4.03S, 39.40E	52	45 yrs bef 1955	79.0	82.4 Mar	75.9 Jul	96	61	91	67	46.85
*Nairobi	1.17S, 36.49E	5453	1910-20, 1929-60	64.4	65.7 Mar	58.8 Jul	87	41	83	45	37.17
LIBERIA											
*Monrovia	6.19N, 10.49W	75	1953-56	78.4	80.6 Mar	75.9 Jul	93	55	91	63	202.01
LIBYA											
*Bengasi	32.07N, 20.04E	82	46 yrs bef 1947	68	78.5 Aug	56.5 Jan	109	37	104	41	10.47
*Tripoli	32.54N, 13.11E	72	31 yrs bef 1941	67.5	79.9 Aug	54.9 Jan	114	33	106	39	15.94
(MADEIRA ISLANDS), PORTUGAL											
*Funchal	32.38N, 16.54W	82	1921-50	65.8	72.1 Aug	60.4 Feb	103	40	88	47	21.77

AFRICA

City	Latitude and longitude	Elev (ft)	Period of record	Temperature (°F) Avg	Avg warmest month	Avg coolest month	Absolute High	Absolute Low	Avg annual High	Avg annual Low	Annual precipitation (in)
MALAGASY REPUBLIC											
*Tananarive	18.55S, 47.31E	4531	44 yrs bef 1954	65.5	70 Dec	58 Jul	95	34	90	38	53.4
MALAWI											
Blantyre	15.48S, 35.01E	3501	1931-60[1]	70.2	75.4 Nov	62.8 Jul	95	41	93	47	45.47
MALI											
*Bamako	12.39N, 8.00W	1089	1941-60	82.6	91.4 Apr	77.5 Jan	117	47	111	52	43.27
Timbuktu	16.46N, 3.01W	978	1951-60	84.7	93.7 May	72.7 Jan	119	41	117	44	8.86
MAURITIUS											
*Port Louis	20.10S, 57.30E	181	1921-50	73.4	78.8 Jan	68.0 Jul	95	50	91	54	50.98
MOROCCO											
Casablanca	33.36N, 7.37W	164	1924-50	63.5	73.4 Aug	54.0 Jan	110	31	99	36	15.83
Fez	34.03N, 4.59W	1368	1925-49	64.0	80.8 Aug	49.6 Jan	119	24	112	28	21.50
Marrakesh	31.37N, 8.00W	1509	1924-50	67.8	84.4 Aug	52.5 Jan	120	27	115	31	9.76
Meknes	33.54N, 5.33W	1831	1925-49	62.8	78.1 Aug	49.5 Jan					22.64
*Rabat-Sale	34.02N, 6.50W	213	1925-49	64.0	73.8 Aug	54.5 Jan	118	32	105	37	20.59
Tangier	35.47N, 5.48W	246	1925-49	63.3	73.6 Aug	54.5 Jan	106	28	94	36	34.25
MOZAMBIQUE											
*Lourenco Marques	25.58S, 32.33E	194	1921-50	72.0	77.9 Feb	64.8 Jul	114	45	105	48	29.68
NIGER											
*Niamey	13.30N, 2.08E	728	1945-60	84.0	92.5 Apr	76.3 Jan	114	47	113	50	25.04

[1] Temperature data for Zomba, nr Blantyre.

AFRICA

City	Latitude and longitude	Elev (ft)	Period of record	Temperature (°F) Avg	Avg warmest month	Avg coolest month	Absolute High	Absolute Low	Avg annual High	Avg annual Low	Annual precipitation (in)
NIGERIA											
Abeokuta	7.10N, 3.20E	220	1909-13, 1916-29	79.0	80.8 Mar	76.6 Aug					46.6
Enugu	6.27N, 7.28E	466	1951-60	80.1	83.5 Mar	77.7 Aug	99	55	97	62	65.39
Ibadan	7.23N, 3.53E	651	24 yrs bef 1955	80.1	83.8 Mar	75.9 Aug	102	50	99	57	49.68
Ilesha	7.38N, 4.45E	1100?	(see Oshogbo)								
Ilorin	8.45N, 4.32E	1079	1916-29, 1951-60	79.2	83.5 Mar	76.1 Aug	104	48	101	53	52.01
Kano	12.00N, 8.30E	1533	1921-50	79.6	88.1 Apr	70.7 Jan	114	43	107	48	32.80
*Lagos	6.26N, 3,23E	9	1921-50	80.2	83.0 Mar	77.1 Aug	104	60	95	67	68.96
Ogbomosho	8.05N, 4.11E	1200	14 yrs bef 1926	77.0	81.3 Feb	73.4 Aug					
Oshogbo	7.50N, 4.35E	990	1937	78.6	84.7 Mar	74.3 Aug			100	50	44.2
Port Harcourt	4.43N, 7.05E	64	1951-60	78.8	80.6 Mar	76.6 Jul	99	60			94.3
Zaria	11.07N, 7.44E	2100	1919-54[1]	77.0	83.5 Apr	73.4 Dec	105	46			44.4
REUNION											
*Saint-Denis	20.52S, 55.28E	36	1951-60	74.3	78.8 Jan	69.6 Jul					55.87
RHODESIA											
Bulawayo	20.09S, 28.36E	4405	1921-50	66.4	72.4 Nov	57.0 Jul	99	28	96	35	22.85
*Salisbury	17.50S, 31.03E	4831	1923-50	65.3	70.8 Oct	56.7 Jul	95	32	91	35	32.64
SENEGAL											
*Dakar	14.40N, 17.26W	79	1899-1913, 1932-40	77	82 Jul	71.5 Jan	109	53	100	58	22.76

[1] Temperature data for Kaduna, nr Zaria.

AFRICA

City	Latitude and longitude	Elev (ft)	Period of record	Temperature (°F) Avg	Avg warmest month	Avg coolest month	Absolute High	Absolute Low	Avg annual High	Avg annual Low	Annual precipitation (in)
SIERRA LEONE											
*Freetown	8.29N, 13.13W	86	1921-50	79.7	81.8 Apr	77.0 Aug	98	62	95	64	141.14
SOMALIA											
*Mogadishu	2.02N, 45.21E	33	1931-60	81.0	84.6 Apr	78.6 Aug	97	59	92	67	16.30
SOUTH AFRICA											
Bloemfontein	29.08S, 26.13E	4678	1880-1940	60.7	73.0 Jan	46.1 Jul	113	12	96	21	20.77
*Cape Town	33.55S, 18.27E	40	1881-1940	63.2	71.1 Feb	55.5 Jul	105	28	97	32	24.65
Durban	29.53S, 31.02E	22	1921-50	70.3	76.3 Feb	63.4 Jul	107	39	95	42	40.20
Germiston	26.15S, 28.10E	5450	1921-50	60.6	67.5 Jan	50.4 Jul	93	19	89	24	29.81
Johannesburg	26.11S, 28.03E	5750	1893-1940	60.8	68.6 Jan	49.3 Jul	96	22	86	27	32.60
Pietermaritzburg	29.37S, 30.23E	2128	1916-40	66.0	73.5 Feb	56.1 Jul	106	26	98	31	36.54
Port Elizabeth	33.58S, 25.37E	176	1881-1940	64.2	70.7 Feb	58.3 Jul	107	31	99	33	22.73
*Pretoria	25.45S, 28.12E	4375	1920-40	63.7	72.3 Jan	51.4 Jul	101	20	92	27	28.28
Vereeniging	26.41S, 27.56E	4725	1903-40	61.5	71.2 Jan	47.7 Jul	100	12	92	18	26.49
SUDAN											
*Khartoum	15.36N, 32.32E	1257	1921-50	84.6	93.0 Jun	73.8 Jan	118	41	114	47	7.05
Omdurman	15.38N, 32.30E		(see Khartoum)								
TANZANIA											
*Dar es Salaam	6.48S, 39.17E	47	44 yrs bef 1955	78	82.5 Feb	74.5 Jul	96	59	92	62	40.98
Zanzibar	6.10S, 39.11E	61	1921-50	79.5	82.6 Feb	76.5 Aug	102	67	98	68	55.54
TOGO											
*Lome	6.08N, 1.13E	66	1951-60	79.5	82.2 Mar	76.3 Aug	98	60			35.16

AFRICA

City	Latitude and longitude	Elev (ft)	Period of record	Temperature (°F) Avg	Avg warmest month	Avg coolest month	Absolute High	Absolute Low	Avg annual High	Avg annual Low	Annual precipitation (in)
TUNISIA											
Sfax	34.44N, 10.46E	69	1901-50	65.8	79.0 Aug	52.5 Jan	111	25	98	36	7.76
*Tunis	36.48N, 10.12E	217	60 yrs bef 1951	64.5	80 Aug	50.5 Jan	118	30	109	35	17.48
UGANDA											
*Kampala	0.19N, 32.35E	3910	1931-50	70.0	72.1 Jan	68.0 Aug	97	53	91	57	45.17
UPPER VOLTA											
*Ouagadougou	12.22N, 1.31W	997	25 yrs bef 1960	83.5	91.4 Apr	77.2 Jan	118	47			34.61
ZAIRE											
Kananga	5.54S, 22.25E	2215	1940-59	76.5	77.2 Mar	74.5 Jul	94	55	94	58	62.76
*Kinshasa	4.18S, 15.18E	951	1940-57	77.5	80.1 Apr	72.0 Jul	100	53	96	59	53.50
Kisangani	0.30N, 25.12E	1362	1927-41, 1951-59	77.5	79.2 Apr	76.1 Jul	97	59	96	65	67.05
Lubumbashi	11.40S, 27.28E	4035	1919-59	68.9	74.7 Oct	61.5 Jul	99	33	97	37	48.90
Mbuji-Mayi	6.09S, 23.36E										
ZAMBIA											
Kitwe	12.49S, 28.13E		10 yrs bef 1968[1]	67.5	73.9 Oct	58.5 Jun	97	28	93	32	45.12
*Lusaka	15.25S, 28.17E	4196	1941-60	69.1	76.5 Oct	61.5 Jun	100	39	95	42	31.22

[1] Climatic data for Ndola, nr Kitiue.

ASIA

City	Latitude and longitude	Elev (ft)	Period of record	Temperature (°F) Avg	Avg warmest month	Avg coolest month	Absolute High	Absolute Low	Avg annual High	Avg annual Low	Annual precipitation (in)
AFGHANISTAN											
Herat	34.22N, 62.09E	3025	1940–44	61.5	86.9 Jul	35.6 Jan					7.91
*Kabul	34.30N, 69.13E	5903	40 yrs bef 1945	57.2	78.6 Jul	30.9 Jan	112	−7	100	2	12.20
Kandahar	31.27N, 65.43E	3462	1940–47	64	84 Jul	43.5 Jan	111	14	108	19	7.0
BAHRAIN											
*Manama	26.13N, 50.35E	3	8 yrs bef 1960	79.5	93.5 Aug	64.0 Jan					2.9
BANGLADESH											
Chittagong	22.20N, 91.50E	46	60 yrs bef 1963	77.2	82.2 May	66.9 Jan	102	45	95	48	107.63
*Dacca	23.43N, 90.25E	27	1950-59	78.2	84.8 May	66.1 Jan					73.35
Khulna	22.48N, 89.33E	16	20 yrs bef 1963	78.9	84.9 May	66.8 Jan	104	45			67.85
Narayanganj	23.37N, 90.30E	26	60 yrs bef 1963	78.5	83.6 Jun	66.7 Jan	105	44	99	49	73.79
BURMA											
Mandalay	22.00N, 96.05E	75	43 yrs bef 1941	81.7	89.6 Apr	70.5 Jan	114	44	108	50	37.56
*Rangoon	16.47N, 96.10E	20	1881-1940	81.3	86.7 Apr	77.2 Jan	107	55	102	59	104.45
CAMBODIA											
*Phnom-Penh	11.33N, 104.55E	36	1941-50	81.5	84.2 Apr	77.7 Dec					56.81
CEYLON											
*Colombo	6.56N, 79.51E	24	1931-60	80.4	82.3 May	79.0 Dec	96	59	92	65	94.3
Kandy	6.18N, 80.38E	1572	1931-60	75.8	78.8 Apr	73.6 Jan			91	55	79.7
CHINA											
Amoy	24.27N, 118.05E	131	1915,1917-42	71.2	84.2 Aug	56.5 Feb	100	39	95	42	46.69
Anking	30.31N, 117.02E	128	1934-37,1942	63.0	85.8 Jul	37.9 Jan	103	18			40.87

ASIA

City	Latitude and longitude	Elev (ft)	Period of record	Temperature (°F) Avg	Avg warmest month	Avg coolest month	Absolute High	Absolute Low	Avg annual High	Avg annual Low	Annual precipitation (in)
Anshan	41.07N, 122.57E	115	? yrs bef 1934	47.3	76.6 Jul	14.2 Jan	100	-21			26.81
Antung	40.08N, 124.24E	20	1924–40, 1949-52	47.3	76.3 Aug	14.7 Jan	100	-25			40.28
Canton	23.07N, 113.15E	59	1912-37, 1943-52	71.4	82.9 Jul	56.5 Jan	100	31	97	36	67.72
Changchih	36.11N, 113.06E	2999	1941–44, 1954-55	48.7	73.8 Jul	19.6 Jan	98	-20			20.00
Changchow (Fukien)	24.31N, 117.40E		(see Amoy)								
Changchow (Kiangsu)	31.47N, 119.58E		(see Wusih)								
Changchun	43.52N, 125.21E	709	1909–42, 1947-52	40.5	74.3 Jul	1.8 Jan	103	-33	94	-23	24.88
Changsha	28.12N, 112.58E	157	1924-38, 1946-50	63.1	83.8 Aug	41.0 Jan	109	17	102	21	52.13
Chefoo	37.32N, 121.24E	15[illegible]	1924–42	54.7	78.4 Jul	28.6 Jan	104	5	97	13	24.13
Chengchow	34.45N, 113.40E	358	1924-37	61.0	85.3 Jul	32.5 Jan	110	1			32.36
Chengtu	30.40N, 104.04E	1634	1932-53	62.6	79.7 Jul	43.2 Jan	104	25	93	32	45.12
Chinchow	41.07N, 121.06E		1920-27[1]	47.3	76.6 Jul	13.8 Jan					
Chinkiang	32.13N, 119.26E	39	1881-1915	60.4	82.9 Aug	37.6 Jan	104	10			40.36
Chinwangtao	39.56N, 119.37E	10	1909-16, 1930-36	49.5	75.9 Aug	21.0 Jan	96	-8			26.26
Chuchow	27.50N, 113.09E		(see Changsha)								
Chungking	29.34N, 106.35E	659	1924-38, 1940-53	65.5	83.8 Aug	46.6 Jan	111	27	105	34	42.87
Foochow	26.05N, 119.18E	289	1924-44, 1951-52	67.6	83.3 Jul	51.3 Feb	104	27			57.09
Foshan	23.02N, 113.07E	50	(see Canton)								

[1] Temperature data for Sungshutsuitzu, nr Chinchow.

ASIA

City	Latitude and longitude	Elev (ft)	Period of record	Temperature (°F) Avg	Avg warmest month	Avg coolest month	Absolute High	Absolute Low	Avg annual High	Avg annual Low	Annual precipitation (in)
Fushun	41.52N, 123.53E		(see Mukden)								
Fusin	42.06N, 121.46E										
Hangchow	30.15N, 120.10E	16	1904–47, 1950–52	61.3	82.9 Jul	39.7 Jan	108	13			58.66
Hantan	36.35N, 114.29E		1939–43[1]	58.5	82.8 Jul	30.0 Jan	111	6			20.91
Harbin	45.45N, 126.39E	476	1909–42, 1949–52	37.9	73.9 Jul	-7.1 Jan	102	-42	92	-31	22.72
Hengyang	26.54N, 112.36E	308	12 yrs bef 1953	64.0	84.4 Jul	42.1 Jan	106	21	105	23	58.19
Hofei	31.51N, 117.17E	85	1953–55	59.9	82.9 Aug	32.9 Jan	100	-5			32.68
Hoihow	20.03N, 110.19E	46	1924–42	76.1	84.7 Jun	64.6 Jan	102	37			60.35
Hokang	47.05N, 130.20E		(see Kiamusze)								
Huhehot	40.47N, 111.37E	3484	1930–43, 1946–50	42.4	72.0 Jul	7.3 Jan	100	-33			14.41
Hwainan	32.40N, 117.00E		(see Pengpu)								
Hwangshih	30.13N, 115.06E		(see Wuhan)								
Ichang	30.42N, 111.17E	436	1924–38	63.5	84.0 Jul	40.3 Jan	111	20	106	26	44.57
Ichun	47.42N, 128.54E										
Ipin	28.46N, 104.34E	938	11 yrs bef 1953	65.7	82.2 Aug	47.1 Jan	108	29			46.66
Kaifeng	34.51N, 114.21E	246	1931–37, 1940–43	58.8	83.1 Jul	30.9 Jan	109	5			24.41
Kalgan	40.50N, 114.56E	2494	1937–43, 1947–52	46.9	73.6 Jul	16.3 Jan	101	-14			14.45
Kashgar	39.29N, 75.58E	4629	49 yrs bef 1941	54.7	80.1 Jul	22.5 Jan	106	-15	102	0	3.07
Kiamusze	46.50N, 130.21E	266	1938–42, 1949–53	38.1	73.2 Jul	-4.4 Jan	98	-39			24.76
Kingtehchen	29.16N, 117.11E										

[1] Climatic data for Anyang, nr Hantan.

ASIA

City	Latitude and longitude	Ele[illegible] (f[illegible]	Period of record	Temperature (°F) Avg	Avg warmest month	Avg coolest month	Absolute High	Absolute Low	Avg annual High	Avg annual Low	Annual precipitation (in)
Kirin	43.51N, 126.33E	6[illegible]	1911-13	39.9	72.9 Jul	1.6 Jan	99	-37			26.38
Kisi	45.18N, 130.58E	7[illegible]	1949-52	38.8	72.3 Jul	0.1 Jan	100	-31			20.98
Kokiu	23.23N, 103.09E	57[illegible]	1928-32[1]	69.4	76.3 May	58.3 Jan	98	26	96	36	37.52
Kunming	25.04N, 102.41E	62[illegible]	39 yrs bef 1953	61.0	70.2 Jul	49.3 Jan	91	22	87	28	39.53
Kweilin	25.17N, 110.17E	5[illegible]	1935-43, 1949-50	66.9	83.1 Jul	48.6 Jan	103	23			77.40
Kweiyang	26.35N, 106.43E	351[illegible]	1920-53	60.1	76.5 Jul	41.0 Jan	103	15	95	23	50.16
Lanchow	36.03N, 103.41E	49[illegible]	1932-52	49.1	73.0 Jul	20.3 Jan	100	-10	98	0	13.31
Lhasa	29.39N, 91.06E	12,00[illegible]	1935-38, 1941-49	47.8	62.6 Jun	31.5 Jan	89	3	82	5	57.52
Liaoyang	41.17N, 123.11E	8[illegible]	(see Mukden)								
Liaoyuan	42.55N, 125.09E		(see Szeping)								
Liuchow	24.19N, 109.24E	32[illegible]	1938-46								57.99
Loyang	34.41N, 112.28E	45[illegible]	1932-37, 1950-52	57.6	82.0 Jul	30.4 Jan	111	-4			18.90
Luchow	28.53N, 105.23E	100[illegible]	(see Ipin)								
Lushun-Talien	38.55N, 121.39E	31[illegible]	1905-40, 1950-52	50.5	76.1 Aug	22.6 Jan	97	-4	91	2	22.05
Malipo	23.09N, 104.44E										
Mukden	41.48N, 123.27E	13[illegible]	1905-42, 1947-52	45.1	76.8 Jul	9.0 Jan	103	-28	98	-18	27.99
Mutankiang	44.35N, 129.36E	76[illegible]	1909-43, 1949-53	37.0	72.0 Jul	-4.2 Jan	99	-49			20.51
Nanchang	28.41N, 115.53E	16[illegible]	1929-33, 1946-52	63.3	85.1 Aug	41.9 Jan	103	21			69.69
Nanchung	30.48N, 106.04E	97[illegible]	1940-46	65.8	84.4 Jul	46.4 Jan	109	29			36.97
Nanking	32.03N, 118.47E	20[illegible]	1905-37, 1947-50	59.5	81.9 Jul	36.0 Jan	109	7	101	13	38.94
Nanning	22.49N, 108.19E	24[illegible]	1922-39, 1941-50	72.0	83.3 Jul	56.5 Jan	102	34			52.05
Nantung	32.02N, 120.53E	36	1917-37, 1949-50	58.5	80.4 Jul	35.2 Jan	108	9			41.02
Neikiang	29.35N, 105.03E	116[illegible]	1936-50	64.9	81.7 Jul	47.1 Jan	105	27			36.89
Ningpo	29.53N, 121.33E	1[illegible]	1881-1915	61.9	82.4 Aug	41.7 Jan	103	14			53.54
Paoki	34.22N, 107.07E	204	1952-55	55.4	77.4 Jul	31.3 Jan	103	2			22.24

[1] Climatic data for Mengtzu, nr Kokiu.

ASIA

City	Latitude and longitude	Elev (ft)	Period of record	Temperature (°F) Avg	Avg warmest month	Avg coolest month	Absolute High	Absolute Low	Avg annual High	Avg annual Low	Annual precipitation (in)
Paoting	38.52N, 115.29E	72	1913-37, 1950	53.8	80.4 Jul	22.1 Jan	109	-12			17.48
Paotow	40.36N, 110.03E	3425	1935-37, 1949-53	43.5	72.9 Jul	10.8 Jan	101	-27			11.97
*Peking	39.56N, 116.24E	171	78 yrs bef 1953	53.2	79.0 Jul	23.5 Jan	109	-9	99	3	24.53
Pengpu	32.57N, 117.21E	66	1926-37	63.1	85.3 Jul	34.3 Jan	105	-3			28.11
Penki	41.20N, 123.45E		(see Mukden)								
Shanghai	31.14N, 121.28E	15	1873-1953	59.5	81.0 Aug	38.1 Jan	105	10	102	16	45.00
Shangkiu	34.23N, 115.37E		1953-55[1]	58.5	80.8 Jul	30.6 Jan	105	-1			25.12
Shaohing	30.00N, 120.35E		(see Hangchow)								
Shaoyang	27.15N, 111.28E	817	1936-44	63.5	81.9 Jul	42.1 Jan	101	24			51.38
Shihkiachwang	38.03N, 114.29E	269	1939-43, 1949-52	55.8	80.4 Jul	25.5 Jan	109	-16			17.09
Shiukwan	24.48N, 113.35E	285	1951-55	68.5	84.0 Jul	50.4 Jan	108	24			59.17
Siakwan	25.34N, 100.14E	5118	1952-55[2]	61.7	69.8 Jun	49.8 Jan	87	30			38.23
Sian	34.16N, 108.54E	1352	1922-25, 1931-52	57.2	82.2 Jul	31.1 Jan	115	-13	107	9	22.68
Siangtan	27.51N, 112.54E	640	(see Changsha)								
Sinhailien	34.36N, 119.13E	13	1951-53	57.9	81.1 Aug	32.5 Jan	102	6			32.20
Sining	36.37N, 101.46E	7363	1936-49	44.4	64.9 Jul	20.5 Jan	90	-10			14.84
Sinsiang	35.19N, 113.52E		(see Chengchow)								
Soochow	31.18N, 120.37E	52	1936-37	61.2	81.9 Jul	40.3 Jan					
Suchow	34.16N, 117.11E	112	1926-43, 1949-52	58.1	81.9 Jul	31.6 Jan	110	-1			27.76
Swatow	23.22N, 116.40E	14	1880-1941	71.1	84.0 Aug	57.0 Jan	101	31	98	40	58.62
Szeping	43.10N, 124.20E	535	1934-44, 1949-52	42.6	75.4 Jul	3.7 Jan	100	-38			27.91
Taichow	32.29N, 119.55E		(see Chinkiang)								
Taiyuan	37.52N, 112.33E	2566	1916-48, 1950-52	50.0	77.0 Jul	18.9 Jan	107	-21	100	-8	15.55
Tangshan	39.38N, 118.11E	187	1922-37	54.3	80.6 Jul	24.3 Jan	104	-9			13.54
Tatung	40.05N, 113.18E	3442	1925-37, 1939-43	44.1	72.9 Jul	11.1 Jan	100	-21			13.89

[1] Climatic data for Pohsien, nr Shangkiu.

[2] Climatic data for Paoshan, nr Siakwan.

ASIA

City	Latitude and longitude	Elev (ft)	Period of record	Temperature (°F) Avg	Avg warmest month	Avg coolest month	Absolute High	Absolute Low	Avg annual High	Avg annual Low	Annual precipitation (in)
Tientsin	39.08N, 117.12E	11	1904–42, 1944–52	54.1	80.2 Jul	24.6 Jan	109	-5	103	3	20.75
Tsamkong	21.12N, 110.23E	85	1921–40	73.9	83.7 Jul	61.3 Jan	100	38			54.45
Tsiaotso	35.15N, 113.13E		(see Chengchow)								
Tsinan	36.40N, 117.00E	180	1919–52	58.6	83.1 Jul	29.8 Jan	109	-3	103	6	24.84
Tsingtao	36.04N, 120.19E	253	1898–1952	53.8	77.2 Aug	30.0 Jan	97	2			25.47
Tsitsihar	47.22N, 123.57E	482	1930–42, 1949–53	36.9	73.4 Jul	-4.9 Jan	99	-39			14.92
Tzekung	29.24N, 104.47E		(see Neikiang)								
Tzepo	36.29N, 117.50E	590	(see Tsinan)								
Urumtsi	43.48N, 87.35E	2996	22 yrs bef 1948	43.0	76.5 Jul	3.2 Jan	112	-43			9.17
Weifang	36.43N, 119.06E	207	1929–37	58.1	82.4 Jul	28.2 Jan	109	1			24.80
Wenchow	28.01N, 120.39E	16	1924–41	64.4	83.8 Jul	46.0 Jan	105	27			67.28
Wuhan	30.32N, 114.18E	75	1905–40, 1951–53	62.2	84.0 Jul	38.8 Jan	108	9	100	23	47.32
Wuhu	31.21N, 118.22E	43	1880–1915	61.3	83.1 Aug	39.2 Jan	106	11			46.26
Wusih	31.35N, 120.18E	23	1936–37	61.2	81.0 Jul	39.7 Jan					
Wutungkiao	29.21N, 103.48E		1936–50[1]	64.0	79.5 Jul	46.9 Jan	105	27			53.82
Yangchow	32.24N, 119.26E		(see Chinkiang)								
Yangchuan	37.54N, 113.36E	2181	(see Taiyuan)								
Yenan	36.38N, 109.27E	3400									
Yinchwan	38.28N, 106.19E	3645	1951–53, 1955	39.0	75.4 Jul	15.6 Jan	103	-23			7.99
Yingkow	40.40N, 122.17E	11	1905–43, 1949–53	47.5	77.0 Jul	14.2 Jan	98	-24	93	-13	26.42
CYPRUS											
*Nicosia	35.11N, 33.23E	508	1921–50	66.6	83.6 Jul	50.0 Jan	116	23	105	31	14.76
GAZA STRIP											
*Gaza	31.30N, 34.28E	157	1921–34	67.5	78.1 Aug	55.4 Jan	112	30	104	38	13.70

[1] Climatic data for Loshan, nr Wutungkiao.

ASIA

City	Latitude and longitude	Elev (ft)	Period of record	Temperature (°F) Avg	Avg warmest month	Avg coolest month	Absolute High	Absolute Low	Avg annual High	Avg annual Low	Annual precipitation (in)
HONG KONG											
*Hong Kong	22.17N, 114.09E	109	1884-1941, 1947-48	72.0	82.0 Jul	59.2 Feb	97	32	93	43	84.92
INDIA											
Agra	27.11N, 78.01E	553	1931-60	78.1	95.0 Jun	58.6 Jan	120	28	114	36	26.18
Ahmedabad	23.02N, 72.37E	180	1931-60	81.1	92.3 May	68.5 Jan	118	36	111	47	30.83
Ajmer	26.27N, 74.38E	1593	1931-60	76.5	92.1 May	58.5 Jan	114	27	110	35	20.47
Aligarh	27.53N, 78.05E	615	29 yrs bef 1961	77.5	93.6 Jun	58.3 Jan	115	33	114	38	24.72
Allahabad	25.27N, 81.51E	322	1931-60	79.0	94.5 May	61.5 Jan	120	34	115	40	37.20
Ambala	30.21N, 76.50E	892	1931-60	76.3	93.0 Jun	56.8 Jan	118	30	114	36	30.20
Amravati	21.29N, 78.11E	1214	1931-60	81.0	95.0 May	71.2 Dec	116	41	113	50	34.49
Amritsar	31.35N, 74.53E	768	1951-60	73.8	91.0 Jun	52.7 Jan	116	27	113	32	22.17
Asansol	23.41N, 86.59E	414	1931-60	79.5	90.9 May	66.0 Jan	117	41	113	46	57.83
Bangalore	12.59N, 77.35E	3021	1931-60	74.5	81.1 Apr	68.9 Dec	102	46	97	53	35.00
Bareilly	28.21N, 79.25E	568	1931-60	77.4	91.8 Jun	59.5 Jan	116	30	113	40	42.36
Baroda	22.18N, 73.12E	115	28 yrs bef 1961	80.6	91.8 May	68.7 Jan	116	30	113	41	39.61
Belgaum	15.52N, 74.30E	2470	1931-60	75.2	81.7 Apr	70.9 Dec	105	44	100	49	51.30
Bhatpara	22.52N, 88.24E		21 yrs bef 1961[1]	79.5	87.4 May	66.7 Jan	109	41	106	47	66.42
Bhavnagar	21.46N, 72.09E	55	1931-60	81.0	91.0 May	66.7 Jan	116	33	112	44	24.41
Bhopal	23.16N, 77.24E	1716	1931-60	77.0	92.3 May	64.4 Jan	114	33	111	40	49.61
Bikaner	28.01N, 73.18E	734	23 yrs bef 1961	78.6	95.9 Jun	56.5 Jan	121	27	115	32	12.05
Bombay	18.58N, 72.50E	37	1931-60	81.1	86.2 May	75.6 Jan	105	53	98	60	71.06
Calcutta	22.32N, 88.22E	21	1931-60	80.4	88.0 May	68.4 Jan	111	44	106	49	63.98
Calicut	11.15N, 75.46E	26	1931-60	81.1	84.7 Apr	78.3 Jul	99	61	94	66	125.12
Chandigarh	30.43N, 76.47E	1300	(see Ambala)								
Coimbatore	11.00N, 76.58E	1341	1931-60	79.5	84.2 Apr	75.6 Dec	104	53	99	60	24.17

[1] Climatic data for Dum Dum, nr Bhatpara.

ASIA

City	Latitude and longitude	Elev (ft)	Period of record	Temperature (°F) Avg	Avg warmest month	Avg coolest month	Absolute High	Absolute Low	Avg annual High	Avg annual Low	Annual precipitation (in)
Cuttack	20.30N, 85.50E	89	1931-60	81.9	91.0 May	71.4 Dec	118	46	112	52	60.94
Dehra Dun	30.19N, 78.02E	2238	1931-60	71.2	84.9 Jun	54.7 Jan	111	30	106	36	84.58
Delhi	28.40N, 77.13E	770	1901-50	(see New Delhi for temperature data)							23.43
Dhanbad	23.48N, 86.27E	843	27 yrs bef 1961	78.3	90.1 May	65.1 Jan	115	41	112	46	53.35
Durg	21.11N, 81.17E	967	1901-50	(see Raipur for temperature data)							50.28
Durgapur	23.30N, 87.20E		(see Asansol)								
Ernakulam	9.59N, 76.17E	10	1931-60[1]	80.8	83.7 Apr	78.6 Jul	100	61	92	69	120.55
Gaya	24.47N, 85.00E	381	1931-60	79.2	93.7 May	62.8 Jan	117	38	114	43	46.65
Gorakhpur	26.45N, 83.22E	254	1931-60	78.3	90.3 May	61.5 Jan	119	35	108	43	49.13
Guntur	16.18N, 80.27E		1931-60[2]	82.0	90.0 May	74.5 Jan	118	57	110	61	35.31
Gwalior	26.13N, 78.10E	681	21 yrs bef 1961	78.1	95.9 Jun	60.1 Jan	119	30	116	34	32.44
Howrah	22.35N, 88.20E		48 yrs bef 1951	(see Calcutta for temperature data)							60.47
Hubli	15.21N, 75.10E	2297	1931-60[3]	78.6	85.8 Apr	73.0 Dec	107	52	104	55	26.34
Hyderabad	17.23N, 78.28E	1788	1931-60	78.4	90.3 May	69.1 Dec	112	43	108	48	30.39
Indore	22.43N, 75.50E	1823	1931-60	75.9	90.1 May	64.0 Jan	114	27	108	38	36.57
Jabalpur	23.10N, 79.57E	1289	1931-60	77.4	93.0 May	64.2 Dec	116	32	113	38	56.34
Jaipur	26.55N, 75.49E	1431	1931-60	77.0	91.8 Jun	59.2 Jan	118	28	113	36	23.54
Jamnagar	22.28N, 70.04E	60	1931-60	78.8	88.7 Jun	65.3 Jan	112	35	106	43	18.35
Jamshedpur	22.48N, 86.11E	423	1931-60	80.6	92.1 May	66.6 Dec	117	39	113	44	56.65
Jhansi	25.26N, 78.35E	848	1931-60	79.2	96.3 May	61.9 Jan	118	33	115	40	37.17
Jodhpur	26.17N, 73.02E	736	1931-60	80.1	93.9 May	62.6 Jan	120	28	115	38	14.41
Jullundur	31.19N, 75.34E		1901-50	(see Amritsar for temperature data)							25.87
Kalyan	19.15N, 73.09E		1901-50	(see Bombay for temperature data)							92.72
Kanpur	26.28N, 80.21E	413	1931-60	78.3	93.9 May	60.3 Jan	117	33	115	39	31.69

[1] Temperature data for Cochin, nr Ernakulam.
[2] Temperature data for Masulipatnam, nr Guntur.
[3] Temperature data for Gadag, nr Hubli.

ASIA

City	Latitude and longitude	Elev (ft)	Period of record	Temperature (°F) Avg	Avg warmest month	Avg coolest month	Absolute High	Absolute Low	Avg annual High	Avg annual Low	Annual precipitation (in)
Kolhapur	16.42N, 74.13E	1880	1951-60	77.4	84.7 Apr	74.1 Dec	107	48	105	51	39.09
Kota	25.11N, 75.50E	843	1931-60	80.6	97.0 May	63.5 Jan	118	35	115	43	30.94
Lucknow	26.51N, 80.55E	364	1931-60	78.4	92.8 May	61.0 Jan	119	34	114	40	40.00
Ludhiana	30.54N, 75.51E	812	1931-60	76.3	93.4 Jun	55.4 Jan	119	29	116	35	25.51
Madras	13.05N, 80.17E	51	1931-60	83.5	90.9 May	76.1 Jan	113	57	107	63	49.92
Madurai	9.56N, 78.07E	437	1931-60	84.0	89.4 May	77.9 Jan	108	60	105	65	35.20
Malegaon	20.33N, 74.32E	1432	1931-60	78.8	90.5 May	69.4 Dec	116	31	110	41	21.34
Mangalore	12.52N, 74.53E	72	1931-60	80.8	84.6 Apr	79.7 Jan	100	60	95	65	133.78
Meerut	28.59N, 77.42E	733	1951-60	76.5	92.1 Jun	57.6 Jan	115	33	112	38	31.93
Moradabad	28.50N, 78.47E	197	1901-50	(see Bareilly for temperature data)							38.66
Mysore	12.18N, 76.39E	2518	1931-60	75.9	81.9 Apr	71.1 Dec	103	51	98	55	31.89
Nagpur	21.09N, 79.06E	1017	1951-60	80.4	96.1 May	68.7 Dec	118	39	115	44	48.90
Nasik	19.59N, 73.48E	1961	1901-50	(see Malegaon for temperature data)							27.44
*New Delhi	28.36N, 77.12E	714	23 yrs bef 1961	77.4	93.7 Jun	57.7 Jan	118	31	113	37	25.98
Patna	25.35N, 85.15E	173	1931-60	79.2	90.3 May	63.1 Jan	115	36	111	44	45.90
Poona	18.32N, 73.52E	1834	1931-60	77.2	85.8 May	69.8 Dec	110	35	109	43	26.02
Raipur	21.14N, 81.38E	971	1931-60	80.4	95.9 May	68.4 Dec	117	39	114	48	53.50
Rajahmundry	16.59N, 81.47E		1931-60[1]	81.9	90.1 May	73.6 Dec	117	57	110	60	41.61
Rajkot	22.18N, 70.47E	453	1931-60	80.1	90.7 May	66.9 Jan	118	31	110	41	23.39
Ranchi	23.21N, 85.20E	2149	1931-60	74.7	87.6 May	62.1 Jan	110	37	107	42	59.57
Saharanpur	29.58N, 77.33E	896	1931-60[2]	74.5	90.0 Jun	55.9 Jan	116	28	111	36	36.85
Salem	11.39N, 78.10E	913	1931-60	82.4	88.0 May	76.6 Dec	109	52	104	60	37.60
Sholapur	17.41N, 75.55E	1570	1931-60	80.8	91.2 May	72.5 Dec	114	40	110	50	26.69
South Suburban	22.30N, 88.19E		(see Calcutta)								
Surat	21.10N, 72.50E	39	1931-60	81.9	88.5 May	73.6 Jan	114	40	109	50	42.17

[1] Temperature data for Kakinada, nr Rajahmundry.

[2] Temperature data for Roorkee, nr Saharanpur.

ASIA

City	Latitude and longitude	Elev (ft)	Period of record	Temperature (°F) Avg	Avg warmest month	Avg coolest month	Absolute High	Absolute Low	Avg annual High	Avg annual Low	Annual precipitation (in)
Tiruchirapalli	10.49N, 78.41E	255	1931-60	83.8	89.1 May	77.5 Dec	111	57	105	63	34.25
Tirunelveli	8.44N, 77.42E		1951-60[1]	84.7	89.1 May	79.5 Dec	108	65	104	68	31.34
Trivandrum	8.29N, 76.55E	210	20 yrs bef 1961	80.8	83.7 Apr	79.0 Jul	100	61	95	67	71.34
Ujjain	23.11N, 75.46E	1680	1951-60[2]	77.9	90.9 May	65.5 Jan	113	41	109	44	35.24
Varanasi	25.20N, 83.00E	250	1931-60	78.8	93.6 May	61.5 Jan	117	35	113	40	42.36
Vijayawada	16.31N, 80.37E	80	1931-60[3]	82.0	90.0 May	74.5 Jan	118	57	110	61	37.76
Visakhapatnam	17.42N, 83.18E	10	1931-60	81.0	87.6 May	72.7 Jan	112	55	103	59	37.56
Warangal	18.18N, 79.35E	883	1931-60	81.9	93.9 May	72.5 Dec	116	47	112	53	36.38
INDONESIA											
Bandjermasin	3.20S, 114.36E	66	1956-65	80.2	81.1 Apr	79.3 Jan					108.46
Bandung	6.54S, 107.36E	2520	1913-38	72.7	73.2 Oct	71.8 Jul	94	52	90	55	85.00
Bogor	6.35S, 106.47E	820	1933-37	77.9	78.3 May	77.0 Jan					166.34
*Djakarta	6.10S, 106.49E	23	1921-50	80.2	81.0 May	79.0 Jan	98	66	92	69	69.68
Jogjakarta	7.48S, 110.22E	377	1933-37[4]	78.6	80.1 Oct	77.0 Jul			96	63	78.82
Makasar	5.07S, 119.24E	7	1956-65	79.5	81.1 Apr	78.3 Dec	95	58	91	64	125.51
Malang	7.59S, 112.38E	1460	1929-38	74.8	76.1 Oct	72.5 Jul	96	50	93	54	
Manado	1.29N, 124.51E	26	1956-65[5]	78.4	79.5 May	76.1 Feb			94	67	131.97
Medan	3.35N, 98.40E	82	1914-32, 1956-65	78.8	80.2 May	77.2 Jan	96	60	95	66	77.09
Padang	0.57S, 100.21E	23	1933-37	79.9	80.6 Apr	78.4 Nov	93	68			187.56
Palembang	3.00S, 104.46E	26	1956-65	79.9	82.0 Apr	78.6 Jan					93.74
Pontianak	0.02S, 109.20E	9	1933-37	81.3	82.2 Jul	79.9 Nov	94	68			120.31
Semarang	6.57S, 110.25E	7	1956-65	80.4	83.8 Nov	79.0 Jul	99	63	97	64	80.04

[1] Tamperature data for Palayamcottai, nr Tirunelveli.

[2] Temperature data for Ratlam, nr Ujjain.

[3] Temperature data for Masulipatnam, nr Vijayawada.

[4] Temperature data for Klaten, nr Jogjakarta.

[5] Temperature data for Mapanget, nr Manado.

ASIA

City	Latitude and longitude	Elev (ft)	Period of record	Temperature (°F) Avg	Avg warmest month	Avg coolest month	Absolute High	Absolute Low	Avg annual High	Avg annual Low	Annual precipitation (in)
Surabaja	7.15S, 112.45E	23	1920–25, 1927–38	80.2	81.9 Nov	78.4 Jul	97	62	94	65	59.76
Surakarta	7.35S, 110.50E	341	1933–37[1]	78.6	80.1 Oct	77.0 Jul			96	63	85.24
Tjirebon	6.44S, 108.34E	13	1937	81.1	83.3 Nov	79.9 Dec			95	68	74.96
IRAN											
Abadan	30.20N, 48.16E	10	9 yrs bef 1954	77.0	96.8 Jul	51.8 Jan	123	24	119	32	6.65
Ahvaz	31.19N, 48.42E	66	11 yrs bef 1954	77.0	96.8 Jul	59.0 Dec					7.48
Hamadan	34.48N, 48.30E	5824	13 yrs bef 1954	53.6	77.0 Aug	33.8 Jan			101	5	15.91
Isfahan	32.40N, 51.38E	5217	38 yrs bef 1947	59.7	82.2 Jul	36.5 Jan	110	-3	104	12	4.61
Kermanshah	34.19N, 47.04E	4337	1936–51	55.5	77.5 Jul	34 Jan	107	-13	105	5	16.3
Meshed	36.18N, 59.36E	3232	33 yrs bef 1948	56.1	77.0 Jul	34.5 Jan	105	-11	102	3	8.23
Shiraz	29.36N, 52.32E	5049	13 yrs bef 1954	60.8	78.8 Jul	41.0 Jan					13.23
Tabriz	38.05N, 46.18E	4469	11 yrs bef 1948	53.2	76.6 Jul	27.7 Jan					11.14
*Teheran	35.40N, 51.26E	3908	51 yrs bef 1948	61.0	83.5 Jul	36.7 Jan	109	-5	104	15	9.84
IRAQ											
*Baghdad	33.21N, 44.25E	111	1938–62	72.1	93.7 Jul	50.2 Jan	123	18	117	25	6.14
Basra	30.30N, 47.47E	8	1937–62	75.7	93.2 Jul	54.0 Jan	123	24	116	31	6.34
Karbala	32.36N, 44.02E	85	(see Baghdad)								
Kirkuk	35.28N, 44.28E	1086	? yrs bef 1964	71.1	94.1 Jul	48.0 Jan					15.47
Mosul	36.20N, 43.08E	730	1927–62	67.3	90.9 Jul	45.0 Jan	124	12	117	23	14.76
ISRAEL											
Haifa	32.49N, 35.00E	16	21 yrs bef 1951	71	83 Aug	57 Jan	112	27	103	41	26.1
*Jerusalem	31.47N, 35.13E	2658	1921–50	62.2	74.1 Aug	46.9 Jan	107	26	101	31	21.10
Tel Aviv–Jaffa	32.05N, 34.46E	10	1951–60	68.0	80.4 Aug	56.5 Jan			102	34	21.06

[1] Temperature data for Klaten, nr Surakarta.

ASIA

City	Latitude and longitude	Elev (ft)	Period of record	Temperature (°F) Avg	Avg warmest month	Avg coolest month	Absolute High	Absolute Low	Avg annual High	Avg annual Low	Annual precipitation (in)
JAPAN											
Akashi	34.38N, 134.59E	20	(see Kobe)								
Akita	39.43N, 140.07E	30	1931-60	51.3	75.6 Aug	30.0 Jan	98	-12	93	6	70.43
Amagasaki	34.43N, 135.25E		(see Osaka)								
Aomori	40.49N, 140.45E	13	1901–45, 1951-60	48.6	72.7 Aug	27.0 Jan	97	-12			54.41
Asahigawa	43.46N, 142.22E	364	1931-60	42.8	70.0 Aug	16.0 Jan	97	-42			45.04
Chiba	35.36N, 140.07E	79	(see Tokyo)								
Fujisawa	35.21N, 139.29E		(see Yokosuka)								
Fukui	36.04N, 136.13E	30	1901–45, 1951-60	56.5	79.0 Aug	36.1 Jan	101	5			92.64
Fukuoka	33.35N, 130.24E	7	1931-60	59.7	80.2 Aug	41.2 Jan	99	17			67.05
Fukushima	37.45N, 140.28E	220	1931-60	53.8	77.0 Aug	32.9 Jan	102	-1			45.51
Fukuyama	34.29N, 133.22E		(see Okayama)								
Funabashi	35.42N, 139.59E		(see Tokyo)								
Gifu	35.25N, 136.45E	43	1931-60	58.1	80.1 Aug	37.6 Jan	101	6			73.11
Hachinohe	40.30N, 141.29E	89	(see Aomori)								
Hachioji	35.39N, 139.20E		(see Tokyo)								
Hakodate	41.45N, 140.43E	108	1941-60	46.6	70.9 Aug	24.6 Jan	92	-7	86	2	46.38
Hamamatsu	34.42N, 137.44E	95	1897-1926	59.2	78.4 Aug	41.2 Jan	99	21			79.45
Higashiosaka	34.39N, 135.35E		(see Osaka)								
Himeji	34.49N, 134.42E	56	(see Kobe)								
Hirakata	34.48N, 135.38E		(see Osaka)								
Hiroshima	34.24N, 132.27E	95	1941-60	58.5	79.9 Aug	39.6 Jan	101	17	95	22	62.83
Hitachi	36.36N, 140.39E	171	1931-60[1]	55.0	76.3 Aug	35.6 Jan	97	10			54.96
Ichikawa	35.44N, 139.55E	75	(see Tokyo)								
Ichinomiya	35.18N, 136.48E		(see Nagoya)								
Ise	34.29N, 136.42E	7	1931-60[2]	58.5	79.7 Aug	39.6 Jan	101	18			67.09

[1] Climatic data for Mito, nr Hitachi.

[2] Climatic data for Tsu, nr Ise.

ASIA

City	Latitude and longitude	Elev (ft)	Period of record	Temperature (°F) Avg	Avg warmest month	Avg coolest month	Absolute High	Absolute Low	Avg annual High	Avg annual Low	Annual precipitation (in)
Iwaki	36.57N, 140.54E	10	? yrs bef 1961	54.7	75.0 Aug	36.9 Jan					55.04
Kagoshima	31.36N, 130.33E	16	1931-60	62.2	80.8 Aug	43.9 Jan	99	20	94	24	92.01
Kamakura	35.19N, 139.33E		(see Yokosuka)								
Kanazawa	36.34N, 136.39E	89	1931-60	56.3	78.6 Aug	36.5 Jan	101	15			100.75
Kawaguchi	35.48N, 139.43E		(see Tokyo)								
Kawasaki	35.32N, 139.43E		(see Yokohama)								
Kitakyushu	33.52N, 130.50E	23	(see Shimonoseki)								
Kobe	34.41N, 135.10E	190	1931-60	59.5	80.8 Aug	40.1 Jan	100	20			52.64
Kochi	33.33N, 133.33E	2	1931-60	60.4	79.3 Aug	41.4 Jan	99	19			104.17
Kofu	35.39N, 138.35E	892	1931-60	56.3	78.1 Aug	34.7 Jan	101	-3			47.52
Koriyama	37.24N, 140.23E	837	(see Fukushima)								
Kumamoto	32.48N, 130.43E	125	1931-60	60.3	80.6 Aug	40.3 Jan	102	15			73.58
Kurashiki	34.35N, 133.46E	10	(see Okayama)								
Kure	34.14N, 132.34E	89	1895-1929	59.2	80.6 Aug	40.8 Jan	100	19			56.42
Kurume	33.19N, 130.31E	43	(see Fukuoka)								
Kushiro	42.58N, 144.23E	108	1910-29	41.4	64.0 Aug	19.8 Jan	87	-19	80	-10	43.66
Kyoto	35.00N, 135.45E	135	1931-60	58.3	80.4 Aug	37.9 Jan	101	11			62.17
Machida	35.33N, 139.28E	318	(see Tokyo)								
Maebashi	36.23N, 139.04E	367	1931-60	56.1	77.5 Aug	36.3 Jan					49.05
Matsudo	35.47N, 139.54E	82	(see Tokyo)								
Matsuyama	33.50N, 132.45E	105	1931-60	59.5	79.9 Aug	41.0 Jan	99	17			54.29
Miyazaki	31.54N, 131.26E	23	1931-60	62.1	80.1 Aug	44.2 Jan	100	18			101.22
Morioka	39.42N, 141.09E	505	1931-60	49.1	73.6 Aug	26.6 Jan	99	0			50.20
Nagano	36.39N, 138.11E	1371	1931-60	52.0	76.3 Aug	29.1 Jan	101	1			39.41
Nagasaki	32.48N, 129.55E	89	1901-45, 1951-60	60.3	79.9 Aug	42.1 Jan	98	22	93	25	76.50
Nagoya	35.10N, 136.55E	167	1931-60	57.9	79.9 Aug	37.2 Jan	104	13			60.87
Nara	34.41N, 135.50E	345	1931-60	59.0	81.3 Aug	38.7 Jan					52.68
Neyagawa	34.46N, 135.38E		(see Osaka)								

ASIA

City	Latitude and longitude	Elev (ft)	Period of record	Temperature (°F) Avg	Avg warmest month	Avg coolest month	Absolute High	Absolute Low	Avg annual High	Avg annual Low	Annual precipitation (in)
Niigata	37.55N, 139.03E	7	1941-60	55.2	78.4 Aug	35.1 Jan	102	9	95	21	72.48
Nikko	36.45N, 139.37E	2001	1916, 1923-25, 1946-50	50.9	72.0 Aug	32.0 Feb	92	-3	88	11	68.82
Nishinomiya	34.43N, 135.20E		(see Osaka)								
Numazu	35.06N, 138.52E	23	1897-1926	59.5	78.6 Aug	41.7 Jan	98	17			82.44
Oita	33.14N, 131.36E	15	1931-60	59.2	78.8 Aug	41.2 Jan	97	16			65.16
Okayama	34.39N, 133.55E	10	1901-45, 1951-60	58.3	80.4 Aug	38.3 Jan	99	17			43.43
Okazaki	34.57N, 137.10E		(see Nagoya)								
Omiya	35.54N, 139.38E		(see Tokyo)								
Omuta	33.02N, 130.27E		(see Kumamoto)								
Osaka	34.40N, 135.30E	23	1941-60	59.9	82.0 Aug	40.1 Jan	100	18	96	25	53.50
Otaru	43.13N, 141.00E	79	(see Sapporo)								
Sagamihara	35.33N, 139.22E		(see Yokohama)								
Sakai	34.35N, 135.28E		(see Osaka)								
Sapporo	43.03N, 141.21E	56	1931-60	45.7	71.1 Aug	22.1 Jan	96	-19	90	-7	44.72
Sasebo	33.10N, 129.43E	43	1894-1929	60.6	81.0 Aug	42.4 Jan	101	23			77.40
Sendai	38.15N, 140.53E	125	1931-60	52.3	74.8 Aug	32.2 Jan					48.50
Shimizu	35.01N, 138.29E	98	(see Shizuoka)								
Shimonoseki	33.57N, 130.57E	151	1931-60	59.7	79.7 Aug	41.7 Jan	97	20			66.97
Shizuoka	34.58N, 138.23E	43	1941-60	60.1	79.2 Aug	42.3 Jan					95.51
Suita	34.45N, 135.32E		(see Osaka)								
Takamatsu	34.20N, 134.03E	30	1951-60	59.2	79.9 Aug	40.6 Jan					48.90
Takasaki	36.20N, 139.01E	312	(see Maebashi)								
Takatsuki	34.51N, 135.37E		(see Osaka)								
Tokushima	34.04N, 134.34E	4	1931-60	59.5	79.7 Aug	40.8 Jan	99	21			63.98
*Tokyo	35.42N, 139.46E	13	1931-60	58.5	79.5 Aug	38.7 Jan	101	17	93	21	61.54
Toyama	36.41N, 137.13E	30	1941-60	55.8	78.3 Aug	35.6 Jan					93.31
Toyohashi	34.46N, 137.23E	98	(see Hamamatsu)								

ASIA

City	Latitude and longitude	Elev (ft)	Period of record	Temperature (°F) Avg	Avg warmest month	Avg coolest month	Absolute High	Absolute Low	Avg annual High	Avg annual Low	Annual precipitation (in)
Toyonaka	34.47N, 135.28E		(see Osaka)								
Toyota	35.05N, 137.09E	246	(see Nagoya)								
Urawa	35.51N, 139.39E	66	(see Tokyo)								
Utsunomiya	36.33N, 139.52E	394	1941-60	54.5	76.6 Aug	33.8 Jan	99	5			59.92
Wakayama	34.13N, 135.11E	46	1931-60	59.9	80.6 Aug	41.0 Jan	100	21			56.50
Yamagata	38.15N, 140.15E	495	1931-60	51.4	75.9 Aug	29.1 Jan	105	-4			48.66
Yao	34.37N, 135.36E		(see Osaka)								
Yokkaichi	34.58N, 136.37E	10	(see Nagoya)								
Yokohama	35.27N, 139.39E	128	1931-60	58.1	78.4 Aug	39.4 Jan	97	17			65.55
Yokosuka	35.18N, 139.40E	39	1894-1929	58.1	77.4 Aug	40.5 Jan	98	20			76.34
JORDAN											
*Amman	31.57N, 35.56E	2513	1931-60	63.5	78.1 Aug	46.8 Jan	109	21	103	29	10.75
KASHMIR-JAMMU											
*Jammu	32.44N, 74.52E	1201	1931-60	75.7	93.2 Jun	55.9 Jan	117	33	113	40	43.94
*Srinagar	34.05N, 74.50E	5205	1931-60	55.9	76.3 Jul	33.8 Jan	101	-4	97	18	25.94
KOREA: NORTH											
Chongjin	41.46N, 129.49E	164	1905-34	45.5	71.1 Aug	21.6 Jan					22.20
Hamhung	39.54N, 127.32E	108	1910-37, 1941-54	49.1	74.1 Aug	21.7 Jan					35.67
Hungnam	39.30N, 127.14E		(see Hamhung)								
Kaesong	37.58N, 126.33E	197	1917-37	50.7	77.4 Aug	21.2 Jan					50.98
Kimchaek	40.41N, 129.12E	13	1905-36	46.2	71.4 Aug	21.2 Jan	99	-12			31.81
*Pyongyang	39.01N, 125.45E	95	1907-54	48.9	75.9 Aug	17.6 Jan	98	-19			37.01
Sinuiju	40.06N, 124.24E	20	1931-54	47.7	75.4 Aug	15.8 Jan					54.49
Wonsan	39.10N, 127.26E	120	1905-54	50.5	73.9 Aug	25.5 Jan	103	-7	96	2	52.8

ASIA

City	Latitude and longitude	Elev (ft)	Period of record	Temperature (° F) Avg	Avg warmest month	Avg coolest month	Absolute High	Absolute Low	Avg annual High	Avg annual Low	Annual precipitation (in)
KOREA: SOUTH											
Chonju	35.49N, 127.09E	167	1919-34	53.8	78.6 Aug	28.6 Jan	99	4			49.72
Inchon	37.28N, 126.38E	226	1905-34	51.3	76.6 Aug	25.2 Jan	98	-6			40.8
Kwangju	35.09N, 126.55E	115	1913-37	54.7	79.5 Aug	30.0 Jan					47.91
Masan	35.11N, 128.34E	89	1916-25	57.0	80.1 Aug	34.3 Jan	97	7	94	12	55.39
Mokpo	34.47N, 126.23E	105	1905-38	55.6	79.0 Aug	34.2 Jan	99	6			42.05
Pusan	35.06N, 129.03E	226	1905-34	56.5	78.1 Aug	35.6 Jan	96	7	91	14	55.6
*Seoul	37.34N, 127.00E	279	1908-34	51.6	77.9 Aug	23.7 Jan	99	-12	96	-4	49.17
Taegu	35.52N, 128.36E	190	1921-50	54.5	79.2 Aug	28.8 Jan	103	-4			37.64
Taejon	36.20N, 127.26E	187	1917-37	53.4	78.8 Aug	24.3 Jan					52.72
KUWAIT											
*Kuwait	29.20N, 47.59E	16	15 yrs bef 1954	77	95 Aug	55 Jan	121	32	115	38	4.69
LAOS											
*Vientiane	17.58N, 102.36E	558	1941-44, 1947-50	77.4	81.5 May	69.4 Jan	104	39	101	47	72.83
LEBANON											
*Beirut	33.53N, 35.30E	79	1881-1935	70.0	83.1 Aug	56.7 Jan	107	30	95	40	34.80
Tripoli	34.26N, 35.51E	26	1951-58	66.0	79.2 Aug	53.6 Jan					30.12
MACAO											
*Macao	22.12N, 113.32E	66	1881-1916	72.7	83.3 Jul	59.5 Feb	101	29			66.69
MALAYSIA											
George Town	5.25N, 100.20E	17	49 yrs bef 1939	82	83 Mar	80.5 Sep	98	65	95	69	107.7
Ipoh	4.35N, 101.05E	126	? yrs bef 1963	81.7	82.6 Jun	80.8 Dec	99	63			101.60
*Kuala Lumpur	3.10N, 101.42E	127	1930-41, 1948-54	81.5	82.5 Mar	80.5 Dec	98	64	96	67	96.1

ASIA

City	Latitude and longitude	Elev (ft)	Period of record	Temperature (°F) Avg	Avg warmest month	Avg coolest month	Absolute High	Absolute Low	Avg annual High	Avg annual Low	Annual precipitation (in)
MONGOLIA											
*Ulan-Bator	47.55N, 106.53E	4295	40 yrs bef 1949	24.8	64.0 Jul	-20.7 Jan	99	-56	91	-41	9.02
NEPAL											
*Katmandu	27.42N, 85.20E	4388	42 yrs bef 1937	65.1	75.6 Jul	49.8 Jan	97	28	94	30	56.2
PAKISTAN											
Gujranwala	32.09N, 74.11E	738	1963-66	73.0	91.7 Jun	52.7 Jan	118	29	114	30	21.53
Hyderabad	25.22N, 68.22E	98	1881-1930, 1935-36	81.0	93.4 Jun	63.1 Jan					7.20
*Islamabad	33.42N, 73.10E	1800	(see Rawalpindi)								
Karachi	24.52N, 67.03E	20	1921-50	78.0	86.3 Jun	66.2 Jan	118	39	107	45	8.13
Lahore	31.35N, 74.18E	702	1921-50	76.3	94.1 Jun	54.0 Jan	120	28	116	32	18.23
Lyallpur	31.25N, 73.05E	605	? yrs bef 1944	75.3	93.8 Jun	53.5 Jan	117	30	115	33	13.18
Multan	30.11N, 71.29E	413	35 yrs bef 1937	79.0	97.0 Jun	56.5 Jan	121	29	118	33	6.6
Peshawar	34.01N, 71.33E	1177	1891-1929, 1931-40	72.5	92.1 Jun	50.7 Jan	122	26	116	31	13.54
Rawalpindi	33.36N, 73.04E	1676	1881-1940	70.9	89.8 Jun	50.2 Jan	117	25	114	29	35.72
Sargodha	32.05N, 72.40E	614	(see Lyallpur)								
Sialkot	32.30N, 74.31E	830	? yrs bef 1921	74.8	92.9 Jun	54.4 Jan					31.83
PHILIPPINES											
Bacolod	10.41N, 122.56E	23	6 yrs bef 1919	80.2	82.9 May	78.6 Jan	101	59	96	64	85.55
Basilan	6.42N, 121.58E	25	(see Zamboanga)								
Caloocan	14.38N, 121.03E		(see Manila)								
Cebu	10.18N, 123.54E	138	1903-18	80.8	82.6 May	78.8 Jan	96	65	93	69	67.05
Davao	7.04N, 125.36E	63	1903-18	80.4	81.7 Apr	79.2 Jan	99	61	96	66	76.47
Iloilo	10.42N, 122.34E	46	15 yrs bef 1938	81.5	84 Apr	79 Jan	98	67	96	69	83.54

ASIA

City	Latitude and longitude	Elev (ft)	Period of record	Temperature (°F) Avg	Avg warmest month	Avg coolest month	Absolute High	Absolute Low	Avg annual High	Avg annual Low	Annual precipitation (in)
Manila	14.36N, 120.59E	51	1887-1940	79.9	83.1 May	76.5 Jan	101	58	98	61	84.92
Pasay	14.33N, 121.00E		(see Manila)								
*Quezon City	14.38N, 121.00E	232	1952-55	80.0	84.4 May	75.4 Dec	101	56			91.62
Zamboanga	6.54N, 122.04E	15	1903-18	79.9	80.4 May	79.3 Feb	94	60	92	67	38.98
RYUKYU ISLANDS											
*Naha	26.13N, 127.40E	89	1901-45	71.8	82.4 Jul	60.6 Feb	96	41	93	45	82.80
SAUDI ARABIA											
*Jidda	21.30N, 39.12E	20	1941-45	82.2	89.1 Jul	75.0 Jan	117	49	110	52	3.15
Mecca	21.27N, 39.49E	853									
Medina	24.28N, 39.36E	1949	1957-60	81.1	94.8 Aug	63.5 Jan					2.44
*Riyadh	24.38N, 46.43E	1938	1941-45	76.7	92.5 Jul	58.1 Jan	113	19	112	29	3.14
SINGAPORE											
*Singapore	1.17N, 103.51E	33	1903-39	80.6	81.5 May	79.0 Jan	97	66	93	69	95.08
SOUTHERN YEMEN											
*Aden	12.46N, 45.01E	12	1921-50	83.9	90.2 Jun	77.8 Jan	106	61	103	63	1.51
SYRIA											
Aleppo	36.10N, 37.10E	1050	1952-61	63.3	84.0 Aug	43.2 Jan	117	9	108	17	12.09
*Damascus	33.30N, 36.18E	2392	1952-61	63.9	81.9 Aug	45.7 Jan	113	21	105	25	8.98
Hama	35.09N, 36.44E	1014	1956-60	64.4	84.0 Aug	45.3 Jan					11.77
Homs	34.44N, 36.43E	1600	(see Hama)								
TAIWAN											
Chiai	23.29N, 120.27E	102	(see Tainan)								

ASIA

City	Latitude and longitude	Elev (ft)	Period of record	Temperature (°F) Avg	Avg warmest month	Avg coolest month	Absolute High	Absolute Low	Avg annual High	Avg annual Low	Annual precipitation (in)
Hsinchu	24.48N, 120.58E	108	1938-52	71.4	82.4 Jul	58.8 Feb	99	37	97	43	69.41
Kaohsiung	22.38N, 120.17E	95	1932-52	75.7	82.2 Jul	66.0 Jan	99	45	95	48	75.71
Keelung	25.08N, 121.44E	10	1903-52	71.1	82.4 Jul	60.1 Jan	100	37	97	46	119.80
Sanchung	25.04N, 121.29E		(see Taipei)								
Taichung	24.09N, 120.41E	253	1897-1952	72.3	82.0 Jul	60.4 Jan	102	30	95	39	70.24
Tainan	23.00N, 120.12E	43	1897-1952	73.9	82.2 Jul	62.8 Jan	100	36	95	43	72.40
*Taipei	25.03N, 121.30E	26	1897-1952	71.2	82.8 Jul	59.0 Feb	102	32	97	41	82.68
THAILAND											
*Bangkok	13,45N, 100.31E	26	1931-60	82.6	86.4 Apr	77.9 Dec	106	52	103	57	58.74
Thon Buri	13.43N, 100.29E		(see Bangkok)								
TURKEY											
Adana	37.01N, 35.18E	66	30 yrs bef 1961	65.5	82.4 Aug	48.4 Jan	114	19	104	25	24.06
*Ankara	39.56N, 32.52E	2959	30 yrs bef 1961	53.1	73.9 Jul	31.6 Jan	104	-13	98	2	14.17
Antioch	36.14N, 36.07E	305	21 yrs bef 1961	64.6	81.9 Aug	46.4 Jan	109	6			44.92
Bursa	40.11N, 29.04E	328	30 yrs bef 1961	57.9	75.6 Jul	41.7 Jan	109	-3	100	16	28.54
Eskisehir	39.46N, 30.32E	2576	30 yrs bef 1961	51.4	70.5 Jul	31.6 Jan	102	-15			14.49
Gaziantep	37.05N, 37.22E	2756	21 yrs bef 1961	57.9	80.8 Jul	36.7 Jan	109	0			21.65
Izmir	38.25N, 27.09E	82	30 yrs bef 1961	63.5	81.7 Jul	47.5 Jan	109	12	103	24	27.28
Kayseri	38.43N, 35.30E	3514	27 yrs bef 1961	51.4	73.0 Jul	28.9 Jan	105	-26			14.41
Konya	37.52N, 32.31E	3366	30 yrs bef 1961	52.7	73.6 Jul	31.6 Jan	100	-19	96	-1	12.40
USSR											
Aktyubinsk	50.17N, 57.10E	719	46 yrs bef 1961	38.5	72.1 Jul	3.9 Jan	109	-54	100	-33	
Alma-Ata	43.15N, 76.57E	2779	1915-60	47.7	73.9 Jul	18.7 Jan	108	-36	99	-15	22.05
Andizhan	40.45N, 72.22E	1565	1931-57	56.3	81.1 Jul	26.6 Jan	111	-20	104	-2	
Angarsk	52.34N, 103.54E	1368	1951-60	29.7	64.0 Jul	-8.1 Jan	99	-60	91	-44	

ASIA

City	Latitude and longitude	Elev (ft)	Period of record	Temperature (° F) Avg	Avg warmest month	Avg coolest month	Absolute High	Absolute Low	Avg annual High	Avg annual Low	Annual precipitation (in)
Ashkhabad	37.57N, 58.23E	745	? yrs bef 1961	60.6	86.7 Jul	33.1 Jan	118	-15	108	3	8.70
Barnaul	53.22N, 83.45E	518	1881-1960	34.0	67.5 Jul	0.1 Jan	100	-62	93	-45	18.90
Biysk	52.34N, 85.15E	745	1934-60	32.9	66.0 Jul	-0.8 Jan	102	-63	93	-45	18.70
Bratsk	56.21N, 101.55E	1243	1957-62	28.0	64.8 Jul	-8.7 Jan	99	-71	91	-49	11.85
Bukhara	39.48N, 64.25E	738	1951-60	57.0	81.5 Jul	30.9 Jan	117	-15	106	1	
Chelyabinsk	55.10N, 61.24E	758	? yrs bef 1960	35.2	65.7 Jul	3.7 Jan	102	-49			15.47
Chimkent	42.18N, 69.36E	1782	1920-60	53.4	79.3 Jul	26.6 Jan	111	-29	104	-11	
Chita	52.03N, 113.30E	2202	1890-1919, 1924-56	27.1	65.8 Jul	-15.9 Jan	106	-65	93	-45	13.70
Dushanbe	38.33N, 68.48E	2697	1937-57	57.6	80.8 Jul	33.1 Jan	111	-18	104	7	23.78
Dzhambul	42.54N, 71.22E	2106	1928-60	48.2	73.9 Jul	21.2 Jan	111	-42	100	-22	11.30
Frunze	42.54N, 74.36E	2480	1927-60	49.6	75.4 Jul	21.9 Jan	108	-36	100	-15	
Irkutsk	52.16N, 104.20E	1536	1881-1960	30.0	63.7 Jul	-5.6 Jan	97	-58	90	-42	15.87
Kamensk-Uralskiy	56.25N, 61.54E		(see Sverdlovsk)								
Karaganda	49.50N, 73.10E	1804	1933-60	36.1	68.5 Jul	4.8 Jan	104	-56	95	-35	12.32
Kemerovo	55.20N, 86.05E	505	1933-60	31.3	65.1 Jul	-2.6 Jan	100	-67	90	-44	
Khabarovsk	48.30N, 135.06E	285	66 yrs bef 1961	34.5	70.0 Jul	-8.1 Jan	104	-45	90	-31	19.2
Kokand	40.30N, 70.57E	1339	1925-60	56.3	81.5 Jul	27.9 Jan	111	-17	104	3	
Komsomolsk-na-Amure	50.35N, 137.02E	66	1932-33, 1935-60	30.7	67.8 Jul	-14.1 Jan	102	-58	88	-44	
Kopeysk	55.07N, 61.37E		(see Chelyabinsk)								
Krasnoyarsk	56.01N, 92.50E	637	? yrs bef 1960	33.4	67.8 Jul	0.7 Jan	103	-56			13.31
Kurgan	55.26N, 65.18E	259	? yrs bef 1948[1]	32.4	65.7 Jul	-0.9 Jan					15.16
Magnitogorsk	53.27N, 59.04E	1263									
Namangan	41.00N, 71.40E	1555	1924-60	56.1	81.7 Jul	25.9 Jan	111	-20	104	0	
Nizhniy Tagil	57.55N, 59.57E	732									
Novokuznetsk	53.45N, 87.06E	771	1931-37, 1944-54	33.3	65.3 Jul	0.0 Jan	100	-62	91	-42	

[1] Climatic data for Staro-Sidorovo, nr Kurgan.

ASIA

City	Latitude and longitude	Elev (ft)	Period of record	Temperature (°F) Avg	Avg warmest month	Avg coolest month	Absolute High	Absolute Low	Avg annual High	Avg annual Low	Annual precipitation (in)
Novosibirsk	55.02N, 82.55E	446	1930–57	31.8	65.7 Jul	-2.2 Jan	100	-58	93	-45	15.12
Omsk	55.00N, 73.24E	410	1930–60	32.0	64.9 Jul	-2.6 Jan	104	-56	93	-40	13.43
Pavlodar	52.18N, 76.57E	387	1906–11, 1922–60	35.4	70.2 Jul	-0.2 Jan	108	-53	97	-38	10.00
Petropavlovsk	54.52N, 69.06E	440	62 yrs bef 1961	32.9	65.8 Jul	-1.7 Jan	106	-63	93	-36	
Petropavlovsk-Kamchatskiy	53.01N, 158.39E	105	48 yrs bef 1961	35.4	56.3 Aug	16.7 Feb	88	-29	77	-8	27.32
Prokopyevsk	53.53N, 86.45E		1925–60[1]	32.7	64.9 Jul	0.1 Jan	100	-58	91	-42	
Samarkand	39.40N, 66.58E	2382	1932–60	55.2	77.9 Jul	31.5 Jan	113	-22	102	0	12.60
Semipalatinsk	50.28N, 80.13E	663	64 yrs bef 1949	37.8	72.0 Jul	2.8 Jan	108	-56	100	-40	10.51
Sverdlovsk	56.51N, 60.36E	925	1921–50	34.7	63.5 Jul	4.8 Jan	99	-45	87	-34	17.68
Tashkent	41.20N, 69.18E	1565	1881–1960	55.9	80.4 Jul	30.4 Jan	111	-22	106	-2	14.65
Temir-Tau	50.05N, 72.56E		(see Karaganda)								
Tomsk	56.30N, 84.58E	456	1881–1960	30.9	64.6 Jul	-2.6 Jan	97	-67	90	-47	21.10
Tselinograd	51.10N, 71.30E	1139	73 yrs bef 1961	34.5	68.4 Jul	0.7 Jan	108	-62	97	-36	12.01
Tyumen	57.09N, 65.26E	249	1884–1942	34.3	65.5 Jul	2.1 Jan	104	-58	93	-35	15.94
Ulan-Ude	51.50N, 107.37E	1686	66 yrs bef 1961	28.9	66.9 Jul	-13.7 Jan	104	-60	95	-44	7.95
Ust-Kamenogorsk	49.58N, 82.40E	932	1921–22, 1926–48	37.4	70.2 Jul	2.8 Jan	106	-54	99	-49	14.21
Vladivostok	43.08N, 131.54E	364	1917–60	39.2	68.0 Aug	6.1 Jan	97	-24	86	-15	29.29
Zlatoust	55.10N, 59.40E	1503	? yrs bef 1959	33.1	61.3 Jul	4.3 Jan	93	-51	85	-38	21.54
VIETNAM: NORTH											
Haiphong	20.52N, 106.41E	381	1904, 1906–30	73.8	82.9 Jul	61.7 Feb			99	48	69.21
*Hanoi	21.02N, 105.51E	56	22 yrs bef 1931	75.2	85.1 Jun	62.8 Feb	109	42	102	46	71.22
VIETNAM: SOUTH											
Da Nang	16.04N, 108.13E	20	1931–44, 1947–62	77.9	84.4 Jun	70.3 Jan					81.61

[1] Temperature data for Kiselevsk, nr Prokopyevsk.

ASIA

City	Latitude and longitude	Elev (ft)	Period of record	Temperature (°F) Avg	Avg warmest month	Avg coolest month	Absolute High	Absolute Low	Avg annual High	Avg annual Low	Annual precipitation (in)
Hue	16.28N, 107.36E	49	1931–44, 1947–62	77.2	84.7 Jun	68.0 Jan			104	54	118.78
*Saigon	10.45N, 106.40E	30	1929–44, 1947–62	80.4	83.8 Apr	78.1 Dec	104	57	98	62	76.26
YEMEN											
*Sana	15.23N, 44.12E	7260	? yrs bef 1936	63.5	71.1 Jun	57.3 Jan					19.68

EUROPE

City	Latitude and longitude	Elev (ft)	Period of record	Temperature (°F) Avg	Avg warmest month	Avg coolest month	Absolute High	Absolute Low	Avg annual High	Avg annual Low	Annual precipitation (in)
ALBANIA											
*Tirane	41.20N, 19.50E	416	1930-58	60.4	77.2 Jul	44.4 Jan	105	13			46.81
AUSTRIA											
Graz	47.04N, 15.27E	1237	1881-1930	47.8	65.5 Jul	27.3 Jan	99	-11	88	5	34.41
Innsbruck	47.16N, 11.24E	1909	1921-55	48.5	66.5 Jul	27 Jan	97	-16	92	0	33.8
Linz	48.18N, 14.18E	853	1881-1930	47.8	65.8 Jul	30.2 Jan	100	-17	92	3	38.50
Salzburg	47.48N, 13.02E	1427	1881-1930	47.5	64.6 Jul	29.5 Jan	97	-23	91	-1	54.29
*Vienna	48.12N, 16.22E	663	1881-1939	48.6	66.7 Jul	30.0 Jan	98	-14	90	7	26.34
BELGIUM											
Anderlecht	50.50N, 4.18E	98	(see Brussels)								
Antwerp	51.13N, 4.25E	16	1901-30	50.2	64.4 Jul	37.6 Jan					28.07
Bruges	51.13N, 3.14E	39	(see Ghent)								
*Brussels	50.50N, 4.20E	328	1901-30	49.8	63.1 Jul	37.8 Jan	98	0	90	13	32.87
Charleroi	50.25N, 4.26E	341	1901-30[1]	49.8	63.0 Jul	38.3 Jan					30.83

[1] Climatic data for Paturages, nr Charleroi.

EUROPE

City	Latitude and longitude	Elev (ft)	Period of record	Temperature (°F) Avg	Avg warmest month	Avg coolest month	Absolute High	Absolute Low	Avg annual High	Avg annual Low	Annual precipitation (in)
Ghent	51.03N, 3.43E	23	1901-30	50.4	64.6 Jul	37.9 Jan					32.28
La Louviere	50.28N, 4.11E		1901-30[1]	49.8	63.0 Jul	38.3 Jan					30.83
Liege	50.38N, 5.34E	377	(see Aachen, West Germany)								
Schaerbeek	50.51N, 4.23E		(see Brussels)								
BULGARIA											
Burgas	42.30N, 27.28E	16	1900-18, 1926-39	54.7	73.8 Jul	35.2 Jan					21.77
Plovdiv	42.09N, 24.45E	525	30 yrs bef 1951	54.5	74.5 Jul	31.5 Jan	104	-25	100	1	20.1
Ruse	43.50N, 25.57E	151	1894-1939	51.1	72.3 Jul	27.1 Jan					22.68
*Sofia	42.41N, 23.19E	1850	1881-82, 1887-1939	50.2	70.2 Jul	28.4 Jan	99	-17	96	-2	24.61
Stara Zagora	42.25N, 25.38E	768	1900-18, 1928-39	55.2	75.7 Jul	34.0 Jan					23.39
Varna	43.13N, 27.55E	157	1892-1919, 1924-39	53.6	72.7 Jul	33.8 Jan	107	-12	96	8	19.76
CZECHOSLOVAKIA											
Bratislava	48.09N, 17.07E	538	1901-50	49.8	68.4 Jul	29.1 Jan	101	-22	93	3	26.38
Brno	49.11N, 16.37E	745	1901-50	47.1	65.1 Jul	28.2 Jan	98	-23	91	1	21.53
Karlovy Vary	50.14N, 12.53E	1263	1901-50	45.1	62.4 Jul	28.2 Jan	97	-18	90	-1	25.94
Kosice	48.44N, 21.15E	676	1901-50	47.1	66.4 Jul	25.9 Jan	99	-23	92	-3	26.10
Ostrava	49.51N, 18.18E	712	1901-50	47.5	65.7 Jul	28.4 Jan	97	-26	92	-7	30.28
Plzen	49.45N, 13.25E	1161	1901-50	46.0	64.0 Jul	28.4 Jan	98	-21	92	-2	20.39
*Prague	50.04N, 14.27E	633	1901-50	48.2	66.2 Jul	30.4 Jan	101	-20	93	1	19.17
DENMARK											
Alborg	57.03N, 9.56E	10	1886-1925[2]	44.1	59.5 Jul	30.9 Feb					
Arhus	56.09N, 10.13E	161	1934-54	46	62 Jul	31 Jan	87	-12	82	10	26.6

[1] Climatic data for Paturages, nr La Louviere.

[2] Temperature data for Skorping, nr Alborg.

EUROPE

City	Latitude and longitude	Elev (ft)	Period of record	Temperature (°F) Avg	Avg warmest month	Avg coolest month	Absolute High	Absolute Low	Avg annual High	Avg annual Low	Annual precipitation (in)
*Copenhagen	55.40N, 12.35E	16	1921-50	46.9	63.9 Jul	31.8 Feb	91	-3	83	11	22.72
Frederiksberg	55.41N, 12.32E		(see Copenhagen)								
Odense	55.24N, 10.23E	49	1926-54	46.5	61.5 Jul	31.5 Feb	90	-11	83	7	23.8
FINLAND											
Espoo	60.13N, 24.40E		(see Helsinki)								
*Helsinki	60.10N, 24.58E	39	1931-60	41.7	64.0 Jul	21.2 Feb	89	-23	82	-11	25.47
Tampere	61.30N, 23.45E	312	1931-60	38.8	62.2 Jul	17.6 Feb	91	-32	85	-16	19.96
Turku	60.27N, 22.17E	52	20 yrs bef 1944	40	62 Jul	21 Feb	97	-29	85	-14	24.0
FRANCE											
Ajaccio	41.55N, 8.44E	125	1921-50	58.5	71.2 Aug	47.1 Jan	103	23	96	29	27.36
Amiens	49.54N, 2.18E	118	1891-1914, 1923-34[1]	49.3	63.3 Jul	36.5 Jan					26.26
Angers	47.28N, 0.33W	154	1901-30	52.7	66.2 Jul	40.6 Jan					25.79
Avignon	43.57N, 4.49E	180	1891-1914, 1921-34	56.7	73.0 Jul	40.8 Jan					24.25
Bayonne	43.29N, 1.29W	10	1901-30[2]	58.1	69.4 Aug	47.8 Jan			96	24	51.34
Besancon	47.15N, 6.02E	1207	1921-50	50.5	66.2 Jul	34.9 Jan					43.39
Bethune	50.32N, 2.38E	98	1891-1914, 1923-34[1]	49.3	63.3 Jul	36.5 Jan					25.67
Bordeaux	44.50N, 0.34W	23	1921-50	54.7	67.5 Jul	42.1 Dec	102	9	96	19	34.61
Boulogne-Billancourt	48.50N, 2.15E	98	(see Paris)								
Brest	48.24N, 4.29W	322	1921-50	51.4	61.0 Aug	43.3 Feb	95	7	86	24	42.91

[1] Temperature data for Arras, nr Amiens and Bethune.

[2] Climatic data for Biarritz, nr Bayonne.

EUROPE

City	Latitude and longitude	Elev (ft)	Period of record	Temperature (°F) Avg	Avg warmest month	Avg coolest month	Absolute High	Absolute Low	Avg annual High	Avg annual Low	Annual precipitation (in)
Bruay-en-Artois	50.29N, 2.33E	131	1891-1914, 1923-34[1]	49.3	63.3 Jul	36.5 Jan					
Caen	49.11N, 0.21W	85	1901-30	50.9	62.8 Jul	40.3 Jan	99	6	91	10	25.79
Cannes	43.33N, 7.01E	10	1921-50	57.9	71.6 Jul	45.1 Jan					31.46
Clermont-Ferrand	45.47N, 3.05E	1335	1921-50	51.8	66.7 Jul	37.6 Jan	107	-10	97	9	22.64
Denain	50.20N, 3.23E	131	1891-1914, 1923-34[1]	49.3	63.3 Jul	36.5 Jan					
Dijon	47.19N, 5.01E	1109	1891-1936, 1946-50	51	67.5 Jul	35 Jan	107	-8	94	11	27.5
Douai	50.22N, 3.04E	79	(see Lille)								
Dunkerque	51.03N, 2.22E	26	1881-1917, 1921-34	50.0	62.6 Aug	38.8 Jan					30.04
Grenoble	45.10N, 5.43E	810	1921-50	51.6	68.2 Jul	35.1 Jan	99	-6	94	10	39.96
Le Havre	49.30N, 0.08E	16	1901-30	51.4	63.3 Aug	40.8 Jan					27.83
Le Mans	48.00N, 0.12E	253	1921-50	52.0	65.8 Jul	39.2 Dec					25.98
Lens	50.26N, 2.50E	131	(see Lille)								
Lille	50.38N, 3.04E	79	1921-50	49.8	63.5 Aug	37.2 Jan	96	0	91	12	26.97
Limoges	45.51N, 1.15E	942	1891-1913, 1921-34	51.4	66.0 Jul	37.8 Jan	102	0	97	11	35.71
Lyons	45.45N, 4.51E	738	1921-50	52.5	69.3 Jul	36.3 Jan	105	-13	95	11	31.93
Marseilles	43.18N, 5.24E	532	1921-50	57.7	73.6 Jul	42.8 Jan	101	9	93	23	21.02
Metz	49.08N, 6.10E	860	1901-30	49.6	65.5 Jul	34.3 Dec					28.39
Montbeliard	47.31N, 6.48E	1207	1901-30	(see Besancon for temperature data)							41.77
Montpellier	43.36N, 3.53E	144	1921-50	57.0	72.3 Jul	42.8 Jan					26.57
Montreuil	48.52N, 2.26E	394	(see Paris)								
Mulhouse	47.45N, 7.20E	787	1921-50	49.8	66.2 Jul	33.4 Jan					28.31

[1] Temperature data for Arras, nr Bruay-en-Artois and Denain.

EUROPE

City	Latitude and longitude	Elev (ft)	Period of record	Temperature (°F) Avg	Avg warmest month	Avg coolest month	Absolute High	Absolute Low	Avg annual High	Avg annual Low	Annual precipitation (in)
Nancy	48.41N, 6.12E	915	1921-50	49.3	64.9 Jul	34.2 Jan	96	-4	89	7	27.91
Nantes	47.13N, 1.33W	62	1921-50	53.2	66.2 Jul	41.4 Dec	102	5	94	17	31.50
Nice	43.42N, 7.15E	151	1921-50	59.4	72.7 Jul	46.9 Jan	98	24	92	31	31.89
Nimes	43.50N, 4.21E	374	1901-30	57.9	74.8 Jul	43.0 Jan					29.61
Orleans	47.55N, 1.54E	381	1921-50	51.4	65.8 Jul	37.9 Dec	105	4	93	15	24.96
*Paris	48.52N, 2.20E	197	1921-50	52.0	66.7 Jul	38.5 Dec	104	4	93	16	25.39
Pau	43.18N, 0.22W	679	1901-30	54.5	67.5 Jul	42.3 Dec					45.24
Perpignan	42.41N, 2.53E	197	1921-50	59.9	75.0 Jul	46.4 Jan	108	12	95	25	23.90
Rennes	48.05N, 1.41W	177	1921-50	52.2	64.4 Jul	41.4 Dec	105	-3	91	16	26.97
Rheims	49.15N, 4.02E	282	1921-50	50.4	65.1 Jul	36.3 Jan	101	-4	93	9	23.90
Roubaix	50.42N, 3.10E	115	(see Lille)								
Rouen	49.26N, 1.05E	72	1921-50	50.5	63.9 Jul	38.3 Jan					27.44
Saint-Denis	48.56N, 2.22E	98	(see Paris)								
Saint-Etienne	45.26N, 4.24E	1772	1921-50	50.7	66.2 Jul	36.1 Jan					27.16
Saint-Nazaire	47.17N, 2.12W	26	(see Nantes)								
Strasbourg	48.35N, 7.45E	932	1921-50	50.0	66.6 Jul	33.6 Jan	99	-8	93	9	24.17
Thionville	49.22N, 6.10E	656	(see Saarbrucken, West Germany)								
Toulon	43.07N, 5.56E	92	1921-50	59.9	73.4 Jul	47.7 Jan	96	14	92	29	26.65
Toulouse	43.36N, 1.26E	456	1921-50	55.4	70.3 Jul	41.5 Jan	111	1	99	16	26.18
Tourcoing	50.43N, 3.09E	148	(see Lille)								
Tours	47.23N, 0.41E	180	1921-50	52.5	66.9 Jul	39.4 Dec					26.81
Troyes	48.18N, 4.05E	361	1881-1917, 1921-34[1]	48.9	64.4 Jul	34.0 Jan					25.59
Valenciennes	50.21N, 3.32E	98	(see Lille)								
Versailles	48.48N, 2.08E	604	(see Paris)								

[1] Temperature data for Chaumont, nr Troyes.

EUROPE

City	Latitude and longitude	Elev (ft)	Period of record	Temperature (°F) Avg	Avg warmest month	Avg coolest month	Absolute High	Absolute Low	Avg annual High	Avg annual Low	Annual precipitation (in)
Villeurbanne	45.46N, 4.53E	581	(see Lyons)								
GERMANY: EAST											
*Berlin (see under Germany: West)											
Brandenburg	52.25N, 12.33E	102	1955-56, 1958-59, 1962	(see Potsdam for temperature data)							21.85
Dessau	51.50N, 12.15E	200	1893-1930	47.8	64.4 Jul	32.0 Jan					
Dresden	51.03N, 13.45E	371	1901-50	47.1	64.0 Jul	30.6 Jan	100	-18	91	5	25.94
Erfurt	50.59N, 11.02E	656	1901-50	46.0	62.2 Jul	30.4 Jan					19.68
Gera	50.52N, 12.05E	673	1881-1930[1]	46.0	62.2 Jul	30.4 Jan					
Halle	51.30N, 12.00E	328	(see Leipzig)								
Karl-Marx-Stadt	50.50N, 12.55E	1014	1901-50	44.6	61.2 Jul	28.6 Jan					25.67
Leipzig	51.18N, 12.20E	387	1901-50	46.9	64.4 Jul	30.9 Jan	97	-15	90	4	22.05
Magdeburg	52.10N, 11.40E	164	1901-50	47.3	63.9 Jul	31.5 Jan					19.92
Potsdam	52.24N, 13.04E	105	1901-50	47.3	64.6 Jul	30.7 Jan					23.03
Rostock	54.05N, 12.08E	43	1901-50	47.3	63.5 Jul	32.7 Jan					22.17
Schwerin	53.38N, 11.23E	131	1901-50	47.1	63.5 Jul	31.8 Jan					24.68
Zwickau	50.44N, 12.30E	876	1881-1930[1]	46.0	62.2 Jul	30.4 Jan					
GERMANY: WEST											
Aachen	50.46N, 6.06E	568	1931-60	49.3	63.5 Jul	35.2 Jan	94	7			33.07
Augsburg	48.22N, 10.53E	1608	1881-1930	46.8	64.2 Jul	29.5 Jan	98	1			33.23
Baden-Baden	48.45N, 8.15E	594	1881-1930	48.7	64.4 Jul	33.4 Jan					43.19
Berlin	52.33N, 13.22E	112	1931-60	48.2	65.7 Jul	30.7 Jan	99	-15	91	6	23.11
Bielefeld	52.02N, 8.32E	387	1881-1930	47.7	62.4 Jul	33.3 Jan					33.03
Bochum	51.29N, 7.13E	328	1957-61	(see Essen for temperature data)							32.28

[1] Temperature data for Crimmitschau, nr Gera and Zwickau.

EUROPE

City	Latitude and longitude	Elev (ft)	Period of record	Temperature (°F) Avg	Avg warmest month	Avg coolest month	Absolute High	Absolute Low	Avg annual High	Avg annual Low	Annual precipitation (in)
*Bonn	50.44N, 7.06E	19[illegible]	1957-61	(see Cologne for temperature data)							26.50
Bottrop	51.31N, 6.55E	19[illegible]	(see Essen)								
Bremen	53.05N, 8.48E	1[illegible]	1931-60	48.2	63.3 Jul	33.1 Jan	94	-7	87	9	26.30
Bremerhaven	53.33N, 8.35E	2[illegible]	1881-1930	47.5	62.6 Jul	33.3 Jan	93	4	84	11	31.97
Brunswick	52.16N, 10.32E	23[illegible]	1893-1930	47.8	63.7 Jul	32.4 Jan	95	-5			26.61
Cologne	50.56N, 6.57E	17[illegible]	1881-1930	50.4	65.1 Jul	36.3 Jan	96	-3	89	14	27.40
Darmstadt	49.52N, 8.39E	47[illegible]	1881-1930	49.1	65.3 Jul	33.3 Jan	94	-2	90	4	25.04
Dortmund	51.31N, 7.27E	24[illegible]	1960-63,1965	48.4	60.8 Jun	33.6 Jan	96	-3	87	6	37.28
Duisburg	51.26N, 6.45E	8[illegible]	1957-61	(see Essen for temperature data)							28.66
Dusseldorf	51.13N, 6.46E	11[illegible]	1957-61	(see Solingen for temperature data)							31.22
Essen	51.27N, 7.01E	24[illegible]	1931-60	49.3	63.5 Jul	34.7 Jan	94	11			35.31
Flensburg	54.47N, 9.26E	6[illegible]	1931-60	46.6	61.9 Jul	32.4 Jan					31.65
Frankfurt am Main	50.07N, 8.41E	32[illegible]	1931-60	50.4	66.9 Jul	33.4 Jan	100	-7	91	9	23.78
Freiburg im Breisgau	48.00N, 7.51E	91[illegible]	1931-60	50.5	66.9 Jul	34.2 Jan	103	-7	91	8	34.80
Furth	49.28N, 11.00E	974	1957-61	(see Nuremberg for temperature data)							25.47
Gelsenkirchen	51.31N, 7.06E	171	1957-61	(see Essen for temperature data)							33.90
Gottingen	51.32N, 9.56E	492	1893-1930	47.3	63.0 Jul	32.0 Jan	92	-14	86	-8	23.90
Hagen	51.21N, 7.28E	348	1957-61	(see Dortmund for temperature data)							37.72
Hamburg	53.33N, 10.00E	20	1931-60	47.5	63.1 Jul	32.0 Jan	94	-4	85	10	29.13
Hannover	52.22N, 9.43E	180	1931-60	48.0	63.7 Jul	32.4 Jan	98	-13	88	7	25.08
Heidelberg	49.25N, 8.42E	374	1881-1930	50.4	66.2 Jul	34.5 Jan					31.46
Heilbronn	49.08N, 9.13E	495	1957-61	(see Heidelberg for temperature data)							28.82
Herne	51.33N, 7.13E	194	(see Essen)								
Hildesheim	52.09N, 9.58E	262	1957-61	(see Hannover for temperature data)							30.43
Kaiserslautern	49.27N, 7.45E	787	1957-61	(see Saarbrucken for temperature data)							28.31
Karlsruhe	49.01N, 8.24E	377	1931-60	50.2	67.1 Jul	33.4 Jan	99	-3			29.76
Kassel	51.19N, 9.30E	548	1931-60	48.2	64.2 Jul	31.8 Jan	99	-16	90	6	23.42
Kiel	54.20N, 10.08E	46	1881-1930	45.7	61.3 Jul	32.0 Jan	92	-4	81	12	28.23

EUROPE

City	Latitude and longitude	Elev (ft)	Period of record	Temperature (°F) Avg	Avg warmest month	Avg coolest month	Absolute High	Absolute Low	Avg annual High	Avg annual Low	Annual precipitation (in)
Koblenz	50.21N, 7.36E	230	1881-1930	50.2	65.3 Jul	35.2 Jan	91	3	89	9	24.29
Krefeld	51.20N, 6.34E	125	1881-1930	48.9	63.7 Jul	35.2 Jan					25.28
Leverkusen	51.01N, 6.59E	144	(see Essen)								
Lubeck	53.52N, 10.42E	43	1931-60	47.7	63.9 Jul	32.2 Jan	96	2			24.88
Ludwigshafen	49.29N, 8.27E	312	1891-1930	(see Mannheim for temperature data)							22.24
Mainz	50.00N, 8.15E	269	1881-1930[1]	48.6	62.4 Jul	35.4 Jan					23.78
Mannheim	49.29N, 8.28E	318	1881-1930	50.0	66.6 Jul	33.6 Jan	99	4			25.55
Monchengladbach	51.12N, 6.26E	197	(see Solingen)								
Mulheim an der Ruhr	51.26N, 6.53E	131	(see Essen)								
Munich	48.09N, 11.35E	1706	1931-60	46.2	63.5 Jul	28.2 Jan	93	-14	86	-1	34.88
Munster	51.58N, 7.38E	197	1931-60	49.1	63.9 Jul	34.3 Jan	96	-17	91	8	30.59
Neuss	51.12N, 6.42E	131	(see Solingen)								
Nuremberg	49.27N, 11.05E	1014	1931-60	47.3	64.8 Jul	29.5 Jan	100	-18	91	1	23.31
Oberhausen	51.28N, 6.51E	131	1957-61	(see Essen for temperature data)							33.50
Offenbach am Main	50.06N, 8.46E	322	(see Frankfurt am Main)								
Oldenburg in Oldenburg	53.10N, 8.12E	16	1893-1930	47.1	62.4 Jul	33.3 Jan					31.38
Osnabruck	52.16N, 8.03E	210	1893-1930	47.8	62.8 Jul	34.0 Jan	93	0	86	4	34.92
Pforzheim	48.53N, 8.42E	896	1957-61	(see Stuttgart for temperature data)							30.16
Recklinghausen	51.37N, 7.12E	358	(see Dortmund)								
Regensburg	49.01N, 12.06E	1112	1881-1930	45.9	63.7 Jul	27.7 Jan	94	-9	91	-1	23.27
Remscheid	51.11N, 7.12E	1198	(see Solingen)								
Rheydt	51.10N, 6.27E	259	(see Solingen)								
Saarbrucken	49.14N, 7.00E	623	1931-60	49.3	64.8 Jul	33.6 Jan	92	-1	89	5	30.94
Salzgitter	52.05N, 10.20E	469	(see Brunswick)								
Solingen	51.11N, 7.05E	725	1881-1930	47.5	61.5 Jul	34.2 Jan	97	12			43.62
Stuttgart	48.46N, 9.11E	804	1931-60	49.8	66.2 Jul	33.4 Jan	102	-13	91	8	26.06

[1] Temperature data for Alzey, nr Mainz.

EUROPE

City	Latitude and longtiude	Elev (ft)	Period of record	Temperature (°F) Avg	Avg warmest month	Avg coolest month	Absolute High	Absolute Low	Avg annual High	Avg annual Low	Annual precipitation (in)
Trier	49.45N, 6.38E	410	1931-60	48.9	64.2 Jul	33.3 Jan	92	2	89	7	28.31
Ulm	48.24N, 10.00E	1568	1931-60	46.8	63.9 Jul	28.8 Jan					27.64
Wanne-Eickel	51.32N, 7.10E	180	(see Essen)								
Wiesbaden	50.05N, 8.15E	381	1957-61	(see Frankfurt am Main for temperature data)							25.75
Wilhelmshaven	53.31N, 8.08E	13	1893-1930	46.9	61.5 Jul	33.4 Jan					27.28
Witten	51.26N, 7.20E	269	(see Essen)								
Wolfsburg	52.26N, 10.48E	184	(see Brunswick)								
Wuppertal	51.16N, 7.11E	525	1881-1930	48.6	63.1 Jul	34.7 Jan					45.16
Wurzburg	49.48N, 9.56E	594	1931-60	48.4	65.1 Jul	30.7 Jan	94	-6	90	2	22.05
GIBRALTAR											
*Gibraltar	36.06N, 5.21W	11	1951-60	64.8	75.4 Aug	55.0 Jan	101	33	96	38	32.09
GREECE											
*Athens	37.58N, 23.43E	453	1900-29	63.3	80.4 Jul	48.4 Jan	109	20	100	29	15.12
Iraklion	35.20N, 25.09E	98	1900-29	66.2	79.3 Aug	54.0 Jan	114	32	99	38	20.08
Patras	38.15N, 21.44E	15	38 yrs bef 1941	65.1	81.5 Jul	50.0 Jan	110	25	100	32	27.95
Peristeri	38.01N, 23.41E		(see Athens)								
Piraeus	37.57N, 23.38E	30	(see Athens)								
Salonika	40.38N, 22.56E	200	1900-29	60.6	79.3 Jul	42.1 Jan	107	15	101	23	19.13
HUNGARY											
*Budapest	47.30N, 19.05E	377	1918-47	51.8	72.0 Jul	30.4 Jan	103	-10	95	8	24.88
Debrecen	47.32N, 21.38E	404	1881-1909, 1916-38	49.6	70.2 Jul	27.1 Jan	102	-22	95	-3	22.83
Miskolc	48.06N, 20.47E	394	1951-60	49.5	69.8 Jul	27.9 Jan					25.08

EUROPE

City	Latitude and longitude	Elev (ft)	Period of record	Temperature (°F) Avg	Avg warmest month	Avg coolest month	Absolute High	Absolute Low	Avg annual High	Avg annual Low	Annual precipitation (in)
Pecs	46.05N, 18.14E	830	29 yrs bef 1939[1]	51.3	71.6 Jul	30.2 Jan					34.49
Szeged	46.15N, 20.10E	269	1881-1901, 1916-38	52.0	72.9 Jul	29.8 Jan	102	-20	96	2	22.52
ICELAND											
*Reykjavik	64.09N, 21.57W	92	1920-50	41.5	53 Jul	32 Jan	74	4	67	10	33.9
IRELAND											
Cork	51.54N, 8.28W	56	27 yrs bef 1951	50.5	60.5 Jul	42.5 Dec	85	15	79	23	41.3
*Dublin	53.20N, 6.15W	51	1921-50	50.0	60.4 Jul	41.9 Jan	86	8	79	19	26.78
ITALY											
Alessandria	44.54N, 8.37E	312	25 yrs bef 1926	54.3	74.8 Jul	32.9 Jan					21.89
Ancona	43.38N, 13.30E	52	1946-55	59	76.5 Jul	45 Jan	98	20	96	27	25.35
Bari	41.08N, 16.51E	16	1931-48, 1951-55	61.5	76.6 Jul	47.5 Jan	111	18			20.71
Bergamo	45.41N, 9.43E	817	1921-50	(see Brescia for temperature data)							48.94
Bologna	44.29N, 11.20E	180	1931-55	57.4	77.9 Jul	36.1 Jan	103	9			23.66
Bolzano	46.31N, 11.22E	860	1946-55	53	71 Jul	32 Jan	100	5			27.05
Brescia	45.33N, 10.15E	489	31 yrs bef 1926	55.8	74.8 Jul	36.0 Jan					34.72
Cagliari	39.13N, 9.07E	13	1931-42, 1945-55	63.9	78.3 Aug	50.9 Jan	104	25			16.97
Catania	37.30N, 15.06E	33	1892-1930	64.4	79.7 Aug	50.5 Jan	112	26			27.40
Como	45.47N, 9.05E	659	1889-1906	54.5	73.4 Jul	36.1 Jan					50.20
Cosenza	39.18N, 16.15E	778	1921-50								40.98
Ferrara	44.50N, 11.35E	30	1921-43, 1946-50	(see Bologna for temperature data)							22.68

[1] Temperature data for Kaposvar, nr Pecs.

EUROPE

City	Latitude and longitude	Elev (ft)	Period of record	Temperature (°F) Avg	Avg warmest month	Avg coolest month	Absolute High	Absolute Low	Avg annual High	Avg annual Low	Annual precipitation (in)
Florence	43.46N, 11.15E	164	1931-55	58.5	76.5 Jul	41.4 Jan	105	11			33.07
Foggia	41.27N, 15.34E	249	1946-55	61	79 Aug	45 Jan	114	14			17.87
Forli	44.13N, 12.03E	112	1921-43, 1946-50	(see Bologna for temperature data)							29.72
Genoa	44.25N, 8.57E	62	1931-55	61.0	76.1 Jul	46.2 Jan	100	18	90	28	45.12
La Spezia	44.07N, 9.50E	10	28 yrs bef 1951	(see Genoa for temperature data)							54.13
Leghorn	43.33N, 10.19E	10	1901-30	59.9	75.6 Jul	45.3 Jan	100	20			32.32
Messina	38.11N, 15.34E	10	1901-30	64.2	78.6 Aug	52.5 Feb	105	28			36.93
Milan	45.28N, 9.12E	397	1931-43, 1946-55	56.7	77.0 Jul	35.6 Jan	101	1			35.91
Modena	44.40N, 10.55E	112	1921-50	(see Bologna for temperature data)							24.84
Monza	45.35N, 9.16E	532	1921-50	(see Milan for temperature data)							44.53
Naples	40.50N, 14.15E	33	1931-55	62.8	77.9 Jul	48.2 Jan	100	24	93	30	33.46
Novara	45.28N, 8.38E	522	1889-1906	55.4	75.0 Jul	36.1 Jan					36.14
Padua	45.25N, 11.53E	39	1921-50	(see Verona for temperature data)							33.31
Palermo	38.07N, 13.22E	46	1931-55	64.9	78.1 Aug	53.1 Jan	113	29			28.78
Parma	44.48N, 10.20E	187	1931-46	(see Bologna for temperature data)							30.20
Perugia	43.08N, 12.22E	1618	1946-55	56.5	73.5 Jul	40.5 Jan	100	9	95	21	34.41
Pescara	42.28N, 14.13E	13	1946-55	58.5	73.5 Jul	44 Jan	105	21			27.24
Piacenza	45.01N, 9.40E	200	30 yrs bef 1926	54.1	74.1 Jul	32.7 Jan	99	-6			31.26
Pisa	43.43N, 10.23E	16	1901-30	57.9	73.0 Aug	43.2 Jan	100	13			38.03
Prato	43.53N, 11.06E	207	1921-50	(see Florence for temperature data)							38.90
Ravenna	44.25N, 12.12E	13	1924-43, 1946-50	(see Bologna for temperature data)							27.56
Reggio di Calabria	38.06N, 15.39E	49	1921-50	(see Messina for temperature data)							23.47
Reggio nell'Emilia	44.43N, 10.36E	190	1921-50	(see Bologna for temperature data)							27.72
Rimini	44.04N, 12.34E	23	1921-43	(see Florence for temperature data)							29.37
*Rome	41.54N, 12.29E	66	1931-55	61.2	77.7 Jul	45.9 Jan	108	15			29.92
Salerno	40.41N, 14.47E	13	1921-50	(see Naples for temperature data)							51.14
Sassari	40.43N, 8.34E	738	1883-1930	59.9	74.5 Aug	46.6 Jan					23.47
Syracuse	37.04N, 15.18E	56	32 yrs bef 1926	64.2	79.0 Aug	51.8 Jan					25.24

EUROPE

City	Latitude and longitude	Elev (ft)	Period of record	Temperature (°F) Avg	Avg warmest month	Avg coolest month	Absolute High	Absolute Low	Avg annual High	Avg annual Low	Annual precipitation (in)
Taranto	40.28N, 17.14E	49	1901-30	62.2	78.3 Aug	47.8 Jan	108	24			17.52
Terni	42.34N, 12.37E	427	1882-1900,1906[1]	57.9	75.7 Jul	41.9 Jan					33.03
Trieste	45.40N, 13.46E	7	1951-60	57.4	74.8 Jul	41.2 Jan	99	6			38.07
Turin	45.03N, 7.40E	784	1898-1915,1926-34	53.2	73.2 Jul	33.3 Jan	100	6	96	15	30.67
Udine	46.03N, 13.14E	371	1923-58	55.6	73.4 Jul	37.4 Jan	99	0	94	20	53.82
Venice	45.27N, 12.21E	3	30 yrs bef 1926	56.5	75.6 Jul	37.4 Jan	96	14			29.80
Verona	45.27N, 11.00E	194	1946-55	55.5	74 Jul	36.5 Jan	100	0			25.35
Vicenza	45.33N, 11.33E	128	1921-43, 1946-50	(see Verona for temperature data)							40.83
LUXEMBOURG											
*Luxembourg	49.36N, 6.07E	984	1931-60	47.8	63.3 Jul	32.5 Jan	99	-10	87	9	29.25
MALTA											
*Valletta	35.54N, 14.32E	233	90 yrs bef 1948	66	79 Aug	55 Jan	105	34	97	42	20.3
MONACO											
*Monaco	43.44N, 7.25E	180	1921-50	61.5	74.8 Aug	50.4 Jan	93	27	86	36	30.1
NETHERLANDS											
*Amsterdam	52.23N, 4.54E	5	1921-50	50	64 Jul	37 Jan	95	3	86	17	25.6
Apeldoorn	52.13N, 5.57E		(see Utrecht)								
Arnhem	52.00N, 5.53E		(see Utrecht)								
Breda	51.35N, 4.46E	23	1931-60[2]	51.1	65.7 Jul	36.3 Jan					29.17
Dordrecht	51.48N, 4.40E	13	1931-60[2]	51.1	65.7 Jul	36.3 Jan					29.17

[1] Climatic data for Teramo, nr Terni.

[2] Climatic data for Oudenbosch, nr Breda and Dordrecht.

EUROPE

City	Latitude and longitude	Elev (ft)	Period of record	Temperature (°F) Avg	Avg warmest month	Avg coolest month	Absolute High	Absolute Low	Avg annual High	Avg annual Low	Annual precipitation (in)
Eindhoven	51.26N, 5.30E	63	1931-60[1]	51.3	66.9 Jul	35.6 Jan					27.32
Enschede	52.13N, 6.55E	95	(see Munster, West Germany)								
Groningen	53.13N, 6.34E	13	1921-50	48.5	63.5 Jul	34.5 Jan	98	-5	90	10	29.4
Haarlem	52.20N, 4.36E	10	(see Amsterdam)								
*Hague	52.04N, 4.19E	12	1931-60[2]	50.9	65.1 Aug	36.7 Jan					29.57
Heerlen	50.53N, 5.59E	377	(see Aachen, West Germany)								
Hilversum	52.14N, 5.10E	13	(see Utrecht)								
Leiden	52.10N, 4.30E	10	1931-60[2]	50.9	65.1 Aug	36.7 Jan					29.57
Maastricht	50.51N, 5.42E	161	1900-36	(see Aachen, West Germany, for temperature data)							25.94
Nijmegen	51.50N, 5.52E	82	1931-60[1]	51.3	66.9 Jul	35.6 Jan					27.32
Rotterdam	51.55N, 4.29E	12	1921-50	50	64 Jul	37 Jan	100	2	90	15	28.6
's Hertogenbosch	51.41N, 5.19E	26	1931-60[3]	51.3	66.9 Jul	35.6 Jan					27.32
Tilburg	51.34N, 5.05E	59	1931-60[3]	51.3	66.9 Jul	35.6 Jan					27.32
Utrecht	52.07N, 5.05E	10	1931-60	50.7	65.7 Jul	35.6 Jan	98	-13			30.12
Zaandam	52.27N, 4.49E	10	(see Amsterdam)								
NORWAY											
Bergen	60.23N, 5.20E	144	1931-60	46.0	59.0 Jul	34.3 Feb	89	3	78	14	77.09
*Oslo	59.55N, 10.45E	315	1931-60	42.6	63.1 Jul	23.5 Jan	93	-21	83	-2	29.13
Stavanger	58.58N, 5.45E	26	1951-60	45.1	58.3 Aug	31.3 Feb	85	12	80	17	39.96
Trondheim	63.25N, 10.25E	417	1885-1935	40.8	57.6 Jul	28.2 Jan	95	-22	82	1	28.86

[1] Climatic data for Gemert, nr Eindhoven and Nijmegen.

[2] Climatic data for Naaldwijk, nr Hague and Leiden.

[3] Climatic data for Gemert, nr 's Hertogenbosch and Tilburg.

EUROPE

City	Latitude and longitude	Elev (ft)	Period of record	Temperature (°F) Avg	Avg warmest month	Avg coolest month	Absolute High	Absolute Low	Avg annual High	Avg annual Low	Annual precipitation (in)
POLAND											
Bialystok	53.09N, 23.10E	456	1931-60	44.4	64.9 Jul	23.2 Jan					21.42
Bielsko-Biala	49.50N, 19.00E	1014	1931-60	45.9	63.5 Jul	26.4 Jan					39.80
Bydgoszcz	53.16N, 17.33E	230	1931-60	46.2	65.7 Jul	27.0 Jan	98	-24			20.83
Bytom	50.22N, 18.53E	935	(see Katowice)								
Chorzow	50.19N, 18.56E	925	(see Katowice)								
Czestochowa	50.49N, 19.07E	856	1931-60	46.0	65.1 Jul	25.9 Jan					25.98
Gdansk	54.20N, 18.40E	43	1931-60	45.1	63.1 Jul	27.7 Jan	96	-18	87	1	23.23
Gdynia	54.31N, 18.30E	7	(see Gdansk)								
Gliwice	50.20N, 18.40E	728	(see Katowice)								
Katowice	50.15N, 18.59E	932	1931-60	46.0	64.4 Jul	26.1 Jan					26.81
Kielce	50.51N, 20.39E	879	1931-60	45.3	64.8 Jul	24.6 Jan					25.55
Krakow	50.05N, 19.55E	778	1931-60	47.5	66.7 Jul	26.8 Jan	96	-28	90	-2	27.09
Lodz	51.46N, 19.25E	614	1931-60	45.7	64.9 Jul	25.7 Jan	97	-24			23.07
Lublin	51.20N, 22.30E	561	1931-60	45.5	65.5 Jul	24.4 Jan					22.20
Olsztyn	53.47N, 20.29E	377	1931-60	44.4	63.9 Jul	24.8 Jan					23.23
Poznan	52.25N, 16.58E	282	1931-60	46.8	65.7 Jul	27.3 Jan	96	-20	93	1	20.67
Radom	51.26N, 21.10E	584	1881-1930	46.4	65.7 Jul	27.3 Jan					23.23
Ruda Slaska	50.18N, 18.51E	938	(see Katowice)								
Sosnowiec	50.16N, 19.07E	820	(see Katowice)								
Szczecin	53.26N, 14.34E	3	1931-60	46.9	64.6 Jul	29.5 Jan	97	-16	88	5	22.36
Torun	53.01N, 18.35E	226	1881-1930	46.0	65.1 Jul	28.0 Jan					19.49
Walbrzych	50.48N, 16.19E	1476	1881-1930[1]	45.1	62.4 Jul	27.7 Jan					
*Warsaw	52.15N, 21.00E	348	1931-60	46.6	66.6 Jul	25.7 Jan	98	-27	90	-3	21.34
Wroclaw	51.07N, 17.02E	394	1931-60	47.3	65.8 Jul	28.4 Jan	98	-26	90	1	22.99
Zabrze	50.18N, 18.47E	820	(see Katowice)								

[1] Temperature data for Klodzko, nr Walbrzych.

EUROPE

City	Latitude and longitude	Elev (ft)	Period of record	Temperature (°F) Avg	Avg warmest month	Avg coolest month	Absolute High	Absolute Low	Avg annual High	Avg annual Low	Annual precipitation (in)
PORTUGAL											
*Lisbon	38.43N, 9.08W	312	1921-50	61.0	71.8 Aug	51.1 Jan	103	29	98	32	24.37
Porto	41.09N, 8.37W	323	1921-50	57.5	67.5 Aug	48 Jan	104	25	97	28	45.5
ROMANIA											
Arad	46.11N, 21.19E	331	1896-1955	51.4	70.5 Jul	30.0 Jan	105	-22			22.72
Bacau	46.34N, 26.54E	597	1896-1955	48.6	69.4 Jul	24.3 Jan	102	-26			21.42
Baia Mare	47.40N, 23.35E	637	1896-1955	48.9	67.8 Jul	27.7 Jan	103	-22			38.43
Braila	45.16N, 27.59E	49	1896-1955	52.0	73.6 Jul	27.9 Jan	105	-16			17.32
Brasov	45.38N, 25.35E	194[illegible]	1896-1955	46.0	64.0 Jul	25.0 Jan	99	-21			29.41
*Bucharest	44.26N, 26.06E	269	1896-1955	51.6	73.2 Jul	27.0 Jan	106	-22	98	-2	22.83
Cluj	46.46N, 23.36E	1027	1896-1955	46.8	66.0 Jul	24.1 Jan	98	-30	92	-9	24.13
Constanta	44.11N, 28.39E	105	1896-1955	52.2	72.0 Jul	31.5 Jan	101	-13			14.92
Craiova	44.19N, 23.48E	345	1896-1955	51.4	72.9 Jul	27.5 Jan	107	-23			20.59
Galati	45.27N, 28.03E	98	1896-1955	50.9	72.7 Jul	26.4 Jan	102	-19			16.77
Hunedoara	45.45N, 22.54E	797	1896-1955	49.5	68.4 Jul	27.0 Jan					24.61
Iasi	47.10N, 27.36E	335	1896-1955	49.3	70.3 Jul	25.5 Jan	104	-23			20.39
Oradea	47.04N, 21.56E	449	1896-1955	50.9	70.2 Jul	29.3 Jan	103	-20			25.00
Petroseni	45.25N, 23.22E	1906	1896-1955	44.2	62.1 Jul	23.9 Jan	96	-22			27.32
Pitesti	44.51N, 24.52E	1004	1896-1955	49.6	69.4 Jul	27.7 Jan	103	-17			27.56
Ploesti	44.57N, 26.01E	505	1896-1955	51.1	71.6 Jul	28.2 Jan	103	-22			23.15
Resita	45.18N, 21.55E	742	1896-1955[1]	51.1	69.8 Jul	30.6 Jan					32.28
Sibiu	45.48N, 24.09E	1365	1896-1955	48.0	67.3 Jul	25.2 Jan	99	-25			26.06
Timisoara	45.45N, 21.13E	295	1896-1955	51.6	70.9 Jul	29.8 Jan	104	-32			24.84
Tirgu Mures	46.33N, 24.34E	1014	1896-1955	47.7	66.9 Jul	24.3 Jan	102	-27			25.04
SPAIN											
Alicante	38.21N, 0.29W	10	1939-60	64.4	79.0 Aug	51.8 Jan	106	24	98	31	13.35
Almeria	36.50N, 2.27W	56	1934-60	64.2	77.5 Aug	53.1 Jan	108	32	99	40	9.09

[1] Temperature data for Caransebes, nr Resita.

EUROPE

City	Latitude and longitude	Elev (ft)	Period of record	Temperature (°F) Avg	Avg warmest month	Avg coolest month	Absolute High	Absolute Low	Avg annual High	Avg annual Low	Annual precipitation (in)
Badajoz	38.53N, 6.58W	604	1931–60	62.1	78.4 Jul	47.5 Jan	113	23	107	27	18.66
Badalona	41.27N, 2.15E	75	(see Barcelona)								
Baracaldo	43.18N, 2.59W	128	(see San Sebastian)								
Barcelona	41.23N, 2.11E	39	1931–60	61.5	75.9 Jul	48.9 Jan	98	20	92	31	23.39
Bilbao	43.15N, 2.58W	10	26 yrs bef 1927	(see San Sebastian for temperature data)							41.93
Burgos	42.21N, 3.42W	2808	1931–47, 1950–60	51.1	66.0 Jul	36.5 Jan	99	0			22.17
Cadiz	36.32N, 6.18W	16	27 yrs bef 1961	64.4	76.8 Aug	52.5 Jan	106	28			20.59
Cartagena	37.36N, 0.59W	20	1881–1901	63.0	76.3 Aug	51.3 Jan					12.60
Cordova	37.53N, 4.46W	328	1931–60	64.2	82.2 Jul	48.4 Jan	112	21			26.14
Elche	38.15N, 0.42W	266	(see Alicante)								
Gijon	43.32N, 5.40W	30	1931–60	57.0	67.3 Jul	48.7 Jan	95	23			40.83
Granada	37.13N, 3.41W	2261	25 yrs bef 1961	59.9	78.3 Jul	44.6 Jan	109	13	100	25	20.83
Hospitalet	41.22N, 2.08E	26	(see Barcelona)								
Huelva	37.16N, 6.57W	13	1931–60	64.4	77.4 Aug	52.0 Jan	110	22			18.31
Jerez de la Frontera	36.41N, 6.08W	161	(see Cadiz)								
La Coruna	43.22N, 8.23W	79	1931–60	57.0	66.0 Aug	49.6 Feb	95	27	85	33	38.15
Leon	42.36N, 5.34W	2697	1938–60	51.8	67.5 Jul	37.0 Jan	100	1			20.75
*Madrid	40.24N, 3.41W	2100	1931–60	57.0	75.6 Jul	40.8 Jan	102	14	97	22	17.24
Malaga	36.43N, 4.25W	33	1931–60	65.3	78.1 Aug	54.5 Jan	105	32	100	37	18.46
Murcia	37.59N, 1.07W	141	1931–60	64.4	79.3 Aug	51.3 Jan	113	14	104	28	11.85
Oviedo	43.22N, 5.50W	705	45 yrs bef 1933	54.1	64.8 Aug	44.8 Jan					36.89
Palma	39.34N, 2.39E	108	1931–60	62.2	76.1 Aug	50.2 Jan	102	25	95	33	17.76
Pamplona	42.49N, 1.38W	1476	1931–60	54.1	68.4 Jul	40.3 Jan	105	5	99	19	42.80
Sabadell	41.33N, 2.06E	617	(see Barcelona)								
Salamanca	40.58N, 5.39W	2553	1931–60	53.4	70.7 Jul	38.7 Jan	103	10	100	16	16.54
San Sebastian	43.19N, 1.59W	26	1931–60	55.6	66.2 Aug	46.0 Jan	100	10			59.29
Santa Coloma de Gramanet	41.27N, 2.13E	59	(see Barcelona)								
Santander	43.28N, 3.48W	13	1931–60	57.0	66.7 Aug	48.6 Feb	104	25	90	32	47.13

EUROPE

City	Latitude and longitude	Elev (ft)	Period of record	Temperature (°F) Avg	Avg warmest month	Avg coolest month	Absolute High	Absolute Low	Avg annual High	Avg annual Low	Annual precipitation (in)
Saragossa	41.38N, 0.53W	656	1931-60	58.5	74.7 Aug	43.0 Jan	108	5	100	22	13.42
Seville	37.23N, 5.59W	20	1931-60	65.8	82.2 Jul	50.9 Jan	117	26	110	31	21.06
Tarrasa	41.34N, 2.01E	909	(see Barcelona)								
Toledo	39.52N, 4.01W	1729	1931-60	59.0	79.0 Jul	42.6 Jan	108	15			14.80
Valencia	39.28N, 0.22W	10	1938-60	62.6	76.1 Aug	50.5 Jan	107	19	96	31	16.50
Valladolid	41.39N, 4.43W	2270	1943-60	53.8	70.3 Jul	37.9 Jan	103	9	99	18	14.25
Vigo	42.14N, 8.43W	66	1931-60	59.0	67.8 Aug	50.4 Jan	102	27			50.20
Vitoria	42.51N, 2.40W	1719	1931-60	53.1	66.9 Aug	40.3 Jan	103	0			33.23
SWEDEN											
Goteborg	57.43N, 11.58E	102	1931-60	45.7	62.6 Jul	29.8 Feb	90	-15	83	6	26.38
Halsingborg	56.03N, 12.42E	131	(see Copenhagen, Denmark)								
Jonkoping	57.47N, 14.11E	325	1931-60	43.2	61.3 Jul	26.8 Feb	92	-28	84	-2	21.10
Linkoping	58.25N, 15.37E	210	1931-60	44.2	63.9 Jul	26.6 Feb	94	-26			20.79
Malmo	55.36N, 13.00E	10	1901-30	45.9	61.9 Jul	32.5 Jan					22.91
Norrkoping	58.36N, 16.11E	33	(see Linkoping)								
Orebro	59.17N, 15.13E	118	1931-60	42.4	62.2 Jul	24.8 Jan	93	-22			25.24
*Stockholm	59.20N, 18.03E	144	1931-60	43.9	64.0 Jul	26.4 Feb	97	-26	83	3	21.85
Uppsala	59.52N, 17.38E	79	1931-60	42.4	63.1 Jul	24.3 Feb	99	-28	86	-8	21.81
Vasteras	59.37N, 16.33E	59	1891-1933, 1935-44	42.3	63.3 Jul	25.0 Jan	97	-24			20.71
SWITZERLAND											
Basel	47.34N, 7.36E	1040	1901-60	48.6	65.1 Jul	32.4 Jan	102	-11	95	7	31.26
*Bern	46.57N, 7.28E	1877	1901-60	46.9	63.7 Jul	29.8 Jan	96	-9	88	8	39.37
Geneva	46.12N, 6.10E	1411	1901-60	48.6	64.9 Jul	32.4 Jan	101	-1	91	13	36.73
Lausanne	46.32N, 6.39E	1831	1901-60	48.9	65.3 Jul	32.7 Jan					41.89
Luzern	47.03N, 8.17E	1634	1901-60	47.3	64.0 Jul	30.4 Jan					45.43

EUROPE

City	Latitude and longitude	Elev (ft)	Period of record	Temperature (°F) Avg	Avg warmest month	Avg coolest month	Absolute High	Absolute Low	Avg annual High	Avg annual Low	Annual precipitation (in)
Winterthur	47.30N, 8.45E	1608	(see Zurich)								
Zurich	47.22N, 8.31E	1539	1901-60	46.8	63.0 Jul	30.2 Jan	99	-11	88	9	44.41
TURKEY											
Edirne	41.40N, 26.34E	157	30 yrs bef 1961	56.1	76.3 Jul	35.6 Jan	107	-8	99	8	23.98
Istanbul	41.01N, 28.58E	131	30 yrs bef 1961	57.0	74.1 Aug	41.9 Jan	100	17	96	23	26.14
UK											
Aberdeen	57.08N, 2.06W	79	1921-47	47.0	57.6 Jul	38.7 Jan	83	12	76	20	32.93
Basildon	51.34N, 0.25E	40	(see London)								
Bath	51.23N, 2.22W	67	1926-50	50.6	62.8 Jul	40.6 Jan					30.93
Belfast	54.36N, 5.56W	66	24 yrs bef 1963	48.8	59.8 Jul	40.0 Jan					38.26
Birkenhead	53.24N, 3.02W	198	1916-50	(see Liverpool for temperature data)							29.01
Birmingham	52.29N, 1.53W	425	1921-50	49.3	62.1 Jul	38.6 Jan	92	11	85	21	29.87
Blackburn	53.45N, 2.29W	310	(see Bolton)								
Blackpool	53.50N, 3.03W	65	1926-49	49.3	60.7 Jul	39.6 Jan					35.11
Bolton	53.35N, 2.26W	342	1921-50	48.5	60.3 Jul	38.5 Jan					46.85
Bournemouth	50.43N, 1.54W	139	1926-50	50.9	62.7 Jul	41.3 Feb					31.2
Bradford	53.48N, 1.45W	439	1921-50	47.9	60.0 Jul	38.0 Jan					34.15
Brighton	50.49N, 0.08W	32	1926-40, 1948-50	51.2	62.9 Aug	41.1 Feb					31.52
Bristol	51.27N, 2.35W	386	1916-50	(see Cardiff for temperature data)							32.20
Cambridge	52.12N, 0.07E	41	1921-50	49.7	62.6 Jul	38.9 Jan	96	1	86	16	21.72
Cardiff	51.29N, 3.10W	203	1921-50	50.2	61.4 Jul	40.6 Jan	91	2	83	21	42.10
Coventry	52.25N, 1.30W	241	1921-50	49.2	62.1 Jul	38.4 Jan					26.54
Derby	52.55N, 1.28W	211	1916-50	(see Nottingham for temperature data)							28.80
Dudley	52.30N, 2.05W	745	1916-50	(see Birmingham for temperature data)							28.68
Dundee	56.27N, 2.58W	147	1921-50	47.2	59.0 Jul	37.5 Jan					31.14
Edinburgh	55.57N, 3.12W	441	1921-50	47.4	58.5 Jul	38.7 Jan	83	15	78	22	27.53

EUROPE

City	Latitude and longitude	Elev (ft)	Period of record	Temperature (°F) Avg	Avg warmest month	Avg coolest month	Absolute High	Absolute Low	Avg annual High	Avg annual Low	Annual precipitation (in)
Exeter	50.43N, 3.31W	110	1921-50[1]	50.5	61.0 Jul	42.2 Jan					31.90
Gateshead	54.58N, 1.35W	510	1921-50[2]	47.0	58.7 Jul	37.2 Jan					27.6
Glasgow	55.51N, 4.16W	180	1921-50	47.0	58.0 Jul	37.9 Jan					38.30
Gloucester	51.53N, 2.14W	33	1926-50[3]	50.1	62.6 Jul	39.7 Jan					25.71
Grimsby	53.35N, 0.05W	14	1921-50	49.4	61.1 Jul	39.4 Jan					25.0
Halifax	53.44N, 1.52W	795	1916-50	(see Huddersfield for temperature data)							38.56
Hartlepool	54.41N, 1.13W	30	1926-50[4]	47.7	59.7 Jul	37.6 Jan					24.5
Havant and Waterloo	50.51N, 0.59W	25	1916-50	(see Portsmouth for temperature data)							28.33
Huddersfield	53.39N, 1.47W	762	1925-50	47.5	59.6 Jul	37.6 Jan					37.62
Hull	53.45N, 0.20W	8	1921-50	49.7	62.3 Jul	39.4 Jan					25.39
Ipswich	52.04N, 1.10E	190	1916-50	(see Norwich for temperature data)							24.4
Leeds	53.48N, 1.32W	307	1916-50	(see Bradford for temperature data)							28.20
Leicester	52.38N, 1.07W	237	1921-50	49.0	61.5 Jul	38.3 Jan					26.39
Liverpool	53.23N, 3.00W	198	1921-50	49.3	60.4 Jul	40.0 Jan	87	15	82	24	35.06
*London	51.31N, 0.05W	149	1921-50	50.6	63.7 Jul	39.8 Jan	99	9	90	20	24.00
Luton	51.53N, 0.25W	381	1921-50	48.9	61.7 Jul	38.4 Jan					25.10
Manchester	53.28N, 2.14W	125	1921-50	49.8	61.6 Jul	40.0 Jan					33.79
Newcastle upon Tyne	54.58N, 1.37W	255	1926-50[4]	47.7	59.7 Jul	37.6 Jan					27.69
Newport	51.35N, 3.00W	265	1921-50	50.3	62.8 Jul	40.6 Jan					43.56
Northampton	52.14N, 0.54W	258	1916-50	(see Leicester for temperature data)							24.65
Norwich	52.38N, 1.18E	110	1921-47	49.7	62.8 Jul	38.6 Jan					25.58
Nottingham	52.51N, 1.08W	192	1921-50	49.5	62.2 Jul	39.1 Jan					24.19

1 Temperature data for Exmouth, nr Exeter.
2 Temperature data for Chopwell, nr Gateshead.
3 Temperature data for Cheltenham, nr Gloucester.
4 Temperature data for Houghall, nr Hartlepool and Newcastle upon Tyne.

EUROPE

City	Latitude and longitude	Elev (ft)	Period of record	Temperature (°F) Avg	Avg warmest month	Avg coolest month	Absolute High	Absolute Low	Avg annual High	Avg annual Low	Annual precipitation (in)
Oldham	53.33N, 2.07W	550	1921-50[1]	48.0	60.3 Jul	37.7 Jan					36.33
Oxford	51.45N, 1.15W	208	1921-50	50.1	62.8 Jul	39.5 Jan	95	3	87	18	25.66
Paisley	55.50N, 4.26W	106	1921-50	48.6	60.0 Jul	39.2 Jan					44.22
Plymouth	50.23N, 4.06W	117	1921-50	51.8	61.6 Aug	43.1 Feb	88	16	80	25	37.76
Poole	50.43N, 1.59W	20	(see Bournemouth)								
Portsmouth	50.48N, 1.06W	7	1926-50	51.9	63.7 Jul	41.7 Feb					27.78
Preston	53.46N, 2.42W	110	1921-50[2]	48.7	60.1 Jul	38.8 Jan					39.47
Reading	51.28N, 0.59W	152	1921-50	50.6	63.2 Jul	39.8 Jan					25.72
Rochdale	53.38N, 2.09W	360	1916-50	(see Bolton for temperature data)							44.2
Saint Helens	53.28N, 2.44W	150	(see Liverpool)								
Salford	53.30N, 2.16W	70	(see Manchester)								
Sheffield	53.23N, 1.28W	428	1921-50	49.2	61.5 Jul	39.2 Jan					31.86
Solihull	52.25N, 1.45W	420	1916-50	(see Birmingham for temperature data)							29.7
Southampton	50.54N, 1.23W	65	1921-50	51.0	62.8 Jul	40.8 Jan	93	12	85	20	31.64
Southend-on-Sea	51.33N, 0.43E	90	1926-40, 1946-50	51.3	64.6 Aug	39.7 Jan					21.15
South Shields	55.00N, 1.25W	40	1921-50[3]	48.5	59.1 Jul	39.9 Jan					26.6
Stockport	53.25N, 2.10W	290	(see Bolton)								
Stoke-on-Trent	53.00N, 2.11W	390	1921-50[4]	47.5	59.8 Jul	37.5 Jan					30.9
Sunderland	54.55N, 1.22W	216	1926-50[5]	47.7	59.7 Jul	37.6 Jan					25.11
Swansea	51.37N, 3.56W	32	1926-50	51.5	62.2 Jul	42.1 Feb					42.16

[1] Climatic data for Macclesfield, nr Oldham.

[2] Temperature data for Hutton, nr Preston.

[3] Temperature data for Tynemouth, nr South Shields.

[4] Temperature data for Mayfield, nr Stoke-on-Trent.

[5] Temperature data for Houghall, nr Sunderland.

EUROPE

City	Latitude and longitude	Elev (ft)	Period of record	Temperature (°F) Avg	Avg warmest month	Avg coolest month	Absolute High	Absolute Low	Avg annual High	Avg annual Low	Annual precipitation (in)
Swindon	51.34N, 1.47W	476	1921-50[1]	48.4	60.4 Jul	38.4 Jan					29.0
Teesside	54.35N, 1.14W	61	1926-50[2]	47.7	59.7 Jul	37.6 Jan					23.62
Thurrock	51.29N, 0.20E	70	(see London)								
Torbay	50.28N, 3.30W	27	1926-50	51.9	62.2 Jul	43.2 Feb					34.98
Wallasey	53.26N, 3.03W	57	1925-35	50.0	62.2 Jul	40.7 Feb					
Walsall	52.35N, 1.58W	530	(see Birmingham)								
Warley	52.30N, 1.58W	610	(see Birmingham)								
West Bromwich	52.31N, 1.59W	543	1916-50	(see Birmingham for temperature data)							28.51
Wolverhampton	52.36N, 2.08W	430	1916-50	(see Birmingham for temperature data)							28.45
York	53.57N, 1.05W	57	1921-50	49.3	61.9 Jul	38.9 Jan	90	7	85	19	24.70
USSR											
Archangel	64.34N, 40.32E	10	1881-1960	33.4	60.1 Jul	9.5 Jan	93	-49	86	-29	19.45
Astrakhan	46.21N, 48.03E	-72	1881-1960	48.9	77.5 Jul	19.8 Jan	104	-29	97	-13	6.89
Baku	40.23N, 49.51E	7	1891-1917, 1921-60	57.9	78.3 Jul	38.8 Jan	104	9	97	23	9.37
Belgorod	50.36N, 36.34E	604	1925-41, 1943-60	43.3	68.4 Jul	18.3 Jan	106	-35	93	-17	
Bryansk	53.15N, 34.22E	528	1936-41, 1947-60	40.8	65.1 Jul	16.7 Jan	100	-44	90	-22	21.93
Cheboksary	56.09N, 47.15E	607	1927-60	37.2	65.5 Jul	8.6 Jan	100	-47	91	-27	
Cherepovets	59.08N, 37.54E	413	1937-60	36.7	63.1 Jul	11.7 Jan	97	-56	86	-27	
Cherkassy	49.26N, 32.04E	308									
Chernigov	51.30N, 31.18E	443	1881-1960	43.7			102	-29			21.22
Chernovtsy	48.18N, 25.56E	1148	1881-1960	46.0			100	-26			24.57
Dneprodzerzhinsk	48.30N, 34.37E		(see Denpropetrovsk)								
Dnepropetrovsk	48.27N, 34.59E	322	1891-1911	48.5	71 Jul	20.5 Jan	101	-25	95	-11	19.4

[1] Temperature data for Marlborough, nr Swindon.
[2] Temperature data for Houghall, nr Teesside.

EUROPE

City	Latitude and longitude	Elev (ft)	Period of record	Temperature (°F) Avg	Avg warmest month	Avg coolest month	Absolute High	Absolute Low	Avg annual High	Avg annual Low	Annual precipitation (in)
Donetsk	48.00N, 37.48E	659	(see Makeyevka)								
Dzerzhinsk	56.15N, 43.24E		(see Gorkiy)								
Gomel	52.25N, 31.00E	453	1928–40								24.17
Gorkiy	56.20N, 44.00E	532	1922–60	37.6	64.6 Jul	10.4 Jan	99	-42	90	-24	23.15
Gorlovka	48.18N, 38.03E		(see Makeyevka)								
Groznyy	43.20N, 45.42E	404	1938–60	50.2	74.8 Jul	25.5 Jan	106	-27	100	-11	19.25
Ivanovo	57.00N, 40.59E	420	1891–1918, 1922–48	37.9	65.3 Jul	11.1 Jan	100	-51	90	-29	23.35
Izhevsk	56.51N, 53.14E	479	1933–60	35.8	65.7 Jul	6.4 Jan	99	-51	91	-33	
Kalinin	56.52N, 35.55E	446	? yrs bef 1948	39.0	64.2 Jul	14.0 Jan					24.29
Kaliningrad	54.43N, 20.30E	20	1921–50	45.0	63.9 Jul	27.3 Feb	97	-24	90	-3	29.25
Kaluga	54.31N, 36.16E	663	20 yrs bef 1912	38.5	64 Jul	12 Jan	94	-36	89	-23	22.9
Kaunas	54.54N, 23.54E	246	1951–60	43.3	64.0 Jul	21.7 Feb	96	-23	89	-13	22.72
Kazan	55.45N, 49.08E	276	1881–1960	38.5	69.0 Jul	9.0 Jan	102	-47	93	-27	17.20
Kerch	45.21N, 36.28E	13									
Kharkov	50.00N, 36.15E	410	1951–60	45.0	70.5 Jul	19.2 Feb	98	-31	92	-19	18.58
Kherson	46.38N, 32.36E	59	? yrs bef 1948	49.9	73.9 Jul	25.9 Jan	102	-26			13.94
Kiev	50.26N, 30.31E	440	1921–50	45.0	67.8 Jul	20.3 Jan	102	-26	93	-12	24.02
Kirov	58.33N, 49.42E	545	1881–1960	34.7	64.0 Jul	6.4 Jan	99	-49	90	-31	19.13
Kirovabad	40.41N, 46.22E	1024	47 yrs bef 1961	55.8	77.7 Jul	34.0 Jan	104	0	99	14	9.76
Kirovograd	48.30N, 32.18E	427	1881–1960	45.5			104	-31			18.66
Kishinev	47.00N, 28.50E	295	1951–60	49.3	72.3 Jul	27.3 Feb					18.54
Klaypeda	55.43N, 21.07E	26	1851–1900	44.2	63.3 Jul	26.8 Jan					
Kostroma	57.46N, 40.55E	456	1925–60	36.9	63.7 Jul	10.8 Jan	99	-51	90	-27	21.97
Kramatorsk	48.43N, 37.32E										
Krasnodar	45.02N, 39.00E	95	1896–1942, 1944–60	51.4	73.8 Jul	28.8 Jan	108	-33	99	-9	25.12
Kremenchug	49.04N, 33.25E										
Krivoy Rog	47.55N, 33.21E	325	1883, 1885–96	49.1	75.6 Jul	21.6 Jan	103	-20	99	-7	16.38
Kursk	51.42N, 36.12E	738	67 yrs bef 1961	41.7	66.7 Jul	16.5 Jan	99	-36	90	-17	23.50

EUROPE

City	Latitude and longitude	Elev (ft)	Period of record	Temperature (°F) Avg	Avg warmest month	Avg coolest month	Absolute High	Absolute Low	Avg annual High	Avg annual Low	Annual precipitation (in)
Kutaisi	42.15N, 42.40E	374									
Kuybyshev	53.12N, 50.09E	446	1935-60	38.8	69.3 Jul	7.2 Jan	102	-45	95	-26	15.33
Leninakan	40.48N, 43.50E	5105	1926-60	42.4	66.7 Aug	13.1 Jan	97	-42	91	-20	18.31
Leningrad	59.55N, 30.15E	7	1881-1960	39.7	64.0 Jul	17.8 Feb	91	-33	86	-15	22.36
Lipetsk	52.37N, 39.35E	541	58 yrs bef 1961	41.2	68.4 Jul	13.5 Jan	102	-36	93	-22	19.61
Lugansk	48.34N, 39.20E	194	? yrs bef 1948	45.7	72.0 Jul	19.4 Jan					18.46
Lvov	49.50N, 24.00E	984	1911-30, 1941-50	46.0	65.5 Jul	25.0 Jan	97	-29	92	-4	23.86
Makeyevka	48.02N, 37.58E	623	? yrs bef 1948	45.0	71.6 Jul	18.5 Jan					17.28
Makhachkala	42.58N, 47.30E	-69	1882-1960	53.2	76.5 Jul	31.3 Jan	99	-15	95	5	16.93
Minsk	53.54N, 27.34E	732	1951-60	41.7	64.4 Jul	19.4 Feb	92	-27	86	-19	22.36
Mogilev	53.54N, 30.21E	499	1881-1930	41.7	64.4 Jul	19.2 Jan	96	-30			25.12
*Moscow	55.45N, 37.35E	548	1921-50	39.6	65.1 Jul	13.5 Jan	100	-43	89	-19	21.77
Murmansk	68.58N, 33.05E	187	1951-60	32.4	55.2 Jul	13.1 Feb					16.14
Nikolayev	46.58N, 32.00E	98	? yrs bef 1960	49.5	73.6 Jul	24.8 Jan	102	-22			15.28
Novgorod	58.31N, 31.17E	79	70 yrs bef 1961	39.0	63.1 Jul	16.5 Jan	93	-49	86	-24	22.44
Novocherkassk	47.25N, 40.06E	341	1922-36	47.5	73.8 Jul	21.0 Jan		-26		-8	
Odessa	46.28N, 30.44E	138	1921-50	49.1	73.2 Jul	26.2 Jan	99	-18	91	-1	14.72
Ordzhonikidze	43.00N, 44.40E	2192	1934-35, 1938-60	46.2	67.5 Jul	23.0 Jan	102	-29	91	-9	32.95
Orel	52.55N, 36.05E	666	1935-41, 1947-60	40.3	65.8 Jul	15.4 Jan	100	-38	91	-22	
Orenburg	51.45N, 55.06E	358	1886-1960	39.0	71.4 Jul	5.4 Jan	108	-44	99	-31	15.12
Orsk	51.12N, 58.34E	673	1925-60	37.4	70.3 Jul	2.5 Jan	108	-47	99	-35	
Penza	53.13N, 45.00E	764	1887-1919, 1923-60	39.0	67.6 Jul	10.2 Jan	100	-45	93	-24	19.21
Perm	58.00N, 56.15E	535	1921-50	35.2	64.6 Jul	5.7 Jan	95	-49	88	-37	24.06
Petrozavodsk	61.49N, 34.20E	361	1949-63	36.0	60.6 Jul	12.9 Jan	93	-40	82	-24	20.94
Podolsk	55.26N, 37.33E		(see Moscow)								
Poltava	49.35N, 34.34E	525	1881-1960	44.6			100	-35			19.09
Riga	56.57N, 24.06E	30	1881-1960	43.2	64.4 Jul	23.9 Jan	95	-24	86	-6	24.96
Rostov-na-Donu	47.14N, 39.42E	217	1886-1960	47.7	73.2 Jul	21.7 Jan	104	-27	97	-11	18.66

EUROPE

City	Latitude and longitude	Elev (ft)	Period of record	Temperature (°F)							Annual precipitation (in)
				Avg	Avg warmest month	Avg coolest month	Absolute High	Absolute Low	Avg annual High	Avg annual Low	
Ryazan	54.38N, 39.44E	512									
Rybinsk	58.03N, 38.50E	341									
Saransk	54.11N, 45.11E	230	1927–42, 1944–60	38.7	66.7 Jul	10.2 Jan	100	-47	91	-38	
Saratov	51.34N, 46.02E	492	1936–55	41.5	71.8 Jul	10.6 Jan	106	-42	97	-22	15.16
Sevastopol	44.36N, 33.32E	23	? yrs bef 1960	54.0	73.9 Jul	35.6 Jan	97	-4	93	6	14.21
Shakhty	47.42N, 40.13E	384	1937-60	46.2	72.5 Jul	19.6 Jan	104	-29	97	-13	
Simferopol	44.57N, 34.06E	669	? yrs bef 1960	50.0	70.9 Jul	29.7 Jan	104	-20			19.72
Smolensk	54.47N, 32.03E	764	1951-60	39.2	63.1 Jul	15.3 Feb	89	-28	86	-18	23.62
Sochi	43.35N, 39.45E	39	1916-51	56.1	73.0 Aug	40.8 Jan	102	5	91	19	53.39
Stavropol	45.03N, 41.58E	1552	1940-60	48.4	71.4 Jul	25.3 Jan	104	-33	95	-4	26.10
Sterlitamak	53.37N, 55.58E	423	? yrs bef 1950	36.7	67.8 Jul	4.3 Jan					
Sumy	50.54N, 34.48E	449	1881-1960	42.8			100	-33			19.96
Syzran	53.11N, 48.27E	187	54 yrs bef 1961	39.9	70.3 Jul	8.6 Jan	106	-47	97	-27	
Taganrog	47.12N, 38.56E	46	1945-60	48.4	74.3 Jul	22.3 Jan	100	-27	95	-11	
Tallin	59.25N, 24.45E	39	1948-60	41.0	61.9 Jul	22.1 Feb	91	-26	85	-8	22.56
Tambov	52.43N, 41.27E	459	1927-60	40.6	68.4 Jul	12.6 Jan	104	-38	93	-24	19.09
Tartu	58.23N, 26.43E	217	1881-1960	40.6	63.1 Jul	20.1 Feb	95	-31	86	-13	22.0
Tbilisi	41.42N, 44.45E	1322	1921-50	55.2	76.1 Jul	33.4 Jan	101	0	93	12	20.20
Tolyatti	53.31N, 49.20E	151	1938–42	39.9	69.6 Jul	9.5 Jan	104	-49	97	-26	
Tula	54.12N, 37.37E	541	? yrs bef 1948	39.7	66.0 Jul	13.5 Jan					22.01
Ufa	54.44N, 55.56E	568	? yrs bef 1960	36.7	66.9 Jul	5.7 Jan	99	-42	90	-31	22.83
Ulyanovsk	54.20N, 48.24E	558	1937-54	37.8	67.3 Jul	7.2 Jan	104	-54	93	-31	16.57
Vilnyus	54.41N, 25.19E	486	1921-50	43.3	64.6 Jul	21.6 Jan					25.94
Vinnitsa	49.14N, 28.29E	791	1881-1960	44.1			100	-33			21.42
Vitebsk	55.12N, 30.11E	545	? yrs bef 1948[1]	39.8	62.2 Jul	17.4 Jan					26.85
Vladimir	56.10N, 40.25E	551	? yrs bef 1948	37.9	64.9 Jul	10.9 Jan					20.08

[1] Climatic data for Novoye Korolevo, nr Vitebsk.

EUROPE

City	Latitude and longitude	Elev (ft)	Period of record	Temperature (°F) Avg	Avg warmest month	Avg coolest month	Absolute High	Absolute Low	Avg annual High	Avg annual Low	Annual precipitation (in)
Volgograd	48.45N, 44.25E	75	44 yrs bef 1943	45.7	75.7 Jul	14.9 Jan	109	-33	100	-17	12.52
Vologda	59.13N, 39.54E	430	1884-1918, 1920-60	36.3	63.0 Jul	11.1 Jan	95	-54	88	-31	20.16
Voronezh	51.38N, 39.12E	482	36 yrs bef 1961	41.7	67.8 Jul	15.3 Jan	106	-40	93	-20	20.43
Yaroslavl	57.37N, 39.52E	322	(see Kostroma)								
Yerevan	40.11N, 44.30E	2986	1935-60	52.9	77.2 Jul	24.8 Jan	106	-24	100	0	12.32
Yoshkar-Ola	56.40N, 47.55E	328	1940-60	36.1	64.8 Jul	7.3 Jan	100	-53	91	-36	
Zaporozhye	47.49N, 35.11E	161	1951-60	48.6	73.6 Jul	24.6 Feb					17.76
Zhdanov	47.06N, 37.33E	10	? yrs bef 1963	47.1	72.7 Jul	22.3 Jan	100	-24			
Zhitomir	50.15N, 28.40E	597	1881-1960	44.2			100	-31			22.44
YUGOSLAVIA											
*Belgrade	44.50N, 20.30E	433	1921-30, 1941-60	53.4	72.5 Jul	32.2 Jan	107	-14	99	4	27.60
Dubrovnik	42.39N, 18.07E	161	1955-64	61.5	76.5 Aug	48.2 Jan					54.76
Ljubljana	46.02N, 14.30E	981	1955-64	49.5	69.1 Jul	29.1 Jan					54.61
Maribor	46.33N, 15.39E	902	1955-64	48.6	66.6 Jul	28.2 Jan					41.10
Nis	43.19N, 21.54E	663	1955-64	52.9	71.4 Aug	32.9 Jan	108	-9	100	4	21.85
Novi Sad	45.15N, 19.50E	433	1955-64	52.5	71.2 Jul	30.4 Jan					24.41
Osijek	45.33N, 18.42E	292	1955-64	51.3	70.2 Jul	28.6 Jan					27.80
Rijeka	45.21N, 14.24E	341	1955-64	56.8	73.0 Jul	41.5 Jan					58.31
Sarajevo	43.50N, 18.25E	2067	1955-64	49.5	66.2 Aug	29.7 Jan	104	-14	96	4	36.42
Skopje	42.00N, 21.29E	787	1955-64	54.1	73.9 Jul	32.7 Jan	105	-11	101	3	19.68
Split	43.31N, 16.26E	400	1955-64	61.2	77.7 Jul	45.9 Jan	100	17	96	24	32.60
Zagreb	45.48N, 16.00E	515	1881-1941	52.2	70.9 Jul	32.2 Jan	94	-4	91	10	34.02

NORTH AMERICA

City	Latitude and longitude	Elev (ft)	Period of record	Temperature (°F) Avg	Avg warmest month	Avg coolest month	Absolute High	Absolute Low	Avg annual High	Avg annual Low	Annual precipitation (in)
BAHAMA ISLANDS											
*Nassau	25.05N, 77.21W	18	1921-50	76.7	82.3 Aug	70.8 Feb	94	41	92	53	42.65
BARBADOS											
*Bridgetown	13.06N, 59.37W	181	1912-48	78.5	80.5 Jun	76 Feb	95	61	90	64	50.2
BERMUDA											
*Hamilton	32.17N, 64.46W	158	1921-50	70.7	80.5 Aug	62.0 Feb	99	40	91	46	57.20
CANADA											
Calgary	51.03N, 114.05W	3428	1921-50	39.0	62.4 Jul	15.8 Jan	97	-49	91	-33	17.47
Chicoutimi	48.26N, 71.06W	19	1956-68	37.8	65.5 Jul	5.7 Jan	104	-47			35.05
Edmonton	53.33N, 113.28W	2188	1921-50	36.8	62.9 Jul	7.7 Jan	99	-57	89	-41	17.63
Halifax	44.39N, 63.36W	57	1921-50	44.6	65.0 Jul	24.4 Jan	99	-21	89	-8	54.26
Hamilton	43.15N, 79.51W	306	46 yrs bef 1947	46	71 Jul	23 Jan					30.93
Kitchener	43.27N, 80.29W	1100	23 yrs bef 1947	45	69 Jul	21 Jan					31.19
Laval	45.33N, 73.43W	130	(see Montreal)								
London	42.59N, 81.14W	809	1921-50	45.8	69.6 Jul	22.5 Jan	106	-27	95	-14	38.24
Longueuil	45.32N, 73.31W	55	(see Montreal)								
Mississauga	43.34N, 79.37W	391	(see Toronto)								
Montreal	45.30N, 73.35W	104	1921-50	43.7	70.4 Jul	15.4 Jan	97	-29	90	-19	41.80
Oshawa	43.54N, 78.51W	325	(see Toronto)								
*Ottawa	45.25N, 75.42W	284	1921-50	41.6	68.6 Jul	12.0 Jan	102	-38	93	-24	33.55
Quebec	46.49N, 71.13W	130	1921-50	40.6	67.6 Jul	12.0 Jan	97	-34	89	-23	41.67
Regina	50.25N, 104.39W	1885	1921-50	36.1	66.6 Jul	2.3 Jan	111	-56	96	-42	15.09
Saint Catharines	43.10N, 79.15W	347	21 yrs bef 1947	48	71 Jul	25 Feb					27.03
Saint John	45.16N, 66.03W	42	1921-50	42.0	61.8 Jul	19.8 Jan	94	-28	83	-13	47.39
Saint John's	47.33N, 52.43W	200	1921-50	41.0	60.0 Jul	24.0 Jan	93	-21	83	-5	53.09

NORTH AMERICA

City	Latitude and longitude	Elev (ft)	Period of record	Temperature (°F) Avg	Avg warmest month	Avg coolest month	Absolute High	Absolute Low	Avg annual High	Avg annual Low	Annual precipitation (in)
Saskatoon	52.07N, 106.38W	1574	1921-50	35.4	66.4 Jul	0.8 Jan	104	-55	95	-41	14.15
Sudbury	46.30N, 81.00W	857	16 yrs bef 1947	39	66 Jul	10 Jan					29.36
Sydney	46.09N, 60.11W	42	1921-50	42.8	65.0 Jul	22.7 Jan	98	-25	87	-11	50.61
Thunder Bay	48.25N, 89.14W	615	1921-50	36.8	63.4 Jul	7.6 Jan	104	-42	89	-30	29.40
Toronto	43.39N, 79.23W	273	1921-50	47.0	70.8 Jul	24.5 Jan	105	-27	93	-11	30.93
Trois-Rivieres	46.21N, 72.34W	51	15 yrs bef 1947	40	68 Jul	10 Jan					40.56
Vancouver	49.17N, 123.07W	38	1921-50	50.8	64.4 Jul	37.6 Jan	92	0	86	13	56.83
Victoria	48.25N, 123.22W	55	1921-50	50.2	60.0 Jul	39.2 Jan	95	-2	86	20	26.18
Windsor	42.18N, 83.01W	602	1921-50	48.8	73.0 Jul	24.5 Jan	101	-27			32.61
Winnipeg	49.53N, 97.09W	757	1921-50	36.6	68.4 Jul	0.6 Jan	108	-54	94	-38	19.72
COSTA RICA											
*San Jose	9.56N, 84.05W	3845	1941-60	68.5	70.5 May	66.2 Jan	92	49	88	51	76.26
CUBA											
Camaguey	21.23N, 77.55W	397	1952-60	77.0	81.3 Aug	70.9 Jan			95	49	52.83
Cienfuegos	22.09N, 80.27W	98	26 yrs bef 1920	76.3	80.4 Aug	70.0 Jan	95	45	94	50	38.31
Guantanamo	20.08N, 75.12W	75	13 yrs bef 1925	77.2	80.2 Jul	73.6 Jan					23.11
*Havana	23.08N, 82.22W	161	1921-50	76.8	81.3 Aug	72.0 Jan	96	50	94	54	44.76
Holguin	20.53N, 76.15W		1952-60[1]	80.1	84.4 Aug	75.2 Jan			93	61	43.94
Marianao	23.05N, 82.26W	164	(see Havana)								
Matanzas	23.03N, 81.35W		16 yrs bef 1925	75.7	81.3 Aug	69.3 Feb			93	53	51.51
San Miguel del Padron	23.05N, 82.19W		(see Havana)								
Santa Clara	22.24N, 79.58W	377	1900-19[2]	73.2	77.7 Aug	67.5 Jan					55.04

[1] Climatic data for Gibara, nr Holguin.

[2] Climatic data for Camajuani, nr Santa Clara.

NORTH AMERICA

City	Latitude and longitude	Elev (ft)	Period of record	Temperature (°F) Avg	Avg warmest month	Avg coolest month	Absolute High	Absolute Low	Avg annual High	Avg annual Low	Annual precipitation (in)
Santiago de Cuba	20.01N, 75.49W	115	16 yrs bef 1925	78.8	82.2 Aug	75.0 Jan	99	54			43.79
DOMINICAN REPUBLIC											
Santiago de los Caballeros	19.27N, 70.42W	728	1951-60[1]	78.8	82.2 Sep	73.4 Jan					37.68
*Santo Domingo	18.28N, 69.54W	46	1921-49	78	80.5 Aug	75 Jan	98	59	95	61	55.8
EL SALVADOR											
San Miguel	13.28N, 88.12W	345	1957-61	81.5	85.5 Apr	78.4 Dec	113	53	108	60	66.69
*San Salvador	13.42N, 89.12W	2290	1921-50	73.9	75.9 Apr	72.3 Jan	105	45	99	51	70.98
Santa Ana	13.59N, 89.34W	2116	1912-57	(see San Salvador for temperature data)							65.63
GUATEMALA											
*Guatemala	14.38N, 90.31W	4928	1931-60	64.6	67.5 May	61.5 Jan	90	41	87	45	50.43
HAITI											
*Port-au-Prince	18.32N, 72.20W	135	1921-50	79.9	82.9 Jul	77.2 Jan	101	60	98	63	51.50
HONDURAS											
San Pedro Sula	15.27N, 88.02W	233	1952-60	79.7	84.0 May	74.1 Dec					52.44
*Tegucigalpa	14.06N, 87.13W	3304	1951-60	70.3	73.4 Apr	66.4 Jan	93	44			37.52
JAMAICA											
*Kingston	18.00N, 76.48W	110	33 yrs bef 1944	79.5	81.5 Jul	76.5 Jan	97	57	94	62	31.5
MARTINIQUE											
*Fort-de-France	14.36N, 61.05W	13	1932-60	77.5	79.3 Sep	75.1 Feb	96	56	91	62	73.19

[1] Temperature data for San Francisco de Macoris, nr Santiago de los Caballeros.

NORTH AMERICA

City	Latitude and longitude	Elev (ft)	Period of record	Temperature (°F)							Annual precipitation (in)
				Avg	Avg warmest month	Avg coolest month	Absolute High	Absolute Low	Avg annual High	Avg annual Low	
MEXICO											
Acapulco	16.50N, 99.55W	13	25 yrs bef 1961	81.3	83.8 Aug	78.8 Jan	96	60			57.36
Aguascalientes	21.53N, 102.18W	6195	17 yrs bef 1940	64.0	72.1 May	55.4 Jan	98	24			26.22
Chihuahua	28.38N, 106.05W	4692	1941-60	65.1	81.5 Jun	50.0 Dec	101	11			12.09
Ciudad Juarez	31.44N, 106.29W	3734	1921-35	62.1	80.6 Jul	41.7 Jan	106	3			7.36
Ciudad Madero	22.16N, 97.50W	377	(see Tampico)								
Ciudad Obregon	27.29N, 109.56W	131	1921-35	79.7	92.7 Aug	64.8 Jan	118	30			8.31
Cuernavaca	18.55N, 99.15W	5059	1921-35	68.5	73.8 May	65.1 Jan	91	44			40.91
Culiacan	24.48N, 107.24W	276	24 yrs bef 1940	76.5	84.7 Jun	67.3 Jan	106	38			21.30
Durango	24.02N, 104.40W	6198	16 yrs bef 1940	63.3	72.9 Jun	53.6 Dec	95	23			17.83
Guadalajara	20.40N, 103.20W	5141	1951-60	66.7	73.0 May	59.4 Jan	97	25			34.84
Gustavo A. Madero	19.29N, 99.07W	7356	(see Mexico)								
Hermosillo	29.04N, 110.58W	778	1921-35	75.6	89.6 Jul	60.1 Dec	113	36			12.60
Irapuato	20.41N, 101.28W	5656	1921-35	66.7	73.6 May	58.3 Jan	101	24			29.13
Jalapa	19.32N, 96.55W	4682	1921-35	64.0	68.4 May	58.1 Jan	94	36			62.56
Leon	21.07N, 101.40W	6185	1931-60	66.7	73.6 May	59.4 Jan	98	27			24.61
Matamoros	25.53N, 97.30W	26	1921-35	73.9	84.7 Aug	61.2 Jan	103	24			29.41
Mazatlan	23.13N, 106.25W	256	1881-1911, 1921-40	74.5	82.4 Jul	65.7 Feb	93	52	90	55	29.84
Merida	20.58N, 89.37W	30	1931-60	78.4	82.0 May	73.4 Jan	106	51	99	56	36.53
Mexicali	32.40N, 115.29W	0	1921-35	72.1	91.2 Jul	53.2 Jan	118	25			2.99
*Mexico	19.24N, 99.09W	7546	1931-60	59.4	63.3 May	54.1 Jan	93	24	85	33	27.99
Monterrey	25.40N, 100.19W	1765	1931-60	72.1	82.4 Jul	59.7 Jan	107	22	102	31	25.79
Morelia	19.42N, 101.07W	6368	33 yrs bef 1961	63.2	68.7 May	57.2 Jan	88	35			29.37
Netzahualcoyotl	19.36N, 99.00W	7474	1921-44	59.9	64.6 Jun	53.4 Jan	93	17			22.32
Nuevo Laredo	27.30N, 99.31W	561	1921-35	76.3	90.5 Jul	57.4 Jan	113	19			16.02
Oaxaca	17.03N, 96.43W	5086	1941-50	70.3	74.5 May	65.8 Dec	100	36			25.24
Orizaba	18.51N 97.06W	4213	1921-35	65.1	69.8 May	59.2 Jan	99	35			83.27

NORTH AMERICA

City	Latitude and longitude	Elev (ft)	Period of record	Temperature (°F) Avg	Avg warmest month	Avg coolest month	Absolute High	Absolute Low	Avg annual High	Avg annual Low	Annual precipitation (in)
Poza Rica	20.33N, 97.27W	197	1921-35[1]	76.3	82.9 Jun	67.1 Jan	105	39			54.41
Puebla	19.03N, 98.12W	7094	1931-60	62.1	66.0 Apr	56.5 Jan	87	29			32.99
Queretaro	20.36N, 100.23W	5528	1921-35	64.0	68.5 Jun	57.0 Jan	97	23			20.39
Reinosa	26.07N, 98.18W	125	(see Matamoros)								
Saltillo	25.25N, 101.00W	5246	33 yrs bef 1961	63.9	72.4 Jun	53.4 Jan	100	15			15.41
San Luis Potosi	22.09N, 100.59W	6158	1921-35	63.7	70.7 May	55.2 Jan	99	27	95	32	14.21
Tampico	22.13N, 97.51W	39	1951-60	75.6	82.8 Aug	67.1 Dec	103	27			43.03
Tepic	21.30N, 104.54W	3002	1921-35	69.6	74.7 Jun	63.0 Jan	102	35			47.09
Tijuana	32.32N, 117.01W	95	1921-35	61.7	70.5 Aug	54.7 Jan	101	26			12.40
Toluca	19.17N, 99.40W	8793	1921-35	51.3	58.8 May	49.8 Jan	80	27			31.14
Torreon	25.33N, 103.26W	3708	1951-60	72.5	83.8 Jun	58.3 Dec					6.50
Veracruz	19.12N, 96.08W	10	1921-35	76.6	81.1 Jun	70.2 Jan	96	49	94	55	63.90
Villahermosa	17.59N, 92.55W	33	1921-35	78.8	83.1 Aug	72.0 Jan	106	54			75.51
NETHERLANDS ANTILLES											
*Willemstad	12.06N, 68.57W	75	1937-46	81.9	84.4 Sep	79.3 Jan	96	63	94	69	17.87
NICARAGUA											
*Managua	12.09N, 86.17W	184	1953-60	80.4	82.9 May	78.3 Jan					47.52
PANAMA											
*Panama	8.57N, 79.32W	118	1951-60[2]	80.4	82.9 Apr	79.0 Oct	97	63	94	67	74.92
PUERTO RICO											
Bayamon	18.24N, 66.09W	76	(see San Juan)								

[1] Climatic data for Tuxpan, nr Poza Rica.

[2] Climatic data for Balboa Heights, Canal Zone, nr Panama.

NORTH AMERICA

City	Latitude and longitude	Elev (ft)	Period of record	Temperature (°F) Avg	Avg warmest month	Avg coolest month	Absolute High	Absolute Low	Avg annual High	Avg annual Low	Annual precipitation (in)
Ponce	18.01N, 66.37W	40	34 yrs bef 1951	78.7	81.5 Aug	75.2 Feb					35.50
*San Juan	18.28N, 66.07W	47	1931-60	78.3	80.8 Aug	75.1 Jan	96	62	92	65	60.36
TRINIDAD AND TOBAGO											
*Port of Spain	10.39N, 61.31W	67	1881-1940	78.1	79.9 May	75.9 Feb	101	52	95	62	63.11
USA											
Abilene	32.28N, 99.43W	1719	1931-60	64.3	83.2 Jul	44.6 Jan	111	-9	102	13	23.32
Akron	41.05N, 81.31W	874	1931-60	49.2	71.5 Jul	27.2 Jan	104	-21			36.43
Albany (Georgia)	31.34N, 84.09W	184	1931-60	67.8	82.5 Jul	52.6 Jan	106	-2			47.84
Albany (New York)	42.39N, 73.45W	20	1931-60	47.6	72.1 Jul	22.7 Jan	104	-26	96	-12	35.08
Albuquerque	35.05N, 106.39W	4945	1931-60	56.6	78.5 Jul	35.0 Jan	103	-7			8.13
Alexandria	38.48N, 77.03W	47	(see Washington)								
Allentown	40.36N, 75.28W	255	1931-60	51.1	74.1 Jul	29.0 Jan	102	-12			44.12
Altoona	40.31N, 78.24W	1180	1931-60	49.6	70.9 Jul	28.5 Jan					43.83
Amarillo	35.12N, 101.50W	3685	1931-60	58.7	80.6 Jul	36.6 Jan	107	-16	102	0	19.67
Anaheim	33.50N, 117.55W	165	(see Santa Ana, USA)								
Anchorage	61.13N, 149.53W	118	1931-60	35.2	57.0 Jul	12.4 Jan	92	-38	81	-32	14.72
Anderson	40.10N, 85.41W	874	1931-60	53.5	75.6 Jul	30.6 Jan					37.12
Ann Arbor	42.17N, 83.45W	880	1931-60[1]	50.0	74.2 Jul	26.6 Jan	100	-13			30.67
Appleton	44.16N, 88.25W	723	1931-60	45.6	72.2 Jul	18.3 Jan					28.92
Arlington (Texas)	32.44N, 97.07W	616	(see Fort Worth)								
Arlington (Virginia)	38.53N, 77.07W	200	(see Washington)								
Asheville	35.36N, 82.33W	1985	1931-60	56.5	74.4 Jul	39.7 Jan	99	-7			37.88
Atlanta	33.45N, 84.24W	1050	1931-60	61.6	78.8 Jul	44.1 Dec	103	-9	96	15	47.14
Atlantic City	39.22N, 74.26W	10	1931-60	54.1	75.1 Jul	34.7 Feb	104	-9			42.36

[1] Climatic data for Willow Run, nr Ann Arbor.

NORTH AMERICA

City	Latitude and longitude	Elev (ft)	Period of record	Temperature (°F) Avg	Avg warmest month	Avg coolest month	Absolute High	Absolute Low	Avg annual High	Avg annual Low	Annual precipitation (in)
Augusta	33.28N, 81.58W	143	1931-60	64.0	80.6 Jul	47.5 Jan	106	3			39.18
Aurora	41.45N, 88.19W	638	1931-60	49.4	73.7 Jul	24.3 Jan					33.80
Austin	30.16N, 97.45W	505	1931-60	68.3	84.5 Jul	50.4 Jan	109	-2	103	21	32.58
Bakersfield	35.22N, 119.01W	420	1931-60	65.1	84.2 Jul	47.4 Jan	118	13			6.36
Baltimore	39.17N, 76.37W	20	1931-60	57.6	79.1 Jul	37.3 Jan	107	-7	98	6	44.21
Baton Rouge	30.27N, 91.11W	57	1931-60	67.6	81.7 Jul	52.4 Jan	110	2			54.46
Bay City	43.36N, 83.53W	595	1931-60	48.6	73.1 Jul	25.0 Jan	109	-25			26.73
Beaumont	30.05N, 94.06W	20	1931-60	69.3	84.4 Jul	54.3 Jan					54.29
Berkeley	37.52N, 122.16W	40	1931-60	57.1	63.4 Sep	49.1 Jan					22.38
Billings	45.47N, 108.30W	3120	1931-60	47.5	73.2 Jul	23.2 Jan	112	-49			13.23
Biloxi	30.24N, 88.53W	22	1931-60	68.1	81.9 Jul	53.6 Jan					58.58
Binghampton	42.06N, 75.55W	865	1931-60	48.8	71.7 Jul	26.5 Jan	103	-28			36.68
Birmingham	33.31N, 86.49W	600	1931-60	64.0	81.7 Jul	46.6 Jan	107	-10	99	12	53.03
Bismarck	46.48N, 100.47W	1670	1931-60	42.2	71.7 Jul	9.9 Jan	114	-45	100	-33	15.15
Bloomington	39.10N, 86.32W	752	1931-60	55.3	77.5 Jul	33.2 Jan					43.97
Boise City	43.37N, 116.12W	2704	1931-60	51.0	75.2 Jul	29.1 Jan	113	-28	104	-3	11.43
Boston	42.21N, 71.03W	21	1931-60	51.4	73.7 Jul	29.9 Jan	104	-18			42.77
Boulder	40.01N, 105.17W	5430	1931-60	51.8	73.6 Jul	32.7 Jan					18.57
Bridgeport	41.11N, 73.11W	10	1931-60	51.5	73.7 Jul	30.1 Jan	102	-20			44.89
Bristol	41.40N, 72.57W	240	(see Hartford)								
Brockton	42.05N, 71.01W	130	1931-60[1]	49.6	71.5 Jul	28.6 Jan					40.96
Brownsville	25.54N, 97.30W	57	1931-60	73.7	84.1 Aug	61.4 Jan	104	12	99	28	26.75
Buffalo	42.53N, 78.52W	585	1931-60	46.7	69.8 Jul	24.1 Feb	99	-20			35.65
Burbank	34.11N, 118.19W	560	1931-60	63.6	73.8 Jul	53.6 Jan	111	21			16.86
Burlington	44.29N, 73.13W	110	1931-60	43.2	69.0 Jul	16.2 Jan	101	-30			33.21
Cambridge	42.22N, 71.06W	20	(see Boston)								

[1] Temperature data for Taunton, nr Brockton.

NORTH AMERICA

City	Latitude and longitude	Elev (ft)	Period of record	Temperature (°F) Avg	Avg warmest month	Avg coolest month	Absolute High	Absolute Low	Avg annual High	Avg annual Low	Annual precipitation (in)
Camden	39.57N, 75.07W	30	(see Philadelphia)								
Canton	40.48N, 81.23W	1030	(see Akron)								
Casper	42.51N, 106.19W	5123	1931-60	46.0	71.7 Jul	23.4 Jan	104	-40			11.80
Cedar Rapids	41.58N, 91.40W	730	1931-60	49.3	74.9 Jul	21.5 Jan					33.33
Champaign	40.07N, 88.15W	740	1931-60[1]	52.7	76.2 Jul	28.7 Jan	109	-25			37.00
Charleston (South Carolina)	32.47N, 79.56W	9	1931-60	65.0	80.1 Jul	50.2 Jan	104	7	98	22	49.16
Charleston (West Virginia)	38.21N, 81.38W	601	1931-60	55.6	74.9 Jul	36.6 Jan	108	-17	99	1	44.43
Charlotte	35.13N, 80.51W	720	1931-60	60.8	79.2 Jul	42.7 Dec	104	-5			43.38
Chattanooga	35.03N, 85.19W	675	1931-60	60.2	79.2 Jul	41.6 Jan	106	-10			51.96
Cheyenne	41.08N, 104.49W	6100	1931-60	45.9	70.0 Jul	25.4 Jan	100	-38	92	-18	15.06
Chicago	41.52N, 87.38W	595	1931-60	50.8	75.6 Jul	26.0 Jan	105	-23	95	-10	33.18
Cincinnati	39.06N, 84.31W	550	1931-60	56.9	78.8 Jul	35.5 Jan	109	-17			39.51
Cleveland	41.30N, 81.42W	660	1931-60	49.2	71.5 Jul	27.6 Jan	103	-19			35.35
Colorado Springs	38.50N, 104.49W	5980	1931-60	48.5	70.4 Jul	28.5 Jan	99	-21			13.19
Columbia (Missouri)	38.57N, 92.20W	748	1931-60	55.0	78.7 Jul	30.3 Jan	113	-23			36.96
Columbia (South Carolina)	34.00N, 81.02W	190	1931-60	64.0	81.6 Jul	46.4 Dec	107	-2	100	16	46.82
Columbus (Georgia)	32.28N, 84.59W	265	1931-60	64.4	81.0 Jul	47.8 Jan	104	3			48.67
Columbus (Ohio)	39.58N, 83.00W	780	1931-60	52.0	74.8 Jul	30.9 Jan	106	-20	96	-5	36.67
Corpus Christi	27.48N, 97.24W	35	1931-60	71.8	84.0 Jul	57.4 Jan	105	11			28.34
Dallas	32.47N, 96.48W	435	1931-60	65.8	85.0 Aug	45.9 Jan	110	-3	102	13	34.55
Davenport	41.31N, 90.35W	590	1931-60	51.3	76.9 Jul	23.8 Jan	111	-27			33.88
Dayton	39.46N, 84.12W	745	1931-60	52.3	75.2 Jul	29.5 Jan	106	-16			36.04
Dearborn	42.19N, 83.10W	604	(see Detroit)								
Decatur	39.51N, 88.57W	682	1931-60	54.1	77.5 Jul	29.8 Jan					37.13
Denver	39.45N, 104.59W	5280	1931-60	49.5	72.9 Jul	28.5 Jan	105	-30			14.81
Des Moines	41.35N, 93.37W	805	1931-60	50.2	77.5 Jul	20.8 Jan	110	-30	100	-14	30.37

[1] Climatic data for Urbana, nr Champaign.

NORTH AMERICA

City	Latitude and longitude	Elev (ft)	Period of record	Temperature (°F) Avg	Avg warmest month	Avg coolest month	Absolute High	Absolute Low	Avg annual High	Avg annual Low	Annual precipitation (in)
Detroit	42.20N, 83.03W	585	1931-60	50.1	74.4 Jul	26.9 Jan	105	-24	94	-5	30.95
Downey	33.56N, 118.07W	118	1931-60	(see Los Angeles for temperature data)							14.51
Dubuque	42.30N, 90.40W	612	1931-60	46.6	72.6 Jul	19.2 Jan	110	-32			35.71
Duluth	46.47N, 92.06W	610	1931-60	37.9	65.5 Jul	8.7 Jan	106	-41	91	-28	28.97
Durham	36.00N, 78.55W	405	1931-60	59.9	78.4 Jul	42.2 Jan					42.65
East Los Angeles	34.01N, 118.09W	280	(see Los Angeles)								
Elgin	42.02N, 88.17W	717	1931-60	(see Aurora for temperature data)							34.14
Elizabeth	40.40N, 74.13W	21	1931-60	54.3	75.8 Jul	32.8 Jan					48.34
El Paso	31.46N, 106.29W	3695	1931-60	63.3	81.9 Jul	42.9 Jan	106	-8	103	14	7.89
Erie	42.07N, 80.05W	685	1931-60	48.7	71.0 Jul	27.2 Jan	98	-16			37.50
Eugene	44.03N, 123.05W	422	1931-60	52.5	66.6 Jul	39.0 Jan	105	-4			39.56
Evansville	37.58N, 87.34W	385	1931-60	57.0	78.7 Jul	34.1 Jan	108	-18			41.45
Fall River	41.42N, 71.09W	40	1931-60	50.7	72.6 Jul	29.7 Jan					45.28
Fargo	46.52N, 96.47W	900	1931-60	41.1	71.4 Jul	7.2 Jan	114	-48			18.45
Fayetteville	35.03N, 78.53W	100	1931-60	62.4	80.3 Jul	44.6 Dec					46.44
Fitchburg	42.35N, 71.48W	458	1931-60	49.0	72.3 Jul	25.9 Jan					45.74
Flint	43.01N, 83.42W	715	1931-60	47.3	71.5 Jul	23.6 Jan	97	-22			30.05
Fort Lauderdale	26.07N, 80.08W	7	1931-60	75.4	82.6 Aug	67.8 Jan					60.29
Fort Smith	35.23N, 94.25W	423	1931-60	61.8	83.0 Jul	39.8 Jan	113	-15			42.22
Fort Wayne	41.04N, 85.08W	790	1931-60	50.1	74.1 Jul	26.5 Jan	106	-24			35.31
Fort Worth	32.45N, 97.20W	670	1931-60	65.8	85.4 Jul	45.4 Jan	112	-8			31.33
Fremont	37.32N, 121.57W	50	(see Oakland)								
Fresno	36.44N, 119.47W	285	1931-60	62.4	80.6 Jul	45.5 Jan	115	17	109	26	11.14
Gainesville	29.40N, 82.20W	185	16 yrs bef 1961	70.2	81.1 Jul	58.0 Jan	104	6			52.45
Galveston	29.18N, 94.48W	5	1931-60	69.9	83.1 Jul	54.9 Jan	101	8			41.81
Garden Grove	33.46N, 117.55W	93	(see Long Beach)								
Gary	41.36N, 87.20W	590	(see Chicago)								
Glendale	34.08N, 118.15W	573	(see Burbank)								

NORTH AMERICA

City	Latitude and longitude	Elev (ft)	Period of record	Temperature (°F) Avg	Avg warmest month	Avg coolest month	Absolute High	Absolute Low	Avg annual High	Avg annual Low	Annual precipitation (in)
Grand Forks	47.55N, 97.03W	830	1931-60	39.4	70.5 Jul	4.5 Jan					20.12
Grand Rapids	42.58N, 85.40W	610	1931-60	47.8	72.3 Jul	24.4 Jan	108	-24			31.19
Great Falls	47.30N, 111.17W	3330	1931-60	44.7	69.4 Jul	22.1 Jan	106	-36			14.07
Green Bay	44.31N, 88.01W	590	1931-60	44.3	70.5 Jul	16.8 Jan	104	-36			25.83
Greensboro	36.04N, 79.47W	839	1931-60	58.2	77.3 Jul	39.7 Jan	104	-7			42.16
Greenville	34.51N, 82.24W	966	1931-60	61.0	78.3 Jul	43.3 Jan	103	4			47.65
Hamilton	39.24N, 84.34W	600	1931-60	54.4	76.3 Jul	33.1 Jan					38.81
Hammond	41.38N, 87.30W	590	(see Chicago)								
Hampton	37.01N, 76.20W	3	1931-60	59.8	79.0 Jul	41.5 Jan					41.95
Harrisburg	40.16N, 76.53W	365	1931-60	53.3	75.6 Jul	31.7 Jan	104	-14			37.65
Hartford	41.46N, 72.41W	40	1931-60	49.9	72.8 Jul	27.4 Jan	101	-26			42.92
Hayward	37.40N, 122.05W	116	(see Oakland)								
Hialeah	25.50N, 80.17W	8	(see Miami)								
High Point	35.57N, 80.00W	940	1931-60	(see Greensboro for temperature data)							45.69
Hollywood	26.01N, 80.09W	10	(see Fort Lauderdale)								
Hot Springs	34.30N, 93.03W	599	1931-60	63.9	83.0 Aug	44.2 Jan	108				55.48
Houston	29.45N, 95.22W	40	1931-60	70.0	84.1 Aug	54.6 Jan	108	5	100	22	45.26
Huntington	38.25N, 82.27W	565	1931-60	55.8	75.1 Jul	36.6 Jan	103	-15			39.53
Huntington Beach	33.40N, 118.05W	35	(see Long Beach)								
Huntsville	34.44N, 86.35W	636	1931-60	62.0	81.1 Jul	43.6 Jan	101	-4			48.67
Independence	39.06N, 94.25W	1051	[see Kansas City (Missouri)]								
Indianapolis	39.46N, 86.10W	710	1931-60	52.1	75.2 Jul	29.1 Jan	106	-25	96	-8	39.25
Inglewood	33.58N, 118.21W	140	(see Los Angeles)								
Irving	32.49N, 96.56W	470	(see Dallas)								
Jackson (Michigan)	42.15N, 84.24W	940	1931-60	48.7	72.4 Jul	25.2 Jan	105	-18			31.15
Jackson (Mississippi)	32.18N, 90.11W	298	1931-60	65.1	81.6 Jul	48.0 Jan	107	-5			49.33
Jacksonville	30.20N, 81.40W	20	1931-60	69.5	82.6 Jul	55.9 Jan	104	10	97	25	53.36

NORTH AMERICA

City	Latitude and longitude	Elev (ft)	Period of record	Temperature (°F) Avg	Avg warmest month	Avg coolest month	Absolute High	Absolute Low	Avg annual High	Avg annual Low	Annual precipitation (in)
Jersey City	40.44N, 74.04W	20	1931-60	53.9	75.3 Jul	32.5 Jan					43.58
Johnstown	40.20N, 78.55W	1185	(see Altoona)								
Joliet	41.32N, 88.05W	607	1942-49	49.2	73.6 Jul	23.7 Jan	101	-20			35.42
Kalamazoo	42.17N, 85.35W	755	1927-56	49.6	73.5 Jul	25.7 Jan	109	-17			34.77
Kansas City (Kansas)	39.07N, 94.38W	750	[see Kansas City (Missouri)]								
Kansas City (Missouri)	39.05N, 94.35W	750	1931-60	56.8	81.5 Jul	31.7 Jan	113	-22	99	-5	34.07
Kenosha	42.36N, 87.50W	610	(see Racine)								
Knoxville	35.58N, 83.55W	890	1931-60	59.6	78.8 Jul	40.8 Jan	104	-16			45.85
La Crosse	43.48N, 91.15W	649	1931-60	46.3	73.8 Jul	16.5 Jan	108	-43			31.16
Lafayette (Indiana)	40.25N, 86.54W	550	1931-60[1]	51.4	74.7 Jul	28.1 Jan					37.78
Lafayette (Louisiana)	30.13N, 92.01W	40	1931-60	68.4	82.2 Jul	53.6 Jan					58.47
Lake Charles	30.14N, 93.13W	16	1931-60	68.6	82.8 Jul	53.2 Jan	106	3			56.04
Lakewood	39.44N, 105.05W	5355	(see Denver)								
Lancaster	40.02N, 76.18W	355	1931-60	52.6	74.4 Jul	31.6 Jan	104	-18			43.29
Lansing	42.44N, 84.33W	830	1931-60	47.6	71.6 Jul	24.2 Jan	102	-25			31.18
Laredo	27.30N, 99.30W	440	1931-60	73.9	87.5 Jul	57.7 Jan	115	5			18.63
Las Vegas	36.10N, 115.09W	2030	1931-60	66.0	90.1 Jul	43.5 Jan	117	8	110	18	3.90
Lawrence	42.42N, 71.10W	65	1931-60	49.1	72.3 Jul	26.0 Jan					40.96
Lawton	34.37N, 98.25W	1111	1931-60	62.7	83.6 Jul	40.7 Jan					30.18
Lewiston	44.06N, 70.13W	196	1931-60	45.6	70.0 Jul	20.7 Jan					43.58
Lexington	38.03N, 84.30W	955	1931-60	55.6	77.3 Jul	34.5 Jan	108	-20			44.73
Lima	40.45N, 84.06W	865	1931-60	51.5	74.2 Jul	29.0 Jan	102	-17			36.43
Lincoln	40.49N, 96.42W	1150	1931-60	52.8	80.1 Jul	25.1 Jan	115	-29	102	-15	27.43
Little Rock	34.45N, 92.17W	300	1931-60	61.7	81.9 Jul	40.6 Jan	110	-12	90	10	48.66
Livonia	42.23N, 83.22W	663	(see Detroit)								

[1] Climatic data for Frankfort, nr Lafayette.

NORTH AMERICA

City	Latitude and longitude	Elev (ft)	Period of record	Temperature (°F)							Annual precipitation (in)
				Avg	Avg warmest month	Avg coolest month	Absolute High	Absolute Low	Avg annual High	Avg annual Low	
Long Beach	33.46N, 118.11W	35	1931-60	62.5	71.9 Jul	52.4 Jan	111	25			9.84
Lorain	41.28N, 82.11W	610	(see Cleveland)								
Los Angeles	34.03N, 118.14W	340	1931-60	64.4	73.0 Jul	55.8 Jan	110	28	100	35	14.69
Louisville	38.15N, 85.46W	450	1931-60	55.7	77.6 Jul	35.0 Jan	107	-20	98	0	41.32
Lowell	42.38N, 71.19W	100	1931-60	50.0	73.6 Jul	26.7 Jan					43.34
Lubbock	33.35N, 101.51W	3195	1931-60	59.7	79.4 Jul	39.2 Jan	107	-16			18.08
Lynchburg	37.25N, 79.09W	517	1931-60	56.7	76.3 Jul	37.6 Jan	106	-7			40.30
Lynn	42.28N, 70.57W	34	(see Boston)								
Macon	32.50N, 83.38W	335	1931-60	65.6	81.9 Jul	49.2 Jan	106	5			44.08
Madison	43.04N, 89.23W	860	1931-60	45.0	71.1 Jul	17.5 Jan	107	-30	93	-18	30.16
Manchester	42.59N, 71.28W	175	1931-60	46.8	70.2 Jul	23.7 Jan					42.43
Mansfield	40.45N, 82.31W	1154	1931-60	49.1	71.7 Jul	27.3 Jan	95	-20			38.16
Memphis	35.09N, 90.03W	275	1931-60	61.5	81.3 Jul	41.5 Jan	106	-13			49.73
Meriden	41.32N, 72.47W	150	(see Hartford)								
Metairie	29.58N, 90.09W	5	(see New Orleans)								
Miami	25.47N, 80.12W	10	1931-60	75.1	82.3 Aug	66.9 Jan	98	27	92	39	59.76
Miami Beach	25.47N, 80.08W	6	1931-60	76.2	82.3 Jul	69.1 Jan	98	30			46.26
Milwaukee	43.02N, 87.54W	635	1931-60	45.1	68.7 Jul	20.6 Jan	105	-25			29.51
Minneapolis	44.59N, 93.16W	815	1931-60	43.7	72.3 Jul	12.4 Jan	108	-41	99	-21	24.76
Mobile	30.42N, 88.03W	5	1931-60	68.2	82.6 Jul	53.0 Jan	103	-1	98	23	68.13
Modesto	37.39N, 121.00W	88	1931-60	60.5	76.3 Jul	45.0 Jan					12.17
Monroe	32.30N, 92.07W	77	1931-60[1]	66.0	82.7 Jul	49.0 Jan					51.19
Montgomery	32.23N, 86.19W	160	1931-60	65.0	81.8 Jul	48.1 Jan	107	-5	99	17	50.69
Muncie	40.11N, 85.23W	950	1931-60	(see Anderson for temperature data)							39.26
Muskegon	43.14N, 86.16W	625	1931-60	48.2	71.2 Jul	26.0 Jan	99	-30			30.07

[1] Climatic data for Calhoun, nr Monroe.

NORTH AMERICA

City	Latitude and longitude	Elev (ft)	Period of record	Temperature (°F) Avg	Avg warmest month	Avg coolest month	Absolute High	Absolute Low	Avg annual High	Avg annual Low	Annual precipitation (in)
Nashua	42.45N, 71.28W	152	1931-60	47.0	70.3 Jul	23.8 Jan					42.29
Nashville	36.10N, 86.47W	450	1931-60	60.0	80.2 Jul	39.9 Jan	107	-15	98	4	45.15
Newark	40.44N, 74.10W	55	1931-60	53.7	76.3 Jul	32.2 Jan	105	-14			42.38
New Bedford	41.38N, 70.56W	15	1931-60	51.4	72.0 Jul	31.7 Jan					41.05
New Britain	41.40N, 72.47W	200	(see Hartford)								
New Haven	41.18N, 72.55W	40	1931-60	50.2	72.0 Jul	29.7 Jan	101	-15			46.02
New Orleans	29.57N, 90.04W	5	1931-60	69.5	82.6 Jul	55.5 Jan	102	7	96	26	62.96
Newport	41.29N, 71.19W	10	1931-60[1]	50.1	69.6 Jul	32.1 Jan	95	-10			40.45
Newport News	36.59N, 76.25W	22	(see Norfolk)								
Newton	42.21N, 71.12W	33	(see Boston)								
New York	40.45N, 74.00W	55	1931-60	54.5	76.8 Jul	33.2 Jan	106	-15	98	2	42.37
Niagara Falls	43.06N, 79.03W	570	(see Buffalo)								
Norfolk	36.51N, 76.17W	10	1931-60	59.7	78.8 Jul	41.2 Jan	105	2	97	14	44.94
Norwalk (California)	33.54N, 118.05W	93	(see Los Angeles)								
Norwalk (Connecticut)	41.07N, 73.22W	60	(see Bridgeport)								
Norwich	41.31N, 72.05W	35	(see New Haven)								
Oakland	37.48N, 122.16W	25	1931-60	57.5	65.1 Sep	48.0 Jan	107	23			17.93
Odessa	31.51N, 102.22W	2890	1931-60[2]	64.3	82.9 Jul	44.0 Jan	109	-1			14.24
Ogden	41.14N, 111.58W	4295	1931-60	50.8	75.5 Jul	26.7 Jan					16.44
Oklahoma City	35.28N, 97.31W	1195	1931-60	60.3	82.8 Aug	37.0 Jan	113	-17	104	5	30.82
Omaha	41.16N, 95.56W	1040	1931-60	51.5	78.5 Jul	22.3 Jan	114	-32	100	-13	27.56
Orlando	28.33N, 81.23W	70	1931-60	71.5	81.4 Jul	60.3 Jan	102	20			51.37
Oshkosh	44.01N, 88.33W	761	1931-60	45.9	72.3 Jul	18.6 Jan					28.37
Oxnard	34.12N, 119.10W	50	1931-60	59.3	65.2 Aug	53.3 Jan					14.75
Parma	41.23N, 81.43W	846	(see Cleveland)								

[1] Climatic data for Block Island, nr Newport.

[2] Climatic data for Midland, nr Odessa.

NORTH AMERICA

City	Latitude and longitude	Elev (ft)	Period of record	Temperature (°F) Avg	Avg warmest month	Avg coolest month	Absolute High	Absolute Low	Avg annual High	Avg annual Low	Annual precipitation (in)
Pasadena	34.09N, 118.09W	830	1931-60	63.2	73.7 Aug	52.9 Jan					20.90
Paterson	40.55N, 74.10W	100	1931-60	53.6	75.7 Jul	31.6 Jan					48.83
Pensacola	30.25N, 87.13W	15	1931-60	68.0	80.9 Jul	54.0 Jan	103	7	95	23	61.60
Peoria	40.42N, 89.36W	470	1931-60	51.4	76.0 Jul	25.7 Jan	113	-27			34.84
Petersburg	37.14N, 77.24W	87	1931-60[1]	60.1	79.2 Jul	41.5 Jan					43.68
Philadelphia	39.57N, 75.09W	100	1931-60	53.5	75.6 Jul	32.3 Jan	106	-11	96	5	42.48
Phoenix	33.27N, 112.04W	1090	1931-60	69.0	89.8 Jul	49.7 Jan	118	16	114	29	7.20
Pittsburgh	40.26N, 80.00W	745	1931-60	50.3	72.1 Jul	28.9 Jan	103	-20	95	-1	36.14
Pittsfield	42.27N, 73.15W	1015	1931-60	44.9	67.8 Jul	21.8 Jan	95	-25			44.42
Pocatello	42.52N, 112.27W	4464	1931-60	47.0	72.4 Jul	22.3 Jan	105	-31			10.85
Pomona	34.04N, 117.45W	861	1931-60	61.5	74.2 Jul	49.6 Jan	117	22			17.78
Port Arthur	29.54N, 93.56W	10	1931-60	68.5	81.8 Jul	53.6 Jan	107	14			53.09
Portland (Maine)	43.40N, 70.15W	25	1931-60	45.0	68.1 Jul	21.8 Jan	103	-39			42.85
Portland (Oregon)	45.31N, 122.41W	77	1931-60	54.6	68.6 Jul	40.2 Jan	107	-2	95	16	42.37
Portsmouth	36.50N, 76.18W	10	(see Norfolk)								
Providence	41.50N, 71.25W	80	1931-60	50.1	72.1 Jul	29.2 Jan	102	-17			42.13
Provo	40.14N, 111.39W	4549	1931-60	(see Salt Lake City for temperature data)							12.87
Pueblo	38.16N, 104.37W	4690	1931-60	52.7	76.4 Jul	30.0 Jan	105	-31	99	-14	11.84
Quincy	42.15N, 71.00W	42	(see Boston)								
Racine	42.44N, 87.47W	630	1931-60	48.6	72.9 Jul	24.4 Jan					32.46
Raleigh	35.47N, 78.38W	365	1931-60	59.5	77.9 Jul	41.6 Jan	105	-2			43.58
Rapid City	44.05N, 103.14W	3231	1931-60	47.3	73.8 Jul	22.0 Jan	109	-34			14.71
Reading	40.20N, 75.56W	265	1931-60	54.3	76.8 Jul	32.7 Jan	105	-14			41.43
Reno	39.31N, 119.49W	4490	1931-60	48.4	67.7 Jul	30.4 Jan	106	-19			7.15
Richmond	37.32N, 77.26W	160	1931-60	58.1	78.1 Jul	38.7 Jan	107	-12	98	10	44.21
Riverside	33.59N, 117.22W	851	1931-60	63.1	75.9 Jul	51.3 Jan	118	19			11.04

[1] Climatic data for Hopewell, nr Petersburg.

NORTH AMERICA

City	Latitude and longitude	Elev (ft)	Period of record	Temperature (°F) Avg	Avg warmest month	Avg coolest month	Absolute High	Absolute Low	Avg annual High	Avg annual Low	Annual precipitation (in)
Roanoke	37.16N, 79.57W	905	1931-60	56.9	76.6 Jul	38.1 Jan	105	-12			41.23
Rochester	43.10N, 77.36W	515	1931-60	48.0	71.6 Jul	25.2 Jan	102	-22			31.50
Rockford	42.17N, 89.06W	715	1931-60	48.6	74.2 Jul	21.9 Jan	103	-20			35.62
Sacramento	38.35N, 121.30W	30	1931-60	60.7	74.0 Jul	46.4 Jan	114	17	104	28	18.02
Saginaw	43.26N, 83.56W	595	1931-60	47.1	71.6 Jul	23.3 Feb	111	-18			28.40
Saint Augustine	29.53N, 81.19W	7	(see Jacksonville)								
Saint Joseph	39.46N, 94.51W	850	1931-60	53.8	79.4 Jul	27.2 Jan	110	-24			34.18
Saint Louis	38.38N, 90.12W	455	1931-60	55.3	78.1 Jul	31.9 Jan	112	-22	99	-8	35.31
Saint Paul	44.57N, 93.06W	780	79 yrs bef 1950	44.5	72.7 Jul	12.8 Jan	108	-41			27.13
Saint Petersburg	27.46N, 82.38W	20	1931-60	73.9	83.0 Aug	63.3 Jan					55.41
Salem (Massachusetts)	42.31N, 70.53W	13	(see Boston)								
Salem (Oregon)	44.56N, 123.02W	163	1931-60	52.4	67.1 Jul	39.0 Jan	108	-10			41.75
Salinas	36.40N, 121.39W	44	1931-60	57.2	63.6 Sep	49.7 Jan	110	18			14.14
Salt Lake City	40.45N, 111.53W	4390	1931-60	50.9	76.9 Jul	27.2 Jan	107	-20	102	-1	13.90
San Antonio	29.26N, 98.29W	650	1931-60	68.7	83.9 Jul	51.9 Jan	107	0			27.84
San Bernardino	34.06N, 117.17W	1080	1931-60	62.8	77.6 Jul	51.4 Jan	116	17			17.71
San Diego	32.43N, 117.09W	20	1931-60	63.0	70.7 Aug	55.6 Jan	111	25	91	36	10.39
San Francisco	37.47N, 122.25W	65	1931-60	56.8	62.0 Sep	50.7 Jan	106	20	90	37	20.78
San Jose	37.20N, 121.53W	90	1931-60	59.4	68.2 Jul	49.2 Jan	104	22	99	26	13.11
Santa Ana	33.46N, 117.52W	133	1931-60	62.6	72.3 Aug	53.0 Jan	112	22			14.58
Santa Barbara	34.25N, 119.42W	100	1931-60	60.3	67.1 Jul	52.6 Jan	115	20			17.68
Santa Fe	35.41N, 105.56W	6950	1931-60	49.9	70.5 Jul	29.9 Jan	97	-13	87	-1	13.76
Santa Monica	34.01N, 118.29W	100	(see Los Angeles)								
Santa Rosa	38.26N, 122.43W	150	1931-60	57.6	66.7 Jul	46.5 Jan	112	15			29.34
Savannah	32.05N, 81.06W	20	1931-60	66.4	81.3 Jul	51.7 Jan	105	8			48.91
Scranton	41.25N, 75.40W	725	1931-60	48.7	71.4 Jul	26.6 Jan	103	-19	96	-3	38.48
Seaside	36.37N, 121.50W	20	(see Salinas)								
Seattle	47.37N, 122.20W	10	1931-60	53.2	65.6 Jul	41.2 Jan	100	3	90	21	34.10

NORTH AMERICA

City	Latitude and longitude	Elev (ft)	Period of record	Temperature (°F) Avg	Avg warmest month	Avg coolest month	Absolute High	Absolute Low	Avg annual High	Avg annual Low	Annual precipitation (in)
Shreveport	32.31N, 93.45W	204	1931-60	65.8	83.2 Jul	47.5 Jan	110	-5			46.28
Sioux City	42.30N, 96.24W	1110	1931-60	49.1	77.3 Jul	18.7 Jan	111	-35	99	-19	24.77
Sioux Falls	43.33N, 96.44W	1395	1931-60	45.7	74.3 Jul	15.2 Jan	110	-42			25.16
Somerville	42.23N, 71.06W	41	(see Boston)								
South Bend	41.41N, 86.15W	710	1931-60	49.4	73.5 Jul	25.5 Jan	109	-22			35.70
Spokane	47.40N, 117.26W	1890	1931-60	47.8	70.5 Jul	25.3 Jan	108	-30	99	-7	17.19
Springfield (Illinois)	39.48N, 89.39W	610	1931-60	53.6	78.0 Jul	28.4 Jan	112	-24			34.83
Springfield (Massachusetts)	42.06N, 72.36W	85	1931-60	51.2	74.0 Jul	28.5 Jan					45.11
Springfield (Missouri)	37.13N, 93.18W	1300	1931-60	56.5	78.7 Jul	33.6 Jan	106	-29	96	-5	41.08
Springfield (Ohio)	39.56N, 83.48W	980	[see Columbus (Ohio)]								
Stamford	41.03N, 73.32W	35	(see Bridgeport)								
Steubenville	40.22N, 80.37W	660	(see Wheeling)								
Stockton	37.57N, 121.17W	20	1931-60	61.3	78.1 Jul	44.7 Jan	113	19			13.37
Sunnyvale	37.23N, 122.02W	130	(see San Jose)								
Syracuse	43.03N, 76.09W	400	1931-60	48.0	72.2 Jul	24.0 Jan	102	-26			37.60
Tacoma	47.15N, 122.26W	110	1931-60	50.7	63.8 Jul	38.3 Jan	99	7	90	18	38.94
Tallahassee	30.27N, 84.17W	216	1931-60	68.0	81.3 Jul	53.9 Jan	104	2			56.86
Tampa	27.57N, 82.27W	15	1931-60	72.2	81.5 Jul	61.1 Jan	98	18	95	31	51.57
Terre Haute	39.28N, 87.24W	496	1931-60	54.3	77.4 Jul	31.1 Jan	110	-18			41.07
Toledo	41.39N, 83.33W	585	1931-60	49.0	72.6 Jul	26.2 Jan	105	-17			30.50
Topeka	39.03N, 95.40W	930	1931-60	54.9	79.8 Jul	28.7 Jan	114	-25			32.36
Torrance	33.49N, 118.18W	75	1931-60	61.0	68.5 Aug	53.0 Jan					12.55
Trenton	40.13N, 74.46W	35	1931-60	53.9	75.9 Jul	33.1 Jan	106	-14			41.28
Tucson	32.13N, 110.58W	2390	1931-60	67.5	86.0 Jul	49.3 Jan	111	16			11.00
Tulsa	36.09N, 96.00W	804	1931-60	60.3	82.1 Jul	37.2 Jan	115	-16			37.08
Tuscaloosa	33.12N, 87.34W	172	1931-60	64.3	81.7 Jul	46.9 Jan					52.46

NORTH AMERICA

City	Latitude and longitude	Elev (ft)	Period of record	Temperature (°F) Avg	Avg warmest month	Avg coolest month	Absolute High	Absolute Low	Avg annual High	Avg annual Low	Annual precipitation (in)
Utica	43.06N, 75.14W	415	1931-60[1]	45.8	70.1 Jul	21.0 Jan					41.31
Virginia Beach	36.51N, 75.58W	13	(see Norfolk)								
Waco	31.33N, 97.08W	405	1931-60	67.2	85.3 Jul	48.0 Jan	111	-5			32.08
Warren	42.30N, 83.02W	619	(see Detroit)								
*Washington	38.54N, 77.01W	25	1931-60	57.0	78.2 Jul	36.9 Jan	106	-15	98	4	40.78
Waterbury	41.33N, 73.03W	260	(see Hartford)								
Waterloo	42.30N, 92.20W	850	1931-60	47.2	73.7 Jul	17.8 Jan	98	-34			31.48
West Palm Beach	26.43N, 80.03W	16	1931-60	75.3	82.5 Jul	66.9 Jan	98	30			61.70
Wheeling	40.04N, 80.43W	650	1931-60	52.8	74.6 Jul	32.0 Jan					38.61
Wichita	37.41N, 97.20W	1290	1931-60	57.1	80.9 Jul	32.0 Jan	114	-22			28.41
Wichita Falls	33.55N, 98.29W	945	1931-60	64.5	85.6 Jul	42.7 Jan	113	-12			26.20
Wilkes-Barre	41.15N, 75.53W	640	(see Scranton)								
Williamsburg	37.16N, 76.42W	81	1931-60[2]	60.1	79.2 Jul	41.5 Jan					43.68
Wilmington (Delaware)	39.45N, 75.33W	135	1931-60	54.1	76.0 Jul	33.4 Jan	102	-4			44.56
Wilmington (North Carolina)	34.14N, 77.55W	32	1931-60	63.8	80.0 Jul	47.9 Jan	104	5			51.29
Winston-Salem	36.06N, 80.15W	860	1931-60	59.1	78.0 Jul	40.6 Jan	100	1			44.13
Woodbridge	40.34N, 74.17W	16	1931-60[3]	53.2	75.0 Jul	32.3 Jan	98	-12			43.98
Worcester	42.16N, 71.48W	475	1931-60	46.8	69.7 Jul	24.0 Jan	93	-19			45.41
Yonkers	40.56N, 73.54W	10	(see New York)								
York	39.58N, 76.44W	370	1931-60	53.9	75.7 Jul	32.8 Jan					42.00
Youngstown	41.06N, 80.39W	840	1931-60	49.5	71.0 Jul	28.3 Jan	100	-18			39.27
VIRGIN ISLANDS (USA)											
*Charlotte Amalie	18.21N, 64.56W	15	1931-60	80.2	82.9 Aug	76.6 Feb					44.75

[1] Climatic data for Little Falls, nr Utica.

[2] Climatic data for Hopewell, nr Williamsburg.

[3] Climatic data for New Brunswick, nr Woodbridge.

OCEANIA

City	Latitude and longitude	Elev (ft)	Period of record	Temperature (°F) Avg	Avg warmest month	Avg coolest month	Absolute High	Absolute Low	Avg annual High	Avg annual Low	Annual precipitation (in)
AUSTRALIA											
Adelaide	34.56S, 138.36E	140	109 yrs bef 1967	62.8	73.5 Jan	51.9 Jul	118	32	110	36	20.86
Brisbane	27.30S, 153.01E	134	79 yrs bef 1967	68.8	76.9 Jan	58.7 Jul	110	36	100	39	44.67
*Canberra	35.20S, 149.10E	1906	38 yrs bef 1967	56.1	69.1 Jan	42.8 Jul	107	18	99	21	25.34
Geelong	38.09S, 144.21E	57	1911–40	58.0	67.1 Feb	49.2 Jul	111	27			21.32
Hobart	42.55S, 147.20E	177	1921–50	54.2	61.5 Feb	46.6 Jul	105	28	96	31	24.84
Melbourne	37.50S, 145.00E	114	110 yrs bef 1967	58.5	67.6 Jan	48.9 Jul	114	27	105	31	25.94
Newcastle	32.55S, 151.45E	106	1911–40	64.4	72.1 Jan	54.5 Jul	112	37			41.36
Perth	31.56S, 115.50E	210	69 yrs bef 1967	64,5	74.6 Feb	55.4 Jul	112	34	105	38	34.87
Sydney	33.53S, 151.12E	138	107 yrs bef 1967	63.3	71.6 Jan	53.3 Jul	114	36	100	39	47.71
Wollongong	34.25S, 150.54E	150	1911–40	63.0	70.8 Feb	54.3 Jul	115	34			44.04
FIJI											
*Suva	18.08S, 178.25E	30	1921–50	77.1	80.5 Feb	73.6 Jul	98	55	93	60	124.41
FRENCH POLYNESIA											
*Papeete	17.32S, 149.34W	7	1941–60	79.2	81.5 Mar	76.6 Jul	95	61	93	64	72.60
(HAWAII), USA											
Hilo	19.43N, 155.05W	60	23 yrs bef 1970	73.1	75.8 Aug	70.8 Jan	93	53			136.62
*Honolulu	21.19N, 157.52W	21	1931–60	75.9	79.4 Aug	72.4 Feb	90	52	86	59	21.89
NEW CALEDONIA											
*Noumea	22.16S, 166.27E	10	1941–60	73.6	79.5 Feb	67.8 Jul	99	52	94	56	42.64
NEW ZEALAND											
Auckland	36.51S, 174.45E	160	1931–60	59.5	66.5 Jan	51.5 Jul	90	33	81	37	48.9

OCEANIA

City	Latitude and longitude	Elev (ft)	Period of record	Temperature (°F) Avg	Avg warmest month	Avg coolest month	Absolute High	Absolute Low	Avg annual High	Avg annual Low	Annual precipitation (in)
Christchurch	43.35S, 172.36E	22	1931-60	52.6	61.5 Jan	42.5 Jul	96	21	88	25	26.3
Dunedin	45.52S, 170.30E	5	1931-60	51.6	59.5 Jan	43.5 Jul	94	23	84	29	31.0
*Wellington	41.28S, 174.51E	415	1931-60	54.3	62.5 Jan	47.5 Jul	88	29	80	32	47.5
PAPUA											
*Port Moresby	9.29S, 147.08E	92	1941-60	80.4	81.9 Dec	78.4 Jul	98	64	95	69	45.73
WESTERN SAMOA											
*Apia	13.50S, 171.44W	7	1921-50	79.5	80.1 Jan	78.4 Jul	93	63	90	66	115.28

SOUTH AMERICA

City	Latitude and longitude	Elev (ft)	Period of record	Temperature (°F) Avg	Avg warmest month	Avg coolest month	Absolute High	Absolute Low	Avg annual High	Avg annual Low	Annual precipitation (in)
ARGENTINA											
Almirante Brown	34.48S, 58.23W	82	(see Buenos Aires)								
Avellaneda	34.39S, 58.23W	23	(see Buenos Aires)								
Bahia Blanca	38.43S, 62.17W	66	1901-50	59.9	74.7 Jan	46.2 Jul	109	18	103	23	21.26
*Buenos Aires	34.36S, 58.27W	82	1901-50	61.7	74.3 Jan	50.0 Jul	110	22	99	27	38.62
Cordoba	31.24S, 64.11W	1450	1901-50	63.0	75.2 Jan	50.5 Jul	114	13	105	21	27.16
Lanus	34.43S, 58.24W	33	(see Buenos Aires)								
La Plata	34.55S, 57.57W	59	1941-50	61.0	72.3 Jan	49.3 Jul	92	23			39.21
Lomas de Zamora	34.46S, 58.24W	69	(see Buenos Aires)								
Mar del Plata	38.00S, 57.33W	79	1901-50	56.7	67.5 Jan	46.6 Jul	106	20			30.83
Mendoza	32.53S, 68.49W	2523	1901-50	60.1	74.3 Jan	45.3 Jun	109	15	102	23	7.76
Merlo	34.40S, 58.45W	56	(see Buenos Aires)								

SOUTH AMERICA

City	Latitude and longitude	Elev (ft)	Period of record	Temperature (°F) Avg	Avg warmest month	Avg coolest month	Absolute High	Absolute Low	Avg annual High	Avg annual Low	Annual precipitation (in)
Parana	31.44S, 60.32W	243	1941-50	64.4	77.2 Jan	52.5 Jul	113	22	103	30	37.44
Quilmes	34.44S, 58.16W	62	(see Buenos Aires)								
Rosario	32.57S, 60.40W	85	1901-50	64.2	76.5 Jan	51.6 Jun	111	13	103	24	36.42
Salta	24.47S, 65.25W	3878	1901-50	63.3	71.4 Dec	52.3 Jul	103	14			27.20
San Isidro	34.27S, 58.30W	75	(see Buenos Aires)								
San Justo	34.40S, 58.33W	89	(see Buenos Aires)								
San Martin	34.34S, 58.32W	69	(see Buenos Aires)								
San Miguel	34.33S, 58.43W	157	1941-50	61.3	73.8 Jan	49.3 Jul	105	18			36.97
Santa Fe	31.38S, 60.42W	121	1941-50[1]	64.6	76.1 Jan	52.3 Jul	111	19			34.41
Seis de Septiembre	34.39S, 58.37W	75	(see Buenos Aires)								
Tres de Febrero	34.36S, 58.33W	85	(see Buenos Aires)								
Tucuman	26.49S, 65.13W	1385	1901-50	66.6	77.0 Jan	54.1 Jul	118	19			37.56
Vicente Lopez	34.32S, 58.28W	62	1941-50	62.1	73.2 Jan	50.4 Jul	93	19			35.28
BOLIVIA											
Cochabamba	17.24S, 66.09W	8390	1941-60	62.8	66.9 Nov	56.7 Jun					20.31
*La Paz	16.30S, 68.09W	11,910	1921-50	50.0	53.4 Nov	45.5 Jul	80	26	75	28	21.93
*Sucre	19.02S, 65.17W	9331	5 yrs bef 1953	54	58 Nov	49 Jul	88	25	87	31	27.8
BRAZIL											
Aracaju	10.55S, 37.04W	16	1911-19	79.2	81.1 Feb	76.6 Jul	97	63	90	65	37.28
Belem	1.27S, 48.29W	46	1893-1910	78.6	79.9 Nov	77.4 Feb	98	64	93	67	86.10
Belo Horizonte	19.55S, 43.56W	2723	1954-62	69.8	73.0 Feb	64.6 Jun	97	36	94	49	56.15
*Brasilia	15.47S, 47.55W	3809	1961-65	69.4	72.7 Sep	64.0 Jun	94	43	91	46	64.02
Campina Grande	7.13S, 35.53W	1804	1923-24,1937	72.9	76.1 Jan	68.0 Jul			95	58	35.24
Campinas	22.54S, 47.05W	2274	? yrs bef 1919	67.6	72.3 Jan	61.0 Jun	98	32			55.04

[1] Temperature data for Angel Gallardo, nr Santa Fe.

SOUTH AMERICA

City	Latitude and longitude	Elev (ft)	Period of record	Temperature (°F) Avg	Avg warmest month	Avg coolest month	Absolute High	Absolute Low	Avg annual High	Avg annual Low	Annual precipitation (in)
Campos	21.45S, 41.18W	46	1912-19	72.7	77.9 Feb	67.8 Jul	102	45			42.64
Curitiba	25.25S, 49.15W	3117	1921-50	61.2	67.6 Jan	54.0 Jul	99	16	90	32	57.17
Duque de Caxias	22.47S, 43.18W	13	(see Rio de Janeiro)								
Feira de Santana	12.15S, 38.57W	820									
Florianopolis	27.35S, 48.34W	7	14 yrs bef 1965	69.3	76.6 Jan	61.7 Jul	97	34	91	44	46.69
Fortaleza	3.43S, 38.30W	82	1954-62	80.8	81.7 Jan	79.7 Jul	90	67	89	69	44.80
Goiania	16.40S, 49.16W	2493	1958-65	73.2	77.2 Sep	67.6 Jun	102	36	98	42	55.16
Guarulhos	23.29S, 46.31W	2493	(see Sao Paulo)								
Jaboatao	8.07S, 35.01W	148	(see Recife)								
Joao Pessoa	7.07S, 34.53W	148	1912-19	77.4	79.0 Dec	74.3 Jul	94	63			69.41
Juiz de Fora	21.45S, 43.20W	2218	1893-1922	67.1	73.9 Feb	59.9 Jul	98	33			57.91
Londrina	23.18S, 51.09W	1969	1932-56	69.1	74.8 Jan	62.2 Jun	104	32			56.69
Maceio	9.40S, 35.43W	16	1956-65	78.4	81.1 Feb	75.6 Aug	92	63	90	66	63.23
Manaus	3.08S, 60.01W	197	1910-29, 1931-40	80.4	82.2 Sep	79.3 Jan	101	64	97	67	71.3
Natal	5.47S, 35.13W	10	1904-21	79.0	81.0 Jan	75.9 Jul	91	59	89	65	54.2
Niteroi	22.53S, 43.07W	8	1954-63	75.2	80.8 Jan	69.3 Jun	104	48	102	53	44.61
Nova Iguacu	22.45S, 43.27W	85	(see Rio de Janeiro)								
Olinda	8.01S, 34.51W	98	1941-60	78.4	81.0 Feb	75.0 Aug	92	64	89	66	68.23
Osasco	23.32S, 46.46W	2366	(see Sao Paulo)								
Pelotas	31.46S, 52.20W	23	1912-19	63.9	73.6 Feb	54.1 Jun	102	28			52.05
Petropolis	22.31S, 43.10W	2667	1913-19	64.8	70.2 Jan	59.5 Jul	92	33			83.54
Porto Alegre	30.04S, 51.11W	13	22 yrs bef 1924	67	77.5 Feb	57.5 Jun	105	25	101	32	49.1
Recife	8.03S, 34.54W	180	1901-33	79.5	81.5 Jan	75.5 Jul	94	64	90	67	63.4
Ribeirao Preto	21.10S, 47.48W	1700	1901-17	70.2	75.0 Feb	62.6 Aug	104	29			55.12
Rio de Janeiro	22.54S, 43.14W	102	1921-50	73.2	78.4 Feb	68.4 Jul	102	50	96	56	40.20
Salvador	12.59S, 38.31W	28	1931-50	76.5	79.3 Feb	73.0 Jul	95	62	91	65	76.06
Santo Andre	23.40S, 46.31W	2438	(see Sao Paulo)								
Santos	23.57S, 46.20W	13	1895-1917	71.4	77.9 Feb	66.0 Aug	107	41	101	49	82.05

SOUTH AMERICA

City	Latitude and longitude	Elev (ft)	Period of record	Temperature (°F) Avg	Avg warmest month	Avg coolest month	Absolute High	Absolute Low	Avg annual High	Avg annual Low	Annual precipitation (in)
Sao Bernardo do Campo	23.42S, 46.33W	2507	(see Sao Paulo)								
Sao Goncalo	22.51S, 43.04W	43	(see Rio de Janeiro)								
Sao Joao de Meriti	22.48S, 43.22W	233	(see Rio de Janeiro)								
Sao Luis	2.31S, 44.16W	13	13 yrs bef 1963	79.7	81.0 Oct	79.0 Apr	96	66	92	70	74.05
Sao Paulo	23.32S, 46.37W	2690	1921-50	64.6	70.0 Feb	58.1 Jul	95	35	92	40	54.41
Teresina	5.05S, 42.49W	213	1956-65	82.6	86.7 Oct	79.7 Mar	105	61	102	63	49.96
Vitoria	20.19S, 40.21W	10	1928-32, 1934-58	75.2	81.0 Feb	71.8 Jul	100	50	95	58	51.02
CHILE											
Concepcion	36.50S, 73.03W	43	? yrs bef 1950	56.3	62.6 Jan	50.0 Jul			90	34	51.57
*Santiago	33.27S, 70.40W	1706	1921-50	57.4	68.7 Jan	46.2 Jul	99	24	92	27	13.90
Valparaiso	33.02S, 71.38W	135	22 yrs bef 1933	57.7	63.1 Jan	52.5 Jul	94	36	86	39	20.94
Vina del Mar	33.02S, 71.34W		(see Valparaiso)								
COLOMBIA											
Barranquilla	10.59N, 74.48W	16	1942-53, 1957-61	82.0			108	55	99	65	29.29
*Bogota	4.36N, 74.05W	8675	1941-60	57.2	58.8 Apr	56.8 Aug	77	32	75	35	35.51
Bucaramanga	7.08N, 73.09W	3035	1946-48, 1950-61	73.9			102	58	90	62	49.92
Cali	3.27N, 76.31W	3432	1942-49, 1952-59	74.8			95	57	90	62	44.09
Cartagena	10.25N, 75.32W	0	1942-50, 1952-61	80.8			107	56	94	68	33.07
Cucuta	7.54N, 72.31W	965	1942-54, 1958-61	81.1			102	52	94	69	17.56
Ibague	4.27N, 75.14W	4098	1941-47, 1949-59, 1961	71.4			95	45	91	55	80.83
Manizales	5.04N, 75.37W	7021	1942, 1944-52	64.6			84	45	80	51	80.91
Medellin	6.15N, 75.35W	5056	1942-55, 1957-61	70.7			102	45	91	50	51.57
Pereira	4.49N, 75.43W	4672	1942, 1944, 1946-53	71.2			97	46	89	54	80.87

SOUTH AMERICA

City	Latitude and longitude	Elev (ft)	Period of record	Temperature (°F) Avg	Avg warmest month	Avg coolest month	Absolute High	Absolute Low	Avg annual High	Avg annual Low	Annual precipitation (in)
ECUADOR											
Guayaquil	2.10S, 79.50W	10	1951-60	77.5	79.9 Apr	75.2 Jul	98	57	96	61	40.24
*Quito	0.13S, 78.30W	9249	1921-50	55.8	56.1 Sep	55.6 Jun	86	32	81	35	48.27
GUYANA											
*Georgetown	6.49N, 58.10W	7	1887-1940	80.6	82.0 Sep	79.3 Jan	93	68	90	70	87.44
PARAGUAY											
*Asuncion	25.16S, 57.40W	210	1921-50	74.7	84.0 Jan	63.7 Jul	110	29	105	35	49.84
PERU											
Arequipa	16.24S, 71.33W	7559	1896-1911, 1921-25	58.3	58.8 Sep	57.5 Jul	80	31			4.31
Callao	12.04S, 77.09W	20	9 yrs bef 1956[1]	67.3	73.6 Feb	61.7 Aug					0.47
Cuzco	13.31S, 71.59W	11,152	1931-43	55	58 Nov	50.5 Jul	84	16	82	23	32.0
*Lima	12.03S, 77.03W	505	1931-60	65.1	72.3 Feb	59.2 Aug	93	49	89	51	1.22
SURINAM											
*Paramaribo	5.50N, 55.13W	12	1931-50	81.1	83.5 Oct	79.5 Jan	99	62	96	67	88.90
URUGUAY											
*Montevideo	34.53S, 56.11W	72	1888-1941	61	72.5 Jan	50.5 Jul	109	25	92	36	37.4
VENEZUELA											
Barquisimeto	10.04N, 69.19W	1857	1951-60	74.8	76.3 Apr	73.6 Jan	97	59			20.04
*Caracas	10.30N, 66.55W	3025	1941-60	69.4	71.1 May	66.2 Jan	92	45	87	49	32.88
Maracaibo	10.40N, 71.37W	20	1938-46, 1951-60	82.4	84.3 Aug	80.5 Jan	102	66	99	69	18.70
Maracay	10.15N, 67.36W	1460	1951-60	76.3	79.2 Apr	73.9 Jan					35.98
Valencia	10.11N, 68.00W	1568	1937-46	76.3	78.1 Apr	75.2 Jan	101	63			45.31

[1] Climatic data for La Punta, nr Callao.

TABULAR GAZETTEER 2, CITIES, BY CONTINENT AND COUNTRY

Part III. Location and Climatic Data (Metric Measure)

AFRICA

City	Latitude and longitude	Elev (m)	Period of record	Temperature (°C) Avg	Avg warmest month	Avg coolest month	Absolute High	Absolute Low	Avg Annual High	Avg Annual Low	Annual Precipitation (mm)
ALGERIA											
*Algiers	36.47N, 3.03E	59	1935–49	19.0	25.9 Aug	12.9 Jan	42	0	39	3	708
Annaba	36.54N, 7.46E	3	1935–49	18.0	25.5 Aug	11.6 Jan	46	0			750
Constantine	36.22N, 6.37E	581	1935–49	15.1	25.1 Aug	6.8 Jan	46	-5	40	-2	446
Oran	35.42N, 0.38W	90	1924–50	17.2	25.1 Aug	10.3 Jan	43	-1	38	4	406
ANGOLA											
*Luanda	8.48S, 13.14E	43	1921–50	24.1	26.7 Mar	20.3 Aug	37	14	33	16	349
BURUNDI											
*Bujumbura	3.23S, 29.22E	783	1951–60	23.2	24.0 Sep	22.5 Jul	35	12			831
CAMEROON											
Douala	4.03N, 9.42E	13	1951–60	26.4	27.6 Feb	24.6 Aug	36	18	33	20	4109
*Yaounde	3.52N, 11.31E	760	1951–60	23.4	24.5 Feb	22.1 Jul	36	13	33	15	1547
(CANARY ISLANDS), SPAIN											
*Las Palmas	28.06N, 15.24W	13	1882–1920, 1943–55	20.2	23.6 Aug	17.8 Jan	37	8	32	11	583
Santa Cruz de Tenerife	28.27N, 16.14W	4	1931–60	20.8	24.7 Jul	17.4 Jan	43	8			251
CENTRAL AFRICAN REPUBLIC											
*Bangui	4.23N, 18,35E	381	1941–60	26.0	27.4 Mar	25.1 Jul	42	7	38	14	1560
CHAD											
*Fort-Lamy	12.07N, 15.03E	300	1951–60	28.0	32.7 Apr	23.5 Jan	46	8	45	10	646

AFRICA

City	Latitude and longitude	Elev (m)	Period of record	Temperature (°C) Avg	Avg warmest month	Avg coolest month	Absolute High	Absolute Low	Avg Annual High	Avg Annual Low	Annual Precipitation (mm)
CONGO											
*Brazzaville	4.16S, 15.17E	513	1941-60	24.9	26.4 Apr	21.4 Jul	37	10	36	13	1371
DAHOMEY											
*Cotonou	6.21N, 2.26E	13	1951-60	26.9	28.6 Mar	25.0 Aug	37	18	34	19	1339
*Porto-Novo	6.29N, 2.37E	20	1897-1909	27.2	28.9 Mar	25.3 Jul					1329
EGYPT											
Alexandria	31.12N, 29.54E	4	1901-34	20.0	25.9 Aug	13.6 Jan	44	3	39	6	188
Aswan	24.05N, 32.53E	132	1913-60	26.9	33.9 Jul	15.7 Jan	51	2	48	5	1
Asyut	27.11N, 31.11E	66	1900-34	21.7	29.4 Jul	11.6 Jan	49	0	44	2	5
*Cairo	30.03N, 31.15E	24	1909-34	20.6	27.5 Aug	12.1 Jan	47	-1	42	4	29
Giza	30.01N, 31.13E	25	1909-34	19.7	26.6 Jul	11.1 Jan	47	-4			28
Luxor	25.41N, 32.39E	78	1941-47	24.6	32.6 Jul	13.5 Jan	49	0	47	1	0.5
Mahalla al Kubra	30.58N, 31.10E		1907-29[1]	19.1	26.5 Jul	10.5 Jan	47	0			61
Mansurah	31.03N, 31.23E	7	1927-34	21.4	28.0 Aug	13.6 Feb	47	0			54
Port Said	31.16N, 32.18E	22	1901-34	20.6	26.8 Aug	13.6 Jan	45	0	38	6	83
Shubra al Khaymah	30.06N, 31.15E		(see Cairo)								
Suez	29.58N, 32.33E	4	1910-34	22.0	28.8 Aug	14.0 Jan	45	1	42	5	22
Tanta	30.47N, 31.00E	14	1927-34	19.9	26.6 Jul	11.8 Jan	47	0			42
Zagazig	30.35N, 31.31E	11	1913-18, 1925-34	19.8	26.6 Jul	11.5 Jan	46	0			30
ETHIOPIA											
*Addis Ababa	9.02N, 38.47E	2408	27 yrs bef 1960	15.8	17.9 Mar	15.0 Jul	34	0	29	2	1246
Asmara	15.19N, 38.55E	2374	1922-39, 1945-52	16.9	18.6 May	15.0 Jan	31	-1	29	2	492

[1] Climatic data for Qurashiyah, nr Mahalla al Kubra.

AFRICA

City	Latitude and longitude	Elev (m)	Period of record	Temperature (°C) Avg	Avg warmest month	Avg coolest month	Absolute High	Absolute Low	Avg Annual High	Avg Annual Low	Annual Precipitation (mm)
GABON											
*Libreville	0.23N, 9.27E	3	1956–60	26.4	27.2 Apr	24.3 Jul	37	17	34	18	2648
GAMBIA											
*Bathurst	13.27N, 16.34W	2	34 yrs bef 1961	25.5	27.1 Oct	23.1 Jan	41	7	40	9	1224
GHANA											
*Accra	5.31N, 0.12W	65	1941–60	26.5	27.8 Mar	24.3 Aug	38	15	34	18	787
Kumasi	6.43N, 1.37W	293	1941–60	25.5	26.9 Mar	23.6 Aug	38	11	36	12	1465
GUINEA											
*Conakry	9.31N, 13.43W	46	29 yrs bef 1961	26.7	27.8 Apr	25.0 Aug	36	17	34	18	4341
IVORY COAST											
*Abidjan	5.19N, 4.02W	7	1941–60	26.5	27.8 Mar	24.3 Aug	36	13	34	18	2144
KENYA											
Mombasa	4.03S, 39.40E	16	45 yrs bef 1955	26.1	28.0 Mar	24.4 Jul	36	16	33	19	1190
*Nairobi	1.17S, 36.49E	1662	1910–20, 1929–60	18.0	18.7 Mar	14.9 Jul	31	5	28	7	944
LIBERIA											
*Monrovia	6.19N, 10.49W	23	1953–56	25.8	27.0 Mar	24.4 Jul	34	13	33	17	5131
LIBYA											
*Bengasi	32.07N, 20.04E	25	46 yrs bef 1947	20.0	25.8 Aug	13.6 Jan	43	3	40	5	266
*Tripoli	32.54N, 13.11E	22	31 yrs bef 1941	19.7	26.6 Aug	12.7 Jan	46	1	41	4	405

AFRICA

City	Latitude and longitude	Elev (m)	Period of record	Temperature (°C) Avg	Avg warmest month	Avg coolest month	Absolute High	Absolute Low	Avg Annual High	Avg Annual Low	Annual Precipitation (mm)
(MADEIRA ISLANDS), PORTUGAL											
*Funchal	32.38N, 16.54W	25	1921-50	18.8	22.3 Aug	15.8 Feb	39	4	31	8	553
MALAGASY REPUBLIC											
*Tananarive	18.55S, 47.31E	1381	44 yrs bef 1954	18.6	21.1 Dec	14.4 Jul	35	1	32	3	1356
MALAWI											
Blantyre	15.48S, 35.01E	1067	1931-60[1]	21.2	24.1 Nov	17.1 Jul	35	5	34	8	1155
MALI											
*Bamako	12.39N, 8.00W	332	1941-60	28.1	33.0 Apr	25.3 Jan	47	8	44	11	1099
Timbuktu	16.46N, 3.01W	298	1951-60	29.3	34.3 May	22.6 Jan	48	5	47	7	225
MAURITIUS											
*Port Louis	20.10S, 57.30E	55	1921-50	23.0	26.0 Jan	20.0 Jul	35	10	33	12	1295
MOROCCO											
Casablanca	33.36N, 7.37W	50	1924-50	17.5	23.0 Aug	12.2 Jan	43	-1	37	2	402
Fez	34.03N, 4.59W	417	1925-49	17.8	27.1 Aug	9.8 Jan	48	-4	44	-2	546
Marrakesh	31.37N, 8.00W	460	1924-50	19.9	29.1 Aug	11.4 Jan	49	-3	46	-1	248
Meknes´	33.54N, 5.33W	558	1925-49	17.1	25.6 Aug	9.7 Jan					575
*Rabat-Sale	34.02N, 6.50W	65	1925-49	17.8	23.2 Aug	12.5 Jan	48	0	41	3	523
Tangier	35.47N, 5.48W	75	1925-49	17.4	23.1 Aug	12.5 Jan	41	-2	34	2	887
MOZAMBIQUE											
*Lourenco Marques	25.58S, 32.33E	59	1921-50	22.2	25.5 Feb	18.2 Jul	46	7	41	9	754

[1] Temperature data for Zomba, nr Blantyre.

AFRICA

City	Latitude and longitude	Elev (m)	Period of record	Temperature (°C) Avg	Avg warmest month	Avg coolest month	Absolute High	Absolute Low	Avg Annual High	Avg Annual Low	Annual Precipitation (mm)
NIGER											
*Niamey	13.30N, 2.08E	222	1945-60	28.9	33.6 Apr	24.6 Jan	46	8	45	10	636
NIGERIA											
Abeokuta	7.10N, 3.20E	67	1909-13, 1916-29	26.1	27.1 Mar	24.8 Aug					1184
Enugu	6.27N, 7.28E	142	1951-60	26.7	28.6 Mar	25.4 Aug	37	13	36	17	1661
Ibadan	7.23N, 3.53E	198	24 yrs bef 1955	26.7	28.8 Mar	24.4 Aug	39	10	37	14	1262
Ilesha	7.38N, 4.45E	335?	(see Oshogbo)								
Ilorin	8.45N, 4.32E	329	1916-29, 1951-60	26.2	28.6 Mar	24.5 Aug	40	9	38	12	1321
Kano	12.00N, 8.30E	467	1921-50	26.4	31.2 Apr	21.5 Jan	46	6	42	9	833
*Lagos	6.26N, 3.23E	3	1921-50	26.8	28.3 Mar	25.1 Aug	40	16	35	19	1752
Ogbomosho	8.05N, 4.11E	366	14 yrs bef 1926	25.0	27.4 Feb	23.0 Aug					
Oshogbo	7.50N, 4.35E	302	1937	25.9	29.3 Mar	23.5 Aug			38	10	1123
Port Harcourt	4.43N, 7.05E	20	1951-60	26.0	27.0 Mar	24.8 Jul	37	16			2395
Zaria	11.07N, 7.44E	640	1919-54[1]	25.0	28.6 Apr	23.0 Dec	41	8			1128
REUNION											
*Saint-Denis	20.52S, 55.28E	11	1951-60	23.5	26.0 Jan	20.9 Jul					1419
RHODESIA											
Bulawayo	20.09S, 28.36E	1343	1921-50	19.1	22.4 Nov	13.9 Jul	37	-2	36	2	580
*Salisbury	17.50S, 31.03E	1472	1923-50	18.5	21.6 Oct	13.7 Jul	35	0	33	2	829
SENEGAL											
*Dakar	14.40N, 17.26W	24	1899-1913,1932-40	25.0	27.8 Jul	21.9 Jan	43	12	38	14	578

[1] Temperature data for Kaduna, nr Zaria.

AFRICA

City	Latitude and longitude	Elev (m)	Period of record	Temperature (°C) Avg	Avg warmest month	Avg coolest month	Absolute High	Absolute Low	Avg Annual High	Avg Annual Low	Annual Precipitation (mm)
SIERRA LEONE											
*Freetown	8.29N, 13.13W	26	1921–50	26.5	27.7 Apr	25.0 Aug	37	17	35	18	3585
SOMALIA											
*Mogadishu	2.02N, 45.21E	10	1931–60	27.2	29.2 Apr	25.9 Aug	36	15	33	19	414
SOUTH AFRICA											
Bloemfontein	29.08S, 26.13E	1426	1880–1940	15.9	22.8 Jan	7.8 Jul	45	-11	36	-6	528
*Cape Town	33.55S, 18.27E	12	1881–1940	17.3	21.7 Feb	13.1 Jul	41	-2	36	0	626
Durban	29.53S, 31.02E	7	1921–50	21.3	24.6 Feb	17.4 Jul	42	4	35	6	1021
Germiston	26.15S, 28.10E	1661	1921–50	15.9	19.7 Jan	10.2 Jul	34	-7	32	-4	757
Johannesburg	26.11S, 28.03E	1753	1893–1940	16.0	20.3 Jan	9.6 Jul	36	-6	30	-3	828
Pietermaritzburg	29.37S, 30.23E	649	1916–40	18.9	23.1 Feb	13.4 Jul	41	-3	37	-1	928
Port Elizabeth	33.58S, 25.37E	54	1881–1940	17.9	21.5 Feb	14.6 Jul	42	-1	37	1	577
*Pretoria	25.45S, 28.12E	1333	1920–40	17.6	22.4 Jan	10.8 Jul	38	-7	33	-3	718
Vereeniging	26.41S, 27.56E	1440	1903–40	16.4	21.8 Jan	8.7 Jul	38	-11	34	-7	673
SUDAN											
*Khartoum	15.36N, 32.32E	383	1921–50	29.2	33.9 Jun	23.2 Jan	48	5	46	8	179
Omdurman	15.38N, 32.30E		(see Khartoum)								
TANZANIA											
*Dar es Salaam	6.48S, 39.17E	14	44 yrs bef 1955	25.6	28.1 Feb	23.6 Jul	36	15	33	17	1041
Zanzibar	6.10S, 39.11E	19	1921–50	26.4	28.1 Feb	24.7 Aug	39	19	37	20	1411
TOGO											
*Lome	6.08N, 1.13E	20	1951–60	26.4	27.9 Mar	24.6 Aug	36	16			893

AFRICA

City	Latitude and longitude	Elev (m)	Period of record	Temperature (°C) Avg	Avg warmest month	Avg coolest month	Absolute High	Absolute Low	Avg Annual High	Avg Annual Low	Annual Precipitation (mm)
TUNISIA											
Sfax	34.44N, 10.46E	21	1901-50	18.8	26.1 Aug	11.4 Jan	44	-4	37	2	197
*Tunis	36.48N, 10.12E	63	50 yrs bef 1951	18.1	26.7 Aug	10.3 Jan	48	-1	43	2	444
UGANDA											
*Kampala	0.19N, 32.35E	1192	1931-50	21.1	22.3 Jan	20.0 Aug	36	12	33	14	1147
UPPER VOLTA											
*Ouagadougou	12.22N, 1.31W	304	25 yrs bef 1960	28.6	33.0 Apr	25.1 Jan	48	8			879
ZAIRE											
Kananga	5.54S, 22.25E	675	1940-59	24.7	25.1 Mar	23.6 Jul	35	13	34	14	1594
*Kinshasa	4.18S 15.18E	290	1940-57	25.3	26.7 Apr	22.2 Jul	38	11	36	15	1359
Kisangani	0.30N, 25.12E	415	1927-41, 1951-59	25.3	26.2 Apr	24.5 Jul	36	15	36	18	1703
Lubumbashi	11.40S, 27.28E	1230	1919-59	20.5	23.7 Oct	16.4 Jul	37	1	36	3	1242
Mbuji-Mayi	6.09S, 23.36E										
ZAMBIA											
Kitwe	12,49S, 28.13E		10 yrs bef 1968[1]	19.7	23.3 Oct	14.7 Jun	36	-2	34	0	1146
*Lusaka	15.25S, 28.17E	1279	1941-60	20.6	24.7 Oct	16.4 Jun	38	4	35	6	793

[1] Climatic data for Ndola, nr Kitwe.

ASIA

City	Latitude and longitude	Elev (m)	Period of record	Temperature (°C) Avg	Avg warmest month	Avg coolest month	Absolute High	Absolute Low	Avg Annual High	Avg Annual Low	Annual Precipitation (mm)
AFGHANISTAN											
Herat	34.22N, 62.09E	922	1940-44	16.4	30.5 Jul	2.0 Jan					201
*Kabul	34.30N, 69.13E	1799	40 yrs bef 1945	14.0	25.9 Jul	-0.6 Jan	44	-22	38	-17	310
Kandahar	31.27N, 65.43E	1055	1940-47	17.8	28.9 Jul	6.4 Jan	44	-10	42	-7	178
BAHRAIN											
*Manama	26.13N, 50.35E	1	8 yrs bef 1960	26.4	34.2 Aug	17.8 Jan					74
BANGLADESH											
Chittagong	22.20N, 91.50E	14	60 yrs bef 1963	25.1	27.9 May	19.4 Jan	39	7	35	9	2734
*Dacca	23.43N, 90.25E	8	1950-59	25.7	29.3 May	18.9 Jan					1863
Khulna	22.48N, 89.33E	5	20 yrs bef 1963	26.1	29.4 May	19.3 Jan	40	7			1723
Narayanganj	23.37N, 90.30E	8	60 yrs bef 1963	25.8	28.7 Jun	19.3 Jan	41	7	37	9	1874
BURMA											
Mandalay	22.00N, 96.05E	23	43 yrs bef 1941	27.6	32.0 Apr	2.14 Jan	46	7	42	10	954
*Rangoon	16.47N, 96.10E	6	1881-1940	27.4	30.4 Apr	25.1 Jan	42	13	39	15	2653
CAMBODIA											
*Phnom-Penh	11.33N, 104.55E	11	1941-50	27.5	29.0 Apr	25.4 Dec					1443
CEYLON											
*Colombo	6.56N, 79.51E	7	1931-60	26.9	27.9 May	26.1 Dec	36	15	33	18	2395
Kandy	7.18N, 80.38E	479	1931-60	24.3	26.0 Apr	23.1 Jan			33	13	2024
CHINA											
Amoy	24.27N, 118.05E	40	1915, 1917-42	21.8	29.0 Aug	13.6 Feb	38	4	35	6	1186
Anking	30.31N, 117.02E	39	1934-37, 1942	17.2	29.9 Jul	3.3 Jan	39	-8			1038

ASIA

City	Latitude and longitude	Elev (m)	Period of record	Temperature (°C) Avg	Avg warmest month	Avg coolest month	Absolute High	Absolute Low	Avg Annual High	Avg Annual Low	Annual Precipitation (mm)
Anshan	41.07N, 122.57E	35	? yrs bef 1934	8.5	24.8 Jul	-9.9 Jan	38	-29			681
Antung	40.08N, 124.24E	6	1924-40, 1949-52	8.5	24.6 Aug	-9.6 Jan	38	-32			1023
Canton	23.07N, 113.15E	18	1912-37, 1943-52	21.9	28.3 Jul	13.6 Jan	38	0	36	2	1720
Changchih	36.11N, 113.06E	914	1941-44, 1954-55	9.3	23.2 Jul	-6.9 Jan	36	-29			508
Changchow (Fukien)	24.31N, 117.40E		(see Amoy)								
Changchow (Kiangsu)	31.47N, 119.58E		(see Wusih)								
Changchun	43.52N, 125.21E	216	1909-42, 1947-52	4.7	23.5 Jul	-16.8 Jan	39	-36	34	-31	632
Changsha	28.12N, 112.58E	48	1924-38, 1946-50	17.3	28.8 Aug	5.0 Jan	43	-8	39	-6	1324
Chefoo	37.32N, 121.24E	46	1924-42	12.6	25.8 Jul	-1.9 Jan	40	-15	36	-11	613
Chengchow	34.45N, 113.40E	109	1924-37	16.1	29.6 Jul	0.3 Jan	43	-17			822
Chengtu	30.40N, 104.04E	498	1932-53	17.0	26.5 Jul	6.2 Jan	40	-4	34	0	1146
Chinchow	41.07N, 121.06E		1920-27[1]	8.5	24.8 Jul	-10.1 Jan					
Chinkiang	32.13N, 119.26E	12	1881-1915	15.8	28.3 Aug	3.1 Jan	40	-12			1025
Chinwangtao	39.56N, 119.37E	3	1909-16, 1930-36	9.7	24.4 Aug	-6.1 Jan	35	-22			667
Chuchow	27.50N, 113.09E		(see Changsha)								
Chungking	29.34N, 106.35E	20[illegible]	1924-38, 1940-53	18.6	28.8 Aug	8.1 Jan	44	-2	41	1	1089
Foochow	26.05N, 119.18E	88	1924-44, 1951-52	19.8	28.5 Jul	10.7 Feb	40	-2			1450
Foshan	23.02N, 113.07E	15	(see Canton)								
Fushun	41.52N, 123.53E		(see Mukden)								
Fusin	42.06N, 121.46E										
Hangchow	30.15N, 120.10E	5	1904-47, 1950-52	16.3	28.3 Jul	4.3 Jan	42	-10			1490
Hantan	36.35N, 114.29E		1939-43[2]	14.7	28.2 Jul	-1.1 Jan	44	-15			531
Harbin	45.45N, 126.39E	145	1909-42, 1949-52	3.3	23.3 Jul	-21.7 Jan	39	-41	33	-35	577
Hengyang	26.54N, 112.36E	94	12 yrs bef 1953	17.8	29.1 Jul	5.6 Jan	41	-6	41	-5	1478
Hofei	31.51N, 117.17E	26	1953-55	15.5	28.3 Aug	0.5 Jan	38	-21			830

[1] Temperature data for Sungshutsuitzu, nr Chinchow.

[2] Climatic data for Anyang, nr Hantan.

ASIA

City	Latitude and longitude	Elev (m)	Period of record	Temperature (°C) Avg	Avg warmest month	Avg coolest month	Absolute High	Absolute Low	Avg Annual High	Avg Annual Low	Annual Precipitation (mm)
Hoihow	20.03N, 110.19E	14	1924–42	24.5	29.3 Jun	18.1 Jan	39	3			1533
Hokang	47.05N, 130.20E		(see Kiamusze)								
Huhehot	40.47N, 111.37E	1062	1930–43, 1946–50	5.8	22.2 Jul	-13.7 Jan	38	-36			366
Hwainan	32.40N, 117.00E		(see Pengpu)								
Hwangshih	30.13N, 115.06E		(see Wuhan)								
Ichang	30.42N, 111.17E	133	1924–38	17.5	28.9 Jul	4.6 Jan	44	-7	41	-3	1132
Ichun	47.42N, 128.54E										
Ipin	28.46N, 104.34E	286	11 yrs bef 1953	18.7	27.9 Aug	8.4 Jan	42	-2			1185
Kaifeng	34.51N, 114.21E	75	1931–37, 1940–43	14.9	28.4 Jul	-0.6 Jan	43	-15			620
Kalgan	40.50N, 114.56E	760	1937–43, 1947–52	8.3	23.1 Jul	-8.7 Jan	38	-25			367
Kashgar	39.29N, 75.58E	1411	49 yrs bef 1941	12.6	26.7 Jul	-5.3 Jan	41	-26	39	-18	78
Kiamusze	46.50N, 130.21E	81	1938–42, 1949–53	3.4	22.9 Jul	-20.2 Jan	36	-40			629
Kingtehchen	29.16N, 117.11E										
Kirin	43.51N, 126.33E	210	1911–13	4.4	22.7 Jul	-16.9 Jan	37	-38			670
Kisi	45.18N, 130.58E	219	1949–52	3.8	22.4 Jul	-17.7 Jan	38	-35			533
Kokiu	23.23N, 103.09E	1740	1928–32[1]	20.8	24.6 May	14.6 Jan	36	-3	35	2	953
Kunming	25.04N, 102.41E	1893	39 yrs bef 1953	16.1	21.2 Jul	9.6 Jan	33	-5	31	-2	1004
Kweilin	25.17N, 110.17E	167	1935–43, 1949–50	19.4	28.4 Jul	9.2 Jan	40	-5			1966
Kweiyang	26.35N, 106.43E	1071	1920–53	15.6	24.7 Jul	5.0 Jan	39	-9	35	-5	1274
Lanchow	36.03N, 103.41E	1508	1932–52	9.5	22.8 Jul	-6.5 Jan	38	-23	37	-18	338
Lhasa	29.39N, 91.06E	3658	1935–38, 1941–49	8.8	17.0 Jun	-0.3 Jan	32	-16	28	-15	1461
Liaoyang	41.17N, 123.11E	26	(see Mukden)								
Liaoyuan	42.55N, 125.09E		(see Szeping)								
Liuchow	24.19N, 109.24E	98	1938–46								1473
Loyang	34.41N, 112.28E	138	1932–37, 1950–52	14.2	27.8 Jul	-0.9 Jan	44	-20			480
Luchow	28.53N, 105.23E	305	(see Ipin)								

[1] Climatic data for Mengtzu, nr Kokiu.

ASIA

City	Latitude and longitude	Elev (m)	Period of record	Temperature (°C) Avg	Avg warmest month	Avg coolest month	Absolute High	Absolute Low	Avg Annual High	Avg Annual Low	Annual Precipitation (mm)
Lushun-Talien	38.55N, 121.39E	96	1905-40, 1950-52	10.3	24.5 Aug	-5.2 Jan	36	-20	33	-17	560
Malipo	23.09N, 104.44E										
Mukden	41.48N, 123.27E	42	1905-42, 1947-52	7.3	24.9 Jul	-12.8 Jan	39	-33	37	-28	711
Mutankiang	44.35N, 129.36E	232	1909-43, 1949-53	2.8	22.2 Jul	-20.1 Jan	37	-45			521
Nanchang	28.41N, 115.53E	49	1929-33, 1946-52	17.4	29.5 Aug	5.5 Jan	39	-6			1770
Nanchung	30.48N, 106.04E	298	1940-46	18.8	29.1 Jul	8.0 Jan	43	-1			939
Nanking	32.03N, 118.47E	61	1905-37, 1947-50	15.3	27.7 Jul	2.2 Jan	43	-14	38	-11	989
Nanning	22.49N, 108.19E	75	1922-39, 1941-50	22.2	28.5 Jul	13.6 Jan	39	1			1322
Nantung	32.02N, 120.53E	110	1917-37, 1949-50	14.7	26.9 Jul	1.8 Jan	42	-13			1042
Neikiang	29.35N, 105.03E	355	1936-50	18.3	27.6 Jul	8.4 Jan	41	-3			937
Ningpo	29.53N, 121.33E	4	1881-1915	16.6	28.0 Aug	5.4 Jan	39	-10			1360
Paoki	34.22N, 107.07E	622	1952-55	13.0	25.2 Jul	-0.4 Jan	40	-17			565
Paoting	38.52N, 115.29E	22	1913-37, 1950	12.1	26.9 Jul	-5.5 Jan	43	-24			444
Paotow	40.36N, 110.03E	1044	1935-37, 1949-53	6.4	22.7 Jul	-11.8 Jan	38	-33			304
*Peking	39.56N, 116.24E	52	78 yrs bef 1953	11.8	26.1 Jul	-4.7 Jan	43	-23	37	-16	623
Pengpu	32.57N, 117.21E	20	1926-37	17.3	29.6 Jul	1.3 Jan	41	-19			714
Penki	41.20N, 123.45E		(see Mukden)								
Shanghai	31.14N, 121.28E	5	1873-1953	15.3	27.2 Aug	3.4 Jan	40	-12	39	-9	1143
Shangkiu	34.23N, 115.37E		1953-55[1]	14.7	27.1 Jul	-0.8 Jan	40	-18			638
Shaohing	30.00N, 120.35E		(see Hangchow)								
Shaoyang	27.15N, 111.28E	249	1936-44	17.5	27.7 Jul	5.6 Jan	38	-4			1305
Shihkiachwang	38.03N, 114.29E	82	1939-43, 1949-52	13.2	26.9 Jul	-3.6 Jan	43	-26			434
Shiukwan	24.48N, 113.35E	87	1951-55	20.3	28.9 Jul	10.2 Jan	42	-4			1503
Siakwan	25.34N, 100.14E	1560	1952-55[2]	16.5	21.0 Jun	9.9 Jan	31	-1			971
Sian	34.16N, 108.54E	412	1922-25, 1931-52	14.0	27.9 Jul	-0.5 Jan	46	-25	42	-13	576

[1] Climatic data for Pohsien, nr Shangkiu.

[2] Climatic data for Paoshan, nr Siakwan.

ASIA

City	Latitude and longitude	Elev (m)	Period of record	Temperature (°C) Avg	Avg warmest month	Avg coolest month	Absolute High	Absolute Low	Avg Annual High	Avg Annual Low	Annual Precipitation (mm)
Siangtan	27.51N, 112.54E	195	(see Changsha)								
Sinhailien	34.36N, 119.13E	4	1951-53	14.4	27.3 Aug	0.3 Jan	39	-15			818
Sining	36.37N, 101.46E	2244	1936-49	6.9	18.3 Jul	-6.4 Jan	32	-23			377
Sinsiang	35.19N 113.52E		(see Chengchow)								
Soochow	31.18N, 120.37E	16	1936-37	16.2	27.7 Jul	4.6 Jan					
Suchow	34.16N, 117.11E	34	1926-43, 1949-52	14.5	27.7 Jul	-0.2 Jan	43	-18			705
Swatow	23.22N, 116.40E	4	1880-1941	21.7	28.9 Aug	13.9 Jan	38	-1	37	4	1489
Szeping	43.10N, 124.20E	163	1934-44, 1949-52	5.9	24.1 Jul	-15.7 Jan	38	-39			709
Taichow	32.29N, 119.55E		(see Chinkiang)								
Taiyuan	37.52N, 112.33E	782	1916-48, 1950-52	10.0	25.0 Jul	-7.3 Jan	41	-30	38	-22	395
Tangshan	39.38N, 118.11E	57	1922-37	12.4	27.0 Jul	-4.3 Jan	40	-23			344
Tatung	40.05N, 113.18E	1049	1925-37, 1939-43	6.7	22.7 Jul	-11.6 Jan	38	-29			353
Tientsin	39.08N, 117.12E	3	1904-42, 1944-52	12.3	26.8 Jul	-4.1 Jan	43	-20	39	-16	527
Tsamkong	21.12N, 110.23E	26	1921-40	23.3	28.7 Jul	16.3 Jan	38	3			1383
Tsiaotso	35.15N, 113.13E		(see Chengchow)								
Tsinan	36.40N, 117.00E	55	1919-52	14.8	28.4 Jul	-1.2 Jan	43	-19	39	-14	631
Tsingtao	36.04N, 120.19E	77	1898-1952	12.1	25.1 Aug	-1.1 Jan	36	-16			647
Tsitsihar	47.22N, 123.57E	147	1930-42, 1949-53	2.7	23.0 Jul	-20.5 Jan	37	-39			379
Tzekung	29.24N, 104.47E		(see Neikiang)								
Tzepo	36.29N, 117.50E	180	(see Tsinan)								
Urumtsi	43.48N, 87.35E	913	22 yrs bef 1948	6.1	24.7 Jul	-16.0 Jan	44	-41			233
Weifang	36.43N, 119.06E	63	1929-37	14.5	28.0 Jul	-2.1 Jan	43	-17			630
Wenchow	28.01N, 120.39E	5	1924-41	18.0	28.8 Jul	7.8 Jan	40	-3			1709
Wuhan	30.32N, 114.18E	23	1905-40, 1951-53	16.8	28.9 Jul	3.8 Jan	42	-13	38	-5	1202
Wuhu	31.21N, 118.22E	13	1880-1915	16.3	28.4 Aug	4.0 Jan	41	-12			1175
Wusih	31.35N, 120.18E	7	1936-37	16.2	27.2 Jul	4.3 Jan					
Wutungkiao	29.21N, 103.48E		1936-50[1]	17.8	26.4 Jul	8.3 Jan	40	-3			1367

[1] Climatic data for Loshan, nr Wutungkiao.

ASIA

City	Latitude and longitude	Elev (m)	Period of record	Temperature (°C) Avg	Avg warmest month	Avg coolest month	Absolute High	Absolute Low	Avg Annual High	Avg Annual Low	Annual Precipitation (mm)
Yangchow	32.24N, 119.26E		(see Chinkiang)								
Yangchuan	37.54N, 113.36E	665	(see Taiyuan)								
Yenan	36.38N, 109.27E	1033									
Yinchwan	38.28N, 106.19E	1111	1951-53, 1955	3.9	24.1 Jul	-9.1 Jan	39	-31			203
Yingkow	40.40N, 122.17E	3	1905-43, 1949-53	8.6	25.0 Jul	-9.9 Jan	37	-31	34	-25	671
CYPRUS											
*Nicosia	35.11N, 33.23E	155	1921-50	19.2	28.7 Jul	10.0 Jan	47	-5	41	-1	375
GAZA STRIP											
*Gaza	31.30N, 34.28E	43	1921-34	19.7	25.6 Aug	13.0 Jan	44	-1	40	3	348
HONG KONG											
*Hong Kong	22.17N, 114.09E	33	1884-1941, 1947-48	22.2	27.8 Jul	15.1 Feb	36	0	34	6	2157
INDIA											
Agra	27.11N, 78.01E	169	1931-60	25.6	35.0 Jun	14.8 Jan	49	-2	46	2	665
Ahmedabad	23.02N, 72.37E	55	1931-60	27.3	33.5 May	20.3 Jan	48	2	44	8	783
Ajmer	26.27N, 74.38E	483	1931-60	24.7	33.4 May	14.7 Jan	46	-3	43	1	520
Aligarh	27.53N, 78.05E	187	29 yrs bef 1961	25.3	34.2 Jun	14.6 Jan	46	1	45	3	628
Allahabad	25.27N, 81.51E	93	1931-60	26.1	34.7 May	16.4 Jan	49	1	46	4	945
Ambala	30.21N, 76.50E	272	1931-60	24.6	33.9 Jun	13.8 Jan	48	-1	46	2	767
Amravati	21.29N, 78.11E	1214	1931-60	27.2	35.0 May	21.8 Dec	47	5	45	10	876
Amritsar	31.35N, 74.53E	234	1951-60	23.2	32.8 Jun	11.5 Jan	47	-3	45	0	563
Asansol	23.41N, 86.59E	123	1931-60	26.4	32.7 May	18.9 Jan	47	5	45	8	1469
Bangalore	12.59N, 77.35E	921	1931-60	23.6	27.3 Apr	20.5 Dec	39	8	36	12	889
Bareilly	28.21N, 79.25E	173	1931-60	25.2	33.2 Jun	15.3 Jan	47	-1	45	4	1076
Baroda	22.18N, 73.12E	35	28 yrs bef 1961	27.0	33.2 May	20.4 Jan	47	-1	45	5	1006

ASIA

City	Latitude and longitude	Elev (m)	Period of record	Temperature (°C)							Annual Precipitation (mm)
				Avg	Avg warmest month	Avg coolest month	Absolute High	Absolute Low	Avg Annual High	Avg Annual Low	
Belgaum	15.52N, 74.30E	753	1931-60	24.0	27.6 Apr	21.6 Dec	41	7	38	10	1303
Bhatpara	22.52N, 88.24E		21 yrs bef 1961[1]	26.4	30.8 May	19.3 Jan	43	5	41	8	1687
Bhavnagar	21.46N, 72.09E	17	1931-60	27.2	32.8 May	19.3 Jan	47	1	44	7	620
Bhopal	23.16N, 77.24E	523	1931-60	25.0	33.5 May	18.0 Jan	46	1	44	5	1260
Bikaner	28.01N, 73.18E	224	23 yrs bef 1961	25.9	35.5 Jun	13.6 Jan	49	-3	46	0	306
Bombay	18.58N, 72.50E	11	1931-60	27.3	30.1 May	24.2 Jan	41	12	37	15	1805
Calcutta	22.32N, 88.22E	6	1931-60	26.9	31.1 May	20.2 Jan	44	7	41	10	1625
Calicut	11.15N, 75.46E	8	1931-60	27.3	29.3 Apr	25.7 Jul	37	16	35	19	3178
Chandigarh	30.43N, 76.47E	396	(see Ambala)								
Coimbatore	11.00N, 76.58E	409	1931-60	26.4	29.0 Apr	24.2 Dec	40	12	37	16	614
Cuttack	20.30N, 85.50E	27	1931-60	27.7	32.8 May	21.9 Dec	48	8	44	11	1548
Dehra Dun	30.19N, 78.02E	682	1931-60	21.8	29.4 Jun	12.6 Jan	44	-1	41	2	2149
Delhi	28.40N, 77.13E	235	1901-50	(see New Delhi for temperature data)							595
Dhanbad	23.48N, 86.27E	257	27 yrs bef 1961	25.7	32.3 May	18.4 Jan	46	5	44	8	1355
Durg	21.11N, 81.17E	295	1901-50	(see Raipur for temperature data)							1277
Durgapur	23.30N, 87.20E		(see Asansol)								
Ernakulam	9.59N, 76.17E	3	1931-60[2]	27.1	28.7 Apr	25.9 Jul	38	16	33	21	3062
Gaya	24.47N, 85.00E	116	1931-60	26.2	34.3 May	17.1 Jan	47	3	46	6	1185
Gorakhpur	26.45N, 83.22E	77	1931-60	25.7	32.4 May	16.4 Jan	48	2	42	6	1248
Guntur	16.18N, 80.27E		1931-60[3]	27.8	32.2 May	23.6 Jan	48	14	43	16	897
Gwalior	26.13N, 78.10E	208	21 yrs bef 1961	25.6	35.5 Jun	15.6 Jan	48	-1	46	1	824
Howrah	22.35N, 88.20E		48 yrs bef 1951	(see Calcutta for temperature data)							1536
Hubli	15.21N, 75.10E	700	1931-60[4]	25.9	29.9 Apr	22.8 Dec	42	11	40	13	669

[1] Climatic data for Dum Dum, nr Bhatpara.

[2] Temperature data for Cochin, nr Ernakulam.

[3] Temperature data for Masulipatnam, nr Guntur.

[4] Temperature data for Gadag, nr Hubli.

ASIA

City	Latitude and longitude	Elev (m)	Period of record	Temperature (°C) Avg	Avg warmest month	Avg coolest month	Absolute High	Absolute Low	Avg Annual High	Avg Annual Low	Annual Precipitation (mm)
Hyderabad	17.23N, 78.28E	545	1931-60	25.8	32.4 May	20.6 Dec	44	6	42	9	772
Indore	22.43N, 75.50E	556	1931-60	24.4	32.3 May	17.8 Jan	46	-3	42	3	929
Jabalpur	23.10N, 79.57E	393	1931-60	25.2	33.9 May	17.9 Dec	47	0	45	3	1431
Jaipur	26.55N, 75.49E	436	1931-60	25.0	33.2 Jun	15.1 Jan	48	-2	45	2	598
Jamnagar	22.28N, 70.04E	18	1931-60	26.0	31.5 Jun	18.5 Jan	44	2	41	6	466
Jamshedpur	22.48N, 86.11E	129	1931-60	27.0	33.4 May	19.2 Dec	47	4	45	7	1439
Jhansi	25.26N, 78.35E	258	1931-60	26.2	35.7 May	16.6 Jan	48	1	46	4	944
Jodhpur	26.17N, 73.02E	224	1931-60	26.7	34.4 May	17.0 Jan	49	-2	46	3	366
Jullundur	31.19N, 75.34E		1901-50	(see Amritsar for temperature data)							657
Kalyan	19.15N, 73.09E		1901-50	(see Bombay for temperature data)							2355
Kanpur	26.28N, 80.21E	126	1931-60	25.7	34.4 May	15.7 Jan	47	1	46	4	805
Kolhapur	16.42N, 74.13E	573	1951-60	25.2	29.3 Apr	22.4 Dec	42	9	40	11	993
Kota	25.11N, 75.50E	257	1931-60	27.0	36.1 May	17.5 Jan	48	2	46	6	786
Lucknow	26.51N, 80.55E	111	1931-60	25.8	33.8 May	16.1 Jan	48	1	45	4	1016
Ludhiana	30.54N, 75.51E	247	1931-60	24.6	34.1 Jun	13.0 Jan	48	-2	46	1	648
Madras	13.05N, 80.17E	16	1931-60	28.6	32.7 May	24.5 Jan	45	14	41	17	1268
Madurai	9.56N, 78.07E	133	1931-60	28.9	31.9 May	25.5 Jan	42	16	40	18	894
Malegaon	20.33N, 74.32E	433	1931-60	26.0	32.5 May	20.8 Dec	47	-1	43	5	542
Mangalore	12.52N, 74.53E	22	1931-60	27.1	29.2 Apr	26.5 Jan	38	16	35	19	3398
Meerut	28.59N, 77.42E	223	1951-60	24.7	33.4 Jun	14.2 Jan	46	1	44	3	811
Moradabad	28.50N, 78.47E	60	1901-50	(see Bareilly for temperature data)							982
Mysore	12.18N, 76.39E	767	1931-60	24.4	27.7 Apr	21.7 Dec	39	11	36	13	810
Nagpur	21.09N, 79.06E	310	1951-60	26.9	35.6 May	20.4 Dec	48	4	46	7	1242
Nasik	19.59N, 73.48E	593	1901-50	(see Malegaon for temperature data)							697
*New Delhi	28.36N, 77.12E	213	23 yrs bef 1961	25.2	34.3 Jun	14.3 Jan	48	-1	45	3	660
Patna	25.35N, 85.15E	53	1931-60	26.2	32.4 May	17.3 Jan	46	2	44	6	1166
Poona	18.32N, 73.52E	553	1931-60	25.1	29.9 May	21.0 Dec	43	2	42	6	661
Raipur	21.14N, 81.38E	293	1931-60	26.9	35.5 May	20.2 Dec	47	4	45	9	1359

ASIA

City	Latitude and longitude	Elev (m)	Period of record	Temperature (°C) Avg	Avg warmest month	Avg coolest month	Absolute High	Absolute Low	Avg Annual High	Avg Annual Low	Annual Precipitation (mm)
Rajahmundry	16.59N, 81.47E		1931-60[1]	27.7	32.3 May	23.1 Dec	47	14	43	16	1057
Rajkot	22.18N, 70.47E	138	1931-60	26.7	32.6 May	19.4 Jan	48	-1	43	5	594
Ranchi	23.21N, 85.20E	655	1931-60	23.7	30.9 May	16.7 Jan	43	3	42	5	1513
Saharanpur	29.58N, 77.33E	273	1931-60[2]	23.6	32.2 Jun	13.3 Jan	47	-2	44	2	936
Salem	11.39N, 78.10E	278	1931-60	28.0	31.1 May	24.8 Dec	43	11	40	15	955
Sholapur	17.41N, 75.55E	479	1931-60	27.1	32.9 May	22.5 Dec	46	4	43	10	678
South Suburban	22.30N, 88.19E		(see Calcutta)								
Surat	21.10N, 72.50E	12	1931-60	27.7	31.4 May	23.1 Jan	46	4	43	10	1071
Tiruchirapalli	10.49N, 78.41E	78	1931-60	28.8	31.7 May	25.3 Dec	44	14	40	17	870
Tirunelveli	8.44N, 77.42E		1951-60[3]	29.3	31.7 May	26.4 Dec	42	18	40	20	796
Trivandrum	8.29N, 76.55E	64	20 yrs bef 1961	27.1	28.7 Apr	26.1 Jul	38	16	35	20	1812
Ujjain	23.11N, 75.46E	512	1951-60[4]	25.5	32.7 May	18.6 Jan	45	5	43	6	895
Varanasi	25.20N, 83.00E	76	1931-60	26.0	34.2 May	16.4 Jan	47	2	45	5	1076
Vijayawada	16.31N, 80.37E	24	1931-60[5]	27.8	32.2 May	23.6 Jan	48	14	43	16	959
Visakhapatnam	17.42N, 83.18E	3	1931-60	27.2	30.9 May	22.6 Jan	44	13	40	15	954
Warangal	18.18N, 79.35E	269	1931-60	27.7	34.4 May	22.5 Dec	47	8	44	11	924
INDONESIA											
Bandjermasin	3.20S, 114.36E	20	1956-65	26.8	27.3 Apr	26.3 Jan					2755
Bandung	6.54S, 107.36E	768	1913-38	22.6	22.9 Oct	22.1 Jul	34	11	32	13	2159

[1] Temperature data for Kakinada, nr Rajahmundry.
[2] Temperature data for Roorkee, nr Saharanpur.
[3] Temperature data for Palayamcottai, nr Tirunelveli.
[4] Temperature data for Ratlam, nr Ujjain.
[5] Temperature data for Masulipatnam, nr Vijayawada.

ASIA

City	Latitude and longitude	Elev (m)	Period of record	Temperature (°C) Avg	Avg warmest month	Avg coolest month	Absolute High	Absolute Low	Avg Annual High	Avg Annual Low	Annual Precipitation (mm)
Bogor	6.35S, 106.47E	250	1933-37	25.5	25.7 May	25.0 Jan					4225
*Djakarta	6.10S, 106.49E	7	1921-50	26.8	27.2 May	26.1 Jan	37	19	33	21	1770
Jogjakarta	7.48S, 110.22E	115	1933-37[1]	25.9	26.7 Oct	25.0 Jul			35	17	2002
Makasar	5.07S, 119.24E	2	1956-65	26.4	27.3 Apr	25.7 Dec	35	15	33	18	3188
Malang	7.59S, 112.38E	445	1929-38	23.8	24.5 Oct	22.5 Jul	35	10	34	12	
Manado	1.29N, 124.51E	8	1956-65[2]	25.8	26.4 May	24.5 Feb			34	19	3352
Medan	3.35N, 98.40E	25	1914-32, 1956-65	26.0	26.8 May	25.1 Jan	36	16	35	19	1958
Padang	0.57S, 100.21E	7	1933-37	26.6	27.0 Apr	25.8 Nov	34	20			4764
Palembang	3.00S, 104.46E	8	1956-65	26.6	27.8 Apr	25.9 Jan					2381
Pontianak	0.02S, 109.20E	3	1933-37	27.4	27.9 Jul	26.6 Nov	34	20			3056
Semarang	6.57S, 110.25E	2	1956-65	26.9	28.8 Nov	26.1 Jul	37	17	36	18	2033
Surabaja	7.15S, 112.45E	7	1920-25, 1927-38	26.8	27.7 Nov	25.8 Jul	36	16	35	18	1518
Surakarta	7.35S, 110.50E	104	1933-37[1]	25.9	26.7 Oct	25.0 Jul			35	17	2165
Tjirebon	6.44S, 108.34E	4	1937	27.3	28.5 Nov	26.6 Dec			35	20	1904
IRAN											
Abadan	30.20N, 48.16E	3	9 yrs bef 1954	25	36 Jul	11 Jan	51	-4	48	0	169
Ahvaz	31.19N, 48.42E	20	11 yrs bef 1954	25	36 Jul	15 Dec					190
Hamadan	34.48N, 48.30E	1775	13 yrs bef 1954	12	25 Aug	1 Jan			38	-15	404
Isfahan	32.40N, 51.38E	1590	38 yrs bef 1947	15.4	27.9 Jul	2.5 Jan	43	-19	40	-11	117
Kermanshah	34.19N, 47.04E	1322	1936-51	13.1	25.3 Jul	1.1 Jan	42	-25	41	-15	414
Meshed	36.18N, 59.36E	985	33 yrs bef 1948	13.4	25.0 Jul	1.4 Jan	41	-24	39	-16	209
Shiraz	29.36N, 52.32E	1539	13 yrs bef 1954	16	26 Jul	5 Jan					336
Tabriz	38.05N, 46.18E	1362	11 yrs bef 1948	11.8	24.8 Jul	-2.4 Jan					283
*Teheran	35.40N, 51.26E	1191	51 yrs bef 1948	16.1	28.6 Jul	2.6 Jan	43	-21	40	-9	250

[1] Temperature data for Klaten, nr Jogjakarta and Surakarta.

[2] Temperature data for Mapanget, nr Manado.

ASIA

City	Latitude and longitude	Elev (m)	Period of record	Temperature (°C) Avg	Avg warmest month	Avg coolest month	Absolute High	Absolute Low	Avg Annual High	Avg Annual Low	Annual Precipitation (mm)
IRAQ											
*Baghdad	33.21N, 44.25E	34	1938-62	22.3	34.3 Jul	10.1 Jan	51	-8	47	-4	156
Basra	30.30N, 47.47E	2	1937-62	24.3	34.0 Jul	12.2 Jan	50	-4	47	-1	161
Karbala	32.36N, 44.02E	26	(see Baghdad)								
Kirkuk	35.28N, 44.28E	331	? yrs bef 1964	21.7	34.5 Jul	8.9 Jan					393
Mosul	36.20N, 43.08E	223	1927-62	19.6	32.7 Jul	7.2 Jan	51	-11	47	-5	375
ISRAEL											
Haifa	32.49N, 35.00E	5	21 yrs bef 1951	21.7	28.3 Aug	13.9 Jan	44	-3	39	5	663
*Jerusalem	31.47N, 35.13E	810	1921-50	16.8	23.4 Aug	8.3 Jan	42	-3	38	-1	536
Tel Aviv-Jaffa	32.05N, 34.46E	3	1951-60	20.0	26.9 Aug	13.6 Jan			39	1	535
JAPAN											
Akashi	34.38N, 134.59E	6	(see Kobe)								
Akita	39.43N, 140.07E	9	1931-60	10.7	24.2 Aug	-1.1 Jan	36	-25	34	-14	1789
Amagasaki	34.43N, 135.25E		(see Osaka)								
Aomori	40.49N, 140.45E	4	1901-45, 1951-60	9.2	22.6 Aug	-2.8 Jan	36	-25			1382
Asahigawa	43.46N, 142.22E	111	1931-60	6.0	21.1 Aug	-8.9 Jan	36	-41			1144
Chiba	35.36N, 140.07E	24	(see Tokyo)								
Fujisawa	35.21N, 139.29E		(see Yokosuka)								
Fukui	36.04N, 136.13E	9	1901-45, 1951-60	13.6	26.1 Aug	2.3 Jan	39	-15			2353
Fukuoka	33.35N, 130.24E	2	1931-60	15.4	26.8 Aug	5.1 Jan	37	-8			1703
Fukushima	37.45N, 140.28E	67	1931-60	12.1	25.0 Aug	0.5 Jan	39	-18			1156
Fukuyama	34.29N, 133.22E		(see Okayama)								
Funabashi	35.42N, 139.59E		(see Tokyo)								
Gifu	35.25N, 136.45E	13	1931-60	14.5	26.7 Aug	3.1 Jan	39	-14			1857
Hachinohe	40.30N, 141.29E	27	(see Aomori)								
Hachioji	35.39N, 139.20E		(see Tokyo)								

City	Latitude and longitude	Elev (m)	Period of record	Temperature (°C) Avg	Avg warmest month	Avg coolest month	Absolute High	Absolute Low	Avg Annual High	Avg Annual Low	Annual Precipitation (mm)
Hakodate	41.45N, 140.43E	33	1941-60	8.1	21.6 Aug	-4.1 Jan	33	-28	30	-17	1178
Hamamatsu	34.42N, 137.44E	29	1897-1926	15.1	25.8 Aug	5.1 Jan	37	-6			2018
Higashiosaka	34.39N, 135.35E		(see Osaka)								
Himeji	34.49N, 134.42E	17	(see Kobe)								
Hirakata	34.48N, 135.38E		(see Osaka)								
Hiroshima	34.24N, 132.27E	29	1941-60	14.7	26.6 Aug	4.2 Jan	38	-9	35	-6	1596
Hitachi	36.36N, 140.39E	52	1931-60[1]	12.8	24.6 Aug	2.0 Jan	36	-12			1396
Ichikawa	35.44N, 139.55E	23	(see Tokyo)								
Ichinomiya	35.18N, 136.48E		(see Nagoya)								
Ise	34.29N, 136.42E	2	1931-60[2]	14.7	26.5 Aug	4.2 Jan	38	-8			1704
Iwaki	36.57N, 140.54E	3	? yrs bef 1961	12.6	23.9 Aug	2.7 Jan					1398
Kagoshima	31.36N, 130.33E	5	1931-60	16.8	27.1 Aug	6.6 Jan	37	-7	34	-4	2337
Kamakura	35.19N, 139.33E		(see Yokosuka)								
Kanazawa	36.34N, 136.39E	27	1931-60	13.5	25.9 Aug	2.5 Jan	38	-10			2559
Kawaguchi	35.48N, 139.43E		(see Tokyo)								
Kawasaki	35.32N, 139.43E		(see Yokohama)								
Kitakyushu	33.52N, 130.50E	7	(see Shimonoseki)								
Kobe	34.41N, 135.10E	58	1931-60	15.3	27.1 Aug	4.5 Jan	38	-6			1337
Kochi	33.33N, 133.33E	0.5	1931-60	15.8	26.3 Aug	5.2 Jan	37	-7			2646
Kofu	35.39N, 138.35E	272	1931-60	13.5	25.6 Aug	1.5 Jan	38	-19			1207
Koriyama	37.24N, 140.23E	255	(see Fukushima)								
Kumamoto	32.48N, 130.43E	38	1931-60	15.7	27.0 Aug	4.6 Jan	39	-9			1869
Kurashiki	34.35N, 133.46E	3	(see Okayama)								
Kure	34.14N, 132.34E	27	1895-1929	15.1	27.0 Aug	4.9 Jan	38	-7			1433
Kurume	33.19N, 130.31E	13	(see Fukuoka)								

[1] Climatic data for Mito, nr Hitachi.
[2] Climatic data for Tsu, nr Ise.

ASIA

City	Latitude and longitude	Elev (m)	Period of record	Temperature (°C) Avg	Avg warmest month	Avg coolest month	Absolute High	Absolute Low	Avg Annual High	Avg Annual Low	Annual Precipitation (mm)
Kushiro	42.58N, 144.23E	33	1910–29	5.2	17.8 Aug	-6.8 Jan	31	-28	27	-23	1109
Kyoto	35.00N. 135.45E	41	1931–60	14.6	26.9 Aug	3.3 Jan	38	-12			1579
Machida	35.33N, 139.28E	97	(see Tokyo)								
Maebashi	36.23N, 139.04E	112	1931–60	13.4	25.3 Aug	2.4 Jan					1246
Matsudo	35.47N, 139.54E	25	(see Tokyo)								
Matsuyama	33.50N, 132.45E	32	1931–60	15.3	26.6 Aug	5.0 Jan	37	-8			1379
Miyazaki	31.54N, 131.26E	7	1931–60	16.7	26.7 Aug	6.8 Jan	38	-7			2571
Morioka	39.42N, 141.09E	154	1931–60	9.5	23.1 Aug	-3.0 Jan	37	-18			1275
Nagano	36.39N, 138.11E	418	1931–60	11.1	24.6 Aug	-1.6 Jan	39	-17			1001
Nagasaki	32.48N, 129.55E	27	1901–45, 1951–60	15.7	26.6 Aug	5.6 Jan	37	-6	34	-4	1943
Nagoya	35.10N, 136.55E	51	1931–60	14.4	26.6 Aug	2.9 Jan	40	-10			1546
Nara	34.41N, 135.50E	105	1931–60	15.0	27.4 Aug	3.7 Jan					1338
Neyagawa	34.46N, 135.38E		(see Osaka)								
Niigata	37.55N, 139.03E	2	1941–60	12.9	25.8 Aug	1.7 Jan	39	-13	35	-6	1841
Nikko	36.45N, 139.37E	610	1916, 1923–25, 1946–50	10.5	22.2 Aug	0.0 Feb	33	-19	31	-12	1748
Nishinomiya	34.43N, 135.20E		(see Osaka)								
Numazu	35.06N, 138.52E	7	1897–1926	15.3	25.9 Aug	5.4 Jan	37	-8			2094
Oita	33.14N, 131.36E	5	1931–60	15.1	26.0 Aug	5.1 Jan	36	-9			1655
Okayama	34.39N, 133.55E	3	1901–45, 1951–60	14.6	26.9 Aug	3.5 Jan	37	-8			1103
Okazaki	34.57N, 137.10E		(see Nagoya)								
Omiya	35.54N, 139.38E		(see Tokyo)								
Omuta	33.02N, 130.27E		(see Kumamoto)								
Osaka	34.40N, 135.30E	7	1941–60	15.5	27.8 Aug	4.5 Jan	38	-7	36	-4	1359
Otaru	43.13N, 141.00E	24	(see Sapporo)								
Sagamihara	35.33N, 139.22E		(see Yokohama)								
Sakai	34.35N, 135.28E		(see Osaka)								
Sapporo	43.03N, 141.21E	17	1931–60	7.6	21.7 Aug	-5.5 Jan	36	-28	32	-22	1136

ASIA

City	Latitude and longitude	Elev (m)	Period of record	Temperature (°C) Avg	Avg warmest month	Avg coolest month	Absolute High	Absolute Low	Avg Annual High	Avg Annual Low	Annual Precipitation (mm)
Sasebo	33.10N, 129.43E	13	1894-1929	15.9	27.2 Aug	5.8 Jan	38	-5			1966
Sendai	38.15N, 140.53E	38	1931-60	11.3	23.8 Aug	0.1 Jan					1232
Shimizu	35.01N, 138.29E	30	(see Shizuoka)								
Shimonoseki	33.57N, 130.57E	46	1931-60	15.4	26.5 Aug	5.4 Jan	36	-6			1701
Shizuoka	34.58N, 138.23E	13	1941-60	15.6	26.2 Aug	5.7 Jan					2426
Suita	34.45N, 135.32E		(see Osaka)								
Takamatsu	34.20N, 134.03E	9	1951-60	15.1	26.6 Aug	4.8 Jan					1242
Takasaki	36.20N, 139.01E	95	(see Maebashi)								
Takatsuki	34.51N, 135.37E		(see Osaka)								
Tokushima	34.04N, 134.34E	1	1931-60	15.3	26.5 Aug	4.9 Jan	37	-6			1625
*Tokyo	35.42N, 139.46E	4	1931-60	14.7	26.4 Aug	3.7 Jan	38	-9	34	-6	1563
Toyama	36.41N, 137.13E	9	1941-60	13.2	25.7 Aug	2.0 Jan					2370
Toyohashi	34.46N, 137.23E	30	(see Hamamatsu)								
Toyonaka	34.47N, 135.28E		(see Osaka)								
Toyota	35.05N, 137.09E	75	(see Nagoya)								
Urawa	35.51N, 139.39E	20	(see Tokyo)								
Utsunomiya	36.33N, 139.52E	120	1941-60	12.5	24.8 Aug	1.0 Jan	37	-15			1522
Wakayama	34.13N, 135.11E	14	1931-60	15.5	27.0 Aug	5.0 Jan	38	-6			1435
Yamagata	38.15N, 140.15E	151	1931-60	10.8	24.4 Aug	-1.6 Jan	41	-20			1236
Yao	34.37N, 135.36E		(see Osaka)								
Yokkaichi	34.58N, 136.37E	3	(see Nagoya)								
Yokohama	35.27N, 139.39E	39	1931-60	14.5	25.8 Aug	4.1 Jan	36	-8			1665
Yokosuka	35.18N, 139.40E	12	1894-1929	14.5	25.2 Aug	4.7 Jan	36	-7			1939
JORDAN											
*Amman	31.57N, 35.56E	766	1931-60	17.5	25.6 Aug	8.2 Jan	43	-6	39	-2	273

ASIA

City	Latitude and longitude	Elev (m)	Period of record	Temperature (°C) Avg	Avg warmest month	Avg coolest month	Absolute High	Absolute Low	Avg Annual High	Avg Annual Low	Annual Precipitation (mm)
KASHMIR-JAMMU											
*Jammu	32.44N, 74.52E	366	1931-60	24.3	34.0 Jun	13.3 Jan	47	1	45	4	1116
*Srinagar	34.05N, 74.50E	1586	1931-60	13.3	24.6 Jul	1.0 Jan	38	-20	36	-8	659
KOREA: NORTH											
Chongjin	41.46N, 129.49E	50	1905-34	7.5	21.7 Aug	-5.8 Jan					564
Hamhung	39.54N, 127.32E	33	1910-37, 1941-54	9.5	23.4 Aug	-5.7 Jan					906
Hungnam	39.30N, 127.14E		(see Hamhung)								
Kaesong	37.58N, 126.33E	60	1917-37	10.4	25.2 Aug	-6.0 Jan					1295
Kimchaek	40.41N, 129.12E	4	1905-36	7.9	21.9 Aug	-6.0 Jan	37	-25			808
*Pyongyang	39.01N, 125.45E	29	1907-54	9.4	24.4 Aug	-8.0 Jan	36	-28			940
Sinuiju	40.06N, 124.24E	6	1931-54	8.7	24.1 Aug	-9.0 Jan					1384
Wonsan	39.10N, 127.26E	37	1905-54	10.3	23.3 Aug	-3.6 Jan	39	-22	36	-17	1341
KOREA: SOUTH											
Chonju	35.49N, 127.09E	51	1919-34	12.1	25.9 Aug	-1.9 Jan	37	-15			1263
Inchon	37.28N, 126.38E	69	1905-34	10.7	24.8 Aug	-3.8 Jan	36	-21			1036
Kwangju	35.09N, 126.55E	35	1913-37	12.6	26.4 Aug	-1.1 Jan					1217
Masan	35.11N, 128.34E	27	1916-25	13.9	26.7 Aug	1.3 Jan	36	-14	34	-11	1407
Mokpo	34.47N, 126.23E	32	1905-38	13.1	26.1 Aug	1.2 Jan	37	-14			1068
Pusan	35.06N, 129.03E	69	1905-34	13.6	25.6 Aug	2.0 Jan	35	-14	33	-10	1412
*Seoul	37.34N, 127.00E	85	1908-34	10.9	25.5 Aug	-4.6 Jan	37	-24	36	-20	1249
Taegu	35.52N, 128.36E	58	1921-50	12.5	26.2 Aug	-1.8 Jan	39	-20			956
Taejon	36.20N, 127.26E	57	1917-37	11.9	26.0 Aug	-4.3 Jan					1339
KUWAIT											
*Kuwait	29.20N, 47.59E	5	15 yrs bef 1954	25.0	35.0 Aug	12.8 Jan	49	0	46	3	119

ASIA

City	Latitude and longitude	Elev (m)	Period of record	Temperature (°C) Avg	Avg warmest month	Avg coolest month	Absolute High	Absolute Low	Avg Annual High	Avg Annual Low	Annual Precipitation (mm)
LAOS											
*Vientiane	17.58N, 102.36E	170	1941–44, 1947–50	25.2	27.5 May	20.8 Jan	40	4	38	8	1850
LEBANON											
*Beirut	33.53N, 35.30E	24	1881–1935	21.1	28.4 Aug	13.7 Jan	42	-1	35	4	884
Tripoli	34.26N, 35.51E	3	1951–58	18.9	26.2 Aug	12.0 Jan					765
MACAO											
*Macao	22.12N, 113.32E	20	1881–1916	22.6	28.5 Jul	15.3 Feb	38	-2			1694
MALAYSIA											
George Town	5.25N, 100.20E	5	49 yrs bef 1939	27.8	28.3 Mar	26.9 Sep	37	18	35	21	2736
Ipoh	4.35N, 101.05E	33	? yrs bef 1963	27.6	28.1 Jun	27.1 Dec	37	17			2581
*Kuala Lumpur	3.10N, 101.42E	39	1930–41, 1948–54	27.5	28.1 Mar	26.9 Dec	37	18	36	19	2441
MONGOLIA											
*Ulan-Bator	47.55N, 106.53E	1309	40 yrs bef 1949	-4.0	17.8 Jul	-29.3 Jan	37	-49	33	-41	229
NEPAL											
*Katmandu	27.42N, 85.20E	1337	42 yrs bef 1937	18.4	24.2 Jul	9.9 Jan	36	-2	34	-1	1427
PAKISTAN											
Gujranwala	32.09N, 74.11E	225	1963–66	22.8	33.2 Jun	11.5 Jan	48	-2	46	-1	547
Hyderabad	25.22N, 68.22E	30	1881–1930, 1935–36	27.2	34.1 Jun	17.3 Jan					183
*Islamabad	33.42N, 73.10E	549	(see Rawalpindi)								
Karachi	24.52N, 67.03E	6	1921–50	25.6	30.2 Jun	19.0 Jan	48	4	42	7	206
Lahore	31.35N, 74.18E	214	1921–50	24.6	34.5 Jun	12.2 Jan	49	-2	47	0	463
Lyallpur	31.25N, 73.05E	184	? yrs bef 1944	24.1	34.3 Jun	11.9 Jan	47	-1	46	1	335

ASIA

City	Latitude and longitude	Elev (m)	Period of record	Temperature (°C) Avg	Avg warmest month	Avg coolest month	Absolute High	Absolute Low	Avg Annual High	Avg Annual Low	Annual Precipitation (mm)
Multan	30.11N, 71.29E	126	35 yrs bef 1937	26.1	36.1 Jun	13.6 Jan	49	-2	48	1	168
Peshawar	34.01N, 71.33E	359	1891–1929, 1931–40	22.5	33.4 Jun	10.4 Jan	50	-3	47	-1	344
Rawalpindi	33.36N, 73.04E	511	1881–1940	21.6	32.1 Jun	10.1 Jan	47	-4	46	-2	907
Sargodha	32.05N, 72.40E	187	(see Lyallpur)								
Sialkot	32.30N, 74.31E	253	? yrs bef 1921	23.8	33.8 Jun	12.4 Jan					808
PHILIPPINES											
Bacolod	10.41N, 122.56E	7	6 yrs bef 1919	26.8	28.3 May	25.9 Jan	38	15	35	18	2173
Basilan	6.42N, 121.58E	8	(see Zamboanga)								
Caloocan	14.38N, 121.03E		(see Manila)								
Cebu	10.18N, 123.54E	42	1903–18	27.1	28.1 May	26.0 Jan	35	18	34	20	1703
Davao	7.04N, 125.36E	19	1903–18	26.9	27.6 Apr	26.2 Jan	37	16	35	19	1942
Iloilo	10.42N, 122.34E	14	15 yrs bef 1938	27.5	28.9 Apr	26.1 Jan	37	19	36	21	2122
Manila	14.36N, 120.59E	16	1887–1940	26.6	28.4 May	24.7 Jan	39	14	37	16	2157
Pasay	14.33N, 121.00E		(see Manila)								
*Quezon City	14.38N, 121.00E	71	1952–55	26.7	29.1 May	24.1 Dec	38	13			2327
Zamboanga	6.54N, 122.04E	5	1903–18	26.6	26.9 May	26.3 Feb	34	16	33	19	990
RYUKYU ISLANDS											
*Naha	26.13N, 127.40E	27	1901–45	22.1	28.0 Jul	15.9 Feb	35	5	34	7	2103
SAUDI ARABIA											
*Jidda	21.30N, 39.12E	6	1941–45	27.9	31.7 Jul	23.9 Jan	47	9	43	11	80
Mecca	21.27N, 39.49E	260									
Medina	24.28N, 39.36E	594	1957–60	27.3	34.9 Aug	17.5 Jan					62
*Riyadh	24.38N, 46.43E	591	1941–45	24.8	33.6 Jul	14.5 Jan	45	-7	44	-2	80

ASIA

City	Latitude and longitude	Elev (m)	Period of record	Temperature (°C) Avg	Avg warmest month	Avg coolest month	Absolute High	Absolute Low	Avg Annual High	Avg Annual Low	Annual Precipitation (mm)
SINGAPORE											
*Singapore	1.17N, 103.51E	10	1903–39	27.0	27.5 May	26.1 Jan	36	19	34	21	2415
SOUTHERN YEMEN											
*Aden	12.46N, 45.01E	4	1921–50	28.8	32.3 Jun	25.4 Jan	41	16	39	17	38
SYRIA											
Aleppo	36.10N, 37.10E	320	1952–61	17.4	28.9 Aug	6.2 Jan	47	-13	42	-8	307
*Damascus	33.30N, 36.18E	729	1952–61	17.7	27.7 Aug	7.6 Jan	45	-6	41	-4	228
Hama	35.09N, 36,44E	309	1956–60	18.0	28.9 Aug	7.4 Jan					299
Homs	34.44N, 36.43E	488	(see Hama)								
TAIWAN											
Chiai	23.29N, 120.27E	31	(see Tainan)								
Hsinchu	24.48N, 120.58E	33	1938–52	21.9	28.0 Jul	14.9 Feb	37	3	36	6	1763
Kaohsiung	22.38N, 120.17E	29	1932–52	24.3	27.9 Jul	18.9 Jan	37	7	35	9	1923
Keelung	25.08N, 121.44E	3	1903–52	21.7	28.0 Jul	15.6 Jan	38	3	36	8	3043
Sanchung	25.04N, 121.29E		(see Taipei)								
Taichung	24.09N, 120.41E	77	1897–1952	22.4	27.8 Jul	15.8 Jan	39	-1	35	4	1784
Tainan	23.00N, 120.12E	13	1897–1952	23.3	27.9 Jul	17.1 Jan	38	2	35	6	1839
*Taipei	25.03N, 121.30E	8	1897–1952	21.8	28.2 Jul	15.0 Feb	39	0	36	5	2100
THAILAND											
*Bangkok	13.45N, 100.31E	8	1931–60	28.1	30.2 Apr	25.5 Dec	41	11	39	14	1492
Thon Buri	13.43N, 100.29E		(see Bangkok)								
TURKEY											
Adana	37.01N, 35.18E	20	30 yrs bef 1961	18.6	28.0 Aug	9.1 Jan	46	-7	40	-4	611

ASIA

City	Latitude and longitude	Elev (m)	Period of record	Temperature (°C) Avg	Avg warmest month	Avg coolest month	Absolute High	Absolute Low	Avg Annual High	Avg Annual Low	Annual Precipitation (mm)
*Ankara	39.56N, 32.52E	902	30 yrs bef 1961	11.7	23.3 Jul	-0.2 Jan	40	-25	37	-17	360
Antioch	36.14N, 36.07E	93	21 yrs bef 1961	18.1	27.7 Aug	8.0 Jan	43	-15			1141
Bursa	40.11N, 29.04E	100	30 yrs bef 1961	14.4	24.2 Jul	5.4 Jan	43	-20	38	-9	725
Eskisehir	39.46N, 30.32E	785	30 yrs bef 1961	10.8	21.4 Jul	-0.2 Jan	39	-26			368
Gaziantep	37.05N, 37.22E	840	21 yrs bef 1961	14.4	27.1 Jul	2.6 Jan	43	-17			550
Izmir	38.25N, 27.09E	25	30 yrs bef 1961	17.5	27.6 Jul	8.6 Jan	43	-11	39	-4	693
Kayseri	38.43N, 35.30E	1071	27 yrs bef 1961	10.8	22.8 Jul	-1.7 Jan	41	-32			366
Konya	37.52N, 32.31E	1026	30 yrs bef 1961	11.5	23.1 Jul	-0.2 Jan	38	-28	36	-18	315
USSR											
Aktyubinsk	50.17N, 57.10E	219	46 yrs bef 1961	3.6	22.3 Jul	-15.6 Jan	43	-48	38	-36	
Alma-Ata	43.15N, 76.57E	847	1915-60	8.7	23.3 Jul	-7.4 Jan	42	-38	37	-26	560
Andizhan	40.45N, 72.22E	477	1931-57	13.5	27.3 Jul	-3.0 Jan	44	-29	40	-19	
Angarsk	52.34N, 103.54E	417	1951-60	-1.3	17.8 Jul	-22.3 Jan	37	-51	33	-42	
Ashkhabad	37.57N, 58.23E	227	? yrs bef 1961	15.9	30.4 Jul	0.6 Jan	48	-26	42	-16	221
Barnaul	53.22N, 83.45E	158	1881-1960	1.1	19.7 Jul	-17.7 Jan	38	-52	34	-43	480
Biysk	52.34N, 85.15E	227	1934-60	0.5	18.9 Jul	-18.2 Jan	39	-53	34	-43	475
Bratsk	56.21N, 101.55E	379	1957-62	-2.2	18.2 Jul	-22.6 Jan	37	-57	33	-45	301
Bukhara	39.48N, 64.25E	225	1951-60	13.9	27.5 Jul	-0.6 Jan	47	-26	41	-17	
Chelyabinsk	55.10N, 61.24E	231	? yrs bef 1960	1.8	18.7 Jul	-15.7 Jan	39	-45			393
Chimkent	42.18N, 69.36E	543	1920-60	11.9	26.3 Jul	-3.0 Jan	44	-34	40	-24	
Chita	52.03N, 113.30E	671	1890-1919, 1924-56	-2.7	18.8 Jul	-26.6 Jan	41	-54	34	-43	348
Dushanbe	38.33N, 68.48E	822	1937-57	14.2	27.1 Jul	0.6 Jan	44	-28	40	-14	604
Dzhambul	42.54N, 71.22E	642	1928-60	9.0	23.3 Jul	-6.0 Jan	44	-41	38	-30	287
Frunze	42.54N, 74.36E	756	1927-60	9.8	24.1 Jul	-5.6 Jan	42	-38	38	-26	
Irkutsk	52.16N, 104.20E	468	1881-1960	-1.1	17.6 Jul	-20.9 Jan	36	-50	32	-41	403
Kamensk-Uralskiy	56.25N, 61.54E		(see Sverdlovsk)								
Karaganda	49.50N, 73.10E	550	1933-60	2.3	20.3 Jul	-15.1 Jan	40	-49	35	-37	313

ASIA

City	Latitude and longitude	Elev (m)	Period of record	Temperature (°C) Avg	Avg warmest month	Avg coolest month	Absolute High	Absolute Low	Avg Annual High	Avg Annual Low	Annual Precipitation (mm)
Kemerovo	55.20N, 86.05E	154	1933-60	-0.4	18.4 Jul	-19.2 Jan	38	-55	32	-42	
Khabarovsk	48.30N, 135.06E	87	66 yrs bef 1961	1.4	21.1 Jul	-22.3 Jan	40	-43	32	-35	488
Kokand	40.30N, 70.57E	408	1925-60	13.5	27.5 Jul	-2.3 Jan	44	-27	40	-16	
Komsomolsk-na-Amure	50.35N, 137.02E	20	1932-33, 1935-60	-0.7	19.9 Jul	-25.6 Jan	39	-50	31	-42	
Kopeysk	55.07N, 61.37E		(see Chelyabinsk)								
Krasnoyarsk	56.01N, 92.50E	194	? yrs bef 1960	0.3	19.9 Jul	-17.4 Jan	39	-49			338
Kurgan	55.26N, 65.18E	79	? yrs bef 1948[1]	0.2	18.7 Jul	-18.3 Jan					385
Magnitogorsk	53.27N, 59.04E	385									
Namangan	41.00N, 71.40E	474	1924-60	13.4	27.6 Jul	-3.4 Jan	44	-29	40	-18	
Nizhniy Tagil	57.55N, 59.57E	223									
Novokuznetsk	53.45N, 87.06E	235	1931-37, 1944-54	0.7	18.5 Jul	-17.8 Jan	38	-52	33	-41	
Novosibirsk	55.02N, 82.55E	136	1930-57	-0.1	18.7 Jul	-19.0 Jan	38	-50	34	-43	384
Omsk	55.00N, 73.24E	125	1930-60	0.0	18.3 Jul	-19.2 Jan	40	-49	34	-40	341
Pavlodar	52.18N, 76.57E	118	1906-11, 1922-60	1.9	21.2 Jul	-17.9 Jan	42	-47	36	-39	254
Petropavlovsk	54.52N, 69.06E	134	62 yrs bef 1961	0.5	18.8 Jul	-18.7 Jan	41	-53	34	-38	
Petropavlovsk-Kamchatskiy	53.01N, 158.39E	32	48 yrs bef 1961	1.9	13.5 Aug	-8.5 Feb	31	-34	25	-22	694
Prokopyevsk	53.53N, 86.45E		1925-60[2]	0.4	18.3 Jul	-17.7 Jan	38	-50	33	-41	
Samarkand	39.40N, 66.58E	726	1932-60	12.9	25.5 Jul	-0.3 Jan	45	-30	39	-18	320
Semipalatinsk	50.28N, 80.13E	202	64 yrs bef 1949	3.2	22.2 Jul	-16.2 Jan	42	-49	38	-40	267
Sverdlovsk	56.51N, 60.36E	282	1921-50	1.5	17.5 Jul	-15.1 Jan	37	-43	31	-37	449
Tashkent	41.20N, 69.18E	477	1881-1960	13.3	26.9 Jul	-0.9 Jan	44	-30	41	-19	372
Temir-Tau	50.05N, 72.56E		(see Karaganda)								
Tomsk	56.30N, 84.58E	139	1881-1960	-0.6	18.1 Jul	-19.2 Jan	36	-55	32	-44	536
Tselinograd	51.10N, 71.30E	347	73 yrs bef 1961	1.4	20.2 Jul	-17.4 Jan	42	-52	36	-38	305
Tyumen	57.09N, 65.26E	76	1884-1942	1.3	18.6 Jul	-16.6 Jan	40	-50	34	-37	405

[1] Climatic data for Staro-Sidorovo, nr Kurgan.

[2] Temperature data for Kiselevsk, nr Prokopyevsk.

ASIA

City	Latitude and longitude	Elev (m)	Period of record	Temperature (°C) Avg	Avg warmest month	Avg coolest month	Absolute High	Absolute Low	Avg Annual High	Avg Annual Low	Annual Precipitation (mm)
Ulan-Ude	51.50N, 107.37E	514	66 yrs bef 1961	-1.7	19.4 Jul	-25.4 Jan	40	-51	35	-42	202
Ust-Kamenogorsk	49.58N, 82.40E	284	1921-22, 1926-48	3.0	21.2 Jul	-16.2 Jan	41	-48	37	-45	361
Vladivostok	43.08N, 131.54E	111	1917-60	4.0	20.0 Aug	-14.4 Jan	36	-31	30	-26	744
Zlatoust	55.10N, 59.40E	458	? yrs bef 1959	0.6	16.3 Jul	-15.4 Jan	34	-46	29	-39	547
VIETNAM: NORTH											
Haiphong	20.52N, 106.41E	116	1904, 1906-30	23.2	28.3 Jul	16.5 Feb			37	9	1758
*Hanoi	21.02N, 105.51E	17	22 yrs bef 1931	24.0	29.5 Jun	17.1 Feb	43	6	39	8	1809
VIETNAM: SOUTH											
Da Nang	16.04N, 108.13E	6	1931-44, 1947-62	25.5	29.1 Jun	21.3 Jan					2073
Hue	16.28N, 107.36E	15	1931-44, 1947-62	25.1	29.3 Jun	20.0 Jan			40	12	3017
*Saigon	10.45N, 106.40E	9	1929-44, 1947-62	26.9	28.8 Apr	25.6 Dec	40	14	37	17	1937
YEMEN											
*Sana	15.23N, 44.12E	2213	? yrs bef 1936	17.5	21.7 Jun	14.2 Jan					500

EUROPE

City	Latitude and longitude	Elev (m)	Period of record	Temperature (°C) Avg	Avg warmest month	Avg coolest month	Absolute High	Absolute Low	Avg Annual High	Avg Annual Low	Annual Precipitation (mm)
ALBANIA											
*Tirane	41.20N, 19.50E	127	1930-58	15.8	25.1 Jul	6.9 Jan	40	-10			1189
AUSTRIA											
Graz	47.04N, 15.27E	377	1881-1930	8.8	18.6 Jul	-2.6 Jan	37	-24	31	-15	874

EUROPE

City	Latitude and longitude	Elev (m)	Period of record	Temperature (°C) Avg	Avg warmest month	Avg coolest month	Absolute High	Absolute Low	Avg Annual High	Avg Annual Low	Annual Precipitation (mm)
Innsbruck	47.16N, 11.24E	582	1921-55	9.2	19.2 Jul	-2.8 Jan	36	-27	33	-18	859
Linz	48.18N, 14.18E	260	1881-1930	8.8	18.8 Jul	-1.0 Jan	38	-27	33	-16	978
Salzburg	47.48N, 13.02E	435	1881-1930	8.6	18.1 Jul	-1.4 Jan	36	-31	33	-18	1379
*Vienna	48.12N, 16.22E	202	1881-1939	9.2	19.3 Jul	-1.1 Jan	37	-26	32	-14	669
BELGIUM											
Anderlecht	50.50N, 4.18E	30	(see Brussels)								
Antwerp	51.13N, 4.25E	5	1901-30	10.1	18.0 Jul	3.1 Jan					713
Bruges	51.13N, 3.14E	12	(see Ghent)								
*Brussels	50.50N, 4.20E	100	1901-30	9.9	17.3 Jul	3.2 Jan	37	-18	32	-11	835
Charleroi	50.25N, 4.26E	104	1901-30[1]	9.9	17.2 Jul	3.5 Jan					783
Ghent	51.03N, 3.43E	7	1901-30	10.2	18.1 Jul	3.3 Jan					820
La Louviere	50.28N, 4.11E		1901-30[1]	9.9	17.2 Jul	3.5 Jan					783
Liege	50.38N, 5.34E	115	(see Aachen, West Germany)								
Schaerbeek	50.51N, 4.23E		(see Brussels)								
BULGARIA											
Burgas	42.30N, 27.28E	5	1900-18, 1926-39	12.6	23.2 Jul	1.8 Jan					553
Plovdiv	42.09N, 24.45E	160	30 yrs bef 1951	12.5	23.6 Jul	-0.3 Jan	40	-32	38	-17	511
Ruse	43.50N, 25.57E	46	1894-1939	10.6	22.4 Jul	-2.7 Jan					576
*Sofia	42.41N, 23.19E	564	1881-82, 1887-1939	10.1	21.2 Jul	-2.0 Jan	37	-27	36	-19	625
Stara Zagora	42.25N, 25.38E	234	1900-18, 1928-39	12.9	24.3 Jul	1.1 Jan					594
Varna	43.13N, 27.55E	48	1892-1919, 1924-39	12.0	22.6 Jul	1.0 Jan	42	-24	36	-13	502

[1] Climatic data for Paturages, nr Charleroi and La Louviere.

EUROPE

City	Latitude and longitude	Elev (m)	Period of record	Temperature (°C) Avg	Avg warmest month	Avg coolest month	Absolute High	Absolute Low	Avg Annual High	Avg Annual Low	Annual Precipitation (mm)
CZECHOSLOVAKIA											
Bratislava	48.09N, 17.07E	164	1901-50	9.9	20.2 Jul	-1.6 Jan	38	-30	34	-16	670
Brno	49.11N, 16.37E	227	1901-50	8.4	18.4 Jul	-2.1 Jan	37	-30	33	-17	547
Karlovy Vary	50.14N, 12.53E	385	1901-50	7.3	16.9 Jul	-2.1 Jan	36	-28	32	-18	659
Kosice	48.44N, 21.15E	206	1901-50	8.4	19.1 Jul	-3.4 Jan	37	-30	33	-19	663
Ostrava	49.51N, 18.18E	217	1901-50	8.6	18.7 Jul	-2.0 Jan	36	-32	33	-21	769
Plzen	49.45N, 13.25E	354	1901-50	7.8	17.8 Jul	-2.0 Jan	37	-29	33	-19	518
*Prague	50.04N, 14.27E	193	1901-50	9.0	19.0 Jul	-0.9 Jan	38	-29	34	-17	487
DENMARK											
Alborg	57.03N, 9.56E	3	1886-1925[1]	6.7	15.3 Jul	-0.6 Feb					
Arhus	56.09N, 10.13E	49	1934-54	7.8	16.7 Jul	-0.6 Jan	31	-24	28	-12	676
*Copenhagen	55.40N, 12.35E	5	1921-50	8.3	17.7 Jul	-0.1 Feb	33	-19	28	-12	577
Frederkisberg	55.41N, 12.32E		(see Copenhagen)								
Odense	55.24N, 10.23E	15	1926-54	8.1	16.4 Jul	-0.3 Feb	32	-24	28	-14	605
FINLAND											
Espoo	60.13N, 24.40E		(see Helsinki)								
*Helsinki	60.10N, 24.58E	12	1931-60	5.4	17.8 Jul	-6.0 Feb	32	-31	28	-24	647
Tampere	61.30N, 23.45E	95	1931-60	3.8	16.8 Jul	-8.0 Feb	33	-36	29	-27	507
Turku	60.27N, 22.17E	16	20 yrs bef 1944	4.4	16.7 Jul	-6.1 Feb	36	-34	29	-26	610
FRANCE											
Ajaccio	41.55N, 8.44E	38	1921-50	14.7	21.8 Aug	8.4 Jan	39	-5	36	-2	695
Amiens	49.54N, 2.18E	36	1891-1914, 1923-34[2]	9.6	17.4 Jul	2.5 Jan					667

[1] Temperature data for Skorping, nr Alborg.

[2] Temperature data for Arras, nr Amiens.

EUROPE

City	Latitude and longitude	Elev (m)	Period of record	Temperature (°C) Avg	Avg warmest month	Avg coolest month	Absolute High	Absolute Low	Avg Annual High	Avg Annual Low	Annual Precipitation (mm)
Angers	47.28N, 0.33W	47	1901-30	11.5	19.0 Jul	4.8 Jan					655
Avignon	43.57N, 4.49E	55	1891-1914, 1921-34	13.7	22.8 Jul	4.9 Jan					616
Bayonne	43.29N, 1.29W	3	1901-30[1]	14.5	20.8 Aug	8.8 Jan			36	-4	1304
Besancon	47.15N, 6.02E	368	1921-50	10.3	19.0 Jul	1.6 Jan					1102
Bethune	50.32N, 2.38E	30	1891-1914, 1923-34[2]	9.6	17.4 Jul	2.5 Jan					652
Bordeaux	44.50N, 0.34W	7	1921-50	12.6	19.7 Jul	5.6 Dec	39	-13	36	-7	879
Boulogne-Billancourt	48.50N, 2.15E	30	(see Paris)								
Brest	48.24N, 4.29W	98	1921-50	10.8	16.1 Aug	6.3 Feb	35	-14	30	-4	1090
Bruay-en-Artois	50.29N, 2.33E	40	1891-1914, 1923-34[2]	9.6	17.4 Jul	2.5 Jan					
Caen	49.11N, 0.21W	26	1901-30	10.5	17.1 Jul	4.6 Jan	37	-14	33	-12	655
Cannes	43.33N, 7.01E	3	1921-50	14.4	22.0 Jul	7.3 Jan					799
Clermont-Ferrand	45.47N, 3.05E	407	1921-50	11.0	19.3 Jul	3.1 Jan	42	-23	36	-13	575
Denain	50.20N, 3.23E	40	1891-1914, 1923-34[2]	9.6	17.4 Jul	2.5 Jan					
Dijon	47.19N, 5.01E	338	1891-1936, 1946-50	10.6	19.7 Jul	1.7 Jan	42	-22	34	-12	698
Douai	50.22N, 3.04E	24	(see Lille)								
Dunkerque	51.03N, 2.22E	8	1881-1917, 1921-34	10.0	17.0 Aug	3.8 Jan					763
Grenoble	45.10N, 5.43E	247	1921-50	10.9	20.1 Jul	1.7 Jan	37	-21	34	-12	1015
Le Havre	49.30N, 0.08E	5	1901-30	10.8	17.4 Aug	4.9 Jan					707
Le Mans	48.00N, 0.12E	77	1921-50	11.1	18.8 Jul	4.0 Dec					660
Lens	50.26N, 2.50E	40	(see Lille)								
Lille	50.38N, 3.04E	24	1921-50	9.9	17.5 Aug	2.9 Jan	36	-18	33	-11	685
Limoges	45.51N, 1.15E	287	1891-1913, 1921-34	10.8	18.9 Jul	3.2 Jan	39	-18	36	-12	907
Lyons	45.45N, 4.51E	225	1921-50	11.4	20.7 Jul	2.4 Jan	41	-25	35	-12	811
Marseilles	43.18N, 5.24E	162	1921-50	14.3	23.1 Jul	6.0 Jan	38	-13	34	-5	534

[1] Climatic data for Biarritz, nr Bayonne.

[2] Temperature data for Arras, nr Bethune, Bruay-en-Artois, and Denain.

EUROPE

City	Latitude and longitude	Elev (m)	Period of record	Temperature (°C) Avg	Avg warmest month	Avg coolest month	Absolute High	Absolute Low	Avg Annual High	Avg Annual Low	Annual Precipitation (mm)
Metz	49.08N, 6.10E	262	1901-30	9.8	18.6 Jul	1.3 Dec					721
Montbeliard	47.31N, 6.48E	368	1901-30	(see Besancon for temperature data)							1061
Montpellier	43.36N, 3.53E	44	1921-50	13.9	22.4 Jul	6.0 Jan					675
Montreuil	48.52N, 2.26E	120	(see Paris)								
Mulhouse	47.45N, 7.20E	240	1921-50	9.9	19.0 Jul	0.8 Jan					719
Nancy	48.41N, 6.12E	279	1921-50	9.6	18.3 Jul	1.2 Jan	36	-20	32	-14	709
Nantes	47.13N, 1.33W	19	1921-50	11.8	19.0 Jul	5.2 Dec	39	-15	34	-8	800
Nice	43.42N, 7.15E	46	1921-50	15.2	22.6 Jul	8.3 Jan	37	-4	33	-1	810
Nimes	43.50N, 4.21E	114	1901-30	14.4	23.8 Jul	6.1 Jan					752
Orleans	47.55N, 1.54E	116	1921-50	10.8	18.8 Jul	3.3 Dec	41	-16	34	-9	634
*Paris	48.52N, 2.20E	60	1921-50	11.1	19.3 Jul	3.6 Dec	40	-16	34	-9	645
Pau	43.18N, 0.22W	207	1901-30	12.5	19.7 Jul	5.7 Dec					1149
Perpignan	42.41N, 2.53E	60	1921-50	15.5	23.9 Jul	8.0 Jan	42	-11	35	-4	607
Rennes	48.05N, 1.41W	54	1921-50	11.2	18.0 Jul	5.2 Dec	41	-19	33	-9	685
Rheims	49.15N, 4.02E	86	1921-50	10.2	18.4 Jul	2.4 Jan	38	-20	34	-13	607
Roubaix	50.42N, 3.10E	35	(see Lille)								
Rouen	49.26N, 1.05E	22	1921-50	10.3	17.7 Jul	3.5 Jan					697
Saint-Denis	48.56N, 2.22E	30	(see Paris)								
Saint-Etienne	45.26N, 4.24E	540	1921-50	10.4	19.0 Jul	2.3 Jan					690
Saint-Nazaire	47.17N, 2.12W	8	(see Nantes)								
Strasbourg	48.35N, 7.45E	284	1921-50	10.0	19.2 Jul	0.9 Jan	37	-22	34	-13	614
Thionville	49.22N, 6.10E	200	(see Saarbrucken, West Germany)								
Toulon	43.07N, 5.56E	28	1921-50	15.5	23.0 Jul	8.7 Jan	36	-10	33	-2	677
Toulouse	43.36N, 1.26E	139	1921-50	13.0	21.3 Jul	5.3 Jan	44	-17	37	-9	665
Tourcoing	50.43N, 3.09E	45	(see Lille)								
Tours	47.23N, 0.41E	55	1921-50	11.4	19.4 Jul	4.1 Dec					681

City	Latitude and longitude	Elev (m)	Period of record	Temperature (°C) Avg	Avg warmest month	Avg coolest month	Absolute High	Absolute Low	Avg Annual High	Avg Annual Low	Annual Precipitation (mm)
Troyes	48.18N, 4.05E	110	1881-1917, 1921-34[1]	9.4	18.0 Jul	1.1 Jan					650
Valenciennes	50.21N, 3.32E	30	(see Lille)								
Versailles	48.48N, 2.08E	184	(see Paris)								
Villeurbanne	45.46N, 4.53E	177	(see Lyons)								
GERMANY: EAST											
*Berlin (see under Germany: West)											
Brandenburg	52.25N, 12.33E	31	1955-56, 1958-59, 1962	(see Potsdam for temperature data)							555
Dessau	51.50N, 12.15E	61	1893-1930	8.8	18.0 Jul	0.0 Jan					
Dresden	51.03N, 13.45E	113	1901-50	8.4	17.8 Jul	-0.8 Jan	38	-28	33	-15	659
Erfurt	50.59N, 11.02E	200	1901-50	7.8	16.8 Jul	-0.9 Jan					500
Gera	50.52N, 12.05E	205	1881-1930[2]	7.8	16.8 Jul	-0.9 Jan					
Halle	51.30N, 12.00E	100	(see Leipzig)								
Karl-Marx-Stadt	50.50N, 12.55E	309	1901-50	7.0	16.2 Jul	-1.9 Jan					652
Leipzig	51.18N, 12.20E	118	1901-50	8.3	18.0 Jul	-0.6 Jan	36	-26	32	-16	560
Magdeburg	52.10N, 11.40E	50	1901-50	8.5	17.7 Jul	-0.3 Jan					506
Potsdam	52.24N, 13.04E	32	1901-50	8.5	18.1 Jul	-0.7 Jan					585
Rostock	54.05N, 12.08E	13	1901-50	8.5	17.5 Jul	0.4 Jan					563
Schwerin	53.38N, 11.23E	40	1901-50	8.4	17.5 Jul	-0.1 Jan					627
Zwickau	50.44N, 12.30E	267	1881-1930[2]	7.8	16.8 Jul	-0.9 Jan					
GERMANY: WEST											
Aachen	50.46N, 6.06E	173	1931-60	9.6	17.5 Jul	1.8 Jan	35	-14			840
Augsburg	48.22N, 10.53E	490	1881-1930	8.2	17.9 Jul	-1.4 Jan	36	-17			844

[1] Temperature data for Chaumont, nr Troyes.

[2] Temperature data for Crimmitschau, nr Gera and Zwickau.

EUROPE

City	Latitude and longitude	Elev (m)	Period of record	Temperature (°C) Avg	Avg warmest month	Avg coolest month	Absolute High	Absolute Low	Avg Annual High	Avg Annual Low	Annual Precipitation (mm)
Baden-Baden	48.45N, 8.15E	181	1881-1930	9.3	18.0 Jul	0.8 Jan					1097
Berlin	52.33N, 13.22E	34	1931-60	9.0	18.7 Jul	-0.7 Jan	37	-26	33	-14	587
Bielefeld	52.02N, 8.32E	118	1881-1930	8.7	16.9 Jul	0.7 Jan					839
Bochum	51.29N, 7.13E	100	1957-61	(see Essen for temperature data)							820
*Bonn	50.44N, 7.06E	60	1957-61	(see Cologne for temperature data)							673
Bottrop	51.31N, 6.55E	60	(see Essen)								
Bremen	53.05N, 8.48E	3	1931-60	9.0	17.4 Jul	0.6 Jan	35	-22	31	-13	668
Bremerhaven	53.33N, 8.35E	7	1881-1930	8.6	17.0 Jul	0.7 Jan	34	-15	29	-11	812
Brunswick	52.16N, 10.32E	70	1893-1930	8.8	17.6 Jul	0.2 Jan	35	-21			676
Cologne	50.56N, 6.57E	53	1881-1930	10.2	18.4 Jul	2.4 Jan	36	-19	32	-10	696
Darmstadt	49.52N, 8.39E	144	1881-1930	9.5	18.5 Jul	0.7 Jan	35	-19	32	-15	636
Dortmund	51.31N, 7.27E	76	1960-63, 1965	9.1	16.0 Jun	0.9 Jan	35	-19	31	-14	947
Duisburg	51.26N, 6.45E	26	1957-61	(see Essen for temperature data)							728
Dusseldorf	51.13N, 6.46E	36	1957-61	(see Solingen for temperature data)							793
Essen	51.27N, 7.01E	76	1931-60	9.6	17.5 Jul	1.5 Jan	34	-11			897
Flensburg	54.47N, 9.26E	20	1931-60	8.1	16.6 Jul	0.2 Jan					804
Frankfurt am Main	50.07N, 8.41E	98	1931-60	10.2	19.4 Jul	0.8 Jan	38	-22	33	-13	604
Freiburg im Breisgau	48.00N, 7.51E	278	1931-60	10.3	19.4 Jul	1.2 Jan	39	-22	33	-13	884
Furth	49.28N, 11.00E	297	1957-61	(see Nuremberg for temperature data)							647
Gelsenkirchen	51.31N, 7.06E	52	1957-61	(see Essen for temperature data)							861
Gottingen	51.32N, 9.56E	150	1893-1930	8.5	17.2 Jul	0.0 Jan	33	-26	30	-22	607
Hagen	51.21N, 7.28E	106	1957-61	(see Dortmund for temperature data)							958
Hamburg	53.33N, 10.00E	6	1931-60	8.6	17.3 Jul	0.0 Jan	35	-20	29	-12	740
Hannover	52.22N, 9.43E	55	1931-60	8.9	17.6 Jul	0.2 Jan	37	-25	31	-14	637
Heidelberg	49.25N, 8.42E	114	1881-1930	10.2	19.0 Jul	1.4 Jan					799
Heilbronn	49.08N, 9.13E	151	1957-61	(see Heidelberg for temperature data)							732
Herne	51.33N, 7.13E	59	(see Essen)								
Hildesheim	52.09N, 9.58E	80	1957-61	(see Hannover for temperature data)							773

EUROPE

City	Latitude and longitude	Elev (m)	Period of record	Temperature (°C) Avg	Avg warmest month	Avg coolest month	Absolute High	Absolute Low	Avg Annual High	Avg Annual Low	Annual Precipitation (mm)
Kaiserslautern	49.27N, 7.45E	240	1957-61	(see Saarbrucken for temperature data)							719
Karlsruhe	49.01N, 8.24E	115	1931-60	10.1	19.5 Jul	0.8 Jan	37	-20			756
Kassel	51.19N, 9.30E	167	1931-60	9.0	17.9 Jul	-0.1 Jan	37	-27	32	-14	595
Kiel	54.20N, 10.08E	14	1881-1930	7.6	16.3 Jul	0.0 Jan	33	-20	27	-11	717
Koblenz	50.21N, 7.36E	70	1881-1930	10.1	18.5 Jul	1.8 Jan	33	-16	32	-13	617
Krefeld	51.20N, 6.34E	38	1881-1930	9.4	17.6 Jul	1.8 Jan					642
Leverkusen	51.01N, 6.59E	44	(see Essen)								
Lubeck	53.52N, 10.42E	13	1931-60	8.7	17.7 Jul	0.1 Jan	36	-16			632
Ludwigshafen	49.29N, 8.27E	95	1891-1930	(see Mannheim for temperature data)							565
Mainz	50.00N, 8.15E	82	1881-1930[1]	9.2	16.9 Jul	1.9 Jan					604
Mannheim	49.29N, 8.28E	97	1881-1930	10.0	19.2 Jul	0.9 Jan	37	-16			649
Monchengladbach	51.12N, 6.26E	60	(see Solingen)								
Mulheim an der Ruhr	51.26N, 6.53E	40	(see Essen)								
Munich	48.09N, 11.35E	520	1931-60	7.9	17.5 Jul	-2.1 Jan	34	-26	30	-18	886
Munster	51.58N, 7.38E	60	1931-60	9.5	17.7 Jul	1.3 Jan	36	-27	33	-13	777
Neuss	51.12N, 6.42E	40	(see Solingen)								
Nuremberg	49.27N, 11.05E	309	1931-60	8.5	18.2 Jul	-1.4 Jan	38	-28	33	-17	592
Oberhausen	51.28N, 6.51E	40	1957-61	(see Essen for temperature data)							851
Offenbach am Main	50.06N, 8.46E	98	(see Frankfurt am Main)								
Oldenburg in Oldenburg	53.10N, 8.12E	5	1893-1930	8.4	16.9 Jul	0.7 Jan					797
Osnabruck	52.16N, 8.03E	64	1893-1930	8.8	17.1 Jul	1.1 Jan	34	-18	30	-15	887
Pforzheim	48.53N, 8.42E	273	1957-61	(see Stuttgart for temperature data)							766
Recklinghausen	51.37N, 7.12E	109	(see Dortmund)								
Regensburg	49.01N, 12.06E	339	1881-1930	7.7	17.6 Jul	-2.4 Jan	34	-23	33	-18	591
Remscheid	51.11N, 7.12E	365	(see Solingen)								
Rheydt	51.10N, 6.27E	79	(see Solingen)								

[1] Temperature data for Alzey, nr Mainz.

EUROPE

City	Latitude and longitude	Elev (m)	Period of record	Temperature (°C) Avg	Avg warmest month	Avg coolest month	Absolute High	Absolute Low	Avg Annual High	Avg Annual Low	Annual Precipitation (mm)
Saarbrucken	49.14N, 7.00E	190	1931-60	9.6	18.2 Jul	0.9 Jan	33	-18	31	-15	786
Salzgitter	52.05N, 10.20E	141	(see Brunswick)								
Solingen	51.11N, 7.05E	221	1881-1930	8.6	16.4 Jul	1.2 Jan	36	-11			1108
Stuttgart	48.46N, 9.11E	245	1931-60	9.9	19.0 Jul	0.8 Jan	39	-25	33	-13	662
Trier	49.45N, 6.38E	125	1931-60	9.4	17.9 Jul	0.7 Jan	33	-17	32	-12	719
Ulm	48.24N, 10.00E	478	1931-60	8.2	17.7 Jul	-1.8 Jan					702
Wanne-Eickel	51.32N, 7.10E	55	(see Essen)								
Wiesbaden	50.05N, 8.15E	116	1957-61	(see Frankfurt am Main for temperature data)							654
Wilhelmshaven	53.31N, 8.08E	4	1893-1930	8.3	16.4 Jul	0.8 Jan					693
Witten	51.26N, 7.20E	82	(see Essen)								
Wolfsburg	52.26N, 10.48E	56	(see Brunswick)								
Wuppertal	51.16N, 7.11E	160	1881-1930	9.2	17.3 Jul	1.5 Jan					1147
Wurzburg	49.48N, 9.56E	181	1931-60	9.1	18.4 Jul	-0.7 Jan	34	-21	32	-17	560
GIBRALTAR											
*Gibraltar	36.06N, 5.21W	3	1951-60	18.2	24.1 Aug	12.8 Jan	38	1	36	3	815
GREECE											
*Athens	37.58N, 23.43E	138	1900-29	17.4	26.9 Jul	9.1 Jan	43	-7	38	-2	384
Iraklion	35.20N, 25.09E	30	1900-29	19.0	26.3 Aug	12.2 Jan	46	0	37	3	510
Patras	38.15N, 21.44E	5	38 yrs bef 1941	18.4	27.5 Jul	10.0 Jan	43	-4	38	0	710
Peristeri	38.01N, 23.41E		(see Athens)								
Piraeus	37.57N, 23.38E	9	(see Athens)								
Salonika	40.38N, 22.56E	61	1900-29	15.9	26.3 Jul	5.6 Jan	42	-9	38	-5	486
HUNGARY											
*Budapest	47.30N, 19.05E	115	1918-47	11.0	22.2 Jul	-0.9 Jan	39	-23	35	-13	632
Debrecen	47.32N, 21.38E	123	1881-1909, 1916-36	9.8	21.2 Jul	-2.7 Jan	39	-30	35	-19	580

EUROPE

City	Latitude and longitude	Elev (m)	Period of record	Temperature (°C) Avg	Avg warmest month	Avg coolest month	Absolute High	Absolute Low	Avg Annual High	Avg Annual Low	Annual Precipitation (mm)
Miskolc	48.06N, 20.47E	12[illegible]	1951–60	9.7	21.0 Jul	-2.3 Jan					637
Pecs	46.05N, 18.14E	25[illegible]	29 yrs bef 1939[1]	10.7	22.0 Jul	-1.0 Jan					876
Szeged	46.15N, 20.10E	8[illegible]	1881–1909, 1916–38	11.1	22.7 Jul	-1.2 Jan	39	-29	36	-17	572
ICELAND											
*Reykjavik	64.09N, 21.57W	2[illegible]	1920–50	5.3	11.7 Jul	0.0 Jan	23	-16	19	-12	861
IRELAND											
Cork	51.54N, 8.28W	1[illegible]	27 yrs bef 1951	10.3	15.8 Jul	5.8 Dec	29	-9	26	-5	1049
*Dublin	53.20N, 6.15W	1[illegible]	1921–50	10.0	15.8 Jul	5.5 Jan	30	-13	26	-7	680
ITALY											
Alessandria	44.54N, 8.37E	9[illegible]	25 yrs bef 1926	12.4	23.8 Jul	0.5 Jan					556
Ancona	43.38N, 13.30E	1[illegible]	1946–55	15.0	24.7 Jul	7.2 Jan	37	-7	36	-3	644
Bari	41.08N, 16.51E	[illegible]	1931–48, 1951–55	16.4	24.8 Jul	8.6 Jan	44	-8			526
Bergamo	45.41N, 9.43E	24[illegible]	1921–50	(see Brescia for temperature data)							1243
Bologna	44.29N, 11.20E	5[illegible]	1931–55	14.1	25.5 Jul	2.3 Jan	40	-13			601
Bolzano	46.31N, 11.22E	26[illegible]	1946–55	11.7	21.7 Jul	0.0 Jan	38	-15			687
Brescia	45.33N, 10.15E	14[illegible]	31 yrs bef 1926	13.2	23.8 Jul	2.2 Jan					882
Cagliari	39.13N, 9.07E	4	1931–42, 1945–55	17.7	25.7 Aug	10.5 Jan	40	-4			431
Catania	37.30N, 15.06E	10	1892–1930	18.0	26.5 Aug	10.3 Jan	44	-4			696
Como	45.47N, 9.05E	201	1889–1906	12.5	23.0 Jul	2.3 Jan					1275
Cosenza	39.18N, 16.15E	237	1921–50								1041
Ferrara	44.50N, 11.35E	9	1921–43, 1946–50	(see Bologna for temperature data)							576
Florence	43.46N, 11.15E	50	1931–55	14.7	24.7 Jul	5.2 Jan	41	-12			840
Foggia	41.27N, 15.34E	76	1946–55	16.1	26.1 Aug	7.2 Jan	46	-10			454

[1] Temperature data for Kaposvar, nr Pecs.

EUROPE

City	Latitude and longitude	Elev (m)	Period of record	Temperature (°C) Avg	Avg warmest month	Avg coolest month	Absolute High	Absolute Low	Avg Annual High	Avg Annual Low	Annual Precipitation (mm)
Forli	44.13N, 12.03E	34	1921–43, 1946–50	(see Bologna for temperature data)							755
Genoa	44.25N, 8.57E	19	1931–55	16.1	24.5 Jul	7.9 Jan	38	-8	32	-2	1146
La Spezia	44.07N, 9.50E	3	28 yrs bef 1951	(see Genoa for temperature data)							1375
Leghorn	43.33N, 10.19E	3	1901–30	15.5	24.2 Jul	7.4 Jan	38	-7			821
Messina	38.11N, 15.34E	3	1901–30	17.9	25.9 Aug	11.4 Feb	40	-2			938
Milan	45.28N, 9.12E	121	1931–43, 1946–55	13.7	25.0 Jul	2.0 Jan	38	-17			912
Modena	44.40N, 10.55E	34	1921–50	(see Bologna for temperature data)							631
Monza	45.35N, 9.16E	162	1921–50	(see Milan for temperature data)							1131
Naples	40.50N, 14.15E	10	1931–55	17.1	25.5 Jul	9.0 Jan	38	-5	34	-1	850
Novara	45.28N, 8.38E	159	1889–1906	13.0	23.9 Jul	2.3 Jan					918
Padua	45.25N, 11.53E	12	1921–50	(see Verona for temperature data)							846
Palermo	38.07N, 13.22E	14	1931–55	18.3	25.6 Aug	11.7 Jan	45	-2			731
Parma	44.48N, 10.20E	57	1931–46	(see Bologna for temperature data)							767
Perugia	43.08N, 12.22E	493	1946–55	13.6	23.1 Jul	4.7 Jan	38	-13	35	-6	874
Pescara	42.28N, 14.13E	4	1946-55	14.7	23.1 Jul	6.7 Jan	41	-6			692
Piacenza	45.01N, 9.40E	61	30 yrs bef 1926	12.3	23.4 Jul	0.4 Jan	37	-21			794
Pisa	43.43N, 10.23E	5	1901–30	14.4	22.8 Aug	6.2 Jan	38	-11			966
Prato	43.53N, 11.06E	63	1921–50	(see Florence for temperature data)							988
Ravenna	44.25N, 12.12E	4	1924–43, 1946–50	(see Bologna for temperature data)							700
Reggio di Calabria	38.06N, 15.39E	15	1921–50	(see Messina for temperature data)							596
Reggio nell'Emilia	44.43N, 10.36E	58	1921–50	(see Bologna for temperature data)							704
Rimini	44.04N, 12.34E	7	1921–43	(see Florence for temperature data)							746
*Rome	41.54N, 12.29E	20	1931–55	16.2	25.4 Jul	7.7 Jan	42	-9			760
Salerno	40.41N, 14.47E	4	1921–50	(see Naples for temperature data)							1299
Sassari	40.43N, 8.34E	225	1883–1930	15.5	23.6 Aug	8.1 Jan					596
Syracuse	37.04N, 15.18E	17	32 yrs bef 1926	17.9	26.1 Aug	11.0 Jan					641
Taranto	40.28N, 17.14E	15	1901–30	16.8	25.7 Aug	8.8 Jan	42	-4			445

EUROPE

City	Latitude and longitude	Elev (m)	Period of record	Temperature (°C) Avg	Avg warmest month	Avg coolest month	Absolute High	Absolute Low	Avg Annual High	Avg Annual Low	Annual Precipitation (mm)
Terni	42.34N, 12.37E	130	1882–1900, 1906[1]	14.4	24.3 Jul	5.5 Jan					839
Trieste	45.40N, 13.46E	2	1951–60	14.1	23.8 Jul	5.1 Jan	37	−14			967
Turin	45.03N, 7.40E	239	1898–1915, 1926–34	11.8	22.9 Jul	0.7 Jan	38	−14	36	−9	779
Udine	46.03N, 13.14E	113	1923–58	13.1	23.0 Jul	3.0 Jan	37	−18	34	−7	1367
Venice	45.27N, 12.21E	1	30 yrs bef 1926	13.6	24.2 Jul	3.0 Jan	36	−10			757
Verona	45.27N, 11.00E	59	1946–55	13.1	23.3 Jul	2.5 Jan	38	−18			644
Vicenza	45.33N, 11.33E	39	1921–43, 1946–50	(see Verona for temperature data)							1037
LUXEMBOURG											
*Luxembourg	49.36N, 6.07E	300	1931–60	8.8	17.4 Jul	0.3 Jan	37	−23	31	−13	743
MALTA											
*Valletta	35.54N, 14.32E	71	90 yrs bef 1948	18.9	26.1 Aug	12.8 Jan	41	1	36	6	516
MONACO											
*Monaco	43.44N, 7.25E	55	1921–50	16.4	23.8 Aug	10.2 Jan	34	−3	30	2	765
NETHERLANDS											
*Amsterdam	52.23N, 4.54E	2	1921–50	10.0	17.8 Jul	2.8 Jan	35	−16	30	−8	650
Apeldoorn	52.13N, 5.57E		(see Utrecht)								
Arnhem	52.00N, 5.53E		(see Utrecht)								
Breda	51.35N, 4.46E	7	1931–60[2]	10.6	18.7 Jul	2.4 Jan					741
Dordrecht	51.48N, 4.40E	4	1931–60[2]	10.6	18.7 Jul	2.4 Jan					741
Eindhoven	51.26N, 5.30E	20	1931–60[3]	10.7	19.4 Jul	2.0 Jan					694

[1] Climatic data for Teramo, nr Terni.

[2] Climatic data for Oudenbosch, nr Breda and Dordrecht.

[3] Climatic data for Gemert, nr Eindhoven.

EUROPE

City	Latitude and longitude	Elev (m)	Period of record	Temperature (°C) Avg	Avg warmest month	Avg coolest month	Absolute High	Absolute Low	Avg Annual High	Avg Annual Low	Annual Precipitation (mm)
Enschede	52.13N, 6.55E	29	(see Munster, West Germany)								
Groningen	53.13N, 6.34E	5	1921-50	9.2	17.5 Jul	1.4 Jan	37	-21	32	-12	747
Haarlem	52.20N, 4.36E	3	(see Amsterdam)								
*Hague	52.04N, 4.19E	4	1931-60[1]	10.5	18.4 Aug	2.6 Jan					751
Heerlen	50.53N, 5.59E	115	(see Aachen, West Germany)								
Hilversum	52.14N, 5.10E	5	(see Utrecht)								
Leiden	52.10N, 4.30E	3	1931-60[1]	10.5	18.4 Aug	2.6 Jan					751
Maastricht	50.51N, 5.42E	49	1900-36	(see Aachen, West Germany, for temperature data)							659
Nijmegen	51.50N, 5.52E	25	1931-60[2]	10.7	19.4 Jul	2.0 Jan					694
Rotterdam	51.55N, 4.29E	4	1921-50	10.0	17.8 Jul	2.8 Jan	38	-17	32	-9	726
's Hertogenbosch	51.41N, 5.19E	8	1931-60[2]	10.7	19.4 Jul	2.0 Jan					694
Tilburg	51.34N, 5.05E	18	1931-60[2]	10.7	19.4 Jul	2.0 Jan					694
Utrecht	52.07N, 5.05E	3	1931-60	10.4	18.7 Jul	2.0 Jan	37	-25			765
Zaandam	52.27N, 4.49E	3	(see Amsterdam)								
NORWAY											
Bergen	60.23N, 5.20E	44	1931-60	7.8	15.0 Jul	1.3 Feb	32	-16	26	-10	1958
*Oslo	59.55N, 10.45E	96	1931-60	5.9	17.3 Jul	-4.7 Jan	34	-29	28	-19	740
Stavanger	58.58N, 5.45E	8	1951-60	7.3	14.6 Aug	-0.4 Feb	29	-11	27	-8	1015
Trondheim	63.25N, 10.25E	127	1885-1935	4.9	14.2 Jul	-2.1 Jan	35	-30	28	-17	733
POLAND											
Bialystok	53.09N, 23.10E	139	1931-60	6.9	18.3 Jul	-4.9 Jan					544

[1] Climatic data for Naaldwijk, nr Hague and Leiden.

[2] Climatic data for Gemert, nr Nijmegen, 's Hertogenbosch, and Tilburg.

EUROPE

City	Latitude and longitude	Elev (m)	Period of record	Temperature (°C) Avg	Avg warmest month	Avg coolest month	Absolute High	Absolute Low	Avg Annual High	Avg Annual Low	Annual Precipitation (mm)
Bielsko-Biala	49.50N, 19.00E	309	1931-60	7.7	17.5 Jul	-3.1 Jan					1011
Bydgoszcz	53.16N, 17.33E	70	1931-60	7.9	18.7 Jul	-2.8 Jan	36	-31			529
Bytom	50.22N, 18.53E	285	(see Katowice)								
Chorzow	50.19N, 18.56E	282	(see Katowice)								
Czestochowa	50.49N, 19.07E	261	1931-60	7.8	18.4 Jul	-3.4 Jan					660
Gdansk	54.20N, 18.40E	13	1931-60	7.3	17.3 Jul	-2.4 Jan	35	-28	31	-17	590
Gdynia	54.31N, 18.30E	2	(see Gdansk)								
Gliwice	50.20N, 18.40E	222	(see Katowice)								
Katowice	50.15N, 18.59E	284	1931-60	7.8	18.0 Jul	-3.3 Jan					681
Kielce	50.51N, 20.39E	268	1931-60	7.4	18.2 Jul	-4.1 Jan					649
Krakow	50.05N, 19.55E	237	1931-60	8.6	19.3 Jul	-2.9 Jan	35	-33	32	-19	688
Lodz	51.46N, 19.25E	187	1931-60	7.6	18.3 Jul	-3.5 Jan	36	-31			586
Lublin	51.20N, 22.30E	17[illegible]	1931-60	7.5	18.6 Jul	-4.2 Jan					564
Olsztyn	53.47N, 20.29E	115	1931-60	6.9	17.7 Jul	-4.0 Jan					590
Poznan	52.25N, 16.58E	86	1931-60	8.2	18.7 Jul	-2.6 Jan					525
Radom	51.26N, 21.10E	178	1881-1930	8.0	18.7 Jul	-2.6 Jan					590
Ruda Slaska	50.18N, 18.51E	286	(see Katowice)								
Sosnowiec	50.16N, 19.07E	250	(see Katowice)								
Szczecin	53.26N, 14.34E	1	1931-60	8.3	18.1 Jul	-1.4 Jan	36	-26	31	-15	568
Torun	53.01N, 18.35E	69	1881-1930	7.8	18.4 Jul	-2.2 Jan					495
Walbrzych	50.48N, 16.19E	450	1881-1930[1]	7.3	16.9 Jul	-2.4 Jan					
*Warsaw	52.15N, 21.00E	106	1931-60	8.1	19.2 Jul	-3.5 Jan	37	-33	32	-19	542
Wroclaw	51.07N, 17.02E	120	1931-60	8.5	18.8 Jul	-2.0 Jan	37	-32	32	-17	584
Zabrze	50.18N, 18.47E	250	(see Katowice)								
PORTUGAL											
*Lisbon	38.43N, 9.08W	95	1921-50	16.1	22.1 Aug	10.6 Jan	39	-2	37	0	619

[1] Temperature data for Klodzko, nr Walbrzych.

EUROPE

City	Latitude longitude	Elev (m)	Period of record	Temperature (°C) Avg	Avg warmest month	Avg coolest month	Absolute High	Absolute Low	Avg Annual High	Avg Annual Low	Annual Precipitation (mm)
Porto	41.09N, 8.37W	100	1921–50	14.2	19.7 Aug	8.9 Jan	40	-4	36	-2	1156
ROMANIA											
Arad	46.11N, 21.19E	101	1896–1955	10.8	21.4 Jul	-1.1 Jan	40	-30			577
Bacau	46.34N, 26.54E	182	1896–1955	9.2	20.8 Jul	-4.3 Jan	39	-32			544
Baia Mare	47.40N, 23.35E	194	1896–1955	9.4	19.9 Jul	-2.4 Jan	39	-30			976
Braila	45.16N, 27.59E	15	1896–1955	11.1	23.1 Jul	-2.3 Jan	40	-26			440
Brasov	45.38N, 25.35E	592	1896–1955	7.8	17.8 Jul	-3.9 Jan	37	-30			747
*Bucharest	44.26N, 26.06E	82	1896–1955	10.9	22.9 Jul	-2.8 Jan	41	-30	37	-19	580
Cluj	46.46N, 23.36E	313	1896–1955	8.2	18.9 Jul	-4.4 Jan	37	-34	33	-23	613
Constanta	44.11N, 28.39E	32	1896–1955	11.2	22.2 Jul	-0.3 Jan	38	-25			379
Craiova	44.19N, 23.48E	105	1896–1955	10.8	22.7 Jul	-2.5 Jan	41	-30			523
Galati	45.27N, 28.03E	30	1896–1955	10.5	22.6 Jul	-3.1 Jan	39	-29			426
Hunedoara	45.45N, 22.54E	243	1896–1955	9.7	20.2 Jul	-2.8 Jan					625
Iasi	47.10N, 27.36E	102	1896–1955	9.6	21.3 Jul	-3.6 Jan	40	-31			518
Oradea	47.04N, 21.56E	137	1896–1955	10.5	21.2 Jul	-1.5 Jan	39	-29			635
Petroseni	45.25N, 23.22E	581	1896–1955	6.8	16.7 Jul	-4.5 Jan	36	-30			694
Pitesti	44.51N, 24.52E	306	1896–1955	9.8	20.8 Jul	-2.4 Jan	39	-27			700
Ploesti	44.57N, 26.01E	154	1896–1955	10.6	22.0 Jul	-2.1 Jan	39	-30			588
Resita	45.18N, 21.55E	226	1896–1955[1]	10.6	21.0 Jul	-0.8 Jan					820
Sibiu	45.48N, 24.09E	416	1896–1955	8.9	19.6 Jul	-3.8 Jan	37	-32			662
Timisoara	45.45N, 21.13E	90	1896–1955	10.9	21.6 Jul	-1.2 Jan	40	-35			631
Tirgu Mures	46.33N, 24.34E	309	1896–1955	8.7	19.4 Jul	-4.3 Jan	39	-33			636
SPAIN											
Alicante	38.21N, 0.29W	3	1939–60	18.0	26.1 Aug	11.0 Jan	41	-4	37	-1	339
Almeria	36.50N, 2.27W	17	1934–60	17.9	25.3 Aug	11.7 Jan	42	0	37	4	231
Badajoz	38.53N, 6.58W	184	1931–60	16.7	25.8 Jul	8.6 Jan	45	-5	42	-3	474
Badalona	41.27N, 2.15E	23	(see Barcelona)								

[1] Temperature data for Caransebes, nr Resita.

EUROPE

City	Latitude and longitude	Elev (m)	Period of record	Temperature (°C) Avg	Avg warmest month	Avg coolest month	Absolute High	Absolute Low	Avg Annual High	Avg Annual Low	Annual Precipitation (mm)
Baracaldo	43.18N, 2.59W	39	(see San Sebastian)								
Barcelona	41.23N, 2.11E	12	1931–60	16.4	24.4 Jul	9.4 Jan	37	-7	33	-1	594
Bilbao	43.15N, 2.58W	3	26 yrs bef 1927	(see San Sebastian for temperature data)							1065
Burgos	42.21N, 3.42W	856	1931–47, 1950–60	10.6	19.0 Jul	2.5 Jan	37	-18			563
Cadiz	36.32N, 6.18W	5	27 yrs bef 1961	18.0	24.9 Aug	11.4 Jan	41	-2			523
Cartagena	37.36N, 0.59W	6	1881–1901	17.2	24.6 Aug	10.7 Jan					320
Cordova	37.53N, 4.46W	100	1931–60	17.9	27.9 Jul	9.1 Jan	45	-6			664
Elche	38.15N, 0.42W	81	(see Alicante)								
Gijon	43.32N, 5.40W	9	1931–60	13.9	19.6 Jul	9.3 Jan	35	-5			1037
Granada	37.13N, 3.41W	689	25 yrs bef 1961	15.5	25.7 Jul	7.0 Jan	43	-10	38	-4	529
Hospitalet	41.22N, 2.08E	8	(see Barcelona)								
Huelva	37.16N, 6.57W	4	1931–60	18.0	25.2 Aug	11.1 Jan	43	-6			465
Jerez de la Frontera	36.41N, 6.08W	49	(see Cadiz)								
La Coruna	43.22N, 8.23W	24	1931–60	13.9	18.9 Aug	9.8 Feb	35	-3	29	1	969
Leon	42.36N, 5.34W	822	1938–60	11.0	19.7 Jul	2.8 Jan	38	-17			527
*Madrid	40.24N, 3.41W	640	1931–60	13.9	24.2 Jul	4.9 Jan	39	-10	36	-6	438
Malaga	36.43N, 4.25W	10	1931–60	18.5	25.6 Aug	12.5 Jan	41	0	38	3	469
Murcia	37.59N, 1.07W	43	1931–60	18.0	26.3 Aug	10.7 Jan	45	-10	40	-2	301
Oviedo	43.22N, 5.50W	215	45 yrs bef 1933	12.3	18.2 Aug	7.1 Jan					937
Palma	39.34N, 2.39E	33	1931–60	16.8	24.5 Aug	10.1 Jan	39	-4	35	1	451
Pamplona	42.49N, 1.38W	450	1931–60	12.3	20.2 Jul	4.6 Jan	40	-15	37	-7	1087
Sabadell	41.33N, 2.06E	188	(see Barcelona)								
Salamanca	40.58N, 5.39W	778	1931–60	11.9	21.5 Jul	3.7 Jan	40	-12	38	-9	420
San Sebastian	43.19N, 1.59W	8	1931–60	13.1	19.0 Aug	7.8 Jan	38	-12			1506
Santa Coloma de Gramanet	41.27N, 2.13E	18	(see Barcelona)								
Santander	43.28N, 3.48W	4	1931–60	13.9	19.3 Aug	9.2 Feb	40	-4	32	0	1197
Saragossa	41.38N, 0.53W	200	1931–60	14.7	23.7 Aug	6.1 Jan	42	-15	38	-6	341
Seville	37.23N, 5.59W	6	1931–60	18.8	27.9 Jul	10.5 Jan	47	-3	43	-1	535

EUROPE

City	Latitude and longitude	Elev (m)	Period of record	Temperature (°C) Avg	Avg warmest month	Avg coolest month	Absolute High	Absolute Low	Avg Annual High	Avg Annual Low	Annual Precipitation (mm)
Tarrasa	41.34N, 2.01E	277	(see Barcelona)								
Toledo	39.52N, 4.01W	527	1931–60	15.0	26.1 Jul	5.9 Jan	42	–9			376
Valencia	39.28N, 0.22W	3	1938–60	17.0	24.5 Aug	10.3 Jan	42	–7	36	–1	419
Valladolid	41.39N, 4.43W	692	1943–60	12.1	21.3 Jul	3.3 Jan	39	–13	37	–8	362
Vigo	42.14N, 8.43W	20	1931–60	15.0	19.9 Aug	10.2 Jan	39	–2			1275
Vitoria	42.51N, 2.40W	524	1931–60	11.7	19.4 Aug	4.6 Jan	39	–18			844
SWEDEN											
Goteborg	57.43N, 11.58E	31	1931–60	7.6	17.0 Jul	–1.2 Feb	32	–26	28	–14	670
Halsingborg	56.03N, 12.42E	40	(see Copenhagen, Denmark)								
Jonkoping	57.47N, 14.11E	99	1931–60	6.2	16.3 Jul	–2.9 Feb	33	–33	29	–19	536
Linkoping	58.25N, 15.37E	64	1931–60	6.8	17.7 Jul	–3.0 Feb	34	–32			528
Malmo	55.36N, 13.00E	3	1901–30	7.7	16.6 Jul	0.3 Jan					582
Norrkoping	58.36N, 16.11E	10	(see Linkoping)								
Orebro	59.17N, 15.13E	36	1931–60	5.8	16.8 Jul	–4.0 Jan	34	–30			641
*Stockholm	59.20N, 18.03E	44	1931–60	6.6	17.8 Jul	–3.1 Feb	36	–32	28	–16	555
Uppsala	59.52N, 17.38E	24	1931–60	5.8	17.3 Jul	–4.3 Feb	37	–33	30	–22	554
Vasteras	59.37N, 16.33E	18	1891–1933, 1935–44	5.7	17.4 Jul	–3.9 Jan	36	–31			526
SWITZERLAND											
Basel	47.34N, 7.36E	317	1901–60	9.2	18.4 Jul	0.2 Jan	39	–24	35	–14	794
*Bern	46.57N, 7.28E	572	1901–60	8.3	17.6 Jul	–1.2 Jan	36	–23	31	–13	1000
Geneva	46.12N, 6.10E	430	1901–60	9.2	18.3 Jul	0.2 Jan	38	–18	33	–11	933
Lausanne	46.32N, 6.39E	558	1901–60	9.4	18.5 Jul	0.4 Jan					1064
Luzern	47.03N, 8.17E	498	1901–60	8.5	17.8 Jul	–0.9 Jan					1154
Winterthur	47.30N, 8.45E	490	(see Zurich)								
Zurich	47.22N, 8.31E	469	1901–60	8.2	17.2 Jul	–1.0 Jan	37	–24	31	–13	1128

EUROPE

City	Latitude and longitude	Elev (m)	Period of record	Temperature (°C)							Annual Precipitation (mm)
				Avg	Avg warmest month	Avg coolest month	Absolute		Avg Annual		
							High	Low	High	Low	
TURKEY											
Edirne	41.40N, 26.34E	43	30 yrs bef 1961	13.4	24.6 Jul	2.0 Jan	41	-22	37	-13	609
Istanbul	41.01N, 28.58E	40	30 yrs bef 1961	13.9	23.4 Aug	5.5 Jan	38	-8	36	-5	664
UK											
Aberdeen	57.08N, 2.06W	24	1921–47	8.3	14.2 Jul	3.7 Jan	28	-11	24	-7	836
Basildon	51.34N, 0.25E	12	(see London)								
Bath	51.23N, 2.22W	20	1926–50	10.3	17.1 Jul	4.8 Jan					786
Belfast	54.36N, 5.56W	20	24 yrs bef 1963	9.3	15.4 Jul	4.4 Jan					972
Birkenhead	53.24N, 3.02W	60	1916–50	(see Liverpool for temperature data)							737
Birmingham	52.29N, 1.53W	130	1921–50	9.6	16.7 Jul	3.7 Jan	33	-12	29	-6	759
Blackburn	53.45N, 2.29W	94	(see Bolton)								
Blackpool	53.50N, 3.03W	20	1926–49	9.6	15.9 Jul	4.2 Jan					892
Bolton	53.35N, 2.26W	104	1921–50	9.2	15.7 Jul	3.6 Jan					1190
Bournemouth	50.43N, 1.54W	42	1926–50	10.5	17.1 Jul	5.2 Feb					792
Bradford	53.48N, 1.45W	134	1921–50	8.8	15.6 Jul	3.3 Jan					867
Brighton	50.49N, 0.08W	10	1926–40, 1948–50	10.7	17.2 Aug	5.1 Feb					801
Bristol	51.27N, 2.35W	118	1916–50	(see Cardiff for temperature data)							818
Cambridge	52.12N, 0.07E	12	1921–50	9.8	17.0 Jul	3.8 Jan	36	-17	30	-9	552
Cardiff	51.29N, 3.10W	62	1921–50	10.1	16.3 Jul	4.8 Jan	33	-17	28	-6	1069
Coventry	52.25N, 1.30W	73	1921–50	9.6	16.7 Jul	3.6 Jan					674
Derby	52.55N, 1.28W	64	1916–50	(see Nottingham for temperature data)							732
Dudley	52.30N, 2.05W	227	1916–50	(see Birmingham for temperature data)							728
Dundee	56.27N, 2.58W	45	1921–50	8.4	15.0 Jul	3.1 Jan					791
Edinburgh	55.57N, 3.12W	134	1921–50	8.6	14.7 Jul	3.7 Jan	28	-9	26	-6	699
Exeter	50.43N, 3.31W	34	1921–50[1]	10.3	16.1 Jul	5.7 Jan					810
Gateshead	54.58N, 1.35W	155	1921–50[2]	8.3	14.8 Jul	2.9 Jan					701

[1] Temperature data for Exmouth, nr Exeter.

[2] Temperature data for Chopwell, nr Gateshead.

EUROPE

City	Latitude and longitude	Elev (m)	Period of record	Temperature (°C) Avg	Avg warmest month	Avg coolest month	Absolute High	Absolute Low	Avg Annual High	Avg Annual Low	Annual Precipitation (mm)
Glasgow	55.51N, 4.16W	55	1921-50	8.3	14.4 Jul	3.3 Jan					973
Gloucester	51.53N, 2.14W	10	1926-50[1]	10.1	17.0 Jul	4.3 Jan					653
Grimsby	53.35N, 0.05W	4	1921-50	9.7	16.2 Jul	4.1 Jan					635
Halifax	53.44N, 1.52W	242	1916-50	(see Huddersfield for temperature data)							979
Hartlepool	54.41N, 1.13W	9	1926-50[2]	8.7	15.4 Jul	3.1 Jan					622
Havant and Waterloo	50.51N, 0.59W	8	1916-50	(see Portsmouth for temperature data)							720
Huddersfield	53.39N, 1.47W	232	1925-50	8.6	15.3 Jul	3.1 Jan					956
Hull	53.45N, 0.20W	2	1921-50	9.8	16.8 Jul	4.1 Jan					645
Ipswich	52.04N, 1.10E	58	1916-50	(see Norwich for temperature data)							620
Leeds	53.48N, 1.32W	94	1916-50	(see Bradford for temperature data)							716
Leicester	52.38N, 1.07W	72	1921-50	9.4	16.4 Jul	3.5 Jan					670
Liverpool	53.23N, 3.00W	60	1921-50	9.6	15.8 Jul	4.4 Jan	31	-9	28	-4	891
*London	51.31N, 0.05W	45	1921-50	10.3	17.6 Jul	4.3 Jan	37	-13	32	-7	610
Luton	51.53N, 0.25W	116	1921-50	9.4	16.5 Jul	3.6 Jan					638
Manchester	53.28N, 2.14W	38	1921-50	9.9	16.4 Jul	4.4 Jan					858
Newcastle upon Tyne	54.58N, 1.37W	78	1926-50[3]	8.7	15.4 Jul	3.1 Jan					703
Newport	51.35N, 3.00W	81	1921-50	10.2	17.1 Jul	4.8 Jan					1106
Northampton	52.14N, 0.54W	79	1916-50	(see Leicester for temperature data)							626
Norwich	52.38N, 1.18E	34	1921-47	9.8	17.1 Jul	3.7 Jan					650
Nottingham	52.51N, 1.08W	59	1921-50	9.7	16.8 Jul	3.9 Jan					614
Oldham	53.33N, 2.07W	168	1921-50[4]	8.9	15.7 Jul	3.2 Jan					923
Oxford	51.45N, 1.15W	63	1921-50	10.1	17.1 Jul	4.2 Jan	35	-16	31	-8	652
Paisley	55.50N, 4.26W	32	1921-50	9.2	15.6 Jul	4.0 Jan					1123
Plymouth	50.23N, 4.06W	36	1921-50	11.0	16.4 Aug	6.2 Feb	31	-9	27	-4	959
Poole	50.43N, 1.59W	6	(see Bournemouth)								

[1] Temperature data for Cheltenham, nr Gloucester.

[2] Temperature data for Houghall, nr Hartlepool.

[3] Temperature data for Houghall, nr Newcastle upon Tyne.

[4] Climatic data for Macclesfield, nr Oldham.

EUROPE

City	Latitude and longitude	Elev (m)	Period of record	Temperature (°C) Avg	Avg warmest month	Avg coolest month	Absolute High	Absolute Low	Avg Annual High	Avg Annual Low	Annual Precipitation (mm)
Portsmouth	50.48N, 1.06W	2	1926-50	11.1	17.6 Jul	5.4 Feb					706
Preston	53.46N, 2.42W	34	1921-50[1]	9.3	15.6 Jul	3.8 Jan					1003
Reading	51.28N, 0.59W	46	1921-50	10.3	17.3 Jul	4.3 Jan					653
Rochdale	53.38N, 2.09W	110	1916-50	(see Bolton for temperature data)							1123
Saint Helens	53.28N, 2.44W	46	(see Liverpool)								
Salford	53.30N, 2.16W	21	(see Manchester)								
Sheffield	53.23N, 1.28W	130	1921-50	9.6	16.4 Jul	4.0 Jan					809
Solihull	52.25N, 1.45W	128	1916-50	(see Birmingham for temperature data)							754
Southampton	50.54N, 1.23W	20	1921-50	10.6	17.1 Jul	4.9 Jan	34	-11	29	-7	804
Southend-on-Sea	51.33N, 0.43E	27	1926-40, 1946-50	10.7	18.1 Aug	4.3 Jan					537
South Shields	55.00N, 1.25W	12	1921-50[2]	9.2	15.1 Jul	4.4 Jan					676
Stockport	53.25N, 2.10W	88	(see Bolton)								
Stoke-on-Trent	53.00N, 2.11W	119	1921-50[3]	8.6	15.4 Jul	3.1 Jan					785
Sunderland	54.55N, 1.22W	66	1926-50[4]	8.7	15.4 Jul	3.1 Jan					638
Swansea	51.37N, 3.56W	10	1926-50	10.8	16.8 Jul	5.6 Feb					1071
Swindon	51.34N, 1.47W	145	1921-50[5]	9.1	15.8 Jul	3.6 Jan					737
Teesside	54.35N, 1.14W	19	1926-50[4]	8.7	15.4 Jul	3.1 Jan					600
Thurrock	51.29N, 0.20E	21	(see London)								
Torbay	50.28N, 3.30W	8	1926-50	11.1	16.8 Jul	6.2 Feb					888
Wallasey	53.26N, 3.03W	17	1925-35	10.0	16.8 Jul	4.8 Feb					
Walsall	52.35N, 1.58W	162	(see Birmingham)								

[1] Temperature data for Hutton, nr Preston.
[2] Temperature data for Tynemouth, nr South Shields.
[3] Temperature data for Mayfield, nr Stoke-on-Trent.
[4] Temperature data for Houghall, nr Sunderland and Teesside.
[5] Temperature data for Marlborough, nr Swindon.

EUROPE

City	Latitude and longitude	Elev (m)	Period of record	Temperature (°C) Avg	Avg warmest month	Avg coolest month	Absolute High	Absolute Low	Avg Annual High	Avg Annual Low	Annual Precipitation (mm)
Warley	52.30N, 1.58W	186	(see Birmingham)								
West Bromwich	52.31N, 1.59W	166	1916–50	(see Birmingham for temperature data)							724
Wolverhampton	52.36N, 2.08W	131	1916–50	(see Birmingham for temperature data)							723
York	53.57N, 1.05W	17	1921–50	9.6	16.6 Jul	3.8 Jan	32	-14	29	-7	627
USSR											
Archangel	64.34N, 40.32E	3	1881–1960	0.8	15.6 Jul	-12.5 Jan	34	-45	30	-34	494
Astrakhan	46.21N, 48.03E	-22	1881–1960	9.4	25.3 Jul	-6.8 Jan	40	-34	36	-25	175
Baku	40.23N, 49.51E	2	1891–1917, 1921–60	14.4	25.7 Jul	3.8 Jan	40	-13	36	-5	238
Belgorod	50.36N, 36.34E	184	1925–41, 1943–60	6.3	20.2 Jul	-7.6 Jan	41	-37	34	-27	
Bryansk	53.15N, 34.22E	161	1936–41, 1947–60	4.9	18.4 Jul	-8.5 Jan	38	-42	32	-30	557
Cheboksary	56.09N, 47.15E	185	1927–60	2.9	18.6 Jul	-13.0 Jan	38	-44	33	-33	
Cherepovets	59.08N, 37.54E	126	1937–60	2.6	17.3 Jul	-11.3 Jan	36	-49	30	-33	
Cherkassy	49.26N, 32.04E	94									
Chernigov	51.30N, 31.18E	135	1881–1960	6.5			39	-34			539
Chernovtsy	48.18N, 25.56E	350	1881–1960	7.8			38	-32			624
Dneprodzerzhinsk	48.30N, 34.37E		(see Dnepropetrovsk)								
Dnepropetrovsk	48.27N, 34.59E	98	1891–1911	9.2	21.7 Jul	-6.4 Jan	38	-32	35	-24	493
Donetsk	48.00N, 37.48E	201	(see Makeyevka)								
Dzerzhinsk	56.15N, 43.24E		(see Gorkiy)								
Gomel	52.25N, 31.00E	138	1928–40								614
Gorkiy	56.20N, 44.00E	162	1922–60	3.1	18.1 Jul	-12.0 Jan	37	-41	32	-31	588
Gorlovka	48.18N, 38.03E		(see Makeyevka)								
Groznyy	43.20N, 45.42E	123	1938–60	10.1	23.8 Jul	-3.6 Jan	41	-33	38	-24	489
Ivanovo	57.00N, 40.59E	128	1891–1918, 1922–48	3.3	18.5 Jul	-11.6 Jan	38	-46	32	-34	593
Izhevsk	56.51N, 53.14E	146	1933–60	2.1	18.7 Jul	-14.2 Jan	37	-46	33	-36	
Kalinin	56.52N, 35.55E	136	? yrs bef 1948	3.9	17.9 Jul	-10.0 Jan					617
Kaliningrad	54.43N, 20.30E	6	1921–50	7.2	17.7 Jul	-2.6 Feb	36	-31	32	-19	743

EUROPE

City	Latitude and longitude	Elev (m)	Period of record	Temperature (°C) Avg	Avg warmest month	Avg coolest month	Absolute High	Absolute Low	Avg Annual High	Avg Annual Low	Annual Precipitation (mm)
Kaluga	54.31N, 36.16E	202	20 yrs bef 1912	3.6	17.8 Jul	-11.1 Jan	34	-38	32	-31	582
Kaunas	54.54N, 23.54E	75	1951-60	6.3	17.8 Jul	-5.7 Feb	36	-31	32	-25	577
Kazan	55.45N, 49.08E	84	1881-1960	3.6	20.0 Jul	-12.8 Jan	39	-44	34	-33	437
Kerch	45.21N, 36.28E	4									
Kharkov	50.00N, 36.15E	125	1951-60	7.2	21.4 Jul	-7.1 Feb	37	-35	33	-28	472
Kherson	46.38N, 32.36E	18	? yrs bef 1948	9.9	23.3 Jul	-3.4 Jan	39	-32			354
Kiev	50.26N, 30.31E	134	1921-50	7.2	19.9 Jul	-6.5 Jan	39	-32	34	-24	610
Kirov	58.33N, 49.42E	166	1881-1960	1.5	17.8 Jul	-14.2 Jan	37	-45	32	-35	486
Kirovabad	40.41N, 46.22E	312	47 yrs bef 1961	13.2	25.4 Jul	1.1 Jan	40	-18	37	-10	248
Kirovograd	48.30N, 32.18E	130	1881-1960	7.5			40	-35			474
Kishinev	47.00N, 28.50E	90	1951-60	9.6	22.4 Jul	-2.6 Feb					471
Klaypeda	55.43N, 21.07E	8	1851-1900	6.8	17.4 Jul	-2.9 Jan					
Kostroma	57.46N, 40.55E	139	1925-60	2.7	17.6 Jul	-11.8 Jan	37	-46	32	-33	558
Kramatorsk	48.43N, 37.32E										
Krasnodar	45.02N, 39.00E	29	1896-1942, 1944-60	10.8	23.2 Jul	-1.8 Jan	42	-36	37	-23	638
Kremenchug	49.04N, 33.25E										
Krivoy Rog	47.55N, 33.21E	99	1883, 1885-96	9.5	24.2 Jul	-5.8 Jan	39	-29	37	-22	416
Kursk	51.42N, 36.12E	225	67 yrs bef 1961	5.4	19.3 Jul	-8.6 Jan	37	-38	32	-27	597
Kutaisi	42.15N, 42.40E	114									
Kuybyshev	53.12N, 50.09E	136	1935-60	3.8	20.7 Jul	-13.8 Jan	39	-43	35	-32	389
Leninakan	40.48N, 43.50E	1556	1926-60	5.8	19.3 Aug	-10.5 Jan	36	-41	33	-29	465
Leningrad	59.55N, 30.15E	2	1881-1960	4.3	17.8 Jul	-7.9 Feb	33	-36	30	-26	568
Lipetsk	52.37N, 39.35E	165	58 yrs bef 1961	5.1	20.2 Jul	-10.3 Jan	39	-38	34	-30	498
Lugansk	48.34N, 39.20E	59	? yrs bef 1948	7.6	22.2 Jul	-7.0 Jan					469
Lvov	49.50N, 24.00E	300	1911-30, 1941-50	7.8	18.6 Jul	-3.9 Jan	36	-34	33	-20	606
Makeyevka	48.02N, 37.58E	190	? yrs bef 1948	7.2	22.0 Jul	-7.5 Jan					439
Makhachkala	42.58N, 47.30E	-21	1882-1960	11.8	24.7 Jul	-0.4 Jan	37	-26	35	-15	430
Minsk	53.54N, 27.34E	223	1951-60	5.4	18.0 Jul	-7.0 Feb	33	-33	30	-28	568

EUROPE

City	Latitude and longitude	Elev (m)	Period of record	Temperature (°C) Avg	Avg warmest month	Avg coolest month	Absolute High	Absolute Low	Avg Annual High	Avg Annual Low	Annual Precipitation (mm)
Mogilev	53.54N, 30.21E	152	1881–1930	5.4	18.0 Jul	-7.1 Jan	35	-34			638
*Moscow	55.45N, 37.35E	167	1921–50	4.2	18.4 Jul	-10.3 Jan	38	-42	32	-28	553
Murmansk	68.58N, 33.05E	57	1951–60	0.2	12.9 Jul	-10.5 Feb					410
Nikolayev	46.58N, 32.00E	30	? yrs bef 1960	9.7	23.1 Jul	-4.0 Jan	39	-30			388
Novgorod	58.31N, 31.17E	24	70 yrs bef 1961	3.9	17.3 Jul	-8.6 Jan	34	-45	30	-31	570
Novocherkassk	47.25N, 40.06E	104	1922–36	8.6	23.2 Jul	-6.1 Jan		-32		-22	
Odessa	46.28N, 30.44E	42	1921–50	9.5	22.9 Jul	-3.2 Jan	37	-28	33	-18	374
Ordzhonikidze	43.00N, 44.40E	668	1934–35, 1938–60	7.9	19.7 Jul	-5.0 Jan	39	-34	33	-23	837
Orel	52.55N, 36.05E	203	1935–41, 1947–60	4.6	18.8 Jul	-9.2 Jan	38	-39	33	-30	
Orenburg	51.45N, 55.06E	109	1886–1960	3.9	21.9 Jul	-14.8 Jan	42	-42	37	-35	384
Orsk	51.12N, 58.34E	205	1925–60	3.0	21.3 Jul	-16.4 Jan	42	-44	37	-37	
Penza	53.13N, 45.00E	233	1887–1919, 1923–60	3.9	19.8 Jul	-12.1 Jan	38	-43	34	-31	488
Perm	58.00N, 56.15E	163	1921–50	1.8	18.1 Jul	-14.6 Jan	35	-45	31	-38	611
Petrozavodsk	61.49N, 34.20E	110	1949–63	2.2	15.9 Jul	-10.6 Jan	34	-40	28	-31	532
Podolsk	55.26N, 37.33E		(see Moscow)								
Poltava	49.35N, 34.34E	160	1881–1960	7.0			38	-37			485
Riga	56.57N, 24.06E	9	1881–1960	6.2	18.0 Jul	-4,5 Jan	35	-31	30	-21	634
Rostov-na-Donu	47.14N, 39.42E	66	1886–1960	8.7	22.9 Jul	-5.7 Jan	40	-33	36	-24	474
Ryazan	54.38N, 39.44E	156									
Rybinsk	58.03N, 38.50E	104									
Saransk	54.11N, 45.11E	70	1927–42, 1944–60	3.7	19.3 Jul	-12.1 Jan	38	-44	33	-39	
Saratov	51.34N, 46.02E	150	1936–55	5.3	22.1 Jul	-11.9 Jan	41	-41	36	-30	385
Sevastopol	44.36N, 33.32E	7	? yrs bef 1960	12.2	23.3 Jul	2.0 Jan	36	-20	34	-14	361
Shakhty	47.42N, 40.13E	117	1937–60	7.9	22.5 Jul	-6.9 Jan	40	-34	36	-25	
Simferopol	44.57N, 34.06E	204	? yrs bef 1960	10.0	21.6 Jul	-1.3 Jan	40	-29			501
Smolensk	54.47N, 32.03E	233	1951–60	4.0	17.3 Jul	-9.3 Feb	32	-33	30	-28	600
Sochi	43.35N, 39.45E	12	1916–51	13.4	22.8 Aug	4.9 Jan	39	-15	33	-7	1356
Stavropol	45.03N, 41.58E	473	1940–60	9.1	21.9 Jul	-3.7 Jan	40	-36	35	-20	663

EUROPE

City	Latitude and longitude	Elev (m)	Period of record	Temperature (°C) Avg	Avg warmest month	Avg coolest month	Absolute High	Absolute Low	Avg Annual High	Avg Annual Low	Annual Precipitation (mm)
Sterlitamak	53.37N, 55.58E	12[illegible]	? yrs bef 1950	2.6	19.9 Jul	-15.4 Jan					
Sumy	50.54N, 34.48E	13[illegible]	1881-1960	6.0			38	-36			507
Syzran	53.11N, 48.27E	5[illegible]	54 yrs bef 1961	4.4	21.3 Jul	-13.0 Jan	41	-44	36	-33	
Taganrog	47.12N, 38.56E	1[illegible]	1945-60	9.1	23.5 Jul	-5.4 Jan	38	-33	35	-24	
Tallin	59.25N, 24.45E	1[illegible]	1948-60	5.0	16.6 Jul	-5.5 Feb	33	-32	29	-22	573
Tambov	52.43N, 41.27E	14[illegible]	1927-60	4.8	20.2 Jul	-10.8 Jan	40	-39	34	-31	485
Tartu	58.23N, 26.43E	6[illegible]	1881-1960	4.8	17.3 Jul	-6.6 Feb	35	-35	30	-25	559
Tbilisi	41.42N, 44.45E	40[illegible]	1921-50	12.9	24.5 Jul	0.8 Jan	38	-18	34	-11	513
Tolyatti	53.31N, 49.20E	4[illegible]	1938-42	4.4	20.9 Jul	-12.5 Jan	40	-45	36	-32	
Tula	54.12N, 37.37E	16[illegible]	? yrs bef 1948	4.3	18.9 Jul	-10.3 Jan					559
Ufa	54.44N, 55.56E	17[illegible]	? yrs bef 1960	2.6	19.4 Jul	-14.6 Jan	37	-41	32	-35	580
Ulyanovsk	54.20N, 48.24E	17[illegible]	1937-54	3.2	19.6 Jul	-13.8 Jan	40	-48	34	-35	421
Vilnyus	54.41N, 25.19E	14[illegible]	1921-50	6.3	18.1 Jul	-5.8 Jan					659
Vinnitsa	49.14N, 28.29E	24[illegible]	1881-1960	6.7			38	-36			544
Vitebsk	55.12N, 30.11E	16[illegible]	? yrs bef 1948[1]	4.3	16.8 Jul	-8.1 Jan					682
Vladimir	56.10N, 40.25E	16[illegible]	? yrs bef 1948	3.3	18.3 Jul	-11.7 Jan					510
Volgograd	48.45N, 44.25E	2[illegible]	44 yrs bef 1943	7.6	24.3 Jul	-9.5 Jan	43	-36	38	-27	318
Vologda	59.13N, 39.54E	13[illegible]	1884–1918, 1920–60	2.4	17.2 Jul	-11.6 Jan	35	-48	31	-35	512
Voronezh	51.38N, 39.12E	14[illegible]	36 yrs bef 1961	5.4	19.9 Jul	-9.3 Jan	41	-40	34	-29	519
Yaroslavl	57.37N, 39.52E	9[illegible]	(see Kostroma)								
Yerevan	40.11N, 44.30E	91[illegible]	1935-60	11.6	25.1 Jul	-4.0 Jan	41	-31	38	-18	313
Yoshkar-Ola	56.40N, 47.55E	10[illegible]	1940-60	2.3	18.2 Jul	-13.7 Jan	38	-47	33	-38	
Zaporozhye	47.49N, 35.11E	4[illegible]	1951-60	9.2	23.1 Jul	-4.1 Feb					451
Zhdanov	47.06N, 37.33E	[illegible]	? yrs bef 1963	8.4	22.6 Jul	-5.4 Jan	38	-31			
Zhitomir	50.15N, 28.40E	18[illegible]	1881-1960	6.8			38	-35			570

[1] Climatic data for Novoye Korolevo, nr Vitebsk.

EUROPE

City	Latitude and longitude	Elev (m)	Period of record	Temperature (°C) Avg	Avg warmest month	Avg coolest month	Absolute High	Absolute Low	Avg Annual High	Avg Annual Low	Annual Precipitation (mm)
YUGOSLAVIA											
*Belgrade	44.50N, 20.30E	132	1921-30, 1941-60	11.9	22.5 Jul	0.1 Jan	42	-26	37	-16	701
Dubrovnik	42.39N, 18.07E	49	1955-64	16.4	24.7 Aug	9.0 Jan					1391
Ljubljana	46.02N, 14.30E	299	1955-64	9.7	20.6 Jul	-1.6 Jan					1387
Maribor	46.33N, 15.39E	275	1955-64	9.2	19.2 Jul	-2.1 Jan					1044
Nis	43.19N, 21.54E	202	1955-64	11.6	21.9 Aug	0.5 Jan	42	-23	38	-16	555
Novi Sad	45.15N, 19.50E	132	1955-64	11.4	21.8 Jul	-0.9 Jan					620
Osijek	45.33N, 18.42E	89	1955-64	10.7	21.2 Jul	-1.9 Jan					706
Rijeka	45.21N, 14.24E	104	1955-64	13.8	22.8 Jul	5.3 Jan					1481
Sarajevo	43.50N, 18.25E	630	1955-64	9.7	19.0 Aug	-1.3 Jan	40	-26	36	-16	925
Skopje	42.00N, 21.29E	240	1955-64	12.3	23.3 Jul	0.4 Jan	41	-24	38	-16	500
Split	43.31N, 16.26E	122	1955-64	16.2	25.4 Jul	7.7 Jan	38	-8	36	-4	828
Zagreb	45.48N, 16.00E	157	1881-1941	11.2	21.6 Jul	0.1 Jan	34	-20	33	-12	864

NORTH AMERICA

City	Latitude and longitude	Elev (m)	Period of record	Temperature (°C) Avg	Avg warmest month	Avg coolest month	Absolute High	Absolute Low	Avg Annual High	Avg Annual Low	Annual Precipitation (mm)
BAHAMA ISLANDS											
*Nassau	25.05N, 77.21W	5	1921-50	24.8	27.9 Aug	21.6 Feb	34	5	33	12	1083
BARBADOS											
*Bridgetown	13.06N, 59.37W	55	1912-48	25.8	26.9 Jun	24.4 Feb	35	16	32	18	1275
BERMUDA											
*Hamilton	32.17N, 64.46W	48	1921-50	21.5	26.9 Aug	16.7 Feb	37	4	33	8	1453

NORTH AMERICA

City	Latitude and longitude	Elev (m)	Period of record	Temperature (°C) Avg	Avg warmest month	Avg coolest month	Absolute High	Absolute Low	Avg Annual High	Avg Annual Low	Annual Precipitation (mm)
CANADA											
Calgary	51.03N, 114.05W	1045	1921-50	3.9	16.9 Jul	-9.0 Jan	36	-45	33	-36	444
Chicoutimi	48.26N, 71.06W	6	1956-68	3.2	18.6 Jul	-14.6 Jan	40	-44			890
Edmonton	53.33N, 113.28W	667	1921-50	2.7	17.2 Jul	-13.5 Jan	37	-49	32	-41	448
Halifax	44.39N, 63.36W	17	1921-50	7.0	18.3 Jul	-4.2 Jan	37	-29	32	-22	1378
Hamilton	43.15N, 79.51W	93	46 yrs bef 1947	7.8	21.7 Jul	-5.0 Jan					786
Kitchener	43.27N, 80.29W	335	23 yrs bef 1947	7.2	20.6 Jul	-6.1 Jan					792
Laval	45.33N, 73.43W	40	(see Montreal)								
London	42.59N, 81.14W	247	1921-50	7.7	20.9 Jul	-5.3 Jan	41	-33	35	-26	971
Longueuil	45.32N, 73.31W	17	(see Montreal)								
Mississauga	43.34N, 79.37W	119	(see Toronto)								
Montreal	45.30N, 73.35W	32	1921-50	6.5	21.3 Jul	-9.2 Jan	36	-34	32	-28	1062
Oshawa	43.54N, 78.51W	99	(see Toronto)								
*Ottawa	45.25N, 75.42W	87	1921-50	5.3	20.3 Jul	-11.1 Jan	39	-39	34	-31	852
Quebec	46.49N, 71.13W	40	1921-50	4.8	19.8 Jul	-11.1 Jan	36	-37	32	-31	1058
Regina	50.25N, 104.39W	575	1921-50	2.3	19.2 Jul	-16.5 Jan	44	-49	36	-41	383
Saint Catharines	43.10N, 79.15W	106	21 yrs bef 1947	8.9	21.7 Jul	-3.9 Feb					687
Saint John	45.16N, 66.03W	13	1921-50	5.6	16.6 Jul	-6.8 Jan	34	-33	28	-25	1204
Saint John's	47.33N, 52.43W	61	1921-50	5.0	15.6 Jul	-4.4 Jan	34	-29	28	-21	1348
Saskatoon	52.07N, 106.38W	480	1921-50	1.9	19.1 Jul	-17.3 Jan	40	-48	35	-41	359
Sudbury	46.30N, 81.00W	261	16 yrs bef 1947	3.9	18.9 Jul	-12.2 Jan					746
Sydney	46.09N, 60.11W	13	1921-50	6.0	18.3 Jul	-5.2 Jan	37	-32	31	-24	1285
Thunder Bay	48.25N, 89.14W	187	1921-50	2.7	17.4 Jul	-13.6 Jan	40	-41	32	-34	747
Toronto	43.39N, 79.23W	83	1921-50	8.3	21.6 Jul	-4.2 Jan	41	-33	34	-24	786
Trois-Rivieres	46.21N, 72.34W	16	15 yrs bef 1947	4.4	20.0 Jul	-12.2 Jan					1030
Vancouver	49.17N, 123.07W	12	1921-50	10.4	18.0 Jul	3.1 Jan	33	-18	30	-11	1443
Victoria	48.25N, 123.22W	17	1921-50	10.1	15.6 Jul	4.0 Jan	35	-19	30	-7	665
Windsor	42.18N, 83.01W	183	1921-50	9.3	22.8 Jul	-4.2 Jan	38	-33			828

NORTH AMERICA

City	Latitude and longitude	Elev (m)	Period of record	Temperature (°C) Avg	Avg warmest month	Avg coolest month	Absolute High	Absolute Low	Avg Annual High	Avg Annual Low	Annual Precipitation (mm)
Winnipeg	49.53N, 97.09W	231	1921-50	2.6	20.2 Jul	-17.4 Jan	42	-48	34	-39	501
COSTA RICA											
*San Jose	9.56N, 84.05W	1172	1941-60	20.3	21.4 May	19.0 Jan	33	9	31	11	1937
CUBA											
Camaguey	21.23N, 77.55W	121	1952-60	25.0	27.4 Aug	21.6 Jan			35	9	1342
Cienfuegos	22.09N, 80.27W	30	26 yrs bef 1920	24.6	26.9 Aug	21.1 Jan	35	7	34	10	973
Guantanamo	20.08N, 75.12W	23	13 yrs bef 1925	25.1	26.8 Jul	23.1 Jan					587
*Havana	23.08N, 82.22W	49	1921-50	24.9	27.4 Aug	22.2 Jan	36	10	34	12	1137
Holguin	20.53N, 76.15W		1952-60[1]	26.7	29.1 Aug	24.0 Jan			34	16	1116
Marianao	23.05N, 82.26W	50	(see Havana)								
Matanzas	23.03N, 81.35W		16 yrs bef 1925	24.3	27.4 Aug	20.7 Feb			34	12	1308
San Miguel del Padron	23.05N, 82.19W		(see Havana)								
Santa Clara	22.24N, 79.58W	115	1900-19[2]	22.9	25.4 Aug	19.7 Jan					1398
Santiago de Cuba	20.01N, 75.49W	35	16 yrs bef 1925	26.0	27.9 Aug	23.9 Jan	37	12			1112
DOMINICAN REPUBLIC											
Santiago de los Caballeros	19.27N, 70.42W	222	1951-60[3]	26.0	27.9 Sep	23.0 Jan					957
*Santo Domingo	18.28N, 69.54W	14	1921-49	25.6	26.9 Aug	23.9 Jan	37	15	35	16	1417
EL SALVADOR											
San Miguel	13.28N, 88.12W	105	1957-61	27.5	29.7 Apr	25.8 Dec	45	12	42	15	1694
*San Salvador	13.42N, 89.12W	698	1921-50	23.3	24.4 Apr	22.4 Jan	41	7	37	11	1803

[1] Climatic data for Gibara, nr Holguin.
[2] Climatic data for Camajuani, nr Santa Clara.
[3] Temperature data for San Francisco de Macoris, nr Santiago de los Caballeros.

NORTH AMERICA

City	Latitude and longitude	Elev (m)	Period of record	Temperature (°C) Avg	Avg warmest month	Avg coolest month	Absolute High	Absolute Low	Avg Annual High	Avg Annual Low	Annual Precipitation (mm)
Santa Ana	13.59N, 89.34W	645	1912–57	(see San Salvador for temperature data)							1667
GUATEMALA											
*Guatemala	14.38N, 90.31W	1502	1931–60	18.1	19.7 May	16.4 Jan	32	5	31	7	1281
HAITI											
*Port-au-Prince	18.32N, 72.20W	41	1921–50	26.6	28.3 Jul	25.1 Jan	38	16	37	17	1308
HONDURAS											
San Pedro Sula	15.27N, 88.02N	71	1952–60	26.5	28.9 May	23.4 Dec					1332
*Tegucigalpa	14.06N, 87.13W	1007	1951–60	21.3	23.0 Apr	19.1 Jan	34	7			953
JAMAICA											
*Kingston	18.00N, 76.48W	34	33 yrs bef 1944	26.4	27.5 Jul	24.7 Jan	36	14	34	17	800
MARTINIQUE											
*Fort-de-France	14.36N, 61.05W	4	1932–60	25.3	26.3 Sep	23.9 Feb	36	13	33	17	1859
MEXICO											
Acapulco	16.50N, 99.55W	4	25 yrs bef 1961	27.4	28.8 Aug	26.0 Jan	36	16			1457
Aguascalientes	21.53N, 102.18W	1888	17 yrs bef 1940	17.8	22.3 May	13.0 Jan	37	-5			666
Chihuahua	28.38N, 106.05W	1430	1941–60	18.4	27.5 Jun	10.0 Dec	38	-11			307
Ciudad Juarez	31.44N, 106.29W	1138	1921–35	16.7	27.0 Jul	5.4 Jan	41	-16			187
Ciudad Madero	22.16N, 97.50W	115	(see Tampico)								
Ciudad Obregon	27.29N, 109.56W	40	1921–35	26.5	33.7 Aug	18.2 Jan	48	-1			211
Cuernavaca	18.55N, 99.15W	1542	1921–35	20.3	23.2 May	18.4 Jan	33	7			1039
Culiacan	24.48N, 107.24W	84	24 yrs bef 1940	24.7	29.3 Jun	19.6 Jan	41	3			541
Durango	24.02N, 104.40W	1889	16 yrs bef 1940	17.4	22.7 Jun	12.0 Dec	35	-5			453

NORTH AMERICA

City	Latitude and longitude	Elev (m)	Period of record	Temperature (°C) Avg	Avg warmest month	Avg coolest month	Absolute High	Absolute Low	Avg Annual High	Avg Annual Low	Annual Precipitation (mm)
Guadalajara	20.40N, 103.20W	1567	1951-60	19.3	22.8 May	15.2 Jan	36	-4			885
Gustavo A. Madero	19.29N, 99.07W	2242	(see Mexico)								
Hermosillo	29.04N, 110.58W	237	1921-35	24.2	32.0 Jul	15.6 Dec	45	2			320
Irapuato	20.41N, 101.28W	1724	1921-35	19.3	23.1 May	14.6 Jan	38	-4			740
Jalapa	19.32N, 96.55W	1427	1921-35	17.8	20.2 May	14.5 Jan	35	2			1589
Leon	21.07N, 101.40W	1885	1931-60	19.3	23.1 May	15.2 Jan	36	-2			625
Matamoros	25.53N, 97.30W	8	1921-35	23.3	29.3 Aug	16.2 Jan	39	-5			747
Mazatlan	23.13N, 106.25W	78	1881-1911, 1921-40	23.6	28.0 Jul	18.7 Feb	34	11	32	13	758
Merida	20.58N, 89.37W	9	1931-60	25.8	27.8 May	23.0 Jan	41	11	37	13	928
Mexicali	32.40N, 115.29W	0	1921-35	22.3	32.9 Jul	11.8 Jan	48	-4			76
*Mexico	19.24N, 99.09W	2300	1931-60	15.2	17.4 May	12.3 Jan	34	-4	29	1	711
Monterrey	25.40N, 100.19W	538	1931-60	22.3	28.0 Jul	15.4 Jan	41	-5	39	-1	655
Morelia	19.42N, 101.07W	1941	33 yrs bef 1961	17.3	20.4 May	14.0 Jan	31	2			746
Netzahualcoyotl	19.36N, 99.00W	2278	1921-44	15.5	18.1 Jun	11.9 Jan	34	-8			567
Nuevo Laredo	27.30N, 99.31W	171	1921-35	24.6	32.5 Jul	14.1 Jan	45	-7			407
Oaxaca	17.03N, 96.43W	1550	1941-50	21.3	23.6 May	18.8 Dec	38	2			641
Orizaba	18.51N, 97.06W	1284	1921-35	18.4	21.0 May	15.1 Jan	37	1			2115
Poza Rica	20.33N, 97.27W	60	1921-35[1]	24.6	28.3 Jun	19.5 Jan	40	4			1382
Puebla	19.03N, 98.12W	2162	1931-60	16.7	18.9 Apr	13.6 Jan	31	-1			838
Queretaro	20.36N, 100.23W	1685	1921-35	17.8	20.3 Jun	13.9 Jan	36	-5			518
Reinosa	26.07N, 98.18W	38	(see Matamoros)								
Saltillo	25.25N, 101.00W	1599	33 yrs bef 1961	17.7	22.4 Jun	11.9 Jan	38	-10			391
San Luis Potosi	22.09N, 100.59W	1877	1921-35	17.6	21.5 May	12.9 Jan	37	-3	35	0	361
Tampico	22.13N, 97.51W	12	1951-60	24.2	28.2 Aug	19.5 Dec	39	-2			1093
Tepic	21.30N, 104.54W	915	1921-35	20.9	23.7 Jun	17.2 Jan	39	2			1196
Tijuana	32.32N, 117.01W	29	1921-35	16.5	21.4 Aug	12.6 Jan	38	-3			315
Toluca	19.17N, 99.40W	2680	1921-35	10.7	14.9 May	9.9 Jan	27	-3			791

[1] Climatic data for Tuxpan, nr Poza Rica.

NORTH AMERICA

City	Latitude and longitude	Elev (m)	Period of record	Temperature (°C) Avg	Avg warmest month	Avg coolest month	Absolute High	Absolute Low	Avg Annual High	Avg Annual Low	Annual Precipitation (mm)
Torreon	25.33N, 103.26W	1130	1951-60	22.5	28.8 Jun	14.6 Dec					165
Veracruz	19.12N, 96.08W	3	1921-35	24.8	27.3 Jun	21.2 Jan	36	10	34	13	1623
Villahermosa	17.59N, 92.55W	10	1921-35	26.0	28.4 Aug	22.2 Jan	41	12			1918
NETHERLANDS ANTILLES											
*Willemstad	12.06N, 68.57W	23	1937-46	27.7	29.1 Sep	26.3 Jan	36	17	34	21	454
NICARAGUA											
*Managua	12.09N, 86.17W	56	1953-60	26.9	28.3 May	25.7 Jan					1207
PANAMA											
*Panama	8.57N, 79.32W	36	1951-60[1]	26.9	28.3 Apr	26.1 Oct	36	17	34	19	1903
PUERTO RICO											
Bayamon	18.24N, 66.09W	23	(see San Juan)								
Ponce	18.01N, 66.37W	12	34 yrs bef 1951	25.9	27.5 Aug	24.0 Feb					902
*San Juan	18.28N, 66.07W	14	1931-60	25.7	27.1 Aug	23.9 Jan	36	17	33	18	1533
TRINIDAD AND TOBAGO											
*Port of Spain	10.39N, 61.31W	20	1881-1940	25.6	26.6 May	24.4 Feb	38	11	35	17	1603
USA											
Abilene	32.28N, 99.43W	524	1931-60	17.9	28.4 Jul	7.0 Jan	44	-23	39	-11	592
Akron	41.05N, 81.31W	266	1931-60	9.6	21.9 Jul	-2.7 Jan	40	-29			925
Albany (Georgia)	31.34N, 84.09W	56	1931-60	19.9	28.1 Jul	11.4 Jan	41	-19			1215
Albany (New York)	42.39N, 73.45W	6	1931-60	8.7	22.3 Jul	-5.2 Jan	40	-32	36	-24	891

[1] Climatic data for Balboa Heights, Canal Zone, nr Panama.

NORTH AMERICA

City	Latitude and longitude	Elev (m)	Period of record	Temperature (°C) Avg	Avg warmest month	Avg coolest month	Absolute High	Absolute Low	Avg Annual High	Avg Annual Low	Annual Precipitation (mm)
Albuquerque	35.05N 106.39W	1507	1931-60	13.7	25.8 Jul	1.7 Jan	39	-22			206
Alexandria	38.48N, 77.03W	14	(see Washington)								
Allentown	40.36N, 75.28W	78	1931-60	10.6	23.4 Jul	-1.7 Jan	39	-24			1121
Altoona	40.31N, 78.24W	360	1931-60	9.8	21.6 Jul	-1.9 Jan					1113
Amarillo	35.12N, 101.50W	1123	1931-60	14.8	27.0 Jul	2.6 Jan	42	-27	39	-18	500
Anaheim	33.50N, 117.55W	50	(see Santa Ana, USA)								
Anchorage	61.13N, 149.53W	36	1931-60	1.8	13.9 Jul	-10.9 Jan	33	-39	27	-36	374
Anderson	40.10N, 85.41W	266	1931-60	11.9	24.2 Jul	-0.8 Jan					943
Ann Arbor	42.17N, 83.45W	268	1931-60[1]	10.0	23.4 Jul	-3.0 Jan	38	-25			779
Appleton	44.16N, 88.25W	220	1931-60	7.6	22.3 Jul	-7.6 Jan					735
Arlington (Texas)	32.44N, 97.07W	188	(see Fort Worth)								
Arlington (Virginia)	38.53N, 77.07W	61	(see Washington)								
Asheville	35.36N, 82.33W	605	1931-60	13.6	23.6 Jul	4.3 Jan	37	-22			962
Atlanta	33.45N, 84.24W	320	1931-60	16.4	26.0 Jul	6.7 Dec	39	-23	36	-9	1197
Atlantic City	39.22N, 74.26W	3	1931-60	12.3	23.9 Jul	1.5 Feb	40	-23			1076
Augusta	33.28N, 81.58W	44	1931-60	17.8	27.0 Jul	8.6 Jan	41	-16			995
Aurora	41.45N, 88.19W	194	1931-60	9.7	23.2 Jul	-4.3 Jan					859
Austin	30.16N, 97.45W	154	1931-60	20.2	29.2 Jul	10.2 Jan	43	-19	39	-6	828
Bakersfield	35.22N, 119.01W	128	1931-60	18.4	29.0 Jul	8.6 Jan	48	-11			162
Baltimore	39.17N, 76.37W	6	1931-60	14.2	26.2 Jul	2.9 Jan	42	-22	37	-14	1123
Baton Rouge	30.27N, 91.11W	17	1931-60	19.8	27.6 Jul	11.3 Jan	43	-17			1383
Bay City	43.36N, 83.53W	181	1931-60	9.2	22.8 Jul	-3.9 Jan	43	-32			679
Beaumont	30.05N, 94.06W	6	1931-60	20.7	29.1 Jul	12.4 Jan					1379
Berkeley	37.52N, 122.16W	12	1931-60	13.9	17.4 Sep	9.5 Jan					568
Billings	45.47N, 108.30W	951	1931-60	8.6	22.9 Jul	-4.9 Jan	44	-45			336
Biloxi	30.24N, 88.53W	7	1931-60	20.1	27.7 Jul	12.0 Jan					1488

[1] Climatic data for Willow Run, nr Ann Arbor.

NORTH AMERICA

City	Latitude and longitude	Elev (m)	Period of record	Temperature (°C) Avg	Avg warmest month	Avg coolest month	Absolute High	Absolute Low	Avg Annual High	Avg Annual Low	Annual Precipitation (mm)
Binghampton	42.06N, 75.55W	264	1931-60	9.3	22.1 Jul	-3.1 Jan	39	-33			932
Birmingham	33.31N, 86.49W	183	1931-60	17.8	27.6 Jul	8.1 Jan	42	-23	37	-11	1347
Bismarck	46.48N, 100.47W	509	1931-60	5.7	22.1 Jul	-12.3 Jan	46	-43	38	-36	385
Bloomington	39.10N, 86.32W	229	1931-60	12.9	25.3 Jul	0.7 Jan					1117
Boise City	43.37N, 116.12W	824	1931-60	10.6	24.0 Jul	-1.6 Jan	45	-33	40	-19	290
Boston	42.21N, 71.03W	6	1931-60	10.8	23.2 Jul	-1.2 Jan	40	-28			1086
Boulder	40.01N, 105.17W	1655	1931-60	11.0	23.1 Jul	0.4 Jan					472
Bridgeport	41.11N, 73.11W	3	1931-60	10.8	23.2 Jul	-1.1 Jan	39	-29			1140
Bristol	41.40N, 72.57W	73	(see Hartford)								
Brockton	42.05N, 71.01W	40	1931-60[1]	9.8	21.9 Jul	-1.9 Jan					1040
Brownsville	25.54N, 97.30W	17	1931-60	23.2	28.9 Aug	16.3 Jan	40	-11	37	-2	679
Buffalo	42.53N, 78.52W	178	1931-60	8.2	21.0 Jul	-4.4 Feb	37	-29			905
Burbank	34.11N, 118.19W	171	1931-60	17.6	23.2 Jul	12.0 Jan	44	-6			428
Burlington	44.29N, 73.13W	34	1931-60	6.2	20.6 Jul	-8.8 Jan	38	-34			844
Cambridge	42.22N, 71.06W	6	(see Boston)								
Camden	39.57N, 75.07W	9	(see Philadelphia)								
Canton	40.48N, 81.23W	314	(see Akron)								
Casper	42.51N, 106.19W	1561	1931-60	7.8	22.1 Jul	-4.8 Jan	40	-40			300
Cedar Rapids	41.58N, 91.40W	223	1931-60	9.6	23.8 Jul	-5.8 Jan					847
Champaign	40.07N, 88.15W	226	1931-60[2]	11.5	24.6 Jul	-1.8 Jan	43	-32			940
Charleston (South Carolina)	32.47N, 79.56W	3	1931-60	18.3	26.7 Jul	10.1 Jan	40	-14	37	-6	1249
Charleston (West Virginia)	38.21N, 81.38W	183	1931-60	13.1	23.8 Jul	2.6 Jan	42	-27	37	-17	1129
Charlotte	35.13N, 80.51W	219	1931-60	16.0	26.2 Jul	5.9 Dec	40	-21			1102
Chattanooga	35.03N, 85.19W	206	1931-60	15.7	26.2 Jul	5.3 Jan	41	-23			1320
Cheyenne	41.08N, 104.49W	1859	1931-60	7.7	21.1 Jul	-3.7 Jan	38	-39	33	-28	383

[1] Temperature data for Taunton, nr Brockton.

[2] Climatic data for Urbana, nr Champaign.

NORTH AMERICA

City	Latitude and longitude	Elev (m)	Period of record	Temperature (°C) Avg	Avg warmest month	Avg coolest month	Absolute High	Absolute Low	Avg Annual High	Avg Annual Low	Annual Precipitation (mm)
Chicago	41.52N, 87.38W	181	1931-60	10.4	24.2 Jul	-3.3 Jan	41	-31	35	-23	843
Cincinnati	39.06N, 84.31W	168	1931-60	13.8	26.0 Jul	1.9 Jan	43	-27			1004
Cleveland	41.30N, 81.42W	201	1931-60	9.6	21.9 Jul	-2.4 Jan	39	-28			898
Colorado Springs	38.50N, 104.49W	1823	1931-60	9.2	21.3 Jul	-1.9 Jan	37	-29			335
Columbia (Missouri)	38.57N, 92.20W	228	1931-60	12.8	25.9 Jul	-0.9 Jan	45	-31			939
Columbia (South Carolina)	34.00N, 81.02W	58	1931-60	17.8	27.6 Jul	8.0 Dec	42	-19	38	-9	1189
Columbus (Georgia)	32.28N, 84.59W	81	1931-60	18.0	27.2 Jul	8.8 Jan	40	-16			1236
Columbus (Ohio)	39.58N, 83.00W	238	1931-60	11.1	23.8 Jul	-0.6 Jan	41	-29	36	-21	931
Corpus Christi	27.48N, 97.24W	11	1931-60	22.1	28.9 Jul	14.1 Jan	41	-12			720
Dallas	32.47N, 96.48W	133	1931-60	18.8	29.4 Aug	7.7 Jan	43	-19	39	-11	878
Davenport	41.31N, 90.35W	180	1931-60	10.7	24.9 Jul	-4.6 Jan	44	-33			861
Dayton	39.46N, 84.12W	227	1931-60	11.3	24.0 Jul	-1.4 Jan	41	-27			915
Dearborn	42.19N, 83.10W	184	(see Detroit)								
Decatur	39.51N, 88.57W	208	1931-60	12.3	25.3 Jul	-1.2 Jan					943
Denver	39.45N, 104.59W	1609	1931-60	9.7	22.7 Jul	-1.9 Jan	41	-34			376
Des Moines	41.35N, 93.37W	245	1931-60	10.1	25.3 Jul	-6.2 Jan	43	-34	38	-26	771
Detroit	42.20N, 83.03W	178	1931-60	10.1	23.6 Jul	-2.8 Jan	41	-31	34	-21	786
Downey	33.56N, 118.07W	36	1931-60	(see Los Angeles for temperature data)							369
Dubuque	42.30N, 90.40W	187	1931-60	8.1	22.6 Jul	-7.1 Jan	43	-36			907
Duluth	46.47N, 92.06W	186	1931-60	3.3	18.6 Jul	-12.9 Jan	41	-41	33	-33	736
Durham	36.00N, 78.55W	123	1931-60	15.5	25.8 Jul	5.7 Jan					1083
East Los Angeles	34.01N, 118.09W	85	(see Los Angeles)								
Elgin	42.02N, 88.17W	219	1931-60	(see Aurora for temperature data)							867
Elizabeth	40.40N, 74.13W	6	1931-60	12.4	24.3 Jul	0.4 Jan					1228
El Paso	31.46N, 106.29W	1126	1931-60	17.4	27.7 Jul	6.1 Jan	41	-22	39	-10	200
Erie	42.07N, 80.05W	209	1931-60	9.3	21.7 Jul	-2.7 Jan	37	-27			952
Eugene	44.03N, 123.05W	129	1931-60	11.4	19.2 Jul	3.9 Jan	41	-20			1005
Evansville	37.58N, 87.34W	117	1931-60	13.9	25.9 Jul	1.2 Jan	42	-28			1053

NORTH AMERICA

City	Latitude and longitude	Elev (m)	Period of record	Temperature (°C) Avg	Avg warmest month	Avg coolest month	Absolute High	Absolute Low	Avg Annual High	Avg Annual Low	Annual Precipitation (mm)
Fall River	41.42N, 71.09W	12	1931-30	10.4	22.6 Jul	-1.3 Jan					1150
Fargo	46.52N, 96.47W	274	1931-60	5.1	21.9 Jul	-13.8 Jan	46	-44			469
Fayetteville	35.03N, 78.53W	30	1931-60	16.9	26.8 Jul	7.0 Dec					1180
Fitchburg	42.35N, 71.48W	140	1931-60	9.4	22.4 Jul	-3.4 Jan					1162
Flint	43.01N, 83.42W	218	1931-60	8.5	21.9 Jul	-4.7 Jan	36	-30			763
Fort Lauderdale	26.07N, 80.08W	2	1931-60	24.1	28.1 Aug	19.9 Jan					1531
Fort Smith	35.23N, 94.25W	129	1931-60	16.6	28.3 Jul	4.3 Jan	45	-26			1072
Fort Wayne	41.04N, 85.08W	241	1931-60	10.1	23.4 Jul	-3.1 Jan	41	-31			897
Fort Worth	32.45N, 97.20W	204	1931-60	18.8	29.7 Jul	7.4 Jan	44	-22			796
Fremont	37.32N, 121.57W	15	(see Oakland)								
Fresno	36.44N, 119.47W	87	1931-60	16.9	27.0 Jul	7.5 Jan	46	-8	43	-3	283
Gainesville	29.40N, 82.20W	56	16 yrs bef 1961	21.2	27.3 Jul	14.4 Jan	40	-14			1332
Galveston	29.18N, 94.48W	2	1931-60	21.1	28.4 Jul	12.7 Jan	38	-13			1062
Garden Grove	33.46N, 117.55W	23	(see Long Beach)								
Gary	41.36N, 87.20W	180	(see Chicago)								
Glendale	34.08N, 118.15W	175	(see Burbank)								
Grand Forks	47.55N, 97.03W	253	1931-60	4.1	21.4 Jul	-15.3 Jan					511
Grand Rapids	42.58N, 85.40W	183	1931-60	8.8	22.4 Jul	-4.2 Jan	42	-31			792
Great Falls	47.30N, 111.17W	1015	1931-60	7.1	20.8 Jul	-5.5 Jan	41	-38			357
Green Bay	44.31N, 88.01W	180	1931-60	6.8	21.4 Jul	-8.4 Jan	40	-38			656
Greensboro	36.04N, 79.47W	253	1931-60	14.6	25.2 Jul	4.3 Jan	40	-22			1071
Greenville	34.51N, 82.24W	294	1931-60	16.1	25.7 Jul	6.3 Jan	39	-16			1210
Hamilton	39.24N, 84.34W	183	1931-60	12.4	24.6 Jul	0.6 Jan					986
Hammond	41.38N, 87.30W	180	(see Chicago)								
Hampton	37.01N, 76.20W	1	1931-60	15.4	26.1 Jul	5.3 Jan					1066
Harrisburg	40.16N, 76.53W	111	1931-60	11.8	24.2 Jul	-0.2 Jan	40	-26			956
Hartford	41.46N, 72.41W	12	1931-60	9.9	22.7 Jul	-2.6 Jan	38	-32			1090
Hayward	37.40N, 122.05W	35	(see Oakland)								

NORTH AMERICA

City	Latitude and longitude	Elev (m)	Period of record	Temperature (°C) Avg	Avg warmest month	Avg coolest month	Absolute High	Absolute Low	Avg Annual High	Avg Annual Low	Annual Precipitation (mm)
Hialeah	25.50N, 80.17W	2	(see Miami)								
High Point	35.57N, 80.00W	287	1931–60	(see Greensboro for temperature data)							1161
Hollywood	26.01N, 80.09W	3	(see Fort Lauderdale)								
Hot Springs	34.30N, 93.03W	183	1931–60	17.7	28.3 Aug	6.8 Jan	42				1409
Houston	29.45N, 95.22W	12	1931–60	21.1	28.9 Aug	12.6 Jan	42	−15	38	−6	1150
Huntington	38.25N, 82.27W	172	1931–60	13.2	23.9 Jul	2.6 Jan	39	−26			1004
Huntington Beach	33.40N, 118.05W	11	(see Long Beach)								
Huntsville	34.44N, 86.35W	194	1931–60	16.7	27.3 Jul	6.4 Jan	38	−20			1236
Independence	39.06N, 94.25W	320	[see Kansas City (Missouri)]								
Indianapolis	39.46N, 86.10W	216	1931–60	11.2	24.0 Jul	−1.6 Jan	41	−32	36	−22	997
Inglewood	33.58N, 118.21W	43	(see Los Angeles)								
Irving	32.49N, 96.56W	143	(see Dallas)								
Jackson (Michigan)	42.15N, 84.24W	287	1931–60	9.3	22.4 Jul	−3.8 Jan	41	−28			791
Jackson (Mississippi)	32.18N, 90.11W	91	1931–60	18.4	27.6 Jul	8.9 Jan	42	−21			1253
Jacksonville	30.20N, 81.40W	6	1931–60	20.8	28.1 Jul	13.3 Jan	43	−12	36	−4	1355
Jersey City	40.44N, 74.04W	6	1931–60	12.2	24.1 Jul	0.3 Jan					1107
Johnstown	40.20N, 78.55W	361	(see Altoona)								
Joliet	41.32N, 88.05W	185	1942–49	9.6	23.1 Jul	−4.6 Jan	38	−29			900
Kalamazoo	42.17N, 85.35W	230	1927–56	9.8	23.1 Jul	−3.5 Jan	43	−27			883
Kansas City (Kansas)	39.07N, 94.38W	229	[see Kansas City (Missouri)]								
Kansas City (Missouri)	39.05N, 94.35W	229	1931–60	13.8	27.5 Jul	−0.2 Jan	43	−30	37	−21	865
Kenosha	42.36N, 87.50W	186	(see Racine)								
Knoxville	35.58N, 83.55W	271	1931–60	15.3	26.0 Jul	4.9 Jan	40	−27			1165
La Crosse	43.48N, 91.15W	198	1931–60	7.9	23.2 Jul	−8.6 Jan	42	−42			791
Lafayette (Indiana)	40.25N, 86.54W	168	1931–60[1]	10.8	23.7 Jul	−2.2 Jan					960

[1] Climatic data for Frankfort, nr Lafayette.

NORTH AMERICA

City	Latitude and longitude	Elev (m)	Period of record	Temperature (°C) Avg	Avg warmest month	Avg coolest month	Absolute High	Absolute Low	Avg Annual High	Avg Annual Low	Annual Precipitation (mm)
Lafayette (Louisiana)	30.13N, 92.01W	12	1931-60	20.2	27.9 Jul	12.0 Jan					1485
Lake Charles	30.14N, 93.13W	5	1931-60	20.3	28.2 Jul	11.8 Jan	41	-16			1423
Lakewood	39.44N, 105.05W	1632	(see Denver)								
Lancaster	40.02N, 76.18W	108	1931-60	11.4	23.6 Jul	-0.2 Jan	40	-28			1100
Lansing	42.44N, 84.33W	253	1931-60	8.7	22.0 Jul	-4.3 Jan	39	-32			792
Laredo	27.30N, 99.30W	134	1931-60	23.3	30.8 Jul	14.3 Jan	46	-15			473
Las Vegas	36.10N, 115.09W	619	1931-60	18.9	32.3 Jul	6.4 Jan	47	-13	43	-8	99
Lawrence	42.42N, 71.10W	20	1931-60	9.5	22.4 Jul	-3.3 Jan					1040
Lawton	34.37N, 98.25W	339	1931-60	17.1	28.7 Jul	4.8 Jan					767
Lewiston	44.06N, 70.13W	60	1931-60	7.6	21.1 Jul	-6.3 Jan					1107
Lexington	38.03N, 84.30W	291	1931-60	13.1	25.2 Jul	1.4 Jan	42	-29			1136
Lima	40.45N, 84.06W	264	1931-60	10.8	23.4 Jul	-1.7 Jan	39	-27			925
Lincoln	40.49N, 96.42W	351	1931-60	11.6	26.7 Jul	-3.8 Jan	46	-34	39	-26	697
Little Rock	34.45N, 92.17W	91	1931-60	16.5	27.7 Jul	4.8 Jan	43	-24	32	-12	1236
Livonia	42.23N, 83.22W	202	(see Detroit)								
Long Beach	33.46N, 118.11W	11	1931-60	16.9	22.2 Jul	11.3 Jan	44	-4			250
Lorain	41.28N, 82.11W	186	(see Cleveland)								
Los Angeles	34.03N, 118.14W	104	1931-60	18.0	22.8 Jul	13.2 Jan	43	-2	38	2	373
Louisville	38.15N, 85.46W	137	1931-60	13.2	25.3 Jul	1.7 Jan	42	-29	37	-18	1050
Lowell	42.38N, 71.19W	30	1931-60	10.0	23.1 Jul	-2.9 Jan					1101
Lubbock	33.35N, 101.51W	974	1931-60	15.4	26.3 Jul	4.0 Jan	42	-27			459
Lynchburg	37.25N, 79.09W	158	1931-60	13.7	24.6 Jul	3.1 Jan	41	-22			1024
Lynn	42.28N, 70.57W	10	(see Boston)								
Macon	32.50N, 83.38W	102	1931-60	18.7	27.7 Jul	9.6 Jan	41	-15			1120
Madison	43.04N, 89.23W	262	1931-60	7.2	21.7 Jul	-8.1 Jan	42	-34	34	-28	766
Manchester	42.59N, 71.28W	53	1931-60	8.2	21.2 Jul	-4.6 Jan					1078
Mansfield	40.45N, 82.31W	351	1931-60	9.5	22.1 Jul	-2.6 Jan	35	-29			969
Memphis	35.09N, 90.03W	84	1931-60	16.4	27.4 Jul	5.3 Jan	41	-25			1263

NORTH AMERICA

City	Latitude and longitude	Elev (m)	Period of record	Temperature (°C) Avg	Avg warmest month	Avg coolest month	Absolute High	Absolute Low	Avg Annual High	Avg Annual Low	Annual Precipitation (mm)
Meriden	41.32N, 72.47W	46	(see Hartford)								
Metairie	29.58N, 90.09W	2	(see New Orleans)								
Miami	25.47N, 80.12W	3	1931-60	23.9	27.9 Aug	19.4 Jan	37	-3	33	4	1518
Miami Beach	25.47N, 80.08W	2	1931-60	24.6	27.9 Jul	20.6 Jan	37	-1			1175
Milwaukee	43.02N, 87.54W	194	1931-60	7.3	20.4 Jul	-6.3 Jan	41	-32			750
Minneapolis	44.59N, 93.16W	248	1931-60	6.5	22.4 Jul	-10.9 Jan	42	-41	37	-29	629
Mobile	30.42N, 88.03W	2	1931-60	20.1	28.1 Jul	11.7 Jan	39	-18	37	-5	1731
Modesto	37.39N, 121.00W	27	1931-60	15.8	24.6 Jul	7.2 Jan					309
Monroe	32.30N, 92.07W	23	1931-60[1]	18.9	28.2 Jul	9.4 Jan					1300
Montgomery	32.23N, 86.19W	49	1931-60	18.3	27.7 Jul	8.9 Jan	42	-21	37	-8	1288
Muncie	40.11N, 85.23W	290	1931-60	(see Anderson for temperature data)							997
Muskegon	43.14N, 86.16W	190	1931-60	9.0	21.8 Jul	-3.3 Jan	37	-34			764
Nashua	42.45N, 71.28W	46	1931-60	8.3	21.3 Jul	-4.6 Jan					1074
Nashville	36.10N, 86.47W	137	1931-60	15.6	26.8 Jul	4.4 Jan	42	-26	37	-16	1147
Newark	40.44N, 74.10W	17	1931-60	12.1	24.6 Jul	0.1 Jan	41	-26			1077
New Bedford	41.38N, 70.56W	5	1931-60	10.8	22.2 Jul	-0.2 Jan					1043
New Britain	41.40N, 72.47W	61	(see Hartford)								
New Haven	41.18N, 72.55W	12	1931-60	10.1	22.2 Jul	-1.3 Jan	38	-26			1169
New Orleans	29.57N, 90.04W	2	1931-60	20.8	28.1 Jul	13.1 Jan	39	-14	36	-3	1599
Newport	41.29N, 71.19W	3	1931-60[2]	10.1	20.9 Jul	0.1 Jan	35	-23			1027
Newport News	36.59N, 76.25W	7	(see Norfolk)								
Newton	42.21N, 71.12W	10	(see Boston)								
New York	40.45N, 74.00W	17	1931-60	12.5	24.9 Jul	0.7 Jan	41	-26	37	-17	1076
Niagara Falls	43.06N, 79.03W	174	(see Buffalo)								
Norfolk	36.51N, 76.17W	3	1931-60	15.4	26.0 Jul	5.1 Jan	41	-17	36	-10	1141

[1] Climatic data for Calhoun, nr Monroe.

[2] Climatic data for Block Island, nr Newport.

NORTH AMERICA

City	Latitude and longitude	Elev (m)	Period of record	Temperature (°C) Avg	Avg warmest month	Avg coolest month	Absolute High	Absolute Low	Avg Annual High	Avg Annual Low	Annual Precipitation (mm)
Norwalk (California)	33.54N, 118.05W	28	(see Los Angeles)								
Norwalk (Connecticut)	41.07N, 73.22W	18	(see Bridgeport)								
Norwich	41.31N, 72.05W	11	(see New Haven)								
Oakland	37.48N, 122.16W	8	1931–60	14.2	18.4 Sep	8.9 Jan	42	-5			455
Odessa	31.51N, 102.22W	881	1931–60[1]	17.9	28.3 Jul	6.7 Jan	43	-18			362
Ogden	41.14N, 111.58W	1309	1931–60	10.4	24.2 Jul	-2.9 Jan					418
Oklahoma City	35.28N, 97.31W	364	1931–60	15.7	28.2 Aug	2.8 Jan	45	-27	40	-15	783
Omaha	41.16N, 95.56W	317	1931–60	10.8	25.8 Jul	-5.4 Jan	46	-36	38	-25	700
Orlando	28.33N, 81.23W	21	1931–60	21.9	27.4 Jul	15.7 Jan	39	-7			1305
Oshkosh	44.01N, 88.33W	232	1931–60	7.7	22.4 Jul	-7.4 Jan					721
Oxnard	34.12N, 119.10W	15	1931–60	15.2	18.4 Aug	11.8 Jan					375
Parma	41.23N, 81.43W	258	(see Cleveland)								
Pasadena	34.09N, 118.09W	253	1931–60	17.3	23.2 Aug	11.6 Jan					531
Paterson	40.55N, 74.10W	30	1931–60	12.0	24.3 Jul	-0.2 Jan					1240
Pensacola	30.25N, 87.13W	5	1931–60	20.0	27.2 Jul	12.2 Jan	39	-14	35	-5	1565
Peoria	40.42N, 89.36W	143	1931–60	10.8	24.4 Jul	-3.5 Jan	45	-33			885
Petersburg	37.14N, 77.24W	27	1931–60[2]	15.6	26.2 Jul	5.3 Jan					1109
Philadelphia	39.57N, 75.09W	30	1931–60	11.9	24.2 Jul	0.2 Jan	41	-24	36	-15	1079
Phoenix	33.27N, 112.04W	332	1931–60	20.6	32.1 Jul	9.8 Jan	48	-9	46	-2	183
Pittsburgh	40.26N, 80.00W	227	1931–60	10.2	22.3 Jul	-1.7 Jan	39	-29	35	-18	918
Pittsfield	42.27N, 73.15W	309	1931–60	7.2	19.9 Jul	-5.7 Jan	35	-32			1128
Pocatello	42.52N, 112.27W	1361	1931–60	8.3	22.4 Jul	-5.4 Jan	41	-35			276
Pomona	34.04N, 117.45W	262	1931–60	16.4	23.4 Jul	9.8 Jan	47	-6			452
Port Arthur	29.54N, 93.56W	3	1931–60	20.3	27.7 Jul	12.0 Jan	42	-10			1348
Portland (Maine)	43.40N, 70.15W	8	1931–60	7.2	20.1 Jul	-5.7 Jan	39	-39			1088

[1] Climatic data for Midland, nr Odessa.

[2] Climatic data for Hopewell, nr Petersburg.

NORTH AMERICA

City	Latitude and longitude	Elev (m)	Period of record	Temperature (°C) Avg	Avg warmest month	Avg coolest month	Absolute High	Absolute Low	Avg Annual High	Avg Annual Low	Annual Precipitation (mm)
Portland (Oregon)	45.31N, 122.41W	23	1931-60	12.6	20.3 Jul	4.6 Jan	42	-19	35	-9	1076
Portsmouth	36.50N, 76.18W	3	(see Norfolk)								
Providence	41.50N, 71.25W	24	1931-60	10.1	22.3 Jul	-1.6 Jan	39	-27			1070
Provo	40.14N, 111.39W	1387	1931-60	(see Salt Lake City for temperature data)							327
Pueblo	38.16N, 104.37W	1430	1931-60	11.5	24.7 Jul	-1.1 Jan	41	-35	37	-26	301
Quincy	42.15N, 71.00W	13	(see Boston)								
Racine	42.44N, 87.47W	192	1931-60	9.2	22.7 Jul	-4.2 Jan					824
Raleigh	35.47N, 78.38W	111	1931-60	15.3	25.5 Jul	5.3 Jan	41	-19			1107
Rapid City	44.05N, 103.14W	985	1931-60	8.5	23.2 Jul	-4.8 Jan	43	-37			374
Reading	40.20N, 75.56W	81	1931-60	12.4	24.9 Jul	0.4 Jan	41	-26			1052
Reno	39.31N, 119.49W	1369	1931-60	9.1	19.8 Jul	-0.9 Jan	41	-28			182
Richmond	37.32N, 77.26W	49	1931-60	14.5	25.6 Jul	3.7 Jan	42	-24	37	-12	1123
Riverside	33.59N, 117.22W	259	1931-60	17.3	24.4 Jul	10.7 Jan	48	-7			280
Roanoke	37.16N, 79.57W	276	1931-60	13.8	24.8 Jul	3.4 Jan	41	-24			1047
Rochester	43.10N, 77.36W	157	1931-60	8.9	22.0 Jul	-3.8 Jan	39	-30			800
Rockford	42.17N, 89.06W	218	1931-60	9.2	23.4 Jul	-5.6 Jan	39	-29			905
Sacramento	38.35N, 121.30W	9	1931-60	15.9	23.3 Jul	8.0 Jan	46	-8	40	-2	458
Saginaw	43.26N, 83.56W	181	1931-60	8.4	22.0 Jul	-4.8 Feb	44	-28			721
Saint Augustine	29.53N, 81.19W	2	(see Jacksonville)								
Saint Joseph	39.46N, 94.51W	259	1931-60	12.1	26.3 Jul	-2.7 Jan	43	-31			868
Saint Louis	38.38N, 90.12W	139	1931-60	12.9	25.6 Jul	-0.1 Jan	44	-30	37	-22	897
Saint Paul	44.57N, 93.06W	238	79 yrs bef 1950	6.9	22.6 Jul	-10.7 Jan	42	-41			689
Saint Petersburg	27.46N, 82.38W	6	1931-60	23.3	28.3 Aug	17.4 Jan					1407
Salem (Massachusetts)	42.31N, 70.53W	4	(see Boston)								
Salem (Oregon)	44.56N, 123.02W	50	1931-60	11.3	19.5 Jul	3.9 Jan	42	-23			1060
Salinas	36.40N, 121.39W	13	1931-60	14.0	17.6 Sep	9.8 Jan	43	-8			359
Salt Lake City	40.45N, 111.53W	1338	1931-60	10.5	24.9 Jul	-2.7 Jan	42	-29	39	-18	353
San Antonio	29.26N, 98.29W	198	1931-60	20.4	28.8 Jul	11.1 Jan	42	-18			707

NORTH AMERICA

City	Latitude and longitude	Elev (m)	Period of record	Temperature (°C) Avg	Avg warmest month	Avg coolest month	Absolute High	Absolute Low	Avg Annual High	Avg Annual Low	Annual Precipitation (mm)
San Bernardino	34.06N, 117.17W	329	1931–60	17.1	25.3 Jul	10.8 Jan	47	–8			450
San Diego	32.43N, 117.09W	6	1931–60	17.2	21.5 Aug	13.1 Jan	44	–4	33	2	264
San Francisco	37.47N, 122.25W	20	1931–60	13.8	16.7 Sep	10.4 Jan	41	–7	32	3	528
San Jose	37.20N, 121.53W	27	1931–60	15.2	20.1 Jul	9.6 Jan	40	–6	37	–3	333
Santa Ana	33.46N, 117.52W	41	1931–60	17.0	22.4 Aug	11.7 Jan	44	–6			370
Santa Barbara	34.25N, 119.42W	30	1931–60	15.7	19.5 Jul	11.4 Jan	46	–7			449
Santa Fe	35.41N, 105.56W	2118	1931–60	9.9	21.4 Jul	–1.2 Jan	36	–25	31	–18	350
Santa Monica	34.01N, 118.29W	30	(see Los Angeles)								
Santa Rosa	38.26N, 122.43W	46	1931–60	15.3	19.3 Jul	8.1 Jan	44	–9			745
Savannah	32.05N, 81.06W	6	1931–60	19.1	27.4 Jul	10.9 Jan	41	–13			1242
Scranton	41.25N, 75.40W	221	1931–60	9.3	21.9 Jul	–3.0 Jan	39	–28	36	–19	977
Seaside	36.37N, 121.50W	6	(see Salinas)								
Seattle	47.37N, 122.20W	3	1931–60	11.8	18.7 Jul	5.1 Jan	38	–16	32	–6	866
Shreveport	32.31N, 93.45W	62	1931–60	18.8	28.4 Jul	8.6 Jan	43	–21			1176
Sioux City	42.30N, 96.24W	338	1931–60	9.5	25.2 Jul	–7.4 Jan	44	–37	37	–28	629
Sioux Falls	43.33N, 96.44W	425	1931–60	7.6	23.5 Jul	–9.3 Jan	43	–41			639
Somerville	42.23N, 71.06W	12	(see Boston)								
South Bend	41.41N, 86.15W	216	1931–60	9.7	23.1 Jul	–3.6 Jan	43	–30			907
Spokane	47.40N, 117.26W	576	1931–60	8.8	21.4 Jul	–3.7 Jan	42	–34	37	–22	437
Springfield (Illinois)	39.48N, 89.39W	186	1931–60	12.0	25.6 Jul	–2.0 Jan	44	–31			885
Springfield (Massachusetts)	42.06N, 72.36W	26	1931–60	10.7	23.3 Jul	–1.9 Jan					1146
Springfield (Missouri)	37.13N, 93.18W	396	1931–60	13.6	25.9 Jul	0.9 Jan	41	–34	36	–21	1043
Springfield (Ohio)	39.56N, 83.48W	299	[see Columbus (Ohio)]								
Stamford	41.03N, 73.32W	11	(see Bridgeport)								
Steubenville	40.22N, 80.37W	201	(see Wheeling)								
Stockton	37.57N, 121.17W	6	1931–60	16.3	25.6 Jul	7.1 Jan	45	–7			340
Sunnyvale	37.23N, 122.02W	40	(see San Jose)								
Syracuse	43.03N, 76.09W	122	1931–60	8.9	22.3 Jul	–4.4 Jan	39	–32			955

NORTH AMERICA

City	Latitude and longitude	Elev (m)	Period of record	Temperature (°C) Avg	Avg warmest month	Avg coolest month	Absolute High	Absolute Low	Avg Annual High	Avg Annual Low	Annual Precipitation (mm)
Tacoma	47.15N, 122.26W	34	1931-60	10.4	17.7 Jul	3.5 Jan	37	-14	32	-8	989
Tallahassee	30.27N, 84.17W	66	1931-60	20.0	27.4 Jul	12.2 Jan	40	-17			1444
Tampa	27.57N, 82.27W	5	1931-60	22.3	27.5 Jul	16.2 Jan	37	-8	35	-1	1310
Terre Haute	39.28N, 87.24W	151	1931-60	12.4	25.2 Jul	-0.5 Jan	43	-28			1043
Toledo	41.39N, 83.33W	178	1931-60	9.4	22.6 Jul	-3.2 Jan	41	-27			775
Topeka	39.03N, 95.40W	283	1931-60	12.7	26.6 Jul	-1.8 Jan	46	-32			822
Torrance	33.49N, 118.18W	23	1931-60	16.1	20.3 Aug	11.7 Jan					319
Trenton	40.13N, 74.46W	11	1931-60	12.2	24.4 Jul	0.6 Jan	41	-26			1049
Tucson	32.13N, 110.58W	728	1931-60	19.7	30.0 Jul	9.6 Jan	44	-9			279
Tulsa	36.09N, 96.00W	245	1931-60	15.7	27.8 Jul	2.9 Jan	46	-27			942
Tuscaloosa	33.12N, 87.34W	52	1931-60	17.9	27.6 Jul	8.3 Jan					1332
Utica	43.06N, 75.14W	126	1931-60[1]	7.7	21.2 Jul	-6.1 Jan					1049
Virginia Beach	36.51N, 75.58W	4	(see Norfolk)								
Waco	31.33N, 97.08W	123	1931-60	19.6	29.6 Jul	8.9 Jan	44	-21			815
Warren	42.30N, 83.02W	189	(see Detroit)								
*Washington	38.54N, 77.01W	8	1931-60	13.9	25.7 Jul	2.7 Jan	41	-26	37	-16	1036
Waterbury	41.33N, 73.03W	79	(see Hartford)								
Waterloo	42.30N, 92.20W	259	1931-60	8.4	23.2 Jul	-7.9 Jan	37	-37			800
West Palm Beach	26.43N, 80.03W	5	1931-60	24.1	28.1 Jul	19.4 Jan	37	-1			1567
Wheeling	40.04N, 80.43W	198	1931-60	11.6	23.7 Jul	0.0 Jan					981
Wichita	37.41N, 97.20W	393	1931-60	13.9	27.2 Jul	0.0 Jan	46	-30			722
Wichita Falls	33.55N, 98.29W	288	1931-60	18.1	29.8 Jul	5.9 Jan	45	-24			665
Wilkes-Barre	41.15N, 75.53W	195	(see Scranton)								
Williamsburg	37.16N, 76.42W	25	1931-60[2]	15.6	26.2 Jul	5.3 Jan					1109
Wilmington (Delaware)	39.45N, 75.33W	41	1931-60	12.3	24.4 Jul	0.8 Jan	39	-20			1132

[1] Climatic data for Little Falls, nr Utica.

[2] Climatic data for Hopewell, nr Williamsburg.

NORTH AMERICA

City	Latitude and longitude	Elev (m)	Period of record	Temperature (°C) Avg	Avg warmest month	Avg coolest month	Absolute High	Absolute Low	Avg Annual High	Avg Annual Low	Annual Precipitation (mm)
Wilmington (North Carolina)	34.14N, 77.55W	10	1931-60	17.7	26.7 Jul	8.8 Jan	40	-15			1303
Winston-Salem	36.06N, 80.15W	262	1931-60	15.1	25.6 Jul	4.8 Jan	38	-17			1121
Woodbridge	40.34N, 74.17W	5	1931-60[1]	11.8	23.9 Jul	0.2 Jan	37	-24			1117
Worcester	42.16N, 71.48W	145	1931-60	8.2	20.9 Jul	-4.4 Jan	34	-28			1153
Yonkers	40.56N, 73.54W	3	(see New York)								
York	39.58N, 76.44W	113	1931-60	12.2	24.3 Jul	0.4 Jan					1067
Youngstown	41.06N, 80.39W	256	1931-60	9.7	21.7 Jul	-2.1 Jan	38	-28			997
VIRGIN ISLANDS (USA)											
*Charlotte Amalie	18.21N, 64.56W	5	1931-60	26.8	28.3 Aug	24.8 Feb					1137

OCEANIA

City	Latitude and longitude	Elev (m)	Period of record	Temperature (°C) Avg	Avg warmest month	Avg coolest month	Absolute High	Absolute Low	Avg Annual High	Avg Annual Low	Annual Precipitation (mm)
AUSTRALIA											
Adelaide	34.56S, 138.36E	43	109 yrs bef 1967	17.1	23.1 Jan	11.1 Jul	48	0	43	2	530
Brisbane	27.30S, 153.01E	41	79 yrs bef 1967	20.4	24.9 Jan	14.8 Jul	43	2	38	4	1135
*Canberra	35.20S, 149.10E	581	38 yrs bef 1967	13.4	20.6 Jan	6.0 Jul	42	-8	37	-6	644
Geelong	38.09S, 144.21E	17	1911-40	14.4	19.5 Feb	9.6 Jul	44	-3			542
Hobart	42.55S, 147.20E	54	1921-50	12.3	16.4 Feb	8.1 Jul	41	-2	36	-1	631
Melbourne	37.50S, 145.00E	35	110 yrs bef 1967	14.7	19.8 Jan	9.4 Jul	46	-3	41	-1	659
Newcastle	32.55S, 151.45E	32	1911-40	18.0	22.3 Jan	12.5 Jul	44	3			1051
Perth	31.56S, 115.50E	64	69 yrs bef 1967	18.1	23.7 Feb	13.0 Jul	45	1	41	3	886

[1] Climatic data for New Brunswick, nr Woodbridge.

OCEANIA

City	Latitude and longitude	Elev (m)	Period of record	Temperature (°C) Avg	Avg warmest month	Avg coolest month	Absolute High	Absolute Low	Avg Annual High	Avg Annual Low	Annual Precipitation (mm)
Sydney	33.53S, 151.12E	42	107 yrs bef 1967	17.4	22.0 Jan	11.8 Jul	45	2	38	4	1212
Wollongong	34.25S, 150.54E	46	1911–40	17.2	21.6 Feb	12.4 Jul	46	1			1119
FIJI											
*Suva	18.08S, 178.25E	9	1921–50	25.1	26.9 Feb	23.1 Jul	37	13	34	16	3160
FRENCH POLYNESIA											
*Papeete	17.32S, 149.34W	2	1941–60	26.2	27.5 Mar	24.8 Jul	35	16	34	18	1844
(HAWAII), USA											
Hilo	19.43N, 155.05W	18	23 yrs bef 1970	22.8	24.3 Aug	21.6 Jan	34	12			3470
*Honolulu	21.19N, 157.52W	6	1931–60	24.4	26.3 Aug	22.4 Feb	32	11	30	15	556
NEW CALEDONIA											
*Noumea	22.16S, 166.27E	3	1941–60	23.1	26.4 Feb	19.9 Jul	37	11	34	13	1083
NEW ZEALAND											
Auckland	36.51S, 174.45E	49	1931–60	15.3	19.2 Jan	10.8 Jul	32	1	27	3	1242
Christchurch	43.35S, 172.36E	7	1931–60	11.4	16.4 Jan	5.8 Jul	36	–6	31	–4	668
Dunedin	45.52S, 170.30E	2	1931–60	10.9	15.3 Jan	6.4 Jul	34	–5	29	–2	787
*Wellington	41.28S, 174.51E	126	1931–60	12.4	16.9 Jan	8.6 Jul	31	–2	27	0	1206
PAPUA											
*Port Moresby	9.29S, 147.08E	28	1941–60	26.9	27.7 Dec	25.8 Jul	37	18	35	21	1162
WESTERN SAMOA											
*Apia	13.50S, 171.44W	2	1921–50	26.4	26.7 Jan	25.8 Jul	34	17	32	19	2928

SOUTH AMERICA

City	Latitude and longitude	Elev (m)	Period of record	Temperature (°C) Avg	Avg warmest month	Avg coolest month	Absolute High	Absolute Low	Avg Annual High	Avg Annual Low	Annual Precipitation (mm)
ARGENTINA											
Almirante Brown	34.48S, 58.23W	25	(see Buenos Aires)								
Avellaneda	34.39S, 58.23W	7	(see Buenos Aires)								
Bahia Blanca	38.43S, 62.17W	20	1901-50	15.5	23.7 Jan	7.9 Jul	43	-8	39	-5	540
*Buenos Aires	34.36S, 58.27W	25	1901-50	16.5	23.5 Jan	10.0 Jul	43	-5	37	-3	981
Cordoba	31.24S, 64.11W	442	1901-50	17.2	24.0 Jan	10.3 Jul	46	-10	41	-6	690
Lanus	34.43S, 58.24W	10	(see Buenos Aires)								
La Plata	34.55S, 57.57W	18	1941-50	16.1	22.4 Jan	9.6 Jul	33	-5			996
Lomas de Zamora	34.46S, 58.24W	21	(see Buenos Aires)								
Mar del Plata	38.00S, 57.33W	24	1901-50	13.7	19.7 Jan	8.1 Jul	41	-7			783
Mendoza	32.53S, 68.49W	769	1901-50	15.6	23.5 Jan	7.4 Jun	43	-9	39	-5	197
Merlo	34.40S, 58.45W	17	(see Buenos Aires)								
Parana	31.44S, 60.32W	74	1941-50	18.0	25.1 Jan	11.4 Jul	45	-6	39	-1	951
Quilmes	34.44S, 58.16W	19	(see Buenos Aires)								
Rosario	32.57S, 60.40W	26	1901-50	17.9	24.7 Jan	10.9 Jun	44	-11	39	-4	925
Salta	24.47S, 65.25W	1182	1901-50	17.4	21.9 Dec	11.3 Jul	39	-10			691
San Isidro	34.27S, 58.30W	23	(see Buenos Aires)								
San Justo	34.40S, 58.33W	27	(see Buenos Aires)								
San Martin	34.34S, 58.32W	21	(see Buenos Aires)								
San Miguel	34.33S, 58.43W	48	1941-50	16.3	23.2 Jan	9.6 Jul	40	-8			939
Santa Fe	31.38S, 60.42W	37	1941-50[1]	18.1	24.5 Jan	11.3 Jul	44	-7			874
Seis de Septiembre	34.39S, 58.37W	23	(see Buenos Aires)								
Tres de Febrero	34.36S, 58.33W	26	(see Buenos Aires)								
Tucuman	26.49S, 65.13W	422	1901-50	19.2	25.0 Jan	12.3 Jul	48	-7			954
Vicente Lopez	34.32S, 58.28W	19	1941-50	16.7	22.9 Jan	10.2 Jul	34	-7			896

[1] Temperature data for Angel Gallardo, nr Santa Fe.

SOUTH AMERICA

City	Latitude and longitude	Elev (m)	Period of record	Temperature (°C) Avg	Avg warmest month	Avg coolest month	Absolute High	Absolute Low	Avg Annual High	Avg Annual Low	Annual Precipitation (mm)
BOLIVIA											
Cochabamba	17.24S, 66.09W	2557	1941-60	17.1	19.4 Nov	13.7 Jun					516
*La Paz	16.30S, 68.09W	3630	1921-50	10.0	11.9 Nov	7.5 Jul	27	-3	24	-2	557
*Sucre	19.02S, 65.17W	2844	5 yrs bef 1953	12.2	14.4 Nov	9.4 Jul	31	-4	31	-1	706
BRAZIL											
Aracaju	10.55S, 37.04W	5	1911-19	26.2	27.3 Feb	24.8 Jul	36	17	32	18	947
Belem	1.27S, 48.29W	14	1893-1910	25.9	26.6 Nov	25.2 Feb	37	18	34	19	2187
Belo Horizonte	19.55S, 43.56W	830	1954-62	21.0	22.8 Feb	18.1 Jun	36	2	34	9	1426
*Brasilia	15.47S, 47.55W	1161	1961-65	20.8	22.6 Sep	17.8 Jun	34	6	33	8	1626
Campina Grande	7.13S, 35.53W	550	1923-24, 1937	22.7	24.5 Jan	20.0 Jul			35	14	895
Campinas	22.54S, 47.05W	693	? yrs bef 1919	19.8	22.4 Jan	16.1 Jun	37	0			1398
Campos	21.45S, 41.18W	14	1912-19	22.6	25.5 Feb	19.9 Jul	39	7			1083
Curitiba	25.25S, 49.15W	950	1921-50	16.2	19.8 Jan	12.2. Jul	37	-9	32	0	1452
Duque de Caxias	22.47S, 43.18W	4	(see Rio de Janeiro)								
Feira de Santana	12.15S, 38.57W	250									
Florianopolis	27.35S, 48.34W	2	14 yrs bef 1965	20.7	24.8 Jan	16.5 Jul	36	1	33	7	1186
Fortaleza	3.43S, 38.30W	25	1954-62	27.1	27.6 Jan	26.5 Jul	32	19	32	20	1138
Goiania	16.40S, 49.16W	760	1958-65	22.9	25.1 Sep	19.8 Jun	39	2	36	6	1401
Guarulhos	23.29S, 46.31W	760	(see Sao Paulo)								
Jaboatao	8.07S, 35.01W	45	(see Recife)								
Joao Pessoa	7.07S, 34.53W	45	1912-19	25.2	26.1 Dec	23.5 Jul	35	17			1763
Juiz de Fora	21.45S, 43.20W	676	1893-1922	19.5	23.3 Feb	15.5 Jul	37	1			1471
Londrina	23.18S, 51.09W	600	1932-56	20.6	23.8 Jan	16.8 Jun	40	0			1440
Maceio	9.40S, 35.43W	5	1956-65	25.8	27.3 Feb	24.2 Aug	34	17	32	19	1606
Manaus	3.08S, 60.01W	60	1910-29, 1931-40	26.9	27.9 Sep	26.3 Jan	38	18	36	19	1811
Natal	5.47S, 35.13W	3	1904-21	26.1	27.2 Jan	24.4 Jul	33	15	32	18	1377
Niteroi	22.53S, 43.07W	2	1954-63	24.0	27.1 Jan	20.7 Jun	40	9	39	11	1133

SOUTH AMERICA

City	Latitude and longitude	Elev (m)	Period of record	Temperature (°C) Avg	Avg warmest month	Avg coolest month	Absolute High	Absolute Low	Avg Annual High	Avg Annual Low	Annual Precipitation (mm)
Nova Iguacu	22.45S, 43.27W	26	(see Rio de Janeiro)								
Olinda	8.01S, 34.51W	30	1941–60	25.8	27.2 Feb	23.9 Aug	33	18	32	19	1733
Osasco	23.32S, 46.46W	721	(see Sao Paulo)								
Pelotas	31.46S, 52.20W	7	1912–19	17.7	23.1 Feb	12.3 Jun	39	−2			1322
Petropolis	22.31S, 43.10W	8[illegible]3	1913–19	18.2	21.2 Jan	15.3 Jul	33	0			2122
Porto Alegre	30.04S, 51.11W	4	22 yrs bef 1924	19.4	25.3 Feb	14.2 Jun	41	−4	38	0	1247
Recife	8.03S, 34.54W	55	1901–33	26.4	27.5 Jan	24.2 Jul	34	18	32	19	1610
Ribeirao Preto	21.10S, 47.48W	5[illegible]8	1901–17	21.2	23.9 Feb	17.0 Aug	40	−1			1400
Rio de Janeiro	22.54S, 43.14W	31	1921–50	22.9	25.8 Feb	20.2 Jul	39	10	36	13	1021
Salvador	12.59S, 38.31W	8	1931–50	24.7	26.3 Feb	22.8 Jul	35	17	33	18	1932
Santo Andre	23.40S, 46.31W	743	(see Sao Paulo)								
Santos	23.57S, 46.20W	4	1895–1917	21.9	25.5 Feb	18.9 Aug	42	5	38	9	2084
Sao Bernardo do Campo	23.42S, 46.33W	764	(see Sao Paulo)								
Sao Goncalo	22.51S, 43.04W	[illegible]3	(see Rio de Janeiro)								
Sao Joao de Meriti	22.48S, 43.22W	[illegible]1	(see Rio de Janeiro)								
Sao Luis	2.31S, 44.16W	4	13 yrs bef 1963	26.5	27.2 Oct	26.1 Apr	35	19	33	21	1881
Sao Paulo	23.32S, 46.37W	820	1921–50	18.1	21.1 Feb	14.5 Jul	35	1	34	4	1382
Teresina	5.05S, 42.49W	65	1956–65	28.1	30.4 Oct	26.5 Mar	40	16	39	17	1269
Vitoria	20.19S, 40.21W	3	1928–32, 1934–58	24.0	27.2 Feb	22.1 Jul	38	10	35	14	1296
CHILE											
Concepcion	36.50S, 73.03W	13	? yrs bef 1950	13.5	17 Jan	10 Jul			32	1	1310
*Santiago	33.27S, 70.40W	520	1921–50	14.1	20.4 Jan	7.9 Jul	37	−5	33	−3	353
Valparaiso	33.02S, 71.38W	41	22 yrs bef 1933	14.3	17.3 Jan	11.4 Jul	34	2	30	4	532
Vina del Mar	33.02S, 71.34W		(see Valparaiso)								
COLOMBIA											
Barranquilla	10.59N, 74.48W	5	1942–53, 1957–61	27.8			42	13	37	18	744

SOUTH AMERICA

City	Latitude and longitude	Elev (m)	Period of record	Temperature (°C) Avg	Avg warmest month	Avg coolest month	Absolute High	Absolute Low	Avg Annual High	Avg Annual Low	Annual Precipitation (mm)
*Bogota	4.36N, 74.05W	2644	1941-60	14.0	14.9 Apr	13.8 Aug	25	0	24	2	903
Bucaramanga	7.08N, 73.09W	925	1946-48, 1950-61	23.3			39	14	32	17	1268
Cali	3.27N, 76.31W	1046	1942-49, 1952-59	23.8			35	14	32	17	1120
Cartagena	10.25N, 75.32W	0	1942-50, 1952-61	27.1			41	13	34	20	840
Cucuta	7.54N, 72.31W	294	1942-54, 1958-61	27.3			39	11	35	21	446
Ibague	4.27N, 75.14W	1249	1941-47, 1949-59, 1961	21.9			35	7	33	13	2053
Manizales	5.04N, 75.37W	2140	1942, 1944-52	18.1			29	7	27	11	2055
Medellin	6.15N, 75.35W	1541	1942-55, 1957-61	21.5			39	7	33	10	1310
Pereira	4.49N, 75.43W	1424	1942, 1944, 1946-53	21.8			36	8	31	12	2054
ECUADOR											
Guayaquil	2.10S, 79.50W	3	1951-60	25.3	26.6 Apr	24.0 Jul	37	14	36	16	1022
*Quito	0.13S, 78.30W	2819	1921-50	13.2	13.4 Sep	13.1 Jun	30	0	27	2	1226
GUYANA											
*Georgetown	6.49N, 58.10W	2	1887-1940	27.0	27.8 Sep	26.3 Jan	34	20	32	21	2221
PARAGUAY											
*Asuncion	25.16S, 57.40W	64	1921-50	23.7	28.9 Jan	17.6 Jul	43	-2	41	2	1266
PERU											
Arequipa	16.24S, 71.33W	2304	1896-1911, 1921-25	14.6	14.9 Sep	14.2 Jul	27	-1			109
Callao	12.04S, 77.09W	6	9 yrs bef 1956[1]	19.6	23.1 Feb	16.5 Aug					12
Cuzco	13.31S, 71.59W	3399	1931-43	12.8	14.4 Nov	10.3 Jul	29	-9	28	-5	813
*Lima	12.03S, 77.03W	154	1931-60	18.4	22.4 Feb	15.1 Aug	34	9	32	11	31

[1] Climatic data for La Punta, nr Callao.

SOUTH AMERICA

City	Latitude and longitude	Elev (m)	Period of record	Temperature (°C) Avg	Avg warmest month	Avg coolest month	Absolute High	Absolute Low	Avg Annual High	Avg Annual Low	Annual Precipitation (mm)
SURINAM											
*Paramaribo	5.50N, 55.13W	4	1931–50	27.3	28.6 Oct	26.4 Jan	37	17	35	19	2258
URUGUAY											
*Montevideo	34.53S, 56.11W	22	1888–1941	16.1	22.5 Jan	10.3 Jul	43	–4	33	2	950
VENEZUELA											
Barquisimeto	10.04N, 69.19W	56[illegible]	1951–60	23.8	24.6 Apr	23.1 Jan	36	15			509
*Caracas	10.30N, 66.55W	92[illegible]	1941–60	20.8	21.7 May	19.0 Jan	33	7	31	9	835
Maracaibo	10.40N, 71.37W	[illegible]	1938–46, 1951–60	28.0	29.1 Aug	26.9 Jan	39	19	37	21	475
Maracay	10.15N, 67.36W	44[illegible]	1951–60	24.6	26.2 Apr	23.3 Jan					914
Valencia	10.11N, 68.00W	47[illegible]	1937–46	24.6	25.6 Apr	24.0 Jan	38	17			1151

TABULAR GAZETTEER 2. CITIES, BY CONTINENT AND COUNTRY

Part IV. Supplemental Information

AFRICA

Algeria

*Algiers: [b] alt Alger; off Jazair. [c] B of Algiers of Mediterranean Sea. [d] Universite d'Alger (1859) 9 – 600? [e] Bibliotheque Nationale (1835) 650; Bibliotheque de l'Universite . . . (1879) 600.

Annaba: [b] for Bone. [c] Mediterranean Sea. [d] none. [e] Bibliotheque Municipale (?) 20.

Constantine: [b] off Qusantina. [c] Rummel R. [d] Universite de Constantine (1961) ? – 118. [e] Bibliotheque Municipale (1862) 35.

Oran: [b] off Ouahran. [c] Mediterranean Sea. [d] Universite d'Oran (1965) ? – ?. [e] Bibliotheque Municipale (1861) 32.

Angola

*Luanda: [b] for Loanda, Sao Paulo de Loanda. [c] Atlantic O. [d] Universidade de Luanda (1962) 2 – 220. [e] Biblioteca Municipal (?) 18; Biblioteca Nacional de Angola (1938) 10.

Burundi

*Bujumbura: [b] for Usumbura. [c] Tanganyika L. [d] Universite Officielle de Bujumbura (1960) 0.3 – 62. [e] Bibliotheque de l'Universite . . . (1960) 29; Bibliotheque Publique (?) 26. [f] 100s (1970e).

Cameroon

Douala: [b] alt Duala. [c] Wouri R. [d] none. [e] Bibliotheque du Centre IFAN du Cameroun (?) 5.

*Yaounde: [b] alt Yaunde. [c] none. [d] Universite Federale du Cameroun (1962) 3 – 248. [e] Bibliotheque de l'Universite . . .- (1962?) 23; Bibliotheque Nationale du Cameroun (?) 10. [f] 166s (1969e).

(Canary Islands), Spain

*Las Palmas: [a] Gran Canaria I. [b] alt Las Palmas de Gran Canaria, Palmas. [c] Atlantic O. [d] none. [e] Biblioteca del Museo Canario (1879) 40; Biblioteca Publica (?) ?

Santa Cruz de Tenerife: [a] Tenerife I. [b] none. [c] Atlantic O. [d] Universidad de La Laguna (at La Laguna, nr Santa Cruz de Tenerife) (1701) 2 – 125. [e] Biblioteca de la Universidad . . . (at La Laguna, nr Santa Cruz de Tenerife) (1701) 61; Biblioteca Municipal (?) ?

Central African Republic

*Bangui: [b] none. [c] Ubangi R. [d] Jean-Bedel Bokassa Universite de Bangui (1970) 0.07 – 9. [e] Bibliotheque Nationale (bef 1966) ?

Chad

*Fort-Lamy: [b] none. [c] Shari R; Logone R. [d] none. [e] Bibliotheque du Centre de Documentation Pedagogique (1962) 2; Bibliotheque de l'Ecole Nationale d'Administration (1963?)?

Congo

*Brazzaville: [b] none. [c] Congo R. [d] none. [e] Bibliotheque du Centre d'Enseignement Superieur (1959) 32; Bibliotheque Publique (1950) 15.

Dahomey

*Cotonou: [b] for Kotonu. [c] G of Guinea of Atlantic O. [d] none. [e] Bibliotheque du Service des Travaux Publiques (?) ?

*Porto-Novo: [b] none. [c] Porto-Novo Lagoon. [d] Universite du Dahomey (1962) 0.5 – ?. [e] Bibliotheque Nationale (1961) 7.

Egypt

Alexandria: [b] off Iskandariyah. [c] Mediterranean Sea; Mareotis (off Maryut) L. [d] University of Alexandria (1942) 34 – 2604 [Alexandria campus: (1942) ? – ?]. [e] University . . . Library (1942) 1000; Municipal Library (1892) 90. [f] 1801 (1966), 227 (1882).

Aswan: [b] alt Assuan. [c] Nile R. [d] none. [f] 128 (1966).

Asyut: [b] alt Assiut; for Siut. [c] Nile R. [d] University of Asyut (1957) 11 – 380. [e] University . . . Library (1957) 60. [f] 154 (1966), 31 (1882).

*Cairo: [b] off Qahirah. [c] Nile R. [d] Ain Shams University (1950) 37 – 1079; Al-Azhar University (970) 21 – 705; American University in Cairo (1919) 1 – 166. [e] Egyptian National Library (alt Dar-ul-Kutub) (1870) 1000; Bibliotheque de l'Institut d'Egypte (1859) 180. [f] 4220 (1966), 375 (1882).

Giza: [b] alt Gizeh; inc Imbabah since 1960; off Jizah. [c] Nile R. [d] University of Cairo (1908) 45 – 2892 [Giza campus: (1908) ? – ?]. [e] University . . . Library (1908) 800. [f] 571 (1966), 11 (1882); Imbabah: 136 (1960), 1 (1947?)

Luxor: [b] off Uqsur. [c] Nile R. [d] none.

Mahalla al Kubra: [b] for Mehallet el Kebir. [c] nr Damietta (off Dumyat) R (Nile R distributary). [d] none. [f] 225 (1966).

Mansurah: [b] alt Mansura. [c] Damietta (off Dumyat) R (Nile R distributary). [d] University of Cairo, Mansurah campus (1960) ? – ? [e] Municipal Library (?) 22. [f] 191 (1966), 27 (1882).

Port Said: [b] off Bur Said. [c] Mediterranean Sea; Manzala Lagoon. [d] none. [f] 283 (1966), 17 (1882).

Shubra al Khaymah: [b] alt Shubra el-Kheima. [c] Nile R. [d] none. [f] 173 (1966).

Suez: [b] off Suways. [c] G of Suez of Red Sea. [d] none. [f] 264 (1966), 11 (1882).

Tanta: [b] none. [c] nr Rosetta (off Rashid) R (Nile R distributary). [d] University of Alexandria, Tanta campus (1963) ? – ? [e] Municipal Library (?) 23. [f] 230 (1966), 34 (1882).

Zagazig: [b] off Zaqaziq. [c] none. [d] none. [e] Sharqiyah Provincial Council Library (?) 15. [f] 151 (1966).

Ethiopia

*Addis Ababa: [b] none. [c] nr Akaki R. [d] Haile Selassie I University (1950) 5 – 581. [e] . . . University Library (1950) 247; National Library of Ethiopia (1944) 90.

Asmara: [a] *Eritrea. [b] none. [c] nr Anseba R. [d] University of Asmara (1958) 1 – 107. [e] University . . . Library (1958?) 32; Public Library (1955) 5.

Gabon

*Libreville: [b] none. [c] G of Guinea of Atlantic O; Gabon (for Gabun) R. [d] none. [e] Bibliotheque du Centre d'Information (1960) 10.

Gambia

*Bathurst: [b] none. [c] Atlantic O; Gambia R. [d] none. [e] British Council Library (1946) 20.

Ghana

*Accra: [b] for Akkra. [c] G of Guinea of Atlantic O. [d] University of Ghana (1927) 3 – 456. [e] Ghana Library Board (1950) 800; Balme Library (alt University . . . Library) (1948) 247.

Kumasi: [b] for Coomassie. [c] none. [d] University of Science and Technology (1951) 1 – 250. [e] University . . . Library (1951) 69; Ashanti Regional Library of the Ghana Library Board (?) 40.

Guinea

*Conakry: [b] for Konakry. [c] Atlantic O. [d] none. [e] Bibliotheque de l'Institut Polytechnique de Conakry (1963) 18; Bibliotheque Nationale (1960) 10. [f] 112s (1960).

Ivory Coast

*Abidjan: [b] none. [c] Ebrie Lagoon. [d] Universite d'Abidjan (1959) 3 – 174? [e] Bibliotheque Municipale (?) 50; Bibliotheque de l'Universite . . . (1963) 30; Bibliotheque Centrale de la Cote d'Ivoire (1963) 14; Bibliotheque Nationale (1968) 7.

Kenya

Mombasa: [b] alt Mvita. [c] Indian O. [d] none. [e] Seif Bin Salim Public Library (1903) 18.

*Nairobi: [b] none. [c] Nairobi R; Mathari R. [d] University of Nairobi (1956) 2 – 201. [e] McMillan Memorial Library. (1931) 120; University . . . Library (1956) 95.

Liberia

*Monrovia: [b] none. [c] Atlantic O. [d] University of Liberia (1862) 1 – 110. [e] University . . . Library (1862) 40; Government Public Library (1959) 20.

Libya

*Bengasi: [a] *Cyrenaica. [b] alt Benghazi; off Banghazi. [c] Mediterranean Sea. [d] University of Libya (1956) 4 – 309 [Bengasi campus: (1956) 2 – 93]. [e] University . . . Library (1955) 77; Public Library (1955) 11.

*Tripoli: [a] *Tripolitania. [b] off Tarabulus. [c] Mediterranean Sea. [d] University of Libya, Tripoli campus (1957) 1 – 216. [e] Public Library (1917) 35; UAR Cultural Center Library (1955) 26.

(Madeira Islands), Portugal

*Funchal: [a] Madeira I. [b] none. [c] Atlantic O. [d] none. [e] Biblioteca Municipal (1838) 35.

Malagasy Republic

*Tananarive: [b] alt Antananarivo. [c] Ikopa R; Anosy L. [d] Universite de Madagascar (1955) 4 – 213? [e] Bibliotheque Nationale (1961) 123; Bibliotheque Universitaire (1960) 85.

Malawi

Blantyre: [b] inc Limbe since 1949. [c] Mudi R. [d] University of Malawi (1962) 1 – 140. [e] British Council Library (1951) 20. [f] Limbe: 9 (1949e).

Mali

*Bamako: [b] none. [c] Niger R. [d] none. [e] Centre Francais de Documentation (1962) 10; Bibliotheque Nationale (1913) 8; Bibliotheque Municipale (1949)?

Timbuktu: [b] off Tombouctou. [c] nr Niger R. [d] none. [e] Centre de Documentation Arabe (1966) ?

Mauritius

*Port Louis: [b] none. [c] Indian O. [d] University of Mauritius (at Reduit, nr Port Louis) (1965) 2 – 33. [e] Mauritius Institute Public Library (1902) 50; Municipal Library (1875) 40. [f] 120s (1962).

Morocco

Casablanca: [b] off Dar al Baida. [c] Atlantic O. [d] none. [e] Bibliotheque Municipale (?) ?

Fez: [b] alt Fes; off Fas. [c] Fez (alt Fes; off Fas) R. [d] Universite Qarawiyine (859) 0.9 – 60? [e] Bibliotheque de l'Universite .. (11 th c) 20; Bibliotheque Publique (?)?

Marrakesh: [b] alt Marrakech; for Morocco; off Marrakush. [c] Issil R. [d] Universite Ben Youssef de Marrakech (14th c) 1 – ? [e] Bibliotheque de l'Universite . . . (14th c?) 18; Bibliotheque Publique (?) ?

Meknes: [b] for Mequinez; off Miknasa. [c] Boufekrane R. [d] none. [e] Bibliotheque de la Grande Mosquee (?) 8; Bibliotheque Publique (?) ?

*Rabat-Sale: [b] Sale: for Sallee; off Sla. [c] Atlantic O; Bou Regreg R. [d] Universite Mohammed V (1912) 11 – 498. [e] Bibliotheque Generale et Archives (1920) 208; Bibliotheque de l'Universite . . . (1957) ? [f] Rabat: 227 (1960), 156 (1952), 53 (1931), 31 (1900e), 28 (1850e), 17 (1800e); Sale: 76 (1960), 47 (1952), 26 (1931), 30 (1900e), 10 (1850e).

Tangier: [b] alt Tanger; off Tanjah. [c] Strait of Gibraltar. [d] University of North Africa (1969) ? – ? [e] Biblioteca Publica Espanola Antonio de Nebrija (1941) 25.

Mozambique

*Lourenco Marques: [b] none. [c] Delagoa B of Indian O. [d] Universidade de Lourenco Marques (1962) 1 – 199. [e] Biblioteca Nacional de Mocambique (1961) 95.

Niger

*Niamey: [b] none. [c] Niger R. [d] none. [e] Centre de Documentation (1965) ?

Nigeria

Abeokuta: [b] none. [c] Ogun R. [d] none.

Enugu: [b] none. [c] Asata R; Aria R. [d] none. [e] Regional Central Library (1956) 134.

Ibadan: [b] none. [c] Ogunpa R. [d] University of Ibadan (1948) 3 – 555. [e] University . . . Library (1948) 260; Western State Library (1954) 78.

Ilesha: [b] none. [c] nr Shasha R. [d] none.

Ilorin: [b] none. [c] Awun R. [d] none.

Kano: [b] none. [c] Jakara R. [d] none. [e] Abdullahi Bayero College Library of Ahmadu Bello University (1964) 11; British Council Library (1950) 11.

*Lagos: [b] none. [c] G of Guinea of Atlantic O; Lagos (for Cradu) Lagoon. [d] University of Lagos (1962) 2 – 420. [e] University . . . Library (1962) 90; Public Library (1946) 69; National Library of Nigeria (1962) 40.

Ogbomosho: [b] none. [c] nr Oba R. [d] none.

Oshogbo: [b] none. [c] Oshun R. [d] none.

Port Harcourt: [b] none. [c] Bonny R (Niger R distributary). [d] University of Science and Technology (planned). [e] British Council Library (?) 3.

Zaria: [b] none. [c] Galma R. [d] Ahmadu Bello University (1946) 3 – 540. [e] Shettima Kashim Library of... University (1962) 102.

Reunion

*Saint-Denis: [b] none. [c] Indian O; Saint-Denis R. [d] none. [e] Bibliotheque Centrale de Pret (1956) 45; Bibliotheque Departementale (1856) 30.

Rhodesia

Bulawayo: [b] none. [c] Matsheumhlope R. [d] none. [e] Public Library (1896) 60; National Free Library of Rhodesia (1944) 40.

*Salisbury: [b] none. [c] Makabusi R. [d] University of Rhodesia (1955) 1 – 200. [e] University... Library (1956) 190; Library of Parliament (1899) 70; Queen Victoria Public Library (1902) 49.

Senegal

*Dakar: [b] none. [c] Atlantic O. [d] Universite de Dakar (1950) 3 – 240. [e] Bibliotheque de l'Universite... (1950) 201; Bibliotheque de l'Institut Fondamental d'Afrique Noire (1936) 55. [f] 23s (1904).

Sierra Leone

*Freetown: [b] none. [c] Atlantic O. [d] University of Sierra Leone (1827) 1 – 191. [e] Sierra Leone Library Board (1959) 380; University... Library (1827) 84.

Somalia

*Mogadishu: [b] alt Mogadiscio; off Hamar. [c] Indian O. [d] Universita Nazionale della Somalia (1954) 0.8 – 23. [e] National Library (1934) 8; Biblioteca dell'Universita... (1954) ?

South Africa

Bloemfontein: [a] *Orange Free State. [b] none. [c] Bloem(spruit) Creek. [d] University of the Orange Free State (alt Universiteit van die Oranje-Vrystaat) (1855) 4 – 321. [e] Orange Free State Provincial Library Service (alt Oranje-Vrystaat Provinsiale Biblioteekdiens) (1948) 744; Public Library (alt Openbare Biblioteek) (1875) 178.

*Cape Town: [a] *Cape of Good Hope. [b] alt Kaapstad. [c] Table B of Atlantic O. [d] University of Cape Town (alt Universiteit van Kaapstad) (1829) 8 – 500. [e] Cape Provincial Library Service (alt Kaapse Provinsiale Biblioteekdiens) (1945) 4073; City Library (alt Stadsbiblioteek) (1952) 739; South African Public Library (alt Suid-Afrikaanse Openbare Biblioteek) (1820) 510; University... Library (alt Universiteit... Biblioteek) (1905) 510.

Durban: [a] Natal. [b] none. [c] Natal B of Indian O. [d] University of Durban-Westville (alt Universiteit van Durban-Westville (1960) 2 – 174; University of Natal, Durban campus (1922) ? – ?. [e] Municipal Library (alt Munisipale Biblioteek) (1853) 550; Durban Campus Library of the University of Natal (1936) 210. [f] 0.5 (1850?e).

Germiston: [a] Transvaal. [b] none. [c] Germiston L. [d] none. [e] Carnegie Public Library (alt Carnegie Openbare Biblioteek) (1909) 88.

Johannesburg: [a] Transvaal. [b] none. [c] none. [d] University of the Witwatersrand (alt Universiteit van Witwatersrand) (1896 at Kimberley, relocated 1904) 10 –?; Rand Afrikaans University (alt Randse Afrikaanse Universiteit) (1966) 1 – 145. [e] Public Library (alt Openbare Biblioteek) (1890) 1182; University... Library (alt Universiteit... Biblioteek) (1922) 450.

Pietermaritzburg: [a] *Natal. [b] none. [c] Umsindusi R. [d] University of Natal (alt Universiteit van Natal) (1909) 7 – 640 [Pietermaritzburg campus: (1909) ? – ?]. [e] Natal Provincial Library Service (alt Natalse Provinsiale Biblioteekdiens) (1951) 831; University... Library (alt Universiteit... Biblioteek) (1912) 330 [Pietermaritzburg campus: (1912) 120].

Port Elizabeth: [a] Cape of Good Hope. [b] none. [c] Algoa B of Indian O. [d] University of Port Elizabeth (alt Universiteit van Port Elizabeth) (1964) 1 – 142. [e] Municipal Library (alt Munisipale Biblioteek) (1848) 271.

*Pretoria: [a] *Transvaal. [b] none. [c] Apies R. [d] University of Pretoria (alt Universiteit van Pretoria) (1908) 13 – 730. [e] Transvaal Provincial Library Service (alt Transvaalse Provinsiale Biblioteekdiens) (1943) 2655; State Library (alt Staatsbiblioteek) (1887) 592.

Vereeniging: [a] Transvaal. [b] none. [c] Vaal R. [d] none. [e] Public Library (alt Openbare Biblioteek) (1912) 23.

Sudan

*Khartoum: [b] off Khurtum. [c] Nile R; Blue Nile R. [d] University of Khartoum (1902) 3 – 360?; University of Cairo, Khartoum campus (1955) 5 – 80. [e] University of Khartoum Library (1945) 200.

Omdurman: [b] off Umm Durman. [c] Blue Nile R. [d] none. [e] Islamic College Library (1912?) 20; Public Library (1951) 20.

Tanzania

*Dar es Salaam: [a] *Tanganyika. [b] none. [c] Indian O. [d] University of Dar es Salaam (1961) 1 – 123. [e] Tanganyika Library Service (1964) 250; University . . . Library (1961) 70. [f] 344 (1970e).

Zanzibar: [a] *Zanzibar; Zanzibar I. [b] alt Unguja. [c] Zanzibar Channel. [d] none. [e] Shree Vanik Library (?) 7; Museum Library (?) 3.

Togo

*Lome: [b] none. [c] G of Guinea of Atlantic O. [d] Universite du Benin (1962) 0.4 – 40? [e] Bibliotheque Nationale (1960) 8.

Tunisia

Sfax: [b] off Safaqis. [c] Mediterranean Sea. [d] none. [e] Bibliotheque Publique (?) ? [f] 216s (1966)

*Tunis: [b] none. [c] Tunis Lagoon. [d] Universite de Tunis (1960) 9 – 596. [e] Bibliotheque Nationale de Tunisie (1883) 359; Bibliotheque Centrale (?) 150. [f] 648s (1966).

Uganda

*Kampala: [b] none. [c] nr Victoria L. [d] Makerere University (1922) 3 – 350. [e] . . . University Library (1948) 250; Uganda Library Service (1964) 140.

Upper Volta

*Ouagadougou: [b] for Wagadugu. [c] nr Ouadmana R. [d] none.

Zaire

Kananga: [b] for Luluabourg. [c] Lulua R. [d] none. [e] Bibliotheque Publique (?) 25.

*Kinshasa: [b] for Leopoldville. [c] Congo R. [d] Universite Lovanium de Kinshasa (1925) 3 – 477. [e] Bibliotheque de l'Universite . . . (1954) 600; Bibliotheque Centrale du Congo (1949) 90.

Kisangani: [b] for Stanleyville. [c] Congo R; Tshope R. [d] Universite Libre du Congo a Kisangani (1963) 0.6 – 75. [e] Bibliotheque Publique (1930) 20.

Lubumbashi: [b] for Elisabethville. [c] Lubumbashi R. [d] Universite Officielle du Congo a Lubumbashi (1956) 1 – 65. [e] Bibliotheque de l'Universite. . . (1956) 60.

Mbuji-Mayi: [b] for Bakwanga. [c] Bushimaie R. [d] none.

Zambia

Kitwe: [b] none. [c] nr Kafue R. [d] none. [e] Central Technical Library of Rhokana Corporation, Ltd (1954) 20; Municipal African Library (1960) 4.

*Lusaka: [b] none. [c] none. [d] University of Zambia (1965) 2 – 200? [e] Zambia Library Service (1962) 250; Public Library (1943) 50.

ASIA

Afghanistan

Herat: [b] none. [c] Hari (Rud) R. [d] none.

*Kabul: [b] for Cabul. [c] Kabul (for Cabul) R. [d] Kabul University (1931) 6 – 924. [e] . . . University Library (1931) 85; Public Library (1920) 65. [f] 489s (1970e), 292, 439s (1965).

Kandahar: [b] alt Qandahar. [c] Arghandab R. [d] none. [e] Teachers' Training School Library (1956) ?

Bahrain

*Manama: [a] Bahrain I. [b] off Manamah. [c] Persian G. [d] none. [e] British Council Library (?) 7

Bangladesh

Chittagong: [b] for Islamabad, Porto Grande. [c] Karnaphuli R. [d] University of Chittagong (1966) 22 – ? [e] University . . . Central Library (1869) 21; Municipal Public Library (1904) 13.

*Dacca: [b] none. [c] Burhi Ganga R (Brahmaputra R distributary). [d] University of Dacca (1910) 45 – ?; Bangladesh University of Engineering and Technology (1961) 2 – 141. [e] University . . . Library (1921) 340; National Assembly Library (1947) 45.

Khulna: [b] none. [c] Bhairab R (Ganges R distributary). [d] none. [e] Brajalal College Library (?) 16.

Narayanganj: [b] none. [c] Dhaleswari R (Brahmaputra R distributary); Lakhya R (Brahmaputra R distributary). [d] none. [e] Rahmatullah Muslim Institute Library (?) 4; Municipal Public Library (?) ?

Burma

Mandalay: [b] off Mandale. [c] Irrawaddy R. [d] Arts and Science University, Mandalay (1923) 7 – 429. [e] . . . University Library (1958) 71.

*Rangoon: [b] off Yangon. [c] Rangoon (off Yangon) R; Pegu R; Myitmaka R. [d] Arts and Science University, Rangoon (1885) 14 – 887. [e] Universities' Central Library (1929) 110; National Library (1952) 49.

Cambodia

*Phnom-Penh: [b] none. [c] Mekong R; Bassac R; Tonle Sap R. [d] Universite de Phnom-Penh (1953) 5 – 346; Universite Technique (1958) 1 – 233?; Universite Bouddhique (1954) 0.2 – 20; Universite des Beaux-Arts (1965) 0.2 – ?; Universite des Sciences Agronomiques (1965) 0.1 – 46. [e] Bibliotheque de l'Institut Bouddhique (1923) 40; Bibliotheque Nationale (1921) 33.

Ceylon

*Colombo: [b] none. [c] Indian O; Colombo L. [d] University of Colombo (1870) 4 – 248; Vidyodaya University of Ceylon (at Gangodawila, nr Colombo) (1873) 3 – 142; Vidyalankara University of Ceylon (at Kelaniya, nr Colombo) (1875) 1 – 152. [e] Public Library (1925) 80; Colombo National Museum Library (1870) 78; University . . . Library (1967) 71.

Kandy: [b] for Candy. [c] Mahaweli Ganga R; Kandy L. [d] University of Ceylon (at Peradeniya, nr Kandy) (1870 at Colombo, relocated from 1952) 5 – 345. [e] University . . . Library (at Peradeniya, nr Kandy) (1942 at Colombo, relocated ?) 185; Municipal Public Library (?) ?

China

Amoy: [a] Fukien. [b] for Szeming; off Hsiamen. [c] Formosa (alt Taiwan) Strait; Kiulung (off Chiulung) R. [d] Amoy University (1921) 3 – 1000? [e] . . . University Library (1921) ?

Anking: [a] Anhwei. [b] for Hwaining; off Anching. [c] Yangtze R. [d] none.

Anshan: [a] Liaoning. [b] for Shaho. [c] nr Taitzu R. [d] none.

Antung: [a] Liaoning. [b] none. [c] Yalu R. [d] none.

Canton: [a] *Kwangtung. [b] alt Kwangchow; off Kuangchou. [c] Pearl R. [d] Chinan University (1958) 2 – ?; Chungshan University (?) ? – ?; South China Technical University (?) ? – ?; Sun Yat-sen University (1924) ? – ? [e] Chungshan Library of Kwangtung Province (1909) 980; Chinan University Library (1958) 400; Sun Yat-sen University Library (1924) ?

Changchih: [a] Shansi. [b] for Luan. [c] nr Chang R. [d] none.

Changchow: [a] Fukien. [b] for Lungki; off Changchou. [c] Lungki (off Lungchi) R. [d] none.

Changchow: [a] Kiangsu. [b] for Wutsin; off Changchou. [c] nr Ho L. [d] none.

Changchun: [a] *Kirin. [b] for Hsinking. [c] Itung R. [d] Kirin University (1958) ? – ? [e] Changchun Library (?) 245; . . . University Library (1958) ?

Changsha: [a] Hunan. [b] none. [c] Siang R. [d] Hunan University (1959) ? – ? [e] Chungshan Library of Hunan Province (1912) 410; . . . University Library (1959) ?

Chefoo: [a] Shantung. [b] off Yentai. [c] G of Chihli [alt Po (Hai) G] of Yellow Sea. [d] none.

Chengchow: [a] *Honan. [b] for Chenghsien; off Chengchou. [c] nr Kialu (off Chialu) R. [d] Chengchow University (?) ? – ? [e] . . . University Library (?) ?

Chengtu: [a] *Szechwan. [b] none. [c] Chin R (arm of Min R). [d] Szechwan University (1931) 4 – 700?; Chengtu Technical University (1954) ? – ? [e] Szechwan Library (1912) 895; Chengtu Technical University Library (1954) ?; Szechwan University Library (1931) ?

Chinchow: [a] Liaoning. [b] off Chinchou. [c] Taling R. [d] none.

Chinkiang: [a] Kiangsu. [b] off Chenchiang. [c] Yangtze R. [d] none.

Chinwangtao: [a] Hopeh. [b] off Chinhuangtao. [c] G of Liaotung of Yellow Sea. [d] none.

Chuchow: [a] Hunan. [b] off Chuchou. [c] Siang R. [d] none.

Chungking: [a] Szechwan. [b] for Pahsien; off Chungching. [c] Yangtze R; Kialing R. [d] Chungking Technical University (?) ? – ?; Chungking University (?) ? – ? [e] Chungking Library (?) 1850; Chungking Technical University Library (?) ?; Chungking University Library (?) ?

Foochow: [a] *Fukien. [b] for Minhow; off Fuchou. [c] Min R. [d] Foochow University (?) ? – ? [e] Fukien Library (1908) 310; . . . University Library (?) ?

Foshan: [a] Kwangtung. [b] alt Fatshan; for Namhoi, Nanhai. [c] Foshan (alt Fatshan) R (Si R distributary). [d] none.

Fushun: [a] Liaoning. [b] none. [c] Hun R. [d] none.

Fusin: [a] Liaoning. [b] off Fouhsinhsien. [c] Hsi R. [d] none.

Hangchow: [a] *Chekiang. [b] off Hangchou. [c] Tsientang R; Hsi (alt West) L. [d] Chekiang University (1927) 6 – ?; Hangchow University (1959?) ? – ? [e] Chekiang Library (1872) 1050; Chekiang University Library (1927) ?; Hangchow University Library (1959) ?

Hantan: [a] Hopeh. [b] none. [c] Fuyang R. [d] none.

Harbin: [a] *Heilungkiang. [b] for Pinkiang; off Haerhpin. [c] Sungari R. [d] Harbin Polytechnic University (1920) 4 – ?; Heilungkiang University (?)? – ? [e] Harbin Library (1950) 430; Harbin Polytechnic University Library (1920)?

Hengyang: [a] Hunan. [b] for Hengchow. [c] Siang R; Lei R; Chen R. [d] none.

Hofei: [a] *Anhwei. [b] for Luchow. [c] Chintou R. [d] Anhwei University (?) ? – ?; Hofei Polytechnic University (?) ? – ? [e] Anhwei Library (?) 330; Anhwei University Library (?) ?; Hofei Polytechnic University Library (?) ?

Hoihow: [a] Kwangtung; Hainan I. [b] off Haikou. [c] Hainan Strait; Nantu R. [d] none.

Hokang: [a] Heilungkiang. [b] off Haoli. [c] Alingta R. [d] none.

Huhehot: [a] *Inner Mongolia. [b] alt Kuku-Khoto; for Kweisui; inc Kweihwating, Suiyuan; off Huhohaote. [c] Tahei R. [d] Inner Mongolian University (1957) ? – ? [e] Library of Inner Mongolia (?) 125;. . . University Library (1957) ?

Hwainan: [a] Anhwei. [b] for Tienkiaan; off Huainan. [c] Hwai R. [d] none.

Hwangshih: [a] Hupeh. [b] inc Hwangshihkang, Shihhweiyao; off Huangshih. [c] Yangtze R. [d] none.

Ichang: [a] Hupeh. [b] none. [c] Yangtze R. [d] none.

Ichun: [a] Heilungkiang. [b] none. [c] Tangwang R. [d] none.

Ipin: [a] Szechwan. [b] for Suchow, Suifu. [c] Yangtze R; Min R. [d] none.

Kaifeng: [a] Honan. [b] none. [c] nr Yellow R. [d] none. [e] Honan Library (1909) 395.

Kalgan: [a] Hopeh. [b] for Wanchuan; off Changchiakou. [c] Chin R. [d] none.

Kashgar: [a] Sinkiang. [b] for Shufu, Sufu; off Koshih. [c] Kashgar (off Kashihkaerh) R. [d] none.

Kiamusze: [a] Heilungkiang. [b] off Chiamussu. [c] Sungari R. [d] none.

Kingtehchen: [a] Kiangsi. [b] for Fowliang; off Chingtechen. [c] Chang R. [d] none.

Kirin: [a] Kirin. [b] for Yungki; off Chilin. [c] Sungari R. [d] none.

Kisi: [a] Heilungkiang. [b] off Chihsi. [c] Muleng R. [d] none.

Kokiu: [a] Yunnan. [b] for Kokiuchang; off Kochiu. [c] nr Hsiao R. [d] none.

Kunming: [a] *Yunnan. [b] for Yunnan. [c] Tien (off Chih) L. [d] Yunnan University (1923) ? – ? [e] Yunnan Library (1909) 810;. . . University Library (1934) ?

Kweilin: [a] Kwangsi. [b] off Kueilin. [c] Kwei (off Kuei) R. [d] none. [e] First Library of Kwangsi (1909) 280.

Kweiyang: [a] *Kweichow. [b] for Kweichu; off Kueiyang. [c] Nanming R; Niulu R. [d] Kweichow University (1958) ? – ?; Kweiyang Technical University (1958) ? – ? [e] People's Library of Kweiyang (?) 280; Kweichow University Library (1958) ?; Kweiyang Technical University Library (1958) ?

Lanchow: [a] *Kansu. [b] for Kaolan; off Lanchou. [c] Yellow R. [d] Lanchow University (1946) 2 – 700? [e] Kansu Library (?) 380; Municipal Library (1957) 380;. . . University Library (1946?) ?

Lhasa: [a] *Tibet. [b] off Lasa. [c] Lasa R. [d] none.

Liaoyang: [a] Liaoning. [b] none. [c] Taitzu R. [d] none.

Liaoyuan: [a] Kirin. [b] for Peifeng, Sian, Tungliao. [c] Tungliao R. [d] none.

Liuchow: [a] Kwangsi. [b] for Maping; off Liuchou. [c] Liu R. [d] none.

Loyang: [a] Honan. [b] for Honan. [c] Lo R. [d] none. [e] Library of the Honan Institute for Agricultural Machinery (?) ?

Luchow: [a] Szechwan. [b] for Luhsien; off Luchou. [c] Yangtze R; To R. [d] none.

Lushun-Talien: [a] Liaoning. [b] alt Luta; Lushun: for Port Arthur, Ryojun; Talien: for Dairen, Dalny. [c] G of Chihli [alt Po (Hai) G] of Yellow Sea; Korea B of Yellow Sea. [d] Talien Technical University (1950)? – ? [e] Lushun-Talien Library (?) 740;. . . University Library (1950) ? [f] Lushun: 34 (1930), 14 (1900?e); Talien: 293 (1930), 40 (1900?e).

Malipo: [a] Yunnan. [b] none. [c] nr Chouyangta R. [d] none.

Mukden: [a] *Liaoning. [b] for Fengtien; off Shenyang. [c] Hun (off Shen) R. [d] Liaoning University (?) ? – ?; Northeastern China Technical University (?) ? – ?. [e] Liaoning Library (1948) 1300; Shenyang Library (1908) 580.

Mutankiang: [a] Heilungkiang. [b] off Mutanchiang. [c] Mutan R. [d] none.

Nanchang: [a] *Kiangsi. [b] none. [c] Kan R. [d] none. [e] Kiangsi Library (1921) 520.

Nanchung: [a] Szechwan. [b] for Shunking. [c] Kialing R. [d] none.

Nanking: [a] *Kiangsu. [b] for Kiangning; off Nanching. [c] Yangtze R. [d] Nanking Technical University (?) ? – ?; Nanking University (1902) ? – ? [e] Nanking Library (1908) 2400; Second Library of Kiangsu (1914?) 210; Nanking Technical University Library (?) ?; Nanking University Library (1902) ?

Nanning: [a] *Kwangsi. [b] for Yungning. [c] Yu R. [d] none. [e] Kwangsi Agricultural Institute Library (?) ?; Kwangsi Medical College Library (?) ?

Nantung: [a] Kiangsu. [b] for Tungchow. [c] Yangtze R. [d] none. [e] Nantung Medical College Library (?) ?

Neikiang: [a] Szechwan. [b] off Neichiang. [c] To R. [d] none.
Ningpo: [a] Chekiang. [b] for Ninghsien. [c] Yung (alt Ningpo) R; Fenghua R; Yao R. [d] none.
Paoki: [a] Shensi. [b] off Paochi. [c] Wei R. [d] none.
Paoting: [a] Hopeh. [b] for Tsingyuan. [c] Fu R. [d] none. [e] Hopeh Library (?) 195.
Paotow: [a] Inner Mongolia. [b] off Paotou. [c] Yellow R. [d] none.
*Peking: [a] (independent city). [b] for Peiping; off Peiching. [c] Pei L; Chung L; Nan L. [d] Tsinghua University (1911) 12 – 1200?; Peking University (1898) 10 – 2000?; China University of Science and Technology (1958) 6 – ?; People's University of China (1953) 1 – ? [e] National Library of Peking (1909) 4600; Central Library of the Chinese Academy of Sciences (1951) 2500; National Capital Library (?) 520; Peking University Library (1902) ?; People's University of China Library (1950) ?; Tsinghua University Library (1911) ?
Pengpu: [a] Anhwei. [b] off Pangfou. [c] Hwai R. [d] none.
Penki: [a] Liaoning. [b] for Penkihu; off Penchi. [c] Taitzu R. [d] none.
Shanghai: [a] (independent city). [b] none. [c] East China Sea; Yangtze R; Whangpoo (off Huangpu) R; Wusung R. [d] Shanghai University (1895) 7 – 1400?; Tung Chi University (1907) 6 – 550?; Futan University (1905) 3 – ?; Chiao Tung University (1896) ? – ? [e] Shanghai Library (1952) 3500; Municipal People's Library (1912) 920; Chiao Tung University Library (1896) ?; Futan University Library (1922) ?; Shanghai University Library (1895) ?
Shangkiu: [a] Honan. [b] for Kweiteh; off Shangchiuhsien. [c] Pao R. [d] none.
Shaohing: [a] Chekiang. [b] off Shaohsing. [c] nr Hangchow B of East China Sea. [d] none.
Shaoyang: [a] Hunan. [b] for Paoking. [c] Tzu R. [d] none.
Shihkiachwang: [a] Hopeh. [b] for Shihmen; off Shihchiachuang. [c] nr Sha R. [d] none.
Shiukwan: [a] Kwangtung. [b] for Chukiang, Kukong, Shaochow, Shiuchow; off Shaokuan. [c] Pei R; Wu R; Cheng R. [d] none.
Siakwan: [a] Yunnan. [b] off Hsiakuan. [c] Yangpi R; Erh L. [d] none.
Sian: [a] *Shensi. [b] for Changan, Siking, Singan; off Hsian. [c] nr Wei R. [d] Northwestern University (1937) 3 – 300?; Shensi University of Science and Technology (1960) ? – ?; Sian University (1884) ? – ? [e] Shensi Library (1909) 380; Northwestern University Library (1937) ?; Shensi University . . . Library (1960) ?
Siangtan: [a] Hunan. [b] off Hsiangtan. [c] Siang R. [d] none.
Sinhailien: [a] Kiangsu. [b] inc Lienyunkang, Sinpu, Tunghai (for Haichow); off Hsinhailien. [c] Yellow Sea; Yen R. [d] none. [f] Lienyunkang: 77 (1946e); Tunghai: 48 (1948e).
Sining: [a] *Tsinghai. [b] off Hsining. [c] Huang (alt Hsining, Sining) R. [d] none. [e] Tsinghai Library (?) 130
Sinsiang: [a] Honan. [b] off Hsinhsiang. [c] Wei R. [d] none.
Soochow: [a] Kiangsu. [b] for Wuhsien; off Suchou. [c] nr Yangcheng L; nr Tushu L. [d] none.
Suchow: [a] Kiangsu. [b] for Tungshan; off Hsuchou. [c] nr Wei Shan L. [d] none.
Swatow: [a] Kwangtung. [b] off Shantou. [c] South China Sea; Han R. [d] none.
Szeping: [a] Kirin. [b] for Szepingkai; off Ssuping. [c] Tiaotzu R. [d] none.
Taichow: [a] Kiangsu. [b] for Taihsien; off Taichou. [c] Tung R; Hsi R. [d] none.
Taiyuan: [a] *Shansi. [b] for Yangku. [c] Fen R. [d] none.
Tangshan: [a] Hopeh. [b] none. [c] Tung R. [d] none.
Tatung: [a] Shansi. [b] none. [c] Yu R. [d] none.
Tientsin: [a] *Hopeh. [b] off Tienching. [c] Hai R; Chinchung R; Hsinkai R; Tzuya R; Weiching R; Yun R. [d] Nankai University (1914) 3 – 460; Hopeh University (1960?) ? – ?;Tientsin University (1895) ? – ? [e] Municipal Library (1908) 880; Hopeh University Library (1960) ?; Nankai University Library (1919) ?
Tsamkong: [a] Kwangtung. [b] for Fort-Bayard, Haikang, Leichow, Siying; off Chanchiang. [c] Kwangchow B of South China Sea. [d] none. [f] 60 (1900?e).
Tsiaotso: [a] Honan. [b] off Chiaotso. [c] Yunliang R. [d] none.
Tsinan: [a] *Shantung. [b] for Licheng; off Chinan. [c] Siaoching (off Hsiaoching) R; Taming L. [d] Tsinan Technical University (?) ? – ? [e] Shantung Library (1909) 680; . . . University Library (?) ?
Tsingtao: [a] Shantung. [b] off Chingtao. [c] Yellow Sea. [d] Shantung University (1926) ? – ?; Tsingtao Technical University (?) ? – ? [e] Tsingtao Library (?) 330; Shantung University Library (1926) ?; Tsingtao Technical University Library (?) ? [f] 527 (1935e).
Tsitsihar: [a] Heilungkiang. [b] for Lungkiang, Pukwei; off Chichihaerh. [c] Nonni R. [d] none.
Tzekung: [a] Szechwan. [b] inc Kungtsing, Tzeliutsing; off Tzukung. [c] Tsin (off Ching) R. [d] none. [f] Tzeliutsing: 100 (1926e).
Tzepo: [a] Shantung. [b] inc Poshan, Tzechwan; off Tzupo. [c] Chenghuang (alt Hsiaofu) R. [d] none. [f] Poshan: 50 (1920?e).
Urumtsi: [a] *Sinkiang. [b] alt Tihwa, Urumchi; off Wulumuchi. [c] Wulumuchi R. [d] Sinkiang University (1960) 2 -? [e] Library of the Sinkiang Uighur Autonomous Region (?) 85; . . . University Library (1960) ?
Weifang: [a] Shantung. [b] for Weihsien. [c] Pailang R. [d] none.
Wenchow: [a] Chekiang. [b] for Yungkia; off Wenchou. [c] Wu (alt Ou) R. [d] none. [e] Chekiang Institute of Forestry Library (?) ?

Wuhan: [a] *Hupeh. [b] inc Hankow, Hanyang, Wuchang. [c] Yangtze R; Han (Shui) R; Tung L. [d] Wuhan University (1913) 4 – 700?; Central China Technical University (?) ? – ?; Hupeh University (?) ? – ? [e] Hupeh Library (1908) 780; Wuhan Library (?) 280; Central China Technical University Library (?) ?; Hupeh University Library (?) ?; Wuhan University Library (1913) ? [f] Hankow: 782 (1935e), 850 (1900?e), 690 (1850e); Hanyang: 137 (1934e), 100 (1900?e), 100 (1850e); Wuchang: 434 (1935e), 550 (1900?e), 206 (1850e).

Wuhu: [a] Anhwei. [b] none. [c] Yangtze R; Chingi R; Suiyang R. [d] none.

Wusih: [a] Kiangsu. [b] off Wuhsi. [c] nr Tai L [d] none.

Wutungkiao: [a] Szechwan. [b] none. [c] Min R. [d] none.

Yangchow: [a] Kiangsu. [b] for Kiangtu; off Yangchou. [c] Nanyun R. [d] none. [e] North Kiangsu Agricultural Institute Library (?) ?

Yangchuan: [a] Shansi. [b] none. [c] Mien (Shui) R. [d] none.

Yenan: [a] Shensi. [b] for Fushih. [c] Yen R. [d] none.

Yinchwan: [a] *Ningsia. [b] for Ningsia; off Yinchuan. [c] nr Yellow R. [d] Ningsia University (bef 1962) 1 – 290. [e] . . . University Library (1962) ?

Yingkow: [a] Liaoning. [b] for Yingtze; off Yingkou. [c] G of Liaotung of Yellow Sea; Liao R. [d] none.

Cyprus

*Nicosia: [b] off Levkosia. [c] Pedias R. [d] none. [e] Library of the Pan-Cyprian Gymnasium (1927) 35. [f] 96s (1960).

Gaza Strip

*Gaza: [b] alt Azzah; off Ghazzah. [c] Mediterranean Sea. [d] none. [f] 10s (1850?e).

Hong Kong

*Hong Kong: [b] alt Hsiangchiang, Hsiangkang; inc Kowloon, New Kowloon, Victoria. [c] South China Sea; Pearl R. [d] University of Hong Kong (1887) 3 – 390?; Chinese University of Hong Kong (1949) 2 – 371. [e] University . . . Library (1912) 375; Public Library (1962) 345. [f] Kowloon: 727s (1961), 232 (1931); New Kowloon: 853s (1961), 23 (1931); Victoria: 522 (1971), 633, 675s (1961), 358 (1931).

India

Agra: [a] Uttar Pradesh. [b] none. [c] Yamuna R. [d] Agra University (1927) 72 – ? [e] . . . University Library (1935) 94; Agra District Central Library (1957) 9. [f] 125 (1853).

Ahmedabad: [a] *Gujarat. [b] alt Ahmadabad. [c] Sabarmati R. [d] Gujarat University (1949) 61 – ?; National University of Gujarat (1920) 0.7 – 45. [e] National University of Gujarat Library (1920) 163; Gujarat University Library (1949) 154; Gujarat State Central Library (1933) 124. [f] 97 (1851).

Ajmer: [a] Rajasthan. [b] none. [c] Ana L. [d] none. [e] City Public Library (1899) 35.

Aligarh: [a] Uttar Pradesh,. [b] inc Koil. [c] none. [d] Aligarh Muslim University (1877) 8 – 539. [e] . . . University Library (1921) 365; Lytton Library (1880) 45 (in 1950).

Allahabad: [a] Uttar Pradesh. [b] none. [c] Ganges R; Yamuna R. [d] University of Allahabad (1887) 10 – 296? [e] University . . . Library (1916) 288; Public Library (1864) 63. [f] 72 (1853).

Ambala: [a] Haryana. [b] for Umballa. [c] nr Ghaggar R. [d] none. [e] Hans Raj Library of D.A.V. College (1886) 24.

Amravati: [a] Maharashtra. [b] alt Amraoti. [c] nr Pedhi R. [d] none. [e] Amravati District Central Library (1923) 40.

Amritsar: [a] Punjab. [b] none. [c] none. [d] Guru Nanak University (1969) ? – ? [e] Pandit Motilal Nehru City Public Library (1900) 42.

Asansol: [a] West Bengal. [b] none. [c] nr Damodar R; nr Barakar R. [d] none. [e] Burdwan District Library (1959) 5.

Bangalore: [a] *Mysore. [b] none. [c] nr Pinikini R. [d] Bangalore University (1864) 39 – 1614; University of Agricultural Sciences (1964) 2 – 150; Indian Institute of Science (univ) (1909) 1 – 214. [e] . . . Institute Library (1909) 135; . . . University Library (1865) 123; Mysore State Central Library (1914) 77.

Bareilly: [a] Uttar Pradesh. [b] for Bareli. [c] Jooah R; Sunkra R. [d] none. [e] Bareilly College Library (1837) 33; Bareilly District Central Library (1957) 7. [f] 111 (1853).

Baroda: [a] Gujarat. [b] none. [c] Vishvamitri R. [d] Maharaja Sayajirao University of Baroda (1881) 15 – 766. [e] . . . University Library (1950) 238; Baroda District Central Library (1910) 162.

Belgaum: [a] Mysore. [b] none. [c] Markandeya R. [d] none. [e] General Library (1848) 11 (in 1950).

Bhatpara: [a] West Bengal. [b] none. [c] Hooghly R (Ganges R distributary). [d] none. [e] Bhatpara Literary Association and Library (?) ?

Bhavnagar: [a] Gujarat. [b] alt Bhaunagar. [c] G of Cambay of Indian O. [d] none. [e] Bhavnagar District Central Library (1959) 30.

Bhopal: [a] *Madhya Pradesh. [b] none. [c] Bess R; Patra R; Pukhta-Pul Talao L. [d] Bhopal University (1970) ? – ? [e] Maulana Azad Central Library (?) 60.

Bikaner: [a] Rajasthan. [b] none. [c] none. [d] none. [e] King Emperor George V Silver Jubilee Library (1937) 37; Dungar College Library (1935) 14 (in 1950); Anup Sanskrit Library (bef 1698) 10.

Bombay: [a] *Maharashtra. [b] none. [c] Arabian Sea of Indian O. [d] University of Bombay (1832) 88 – ?; Shreemati Nathibai Damodar Thackersey Women's University (1916) 13 – 395; Indian Institute of Technology, Bombay (univ) (1958) 2 – 200. [e] Asiatic Society of Bombay Library (alt Maharashtra State Central Library) (1804) 382; University . . . Library (1869) 333. [f] 70 (1744e), 10 (1698e).

Calcutta: [a] *West Bengal. [b] none. [c] Hooghly R (Ganges R distributary). [d] University of Calcutta (1817) 196 – ?; Jadavpur University (1906) 5 – 398; Rabindra Bharati University (1962) 4 – 97. [e] National Library (1836) 1308; University . . . Library (1857) 434. [f] 413 (1850), 117 (1752e), 12 (1700e).

Calicut: [a] Kerala. [b] alt Kozhikode. [c] Arabian Sea of Indian O; Kallayi R. [d] University of Calicut (1968) 50 – ? [e] Zamorin's College High School Library (?) 6; City Public Library (?) ?

Chandigarh: [a] Chandigarh (*Haryana; *Punjab). [b] none. [c] nr Ghaggar R. [d] Panjab University (1947 at Solon, relocated 1957?) 166 – ? [e] . . . University Library (1947 at Solon, relocated 1957?) 284; Punjab State Central Library (?) 50.

Coimbatore: [a] Tamil Nadu. [b] none. [c] Noyil R. [d] none. [e] Agricultural College and Research Institute Library (1876) 65; Coimbatore District Central Library (1952) 20.

Cuttack: [a] Orissa. [b] none. [c] Mahanadi R. [d] none. [e] Kanika Library of Ravenshaw College (1919) 67.

Dehra Dun: [a] Uttar Pradesh. [b] for Dehra. [c] Rispana R; Bindal R. [d] none. [e] Forest Research Institute Central Library (1906) 62; Mahatma Kushiram Public Library and Reading Room (1921) 5 (in 1950).

Delhi: [a] *Delhi. [b] none. [c] Yamuna R. [d] University of Delhi (1881) 56 – ? [e] Public Library (1951) 674; University . . . Library (1922) 361. [f] 152 (1853).

Dhanbad: [a] Bihar. [b] none. [c] nr Damodar R. [d] none. [e] Central Fuel Research Institute Library (1955) 16; Dhanbad District Central Library (1956) 11; Indian School of Mines Library (1926) 10.

Durg: [a] Madhya Pradesh. [b] for Drug. [c] nr Seonath R. [d] none.

Durgapur: [a] West Bengal. [b] none. [c] Damodar R. [d] none.

Ernakulam: [a] Kerala. [b] none. [c] Vembanad Lagoon. [d] none. [e] Maharajah's College Library (1875?) ?; Public Library (?) ?

Gaya: [a] Bihar. [b] none. [c] Phalgu R. [d] Magadh University (at Bodh Gaya, nr Gaya) (1942) 35 – ?. [e] . . . University Library (at Bodh Gaya, nr Gaya) (1962?) 34; Mannulal Library (1911) 24 (in 1950); Gaya District Central Library (1855) 14.

Gorakhpur: [a] Uttar Pradesh. [b] none. [c] Rapti R. [d] University of Gorakhpur (1933) 31 – ?. [e] University . . . Library (1957) 86; Gorakhpur District Central Library (1957) 9. [f] 55 (1853).

Guntur: [a] Andhra Pradesh. [b] for Guntoor. [c] none. [d] none. [e] Guntur District Central Library (1952) 15.

Gwalior: [a] Madhya Pradesh. [b] inc Lashkar since 1951. [c] Sonrekha (Nadi) Creek. [d] Jiwaji University (1887) 29 – 708? [e] Government Central Library (1928) 77;. . . University Library (1964) 25. [f] Lashkar: 151 (1951), 79 (1931), 89 (1901), 88 (1881).

Howrah: [a] West Bengal. [b] inc Bally (alt Baly) since 1969. [c] Hooghly R (Ganges R distributary). [d] none. [e] Sibpur Public Library (?) 21; Bally Public Library (?) 20. [f] Bally: 131 (1961), 63 (1951), 30 (1931), 19 (1901), 14 (1872).

Hubli: [a] Mysore. [b] none. [c] nr Bedti R. [d] Karnatak University (at Dharwar, nr Hubli) (1917) 58 – ? [e] . . . University Library (at Dharwar, nr Hubli) (1950) 129; Hubli-Dharwar City Central Library (1948) 50.

Hyderabad: [a] *Andhra Pradesh. [b] for Bhagnagar, Haidarabad; inc Secunderabad since 1951. [c] Musi R; Hussain L. [d] Osmania University (1887) 62 – 2543; Andhra Pradesh Agricultural University (1964) ? – ? [e] Osmania University Library (1919) 219; Andhra Pradesh State Central Library (1891) 157. [f] Secunderabad: 225 (1951), 121 (1931), 96 (1901).

Indore: [a] Madhya Pradesh. [b] none. [c] Katki R. [d] University of Indore (1884) 20 – 677? [e] University . . . Library (1964) 34; Indore Christian College Library (1884?) 22; General Library (1854) 21 (in 1950). [f] 573s (1971), 15 (1850?e).

Jabalpur: [a] Madhya Pradesh. [b] for Jubbulpore. [c] nr Narmada R. [d] University of Jabalpur (1933) 16 – 683?; Jawaharlal Nehru Agricultural University (1948) 2 – ? [e] University . . . Library (1957) 64.

Jaipur: [a] *Rajasthan. [b] none. [c] nr Dhund (Nadi) Creek. [d] University of Rajasthan (1873) 63 – 2433. [e] University . . . Library (1947) 166; Public Library (1866) 34 (in 1950).

Jamnagar: [a] Gujarat. [b] for Navanagar. [c] G of Cutch of Indian O. [d] Gujarat Ayurved University (1966) 2 – ? [e] Jamnagar District Central Library (1956) 34;. . . University Library (1966?) 17.

Jamshedpur: [a] Bihar. [b] none. [c] Subarnarekha R. [d] none. [e] National Metallurgical Laboratory Library (1950) 14.

Jhansi: [a] Uttar Pradesh. [b] none. [c] nr Betwa R. [d] none. [e] Jhansi District Central Library (1957) 7.

Jodhpur: [a] Rajasthan. [b] none. [c] nr Umed L. [d] University of Jodhpur (1962) 9 – 425. [e] University . . . Library (1962) 83; Sumer Public Library (1915) 40. [f] 60 (1850?e).

Jullundur: [a] Punjab. [b] none. [c] nr East Bein (alt White Bein) R. [d] none. [e] Lajpat Rai Library (1918) 12 (in 1950).

Kalyan: [a] Maharashtra. [b] none. [c] Ulhas R. [d] none.

Kanpur: [a] Uttar Pradesh. [b] for Cawnpore. [c] Ganges R. [d] Kanpur University (1966) 58 – ?; Indian Institute of Technology, Kanpur (univ) (1960) 2 – 162. [e] . . . Institute Library (1960?) 99; Government Agricultural Library (1904) 62; Kanpur District Central Library (1957) 7. [f] 118 (1853).

Kolhapur: [a] Maharashtra. [b] none. [c] Panchaganga R. [d] Shivaji University (1962) 42 – 1712. [e] . . . University Library (1962) 58; Rajaram College Library (1880) 49; Kolhapur District Central Library (1850) 25.

Kota: [a] Rajasthan. [b] alt Kotah. [c] Chambal R. [d] none. [e] Government Girls Higher Secondary School Library (?) 4; Herbert College Library (?) ?

Lucknow: [a] *Uttar Pradesh. [b] none. [c] Gumti R. [d] University of Lucknow (1911) 25 – 597. [e] University . . . Library (1921) 247; Uttar Pradesh Legislative Library (1931) 160; Amir-ud-Daula Government Public Library (alt Uttar Pradesh State Central Library) (1910) 48.

Ludhiana: [a] Punjab. [b] none. [c] none. [d] Punjab Agricultural University (1947) 2 – ? [e] . . . University Library (1962) 48.

Madras: [a] *Tamil Nadu. [b] none. [c] B of Bengal of Indian O; Cooum R; Adyar R. [d] University of Madras (1794) 118 – ?; Indian Institute of Technology, Madras (univ) (1959) 2 – 186. [e] University . . . Library (1857) 327; Connemara Public Library (alt Tamil Nadu State Central Library) (1896) 214.

Madurai: [a] Tamil Nadu. [b] alt Madura. [c] Vaigai R. [d] Madurai University (1958) 54 – ? [e] . . . University Library (1958) 45; American College Library (1842?) 27; Madurai District Central Library (1952) 14.

Malegaon: [a] Maharashtra. [b] none. [c] Girna R. [d] none.

Mangalore: [a] Mysore. [b] none. [c] Arabian Sea of Indian O; Netravati R; Gurpur R. [d] none. [e] South Kanara District Central Library (1950) 74; Saint Aloysius College Library (1880) 49 (in 1950).

Meerut: [a] Uttar Pradesh. [b] none. [c] nr Kali (Nadi) Creek. [d] Meerut University (1966) 44 – 1942. [e] Meerut College Library (1892) 79; . . . University Library (1966?) 10; Meerut District Central Library (1957) 7.

Moradabad: [a] Uttar Pradesh. [b] none. [c] Ramganga R. [d] none. [e] K. G. K. College Library (1940?) 19. [f] 57 (1853).

Mysore: [a] Mysore. [b] none. [c] nr Kaveri R. [d] University of Mysore (1833) 70 – ? [e] University . . . Library (1916) 197; Oriental Research Institute Library (1891) 48; City Central Library (1915) 14 (in 1950).

Nagpur: [a] Maharashtra. [b] none. [c] Nag R; Chamar R. [d] Nagpur University (1923) 67 – 2480. [e] . . . University Library (1927) 228; Nagpur District Central Library (1955) 67.

Nasik: [a] Maharashtra. [b] none. [c] Godavari R. [d] none. [e] Nasik District Central Library (1840) 35; Hansraj Pragji Thackersey College Library (1924) 27. [f] 22 (1850).

*New Delhi: [a] Delhi. [b] none. [c] Yamuna R. [d] Indian Institute of Technology, Delhi (univ) (1961) 2 – 164; Jawaharlal Nehru University (1969) 0.3 – 65. [e] Central Secretariat Library (1900) 280; Parliament Library (1921) 270.

Patna: [a] *Bihar. [b] none. [c] Ganges R. [d] Patna University (1863) 13 – 735. [e] . . . University Library (1917) 165; Shrimati Radhika Sinha Institute and Sachchidananda Sinha Library (alt Bihar State Central Library)(1924) 75. [f] 490s (1971), 284 (1837).

Poona: [a] Maharashtra. [b] none. [c] Mutha Mula R; Mutha R; Mula R. [d] University of Poona (1885) 58 – ? [e] University . . . Library (1950) 147; Bai Jerbai Wadia Library of Fergusson College (1885) 120; Poona District Central Library (1947) 62. [f] 73 (1851).

Raipur: [a] Madhya Pradesh. [b] none. [c] Karun R. [d] Ravishankar University (1948) 19 – 1024. [e] . . . University Library (1948) 19. [f] 206s (1971).

Rajahmundry: [a] Andhra Pradesh. [b] none. [c] Godavari R. [d] none. [e] Gauthami Library (1898) 70. [f] 189s (1971).

Rajkot: [a] Gujarat. [b] none. [c] Aji R. [d] Saurashtra University (1967) 23 – ? [e] Rajkot District Central Library (1956) 34; . . . University Library (1967?) 29.

Ranchi: [a] Bihar. [b] none. [c] Subarnarekha R. [d] Ranchi University (1899) 37 – 1571. [e] . . . University Library (1899?) 34; British Council Library (1962) 14; Ranchi Distiict Central Library (1953) 13.

Saharanpur: [a] Uttar Pradesh. [b] none. [c] Dhamola R. [d] none. [e] City Library (?) ? [f] 32 (1853).

Salem: [a] Tamil Nadu. [b] none. [c] Tirumanimutar (alt Salem) R. [d] none. [e] Salem District Central Library (1953) 10.

Sholapur: [a] Maharashtra. [b] none. [c] nr Ekruk L. [d] none. [e] Dayanand College Library (1940?) 33; Sholapur District Central Library (1857) 26.

South Suburban: [a] West Bengal. [b] inc Behala. [c] nr Hooghly R (Ganges R distributary.). [d] none. [e] Behala Library (?) ?

Surat: [a] Gujarat. [b] none. [c] Tapti R. [d] South Gujarat University (1966) 19 – ? [e] Maganlal Thakordas Balmukandas College Library (1918) 24; Andrews Library (alt Surat District Central Library) (1850) 15. [f] 493s (1971), 90 (1851).

Tiruchirapalli: [a] Tamil Nadu. [b] for Trichinopoly. [c] Kaveri R. [d] none. [e] National College Library (1919) 17; Tiruchirapalli District Central Library (1952) 7.

Tirunelveli: [a] Tamil Nadu. [b] for Tinnevelly. [c] Tambraparni R. [d] none. [e] Saint John's College Library (at Palayamcottai, nr Tirunelveli) (1878?) 14; Madura Diraviyam Thayumanavar Hindu College Library (1861) 10 (in 1950); Tirunelveli District Central Library (1952) 10.

Trivandrum: [a] *Kerala. [b] none. [c] Arabian Sea of Indian O. [d] University of Kerala (1937) 114 – ? [e] University . . . Library (1943) 140; Kerala State Central Library (1851) 95.

Ujjain: [a] Madhya Pradesh. [b] none. [c] Sipra R. [d] Vikram University (1896) 33 – ? [e] . . . University Library (1896?) 50; Madhav College Library (1896?) 26; Yuvraj General Library (1913) 10 (in 1950). [f] 209s (1971).

Varanasi: [a] Uttar Pradesh. [b] alt Banaras; for Benares. [c] Ganges R. [d] Varanaseya Sanskrit University (1958) 20 – ?; Banaras Hindu University (1898) 11 – 1068. [e] Banaras Hindu University Library (1916) 432; Varanasi District Central Library (1957) 6. [f] 186 (1853).

Vijayawada: [a] Andhra Pradesh. [b] alt Vijayavada; for Bezwada. [c] Krishna R. [d] none. [e] Ram Mohan Free Reading Room and Library (1911) 31. [f] 344s (1971).

Visakhapatnam: [a] Andhra Pradesh. [b] alt Vishakhapatnam; for Vizagapatam. [c] B of Bengal of Indian O. [d] Andhra University (at Waltair, nr Visakhapatnam) (1926) 113 – ? [e] . . . University Library (at Waltair, nr Visakhapatnam) (1927) 172. [f] 362s (1971).

Warangal: [a] Andhra Pradesh. [b] alt Hanamkonda. [c] none. [d] none. [e] Warangal District Central Library (1958) 8.

Indonesia

Bandjermasin: [a] Borneo I. [b] alt Bandjarmasin, Banjermasin. [c] Barito R; Martapura R. [d] Universitas Lambung Mangkurat (1961) ? – ? [e] Perpustakaan Negara (?) ?; Perpustakaan Universitas (1960) ?

Bandung: [a] Java I. [b] for Bandoeng. [c] (Tji)kapundung R. [d1] Universitas Negeri Padjadjaran (1952) 10 – 1789; Institut Teknologi Bandung (univ) (1959) 5 – 300; Universitas Katolik Parahyangan (1955) 4 – 200. [e] Pusat Perpustakaan Institut . . . (1959) 100; Perpustakaan Universitas Negeri Padjadjaran (1957) 95.

Bogor: [a] Java I. [b] for Buitenzorg. [c] (Tji)liwung R. [d] Institut Pertanian Bogor (univ) (1963) 2 – 417; Universitas Bogor (1958) 0.3 – 64; Universitas Ibnu Chaldun Bogor (1958) ? – ? [e] Bibliotheca Bogoriensis (1842) 300.

*Djakarta: [a] Java I. [b] alt Jakarta; for Batavia. [c] Java Sea; (Tji)liwung R. [d1] Universitas Indonesia (1920) 7 – 1535; Universitas Trisakti (1965) 4 – 449; Universitas Kristen Indonesia (1953) 3 – 401; Universitas Krisnadwipajana (1952) 2 – 128; Universitas Tarumanegara (1959) 2 – 214; Universitas Ibnu Chaldun (1956) 1 – 80; Universitas Katolik Indonesia Atma Jaya (1960) 1 – 180. [e] Perpustakaan Museum Pusat (1778) 400.

Jogjakarta: [a] Java I. [b] alt Djokjakarta. [c] Tjodeh R. [d] Universitas Gadjah Mada (1949) 17 – 1344; Universitas Islam Indonesia (1945) 5 – 246 [Jogjakarta campus: (1945) ? – ?]; Universitas Janabadra (1958) ? – ?; Universitas Proklamasi (1964) ? – ?; Universitas Taman Siswa (?) ? – ? [e] Perpustakaan Negara (1949) 75.

Makasar: [a] Celebes I. [b] alt Macassar, Makassar. [c] Makassar Strait. [d] Universitas Hasanuddin (1949) 7 – 825; Universitas Veteran Republik Indonesia (1959) 2 – 224; Universitas Sawerigadang (1945) 1 – 158. [e] Perpustakaan Universitas Hasanuddin (1949) 55.

Malang: [a] Java I. [b] for Singasari. [c] Brantas R. [d] Universitas Brawidjaja (1957) 4 – 497; Universitas Merdeka (1964) ? – ?

Manado: [a] Celebes I. [b] alt Menado. [c] Celebes Sea; Manado (alt Menado) R. [d] Universitas Sulawesi Utara (1961) ? – ?; Universitas Sam Ratulangi (1961) ? – ?

Medan: [a] Sumatra I. [b] none. [c] Deli R. [d] Universitas Sumatera Utara (1952) 4 – 153; Universitas Islam Sumatera Utara (1952) 3 – 89; Universitas Tjut Nja' Dhien (1956) 0.6 – 149. [e] Perpustakaan Negara (?) 4; Perpustakaan Universitas Islam Sumatera Utara (1952?) ?

Padang: [a] Sumatra I. [b] none. [c] Indian O; Padang R. [d] Universitas Andalas (1956) 4 – 487.

Palembang: [a] Sumatra I. [b] none. [c] Musi (for Moesi) R. [d] Universitas Negeri Sriwidjaja (1953) 4 – 516.

Pontianak: [a] Borneo I. [b] none. [c] Kapuas-Ketjil R (Kapuas R distributary); Landak R. [d] Universitas Tandjungpura Pontianak (1963) 0.9 – 154; Universitas Kalimantan Barat (?) ? – ?

Semarang: [a] Java I. [b] alt Samarang. [c] Java Sea; Semarang (alt Samarang) R. [d] Universitas Diponegoro (1956) 5 – 215; Universitas Islam Sultan Agung (1962) 0.9 – 265. [e] Perpustakaan Negara (?) ?

Surabaja: [a] Java I. [b] alt Surabaya; for Soerabaja. [c] Surabaja (alt Surabaya) Strait; Mas R. [d] Universitas Airlangga (1954) 7 – 456; Institut Teknologi 10 Nopember Surabaja (univ) (1960) 3 – 304; Universitas Kristen Petra (1965) 0.6 – 72. [e] Perpustakaan Universitas Airlangga (1954) 55.

Surakarta: [a] Java I. [b] alt Solo; for Soerakarta. [c] Solo R; Pepe R. [d] Universitas Tjokroaminoto Surakarta (1955) 4 – 100.

Tjirebon: [a] Java I. [b] for Cheribon. [c] Java Sea. [d] Universitas Islam Sjarief Hidajatullah Tjirebon (?) ? – ?

Iran

Abadan: [b] none. [c] (Shatt al) Arab R. [d] none. [e] Abadan Institute of Technology Library (1938?) 20.

Ahvaz: [b] alt Ahwaz. [c] Karun R. [d] Jundi Shapur University (1955) 1 – 132. [e] . . . University Library (1955) ?

Hamadan: [b] none. [c] nr Qareh (Su) [alt Qara (Chai)] R. [d] none.

Isfahan: [b] alt Ispahan; off Esfahan. [c] Zayandeh R. [d] University of Isfahan (1949) 3 – 190. [e] University . . . Library (1958) 102; Municipal Library (?) 31.

Kermanshah: [b] none. [c] nr Qareh (Su) [alt Qara (Chai)] R. [d] none. [e] Public Library (bef 1969) ?

Meshed: [b] off Mashhad. [c] nr Kashaf R. [d] University of Meshed (1938) 3 – 269. [e] Astaneh Razavy Library (15th c?) 43; University . . . Library (1925?) 22; Public Library (?) 18.

[1] Universities with 1000 or more students.

Shiraz: [b] none. [c] Khoshk R. [d] Pahlavi University (1945) 3 – 310. [e] . . . University Library (1948) 103; Fars National Library (?) 14.

Tabriz: [b] none. [c] Talkheh (alt Aji) R. [d] University of Tabriz (1946) 4 – 359. [e] University . . . Library (1947) 45; Public Library (?) 13.

*Teheran: [b] off Tehran. [c] none. [d] University of Teheran (1934) 17 – 1325; National University of Iran (1960) 5 – 195; Arya-Mehr University of Technology (1965) 2 – 192. [e] Library of the Faculty of Arts of the University . . . (1932) 90; National Library (1935) 80; Parliament Library (1924) 65.

Iraq

*Baghdad: [b] alt Bagdad. [c] Tigris R. [d] University of Baghdad (1908) 20 – 1418; Al-Mustansiriya University (1963) 10 – 450; Al-Hikma University of Baghdad (1956) 0.6 – 65. [e] University . . . Central Library (1958) 220; University . . . College of Medicine Library (1927) 62; National Library (1955) 51; Al-Hikma University of Baghdad Library (1956?) 50; National Library of the Iraq Museum (1934) 37.

Basra: [b] off Basrah. [c] (Shatt al) Arab R. [d] Basra University (1967) 3 – 135. [e] Bashayan el Abbasi Library (16th c) 11; Public Library (?) ?. [f] 311s (1965).

Karbala: [b] alt Kerbela. [c] Jadwal R. [d] none. [e] Public Library (?) ? [f] 123s (1965).

Kirkuk: [b] alt Kerkuk; for Zor. [c] Qada (alt Qadha) (Chai) Creek. [d] none. [e] Public Library (?) ? [f] 184s (1965).

Mosul: [b] off Mawsil. [c] Tigris R. [d] Mosul University (1967) 3 – 149? [e] Public Library (1930) 66. [f] 264s (1965).

Israel

Haifa: [b] none. [c] B of Acre of Mediterranean Sea; Kishon R. [d] Technion, Israel Institute of Technology (univ) (1912) 8 – 1271; Haifa University (1964) 4 – 410. [e] . . . University Library (1951) 180; Central Library of Technion (1925) 109; Borochov Library (1921) 105. [f] 448s (1968e).

*Jerusalem: [b] alt Quds ash Sharif; inc Jordanian Jerusalem; off Yerushalayim. [c] nr Dead (Sea) L. [d] Hebrew University (1925) 16 – 1955. [e] Jewish National and University Library (1884) 2000; City Library (1961) 250. [f] Jordanian Jerusalem: 60 (1961), 70 (1952).

Tel Aviv-Jaffa: [b] Jaffa: off Yafo. [c] Mediterranean Sea. [d] Tel Aviv University (1935) 13 – 2019; Bar-Ilan University (at Ramat Gan, nr Tel Aviv-Jaffa) (1953) 5 – 814. [e] Municipal Library (1885) 418; Tel Aviv University Library (1953) 250. [f] 838s (1968e); Jaffa: 51 (1931), 21 (1900e), 5 (1850e).

Japan

Akashi: [a] Honshu I. [b] none. [c] Akashi Channel. [d] none.

Akita: [a] Honshu I. [b] none. [c] Sea of Japan; Omono R. [d] Akita University (college) (1875) 2 – 226. [e] Akita Prefectural Library (1899) 219; . . . University Library (1911) 76.

Amagasaki: [a] Honshu I. [b] none. [c] Osaka B of Inland (alt Seto) Sea; Yodo R. [d] none. [e] Municipal Library (1919) 68.

Aomori: [a] Honshu I. [b] none. [c] Aomori B of Tsugaru Strait. [d] none. [e] Aomori Prefectural Library (1928) 85.

Asahigawa: [a] Hokkaido I. [b] alt Asahikawa. [c] Ishikari R. [d] none. [e] Shimomura Bunko Library (1918) 10 (in 1946).

Chiba: [a] Honshu I. [b] none. [c] Tokyo B of Pacific O. [d] Chiba University (1872) 6 – 845? [e] . . . University Library (1949) 310; Chiba Prefectural Library (1924) 199.

Fujisawa: [a] Honshu I. [b] none. [c] Sagami B of Pacific O. [d] none.

Fukui: [a] Honshu I. [b] none. [c] Asuwa R. [d] Fukui University (bef 1943) 2 – 306. [e] . . . University Library (1943?) 128; Fukui Prefectural Library (1909) 65.

Fukuoka: [a] Kyushu I. [b] inc Hakata. [c] Hakata B of East China Sea; Naka R. [d] Fukuoka University (1934) 13 – 379; Kyushu University (1903) 10 – 1952. [e] Kyushu University Library (1911) 1670.

Fukushima: [a] Honshu I. [b] none. [c] Abukuma R. [d] Fukushima University (college) (1949) 2 – 146; Fukushima Prefectural Medical College (univ) (1944) 0.5 – 209. [e] Fukushima Prefectural Library (1929) 120.

Fukuyama: [a] Honshu I. [b] none. [c] Inland (alt Seto) Sea; Ashida R. [d] none. [e] Library of the Faculty of Fisheries and Animal Husbandry of Hiroshima University (1949) 11; Yoshikura Library (1910) ?

Funabashi: [a] Honshu I. [b] none. [c] Tokyo B of Pacific O. [d] none.

Gifu: [a] Honshu I. [b] for Imaizumi. [c] Nagara R. [d] Gifu University (1875) 4 – 907; Gifu College of Pharmacy (univ) (1932) 0.5 – 59. [e] Gifu Prefectural Library (1909) 174.

Hachinohe: [a] Honshu I. [b] none. [c] Mabechi R. [d] none. [e] Municipal Library (1913) 21 (in 1946).

Hachioji: [a] Honshu I. [b] none. [c] Asa R; Kawaguchi R. [d] none. [e] Tokyo Metropolitan Hachioji Library (1911) 2 (in 1946).

Hakodate: [a] Hokkaido I. [b] none. [c] Tsugaru Strait. [d] none. [e] Municipal Library (1926) 125.

Hamamatsu: [a] Honshu I. [b] none. [c] Pacific O. [d] none. [e] Hamamatsu Technical College Library (1924) 35 (in 1946); Municipal Library (1920) 16 (in 1946).

Higashiosaka: ^{a} Honshu I. ^{b} for Fuse. ^{c} nr Yodo R. ^{d} Kinki University (1925) 24 – 527. ^{e} ... University Library (1925?) 212.

Himeji: ^{a} Honshu I. ^{b} none. ^{c} Ichi R. ^{d} none. ^{e} Himeji Higher School Library (1923) 41 (in 1946); Municipal Library (1912) 20 (in 1946).

Hirakata: ^{a} Honshu I. ^{b} none. ^{c} Yodo R. ^{d} none. ^{e} Osaka College of Dental Medicine Library (1931) 5 (in 1946); Osaka Women's Higher Medical College Library (1915) 5 (in 1946).

Hiroshima: ^{a} Honshu I. ^{b} none. ^{c} Hiroshima B of Inland (alt Seto) Sea. ^{d} Hiroshima University (1902) 8 – 1114. ^{e} ... University Library (1949) 835; Hiroshima Prefectural Library (?) 100.

Hitachi: ^{a} Honshu I. ^{b} none. ^{c} Pacific O. ^{d} none.

Ichikawa: ^{a} Honshu I. ^{b} none. ^{c} Edo R. ^{d} none.

Ichinomiya: ^{a} Honshu I. ^{b} none. ^{c} nr Kiso R. ^{d} none. ^{e} Municipal Library (1915) 6 (in 1946).

Ise: ^{a}Honshu I. ^{b} for Uji-Yamada. ^{c} Ise B of Pacific O. ^{d} none. ^{e} Mie Shinto Library (1928) 195.

Iwaki: ^{a} Honshu I. ^{b} for Onahama; inc Taira since 1965. ^{c} Pacific O; Kamata R. ^{d} none. ^{f} Taira: 71 (1965), 71 (1960), 43 (1950), 25 (1930), 11 (1898), 4 (1874).

Kagoshima: ^{a} Kyushu I. ^{b} none. ^{c} Kagoshima B of East China Sea. ^{d} Kagoshima University (1949) 6 – 1206. ^{e} ... University Library (1949) 428; Kagoshima Prefectural Library (1912) 222.

Kamakura: ^{a} Honshu I. ^{b} none. ^{c} Sagami B of Pacific O. ^{d} none. ^{e} Municipal Library (1911) 10 (in 1946).

Kanazawa: ^{a} Honshu I. ^{b} none. ^{c} Sea of Japan; Ono R. ^{d} Kanazawa University (1949) 5 – 965. ^{e} ... University Library (1949) 580; Central Library of Ishikawa Prefecture (1912) 165; Municipal Library (1929) 157.

Kawaguchi: ^{a} Honshu I. ^{b} none. ^{c} Ara R. ^{d} none.

Kawasaki: ^{a} Honshu I. ^{b} none. ^{c} Tokyo B of Pacific O. ^{d} none. ^{e} Mukigaoka Library (1923) 5 (in 1946); Municipal Library (1924) 3 (in 1946); Daishi Library (1926) ?

Kitakyushu: ^{a} Kyushu I. ^{b} inc Kokura, Moji, Tobata, Wakamatsu, Yahata (alt Yawata). ^{c} Kammon Strait. ^{d} Kyushu Institute of Technology (univ) (1907) 2 – 203. ^{e} Yawata Iron and Steel Works Company Library (?) 145; ... Institute Library (1909) 85. ^{f}:

	1960	1950	1930	1898	1874
Kokura	286	199	88	28	7
Moji	152	124	108	25	
Tobata	109	88	52	3	
Wakamatsu	107	90	57	29	
Yahata	332	210	168	3	

Kobe: ^{a} Honshu I. ^{b} inc Hyogo (alt Hiogo) since 1878. ^{c} Osaka B of Inland (alt Seto) Sea; Minato R. ^{d} Kobe University (1903) 9 – 1209; Konan University (1918) 6 – 302; Kobe Women's College of Pharmacy (univ) (1920) 1 – 97. ^{e} Kobe University Library (1903) 898; Municipal Library (1911) 240. ^{f} Hyogo: 30 (1877).

Kochi: ^{a} Shikoku I. ^{b} none. ^{c} Tosa B of Pacific O; Kagami R. ^{d} Kochi University (college) (1874) 2 – 357. ^{e} Kochi Prefectural Library (1915) 142; ... University Library (1925) 120.

Kofu: ^{a} Honshu I. ^{b} none. ^{c} Ara R. ^{d} Yamanashi University (bef 1949) 2 – 409. ^{e} Yamanashi Prefectural Library (1931) 138; ... University Library (1949?) 116.

Koriyama: ^{a} Honshu I. ^{b} none. ^{c} Abukuma R. ^{d} none. ^{e} Municipal Library (1944) 8 (in 1946).

Kumamoto: ^{a} Kyushu I. ^{b} none. ^{c} Shira R. ^{d} Kumamoto University (1874) 6 – 955. ^{e} ... University Library (1949) 459.

Kurashiki: ^{a} Honshu I. ^{b} none. ^{c} Kurashiki R. ^{d} none. ^{e} Library of the Ohara Institute of Agricultural Biology of Okayama University (1921) 38.

Kure: ^{a} Honshu I. ^{b} none. ^{c} Hiroshima B of Inland (alt Seto) Sea. ^{d} none. ^{e} Municipal Library (1924) 32 (in 1946).

Kurume: ^{a} Kyushu I. ^{b} none. ^{c} Chikugo R. ^{d} Kurume University (1928) 3 – 334. ^{e} ... University Library (1928?) 125.

Kushiro: ^{a} Hokkaido I. ^{b} none. ^{c} Pacific O; Kushiro R. ^{d} none. ^{e} Municipal Popular Library (1925) 7 (in 1946).

Kyoto: ^{a} Honshu I. ^{b} alt Kioto; for Miyako. ^{c} Kamo R. ^{d}[1] Ritsumeikan University (1900) 21 – 596; Doshisha University (1875) 20 – 779; Kyoto University (1897) 15 – 3458; Kyoto Industrial College (univ) (1965) 5 – 240?; Ryukoku University (1639) 4 – 217; Kyoto University of Industrial Arts and Textiles (1889) 2 – 348; University of Buddhism (1903) 1 – 67. ^{e} Kyoto University Library (1899) 2917; Doshisha University Library (1875) 559; Ryukoku University Library (1639) 322; Kyoto Prefectural Library (1909) 320. ^{f} 478 (1850?).

Machida: ^{a} Honshu I. ^{b} none. ^{c} Sakai R. ^{d} Tamagawa University (1929) 5 – 832. ^{e} ... University Library (1929) 200.

Maebashi: ^{a} Honshu I. ^{b} for Umayabashi. ^{c} Tone R. ^{d} Gumma University (1876) 5 – 506? ^{e} ... University Library (1949) 180; Municipal Library (1915) 92.

[1] Universities with 1000 or more students.

Matsudo: [a] Honshu I. [b] none. [c] Edo R. [d] none. [e] Library of the Faculty of Horticulture of Chiba University (1909) 12.

Matsuyama: [a] Shikoku I. [b] none. [c] nr Inland (alt Seto) Sea. [d] Ehime University (college) (1896) 4 – 553. [e] . . . University Library (1949) 310; Matsuyama College of Commerce Library (1923) 120; Ehime Prefectural Library (1935) 82.

Miyazaki: [a] Kyushu I. [b] none. [c] Oyodo R. [d] Miyazaki University (1923) 2 – 403. [e] . . . University Library (1926) 120; Miyazaki Prefectural Library (1902) 78.

Morioka: [a] Honshu I. [b] none. [c] Kitakami R. [d] Iwate University (bef 1949) 3 – 291; Iwate Medical University (1928) 1 – 333. [e] Iwate University Library (1902) 198; Iwate Prefectural Library (1922) 132.

Nagano: [a] Honshu I. [b] for Zenkoji. [c] Sai R. [d] none. [e] Nagano Prefectural Library (1929) 174.

Nagasaki: [a] Kyushu I. [b] none. [c] East China Sea. [d] Nagasaki University (1857) 4 – 699. [e] Nagasaki Prefectural Library (1912) 780; . . . .University Library (1949) 320.

Nagoya: [a] Honshu I. [b] none. [c] Ise B of Pacific O; Shonai R; Yata R. [d] Meijo University (1924) 18 – 470; Nagoya University (1871) 9 – 2292; Nanzan University (1932) 4 – 140; Nagoya Institute of Technology (univ) (1905) 4 – 586; Nagoya Municipal University (1931) 2 – 353; Aichi Gakuin University (1876) 1 – 139. [e] Nagoya University Library (1939) 835; Municipal Library (1920) 247.

Nara: [a] Honshu I. [b] none. [c] Saho R; Noto R. [d] Tenri University (college) (at Tenri, nr Nara) (1925) 2 – 244?; Nara Women's University (1908) 1 – 306. [e] Tenri Central Library (at Tenri, nr Nara) (1930) 1083; Nara Women's University Library (1909) 200; Todaiji Library (1903) 165; Nara Prefectural Library (1908) 143.

Neyagawa: [a] Honshu I. [b] alt Neyakawa. [c] nr Yodo R. [d] none.

Niigata: [a] Honshu I. [b] for Kambaratsu. [c] Sea of Japan; Shinano R. [d] Niigata University (1910) 6 – 1088. [e] . . . University Library (1949) 409; Niigata Prefectural Library (1915) 230.

Nikko: [a] Honshu I. [b] none. [c] Daiya R. [d] none. [e] Nikko Bunko Library (1924) 16 (in 1946).

Nishinomiya: [a] Honshu I. [b] none. [c] Osaka B of Inland (alt Seto) Sea. [d] Kwansei Gakuin University (1889) 12 – 556; Kobe Jogakuin College (univ) 1 – 165. [e] . . . University Library (1889) 367.

Numazu: [a] Honshu I. [b] none. [c] Suruga B of Pacific O; Kano R. [d] none. [e] Numazu Bunko Library (1898) 9 (in 1946).

Oita: [a] Kyushu I. [b] for Funai. [c] Beppu B of Hoyo Strait; Oita R. [d] Oita University (college) (1875) 1 – 158. [e] . . . University Library (1922) 128; Oita Prefectural Library (1902) 65.

Okayama: [a] Honshu I. [b] none. [c] Asahi R. [d] Okayama University (1874) 5 – 1177. [e] . . . University Library (1949) 682.

Okazaki: [a] Honshu I. [b] none. [c] Yahagi R. [d] Aichi Gakugei University (college) (1945) 2 – 282. [e] . . . University Library (1945?) 125.

Omiya: [a] Honshu I. [b] none. [c] nr Shiba R. [d] none. [e] Municipal Library (1921) 4 (in 1946).

Omuta: [a] Kyushu I. [b] none. [c] Ariakeno G of Amakusa Sea. [d] none.

Osaka: [a] Honshu I. [b] none. [c] Osaka B of Inland (alt Seto) Sea; Yodo R. [d1] Osaka University (1843) 8 – 1243; Osaka Municipal University (1928) 7 – 1088; Osaka University of Education (1949?) 4 – 285?; Osaka University of Foreign Studies (1921) 3 – 123; Osaka Dental College (univ) (1912) 1 – 300? [e] Osaka University Library (1931) 839; Osaka Prefectural Library (1903) 750; Osaka Municipal University Library (1928) 718.

Otaru: [a] Hokkaido I. [b] none. [c] Ishikari (alt Otaru) B of Sea of Japan. [d] Otaru University of Commerce (college) (1910) 1 – 50. [e] . . . University Library (1911) 115.

Sagamihara: [a] Honshu I. [b] inc Kami-Mizo, Ono. [c] Sakai R. [d] none. [e] Azabu Veterinary College Library (1949) 22.

Sakai: [a] Honshu I. [b] none. [c] Osaka B of Inland (alt Seto) Sea; Yamato R. [d] University of Osaka Prefecture (1949) 4 – 715. [e] University . . . Library (1949?) 403; Municipal Library (1872) 62.

Sapporo: [a] Hokkaido I. [b] none. [c] Toyohira R. [d] Hokkaido University (1876) 11 – 1726; Sapporo Medical College (univ) (1945) 0.5 – 296. [e] . . . University Library (1918) 1320; Hokkaido Prefectural Library (1924) 92.

Sasebo: [a] Kyushu I. [b] none. [c] East China Sea. [d] none. [e] Municipal Library (1918) 5 (in 1946).

Sendai: [a] Honshu I. [b] none. [c] Hirose R. [d] Tohoku University (1907) 11 – 2690; Tohoku Gakuin University (1886) 9 – 353; Tohoku Pharmaceutical College (univ) (1939) 0.8 – 80? [e] Tohoku University Library (1911) 1180; Tohoku Gakuin University Library (1890) 120; Miyagi Prefectural Library (1881) 110.

Shimizu: [a] Honshu I. [b] none. [c] Suruga B of Pacific O. [d] none [e] Nautical College Library (1943) 20 (in 1946); Municipal Library (1931) 1 (in 1946).

Shimonoseki: [a] Honshu I. [b] for Akamagaseki, Bakwan. [c] Kammon Strait. [d] none. [e] Municipal Library (1882) 26 (in 1946).

Shizuoka: [a] Honshu I. [b] for Fuchu, Shunpei, Sumpu. [c] Suruga B of Pacific O. [d] Shizuoka University (1875) 5 – 597; Shizuoka College of Pharmacy (univ) (1916) 0.4 – 90. [e] . . . University Library (1949) 210; Central Library of Shizuoka Prefecture (1922) 146.

Suita: [a] Honshu I. [b] none. [c] Yodo R. [d] Kansai University (1886) 24 – 650. [e] . . . University Library (1886) 630.

Takamatsu: [a] Shikoku I. [b] none. [c] Inland (alt Seto) Sea. [d] Kagawa University (college) (1924) 2 – 594? [e] . . . University Library (1924) 128; Kagawa Prefectural Library (1934) ?

[1] Universities with 1000 or more students.

Takasaki: [a] Honshu I. [b] none. [c] Karasu R. [d] none. [e] Municipal Library (1910) 32 (in 1946).

Takatsuki: [a] Honshu I. [b] none. [c] Yodo R. [d] none.

Tokushima: [a] Shikoku I. [b] none. [c] Kii Channel; Yoshino R. [d] Tokushima University (1949?) 3 – 718. [e] . . . University Library (1949) 125; Tokushima Prefectural Library (1916) 88.

*Tokyo: [a] Honshu I. [b] alt Tokio; for Edo, Yedo. [c] Tokyo B of Pacific O; Sumida R; Ara R. [d][1] Nihon University (1889) 72 – 3077; Waseda University (1882) 46 – 2037; Chuo University (1885) 33 – 1235; Meiji University (1881) 32 – 1083; Hosei University (1880) 30 – 911; Keio University (1858) 26 – 1221; Toyo University (1887) 20 – 438; Komazawa University (1759) 19 – 362?; Aoyama Gakuin University (1874) 17 – 788; University of Tokyo (1789?) 16 – 3558; Senshu University (1880) 15 – 470; Kokugakuin University (1882) 13 – 480; Meiji Gakuin University (1877) 12 – 365; Rikkyo (alt Saint Paul's) University (1874) 12 – 683. [e] National Diet Library (1948) 5840; University of Tokyo Library (1893) 3300; Waseda University Library (1882) 911; Keio University Library (1858) 760; Meiji University Library (1903) 731; Nihon University Library (1889) 707.

Toyama: [a] Honshu I. [b] none. [c] Jintsu R. [d] Toyama University (1949) 4 – 376. [e] Toyama Prefectural Library (?) 164; . . . University Library (1949?) 160.

Toyohashi: [a] Honshu I. [b] for Yoshida. [c] Atsumi B of Pacific O. [d] Aichi University (1946) 8 – 113. [e] . . . University Library (1946?) 160; Municipal Library (1912) 78.

Toyonaka: [a] Honshu I. [b] none. [c] Yodo R. [d] none. [e] Naniwa Higher School Library (1926) 27 (in 1946).

Toyota: [a] Honshu I. [b] for Koromo. [c] Yahagi R. [d] none.

Urawa: [a] Honshu I. [b] none. [c] Ara R. [d] Saitama University (college) (1921) 5 – 701. [e] Saitama Prefectural Library (1924) 120; . . . University Library (1924) 95.

Utsunomiya: [a] Honshu I. [b] none. [c] Ta R. [d] Utsunomiya University (1922) 2 – 330. [e] Tochigi Prefectural Library (?) 197; . . . University Library (1922) 120.

Wakayama: [a] Honshu I. [b] none. [c] Kitan Strait; Kino R. [d] Wakayama University (college) (1871) 2 – 210; Wakayama Prefectural Medical College (univ) (1945) 0.4 – 243. [e] . . . University Library (1923) 210; Wakayama Prefectural Library (1908) 68.

Yamagata: [a] Honshu I. [b] none. [c] nr Mogami R. [d] Yamagata University (1949) 5 – 562. [e] . . . University Library (1949) 311; Yamagata Prefectural Library (1910) 108.

Yao: [a] Honshu I. [b] none. [c] nr Yamato R. [d] none.

Yokkaichi: [a] Honshu I. [b] none. [c] Ise B of Pacific O. [d] none. [e] Municipal Library (1908) 6 (in 1946).

Yokohama: [a] Honshu I. [b] none. [c] Tokyo B of Pacific O. [d] Kanagawa University (college) (1929) 9 – 333; Kanto Gakuin University (1884) 8 – 409; Yokohama National University (1876) 6 – 1020; Yokohama Municipal University (1928) 3 – 412. [e] Yokohama National University Library (1949) 312; Kanagawa Prefectural Library (1930) 234; Municipal Library (1925) 140.

Yokosuka: [a] Honshu I. [b] none. [c] Tokyo B of Pacific O. [d] none.

Jordan

*Amman: [b] none. [c] Zerqa R. [d] University of Jordan (1962) 3 – 170. [e] Municipal Public Library (1960) 30; University . . . Library (1962?) 21.

Kashmir-Jammu

*Jammu: [b] none. [c] Tawi R. [d] none. [e] Shri Ranbir Library (1879) 18 (in 1950).

*Srinagar: [b] for Cashmere. [c] Jhelum R. [d] University of Kashmir (1948) 13 – 1018. [e] University . . . Library (1948) 77. [f] 295s (1961).

Korea: North

Chongjin: [b] for Seishin. [c] Sea of Japan. [d] none. [e] City Library (?) 23; North Hamgyong Provincial Library (?) ?

Hamhung: [b] for Kanko. [c] Tongsong R. [d] none. [e] South Hamgyong Provincial Library (?) 40; City Library (?) ?

Hungnam: [b] for Konan. [c] Sea of Japan; Tongsong R. [d] none.

Kaesong: [b] for Kaijo, Songdo. [c] nr Han R; nr Yesong R. [d] none. [e] City Library (?) 28.

Kimchaek: [b] for Joshin, Songjin. [c] Sea of Japan; Susong R. [d] none.

*Pyongyang: [b] for Heijo. [c] Taedong R. [d] Kim Il-song Comprehensive University (1946) 16 – 900? [e] State Central Library (1964) 1520; University Library (1946) 60; South Pyongan Provincial Library (?) ?

Sinuiju: [b] for Shingishu. [c] Yalu R. [d] none. [e] North Pyongan Provincial Library (?) ?

Wonsan: [b] for Gensan. [c] Sea of Japan. [d] none. [e] Kangwon Provincial Library (?) ?

[1] Universities with 10,000 or more students.

Korea: South

Chonju: [b] alt Jeonju; for Zenshu. [c] Chonju (alt Jeonju) R. [d] Chunpuk National University (1951) 4 – ? [e] ... University Library (1952) 66.

Inchon: [b] alt Incheon; for Chemulpo, Zinsen. [c] Yellow Sea. [d] none. [e] Inha Institute of Technology Library (1955) 31 (in 1959); Public Library (1921) 18 (in 1959).

Kwangju: [b] alt Gwangju; for Koshu. [c] nr Yongsan R. [d] Chonnam National University (1951) 6 – 321; Chosun University (1946) 4 – 247. [e] Chosun University Library (1950) 158; Chonnam National University Library (1952) 58.

Masan: [b] for Masampo. [c] Chinhae B of Korea Strait. [d] none. [e] Masan College Library (?) ?

Mokpo: [b] for Moppo. [c] Yellow Sea. [d] none. [e] Commerce College Library of Chonnam National University (?) ?

Pusan: [b] alt Busan; for Fusan. [c] Korea Strait. [d] Dong A University (1945) 4 – 337; Pusan National University (1945) 3 – 264. [e] Dong A University Library (1950) 127; Pusan National University Library (1955) 79.

*Seoul: [b] alt Kyongsong; for Keijo; off Soul. [c] Han R. [d][1] Seoul National University (1946) 14 – 1725; Hanyang University (1939) 10 – 638; Chungang University (1919) 9 – 315; Konkuk University (1946) 8 – 397; Yonsei University (1884) 8 – 725; Ewha Women's University (1886) 8 – 594; Korea University (1905) 6 – 506. [e] Seoul National University Library (1946) 882; National Central Library (1923) 450.

Taegu: [b] alt Daegu; for Taikyu. [c] Tae R. [d] Yeungnam University (1948) 7 – 154; Kyongbuk National University (1951) 4 – 421. [e] Kyongbuk National University Library (1952) 130.

Taejon: [b] alt Daejeon; for Taiden. [c] Taejon (alt Daejeon) R. [d] Chungnam National University (1952) 2 – 130. [e] ... University Library (1955) 43.

Kuwait

*Kuwait: [b] alt Kuweit; off Kuwayt. [c] Persian G. [d] Kuwait University (1962) 2 – 159?. [e] ... University Library (1966) 100; Kuwait Central Library (1963) 95. [f] 100 (1965).

Laos

*Vientiane: [b] none. [c] Mekong R. [d] Sisavangvong University (planned). [e] Bibliotheque de l'Alliance Francaise (?) 10; British Council Library (?) 10; Bibliotheque Nationale (?) ?

Lebanon

*Beirut: [b] for Beyrouth; off Bayrut. [c] Mediterranean Sea. [d] Beirut Arab University (1960) 17 – 120?; Universite Libanaise (1951) 10 – 529; American University of Beirut (1866) 4 – 593; Universite Saint-Joseph (1846) 3 – 342. [e] American University of Beirut Library (1866) 340; Bibliotheque Orientale de l'Universite Saint-Joseph (1881) 150; Bibliotheque Nationale du Liban (1921) 120.

Tripoli: [b] off Tarabulus. [c] Mediterranean Sea. [d] none.

Macao

*Macao: [b] alt Aomen; off Macau. [c] South China Sea; Pearl R. [d] none. [e] Biblioteca Nacional de Macau (1929) 60.

Malaysia

George Town: [a] West Malaysia; Penang (off Pinang) I. [b] alt Penang; off Pinang. [c] Strait of Malacca. [d] University of Penang (1969) 0.7 – 33. [e] Penang Library (1817) 36. [f] 52 (1891).

Ipoh: [a] West Malaysia. [b] none. [c] Kinta R. [d] none. [e] Public Library (1951) 60.

*Kuala Lumpur: [a] *West Malaysia. [b] none. [c] Klang R. [d] University of Malaya (1905) 8 – 237; Kebangsaan National University (1970) 0.2 – 36. [e] University ... Library (1957) 333; Kuala Lumpur Book Club (1900) 135; Public Library (1966) 45. [f] 876s (1970).

Mongolia

*Ulan-Bator: [b] alt Ulaan Baatar; for Kulun, Urga. [c] Tola (off Tuula) R. [d] Mongolian State University (1942) 3 – 355. [e] State Public Library (1921) 1100; ... University Library (1942) 350.

Nepal

*Katmandu: [b] alt Kathmandu. [c] Baghmati R. [d] Tribhuvan University (1959) 0.7 – 142. [e] Nepal National Library (?) 20; Indian Library (1952) 13.

[1] Universities with 5000 or more students.

Pakistan

Gujranwala: [b] none. [c] none. [d] none. [e] Islamia College Library (?) 11; Municipal Public Library (?) 6.

Hyderabad: [b] for Nerankot. [c] Indus R. [d] University of Sind (1947 at Karachi, relocated 1951) 12 – ?. [e] University . . . Library (1947) 102; Hayat-e-Adab Library (?) 38.

*Islamabad: [b] none. [c] Soan R; Rawal L; Lohi Shir L. [d] University of Islamabad (1965) 0.08 – 42. [e] University . . . Library (1967) 10; National Library (planned).

Karachi: [b] none. [c] Arabian Sea of Indian O. [d] University of Karachi (1950) 23 – ? [e] University . . . Library (1950) 200; Liaquat Memorial Library (1950) 70; Anjuman Taraqqi-e-Urdu Library (1948) 55. [f] 22s (1853).

Lahore: [b] none. [c] Ravi R. [d] University of the Punjab (1858) 42 – ?; West Pakistan University of Engineering and Technology (1923) 2 – 145. [e] University . . . Library (1882) 250; Punjab Public Library (1884) 200.

Lyallpur: [b] none. [c] none. [d] West Pakistan Agricultural University (1909) 2 – 330. [e] . . . University Library (1909) 57.

Multan: [b] none. [c] nr Chenab R. [d] none. [e] Emerson College Library (?) 18; Public Library (?) 10.

Peshawar: [b] none. [c] nr Bara R. [d] University of Peshawar (1913) 21 – ? [e] University . . . Library (1950) 95.

Rawalpindi: [b] none. [c] Leh R. [d] none. [e] National Assembly Library (?) 48; Gordon College Library (1893?) 37.

Sargodha: [b] none. [c] none. [d] none. [e] Municipal Public Library (?) 13; De Montmorency College Library (1934?) 12.

Sialkot: [b] for Sealkote. [c] Aik (Nala) Creek. [d] none. [e] Murray College Library (1889?) 26; Municipal Library (?) 5

Philippines

Bacolod: [a] Negros I. [b] none. [c] Guimaras Strait; Lupit R. [d] University of Negros Occidental-Recoletos (1941) 8 – 210. [e] University . . . Library (1941) 60.

Basilan: [a] Basilan I. [b] inc Isabela. [c] Basilan Strait. [d] none. [f] Isabela: 48 (1960), 34 (1948), 12 (1939), 1 (1903), 1 (1887).

Caloocan: [a] Luzon I. [b] none. [c] Manila B of South China Sea. [d] Araneta University (at Malabon, nr Caloocan) (1946) 4 – 180. [e] . . . University Library (at Malabon, nr Caloocan) (1946?) 19.

Cebu: [a] Cebu (for Zebu) I. [b] for Zebu. [c] Bohol Strait. [d] University of the Visayas (1919) 20 – 508; Southwestern University (1946) 15 – 350; University of San Carlos (1595) 9 – 320; University of Southern Philippines (1927) 3 – 85. [e] University of San Carlos Library (1945) 120.

Davao: [a] Mindanao I. [b] none. [c] Davao G of Pacific O. [d] University of Mindanao (1946) 11 – 205; International Harvardian University (1951) ? – ? [e] City Library (?) 19. [f] 3 (1887).

Iloilo: [a] Panay I. [b] none. [c] Iloilo Strait; Iloilo R. [d] University of San Agustin (1904) 11 – 301; Central Philippine University (1905) 5 – 249; University of Iloilo (1947) ? – ? [e] University of San Agustin Library (1904?) 55; . . . University Library (1903) 49. [f] 12 (1887).

Manila: [a] Luzon I. [b] none. [c] Manila B of South China Sea; Pasig R. [d][1] University of the East (1946) 55 – 1422; Far Eastern University (1928) 38 – 1300; University of Santo Tomas (1611) 32 – 1260; Feati University (1946) 26 – 595; Centro Escolar University (1907) 11 – 308; University of Manila (1913) 11 – 356; Adamson University (1932) 10 – 320; Arellano University (1938) 8 – 203; Manuel L. Quezon University (1947) 8 – 489; National University (1900) 6 – 230; Philippine Women's University (1919) 6 – 586 [Manila campus: (1919) ? – ?]. [e] Bureau of Public Libraries (1900) 280; University of Santo Tomas Library (1611) 210; Far Eastern University Library (1928) 117. [f] 2989s (1969e).

Pasay: [a] Luzon I. [b] for Pineda, Rizal. [c] Manila B of South China Sea. [d] none.

*Quezon City: [a] Luzon I. [b] none. [c] Marikina R; Dario R. [d] University of the Philippines (1908 at Manila, relocated 1948) 20 – 1920; Ateneo de Manila University (1859 at Manila, relocated 1945?) 7 – 420. [e] University . . . Library (1908? at Manila, relocated 1948) 614.

Zamboanga: [a] Mindanao I. [b] for Samboangan. [c] Basilan Strait. [d] none. [e] Public Library (?) ?

Ryukyu Islands

*Naha: [a] Okinawa I. [b] alt Nawa. [c] East China Sea. [d] University of the Ryukyus (1950) 4 – 509; Okinawa University (1956) 3 – ? [e] Shikiya Memorial Library (alt University . . . Library) (1950) 200; Government of the Ryukyus Central Library (1950) 46.

Saudi Arabia

*Jidda: [a] Hejaz. [b] alt Jedda; off Juddah. [c] Red Sea. [d] King Abdul Aziz University (1967) 0.4 – 40. [e] Educational Library (?) 4.

Mecca: [a] *Hejaz. [b] alt Mekka; off Makkah. [c] nr (Wadi) Shayi R. [d] none. [e] Abbas Kattan Library (?) 10; Library of Alharam (?) 7.

Medina: [a] Hejaz. [b] off Madinah. [c] (Wadi) Buthan R. [d] Islamic University (1961) 1 – 57. [e] . . . University Library (1961) 30.

[1] Universities with 5000 or more students.

*Riyadh: [a] *Nejd. [b] off Riyad. [c] (Wadi) Hanifah R. [d] University of Riyadh (1951) 3 – 353. [e] University . . . Library (1957) 76; Saudi Library (?) 18.

Singapore

*Singapore: [b] off Singapura. [c] Singapore Strait; Johore Strait. [d] University of Singapore (1905) 4 – 325; Nanyang University (1953) 2 – 162. [e] University . . . Library (1962) 474; National Library (1884) 470.

Southern Yemen

*Aden: [b] none. [c] G of Aden of Indian O. [d] none. [e] Miswat Library (1951) 30. [f] 225s (1964e), 23 (1901?).

Syria

Aleppo: [b] off Halab. [c] Quwayq (alt Kuweik) R. [d] University of Aleppo (1946) 6 – 522. [e] National Library (1924) ?; University . . . Library (1960) ?

*Damascus: [b] off Dimashq. [c] Barada R. [d] Damascus University (1902) 31 – 677. [e] . . . University Library (1924) 103; Library of the Academy of Damascus (1881) 90; National Library (1880) 80.

Hama: [b] off Hamah. [c] Orontes R. [d] none.

Homs: [b] alt Hums; for Lebda; off Hims. [c] nr Orontes R. [d] none. [e] National Library (?) ?

Taiwan

Chiai: [b] alt Chiayi, Kiayi; for Kagi. [c] Pachang R. [d] none. [e] Chiai County Library (?) 13. [f] 22 (1911).

Hsinchu: [b] alt Sinchu; for Chuchien, Shinchiku. [c] Formosa (alt Taiwan) Strait. [d] National Tsing Hua University (1956) 0.8 – 141. [e] . . . University Library (1956) 8.

Kaohsiung: [b] for Takao; inc Kigo. [c] Formosa (alt Taiwan) Strait; Kaohsiung R. [d] none. [e] City Library (?) 28. [f] 672 (1966); Kigo: 7 (1911).

Keelung: [b] alt Chilung; for Kiirun. [c] East China Sea; Keelung (alt Chilung) R. [d] none. [e] City Library (?) 12. [f] 294 (1966), 18 (1911).

Sanchung: [b] none. [c] Tanshui (for Tamsui) R. [d] none.

Taichung: [b] for Taichu. [c] Yanagi R; Midori R. [d] Taiwan Provincial Chung Hsing University (1946) 8 – 546; Tunghai (Christian) University (1955) 1 – 220. [e] Providence College Library (1963?) 240; Tunghai University Library (1955) 73; Taiwan Provincial Chung Hsing University Library (1961) 72; Provincial Taichung Library (?) 58. [f] 382 (1966), 13 (1911).

Tainan: [b] for Taiwan. [c] Formosa (alt Taiwan) Strait. [d] Taiwan Provincial Cheng Kung University (1927) 5 – 575. [e] . . . University Library (1927) 110; City Library (?) 42. [f] 425 (1966), 60 (1911).

*Taipei: [b] for Taihoku; inc Daitotei, Moko (alt Banka, Manka). [c] Tanshui (for Tamsui) R; Keelung (alt Chilung) R. [d] National Taiwan University (1928) 12 – 2116; National Taiwan Normal University (1946) 8 – 781; National Chengchi University (1927 at Nanking, China; relocated 1954) 5 – 590; Fu Jen Catholic University (1961) 3 – 494; Soochow University (1901 at Soochow, China; relocated 1951) 2 – 249. [e] National Taiwan University Library (1945) 859; National Central Library (1954) 367; Provincial Taipei Library (1915) 340. [f] 1203 (1966), 95 (1911); Daitotei: 49 (1911), 50 (1901); Moko: 33 (1911), 29 (1901). 50 (1864e).

Thailand

*Bangkok: [b] off Krung Thep. [c] Chao Phraya R. [d1] Thammasat University (1933) 16 – 651; Chulalongkorn University (1902) 11 – 1113; Kasetsart University (1904) 4 – 551. [e] National Library (1905) 709; Thammasat University Library (1933) 152.

Thon Buri: [b] included in Bangkok until 1937. [c] Chao Phraya R. [d] Mahidol University (1880) 4 – 1357. [e] Siriraj Medical Library (?) 40.

Turkey

Adana: [b] for Seyhan. [c] Seyhan R. [d] none. [e] Merkez Ramazanoglu Kutuphane (?) 9.

*Ankara: [b] for Angora. [c] Ankara R; Cubuk R. [d] Ankara Universitesi (1925) 18 – 1616; Hacettepe Universitesi (1967) 8 – 825; Orta Dogu Teknik Universitesi (1956) 6 – 585. [e] Milli Kutuphane (1946) 524; Ankara Universitesi Kutuphane (1925?) 465.

Antioch: [b] off Antakya. [c] Orontes R. [d] none.

Bursa: [b] alt Brusa. [c] Gok R. [d] none. [e] Merkez Genel Kutuphane (?) 31.

Eskisehir: [b] alt Eskishehir. [c] Porsuk R. [d] none. [e] Merkez Genel Kutuphane (?) 14.

[1] Universities with 1000 or more students.

Gaziantep: [b] for Aintab, Antep. [c] Kavaklik Creek; Ainleben Creek. [d] none. [e] Merkez Genel Kutuphane (?) 9.
Izmir: [b] for Smyrna. [c] G of Izmir of Aegean Sea. [d] Ege Universitesi (1955) 6 – 755. [e] Merkez Milli Kutuphane (1912) 97. [f] 27 (1701e).
Kayseri: [b] none. [c] Kizil (Irmak) R. [d] none. [e] Merkez Genel Kutuphane (?) 15.
Konya: [b] alt Konia. [c] none. [d] none. [e] Merkez Genel Kutuphane (1947) 34.

USSR

Aktyubinsk: [a] Kazakhstan. [b] none. [c] Ilek R. [d] none. [e] Aktyubinsk Province Library (1932) 109.
Alma-Ata: [a] *Kazakhstan. [b] for Vernyy. [c] Bolshaya Almatinka R. [d] Kazakh S. M. Kirov State University (1934) 10 – 600. [e] Central Scientific Library of the Kazakh SSR Academy of Sciences (1933) 2866; National A. S. Pushkin State Library of the Kazakh SSR (1931) 2317; Central Library of the . . . University (1934) 806.
Andizhan: [a]Uzbekistan. [b] none. [c] Andizhan(-Say) R. [d] none. [e] Andizhan Province Library (1906) 196.
Angarsk: [a] Russia in Asia. [b] none. [c] Angara R. [d] none. [e] City Library (1951) 83.
Ashkhabad: [a] *Turkmenia. [b] for Poltoratsk. [c] Geami R. [d] Turkmen A. M. Gorkiy State University (1950) 4 – ? [e] Karl Marx State Library of the Turkmen SSR (1895) 2555;. . . University Library (1950) 363; Central Scientific Library of the Turkmen SSR Academy of Sciences (1941) 271.
Barnaul: [a] Russia in Asia. [b] none. [c] Ob R; Barnaulka R. [d] none. [e] Altai Regional Library (1888) 578.
Biysk: [a] Russia in Asia. [b] alt Biisk, Bisk. [c] Biya R. [d] none. [e] Biysk Pedagogic Institute Library (1931) 174; Central City Library (1899) 111.
Bratsk: [a] Russia in Asia. [b] none. [c] Angara R. [d] none. [e] City Library (1957) 24.
Bukhara: [a] Uzbekistan. [b] alt Bokhara. [c] nr Zeravshan R. [d] none. [e] Bukhara Province Library (?) 200.
Chelyabinsk: [a] Russia in Asia. [b] none. [c] Miass R. [d] none. [e] Chelyabinsk Province 50th Anniversary of the October Revolution Public Library (1898) 1375.
Chimkent: [a] Kazakhstan. [b] none. [c] Badam R. [d] none. [e] Chimkent Province A. S. Pushkin Library (1815) 111; Kazakh Technological Institute Library (1943?) 102.
Chita: [a] Russia in Asia. [b] none. [c] Ingoda R. [d] none. [e] Chita Province A. S. Pushkin Library (1895) 402.
Dushanbe: [a] *Tadzhikistan. [b] for Dyushambe, Stalinabad. [c] Kafirnigan R; Dushanbinka R. [d] Tadzhik V. I. Lenin State University (1948) 11 – 600. [e] National Firdousi State Library of the Tadzhik SSR (1933) 1962; Central Scientific Library of the Tadzhik SSR Academy of Sciences (1933) 657.
Dzhambul: [a] Kazakhstan. [b] for Auliye-Ata. [c] Talas R. [d]none. [e] Dzhambul Province C. Valichanov Library (1914) 98.
Frunze: [a] *Kirgizia. [b] for Pishpek. [c] Alamedin R; Alarcha R; Dzhirgozar R. [d] Kirgiz State University (1951) 12 – 550. [e] National N. G. Chernyshevskiy State Library of the Kirgiz SSR (1934) 2261; Scientific Library of the . . . University (1932) 623; Central Scientific Library of the Kirgiz SSR Academy of Sciences (1943) 496.
Irkutsk: [a] Russia in Asia. [b] none. [c] Angara R; Irkut R. [d] Irkutsk A. A. Zhdanov State University (1918) 9 – 500. [e] Scientific Library of the . . . University (1918) 2215; Irkutsk Province I. I. Molchanov-Sibirskiy Library (1861) 809.
Kamensk-Uralskiy: [a] Russia in Asia. [b] for Kamensk. [c] Iset R; Kamenka R. [d] none. [e] Technical Library of the Ural Aluminum Works (1936) 70.
Karaganda: [a] Kazakhstan. [b] none. [c] nr Nura R. [d] none. [e] Karaganda Province N. V. Gogol Library (1937) 202.
Kemerovo: [a] Russia in Asia. [b] for Shcheglovsk. [c] Tom R. [d] none. [e] Kemerovo Province Scientific Library (1920) 800.
Khabarovsk: [a] Russia in Asia. [b] none. [c] Amur R. [d] none. [e] Khabarovsk Region Scientific Library (1894) 1487.
Kokand: [a] Uzbekistan. [b] alt Khokand. [c] Sokh R. [d] none. [e] Kokand Mukimi Pedagogic Institute Library (1930) 129.
Komsomolsk-na-Amure: [a] Russia in Asia. [b] for Permskoye. [c] Amur R. [d] none. [e] Komsomolsk-na-Amure Pedagogic Institute Library (1954) 133; Central City N. Ostrovskiy Library (1934) 82.
Kopeysk: [a] Russia in Asia. [b] alt Kopeisk; for Kopi. [c] nr Miass R. [d] none.
Krasnoyarsk: [a] Russia in Asia. [b] none. [c] Yenisey R. [d] Krasnoyarsk University (1969) ? – ? [e] Krasnoyarsk Regional Library (1935) 1042.
Kurgan: [a] Russia in Asia. [b] none. [c] Tobol R. [d] none. [e] Kurgan Province Library (1943) 471.
Magnitogorsk: [a] Russia in Asia. [b] none. [c] Ural R. [d] none. [e] Scientific-Technical Library of the Magnitogorsk Metallurgical Combine (1931) 307.
Namangan: [a] Uzbekistan. [b] none. [c] nr Naryn R. [d] none. [e] Namangan Pedagogic Institute Library (1946) 85.
Nizhniy Tagil: [a] Russia in Asia. [b] alt Nizhni Tagil. [c] Tagil R. [d] none. [e] Nizhniy Tagil Pedagogic Institute Library (1952) 214; Scientific-Technical Library of the Ural Car-Building Works (1932) 187; Scientific-Technical Library of the Nizhniy Tagil V. I. Lenin Metallurgical Combine (1934) 178.
Novokuznetsk: [a] Russia in Asia. [b] for Stalinsk. [c] Tom R; Kondoma R; Aba R. [d] none. [e] Academician I. P. Bardin Scientific-Technical Library of the Kuznetsk Metallurgical Combine (1927) 1014; Metallurgical Palace of Culture Library of the Kuznetsk Metallurgical Combine (1931) 261.

Novosibirsk: [a] Russia in Asia. [b] for Novonikolayevsk. [c] Ob R; Inya R; Yeltsovka R. [d] Novosibirsk State University (1959) 5 – 500. [e] State Public Scientific-Technical Library of the Siberian Department of the USSR Academy of Sciences (1918) 5021; Novosibirsk Province Library (1929) 1019;... University Library (1959) 1000.

Omsk: [a] Russia in Asia. [b] none. [c] Irtysh R; Om R. [d] none. [e] Omsk Province A. S. Pushkin Library (1899) 1071; Omsk M. I. Kalinin Medical Institute Library (1920) 822.

Pavlodar: [a] Kazakhstan. [b] none. [c] Irtysh R. [d] none. [e] Pavlodar General Industrial Institute Library (1960?) 250; Pavlodar Province N. Ostrovskiy Library (1947) 126.

Petropavlovsk: [a] Kazakhstan. [b] none. [c] Ishim R. [d] none. [e] Petropavlovsk K. D. Ushinskiy Pedagogic Institute Library (1937) 157; North Kazakhstan Province Library (1919) 134.

Petropavlovsk-Kamchatskiy: [a] Russia in Asia. [b] for Petropavlovsk. [c] Ayacha B of Pacific O. [d] none. [e] Kamchatka Province Library (1914) 167.

Prokopyevsk: [a] Russia in Asia. [b] alt Prokopevsk. [c] Aba R. [d] none. [e] Technical Library of the Kuznetsk Coal Scientific Research Institute (1945) 54.

Samarkand: [a] Uzbekistan. [b] none. [c] nr Zeravshan R. [d] Samarkand Alisher Navoi State University (1927) 6 – 600. [e] Central Library of the... University (1927) 1195; Samarkand V. V. Kuybyshev Agricultural Institute Library (1948) 199; Samarkand Province A. S. Pushkin Library (1911) 167.

Semipalatinsk: [a] Kazakhstan. [b] none. [c] Irtysh R. [d] none. [e] Semipalatinsk Province N. V. Gogol Library (1883) 214.

Sverdlovsk: [a] Russia in Asia. [b] for Ekaterinburg, Yekaterinburg. [c] Iset R. [d] Ural A. M. Gorkiy State University (1920) 6 – 425. [e] Sverdlovsk V. G. Belinskiy State Public Library (1899) 1659; Ural S. M. Kirov Polytechnic Institute Library (1920) 1548; Scientific Library of the... University (1920) 687.

Tashkent: [a] *Uzbekistan. [b] alt Tashkend. [c] Chirchik R. [d] Tashkent V. I. Lenin State University (1920) 13 – 1100. [e] Alisher Navoi State Library of the Uzbek SSR (1870) 3410; Central Library of the Uzbek SSR Academy of Sciences (1933) 1554; Central Library of the... University (1918) 1535.

Temir-Tau: [a] Kazakhstan. [b] for Samarkandskiy. [c] Nura R. [d] none.

Tomsk: [a] Russia in Asia. [b] none. [c] Tom R. [d] Tomsk V. V. Kuybyshev State University (1888) 10 – ? [e] Scientific Library of the... University (1888) 2677; Scientific Library of the Tomsk S. M. Kirov Polytechnic Institute (1900) 628; Tomsk Province A. S. Pushkin Library (1899) 336.

Tselinograd: [a] Kazakhstan. [b] for Akmolinsk. [c] Ishim R. [d] none. [e] Tselinograd Province Saken Seyfullin Library (1941) 350.

Tyumen: [a] Russia in Asia. [b] alt Tiumen. [c] Tura R. [d] none. [e] Tyumen Province Library (1875) 378.

Ulan-Ude: [a] Russia in Asia; *Buryat ASSR. [b] for Verkhne-Udinsk. [c] Selenga R; Uda R. [d] none. [e] National M. Gorkiy Library of the Buryat ASSR (1881) 521.

Ust-Kamenogorsk: [a] Kazakhstan. [b] for Zashchita. [c] Irtysh R; Ulba R. [d] none. [e] East Kazakhstan Province A. S. Pushkin Library (1896) 167; Ust-Kamenogorsk Pedagogic Institute Library (1952) 160.

Vladivostok: [a] Russia in Asia. [b] none. [c] Sea of Japan. [d] Far Eastern State University (1923) 7 – 400. [e] Maritime Region A. M. Gorkiy Library (1887) 488; Far Eastern V. V. Kuybyshev Polytechnic Institute Library (1930) 348;... University Library (1956) 298.

Zlatoust: [a] Russia in Asia. [b] none. [c] Ay R. [d] none. [e] Scientific-Technical Library of the Zlatoust Metallurgical Works (1933) 114.

Vietnam: North

Haiphong: [b] none. [c] (Cua) Cam R; Kinh Thay R; Tram Bac (alt Tambac) R. [d] none. [f] 369s (1960).

*Hanoi: [b] for Kecho. [c] Red R; Tay L; Truc Bach L. [d] University of Hanoi (1904) 1 – 144. [e] Bibliotheque Nationale (1918) 1000. [f] 644s (1960).

Vietnam: South

Da Nang: [b] for Tourane. [c] South China Sea; Da Nang R. [d] none.

Hue: [b] none. [c] Huong (alt Parfums) R. [d] Universite de Hue (1957) 3 – 261. [e] Bibliotheque de l'Universite... (1957) 21.

*Saigon: [b] inc Cholon. [c] Sai Gon R; (Arroyo) Chinois Creek. [d] University of Saigon (1917 at Hanoi, relocated 1954) 24 – 677; Van Hanh University (1964) 4 – 108. [e] Bibliotheque Nationale (?) 121. [f] Cholon: 481 (1948e), 145 (1936), 122 (1900).

Yemen

*Sana: [b] alt Sanaa. [c] (Wadi) Alaf R; (Wadi) Shaub R. [d] none. [e] Great Mosque Library (1925) 4.

EUROPE

Albania

*Tirane: [b] alt Tirana. [c] nr Ishm R. [d] Universiteti Shteteror i Tiranes (1957) 7 – 807. [e] Biblioteka Kombetare (1922) 550; Biblioteka Shkencore e Universitetit . . . (1957) 360.

Austria

Graz: [b] none. [c] Mur (alt Mura) R. [d] Karl-Franzens-Universitat (1586) 6 – 626; Technische Hochschule in Graz (univ) (1811) 4 – 333. [e] Universitatsbibliothek (1586) 730; Steiermarkische Landesbibliothek am Joanneum (1811) 437. [f] 63 (1857).

Innsbruck: [b] none. [c] Inn R; Sill R. [d] Leopold-Franzens-Universitat (1669) 6 – 253. [e] Universitatsbibliothek (1746) 737. [f] 14 (1857).

Linz: [b] none. [c] Danube R. [d] none. [e] Bundesstaatliche Studienbibliothek (1774) 178. [f] 28 (1857).

Salzburg: [b] none. [c] Salzach R. [d] Universitat Salzburg (1622) 2 – 403. [e] Universitatsbibliothek (1623) 296. [f] 17 (1857).

*Vienna: [b] off Wien. [c] Danube R. [d] Universitat Wien (1365) 21 – 1943; Technische Hochschule in Wien (univ) (1815) 6 – 572? [e] Osterreichische Nationalbibliothek (1526) 2040; Universitatsbibliothek (1365) 1686. [f] 476 (1857), 175 (1754).

Belgium

Anderlecht: [b] none. [c] Senne (alt Zenne) R. [d] none.

Antwerp: [b] off Antwerpen, Anvers. [c] Scheldt R. [d] Rijksuniversitair Centrum te Antwerpen (1852) 2 – 215. [e] Stadsbibliotheek (1470) 800.

Bruges: [b] alt Brugge. [c] Rei (alt Reye, Roye) R. [d] none. [e] Bibliotheque du Grand Seminaire (1833) 110; Stadsbibliotheek (1796) 66.

*Brussels: [b] off Brussel, Bruxelles. [c] Senne (alt Zenne) R. [d] Universite Libre de Bruxelles (1834) 13 – 2009; Vrije Universiteit Brussel (1834) 3 – 365? [e] Bibliotheque Royale de Belgique (1837) 2600; Bibliotheque de l'Universite . . . (1846) 780. [f] 57 (1755).

Charleroi: [b] none. [c] Sambre R. [d] none. [e] Bibliotheque Communale (?) 40.

Ghent: [b] off Gand, Gent. [c] Scheldt R; Lys R. [d] Rijksuniversiteit te Gent (1816) 12 – 1004. [e] Bibliotheek der Universiteit (1817) 1550; Bibliotheque Publique Municipale (1945) 100.

La Louviere: [b] alt Louviere. [c] nr Sambre R. [d] Centre Universitaire de l'Etat a Mons (at Mons, nr La Louviere) (1965) 0.9 – 183. [e] Bibliotheque Centrale du Centre Universitaire . . . (at Mons, nr La Louviere) (1797) 300; Bibliotheque Centrale du Hainaut (1958) 60.

Liege: [b] alt Luik. [c] Meuse R; Ourthe R. [d] Universite de l'Etat a Liege (1816) 9 – 302. [e] Bibliotheque de l'Universite . . . (1817) 1328; Bibliotheque Centrale (1862) 250.

Schaerbeek: [b] alt Schaarbeek. [c] Woluwe R. [d] none.

Bulgaria

Burgas: [b] none. [c] G of Burgas of Black Sea. [d] none. [e] District Library (1890) 248. [f] 106 (1965).

Plovdiv: [b] for Philippopolis. [c] Maritsa R. [d] none. [e] National Ivan Vazov Library (1882) 665. [f] 223 (1965).

Ruse: [b] for Ruschuk. [c] Danube R. [d] none. [e] L. Karavelov District Library (1888) 300. [f] 128 (1965).

*Sofia: [b] off Sofiya. [c] Bogana R. [d] Saint Kliment of Okhrid University of Sofia (1888) 12 – 745. [e] National Cyril and Methodius Library (1878) 1032; Bulgarian Academy of Sciences Library (1869) 857; . . . University Library (1888) 834; City Library (1928) 453. [f] 801, 894s (1965).

Stara Zagora: [b] for Eski Zagra. [c] nr Syuyutliyka R. [d] none. [e] District Library (1955) 207. [f] 89 (1965).

Varna: [b] for Stalin. [c] Black Sea; Varna L. [d] none. [e] National City Library (1883) 322. [f] 180 (1965).

Czechoslovakia

Bratislava: [a] Slovakia. [b] for Pozsony, Pressburg. [c] Danube R. [d] Universita Komenskeho (1919) 14 – 1743; Slovenska Vysoka Skola Technicka (univ) (1938) 9 – 1504. [e] Universitni Kniznica (1919) 1248; Slovenska Technicka Kniznica (1938) 1100. [f] 44 (1857).

Brno: [a] Moravia. [b] for Brunn. [c] Svratka R; Svitava R. [d] Vysoke Uceni Technicke v Brne (univ) (1849) 9 – 1042; Universita Jana Evangelisty Purkyne (1919) 6 – 868. [e] Statni Vedecka Knihovna (1899) 2973; Universitni Knihovna (1770) 1564. [f] 59 (1857).

Karlovy Vary: [a] Bohemia. [b] alt Carlsbad; for Karlsbad. [c] Ohre (alt Eger) R; Tepla (for Tepl) R. [d] none. [e] Mestska Knihovna (1825) 65.

Kosice: [a] Slovakia. [b] for Kaschau, Kassa. [c] Hornad R. [d] Universita Pavla Jozefa Safarika (1959) 5 – 600; Vysoka Skola Technicka v Kosiciach (univ) (1952) 2 – ? [e] Statna Vedecka Kniznica (1657) 988. [f] 16 (1857).

Ostrava: [a] Moravia. [b] for Mahrisch-Ostrau, Moravska Ostrava. [c] Oder R; Ostravice R. [d] none. [e] Statni Vedecka Knihovna (1951) 432.

Plzen: [a] Bohemia. [b] for Pilsen. [c] Berounka R; Mze R; Radbuza R; Uhlava R; Uslava R. [d] none. [e] Statni Vedecka Knihovna (1950) 816. [f] 14 (1857).

*Prague: [a] Bohemia. [b] for Prag; off Praha. [c] Vltava R. [d] Universita Karlova (1348) 19 – 2842; Ceske Vysoke Uceni Technicke v Praze (univ) (1707) 12 – 1508; Universita 17. Listopadu (1961) 1 – 193. [e] Statni Knihovna (1366?) 4213; Narodniho Muzea Knihovna (1818) 1700; Mestska Lidova Knihovna (1891) 1436; Ceskoslovenske Akademie ved Zakladni Knihovna (1890) 1000. [f] 143 (1857), 78 (1770e).

Denmark

Alborg: [b] alt Aalborg. [c] Lim Fjord of Kattegat Strait. [d] none. [e] Nordjyske Landsbibliotek (1895) 331.

Arhus: [b] alt Aarhus. [c] Kattegat Strait. [d] Arhus Universitet (1928) 10 – 1439. [e] Statsbiblioteket (1902) 1060; Kommunes Biblioteker (1934) 502.

*Copenhagen: [b] off Kobenhavn. [c] Oresund Strait. [d] Kobenhavns Universitet (1479) 24 – 2161; Polytekniske Laereanstalt, Danmarks Tekniske Hojskole (univ) (at Lyngby, nr Copenhagen) (1829) 3 – 576? [e] Kongelige Bibliotek (1661) 1800; Universitetsbiblioteket (1482) 1306; Kommunes Biblioteker (1885) 1138. [f] 93 (1769).

Frederiksberg: [b] none. [c] nr Oresund Strait. [d] none. [e] Kommunes Biblioteker (1887) 525.

Odense: [b] none. [c] Odense R. [d] Odense Universitet (1964) 1 – 186. [e] Universitetsbiblioteket (1966?) 309; Centralbibliotek (1924) 300.

Finland

Espoo: [b] alt Esbo. [c] G of Finland of Baltic Sea. [d] none. [e] Kaupunginkirjasto (?) 90.

*Helsinki: [b] alt Helsingfors. [c] G of Finland of Baltic Sea. [d] Helsingin Yliopisto (1640 at Turku, relocated 1828) 23 – 1813; Teknillinen Korkeakoulu (univ) (1849) 6 – 559; Kuopion Korkeakoulu (univ) (1966) ? – ? [e] . . . Yliopiston Kirjasto (1640 at Turku, relocated 1828) 1400; Kaupunginkirjasto (1860) 874.

Tampere: [b] alt Tammerfors. [c] Tammer Rapids; Nasi L; Pyha L. [d] Tampereen Yliopisto (1925) 6 – 185; Tampereen Teknillinen Korkeakoulu (univ) (1966) 0.5 – 118. [e] Kaupunginkirjasto (1861) 427; . . . Yliopiston Kirjasto (1925) 215. [f] 220s (1970).

Turku: [b] alt Abo. [c] G of Bothnia of Baltic Sea; Aura R. [d] Turun Yliopisto (1920) 8 – 603; Abo Akademi (univ) (1917) 2 – 183. [e] . . . Akademis Bibliotek (1918) 710; . . . Yliopiston Kirjasto (1919) 640. [f] 203s (1970).

France

Ajaccio: [a] Provence-Cote d'Azur-Corse; *Corsica I. [b] none. [c] Mediterranean Sea. [d] none. [e] Bibliotheque Municipale (1801) 60.

Amiens: [a] Picardie. [b] none. [c] Somme R. [d] Universite d'Amiens (1964) 6 – 206. [e] Bibliotheque Municipale (1791) 99.

Angers: [a] Pays de la Loire. [b] none. [c] Maine R. [d] Universite Catholique de l'uest (1875) 3 – 306; Universite d'Etat d'Angers (1969) ? – ? [e] Bibliotheque Lamoriciere de l'Universite Catholique de l'Ouest (1875) 200; Bibliotheque Municipale (1848) 135.

Avignon: [a] Provence-Cote d'Azur-Corse. [b] none. [c] Rhone R. [d] none. [e] Bibliotheque du Museum Calvet (1810) 231. [f] 139s (1968).

Bayonne: [a] Aquitaine. [b] none. [c] Adour R; Nive R. [d] none. [e] Bibliotheque Municipale (1850) 62. [f] 110s (1968).

Besancon: [a] Franche-Comte. [b] none. [c] Doubs R. [d] Universite de Besancon (1422 at Dole, relocated 1691) 9 – 250? [e] Bibliotheque Universitaire (1891) 350; Bibliotheque Municipale (1694) 250. [f] 116s (1968).

Bethune: [a] Nord. [b] none. [c] Lawe R. [d] none. [e] Bibliotheque Municipale (?) 13. [f] 145s (1968).

Bordeaux: [a] Aquitaine. [b] none. [c] Garonne R. [d] Universite de Bordeaux (1441) 34 – 736. [e] Bibliotheque de l'Universite . . . (1879) 870; Bibliotheque Municipale (1736) 399.

Boulogne-Billancourt: [a] Region Parisienne. [b] for Boulogne-sur-Seine. [c] Seine R. [d] none. [e] Bibliotheque Municipale (1864) 56.

Brest: [a] Bretagne. [b] none. [c] Atlantic O. [d] none. [e] Bibliotheque Municipale (1853) 86. [f] 169s (1968).

Bruay-en-Artois: [a] Nord. [b] for Bruay. [c] Lawe R. [d] none.

Caen: [a] Basse-Normandie. [b] none. [c] Orne R; Odon R. [d] Universite de Caen (1432) 13 – 718. [e] Bibliotheque Universitaire (1432) 500; Bibliotheque Municipale (1872) 132.

Cannes: [a] Provence-Cote d'Azur-Corse. [b] none. [c] Mediterranean Sea. [d] none. [e] Bibliotheque Municipale (1868) 90.

Clermont-Ferrand: [a] Auvergne. [b] none. [c] nr Sioule R. [d] Universite de Clermont-Ferrand (1810) 13 – 532. [e] Bibliotheque Municipale et Universitaire (18th c) 230.

Denain: [a] Nord. [b] none. [c] Scheldt R. [d] none. [f] 127s (1968).

Dijon: [a] Bourgogne. [b] none. [c] Ouche R; Suzon R. [d] Universite de Dijon (1722) 11 – 535. [e] Bibliotheque de l'Universite . . . (1880) 325; Bibliotheque Municipale (1701) 180.

Douai: [a] Nord. [b] for Douay. [c] Scarpe R. [d] none. [e] Bibliotheque Municipale (1767) 81.

Dunkerque: [a] Nord. [b] alt Dunkirk. [c] North Sea. [d] none. [e] Bibliotheque Municipale (18th c) 31.

Grenoble: [a] Rhone-Alpes. [b] none. [c] Isere R. [d] Universite de Grenoble (1339) 24 – 1232. [e] Bibliotheque Universitaire (1879) 469; Bibliotheque Municipale (1772) 294.

Le Havre: [a] Haute-Normandie. [b] alt Havre. [c] English Channel; Seine R. [d] none. [e] Bibliotheque Municipale (1800) 148.

Le Mans: [a] Pays de la Loire. [b] alt Mans. [c] Sarthe R. [d] none. [e] Bibliotheque Municipale (1931) 110.

Lens: [a] Nord. [b] none. [c] Deule R. [d] none.

Lille: [a] Nord. [b] none. [c] Deule R. [d] Universite de Lille (1562 at Douai, relocated 1887) 28 – 1253. [e] Bibliotheque Universitaire (1880) at Douai, relocated 1887) 700; Bibliotheque Municipale (1726) 310.

Limoges: [a] Limousin. [b] none. [c] Vienne R. [d] Universite de Limoges (1808) 5 – 261. [e] Bibliotheque Municipale (1804) 220.

Lyons: [a] Rhone-Alpes. [b] off Lyon. [c] Rhone R; Saone R. [d] Universite de Lyon (1809) 38 – 2433. [e] Bibliotheque Municipale (1693) 780; Bibliotheque Universitaire, Section Droit-Lettres (1896) 432.

Marseilles: [a] Povence-Cote d'Azur-Corse. [b] off Marseille. [c] G of Lions of Mediterranean Sea. [d] Universite d'Aix-Marseille (at Aix-en-Provence and Marseilles) (1409) 37 – 2225 [Marseilles campus: (1854) ? – ?]. [e] Bibliotheque Universitaire, Section Medecine-Pharmacie (1891) 252; Bibliotheque Municipale (1799) 230.

Metz: [a] Lorraine. [b] none. [c] Moselle R; Seille R. [d] none. [e] Bibliotheque Municipale (1811) 115.

Montbeliard: [a] Franche-Comte. [b] none. [c] Allaine R; Luzine R. [d] none. [e] Bibliotheque Municipale (1765) 56. [f] 115s (1968).

Montpellier: [a] Languedoc. [b] none. [c] Lez R. [d] Universite de Montpellier (1181) 27 – 1200. [e] Bibliotheque Universitaire Centrale (1890) 713; Bibliotheque de la Ville et du Musee Fabre (1800) 350; Bibliotheque Universitaire, Section Medecine (1767) 350.

Montreuil: [a] Region Parisienne. [b] alt Montreuil-sous-Bois. [c] nr Seine R. [d] none. [e] Bibliotheque Municipale (1879) 40.

Mulhouse: [a] Alsace. [b] for Mulhausen. [c] Ill R. [d] none. [e] Bibliotheque Municipale (1840) 158.

Nancy: [a] Lorraine. [b] none. [c] Meurthe R. [d] Universite de Nancy (1572) 20 – 744. [e] Bibliotheque de l'Universite . . . (1855) 705; Bibliotheque Municipale (1750) 200.

Nantes: [a] Pays de la Loire. [b] none. [c] Loire R; Sevre Nantaise R; Erdre R. [d] Universite de Nantes (1808) 14 – ? [e] Bibliotheque Municipale (1753) 326.

Nice: [a] Provence-Cote d'Azur-Corse. [b] for Nizza. [c] Mediterranean Sea; Paillon R. [d] Universite de Nice (1965) 12 – 413. [e] Bibliotheque Municipale (bef 1787) 154.

Nimes: [a] Languedoc. [b] none. [c] nr Gard R. [d] none. [e] Bibliotheque Municipale Dite Seguier (1794) 171. [f] 125s (1968).

Orleans: [a] Centre. [b] none. [c] Loire R. [d] Universite d'Orleans-Tours (at Orleans and Tours) (1306) 12 – 420 [Orleans campus: (1306) ? – ?]. [e] Bibliotheque Municipale (1714) 245.

*Paris: [a] Region Parisienne. [b] none. [c] Seine R. [d] Universite de Paris (1200) 166 – 5848; Institut Catholique de Paris (univ) (1875) 10 – 741. [e] Bibliotheque Nationale (1480) 7000; Bibliotheque de l'Universite . . . (1570?) 6076, inc Bibliotheque Sainte-Genevieve (1624) 3000, and Bibliotheque de la Sorbonne (1762) 1600; Bibliotheque de l'Arsenal (1797) 1530; Bibliotheque de l'Institut de France (1796) 1500; Bibliotheque Pedagogique (1879) 1000. [f] 510 (1719).

Pau: [a] Aquitaine. [b] none. [c] (Gave de) Pau R. [d] none. [e] Bibliotheque Municipale (1789) 150. [f] 110s (1968).

Perpignan: [a] Languedoc. [b] none. [c] Tet R. [d] none. [e] Bibliotheque Municipale (1349) 72. [f] 107s (1968).

Rennes: [a] Bretagne. [b] none. [c] Vilaine R; Ille R. [d] Universite de Rennes (1461 at Nantes, relocated 1735) 22 – 828. [e] Bibliotheque de l'Universite . . . (1855) 665; Bibliotheque Municipale (1790) 259.

Rheims: [a] Champagne. [b] off Reims. [c] Vesle R. [d] Universite de Reims (1550) 8 – 681. [e] Bibliotheque Municipale Dite Carnegie (1809) 198.

Roubaix: [a] Nord. [b] none. [c] nr Scheldt R. [d] none. [e] Bibliotheque de l'Agence Univers (1934 at Lille, relocated 1952) 67; Bibliotheque Municipale (1833) 57.

Rouen: [a] Haute-Normandie. [b] none. [c] Seine R. [d] Universite de Rouen (1828) 9 – 294. [e] Bibliotheque Municipale (1791) 300.

Saint-Denis: [a] Region Parisienne. [b] none. [c] Seine R. [d] none. [e] Bibliotheque Municipale (1792) 120.

Saint-Etienne: [a] Rhone-Alpes. [b] none. [c] Furens R. [d] none. [e] Bibliotheque Municipale (1842) 107.

Saint-Nazaire: [a] Pays de la Loire. [b] none. [c] B of Biscay of Atlantic O; Loire R. [d] none. [e] Bibliotheque Municipale (1889) 61. [f] 111s (1968).

Strasbourg: [a] Alsace. [b] for Strassburg. [c] Ill R. [d] Universite de Strasbourg (1537) 23 – 1437. [e] Bibliotheque Nationale et Universitaire (1872) 3000; Bibliotheque Municipale (1765) 218.

Thionville: [a] Lorraine. [b] for Diedenhofen. [c] Moselle R. [d] none. [e] Bibliotheque Municipale (1842) 12.

Toulon: [a] Provence-Cote d'Azur-Corse. [b] none. [c] Mediterranean Sea. [d] none. [e] Bibliotheque Municipale (1790) 78.

Toulouse: [a] Midi-Pyrenees. [b] none. [c] Garonne R. [d] Universite de Toulouse (1229) 35 – 1127. [e] Bibliotheque Universitaire Centrale (1879) 900; Bibliotheque Municipale (1782) 259.

Tourcoing: [a] Nord. [b] none. [c] nr Scheldt R. [d] none. [e] Bibliotheque Municipale (1880) 16.

Tours: [a] Centre. [b] none. [c] Loire R; Cher R. [d] Universite d'Orleans-Tours (at Orleans and Tours) (1306) 12 – 420 [Tours campus: (1948) ? – ?]. [e] Bibliotheque Municipale (1791) 220. [f] 33 (1856), 25 (1841).

Troyes: [a] Champagne. [b] none. [c] Seine R. [d] none. [e] Bibliotheque Municipale (1651) 253. [f] 114s (1968).

Valenciennes: [a] Nord. [b] none. [c] Scheldt R; Rhonelle R. [d] none. [e] Bibliotheque Municipale (1765) 96.

Versailles: [a] Region Parisienne. [b] none. [c] nr Seine R. [d] none. [e] Bibliotheque Municipale (1803) 403. [f] 44 (1789).

Villeurbanne: [a] Rhone-Alpes. [b] none. [c] nr Rhone R. [d] none. [e] Bibliotheque Universitaire, Section Centrale et Sciences (of the Universite de Lyon) (1964) 143; Bibliotheque Municipale (1934) 100.

Germany: East

*Berlin (see under Germany: West).

Brandenburg: [b] alt Brandenburg an der Havel. [c] Havel R. [d] none. [e] Stadtbibliothek (1892) 77.

Dessau: [b] none. [c] Mulde R. [d] none. [e] Stadtbibliothek (1897) 188.

Dresden: [b] none. [c] Elbe R; Weisseritz R. [d] Technische Universitat Dresden (1828) 12 – 2388. [e] Sachsische Landesbibliothek (1556) 1002; Universitatsbibliothek (1833) 352; Stadt-und Bezirksbibliothek (1910) 314. [f] 63 (1755), 40 (1697e).

Erfurt: [b] none. [c] Gera R. [d] none. [e] Wissenschaftliche Allgemeinbibliothek (1392) 447.

Gera: [b] none. [c] White Elster (off Weisse Elster) R. [d] none. [e] Stadt- und Bezirksbibliothek (1920) 118.

Halle: [b] none. [c] Saale R. [d] Martin-Luther-Universitat Halle-Wittenberg [1502 at Wittenberg, united with Universitat Halle (1694) in 1817] 6 – 1445. [e] Universitats- und Landesbibliothek Sachsen-Anhalt (1696) 1845; Stadt- und Bezirksbibliothek (1874) 188.

Karl-Marx-Stadt: [b] for Chemnitz. [c] Chemnitz R. [d] Technische Hochschule Karl-Marx-Stadt (univ) (1836) 8 – 1029. [e] Stadt- und Bezirksbibliothek (1869) 338; Bibliothek der Technischen Hochschule . . . (1836) 243.

Leipzig: [b] none. [c] White Elster (off Weisse Elster) R; Pleisse R; Parthe R. [d] Karl-Marx-Universitat Leipzig (1409) 13 – 2189. [e] Deutsche Bucherei (1912) 3151; Universitatsbibliothek (1543) 2035; Stadt- und Bezirksbibliothek (1914) 457.

Magdeburg: [b] none. [c] Elbe R. [d] Technische Hochschule Otto von Guericke Magdeburg (univ) (1953) 3 – 627. [e] Stadt- und Bezirksbibliothek (1525) 266.

Potsdam: [b] none. [c] Havel R; Templiner L; Jungfern L; Heiliger L. [d] none. [e] Wissenschaftliche Allgemeinbibliothek des Bezirkes Potsdam (1946) 423; Bibliothek der Deutschen Akademie fur Staats- und Rechtswissenschaft Walter Ulbricht (1949) 292.

Rostock: [b] none. [c] Warnow R. [d] Universitat Rostock (1419) 6 – 1283. [e] Universitatsbibliothek (1419) 1004; Stadt- und Bezirksbibliothek Willi Bredel (1894) 135.

Schwerin: [b] none. [c] Schweriner L. [d] none. [e] Wissenschaftliche Allgemeinbibliothek des Bezirkes Schwerin (1779) 539.

Zwickau: [b] none. [c] Zwickauer Mulde R. [d] none. [e] Ratsschulbibliothek (1500?) 76; Stadtbibliothek (1923) 45.

Germany: West

Aachen: [a] Nordrhein-Westfalen. [b] for Aix-la-Chapelle. [c] Wurm(bach) Creek. [d] Rheinisch-Westfalische Technische Hochschule (univ) (1870) 13 – 1253. [e] Bibliothek der . . . Technischen Hochschule (1870) 341; Stadtbibliothek (1828) 223.

Augsburg: [a] Bayern. [b] none. [c] Lech R. [d] Universitat Augsburg (1970) 0.3 – 74. [e] Staats- und Stadtbibliothek (1537) 354. [f] 26 (1703).

Baden-Baden: [a] Baden-Wurttemberg. [b] alt Baden. [c] Oos(bach) Creek. [d] none. [e] Stadtbucherei (1900) 43.

Berlin: [a] West Berlin: *West-Berlin. [b] inc Charlottenburg since 1920, East Berlin (off Ost-Berlin), West Berlin (off West-Berlin). [c] Havel R; Spree R. [d] East Berlin: Humboldt-Universitat zu Berlin (1809) 14 – 2726; West Berlin: Freie Universitat Berlin (1948) 13 – 1744; Technische Universitat Berlin (1799) 8 – 1549? [e] East Berlin: Deutsche Staatsbibliothek (1661) 3024; Universitatsbibliothek der Humboldt-Universitat zu Berlin (1831) 1944; Stadtbibliothek (1901) 924; West Berlin: Staatsbibliothek Preussischer Kulturbesitz (1661) 2270; Universitatsbibliothek der Freien Universitat Berlin (1952) 571. [f] 91 (1740), 29 (1700); Charlottenburg: 189 (1900), 12 (1861), 3 (1800); East Berlin: 1085 (1971), 1071 (1964), 1189 (1950); West Berlin: 2122 (1970), 2197 (1961), 2147 (1950).

Bielefeld: [a] Nordrhein-Westfalen. [b] none. [c] Lutter(bach) Creek. [d] Universitat Bielefeld (1966) 0.4 – 25. [e] Stadtbibliothek (1905) 202; Universitatsbibliothek (1966?) 181.

Bochum: [a] Nordrhein-Westfalen. [b] none. [c] nr Ruhr R. [d] Ruhr-Universitat Bochum (1961) 11 – 398. [e] Universitatsbibliothek (1965) 480; Stadtbucherei (1905) 258.

*Bonn: [a] Nordrhein-Westfalen. [b] inc Bad Godesberg (alt Godesberg) since 1968. [c] Rhine R. [d] Rheinische Friedrich-Wilhelms-Universitat Bonn (1777) 17 – 800. [e] Universitatsbibliothek (1818) 1010; Abteilung Wissenschaftliche Dokumentation des Deutschen Bundestages (1949) 473. [f] Bad Godesberg: 75 (1968e), 65 (1961), 45 (1950), 24 (1933), 9 (1900), 0.9 (1850?).

Bottrop: [a] Nordrhein-Westfalen. [b] none. [c] nr Emscher R. [d] none. [e] Stadtbucherei (1934) 70.

Bremen: [a] *Bremen. [b] none. [c] Weser R. [d] Universitat Bremen (1964) ? – ? [e] Staatsbibliothek und Universitatsbibliothek (1660) 804; Stadtbibliothek (1902) 438.

Bremerhaven: [a] Bremen. [b] none. [c] Weser R. [d] none. [e] Stadtbibliothek (1873) 149.

Brunswick: [a] Niedersachsen. [b] off Braunschweig. [c] Oker R. [d] Technische Universitat Carolo-Wilhelmina (1745) 5 – 300. [e] Bibliothek der . . . Universitat (1748) 335; Stadtarchiv und Stadtbibliothek (1861) 218.

Cologne: [a] Nordrhein-Westfalen. [b] off Koln. [c] Rhine R. [d] Universitat zu Koln (1388) 19 – 778. [e] Universitats- und Stadtbibliothek (1602) 1102.

Darmstadt: [a] Hessen. [b] none. [c] nr Gersprenz R. [d] Technische Universitat Darmstadt (1836) 6 – 617. [e] Hessische Landes- und Universitatsbibliothek (1567) 852.

Dortmund: [a] Nordrhein-Westfalen. [b] none. [c] Emscher R. [d] Universitat Dortmund (1966) 0.6 – 113. [e] Stadt- und Landesbibliothek (1907) 282; Stadtische Volksbucherei (1897) 260.

Duisburg: [a] Nordrhein-Westfalen. [b] inc Hamborn since 1929. [c] Rhine R; Ruhr R. [d] none. [e] Stadtbucherei (1901) 446. [f] Hamborn: 127 (1925), 33 (1900), 1 (1871).

Dusseldorf: [a] *Nordrhein-Westfalen. [b] none. [c] Rhine R. [d] Universitat Dusseldorf (1708) 2 – 605. [e] Universitatsbibliothek (1770) 806; Hauptstaatsarchiv (1832) 400; Stadtbucherei (1886) 307.

Essen: [a] Nordrhein-Westfalen. [b] none. [c] Ruhr R; Emscher R; Baldeney L. [d] none. [e] Stadtbibliothek (1902) 574.

Flensburg: [a] Schleswig-Holstein. [b] for Flensborg. [c] Flensburger (Forde) Inlet of Baltic Sea. [d] none. [e] Dansk Centralbibliotek for Sydslesvig (1920) 85; Stadtbucherei (1904) 66.

Frankfurt am Main: [a] Hessen. [b] alt Frankfort, Frankfurt. [c] Main R. [d] Johann Wolfgang Goethe-Universitat (1914) 15 – 1136. [e] Stadt- und Universitatsbibliothek (1668) 1500; Deutsche Bibliothek (1946) 1376; Senckenbergische Bibliothek (1763) 630.

Freiburg im Breisgau: [a] Baden-Wurttemberg. [b] alt Freiburg. [c] Dreisam R. [d] Albert-Ludwigs-Universitat (1457) 12 – 493. [e] Universitatsbibliothek (1457) 1021.

Furth: [a] Bayern. [b] none. [c] Regnitz R; Pegnitz R; Rednitz R. [d] none. [e] Stadtische Bibliothek (1906) 30.

Gelsenkirchen: [a] Nordrhein-Westfalen. [b] none. [c] Emscher R. [d] none. [e] Stadtbucherei (1911) 219.

Gottingen: [a] Niedersachsen. [b] none. [c] Leine R. [d] Georg-August-Universitat (1736) 11 – 621. [e] Niedersachsische Staats- und Universitatsbibliothek (1735) 1544.

Hagen: [a] Nordrhein-Westfalen. [b] none. [c] Ennepe R; Volme R. [d] none. [e] Stadtbucherei (1899) 80. [f] 1 (1750).

Hamburg: [a] *Hamburg. [b] inc Altona since 1933. [c] Elbe R. [d] Universitat Hamburg (1919) 21 – 1874. [e] Staats- und Universitatsbibliothek (1479) 1258; Hamburgisches Weltwirtschafts-Archiv (1908) 550. [f] 54 (1756), 5 (1700?e); Altona: 242 (1933), 162 (1900), 41 (1855), 23 (1803).

Hannover: [a] *Niedersachsen. [b] alt Hanover. [c] Leine R. [d] Technische Universitat Hannover (1831) 7 – 432; Tierarztliche Hochschule Hannover (univ) (1778) 0.9 – 214; Medizinische Hochschule Hannover (univ) (1961) 0.4 – 97. [e] Niedersachsische Landesbibliothek (1665) 580; Bibliothek der . . . Universitat (1831) 362; Stadtbibliothek (1440) 354.

Heidelberg: [a] Baden-Wurttemberg. [b] none. [c] Neckar R. [d] Ruprecht-Karl-Universitat Heidelberg (1386) 13 – 983. [e] Universitatsbibliothek (1706) 1075.

Heilbronn: [a] Baden-Wurttemberg. [b] none. [c] Neckar R. [d] none. [e] Stadtbucherei (?) 53.

Herne: [a] Nordrhein-Westfalen. [b] none. [c] nr Emscher R. [d] none. [e] Stadtische Bucherei (1910) 110.

Hildesheim: [a] Niedersachsen. [b] none. [c] Innerste R. [d] none. [e] Stadtarchiv und Stadtbibliothek (?) 107.

Kaiserslautern: [a] Rheinland-Pfalz. [b] none. [c] Lauter R. [d] Universitat Trier-Kaiserslautern (at Trier and Kaiserslautern) (1970) ? – ? [Kaiserslautern campus: (1970) ? – ?]. [e] Stadtbucherei (?) 34; Bibliothek der Pfalzischen Landesgewerbeanstalt Kaiserslautern (1882) 32.

Karlsruhe: [a] Baden-Wurttemberg. [b] for Carlsruhe. [c] nr Rhine R. [d] Universitat Fridericiana (1825) 8 – 650. [e] Badische Landesbibliothek (1500 at Pforzheim, relocated 1765) 458; Universitatsbibliothek (1840) 337. [f] 2 (1738).

Kassel: [a] Hessen. [b] for Cassel. [c] Fulda R. [d] Gesamthochschule Kassel (univ) (1970) ? – ? [e] Murhardsche Bibliothek der Stadt und Landesbibliothek (1863) 230.

Kiel: [a]*Schleswig-Holstein. [b] none. [c] Baltic Sea. [d] Christian-Albrechts-Universitat Kiel (1665) 8 – 889. [e] Bibliothek des Instituts fur Weltwirtschaft an der . . . Universitat (1910) 1012; Universitatsbibliothek (1665) 576.

Koblenz: [a] Rheinland-Pfalz. [b] alt Coblenz. [c] Rhine R; Moselle R. [d] none. [e] Stadtbibliothek (1827) 196.

Krefeld: [a] Nordrhein-Westfalen. [b] for Crefeld. [c] Rhine R. [d] none. [e] Stadtbibliothek (1900) 82.

Leverkusen: [a] Nordrhein-Westfalen. [b] for Wiesdorf. [c] Rhine R; Wupper R. [d] none. [e] Kekule-Bibliothek (1897) 330.

Lubeck: [a] Schleswig-Holstein. [b] none. [c] Trave R; Wakenitz R. [d] none. [e] Bibliothek der Hansestadt Lubeck (1616) 372.

Ludwigshafen: [a] Rheinland-Pfalz. [b] alt Ludwigshafen am Rhein. [c] Rhine R. [d] none. [e] Stadtbucherei (1875) 171.

Mainz: [a] *Rheinland-Pfalz. [b] for Mayence. [c] Rhine R; Main R. [d] Johannes-Gutenberg-Universitat (1477) 12 – 753. [e] Universitatsbibliothek (1946?) 726; Stadtbibliothek (1477) 400.

Mannheim: [a] Baden-Wurttemberg. [b] none. [c] Rhine R; Neckar R. [d] Universitat Mannheim (1907) 5 – 291. [e] Universitatsbibliothek (1907?) 470; Wissenschaftliche Stadtbibliothek (1869) 232; Stadtische Volks- und Musikbucherei (1895) 170.

Monchengladbach: [a] Nordrhein-Westfalen. [b] for Munchen-Gladbach. [c] Niers R. [d] none. [e] Stadtbibliothek (1904) 223.
Mulheim an der Ruhr: [a] Nordrhein-Westfalen. [b] alt Mulheim. [c] Ruhr R. [d] none. [e] Stadtbucherei (1887) 187.
Munich: [a] *Bayern. [b] off Munchen. [c] Isar R. [d] Ludwig-Maximilians-Universitat Munchen (1472) 24 – 2500?; Technische Universitat Munchen (1827) 10 – 575. [e] Bayerische Staatsbibliothek (1558) 3200; Universitatsbibliothek (1472) 1042; Bibliothek des Deutschen Museums (1903) 540; Stadtbibliothek (1843) 461.
Munster: [a] Nordrhein-Westfalen. [b] none. [c] Aa R. [d] Westfalische Wilhelms-Universitat Munster (1780) 19 – 665. [e] Universitatsbibliothek (1906) 668.
Neuss: [a] Nordrhein-Westfalen. [b] none. [c] Rhine R; Erft R. [d] none. [e] Stadtbucherei (1907) 62.
Nuremberg: [a] Bayern. [b] off Nurnberg. [c] Pegnitz R. [d] Friedrich-Alexander-Universitat Erlangen-Nurnberg (at Erlangen, nr Nuremberg) (1743) 11 – 505. [e] Universitatsbibliothek (at Erlangen, nr Nuremberg (1743) 750; Stadtbibliothek (1371) 375; Bibliothek des Germanischen Nationalmuseums (1852) 296.
Oberhausen: [a] Nordrhein-Westfalen. [b] none. [c] nr Emscher R. [d] none. [e] Stadtbucherei (1905) 145.
Offenbach am Main: [a] Hessen. [b] alt Offenbach. [c] Main R. [d] none. [e] Bibliothek des Deutschen Wetterdienstes (1848) 100.
Oldenburg in Oldenburg: [a] Niedersachsen. [b] alt Oldenburg. [c] Hunte R. [d] none. [e] Landesbibliothek (1792) 274.
Osnabruck: [a] Niedersachsen. [b] none. [c] Haase R. [d] none. [e] Stadtbibliothek (1902) 113.
Pforzheim: [a] Baden-Wurttemberg. [b] none. [c] Enz R; Nagold R; Wurm R. [d] none. [e] Stadtbucherei (1893) 70.
Recklinghausen: [a] Nordrhein-Westfalen. [b] none. [c] nr Emscher R. [d] none. [e] Stadtbucherei (1937) 42.
Regensburg: [a] Bayern. [b] alt Ratisbon. [c] Danube R. [d] Universitat Regensburg (1962) 2 – 423. [e] Universitatsbibliothek (1964) 824; Furstlich Thurn und Taxissche Hofbibliothek (1773) 172; Staatliche Bibliothek (1816) 140.
Remscheid: [a] Nordrhein-Westfalen. [b] none. [c] Wupper R. [d] none. [e] Stadtbucherei (1902) 99.
Rheydt: [a] Nordrhein-Westfalen. [b] none. [c] Niers R. [d] none. [e] Stadtbucherei (1905) 46.
Saarbrucken: [a] *Saarland. [b] for Sarrebruck. [c] Saar (alt Sarre) R; Sulz R. [d] Universitat des Saarlandes (1948) 9 – 659. [e] Universitatsbibliothek (1950) 589; Stadtbucherei (1924) 141.
Salzgitter: [a] Niedersachsen. [b] for Watenstedt-Salzgitter. [c] Fuhse R. [d] none. [e] Stadtbucherei (1945) 40. [f] 46 (1939).
Solingen: [a] Nordrhein-Westfalen. [b] none. [c] Wupper R. [d] none. [e] Stadtbucherei (1926) 132.
Stuttgart: [a] *Baden-Wurttemberg. [b] none. [c] Neckar R. [d] Universitat Stuttgart (1829) 8 – 2610; Universitat Hohenheim (1818) 1 – 230. [e] Wurttembergische Landesbibliothek (1765) 1083; Stadtbucherei (1897) 433; Universitatsbibliothek (of the Universitat Stuttgart) (1829) 368.
Trier: [a] Rheinland-Pfalz. [b] for Treves. [c] Moselle R. [d] Universitat Trier-Kaiserslautern (at Trier and Kaiserslautern) (1970) ? – ? [Trier campus: (1970) ? – ?]. [e] Stadtbibliothek (1775) 261.
Ulm: [a] Baden-Wurttemberg. [b] none. [c] Danube R. [d] Universitat Ulm (1967) 0.1 – 74. [e] Universitatsbibliothek (1964) 200; Stadtbibliothek (1516) 134.
Wanne-Eickel: [a] Nordrhein-Westfalen. [b] Wanne: for Bickern. [c] nr Emscher R. [d] none. [e] Stadtbucherei (1902) 75. [f] Eickel: 17 (1900), 0.5 (1849?); Wanne: 24 (1900), 0.1 (1849?).
Wiesbaden: [a] *Hessen. [b] none. [c] Rhine R. [d] none. [e] Hessische Landesbibliothek (1813) 437.
Wilhelmshaven: [a] Niedersachsen. [b] none. [c] Jade B of North Sea. [d] none. [e] Stadtbucherei (1872) 59.
Wolfsburg: [a] Niedersachsen. [b] none. [c] Aller R. [d] none. [e] Stadtbucherei (?) 97.
Witten: [a] Nordrhein-Westfalen. [b] none. [c] Ruhr R. [d] none. [e] Stadtbucherei (1911) 45.
Wuppertal: [a] Nordrhein-Westfalen. [b] inc Barmen, Elberfeld. [c] Wupper R. [d] none. [e] Stadtbibliothek und Stadtbucherei (1852) 247. [f] Barmen: 142 (1900), 36 (1849), 19 (1816); Elberfeld: 157 (1900), 40 (1851), 16 (1816).
Wurzburg: [a] Bayern. [b] none. [c] Main R. [d] Bayerische Julius-Maximilians-Universitat (1402) 10 – 526. [e] Universitatsbibliothek (1619) 435; Stadtbucherei (1872) 62.

Gibraltar

*Gibraltar: [b] none. [c] Strait of Gibraltar. [d] none. [e] Gibraltar Garrison Library (1793) 45.

Greece

*Athens: [b] off Athinai. [c] Kifisos R; Ilissos R. [d] National and Capodistrian University of Athens (1835) 19 – 500; National Technical University (1836) 4 – 357. [e] Chamber of Deputies Library (1844) 1100; National Library of Greece (1828) 1000.
Iraklion: [b] alt Herakleion; for Candia. [c] Sea of Crete. [d] none. [e] Vikelaia Municipal Library (?) 35.
Patras: [b] off Patrai. [c] G of Patras of Ionian Sea. [d] University of Patras (1966) 1 – ? [e] Municipal Library (?) ?
Peristeri: [b] alt Peristerion. [c] nr Kifisos R. [d] none.
Piraeus: [b] off Piraievs. [c] Saronic G of Aegean Sea. [d] none. [e] Institute of Advanced Industrial Studies Library (?) 14; Municipal Library (1926) ?
Salonika: [b] alt Salonica; off Thessaloniki. [c] G of Salonika of Aegean Sea. [d] Aristotelian University of Salonika (1925) 29 – 893. [e] . . . University Library (1925) 700.

Hungary

*Budapest: [b] inc Buda (for Ofen), Pest. [c] Danube R. [d] Budapesti Muszaki Egyetem (1782) 11 – 1471; Eotvos Lorand Tudomanyegyetem (1561) 7 – 834; Marx Karoly Kozgazdasagtudomanyi Egyetem (1948) 4 – 267; Semmelweis Orvostudomanyi Egyetem (1769) 3 – 1117; Allatorvostudomanyi Egyetem (1787) 0.5 – 108. [e] Fovarosi Szabo Ervin Konyvtar (1904) 2535; Orszagos Szechenyi Konyvtar (1802) 2150; Egyetemi Konyvtara (of Eotvos Lorand Tudomanyegyetem) (1635) 1206. [f] 1571s (1949), 187 (1857); Buda: 55 (1857), 50 (1850), 24 (1799), 25 (1787), 10 (1720); Pest: 132 (1857), 128 (1850), 30 (1799), 22 (1787), 3 (1720).

Debrecen: [b] for Debreczin. [c] nr Berettyo R. [d] Kossuth Lajos Tudomanyegyetem (1538) 2 – 277; Debreceni Orvostudomanyi Egyetem (1912) 1 – 423. [e] Egyetemi Konyvtara (of Kossuth Lajos Tudomanyegyetem (1916) 880; Tiszantuli Reformatus Egyhazkerulet Nagykonyvtara (1549) 551. [f] 36 (1857).

Miskolc: [b] none. [c] Szvinva R. [d] Nehezipari Muszaki Egyetem (1763 at Banska Stiavnica, Czechoslovakia; relocated 1949) 3 – 365. [e] . . . Egyetem Kozponti Konyvtara (1763) at Banska Stiavnica, Czechoslovakia; relocated 1949) 328. [f] 17 (1857).

Pecs: [b] for Funfkirchen. [c] Pecsi (Viz) Creek. [d] Pecsi Orvostudomanyi Egyetem (1923) 1 – 355; Pecsi Tudomanyegyetem (1367) 0.8 – 44. [e] Pecsi Tudomanyegyetem Konyvtara (1774) 300; Baranya Megyei Konyvtar (1941) 90. [f] 17 (1857).

Szeged: [b] for Szegedin. [c] Tisza R; Maros R. [d] Jozsef Attila Tudomanyegyetem Szeged (1872) 3 – 379; Szegedi Orvostudomanyi Egyetem (1921) 2 – 452. [e] Jozsef Attila Tudomanyegyetem Kozponti Konyvtara (1872) 576; Varosi Somogyi Konyvtar (1880) 400. [f] 63 (1857).

Iceland

*Reykjavik: [b] none. [c] Faxa B of Atlantic O. [d] Haskoli Islands (1911) 2 – 233. [e] Landsbokasafn Islands (1818) 288; Borgarbokasafn (1923) 175; Haskolabokasafn (1940) 150.

Ireland

Cork: [b] off Corcaigh. [c] Lee R; Mahon L. [d] University College, Cork (of the National University or Ireland) (1845) 3 – 376. [e] University College Library (1845) 510; City Public Library (1790) 76.

*Dublin: [b] off Baile Atha Cliath. [c] Dublin B of Irish Sea; Liffey R. [d] National University of Ireland (1795) 16 – 1095? [University College, Dublin (1851) 10 – 500?]; Trinity College, University of Dublin (1591) 4 – 386. [e] Trinity College Library (1591) 1000; Public Library (1884) 836; National Library of Ireland (1877) 550. [f] 129 (1753), 64 (1682).

Italy

Alessandria: [a] Piemonte. [b] none. [c] Tanaro R. [d] none. [e] Biblioteca Civica (1806) 81. [f] 52 (1861), 22 (1741).

Ancona: [a] Marche. [b] none. [c] Adriatic Sea. [d] Universita degli Studi di Ancona (1970) ? – ? [e] Biblioteca Comunale Luciano Benincasa (1669) 88. [f] 47 (1861).

Bari: [a] Puglia. [b] alt Bari delle Puglie. [c] Adriatic Sea. [d] Universita degli Studi di Bari (1924) 35 – 2506. [e] Biblioteca Universitaria (1924?) 289; Biblioteca Nazionale Sagarriga-Visconti-Volpi (1865) 212.

Bergamo: [a] Lombardia. [b] none. [c] Serio R; Brembo R. [d] none. [e] Biblioteca Civica A. Mai (1760) 550.

Bologna: [a] Emilia-Romagna. [b] none. [c] nr Reno R; nr Savena R. [d] Universita degli Studi di Bologna (11th c) 35 – 2095. [e] Biblioteca Comunale dell'Archiginnasio (1801) 700; Biblioteca Universitaria (1712) 638. [f] 113 (1861).

Bolzano: [a] Trentino-Alto Adige. [b] for Bozen. [c] Isarco R. [d] none. [e] Biblioteca Civica Cesare Battisti (1928) 90.

Brescia: [a] Lombardia. [b] none. [c] Garza R. [d] none. [e] Biblioteca Civica Queriniana (1747) 300. [f] 39 (1861).

Cagliari: [a] Sardegna; *Sardinia I. [b] none. [c] G of Cagliari of Mediterranean Sea. [d] Universita degli Studi di Cagliari (1606) 12 – 816. [e] Biblioteca Universitaria (1606) 463. [f] 32 (1861), 15 (1720e).

Catania: [a] Sicilia; Sicily I. [b] none. [c] G of Catania of Mediterranean Sea. [d] Universita degli Studi di Catania (1434) 19 – 653. [e] Biblioteca Universitaria (1755) 250; Biblioteca Riunite Civica e A. Ursino Recupero (1693) 125. [f] 70 (1861).

Como: [a] Lombardia. [b] none. [c] Como L. [d] none. [e] Biblioteca Comunale (1673) 180. [f] 23 (1861).

Cosenza: [a] Calabria. [b] none. [c] Crati R; Busente R. [d] none. [e] Biblioteca Civica Cosentina (1520) 145.

Ferrara: [a] Emilia-Romagna. [b] none. [c] Po di Volano R. [d] Universita degli Studi di Ferrara (1391) 4 – 382. [e] Biblioteca Comunale Ariostea (1753) 150. [f] 69 (1861), 27 (1768), 25 (1701).

Florence: [a] Toscana. [b] off Firenze. [c] Arno R. [d] Universita degli Studi di Firenze (1321) 19 – 3035. [e] Biblioteca Nazionale Centrale (1747) 3831; Biblioteca della Facolta di Lettre e Filosofia dell'Universita . . . (1859) 1537; Biblioteca Marucelliana (1752) 408; . . . Biblioteca Medicea-Laurenziana (1571) 60. [f] 96 (1861).

Foggia: [a] Puglia. [b] none. [c] nr Celone R. [d] none. [e] Biblioteca Provinciale Gaetano Postiglione (1936) 135.

Forli: [a] Emilia-Romagna. [b] none. [c] Montone R. [d] none. [e] Biblioteca Comunale Aurelio Saffi (1750) 250.

Genoa: [a] Liguria. [b] off Genova. [c] G of Genoa of Ligurian Sea. [d] Universita degli Studi di Genova (1471) 16 – 1557. [e] Biblioteca Universitaria (1773) 357; Biblioteca Civica Berio (1775) 203. [f] 131 (1861), 100 (1766e).

La Spezia: [a] Liguria. [b] alt Spezia. [c] G of Spezia of Ligurian Sea. [d] none. [e] Biblioteca Comunale Ubaldo Mazzini (1898) 110.

Leghorn: [a] Toscana. [b] off Livorno. [c] Ligurian Sea. [d] none. [e] Biblioteca Comunale Labronica Francesco Domenico Guerrazzi (1816) 150. [f] 95 (1861).

Messina: [a] Sicilia; Sicily I. [b] none. [c] Strait of Messina. [d] Universita degli Studi di Messina (1548) 19 – ? [e] Biblioteca Universitaria (1548) 168. [f] 103 (1861).

Milan: [a] Lombardia. [b] for Mailand; off Milano. [c] Olona R. [d] Universita Cattolica del Sacro Cuore (1920) 23 – 1072; Universita degli Studi di Milano (1923) 20 – 3696; Politecnico di Milano (univ) (1862) 10 – 1443; Universita Commerciale Luigi Bocconi (1902) 6 – 233. [e] Biblioteca Comunale (1890) 930; Biblioteca Ambrosiana (1609) 850; Biblioteca dell'Universita Cattolica del Sacro Cuore (1918) 807; Biblioteca Nazionale Braidense (1763) 785. [f] 192 (1861), 110 (1760e).

Modena: [a] Emilia-Romagna. [b] none. [c] nr Secchia R. [d] Universita degli Studi di Modena (1175) 5 – 639? [e] Biblioteca Estense e Universitaria (14th c) 493.

Monza: [a] Lombardia. [b] none. [c] Lambro R. [d] none. [e] Biblioteca Civica (1870) 65.

Naples: [a] Campania. [b] off Napoli. [c] B of Naples of Tyrrhenian Sea. [d] Universita degli Studi di Napoli (1224) 44 – 3000? [e] Biblioteca Nazionale Vittorio Emanuele III (1804) 1518; Biblioteca Universitaria di Napoli Statale (1615) 686; Biblioteca del Conservatorio di Musica Santo Pietro a Maiella (1792) 500. [f] 440 (1861), 300 (1742e), 185 (1688e).

Novara: [a] Piemonte. [b] none. [c] Agogna R; Terdoppio R. [d] none. [e] Biblioteca Civica e Negroni (1852) 174.

Padua: [a] Veneto. [b] off Padova. [c] Bacchiglione R. [d] Universita degli Studi di Padova (1222) 32 – 3293. [e] Biblioteca Universitaria (1629) 457; Biblioteca Civica (1839) 330.

Palermo: [a] Sicilia; *Sicily I. [b] none. [c] G of Palermo of Tyrrhenian Sea. [d] Universita degli Studi di Palermo (1777) 23 – 1300? [e] Biblioteca Nazionale (1782) 508; Biblioteca Comunale (1760) 400. [f] 197 (1861), 141 (1775).

Parma: [a] Emilia-Romagna. [b] none. [c] Parma R. [d] Universita degli Studi di Parma (1065) 15 – 849. [e] Biblioteca Palatina (1762) 369. [f] 44 (1861).

Perugia: [a] Umbria. [b] none. [c] nr Tiber R. [d] Universita degli Studi di Perugia (1200) 16 – 280?; Universita Italiana per Stranieri (1925) 5 – 105. [e] Biblioteca Augusta (1582) 190; Biblioteca dell'Universita . . . (1848) 180. [f] 16 (1701).

Pescara: [a] Abruzzi e Molise. [b] none. [c] Adriatic Sea; Pescara R. [d] none. [e] Biblioteca Provinciale Gabriele D'Annunzio (1929) 106.

Piacenza: [a] Emilia-Romagna. [b] none. [c] Po R. [d] none. [e] Biblioteca Comunale Passerini Landi (1791) 200.

Pisa: [a] Toscana. [b] none. [c] Arno R. [d] Universita degli Studi di Pisa (1343) 18 – 1280? [e] Biblioteca Universitaria (1742) 306.

Prato: [a] Toscana. [b] none. [c] Bisenzio R. [d] none. [e] Biblioteca Lazzariniana Comunale e Biblioteca Roncioniana (1676) 55.

Ravenna: [a] Emilia-Romagna. [b] none. [c] nr Adriatic Sea. [d] none. [e] Biblioteca Comunale Classense (1710?) 200. [f] 57 (1861).

Reggio di Calabria: [a] Calabria. [b] none. [c] Strait of Messina. [d] none. [e] Biblioteca Comunale Pietro De Nava (1819) 50; Biblioteca Sandicchi (1957) 50.

Reggio nell'Emilia: [a] Emilia-Romagna. [b] none. [c] Crostolo R. [d] none. [e] Biblioteca Municipale (1797) 230.

Rimini: [a] Emilia-Romagna. [b] none. [c] Adriatic Sea; Marecchia R. [d] none. [e] Biblioteca Civica Gambalunga (1619) 129.

*Rome: [a] Lazio. [b] off Roma. [c] Tiber R. [d][1] Universita degli Studi di Roma (1303) 66 – 4955; Pontificia Universitas Gregoriana[2] (1553) 3 – 171; Libera Universita Internazionale degli Studi Sociali pro Deo (1945) 3 – 433; Pontificia Universitas Lateranensis[2] (1774) 2 – 229. [e] Biblioteca Nazionale Centrale Vittorio Emanuele II (1876) 2038; Biblioteca Apostolica Vaticana[2] (15th c) 1008; Biblioteca Universitaria Alessandrina (1661) 828; Biblioteca del Ministero dell'Agricoltura e delle Foreste (1860) 800; Biblioteca della Pontificia Universitas Gregoriana[2] (1551) 510; Biblioteca dell'Accademia Nazionale dei Lincei (1730) 399; Biblioteca Casanatense (1700) 301. [f] 146 (1740), 149 (1700).

Salerno: [a] Campania. [b] none. [c] G of Salerno of Tyrrhenian Sea. [d] Universita degli Studi di Salerno (1969?) 7 – ? [e] Biblioteca Provinciale (1845) 90. [f] 27 (1861).

Sassari: [a] Sardegna; Sardinia I. [b] none. [c] nr G of Asinara of Mediterranean Sea. [d] Universita degli Studi di Sassari (1562) 2 – 274? [e] Biblioteca Universitaria (1560?) 128; Biblioteca Comunale (1934) 70.

Syracuse: [a] Sicilia; Sicily I. [b] off Siracusa. [c] Ionian Sea. [d] none. [e] Biblioteca Comunale (1857) 50.

Taranto: [a] Puglia. [b] none. [c] G of Taranto of Ionian Sea. [d] none. [e] Biblioteca Comunale Pietro Acclavio (1893) 57.

Terni: [a] Umbria. [b] none. [c] Nera R. [d] none. [e] Biblioteca Comunale (1885) 40.

Trieste: [a] Friuli-Venezia Giulia. [b] for Triest. [c] G of Trieste of Adriatic Sea. [d] Universita degli Studi di Trieste (1877) 9 – 910. [e] Biblioteca Civica (1793) 310. [f] 105 (1857).

Turin: [a] Piemonte. [b] off Torino. [c] Po R; Dora Riparia R. [d] Universita degli Studi di Torino (1404) 18 – 2103; Politecnico di Torino (univ) (1859) 6 – 850. [e] Biblioteca Nazionale (1720) 705; Biblioteche Civiche e Raccolte Storiche (1869) 350. [f] 173 (1861).

Udine: [a] Friuli-Venezia Giulia. [b] none. [c] Torre R. [d] none. [e] Biblioteca Comunale Joppi (1866) 360.

[1] Universities with 1000 or more students.

[2] At Vatican City, nr Rome.

Venice: [a] Veneto. [b] for Venedig; off Venezia. [c] G of Venice of Adriatic Sea. [d] Universita degli Studi di Venezia (1868) 4 – ? [e] Biblioteca Nazionale Marciana (1468) 661. [f] 118 (1857), 140 (1775), 140 (1706).
Verona: [a] Veneto. [b] none. [c] Adige R. [d] none. [e] Biblioteca Civica (1792) 720. [f] 59 (1857).
Vicenza: [a] Veneto. [b] none. [c] Bacchiglione R; Retrone R; Astichello R. [d] none. [e] Biblioteca Civica Bertoliana (1696) 370.

Luxembourg

*Luxembourg: [b] alt Lutzelburg, Luxemburg. [c] Alzette R. [d] Universite Internationale de Sciences Comparees (1958) 0.06 – 12. [e] Bibliotheque Nationale (1798) 650.

Malta

*Valletta: [a] Malta I. [b] alt Valetta. [c] Mediterranean Sea. [d] Royal University of Malta (at Msida, nr Valletta) (1592 at Valletta, relocated from 1967?) 1 – 190. [e] . . . University Library (at Msida, nr Valletta) (1592 at Valletta, relocated 1967?) 100; Royal Malta Library (1796) 61.

Monaco

*Monaco: [b] inc Monte-Carlo. [c] Mediterranean Sea. [d] none. [e] Bibliotheque Communale (1909) 150.

Netherlands

*Amsterdam: [b] none. [c] Amstel R; IJssel(meer) L. [d] Universiteit van Amsterdam (1632) 17 – 1824; Vrije Universiteit (1880) 8 – 641? [e] Universiteitsbibliotheek (of the Universiteit . . .) (1578) 2000; Openbare Leeszaal en Bibliotheek (1919) 480. [f] 105 (1622).
Apeldoorn: [b] none. [c] IJssel R. [d] none. [e] Openbare Leeszaal en Bibliotheek (1911) 40.
Arnhem: [b] for Arnheim. [c] Nederrijn R (Rhine R distributary). [d] none. [e] Stichting Arnhemse Openbare en Gelderse Wetenschappelijke Bibliotheek (1856) 225.
Breda: [b] none. [c] Mark R; Aa of Weerijs R. [d] none. [e] Katholieke Provinciale Bibliotheekcentrale voor Noord-Brabant (1915) 112; Bibliotheek Koninklijke Militaire Academie (1828) 95.
Dordrecht: [b] alt Dort. [c] Lower Merwede (off Beneden Merwede) R. [d] none. [e] Openbare Leeszaal en Bibliotheek (1899) 80. [f] 169s (1970e).
Eindhoven: [b] none. [c] Dommel R; Gender R. [d] Technische Hogeschool te Eindhoven (univ) (1956) 4 – 573. [e] Openbare Leeszaal en Boekerij Sint Catharina (1916) 250.
Enschede: [b] none. [c] nr Almeloosche R. [d] Technische Hogeschool Twente (univ) (1961) 1 – 257? [e] Openbare Leeszaal en Bibliotheek (1920) 115. [f] 230s (1970e).
Groningen: [b] none. [c] Drentse A (Riviertje) Creek; Hunze (Riviertje) Creek. [d] Rijksuniversiteit te Groningen (1614) 10 – 1395. [e] Bibliotheek der Rijksuniversiteit . . . (1615) 630; Openbare Bibliotheek (1903) 140.
Haarlem: [b] none. [c] Spaarne R. [d] none. [e] Stadsbibliotheek en Leeszaal (1596) 218.
*Hague: [b] alt The Hague; off 's Gravenhage. [c] North Sea. [d] Technische Hogeschool te Delft (univ) (at Delft, nr Hague) (1842) 10 – 1726. [e] Koninklijke Bibliotheek (1798) 900; Bibliotheek van het Vredespaleis (1913) 500; Openbare Bibliotheek (1906) 420; Bibliotheek der Technische Hogeschool . . . (at Delft, nr Hague) (1842) 375.
Heerlen: [b] none. [c] Geleen R. [d] none. [e] Openbare Leeszaal en Bibliotheek (1913) 38. [f] 264s (1970e).
Hilversum: [b] none. [c] nr IJssel(meer) L. [d] none. [e] Openbare Leeszaal en Bibliotheek (1909) 95. [f] 115s (1970e).
Leiden: [b] alt Leyden. [c] Rhine R. [d] Rijksuniversiteit te Leiden (1575) 11 – 1179. [e] Bibliotheek der Rijksuniversiteit . . . (1575) 1930.
Maastricht: [b] for Maestricht. [c] Meuse R; Geer R. [d] none. [e] Bibliotheek Theologische Hogeschool (1852) 300; Stadsarchief en-Bibliotheek (1662) 125. [f] 143S (1970e).
Nijmegen: [b] alt Nimeguen, Nimwegen. [c] Waal R (Rhine R distributary). [d] Katholieke Universiteit te Nijmegen (1923) 9 – 1002? [e] Bibliotheek van de . . . Universiteit (1923) 500.
Rotterdam: [b] none. [c] Nieuwe Maas R (Rhine R distributary). [d] none. [e] Bibliotheek en Leeszalen der Gemeente (1604) 510.
's Hertogenbosch: [b] for Bois-le-Duc. [c] Dieze R; Dommel R; Aa R. [d] none. [e] Bibliotheekcentrale van de Nederlandse Capucijnen (?) 110. [f] 167s (1970e).
Tilburg: [b] none. [c] Leij R. [d] none. [e] Bibliotheek der Katholieke Hogeschool (1927) 150; Openhare Bibliotheek (1845) 85. [f] 203s (1970e).
Utrecht: [b] none. [c] Rhine R. [d] Rijksuniversiteit te Utrecht (1636) 14 – 2122. [e] Bibliotheek der Rijksuniversiteit . . . (1584) 1600; Stichting Openbare Bibliotheken (1892) 340.
Zaandam: [b] none. [c] Zaan R. [d] none. [e] Openbare Bibliotheek (1913) 45. [f] 127s (1970e).

Norway

Bergen: [b] none. [c] North Sea. [d] Universitetet i Bergen (1948) 6 – 623. [e] Universitetsbiblioteket (1825) 610; Bergens Offentlige Bibliotek (1874) 338.

*Oslo: [b] for Christiania, Kristiania. [c] Oslo Fjord of Skagerrak Strait. [d] Universitetet i Oslo (1811) 14 – 1240. [e] Universitetsbiblioteket (1811) 2836; Deichmanske Bibliotek (1785) 880.

Stavanger: [b] none. [c] Bokn Fjord of North Sea. [d] none. [e] Stavanger Bibliotek (1885) 185.

Trondheim: [b] for Nidaros, Trondhjem. [c] Trondheim Fjord of Norwegian Sea. [d] Norges Tekniske Hogskole (univ) (1900) 4 – 371; Universitetet i Trondheim (1969) ? – ? [e] Norges Tekniske Hogskole Hovedbiblioteket (1911) 409; Kongelige Norske Videnskabers Selskabs Bibliotek (1760) 375.

Poland

Bialystok: [b] for Belostok. [c] Suprasl (alt Biala) R. [d] none. [e] Akademia Medycznej Biblioteka (1950) 190; Powiatowa Biblioteka Publiczna (?) 100.

Bielsko-Biala: [b] Bielsko: for Bielitz. [c] Biala R. [d] none. [e] Powiatowa Biblioteka Publiczna (?) 105; Miejska Biblioteka Publiczna (?) 75. [f] Biala: 23 (1931), 8 (1900), 4 (1850?); Bielsko: 22 (1931), 17 (1900), 9 (1857).

Bydgoszcz: [b] for Bromberg. [c] Brda R. [d] none. [e] Miejska Biblioteka Publiczna (1903) 480.

Bytom: [b] for Beuthen; inc Rossberg since 1927. [c] Bytomka R. [d] none. [e] Muzeum Gornoslaskie Biblioteka (?) 20. [f] Rossberg: 14 (1900), 3 (1871).

Chorzow: [b] for Konigshutte, Krolewska Huta. [c] Rawa R. [d] none. [e] Huta Batory Biblioteka (?) 16.

Czestochowa: [b] for Chenstokhov. [c] Warta R; Stradomka R. [d] Politechnika Czestochowska (univ) (1949) 3 – 291. [e] Miejska Biblioteka Publiczna imienia Wladyslawa Bieganskiego (1917) 188; Powiatowa Biblioteka Publiczna (?) 137. [f] 14 (1867).

Gdansk: [b] for Danzig. [c] G of Danzig of Baltic Sea; Vistula R. [d] Politechnika Gdanska (univ) (1904) 9 - 916; Uniwersytet Gdanska (1970) ? – ? [e] Biblioteka Gdanska Polska Akademia Nauk (1596) 464; Biblioteka Glowna Politechniki Gdnaskiej (1945) 400.

Gdynia: [b] none. [c] G of Danzig of Baltic Sea. [d] none. [e] Wyzsza Szkola Marynarki Wojennej Biblioteka (?) 80.

Gliwice: [b] for Gleiwitz. [c] Klodnica R. [d] Politechnika Slaska imienia W. Pstrowskiego (univ) (1945) 17 – 1800. [e] Biblioteka Glowna Politechniki Slaskiej (1945) 366; Powiatowa Biblioteka Publiczna (?) 88.

Katowice: [b] for Kattowitz, Stalinogrod. [c] Rawa R. [d] Uniwersytet Slaski (1968) 7 – ? [e] Biblioteka Slaska (1922) 606.

Kielce: [b] for Keltsy. [c] nr Czarna Nida R. [d] none. [e] Powiatowa Biblioteka Publiczna (?) 160; Wojewodzka i Miejska Biblioteka Publiczna (1909) 160.

Krakow: [b] alt Cracow; for Krakau. [c] Vistula R. [d] Uniwersytet Jagiellonski (1364) 9 – 826; Politechnika w Krakowie (univ) (1835) 7 – 866. [e] Biblioteka Jagiellonska (1364) 1448; Miejska Biblioteka Publiczna (1946) 712; Biblioteka Glowna Akademii Gorniczo-Hutniczej w Krakowie (1919) 527.

Lodz: [b] none. [c] Lodka R. [d] Uniwersytet Lodzki (1945) 11 – 693; Politechnika Lodzka (univ) (1945) 10 – 937. [e] Miejska Biblioteka Publiczna imienia L. Warynskiego (1917) 855; Biblioteka Uniwersytet . . . (1945) 711.

Lublin: [b] for Lyublin. [c] Bystrzyca R. [d] Uniwersytet Marii Curie-Sklodowskiej (1944) 5 – 591; Katolicki Uniwersytet Lubelski (1918) 2 – 223? [e] Biblioteka . . . Uniwersytet (1918) 640; Biblioteka Glowna Uniwersytet . . . (1944) 575.

Olsztyn: [b] for Allenstein. [c] Lyna R. [d] none. [e] Biblioteka Glowna Wylsza Szkoza Rolnicza (1950) 132; Wojewodzka Instytet Miejska Biblioteka Publiczna (?) 105.

Poznan: [b] for Posen. [c] Warta R; Cybina R. [d] Uniwersytet imienia Adama Mickiewicza w Poznaniu (1919) 12 – 590; Politechnika Poznanska (univ) (1918) 4 – 821. [e] Biblioteka Glowna Uniwersytet . . . (1902) 2195; Miejska Biblioteka Publiczna imienia Edwarda Raczynskiego (1829) 612.

Radom: [b] none. [c] Mleczna R. [d] none. [e] Powiatowa Biblioteka Publiczna (?) 120.

Ruda Slaska: [b] for Ruda. [c] nr Bytomka R. [d] none.

Sosnowiec: [b] for Sosnovets. [c] Czarna Przemsza R. [d] none.

Szczecin: [b] for Stettin. [c] Oder R. [d] Politechnika Szczecinska (univ) (1946) 3 – 412. [e] Wojewodzka i Miejska Biblioteka Publiczna (1902) 650.

Torun: [b] for Thorn. [c] Vistula R. [d] Uniwersytet Mikolaja Kopernika w Toruniu (1945) 5 – 489 [e] Biblioteka Glowna Uniwersytet . . . (1945) 1186; Ksiaznica Miejska imienia M. Kopernika (1923) 410.

Walbrzych: [b] for Waldenburg, Waldenburg in Schlesien. [c] Strzegomka R. [d] none. [e] Miejska Biblioteka Publiczna (?) 82; Powiatowa Biblioteka Publiczna (?) 75.

*Warsaw: [b] off Warszawa. [c] Vistula R. [d] Politechnika Warszawska (univ) (1826) 23 – 2138; Uniwersytet Warszawski (1808) 21 – 1528. [e] Biblioteka Narodowa (1928) 2416; Biblioteka Publiczna (1907) 2258; Biblioteka Uniwersytecka w Warszawie (1817) 1693; Glowna Biblioteka Lekarska (1945) 1027.

Wroclaw: [b] for Breslau. [c] Oder R; Olawa R; Sleza R. [d] Politechnika Wroclawska (univ) (1910) 11 – 1300; Uniwersytet Wroclawski imienia Boleslawa Bieruta (1505) 6 – 810. [e] Biblioteka Uniwersytecka (1811) 1100; Biblioteka Zakladu Narodowego imienia Ossolinskich (1817 at Lvov, USSR; relocated 1946) 437. [f] 55 (1756), 41 (1710e).

Zabrze: [b] for Hindenburg. [c] Bytomka R. [d] none. [e] Slaska Akademia Medyczna Biblioteka (1948) 70.

Portugal

*Lisbon: [b] off Lisboa. [c] Tagus R. [d] Universidade de Lisboa (1290) 15 – 560; Universidade Tecnica de Lisboa (1759) 8 – 410; Universidade Catolica de Lisboa (1968) ? – ? [e] Biblioteca Nacional (1796) 1300; Biblioteca da Universidade de Lisboa (1837) 500. [f] 1335s (1960), 126 (1626).

Porto: [b] alt Oporto [c] Douro R. [d] Universidade do Porto (1762) 4 – 220. [e] Biblioteca Publica Municipal (1833) 1325. [f] 746s (1960), 41 (1766), 16 (1706).

Romania

Arad: [b] none. [c] Maros R. [d] none. [e] Biblioteca Municipala (1888) 235. [f] 159s (1970e), 126, 137s (1966), 27 (1857).

Bacau: [b] none. [c] Bistrita R. [d] none. [e] Biblioteca Municipala (1950) 150. [f] 114s (1970e), 73, 87s (1966).

Baia Mare: [b] for Nagybanya. [c] nr Lapusul R. [d] none. [e] Biblioteca Municipala (1951) 100. [f] 94s (1970e), 63, 109s (1966), 7 (1857).

Braila: [b] for Ibraila. [c] Danube R. [d] none. [e] Biblioteca Municipala (1881) 100. [f] 158s (1970e), 139, 144s (1966).

Brasov: [b] for Brasso, Kronstadt, Orasul Stalin, Stalin. [c] Timis R. [d] Institutul Politehnic Brasov (univ) (1948) 4 – 332. [e] Biblioteca Municipala (1926) 350; Biblioteca Institutul . . . (1949) 274. [f] 186s (1970e), 163, 263s (1966), 27 (1857).

*Bucharest: [b] off Bucuresti. [c] Dimbovita R; Colentina R. [d] Universitatea din Bucuresti (1694) 20 – 1500; Institutul Politehnic Gheorghe Gheorghiudej Bucuresti (univ) (1867) 14 – 1146. [e] Biblioteca Academiei Republicii Socialiste Romania (1867) 6624; Biblioteca Centrala de Stat (1955) 5642; Biblioteca Centrala Universitara (1864) 1661. [f] 1366, 1511s (1966), 59 (1831).

Cluj: [b] for Klausenburg, Kolozsvar. [c] Somesul Mic R; Nadasul R. [d] Universitatea Babes Bolyai (1872) 7 – 852; Institutul Politehnic din Cluj (univ) (1948) 3 – 322. [e] Biblioteca Centrala Universitara Cluj (1872) 2401; Biblioteca Filialei Cluj a Academiei Republicii Socialiste Romania (1950) 500; Biblioteca Municipala (1945) 170. [f] 203s (1970e), 186, 223s (1966), 21 (1857).

Constanta: [b] alt Constantsa; for Kustendje. [c] Black Sea. [d] none. [e] Biblioteca Municipala (1935) 130. [f] 150, 199s (1966).

Craiova: [b] none. [c] Jiu R. [d] Universitatea Craiova (1966) 4 – 362? [e] Biblioteca Municipala (1908) 180; Biblioteca Centrala Universitara Craiova (1966) 170. [f] 202s (1970e), 149, 173s (1966).

Galati: [b] for Galatz. [c] Danube R; Brates L. [d] Institutul Politehnic din Galati (univ) (1948) 2 – 193. [e] Biblioteca V. A. Urechia (1890) 303. [f] 186s (1970e), 151, 151s (1966).

Hunedoara: [b] for Eisenmarkt, Vajdahunyad. [c] nr Cerna R. [d] none. [e] Biblioteca Clubului Sindicatului Combinatului Siderurgic Hunedoara (1950) 71; Biblioteca Municipala (1951) 32. [f] 89s (1970e), 68, 101s (1966).

Iasi: [b] for Jassy. [c] Bahlui R. [d] Universitatea Alexandru Ioan Cuza din Iasi (1860) 13 – 694; Institutul Politehnic Gheorghe Asachi din Iasi (univ) (1912) 7 – 600. [e] Biblioteca Centrala Universitara M. Eminescu (1640) 1450; Biblioteca Institutului Politehnic (1937) 280; Biblioteca Municipala Gheorghe Asachi (1950) 205; Biblioteca Filialei Iasi a Academiei Republicii Socialiste Romania (1949) 200. [f] 202s (1970e), 161, 195s (1966).

Oradea: [b] alt Oradea Mare; for Grosswardein, Nagy-Varad. [c] Sebes Koros (alt Crisul-Repede) R. [d] none. [e] Biblioteca Municipala (1882) 260. [f] 148s (1970e), 123, 135s (1966), 22 (1857).

Petroseni: [b] alt Petrosani; for Petrozseny. [c] Jiul Transilvan R. [d] none. [e] Biblioteca Institutului de Mine Gheorghiu-Dej (1948) 149. [f] 141s (1970e), 35, 130s (1966).

Pitesti: [b] none. [c] Arges (alt Argesul) R. [d] none. [e] Biblioteca Municipala (1950) 130. [f] 110s (1970e), 60, 79s (1966).

Ploesti: [b] alt Ploiesti. [c] nr Teleajen R. [d] none. [e] Biblioteca Municipala (1921) 138. [f] 217s (1970e), 147, 191s (1966).

Resita: [b] for Resiczabanya. [c] Birzava (alt Brzava) R. [d] none. [e] Biblioteca Casei de Cultura a Sindicatelor (?) 78; Biblioteca Municipala (1952) 30. [f] 68s (1970e), 57, 121s (1966).

Sibiu: [b] for Hermannstadt, Nagyszeben. [c] Cibin R. [d] none. [e] Biblioteca Municipala Astra (1861) 370; Biblioteca Muzeului Brukenthal (1815) 270. [f] 138s (1970e), 110, 110s (1966), 19 (1857).

Timisoara: [b] for Temesvar. [c] Bega R. [d] Institutul Politehnic din Timisoara (univ) (1920) 6 – 605; Universitatea din Timisoara (1948) 3 – 375? [e] Biblioteca Municipala (1904) 300; Biblioteca Centrala Universitara (1948) 228. [f] 206s (1970e), 174, 193s (1966).

Tirgu Mures: [b] alt Targu Mures; for Maros-Vasarhely. [c] Maros R. [d] none. [e] Biblioteca Municipala (1913) 300; Biblioteca Documentara Teleki-Bolyai (1557) 200. [f] 121s (1970e), 86, 105s (1966), 11 (1857).

Spain

Alicante: [a] Valencia. [b] none. [c] Mediterranean Sea. [d] none. [e] Biblioteca Publica Provincial (?) 24.

Almeria: [a] Andalucia. [b] none. [c] G of Almeria of Mediterranean Sea. [d] none. [e] Biblioteca Publica Provincial (?) 22

Badajoz: [a] Extremadura. [b] none. [c] Guadiana R. [d] none. [e] Biblioteca Publica Provincial (?) 21.

Badalona: [a] Cataluna. [b] none. [c] Mediterranean Sea. [d] none.

Baracaldo: [a] Vascongadas y Navarra. [b] alt San Vicente de Baracaldo. [c] Nervion R. [d] none.

Barcelona: [a] Cataluna. [b] none. [c] Mediterranean Sea; Besos R. [d] Universidad de Barcelona (1450) 25 – 2106; Universidad Autonoma de Barcelona (1968) 3 – 295. [e] Biblioteca Central de la Diputacion Provincial de Barcelona (alt Biblioteca de Cataluna) (1914) 622; Biblioteca Universitaria y Provincial (1837) 350. [f] 115 (1773), 37 (1715e).

Bilbao: [a] Vascongadas y Navarra. [b] none. [c] Nervion R. [d] Universidad de Bilbao (1968) 5 – 225; Universidad de Deusto (1886) 5 – 416. [e] Biblioteca de la Universidad de Deusto (1916) 38; Biblioteca Municipal (?) ?; Biblioteca Provincial(?) ?

Burgos: [a] Castilla la Vieja. [b] none. [c] Arlanzon R. [d] none. [e] Biblioteca del Colegio Maximo de San Francisco (1880) 100; Biblioteca Publica (1871) 60.

Cadiz: [a] Andalucia. [b] none. [c] G of Cadiz of Atlantic O. [d] none. [e] Biblioteca Popular (?) 40.

Cartagena: [a] Murcia. [b] none. [c] Mediterranean Sea. [d] none. [e] Biblioteca Popular (?) 30. [f] 54 (1860).

Cordova: [a] Andalucia. [b] off Cordoba. [c] Guadalquivir R. [d] none. [e] Biblioteca Publica Provincial (?) 60

Elche: [a] Valencia. [b] none. [c] Vinalapo R. [d] none.

Gijon: [a] Asturias. [b] none. [c] B of Biscay of Atlantic O. [d] none.

Granada: [a] Andalucia. [b] none. [c] Genil R. [d] Universidad de Granada (1531) 12 – 670. [e] Biblioteca de la Universidad . . . (1532) 267; Biblioteca Publica (?) ?

Hospitalet: [a] Cataluna. [b] none. [c] nr Llobregat R. [d] none.

Huelva: [a] Andalucia. [b] none. [c] Odiel R; Tinto R. [d] none. [e] Biblioteca Publica Provincial (?) 18.

Jerez de la Frontera: [a] Andalucia. [b] alt Jerez; for Xeres. [c] nr Guadalete R. [d] none. [e] Biblioteca, Archivo y Coleccion Arquelogica Municipal (1873) 29.

La Coruna: [a] Galicia. [b] alt Coruna, Corunna. [c] Atlantic O. [d] none. [e] Biblioteca Publica Provincial (?) 40.

Leon: [a] Leon. [b] none. [c] Bernesga R; Torio R. [d] none. [e] Biblioteca Publica Provincial la Reina (1844) 28.

*Madrid: [a] Castilla la Nueva. [b] none. [c] Manzanares R. [d] Universidad Complutense de Madrid (1498 at Alcala de Henares, relocated 1836) 42 – 2200; Universidad Autonoma de Madrid (1968) 3 – 461; Universidad Pontificia de Comillas (1890 at Comillas, relocated from 1960) 0.9 – 117. [e] Biblioteca Nacional (1712) 2923; Biblioteca de la Universidad Complutense de Madrid (1498 at Alcala de Henares, relocated 1841) 665.

Malaga: [a] Andalucia. [b] none. [c] Mediterranean Sea. [d] none. [e] Biblioteca Publica (1933) 27.

Murcia: [a] Murcia. [b] none. [c] Segura R. [d] Universidad de Murcia (1915) 4 – 182. [e] Biblioteca de la Universidad . . . (1915) 50; Biblioteca Publica (19th c) 25. [f] 87 (1860).

Oviedo: [a] Asturias. [b] none. [c] nr Nalon R; nr Nora R. [d] Universidad de Oviedo (1604) 5 – 300. [e] Biblioteca de la Universidad . . . (1608) 120.

Palma: [a] Baleares; Majorca I; *Balearic Islands (off Islas Baleares). [b] alt Palma de Mallorca. [c] Mediterranean Sea. [d] none. [e] Biblioteca Publica Provincial (?) 80. [f] 39 (1700e).

Pamplona: [a] Vascongadas y Navarra. [b] for Pampeluna. [c] Arga R. [d] Universidad de Navarra (1952) 6 – 801. [e] Biblioteca de la Universidad . . . (1952) 150.

Sabadell: [a] Cataluna. [b] none. [c] Ripoll R. [d] none. [e] Biblioteca del Archivo Historico (1793) 6.

Salamanca: [a] Leon. [b] none. [c] Tormes R. [d] Universidad de Salamanca (1218) 8 – 473; Universidad Pontificia de Salamanca (1940) 0.8 – 165. [e] Biblioteca de la Universidad de Salamanca (1254) 230.

San Sebastian: [a] Vascongadas y Navarra. [b] none. [c] B of Biscay of Atlantic O; Urumea R. [d] none. [e] Biblioteca de los Estudios Universitarios y Tecnicos de Guipuzcoa (1956) ?

Santa Coloma de Gramanet: [a] Cataluna. [b] none. [c] Besos R. [d] none.

Santander: [a] Castilla la Vieja. [b] none. [c] B of Biscay of Atlantic O. [d] none. [e] Biblioteca de Menendez Pelayo (1908) 120; Biblioteca Municipal (?) 60.

Saragossa: [a] Aragon. [b] off Zaragoza. [c] Ebro R; Huerva R. [d] Universidad de Zaragoza (1474) 8 – 450. [e] Biblioteca de la Universidad . . . (1542) 207; Biblioteca Publica (?) 48.

Seville: [a] Andalucia. [b] off Sevilla. [c] Guadalquivir R. [d] Universidad de Sevilla (1502) 9 – 974. [e] Biblioteca de la Universidad . . . (1502) 200; Biblioteca Capitular Colombina (1450) 92.

Tarrasa: [a] Cataluna. [b] none. [c] nr Ripoll R. [d] none. [e] Biblioteca de la Escuela Tecnica Superior de Ingenieros Industriales (1962) 3.

Toledo: [a] Castilla la Nueva. [b] none. [c] Tagus R. [d] none. [e] Biblioteca Provincial de Toledo (1775) 98. [f] 5 (1752).

Valencia: [a] Valencia. [b] none. [c] Turia R. [d] Universidad de Valencia (1500) 11 – 632. [e] Biblioteca de la Universidad . . . (1500) 300; Biblioteca Publica Provincial (?) 12.

Valladolid: [a] Castilla la Vieja. [b] none. [c] Pisuerga R; Esgueva R. [d] Universidad de Valladolid (1346) 7 – 424. [e] Biblioteca de la Universidad . . . (1484) 134; Biblioteca Publica Provincial (?) 10.

Vigo: [a] Galicia. [b] none. [c] Vigo B of Atlantic O. [d] none. [e] Biblioteca Publica Municipal (?)8.

Vitoria: [a] Vascongadas y Navarra. [b] none. [c] Zapardiel R. [d] none. [e] Biblioteca Publica Provincial (?) 32.

Sweden

Goteborg: [b] alt Gothenburg. [c] Kattegat Strait; Gota R. [d] Goteborgs Universitet (1891) 8 – 1080; Chalmers Tekniska Hogskola (univ) (1829) 4 – 280. [e] . . . Universitetsbibliotek (1861) 1200; Stadsbibliotek (1861) 1000.

Halsingborg: [b] alt Helsingborg. [c] Oresund Strait. [d] none. [e] Stadsbibliotek (1866) 220.

Jonkoping: [b] none. [c] Vattern L; Munksjon L; Rocksjon L. [d] none. [e] Stadsbibliotek (1916) 171.

Linkoping: [b] none. [c] Stangan R. [d] Linkopings Hogskola (univ) (1970) 3 – 40. [e] Stifts- och Landsbiblioteket i Linkoping (1926) 439.

Malmo: [b] none. [c] Oresund Strait. [d] Kungliga Universitetet i Lund (at Lund, nr Malmo) (1666) 21 – 795; Tekniska Hogskolan i Lund (univ) (at Lund, nr Malmo) (1961) 2 – 99. [e] . . . Universitetsbibliotek (at Lund, nr Malmo) (1671) 2000; Stadsbibliotek (1905) 753.

Norrkoping: [b] none. [c] Motala R. [d] none. [e] Stadsbibliotek (1913) 275.

Orebro: [b] none. [c] Svartan R. [d] Uppsala Universitet, Orebro campus (1970) ? – ? [e] Stadsbibliotek (1862) 315.

*Stockholm: [b] none. [c] Baltic Sea; Malaren L. [d] Kungliga Universitetet i Stockholm (1877) 30 – 995; Kungliga Tekniska Hogskolan (univ) (1827) 6 – 1300. [e] Stadsbibliotek (1927) 1285; Kungliga Biblioteket (17th c) 1000. [f] 54 (1750).

Uppsala: [b] alt Upsala. [c] Fyris R. [d] Uppsala Universitet (1477) 25 – 600 [Uppsala campus: (1477) ? – ?]. [e] . . . Universitetsbibliotek (1620) 1800; Stadsbibliotek (1906) 287.

Vasteras: [b] for Vesteras. [c] Svart R; Malaren L. [d] none. [e] Stifts- och Landsbiblioteket i Vasteras (1952) 439.

Switzerland

Basel: [b] alt Bale, Basilea. [c] Rhine R; Birs R; Wiese R. [d] Universitat Basel (1460) 4 – 435. [e] Offentliche Bibliothek der Universitat . . . (1460) 1903; Schweizerisches Wirtschaftsarchiv (alt Archives Economiques Suisses) (1910) 750.

*Bern: [b] alt Berna, Berne. [c] Aar R. [d] Universitat Bern (1528) 6 – 450. [e] Schweizerische Landesbibliothek (alt Bibliotheque Nationale Suisse) (1895) 1210; Stadt- und Universitatsbibliothek (1528) 1000.

Geneva: [b] off Geneve, Genf, Ginevra. [c] Rhone R; Geneva L. [d] Universite de Geneve (1559) 6 – 695. [e] Bibliotheque Publique et Universitaire (1561) 1200; International Labour Office Library (1920) 660; Bibliotheque des Nations Unies (alt Library of the United Nations) (1920) 654. [f] 18 (1715e).

Lausanne: [b] alt Losanna. [c] Geneva L. [d] Universite de Lausanne (1537) 3 – 340; Ecole Polytechnique Federale de Lausanne (univ) (1853) 1 – 281. [e] Bibliotheque Cantonale et Universitaire (1537) 650.

Luzern: [b] alt Lucerna, Lucerne. [c] Reuss R; Lucerne L. [d] none. [e] Zentralbibliothek (1812) 375.

Winterthur: [b] none. [c] Toss R. [d] none. [e] Stadtbibliothek (1660) 380.

Zurich: [b] alt Zurigo. [c] Limmat R; Sihl R; Zurich(see) L. [d] Universitat Zurich (1523) 9 – 751; Eidgenossische Technische Hochschule (univ) (1855) 7 – 470. [e] Zentralbibliothek (1629) 1600; Bibliothek der . . . Technische Hochschule (1855) 1250; Universitatsbibliothek (1523?) 1000. [f] 18 (1700), 14 (1637).

Turkey

Edirne: [b] for Adrianople. [c] Maritsa R. [d] none. [e] Merkez Selimiye Kutuphane (1575) 9.

Istanbul: [b] for Constantinople. [c] Sea of Marmara; Bosporus Strait. [d] Istanbul Universitesi (1453) 35 – 1327; Istanbul Teknik Universitesi (1773) 6 – 437. [e] Istanbul Universitesi Kutuphane (1453?) 210; Merkez Beyázit Genel Kutuphane (?) 118; Robert College Library (1863) 105.

UK

Aberdeen: [a] Scotland. [b] none. [c] North Sea; Dee R; Don R. [d] University of Aberdeen (1494) 6 – 939. [e] University . . . Library (1495) 500; Public Library (1885) 384. [f] 16 (1755), 6 (1707).

Basildon: [a] England. [b] for Billericay. [c] nr Thames R. [d] none. [e] Basildon Branch of Essex County Library (?) ?

Bath: [a] England. [b] none. [c] Avon R. [d] University of Bath (1856) 2 – 260. [e] Public Library (1900) 221.

Belfast: [a] *Northern Ireland. [b] none. [c] North Channel; Lagan R. [d] Queen's University of Belfast (1845) 7 – 566. [e] Public Library (1888) 650; . . . University Library (1848) 615. [f] 9 (1758).

Birkenhead: [a] England. [b] none. [c] Mersey R. [d] none. [e] Public Library (1856) 227.

Birmingham: [a] England. [b] none. [c] Tame R; Rea R. [d] University of Birmingham (1880) 7 – 1010; University of Aston in Birmingham (1895) 3 – 390. [e] Public Library (1866) 2137; University of Birmingham Library (1880) 790.

Blackburn: [a] England. [b] none. [c] Darwen R. [d] none. [e] Public Library (1862) 262.

Blackpool: [a] England. [b] none. [c] Irish Sea. [d] none. [e] Public Library (1880) 219.

Bolton: [a] England. [b] none. [c] Croal R. [d] none. [e] Public Library (1853) 283.

Bournemouth: [a] England. [b] none. [c] English Channel. [d] none [e] Public Library (1895) 271.

Bradford: [a] England. [b] none. [c] Bradford (Beck) Creek. [d] University of Bradford (1957) 4 – 378. [e] Public Library (1872) 519.

Brighton: [a] England. [b] none. [c] English Channel. [d] University of Sussex (1961) 4 – 426. [e] Public Library (1873) 596; University . . . Library (1961) 300.

Bristol: [a] England. [b] none. [c] Avon R; Frome R. [d] University of Bristol (1876) 7 – 1900. [e] Public Library (1876) 787; University . . . Library (1923) 500.

Cambridge: [a] England. [b] none. [c] Cam R. [d] University of Cambridge (1209?) 11 – 1200? [e] University . . . Library (1400) 3000; Public Library (1855) 240.

Cardiff: [a] *Wales. [b] alt Caerdydd. [c] Bristol Channel; Taff R. [d] University of Wales (1822) 15 – 1874 [Cardiff campus: (1866) 6 – 834]. [e] Public Library (1861) 935; Cardiff Campus Library of the University . . . (1931?) 348.

Coventry: [a] England. [b] none. [c] Sherbourne R. [d] University of Warwick (1965) 2 – 230. [e] Public Library (1868) 393.

Derby: [a] England [b] none. [c] Derwent R. [d] none. [e] Public Library (1871) 400.

Dudley: [a] England. [b] none. [c] nr Stour R. [d] none. [e] Public Library (1884) 369.

Dundee: [a] Scotland. [b] none. [c] Tay R. [d] University of Dundee (1881) 3 – 430; University of Saint Andrews (at Saint Andrews, nr Dundee) (1410) 3 - 274. [e] University of Saint Andrews Library (at Saint Andrews, nr Dundee) (1456) 580; Public Library (1869) 386; University of Dundee Library (1883) 215.

Edinburgh: [a] *Scotland. [b] none. [c] Forth R. [d] University of Edinburgh (1583) 10 – 1300; Heriot-Watt University (1821) 3 – 234. [e] National Library of Scotland (1682) 3000; Public Library (1890) 1061; University . . . Library (1580) 1000. [f] 57 (1755), 36 (1705e).

Exeter: [a] England. [b] none. [c] Exe R. [d] Exeter University (1855) 3 – 370? [e] Devon County Library (1924) 868; Public Library (1868) 333; . . . University Library (1933) 245.

Gateshead: [a] England. [b] none. [c] Tyne R. [d] none. [e] Public Library (1885) 167.

Glasgow: [a] Scotland. [b] none. [c] Clyde R; Kelvin R. [d] University of Glasgow (1451) 9 – 1717; University of Strathclyde (1796) 5 – 640. [e] Public Library (1877) 1853; University of Glasgow Library (1577) 880. [f] 24 (1755), 13 (1708).

Gloucester: [a] England. [b] none. [c] Severn R. [d] none. [e] Gloucestershire County Library (1917) 856; Public Library (1900) 214.

Grimsby: [a] England. [b] for Great Grimsby. [c] Humber R. [d] none. [e] Public Library (1901) 164.

Halifax: [a] England. [b] none. [c] Hebble R. [d] none. [e] Public Library (1883) 250.

Hartlepool: [a] England. [b] inc West Hartlepool. [c] North Sea. [d] none. [e] Public Library (1895) 143. [f] West Hartlepool: 77 (1961), 73 (1951), 68 (1931), 63 (1901).

Havant and Waterloo: [a] England. [b] for Havant. [c] nr English Channel. [d] none. [e] Plessey Company, Ltd, Library (1959) 6; Havant and Waterloo Branch of Hampshire County Library (?) ?

Huddersfield: [a] England. [b] none. [c] Colne R. [d] none. [e] Public Library (1898) 267.

Hull: [a] England. [b] off Kingston upon Hull. [c] Humber R; Hull R. [d] University of Hull (1927) 4 – 439. [e] Public Library (1889) 877; University . . . Library (1928) 333.

Ipswich: [a] England. [b] none. [c] Orwell R; Gipping R. [d] none. [e] East Suffolk County Library (1925) 387; Public Library (1852) 245.

Leeds: [a] England. [b] none. [c] Aire R. [d] University of Leeds (1831) 9 – ? [e] Public Library (1871) 972; Brotherton Library (alt University . . . Library) (1874) 710.

Leicester: [a] England. [b] none. [c] Soar R. [d] University of Leicester (1918) 3 – 362; Loughborough University of Technology (at Loughborough, nr Leicester) (1952) 3 – 280. [e] Leicestershire County Library (1922) 800; Public Library (1871) 389; University . . . Library (1921) 300.

Liverpool: [a] England. [b] none. [c] Mersey R. [d] University of Liverpool (1881) 7 – 1186. [e] Public Library (1852) 2245; University . . . Library (1881) 700.

*London: [a] *England. [b] none. [c] Thames R; Lea R. [d] University of London (13th c) 39 – 3000?; City University (1891) 3 – 320; University of Surrey (1891) 3 – 284?; Brunel University (1957) 2 – 220; Royal College of Arts (univ) (1837) 0.6 – 108. [e] British Museum Library (1753) 8000; Westminster Public Library (1857) 1073; University of London Library (1838) 1000; Lambeth Public Library (1887) 936. [f] 676 (1750), 674 (1701).

Luton: [a] England. [b] none. [c] Lea R. [d] none. [e] Public Library (1910) 349.

Manchester: [a] England. [b] none. [c] Irwell R. [d] Victoria University of Manchester (1851) 12 – 1618? [e] Public Library (1852) 1710; . . . University Library (1851) 900; John Rylands Library (1899) 600. [f] 20 (1757).

Newcastle upon Tyne: [a] England. [b] alt Newcastle. [c] Tyne R. [d] University of Newcastle upon Tyne (1834) 6 – 935. [e] Public Library (1880) 687; University . . . Library (1871) 345.

Newport: [a] Wales. [b] alt Casnewydd-ar-Wysg. [c] Usk (alt Wysg) R. [d] none. [e] Monmouthshire County Library (1927) 473; Public Library (1870) 191.

Northampton: [a] England. [b] none. [c] Nene R. [d] none. [e] Northamptonshire County Library (1926) 566; Public Library (1876) 224.

Norwich: [a] England. [b] none. [c] Wensum R. [d] University of East Anglia (1961) 3 – 267. [e] Norfolk County Library (1925) 941; Public Library (1857) 395.

Nottingham: [a] England. [b] none. [c] Trent R. [d] University of Nottingham (1881) 5 – 743. [e] Nottinghamshire County Library (1920) 1208; Public Library (1867) 759. [f] 18 (1779).

Oldham: [a] England. [b]none. [c] Medlock R. [d]none. [e] Public Library (1883) 206.

Oxford: [a] England. [b] none. [c] Thames R; Cherwell R. [d] University of Oxford (1200?) 11 – 1100? [e] Bodleian Library (alt University . . . Library) (1602) 3000; Rhodes House Library (1928) 500; Oxfordshire County Library (1924) 440; Public Library (1854) 254.

Paisley: [a] Scotland. [b] none. [c] White Cart R. [d] none. [e] Renfrew County Library (1921) 506; Public Library (1871) 155.

Plymouth: [a] England. [b] none. [c] Plymouth Sound of English Channel; Tamar R; Plym R. [d] none. [e] Public Library (1876) 501.

Poole: [a] England. [b] none. [c] English Channel. [d] none. [e] Public Library (1887) 204.

Portsmouth: [a] England. [b] none. [c] English Channel. [d] none. [e] Public Library (1883) 321.

Preston: [a] England. [b] none. [c] Ribble R. [d] none. [e] Lancashire County Library (1925) 3731; Harris Public Library (1879) 294.

Reading: [a] England. [b] none. [c] Thames R; Kennet R. [d] University of Reading (1892) 5 – 558. [e] Berkshire County Library (1924) 590; University . . . Library (1893) 345; Public Library (1882) 241.

Rochdale: [a] England. [b] none. [c] Roch R. [d] none. [e] Public Library (1872) 190.

Saint Helens: [a] England. [b] none. [c] Sankey Brook. [d] none. [e] Public Library (1872) 193.

Salford: [a] England. [b] none. [c] Irwell R. [d] University of Salford (1896) 3 – 449. [e] Public Library (1850) 197.

Sheffield: [a] England. [b] none. [c] Don R. [d] University of Sheffield (1828) 6 – 779? [e] Public Library (1856) 1187; University . . . Library (1897) 430. [f] 10 (1736).

Solihull: [a] England. [b] none. [c] Blythe R. [d] none. [e] Public Library (bef 1952) 191.

Southampton: [a] England. [b] none. [c] English Channel; Test R; Itchen R. [d] University of Southampton (1862) 4 – 575. [e] Public Library (1889) 355; University . . . Library (1862) 316.

Southend-on-Sea: [a] England. [b] alt Southend. [c] North Sea; Thames R. [d] none. [e] Public Library (1906) 355.

South Shields: [a] England. [b] none. [c] North Sea; Tyne R. [d] none. [e] Public Library (1873) 225.

Stockport: [a] England. [b] none. [c] Mersey R; Tame R; Goyt R. [d] none. [e] Public Library (1875) 280.

Stoke-on-Trent: [a] England. [b] inc Burslem, Fenton, Hanley, Longton, Stoke-upon-Trent, Tunstall. [c] Trent R. [d] none. [e] Public Library (1863) 462. [f] Burslem: 39 (1901), 20 (1851), 7 (1801); Fenton: 23 (1901), 4 (1851); Hanley: 62 (1901), 25 (1851); Longton: 36 (1901), 15 (1851); Stoke-upon-Trent: 30, 89s (1901), 58s (1851), 16s (1801); Tunstall: 19 (1901), 10 (1851).

Sunderland: [a] England. [b] none. [c] North Sea; Wear R. [d] none. [e] Public Library (1866) 300.

Swansea: [a] Wales. [b] alt Abertawe. [c] Swansea B of Bristol Channel; Tawe R. [d] University College of Swansea of the University of Wales (1920) 3 – 390. [e] University College . . . Library (1920) 240; Public Library (1876) 207.

Swindon: [a] England. [b] none. [c] nr Cole R. [d] none. [e] Public Library (1943) 229.

Teesside: [a] England. [b] inc Billingham, Eston, Middlesbrough, Redcar, Stockton-on-Tees, Thornaby-on-Tees. [c] North Sea; Tees R. [d] none. [e] Public Library (1871) 365. [f] :

	1961	1951	1931	1901	1851	1801
Billingham	32	24	19	1	0.7	0.3
Eston	37	33	31	11	0.5	0.3
Middlesbrough	157	147	139	91	7	0.02
Redcar	31	28	20	8	1	0.4
Stockton-on-Tees	81	74	68	51	10	4
Thornaby-on-Tees	23	23	21	16	2	0.2

Thurrock: [a] England. [b] inc Grays Thurrock, Tilbury. [c] Thames R. [d] none. [e] Public Library (1904) 215. [f] Grays Thurrock: 18 (1931), 14 (1901), 2 (1851), 0.7 (1801); Tilbury: 17 (1931), 5 (1901).

Torbay: [a] England. [b] for Torquay. [c] English Channel. [d] none. [e] Public Library (1907) 90.

Wallasey: [a] England. [b] none. [c] Mersey R. [d] none. [e] Public Library (1900) 156.

Walsall: [a] England. [b] none. [c] nr Tame R. [d] none. [e] Public Library (1859) 153.

Warley: [a] England. [b] inc Oldbury, Rowley Regis, Smethwick. [c] nr Tame R. [d] none. [e] Public Library (1877) 333. [f] Oldbury: 54 (1961), 54 (1951), 36 (1931), 25 (1901); Rowley Regis: 48 (1961), 49 (1951), 41 (1931), 35 (1901); Smethwick: 68 (1961), 76 (1951), 84 (1931), 55 (1901), 8 (1851), 1 (1801).

West Bromwich: [a] England. [b] none. [c] Tame R. [d] none. [e]Public Library (1875) 360.

Wolverhampton: [a] England. [b] none. [c] nr Smestow R. [d] none. [e] Public Library (1869) 438.

York: [a] England. [b] none. [c] Ouse R; Foss R. [d] University of York (1963) 3 – 250. [e] Public Library (1893) 229; University . . . Library (1963) 150.

USSR

Archangel: [a] Russia in Europe. [b] off Arkhangelsk. [c] Northern Dvina R. [d] none. [e] Archangel Province N.A. Dobrolyubov Library (1833) 737.

Astrakhan: [a] Russia in Europe. [b] none. [c] Volga R. [d] none. [e] Astrakhan Province N. K. Krupskaya Scientific Library (1838) 566.

Baku: [a] *Azerbaijan. [b] none. [c] Caspian (Sea) L. [d] Azerbaijan S. M. Kirov State University (1920) 11 – 700. [e] Azerbaijan National M. F. Akhundov Library (1923) 2013; Central Library of the . . . University (1919) 1094; Central Scientific Library of the Azerbaijan SSR Academy of Sciences (1934) 753.

Belgorod: [a] Russia in Europe. [b] none. [c] Donets R. [d] none. [e] Belgorod Province Library (1955) 254.

Bryansk: [a] Russia in Europe. [b] alt Briansk. [c] Desna R. [d] none. [e] Bryansk Province Library (1944) 427.

Cheboksary: [a] Russia in Europe; *Chuvash ASSR. [b] none. [c] Volga R. [d] Chuvash I. N. Ulyanov State University (1967) 6 – 300. [e] Chuvash National M. Gorkiy Library (1871) 543.

Cherepovets: [a] Russia in Europe. [b] none. [c] Sheksna R. [d] none. [e] Cherepovets Pedagogic Institute Library (1875) 140.

Cherkassy: [a] Ukraine. [b] none. [c] Dnieper R. [d] none. [e] Cherkassy 300th Anniversary of the Union of Russia and the Ukraine Pedagogic Institute Library (1930) 334; Cherkassy Province V. V. Mayakovskiy Library (1954) 312.

Chernigov: [a] Ukraine. [b] none [c] Desna R. [d] none. [e] Chernigov Province V. G. Korolenko State Library (1877) 236.

Chernovtsy: [a] Ukraine. [b] for Cernauti, Czernowitz. [c] Prut R. [d] Chernovtsy State University (1875) 9 – 450. [e] Scientific Library of the . . . University (1875) 1630; Chernovtsy Province Library (1940) 334.

Dneprodzerzhinsk: [a] Ukraine. [b] for Kamenskoye. [c] Dnieper R. [d] none. [e] Dneprodzerzhinsk Arsenichev Industrial Institute Library (bef 1944) ?; Palace of Culture Library (?) ?

Dnepropetrovsk: [a] Ukraine. [b] for Ekaterinoslav, Yekaterinoslav. [c] Dnieper R; Samara R. [d] Dnepropetrovsk 300th Anniversary of the Union of Russia and the Ukraine University (1919) 13 – 700. [e] Dnepropetrovsk Province October Revolution Library (1887) 1062; Scientific Library of the . . . University (1918) 818.

Donetsk: [a] Ukraine. [b] for Stalino, Yuzovka, Yuzovo. [c] Kalmius R. [d] Donetsk State University (1965) ? – ? [e] Donetsk Province N. K. Krupskaya State Library (1926) 1211; Donetsk Polytechnic Institute Library (1921) 700.

Dzerzhinsk: [a] Russia in Europe. [b] for Chernorechye, Rastyapino. [c] Oka R. [d] none. [e] Scientific-Technical Library of the Chernorechen M. I. Kalinin Chemical Works (1929) 106; N. K. Krupskaya City Library (1927) 52.

Gomel: [a] White Russia. [b] none. [c] Sozh R. [d] Gomel State University (1969) 5 – 250. [e] Gomel Province V. I. Lenin Library (1934) 402; . . . University Library (1969?) 250.

Gorkiy: [a] Russia in Europe. [b] alt Gorki, Gorky; for Nizhniy Novgorod. [c] Volga R; Oka R. [d] Gorkiy N. I. Lobachevskiy State University (1920) 8 – 700. [e] Gorkiy Province V. I. Lenin Library (1930) 2572; Gorkiy A. A. Zhdanov Polytechnic Institute Library (1930) 615; Central Library of the . . . University (1931) 477.

Gorlovka: [a] Ukraine. [b] none. [c] nr Lugan R. [d] none. [e] Foreign-Language Pedagogic Institute Library (1949) 107.

Groznyy: [a] Russia in Europe; *Chechen-Ingush ASSR. [b] alt Grozny. [c] Sunzha R. [d] none. [e] Chechen-Ingush National A. P. Chekhov Library (1905) 834.

Ivanovo: [a] Russia in Europe. [b] for Ivanovo-Voznesensk. [c] Uvod R. [d] none. [e] Ivanovo Province Library (1919) 1100.

Izhevsk: [a] Russia in Europe; *Udmurt ASSR. [b] for Izhevskiy Zavod. [c] Izh R. [d] none. [e] National V. I. Lenin Library of the Udmurt ASSR (1919) 587.

Kalinin: [a] Russia in Europe. [b] for Tver. [c] Volga R; Tvertsa R; Tmaka R. [d] none. [e] Kalinin Province A. M. Gorkiy Library (1860) 1038.

Kaliningrad: [a] Russia in Europe. [b] for Konigsberg. [c] Pregolya (for Pregel) R. [d] Kaliningrad State University (1544) 4 – 200. [e] Kaliningrad Province Library (1946) 633. [f] 306s (1970).

Kaluga: [a] Russia in Europe. [b] none. [c] Oka R. [d] none. [e] Kaluga Province V. G. Belinskiy Library (1944) 319.

Kaunas: [a] Lithuania. [b] alt Kovno. [c] Neman R; Viliya R. [d] Kaunas Polytechnic Institute (univ) (1920) 20 – 1653. [e] . . . Institute Library (1920?) 1200; Public Library (1919) 1000.

Kazan: [a] Russia in Europe; *Tatar ASSR. [b] for Kasan. [c] Kazanka R. [d] Kazan V. I. Ulyanov-Lenin State University (1804) 10 – 700. [e] N. I. Lobachevskiy Scientific Library of the . . . University (1798) 3858; National V. I. Lenin Library of the Tatar ASSR (1865) 1205.

Kerch: [a] Ukraine. [b] none. [c] Kerch Strait. [d] none.

Kharkov: [a] Ukraine. [b] none. [c] Kharkov R; Lopan R; Netetcha R; Gnilopiat R; Udi R. [d] Kharkov A. M. Gorkiy State University (1805) 7 – ? [e] V. G. Korolenko State Scientific Library (1886) 3760; Central Scientific Library of the . . . . University(1805) 2552; Kharkov V. I. Lenin Polytechnic Institute Library (1885) 1688.

Kherson: [a] Ukraine. [b] none. [c] Dnieper R. [d] none. [e] Kherson Province A. M. Gorkiy State Library (1872) 526.

Kiev: [a] *Ukraine. [b] off Kiyev. [c] Dnieper R. [d] Kiev T. G. Shevchenko State University (1834) 20 – 1720. [e] Central Scientific Library of the Ukrainian SSR Academy of Sciences (1919) 6051; National CPSU State Library of the Ukrainian SSR (1866) 2000; Scientific Library of the . . . University (1834) 1751; Scientific Library of the Kiev Polytechnic Institute (1898) 1107.

Kirov: [a] Russia in Europe. [b] for Khlynov, Viatka, Vyatka. [c] Vyatka R. [d] none. [e] Kirov Province A. I.Herzen Library (1837) 1615.

Kirovabad: [a] Azerbaijan. [b] for Elisavetpol, Gandzha, Yelisavetpol. [c] Gyandzhachay R. [d] none. [e] Azerbaijan Agricultural Machine Construction Institute Library (1932) 180; Kirovabad G. B. Zardabi Pedagogic Institute Library (1943) 160.

Kirovograd: [a] Ukraine. [b] for Elisavetgrad, Yelisavetgrad, Zinovyevsk. [c] Ingul R. [d] none. [e] Kirovograd Province N. K. Krupskaya Library (1898) 688.

Kishinev: [a] *Moldavia. [b] for Chisinau. [c] Byk R. [d] Kishinev State University (1945) 8 – 513. [e] National N. K. Krupskaya State Library of the Moldavian SSR (1832) 1532;. . . University Library (1946) 952; Central Scientific Library of the Moldavian SSR Academy of Sciences (1939) 505.

Klaypeda: [a] Lithuania. [b] alt Klaipeda; for Memel. [c] Baltic Sea; Neman R. [d] none.

Kostroma: [a] Russia in Europe. [b] none. [c] Volga R; Kostroma R. [d] none. [e] Kostroma Province N. K. Krupskaya Library (1918) 711.

Kramatorsk: [a] Ukraine. [b] for Kramatorskaya. [c] Kazennyy Torets R. [d] none. [e] Technical Library of the Kramatorsk Industrial Institute (1953) 120.

Krasnodar: [a] Russia in Europe. [b] for Ekaterinodar, Yekaterinodar. [c] Kuban R. [d] none. [e] Krasnodar Region A. S. Pushkin Library (1900) 1045.

Kremenchug: [a] Ukraine. [b] alt Kremenchuk. [c] Dnieper R. [d] none.

Krivoy Rog: [a] Ukraine. [b] alt Krivoi Rog. [c] Ingulets R; Saksagan R. [d] none. [e] Krivoy Rog Pedagogic Institute Library (1930) 195; Krivoy Rog Ore-Mining Institute Library (1944?) 185.

Kursk: [a] Russia in Europe. [b] none. [c] Tuskor R; Kur R. [d] none. [e] Kursk Province N. N. Aseyev Library (1935) 462.

Kutaisi: [a] Georgia. [b] for Kutais. [c] Rioni R. [d] none. [e] Scientific Library of the Kutaisi A. Tsulukidze Pedagogic Institute (1933) 332.

Kuybyshev: [a] Russia in Europe. [b] alt Kuibyshev; for Samara. [c] Volga R; Samara R. [d] Kuybyshev University (1969) ? – ? [e] Kuybyshev Province Library (1860) 1600; Kuybyshev V. V. Kuybyshev Polytechnic Institute Library (1934) 534.

Leninakan: [a] Armenia. [b] for Aleksandropol, Gyumri. [c] Akhuryan [alt Arpa (Cayi)] R. [d] none.

Leningrad: [a] Russia in Europe. [b] for Petrograd, Saint Petersburg. [c] G of Finland of Baltic Sea; Neva R. [d] Leningrad A. A. Zhdanov State University (1819) 20 – 1700. [e] M. E. Saltykov-Shchedrin State Public Library (1795) 15,144; USSR Academy of Sciences Library (1714) 10,343; M. Gorkiy Scientific Library of the . . . University (1819) 3867; Central Library of the Leningrad M. I. Kalinin Polytechnic Institute (1902) 2000; Leningrad A. I. Herzen Pedagogic Institute Library (1918) 1503. [f] 150 (1760?e), 70 (1725e).

Lipetsk: [a] Russia in Europe. [b] none. [c] Voronezh R. [d] none. [e] Lipetsk Province Library (1955) 556.

Lugansk: [a] Ukraine. [b] for Voroshilovgrad. [c] Lugan R. [d] none. [e] Lugansk Province A. M. Gorkiy Library (1898) 969.

Lvov: [a] Ukraine. [b] for Lemberg, Lwow. [c] Peltev R. [d] Lvov Ivan Franko State University (1661) 13 – 700. [e] Lvov State Scientific Library (1940) 4371; Scientific Library of the . . . University (1608) 1966.

Makeyevka: [a] Ukraine. [b] alt Makeevka; for Dmitriyevsk. [c] Gruzskaya R. [d] none.

Makhachkala: [a] Russia in Europe; *Daghestan ASSR. [b] for Petrovsk. [c] Caspian (Sea) L. [d] Daghestan V. I. Lenin State University (1957) 8 – 450. [e] Daghestan National A. S. Pushkin Library (1900) 336;. . . University Library (1957) 243.

Minsk: [a] *White Russia. [b] none. [c] Svisloch R. [d] White Russian V. I. Lenin State University (1920) 10 – 370. [e] V. I. Lenin State Library of the White Russian SSR (1922) 4513; Yakuba Kolasa Central Library of the White Russian SSR Academy of Sciences (1925) 1102;. . . University Library (1921) 783. [f] 916s (1970).

Mogilev: [a] White Russia. [b] none. [c] Dnieper R. [d] none. [e] Mogilev Province V. I. Lenin Library (1935) 364.

*Moscow: [a] Russia in Europe; *Russia. [b] off Moskva. [c] Moscow (off Moskva) R; Yauza R. [d] Moscow M. V. Lomonosov State University (1755) 29 – 4961; Patrice Lumumba People's Friendship University (1960) 4 – 907; Moscow I. M. Sechenov Medical Institute (univ) (1755) 1 – 680. [e] V. I. Lenin State Library of the USSR (1828 at Leningrad, relocated 1862) 25,226; Institute of Scientific Information and Central Library of Social Sciences of the USSR Academy of Sciences (1918) 6723; A. M. Gorkiy Scientific Library of the Moscow M. V. Lomonosov State University (1755) 5995; State Public Scientific-Technical Library (1958) 5500; All-Union State Library of Foreign Literature (1921) 3547; Central House of the Soviet Army Library (?) 3000; Central State Medical Library (1919) 3000; Central Scientific Agricultural Library of the All-Union Lenin Academy of Agricultural Sciences (1930) 2500; Central Polytechnic Library of the All-Union Society for the Dissemination of Political and Scientific Knowledge (1864) 2500; State Public Historical Library of the Russian SFSR (1938) 2214; Institute of Marxism-Leninism Library (1931) 2000. [f] 7061s (1970), 150 (1700e).

Murmansk: [a] Russia in Europe. [b] none. [c] Barents Sea. [d] none. [e] Murmansk Province Library (1938) 463.

Nikolayev: [a] Ukraine. [b] alt Nikolaev; for Vernoleninsk. [c] Southern Bug R; Ingul R. [d] none. [e] Nikolayev Province Library (1881) 431.

Novgorod: [a] Russia in Europe. [b] none. [c] Volkhoy R. [d] none. [e] Novgorod Province Library (1944) 363.

Novocherkassk: [a] Russia in Europe. [b] none. [c] Ak(say) R. [d] none. [e] Central City A. S. Pushkin Library (1869) 212.

Odessa: [a] Ukraine. [b] none. [c] Black Sea. [d] Odessa I. I. Mechnikov State University (1807) 12 – 600 [e] Odessa A. M. Gorkiy State Scientific Library (1830) 3140; Scientific Library of the . . . University (1817) 2500.

Ordzhonikidze: [a] Russia in Europe; *North Ossetian ASSR. [b] for Dzaudzhikau, Vladikavkaz. [c] Terek R. [d] North Ossetian K. L. Khetagurov State University (1967) ? – ? [e] North Ossetian National S. M. Kirov State Scientific Library (1895) 487; Central Library of the . . . University (1920) 459.

Orel: [a] Russia in Europe. [b] none. [c] Oka R; Orlik R. [d] none. [e] Orel Province N. K. Krupskaya Library (1919) 569.

Orenburg: [a] Russia in Europe. [b] for Chkalov. [c] Ural R; Sakmara R. [d] none. [e] Orenburg Province N. K. Krupskaya Library (1896) 641.

Orsk: [a] Russia in Europe. [b] none. [c] Ural R; Or R. [d] none. [e] Orsk T. G. Shevchenko State Pedagogic Institute Library (1949) 128.

Penza: [a] Russia in Europe. [b] none. [c] Sura R; Penza R. [d] none. [e] Penza Province M. Y. Lermontov Scientific Library (1892) 698.

Perm: [a] Russia in Europe. [b] for Molotov. [c] Kama R. [d] Perm A. M. Gorkiy State University (1916) 12 – 600. [e] Perm Province M. Gorkiy Library (1831) 1384; Central Library of the . . . University (1916) 896.

Petrozavodsk: [a] Russia in Europe; *Karelian ASSR. [b] for Kalininsk. [c] Onega L. [d] Petrozavodsk O. V. Kuusinen State University (1940) 7 – 450. [e] State Public Library of the Karelian ASSR (1860) 1445; Central Library of the . . . University (1940) 377.

Podolsk: [a] Russia in Europe. [b] none. [c] Pakhra R. [d] none. [e] Scientific-Technical Library of the Podolsk M. I. Kalinin Mechanical Works (1932) 115.

Poltava: [a] Ukraine. [b] none. [c] Vorskla R; Kolomak R. [d] none. [e] Poltava Province I. P. Kotlyarevskiy State Scientific Library (1894) 329.

Riga: [a] *Latvia. [b] none. [c] G of Riga of Baltic Sea; Western Dvina R. [d] Latvian Pyetr Stuchka State University (1861) 8 – 500. [e] Vilis Lacis State Library of the Latvian SSR (1919) 3352; Central Library of the Latvian SSR Academy of Sciences (1524) 2079; Scientific Library of the . . . University (1862) 1432. [f] 25 (1782).

Rostov-na-Donu: [a] Russia in Europe. [b] alt Rostov, Rostov-on-Don. [c] Don R. [d] Rostov-na-Donu State University (1915) 6 – ? [e] Rostov K. Marx State Scientific Library (1920) 1758; Scientific Library of the . . . University (1915) 1131.

Ryazan: [a] Russia in Europe. [b] alt Riazan. [c] Oka R; Trobezh R. [d] none. [e] Ryazan Province A. M. Gorkiy Library (1858) 786.

Rybinsk: [a] Russia in Europe. [b] for Shcherbakov. [c] Volga R; Cheremukha R; Sheksna R. [d] none. [e] Central City F. Engels Library (1919) 113.

Saransk: [a] Russia in Europe; *Mordvinian ASSR. [b] none. [c] Insar R. [d] Mordvinian State University (1957) 4 – ? [e] . . . University Library (1931) 428; Mordvinian National A. S. Pushkin Library (1899) 410.

Saratov: [a] Russia in Europe. [b] none. [c] Volga R. [d] Saratov N. G. Chernyshevskiy State University (1909) 10 – 700. [e] Scientific Library of the . . . University (1909) 2150; Saratov Province Library (1831) 900.

Sevastopol: [a] Ukraine. [b] for Sebastopol. [c] Black Sea. [d] none. [e] A. O. Kovalevskiy Biological Research Station Library (1871?) 40; Central City L. N. Tolstoy Library (?) ?; Maritime Library (1844) ?

Shakhty: [a] Russia in Europe. [b] for Aleksandrovsk-Grushevskiy. [c] Grushevka R. [d] none. [e] Central City A. S. Pushkin Library (1915) 257.

Simferopol: [a] Ukraine. [b] none. [c] Salgir R. [d] none. [e] Crimean Province I. Y. Franko Library (1890) 576; Central Library of the Crimean M. V. Frunze Pedagogic Institute (1918) 416.

Smolensk: [a] Russia in Europe. [b] none. [c] Dnieper R. [d] none. [e] Smolensk Province V. I. Lenin Library (1922) 729.

Sochi: [a] Russia in Europe. [b] none. [c] Black Sea; Sochi R. [d] none. [e] Central City Library (1963) 60.

Stavropol: [a] Russia in Europe. [b] for Voroshilovsk. [c] Tashla R. [d] none. [e] Stavropol Region M. Y. Lermontov Library (1853) 762.

Sterlitamak: [a] Russia in Europe; Bashkir ASSR. [b] none. [c] Belaya R; Sterlya R. [d] none. [e] Sterlitamak Pedagogic Institute Library (1944) 99.

Sumy: [a] Ukraine. [b] none. [c] Psel R. [d] none. [e] Sumy Province N. K. Krupskaya Library (1939) 220.

Syzran: [a] Russia in Europe. [b] none. [c] Volga R; Syzran R. [d] none.

Taganrog: [a] Russia in Europe. [b] none. [c] G of Taganrog of Sea of Azov. [d] none. [e] Taganrog Institute of Radio Engineering Library (1952?) 283; City A. P. Chekhov Library (1876) 173.

Tallin: [a] *Estonia. [b] alt Tallinn; for Reval, Revel. [c] G of Finland of Baltic Sea. [d] Tallin Polytechnic Institute (univ) (1936) 9 – 569. [e] F. R. Kreutzwald State Library of the Estonian SSR (1940) 2434; Scientific Library of the Estonian SSR Academy of Sciences (1947) 1631.

Tambov: [a] Russia in Europe. [b] none. [c] Tsna R. [d] none. [e] Tambov Province A. S. Pushkin Library (1830) 560.

Tartu: [a] Estonia. [b] for Derpt, Dorpat, Yurev. [c] Ema R. [d] Tartu State University (1802) 4 – 578. [e] Scientific Library of the . . . University (1802) 2779.

Tbilisi: [a] *Georgia. [b] alt Tiflis. [c] Kura R. [d] Tbilisi State University (1918) 14 – 1288. [e] National K. Marx State Library of the Georgian SSR (1846) 9720; Scientific Library of the . . . University (1918) 2143; Central Scientific Library of the Georgian SSR Academy of Sciences (1941) 1700.

Tolyatti: [a] Russia in Europe. [b] alt Togliatti; for Stavropol. [c] Volga R. [d] none. [e] Library of the Kuybyshev Biological Station of the USSR Academy of Sciences Institute of Inland-Water Biology (1958) 11.

Tula: [a] Russia in Europe. [b] none. [c] Upa R; Tulitsa R. [d] none. [e] Tula Province V. I. Lenin Library (1919) 720.

Ufa: [a] Russia in Europe; *Bashkir ASSR. [b] none. [c] Belaya R; Ufa R. [d] Bashkir 40th Anniversary of the October Revolution State University (1957) 6 – 215. [e] Bashkir National N. K. Krupskaya Library (1921) 1074; Library of the . . . University (1908) 380.

Ulyanovsk: [a] Russia in Europe. [b] alt Ulianovsk; for Simbirsk. [c] Volga R; Sviyaga R. [d] none. [e] Ulyanovsk Province Library – V. I. Lenin Book Palace (1848) 802.

Vilnyus: [a] *Lithuania. [b] alt Vilna, Vilnius; for Wilno [c] Viliya R; Vilnia R. [d] Vilnyus V. Kapsukas State University (1578) 6 – 1230. [e] Scientific Library of the . . . University (1570) 2407; National Library of the Lithuanian SSR (1919) 2224; Central Library of the Lithuanian SSR Academy of Sciences (1941) 1800.

Vinnitsa: [a] Ukraine. [b] none. [c] Southern Bug R. [d] none. [e] Vinnitsa Province K. A. Timiryazev Library (1907) 463.

Vitebsk: [a] White Russia. [b] none. [c] Western Dvina R; Luchesa R. [d] none. [e] Vitebsk Province V. I. Lenin Library (1925) 310.

Vladimir: [a] Russia in Europe. [b] none. [c] Klyazma R; Lybed R. [d] none. [e] Vladimir Province M. Gorkiy Library (1834) 633.

Volgograd: [a] Russia in Europe. [b] for Stalingrad, Tsaritsyn. [c] Volga R; Tsaritsa R. [d] none. [e] Volgograd Province M. Gorkiy Library (1934) 801.

Vologda: [a] Russia in Europe. [b] none. [c] Vologda R. [d] none. [e] Vologda Province I. V. Babushkin Library (1919) 426; Vologda Dairy Institute Library (1912) 240.

Voronezh: [a] Russia in Europe. [b] none. [c] Voronezh R. [d] Voronezh State University (1918) 8 – 507. [e] Central Library of the . . . University (1918) 1139; Voronezh Province I. S. Nikitin Library (1864) 1008.

Yaroslavl: [a] Russia in Europe. [b] none. [c] Volga R; Kotorosl R. [d] Yaroslavl University (1970) ? – ? [e] Yaroslavl Province N. A. Nekrasov Library (1902) 953; Central Library of the Yaroslavl K. D. Ushinskiy Pedagogic Institute (1918) 650.

Yerevan: [a] *Armenia. [b] alt Erevan; for Erivan. [c] Zanga R. [d] Yerevan State University (1920) 7 – 384. [e] National A. F. Myashnikyan State Library of the Armenian SSR (1921) 5698; Central Library of the Armenian SSR Academy of Sciences (1935) 1374; Scientific Library of the . . . University (1921) 1097.

Yoshkar-Ola: [a] Russia in Europe; *Mari ASSR. [b] alt Ioshkar-Ola; for Krasnokokshaysk, Tsarevokokshaysk. [c] Malaya Kokshaga R. [d] none. [e] National Scientific Library of the Mari ASSR (1922) 595.

Zaporozhye: [a] Ukraine. [b] alt Zaporozhe; for Aleksandrovsk. [c] Dnieper R. [d] none. [e] Zaporozhye Province A. M. Gorkiy Library (1905) 676.

Zhdanov: [a] Ukraine. [b] for Mariupol. [c] Sea of Azov; Kalmius R. [d] none. [e] Zhdanov Metallurgical Institute Library (1929?) 167; Gorkiy Library (?) ?; Korolenko Library (?) ?; Krupskaya Library (?) ?

Zhitomir: [a] Ukraine. [b] none. [c] Teterev R; Kamenka R. [d] none. [e] Zhitomir Province October Revolution Library (1866) 344.

Yugoslavia

*Belgrade: [a] *Serbia. [b] off Beograd. [c] Danube R; Sava R. [d] Univerzitet u Beogradu (1808) 41 – 2876. [e] Univerzitetska Biblioteka Svetozar Markovic (1844) 700; Narodna Biblioteka Socijalisticke Republike Srbije (1832) 655; Centralna Biblioteka Srpske Akademije Nauka i Umetnosti (1842) 600.

Dubrovnik: [a] Croatia. [b] for Ragusa. [c] Adriatic Sea. [d] none. [e] Naucna Biblioteka (1950) 118.

Ljubljana: [a] *Slovenia. [b] for Laibach. [c] Ljubljanica R. [d] Univerza v Ljubljani (1595) 10 – 1107. [e] Narodna in Univerzitetna Knjiznica (1774) 800.

Maribor: [a] Slovenia. [b] for Marburg. [c] Drava R. [d] none. [e] Visokoskolska in Studijska Knjiznica (1903) 195; Mestna Knjiznica (1949) 65.

Nis: [a] Serbia. [b] alt Nish; for Nissa. [c] Nisava R. [d] Univerzitet u Nisu (1965) 8 – 458. [e] Visa Pedagoska Skola Biblioteka (1904) 95; Narodna Biblioteka (1903) 90.

Novi Sad: [a] Serbia. [b] for Neusatz, Ujvidek. [c] Danube R. [d] Univerzitet u Novom Sadu (1960) 8 – 699. [e] Biblioteka Matice Srpske (1838 at Budapest, Hungary; relocated 1864) 470. [f] 16 (1857).

Osijek: [a] Croatia. [b] for Esseg, Eszek. [c] Drava R. [d] none. [e] Gradska Knjiznica (1946) 40. [f] 14 (1857).

Rijeka: [a] Croatia. [b] for Fiume. [c] Kvarner G of Adriatic Sea. [d] none. [e] Naucna Biblioteka (1627) 295. [f] 15 (1857).

Sarajevo: [a] *Bosnia and Herzegovina. [b] alt Serajevo. [c] Miljacka R. [d] Univerzitet u Sarajevu (1946) 12 – 1357. [e] Narodna Biblioteka NR Bosne i Hercegovine (1945) 575.

Skopje: [a] *Macedonia. [b] alt Skoplje; for Uskub. [c] Vardar R. [d] Univerzitet Kiril i Metodij vo Skopje (1946) 21 – 892. [e] Narodna i Univerzitetska Biblioteka Kliment Ohridski (1944) 551.

Split: [a] Croatia. [b] for Spalato, Spalatro. [c] Adriatic Sea. [d] none. [e] Gradska Biblioteka (1903) 200. [f] 16 (1857).

Zagreb: [a] *Croatia. [b] for Agram, Zagrab. [c] Sava R. [d] Sveuciliste u Zagrebu (1669) 30 – 4409. [e] Nacionalna i Sveucilisna Biblioteka (1607) 900.

NORTH AMERICA

Bahama Islands

*Nassau: [a] New Providence I. [b] none. [c] Northeast Providence Channel. [d] none. [e] Public Library (1847) 28 (in 1938).

Barbados

*Bridgetown: [b] none. [c] Carlisle B of Atlantic O. [d] University of the West Indies, Barbados campus (1963) 0.4 – 45. [e] Public Library (1847) 105.

Bermuda

*Hamilton: [b] none. [c] Atlantic O. [d] none. [e] Bermuda Library (1839) 95.

Canada

Calgary: [a] Alberta. [b] none. [c] Bow R; Elbow R. [d] University of Calgary (1945) 12 – 880. [e] Public Library (1911) 415; University . . . Library (1957) 335.

Chicoutimi: [a] Quebec. [b] none. [c] Saguenay R; Chicoutimi R. [d] Universite du Quebec (alt University of Quebec), Chicoutimi campus (1969) 2 – 126. [e] Bibliotheque du Petit Seminaire de Chicoutimi (1873) 64; Bibliotheque de l'Universite du Quebec a Chicoutimi (1969) 50; Municipal Library (bef 1954) 23.

Edmonton: [a] *Alberta. [b] none. [c] North Saskatchewan R. [d] University of Alberta (1906) 22 – 1884. [e] D. E. Cameron Library of the University . . . (1909) 900; Public Library (1913) 564.

Halifax: [a] *Nova Scotia. [b] none. [c] Atlantic O. [d] Dalhousie University (1818) 7 – 702; Saint Mary's University (1802) 3 – 161; Mount Saint Vincent University (1914) 1 – 79. [e] Dalhousie University Library (1867) 278; Halifax City Regional Library (1873) 147. [f] 30 (1871).

Hamilton: [a] Ontario. [b] none. [c] Ontario L. [d] McMaster University (1887) 14 – 576. [e] Public Library (1889) 616; Mills Memorial Library of . . . University (1887) 507. [f] 27 (1871).

Kitchener: [a] Ontario [b] for Berlin. [c] Grand R. [d] University of Waterloo (at Waterloo, nr Kitchener) (1864) 14 – 600; Waterloo Lutheran University (at Waterloo, nr Kitchener) (1910) 7 – 135. [e] University . . . Library (at Waterloo, nr Kitchener) (1957) 320; Public Library (1884) 226. [f] 3 (1871).

Laval: [a] Quebec. [b] inc Chomedey, Laval-des-Rapides, Sainte-Rose. [c] Ottawa R. [d] none. [e] Bibliotheque de l'Institut de Microbiologie et d'Hygiene de l'Universite de Montreal (1948) 26. [f] 9s (1871); Chomedey: 30 (1961); Laval-des--Rapides: 19 (1961), 5 (1951), 3 (1931), 1 (1911); Sainte-Rose: 8 (1961), 4 (1951), 2 (1931), 1 (1901), 0.7 (1871).

London: [a] Ontario. [b] none. [c] Thames R. [d] University of Western Ontario (1878) 17 – 750. [e] University . . . Library (1908) 706; Public Library and Art Museum (1893) 363. [f] 16 (1871).

Longueuil: [a] Quebec. [b] inc Jacques-Cartier since 1970. [c] Saint Lawrence R. [d] none. [e] Bibliotheque du College Edouard-Montpetit (1960) 45. [f] 2 (1871); Jacques-Cartier: 41 (1961), 22 (1951).

Mississauga: [a] Ontario. [b] inc Cooksville. [c] Cooksville Creek. [d] none. [e] Public Library (bef 1953) 119. [f] 6s (1871).

Montreal: [a] Quebec. [b] none. [c] Saint Lawrence R; Ottawa R. [d] Universite de Montreal (1876) 36 – 3585; McGill University (1821) 30 – 2227; Sir George Williams University (1929) 18 – 560; Universite du Quebec (alt University of Quebec), Montreal campus (1969) 10 – 338. [e] McLennan Library of McGill University (1821) 1320; Bibliotheque de l'Universite de Montreal (1876?) 850; Bibliotheque de la Ville (alt City Library) (1902) 775. [f] 107 (1871).

Oshawa: [a] Ontario. [b] none. [c] Ontario L. [d] none. [e] McLaughlin Public Library (1887) 148. [f] 3 (1871).

*Ottawa: [a] Ontario. [b] for Bytown. [c] Ottawa R. [d] Carleton University (1942) 14 – 436; University of Ottawa (1848) 14 – 775. [e] National Library of Canada (1953) 760; National Science Library (1925) 683; Public Library (1906) 430; Library of Parliament (1849) 350. [f] 22 (1871)

Quebec: [a] *Quebec. [b] none. [c] Saint Lawrence R; Saint-Charles R. [d] Universite du Quebec (alt University of Quebec) (1968) 18 – 727 (no campus at Quebec); Universite Laval (1852) 17 – 1750. [e] Bibliotheque de l'Universite Laval (1852) 797; Bibliotheque de la Legislature (1867) 235; Bibliotheque Municipale (?) 107. [f] 60 (1871).

Regina: [a] *Saskatchewan. [b] none. [c] Waskana Creek. [d] University of Saskatchewan, Regina campus (1911) 5 – 328. [e] Public Library (1909) 223; Regina Campus Library of the University . . . (1934) 161. [f] 141s (1971).

Saint Catharines: [a] Ontario. [b] none. [c] Twelve Mile Creek. [d] Brock University (1962) 4 – 105. [e] Public Library (1883) 140; . . . University Library (1962?) 125. [f] 8 (1871).

Saint John: [a] New Brunswick. [b] none. [c] B of Fundy of Atlantic O; Saint John R. [d] none. [e] Saint John Regional Library (1883) 116. [f] 29 (1871).

Saint John's: [a] *Newfoundland. [b] none. [c] Atlantic O. [d] Memorial University of Newfoundland (1925) 9 –367. [e] Newfoundland Public Library Services (1936) 449; Henrietta Harvey Library of the . . . University (1925) 200.

Saskatoon: [a] Saskatchewan. [b] none. [c] South Saskatchewan R. [d] University of Saskatchewan (1907) 18 – 956 [Saskatoon campus: (1907) 12 – 628]. [e] Murray Memorial Library of the University . . . (1909) 448; Public Library (1913) 246. [f] 126s (1971).

Sudbury: [a] Ontario. [b] none. [c] Junction Creek; Ramsey L. [d] Laurentian University of Sudbury (1960) 4 – 266. [e] . . . University Library (1960) 126; Public Library (1896) 120.

Sydney: [a] Nova Scotia; Cape Breton I. [b] none. [c] Sydney Harbor of Atlantic O. [d] none. [e] Cape Breton Regional Library (bef 1925) 77.

Thunder Bay: [a] Ontario. [b] inc Fort William, Port Arthur. [c] Kaministikwia R; Thunder B of Superior L. [d] Lakehead University (1946) 4 – 288. [e] Public Library (1881) 187; . . . University Library (1948) 120. [f] Fort William: 45 (1961), 35 (1951), 26 (1931), 4 (1901), 0.7 (1881); Port Arthur: 45 (1961), 31 (1951), 20 (1931), 3 (1901), 1 (1881).

Toronto: [a] *Ontario. [b] for York. [c] Humber R; Ontario L. [d] University of Toronto (1827) 36 – 4700; York University (1959) 17 – 930. [e] University . . . Library (1842) 3088; Public Library (1884) 708. [f] 56 (1871).

Trois-Rivieres: [a] Quebec. [b] alt Three Rivers. [c] Saint Lawrence R; Saint-Maurice R; Sainte-Marguerite R. [d] Universite du Quebec (alt University of Quebec), Trois-Rivieres campus (1969) 5 – 213. [e] Bibliotheque de l'Universite du Quebec a Trois-Rivieres (1963) 105; Bibliotheque du Seminaire Saint-Joseph (1860) 59; Bibliotheque des Trois-Rivieres (?) 59. [f] 8 (1871).

Vancouver: [a] British Columbia. [b] none. [c] Burrard Inlet of Strait of Georgia; Fraser R. [d] University of British Columbia (1908) 23 – 1569; Simon Fraser University (1963) 5 – 726. [e] University . . . Library (1912) 1200; Public Library (1887) 630.

Victoria: [a] *British Columbia; Vancouver I. [b] none. [c] Juan de Fuca Strait. [d] University of Victoria (1902) 6 – 339. [e] Provincial Library (1863) 400; McPherson Library of the University . . . (1902) 375; Library Development Commission (?) 303; Public Library (1864) 253.

Windsor: [a] Ontario. [b] none. [c] Detroit R. [d] University of Windsor (1857) 9 – 450. [e] University . . . Library (1857) 320; Public Library (1894) 286. [f] 4 (1871).

Winnipeg: [a] *Manitoba. [b] none. [c] Red R; Assiniboine R. [d] University of Manitoba (1877) 18 – 1040; University of Winnipeg (1871) 5 – 160. [e] Elizabeth Dafoe Library of the University of Manitoba (1885) 750; Public Library (1905) 400.

Costa Rica

*San Jose: [b] none. [c] Torres R. [d] Universidad de Costa Rica (1814) 7 – 530. [e] Biblioteca Nacional (1888) 175; Biblioteca de la Universidad . . . (1946) 100.

Cuba

Camaguey: [b] for Puerto Principe. [c] Jatibonico R; Tinima R. [d] none. [e] Biblioteca de las Escuelas Pias (?) 10; Biblioteca Municipal (1938)?

Cienfuegos: [b] none. [c] Cienfuegos B of Caribbean Sea. [d] none. [e] Biblioteca Pedro Modesto Hernandez del Instituto de Segunda Ensenanza (1937) 5; Biblioteca Publica Municipal Jose Marti (1931) l.

Guantanamo: [b] none. [c] Guaso R. [d] none. [e] Biblioteca Popular Enrique Jose Varona (1938)?

*Havana: [b] alt Habana; off La Habana. [c] G of Mexico. [d] Universidad de La Habana (1728) 24 – 3145. [e] Biblioteca Nacional Jose Marti (1901) 800; Biblioteca del Instituto de Literatura y Linguistica (1793) 360; Biblioteca Central Ruben Martinez Villena de la Universidad . . . (1728) 208.

Holguin: [b] none. [c] nr Maranon R. [d] none. [e] Biblioteca Jose Marti del Instituto de Segunda Ensenanza (1938) 3; Biblioteca Alex Urquiola (?) ?

Marianao: [b] none. [c] G of Mexico. [d] none. [e] Biblioteca del Colegio de Belen (1854) 37; Biblioteca Municipal Enrique Jose Varona (1945) 10.

Matanzas: [b] none. [c] Matanzas B of G of Mexico; San Juan R; Yumuri R. [d] none. [e] Biblioteca Publica Gener y del Monte (1835) 24.

San Miguel del Padron: [b] none. [c] nr G of Mexico. [d] none. [e] Biblioteca Doctor Tomas Tuna Iza(?) ?

Santa Clara: [b] for Villa Clara. [c] Monte R; Sabana R. [d] Universidad Central de Las Villas (1949) 4 – 814. [e] Biblioteca General de la Universidad . . . (1953) 82; Biblioteca Provincial Marti (1927) 9.

Santiago de Cuba: [b] alt Santiago. [c] Caribbean Sea. [d] Universidad de Oriente (1947) 6 – 764? [e] Biblioteca de la Universidad . . . (1948) 125; Biblioteca del Instituto Pedagogico (1916) 32; Biblioteca Municipal Elvira Cape de Bacardi (1899) 18.

Dominican Republic

Santiago de los Caballeros: [b] alt Santiago. [c] Yaque del Norte R. [d] Universidad Catolica Madre y Maestra (1962) 1 – 153. [e] Biblioteca de la Universidad . . . (1962) 13; Biblioteca del Ateneo Amantes de la Luz (1873) 8.

*Santo Domingo: [b] for Ciudad Trujillo, Trujillo. [c] Caribbean Sea; Ozama R. [d] Universidad Autonoma de Santo Domingo (1538) 12 – 385; Universidad Nacional Pedro Henriquez Urena (1966) 3 – 301. [e] Biblioteca de la Universidad Autonoma de Santo Domingo (1538) 250; Biblioteca Municipal (1914) 35.

El Salvador

San Miguel: [b] none. [c] Grande de San Miguel R. [d] none.

*San Salvador: [b] none. [c] Acelhuate R; Urbina R; Aseseco R. [d] Universidad de El Salvador (1841) 4 – 616; Universidad Centroamericana Jose Simeon Canas (1965) 2 – 79.[e] Biblioteca Nacional (1870) 95; Biblioteca Central de la Universidad de El Salvador (1847) 95.

Santa Ana: [b] none. [c] (Quebrada) Santa Lucia Creek. [d] none. [e] Biblioteca Municipal Camilo Arevalo (1896) 5.

Guatemala

*Guatemala: [b] alt Guatemala City. [c] Barranquila R; Barranca R. [d] Universidad de San Carlos de Guatemala (1676 at Antigua, relocated 1773) 9 – 665; Universidad Rafael Landivar (1961) 3 – 229; Universidad Doctor Mariano Galvez de Guatemala (1966) 0.4 – 48; Universidad del Valle de Guatemala (1961) 0.2 – 46. [e] Biblioteca Nacional de Guatemala (1879) 351.

Haiti

*Port-au-Prince: [b] none. [c] G of Gonaives of Caribbean Sea. [d] Universite d'Etat d'Haiti (1944) 2 – 183. [e] Bibliotheque de l'Institut Francais d'Haiti (1945) 32; Bibliotheque Nationale d'Haiti (1940) 25.

Honduras

San Pedro Sula: [b] none. [c] Piedras R. [d] none.

*Tegucigalpa: [b] none.[c] Choluteca R; Chiquito R.[d] Universidad Nacional Autonoma de Honduras (1845) 4 – 460. [e] Biblioteca Nacional de Honduras (1880) 60; Biblioteca de la Universidad . . . (1848) 25.

Jamaica

*Kingston: [b] none. [c] Caribbean Sea. [d] University of the West Indies (at Mona, nr Kingston) (1921) 5 – 396 [Mona campus: (1921) 3 – 141]; [e] Jamaica Library Service (1948) 606; University . . . Library (at Mona, nr Kingston) (1948) 220.

Martinique

*Fort-de-France: [b] for Fort-Royal. [c] Caribbean Sea; Madame R. [d] none. [e] Bibliotheque Schoelcher (1884) 12 (in 1938).

Mexico

Acapulco: [a] Guerrero. [b] off Acapulco de Juarez. [c] Pacific O. [d] none. [e] Biblioteca Publica Doctor Alfonso G. Alarcon (1960) 6.

Aguascalientes: [a] *Aguascalientes. [b] none. [c] nr San Pedro (alt Aguascalientes, Verde) R. [d] none. [e] Biblioteca Publica del Estado de Aguascalientes (1953) 4.

Chihuahua: [a] *Chihuahua. [b] none. [c] Chuviscar R. [d] Universidad de Chihuahua (1954) 4 – 365. [e] Biblioteca Publica Municipal (1943) 14; Biblioteca de la Universidad . . . (1954)?

Ciudad Juarez: [a] Chihuahua. [b] alt Juarez; for Paso del Norte. [c] Rio Grande R. [d] Universidad Autonoma de Ciudad Juarez (1968)? – ? [e] Biblioteca Publica Municipal Arturo Tolentino (1945) 23.

Ciudad Madero: [a] Tamaulipas. [b] for Dona Cecilia, Villa de Cecilia. [c] Panuco R. [d] none. [e] Biblioteca del Instituto Tecnologico Regional (1955) 1; Biblioteca Publica de la Sociedad Cultural Amado Nervo (1920) 1.

Ciudad Obregon: [a] Sonora. [b] alt Obregon; for Cajeme. [c] nr Yaqui R. [d] none. [e] Biblioteca Popular (1958) 2.

Cuernavaca: [a] *Morelos. [b] none. [c] Cuernavaca R; Amatitlan R. [d] Universidad Autonoma de Morelos (1938) 4 – 231. [e] Biblioteca Central Universitaria (1887) 15.

Culiacan: [a] *Sinaloa. [b] none. [c] Culiacan R. [d] Universidad Autonoma de Sinaloa (1873) 6 – 403. [e] Biblioteca Central de la Universidad . . . (1875) 30; Biblioteca Publica del Estado de Sinaloa (1940) 15.

Durango: [a] *Durango. [b] for Ciudad de Victoria; off Victoria de Durango. [c] Tunal R. [d] Universidad Juarez del Estado de Durango (1856) 2 – 298. [e] Biblioteca Publica del Estado de Durango (1853) 20; Biblioteca de la Universidad . . . (1957) 16.

Guadalajara: [a] *Jalisco. [b] none. [c] San Juan de Dios R; Agua Azul L. [d] Universidad de Guadalajara (1791) 15 – 1128; Universidad Autonoma de Guadalajara (1935) 7 – 452. [e] Biblioteca Publica del Estado de Jalisco (1861) 300. [f] 1487s (1970).

Gustavo A. Madero: [a] Distrito Federal. [b] alt Madero; inc Guadalupe Hidalgo. [c] Remedias R. [d] none. [e] Biblioteca Boturini de la Basilica de Guadalupe (1707?) 10.

Hermosillo: [a] *Sonora. [b] none. [c] Sonora R. [d] Universidad de Sonora (1942) 6 – 297. [e] Biblioteca Central de la Universidad . . . (1949) 56; Biblioteca y Museo de Sonora (1949) 40.

Irapuato: [a] Guanajuato. [b] none. [c] Irapuato R. [d] none. [e] Biblioteca de la Escuela Preparatoria de la Universidad de Guanajuato (1947) 5; Biblioteca Publica Municipal (1950) 2.

Jalapa: [a] *Veracruz. [b] alt Xalapa; off Jalapa Enriquez. [c] (Arroyo de) Santiago Creek. [d] Universidad Veracruzana (1846) 41 – 4103 [Jalapa campus: (1846) ? – ?]. [e] Biblioteca Central de la Universidad . . . (1959) 30; Biblioteca de la Escuela Normal Veracruzana Enrique C. Rebsamen (1893) 11; Biblioteca Publica Juan Diaz Covarrubias (1948) 7.

Leon: [a] Guanajuato. [b] alt Leon de los Aldamas. [c] Turbio R. [d] none. [e] Biblioteca de la Escuela Preparatoria (1877) 33; Biblioteca del Instituto America (1954) 6; Biblioteca Publica Municipal (1924) 2.

Matamoros: [a] Tamaulipas. [b] for Nueva Santander. [c] Rio Grande R. [d] none. [e] Biblioteca Professor Juan B. Tijerina (1958) 6.

Mazatlan: [a] Sinaloa. [b] none. [c] Pacific O. [d] none. [e] Biblioteca de la Escuela Preparatoria de la Universidad Autonoma de Sinaloa (1958) 9; Biblioteca Publica Municipal (1946) 5.

Merida: [a] *Yucatan. [b] none. [c] none. [d] Universidad de Yucatan (1624) 5 – 224. [e] Biblioteca Central de la Universidad . . . (1922) 38; Biblioteca Publica del Estado de Yucatan (1867) 16.

Mexicali: [a] *Baja California. [b] none. [c] Nuevo R. [d] Universidad Autonoma del Estado de Baja California (1957) 2 – 287. [e] Biblioteca Publica del Estado de Baja California (?) 2; Biblioteca Publica Municipal Esperanza Lopez Mateos (1961) 1.

*Mexico: [a] *Distrito Federal. [b] alt Mexico City. [c] Piedad R; Tacubaya R. [d][1] Universidad Nacional Autonoma de Mexico (1551) 105 – 10,500; Instituto Politecnico Nacional (univ) (1931) 80 – 5996; Universidad Iberoamericana (1943) 5 – 527; Universidad del Valle de Mexico (1960) 4 – 250; Universidad Femenina de Mexico (1943) 2 – 160; Universidad Tecnologica de Mexico (1946) 2 – ?; Universidad de las Americas (alt University of the Americas) (1940) 1 – 120; Universidad Anahuac (1964) 1 – 229. [e] Biblioteca Nacional de Mexico (1844) 570; Biblioteca Central del Instituto Nacional de Antropologia e Historia (1825) 250; Biblioteca Publica Miguel Lerdo de Tejada (1928) 230.

Monterrey: [a] *Nuevo Leon. [b] none. [c] Santa Catarina R; Silla R. [d] Universidad de Nuevo Leon (1857) 18 – 1380; Instituto Tecnologico y de Estudios Superiores de Monterrey (univ) (1943) 12 – 746; Universidad de Monterrey (1969?) 2 – 147; Universidad Labastida (1932) 0.3 – 43. [e] Biblioteca de la Universidad de Nuevo Leon (1933) 136; Biblioteca del Instituto . . . (1943) 105; Biblioteca Alfonso Reyes (1934) 54. [f] 1777s (1970).

Morelia: [a] *Michoacan. [b] for Valladolid. [c] Grande R; Chiquito R. [d] Universidad Michoacana de San Nicolas de Hidalgo (1541) 9 – 510. [e] Biblioteca Publica Universitaria (1874) 37.

Netzahualcoyotl: [a] Mexico. [b] none. [c] nr Ixtapan R. [d] none.

Nuevo Laredo: [a] Tamaulipas. [b] none. [c] Rio Grande R. [d] none. [e] Biblioteca Benito Juarez (1941) 4; Biblioteca Publica Municipal (1945) 2.

Oaxaca: [a] *Oaxaca. [b] off Oaxaca de Juarez. [c] Jalatlaco R. [d] Universidad Benito Juarez de Oaxaca (1825) 3 – 265. [e] Biblioteca General de la Universidad . . . (1826) 40.

Orizaba: [a] Veracruz. [b] none. [c] Blanco R. [d] none. [e] Biblioteca Rafael Delgado (1929) 2.

Poza Rica: [a] Veracruz. [b] alt Poza Rica de Hidalgo. [c] Cazones R. [d] none. [e] Biblioteca de la Sociedad Cultural Minerva (bef 1963) 0.4.

Puebla: [a] *Puebla. [b] off Puebla de Zaragoza. [c] Atoyac R; Alseseca R; San Francisco R. [d] Universidad Autonoma de Puebla (1578) 10 – 620; Universidad Femenina de Puebla (1964) ? – ? [e] Biblioteca Central Doctor Rafael Serrano de la Universidad Autonoma de Puebla (1885) 117; Biblioteca Publica del Estado de Puebla (1648) 43.

Queretaro: [a] *Queretaro. [b] none. [c] nr Queretaro R. [d] Universidad Autonoma de Queretaro (1765) 2 – 135. [e] Biblioteca Central de la Universidad . . . (1963) 23; Biblioteca del Museo Regional (1944) 12; Biblioteca Publica Josefa Ortiz de Dominguez (1963) 6.

Reinosa: [a] Tamaulipas. [b] alt Reynosa. [c] Rio Grande R. [d] none. [e] Biblioteca Publica Municipal Amalia de Castillo Ledon (1955) 5.

Saltillo: [a] *Coahuila. [b] none. [c] (Arroyo) Barranca Creek; (Arroyo) Tortola Creek. [d] Universidad de Coahuila (1867) 11 – 542; Universidad Jaime Balmes de Saltillo (1960) 0.5 – 50; Universidad Interamericana (1943) ? – ? [e] Biblioteca Publica del Estado de Coahuila (1942) 12.

San Luis Potosi: [a] *San Luis Potosi. [b] none. [c] Santiago R. [d] Universidad Autonoma de San Luis Potosi (1624) 8 – 671. [e] Biblioteca Publica de la Universidad . . . (1877) 40.

Tampico: [a] Tamaulipas. [b] none. [c] Panuco R. [d] none. [e] Biblioteca Publica Municipal (1941) 10.

Tepic: [a] *Nayarit. [b] none. [c] Mololoa R. [d] none. [e] Biblioteca Publica Municipal Francisco I. Madero (1925) 5.

Tijuana: [a] Baja California. [b] none. [c] Tijuana R. [d] none. [e] Biblioteca del Banco de Baja California (1964) 10; Biblioteca Miguel de Cervantes Saavedra (1926) 2.

Toluca: [a] *Mexico. [b] off Toluca de Lerdo. [c] Xicualtenco R. [d] Universidad Autonoma del Estado de Mexico (1828) 4 – 412. [e] Biblioteca Publica Central del Estado de Mexico (1827) 40.

Torreon: [a] Coahuila. [b] none. [c] Nazas R. [d] none. [e] Biblioteca Municipal Jose Garcia de Letona (1945) 11.

Veracruz: [a] Veracruz. [b] off Veracruz Llave. [c] G of Mexico. [d] Universidad Veracruzana, Veracruz campus (?) ? – ? [e] Biblioteca Publica Municipal Venustiano Carranza (1872) 15.

[1] Universities with 1000 or more students.

Villahermosa: [a] *Tabasco. [b] for San Juan Bautista. [c] Grijalva R. [d] Universidad Autonoma Juarez de Tabasco (1875) 3 – 269. [e] Biblioteca Jose Marti de la Universidad . . . (1944) 23.

Netherlands Antilles

*Willemstad: [a] Curacao I. [b] none. [c] Caribbean Sea. [d] none. [e] Openbare Leeszaal en Bibliotheek (1920) 67. [f] 94s (1960).

Nicaragua

*Managua: [b] none. [c] Managua L. [d] Universidad Centroamericana (1960) 3 – 164. [e] Biblioteca Nacional (1882) 75.

Panama

*Panama: [b] alt Panama City. [c] B of Panama of Pacific O. [d] Universidad de Panama (1935) 7 – 510; Universidad Santa Maria la Antigua (1965) 1 – 240. [e] Biblioteca de la Universidad de Panama (1935) 250; Biblioteca Nacional (1892) 200.

Puerto Rico

Bayamon: [b] none. [c] Bayamon R. [d] none. [e] Biblioteca Central de los Padres Dominicos de Puerto Rico (1963) 14.

Ponce: [b] none. [c] Caribbean Sea. [d] Universidad Catolica de Puerto Rico (college) (1948) 7 – 536. [e] Biblioteca de la Universidad . . . (1948) 123; Biblioteca Publica (1890) 25.

*San Juan: [b] inc Rio Piedras since 1950. [c] Atlantic O. [d] Universidad de Puerto Rico (alt University of Puerto Rico) (1903) 43 – 2785 [San Juan campus: (1903) 29 – ?]. [e] Biblioteca de la Universidad . . . (alt University . . . Library) (1903) 950; Biblioteca Carnegie (alt Carnegie Public Library) (1903) 106. [f] Rio Piedras: 132 (1950), 13 (1930), 2 (1899).

Trinidad and Tobago

*Port of Spain: [a] Trinidad I. [b] none. [c] G of Paria of Caribbean Sea. [d] University of the West Indies, Trinidad campus (at Saint Augustine, nr Port of Spain) (1960) 1 – 210. [e] Central Library of Trinidad and Tobago (1851) 447.

USA

Abilene: [a] Texas. [b] none. [c] Kirby L; Lytle L. [d] Abilene Christian College (univ) (1906) 3 – 174; Hardin-Simmons University (1891) 2 – 107. [e] . . . University Library (1892) 181; . . . College Library (1906) 153; Public Library (1909) 104.

Akron: [a] Ohio. [b] none. [c] Cuyahoga R; Little Cuyahoga R. [d] Kent State University (at Kent, nr Akron) (1910) 29 – 1911 [Kent campus: (1910) 21 – ?]; University of Akron (1870) 18 – 1164. [e] Public Library (1874) 707; . . . University Library (at Kent, nr Akron) (1913) 650.

Albany: [a] Georgia. [b] none. [c] Flint R. [d] none. [e] Public Library (1906) 92.

Albany: [a] *New York. [b] for Fort Orange. [c] Hudson R. [d] State University of New York (1844) 314 – 12,435 [Albany campus: (1844) 13 – 758]; Rensselaer Polytechnic Institute (univ) (at Troy, nr Albany) (1824) 6 – 534 [Troy campus: (1824) 5 – ?]; Union College and University (at Schenectady, nr Albany) (1785) 5 – 162; Russell Sage College (univ) (at Troy, nr Albany) (1916) 4 – 178; College of Saint Rose (univ) (1920) 1 – 111. [e] State University of New York Library (1844) 5579 [Albany campus: (1844) 543]; New York State Library (1818) 4000; Schaffer Library of Union College (at Schenectady, nr Albany) (1795) 264; Schenectady County Public Library (at Schenectady, nr Albany) (1894) 255; Public Library (1792?) 228. [f] 1 (1714).

Albuquerque: [a] New Mexico. [b] none. [c] Rio Grande R. [d] University of New Mexico (1889) 18 – 1026; University of Albuquerque (college) (1920) 2 – 90. [e] Zimmerman Library of the University of New Mexico (1892) 628; Public Library (1891) 301. [f] 1 (1749e).

Alexandria: [a] Virginia. [b] none. [c] Potomac R. [d] none. [e] Alexandria Library (1794) 130.

Allentown: [a] Pennsylvania. [b] for Northampton. [c] Lehigh R. [d] Lehigh University (at Bethlehem, nr Allentown) (1865) 5 – 531. [e] Lucy Packer Linderman Memorial Library of . . . University (at Bethlehem, nr Allentown) (1877) 498; John A. W. Haas Library of Muhlenberg College (1867) 145; Public Library (1912) 138.

Altoona: [a] Pennsylvania. [b] none. [c] Little Juniata R. [d] none. [e] Altoona Area Public Library (1927) 60.

Amarillo: [a] Texas. [b] none. [c] Amarillo L. [d] none. [e] Mary E. Bivins Memorial Library (1905) 186.

Anaheim: [a] California. [b] none. [c] Santa Ana R. [d] California State College at Fullerton (univ) (at Fullerton, nr Anaheim) (1959) 16 – 465. [e] Public Library (1908) 221; . . . College Library (at Fullerton, nr Anaheim) (1959) 217.

Anchorage: [a] Alaska. [b] none. [c] Cook Inlet of Pacific O. [d] Alaska Methodist University (1957) 1 – 58. [e] Z. L. Loussac Public Library (1945) 105.

Anderson: [a] Indiana. [b] none. [c] West Fork of White R. [d] Anderson College (univ) (1917) 2 – 102. [e] Public Library (1890) 112; Charles E. Wilson Library of . . . College (1931) 74. [f] 81s (1970).

Ann Arbor: [a] Michigan. [b] none. [c] Huron R. [d] University of Michigan (1817 at Detroit, relocated 1837) 40 – 4469 [Ann Arbor campus: (1837) 37 – 4154]; Eastern Michigan University (at Ypsilanti, nr Ann Arbor) (1849) 23 – 849. [e] University . . . Library (1838) 3365; . . . University Library (at Ypsilanti, nr Ann Arbor) (1849) 267; Public Library (1856) 153.

Appleton: [a] Wisconsin. [b] none. [c] Fox R. [d] Lawrence University (1847) 1 – 134. [e] Samuel Appleton Library of ... University (1847) 182; Public Library (1897) 119. [f] 130s (1970).

Arlington: [a] Texas. [b] none. [c] nr West Fork of Trinity R. [d] University of Texas, Arlington campus (1895) 14 – 528. [e] Arlington Campus Library of the University of Texas (1917) 306; Public Library (bef 1962) 81.

Arlington: [a] Virginia. [b] none. [c] Potomac R. [d] none. [e] Arlington County Department of Libraries (1930) 319; Army Library (1944) 280.

Asheville: [a] North Carolina. [b] none. [c] French Broad R. [d] none. [e] Pack Memorial Public Library (1879) 135.

Atlanta: [a] *Georgia. [b] none. [c] Chattahoochee R. [d] Georgia State University (1913) 15 – 742; Georgia Institute of Technology (univ) (1885) 10 – 800; [Atlanta campus: (1885) 8 – ?]; Emory University (1836) 6 – 1686 [Atlanta campus: (1836) 5 – ?]; Atlanta University (1865) 1 – 132. [e] Emory University Library (1836) 898; Public Library (1867) 667; Price Gilbert Memorial Library of ... Institute (1901) 612.

Atlantic City: [a] New Jersey. [b] none. [c] Atlantic O. [d] none. [e] Free Public Library (1900) 67.

Augusta: [a] Georgia. [b] none. [c] Savannah R. [d] none. [e] Augusta-Richmond County Public Library (1848) 229.

Aurora: [a] Illinois. [b] none. [c] Fox R. [d] none. [e] Public Library (1882) 144.

Austin: [a] *Texas. [b] none. [c] Colorado R. [d] University of Texas (1881) 74 – 4525 [Austin campus: (1881) 45 – 2724]; Saint Edward's University (college) (1881) 1 – 78. [e] Mirabeau B. Lamar Library of the University ... (1883) 3209 [Austin campus: (1883) 2166]; Texas State Library (1891) 299; Public Library (1925) 285.

Bakersfield: [a] California. [b] none. [c] Kern R. [d] none. [e] Kern County Library (1900) 498.

Baltimore: [a] Maryland. [b] none. [c] Patapsco R. [d1] Johns Hopkins University (1867) 10 – 1950; Towson State College (univ) (at Towson, nr Baltimore) (1866) 10 – 430; University of Maryland, Baltimore campus (1807) 6 – 645; University of Baltimore (college) (1925) 5 – 238; Morgan State College (univ) (1867) 5 – 279. [e] Enoch Pratt Free Library (1886) 1893; ... University Library (1876) 1870. [f] 0.2 (1752e).

Baton Rouge: [a]*Louisiana. [b] none. [c] Mississippi R. [d] Louisiana State University (1853 at Alexandria, relocated 1869) 35 – 4508 [Baton Rouge campus: (1869) 20 – 2500]; Southern University and Agricultural and Mechanical College (1880 at New Orleans, relocated 1914) 10 – 383 [Baton Rouge campus: (1914) 7 – ?]. [e] Louisiana State University Library (1860 at Alexandria, relocated 1869?) 1085; East Baton Rouge Parish Public Library (bef 1923) 238; Southern University Library (1928) 218; Louisiana State Library (1925) 172.

Bay City: [a] Michigan. [b] none. [c] Saginaw R. [d] none. [e] Sage Public Library (1884) 98; Bay City Public Library (1869) 96.

Beaumont: [a] Texas. [b] none. [c] Neches R; Brakes Bayou. [d] Lamar University (1923) 11 – 396. [e] ... University Library (1923) 177; Tyrrell Public Library (1926) 92.

Berkeley: [a] California. [b] none. [c] San Francisco B of Pacific O. [d] University of California (1855 at Oakland, relocated 1873) 147 – 13,582 [Berkeley campus: (1873) 29 – 3648]. [e] University ... Library (1868 at Oakland, relocated 1873?) 10,072 [Berkeley campus: (1873?) 3635]; Public Library (1893) 318.

Billings: [a] Montana. [b] none. [c] Yellowstone R. [d] Eastern Montana College (univ) (1925) 4 – 156. [e] ... College Library (1927) 155; Public Library (1901) 124.

Biloxi: [a] Mississippi. [b] none. [c] Mississippi Sound of G of Mexico; B of Biloxi of G of Mexico. [d] none. [e] Public Library (bef 1918) 23. [f] 122 s (1970).

Binghamton: [a] New York. [b] none. [c] Susquehanna R; Chenango R. [d] State University of New York, Binghamton campus (1946) 7 – 353. [e] Harpur College Library of the ... University (1950) 450; Public Library (1904) 234.

Birmingham: [a] Alabama. [b] none. [c] Village Creek. [d] University of Alabama, Birmingham campus (1966) 6 – 728; Samford University (1841) 3 – 175; Birmingham-Southern College (univ) (1856) 1 – 88. [e] Birmingham Public and Jefferson County Free Library (1886) 791.

Bismarck: [a] *North Dakota. [b] none. [c] Missouri R. [d] none. [e] North Dakota State Library Commission (1908) 81; Public Library (bef 1928) 53.

Bloomington: [a] Indiana. [b] none. [c] nr Salt Creek. [d] Indiana University (1820) 59 – 5375 [Bloomington campus: (1820) 30 – ?]. [e] ... University Library (1824) 1966; Monroe County Public Library (1918) 99.

Boise City: [a] *Idaho. [b] alt Boise. [c] Boise R. [d] none. [e] Public Library (1894) 127; Idaho State Library (1901) 109. [f] 85s (1970).

Boston: [a] *Massachusetts. [b] none. [c] Massachusetts B of Atlantic O; Charles R. [d1] Northeastern University (1898) 38 – 2345; Boston University (1839 at Newbury, Vermont; relocated 1867) 25 – 2500; Massachusetts State College at Boston (univ) (1852) 8 – 428. [e] Public Library (1854) 3784; Massachusetts State Library (1826) 900; Boston University Library (1870) 671. [f] 16 (1752), 11 (1722).

Boulder: [a] Colorado. [b] none. [c] Boulder Creek. [d] University of Colorado (1861) 32 – 2689 [Boulder campus: (1861) 21 – ?]. [e] University ... Library (1876) 1299; Public Library (1882) 110. [f] 69s (1970).

[1] Universities with 5000 or more students.

Bridgeport: [a] Connecticut. [b] none. [c] Long Island Sound of Atlantic O; Pequennock R. [d] University of Bridgeport (1927) 9 – 557; Fairfield University (at Fairfield, nr Bridgeport) (1942) 4 – 141; Sacred Heart University (college) (1963) 2 – 109. [e] Public Library (1882) 446.

Bristol: [a] Connecticut. [b] none. [c] Pequabuck R. [d] none. [e] Public Library (1892) 132. [f] 72s (1970).

Brockton: [a] Massachusetts. [b] none. [c] Salisbury Plain R. [d] Massachusetts State College at Bridgewater (univ) (at Bridgewater, nr Brockton) (1840) 5 – 363. [e] Public Library (1867) 191.

Brownsville: [a] Texas. [b] none. [c] Rio Grande R. [d] none. [e] Texas Southmost College Library (1948) 51. [f] 53s (1970).

Buffalo: [a] New York. [b] none. [c] Niagara R; Erie L. [d] State University of New York, Buffalo campus (1846) 41 – 2818?; Canisius College (univ) (1870) 4 – 274. [e] Buffalo and Erie County Public Library (1836) 2478; Buffalo Campus Library of the . . . University (1922) 1111.

Burbank: [a] California. [b] none. [c] Los Angeles R. [d] none. [e] Public Library (1938) 230.

Burlington: [a] Vermont. [b] none. [c] Winooski R., Champlain L. [d] University of Vermont and State Agricultural College (1791) 9 – 1221; Saint Michael's College (univ) (at Winooski, nr Burlington) (1903) 1 – 99. [e] Guy W. Bailey Memorial Library of the University . . . (1800) 457; . . . College Library (at Winooski, nr Burlington) (1904) 68; Fletcher Free Library (1873) 46.

Cambridge: [a] Massachusetts. [b] none. [c] Charles R. [d] Harvard University (1636) 18 – 5295; Massachusetts Institute of Technology (univ) (1861) 8 – 1915. [e] . . . University Library (1638) 8088; . . . Institute Library (1862) 1134; Public Library (1857) 262.

Camden: [a] New Jersey. [b] none. [c] Delaware R. [d] none. [e] Camden County Free Library (1922 at Haddonfield, relocated 1931) 178; Free Public Library (1898) 124.

Canton: [a] Ohio. [b] none. [c] Nimishillen Creek. [d] none. [e] Public Library Association (1885) 376.

Casper: [a] Wyoming. [b] none. [c] North Platte R. [d] none. [e] Natrona County Public Library (1910) 65.

Cedar Rapids: [a] Iowa. [b] none. [c] Cedar R; Cedar L. [d] none. [e] Public Library (1897) 183.

Champaign: [a] Illinois. [b] none. [c] nr Kaskaskia R; nr Embarrass (alt Embarras) R. [d] University of Illinois (at Urbana, nr Champaign, and Champaign) (1867) 58 – 8169 [Urbana-Champaign campus: (1867) 36 – 4887]. [e] University of Illinois Library (1868) 4429 [Urbana-Champaign campus: (1868) 4089]; Public Library (bef 1912) 92.

Charleston: [a] South Carolina. [b] none. [c] Atlantic O; Ashley R; Cooper R. [d] none. [e] Charleston County Library (1924?) 229. [f] 4 (1705e).

Charleston: [a] *West Virginia. [b] none. [c] Kanawha R; Elk R. [d] none. [e] West Virginia Library Commission (1929) 466; Kanawha County Public Library (1909) 286.

Charlotte: [a] North Carolina. [b] none. [c] Little Sugar Creek; Irwin Creek. [d] University of North Carolina, Charlotte campus (1946) 4 – 230; Johnson C. Smith University (college) (1867) 1 – 81. [e] Public Library of Charlotte and Mecklenburg County (1891) 506.

Chattanooga: [a] Tennessee. [b] none. [c] Tennessee R. [d] University of Tennessee, Chattanooga campus (1886) 4 – 256. [e] Public Library (1905) 207; John Storrs Fletcher Library of the University . . . (1886) 110.

Cheyenne: [a] *Wyoming. [b] none. [c] Crow Creek. [d] none. [e] Wyoming State Library (1887) 125; Laramie County Library (1872?) 95.

Chicago: [a] Illinois. [b] none. [c] Chicago R; Des Plaines R; Michigan L. [d][1] University of Illinois, Chicago campus (1881) 22 – 3282; Loyola University (1869) 17 – 1889; Northwestern University (at Evanston, nr Chicago) (1851) 16 – 2375 [Evanston campus: (1851) 9 – 785] [Chicago campus: (1920?) 8 – 1523]; University of Chicago (1890) 9 – 1157; DePaul University (1898) 9 – 515; Illinois Institute of Technology (univ) (1892) 8 – 694; Northeastern Illinois State College (univ) (1961) 8 – 396; Chicago State University (1869) 7 – 278; Roosevelt University (1945) 7 – 153. [e] Public Library (1873) 4184; University of Chicago Library (1891) 2854; Center for Research Library (1949) 2750; Northwestern University Library (at Evanston, nr Chicago) (1856) 1996 [Evanstan campus: (1856) 1381] [Chicago campus: (1920?) 615]; John Crerar Library (1895) 1100; Newberry Library (1887) 908.

Cincinnati: [a] Ohio. [b] none. [c] Ohio R. [d] University of Cincinnati (1819) 34 – 2763 [Cincinnati campus: (1819) 32 – ?]; Xavier University (1831) 6 – 299; Athenaeum of Ohio (univ) (at Norwood, nr Cincinnati) (1829) 0.3 – 46. [e] Public Library of Cincinnati and Hamilton County (1856) 2615; University . . . Library (1840) 1068.

Cleveland: [a] Ohio. [b] none. [c] Cuyahoga R; Erie L. [d] Cleveland State University (1881) 14 – 643; Case Western Reserve University (1826) 9 – 1689; John Carroll University (1886) 4 – 300; Saint John College of Cleveland (univ) (1928) 0.9 – 87. [e] Public Library (1869) 3217; Cuyahoga County Public Library (1942) 1104; Case Western Reserve University Library (1856) 1085.

Colorado Springs: [a] Colorado. [b] none. [c] Fountain R. [d] Colorado College (univ) (1874) 2 – 165; University of Colorado, Colorado Springs campus (1955) 2 – ? [e] United States Air Force Academy Library (1955) 276; Charles Leaming Tutt Library of . . . College (1874) 234; Penrose Public Library (1885) 196.

[1] Universities with 5000 or more students.

Columbia: [a] Missouri. [b] none. [c] nr Missouri R. [d] University of Missouri (1839) 49 – 4557 [Columbia campus: (1839) 23 – 3029]. [e] University . . . Library (1841) 1400; Daniel Boone Regional Library (1900) 114. [f] 59s (1970).

Columbia: [a] *South Carolina. [b] none. [c] Congaree R; Saluda R; Broad R. [d] University of South Carolina (1801) 17 – 743 [Columbia campus: (1801) 14 – ?]; Allen University (college) (1870) 0.6 – 52. [e] University . . . Library (1805) 929; South Carolina State Library (1943) 246; Richland County Library (1896) 237.

Columbus: [a] Georgia. [b] none. [c] Chattahoochee R. [d] none. [e] W. C. Bradley Memorial Library (bef 1904) 305.

Columbus: [a] *Ohio. [b] none. [c] Scioto R; Olentangy R. [d] Ohio State University (1870) 51 – 5754 [Columbus campus: (1870) 46 – ?]; Franklin University (college) (1902) 3 – 83; Capital University (college) (1850) 2 – 162. [e] Ohio State University Library (1873) 2246; State Library of Ohio (1817) 1289; Public Library (1872) 939.

Corpus Christi: [a] Texas. [b] none. [c] G of Mexico. [d] University of Corpus Christi (college) (1947) 0.6 – 40. [e] La Retama Public Library (1909) 257.

Dallas: [a] Texas. [b] none. [c] Trinity R. [d] Southern Methodist University (1911) 10 – 741; Baylor University, Dallas campus (1905) 0.5 – ? [e] Public Library (1901) 1047; Southern Methodist University Library (1915) 1047.

Davenport: [a] Iowa. [b] none. [c] Mississippi R. [d] none. [e] Public Library (1874) 201.

Dayton: [a] Ohio [b] none. [c] Miami (alt Great Miami) R; Stillwater R; Mad R. [d] Wright State University (1964) 11 – 510 [Dayton campus: (1964) 10 – ?]; University of Dayton (1850) 9 – 602. [e] Dayton and Montgomery County Public Library (1847) 1143.

Dearborn: [a] Michigan. [b] none. [c] Rouge R. [d] none. [e] Public Library (1921) 257.

Decatur: [a] Illinois. [b] none. [c] Sangamon R. [d] Millikin University (1901) 2 – 125. [e] Public Library (1868) 190.

Denver: [a] *Colorado. [b] none. [c] South Platte R. [d] University of Colorado, Denver campus (1883) 9 – 392; University of Denver (1864) 9 – 823. [e] Public Library (1859) 1171; Mary Reed Library of the University of Denver (1933) 744; Colorado State Library (1862) 413.

Des Moines: [a] *Iowa. [b] none. [c] Des Moines R; Raccoon R. [d] Drake University (1881) 8 – 453. [e] Public Library (1866) 374; Cowles Library of . . . University (1908) 270.

Detroit: [a] Michigan. [b] none. [c] Detroit R. [d] Wayne State University (1868) 36 – 2700; University of Detroit (1877) 10 – 834; Marygrove College (univ) (1910) 0.9 – 84. [e] Public Library (1865) 2116; . . . University Library (1923) 1819.

Downey: [a] California. [b] none. [c] San Gabriel R; Hondo R. [d] none. [e] City Library (1958?) 77.

Dubuque: [a] Iowa. [b] none. [c] Mississippi R. [d] Loras College (univ) (1839) 2 – 115; University of Dubuque (1852) 1 – 77; Clarke College (univ) (1843) 0.8 – 78. [e] Wahlert Memorial Library of Loras College (1839) 186; Carnegie-Stout Public Library (1902) 117.

Duluth: [a] Minnesota. [b] none. [c] Saint Louis R; Superior L. [d] University of Minnesota, Duluth campus (1895) 6 – 300; University of Wisconsin, Superior campus (at Superior, Wisconsin, nr Duluth) (1893) 3 – 188. [e] Public Library (1869) 168; Jim Dan Hill Library of University . . . (at Superior, Wisconsin, nr Duluth) (1896) 136.

Durham: [a] North Carolina. [b] none. [c] nr Eno R. [d] Duke University (1838 at High Point, relocated 1892) 8 – 1042; North Carolina Central University (1909) 4 – 279. [e] Duke University Library (1838 at High Point, relocated 1892?) 2036; North Carolina Central University Library (1910) 200; Durham City-County Public Library (1897) 166.

East Los Angeles: [a] California. [b] none. [c] nr Hondo R. [d] none. [e] East Los Angeles College Library (1945) 59.

Elgin: [a] Illinois. [b] none. [c] Fox R. [d] none. [e] Gail Borden Public Library (1874) 96.

Elizabeth: [a] New Jersey. [b] none. [c] Newark B of Atlantic O; Arthur Kill. [d] none. [e] Free Public Library (1755) 273.

El Paso: [a] Texas. [b] for Franklin. [c] Rio Grande R. [d] University of Texas, El Paso campus (1913) 11 – 468. [e] Public Library (1894) 345; El Paso Campus Library of the University . . . (1913) 294.

Erie: [a] Pennsylvania. [b] none. [c] Erie L. [d] Gannon College (univ) (1944) 4 – 195. [e] Public Library (1899) 251.

Eugene: [a] Oregon. [b] none. [c] Willamette R. [d] University of Oregon (1872) 17 – 1374 [Eugene campus: (1872) 15 – ?]. [e] University . . . Library (1881) 1030; Public Library (1895) 121.

Evansville: [a] Indiana. [b] none. [c] Ohio R. [d] University of Evansville (1854) 5 – 265. [e] Evansville Public Library and Vanderburgh County Public Library (1875) 429.

Fall River: [a] Massachusetts. [b] none. [c] Mount Hope B of Atlantic O; Taunton R; Fall R. [d] none. [e] Public Library (1861) 208.

Fargo: [a] North Dakota. [b] none. [c] Red R. [d] North Dakota State University (1890) 7 – 569; Moorhead State College (univ) (at Moorhead, Minnesota, nr Fargo) (1887) 5 – 332. [e] . . . University Library (1889) 200; Livingston Lord Library of . . . College (at Moorhead, Minnesota, nr Fargo) (1888) 121; Public Library (1900) 88.

Fayetteville: [a] North Carolina. [b] none. [c] Cape Fear R. [d] Fayetteville State University (1867) 1 – 94. [e] Cumberland County Public Library (1907) 86. [f] 161s (1970).

Fitchburg: [a] Massachusetts. [b] none. [c] North Nashua R. [d] Massachusetts State College at Fitchburg (univ) (1894) 5 – 216. [e] Public Library (1859) 138.

Flint: [a] Michigan. [b] none. [c] Flint R. [d] none. [e] Public Library (1851) 343; Genesee County Library (bef 1949) 248.

Fort Lauderdale: [a] Florida. [b] none. [c] Atlantic O. [d] Florida Atlantic University (at Boca Raton, nr Fort Lauderdale) (1961) 7 – 356; Fort Lauderdale University (college) (1945) 0.9 – 41; Nova University (1964) 0.06 – 15. [e] Florida Atlantic University Library (at Boca Raton, nr Fort Lauderdale) (1963) 226; Public Library (bef 1931) 169.

Fort Smith: [a] Arkansas. [b] none. [c] Arkansas R. [d] none. [e] Public Library (1906) 52.

Fort Wayne: [a] Indiana. [b] none. [c] Maumee R; Saint Mary's R; Saint Joseph R. [d] Saint Francis College (univ) (1890) 2 – 104. [e] Public Library of Fort Wayne and Allen County (1893) 1367.

Fort Worth: [a] Texas. [b] none. [c] Trinity R. [d] Texas Christian University (1873) 6 – 451. [e] Mary Couts Burnett Library of . . . University (1910) 683; Public Library (1902) 621.

Fremont: [a] California. [b] none. [c] Alameda Creek. [d] none. [e] Centerville Branch of Alameda County Public Library (1947?) 46 (all Fremont branches: 99).

Fresno: [a] California. [b] none. [c] nr San Joaquin R. [d] Fresno State College (univ) (1911) 17 – 701. [e] Fresno County Free Library (1909) 646; . . . College Library (1911) 302.

Gainesville: [a] Florida. [b] none. [c] nr Newnan L. [d] University of Florida (1853) 24 – 5444. [e] University . . . Library (1889) 1346; Public Library (1917) 76. [f] 69s (1970).

Galveston: [a] Texas. [b] none. [c] G of Mexico. [d] none. [e] Rosenberg Library (1904) 144.

Garden Grove: [a] California. [b] none. [c] Santa Ana R. [d] none. [e] Garden Grove Branch of Orange County Public Library (1921?) 107.

Gary: [a] Indiana. [b] none. [c] Calumet (alt Grand Calumet) R; Little Calumet R; Michigan L. [d] none. [e] Public Library (1908) 400.

Glendale: [a] California. [b] none. [c] Los Angeles R. [d] none. [e] Public Library (1906) 290.

Grand Forks: [a] North Dakota. [b] none. [c] Red R. [d] University of North Dakota (1883) 9 – 400. [e] Chester Fritz Library of the University . . . (1883) 335; Public Library (1899) 65.

Grand Rapids: [a] Michigan. [b] none. [c] Grand R. [d] Aquinas College (univ) (1886) 1 – 118. [e] Public Library (1904) 554.

Great Falls: [a] Montana. [b] none. [c] Missouri R; Sun R. [d] none. [e] Public Library (1889) 149.

Green Bay: [a] Wisconsin. [b] none. [c] Fox R; Green B of Michigan L. [d] none. [e] Brown County Library (1889) 285.

Greensboro: [a] North Carolina. [b] none. [c] Buffalo Creek. [d] University of North Carolina, Greensboro campus (1891) 7 – 462; North Carolina Agricultural and Technical State University (1891) 4 – 274; Guilford College (univ) (1834) 2 – 125. [e] Walter Clinton Jackson Library of the University . . . (1892) 428; F. D. Bluford Library of . . . University (1891) 275; Public Library (1902) 275.

Greenville: [a] South Carolina. [b] for Pleasantburg. [c] Reedy R. [d] Furman University (1825 at Edgefield, relocated 1851) 2 – 145. [e] Greenville County Library (1921) 190; . . . University Library (1826 at Edgefield, relocated 1851?) 164.

Hamilton: [a] Ohio. [b] none. [c] Miami (alt Great Miami) R. [d] Miami University (at Oxford, nr Hamilton) (1809) 16 – 665 [Oxford campus: (1809) 12 – ?]. [e] Alumni Library of . . . University (at Oxford, nr Hamilton) (1824) 537; Lane Public Library (1866) 203.

Hammond: [a] Indiana. [b] none. [c] Calumet (alt Grand Calumet) R; Wolf L. [d] Purdue University, Calumet campus (1945) 5 – 165. [e] Public Library (1903) 244.

Hampton: [a] Virginia. [b] none. [c] Chesapeake B of Atlantic O; James R. [d] Hampton Institute (univ) (1868) 3 – 214. [e] Collis P. Huntington Memorial Library of . . . Institute (1903) 121; Charles H. Taylor Memorial Library (1926) 89.

Harrisburg: [a] *Pennsylvania. [b] none. [c] Susquehanna R. [d] Pennsylvania State University, Capitol campus (at Middletown, nr Harrisburg) (1966) 2 – 68. [e] Pennsylvania State Library (1854) 700; Public Library (1890) 225.

Hartford: [a] *Connecticut. [b] none. [c] Connecticut R. [d] University of Hartford (at West Hartford, nr Hartford) (1877) 10 – 531; Trinity College (univ) (1823) 2 – 130. [e] Connecticut State Library (1854) 550; . . . College Library (1823) 473; Public Library (1893) 459. [f] 3 (1756).

Hayward: [a] California. [b] none. [c] nr San Francisco B of Pacific O. [d] California State College at Hayward (univ) (1957) 16 – 435. [e] Alameda County Public Library (1910 at Oakland, relocated bef 1958) 343; . . . College Library (1959) 303; Public Library (1898) 102.

Hialeah: [a] Florida. [b] none. [c] nr Biscayne B of Atlantic O. [d] none. [e] John F. Kennedy Memorial Library (bef 1949) 100.

High Point: [a] North Carolina. [b] none. [c] nr Uwharrie (alt Uharie) R. [d] none. [e] Public Library (1926) 121.

Hollywood: [a] Florida. [b] none. [c] Atlantic O. [d] none. [e] Public Library (1942?) 45.

Hot Springs: [a] Arkansas. [b] none. [c] nr Ouachita R. [d] none. [e] Garland-Montgomery Regional Library (bef 1928) 61.

Houston: [a] Texas. [b] none. [c] Buffalo Bayou. [d] University of Houston (1927) 26 – 1360; Texas Southern University (1947) 5 – 265; Rice University (1891) 3 – 405; University of Saint Thomas (1946) 1 – 101; University of Texas, Houston campus (1905) 0.6 – 234. [e] Public Library (1848) 1153; Fondren Library of Rice University (1912) 578; M. D. Anderson Memorial Library of the University of Houston (1927) 521.

Huntington: [a] West Virginia. [b] none. [c] Ohio R. [d] Marshall University (1837) 10 – 450 [Huntington campus: (1837) 9 – ?]. [e] . . . University Library (1837) 188; Cabell County Public Library (1902) 136.

Huntington Beach: [a] California. [b] none. [c] Pacific O. [d] none. [e] Public Library (bef 1923) 89.

Huntsville: [a] Alabama. [b] none. [c] Indian Creek. [d] University of Alabama, Huntsville campus (1966) 3 – 180; Alabama Agricultural and Mechanical University (at Normal, nr Huntsville) (1875) 2 – 172. [e] Redstone Scientific Information Center (1949) 152; Public Library (1915?) 133; Joseph F. Drake Library of ... University (at Normal, nr Huntsville) (1904) 102.

Independence: [a] Missouri. [b] none. [c] Missouri R. [d] none. [e] Mid-Continent Public Library Service (1894) 616.

Indianapolis: [a] *Indiana. [b] none. [c] White R. [d] Indiana University, Indianapolis campus (1908) 11 – ?; Butler University (1850) 4 – 204. [e] Indiana State Library (1825) 967; Indianapolis-Marion County Public Library (1873) 875.

Inglewood: [a] California. [b] none. [c] nr Santa Monica B of Pacific O. [d] none. [e] Public Library (1917) 152.

Irving: [a] Texas. [b] none. [c] West Fork of Trinity R. [d] University of Dallas (1955) 1 – 116. [e] Blakely Library of the University ... (1956) 71; Municipal Library (bef 1966) 45.

Jackson: [a] Michigan. [b] none. [c] Grand R. [d] none. [e] Jackson County Library (bef 1935) 122; Public Library (1883) 112.

Jackson: [a] *Mississippi. [b] none. [c] Pearl R. [d] Jackson State College (univ) (1877) 5 – 279. [e] Mississippi Library Commission (1926) 275; Municipal Library (1914) 225.

Jacksonville: [a] Florida. [b] none. [c] Saint Johns R. [d] Jacksonville University (1934) 3 – 155. [e] Public Library (1905) 599.

Jersey City: [a] New Jersey. [b] none. [c] Hudson R; Hackensack R. [d] Jersey City State College (univ) (1927) 9 – 504; Stevens Institute of Technology (univ) (at Hoboken, nr Jersey City) (1870) 3 – 307. [e] Free Public Library (1891) 526.

Johnstown: [a] Pennsylvania. [b] none. [c] Conemaugh R. [d] none. [e] Cambria Public Library (1870) 199.

Joliet: [a] Illinois. [b] for Juliet. [c] Des Plaines R. [d] College of Saint Francis (univ) (1874) 0.8 – 60. [e] Public Library (1875) 96.

Kalamazoo: [a] Michigan. [b] none. [c] Kalamazoo R. [d] Western Michigan University (1903) 22 – 1200; Kalamazoo College (univ) (1833) 1 – 99. [e] ... University Library (1903) 610; Kalamazoo Library (1893) 201.

Kansas City: [a] Kansas. [b] none. [c] Missouri R; Kansas R. [d] none. [e] Public Library (1892) 200.

Kansas City: [a] Missouri. [b] none. [c] Missouri R. [d] University of Missouri, Kansas City campus (1881) 10 – 493. [e] Public Library (1873) 1157.

Kenosha: [a] Wisconsin. [b] none. [c] Michigan L. [d] none. [e] Gilbert M. Simmons Public Library (1897) 194.

Knoxville: [a] Tennessee. [b] none. [c] Tennessee R; Holston R. [d] University of Tennessee (1794) 38 – 2597 [Knoxville campus: (1794) 28 – 1456]. [e] James D. Hoskins Library of the University ... (1838) 961; Public Library of Knoxville and Knox County (1879) 411.

La Crosse: [a] Wisconsin. [b] none. [c] Mississippi R; La Crosse R. [d] University of Wisconsin, La Crosse campus (1909) 7 – 370. [e] Murphy Library of the University ... (1909) 183; Public Library (1888) 129. [f] 63s (1970).

Lafayette: [a] Indiana. [b] none. [c] Wabash R. [d] Purdue University (1869) 38 – 4303 [Lafayette campus: (1869) 26 – ?]. [e] ...University Library (1874) 969; Albert A. Wells Memorial Library (1882) 92. [f] 79s (1970).

Lafayette: [a] Louisiana. [b] none. [c] Vermilion R. [d] University of Southwestern Louisiana (1898) 10 – 648. [e] Dupre Library of the University ... (1901) 336; Public Library (bef 1939) 101. [f] 79s (1970).

Lake Charles: [a] Louisiana. [b] none. [c] Calcasieu R. [d] McNeese State University (1939) 6 – 285. [e] Calcasieu Parish Public Library (bef 1903) 99; Lether E. Frazar Library of ... University (1939) 97.

Lakewood: [a] Colorado. [b] none. [c] nr South Platte R. [d] Colorado School of Mines (univ) (at Golden, nr Lakewood) (1869) 2 – 194. [e] Arthur Lakes Library of ... School (at Golden, nr Lakewood) (1874) 137; Lakewood Branch of Jefferson County Public Library (?) ?

Lancaster: [a] Pennsylvania. [b] none. [c] Conestoga Creek. [d] Millersville State College (univ) (at Millersville, nr Lancaster) (1854) 5 – 330; Franklin and Marshall College (univ) (1787) 3 – 157. [e] Fackenthal Library of Franklin and Marshall College (1787) 198; Free Public Library (1759) 179. [f] 2 (1754e).

Lansing: [a] *Michigan. [b] none. [c] Grand R; Red Cedar R. [d] Michigan State University (at East Lansing, nr Lansing) (1855) 44 – 3450. [e] ... University Library (at East Lansing, nr Lansing) (1855) 1500; Michigan State Library (1837) 1150; Public Library (1871?) 229.

Laredo: [a] Texas. [b] none. [c] Rio Grande R. [d] none. [e] Harold R. Yeary Library of Laredo Junior College (1946) 30; Public Library (bef 1939) 22.

Las Vegas: [a] Nevada. [b] none. [c] Las Vegas Creek. [d] University of Nevada, Las Vegas campus (1951) 6 – 241. [e] Las Vegas Campus Library of the University ... (1957) 189; Public Library (bef 1928) 70.

Lawrence: [a] Massachusetts. [b] none. [c] Merrimack R. [d] none. [e] Free Public Library (1847) 191.

Lawton: [a] Oklahoma. [b] none. [c] Cache Creek. [d] none. [e] Carnegie Public Library (1903) 51.

Lewiston: [a] Maine. [b] none. [c] Androscoggin R. [d] none. [e] Coram Library of Bates College (1863) 139; Public Library (1903) 95.

Lexington: [a] Kentucky. [b] none. [c] Town Branch Creek. [d] University of Kentucky (1865) 28 – 1618 [Lexington campus: (1865) 18 – 1273]. [e] Margaret I. King Library of the University ... (1909) 1116; Public Library (1795) 100.

Lima: [a] Ohio. [b] none. [c] Ottawa R. [d] none. [e] Public Library (1901) 194.

Lincoln: [a] *Nebraska. [b] none. [c] Salt Creek; Antelope Creek. [d] University of Nebraska (1869) 35 – 1518 [Lincoln campus: (1869) 21 – 1000]; Nebraska Wesleyan University (1887) 1 – 116. [e] Don L. Love Memorial Library of the University . . . (1869) 952; Bennett Martin Public Library (1876) 351.

Little Rock: [a] *Arkansas. [b] none. [c] Arkansas R. [d] University of Arkansas, Little Rock campus (1927) 4 – 150. [e] Arkansas Library Commission (1935) 364; Public Library (1910) 193.

Livonia: [a] Michigan. [b] none. [c] Middle Rouge R. [d] none. [e] Public Library (bef 1960) 81.

Long Beach: [a] California. [b] none. [c] San Pedro B of Pacific O; Los Angeles R. [d] California State College at Long Beach (univ) (1949) 26 – 1057. [e] Public Library (1909?) 535;. . . College Library (1949) 377.

Lorain: [a] Ohio. [b] for Charleston. [c] Black R; Erie L. [d] Oberlin College (univ) (at Oberlin, nr Lorain) (1833) 3 – 239. [e] Carnegie Library of. . .College (at Oberlin, nr Lorain) (1833) 656; Public Library (1900) 208.

Los Angeles: [a] California. [b] inc Hollywood. [c] San Pedro B of Pacific O; Los Angeles R. [d][1] University of California, Los Angeles campus (1881) 29 – 3587; California State College at Los Angeles (univ) (1947) 26 – 889; San Fernando Valley State College (univ) (1956) 22 – 798; University of Southern California (1880) 21 – 2100; Pepperdine University (1937) 7 – 128. [e] Public Library (1872) 3371; Los Angeles County Public Library (1912) 3080; Los Angeles Campus Library of the University of California (1919) 2793; University of Southern California Library (1880) 1347.

Louisville: [a] Kentucky. [b] none. [c] Ohio R. [d] University of Louisville (1798) 10 – 1403; Spalding College (univ) (1920) 1 – 127. [e] Free Public Library (1872) 842; University . . . Library (1798) 522.

Lowell: [a] Massachusetts. [b] none. [c] Merrimack R; Concord R. [d] Lowell Technological Institute (univ) (1895) 7 – 311; Massachusetts State College at Lowell (univ) (1894) 2 – 234. [e] City Library (1845) 272;. . . Institute Library (1897) 134.

Lubbock: [a] Texas. [b] none. [c] Double Mountain Fork of Brazos R. [d] Texas Technological University (1923) 20 – 1349. [e] . . . University Library (1925) 920; Lubbock City-County Library (1923) 136.

Lynchburg: [a] Virginia. [b] none. [c] James R. [d] Lynchburg College (univ) (1903) 2 – 116. [e] Jones Memorial Library (1908) 71;. . . College Library (1903) 65.

Lynn: [a] Massachusetts. [b] none. [c] Massachusetts B of Atlantic O. [d] none. [e]Public Library (1862) 244.

Macon: [a] Georgia. [b] none. [c] Ocmulgee R. [d] Mercer University (1833 at Penfield, relocated 1871) 2 – 131. [e] Washington Memorial Library and Middle Georgia Regional Library (bef 1880) 319.

Madison: [a] *Wisconsin. [b] none. [c] Yahara R; Mendota L; Monona L; Waubesa L. [d] University of Wisconsin (1849) 137 – 7369 [Madison campus: (1849) 34 – 2119]. [e] University . . . Library (1850) 2990 [Madison campus: (1850) 2160]; State Historical Society of Wisconsin Library (1854) 388; Public Library (1875) 311.

Manchester: [a] New Hampshire. [b] for Derryfield. [c] Merrimack R. [d] none. [e] City Library (1854) 195.

Mansfield: [a] Ohio. [b] none. [c] Rocky Fork of Mohican R. [d] none. [e] Public Library (1887) 190. [f] 78s (1970).

Memphis: [a] Tennessee. [b] none. [c] Mississippi R; Wolf R. [d] Memphis State University (1912) 19 – 1017; University of Tennessee, Memphis campus (1851) 2 – 498. [e] Public Library (1893) 845; John Willard Brister Library of . . . University (1912?) 397.

Meriden: [a] Connecticut. [b] none. [c] Quinnipiac R. [d] none. [e] Curtis Memorial Library (1903) 114.

Metairie: [a] Louisiana. [b] none. [c] Pontchartrain L. [d] none. [e] Jefferson Parish Library (bef 1953) 313.

Miami: [a] Florida. [b] none. [c] Biscayne B of Atlantic O. [d] University of Miami (at Coral Gables, nr Miami) (1925) 16 – 1248; Barry College (univ) (1940) 1 – 129; Florida International University (planned). [e] Otto G. Richter Library of the University . . . (at Coral Gables, nr Miami) (1926) 862; Public Library (1900) 726.

Miami Beach: [a] Florida. [b] none. [c] Atlantic O; Biscayne B of Atlantic O. [d] none. [e] Public Library (bef 1935) 142.

Milwaukee: [a] Wisconsin. [b] none. [c] Milwaukee R; Menomonee R; Michigan L. [d] University of Wisconsin, Milwaukee campus (1955) 21 – 1076; Marquette University (1857) 11 – 939. [e] Public Library (1847) 2040.

Minneapolis: [a] Minnesota. [b] none. [c] Mississippi R. [d] University of Minnesota (1851) 69 – 7593 [Minneapolis campus: (1851) 61 – 7228]. [e] University . . .Library (1851) 2813 [Minneapolis campus: (1851) 2489]; Public Library (1860) 1111.

Mobile: [a] Alabama. [b] none. [c] Mobile B of G of Mexico; Mobile R. [d] University of South Alabama (1963) 5 – 236; Spring Hill College (univ) (1830) 1 – 96. [e] Public Library (bef 1902) 227; University . . . Library (1963) 150.

Modesto: [a] California. [b] none. [c] Tuolumne R. [d] none. [e] Stanislaus County Free Public Library (1907) 245. [f] 106s (1970).

Monroe: [a] Louisiana. [b] none. [c] Ouachita R. [d] Northeast Louisiana University (1928) 8 – 440. [e] Ouachita Parish Public Library (bef 1923) 135; Sandel Library of . . . University (1931) 125.

Montgomery: [a] *Alabama. [b] none. [c] Alabama R. [d] Alabama State University (1873) 3 – 109. [e] Alabama Public Library Service (bef 1955) 380; Public Library (1899) 159; George W. Trenholm Memorial Library of . . . University (1921) 115.

Muncie: [a] Indiana. [b] none. [c] West Fork of White R. [d] Ball State University (1918) 18 – 924. [e] . . . University Library (1918) 398; Public Library (1875) 208.

[1] Universities with 5000 or more students.

Muskegon: [a] Michigan. [b] none. [c] Muskegon R; Michigan L; Muskegon L. [d] none. [e] Hackley Public Library (1890) 171.

Nashua: [a] New Hampshire. [b] for Dunstable. [c] Merrimack R; Nashua R. [d] Rivier College (univ) (1933) 0.7 – 56. [e] Public Library (1867) 139. [f] 61s (1970).

Nashville: [a] *Tennessee. [b] none. [c] Cumberland R. [d] Vanderbilt University (1872) 6 – 1236; Tennessee State University (1909) 4 – 280; George Peabody College for Teachers (univ) (1785) 2 – 181; Fisk University (1865) 1 – 118. [e] Joint University Library (1936) 1204; Public Library of Nashville and Davidson County (1904) 336; Tennessee State Library and Archives (1854) 250.

Newark: [a] New Jersey. [b] none. [c] Newark B of Atlantic O; Passaic R. [d] Newark State College (univ) (at Union, nr Newark) (1855) 12 – 293; Seton Hall University (at South Orange, nr Newark) (1856) 9 – 601; Newark College of Engineering (univ) (1881) 6 – 380; Rutgers, the State University, Newark campus (1892) 6 – ?; Fairleigh Dickinson University, Madison campus (at Madison, nr Newark) (1942) 3 – ?; Drew University (at Madison, nr Newark) (1866) 2 – 158. [e] Public Library (1888) 1025. [f] 0.8 (1760e).

New Bedford: [a] Massachusetts. [b] none. [c] Buzzards B of Atlantic O; Acushnet R. [d] Southeastern Massachusetts University (at North Dartmouth, nr New Bedford) (1895) 5 – 226. [e] Free Public Library (1852) 314.

New Britain: [a] Connecticut. [b] none. [c] nr Quinnipiac R; nr Mattabessett R. [d] Central Connecticut State College (univ) (1849) 12 – 685. [e] Public Library (1868) 171; Elihu Burritt Library of . . . College (1849) 160.

New Haven: [a] Connecticut. [b] none. [c] Long Island Sound of Atlantic O; Quinnipiac R; Mill R; West R. [d] Southern Connecticut State College (univ) (1893) 13 – 636; Yale University (1701) 9 – 2740. [e] . . . University Library (1701) 5453; Free Public Library (1887) 451.

New Orleans: [a] Louisiana. [b] none. [c] Mississippi R; Pontchartrain L; Borgne L. [d] Louisiana State University, New Orleans campus (1931) 12 – 550; Tulane University of Louisiana (1834) 8 – 830; Loyola University (1849) 5 – 350; Dillard University (college) (1869) 1 – 99; Xavier University of Louisiana (1915) 1 – 133. [e] Howard-Tilton Memorial Library of Tulane University of Louisiana (1834) 1028; Public Library (1843) 631. [f] 3 (1769).

Newport: [a] Rhode Island. [b] none. [c] Atlantic O; Narragansett B of Atlantic O. [d] none. [e] United States Naval War College Library (1885) 235; Redwood Library and Athenaeum (1747) 126; Public Library (1869) 50.

Newport News: [a] Virginia. [b] none. [c] Chesapeake B of Atlantic O; James R. [d] none. [e] Public Library (1908) 125.

Newton: [a] Massachusetts. [b] none. [c] Charles R. [d] Boston College (univ) (1863) 11 – 941; Brandeis University (at Waltham, nr Newton) (1948) 3 – 397; Wellesley College (univ) (at Wellesley, nr Newton) (1870) 2 – 211. [e] Boston College Library (1863) 752; Wellesley College Library (at Wellesley, nr Newton) (1875) 422; Goldfarb Library of . . . University (at Waltham, nr Newton) (1948) 399; Free Library (1870) 304.

New York: [a] New York. [b] alt New York City; for New Amsterdam; inc Brooklyn since 1898. [c] New York B of Atlantic O; Raritan B of Atlantic O; Jamaica B of Atlantic O; Hudson R; East R; Arthur Kill; Harlem R; Kill van Kull. [d1] City University of New York (1847) 123 – 12,350; New York University (1831) 32 – 6100; Columbia University (1754) 24 – 4003; Long Island University (at Greenvale, nr New York) (1886 at New York, relocated 1948) 21 – 1189 [Greenvale campus: (1948) 11 – ?] [New York campus: (1886) 8 – ?]; Saint John's University (1870) 14 – 642; Fordham University (1841) 13 – 769; Hofstra University (at Hempstead, nr New York) (1935) 13 – 703; Pace College (univ) (1906) 10 – 500. [e] New York Public Library (1848) 7179; Columbia University Library (1761) 4014; Brooklyn Public Library (1897) 2745; City University of New York Library (1849) 2694; Queens Borough Public Library (1896) 2464; New York University Library (1835) 2179. . .Pierpont Morgan Library (1924) 67. [f] 10 (1756), 5 (1698); Brooklyn: 806 (1890), 97 (1850), 4 (1800), 0.7 (1738).

Niagara Falls: [a] New York. [b] none. [c] Niagara R. [d] Niagara University (1856) 4 – 207. [e] Public Library (1895) 181; . . . University Library (1878) 107.

Norfolk: [a] Virginia. [b] none. [c] Chesapeake B of Atlantic O; Elizabeth R. [d] Old Dominion University (1930) 10 – 681. [e] Public Library (1872) 381.

Norwalk: [a] California. [b] none. [c] nr San Gabriel R. [d] none. [e] Norwalk Branch of Los Angeles County Public Library (1913) 122.

Norwalk: [a] Connecticut. [b] none. [c] Long Island Sound of Atlantic O; Norwalk R. [d] none. [e] Public Library (1879) 55.

Norwich: [a] Connecticut. [b] none. [c] Thames R; Shetucket R; Yantic R. [d] none. [e] Otis Library (1850) 78.

Oakland: [a] California. [b] none. [c] San Francisco B of Pacific O. [d] California College of Arts and Crafts (univ) (1907) 2 – 120. [e] Public Library (1868) 750.

Odessa: [a] Texas. [b] none. [c] nr Johnson Draw. [d] none. [e] Ector County Public Library (1938) 110.

Ogden: [a] Utah. [b] none. [c] Weber R; Ogden R. [d] none. [e] Weber State College Library (1888) 130; Weber County Library (1903?) 117.

Oklahoma City: [a] *Oklahoma. [b] none. [c] North Canadian R; Hefner L. [d] Central State University (at Edmond, nr Oklahoma City) (1890) 11 – 368; Bethany Nazarene College (univ) (at Bethany, nr Oklahoma City) (1909) 2 – 92; Oklahoma City

[1] Universities with 10,000 or more students.

University (1904) 2 – 179; University of Oklahoma, Oklahoma City campus (1968) 1 – ?. [e] Oklahoma County Library (1901) 560; Oklahoma Department of Libraries (1890) 193; Central State College Library (at Edmond, nr Oklahoma City) (1890) 181.

Omaha: [a] Nebraska. [b] none. [c] Missouri R. [d] University of Nebraska, Omaha campus (1908) 14 – 518; Creighton University (1878) 4 – 671. [e] Public Library (1872) 420;... University Library (1878) 261; Gene Eppley Library of the University ... (1908) 235.

Orlando: [a] Florida. [b] none. [c] Clear L; Holden L; Ivanhoe L; Sue L; Concord L; Lancaster L. [d] Florida Technological University (1963) 5 – 170; Rollins College (univ) (at Winter Park, nr Orlando) (1885) 3 – 172. [e] Public Library (1923) 318; Mills Memorial Library of ... College (at Winter Park, nr Orlando) (1885) 149.

Oshkosh: [a] Wisconsin. [b] none [c] Fox R; Winnebago L. [d] University of Wisconsin, Oshkosh campus (1871) 12 – 640. [e] Forrest R. Polk Library of the University ... (1871) 251; Public Library (1900) 183. [f] 55s (1970).

Oxnard: [a] California. [b] none. [c] nr Santa Clara R. [d] none. [e] Ventura County-City Free Library (at Ventura, nr Oxnard) (1915) 369; Public Library (1906) 89. [f] 245s (1970).

Parma: [a] Ohio. [b] none. [c] nr Cuyahoga R. [d] none. [e] Parma Branch of Cuyahoga County Public Library (bef 1964) 185.

Pasadena: [a] California. [b] none. [c] Arroyo Seco Creek. [d] California Institute of Technology (univ) (1891) 2 – 654; Pasadena College (univ) (1884) 1 – 60. [e] Public Library (1884) 423; Robert A. Millikan Memorial Library of ... Institute (1891) 207.

Paterson: [a] New Jersey. [b] none. [c] Passaic R. [d] Fairleigh Dickinson University (at Rutherford, nr Paterson) (1941) 20 – 1289 [Rutherford campus: (1941) 4 – ?] [Teaneck campus (at Teaneck, nr Paterson): (1954) 12 – ?]; Montclair State College (univ) (at Upper Montclair, nr Paterson) (1908) 10 – 461; William Paterson College of New Jersey (univ) (at Wayne, nr Paterson) (1855) 7 – 407. [e] ... University Library (1941) 376 [Rutherford campus: (1941) 140] [Teaneck campus: (1954) 146]; Free Public Library (1885) 260.

Pensacola: [a] Florida. [b] none. [c] Pensacola B of G of Mexico. [d] University of West Florida (1967) 4 – 215. [e] John C. Pace Library of the University ... (1966) 211; Public Library (bef 1940) 126; Naval Air Station Library (1914) 122.

Peoria: [a] Illinois. [b] none. [c] Illinois R; Peoria L. [d] Bradley University (1896) 6 – 428. [e] Public Library (1855) 371; Cullom-Davis Library of ... University (1897) 185.

Petersburg: [a] Virginia. [b] none. [c] Appomattox R. [d] Virginia State College (univ) (1882)3 – 233. [e] Johnston Memorial Library of ... College (1882) 123; Public Library (1924) 56. [f] 101s (1970).

Philadelphia: [a] Pennsylvania. [b] none. [c] Delaware R; Schuylkill R. [d][1] Temple University (1884) 32 – 3318; University of Pennsylvania (1740) 20 – 4697; Drexel University (1891) 9 – 662; Villanova University (at Villanova, nr Philadelphia) (1842) 9 – 543; La Salle College (univ) (1863) 7 – 343; Saint Joseph's College (univ) (1851) 7 – 289. [e] Free Library (1891) 2535; University ... Library (1750) 2182; Temple University Library (1892) 905. [f] 24 (1760), 4 (1700e).

Phoenix: [a] *Arizona. [b] none. [c] Salt R. [d] Arizona State University (at Tempe, nr Phoenix) (1885) 30 – 1377. [e] Charles Trumbull Hayden Library of ... University (at Tempe, nr Phoenix) (1891) 1200; Arizona State Department of Libraries and Archives (1864 at Prescott, relocated 1889?) 809; Public Library (1908) 657.

Pittsburgh: [a] Pennsylvania. [b] for Pittsburg; inc Allegheny since 1906. [c] Ohio R; Allegheny R; Monongahela R. [d] University of Pittsburgh (1787) 32 – 2532 [Pittsburgh campus: (1787) 28 – ?]; Duquesne University (1878) 8 – 461; Carnegie-Mellon University (1900) 5 – 688. [e] Carnegie Library (1895) 2074; Hillman Library of the University ... (1873) 1242. [f] Allegheny: 130 (1900), 21 (1850), 3 (1830).

Pittsfield: [a] Massachusetts. [b] none. [c] Housatonic R. [d] none. [e] Berkshire Athenaeum (1871) 131.

Pocatello: [a] Idaho. [b] none. [c] Portneuf R. [d] Idaho State University (1901) 8 – 469. [e] ... University Library (1902) 482; Public Library (1906) 69.

Pomona: [a] California. [b] none. [c] Chino Creek. [d] Claremont Colleges (univ) (at Claremont, nr Pomona) (1887) 5 – 396. [e] Honnold Library of ... Colleges (at Claremont, nr Pomona) (1952) 652; Public Library (1883) 221.

Port Arthur: [a] Texas. [b] none. [c] Sabine L. [d] none. [e] Gates Memorial Library (1918) 78.

Portland: [a] Maine. [b] none. [c] Casco B of Atlantic O; Presumpscot R. [d] University of Maine, Portland-Gorham campus (1933) 7 – 263. [e] Public Library (1868) 210. [f] 0.7 (1753e).

Portland: [a] Oregon. [b] none. [c] Willamette R. [d] Portland State University (1946)11 – 690; Lewis and Clark College (univ) (1867) 2 – 135; University of Portland (1901) 2 – 181; Reed College (univ) (1908)1 – 138; University of Oregon, Portland campus (1887) 1 – ?. [e] Library Association of Portland (1864) 980.

Portsmouth: [a] Virginia. [b] none. [c] Elizabeth R. [d] none. [e] Public Library (1916) 85.

Providence: [a] *Rhode Island. [b] none. [c] Providence R; Seekonk R. [d] Brown University (1764) 6 – 1076; Rhode Island College (univ) (1854) 6 – 324; Providence College (univ) (1917) 3 – 206; Rhode Island School of Design (univ) (1877) 1 – 120. [e] ... University Library (1767) 1292; Public Library (1878) 587. [f] 1 (1703e).

[1] Universities with 5000 or more students.

Provo: [a] Utah. [b] none. [c] Provo R. [d] Brigham Young University (1875) 27 – 1590. [e] . . . University Library (1876) 950; Public Library (1906) 64.

Pueblo: [a] Colorado. [b] none. [c] Arkansas R. [d] none. [e] Pueblo Regional Library (1904?) 110.

Quincy: [a] Massachusetts. [b] none. [c] Massachusetts B of Atlantic O; Neponset R; Fore R. [d] none. [e] Thomas Crane Public Library (1871) 230.

Racine: [a] Wisconsin. [b] none. [c] Root R; Michigan L. [d] none. [e] Public Library (1897) 227.

Raleigh: [a] *North Carolina. [b] none. [c] Crabtree Creek. [d] North Carolina State University of the University of North Carolina (1887) 14 – 1307 [Raleigh campus: (1887) 13 – ?]; Shaw University (college) (1865) 1 – 81. [e] D. H. Hill Library of North Carolina State University (1889) 459; Wake County Public Library (1900) 189; North Carolina State Library (1837) 168.

Rapid City: [a] South Dakota. [b] none. [c] Rapid Creek. [d] South Dakota School of Mines and Technology (univ) (1885) 2 – 167. [e] Public Library (1904) 75; . . . School Library (1904) 66.

Reading: [a] Pennsylvania. [b] none. [c] Schuylkill R. [d] none. [e] Public Library (1808) 211.

Reno: [a] Nevada. [b] none. [c] Truckee R. [d] University of Nevada (1864 at Elko, relocated 1886) 13 – 716 [Reno campus: (1886) 7 – 475]. [e] Noble H. Getchell Library of the University . . . (1886) 359; Washoe County Library (1903) 187.

Richmond: [a] *Virginia. [b] none. [c] James R. [d] Virginia Commonwealth University (1838) 14 – 1836; University of Richmond (1830) 5 – 314; Virginia Union University (college) (1865) 1 – 87. [e] Virginia State Library (1823) 495; Public Library (1891) 424.

Riverside: [a] California. [b] none. [c] Santa Ana R. [d] University of California, Riverside campus (1907) 6 – 560; Loma Linda University, Riverside campus (1922) 2 – 139. [e] Riverside Public Library and Riverside County Free Library (1876) 600; Riverside Campus Library of the University . . . (1954) 520.

Roanoke: [a] Virginia. [b] for Big Lick. [c] Roanoke R. [d] Hollins College (univ) (at Hollins, nr Roanoke) (1842) 1 – 92. [e] Public Library (1921) 208.

Rochester: [a] New York. [b] none. [c] Genesee R. [d] Rochester Institute of Technology (univ) (1830) 11 – 763; University of Rochester (1850) 9 – 1900; State University of New York, Brockport campus (at Brockport, nr Rochester) (1866) 8 – 350; Nazareth College of Rochester (univ) (1924) 1 – 93. [e] Monroe County Library (bef 1949) 1307; University . . . Library (1850) 1197; Public Library (1886) 753.

Rockford: [a] Illinois. [b] none. [c] Rock R. [d] Rockford College (univ) (1847) 1 – 101. [e] Public Library (1873) 241.

Sacramento: [a] *California. [b] none. [c] Sacramento R; American R. [d] Sacramento State College (univ) (1947) 20 – 654; University of California, Davis campus (at Davis, nr Sacramento) (1906) 13 – 1413. [e] California State Library (1850) 772; Davis Campus Library of the University . . . (at Davis, nr Sacramento) (1909) 726; Sacramento City-County Library (1857) 582.

Saginaw: [a] Michigan. [b] none. [c] Saginaw R. [d] none. [e] Public Library (1890) 286.

Saint Augustine: [a] Florida. [b] none. [c] Atlantic O. [d] none. [e] Jonathan Sewell Library of Florida Memorial College (1892) 30; Wise Library of Flagler College (1968) 23; Free Public Library (1874) 22.

Saint Joseph: [a] Missouri, [b] none. [c] Missouri R. [d] none. [e] Public Library (1890) 164.

Saint Louis: [a] Missouri. [b] none. [c] Mississippi R. [d] Washington University (1853) 11 – 2179; University of Missouri, Saint Louis campus (1960) 10 – 452; Saint Louis University (1818) 10 – 1318 [Saint Louis campus: (1818) 9 – ?] [e] Public Library (1865) 1325; Washington University Library (1853) 1144; Saint Louis County Library (1946) 946; Pius XII Memorial Library of Saint Louis University (1818) 607. [f] 0.9 (1769).

Saint Paul: [a] *Minnesota. [b] none. [c] Mississippi R. [d] Macalester College (univ) (1853) 2 – 192; College of Saint Thomas (univ) (1885) 2 – 146; Hamline University (college) (1854 at Red Wing, relocated 1880) 1 – 120. [e] Public Library (1863) 691.

Saint Petersburg: [a] Florida. [b] none. [c] Tampa B of G of Mexico; Boca Ciego B of G of Mexico. [d] none. [e] Public Library (1915) 252.

Salem: [a] Massachusetts. [b] none. [c] Atlantic O. [d] Massachusetts State College at Salem (univ) (1854) 7 – 281. [e] James Duncan Phillips Library of Essex Institute (1821) 400; Public Library (1888) 118.

Salem: [a] *Oregon. [b] none. [c] Willamette R. [d] Willamette University (1842) 2 – 142. [e] Oregon State Library (1848) 766; . . . University Library (1844) 123; Public Library (1904) 104. [f] 93s (1970).

Salinas: [a] California. [b] none. [c] Salinas R. [d] none. [e] Monterey County Library (1913) 213; Public Library (1900) 94. [f] 62s (1970).

Salt Lake City: [a] *Utah. [b] for Great Salt Lake City. [c] Jordan R. [d] University of Utah (1850) 22 – 1678. [e] University . . . Library (1850) 1158; Public Library (1898) 418.

San Antonio: [a] Texas. [b] none. [c] San Antonio R; San Pedro R; Acequia R. [d] Saint Mary's University of San Antonio (1852) 4 – 223; Trinity University (1869) 3 – 225; Our Lady of the Lake College (univ) (1896) 2 – 128; Incarnate Word College (univ) (1881) 1 – 121. [e] Public Library (1903) 651; George Storch Memorial Library of Trinity University (1869) 268.

San Bernardino: [a] California. [b] none. [c] Santa Ana R. [d] Loma Linda University (at Loma Linda, nr San Bernardino) (1905) 3 – 1209 [Loma Linda campus: (1905) 1 – 1061]; University of Redlands (at Redlands, nr San Bernardino)(1907) 2 – 138. [e] San Bernardino County Free Library (1914) 573;... University Library (at Loma Linda, nr San Bernardino) (1907) 266 [Loma Linda campus: (1907)156]; Public Library (1904) 174.

San Diego: [a] California. [b] none. [c] San Diego B of Pacific O; San Diego R. [d] San Diego State College (univ) (1897) 35 – 978; University of California, San Diego campus (1901) 6 – 880; United States International University (1952) 4 – 130; University of San Diego (1949) 2 – 114. [e] Public Library (1882) 973;... College Library (1897) 705; San Diego Campus Library of the University of California (1913) 700.

San Francisco: [a] California. [b] none. [c] Pacific O; San Francisco B of Pacific O; Merced L. [d] San Francisco State College (univ) (1899) 18 – 874; University of San Francisco (1855) 7 – 421; Golden Gate College (univ) (1881) 4 – 226; University of California, San Francisco campus (1864) 3 – 1079. [e] Public Library (1879) 1262.

San Jose: [a] California. [b] none. [c] Guadalupe R; Coyote R. [d] San Jose State College (univ) (1857 at San Francisco, relocated 1871) 34 – 874; University of Santa Clara (at Santa Clara, nr San Jose) (1851) 6 – 271. [e] Santa Clara County Free Library (1914) 885;... College Library (1872) 645; Public Library (1872) 503.

Santa Ana: [a] California. [b] none. [c] Santa Ana R. [d] University of California, Irvine campus (at Irvine, nr Santa Ana) (1960) 7 – 662. [e] Irvine Campus Library of the University ... (1965) 266; Public Library (1878) 211.

Santa Barbara: [a] California. [b] none. [c] Santa Barbara Channel. [d] University of California, Santa Barbara campus (1891) 14 – 1419. [e] Santa Barbara Campus Library of the University ... (1909) 668; Public Library (1882) 237.

Santa Fe: [a] *New Mexico. [b] none. [c] Santa Fe R. [d] none. [e] New Mexico State Library (1929) 243; Law Library of the New Mexico Supreme Court (1851) 85; Public Library (1907) 58. [f] 2 (1749e).

Santa Monica: [a] California. [b] none. [c] Santa Monica B of Pacific O. [d] none. [e] Public Library (1890) 248.

Santa Rosa: [a] California. [b] none. [c] nr Russian R. [d] Sonoma State College (univ) (at Rohnert Park, nr Santa Rosa) (1960) 7 – 250. [e] Santa Rosa-Sonoma County Free Public Library (1869) 230. [f] 75s (1970).

Savannah: [a] Georgia. [b] none. [c] Savannah R. [d] none. [e] Savannah Public and Chatham-Effingham-Liberty Regional Library (1809) 287.

Scranton: [a] Pennsylvania. [b] none. [c] Lackawanna R. [d] University of Scranton (1888) 3 – 182; Marywood College (univ) (1915) 2 – 166. [e] Public Library (1893?) 176; University ... Library (1926) 121.

Seaside: [a] California. [b] none. [c] Monterey B of Pacific O. [d] Monterey Institute of Foreign Studies (univ) (at Monterey, nr Seaside) (1955) 0.3 – 45. [e] United States Naval Postgraduate School Library (at Monterey,nr Seaside) (1946) 260; Monterey Public Library (at Monterey, nr Seaside) (1901) 112. [f] 93s (1970).

Seattle: [a] Washington, [b] none. [c] Puget Sound of Pacific O; Washington L; Union L. [d] University of Washington (1861) 33 – 3146; Seattle University (1891) 3 – 209; Seattle Pacific College (univ) (1891) 2 – 147. [e] University ... Library (1861) 1705; Public Library (1873) 1330; King County Library (bef 1949) 777.

Shreveport: [a] Louisiana. [b] none. [c] Red R; Cross L. [d] Louisiana State University, Shreveport campus (1967) 1 – 75. [e] Shreve Memorial Library (1923) 218.

Sioux City: [a] Iowa. [b] none. [c] Missouri R; Big Sioux R; Floyd R. [d] none. [e] Public Library (1870) 178.

Sioux Falls: [a] South Dakota. [b] none. [c] Big Sioux R. [d] Augustana College (univ) (1860 at Chicago, Illinois; relocated 1918) 2 – 151. [e] Carnegie Free Public Library (1886) 106; Mikkelsen Library of ... College (1860 at Chicago, Illinois; relocated 1918?) 91

Somerville: [a] Massachusetts. [b] none. [c] Mystic R. [d] Tufts University (at Medford, nr Somerville) (1852) 5 – 1824. [e] Nils Yngve Wessell Library of ... University (at Medford, nr Somerville) (1854) 276; Public Library (1873) 176.

South Bend: [a] Indiana. [b] none. [c] Saint Joseph R. [d] University of Notre Dame (1842) 8 – 871; Saint Mary's College (univ) (1844 at Bertrand, Michigan; relocated 1855) 2 – 137. [e] Memorial Library of the University ... (1873) 918; Public Library (1888) 260.

Spokane: [a] Washington. [b] none. [c] Spokane R. [d] Gonzaga University (1887) 3 – 195; Whitworth College (univ) (1890) 2 – 96. [e] Public Library (1891) 389; Crosby Library of ... University (1887) 178.

Springfield: [a] *Illinois. [b] none. [c] Spring Creek; Sugar Creek; Springfield L. [d] Sangamon State University (1970) 0.8 – ? [e] Illinois State Library (1839) 1234; Lincoln Library (1867) 238.

Springfield: [a] Massachusetts. [b] none. [c] Connecticut R; Chicopee R. [d] Massachusetts State College at Westfield (univ) (at Westfield, nr Springfield) (1839) 4 – 158; American International College (univ) (1855) 3 – 133; Springfield College (univ) (1885) 3 – 127; Western New England College (univ) (1919) 3 – 227; Mount Holyoke College (univ) (at South Hadley, nr Springfield) (1836) 2 – 191; Smith College (univ) (at Northampton, nr Springfield) (1871) 2 – 288. [e] William Allan Neilson Library of Smith College (at Northampton, nr Springfield) (1909) 743; City Library (1857) 574.

Springfield: [a] Missouri. [b] none. [c] nr James R. [d] Drury College (univ) (1873) 2 – 161. [e] Public Library of Springfield and Greene County (1905?) 208.

Springfield: [a] Ohio. [b] none. [c] Mad R. [d] Antioch College (univ) (at Yellow Springs, nr Springfield) (1852) 3 – 154; Wittenberg University (1845) 3 – 272. [e] Warder Public Library of Springfield and Clark County (1872) 440; Thomas Library of ... University (1845) 200.

Stamford: [a] Connecticut. [b] none. [c] Long Island Sound of Atlantic O; Rippowam R. [d] none. [e] Public Library (1880) 268.

Steubenville: [a] Ohio. [b] none. [c] Ohio R. [d] none. [e] Public Library of Steubenville and Jefferson County (1902) 134.

Stockton: [a] California. [b] none. [c] San Joaquin R; Calaveras R. [d] University of the Pacific (1851 at San Jose, relocated 1924) 5 – 309. [e] Public Library of Stockton and San Joaquin County (1895) 621.

Sunnyvale: [a] California. [b] none. [c] nr San Francisco B of Pacific O. [d] Stanford University (at Palo Alto, nr Sunnyvale) (1885) 12 – 1297. [e] . . . University Library (at Palo Alto, nr Sunnyvale) (1891) 3275; Public Library (bef 1923) 131.

Syracuse: [a] New York. [b] none. [c] Onondaga Creek; Onondaga L. [d] Syracuse University (1870) 15 – 1704. [e] . . . University Library (1871) 1387; Public Library (1852) 354.

Tacoma: [a] Washington. [b] none. [c] Puget Sound of Pacific O; Puyallup R. [d] University of Puget Sound (1888) 4 – 213; Pacific Lutheran University (1890) 3 – 195. [e] Public Library (1886) 476.

Tallahassee: [a] *Florida. [b] none. [c] nr Ochlockonee R. [d] Florida State University (1851) 17 – 1087; Florida Agricultural and Mechanical University (1887) 5 – 292. [e] Robert Manning Strozier Library of Florida State University (1853) 820; Florida State Library (bef 1855) 192; Samuel H. Coleman Memorial Library of Florida Agricultural and Mechanical University (1909) 175; Leon County Public Library (1906) 84. [f] 78s (1970).

Tampa: [a] Florida. [b] none. [c] Tampa B of Gulf of Mexico; Hillsborough R. [d] University of South Florida (1956) 18 – 768; University of Tampa (college) (1930) 2 – 120. [e] Public Library (1917) 374; University of South Florida Library (1960) 226.

Terre Haute: [a] Indiana. [b] none. [c] Wabash R. [d] Indiana State University (1865) 17 – 850 [Terre Haute campus: (1865) 14 – ?]; Rose-Hulman Institute of Technology (univ) (1874) 1 – 63. [e] Cunningham Memorial Library of . . . University (1870) 395; Vigo County Public Library (1882) 204.

Toledo: [a] Ohio. [b] none. [c] Maumee R; Erie L. [d] University of Toledo (1872) 15 – 1006; Mary Manse College (univ) (1873) 0.6 – 61. [e] Toledo-Lucas County Public Library (1838) 1343.

Topeka: [a] *Kansas. [b] none. [c] Kansas R. [d] Washburn University of Topeka (1865) 5 – 171. [e] Kansas State Library (1861) 800; Kansas State Historical Society Library (1875) 300; Public Library (1882) 220.

Torrance: [a] California. [b] none. [c] Pacific O. [d] none. [e] Public Library (1935?) 133.

Trenton: [a] * New Jersey. [b] none. [c] Delaware R. [d] Trenton State College (univ) (1855) 10 – 523; Rider College (univ) (1865) 6 – 331; Princeton University (at Princeton, nr Trenton) (1746) 5 – 1124. [e] . . . University Library (at Princeton, nr Trenton) (1746) 2436; New Jersey State Library (1822?) 701; Free Public Library (1852) 228.

Tucson: [a] Arizona. [b] none. [c] Santa Cruz R. [d] University of Arizona (1885) 26 – 2180. [e] University . . . Library (1891) 1469; Public Library (1879) 354.

Tulsa: [a] Oklahoma. [b] none. [c] Arkansas R. [d] University of Tulsa (1894 at Muskogee, relocated 1907) 6 – 371; Oral Roberts University (college) (1963) 1 – 72. [e] Tulsa City-County Library (1912) 538; McFarlin Library of the University . . . (1894 at Muskogee, relocated 1907?) 363.

Tuscaloosa: [a] Alabama. [b] none. [c] Black Warrior R. [d] University of Alabama (1820) 22 – 1838 [Tuscaloosa campus: (1820) 13 – 930]. [e] Amelia Gayle Gorgas Library of the University . . . (1831) 1258 [Tuscaloosa campus: (1831) 1076]; Friedman Library (1923?) 82.

Utica: [a] New York. [b] none. [c] Mohawk R. [d] none. [e] Mid-York Library (bef 1970) 147; Public Library (1842) 110.

Virginia Beach: [a] Virginia. [b] none. [c] Atlantic O. [d] none. [e] Public Library (bef 1960) 43.

Waco: [a] Texas. [b] none. [c] Brazos R. [d] Baylor University (1845 at Independence, Texas; relocated 1887) 7 – 377 [Waco campus: (1887) 6 – ?]. [e] Moody Memorial Library of . . . University (1901) 453; Waco-McLennan County Library (1904) 145.

Warren: [a] Michigan. [b] none. [c] nr Clinton R. [d] none. [e] Public Library (bef 1940) 216.

*Washington: [a] *District of Columbia. [b] none. [c] Potomac R; Anacostia R. [d][1] University of Maryland (at College Park, Maryland, nr Washington) (1807 at Baltimore, relocated 1856) 52 – 3363 [College Park campus: (1856) 45 – 2718]; George Washington University (1821) 21 – 1982; American University (1893) 15 – 750; Howard University (1867) 9 – 1060; Georgetown University (1789) 8 – 1755; Catholic University of America (1889) 6 – 822; Federal City College (univ) (1968) 6 – 300. [e] Library of Congress (1800) 14,846; Veterans Administration Library Service (1923) 2009; Public Library of the District of Columbia (1896) 1939; National Agricultural Library (at Beltsville, Maryland, nr Washington) (1862 at Washington, relocated 1969) 1500; National Library of Medicine (at Bethesda, Maryland, nr Washington) (1836 at Washington, relocated 1962) 1300; McKeldin Library of the University . . . (at College Park, Maryland, nr Washington) (1891?) 1092; . . . Folger Shakespeare Library (1932) 260.

Waterbury: [a] Connecticut. [b] none. [c] Naugatuck R; Mad R. [d] none. [e] Silas Bronson Public Library (1869) 157.

Waterloo: [a] Iowa. [b] none. [c] Cedar R. [d] University of Northern Iowa (at Cedar Falls, nr Waterloo) (1876) 11 – 506. [e] University . . . Library (at Cedar Falls, nr Waterloo) (1876) 299; Public Library (1896) 175.

West Palm Beach: [a] Florida. [b] none. [c] Worth Lagoon. [d] none. [e] Public Library (1895) 50.

[1] Universities with 5000 or more students.

Wheeling: [a] West Virginia. [b] none. [c] Ohio R. [d] none. [e] Ohio County Public Library (1883) 102.

Wichita: [a]Kansas. [b] none. [c] Arkansas R; Little Arkansas R. [d] Wichita State University (1892) 12 – 724; Friends University (college) (1898) 1 – 60. [e] Ablah Library of Wichita State University (1896) 330; Public Library (1877?) 289.

Wichita Falls: [a] Texas. [b] none. [c] Wichita R. [d] Midwestern University (1922) 4 – 200. [e] George Moffett Library of . . . University (1924) 118; Kemp Public Library (1918?) 85.

Wilkes-Barre: [a] Pennsylvania. [b] none. [c] Susquehanna R. [d] Wilkes College (univ) (1933) 4 – 198. [e] Osterhout Free Library (1889) 130; . . . College Library (1932) 100.

Williamsburg: [a] Virginia. [b] none. [c] nr James R; nr York R. [d] College of William and Mary (univ) (1693) 10 – 408 [Williamsburg campus: (1693) 7 – ?]. [e] Earl Gregg Swem Library of the College . . . (1729) 420. [f] 2 (1779).

Wilmington: [a] Delaware. [b] none. [c] Delaware R; Christina R. [d] University of Delaware (at Newark, nr Wilmington) (1743 at New London, Pennsylvania; relocated 1765) 16 – 947. [e] Hugh M. Morris Library of the University . . . (at Newark, nr Wilmington) (1834) 792; Wilmington Institute Free Library and Newcastle County Free Library (1788) 396. [f] 0.6 (1740e).

Wilmington: [a] North Carolina. [b] none. [c] Cape Fear R. [d] none. [e] Public Library (1907) 103. [f] 58s (1970).

Winston-Salem: [a] North Carolina. [b] inc Salem, Winston. [c] Salem Creek. [d] Wake Forest University (1833 at Wake Forest, relocated 1956) 3 – 520. [e] . . . University Library (1879 at Wake Forest, relocated 1956?) 378; Forsyth County Public Library (1905) 258.

Woodbridge: [a] New Jersey. [b] none. [c] Arthur Kill. [d] Rutgers, the State University (at New Brunswick, nr Woodbridge) (1766) 33 – 4442 [New Brunswick campus: (1766) 24 – ?]. [e] . . . University Library (at New Brunswick nr Woodbridge) (1766) 1656; Free Public Library (1879) 203.

Worcester: [a] Massachusetts. [b] none. [c] Blackstone R; Quinsigamond L; Indian L. [d] Massachusetts State College at Worcester (univ) (1874) 4 – 136; Clark University (1887) 3 – 287; Assumption College (univ) (1904) 2 – 101; College of the Holy Cross (univ) (1843) 2 – 199; Worcester Polytechnic Institute (univ) (1865) 2 – 247. [e] American Antiquarian Society Library (1813) 750; Worcester Public Library and Central Massachusetts Regional Library (1860) 663.

Yonkers: [a] New York. [b] none. [c] Hudson R. [d] Manhattanville College of the Sacred Heart (univ) (at Purchase, nr Yonkers) (1841) 1 – 153; Sarah Lawrence College (univ) (at Bronxville, nr Yonkers) (1926) 0.8 – 146. [e] Public Library (1893) 302.

York: [a] Pennsylvania. [b] none. [c] Codorus Creek. [d] none. [e] Martin Memorial Library (1885) 110.

Youngstown: [a] Ohio. [b] none. [c] Mahoning R. [d] Youngstown State University (1908) 15 – 750. [e] Public Library of Youngstown and Mahoning County (1878) 588.

Virgin Islands (USA)

*Charlotte Amalie: [a] Saint Thomas I. [b] for Saint Thomas. [c] Caribbean Sea. [d] none. [e] Saint Thomas Public Library (1920) 37; College of the Virgin Islands Library (1963) 25.

OCEANIA

Australia

Adelaide: [a] *South Australia. [b] none. [c] Saint Vincent G of Indian O; Torrens R; Sturt R. [d] University of Adelaide (1874) 8 – 1287; Flinders University of South Australia (1963) 2 – 254. [e] State Library of South Australia (1884) 760; Barr Smith Library of the University . . . (1876) 525.

Brisbane: [a] *Queensland. [b] none. [c] Brisbane R. [d] University of Queensland (1909) 16 – 1718. [e] University . . . Library (1911) 658; Public Library of Queensland (1896) 342.

*Canberra: [a] *Australian Capital Territory. [b] none. [c] Molonglo R. [d] Australian National University (1929) 5 – 396. [e] National Library of Australia (1902 at Melbourne, relocated 1927) 1250; . . . University Library (1948) 505.

Geelong: [a] Victoria. [b] none. [c] Port Phillip B of Bass Strait; Barwon R. [d] none. [e] Regional Library Service (?) 65.

Hobart: [a] *Tasmania. [b] none. [c] Derwent R. [d] University of Tasmania (1890) 3 – 416. [e] State Library of Tasmania (1849) 242; University . . . Library (1889) 210.

Melbourne: [a] *Victoria. [b] none. [c] Port Phillip B of Bass Strait; Yarra R. [d] University of Melbourne (1853) 15 – 2020; Monash University (1958) 10 – 1117; La Trobe University (1964) 3 – 337. [e] State Library of Victoria (1853) 1080; University . . . Library (1855) 564. [f] 39s (1851).

Newcastle: [a] New South Wales. [b] none. [c] Pacific O; Hunter R. [d] University of Newcastle (1951) 3 – 360. [e] Public Library (1948) 190; University . . . Library (1951) 158. [f] 1 (1851).

Perth: [a] *Western Australia. [b] none. [c] Swan R. [d] University of Western Australia (1911) 8 – 1025. [e] Library Board of Western Australia (1887) 1011; Library of the University . . . (1913) 384.

Sydney: [a] *New South Wales. [b] none. [c] Pacific O; Parramatta R. [d] University of New South Wales (1949) 17 – 1939 [Sydney campus: (1949) 15 – 1768]; University of Sydney (1850) 17 – 2279; Macquarie University (1964) 4 – 482. [e]

Fisher Library (alt University of Sydney Library) (1852) 1296; Library of New South Wales (1826) 977; Library of the University of New South Wales (1949) 560; Macquarie University Library (1965) 242; Public Library (1909) 225.[f] 44, 54s (1851).

Wollongong: [a] New South Wales. [b] off Greater Wollongong. [c] Pacific O; Nepean R. [d] Wollongong University College of the University of New South Wales (1961) 1 – 102.[e] Public Library (?) 290.

Fiji

*Suva: [a] Viti Levu I. [b] none. [c] Pacific O. [d] University of the South Pacific (1968) 0.4 – 52. [e] City Library (?) 35.

French Polynesia

*Papeete: [a] Tahiti I. [b] none. [c] Pacific O. [d] none.

(Hawaii), USA

Hilo: [a] Hawaii I. [b] none. [c] Hilo B of Pacific O; Wailuku R. [d] none. [e] Hawaii Public Library (1899) 115.

*Honolulu: [a] Oahu I. [b] none. [c] Pacific O. [d] University of Hawaii (1907) 33 – 2109 [Honolulu campus: (1907) 23 – ?]. [e] Hawaii State Library (1879?) 1118; Gregg M. Sinclair Library of the University . . . (1907) 657.

New Caledonia

*Noumea: [b] for Port-de-France. [c] Pacific O. [d] none. [e] Bibliotheque de la Commission du Pacifique Sud (alt South Pacific Commission Library) (?) 25; Bibliotheque Bernheim (1905) 24. [f] 48s (1969), 35 (1963).

New Zealand

Auckland: [a] North I. [b] none. [c] Tasman Sea; Hauraki G of Pacific O. [d] University of Auckland (1882) 9 – 478? [e] Public Library (1880) 535; University . . . Library (1882) 425.

Christchurch: [a] South I. [b] none. [c] Avon R. [d] University of Canterbury (1873) 7 – 414. [e] University . . . Library (1873) 260; Canterbury Public Library (1859) 240.

Dunedin: [a] South I. [b] none. [c] Pacific O. [d] University of Otago (1869) 6 – 440? [e] Hocken Library of the University . . . (1870) 400; Public Library (1908) 247.

*Wellington: [a] North I. [b] none. [c] Cook Strait. [d] Victoria University of Wellington (1897) 6 – 390? [e] National Library of New Zealand (1856) 3484; Public Library (1841) 324; . . . University Library (1897) 284.

Papua

*Port Moresby: [b] none. [c] G of Papua of Coral Sea. [d] University of Papua and New Guinea (1965) 0.8 – 107. [e] University . . . Library (1965?) 80.

Western Samoa

*Apia: [a] Upolu I. [b] none. [c] Pacific O. [d] none. [e] Nelson Memorial Public Library (1959) 36.

SOUTH AMERICA

Argentina

Almirante Brown: [a] Buenos Aires. [b] inc Adrogue. [c] (Arroyo) San Francisco Creek. [d] none.

Avellaneda: [a] Buenos Aires. [b] for Barracas al Sud. [c] Plata R; Riachuelo R. [d] none. [e] Biblioteca Obreros y Empleados Municipales(?) 30.

Bahia Blanca: [a] Buenos Aires. [b] none. [c] Naposta Grande R. [d] Universidad Nacional del Sur (1948) 5 – 931. [e] Biblioteca Popular de la Asociacion Bernardino Rivadavia (1882) 100; Biblioteca Central de la Universidad . . . (1948) 60.

*Buenos Aires: [a] *Distrito Federal. [b] for Buenos Ayres. [c] Plata R; Riachuelo R. [d][1] Universidad de Buenos Aires (1821) 80 – 8408; Universidad Tecnologica Nacional (1953) 10 – 893; Pontificia Universidad Catolica Argentina Santa Maria de los Buenos Aires (1958) 9 – 1182; Universidad de Belgrano (1964) 6 – 444; Universidad Argentina de la Empresa (1962) 4 – 603; Universidad del Salvador (1944) 4 – 1065; Universidad Argentina John F. Kennedy (1961) 1 – 238. [e] Biblioteca de la Universidad de Buenos Aires (1863) 1150; Biblioteca Nacional (1810) 700. [f] 92 (1855), 11 (1744).

Cordoba: [a] *Cordoba. [b] none. [c] Primero R. [d] Universidad Nacional de Cordoba (1613) 25 – 1236; Universidad Catolica de Cordoba (1956) 3 – 710. [e] Biblioteca Mayor de la Universidad Nacional de Cordoba (1614) 100; Biblioteca de la Universidad Catolica de Cordoba (1956) 80.

[1] Universities with 1000 or more students.

Lanus: [a] Buenos Aires. [b] none. [c] nr Plata R. [d] none. [e] Biblioteca Jose Maria Cao (1919) 7.

La Plata: [a] *Buenos Aires. [b] alt Plata; for Eva Peron. [c] Plata R. [d] Universidad Nacional de la Plata (1884) 47 – 1209; Universidad Notarial Argentina (1968) 0.9 – 36; Universidad Catolica de la Plata (1968) ? – ? [e] Biblioteca Publica de la Universidad Nacional de la Plata (1884) 450.

Lomas de Zamora: [a] Buenos Aires. [b] none. [c] (Arroyo) Santa Catalina Creek. [d] none. [e] Biblioteca del Maestro de la Sociedad Popular de Educacion Antonio Mentruit (1900) 28.

Mar del Plata: [a] Buenos Aires. [b] for General Pueyrredon, Pueyrredon. [c] Atlantic O. [d] Universidad Catolica de Mar del Plata Stella Maris (?) ? – ?; Universidad Provincial de Mar del Plata (?) ? – ? [e] Biblioteca Municipal Publica de General Pueyrredon (?) 30.

Mendoza: [a] *Mendoza. [b] none. [c] Tulumaya R. [d] Universidad Nacional de Cuyo (1939) 6 – 460; Universidad Privada Juan Agustin Maza (1960) 0.7 – 95; Universidad de Mendoza (1962) ? – ?; Universidad Privada del Aconcagua (1968) ? – ? [e] Biblioteca Central de la Universidad Nacional de Cuyo (1939) 80; Biblioteca Publica General San Martin (1814) 75.

Merlo: [a] Buenos Aires. [b] none. [c] Reconquista R. [d] none.

Parana: [a] *Entre Rios. [b] for Bajada de Santa Fe. [c] Parana R. [d] Universidad Nacional de Entre Rios (planned). [e] Biblioteca Popular (?) 51; Biblioteca del Museo de Entre Rios (1917) 21.

Quilmes: [a] Buenos Aires. [b] none. [c] Plata R. [d] none. [e] Biblioteca Publica Municipal Domingo Faustino Sarmiento (1872) 29.

Rosario: [a] Santa Fe. [b] none. [c] Parana R. [d] Universidad Nacional de Rosario (1889) 16 – 2053. [e] Biblioteca Argentina Doctor Juan Alvarez (1910) 120; Biblioteca de la Universidad . . . (1910) 100. [f] 10 (1858).

Salta: [a] *Salta. [b] for Lerma. [c] Arias R. [d] Universidad Catolica de Salta (1963) 0.5 – 94. [e] Biblioteca de la Universidad . . . (1963?) 18.

San Isidro: [a] Buenos Aires. [b] none. [c] Plata R. [d] none. [e] Biblioteca del Instituto de Botanica Darwinion (1908) 65.

San Justo: [a] Buenos Aires. [b] for Matanza. [c] Matanza R. [d] none. [e] Biblioteca Juan Bautista Alberdi de la Escuela Normal Mixta Republica de Mexico (?) 4; Biblioteca Bartolome Mitre (?) ?

San Martin: [a] Buenos Aires. [b] alt General San Martin. [c] nr Plata R. [d] none. [e] Biblioteca Popular (1904) 12.

San Miguel: [a] Buenos Aires. [b] for General Sarmiento, Sarmiento. [c] Reconquista R. [d] none. [e] Biblioteca de las Facultades de Filosofia y Teologia S. I. (1931) 105.

Santa Fe: [a] *Santa Fe. [b] none. [c] Salado (alt Salado del Norte) R. [d] Universidad Nacional del Litoral (1889) 6 – 1047; Universidad Catolica de Santa Fe (1957) 2 – 491. [e] Biblioteca de la Universidad Nacional del Litoral (1920) 96; Biblioteca Publica Municipal Bernardino Rivadavia (1945) 10. [f] 6 (1858).

Seis de Septiembre: [a] Buenos Aires. [b] for Moron. [c] (Arroyo) Moron Creek. [d] Universidad de Moron (1960) 2 – 362; Universidad del Oeste (?) ? – ? [e] Biblioteca Municipal Domingo Faustino Sarmiento (1912) 20.

Tres de Febrero: [a] Buenos Aires. [b] for Caseros. [c] Reconquista R. [d] none. [e] Biblioteca Popular Juan Bautista Alberdi (1914) 32.

Tucuman: [a] *Tucuman. [b] off San Miguel de Tucuman. [c] Dulce R. [d] Universidad Nacional de Tucuman (1912) 12 – 1701; Universidad del Norte Santo Tomas de Aquino (1965) 0.9 – 196. [e] Biblioteca Central de la Universidad Nacional de Tucuman (1917) 100; Biblioteca Alberdi (1903) 44.

Vicente Lopez: [a] Buenos Aires. [b] inc Olivos. [c] Plata R. [d] Universidad Bartolome Mitre de Olivos (?) ? – ? [e] Biblioteca Popular (1921) 10; Biblioteca Vicente Lopez de la Asociacion de Cultura (?) ? [f] Olivos: 6 (1914).

Bolivia

Cochabamba: [b] none. [c] Rocha R. [d] Universidad Mayor de San Simon de Cochabamba (1832) 5 – 365; Universidad Catolica de Cochabamba (1965) ? – ? [e] Biblioteca Municipal (?) 30; Biblioteca Central de la Universidad Mayor de San Simon de Cochabamba (1832) 25.

*La Paz: [b] alt Paz; off La Paz de Ayacucho. [c] Choqueyapo R. [d] Universidad Mayor de San Andres (1830) 7 – 824. [e] Biblioteca de la Direccion de Cultura (1832) 140; Biblioteca Municipal Mariscal Andres de Santa Cruz (1836) 85; Biblioteca Central de la Universidad . . . (1830) 75. [f] 76 (1861).

*Sucre: [b] for Chuquisaca. [c] Quirpinchaca R. [d] Universidad Mayor, Real y Pontificia de San Francisco Xavier de Chuquisaca (1624) 2 – 240. [e] Biblioteca de la Universidad . . . (1624?) 62; Biblioteca y Archivo Nacional de Bolivia (1836) 28; Biblioteca Municipal (?) ?

Brazil

Aracaju: [a] *Sergipe. [b] none. [c] Cotinguiba R. [d] Universidade Federal de Sergipe (1948) 0.5 – 175. [e] Biblioteca Publica do Estado de Sergipe (1851) 160.

Belem: [a] *Para. [b] for Para. [c] Para R; Guama R; Guajara R. [d] Universidade Federal do Para (1902) 5 – 587. [e] Biblioteca e Arquivo Publico do Para (1871) 55; Biblioteca da Universidade . . . (1962) 42.

Belo Horizonte: [a] *Minas Gerais. [b] none. [c] Arrudas R. [d] Universidade Federal de Minas Gerais (1892) 14 – 1877; Universidade Catolica de Minas Gerais (1943) 6 – 843; Universidade Mineira de Arte (1957) 0.1 – 74. [e] Biblioteca da Universidade Federal de Minas Gerais (1892) 333; Biblioteca Publica (1898) 28.

*Brasilia: [a] *Distrito Federal. [b] none. [c] Torto R; Fundo R. [d] Universidade de Brasilia (1962) 4 – 498. [e] Biblioteca da Camara dos Deputados (1866 at Rio de Janeiro, relocated 1960?) 181; Biblioteca Central da Universidade . . . (1962) 129.

Campina Grande: [a] Paraiba. [b] none. [c] nr Mamanguape R. [d] Fundacao Universidade Regional do Nordeste (1967?) 0.4 – 71. [e] Biblioteca Central da . . . Universidade (1968) 9; Biblioteca Publica (1936) 5 (in 1952).

Campinas: [a] Sao Paulo. [b] none. [c] Atibaia R. [d] Universidade Catolica de Campinas (1941) 6 – 371; Universidade de Campinas (1962) 1 – 219. [e] Biblioteca Publica do Centro de Ciencias, Letras e Artes (1901) 30; Biblioteca da Universidade Catolica de Campinas (1945) 20.

Campos: [a] Rio de Janeiro. [b] for Sao Salvador. [c] Paraiba R. [d] none. [e] Biblioteca Municipal (1872) 13.

Curitiba: [a] *Parana. [b] for Corityba. [c] nr Iguazu R. [d] Universidade Federal do Parana (1912) 7 – 905; Universidade Catolica do Parana (1937) 4 – 495. [e] Biblioteca Publica do Parana (1857) 120; Biblioteca da Universidade Federal do Parana (1912) 118.

Duque de Caxias: [a] Rio de Janeiro. [b] for Caxias. [c] Guanabara B of Atlantic O. [d] none. [e] Biblioteca da Refinaria Duque de Caxias da Petrobras (1965) 4.

Feira de Santana: [a] Bahia. [b] for Feira de Sant'Anna. [c] Jacuipe R. [d] none. [e] Biblioteca Publica Municipal Arnold Silva (1890) 7.

Florianopolis: [a] *Santa Catarina. [b] for Desterro. [c] Norte B of Atlantic O; Sul B of Atlantic O. [d] Universidade Federal de Santa Catarina (1932) 3 – 530. [e] Biblioteca da Universidade . . . (1951) 56; Biblioteca Publica do Estado de Santa Catarina (1885) 45.

Fortaleza: [a] *Ceara. [b] for Ceara. [c] Atlantic O. [d] Universidade Federal do Ceara (1903) 8 – 568. [e] Biblioteca da Universidade . . . (1918) 89; Biblioteca Publica do Ceara (1867) 60.

Goiania: [a] *Goias. [b] none. [c] nr Meia Ponte R. [d] Universidade Federal de Goias (1947) 5 – 560; Universidade de Goias (1898 at Goias, relocated 1935?) 2 – 184. [e] Biblioteca da Universidade Federal de Goias (1948) 21.

Guarulhos: [a] Sao Paulo. [b] none. [c] Tiete R. [d] none. [e] Biblioteca Publica Municipal (1940) ?

Jaboatao: [a] Pernambuco. [b] none. [c] Jaboatao R. [d] none. [e] Biblioteca Publica Municipal (1952) ?

Joao Pessoa: [a] *Paraiba. [b] for Parahyba. [c] Paraiba do Norte (alt Paraiba) R. [d] Universidade Federal da Paraiba (1947) 3 –345. [e] Biblioteca da Universidade . . . (1955) 27; Biblioteca Publica do Estado da Paraiba (1859) 12.

Juiz de Fora: [a] Minas Gerais. [b] for Parahybuna. [c] Paraibuna R. [d] Universidade Federal de Juiz de Fora (1915) 2 – 343. [e] Biblioteca da Universidade . . . (1914) 32.

Londrina: [a] Parana. [b] none. [c] nr Tibagi R. [d] none. [e] Biblioteca da Faculdade Estadual de Filosofia, Ciencias e Letras de Londrina (1958) 9; Biblioteca Municipal (1940) ?

Maceio: [a] *Alagoas. [b] none. [c] Atlantic O; Mundau R. [d] Universidade Federal de Alagoas (1931) 3 – 235. [e] Biblioteca do Instituto Historico de Alagoas (1869) 9; Biblioteca da Universidade . . . (1950) 8; Biblioteca Publica do Estado de Alagoas (1937) ?

Manaus: [a] *Amazonas. [b] alt Manaos. [c] Negro R. [d] Universidade do Amazonas (1909) 1 – 157. [e] Biblioteca Publica do Amazonas (1873) 45 (in 1947).

Natal: [a] *Rio Grande do Norte. [b] none. [c] Atlantic O; Potengi R. [d] Universidade Federal do Rio Grande do Norte (1948) 4 – 289. [e] Biblioteca da Universidade . . . (1945) 34; Biblioteca Municipal (1948) ?

Niteroi: [a] *Rio de Janeiro. [b] for Nictheroy. [c] Guanabara B of Atlantic O. [d] Universidade Federal Fluminense (1912) 6 – 988. [e] Biblioteca Publica do Estado do Rio de Janeiro (1927) 90; Biblioteca da Universidade . . . (1947) 40.

Nova Iguacu: [a] Rio de Janeiro. [b] for Maxambomba. [c] nr Sarapui R. [d] none. [e] Biblioteca Publica Municipal (1944) ?

Olinda: [a] Pernambuco. [b] none. [c] Atlantic O. [d] none. [e] Biblioteca do Mosteiro de Sao Bento (1917) 7 (in 1939).

Osasco: [a] Sao Paulo. [b] none. [c] Tiete R. [d] none.

Pelotas: [a] Rio Grande do Sul. [b] none. [c] Sao Goncalo R. [d] Universidade Catolica de Pelotas (1939) 3 – 350; Universidade Federal de Pelotas (1883) 1 – 271; Universidade Rural do Sul (1968) 0.2 – 93. [e] Biblioteca Publica Pelotense (1875) 130.

Petropolis: [a] Rio de Janeiro. [b] none. [c] Piabanha R; Quitandinha R; Palatinado R. [d] Universidade Catolica de Petropolis (1954) 1 – 157. [e] Biblioteca Municipal (1871) 100; Biblioteca Premonstratense (1908) 50 (in 1952).

Porto Alegre: [a] *Rio Grande do Sul. [b] none. [c] Guaiba R; Patos Lagoon. [d] Universidade Federal do Rio Grande do Sul (1896) 9 – 1415; Pontificia Universidade Catolica do Rio Grande do Sul (1931) 8 – 833. [e] Biblioteca da Universidade . . . (1898) 210; Biblioteca Publica do Estado do Rio Grande do Sul (1877) 85; Biblioteca da . . . Universidade (1942) 80.

Recife: [a] *Pernambuco. [b] for Pernambuco. [c] Atlantic O; Capiberibe R; Beberibe R. [d] Universidade Federal de Pernambuco (1827) 8 – 2707; Universidade Catolica de Pernambuco (1912) 2 – 202; Universidade Federal Rural de Pernambuco (1914) 0.5 – 147. [e] Biblioteca da Universidade Federal de Pernambuco (1830) 151; Biblioteca Publica do Estado de Pernambuco (1852) 85.

Ribeirao Preto: [a] Sao Paulo. [b] none. [c] Preto R. [d] none. [e] Biblioteca da Faculdade de Medicina de Ribeirao Preto da Universidade de Sao Paulo (1952) 9; Biblioteca Publica da Sociedade Legiao Brasileira (1905) 3 (in 1943).

Rio de Janeiro: [a] *Guanabara. [b] off Sao Sebastiao do Rio de Janeiro. [c] Atlantic O; Guanabara B of Atlantic O; Rodrigo de Freitas Lagoon. [d] Universidade Federal do Rio de Janeiro (1808) 20 – 2718; Universidade do Estado da Guanabara (1950) 7 – 601; Pontificia Universidade Catolica do Rio de Janeiro (1937) 4 – 549. [e] Biblioteca Nacional (1810) 1617; Biblioteca da Universidade Federal do Rio de Janeiro (1833) 557, inc Biblioteca do Museu Nacional (1863) 290; Biblioteca do Instituto Historico e Geografico Brasileiro (1839) 260. [f] 266s (1849).

Salvador: [a] *Bahia. [b] for Bahia, Sao Salvador da Bahia. [c] Todos os Santos B of Atlantic O. [d] Universidade Federal da Bahia (1808) 6 – 1155; Universidade Catolica de Salvador (1961) 1 – 118. [e] Biblioteca da Universidade Federal da Bahia (1909) 193; Biblioteca Publica da Bahia (1811) 72.

Santo Andre: [a] Sao Paulo. [b] none. [c] Tamanduatei R. [d] none. [e] Biblioteca da Faculdade Municipal de Ciencias Economicas de Santo Andre (1954) 1.

Santos: [a] Sao Paulo. [b] none. [c] Santos R. [d] none. [e] Biblioteca da Sociedade Humanitaria dos Empregados no Comercio de Santos (1888) 18; Biblioteca da Faculdade de Filosofia, Ciencias e Letras de Santos (1969) 15; Biblioteca Publica Municipal (1876) 5 (in 1940).

Sao Bernardo do Campo: [a] Sao Paulo. [b] none. [c] nr Grande R. [d] none. [e] Biblioteca George Brett Junior da Faculdade de Engenharia Industrial do Fundacao de Ciencias Aplicadas (1946) 2.

Sao Goncalo: [a] Rio de Janeiro. [b] none. [c] (Riacho) Imbuacu Creek. [d] none. [e] Biblioteca Municipal (1940) ?

Sao Joao de Meriti: [a] Rio de Janeiro. [b] for Mirity. [c] Sao Joao de Meriti R. [d] none. [e] Biblioteca Sao Boaventura (1940) 1 (in 1949).

Sao Luis: [a] *Maranhao. [b] for Maranhao, Sao Luiz. [c] Sao Marcos B of Atlantic O; Itapecuru R; Mearim R. [d] Universidade do Maranhao (1945) 4 – 408. [e] Biblioteca Publica do Estado do Maranhao (1829) 45; Biblioteca da Universidade . . . (1914) 20.

Sao Paulo: [a] *Sao Paulo. [b] none. [c] Tiete R. [d] Universidade de Sao Paulo (1827) 20 – 2707 [Sao Paulo campus: (1827) ? – ?]; Pontificia Universidade Catolica de Sao Paulo (1908) 13 – 700; Universidade Mackenzie (1870) 6 – 836. [e] Biblioteca da Universidade de Sao Paulo (1827) 736 [Sao Paulo campus: (1827) 677]; Biblioteca Municipal Mario de Andrade (1925) 400.

Teresina: [a] *Piaui. [b] for Therezina. [c] Parnaiba R; Poti R. [d] none. [e] Biblioteca Publica do Estado do Piaui (1937) 9 (in 1940); Biblioteca da Faculdade Catolica de Filosofia do Piaui (1957) 4.

Vitoria: [a] *Espirito Santo. [b] for Victoria. [c] Vitoria B of Atlantic O; Santa Maria da Vitoria R. [d] Universidade Federal do Espirito Santo (1955) 2 – 320. [e] Biblioteca Estadual (1885) 32; Biblioteca da Universidade . . . (1933) 17; Biblioteca Municipal (1941) 13.

Chile

Concepcion: [b] none. [c] Bio-Bio R. [d] Universidad de Concepcion (1919) 5 – 1112. [e] Biblioteca Central de la Universidad . . . (1920) 180.

*Santiago: [b] alt Santiago de Chile. [c] Mapocho R. [d] Universidad de Chile (1738) 51 – 9220; Universidad Tecnica del Estado (1849) 16 – 1000?; Universidad Catolica de Chile (1888) 10 – 1648. [e] Biblioteca Nacional de Chile (1813) 1200; Biblioteca de la Universidad de Chile (1738?) 1200; Biblioteca de la Universidad Catolica de Chile (1895) 400.

Valparaiso: [b] none. [c] Pacific O. [d] Universidad Catolica de Valparaiso (1928) 3 – 599; Universidad Tecnica Federico Santa Maria (1926) 2 – 112. [e] Biblioteca de la Universidad Catolica de Valparaiso (1928) 155; Biblioteca Severin (1875) 110. [f] 70 (1865).

Vina del Mar: [b] none. [c] Pacific O; Marga Marga R. [d] none. [e] Biblioteca del Estacion de Biologia Marina de Montemar (1941) 11.

Colombia

Barranquilla: [b] none. [c] Magdalena R. [d] Universidad del Atlantico (1941) 2 – 145; Universidad Libre, Barranquilla campus (1956) ? – ? [e] Biblioteca Publica Departamental (1923) 32.

*Bogota: [b] for Santa Fe de Bogota. [c] San Agustin R; San Francisco R. [d][1] Universidad Nacional de Colombia (1563) 12 – 1614; Pontificia Universidad Javeriana (1604) 5 – 841; Fundacion Universidad de Bogota Jorge Tadeo Lozano (1954) 4 – 401; Universidad de los Andes (1948) 3 – 362; Universidad la Gran Colombia (1951) 3 – ?; Fundacion Universidad de America (1952) 2 – 261; Universidad Libre (1923) 2 – 220 [Bogota campus: (1923) ? – ?]; Universidad Pedagogica Nacional (1928) 2 – 144; Universidad Externado de Colombia (1886) 1 – 194; Colegio Mayor de Nuestra Senora del Rosario (univ) (1653) 1 – 249. [e] Biblioteca Nacional de Colombia (1777) 360; Biblioteca de la Pontificia Universidad Javeriana (1604?) 273. [f] 2294s (1969e), 100 (1905), 20 (1723).

Bucaramanga: [b] none. [c] nr Oro R; nr Surata R. [d] Universidad Industrial de Santander (1948) 3 – 195; Universidad Femenina de Santander (1964) ? – ? [e] Biblioteca Departamental (1898) 28.

[1] Universities with 1000 or more students.

Cali: [b] none. [c] Cali R. [d] Universidad del Valle (1945) 3 – 521; Universidad Santiago de Cali (1958) 0.1 – ? [e] Biblioteca de la Universidad del Valle (1946) 80; Biblioteca Municipal del Centenario (1910) 25.

Cartagena: [b] none. [c] B of Cartagena of Caribbean Sea. [d] Universidad de Cartagena (1824) 2 – 197. [e] Biblioteca Universitaria Fernandez Madrid (1827) 23.

Cucuta: [b] off San Jose de Cucuta. [c] Pamplonita R. [d] Universidad Francisco de Paula Santander (1962) ? – 50. [e] Biblioteca Julio Perez Ferrero (1912) 4; Biblioteca del Centro de Historia (?) 3.

Ibague: [b] off San Bonifacio de Ibague. [c] nr Chipalo R; nr Combeima R. [d] Universidad del Tolima (1954) 2 – 145. [e] Biblioteca General de la Universidad . . . (1963) 5; Biblioteca Departamental del Tolima (1954) 2.

Manizales: [b] none. [c] nr Chinchina R. [d] Universidad de Caldas (1937) 2 – 192. [e] Biblioteca Central de la Universidad . . . (1958) 16; Biblioteca Departamental de Caldas (1954) 14.

Medellin: [b] none. [c] Porce R. [d] Universidad Pontificia Bolivariana (1936) 9 – 560; Universidad de Antioquia (1803) 4 – 570; Universidad de Medellin (1950) 3 – 193; Universidad Autonoma Latinoamericana (1966) 2 – 170. [e] Biblioteca General de la Universidad de Antioquia (1935) 150; Biblioteca Publica Piloto de Medellin para la America Latina (1954) 65.

Pereira: [b] none. [c] Otun R. [d] Universidad Tecnologica de Pereira (1960) 1 – 128. [e] Biblioteca de la Universidad . . . (1960) 6; Biblioteca Jesus Maria Ormaza (?) 4.

Ecuador

Guayaquil: [b] for Santiago de Guayaquil. [c] Guayas R. [d] Universidad de Guayaquil (1867) 5 – 447; Universidad de Santiago de Guayaquil (1962) 2 – 250; Escuela Superior Politecnica del Litoral (univ) (1958) 0.5 – 48. [e] Museo y Biblioteca Municipal (1862) 85.

*Quito: [b] none. [c] Machangara R. [d] Universidad Central del Ecuador (1594) 9 – 600; Pontificia Universidad Catolica del Ecuador (1946) 2 – 150; Escuela Politecnica Nacional (univ) (1870) 0.8 – 64. [e] Biblioteca Ecuatoriana y Archivo (1928) 65; Biblioteca Nacional (1792) 60; Biblioteca de la Universidad . . . (1769?) 45.

Guyana

*Georgetown: [b] none. [c] Atlantic O; Demerara R. [d] University of Guyana (1963) 1 – 86. [e] Public Free Library (1909) 140.

Paraguay

*Asuncion: [b] for Nuestra Senora de la Asuncion. [c] Paraguay R. [d] Universidad Nacional de Asuncion (1883) 3 – 500; Universidad Catolica Nuestra Senora de la Asuncion (1959) 3 – 260. [e] Biblioteca, Museo y Archivo Nacionales (1869) 45.

Peru

Arequipa: [b] none. [c] Chili R. [d] Universidad Nacional de San Agustin (1821) 7 – 420; Universidad de Santa Maria (1961) ? – ? [e] Biblioteca de la Universidad Nacional de San Agustin (1828) 126; Biblioteca Publica Municipal (1821) 28.

Callao: [b] none. [c] Pacific O. [d] none. [e] Biblioteca Municipal Piloto (1936) 35.

Cuzco: [b] for Cusco. [c] Chunchulmayu R; Huatanay R; Tullamayo R. [d] Universidad Nacional de San Antonio Abad del Cuzco (1598) 6 – 479? [e] Biblioteca Central de la Universidad . . . (1696) 55. [f] 18 (1876).

*Lima: [b] none. [c] Pacific O; Rimac R. [d][1] Universidad Nacional Mayor de San Marcos de Lima (1551) 20 – 2052; Universidad Nacional Federico Villarreal (1963) 10 – 1300; Universidad Nacional de Ingenieria (1876) 7 – 779; Pontificia Universidad Catolica del Peru (1917) 5 – 670; Universidad Particular Inca Garcilaso de la Vega (1964) 5 – 173; Universidad Nacional Agraria (1902 at Santa Beatriz, relocated 1933) 2 – 378. [e] Biblioteca Nacional (1821) 600; Biblioteca Central de la Universidad Nacional Mayor de San Marcos de Lima (1551) 400. [f] 101 (1876).

Surinam

*Paramaribo: [b] none. [c] Surinam (off Suriname) R. [d] Universiteit van Suriname (1968) 0.6 – ? [e] Bibliotheek Cultureel Centrum Suriname (1947) 38. [f] 182s (1964).

Uruguay

*Montevideo: [b] none. [c] Plata R. [d] Universidad de la Republica (1849) 16 – 2982; Universidad del Trabajo del Uruguay (1942) ? – ? [e] Biblioteca Nacional del Uruguay (1816) 500; Biblioteca de la Facultad de Medicina de la Universidad de la Republica (1884) 225; Biblioteca del Poder Legislativo (?) 180.

[1] Universities with 1000 or more students.

Venezuela

Barquisimeto: [b] none. [c] Cojedes R. [d] Universidad de la Region Centro-Occidental (1962) 2 – 200. [e] Biblioteca Publica Pio Tamayo (1911) 22.

*Caracas: [b] for Santiago de Leon de Caracas.[c] Guaire R [d1] Universidad Central de Venezuela (1696) 30 – 3060; Universidad Catolica Andres Bello (1953) 5 – 457; Universidad Santa Maria (1953) 3 – 250. [e] Biblioteca Nacional (1841) 438; Biblioteca de la Universidad Catolica Andres Bello (1953) 100; Biblioteca Central de la Universidad Central de Venezuela (1850) 86.

Maracaibo: [b] none. [c] Maracaibo L. [d] Universidad Nacional del Zulia (1891) 11 – 909. [e] Biblioteca Baralt (1961) 20; Biblioteca de la Universidad . . . (1946) 19.

Maracay: [b] none. [c] nr Valencia L. [d] none. [e] Biblioteca del Centro de Investigaciones Agronomicas (1938) 26.

Valencia: [b] none. [c] Cabriales R. [d] Universidad de Carabobo (1833) 12 – 217. [e] Biblioteca Central de la Universidad . . . (1852) 12; Biblioteca Publica del Estado (1876) 4.

[1] Universities with 1000 or more students.

Selected Bibliography

Of the thousands of books and periodical articles consulted in the preparation of *The World in Figures,* 244 of the most useful sources of information are listed here. For the convenience of readers who seek more detailed information on a particular subject than can be given in this book,these sources are listed,alphabetically by author (title if the authorship is anonymous), under the following twenty-five headings:

- Encyclopedias
  - Universal
  - National
- Official statistical yearbooks
- Unofficial yearbooks and almanacs
- Gazetteers
  - Universal
  - National
- Atlases
- Geography
  - Universal
  - National
- Physiography
  - Oceans and seas
  - Islands
  - Rivers
  - Mountains
  - Lakes
  - Waterfalls
- Climate
  - Universal
  - National and regional
- Civil engineering
  - Bridges
  - Tunnels
  - Dams
  - Roads and railroads
- Universities
  - Universal
  - National and regional
- Libraries
  - Universal
  - National and regional

Encyclopedias: Universal

1. *Aschehougs Konversasjons Leksikon.* Oslo, 1954-1961. 18 v.
2. *Bertelsmann Lexikon.* Gutersloh, West Germany, 1966. 7 v.
3. *Bolshaya Sovetskaya Entsiklopediya.* Moscow, 1949-1958. 53 v.
4. Idem. Moscow, 1926-1931. 65 v.
5. *Brockhaus Enzyklopadie.* Wiesbaden, 1966-. v 1-15: A-Ris.
6. *Chambers's Encyclopaedia.* Oxford, 1966. 15 v.
7. *Collier's Encyclopedia.* [New York], 1971. 24 v.
8. *Columbia Encyclopedia.* 3rd ed. New York, 1963. 2388 pp.
9. *Diccionario Enciclopedico Salvat.* Barcelona, 1964. 12 v.
10. *Diccionario Enciclopedico U.T.E.H.A.* Mexico, 1950–1952. 10 v.
11. Idem; *Apendice.* Mexico, 1964. 2 v.
12. *Dizionario Enciclopedico Italiano.* Rome, 1955-1961. 12 v.
13. *Enciclopedia Italiana di Scienze, Lettere ed Arti.* [Rome], 1929-1939. 36 v.

14. *Enciclopedia Universal.* Sao Paulo, 1969. 10 v.
15. *Enciclopedia Universal Ilustrada Europeo-Americana* (short title: *Espasa*). Barcelona, [1907]-1930. 70 v.
16. Idem; *Apendice.* Madrid, 1930-1933. 10 v.
17. *Encyclopaedia Britannica.* Chicago, 1971. 24 v.
18. Idem; 11th ed. New York, 1910-1911. 29 v.
19. Idem; 8th ed. Boston, 1860. 22 v.
20. *Encyclopedia Americana.* New York, 1970. 30 v.
21. *Grande Encyclopedie.* Paris, [1886-1902]. 31 v.
22. *Grand Larousse Encyclopedique.* Paris, 1960-1964. 10 v.
23. *Gran Enciclopedia del Mundo.* Barcelona, 1961-1964. 20 v.
24. *Grosse Brockhaus.* Wiesbaden, 1952-1957. 12 v.
25. Idem. Leipzig, 1928-1935. 20 v.
26. *Grote Winkler Prins.* Amsterdam, 1966-. v 1-14: A-Paga.
27. *Malaya Sovetskaya Entsiklopediya.* [Moscow], 1958-[1961]. 11 v.
28. *Meyers Grosses Konversations-Lexikon.* Leipzig, 1909. 20 v.
29. *Revai Nagy Lexikona.* Budapest, [1911-1926]. 19 v.
30. *Schweizer Lexikon.* Zurich, 1945-1948. 7 v.
31. *Svensk Upplagsbok.* Malmo, 1947-1955. 32 v.
32. *Uj Magyar Lexikon.* Budapest, 1961-1962. 6 v.
33. *Wielka Encyklopedia Powszechna PWN.* Warsaw, 1962-1969. 12 v.
34. *Winkler Prins Encyclopaedie.* Amsterdam, 1947-1955. 19 v.

Encyclopedias: National

35. *Australian Encyclopaedia.* Sydney, 1958. 10 v.
36. *Diccionario Porrua.* Mexico, 1964. 1777 pp.
37. Idem; *Suplemento.* Mexico, 1966. 496 pp.
38. *Enciklopedija Jugoslavije.* Zagreb, 1955-1971. 8 v.
39. *Encyclopaedia of New Zealand.* Wellington, 1966. 3 v.
40. *Encyclopaedie van Nederlandsch-Indie.* Hague, 1917-1939. 8 v.
41. *Encyclopedia Canadiana.* Toronto, 1970. 10 v.
42. *Encyclopedia of Canada.* Toronto, 1935-1937. 6 v.
43. *Gran Enciclopedia Argentina.* Buenos Aires, 1956-1963. 8 v.
44. *Modern Encyclopaedia of Australia and New Zealand.* Sydney, 1964. 1199 pp.

Official Statistical Yearbooks

45. [Australia], Bureau of Census and Statistics. *Official Year Book of the Commonwealth of Australia . . . 1971.* Canberra, 1971. 1106 pp.
46. [Austria], Statistisches Zentralamt. *Statistisches Handbuch fur die Republik Osterreich . . . 1971.* Vienna, 1971. 592 pp.
47. Belgium, Institut National de Statistique. *Annuaire Statistique de la Belgique . . . 1970.* Brussels, ND. 787 pp.
48. [Brazil], Instituto Brasileiro de Estatistica. *Anuario Estatistico do Brasil – 1971.* Rio de Janeiro, 1971. 831 pp.
49. Bulgaria, Tsentralno Statistichesko Upravlenie. *Statisticheski Godishnik na Narodna Republika Bulgariya, 1971.* Sofia, 1971. 605 pp.
50. [Canada], Dominion Bureau of Statistics. *(1970–71) Canada Year Book.* Ottawa. 1971. 1408 pp.
51. Ceylon, Department of Census and Statistics. *Statistical Abstract of Ceylon, 1969.* Colombo, 1970. 400 pp.
52. [Colombia], Departamento Administrativo Nacional de Estadistica. *Anuario General de Estadistica, Colombia – 1963.* [Bogota], 1965. 861 pp.
53. Czechoslovakia, Federalni Statisticky Urad. *Statisticka Rocenka Ceskoslovenske Socialisticke Republiky, 1971.* Prague, 1971. 618 pp.
54. [Denmark], Danmarks Statistik. *Statistisk Arbog, 1971.* Copenhagen, 1971. 600 pp.
55. [East Germany], Staatliche Zentralverwaltung fur Statistik. *Statistisches Jahrbuch der Deutschen Demokratischen Republik, 1972.* Berlin, 1972. 520+96+20 pp.

56. Ethiopia, Central Statistical Office. *Ethiopia Statistical Abstract, 1969.* Addis Ababa, ND. 206 pp.

57. Finland, Tilastollinen Paatoimisto. *Suomen Tilastollinen Vuosikirja . . . 1968.* Helsinki, 1969. 518 pp.

58. [France], Institut National de la Statistique et des Etudes Economiques. *Annuaire Statistique de la France, 1970/71.* [Paris], ND. 664+87 pp.

59. Greece, Ethnike Statistike Iperesia. *Statistike Epeteris tes Ellados. . . . 1969.* Athens, 1969. 373 pp.

60. [Hungary], Kozponti Statisztikai Hivatal. *Statisztikai Evkonyv, 1970.* Budapest, 1971. 573 pp.

61. India, Central Statistical Organisation. *Statistical Abstract, India, 1969.* Delhi, 1970. 774 pp.

62. Indonesia, Biro Pusat Statistik. *Statistik Indonesia . . . 1968 & 1969.* Djakarta, 1971. 469 pp.

63. Iraq, Central Statistical Organization. *Annual Abstract of Statistics, 1969.* Baghdad, ND. 496 pp.

64. Ireland, Central Statistics Office. *Statistical Abstract of Ireland, 1967.* Dublin, 1967. 381 pp.

65. [Israel], Central Bureau of Statistics. *Statistical Abstract of Israel, 1969.* Jerusalem, 1969. 645 pp.

66. [Italy], Istituto Centrale di Statistica. *Annuario Statistico Italiano . . . 1971.* Rome, 1971. 443 pp.

67. [Japan], Bureau of Statistics. *Japan Statistical Yearbook, 1971.* Tokyo, 1972. 683 pp.

68. League of Nations. *Statistical Year-Book, 1926-42/44.* Geneva, 1927–1945. 17 v.

69. [Mexico], Direccion General de Estadistica. *Anuario Estadistico de los Estados Unidos Mexicanos, 1968-1969.* Mexico, 1971. 656 pp.

70. [Netherlands], Centraal Bureau voor de Statistiek. *Jaarcijfers voor Nederland, 1967-1968.* Hague, 1970. 469 pp.

71. [New Zealand], Department of Statistics. *New Zealand Official Yearbook, 1971.* Wellington, 1971. 1177 pp.

72. [North Korea]. *Choson Chungang Yongam. 1965 (Korean Central Yearbook, 1965).* Pyongyang, 1965. 361 pp. (US Joint Publications Research Service, number 35,146.)

73. [Norway], Statistisk Sentralbyra. *Statistisk Arbok, 1971.* Oslo, 1971. 416 pp.

74. Pakistan, Central Statistical Office. *Pakistan Statistical Yearbook, 1967.* Karachi, 1968. 527 pp.

75. [Poland], Glowny Urzad Statystyczny. *Rocznik Statystyczny, 1969.* Warsaw, 1969. 716 pp.

76. Portugal, Instituto Nacional de Estatistica. *Anuario Estatistico . . . 1968.* Lisbon, 1969. 2 v.

77. [Romania], Directia Centrala de Statistica. *Anuarul Statistic al Republicii Socialiste Romania, 1971.* [Bucharest], ND. 846 pp.

78. South Africa, Departement van Statistiek. *Suid-Afrikaanse Statistieke, 1970.* Pretoria, 1971. unp.

79. [South Korea], Economic Planning Board. *Korea Statistical Yearbook, 1971.* Seoul, 1971. 493 pp.

80. [South Vietnam], National Institute of Statistics. *Viet Nam Statistical Yearbook, 1970.* Saigon, ND. 408 pp.

81. [Spain], Instituto Nacional de Estadistica. *Anuario Estadistico de Espana . . . 1970.* Madrid, ND. 742 pp.

82. [Sweden], Statistiska Centralbyran. *Statistisk Arsbok for Sverige . . . 1971.* Stockholm, 1971. 543 pp.

83. Switzerland, Eidgenossisches Statistisches Amt. *Statistisches Jahrbuch der Schweiz . . . 1971.* Bern, 1971. 663 pp

84. Syria, Central Bureau of Statistics. *Statistical Abstract . . . 1971.* Damascus, 1971. 499 pp.

85. [Taiwan], Directorate-General of Budgets, Accounts and Statistics. *Statistical Abstract of the Republic of China, 1971.* [Taipei], ND. 812 pp.

86. [Thailand], National Statistical Office. *Statistical Yearbook, Thailand . . . 1970-1971.* [Bangkok], ND. 551 pp.

87. Turkey, Devlet Istatistik Enstitusu. *Turkiye Istatistik Yilligi, 1968.* Ankara, 1969. 459 pp.

88. [UK], Central Statistical Office. *Annual Abstract of Statistics . . . 1971.* London, 1971. 408 pp.

89. United Nations, Statistical Office. *Demographic Yearbook, 1948-70.* New York, 1949-1971. 23 v.

90. United Nations, Statistical Office. *Statistical Yearbook, 1948-71.* New York, 1949-1972. 24 v.

91. US, Bureau of the Census. *Statistical Abstract of the United States, 1972.* Washington, 1972. 1017 pp.

92. [USSR], Tsentralnoye Statisticheskoye Upravleniye. *Narodnoye Khozyaistvo SSSR v 1971 G.* Moscow, 1971. 822 pp.

93. Venezuela, Direccion General de Estadistica y Censos Nacionales. *Anuario Estadistico de Venezuela, 1969.* Caracas, 1972. 733 pp.

94. [West Germany], Statistisches Bundesamt. *Statistisches Jahrbuch fur die Bundesrepublik Deutschland, 1972.* Wiesbaden, 1972. 570+144+47 pp.

95. Yugoslavia, Savezni Zavod za Statistiku. *Statisticki Godisnjak Jugoslavije, 1971.* Belgrade, 1971. 692 pp.

Unofficial Yearbooks and Almanacs

96. *Almanach de Gotha, 1763-1944.* Gotha, East Germany, 1763-1944. 181v.
97. *(1971) Almanaque Mundial.* New York, 1970. 511 pp.
98. *Bevolkerung der Erde* (in *Petermanns Geographische Mitteilungen).* Gotha, East Germany, 1872-1931. 14 v.
99. *China Yearbook, 1969-70.* Taipei, [1970]. 871 pp.
100. Hassel, G. *Statistische Uebersichts-Tabellen der Sammtlichen Europaischen und Einiger Aussereuropaischen Staaten.* Gottingen, 1809. 106 pp.
101. *Hubner's Weltstatistik . . . 1939.* Vienna, [1939]. 327 pp.
102. *Information Please Almanac . . . 1972.* New York, 1971. 976 pp.
103. *Iran Almanac and Book of Facts, 1970.* Teheran, 1970. 787 pp.
104. *New York Times Encyclopedic Almanac, 1972.* New York, 1971. 956 pp.
105. Nugroho. *Indonesia, Facts and Figures.* Djakarta, 1967. 608 pp.
106. *Pacific Islands Year Book,* 11th ed. Sydney, 1972. 542 pp.
107. *(1971) South American Handbook.* London, 1970. 938 pp.
108. *Statesman's Year-Book, 1864-1972/73.* London, 1864-1972. 109 v.
109. *Statistique Internationale des Grandes Villes . . . 1931.* Hague, 1931. 708+26 pp.
110. *(1972) . . . West Indies & Caribbean Year Book.* Croydon (i.e., London), 1971. 973 pp.
111. Whitaker, Joseph. *Almanack for the Year of Our Lord 1972.* London, 1971. 1220 pp.
112. *World Almanac and Book of Facts, 1867-1972.* New York, 1868-1971. 105 v.

Gazetteers: Universal

113. Brookes, R. *General Gazetteer; or, Compendious Geographical Dictionary.* London, 1815. unp.
114. Chisholm, George G., Ed. *Times [of London] Gazetteer of the World.* London, 1899. 1787 pp.
115. *Columbia Lippincott Gazetteer of the World.* New York, 1952. 2148 pp.
116. *Edinburgh Gazetteer, or Geographical Dictionary.* Edinburgh, 1822. 6 v.
117. *Gazetteer of the World, or, Dictionary of Geographical Knowledge.* Edinburgh, [1850]-1856. 7 v.
118. *Harper's Statistical Gazetteer of the World.* New York, 1855. 1952 pp.
119. *Imperial Gazetteer.* Glasgow, 1855. 2 v.
120. Johnston, Alex. Keith. *Dictionary of Geography, Descriptive, Physical, Statistical, and Historical.* London, 1851. 1432 pp.
121. *Kratkaya Geograficheskaya Entsiklopediya.* Moscow, 1960-1966. 5 v.
122. *Lippincott's Gazetteer of the World.* Philadelphia, 1902, 2636 pp.
123. *Lippincott's Pronouncing Gazetteer.* Philadelphia, 1855. 2182 pp.
124. M'Culloch, J. R. *Dictionary Geographical, Statistical, and Historical of the Various Countries, Places and Principal Natural Objects in the World.* London, 1866. 4 v.
125. *Ritters Geographisch-Statistisches Lexikon.* Leipzig, 1910. 2 v.
126. US, Office of Geography. *Gazetteer [s of individual countries and regions].*[1] Washington, 1955. v 1-115.
127. *Webster's Geographical Dictionary.* Springfield, Mass., 1969. 1293 pp.
128. Worcester, J. E. *Geographical Dictionary, or Universal Gazetteer, Ancient and Modern.* Boston, 1823. 2 v.

Gazetteers: National

129. Canada, Board on Geographical Names. *Gazetteer[s of individual provinces].* Ottawa, 1952-1962. 10 v.
130. *Diccionario Geografico de Espana.* Madrid, 1956-1961. 17 v.
131. *Dicionario Geografico Brasileiro.* Porto Alegre, 1966. 559 pp.
132. *Imperial Gazetteer of India.* Oxford, 1907-1909. 26 v.
133. Orth, Donald J. *Dictionary of Alaska Place Names.* Washington, 1967. 1084 pp.
134. Papinot, E. *Historical and Geographical Dictionary of Japan.* Tokyo, [1909]. 842 pp.

[1] By November 1970, 115 separate gazetteers in this series had been published, and many of these had been revised. Since March 1968 they have been prepared by the Geographic Names Division of the Army Topographic Command, which has assumed the functions of the Office of Geography.

135. Playfair, G.M.H. *Cities and Towns of China; a Geographical Dictionary,* 2nd ed. Shanghai, 1910. 582+76 pp.

Atlases

136. *Chungkuo Fensheng Titu (Provincial Atlas of China).* Peking, 1963. 142 pp. (US Joint Publications Research Service, number 27,071.)

137. *Pergamon World Atlas.* Warsaw, 1968. 525 pp.

138. Rand McNally & Company. *(1972) Commercial Atlas & Marketing Guide.* Chicago, 1972. 667 pp.

139. *Rand McNally International Atlas.* Chicago, 1969. 280+223 pp.

140. *Stielers Hand-Atlas*. Gotha, East Germany, 1925. 108 leaves.

141. Idem; *Namenverzeichnis.* Gotha, East Germany, 1925. 315 pp.

142. *Times [of London] Atlas of the World.* London, 1967. 123 plates + 272 pp.

143. Touring Club Italiano. *Atlante Internazionale.* Milan, 1968. 173 leaves.

144. Idem; *Indice dei Nomi.* Milan, 1968. 1032 pp.

145. US, Geological Survey. *National Atlas of the United States of America.* Washington, 1970. 417 pp.

Geography: Universal

146. Dibo, Dulcidio. *Grande Enciclopedia Geografica Mundial.* Sao Paulo, 1968. 4 v.

Geography: National

147. *Anuario Geografico Argentino.* Buenos Aires, 1941. 650 pp.

148. Arango Cano, Jesus. *Geografia Fisica y Economica de Colombia.* Bogota, 1956. 338 pp.

149. *Argentina, Suma de Geografia.* Buenos Aires, 1958-1963. 9 v.

150. [Brazil], Conselho Nacional de Geografia, *Geografia do Brasil.* Rio de Janeiro, 1959-1960. v 1-2.

151. Federal Writers' Project (or Writers' Program). *Alabama [etc] (American Guide Series) [guidebooks to individual US states].* Various places, 1937-1949. 50 v.

152. *New Official Guide: Japan.* Tokyo, 1966. 1102 pp.

153. Philippines, Bureau of Coast and Geodetic Survey. *Geographical Data of the Philippines.* Manila, 1962. 22 pp.

154. Sociedade de Geographia do Rio de Janeiro. *Geographia do Brasil.* Rio de Janeiro, [1922-1923]. v 1-2, 10.

155. Spate, O. H. K., and A. T. A. Learmonth. *India and Pakistan.* London, 1967. 877 pp.

156. [UK], Central Office of Information. *Britain 1971, an Official Handbook.* London, 1971. 522 pp.

157. US, Bureau of the Census. *County and City Data Book, 1967.* Washington, 1967. 673 pp.

158. Vila, Pablo. *Geografia de Venezuela.* Caracas, 1960-. v 1. 454 pp.

159. Zaychikov, V. T., Ed. *Fizicheskaya Geografiya Kitaya (Physical Geography of China).* Moscow, 1964. 650 pp. (US Joint Publications Research Service, number 32,119.)

Physiography: Oceans and Seas

160. Fairbridge, Rhodes W., Ed. *Encyclopedia of Geomorphology.* New York, 1968. 1295 pp.

161. Fairbridge, Rhodes W., Ed. *Encyclopedia of Oceanography.* New York, 1966. 1021 pp.

162. International Hydrographic Bureau. *Limits of Oceans and Seas (Special Publication number 23).* Monte Carlo, Monaco, [1953]. 35 pp.

163. Menard, H. W., and Stuart M. Smith, "Hypsometry of Ocean Basin Provinces," *Journal of Geophysical* Research, v 71, pp 4305-4325, 15 Sep 1966.

Physiography: Islands

164. Huxley, Anthony, Ed. *Standard Encyclopedia of the World's Oceans and Islands.* New York, 1962. 383 pp.

165. Pemberton Nancy A. *America's Islands (unpublished manuscript prepared for US Coast and Geodetic Survey).* 25 pp.

Physiography: Rivers

166. Akademiya Nauk SSSR, Institut Geografii. *Ocherki po Gidrografii Rek SSSR.* Moscow, 1953. 323 pp.

167. Grande, Jose Carlos P. "Maior Rio do Mundo," *Boletim Geografico [Rio de Janeiro],* v 13, pp 183-192, Mar-Apr 1955.

168. Gresswell, R. Kay, and Anthony Huxley, Ed. *Standard Encyclopedia of the World's Rivers and Lakes.* New York, 1965. 384 pp.

169. Parde, Maurice, and Roy E.Oltman. "Nouvelles Donnees Experimentales et Evaluations sur les Debits de l'Amazone," *Comptes Rendus . . . de l'Academie des Sciences,* v 264 (series D), pp 1401-1406, 13 Mar 1967.

170. Voskresenskiy, K. P. *Norma i Izmenchivost Godovogo Stoka Rek Sovetskogo Soyuza.* Leningrad, 1962. 546 pp.

Physiography: Mountains

171. *Alpinistes Celebres.* Paris, 1956. 416 pp.

172. Bere, Rennie. *Way to the Mountains of the Moon.* London, 1966. 147 pp.

173. Bolinder, Anders, and G. O. Dyhrenfurth. "List of the World's Known Peaks of Over 7,400 Metres (24,280 Feet)," *Mountain World, 1964-1965* [London, 1966], pp 196-199.

174. Burrard, S. G., et al. *Sketch of the Geography and Geology of the Himalaya Mountains and Tibet.* Delhi, 1933. 359 + 32 pp.

175. Carter, Adams. "American Alpine Club Expedition to the Ojos del Salado," *Geographical Review,* v 47, pp 240-250, Apr 1957.

176. Echevarria C., Evelio. "Survey of Andean Ascents," *American Alpine Journal,* v 13, pp 155-192, 425-452, 1962-1963.

177. Filippi, Filippo de. *Ruwenzori.* London, 1909. 407 pp.

178. Freshfield, Douglas William. *Exploration of the Caucasus,* 2nd ed. London, 1902. 2 v.

179. Gansser, Augusto. *Geology of the Himalayas.* London, 1964. 289 pp.

180. Huxley, Anthony, Ed. *Standard Encyclopedia of the World's Mountains.* New York, 1962. 383 pp.

181. International Volcanological Association, Ed. *Catalogue of the Active Volcanoes of the World Including Solfatara Fields.* Naples, 1951-1966. 19 parts.

182. *K Vershinam Sovetskoy Zemli.* Moscow, 1949. 575 pp.

183. Noyce, Wilfrid, and Ian McMorrin. *World Atlas of Mountaineering.* London, 1969. 224 pp.

184. Spencer, Sydney, Ed. *Mountaineering.* London [1934]. 383 pp.

185. Thomas, Lowell. . . .*Book of the High Mountains.* New York, 1964. 512 pp.

Physiography: Lakes

186. Bue, Conrad D. *Principal Lakes of the United States (Geological Survey Circular number 476).* Washington, 1963. 22 pp.

187. Halbfass, Wilhelm. *Seen der Erde.* Gotha, East Germany, 1922. 169 pp.

Physiography: Waterfalls

188. Rashleigh, Edward C. *Among the Waterfalls of the World.* London, 1935. 288 pp.

Climate: Universal

189. Sokhrina, R. F., et al. *Davieniye Vezdukha, Temperatura Vezdukha i Atmosfernyye Osadki Severnogo Polushariya.* Leningrad, 1959. 473 pp.

190. Tokyo Temmondai. *Rika Nempyo, 1970.* Tokyo, 1969. unp.

191. [UK], Meteorological Office. *Tables of Temperature, Relative Humidity and Precipitation for the World.* London, 1958. 6 v.

192. *World Weather Records, 1921-60.* Washington, 1934-1968. 9v.

Climate: National and Regional

193. Argentina, Servicio Meteorologico Nacional. *Estadisticas Climatologicas, 1901-1950.* Buenos Aires, 1958. 44 pp.

194. Argentina, Servicio Meteorologico Nacional. *Estadisticas Climatologicas, 1941-1950.* Buenos Aires, 1958. 161 pp.

195. Canada, Meteorological Division. *Climatic Summaries for Selected Meteorological Stations in the Dominion of Canada.* Toronto, [1947]. 3 v.

196. China, Office of Climatological Research. *Chungkuo Chihou Tu (Atlas of Chinese Climatology).* Peking, 1960. 601 pp. (US Joint Publications Research Service, number 16,321.)

197. Czechoslovakia, Vydava Hydrometeorologicky Ustav. *Podnebi Ceskoslovenske Socialisticke Republiky — Tabulky.* Prague, 1961. 379 pp.

198. Gherzi, E. *Meteorology of China.* Macao, 1951. 2 v.

199. India, Meteorological Department. *Climatological Tables of Observatories (1931-1960).* NP, ND. 470 pp.

200. *Klimaticheskiy Spravochnik Afriki.* Leningrad, 1968. 2 v.

201. [Leningrad], Glavnaya Geofizicheskaya Observatoriya. *Klimat SSSR.* Leningrad, 1958-1963. 8 v.

202. *Spravochnik po Klimatu SSSR.* Leningrad, 1964-. 34 v.

203. Tokyo, Central Meteorological Observatory. *Climatographic Atlas of Japan; 1st series (v 1).* Tokyo, 1948. 42 plates + 12 pp.

204. [UK], Meteorological Office. *Averages of Rainfall for Great Britain and Northern Ireland, 1916-1950.* London, 1958. 36 pp.

205. [UK], Meteorological Office. *Averages of Temperature for Great Britain and Northern Ireland, 1921-50.* London, 1953. 36 pp.

206. US, Environmental Data Service. *Climatological Data; Annual Summary, 1969.* Asheville, 1970. unp.

207. Vivo, Jorge A., and Jose C. Gomez. *Climatologia de Mexico.* Mexico, 1946. 11+73 pp.

Civil Engineering: Bridges

208. Gies, Joseph. *Bridges and Men.* New York, 1963. 343 pp.

209. Smith, H. Shirley. *World's Great Bridges.* New York, 1964. 250 pp.

210. Virola, Juhani. "World's Greatest Bridges," *Civil Engineering [New York]*, v. 38, pp 52-55, Oct 1968.

Civil Engineering: Tunnels

211. Pequignot, G. A. *Tunnels and Tunnelling.* London, 1963. 555 pp.

Civil Engineering: Dams

212. International Commission on Large Dams. *World Register of Dams.* Paris, ND. 4 v.

Civil Engineering: Roads and Railroads

213. International Road Federation. *World Road Statistics, 1965-1969.* Geneva, 1970. 192 pp.

214. *Jane's World Railways . . . 1970-71.* London, 1970. 686 pp.

215. [Moscow], Institut Kompleksnykh Transportnykh Problem. *Zarubezhnyy Transport.* Moscow, 1966. 366 pp.

216. *Railway Directory & Year Book, 1971.* London, 1970. 740 pp.

Universities: Universal

217. *International Handbook of Universities,* 5th ed. Paris, 1971. 1216 pp.

218. *Minerva; Jahrbuch der Gelehrten Welt.* Berlin, 1966-1969. 3 v.

219. *UNESCO World Survey of Education;* v 4, *Higher Education.* Paris, 1966. 1433 pp.

220. *World of Learning, 1971-72.* London, 1972. 2 v. 1899 pp.

Universities: National and Regional

221. *American Universities and Colleges,* 10th ed. Washington, 1968. 1782 pp.

222. *Commonwealth Universities Yearbook, 1970.* London, 1970. 1874 pp.

223. *Japanese Universities and Colleges, 1965-6.* Tokyo, 1965. 475 pp.

224. Parker, Garland G. "Statistics of Attendance in American Universities and Colleges," *School & Society,* v 99, pp 105-126, Feb 1971.

225. *(1972) Universities and Colleges of Canada.* Ottawa, 1972. 710 pp.

226. *Universities Handbook, India & Ceylon.* New Delhi, 1971. 970 pp.

227. US, National Center for Educational Statistics. *Education Directory, 1970-1971; Higher Education.* Washington, 1971. 515 pp.

228. US, National Center for Educational Statistics. *Opening Fall Enrollment in Higher Education, 1970.* Washington, 1970 (i.e., 1971). 84 pp.

Libraries: Universal

229. *International Library Directory,* 3rd ed. London, 1968. 1222 pp.

230. *World Guide to Libraries; Internationales Bibliotheks-Handbuch,* 3rd ed. New York, 1970. 4 v.

Libraries: National and Regional

231. *American Library Directory,* 27th ed. New York, 1970. 1174 pp.

232. *Biblioteki SSSR . . . Spravochnik.* Moscow, 1969. 343 pp.

233. *Bibliotheek- en Documentatiegids voor Nederland, Suriname en de Nederlandse Antillen.* Hague, 1966. 442 pp.

234. [Brazil], Instituto Nacional do Livro. *Guia das Bibliotecas Brasileiras.* Rio de Janeiro, 1955. 681 pp.

235. [France], Direction des Bibliotheques et de la Lecture Publique. *Repertoire des Bibliotheques et Organismes de Documentation.* Paris, 1971. 733 pp.

236. [Italy], Direzione Generale delle Academie e Biblioteche. *Annuario delle Biblioteche Italiane.* Rome, 1956-[1960]. 3 v.

237. *Jahrbuch der Bibliotheken, Archive und Informationsstellen der Deutschen Demokratischen Republik.* Leipzig, 1971. 499 pp.

238. *Jahrbuch der Deutschen Bibliotheken,* 44th ed. Wiesbaden, 1971. 505 pp.

239. *Libraries, Museums and Art Galleries Year Book, 1971.* Cambridge, UK, 1971. 694 pp.

240. [Mexico], Departamento de Bibliotecas. *Directorio de Bibliotecas de la Republica Mexicana,* 3rd ed. [Mexico], 1968. 253 pp.

241. Moldoveanu, Valeriu, et al. *Ghidul Bibliotecilor din Romania.* Bucharest, 1970. 475 pp.

242. Pan American Union, Columbus Memorial Library. *Guia de Bibliotecas de la America Latina.* Washington, 1963. 165 pp.

243. Pretoria, State Library. *Handbook of Southern African Libraries.* Pretoria, 1970. 939 pp.

244. Rio de Janeiro, Instituto Brasileiro de Bibliografia e Documentacao. *Bibliotecas Especializadas Brasileiras,* 2nd ed. Rio de Janeiro, 1969. 605 pp.

Index

ARCTIC OCEAN
GREENLAND
GREENLAND SEA
BARENTS SEA
NOVAYA ZEMLYA
KARA SEA
BAFFIN BAY
LABRADOR SEA
NORWEGIAN SEA
BRITISH ISLES
UNION OF SOVIET SOCIALIST REPUBLICS
NORTH ATLANTIC OCEAN
MAURITANIA
UNITED ARAB REPUBLIC
LIBYA
BLACK SEA
ARABIAN SEA
BAY OF BENGAL
CEYLON
CARIBBEAN SEA
BRAZIL
SOUTH ATLANTIC OCEAN
DEMOCRATIC REPUBLIC OF THE
MALAGASY REPUBLIC
INDIAN OCEAN
SCOTIA SEA
ANTARCTIC PENINSULA
ANTARCTICA
75° 60° 45° 30° 15° 0° 15° 30° 45° 60° 75° 90° 105°
84° 80° 75° 70° 60° 45° 30° 15° 0° 15° 30° 45° 60° 70°